A PREFACE TO OUR TIMES

Contemporary Thought in Traditional Rhetorical Forms

William E. Buckler

New York University

AMERICAN BOOK COMPANY

Grateful acknowledgment is made to the following publishers and individuals for permission to reprint material which is in copyright or of which they are the authorized publishers:

HARRY N. ABRAMS, INC.: Introduction to the *History of Art,* by H. W. Janson.

APPLETON-CENTURY-CROFTS: from: *The Study of Man* by Ralph Linton. Copyright, 1936, by D. Appleton-Century Co., Inc.

BASIC BOOKS, INC.: *Collected Papers of Sigmund Freud,* edited by Ernest Jones, Vol. 4, Chapter V, "Repression," New York, 1959.

GEORGE BRAZILLER, INC.: from *Letters of James Agee to Father Flye.* Reprinted with the permission of the publisher. Copyright © by James Harold Flye and The James Agee Trust 1962.

CAMBRIDGE UNIVERSITY PRESS: from Sir Arthur Eddington's *The Nature of the Physical World.*

COLUMBIA UNIVERSITY FORUM: "The Rhetoric of Malcolm X," Spring 1966, Vol. IX, No. 2. Reprinted by permission of John Illo.

COMMON FACTOR: from *Common Factor Monographs,* Number 3, Freewill, Editor Paule Hodgson, Cumnor, Oxford, England.

J. M. DENT & SONS LTD: "An Outpost of Progress" from *Tales of Unrest* by Joseph Conrad, by permission of the Trustees of the Joseph Conrad Estate.

THE DIAL PRESS, INC.: Reprinted from *Going to Meet The Man* by James Baldwin. Copyright © 1948, 1951, 1957, 1958, 1960, 1965 by James Baldwin and used by permission of the publisher.

DOUBLEDAY & COMPANY, INC.: "Over the Edge of the Universe," copyright © 1967 by Harper's Magazine, Inc., from *Is Anyone There?* by Isaac Asimov.

E. P. DUTTON & CO., INC.: from the book *The Flowering of New England* by Van Wyck Brooks. Copyright, 1936, 1952, by Van Wyck Brooks, Renewal, ©, 1964 by Gladys Brooks, Inc.

FARRAR, STRAUS AND GIROUX, INC.: from *On the Contrary* by Mary McCarthy. Copyright 1947 by Mary McCarthy.

FRENCH REPRODUCTION RIGHTS, INC.: Pablo Picasso, *Bull's Head* (1943) Spadem 1967.

GOLDEN PRESS; ODYSSEY BOOKS: from *Peace on Earth,* an encyclical letter of Pope John XXIII as published by Odyssey Press, Inc. © copyright 1964 by Odyssey Press, Inc. and the Ridge Press, Inc.

HARCOURT, BRACE & WORLD, INC.: from *The Well Wrought Urn,* copyright, 1947, by Cleanth Brooks; from *A Walker in the City,* copyright, 1951, by Alfred Kazin; from *The Seven Storey Mountain* by Thomas Merton, copyright, 1948, by Harcourt, Brace &

Prefatory Note

A Preface to Our Times rests on the following basic convictions: (1) that in our time both teachers and students wish to be confronted with serious issues seriously pondered by authoritative, though not authoritarian, voices; (2) that important subjects become even more compelling when they are presented in writing that is clear and forceful; and (3) that serious reading can, with the help of a few well conceived guidelines, be significantly correlated with a student's efforts to extend his mastery over the writer's craft. The selections are numerous and varied, with special though not exclusive emphasis on contemporay thinking and writing; and the editorial apparatus is principally devoted to making the selections relevant to the student's problems as a writer.

This is not a rhetoric, but an omnibus of readings rhetorically oriented. Thus the brief introduction deals with the relationship between reading and writing; and the selections are organized under broad, valid, but permissive rhetorical headings:

A. Exposition and Argument, including Persuasion
B. Narrative, including Description
   1. Factual Narrative
   2. Fictional Narrative

The "permissiveness" of the organization of the selections—the fact that they are arranged under two broad headings rather than under four or even five—needs a word or two of justification. In the first place, this is primarily an omnibus of relevant readings, not a set of rhetorical exempla. Secondly, it is impossible, in a whole volume of extended selections, to provide many "pure" illustrations of exposition which do not include elements of argument, or of argument which ignores exposition, or of persuasion without argument. To *isolate* description is equally artificial: although describing a person, place, or thing is an important technique, an author seldom devotes a whole piece to it, seldom makes it a prime object of his over-all effort. Hence the more permissive organizational plan.

The "Glossary of Rhetorical Terms" is more severe. There the principal techniques of the writer-rhetorician are identified, defined, and generously illustrated from the selections in this volume. By studying this glossary and the illustrations to which it draws attention, the student can acquire a sophisticated and solid understanding of the major techniques of writing. Further, with a little additional effort, he can identify several of the rhetorical techniques used in a single selection and relate them to the over-all effects of the selection.

The headnotes to each selection are intended to identify the author and to give the student a brief critical orientation toward him; the questions at the end of the text (pp. 1005) are principally designed as instruments of self-evaluation, as a means by which the student can test his comprehension of the selection in preparation for classroom discussion.

WILLIAM E. BUCKLER

Contents

NARRATIVE INCLUDING
DESCRIPTION   *Fictional Narrative*

Reading and Writing

AN INTRODUCTION

"Read not to contradict and confute, nor to believe and take for granted, nor to find talk and discourse, but to weigh and consider. Some books are to be tasted, others to be swallowed, and some few to be chewed and digested; that is, some books are to be read only in parts; others to be read but not curiously; and some few to be read wholly, and with diligence and attention. Some books also may be read by deputy, and extracts made of them by others; but that would be only in the less important arguments and the meaner sort of books; else distilled books are, like common distilled water, flashy things. Reading maketh a full man; conference a ready man; and writing an exact man. And, therefore, if a man write little, he had need have a great memory; if he confer little, he had need have a present wit; and if he read little, he had need have much cunning, to seem to know that he doth not." These five sentences from Sir Francis Bacon's essay *Of Studies* still stand, after more than three and a half centuries, as the most famous pronouncements in English on the subject of reading and writing. And they are impressive sentences indeed—meaty in their substance, austere in their brevity, memorable in their aphoristic style.

It is not surprising that Bacon makes reading and writing the central topics of his brief essay. Unless a man reads well, his access to learning is severely circumscribed. Unless he writes well, he will be denied the subtle pleasure of communicating to others, clearly and persuasively, his observations on the men and events around him. Even if he achieves noteworthy mastery of a specialized subject—high energy physics, for example, or molecular biology—he will be relatively inarticulate on the broad subjects of perennial interest to human beings.

Bacon emphasizes the different roles which reading and writing play in the educational process. Reading makes "a full man" because reading is one of man's most economical ways of obtaining knowledge and understanding: the book which one can read "with diligence and attention" in a few days or even a few hours is almost always the product of many years of disciplined study. When we read a good book, we borrow for a while the mind and spirit of another; for a good book is, as John Milton said soon after Bacon's death, "the precious life-blood of a master-spirit, embalmed and treasured up on purpose to life beyond life." Writing makes "an exact man" in at least two important senses. In the first place, writing is an "exacting" process—as distinct, for example, from speaking—in that, once written, it has a life or existence of its own. When one writes, he assumes responsibility, not for what he meant to say or might have said or wished vaguely to suggest, but for what certain words in the public domain do in fact mean. Speaking is fluid; writing is fixed. Be the written document a brief will or a briefer poem, it will be read and interpreted literally. Hence the writer must say exactly what he means. Secondly, writing is, like all crafts regularly practiced, a habit-forming process; and the habitual writer becomes habitually more exact. At first, he may hesitate to put the mark of his own view of things upon his work—may avoid the issue through an emotive rhetorical circumlocution. But he will gradually find that he either has something particular to say or he doesn't, and that he can command the sustained attention of his reader only when he does have something particular to say. From that critical point onward, he will give up all attempts at serious writing or he will strive unremittingly for clear and economical exposition of his ideas.

It is in no way dismissive of Bacon to say that there are one or two functional relationships between reading and writing not mentioned in his brief essay. These are relationships of what one might call a professional kind, relationships which become functional when the reader goes to a piece of writing not only for its substance but also for its technique.

To read for technique, or craftsmanship, is to read from a writer's point of view, and it requires special effort, conscious and disciplined. Assuming that a given piece of writing is clear and forceful, the reader asks the writer's question: upon what rhetorical techniques does its effectiveness depend? Why is it good? The first stage in reading from a writer's point of view, then, is an analytical, critical stage; and it requires a relatively small but specialized vocabulary, a commonly accepted set of terms for fruitful identification and discussion of the effective use of words, sentences, and paragraphs and of major organizational methods—exposition, argument, narration, description. (The basic terms, as the "Glossary of Rhetorical Terms" at the end of the text shows, do not exceed *in number* the signals a college football player must learn in a single season or the capitols of the hundred states and nations which a pupil masters in the sixth grade.)

The second stage in reading from a writer's point of view is a creative stage: having identified the techniques by which clarity and forcefulness are achieved in the work of another, he consciously translates those techniques, through careful practice, into his own craft as a writer. In other words, he employs the Aristotelian concept of creative imitation. The contemporary student is frequently contemptuous of imitation, feeling it an impediment to the free outpouring of his insights and feelings. And to this point, two admissions must be made: initially, at least, imitation *is* an impediment to formless self-expression; and if it were an end in itself, imitation would hardly be worth the effort. But as a temporary device for learning to exploit the resources of one's language, imitation is one of the best proved methods available to the developing writer. The point does not need extended elaboration: the technique of every craft is learned in large part from informed imitation. Improvisation is inevitable with original people, but even originality requires a standard point of departure.

There is, of course, a quality to writing which goes beyond the separate or combined rhetorical techniques which every accomplished writer uses, a quality which is greater and more distinctive than a sum total of the separable parts of a superior piece of writing. And this all-encompassing quality is known by an all-encompassing name—*style*.

Style is unquestionably the most elusive quality of writing to talk about, as it is the most difficult to define. Thus a recent author has expressed his despair in the matter: "Style is not an isolable quality of writing; it is writing itself"; thus the French naturalist Buffon went even further and made commensurate, not with writing, but with the writer: "Style is the man himself." Several other noteworthy definitions may help to give focus to the meaning of the term. *William Wordsworth:* "style is the incarnation of thoughts"; *Thomas De Quincey:* style is thought and language "united" as "a mysterious incarnation." *John Henry Newman:* "Matter and expression are parts of one; style is a thinking out into language." *Bonamy Dobree:* "It is this voice [of the writer] which we roughly call style, and however much a writer may ignore his personality, even seek to conceal it, he cannot disguise his voice, his style, unless he is deliberately writing a parody." *Herbert Read:* "The thought seems to mold and accentuate the style, the style reacts to mold and accentuates the thought. It is one process of creation, one art, one aim." *Cleanth Brooks and Robert Penn Warren:* "form and content interpenetrate each other and are inseparable."

Style, then, all seem to agree, is the most individually distinctive mark of the writer upon his work, including, besides rhetorical devices, his total personality—his enthusiasms, his attitudes, his tone of voice and sense of rhythm, his hard-headedness and his clear-sightedness, his urbanity or, perhaps, his provincialism.

If style is such an individual, personal matter, then how can one hope to improve his style? The answer is inevitable: by improving himself. He can increase his knowledge, enlarge his point of view, winnow his experience, master the techniques and nuances of the language through which he will gain visibility. These are all aspects of style, and reading the best authors is the most fruitful means of accomplishing them. In the meantime, however, the aspiring writer should strive to perfect in his writing three qualities which Somerset Maugham set himself to accomplish in his own writing: lucidity, simplicity, and euphony. Lucid prose is prose with a perfectly clear meaning; simple prose is prose which has its say without verbal ostentation, is direct and natural; euphonious prose, recognizing that words represent sounds as well as meanings, tries to put words together in harmonious as well as meaningful combinations. As Maugham said, "If you could write lucidly, simply, euphoniously and yet with liveliness, you would write perfectly. . . ."

EXPOSITION
AND ARGUMENT

Including Persuasion

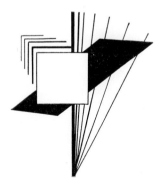

EXPOSITION
AND ARGUMENT

Including Persuasion

Walter Prescott Webb

(1888–1963)

WEBB was a Texan by birth, education, and professional service. He took his three basic degrees at the University of Texas and was a member of its faculty, with brief interruptions, from 1918 onwards. He also served for a term as Harkness Lecturer in American History at London University (1938) and as Harmsworth Professor of American History at Oxford (1942–1943). He won numerous prizes and awards and was elected president of both the Mississippi Valley Historical Association (1953) and the American Historical Association (1958). Besides The Great Frontier *(1952), his books include* The Great Plains *(1931) and* The Texas Rangers *(1935), the latter being screened by Paramount in 1936.*

◼ *The Boom Hypothesis of Modern History*

In order to appreciate the influence of the great frontier it is necessary to examine the inherent quality of the new historical ingredient. What was the essential character of the frontier? *It was inherently a vast body of wealth without proprietors.* It was an empty land five to six times the size of western Europe, a land whose resources had not been exploited. When this great area was made available to the crowded and impoverished people of the Metropolis, they swarmed out like bees to suck up the nectar of wealth, much of which they brought home to the mother hive. *This sudden, contin-*

3

uing, and ever-increasing flood of wealth precipitated on the Metropolis a business boom such as the world had never known before and probably never can know again. The Metropolis seethed with excitement. What with all the coming and going, the wharves were piled high with new strange goods, the tables were set with exotic foods of delightful flavors, and new-minted coins of gold and silver rattled in the coffers of the marketplace. This boom began when Columbus returned from his first voyage, rose slowly, and continued at an ever-accelerating pace until the frontier which fed it was no more. *Assuming that the frontier closed in 1890 or 1900, it may be said that the boom lasted about four hundred years.*   (1)

A hypothesis such as this cannot be presented like dogma to critical thinkers. They must have the supporting facts before they can accept such a radical doctrine as the boom theory of modern history. Before presenting the supporting facts, a corollary of the boom hypothesis should be examined. Assuming that there was a boom, and that it lasted four hundred years or more, it follows that a set of institutions, economic, political, and social, would in that time evolve to meet the needs of a world in boom. It is generally accepted that a set of institutions has developed since 1500, and we speak of them as modern to distinguish them from medieval institutions. Therefore, these boom-born institutions, economic systems, political systems, social systems—in short, the present superstructure of Western civilization—are today founded on boom conditions.   (2)

The boom hypothesis has implications that are far-reaching and important. It means that the modern age was an abnormal age, and not a progressive orderly development which mankind was destined to make anyway. It means that the institutions developed in this exceptional period are exceptional institutions, something out of the ordinary, and something quite different from what might be expected in the course of human affairs. They and their attendant ideas about human beings, government, and economics are very highly specialized to meet boom conditions, and may be expected to undergo much change when those conditions have passed away and history returns to normal. It is too early to guess what the changes will be, for the boom is not yet quite over everywhere, but the end of it is near enough to promote tendencies which give some hint of tomorrow. So much for the hypothesis; let us now return to proof of the boom on which it rests. (3)

If all the problems connected with this study could be proved as conclusively as the existence of the boom in modern times, the task would be less difficult and the conclusions more satisfying. It is a matter of common knowledge that since 1500 Western man's condition has improved, not in a moderate way but extraordinarily. Any table of national wealth for any Western nation would show a constant upward curve until comparatively recent times, and of course the total for all nations would show the same trend. In certain periods and for the most forward nations, the advance would be spectacular. Paralleling the upward curve of material well-being there has been comparable progress in science, arts and letters, and a general admission of more and more people to the possession of property and to the benefits of learning once reserved for the few. Our failure, or refusal, to think of this extraordinary era as an abnormal period of boom, our natural preference to think of it as merely another logical step in the orderly progress of an endowed people, detracts nothing from the reality of the boom, the most naked reality of the modern age.   (4)

The causes which created it are another matter. The idea advanced here is that the frontier furnished directly the major factor of material wealth upon which the boom was founded, and indirectly contributed much to the subsidiary accompaniments in the realm of culture.[1] Our task then is to supply evidence that powerful factors favorable to a boom did exist after the discoveries and because of them, and that those factors which were most potent derived their strength from the frontier. The factors involved, though gigantic in magnitude, are simple in nature and in their relation to one another. There are three of them to deal with, and when they are brought together in proper proportion, a boom is of high probability. Given the social and economic situation of Europe in 1500, it was almost certainly inevitable. The factors are population, land, and capital. Before examining each of these separately, it should be said that all three were present prior to the discovery, but the proportions, the ratios were wrong for a boom. It was the change of ratios which set off the spark for the electric upsurge of modern prosperity. The Metropolis furnished the population and the labor, but the frontier upset the ratios by supplying a *surplus* of land and a *surplus* of capital. It was the union of these factors, two of them radically modified by the frontier, and the opportunity for them to interact on one another, that made the transformation of Western civilization possible.   (5)

The population of the Metropolis in the year 1500 was, according to the best estimates, about 100,000,000 people. These people were crowded into an area of some 3,750,000 square miles. This means that there was an average density of 26.7 persons per square mile, an average of about 24 acres, good or bad, for each individual. The population was fairly stable, varying

---

1 It should be said that the academic argument as to the source of culture and institutions can probably never be settled to the satisfaction of those who must argue. One theory is that all ideas and institutions come from the brain and thought processes of man. The argument must be accepted. The opponents contend that environment presses man in certain directions, and compels him to do what he does. This argument cannot be denied. If man could exist entirely apart from environment, he could receive full credit for all that he does, which would be nothing. If environment existed without man (and it can exist) there would be no human institutions at all, no ideas, no culture. In either extreme we come out with the same result, which is nothing. But historically we never deal with the extremes; we always deal with man in an environment, and we believe that the two are reciprocal factors which complement and adjust themselves to each other. To the historian, at least to me, any argument as to which is the more important smacks of medieval scholasticism. I shall doubtless be charged with attributing too much to the environment, but the reason is not difficult to see. The environment I am dealing with is the *new* ingredient, the special factor whose influence is being followed on special assignment. The historian should have the choice of working the side of the street he sets out to work. The other side has been well canvassed.

little between 1300 and 1650. The scarcity of land in relation to population was reflected in inheritance laws, in late marriage, and in enforced celibacy on those who lacked inheritance and dowery.[2] Primogeniture grew out of it. It is not an exaggeration to say that the land was saturated with people, with a labor supply.   (6)

It is inconceivable that this many people, confined to this small area, could by any stretch of their genius or by any invention they might make produce the wealth and create the boom which they enjoyed during the four following centuries. Even with all the advances they have made, Europeans of the same number could not from their own resources maintain the standards which they have enjoyed, and which but for their own foolish wars they might still enjoy. The essential truth was stated by William Graham Sumner when he said, "It is this ratio of population to land which determines what are the possibilities of human development or the limits of what men can attain in civilization and comfort."[3]   (7)

It was the opening of the frontier which upset the whole European situation by altering the balance that had been struck between the amount of land and the number of people. The effects would have been readily apparent if by some magic the land, clothed with all its resources, could have risen out of the sea adjacent to what is present in Europe, but the distant position of the land, the fact that it lay over the seas, does not in final analysis matter. What does matter is that it was *additional* land, something extra, a great surplus.[4] To the 100,000,000 people of the Metropolis was suddenly made available nearly 20,000,000 square miles of fabulously rich land practically devoid of population, an area more than five times as great as all Europe. Adding this area to that of Europe, the population density was reduced to less than five persons per square mile, and each individual could

---

2 For a discussion of the limitation on marriage and the custom of inheritance, see George Caspar Homans, *English Villagers of the Thirteenth Century* (Cambridge, Mass.: Harvard University Press, 1941). Homans says (p. 159):

"The working rule, no land, no marriage, had two aspects. First, men and women who were not to inherit a family tenement did not marry unless they could secure land for themselves. Second, in many places, the man who was to inherit the tenement did not marry until its last holder was ready to turn it over to him. In this manner the sentiments and customs of men secured a stable adaption of society to its economic conditions. Despite the logic of Malthus, they limited the number of persons who pressed on the land for subsistence."

3 William Graham Sumner, "Earth-Hunger or the Philosophy of Land Grabbing," in Albert G. Keller (ed.), *Earth-Hunger and other Essays* (New Haven: Yale University Press, 1913), p. 31.

4 On November 21, 1882, Robert Griffin, Esq., President of the Statistical Society, London, read as his inaugural address a paper entitled "The Utility of Common Statistics," which appeared in *The Journal of the Statistical Society* for December, 1882, pp. 517–46. In this paper the author anticipated Turner by ten years and predicted that the disappearance of free land which would come by 1900 would alter the history of both Europe and the United States. "The history of Europe we may well say would have been entirely different from what it has been during the last century but for the new countries. It is difficult indeed to over-estimate the extent to which the existence of a new field for population has dominated the recent economic history of Europe. We are so accustomed to a set of economic circumstances in which population . . . finds practically unlimited means of expansion, that we can hardly understand economists like Malthus who were oppressed by the only too evident limits which nature, at the time he wrote, had apparently set.

"It seems impossible, however, not to see that a period in which the pressure of limits to growth and expansion may again be felt is not far off. . . . We are in measurable distance of very great changes."—Pp. 536–37.

have an average of 148 acres instead of 24. One of the important aspects of modern times has been the flow of population from the Metropolis into the frontiers with the result that the population increased and the man-land ratio began to climb from its low of less than 5 to 1, slowly at first but more rapidly as time went on, until in the decade from 1920 to 1930 it passed the point it registered in Europe prior to 1500. The surplus of land is no more, and noting this led Dean Inge in 1938 to remark that "the house is full." By 1940 the big house was much fuller than the little house was in 1500.[5]   (8)

Capital, the third factor in the boom, will be considered in two forms, as gold and silver and as Things, meaning goods and commodities. Our task is to show that here, as in land, the surplus came largely from the frontier. At the starting point in 1500 the Metropolis was short of both these forms of wealth. There is no way of knowing the exact amount of gold and silver in the Metropolis, but we do know that the production was small, and the scanty supply of precious metals had a way of drifting off to the Orient never to return. It is estimated by Michel Chevalier that all Europe had a little less than $200,000,000.[6] Certainly there was not enough to serve the needs of exchange much of which was carried on by barter or to give rise to erudite theories of a money economy. By 1500 the Spaniards had cracked the treasure houses of the New World and set a stream of gold and silver flowing into the Metropolis that continued without abatement for 150 years and that still continues. The results were instantaneous. This flood of treasure, the amount of which will be noticed shortly, changed all the relations that had existed between man and money, between gold and a bushel of wheat or a *fanega* of barley. It set the whole Metropolis in a frenzy of daring and adventure which gave character to the age. But, even so, the gold and silver were of less importance than the form of wealth that was to follow.   (9)

Fortunately, the data on the amount of gold and silver produced in the

---

[5] Man-land ratio in the Metropolis was 26.7 people per square mile. In the Metropolis plus the frontier after 1500, the man-land ratio was as follows:

1650	4.8
1750	6.5
1800	9.0
1850	13.9
1900	23.5
1930	29.5
1940	34.8

A comparison of the figures after 1500 and for 1930 is significant. It is interesting to observe that at the last date the Western World was gripped in depression—a coincidence no doubt, but perhaps of some significance. The above ratios are based on a study by Betty Brooke Eakle, "The Frontier and Population: A Study of the Influence of the New World on Population Growth," unpublished Master's thesis, University of Texas, 1948, p. 70.

[6] Michel Chevalier, *Remarks on the Production of the Precious Metals and on the Depreciation of Gold* (London: Smith Elder & Co., 1853), p. 21. Chevalier's estimate of the total supply of gold and silver in 1492 was slightly less than $200,000,000:

Gold	$ 56,843,000
Silver	139,756,050
Total	$196,599,050

world since 1493 is available. Compared with the pre-Columbian period, the amount is so great that it has been commented on by historians and economists of all Western nations. What is important for the present study is the place of origin, the geographical source of the surplus. The total production of gold in ounces up to 1940 is 1,374,941,037. The total of silver for the same period is 17,253,108,920 ounces. The modern value up to 1934 may be arrived at in dollars by multiplying the number of ounces of gold by $20.67, and the number of ounces of silver by $1.38 per ounce until 1701, after which market values are used. After the devaluation of the dollar in 1934, the value in dollars is obtained by multiplying the number of ounces of gold by $35.00. If we accept the old basis, the amount of gold produced since 1493 would be worth $28,415,448,098; but if we accept the new basis adopted in 1934, the same amount at $35.00 per ounce would have a value of $48,122,936,295. Actual value used here is $31,927,983,709. This is arrived at by taking gold produced prior to 1934 at $20.67 per ounce and that produced since 1934 at $35.00 per ounce. The production of silver would, at $0.8958 per ounce, have a value of $15,454,326,543. The total value of both gold and silver would be $47,382,310,252, an increase on the estimated value for 1500 of 24,101 per cent. Assuming that the Western World today has $31.98 billion of gold, each of the 800,000,000 inhabitants could have on an average of $39.975. Each individual could have about twenty times the amount of money in gold dollars that he had in 1500. If the silver is added, each of the 800,000,000 inhabitants would have approximately $60 or thirty times the amount per individual in 1500.   (10)

The spectacular nature of the first influx of wealth in the form of precious metals should not obscure the fact that it was but the initial wave of wealth or capital washing back from the Great Frontier onto the Metropolis. Wave followed wave in endless succession in the form of material things, and each deposit left the Metropolis richer than before. Unfortunately the amount of material goods cannot be measured because men were not so careful of their records here as they were in respect to gold and silver. It is known that prior to 1500 the people of the Metropolis had little to wear and hardly enough to eat, and that after 1500 their condition gradually and constantly improved until quite recent times. South America sent them coffee and Africa cocoa and the West Indies sent them sugar to sweeten it. Strange and flavorsome fruits came from the tropics. From primeval forests came ship timbers, pitch and tar with which to build the fleets for merchants and warriors. North America sent furs for the rich and cotton for the poor so that all could have more than one garment. It sent the potato which, adapted to the Metropolis, became second to bread as the staff of life. It gave corn, or Indian maize, and rich lands on which to grow it, and in time hides and beef from the plains and pampas of the New World. Everywhere in Europe from the royal palaces to the humble cottages men smoked

American tobacco and in the soothing smoke they dreamed of far countries, wealth, and adventure. Scientists brought home strange plants and herbs and made plant experiment stations in scores of European gardens. In South America they found the bark of a tree from which quinine was derived to cure the plague of malaria and another plant which was sent to the East Indies to establish the rubber industry and add to the fortunes of Holland and Britain. No, it is not possible to measure the amount of goods flowing from the frontier into the Metropolis, but it can be said that the frontier hung like a horn of plenty over the Metropolis and emptied out on it an avalanche of wealth beyond human comprehension, almost beyond the dreams of the most avaricious. Men have not seen this great interplay because they have insisted on cutting the Metropolis up into fragments which they called nations and states, insisted on cutting the frontier up into fragments called colonies and empires. What they have not seen is that the influence of the frontier on the Metropolis was indivisible, having little relation to who claimed what. The Spanish gold prospered England and Holland and France, and English sugar sweetened coffee and tea all over the continent.[7] (11)

We have now examined each of the three factors involved in the boom of the modern Western world. We have shown that the Metropolis furnished the population, and that the population did not increase rapidly until near the opening of the nineteenth century. The frontier furnished the *excess* of the other two factors, land and capital, and it was this excess, this additional amount of real and potential wealth, which incited the acts of appropriation that created a boom condition. It is the ratio between the quantity of land and capital of all kinds and the number of people which furnishes indisputable proof that conditions were highly favorable to an era of exceptional prosperity and economic progress. This excess of wealth over population does not mean that a boom was inevitable, but it does mean that if the society had the acquisitive instinct and the necessary skills and techniques, it would find in the new abundance unusual opportunities to satisfy its acquisitive desires and to develop its techniques through experienced practice. It happened that in Europe at that period, the acquisitive instinct was highly developed, the techniques for a beginning were present, and so the boom got promptly under way. (12)

If we assume that the boom came about because wealth suddenly be-

---

[7] For an account of the effects of the New World on one European country, the reader should consult James E. Gillespie's excellent study, *The Influence of Oversea Expansion on England to 1700* (New York: Columbia University Press, 1920). Gillespie takes into account the influence of the Orient as well as that of the frontier as defined in this study.

Cornelius Walford has found that from the year 1000 to 1600 there was an average of thirteen famines per year. By contrast, he records three in the seventeenth century, four in the eighteenth century, and two in the nineteenth century, prior to 1879.—Cornelius Walford, *The Famines of the World: Past and Present* (London: 1879).

There is no famine recorded for England between 1880 and 1900.

came available, increasing in quantity out of all proportion to increase in population, then we may assume that the boom will continue as long as the quantity of wealth to be had is abundant and out of proportion to the number of people. To tell the story of the relationship between wealth and population over a period of more than four centuries would be a complicated task. We can, however, show graphically what the relationship has been between population and land and between population and capital in the form of gold and silver, all of which factors can be measured with reasonable accuracy. What we cannot measure is the quantity of goods (Things) *produced* at a given time because the records on annual production of goods are not available. Even though we cannot measure the annual production of that form of wealth classed as Things or commodities, we can make some reasonable guesses as to the relative volume of this production by examining the economic theory that dominated economic thought in a given age.   (13)

Let us then set up four categories, each of which will be represented quantitatively by the height of the column. The categories are:

1. Population (measurable)
2. Land (measurable)
3. Gold and Silver (measurable)
4. Things, Goods or Commodities (not measurable)

The quantity of each of the above categories may be indicated by a column, and the heights of the respective columns at any date will reveal a certain relationship or ratio. It should be noted that categories 2, 3, and 4 represent wealth in some form, and the main relationship we are after is that between category 1 and the other three, i.e., between population and the total quantity of wealth. It should be observed that the land area remains the same throughout. The other three categories show a constant increase, and it is the difference in the *rate* of increase that is important. The base for beginning the calculation is 1500, and the amount of population, land, gold and silver, and Things on hand in 1500 is the unit of measurement. The height of a column is a multiple of this base, rather than the absolute amount. The land column rises quickly to about six times the original base, and remains fixed throughout the period. The population column represents the total population of European origin in the Western World at given dates. The gold and silver column is accumulative, no deduction being made for loss or destruction of these metals. There was, of course, some loss, but when we take into consideration the total amount of gold on hand at any given time, and compare it with the accumulated production up to that time, it appears that the actual loss was inconsiderable. The unrecorded gold probably more than compensates for the loss and destruction. At any rate, the loss, whatever it was, would not change to any extent the relationship of gold and silver to people. We saw that in 1500 each individual would have only $2, but the gold supply of $24,000,000,000 now buried in Kentucky would give each of the 80,000,000 people in the Western World $30 each, not to mention gold reserves in other nations and that absorbed by industry. (14)

With this explanation we are ready to examine the relationship between the population and the three categories of wealth. They are each represented in 1500 by small rectangles, the Things rectangle being in special design to show that we have no knowledge as to the amount of production. We only assume the amount in 1500 to represent 100 per cent. Therefore our graph would appear in this form:

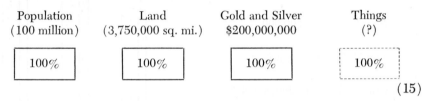

Population (100 million)	Land (3,750,000 sq. mi.)	Gold and Silver $200,000,000	Things (?)
100%	100%	100%	100%

(15)

The four symbols, which merely represent 100 per cent of what was on hand, imply that a balance had been struck prior to the opening of the New World. In the preceding figure, the disturbance of this balance is apparent as we record the situation at intervals throughout modern history. By 1600 the population had not changed appreciably. The land area had increased to more than 600 per cent, and the gold and silver had increased to 855 per cent.[8] Since we have no knowledge of the production of Things, we cannot be certain as to the height the fourth column should be. It is safe to assume that it would stand below the land column, and, as indicated by the price revolution, far below the precious metals column. The popularity, and the practicality, of the mercantile theory until well into the eighteenth century, may be explained by the fact that Things had not yet begun to flow from the frontiers in sufficient quantity to free the people from an intense desire to have the luxuries from the Orient, luxuries which could be obtained only in return for gold and silver.[9] (16)

The situation in 1700 shows no significant change. The population column is beginning to creep upward, the land column remains the same, but the gold and silver column rises to 1,984 per cent of what it was in 1500. The Things column is mounting, but probably is still only a little ahead of land. By 1800 the population column has a little more than doubled, the precious metals have shot up to 3,786 per cent, and the Things column was

---

[8] The percentage figures for land and precious metals are arrived at by adding the new land and the new treasure to what was on hand. Population is, of course, not subject to this treatment.

[9] It will surprise some economists, and many historians, to find the much abused mercantile theory treated as a sound and practical one for the age it served.

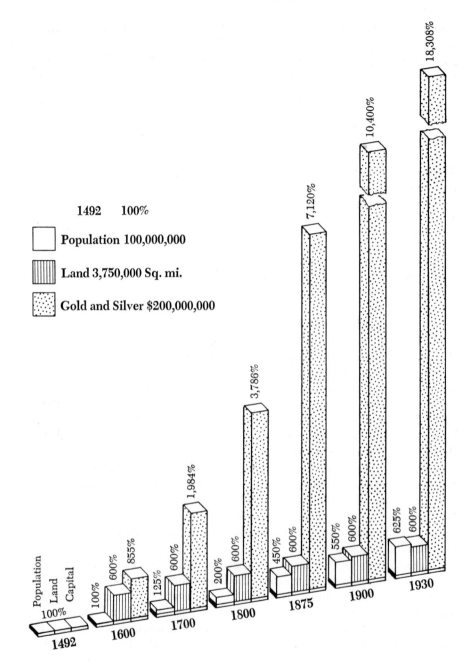

From Harper's Magazine

The Relation of Population to Land and Wealth

The chart illustrates the manner in which the Great Frontier changed the ratio between the number of people on the one hand and the amount of land and of the precious metals on the other at different periods throughout the modern age. A study of these ratios will indicate clearly that a boom was in progress as measured by the excess of land and the excess of precious metals in proportion to population. It will be noted that by 1930 the population column had risen above the land column, indicating that the excess of land has passed away. In the text reference is made to a fourth column, representing Things or commodities, the real wealth. Since the height of this column cannot be determined, it is not included in the chart, but may be imagined in relation to the others. It is suggested that its height was a strong factor in determining the prevailing economic theory of a given time. It is probable that prior to 1700 the Things column was lower than the precious-metals column, explaining the price revolution and making valid the mercantile theory. In the eighteenth century it rose above the precious-metals column, introducing an age of abundance, and making tenable for a long period the theory of laissez faire. The theory of laissez faire was in its turn rendered untenable by the recent rise of the population column above the land column.

almost certainly much higher, and had been since about 1720. This tremendous increase in Things made the old money supply inadequate, even with all its increases, led to the wide adoption of credit to supplement hard money, and prepared the way for the abandonment of the mercantile theory and the adoption of the economic theory of laissez faire. It is only when Things are abundant that the principle of laissez faire can be applied with practicality. By 1875 there was no change in the relation of population to land and capital, except that the excess of land had been reduced and the excess of gold and silver had continued to increase. By this time the industrial revolution had speeded up the production of Things enormously so that the Things column must have been very high indeed. This was the Victorian age when the white man's burden was a real joy.   (17)

By 1900 something of great significance was in the offing, and that was the fact that population had risen almost to the height of the land column, 550 as against 600. The gold and silver column stood at 10,400 per cent, and without doubt the Things column was much higher. By 1930 the significant thing had happened. The population column stood *above* the land column, at 625. This meant many things: That the excess of land furnished by the frontier no longer existed in relation to population; that the bars to immigration from the Metropolis to the frontier countries would go up everywhere; and that the excluded nations who had formerly had an outlet for their surplus populations would demand living room, and failing to find it, would radically alter their forms of government and undertake to gain by force the privileges to which they had long been accustomed. It meant that so far as the Western World was concerned it was back to the man-land ratio which obtained in Europe prior to the opening of the frontiers. It meant more than that, because population was increasing at breakneck speed with the result that by 1940 there were about 34.8 people per square mile instead of 26.7 as in 1500. It meant that in terms of 1500 the big house was fuller than the small house had been four centuries earlier. It may be an accident that the world depression came in 1929, just before the 1930 census revealed the return of the land-man ratio to approximately what it was just before the frontier precipitated the boom.   (18)

It is quite clear that if the existence of an excess of land in proportion to population was a factor in producing the boom, then after 1930 that factor ceased to operate in that direction. Where else could the boom come from? Superficially, it might seem to come from the excess of gold and silver which in 1930 had risen to the astronomical figure of 18,308 per cent of what it was in 1500. A knowledge of elementary economics, or plain common sense, tells us that this is not true, that gold and silver are practically useless except for what they will procure. Things are of utmost importance, such things as food, clothing, and shelter, and therefore we must come at last to our column of Things. The boom, if it continues, can exist and continue only if the column of Things remains high above population so that there will be enough for everybody.   (19)

The abundance of Things, and our great facility in making them available, obscures a fundamental truth which we need to see very clearly if we are to have any hope of meeting the main problem confronting Western civilization today. That basic truth is that the Things which are so abundant, even the gold and silver itself, rest upon the land and are derived from it. The land has only so much to offer, and when it is crowded, it has less to offer each one than when it exists in excess. Regardless of any techniques which may be developed to extract more from the land, there is a limit beyond which we cannot go; and if our techniques speed up the process of utilization and destruction, as they are now doing, they hasten the day when the substance on which they feed and on which a swollen population temporarily subsists will approach scarcity or exhaustion. Then the scholars will look back on the age when the Golden Door opened, and men marched out to the Great Frontier to create the greatest boom that the world has known; they will make myths and legends about it, and in poetry and literature express their poignant yearning for New Frontiers. They will see the frontier as the great factor in the age called modern, see it clearly as the lost factor which they would so love to find.   (20)

Sir Dennis William Brogan

(1900–   )

BROGAN is a professor of political science at Cambridge University and Fellow of Corpus Christi College, Oxford. A member of numerous social and professional associations in England, France, and the United States, he has written mainly on contemporary France and contemporary America—for example, The French Nation *(1957) and* American Aspects *(1964).*

■ *America Is Made*

IN THE COURSE of conquering America and so making Americans, habits were adopted out of urgent necessity which may have survived that necessity. There was, for example, the need for overstatement. To get settlers to move to America it was necessary to paint "America the golden" in very golden colors indeed. Very skilled hands undertook this necessary task: good prose writers like Richard Hakluyt; good or goodish poets like Michael Drayton; good story-tellers of the "when I was in Transylvania" school like Captain John Smith.   (1)

And once the voyage was made, the hazard of new fortunes undertaken, pride, exultation at one's own daring, recurrent optimism as new dreams replaced the old, led to the constant "sale" of America to the old world. For the genuinely adventurous type, for the man and woman whom nature had made ready for America, the exultation and the pride were genuine. Those who did not share in this pride and exultation were probably ill adapted anyway; they died or returned home or kept quiet. They had better, for from the beginning the settlers had no use for "knockers," for anybody who committed the crime of what was to be described in a later age as "selling America short."   (2)

The pioneer American had a real economic as well as emotional interest in growth, in encouraging the booster spirit. If he wanted to stay in the new settlement which he had chosen, he had an interest in other people's staying too. Only so could the profitable rise in values which he counted on be realized. Only so could money be borrowed on the future prosperity of the settlement. If the town refused to grow, if it, in fact, was written off as a failure and abandoned by any serious number of its residents, not only were the anticipated gains lost but real losses were suffered, especially after the Supreme Court put the federal government's power behind the claims of the buyers of municipal and county securities. It mattered little or nothing whether the loans had been prudently or even legally contracted; the Supreme Court, over the protests of that great Iowa jurist, Mr. Justice Miller, insisted on collection from the remaining inhabitants. And while the ingenious borrowers might be enjoying their capital gains in the interesting little town of Los Angeles, the less foresighted inhabitants of a town or county on the prairie were forced to pay or be sold up. They were in the position of a Russian village community under the Tsar from which a number of freed serfs had vanished, refusing to pay their share of the redemption price. Pessimism in such a world was treason. And as long as this boom spirit was flourishing, treason it remained. Thus, in a later age when the Florida land boom was collapsing, many communities made desperate, indeed magical efforts to persuade themselves and the world that values were holding up. And on July 4th, 1926, the city of St. Augustine, the oldest settlement in the United States, formally buried as an embodiment of that treasonable pessimism, "J. Fuller Gloom," with a funeral ceremony conducted according to the rites of the Chamber of Commerce.   (3)

But magic notwithstanding, land booms always burst. There have been few American cities in the last twenty years that have not had on their outskirts ambitious "developments" that have not come off at all, or have come off only after a long period of holding on. Sometimes, the holding on was no great strain. It may be assumed that the losses incurred during the period when only handsome street lamps and magnificent pavements marked most of the development of the old Rockefeller farm in Shaker Heights on the outskirts of Cleveland were no great strain on the Rockefeller fortune. But for less well-financed speculations, the period of holding on might be fatal. The first speculator has so often taken the rap. How few American railroads, how few New York hotels have not gone through the wringer! How profitable has been the job of receiver! Indeed, there have been times when the innocent investors have been forced to wonder whether "receiver"—meaning the recipient of stolen goods—was not merely a special case of "receiver" meaning the officer appointed by a complaisant court to take over and administer the bankrupt assets of great and small concerns alike. It would be unkind to say on what American railroad this incident occurred, but when I complimented a friend of mine on the improved service on his local railroad, he replied, with no conscious irony: "Oh, service has been swell since it went into receivership; the management can afford to spend money now that it hasn't got to worry about the stockholders." This was a commuter's view, not a stockholder's, but there has always been among Americans, including the luckless investors themselves, a philosophical acceptance of the fact that somebody must hold the bag for the great economic improvements of modern America. (4)

The American farmer is perhaps rather less philosophical than the urban investor. He thinks he has a right to expect not a good living or a good cash income but a permanent and certain increase in the selling value of his land. It is this expectation that makes him hold on through drought and storm flood and tornado. On this expectation he borrows money and, as a permanent borrower, he has no fear of inflation; like the small boy in the story, far from being troubled by the thought he simply loves it. He knows, in a general, intellectual way, that somebody will have to be the last buyer, but he hopes and trusts that it won't be he. He will be living off the profits, perhaps invested in new lands, perhaps taken out in mortgages or in a rent that takes full account of the presumed value of the land, future as well as present. And the American absentee owner is not necessarily somebody like the late Lord Clanricarde, celebrated miser, tyrant, and last chief of the elder line of the Burkes, but a mild, modest ex-farmer living in decent comfort in the neighborhood of Los Angeles, raising the moral tone of the neighborhood and swelling the crowds at Iowa picnics. He may be simply a resident in a small Iowa town, able to afford a trip to St. Petersburg to pitch horseshoes in the winter sun of Florida. Or he may be like the Vermont farmer who, when asked by a scornful Midwestern visitor what crops were raised on those stony hills, replied: "The chief crop is those good five per cent Iowa mortgages we hold." The web of speculation, of optimism, of boosting is cast over all the nation. (5)

But, of course, there was a real interest in persuading people to stay. The local banker made his money by backing rising values; he lost if they *all* fell. The local doctor who, like John Hay's father, chose the wrong town to settle in, paid for it in a life of comparative shallows and miseries. Hence the importance of prophetic statistics. "Albuquerque 40,000 by 1930." "Hamlet is a fine town, population 800." I don't think Albuquerque made it by 1930, and I suspect that Hamlet had slightly inflated its figures. But editors of encyclopedias and guide-books have got to accept the necessity of printing not only the federal census figures, but the local estimate—which is always larger; millions of Americans appear to sleep out of town on census day. (6)

One way of anchoring a settler is to get him married and settled down to raising a family. Hence the emphasis on good schools; lavish expenditure on school buildings is not necessarily a totally disinterested tribute to education; it is a bribe to wandering parents. But of course it would not be a bribe to parents who had not the inherited or acquired New England belief in education as a good thing. Even more effective anchorage was investment in a house—or, as the Americans say, a home. And expensive, highly ornamental homes were proof that the settlement was taking root. As Mark Twain put it long ago (in *Life on the Mississippi*): "Every town and village along that vast stretch of double river frontage had a best dwelling, finest dwelling, mansion—the home of its wealthiest and most conspicuous citizen." They still have, although today one would hardly expect to be believed if he asserted what Mark Twain asserted with no apparent fear of contradiction: "Not a bathroom in the house; and no visitor likely to come along who has ever seen one."   (7)

These optimistic exhibitions of civic pride have long been a British jest, a jest which sophisticated Americans have more recently joined in. But most Americans are still touchy on the subject of local improvements, as I discovered when I made an innocent joke about the Chicago drainage canal in a London paper. The European visitor lacks the eye of faith. Thus Dickens made Cairo, Illinois, the butt of his angry wit in his picture of "Eden" in *Martin Chuzzlewit;* but twenty years later, Anthony Trollope found that picture too flattering. "I doubt whether that author ever visited Cairo in mid-winter, and I am sure he never visited Cairo when Cairo was the seat of an American army. Had he done so, his love of truth would have forbidden him to presume that even Mark Tapley could have enjoyed himself in such an Eden.[1] But only a quarter of a century after Trollope played the sourpuss, Cairo was given a big hand by a local resident. "Three years ago people said all the hateful things they could about Cairo. Now they are lavish in their praises. The paper says we'll monopolize all the trade of the Mississippi, Ohio, Tennessee and Cumberland Rivers. Our new grain elevator is one of the largest in the world, new railroads are constantly striking us. We've the most magnificent hotel (run on the grandest scale) in this part of the country, telephone system, new Opera House, elegant one, going up, street-cars soon to be running, and we are altogether citified."[2] So wrote a very bright, very nice local girl, a girl nicer and certainly much brighter than any Dickens or Trollope heroine I can remember. Cairo did not become a new St. Louis or Chicago, but "Maud" liked it and believed in it and what was good enough for her should have been good enough for any reasonable body.   (8)

This conception of growth as everybody's business, everybody's interest, is deep-rooted in the American national psychology. The bulky real estate

---

1 Anthony Trollope: *North America*, Vol. II, p. 121.
2 *Maud*, edited and arranged for publication by Richard Lee Strout (Macmillan), p. 22.

supplements of the Sunday papers are no doubt largely kept going as an advertising revenue producer, but they would produce no advertising and no revenue if no one read them. The Englishman, hidden behind his hedge or wall, is not interested in his neighbor's house, and the idea of wanting to read about houses bought, sold, or built by total strangers is not even funny; it is merely absurd. But to an American, it is not only important, it is comforting, it is gratifying to know that other people are improving your home town; even people who have no personal economic stake in the rise of real estate values feel the same kind of interest that makes a motherly woman smile with genuine amiability on the children of total strangers. The very linguistic difference between "house" and "home" is significant. All Americans who live in houses, not apartments, live in homes; the Englishman lives in *his* home, but all his neighbors live in houses or flats. (9)

The interest of the American in community growth is not confined to homes. He is far more aware of the size and importance of public and business buildings than anybody in England is. To the inhabitants of Minneapolis, the Foshay Tower was a symbol of growth, of maturity, that did not lose its value when the too enterprizing *entrepreneur* went to jail. But in London, people do not long notice what new buildings have gone up and, after a month or two, find it hard to remember what stood on the site cleared by a German bomb. The idle, the curious are no more numerous in America than elsewhere, but those gazers on men-at-work on a new building whom the Americans call "sidewalk superintendents" are a more representative class of citizen than their English fellows. When John D. Rockefeller, Jr., built a covered-in observation post for the comfort of these spectators during the winter when Rockefeller Center was being built, he was not only acting with genuine American hospitality, he was recognizing a genuine and generous American interest in building as such. It is not at all unlikely that, among the spectators who watched with approving interest the new buildings which were rising with a speed that, by our standards, is really not very much slower than the speed with which Aladdin built his palace for the Princess, were stockholders in the Empire State Building. And they had nothing but a truly American tradition to encourage them to cheer the progress of a rival monument to the passion for the bigger and better —or, at any rate, bigger. (10)

In pioneering conditions, personal credit—credit for courage, for competence, for industry, for economic promise—was all important. A pioneering community was composed of people all of whom were extending credit to each other as well as to the locality. When conditions were a little better, a little more settled, credit in the ordinary sense became important, but it was personal, too. The village banker in America was not in the position of the village usurer in Europe. His debtors could walk out on him; they were not anchored to the spot by tradition, by hereditary investment in land and family pride, by the difficulty of finding any place to go—except America. Indeed in Ireland, classic land of the village usurer, lending money to pay fares to America was one of the chief business opportunities—and risks. So there was a mutual assessment of need and greed. But the village banker, unlike the European village moneylender, was himself living on credit; and when it failed him, he might be the sudden migrant, leaving his debtors legally tied to his creditors, while he sought fresh woods and pastures new. Altogether, moneylending and borrowing was more of a sport in America than it was in Europe, and banking, in the West at any rate, called for rather different qualities from what it demands from a citizen of London or a financier of Wall Street. Mr. Ogden Nash's gloomy reflections on the parentage of great American bankers are not, as far as I know, borne out by the facts, but they fit the national tradition of classing bankers with the other robber barons—though it must be remembered that these robber barons were highly popular as long as they shared or were believed to be sharing the spoil.   (11)

But one result of this necessity for and acceptance of the conditions of credit is that publicity must be accepted. If you want (as most American women do want) to have a charge account or a series of charge accounts, you must submit your husband's credit rating to professional and competent investigation. It is of little use for the American husband to try to obey the old maxim of folk-wisdom that bids a husband keep secret from his wife the amount of money he has, if she can, in effect, make a pretty good guess by trying to stretch his credit at a department store. The general acceptance of debt, however disguised, as a normal state of existence for many worthy people no doubt leads to ostentatious expenditure, to conspicuous waste, as it leads to non-functional automobile design and other specimens of art for show's sake. But it also leads to a fish-bowl existence in which the English passion for privacy would offend public opinion and constitute a luxury that only a very large independent income could support. What I have been told of life in official circles in India—that the public knowledge of the incomes of all the nice people cuts out certain kinds of ostentatious expenditure—applies to many American communities, too. They all try to keep up with the Joneses, but they are local Joneses, with accounts at local banks and stores. The attempt to keep up with remote Joneses, to ape the manners and expenditure of remote social circles, and the refusal to admit that there is in that community anybody with whom it is really possible to associate on terms of equality—this is more common in Streatham than in Bronxville. American life imposes respect for the human interest of the community in your private affairs; a refusal to conform at that level is, in fact, a vote of censure on the community which it has no intention of submitting to. You can defy it, but at the cost of being laughed at, not admired—and possibly at the cost of having the local bank wonder if anybody so high hat can be a good risk. (12)

It has to be admitted that this national spirit was often hard on dissenters—dissenters, that is, from the religion of economic and political optimism. A pioneer community could afford to house very hard citizens; it often benefited by the energies of persons who, to use modern terms, "cut their ethical corners rather fine." Courage, enterprise, ingenuity—these were qualities from which everybody benefited, or nearly everybody. So, in many ways, the frontier settlement was very tolerant. But it was not tolerant of the man whose arrogance or pride or morbid pessimism made him a nuisance in a society where all had to hang together if they were not to starve or be scalped separately. Pennsylvania could afford some Quakers, but not too many, in a great crisis like the French and Indian War; but the Revolutionary party in 1776 could not afford to be tolerant of too many Tories (i.e., Loyalists), since it was by no means certain how the majority would react to a strong lead. It was necessary, therefore, by legal or illegal violence, to give them a strong lead—and on one side only. (13)

Religious dissent was more tolerable—as long as it was not dissent from the social creed of the growing nation, or disbelief in economic prosperity, or objection to military service, or real belief in the imminent end of the world. And dissenters or even "atheists" or "deists" were often very energetic and valuable citizens, promoters, and fighters. Indeed, it is possible that as things settled down, as communities acquired more coherence, the role of the religious or political dissenter got harder, since his other qualities became less necessary. But there remained legitimate grounds of dissent. After the Civil War any well-established village in New England or the northern Middle West could afford a town drunkard, a town atheist, and a few Democrats. (14)

But a habit grew up in which it was necessary to call on some courage and perhaps on some independent economic resources before defying the local folkways. The very friendliness of American life made the dissenter more conspicuous. In a country where minding your own business is *de rigueur*, nobody need care what that business is. But in a country where all life is or should be lived pretty publicly, there is more intolerance of an individual eccentricity which is being continually thrust under the eyes of your neighbors. The high degree of social integration of a small American city (above a certain income level) plays its part, too. The tragedy of Mr. John O'Hara's *Appointment in Samarra* involves more than the weakness of the hero; it involves a life made intolerable if the country club and the local business community are mobilized against you. The highly individual character is a misfit in a community in any country, whether his weakness is genius or madness. If he has a private income like Cézanne, he may pursue his vision unmolested. But what Cézanne called *"les grappins"* are more tenaciously extended in America than elsewhere; they put out their tentacles more determinedly and a persistent evasion of their embraces is more offensive than it would be in a French or English town with no common social life anyway. There is truth in the picture of the Faustlike Professor in the film *On the Avenue:*

> *He attracted some attention*
> *When he found the fourth dimension.*
> *But he ain't got rhythm*
> *No one's with him.*
> *He's the lonesomest man in town.* (15)

And since the common interest of the community is still assumed to be economic growth, attained by the "American way," the dissenter from the end, or the means, is especially open to suspicion. But 1929 wrought a great change, probably a permanent one. The sponsors of the old programs have not quite the same confident ring in their voices; too many things have been tried and have failed; the "American way" has been found to be a term less precise than it seemed in the presidential election of 1928 when the problem of poverty was solved and when the good citizens should have been busily expanding their garages to take the second car that was coming along with tomorrow's sunrise. Senator Robert Taft can, with a clear conscience, advocate the putting of the fiscal policy of the nation in the hands of practical men, since the last two Republican Secretaries of the Treasury are dead, but the memory of 1929–33 is a ghost that still walks. New Mellons and new Millses are ready in the wings, but the call has not yet come. (16)

Nevertheless, the strident tone of American controversy, though not unparalleled in modern British history, is a reminder of a national tradition, pragmatically justified, in which dissent, especially continuous pessimistic crabbing, was near to treason. So the High School of Muncie teaches loyalty to Muncie as well as to the United States, and in less straightforward communities something of the same spirit prevails in more sophisticated forms. (17)

Mary McCarthy

(1912–   )

MARY McCARTHY, twice holder of Guggenheim Fellowships, is an editor, teacher, drama critic, traveller, social commentator, novelist, and mistress of one of the sprightliest contemporary prose styles. Her travel books include Venice Observed *(1956) and* The Stones of Florence *(1959). A graduate of Vassar, her novel* The Group *(1963) started the telephones of alumnae (and others) ringing. She has taught for brief periods at Bard College and at Sarah Lawrence.*

■ *America the Beautiful:*
The Humanist in the Bathtub

A VISITING EXISTENTIALIST wanted recently to be taken to dinner at a really American place. This proposal, natural enough in a tourist, disclosed a situation thoroughly unnatural. Unless the visiting lady's object was suffering, there was no way of satisfying her demand. Sukiyaki joints, chop suey joints, Italian table d'hôte places, French provincial restaurants with the menu written on a slate, Irish chophouses, and Jewish delicatessens came abundantly to mind, but these were not what the lady wanted. Schrafft's or the Automat would have answered, yet to take her there would have been to turn oneself into a tourist and to present America as a spectacle—a *New Yorker* cartoon or a savage drawing in the *New Masses*. It was the beginning of an evening of humiliations. The visitor was lively and eager; her mind lay open and orderly, like a notebook ready for impressions. It was not long, however, before she shut it up with a snap. We had no recommendations to make to her. With movies, plays, current books, it was the same

story as with the restaurants. *Open City, Les Enfants du Paradis*, Oscar
Wilde, a reprint of Henry James were *paté de maison* to this lady who
wanted the definitive flapjack. She did not believe us when we said that
there were no good Hollywood movies, no good Broadway plays—only
curios; she was merely confirmed in her impression that American intellectuals were "negative."   (1)

Yet the irritating thing was that we did not feel negative. We admired
and liked our country; we preferred it to that imaginary America, land of
the *peaux rouges* of Caldwell and Steinbeck, dumb paradise of violence and
the detective story, which had excited the sensibilities of our visitor and of
the up-to-date French literary world. But to found our preference, to locate
it materially in some admirable object or institution, such as Chartres, say,
or French café life, was for us, that night at any rate, an impossible undertaking. We heard ourselves saying that the real America was elsewhere, in
the white frame houses and church spires of New England; yet we knew that
we talked foolishly—we were not Granville Hicks and we looked ludicrous
in his opinions. The Elevated, half a block away, interrupting us every time
a train passed, gave us the lie on schedule, every eight minutes. But if the
elm-shaded village green was a false or at least an insufficient address for the
genius loci we honored, where then was it to be found? Surveyed from the
vantage point of Europe, this large continent seemed suddenly deficient in
objects of virtue. The Grand Canyon, Yellowstone Park, Jim Hill's mansion
in St. Paul, Jefferson's Monticello, the blast furnaces of Pittsburgh, Mount
Rainier, the yellow observatory at Amherst, the little-theater movement in
Cleveland, Ohio, a Greek revival house glimpsed from a car window in a
lost river-town in New Jersey—these things were too small for the size of
the country. Each of them, when pointed to, diminished in interest with
the lady's perspective of distance. There was no sight that in itself seemed
to justify her crossing of the Atlantic.   (2)

If she was interested in "conditions," that was a different matter. There
are conditions everywhere; it takes no special genius to produce them. Yet
would it be an act of hospitality to invite a visitor to a lynching? Unfortunately, nearly all the "sights" in America fall under the head of conditions. Hollywood, Reno, the sharecroppers' homes in the South, the mining
towns of Pennsylvania, Coney Island, the Chicago stockyards, Macy's, the
Dodgers, Harlem, even Congress, the forum of our liberties, are spectacles
rather than sights, to use the term in the colloquial sense of "Didn't he
make a holy spectacle of himself?" An Englishman of almost any political
opinion can show a visitor through the Houses of Parliament with a sense
of pride or at least of indulgence toward his national foibles and traditions.
The American, if he has a spark of national feeling, will be humiliated by
the very prospect of a foreigner's visit to Congress—these, for the most part,
illiterate hacks whose fancy vests are spotted with gravy, and whose speeches,

hypocritical, unctuous, and slovenly, are spotted also with the gravy of political patronage, these persons are a reflection on the democratic process rather than of it; they expose it in its underwear. In European legislation, we are told, a great deal of shady business goes on in private, behind the scenes. In America, it is just the opposite, anything good, presumably, is accomplished *in camera*, in the committee rooms.   (3)

It is so with all our institutions. For the visiting European, a trip through the United States has, almost inevitably, the character of an exposé, and the American, on his side, is tempted by love of his country to lock the inquiring tourist in his hotel room and throw away the key. His contention that the visible and material America is not the real or the only one is more difficult to sustain than was the presumption of the "other" Germany behind the Nazi steel.   (4)

To some extent a citizen of any country will feel that the tourist's view of his homeland is a false one. The French will tell you that you have to go into their homes to see what the French people are really like. The intellectuals in the Left Bank cafés are not the real French intellectuals, etc., etc. In Italy, they complain that the tourist must not judge by the *ristorantes;* there one sees only black-market types. But in neither of these cases is the native really disturbed by the tourist's view of his country. If Versailles or Giotto's bell-tower in Florence do not tell the whole story, they are still not incongruous with it; you do not hear a Frenchman or an Italian object when these things are noticed by a visitor. With the American, the contradiction is more serious. He must, if he is to defend his country, repudiate its visible aspect almost entirely. He must say that its parade of phenomenology, its billboards, superhighways, even its skyscrapers, not only fail to represent the inner essence of his country but in fact contravene it. He may point, if he wishes, to certain beautiful objects, but here too he is in difficulties, for nearly everything that is beautiful and has not been produced by Nature belongs to the eighteenth century, to a past with which he has very little connection, and which his ancestors, in many or most cases, had no part in. Beacon Street and the Boston Common are very charming in the eighteenth-century manner, so are the sea captains' houses in the old Massachusetts ports, and the ruined plantations of Louisiana, but an American from Brooklyn or the Middle West or the Pacific Coast finds the style of life embodied in them as foreign as Europe; indeed, the first sensation of a Westerner, coming upon Beacon Hill and the gold dome of the State House, is to feel that at last he has traveled "abroad." The American, if he is to speak the highest truth about his country, must refrain from pointing at all. The virtue of American civilization is that it is unmaterialistic.   (5)

This statement may strike a critic as whimsical or perverse. Everybody knows, it will be said, that America has the most materialistic civilization in the world, that Americans care only about money, they have no time or talent for living; look at radio, look at advertising, look at life insurance, look at the tired businessman, at the Frigidaires and the Fords. In answer, the reader is invited first to look instead into his own heart and inquire whether he personally feels himself to be represented by these things, or whether he does not, on the contrary, feel them to be irrelevant to him, a necessary evil, part of the conditions of life. Other people, he will assume, care about them very much: the man down the street, the entire population of Detroit or Scarsdale, the back-country farmer, the urban poor or the rich. But he himself accepts these objects as imposed on him by a collective "otherness" of desire, an otherness he has not met directly but whose existence he infers from the number of automobiles, Frigidaires, or television sets he sees around him. Stepping into his new Buick convertible, he knows that he would gladly do without it, but imagines that to his neighbor, who is just backing *his* out of the driveway, this car is the motor of life. More often, however, the otherness is projected farther afield, onto a different class or social group, remote and alien. Thus the rich, who would like nothing better, they think, than for life to be a perpetual fishing trip with the trout grilled by a native guide, look patronizingly upon the whole apparatus of American civilization as a cheap Christmas present to the poor, and city people see the radio and the washing machine as the farm-wife's solace.   (6)

It can be argued, of course, that the subjective view is prevaricating, possession of the Buick being nine-tenths of the social law. But who has ever met, outside of advertisements, a true parishioner of this church of Mammon? A man may take pride in a car, and a housewife in her new sink or wallpaper, but pleasure in new acquisitions is universal and eternal; an Italian man with a new gold tooth, a French bibliophile with a new edition, a woman with a new baby, a philosopher with a new thought, all these people are rejoicing in progress, in man's power to enlarge and improve. Before men showed off new cars, they showed off new horses; it is alleged against modern man that he as an individual craftsman did not make the car; but his grandfather did not make the horse either. What is imputed to Americans is something quite different, an abject dependence on material possessions, an image of happiness as packaged by the manufacturer, content in a can. This view of American life is strongly urged by advertising agencies. We know the "others," of course, because we meet them every week in full force in *The New Yorker* or the *Saturday Evening Post,* those brightly colored families of dedicated consumers, waiting in unison on the porch for the dealer to deliver the new car, gobbling the new cereal ("Gee, Mom, is it good for you too?"), lining up to bank their paychecks, or fearfully anticipating the industrial accident and the insurance check that will "compen-sate" for it. We meet them also, more troll-like underground, in the subway placards, in the ferociously complacent One-A-Day family, and we hear their courtiers sing to them on the radio of Ivory or Supersuds. The thing, however, that repels us in these advertisements is their naïve falsity to life. Who are these advertising men kidding, besides the European tourist? Be-tween the tired, sad, gentle faces of the subway riders and the grinning Holy Families of the Ad-Mass, there exists no possibility of even a wishful identification. We take a vitamin pill with the hope of feeling (possibly) a little less tired, but the superstition of buoyant health emblazoned in the bright, ugly pictures has no more power to move us than the blood of St. Januarius. (7)

Familiarity has perhaps bred contempt in us Americans: until you have had a washing machine, you cannot imagine how little difference it will make to you. Europeans still believe that money brings happiness, witness the bought journalist, the bought politician, the bought general, the whole venality of European literary life, inconceivable in this country of the dol-lar. It is true that America produces and consumes more cars, soap, and bathtubs than any other nation, but we live among these objects rather than by them. Americans build skyscrapers; Le Corbusier worships them. Ehren-burg, our Soviet critic, fell in love with the Check-O-Mat in American rail-way stations, writing home paragraphs of song to this gadget—while de-ploring American materialism. When an American heiress wants to buy a man, she at once crosses the Atlantic. The only really materialistic people I have ever met have been Europeans. (8)

The strongest argument for the unmaterialistic character of American life is the fact that we tolerate conditions that are, from a materialistic point of view, intolerable. What the foreigner finds most objectionable in American life is its lack of basic comfort. No nation with any sense of ma-terial well-being would endure the food we eat, the cramped apartments we live in, the noise, the traffic, the crowded subways and buses. American life, in large cities, at any rate, is a perpetual assault on the senses and the nerves; it is out of asceticism, out of unworldliness, precisely, that we bear it. (9)

This republic was founded on an unworldly assumption, a denial of "the facts of life." It is manifestly untrue that all men are created equal; interpreted in worldly terms, this doctrine has resulted in a pseudo-equality, that is, in standardization, in an equality of things rather than of persons. The inalienable rights to life, liberty, and the pursuit of happiness appear, in practice, to have become the inalienable right to a bathtub, a flush toilet, and a can of Spam. Left-wing critics of America attribute this result to the intrusion of capitalism; right-wing critics see it as the logical dead end of democracy. Capitalism, certainly, now depends on mass production, which depends on large-scale distribution of uniform goods, till the consumer to-day is the victim of the manufacturer who launches on him a regiment of products for which he must make house-room in his soul. The buying impulse, in its original force and purity, was not nearly so crass, however, or so meanly acquisitive as many radical critics suppose. The purchase of a bathtub was the exercise of a spiritual right. The immigrant or the poor native American bought a bathtub, not because he wanted to take a bath, but because he wanted to be in a *position* to do so. This remains true in many fields today; possessions, when they are desired, are not wanted for their own sakes but as tokens of an ideal state of freedom, fraternity, and franchise. "Keeping up with the Joneses" is a vulgarization of Jefferson's concept, but it too is a declaration of the rights of man, and decidedly unfeasible and visionary. Where for a European, a fact is a fact, for us Americans, the real, if it is relevant at all, is simply symbolic appearance. We are a nation of twenty million bathrooms, with a humanist in every tub. One such humanist I used to hear of on Cape Cod had, on growing rich, installed two toilets side by side in his marble bathroom, on the model of the two-seater of his youth. He was a clear case of Americanism, hospitable, gregarious, and impractical, a theorist of perfection. Was his dream of the conquest of poverty a vulgar dream or a noble one, a material demand or a spiritual insistence? It is hard to think of him as a happy man, and in this too he is characteristically American, for the parity of the radio, the movies, and the washing machine has made Americans sad, reminding them of another parity of which these things were to be but emblems.   (10)

The American does not enjoy his possessions because sensory enjoyment was not his object, and he lives sparely and thinly among them, in the monastic discipline of Scarsdale or the barracks of Stuyvesant Town. Only among certain groups where franchise, socially speaking, has not been achieved, do pleasure and material splendor constitute a life-object and an occupation. Among the outcasts—Jews, Negroes, Catholics, homosexuals—excluded from the communion of ascetics, the love of fabrics, gaudy show, and rich possessions still anachronistically flaunts itself. Once a norm has been reached, differing in the different classes, financial ambition itself seems to fade away. The self-made man finds, to his anger, his son uninterested in money; you have shirtsleeves to shirtsleeves in three generations. The great financial empires are a thing of the past. Some recent immigrants —movie magnates and gangsters particularly—retain their acquisitiveness, but how long is it since anyone in the general public has murmured, wonderingly, "as rich as Rockefeller"?   (11)

If the dream of American fraternity had ended simply in this, the value of humanistic and egalitarian strivings would be seriously called into question. Jefferson, the Adamses, Franklin, Madison, would be in the position of Dostoevsky's Grand Inquisitor, who, desiring to make the Kingdom of God incarnate on earth, inaugurated the kingdom of the devil. If the nature of matter is such that the earthly paradise, once realized, becomes always the paradise of the earthly, and a spiritual conquest of matter becomes an enslavement of spirit, then the atomic bomb is, as has been argued, the logical result of the Enlightenment, and the land of opportunity is, pre-cisely, the land of death. This position, however, is a strictly materialist one, for it asserts the Fact of the bomb as the one tremendous truth: subjective attitudes are irrelevant; it does not matter what we think or feel; possession again in this case is nine-tenths of the law.   (12)

It must be admitted that there is a great similarity between the nation with its new bomb and the consumer with his new Buick. In both cases, there is a disinclination to use the product, stronger naturally in the case of the bomb, but somebody has manufactured the thing, and there seems to be no way *not* to use it, especially when everybody else will be doing so. Here again the argument of the "others" is invoked to justify our own pro-cedures: if we had not invented the bomb, the Germans would have; the Soviet Union will have it in a year, etc., etc. This is keeping up with the Joneses indeed, our national propagandists playing the role of the advertis-ing men in persuading us of the "others'" intentions.   (13)

It seems likely at this moment that we will find no way of not using the bomb, yet those who argue theoretically that this machine is the true ex-pression of our society leave us, in practice, with no means of opposing it. We must differentiate ourselves from the bomb if we are to avoid using it, and in private thought we do, distinguishing the bomb sharply from our daily concerns and sentiments, feeling it as an otherness that waits outside to descend on us, an otherness already destructive of normal life, since it prevents us from planning or hoping by depriving us of a future. And this inner refusal of the bomb is also a legacy of our past; it is a denial of the given, of the power of circumstances to shape us in their mold. Unfortu-nately, the whole asceticism of our national character, our habit of living in but not through an environment, our alienation from objects, prepares us to endure the bomb but not to confront it.   (13)

Passivity and not aggressiveness is the dominant trait of the American character. The movies, the radio, the superhighway have softened us up for the atom bomb; we have lived with them without pleasure, feeling them as a coercion on our natures, a coercion seemingly from nowhere and ex-pressing nobody's will. The new coercion finds us without the habit of pro-test; we are dissident but apart.   (15)

The very "negativeness," then, of American intellectuals is not a mark of their separation from our society, but a true expression of its separation from itself. We too are dissident but inactive. Intransigent on paper, in "real life" we conform; yet we do not feel ourselves to be dishonest, for to us the real life is rustling paper and the mental life is flesh. And even in our mental life we are critical and rather unproductive; we leave it to the "others," the best-sellers, to create.   (16)

The fluctuating character of American life must, in part, have been responsible for this dissociated condition. Many an immigrant arrived in this country with the most materialistic expectations, hoping, not to escape from a world in which a man was the sum of his circumstances, but to become a new sum of circumstances himself. But this hope was self-defeating; the very ease with which new circumstances were acquired left insufficient time for a man to live into them: all along a great avenue in Minneapolis the huge stone chateaux used to be dark at night, save for a single light in each kitchen, where the family still sat, Swedish-style, about the stove. The pressure of democratic thought, moreover, forced a rising man often, unexpectedly, to recognize that he was *not* his position: a speeding ticket from a village constable could lay him low. Like the agitated United Nations delegates who got summonses on the Merritt Parkway, he might find the shock traumatic: a belief had been destroyed. The effect of these combined difficulties turned the new American into a nomad, who camped out in his circumstances, as it were, and was never assimilated to them. And, for the native American, the great waves of internal migration had the same result. The homelessness of the American, migrant in geography and on the map of finance, is the whole subject of the American realists of our period. European readers see in these writers only violence and brutality. They miss not only the pathos but the nomadic virtues associated with it, generosity, hospitality, equity, directness, politeness, simplicity of relations—traits which, together with a certain gentle timidity (as of very *unpracticed* nomads), comprise the American character. Unobserved also is a peculiar nakedness, a look of being shorn of everything, that is very curiously American, corresponding to the spare wooden desolation of a frontier town and the bright thinness of the American light. The American character looks always as if it had just had a rather bad haircut, which gives it, in our eyes at any rate, a greater humanity than the European, which even among its beggars has an all too professional air.   (17)

The openness of the American situation creates the pity and the terror; status is not protection; life for the European is a career; for the American, it is a hazard. Slaves and women, said Aristotle, are not fit subjects for tragedy, but kings, rather, and noblemen, men, that is, not defined by circumstance but outside it and seemingly impervious. In America we have, subjectively speaking no slaves and no women; the efforts of *PM* and the Stalinized playwrights to introduce, like the first step to servitude, a national psychology of the "little man" have been, so far, unrewarding. The little man is one who is embedded in status; things can be done for and to him generically by a central directive; his happiness flows from statistics. This conception mistakes the national passivity for abjection. Americans will not eat this humble pie; we are still nature's noblemen. Yet no tragedy results, though the protagonist is everywhere; dissociation takes the place of conflict, and the drama is mute. (18)

This humanity, this plain and heroic accessibility, was what we would have liked to point out to the visiting Existentialist as our national glory. Modesty perhaps forbade and a lack of concrete examples—how could we point to ourselves? Had we done so she would not have been interested. To a European, the humanity of an intellectual is of no particular moment; it is the barber pole that announces his profession and the hair oil dispensed inside. Europeans, moreover, have no curiosity about American intellectuals; we are insufficiently representative of the brute. Yet this anticipated and felt disparagement was not the whole cause of our reticence. We were silent for another reason: we were waiting to be discovered. Columbus, however, passed on, and this, very likely, was the true source of our humiliation. But this experience also was peculiarly American. We all expect to be found in the murk of otherness; it looks to us very easy since *we* know we are there. Time after time, the explorers have failed to see us. We have been patient, for the happy ending is our national belief. Now, however, that the future has been shut off from us, it is necessary for us to declare ourselves, at least for the record. (19)

What it amounts to, in verity, is that we are the poor. This humanity we would claim for ourselves is the legacy, not only of the Enlightenment, but of the thousands and thousands of European peasants and poor townspeople who came here bringing their humanity and their sufferings with them. It is the absence of a stable upper class that is responsible for much of the vulgarity of the American scene. Should we blush before the visitor for this deficiency? The ugliness of American decoration, American entertainment, American literature—is not this the visible expression of the impoverishment of the European masses, a manifestation of all the backwardness, deprivation, and want that arrived here in boatloads from Europe? The immense popularity of American movies abroad demonstrates that Europe is the unfinished negative of which America is the proof. The European traveler, viewing with distaste a movie palace or a Motorola, is only looking into the terrible concavity of his continent of hunger inverted startlingly into the convex. Our civilization, deformed as it is outwardly, is still an accomplishment; all this had to come to light. (20)

America is indeed a revelation, though not quite the one that was planned. Given a clean slate, man, it was hoped, would write the future. Instead, he has written his past. This past, inscribed on billboards, ball parks, dance halls, is not seemly, yet its objectification is a kind of disburdenment. The past is at length outside. It does not disturb us as it does Europeans, for our relation with it is both more distant and more familiar. We cannot hate it, for to hate it would be to hate poverty, our eager ancestors, and ourselves.   (21)

If there were time, American civilization could be seen as a beginning, even a favorable one, for we have only to look around us to see what a lot of sensibility a little ease will accrue. The children surpass the fathers and Louis B. Mayer cannot be preserved intact in his descendants. . . . Unfortunately, as things seem now, posterity is not around the corner.   (22)

Lewis Mumford

(1895–   )

MUMFORD, although he did not himself earn a college degree, has held distinguished teaching and research appointments at Stanford, The University of Pennsylvania, M.I.T., and Wesleyan University in Middletown, Connecticut. He has been the principal spokesman in our time for enlightened city planning, especially in such books as The Culture of Cities *(1938),* The City in History *(for which he received the National Book Award, 1961), and* The Highway and the City *(1963).*

◼ *The Suburban Way of Life*

AT THE BEGINNING the suburb was the expression of a new way of life, less effortful, less regimented, less sterile, less formalized in every way than that of the production-minded urban centers; and as the emphasis has, with further gains in production, shifted to consumption, this new way of life has tended to become more universal and is no longer purely an expression of discontent with the disordered city; for even tiny historic towns, like Villeneuve-les-Avignon, now have their new suburban fringe.   (1)

By the very nature of the retreat, the suburb could be identified by a number of related social characteristics. And first, it was a segregated community, set apart from the city, not merely by space but by class stratification: a sort of green ghetto dedicated to the elite. That smug Victorian phrase, "We keep ourselves to ourselves," expresses the spirit of the suburb, in contrast to the city; for the city, by its nature, is a multi-form non-segregated environment. Little groups may indeed form social islands within a city, as the various tribes tended to do in the early cities of Islam, or again as people from a Greek or a Polish village might form temporary nests together in the same block in Chicago or New York. But the metropolis was a mixture of people who came from different places, practiced different occupations, encountered other personalities, meeting and mingling, co-operating and clashing, the rich with the poor, the proud with the humble.   (2)

Except where the suburb enclosed an original small town core, it tended to remain a one-class community, with just a sufficient fringe of tradesmen and servants to keep it going—the latter often condemned to use the central metropolis as their dormitory. Segregation, in practice, means compulsory association, or at least cohabitation; for if there are any choices, they lie outside the immediate community. Hence the great residual freedom of the suburbanite is that of locomotion. For esthetic and intellectual stimulus, the suburb remains dependent upon the big city: the theater, the opera, the orchestra, the art gallery, the university, the museum are no longer part of the daily environment. The problem of re-establishing connections, on a regional rather than a metropolitan basis, is one of the main problems of city planning in our time.   (3)

Not merely did the suburb keep the busier, dirtier, more productive enterprises at a distance, it likewise pushed away the creative activities of the city. Here life ceased to be a drama, full of unexpected challenges and tensions and dilemmas: it became a bland ritual of competitive spending. "Half your trouble," Rudyard Kipling wrote to William James in 1896, "is the curse of America—sheer, hopeless, well-ordered boredom; and that is going some day to be the curse of the world." Kipling put his finger, at that early date, upon the weakness of the suburban way of life.   (4)

Thus the genuine biological benefits of the suburb were undermined by its psychological and social defects: above all, the irreality of its retreat. In the town poor men demonstrated: beggars held out their hands in the street: disease spread quickly from poor quarters to the residences of the comfortable, via the delivery boy, the washerwoman, the seamstress, or other necessary menials: the eye, if not carefully averted, would, on a five-minute walk in any direction, behold a slum, or at least a slum child, ragged and grimy.   (5)

Even in the heyday of Coketown, sensitive and intelligent souls could not remain long in such an environment without banding together to do something about it: they would exhort and agitate, hold meetings and form parades, draw up petitions and besiege legislators, extract money from the rich and dispense aid to the poor, founding soup kitchens and model tenements, passing housing legislation and acquiring land for parks, establishing hospitals and health centers, libraries and universities, in which the whole community played a part and benefited.   (6)

In the suburb one might live and die without marring the image of an innocent world, except when some shadow of its evil fell over a column in the newspaper. Thus the suburb served as an asylum for the preservation of illusion. Here domesticity could flourish, forgetful of the exploitation on which so much of it was based. Here individuality could prosper, oblivious of the pervasive regimentation beyond. This was not merely a child-centered environment: it was based on a childish view of the world, in which reality was sacrificed to the pleasure principle.   (7)

As an attempt to recover what was missing in the city, the suburban exodus could be amply justified, for it was concerned with primary human needs. But there was another side: the temptation to retreat from unpleasant realities, to shirk public duties, and to find the whole meaning of life in the most elemental social group, the family, or even in the still more isolated and self-centered individual. What was properly a beginning was treated as an end.   (8)

In many places, the change toward playful emptiness and civic irresponsibility can be dated. In private conversation Mr. Justice Brandeis once observed to me that he remembered the time, at the turn of the century, when the wealthy citizens of Boston told their sons, when they reached maturity: "Boston holds nothing for you except heavy taxes and political misrule. When you marry, pick out a suburb to build a house in, join the Country Club, and make your life center about your club, your home, and your children."   (9)

That advice was widely followed, not merely by the patricians of Boston and Philadelphia, but by their counterparts in many other big cities in the Western World. Though the result was a wide scattering of upper-class suburbs in the first and second wave of the metropolitan outflow, the exodus also quickened the inner corruption of the city and worked toward its destruction.   (10)

Only as a nursery for bringing up children did the suburb prove a more adequate environment, particularly in the early days of the railroad suburb, when each settlement was surrounded by a broad greenbelt of woods and fields. Here children could gambol safely, without supervision; and around the suburban schools was play-space so ample that it became the ideal requirement for all future schools: space for lawn tennis and croquet, for cricket or baseball, football or bowls. Emerson had noted these advantages clearly in his 'Journal,' in 1865: "There is no police so effective as a good hill and wide pasture in the neighborhood of a village, where the boys can run and play and dispose of their superfluous strength and spirits." The suburb established such play space as an essential part of the city: not to be crowded out by high land values. That was a permanent contribution. (11)

But too soon, in breaking away from the city, the part became a substitute for the whole, even as a single phase of life, that of childhood, became the pattern for all the seven ages of man. As leisure generally increased, play became the serious business of life; and the golf course, the country club, the swimming pool, and the cocktail party became the frivolous counterfeits of a more varied and significant life. Thus in reacting against the disadvantages of the crowded city, the suburb itself became an over-specialized community, more and more committed to relaxation and play as ends in themselves. Compulsive play fast became the acceptable alternative to compulsive work: with small gain either in freedom or vital stimulus. Accordingly, the two modes of life blend into each other; for both in suburb and in metropolis, mass production, mass consumption, and mass recreation produce the same kind of standardized and denatured environment. (12)

Even children suffered from this transformation of the whole community into a mere recreation area. For such a segregated community, composed of segregated economic strata, with little visible daily contact with the realities of the workaday world, placed an undue burden of education on the school and family. The smallest village where people still farm and fish and hunt, the drabbest industrial town whose population still engages in essential productive enterprises, has educational possibilities that the suburb lacks. In the end, the operative differences between the contemporary suburb and the big city become increasingly minimal: for in these seemingly different environments reality has been progressively reduced to what filters through the screen of the television set. (13)

But both childhood and the suburb are transitional stages: so a well-planned urban community must have a place for other phases of life and other modes of living. A universal suburb is almost as much of a nightmare, humanly speaking, as a universal megalopolis: yet it is toward this proliferating nonentity that our present random or misdirected urban growth has been steadily tending. A large scale pattern of expressways and airfields and sprawling car parks and golf-courses envelops a small scale, increasingly shrunken mode of life. (14)

Yet in its original effort, when the suburb approached nearest the romantic goal, it made a positive contribution to the emerging conception of the city as a mixed environment, interwoven in texture with the country; and many of these contributions need to be appraised and selectively adapted and improved, not discarded. (15)

Phyllis McGinley

(1905–   )

PHYLLIS McGINLEY (Mrs. Charles Hayden), winner of the Pulitzer prize for poetry in 1961, is the prolific author of light verse, literary criticism, and articles of general interest. Her literary visibility has been recognized by the academic community through numerous honorary doctorates, including three in one year (1964). Representative and indicative titles are these: Pocketful of Wry *(1940),* Merry Christmas, Happy New Year *(1938),* Mince Pie and Mistletoe *(1961).*

■ *Suburbia: Of Thee I Sing*

Twenty miles east of New York City as the New Haven Railroad flies sits a village I shall call Spruce Manor. The Boston Post Road, there, for the length of two blocks, becomes Main Street and on one side of that thundering thoroughfare are the grocery stores and the drug stores and the Village Spa where teen-agers gather of an afternoon to drink their cokes and speak their curious confidences. There one finds the shoe repairers and the dry cleaners and the secondhand stores which sell "antiques" and the stationery stores which dispense comic books to ten-year-olds and greeting cards and lending library masterpieces to their mothers. On the opposite side stand the bank, the Fire House, the Public Library. The rest of this town of perhaps four or five thousand people lies to the south and is bounded largely by Long Island Sound, curving protectively on three borders. The movie theater (dedicated to the showing of second-run, single-feature pictures) and the grade schools lie north, beyond the Post Road, and that is a source of worry to Spruce Manorites. They are always a little uneasy about the chil-

dren, crossing, perhaps, before the lights are safely green. However, two excellent policemen—Mr. Crowley and Mr. Lang—station themselves at the
intersections four times a day and so far there have been no accidents.   (1)

Spruce Manor in the spring and summer and fall is a pretty town, full of
gardens and old elms. (There are few spruces but the village Council is considering planting a few on the station plaza, out of sheer patriotism.) In the
winter, the houses reveal themselves as comfortable, well-kept, architecturally insignificant. Then one can see the town for what it is and has been
since it left off being farm and woodland some sixty years ago—the epitome
of Suburbia, not the country and certainly not the city. It is a commuter's
town, the living center of a web which unrolls each morning as the men
swing aboard the locals, and contracts again in the evening when they return. By day, with even the children pent in schools, it is a village of
women. They trundle mobile baskets at the A & P, they sit under driers at
the hairdressers, they sweep their porches and set out bulbs and stitch up
slip-covers. Only on weekends does it become heterogeneous and lively, the
parking places difficult to find.   (2)

Spruce Manor has no country club of its own, though devoted golfers
have their choice of two or three not far away. It does have a small yacht
club and a beach which can be used by anyone who rents or owns a house
here. The village supports a little park with playground equipment and a
counselor, where children, unattended by parents, can spend summer days
if they have no more pressing engagements.   (3)

It is a town not wholly without traditions. Residents will point out the
two-hundred-year-old Manor house, now a minor museum; and in the autumn they line the streets on a scheduled evening to watch the Volunteer
Firemen parade. That is a fine occasion, with so many heads of households
marching in their red blouses and white gloves, some with flaming helmets,
some swinging lanterns, most of them genially out of step. There is a bigger
parade on Memorial Day with more marchers than watchers and with the
Catholic priest, the rabbi, and the Protestant ministers each delivering a
short prayer when the paraders gather near the War Memorial. On the
whole, however, outside of contributing generously to the Community
Chest, Manorites are not addicted to municipal get-togethers.   (4)

No one is very poor here and not many families rich enough to be awe-
some. In fact, there is not much to distinguish Spruce Manor from any
other of a thousand suburbs outside of New York City or San Francisco or
Detroit or Chicago or even Stockholm, for that matter. Except for one
thing. For some reason, Spruce Manor has become a sort of symbol to writers and reporters familiar only with its name or trivial aspects. It has become a symbol of all that is middle-class in the worst sense, of settled-
downness or rootlessness, according to what the writer is trying to prove; of

smug and prosperous mediocrity—or even, in more lurid novels, of lechery at the country club and Sunday morning hangovers.   (5)

To condemn Suburbia has long been a literary cliché, anyhow. I have yet to read a book in which the suburban life was pictured as the good life or the commuter as a sympathetic figure. He is nearly as much a stock character as the old stage Irishman: the man who "spends his life riding to and from his wife," the eternal Babbitt who knows all about Buicks and nothing about Picasso, whose sanctuary is the club locker room, whose ideas spring ready-made from the illiberal newspapers. His wife plays politics at the P.T.A. and keeps up with the Joneses. Or—if the scene is more gilded and less respectable—the commuter is the high-powered advertising executive with a station wagon and an eye for the ladies, his wife a restless baggage given to too many cocktails in the afternoon.   (6)

These clichés I challenge. I have lived in the country, I have lived in the city. I have lived in an average Middle Western small town. But for the best eleven years of my life I have lived in Suburbia and I like it.   (7)

"Compromise!" cried our friends when we came here from an expensive, inconvenient, moderately fashionable tenement in Manhattan. It was the period in our lives when everyone was moving somewhere. Farther uptown, farther downtown, across town to Sutton Place, to a half-dozen rural acres in Connecticut or New Jersey or even Vermont. But no one in our rather rarefied little group was thinking of moving to the suburbs except us. They were aghast that we could find anything appealing in the thought of a middle-class house on a middle-class street in a middle-class village full of middle-class people. That we were tired of town and hoped for children, that we couldn't afford both a city apartment and a farm, they put down as feeble excuses. To this day they cannot understand us. You see, they read the books. They even write them.   (8)

Compromise? Of course we compromise. But compromise, if not the spice of life, is its solidity. It is what makes nations great and marriages happy and Spruce Manor the pleasant place it is. As for its being middle-class, what is wrong with acknowledging one's roots? And how free we are! Free of the city's noise, of its ubiquitous doormen, of the soot on the windowsill and the radio in the next apartment. We have released ourselves from the seasonal hegira to the mountains or the seashore. We have only one address, one house to keep supplied with paring knives and blankets. We are free from the snows that block the countryman's roads in winter and his electricity which always goes off in a thunderstorm. I do not insist that we are typical. There is nothing really typical about any of our friends and neighbors here, and therein lies my point. The true suburbanite needs to conform less than anyone else; much less than the gentleman farmer with his remodeled salt-box or than the determined cliff dweller with his necessity for living at the right address. In Spruce Manor all addresses are right. And since we are fairly numerous here, we need not fall back on the people nearest us for total companionship. There is not here, as in a small city away from truly urban centers, some particular family whose codes must be ours. And we could not keep up with the Joneses even if we wanted to, for we know many Joneses and they are all quite different people leading the most various lives.   (9)

The Albert Joneses spend their weekends sailing, the Bertram Joneses cultivate their delphinium, the Clarence Joneses—Clarence being a handy man with a cello—are enthusiastic about amateur chamber music. The David Joneses dote on bridge, but neither of the Ernest Joneses understands it and they prefer staying home of an evening so that Ernest Jones can carve his witty caricatures out of pieces of old fruit wood. We admire each other's gardens, applaud each other's sailing records; we are too busy to compete. So long as our clapboards are painted and our hedges decently trimmed, we have fulfilled our community obligations. We can live as anonymously as in a city or we can call half the village by their first names. (10)

On our half-acre or three-quarters, we can raise enough tomatoes for our salads and assassinate enough beetles to satisfy the gardening urge. Or we can buy our vegetables at the store and put the whole place to lawn without feeling that we are neglecting our property. We can have privacy and shade and the changing of the seasons and also the Joneses next door from whom to borrow a cup of sugar or a stepladder. Despite the novelists, the shadow of the Country Club rests lightly on us. Half of us wouldn't be found dead with a golf stick in our hands, and loathe Saturday dances. Few of us expect to be deliriously wealthy or world-famous or divorced. What we do expect is to pay off the mortgage and send our healthy children to good colleges.   (11)

For when I refer to life here, I think, of course, of living with children. Spruce Manor without children would be a paradox. The summer waters are full of them, gamboling like dolphins. The lanes are alive with them, the yards overflow with them, they possess the tennis courts and the skating pond and the vacant lots. Their roller skates wear down the asphalt and their bicycles make necessary the twenty-five mile speed limit. They converse interminably on the telephones and make rich the dentist and the pediatrician. Who claims that a child and a half is the American middle-class average? A nice medium Spruce Manor family runs to four or five and we count proudly, but not with amazement, the many solid households running to six, seven, eight, nine, even up to twelve. Our houses here are big and not new, most of them, and there is a temptation to fill them up, let the *décor* fall where it may.   (12)

Besides, Spruce Manor seems designed by providence and town planning for the happiness of children. Better designed than the city; better, I say defiantly, than the country. Country mothers must be constantly arranging and contriving for their children's leisure time. There is no neighbor child next door for playmate, no school within walking distance. The ponds are dangerous to young swimmers, the woods full of poison ivy, the romantic dirt roads unsuitable for bicycles. An extra acre or two gives a fine sense of possession to an adult; it does not compensate children for the give-and-take of our village where there is always a contemporary to help swing the skipping rope or put on the catcher's mitt. Where in the country is the Friday evening dancing class or the Saturday morning movie (approved by the P.T.A.)? It is the greatest fallacy of all time that children love the country as a year-around plan. Children would take a dusty corner of Washington Square or a city sidewalk, even, in preference to the lonely sermons in stones and books in running brooks which their contemporaries cannot share. (13)

As for the horrors of bringing up progeny in the city, for all its museums and other cultural advantages (so perfectly within reach of suburban families if they feel strongly about it), they were summed up for me one day last winter. The harried mother of one, speaking to me on the telephone just after Christmas, sighed and said, "It's been a really wonderful time for me, as vacations go. Barbara has had an engagement with a child in our apartment house every afternoon this week. I have had to take her almost nowhere." Barbara is eleven. For six of those eleven years, I realized, her mother must have dreaded Christmas vacation, not to mention spring, as a time when Barbara had to be entertained. I thought thankfully of my own daughters whom I had scarcely seen since school closed, out with their skis and their sleds and their friends, sliding down the roped-off hill half a block away, coming in hungrily for lunch and disappearing again, hearty, amused, and safe—at least as safe as any sled-borne child can be.   (14)

Spruce Manor is not Eden, of course. Our taxes are higher than we like and there is always that eight-eleven in the morning to be caught and we sometimes resent the necessity of rushing from a theater to a train on a weekday evening. But the taxes pay for our really excellent schools and for our garbage collections (so that the pails of orange peels need not stand in the halls overnight as ours did in the city) and for our water supply which does not give out every dry summer as it frequently does in the country. As for the theaters—they are twenty miles away and we don't get to them more than twice a month. But neither, I think, do many of our friends in town. The eight-eleven is rather a pleasant train, too, say the husbands; it gets them to work in thirty-four minutes and they read the papers restfully on the way.   (15)

"But the suburban mind!" cry our die-hard friends in Manhattan and

Connecticut. "The suburban conversation! The monotony!" They imply that they and I must scintillate or we perish. Let me anatomize Spruce Manor, for them and for the others who envision Suburbia as a congregation of mindless housewives and amoral go-getters.   (16)

From my window, now, on a June morning, I have a view. It contains neither solitary hills nor dramatic skyscrapers. But I can see my roses in bloom, and my foxglove, and an arch of trees over the lane. I think comfortably of my friends whose houses line this and other streets rather like it. Not one of them is, so far as I know, doing any of the things that suburban ladies are popularly supposed to be doing. One of them, I happen to know, has gone bowling for her health and figure, but she has already tidied up her house and arranged to be home before the boys return from school. Some, undoubtedly, are ferociously busy in the garden. One lady is on her way to Ellis Island, bearing comfort and gifts to a Polish boy—a seventeen-year-old stowaway who did slave labor in Germany and was liberated by a cousin of hers during the war—who is being held for attempting to attain the land of which her cousin told him. The boy has been on the Island for three months. Twice a week she takes this tedious journey, meanwhile besieging courts and immigration authorities on his behalf. This lady has a large house, a part-time maid, and five children.   (17)

My friend around the corner is finishing her third novel. She writes daily from nine-thirty until two. After that her son comes back from school and she plunges into maternity; at six, she combs her pretty hair, refreshes her lipstick, and is charming to her doctor husband. The village dancing school is run by another neighbor, as it has been for twenty years. She has sent a number of ballerinas on to the theatrical world as well as having shepherded for many a successful season the white-gloved little boys and full-skirted little girls through their first social tasks.   (18)

Some of the ladies are no doubt painting their kitchens or a nursery; one of them is painting the portrait, on assignment, of a very distinguished personage. Some of them are nurses' aides and Red Cross workers and supporters of good causes. But all find time to be friends with their families and to meet the 5:32 five nights a week. They read something besides the newest historical novel, Braque is not unidentifiable to most of them, and their conversation is for the most part as agreeable as the tables they set. The tireless bridge players, the gossips, the women bored by their husbands live perhaps in our suburb, too. Let them. Our orbits need not cross.   (19)

And what of the husbands, industriously selling bonds or practicing law or editing magazines or looking through microscopes or managing offices in the city? Do they spend their evenings and their weekends in the gaudy bars of 52nd Street? Or are they the perennial householders, their lives a dreary round of taking down screens and mending drains? Well, screens they have always with them, and a man who is good around the house can spend happy hours with the plumbing even on a South Sea island. Some of them cut their own lawns and some of them try to break par and some of them sail their little boats all summer with their families for crew. Some of them are village trustees for nothing a year and some listen to symphonies and some think Milton Berle ought to be President. There is a scientist who plays wonderful bebop, and an insurance salesman who has bought a big old house nearby and with his own hands is gradually tearing it apart and re-shaping it nearer to his heart's desire. Some of them are passionate hedge-clippers and some read Plutarch for fun. But I do not know many—though there may be such—who either kiss their neighbors' wives behind doors or whose idea of sprightly talk is to tell you the plot of an old movie.   (20)

It is June, now, as I have said. This afternoon my daughters will come home from school with a crowd of their peers at their heels. They will eat up the cookies and drink up the ginger ale and go down for a swim at the beach if the water is warm enough, that beach which is only three blocks away and open to all Spruce Manor. They will go unattended by me, since they have been swimming since they were four and besides there are life guards and no big waves. (Even our piece of ocean is a compromise.) Presently it will be time for us to climb into our very old Studebaker—we are not car-proud in Spruce Manor—and meet the 5:32. That evening expedition is not vitally necessary, for a bus runs straight down our principal avenue from the station to the shore, and it meets all trains. But it is an event we enjoy. There is something delightfully ritualistic about the moment when the train pulls in and the men swing off, with the less sophisticated children running squealing to meet them. The women move over from the driver's seat, surrender the keys, and receive an absent-minded kiss. It is the sort of picture that wakes John Marquand screaming from his sleep. But, deluded people that we are, we do not realize how mediocre it all seems. We will eat our undistinguished meal, probably without even a cocktail to enliven it. We will drink our coffee at the table, not carry it into the living room; if a husband changes for dinner here it is into old and spotty trousers and more comfortable shoes. The children will then go through the regular childhood routine—complain about their homework, grumble about going to bed, and finally accomplish both ordeals. Perhaps later the Gerard Joneses will drop in. We will talk a great deal of unimportant chatter and compare notes on food prices; we will also discuss the headlines and disagree. (Some of us in the Manor are Republicans, some are Democrats, a few lean plainly leftward. There are probably anti-Semites and anti-Catholics and even anti-Americans. Most of us are merely anti-antis.) We will all have one highball and the Joneses will leave early. To-

morrow and tomorrow and tomorrow the pattern will be repeated. This is
Suburbia.   (21)

But I think that some day people will look back on our little interval
here, on our Spruce Manor way of life, as we now look back on the Currier
and Ives kind of living, with nostalgia and respect. In a world of terrible
extremes, it will stand out as the safe, important medium.   (22)

Suburbia, of thee I sing!   (23)

Hans J. Morgenthau

(1904–   )

*MORGENTHAU, Albert A. Michelson Distinguished Service Professor at the
University of Chicago, is an authoritative analyst of the role of politics in
modern history. Trained in Germany in the law, he began his American
academic career at Brooklyn College in 1937. His major works include* Principles and Problems of International Politics *(1950),* Dilemmas of Politics
(1948), Politics in the Twentieth Century, *3 vols. (1962).*

◼ *Why Nations Decline*

LET ME SAY, first of all, in contrast to what some philosophers of history
have proclaimed, that there is no iron law according to which nations
must decline. Much has been written in the last 100 years or so about the
biological analogy between the development of societies and the development of living organisms. As a living organism grows, reaches maturity, declines and dies, so, it is said, societies, nations, civilizations grow, reach a
period of flowering, decline, and disappear. It is certainly true that most nations which once were prominent in the affairs of the world have either declined or disappeared altogether. But not all of them have. Think of Japan
and China, to mention only two outstanding examples of nations who have

maintained themselves as great powers over thousands of years, while all around them, and more particularly in Europe, nations declined and faded away continuously. So, it seems to me, it is important to realize, first of all, that any analogy with biological or other natural-science data is very much misleading. There is no iron law according to which a nation must decline after a certain period of greatness. However, it is an unequivocal fact that most nations actually have declined and disappeared.   (1)

The second point I would like to make is that there is a kind of mystery about the rise and fall of nations, as there is a kind of mystery about the rise and fall of individuals, a mystery which some might try to explain in the fashionable terms of the day, particularly in psychological, psycho-analytical, or behaviorist terms. In actuality we are really confronted with a mystery. Take, for instance, the example of Spain.   (2)

Why was it that in the sixteenth century what is called the *siglo del oro*, the golden century of Spain, started with an enormous flowering in the fields of literature, art, statesmanship, and all other human endeavors? And why was it that after a hundred years or so this flowering suddenly stopped, and from then on to this day Spain has lived in a kind of somnolescent stupor, never being able even to approach the greatness which it had reached for a short span of time?   (3)

Why is it, for instance, that the Low Countries for a considerable period of history were prominent not only in warfare and foreign policy but also in art, science, and other endeavors, and all of a sudden this development stopped? Why is it that the empires of the Huns and the Mongols fell and left no trace after them?   (4)

All those are questions which many have tried to answer but to which there is really no satisfactory rational answer. I would suggest that, when we approach so great a topic, we ought to approach it with a considerable de-gree of humility, with an awareness of our ignorance. We are here sur-rounded by developments which transcend our understanding.   (5)

The third point I want to make is the enormous extent to which the rise and fall of nations is a result of circumstances over which the nations have no control. The rise of a great man may bring about the rise of a na-tion and his disappearance may bring about its downfall. Take the short flowering of Macedon under Alexander. When he died after a very short reign, the Macedonian Empire disintegrated. Nobody can say what would have happened if Alexander had died of the measles as a child. In all prob-ability there never would have been a Macedonian Empire. And nobody can say what would have happened had Alexander not died as a young man without heirs but had reached a ripe old age, being able to consolidate his empire.   (6)

Take, in more recent history, the rise of France under Napoleon, the rise of bolshevism under Lenin, the rise of fascism in Italy under Mussolini, is the result of comparison. Let me give you two examples from military history. (20)

When the army of Prussia met the army of Napoleon in 1806 in the battle of Jena and Auerstädt, the Prussian generals were confident that the power of their army was superior to that of Napoleon. On what was that erroneous evaluation of their power based? Upon the fact that the Prussian army of 1806 was as good as the army of Frederick the Great had been thirty or forty years earlier. The military might of Prussia, taken by itself, had not only not declined, it might even have increased. What the Prussian generals should have done was to compare the power of the Prussian army of 1806 not with the power of the Prussian army of 1760 or 1770 but with the power of the French army of 1806. (21)

A very similar situation arose from the estimates of French military power immediately preceding the Second World War and during the period of the so-called "phony" war. The French army was then regarded to be the most powerful instrument of land power existing in 1940. I remember very vividly hearing Mr. Churchill say in Paris in 1937 that nothing stands between barbarism and civilization but the French army. (22)

The events of 1940 showed very clearly how completely mistaken this estimate of French power was. On what was it based? It was based upon the same erroneous mental operation which had led in 1806 to the miscalculation of Prussian as over against Napoleonic power. That is to say, we compared the power of the French army of 1940 with the power of the French army, say, of 1920; and we found the results of the comparison extremely satisfactory. Conversely, we had still the mental picture of a German army in 1940 which somehow resembled the insufficient German army of ten years earlier. In other words, we regarded the military weakness of Germany as an absolute, as we regarded the French military superiority as an absolute; and, in consequence, we miscalculated completely the distribution of military power between the two nations. (23)

The second typical error which is frequently made in evaluating the power of a nation lies not so much in believing in its absolute character but in believing in its permanency. Here we refuse to make a projection in time, and we regard the power of a nation in a particular period of history as a permanent attribute which is not subject to change in itself. Remember, for instance, the shock which we all experienced when the Russian Sputniks went up. In what did this shock actually exist? It existed in the sudden awareness that the technological superiority of the United States which we had taken for granted, which we had taken to be a permanent attribute, as it were, of America, like the Rocky Mountains, something which nobody could take away from us, was only a temporary advantage which could be taken away from us by a more determined competitor. (24)

Take as another example Great Britain's reliance at the beginning of

and the rise of naziism under Hitler. If those men had not existed, certainly history would have been different. And it is a good bet that the temporary rise of some of those nations and the permanent rise of others would not have occurred without the presence and activities of those outstanding men. (7)

The factors over which nations have no control and which determine their fate are not only and primarily of a personal nature; they are to a very great extent of a technological and geographic nature. (8)

Take, for instance, the example, which has been correctly mentioned in your "Syllabus," the decline of the power of Great Britain, and the question asked in your "Syllabus" whether different policies pursued by British governments could have prevented that decline of British power. Now, let me ask: In what did British power consist? What brought about the greatness of Great Britain as a world power from Henry VIII at the beginning of the sixteenth century to, say, Sir Edward Grey at the outbreak of the First World War? It was in essence the concatenation of two circumstances, the insular position of Great Britain in close proximity of the European continent and the decisive importance of sea power for world politics, together, of course (and this is the third factor which one should not forget), with the effective exploitation of those factors by British statesmanship. (9)

With sea power having been replaced as the decisive factor in world politics, especially for an insular nation, and with the insular position in the proximity of the European continent having been transformed from a factor of safety into a factor of extreme exposure to danger, the power of Great Britain was bound to decline. While fifty years ago Britannia still ruled the waves, today intermediate ballistic missiles placed anywhere on the European continent rule Great Britain. While experts differ on how many H-bombs are necessary to reduce the British Isles to a heap of radioactive rubble, there is no doubt that a few are sufficient within a couple of minutes to wipe out the very physical existence of the British Isles. (10)

This drastic change in the objective conditions of British existence, no British statesman, no British foreign policy could have altered. Perhaps under certain favorable circumstances, the consequences of these conditions might have been postponed; their effects even today might be mitigated by wise statesmanship. But essentially the indefensibility of the British Isles under modern technological conditions of warfare is a fundamental fact which no British statesman could have changed and over which no British foreign policy could have had any control. This impossibility for foreign policy to change the fundamental conditions of a nation's existence became obvious in that famous episode of 1938, which has gone into history as the surrender at Munich. (11)

We all realize today, of course, the fateful consequences of Mr. Chamberlain's surrender of Czechoslovakia to Germany. But we are less aware today than, as I can readily remember, the contemporaries were in 1938 of the inescapable dilemma that confronted Mr. Chamberlain. It is easy to say today that Mr. Chamberlain was wrong. But what was the alternative? Mr. Chamberlain realized that the objective conditions of British existence had changed to such an extent that any kind of war, even a war from which Great Britain would emerge victorious, would mean the end of Great Britain as a first-rate power. And this prognosis was, of course, proved correct by the results of the Second World War. So Mr. Chamberlain was confronted with an inescapable dilemma which no British foreign policy could have eliminated. It is a matter of judgment as to which horn of the dilemma Mr. Chamberlain should have chosen. I myself believe that he chose the wrong horn. But, even if he had chosen the other one, he could not have escaped the final decline of British power, a decline which was a result not of deficient British statesmanship but of the inescapable objective conditions of British existence.   (12)

Take another example closer to home which again exemplifies the enormous weight which the objective conditions of their existence have for the fate of nations. The unique and privileged position which the United States occupied during the first century and a half of its history was the result primarily of the objective geographic and military conditions under which the United States lived, those conditions again being exploited by wise statesmanship, especially at the very beginning of American history. It is the actual fact of isolation from the great conflicts in which other nations were continuously involved which determined the foreign policy and the advantageous consequences of that foreign policy for the United States.   (13)

The contrary fact, the disappearance of that privileged position, the disappearance of isolation, the involvement of the United States into the affairs of the world is not the result, as some have thought it to be, of an act of will on the part of American statesmen, but it is again the result of the objective conditions of the world over which no American statesman had any control. American statesmen after the First World War could recognize the end of isolation or they could refuse to recognize it; they could base their foreign policies upon the assumption that the United States was still isolated or they could base their foreign policies on the contrary assumption that the United States was no longer isolated, but the objective fact of isolation or non-isolation was beyond the control of American statesmen. Thus, when we deal with the topic of this lecture, the reasons for the decline of nations, we must be aware of the enormous importance which objective factors have upon the decline of nations, factors over which nations themselves have no control.   (14)

Look at the American situation from still a different point of view. The rise of the United States to the position of a colonial power in consequence of the Spanish-American War was of nobody's making. Once the United

States became involved in the Spanish-American War and won most naturally heir to the Asian and American fragments of empire. President McKinley, in his famous account of how he decision to annex the Philippines, made exactly this point whe that we could not give them back to the Spaniards; we could not over to a rival power; we could not leave them to the natives—"t nothing left for us to do but take them all. . . ." Here you have plicit recognition of the power which objective factors have upon policy and their consequences.

Take the rise of the United States, in consequence of the Second War, to world power, to the position of the other great power in the No American statesman planned it that way. It was again the concaten of objective conditions which brought about, very much against the i tions and against the preferences of American statesmen and of Amer people, this rise to power, responsibility, and liability.   (

Once one has said all this—leaving in the dark, as it were, that broa arena over which statesmen have no control, where, in other words, fa reigns over nations—we must consider that area which is subject to human control. Within those predetermined limits, what are the factors through which human action typically contributes to the decline of nations?   (17)

Here the greatest single factor which throughout history has brought about or has contributed to the decline of nations has been the lack of the correct evaluation of the power of one's own nation as over agains power of other nations. Nations, when they devise their foreign po must, of course, evaluate their own powers as over against the pow other nations; and it is in good measure upon the correctness of that ation that success and failure of foreign policy depends. Frequentl typically, nations have fallen because they had an erroneous concep their own power in comparison with the power of other nations. Her typical mistakes must be considered. First, nations tend to believe absolute character of power—that is to say, a nation which has pr be powerful in one period of history is tempted to believe that this s ity of power is a kind of natural quality that exists irrespective of th of other nations.

Power in actuality is a relative thing, of course, as you all kr United States can be said to be powerful compared with the powe nations. You can say the power of the United States is unchalle the Western Hemisphere—which means, compare the power of t States with that of the nations of Latin America, either singly tively, and you arrive at the conclusion that the power of the Ur is superior to that of the nations of Latin America.

There is a tendency in all nations to look at the power of or tion as a kind of absolute, to take it for granted, and not to re

the war against Japan upon traditional sea power unprotected by air power and the catastrophe which befell the Pacific fleet of Great Britain at the beginning of that war, some of her best ships being sunk by Japanese air power in a matter of minutes. This catastrophe was the result of the same mistake of believing that since British sea power had proven to be the unchallengeable main element of British power in the past, it was bound to be so forever. Especially in a period of rapid technological change, in a period of not one revolution in the technology of warfare but a continuous succession of such revolutions, there is very great danger in fixing one's gaze upon one particular period and projecting the distribution of power of that period into the future. The survival of a nation and the continuation of its greatness may well depend upon its ability to project correctly, or at least without making disastrous mistakes, the distribution of power of today into the future, five or ten years hence. (25)

The third typical mistake which nations make in the evaluation of their power and which in the past has frequently led to their decline is the error of the single factor. That is to say, nations have a tendency, as do individuals as well, to put their bets upon one factor which is particularly advantageous to them and to forget about all the other factors which are not so advantageous to them. Take, for instance, the isolation of the United States which as a concept, as a myth, as an idea determining American foreign policy survived for a considerable stretch of time the actual isolation of the United States. (26)

What we call "militarism" is a particular manifestation of this error, the idea that a particular type of weapon or a particular military service or military preparedness itself is the only and the most decisive element in a nation's power, although military power is certainly the indispensable foundation of national power. But anybody, especially in the Free World, who would overlook the vital importance of diplomacy and of what is called "the struggle for the minds of men" through propaganda, foreign aid, and all the other factors which go into that struggle would certainly misunderstand the power of one's own nation and the requirements, in terms of power, of the foreign policy of one's own nation. Nations who try to determine their power in comparison with other nations in terms of the number of their divisions or of their airplanes make a fundamental mistake when they equate the totality of their power with material military might. (27)

Another manifestation of this fallacy of the single factor lies in the field of what has been called "geopolitics"—that is to say, the belief that the power of the nation is predetermined by its geography. The American isolationism of the twenties and thirties comes of course again to mind. As you know, there has been a whole school of thought, particularly in England and Germany, which has tried to develop a theory of foreign policy on the basis of the geographic factor. Nobody will doubt that geography is the

most fundamental and the most permanent of all the factors which go into
the making of national power; but it is by no means the only one. Certain
nations have been greatly favored by the geographic factor, and the geographic factor has by no means prevented their decline. Others have not
been favored at all and have risen to heights of greatness because of the intangible factors which go into the making of a nation's greatness. So here in
the metaphysics of geography you have another fallacy against which one
has to be on guard.   (28)

Finally, there is the fallacy of another single factor, and that is nationalism, conceived as chauvinism, which attributes all the good qualities to
one's own nation and deprives all other nations, especially the enemy, of all
good qualities—which bestows all bad qualities, in other words, upon the
enemy. This psychological tendency has proven to be a disaster for nations
which surrendered to it without reservations and qualifications. The downfall of Germany in recent history resulted in good measure from this chauvinistic overestimation of one's own nation's qualities and the underestimation of the qualities of other nations.   (29)

Take, for instance, the consistent underestimation and, in certain periods, overestimation of Russian power. Certainly this fallacy has done great
harm either way, by either overestimation or underestimation, to the interests of the nations which have indulged in this kind of error. There is great
need for a nation, if it wants to preserve its standing in the world and increase its greatness, its power, and whatever else goes into its greatness, to
look at itself and at its competitors in the world with a certain detachment,
with a certain critical faculty, the absence of which will lead to errors which
in turn will be detrimental to a nation's greatness. Throughout history,
many nations have fallen because they believed too strongly in their superiority.   (30)

I think nobody has phrased this problem better than the great British
political philosopher Edmund Burke who said in 1793, when Great Britain
was engaged in the War of the First Coalition against Napoleon: "Among
precautions against ambition, it may not be amiss to take one precaution
against our own. I must fairly say I dread our own power and our own ambition. I dread our being too much dreaded. It is ridiculous to say that we
are not men and that as men we shall never wish to aggrandize ourselves in
some way or another. Can we say that even at this very hour we are not
invidiously aggrandized? We are already in possession of almost all the commerce of the world. Our empire in India is an awful thing. If we should
come to be in a condition not only to have all this ascendant in commerce,
but to be absolutely able, without the least control, to hold the commerce
of all other nations totally dependent upon our good pleasure, we may say
that we shall not abuse this astonishing and hitherto unheard-of-power. But

every other nation will think we shall abuse it. It is impossible but that, sooner or later, this state of things must produce a combination against us which may end in our ruin." (31)

This is a very wise observation, one that is borne out by historic experience. Nations which have acquired enormous power—too great a power, as it were, for their own good—have frequently declined at the very moment they reached such heights of power. Again a certain humility, here in terms of judging how far one wants to go in aggrandizing one's self, is, it seems to me, in order. (32)

Let me say finally that there is another area which is important for the preservation of a nation's greatness, and the absence of certain qualities here has frequently led to a nation's decline. That area is in the field of domestic government. Nations, especially in our age, are continuously confronted with new tasks, new challenges. In order to meet them they must use institutions, ideas, concepts, policies which had been framed for different tasks and different challenges. So there is always a gap between the experiences of a nation and the institutions and ideas and policies which have been formed by the experiences of the past, on the one hand, and the tasks of the present, on the other. (33)

The continuing greatness of a nation depends in good measure upon its ability to readjust its institutions, to redevise its policies, to reformulate its ideas in the light of new tasks, new conditions, new challenges. The pages of history are full of great empires which became ossified, which because they had solved the problems of the past with institutions, ideas, and policies of the past, thought that they could apply the same institutions, the same ideas, the same policies to the new tasks of the present and of the future. And when those tasks became too great to be dealt with successfully by those institutions, ideas, and policies, those nations declined and disappeared. There is, I think, an analogy between those ossified empires who were unable to move, as it were, with the times and the dinosaur whose biological structure was perfectly adapted to one kind of environment, and, since he could not adapt it to another kind of environment, he had to perish. (34)

In view of the tasks before us, I must say, if I may come to the present and close to home, I cannot look with equanimity at the procedures of our government, especially of our executive branch, of what I have recently called "government by committee." This system, I think, is totally inadequate to the tasks of the present and of the foreseeable future. Our government has been divided into what you might call "a multitude of security councils of the United Nations," where each member has a veto and can forestall action. I have been told that the State Department is a member of about 700 interdepartmental committees which deal with different problems of defense and foreign policy, and this does not include, of course, the committees within the State Department itself. This cumbersome, almost monstrous establishment of the executive branch, this slow-moving, if moving at all, establishment constitutes great danger to the greatness of the United States in an age which requires swift, audacious, and radically new decisions.   (35)

I do not know whether I have answered the question which was posed in the topic. I am quite sure I have not answered it, but I hope I have made a small contribution to showing how difficult and how essentially unanswerable a question it is.   (36)

Michael Harrington

(1928–   )

HARRINGTON has dedicated himself to the civil liberties and economic welfare of the poorest working classes since the early 1950's. He was associate editor of The Catholic Worker *(1951–1952) and has been a member of the national executive committee of the Socialist Party since 1960. His books include* The Other America *(1963),* The Retail Clerks *(1963), and* The Accidental Century *(1964).*

◼ *The Two Nations*

THE UNITED STATES in the sixties contains an affluent society within its borders. Millions and tens of millions enjoy the highest standard of life the world has ever known. This blessing is mixed. It is built upon a peculiarly distorted economy, one that often proliferates pseudo-needs rather than satisfying human needs. For some, it has resulted in a sense of spiritual emptiness, of alienation. Yet a man would be a fool to prefer hunger to satiety, and the material gains at least open up the possibility of a rich and full existence.   (1)

At the same time, the United States contains an underdeveloped nation, a culture of poverty. Its inhabitants do not suffer the extreme privation of the peasants of Asia or the tribesmen of Africa, yet the mechanism of the misery is similar. They are beyond history, beyond progress, sunk in a paralyzing, maiming routine. (2)

The new nations, however, have one advantage: poverty is so general and so extreme that it is the passion of the entire society to obliterate it. Every resource, every policy, is measured by its effect on the lowest and most impoverished. There is a gigantic mobilization of the spirit of the society: aspiration becomes a national purpose that penetrates to every village and motivates a historic transformation. (3)

But this country seems to be caught in a paradox. Because its poverty is not so deadly, because so many are enjoying a decent standard of life, there are indifference and blindness to the plight of the poor. There are even those who deny that the culture of poverty exists. It is as if Disraeli's famous remark about the two nations of the rich and the poor had come true in a fantastic fashion. At precisely that moment in history where for the first time a people have the material ability to end poverty, they lack the will to do so. They cannot see; they cannot act. The consciences of the well-off are the victims of affluence; the lives of the poor are the victims of a physical and spiritual misery. (4)

The problem, then, is to a great extent one of vision. The nation of the well-off must be able to see through the wall of affluence and recognize the alien citizens on the other side. And there must be vision in the sense of purpose, of aspiration: if the word does not grate upon the ears of a gentile America, there must be a passion to end poverty, for nothing less than that will do. (5)

I hope I can supply at least some of the material for such a vision. Let us try to understand the other America as a whole, to see its perspective for the future if it is left alone, to realize the responsibility and the potential for ending this nation in our midst. (6)

But, when all is said and done, the decisive moment occurs after all the sociology and the description is in. There is really no such thing as "the material for a vision." After one reads the facts, either there are anger and shame, or there are not. And, as usual, the fate of the poor hangs upon the decision of the better-off. If this anger and shame are not forthcoming, someone can write a book about the other America a generation from now and it will be the same, or worse. (7)

I

Perhaps the most important analytic point to have emerged in this description of the other America is the fact that poverty in America forms a culture, a way of life and feeling, that it makes a whole. It is crucial to generalize this idea, for it profoundly affects how one moves to destroy poverty.   (8)

The most obvious aspect of this interrelatedness is in the way in which the various subcultures of the other America feed into one another. This is clearest with the aged. There the poverty of the declining years is, for some millions of human beings, a function of the poverty of the earlier years. If there were adequate medical care for everyone in the United States, there would be less misery for old people. It is as simple as that. Or there is the relation between the poor farmers and the unskilled workers. When a man is driven off the land because of the impoverishment worked by technological progress, he leaves one part of the culture of poverty and joins another. If something were done about the low-income farmer, that would immediately tell in the statistics of urban unemployment and the economic underworld. The same is true of the Negroes. Any gain for America's minorities will immediately be translated into an advance for all the unskilled workers. One cannot raise the bottom of a society without benefiting everyone above. (9)

Indeed, there is a curious advantage in the wholeness of poverty. Since the other America forms a distinct system within the United States, effective action at any one decisive point will have a "multiplier" effect; it will ramify through the entire culture of misery and ultimately through the entire society.   (10)

Then, poverty is a culture in the sense that the mechanism of impoverishment is fundamentally the same in every part of the system. The vicious circle is a basic pattern. It takes different forms for the unskilled workers, for the aged, for the Negroes, for the agricultural workers, but in each case the principle is the same. There are people in the affluent society who are poor because they are poor; and who stay poor because they are poor. (11)

To realize this is to see that there are some tens of millions of Americans who are beyond the welfare state. Some of them are simply not covered by social legislation: they are omitted from Social Security and from minimum wage. Others are covered, but since they are so poor they do not know how to take advantage of the opportunities, or else their coverage is so inadequate as not to make a difference.   (12)

The welfare state was designed during that great burst of social creativity that took place in the 1930's. Its structure corresponds to the needs of those who played the most important role in building it: the middle third, the organized workers, the forces of urban liberalism, and so on. At the worst, there is "socialism for the rich and free enterprise for the poor," as when the huge corporation farms are the main beneficiaries of the farm program while the poor farmers get practically nothing; or when public funds are directed to aid in the construction of luxury housing while the slums are left to themselves (or become more dense as space is created for the well-off). (13)

So there is the fundamental paradox of the welfare state: that it is not built for the desperate, but for those who are already capable of helping themselves. As long as the illusion persists that the poor are merrily free-loading on the public dole, so long will the other America continue un-threatened. The truth, it must be understood, is the exact opposite. The poor get less out of the welfare state than any group in America. (14)

This is, of course, related to the most distinguishing mark of the other America: its common sense of hopelessness. For even when there are pro-grams designed to help the other Americans, the poor are held back by their own pessimism. (15)

On one level this fact has been described as a matter of "aspirations." Like the Asian peasant, the impoverished American tends to see life as a fate, an endless cycle from which there is no deliverance. Lacking hope (and he is realistic to feel this way in many cases), that famous solution to all problems—let us educate the poor—becomes less and less meaningful. A person has to feel that education will do something for him if he is to gain from it. Placing a magnificent school with a fine faculty in the middle of a slum is, I suppose, better than having a run-down building staffed by incom-petents. But it will not really make a difference so long as the environment of the tenement, the family, and the street counsels the children to leave as soon as they can and to disregard schooling. (16)

On another level, the emotions of the other America are even more pro-foundly disturbed. Here it is not lack of aspiration and of hope; it is a mat-ter of personal chaos. The drunkenness, the unstable marriages, the violence of the other America are not simply facts about individuals. They are the description of an entire group in the society who react this way because of the conditions under which they live. (17)

In short, being poor is not one aspect of a person's life in this country; it is his life. Taken as a whole, poverty is a culture. Taken on the family level, it has the same quality. These are people who lack education and skill, who have bad health, poor housing, low levels of aspiration and high levels of mental distress. They are, in the language of sociology, "multi-problem" families. Each disability is the more intense because it exists within a web of disabilities. And if one problem is solved, and the others are left constant, there is little gain. (18)

One might translate these facts into the moralistic language so dear to those who would condemn the poor for their faults. The other Americans are those who live at a level of life beneath moral choice, who are so sub-merged in their poverty that one cannot begin to talk about free choice. The point is not to make them wards of the state. Rather, society must help them before they can help themselves.

There is another view about the culture of poverty in America: that by
the end of the seventies it will have been halved.   (20)

It is important to deal in some detail with this theory. To begin with,
it is not offered by reactionaries. The real die-hards in the United States
do not even know the poor exist. As soon as someone begins to talk on the
subject, that stamps him as a humanitarian. And this is indeed the case with
those who look to a relatively automatic improvement in the lot of the other
America during the next twenty years or so.   (21)

The second reason why this view deserves careful consideration is that it
rests, to a considerable extent, upon the projection of inevitable and automatic change. Its proponents are for social legislation and for speeding up
and deepening this process. But their very arguments could be used to justify a comfortable, complacent inaction.   (22)

So, does poverty have a future in the United States?   (23)

One of the most reasonable and sincere statements of the theme that
poverty is coming to an end in America is made by Robert Lampman in
the Joint Committee Study Paper "The Low-Income Population and Economic Growth." Lampman estimates that around 20 per cent of the nation,
some 32,000,000 people, are poor. And he writes, "By 1977–87 we would expect about 10 percent of the population to have low income status as compared to about 20 percent now."   (24)

The main point in Lampman's relatively optimistic argument is that
poverty will decline naturally with a continuing rate of economic growth.
As the sixties begin, however, this assumption is not a simple one. In the
postwar period, growth increased until about the mid-fifties. Then a falling
off occurred. In each of the postwar recessions, the recovery left a larger
reservoir of "normal" prosperity unemployment. Also, long-term unemployment became more and more of a factor among the jobless. There were
more people out of work, and they stayed out of work longer.   (25)

In the first period of the Kennedy Administration, various economists
presented figures as to what kind of Government action was necessary so as
really to attack the problem of depressed areas and low-income occupations.
There were differences, of course, but the significant fact is that the legislation finally proposed was usually only a percentage of the need as described
by the Administration itself. There is no point now in becoming an economic prophet. Suffice it to say that serious and responsible economists feel
that the response of the society has been inadequate.   (26)

This has led to a paradoxical situation, one that became quite obvious
when economic recovery from the recession began in the spring of 1961. The
business indicators were all pointing upward: production and productivity

were on the increase. Yet the human indexes of recession showed a tenacity despite the industrial gain. Unemployment remained at high levels. An extreme form of the "class unemployment" described earlier seemed to be built into the economy.   (27)

At any rate, one can say that if this problem is not solved the other America will not only persist; it will grow. Thus, the first point of the optimistic thesis strikes me as somewhat ambiguous, for it too quickly assumes that the society will make the needed response.   (28)

But even if one makes the assumption that there will be steady economic growth, that will not necessarily lead to the automatic elimination of poverty in the United States. J. K. Galbraith, it will be remembered, has argued that the "new" poverty demonstrates a certain immunity to progress. In making his projection of the abolition of half of the culture of poverty within the next generation, Lampman deals with this point, and it is important to follow his argument.   (29)

Lampman rejects the idea that insular (or depressed-areas) poverty will really drag the poor down in the long run. As an example of this point, he cites the fact that the number of rural farm families with incomes of under $2,000 fell during the 1947–1957 period from 3.3 million to 2.4 million because of a movement off the farm.   (30)

This point illustrates the problem of dealing with simple statistics. A movement from the farm to the city, that is, from rural poverty to urban poverty, will show an upward movement in money income. This is true, among other reasons, because the money income of the urban poor is higher than that of the country poor. But this same change does not necessarily mean that a human being has actually improved his status, that he has escaped from the culture of poverty. These people who are literally driven off the land are utterly unprepared for city life. They come to the metropolis in a time of rising skill requirements and relatively high levels of unemployment. They will often enter the economic underworld. Statistically, they can be recorded as a gain, because they have more money. Socially, they have simply transferred from one part of the culture of poverty to another. (31)

At the same time, it should be noted that although there has been this tremendous exodus of the rural poor, the proportion of impoverished farms in America's agriculture has remained roughly the same.   (32)

Then Lampman deals with Galbraith's theory of "case poverty," of those who have certain disabilities that keep them down in the culture of poverty. Here it should be noted again that Galbraith himself is somewhat optimistic about case poverty. He tends to regard the bad health of the poor, physical as well as mental, as being facts about them that are individual and personal. If my thesis is right, particularly in the discussion of the twisted spirit within the culture of poverty, that is not the case. The per-

sonal ills of the poor are a social consequence, not a bit of biography about
them. They will continue as long as the environment of poverty persists.
(33)

But Lampman's optimism goes beyond that of Galbraith. He believes
that disabilities of case poverty ("mental deficiency, bad health, inability to
adapt to the discipline of modern economic life, excessive procreation, alcohol, insufficient education") are "moderated over time." And he takes as
his main case in point education. "For example, average educational attainment levels will rise in future years simply because younger people presently
have better education than older people. Hence, as the current generation
of old people pass from the scene, the percent of persons with low educational attainment will fall."   (34)

This is true, yet it is misleading if it is not placed in the context of the
changes in the society as a whole. It is much more possible today to be poor
with a couple of years of high school than it was a generation ago. The skill
level of the economy has been changing, and educational deficiency, if
anything, becomes an even greater burden as a result. In this case, saying
that people will have more education is not saying that they will escape the
culture of poverty. It could have a much more ironic meaning: that America will have the most literate poor the world has ever known.   (35)

Lampman himself concedes that the aged are "immune" to economic
growth. If this is the case, and in the absence of ranging and comprehensive
social programs, the increase in the number and percentage of the poor
within the next generation will actually increase the size of the other America. Lampman also concedes that families with female heads are immune to
a general prosperity, and this is another point of resistance for the culture
of poverty.   (36)

Finally, Lampman is much more optimistic about "nonwhite" progress
than this discussion would justify. I will not repeat the argument that has
already been given. Let me simply state the point baldly: the present rate
of economic progress among the minorities is agonizingly slow, and one cannot look for dramatic gains from this direction.   (37)

Thus, I would agree with Galbraith that poverty in the sixties has qualities that give it a hardiness in the face of affluence heretofore unknown.
There are many special factors keeping the unskilled workers, the minorities, the agricultural poor, and the aged in the culture of poverty. If there
is to be a way out, it will come from human action, from political change,
not from automatic processes.   (38)

But finally, let us suppose that Lampman is correct on every point. In
that case a generation of economic growth coupled with some social legislation would find America in 1987 with "only" 10 per cent of the nation
impoverished. If, on the other hand, a vast and comprehensive program attacking the culture of poverty could speed up this whole development, and

perhaps even abolish poverty within a generation, what is the reason for holding back? This suffering is such an abomination in a society where it is needless that anything that can be done should be done. (39)

In all this, I do not want to depict Robert Lampman as an enemy of the poor. In all seriousness, the very fact that he writes about the subject does him credit: he has social eyes, which is more than one can say for quite a few people in the society. And second, Lampman puts forward "A Program to Hasten the Reduction of Poverty" because of his genuine concern for the poor. My argument with him is not over motive or dedication. It is only that I believe that his theory makes the reduction of poverty too easy a thing, that he has not properly appreciated how deeply and strongly entrenched the other America is. (40)

In any case, and from any point of view, the moral obligation is plain: there must be a crusade against this poverty in our midst. (41)

III

If this research makes it clear that a basic attack upon poverty is necessary, it also suggests the kind of program the nation needs. (42)

First and foremost, any attempt to abolish poverty in the United States must seek to destroy the pessimism and fatalism that flourish in the other America. In part, this can be done by offering real opportunities to these people, by changing the social reality that gives rise to their sense of hopelessness. But beyond that (these fears of the poor have a life of their own and are not simply rooted in analyses of employment chances), there should be a spirit, an élan, that communicates itself to the entire society. (43)

If the nation comes into the other America grudgingly, with the mentality of an administrator, and says, "All right, we'll help you people," then there will be gains, but they will be kept to the minimum; a dollar spent will return a dollar. But if there is an attitude that society is gaining by eradicating poverty, if there is a positive attempt to bring these millions of the poor to the point where they can make their contribution to the United States, that will make a huge difference. The spirit of a campaign against poverty does not cost a single cent. It is a matter of vision, of sensitivity. (44)

Let me give an example to make this point palpable. During the Montgomery bus boycott, there was only one aim in the Negro community of that city: to integrate the buses. There were no speeches on crime or juvenile delinquency. And yet it is reported that the crime rate among Negroes in Montgomery declined. Thousands of people had been given a sense of purpose, of their own worth and dignity. On their own, and without any special urging, they began to change their personal lives; they became a different people. If the same élan could invade the other America, there would be similar results. (45)

Second, poverty forms a culture, an interdependent system. In case after case, it has been documented that one cannot deal with the various components of poverty in isolation, changing this or that condition but leaving the basic structure intact. Consequently, a campaign against the misery of the poor should be comprehensive. It should think, not in terms of this or that aspect of poverty, but along the lines of establishing new communities, of substituting a human environment for the inhuman one that now exists. (46)

Here, housing is probably the basic point of departure. If there were the funds and imagination for a campaign to end slums in the United States, most of the other steps needed to deal with poverty could be integrated with it. The vision should be this one: the political, economic, and social integration of the poor with the rest of the society. The second nation in our midst, the other America, must be brought into the Union.   (47)

In order to do this, there is a need for planning. It is literally incredible that this nation knows so much about poverty, that it has made so many inventories of misery, and that it has done so little. The material for a comprehensive program is already available. It exists in congressional reports and the statistics of Government agencies. What is needed is that the society make use of its knowledge in a rational and systematic way. There are proposals for a Department of Urban Affairs in the Cabinet (and it will probably be a reality by the time these words are published). Such an agency could be the coordinating center for a crusade against the other America. In any case, if there is not planning, any attempt to deal with the problem of poverty will fail, at least in part.   (48)

Then there are some relatively simple things that could be done, involving the expansion of existing institutions and programs. Every American should be brought under the coverage of social security, and the payments should be enough to support a dignified old age. The principle already exists. Now it must be extended to those who need help the most. The same is true with minimum wage. The spectacle of excluding the most desperate from coverage must come to an end. If it did, there would be a giant step toward the elimination of poverty itself.   (49)

In every subculture of the other America, sickness and disease are the most important agencies of continuing misery. The New York *Times* publishes a list of the "neediest cases" each Christmas. In 1960 the descriptions of personal tragedy that ran along with this appeal involved in the majority of cases the want of those who had been struck down by illness. If there were adequate medical care, this charity would be unnecessary.   (50)

Today the debate on medical care centers on the aged. And indeed, these are the people who are in the most desperate straits. Yet it would be an error of the first magnitude to think that society's responsibility begins with those sixty-five years of age. The ills of the elderly are often the inheritance of the earlier years. A comprehensive medical program, guaranteeing decent care to every American, would actually reduce the cost of caring for the aged. That, of course, is only the hardheaded argument for such an approach. More importantly, such a program would make possible a human kind of existence for everyone in the society. (51)

And finally, it must be remembered that none of these objectives can be accomplished if racial prejudice is to continue in the United States. Negroes and other minorities constitute only 25 per cent of the poor, yet their degradation is an important element in maintaining the entire culture of poverty. As long as there is a reservoir of cheap Negro labor, there is a means of keeping the poor whites down. In this sense, civil-rights legislation is an absolutely essential component in any campaign to end poverty in the United States. (52)

In short, the welfare provisions of American society that now help the upper two-thirds must be extended to the poor. This can be done if the other Americans are motivated to take advantage of the opportunities before them, if they are invited into the society. It can be done if there is a comprehensive program that attacks the culture of poverty at every one of its strong points. (53)

But who will carry out this campaign? (54)

There is only one institution in the society capable of acting to abolish poverty. That is the Federal Government. In saying this, I do not rejoice, for centralization can lead to an impersonal and bureaucratic program, one that will be lacking in the very human quality so essential in an approach to the poor. In saying this, I am only recording the facts of political and social life in the United States. (55)

The cities are not now capable of dealing with poverty, and each day they become even less capable. As the middle class flees the central urban area, as various industries decentralize, the tax base of the American metropolis shrinks. At the same time, the social and economic problems with which the city must deal are on the rise. Thus, there is not a major city in the United States that is today capable of attacking poverty on its own. On the contrary, the high cost of poverty is dragging the cities down. (56)

The state governments in this country have a political peculiarity that renders them incapable of dealing with the problem of poverty. They are, for the most part, dominated by conservative rural elements. In every state with a big industrial population, the gerrymander has given the forces of rural conservatism two or three votes per person. So it is that the state legislatures usually take more money out of the problem areas than they put back into them. So it is that state governments are notoriously weighted in the direction of caution, pinchpenny economics, and indifference to the plight of the urban millions. (57)

The various private agencies of the society simply do not have the funds to deal with the other America. And even the "fringe benefits" negotiated by unions do not really get to the heart of the problem. In the first place, they extend to organized workers in a strong bargaining position, not to the poor. And second, they are inadequate even to the needs of those who are covered.   (58)

It is a noble sentiment to argue that private moral responsibility express-ing itself through charitable contributions should be the main instrument of attacking poverty. The only problem is that such an approach does not work.   (59)

So, by process of elimination, there is no place to look except toward the Federal Government. And indeed, even if there were alternate choices, Wash-ington would have to play an important role, if only because of the need for a comprehensive program and for national planning. But in any case there is no argument, for there is only one realistic possibility: only the Federal Government has the power to abolish poverty.   (60)

In saying this, it is not necessary to advocate complete central control of such a campaign. Far from it. Washington is essential in a double sense: as a source of considerable funds needed to mount a campaign against the other America, and as a place for coordination, for planning, and the estab-lishment of national standards. The actual implementation of a program to abolish poverty can be carried out through myriad institutions, and the closer they are to the specific local area, the better the results. There are housing administrators, welfare workers, and city planners with dedication and vision. They are working on the local level, and their main frustration is the lack of funds. They could be trusted actually to carry through on a national program. What they lack now is money and the support of the American people.   (61)

There is no point in attempting to blueprint or detail the mechanisms and institutions of a war on poverty in the United States. There is informa-tion enough for action. All that is lacking is political will.   (62)

Thus the difficult, hardheaded question about poverty that one must an-swer is this: Where is the political will coming from? The other America is systematically underrepresented in the Government of the United States. It cannot really speak for itself. The poor, even in politics, must always be the object of charity (with the major exception of the Negroes, who, in recent times, have made tremendous strides forward in organization).   (63)

As a result of this situation, there is no realistic hope for the abolition of poverty in the United States until there is a vast social movement, a new period of political creativity. In times of slow change or of stalemate, it is always the poor who are expendable in the halls of Congress. In 1961, for instance, the laundry workers were dropped out of the minimum wage as part of a deal with the conservatives. Precisely because they are so poor and cruelly exploited, no one had to fear their political wrath. They, and others from the culture of poverty, will achieve the protection of the welfare state when there is a movement in this land so dynamic and irresistible that it need not make concessions. (64)

For that matter, it is much easier to catalogue the enemies of the poor than it is to recite their friends. (65)

All the forces of conservatism in this society are ranged against the needs of the other America. The ideologues are opposed to helping the poor because this can be accomplished only through an expansion of the welfare state. The small businessmen have an immediate self-interest in maintaining the economic underworld. The powerful agencies of the corporate farms want a continuation of an agricultural program that aids the rich and does nothing for the poor. (66)

And now the South is becoming increasingly against the poor. In the days of the New Deal, the Southern Democrats tended to vote for various kinds of social legislation. One of the most outspoken champions of public housing, Burnet Maybank, was a senator from South Carolina. For one thing, there is a Southern tradition of being against Wall Street and big business; it is part of the farmers' hostility to the railroads and the Babylons of the big city. For another, the New Deal legislation did not constitute a challenge to the system of racial segregation in the South. (67)

But in the postwar period, this situation began to change. As industrialization came to the South, there was a growing political opposition to laws like minimum wage, to unions, and to other aspects of social change. The leaders of this area saw their depressed condition as an advantage. They could lure business with the promise of cheap, unorganized labor. They were interested in exploiting their backwardness. (68)

The result was the strengthening of the coalition of Southern Democrats and conservative Northern Republicans. The Northern conservatives went along with opposition to Civil Rights legislation. The Southerners threw their votes into the struggle against social advance. It was this powerful coalition that exacted such a price in the first period of the Kennedy Administration. Many of the proposals that would have benefited the poor were omitted from bills in the first place, and other concessions were made in the course of the legislative battle. Thus poverty in the United States is supported by forces with great political and economic power. (69)

On the other side, the friends of the poor are to be found in the American labor movement and among the middle-class liberals. The unions in the postwar period lost much of the élan that had characterized them in the thirties. Yet on questions of social legislation they remained the most powerful mass force committed to change in general, and to bettering the lot of the poor in particular. On issues like housing, medical care, minimum wage, and social security, the labor movement provided the strongest voice stating the cause of the poor. (70)

Yet labor and the liberals were caught in the irrationalities of the American party system, and this was an enormous disadvantage to the other America. The unionists and their liberal allies are united in the Democratic party with the Southern conservatives. A Democratic victory was usually achieved by appealing to those who were concerned for social change. But at the same time it brought the forces of conservatism powerful positions on the standing committees of the Congress.   (71)

Indeed, part of the invisibility of poverty in American life is a result of this party structure. Since each major party contained differences within itself greater than the differences between it and the other party, politics in the fifties and early sixties tended to have an issueless character. And where issues were not discussed, the poor did not have a chance. They could benefit only if elections were designed to bring new information to the people, to wake up the nation, to challenge, and to call to action.   (72)

In all probability there will not be a real attack on the culture of poverty so long as this situation persists. For the other America cannot be abolished through concessions and compromises that are almost inevitably made at the expense of the poor. The spirit, the vision that are required if the nation is to penetrate the wall of pessimism and despair that surrounds the impoverished millions cannot be produced under such circumstances. (73)

What is needed if poverty is to be abolished is a return of political debate, a restructuring of the party system so that there can be clear choices, a new mood of social idealism.   (74)

These, then, are the strangest poor in the history of mankind.   (75)

They exist within the most powerful and rich society the world has ever known. Their misery has continued while the majority of the nation talked of itself as being "affluent" and worried about neuroses in the suburbs. In this way tens of millions of human beings became invisible. They dropped out of sight and out of mind; they were without their own political voice.
                                                                   (76)

Yet this need not be. The means are at hand to fulfill the age-old dream: poverty can now be abolished. How long shall we ignore this underdeveloped nation in our midst? How long shall we look the other way while our fellow human beings suffer? How long?   (77)

John Kenneth Galbraith

(1908–   )

■ *The Concept of the Conventional Wisdom*

THE FIRST REQUIREMENT for an understanding of contemporary economic and social life is a clear view of the relation between events and the ideas which interpret them. For each of these has a life of its own, and much as it may seem a contradiction in terms each is capable for a considerable period of pursuing an independent course.   (1)

The reason is not difficult to discover. Economic, like other social life, does not conform to a simple and coherent pattern. On the contrary, it often seems incoherent, inchoate, and intellectually frustrating. But one must have an explanation or interpretation of economic behavior. Neither man's curiosity nor his inherent ego allows him to remain contentedly oblivious to anything that is so close to his life.   (2)

Because economic and social phenomena are so forbidding, or at least so seem, and because they yield few hard tests of what exists and what does not, they afford to the individual a luxury not given by physical phenomena.

Within a considerable range he is permitted to believe what he pleases. He may hold whatever view of this world he finds most agreeable or otherwise to his taste.   (3)

As a consequence in the interpretation of all social life, there is a persistent and never-ending competition between what is relevant and what is merely acceptable. In this competition, while a strategic advantage lies with what exists, all tactical advantage is with the acceptable. Audiences of all kinds most applaud what they like best. And in social comment the test of audience approval, far more than the test of truth, comes to influence comment. The speaker or writer who addresses his audience with the proclaimed intent of telling the hard, shocking facts invariably goes on to expound what the audience most wants to hear.   (4)

Just as truth ultimately serves to create a consensus, so in the short run does acceptability. Ideas come to be organized around what the community as a whole or particular audiences find acceptable. And as the laboratory worker devotes himself to discovering scientific verities, so the ghost writer and the public relations man concern themselves with identifying the acceptable. If their clients are rewarded with applause, these artisans are qualified in their craft. If not they have failed. However, by sampling audience reaction in advance, or by pretesting speeches, articles, and other communications, the risk of failure can now be greatly minimized.   (5)

Numerous factors contribute to the acceptability of ideas. To a very large extent, of course, we associate truth with convenience—with what most closely accords with self-interest and individual well-being or promises best to avoid awkward effort or unwelcome dislocation of life. We also find highly acceptable what contributes most to self-esteem. Speakers before the United States Chamber of Commerce rarely denigrate the businessman as an economic force. Those who appear before the AFL-CIO are prone to identify social progress with a strong trade union movement. But perhaps most important of all, people approve most of what they best understand. Economic and social behavior are complex and mentally tiring. Therefore we adhere, as though to a raft, to those ideas which represent our understanding. This is a prime manifestation of vested interest. For a vested interest in understanding is more preciously guarded than any other treasure. It is why men react, not infrequently with something akin to religious passion, to the defense of what they have so laboriously learned. Familiarity may breed contempt in some areas of human behavior, but in the field of social ideas it is the touchstone of acceptability.   (6)

Because familiarity is such an important test of acceptability, the acceptable ideas have great stability. They are highly predictable. It will be convenient to have a name for the ideas which are esteemed at any time for their acceptability, and it should be a term that emphasizes this predictability. I shall refer to these ideas henceforth as the conventional wisdom. (7)

II

The conventional wisdom is not the property of any political group. On a great many modern social issues, as we shall see in the course of this essay, the consensus is exceedingly broad. Nothing much divides those who are liberals by common political designation from those who are conservatives. The test of what is acceptable is much the same for both. On some questions, however, ideas must be accommodated to the political preferences of the particular audience. The tendency to make this adjustment, either deliberately or more often unconsciously, is not greatly different for different political groups. The conservative is led by disposition, not unmixed with pecuniary self-interest, to adhere to the familiar and the established. These underlie his test of acceptability. But the liberal brings moral fervor and passion, even a sense of righteousness, to the ideas with which he is most familiar. While the ideas he cherishes are different from those of the conservative, he is not likely to be much less emphatic in making familiarity a test of acceptability. Deviation in the form of originality is condemned as faithlessness or backsliding. A "good" liberal or a "tried and true" liberal or a "true blue" liberal is one who is adequately predictable. This means that he forswears any serious striving toward originality. In both the United States and Britain, in recent times, liberals and their British counterparts of the left have proclaimed themselves in search of new ideas. To proclaim the need for new ideas has served, in some measure, as a substitute for them.   (8)

Thus we may, as necessary, speak of the conventional wisdom of conservatives or the conventional wisdom of liberals.   (9)

The conventional wisdom is also articulated on all levels of sophistication. At the highest levels of social science scholarship some novelty of formulation or statement is not resisted. On the contrary, considerable store is set by the device of putting an old truth in a new form, and minor heresies are much cherished. And the very vigor of minor debate makes it possible to exclude as irrelevant, and without seeming to be unscientific or parochial, any challenge to the framework itself. Moreover, with time and aided by the debate, the accepted ideas become increasingly elaborate. They have a large literature, even a mystique. The defenders are able to say that the challengers of the conventional wisdom have not mastered their intricacies. Indeed these ideas can be appreciated only by a stable, orthodox, and patient man—in brief, by someone who closely resembles the man of conventional wisdom. The conventional wisdom having been made more or less identical with sound scholarship, its position is virtually impregnable. The skeptic is disqualified by his very tendency to go brashly from the old to the new. Were he a sound scholar he would remain with the conventional wisdom.
(10)

At the same time in the higher levels of the conventional wisdom originality remains highly acceptable in the abstract. Here again the conventional wisdom often makes vigorous advocacy of originality a substitute for originality itself.   (11)

III

As noted, the hallmark of the conventional wisdom is acceptability. It has the approval of those to whom it is addressed. There are many reasons why people like to hear articulated that which they approve. It serves the ego: the individual has the satisfaction of knowing that other and more famous people share his conclusions. To hear what he believes is also a source of reassurance. The individual knows that he is supported in his thoughts—that he has not been left behind and alone. Further, to hear what one approves serves the evangelizing instinct. It means that others are also hearing and are thereby in process of being persuaded.   (12)

In some measure the articulation of the conventional wisdom is a religious rite. It is an act of affirmation like reading aloud from the Scriptures or going to church. The business executive listening to a luncheon address on the virtues of free enterprise and the evils of Washington is already persuaded, and so are his fellow listeners, and all are secure in their convictions. Indeed, although a display of rapt attention is required, the executive may not feel it necessary to listen. But he does placate the gods by participating in the ritual. Having been present, maintained attention, and having applauded, he can depart feeling that the economic system is a little more secure. Scholars gather in scholarly assemblages to hear in elegant statement what all have heard before. Yet it is not a negligible rite, for its purpose is not to convey knowledge but to beatify learning and the learned.
                                                                        (13)

With so extensive a demand, it follows that a very large part of our social comment—and nearly all that is well regarded—is devoted at any time to articulating the conventional wisdom. To some extent this has been professionalized. Individuals, most notably the great television and radio commentators, make a profession of knowing and saying with elegance and unction what their audience will find most acceptable. But in general the articulation of the conventional wisdom is a prerogative of academic, public, or business position. Thus any individual, on being elected president of a college or university, automatically wins the right to enunciate the conventional wisdom should he choose to do so. It is one of the rewards of high academic rank, although such rank is also a reward for expounding the conventional wisdom at a properly sophisticated level.   (14)

The high public official is expected, and indeed is to some extent required, to expound the conventional wisdom. His, in many respects, is the purest case. Before assuming office he ordinarily commands little attention.

But on taking up his position he is immediately assumed to be gifted with deep insights. He does not, except in the rarest instances, write his own speeches or articles; and these are planned, drafted, and scrupulously examined to insure their acceptability. The application of any other test, e.g., their effectiveness as a simple description of the economic or political reality, would be regarded as eccentric in the extreme.   (15)

Finally, the expounding of the conventional wisdom is the prerogative of business success. The head of almost any large corporation—the United States Steel Corporation, General Motors, the Radio Corporation of America—is entitled to do so. And he is privileged to speak not only on business policy and economics but also on the role of government in the society, the foundations of foreign policy, and the nature of a liberal education. In recent years it has been urged that to expound the conventional wisdom is not only the privilege but also the obligation of the businessman. "I am convinced that businessmen must write as well as speak, in order that we may bring to people everywhere the exciting and confident message of our faith in the free enterprise way of life . . . What a change would come in this struggle for men's minds if suddenly there could pour out from the world of American business a torrent of intelligent, forward-looking thinking."[1] (16)

IV

The enemy of the conventional wisdom is not ideas but the march of events. As I have noted, the conventional wisdom accommodates itself not to the world that it is meant to interpret, but to the audience's view of the world. Since the latter remains with the comfortable and the familiar, while the world moves on, the conventional wisdom is always in danger of obsolescence. This is not immediately fatal. The fatal blow to the conventional wisdom comes when the conventional ideas fail signally to deal with some contingency to which obsolescence has made them palpably inapplicable. This, sooner or later, must be the fate of ideas which have lost their relation to the world. At this stage the irrelevance will often be dramatized by some individual. To him will accrue the credit for overthrowing the conventional wisdom and for installing the new ideas. In fact, he will have only crystallized in words what the events have made clear, although this function is not a minor one. Meanwhile, like the Old Guard, the conventional wisdom dies but does not surrender. Society with intransigent cruelty may transfer its exponents from the category of wise man to that of old fogy or even stuffed shirt.   (17)

This sequence can be illustrated from scores of examples, ancient and modern. For decades prior to 1776 men had been catching the vision of the

1 Clarence B. Randall, *A Creed for Free Enterprise* (Boston: Atlantic-Little, Brown, 1952), pp. 3, 5.

liberal state. Traders and merchants in England and in the adjacent Low
Countries, and in the American colonies, had already learned that they were
served best by a minimum of government restriction rather than, as in the
conventional wisdom, by a maximum of government guidance and protection. It had become plain, in turn, that liberal trade and commerce, not the
accumulation of bullion, as the conventional wisdom held, was the modern
source of national power. Men of irresponsible originality had made the
point. Voltaire had observed that "It is only because the English have become merchants and traders that London has surpassed Paris in extent and
in the number of its citizens; that the English can place 200 warships on the
sea and subsidize allies."[2] These views were finally crystallized by Adam
Smith in the year of American independence. *The Wealth of Nations*, however, continued to be viewed with discontent and alarm by the men of the
older wisdom. In the funeral elegy for Alexander Hamilton in 1804, James
Kent complimented his deceased friend on having resisted the "fuzzy philosophy" of Smith. For another generation or more in all western countries
there would be solemn warnings that the notion of a liberal society was a
reckless idea.   (18)

Through the nineteenth century, liberalism in its classical meaning having become the conventional wisdom, there were solemn warnings of the
irreparable damage that would be done by Factory Acts, trade unions, social
insurance, and other social legislation. Liberalism was a fabric which could
not be raveled without being rent. Yet the desire for protection and security
and some measure of equality in bargaining power would not down. In the
end it became a fact with which the conventional wisdom could not deal.
The Webbs, Lloyd George, LaFollette, Roosevelt, Beveridge, and others crystallized the acceptance of the new fact. The result is what we call the welfare state. The conventional wisdom now holds that these measures softened
and civilized capitalism and made it tenable. There have never ceased to be
warnings that the break with classical liberalism was fatal.   (19)

Another interesting instance of the impact of circumstance on the conventional wisdom was that of the balanced budget in times of depression.
Almost from the beginning of organized government the balanced budget
or its equivalent has been the *sine qua non* of sound and sensible management of the public purse. The spendthrift tendencies of princes and repub-
lics alike were curbed by the rule that they must unfailingly take in as much
money as they paid out. The consequences of violating this rule had always
been unhappy in the long run and not infrequently in the short. Anciently
it was the practice of states to cover the deficit by clipping or debasing the
coins and spending the metal so saved. The result invariably was to raise
prices and lower national self-esteem. In modern times the issue of paper

2 "Tenth Philosophical Letter." Quoted by Henri Sée, *Modern Capitalism* (New York: Adelphi, 1928),
p. 87.

money or the obtaining of soft loans from banks had led to the same results. As a result, the conventional wisdom had never emphasized anything more strongly than the importance of an annually balanced budget.   (20)

But meanwhile the underlying reality had gradually changed. The rule requiring a balanced budget was designed for governments that were inherently or recurrently irresponsible on fiscal matters. Until the last century there had been no other. Then in the United States, England and the British Commonwealth, and elsewhere governments began to calculate the fiscal consequences of their actions. Safety no longer depended on confining them within arbitrary rules.   (21)

At about the same time, there appeared the phenomenon of the truly devastating depression. In such a depression men, plant, and materials were unemployed *en masse;* the extra demand from the extra spending induced by the deficit—the counterpart of the extra metal made available from the clipped coinage—did not raise prices uniquely. Rather it mostly returned idle men and plant to work. The effect, as it were, was horizontally on production rather than vertically on prices. And such price increases as did occur were far from being an unmitigated misfortune; on the contrary, they retrieved a previous, painful decline.   (22)

The conventional wisdom continued to emphasize the balanced budget. Audiences continued to respond to the warnings of the disaster which would befall were this rule not respected. The shattering circumstance was the Great Depression. This led to a severe reduction in the revenues of the federal government; it also brought increased pressure for a variety of relief and welfare expenditures. A balanced budget meant increasing tax rates and reducing public expenditure. Viewed in retrospect, it would be hard to imagine a better design for reducing both the private and the public demand for goods, aggravating deflation, increasing unemployment, and adding to the general suffering. In the conventional wisdom, nonetheless, the balanced budget remained of paramount importance. President Hoover in the early thirties called it an "absolute necessity," "the most essential factor to economic recovery," "the imperative and immediate step," "indispensable," "the first necessity of the Nation," and "the foundation of all public and private financial stability."[3] Economists and professional observers of public affairs agreed almost without exception. Almost everyone called upon for advice in the early years of the depression was impelled by the conventional wisdom to offer proposals designed to make things worse. The consensus embraced both liberals and conservatives. The Roosevelt Administration was also elected in 1932 with a strong commitment to reduced expenditures and a balanced budget. In his acceptance speech in 1932 Roosevelt said, "Revenue must cover expenditures by one means or another. Any

3 Arthur M. Schlesinger, Jr., *The Crisis of the Old Order* (Boston: Houghton Mifflin, 1956), p. 232.

government, like any family, can for a year spend a little more than it earns. But you and I know that a continuation of that habit means the poorhouse." One of the early acts of his Administration was an economy drive which included a horizontal slash in public pay. Mr. Lewis W. Douglas, through a distinguished life a notable exemplar of the conventional wisdom, made the quest for a balanced budget into a personal crusade and ultimately broke with the Administration on the issue.   (23)

In fact, circumstances had already triumphed over the conventional wisdom. By the second year of the Hoover Administration the budget was irretrievably out of balance. In the fiscal year ending in 1932, receipts were much less than half of spending. The budget was never balanced during the depression. But not until 1936 did both the necessities and advantages of this course begin to triumph in the field of ideas. In that year, John Maynard Keynes launched his formal assault in *The General Theory of Employment, Interest and Money.* Thereafter the conventional insistence on the balanced budget under all circumstances and at all levels of economic activity was in retreat. Keynes was also on his way to constructing a new body of conventional wisdom, the obsolescence of some parts of which, in its turn, is now well advanced.   (24)

v

In the following pages there will be frequent occasion to advert to the conventional wisdom—to the structure of ideas that is based on acceptability—and to those who articulate it. These references must not be thought to have a wholly invidious connotation. (The warning is necessary because, as noted, we set great ostensible store by intellectual innovation though in fact we resist it. Hence, though we value the rigorous adherence to conventional ideas, we never acclaim it.) Few men are unuseful and the man of conventional wisdom is not. Every society must be protected from a too facile flow of thought. In the field of social comment a great stream of intellectual novelties, if all were taken seriously, would be disastrous. Men would be swayed to this action or that; economic and political life would be erratic and rudderless. In the Communist countries stability of ideas and social purpose is achieved by formal adherence to an officially proclaimed doctrine. In our society a similar stability is enforced far more informally by the conventional wisdom. Ideas need to be tested by their ability, in combination with events, to overcome inertia and resistance. This inertia and resistance the conventional wisdom provides.   (25)

Nor is it to be supposed that the man of conventional wisdom is an object of pity. Apart from his socially useful role, he has come to good terms with life. He can think of himself with justice as socially elect, for society in fact accords him the applause which his ideas are so arranged as to evoke.

Secure in this applause he is well armed against the annoyance of dissent. His bargain is to exchange a strong and even lofty position in the present for a weak one in the future. In the present he is questioned with respect, if not at great length, by Congressional Committees; he walks near the head of the academic processions; he appears on symposia; he is a respected figure at the American Assembly; he is hailed at testimonial banquets. He risks being devastated by hostile events. But by then he may be dead. Only posterity is unkind to the man of conventional wisdom, and all posterity does is bury him in a blanket of neglect.   (26)

VI

No society seems ever to have succumbed to boredom. Man has developed an obvious capacity for surviving the pompous reiteration of the commonplace. The conventional wisdom protects the continuity in social thought and action. But there are also grave drawbacks and even dangers in a system of thought which by its very nature and design avoids accommodation to circumstances until change is dramatically forced upon it. In large areas of economic affairs the march of events—above all, the increase in our wealth and popular well-being—has again left the conventional wisdom sadly obsolete. It may have become inimical to our happiness. It has come to have a bearing on the larger questions of civilized survival. So while it would be much more pleasant (and also vastly more profitable) to articulate the conventional wisdom, this book involves the normally unfruitful effort of an attack upon it. I am not wholly barren of hope, for circumstances have been dealing the conventional wisdom a new series of heavy blows. It is only after such damage has been done, as we have seen, that ideas have their opportunity.   (27)

Keynes, in his most famous observation, noted that we are ruled by ideas and by very little else. In the immediate sense this is true. And he was right in attributing importance to ideas as opposed to the simple influence of pecuniary vested interest. But the rule of ideas is only powerful in a world that does not change. Ideas are inherently conservative. They yield not to the attack of other ideas but to the massive onslaught of circumstance with which they cannot contend.   (28)

David Riesman

(1909–   )

RIESMAN turned first to law before developing his deep and broad interest in the social sciences: he served as law clerk to Mr. Justice Brandeis, U.S. Supreme Court, 1935–1936; practiced law for a year in Boston; taught law for four years at the University of Buffalo, and was deputy assistant district attorney of New York County for a year (1942–1943). After World War II, he joined the faculty in the social sciences at the University of Chicago and since 1958 has been Henry Ford II professor of social sciences at Harvard. His most widely acclaimed book was The Lonely Crowd: A Study of the Changing American Character *(1950), but all of his work continues to command professional attention.*

■ *New Standards for Old: From Conspicuous Consumption to Conspicuous Production*

I

In a recent column, John Crosby affectionately quoted a remark of Sylvester L. Weaver, vice-chairman of the board of NBC: "The kids," said Weaver, "are already getting the full picture. 'The kids running around in space suits are smarter than the adults who are laughing at them.'" The parents' imagination, Weaver implied, is localized, whereas that of their children floats free even of planetary boundaries. A recent story in the science-fiction magazine *Galaxy* preaches a similar moral. It is a tale of two children, aged ten, who take off on a Moebius ring for other times and places. These children, at home in an Einsteinian universe, patronize their parents, are sorry for them, and obey them, not out of fear or favor, but lest they cause them pain. The parents are bound to a specific time and place, a specific job, whereas the children, free of chores for the most part both at home and school, are not hindered, as they would have been in an earlier day, from rapidly overtaking and surpassing their parents' know-how on the frontiers of consumption. It would be my guess, for instance, that more children than parents today favor "modern design" not only in space suits but in cars, bars, houses, and furniture.   (1)

Margaret Mead and others have pointed out that immigrant parents in America have always been on the defensive, because their children were more "American" than they. But the tendencies I am discussing seem to extend beyond this country, for they are the consequences of industrialization and urbanization and the growing leisure that, in later stages, accompany these developments. Indeed, when countries without a long Christian and Puritan heritage adopt the techniques of modern industry, they may appear more "American" than America in their readiness to slough off older ideologies of thrift and workmanship; they may hanker for leisure and consumption before they have solved the problems of production. The Coca-Cola bottlers, the Hollywood film distributors, and other consumption missionaries preach a gospel that may be premature in Thailand or Egypt. But whatever the gospel, it is doubtless the young—lacking the trained incapacities of their elders—who catch on to it most quickly, but at times, as I myself think may be true with space suits, most shallowly.   (2)

II

I am going to illustrate some of these matters by referring to a play many of you have doubtless seen: *Death of a Salesman*. Whereas in 19th-century literature, children often fear that their parents will catch them out in some frivolity, it is Willy Loman, the father in *Death of a Salesman*, who is caught out by his son in a hotel room. And the other son, Happy Loman, openly ridicules his father as a fool for working hard; Happy—how meaningful his nickname!—has latched on to American consumption know-how at its most garish: his eyes are on the pleasure frontier while his father's are still on the production-achievement frontier. Not that Biff or Happy escape defensiveness towards their father—today as in an earlier day sons are still trapped by the irrelevance of their parents' hopes and fears for them—but the initiative is certainly changed.   (3)

The changes that have taken place can scarcely be fitted into a simple chronology of parent-child relations. Too many other factors are involved. The east coast is different from the middle west—and the differences, de-

spite our stereotypes, are not well understood. There are very great differences in social class. It has been said that the upper class is oriented to the
past, the lower class to the present, the middle class to the future. The upper class therefore tends to be strongly family-centered—think of the social
memories of the Apleys, cemented by estates, portraits, memoirs, family
names, and other impedimenta, as these are portrayed in Marquand's
novel. Willy Loman, by contrast, seems to live always in the future, even
though he spends much time listening to voices out of the past which point
him to a future he didn't take or that didn't take him. Willy, in fact, appears to have no past, which is part of his pathos. . . . And Willy faces the
problem that he is not really identified with salesmen but—as happens
among some particularly outstanding salesmen—with the customers. It is
often taken for granted that the good salesman should identify with the
customers on whom he is dependent. Actually, the motives of men in business are more complex, and ambivalence towards the customer is common.
Recently, a friend of mine, a market researcher, told me how a shaving
lotion manufacturer stubbornly refused to alter his product, even to meet
complaints of customers: it was the best on the market, and that was that.
Similarly, another client, a pie-mix maker, while steadily losing business,
would not agree to change his advertising to suit what market research had
uncovered as to its effects: if potential customers who read his copy were
"biased," that was their hard luck. Here, strikingly enough, resentment of
the customer survives in firms highly dependent on sensitivity to consumers, companies which go so far as to employ market researchers but not far
enough to cater to what they regard as customer prejudice. . . .   (4)

   Willy Loman, however, failed to establish such emotional distance from
his clients, and lacking support from his own occupational group, he became something of an anomaly among salesmen, exceptionally vulnerable,
without the occupation's long-built-up defenses against the demands of
work. In his ignorance of the ropes, Willy again strikes me as unusually deracinated—something Arthur Miller mislocates, I suggest, in the intangible
nature of the occupation.   (5)

                                    III

So much may be regarded as an overture to a somewhat more systematic
account of why some of these developments have come about, why our work
and leisure have changed so considerably. Naturally, such an account must
be speculative and abbreviated; I will have to confine myself to institutional changes and to such intellectual currents as *Babbitt* or *Death of a
Salesman* represent.   (6)

   Let me emphasize, first of all, that such changes are never wholesale.
Thus, the attitude towards the middleman in *Death of a Salesman* is noth-

ing new. The idea that the middleman doesn't produce anything can be found in medieval thought and in the Reformation; the idea was very strong in 19th-century American populism. Populism, though it appears to have vanished, has left its mark. For example, nostalgia for a rural past is still very strong in America. Even so urban a writer as Arthur Miller is obsessed in *Death of a Salesman* with the fencing in of a once-rural Brooklyn and with the virtuousness of working with one's hands close to the soil. What is interpreted as "close to the soil" is, to be sure, partly a matter of cultural definition; thus, in Kansas City the leading annual social event, at which debutantes are presented, is the American Royal, a stock show at which grain traders and cattle buyers parade around under huge Stetsons —perhaps believing for a moment that they can identify with ranch life although they make their living as down-town brokers, and although ranchers themselves would seldom wear such head-gear. These identifications, as they become ritualized, have much more influence on our conceptions of our work than anything "intrinsic" to that work (such as the soil itself) or to man's biological potentiality for work and for avoiding work.   (7)

An illustration of the slow way in which cultural definitions change lies in the fact that, as Americans have sloughed off to a considerable extent the Puritan's exalted valuations of work, we have nevertheless not on the whole sought jobs that would provide a maximum of income with a minimum of work. Rather, what has happened is that our aims have become more complex: we now seek "the right kind" of work, including the right blend of leisure with work and inside work. For instance, a recent series of articles in *Fortune* indicates that we are witnessing the death of our salesmen in general: companies are finding it more and more difficult to recruit salesmen, even or especially when they work on a commission basis. The old-fashioned salesman set his own pace; he had a great deal of leisure, and, if he was good and business was good, he could make money. But today such opportunities seem often to go begging, and corporations engage in all kinds of semantic niceties, such as redefining sales jobs as sales engineering to get around the problem; they try to replace direct selling by advertising, and by using the retail store as the point-of-sale as in the Supermarket. College graduates today want jobs in personnel work or other "service" occupations, rather than in the exposed and isolated position of the salesman. For one thing, their wives make more demands of them than Willy's wife did: they want them home, and free of ulcers—and these new-style wives are more help to their men than the neutral misery of Mrs. Loman was any comfort to Willy. In the old days, Biff might have become a salesman without afterthought, but his ambitions are confused by some of the newer currents.   (8)

One reason for this is that young people seem to be increasingly choosing the role of an employee in a large organization, with pensions and perquisites, rather than the chance to make a quick killing by commission selling or other risky entrepreneurial jobs. One company reported to *Fortune* that they now look for salesmen among Greeks—an ethnic group not yet acculturated to the newer American values; another, that they do their recruiting for sales in Texas and Oklahoma—states where also old-fashioned crazy millionaires can still be found. Sometimes people refer to high income taxes as a determining factor, but I think taxes, though certainly an element, are frequently used as rationalizations by men who don't want to take risks. Taxes are simply part of the managerial climate in which enterprise is now carried on, in which innovation is entrusted to a research and development staff trained at the Columbia School of Industrial Management and the Harvard Business School—men who take courses which deal with human relations in order that they will be able to get along with their colleagues in the office, or at least to discuss problems of human relations at American Management Association meetings.   (9)

And this leads me to a further reflection on *Death of a Salesman*. You will remember the terrible scene in which Howard Wagner fires Willy, while listening to an idiotic recording. Some of my colleagues at Chicago have recently been studying retirement practices and find that one reason many companies have a firm rule compelling retirement at, let us say, 65 is that people today are too soft-hearted to fire other people. At one large steel company, a number of older men have jobs which are make-work because no one can bring himself to discharge them. A retirement rule locates the responsibility elsewhere, makes it impersonal. This is true of the retirement regulations in universities also. Indeed, wherever I have observed such matters—in business, in government, in academic life—I have noticed the lengths to which people will go before firing somebody. Howard Wagners are hard to come by. (Now again you will notice that I am criticizing the play on the basis of a sociological estimate, but I must say that the play invites such criticism by its own effort at documentary realism.)   (10)

IV

So far, I have spoken as if fear of risk was the chief factor in the actual dearth of entrepreneurs and of salesmen in the American economy at present. But there is also a growing desire to be serviceable to others—this is one reason for the current high prestige of the medical profession. The attraction of personnel work for many college graduates rests on their urge to work *with* people (the fact is, they more often work with files—but that is in a way beside the point) rather than, as they interpret selling, *against* people. People want to be part of a team, part of a group. Work is done in groups, research is done in groups. It is this security which is often more important than pension plans. (I am discussing at such length the problem of work and the salesman today, because in order to see clearly the changes in the standards for judging consumption, we have to see how work itself has changed. For work and play seem to be fundamental dualities in culture, like day and night, male and female, parent and child, self and not-self.) (11)

It may be that the changes I have been discussing are partly kept from clearer view by the American belief that men must be tough, not soft and sentimental; thus, we tend to conceal from ourselves as well as from others our conciliatory attitudes, our moods of fearing success and display, our sensitivity to envy. And so we continue to talk about free enterprise, about getting ahead—about all the older values which the Loman family, in its several ways, has taken so literally. But often this talk is big talk, or whistling to keep up our courage. (12)

Such interpretation of contemporary talk, in fact, requires us to go back historically and raise the question whether in the 19th century, underneath all the Horatio Alger talk and the Samuel Smiles talk, similar ambivalences towards an all-out individualism were not present. The Christian values which are so strong in Mr. Gosse's group of Plymouth Brethren not only helped to spur the rise of a competitive, individualistic capitalism, but also moderated that capitalism by feelings of social responsibility, of concern for the other—after all, they were called "Brethren." And Christianity always contains the latent dynamic of a potential return to the values of the early Christian era, before the Church became a great going concern; in other words, there is always the available material for a reformation—within Catholicism as well as within Protestantism. Christianity may have become something of a shell in the 19th century, for many pious frauds, but it was always more than that and was not for long successfully allied with the more ferocious forms of competitiveness. Bruce Barton's notion of a generation ago that Jesus was really a big advertising man would hardly go over today among people of Babbitt's station, let alone among the advertising men who relish Mead's satiric *How to Get Ahead in Business without Really Trying*. (13)

By the same evidence, we may conclude that there *have* been changes, very profound ones, although their origins can be traced back to an earlier day. Values once confined to a small elite group, or to an elite place within the hearts of many people—a kind of Sunday rather than weekday place—have now become much more widespread. For example, we can see this in attitudes towards conspicuous consumption. Veblen noticed in his book on the leisure class, published in 1899, that some small groups among the very rich were learning to be offended by conspicuous display, they were going in for "natural-looking" estates, "natural-looking" contrivances, and presumably "natural-looking" dress, too. He realized that when a leisure class gets large enough, and sufficiently in touch with itself, it can depart from

grossly vulgar display—it can whisper rather than shout. And he saw how
renewed attitudes of "workmanship," as against the earlier "wastemanship"
at the top of the social pyramid, could spread downwards, as more people
gained leisure, and as more came in contact with leisure class values. (14)

Yet even he, perhaps because of his farm origin and midwest experience, did not see fully the extent to which nonconspicuous nonconsump-
tion (or, as one of my friends more appropriately terms it, "conspicuous
under-consumption") was already a powerful American pattern. He seems
to have escaped contact with Boston Unitarians or Philadelphia Quakers
whose display was much more veiled. Although in Henry Adams' novel,
Democracy, we are treated to an inauguration ball more gaudy than the
un-top-hatted one of a few weeks ago [January, 1953], when we read Henry
James' *The Bostonians*, which appeared in 1876, we are confronted with
wealthy young women who were plain of dress and disdainful of display.
For them, good intangible causes took the place of good commodities. (15)

I should add, in fairness to Veblen, that he saw some of this. But he
largely overlooked the possibility that these attitudes were being shaped by
intellectual as well as by merely technological currents. Thus it would not
have occurred to him that his own books would influence people's attitudes
towards consumption, that he would be the godfather of the consumers'
movement—that, indeed, a whole series of books, including his own and
coming right down to Marquand's novels or *Death of a Salesman*, have
helped inter certain American values with irony and sarcasm. For him, as
for Marx, men always conform eventually to economic necessity, not to cultural or ideological necessity.   (16)

Nevertheless, Veblen's *Theory of the Leisure Class* fitted not too badly
the American scene from the gay 90s to the not quite so gay 20s. The hero
in the novel *Jefferson Selleck* who suffers agonies on his wedding night because he is of lower social origin than his bride; the drama of *The Great
Gatsby*, and the miseries of Charlie Gray in *Point of No Return* and of
Mary Monahan and her intimidated Beacon Street lover in the *Late George
Apley*, are so many testimonies to the Veblenian cruelties of the American
status system, with its unmerry emulative chase. And yet the last novels I
mentioned are testimony also to a newer note in American life and literature, that of the failure of success, rather than, as in *Death of a Salesman*,
the failure of failure.   (17)

                                v

It has, I believe, been the bounteousness of modern industry, especially in
America, which has done more than almost anything else to make conspicuous consumption obsolete here. It would go much too far to say that consumption bores us, but it no longer has the old self-evident quality; it no

longer furnishes our lives with a kind of simple structure or chronology of motives, as it did for William Randolph Hearst, for instance. To collect objects in Hearst's manner required a certain confidence, even arrogance, a certain imperviousness to ridicule and criticism. Hearst's "whim of iron" appears to be a thing of the past.   (18)

It is not only or primarily, however, that our interest in goods has been drowned by the boundless cornucopia of goods, by analogy with Engel's law that food consumption declines proportionately as income rises. The same expansion of the economy has created new fortunes much faster than their possessors could possibly be tutored by the old rich in the proper consumption values of the latter. No mere "400" located in a single city can any longer dictate appropriate leisure-class behavior in terms of what estates, houses, furniture, and so on to collect. The absence of titles in America, and of many old-family names equivalent to titles (judging by names, many Negroes and onetime Kabotskys belong to some of the best families), also makes such hegemony very difficult—indeed, from the point of view of an Italian count (unfamiliar with American distinctions even in the days of Daisy Miller), a Dallas oil heiress in seven figures and Neiman-Marcus clothes may be preferable to a Saltonstall in six figures and Jordan Marsh clothes. In this situation, the more established wealth and its auxiliary leaders of high taste have sought to fight back, not by a futile outspending, but by a conspicuous underspending. A Hearst has been ridiculed, not only for poor taste in *what* he bought, but *that* he bought in such quantity. (19)

No doubt, universal education—itself part of our bonanza of good fortune—has exposed many people who later have come into means to tasteful critiques of working-class extravagance. The mass media, too, carry along with the prodigality of their advertising the relative emaciation of their judgments on expenditure: the *Vogue* style of restrained elegance is made an accessible model for millions. However, the movement of style has not only been from the top down—and how could it be when people can't tell, for reasons already indicated, where the top is? A relaxation of standards has spread upwards: the new rich gentleman needs no longer to struggle into a dress suit to hear Mary Garden at the Opera House, nor need he learn to ride to hounds or to send his sons to Groton or St. Marks. All he has to learn to do—and this, as Robert L. Steiner and Joseph Weiss point out in "Veblen Revised in the Light of Counter-Snobbery," is not easy for him—is to mute the wish for wild and gaudy spending that he learned as a lower-class lad, the very wish that may have helped propel him into the millionaire ranks. Frictions on this score are indicated by the concern of the Cadillac people with the consequences for their older clients of the fact that the Cadillac (rather than, as some years ago, the Buick) has become "the" car for well-off Negroes.   (20)

Today, men of wealth, fearful of making a wrong move, harried not only by taxes but by public relations and their own misgivings, are apt to give over the now-dreaded responsibilities for spending to a foundation, which then on their behalf can collect research projects or artistic works— protected by bureaucratic organization and corporate responsibility from imputations of extravagance. (As I write this, however, the big foundations such as Ford and Rockefeller are under Congressional Committee scrutiny —there seems to be no escape from money save anonymity!)   (21)

Another form of putting spending at arm's length is to delegate it to one's children. Whether for toys or for schools, for space in the home or advice on child management, more money is being spent on children and by them than ever before. The trouble with children, of course, is that they grow up—unlimited amounts cannot be spent on them. Before too long, in the same strata that Veblen and Arthur Miller have influenced, the children now grown up are denouncing advertising and disdainful of waste and extravagance. The parents, of course, can have more children, and as you may know, this is what has happened to the country in the last decade, much to the bewilderment of the demographers, who thought that the American urban middle classes would continue to have fewer and fewer children and more and more commodities. Demographers do not know, and I do not know, why the shift has occurred; doubtless the causes are complex and ramified—the same thing has happened in France and elsewhere. But I do suspect that the changes in value-patterns we have been discussing have been among the factors. I started several years ago reading college class books for the light they might shed on subtle shifts in attitude. I was struck by the emphasis on the family that began to appear in my own and other college classes of a few years back. People in writing about themselves no longer started off by saying they were Vice-President of Ozark Air Lines and a director of the Tulsa National Bank, and so forth; they began by telling about the wife and five kids and how they had a home in the suburbs where they all enjoyed barbecues in the back yard. The occupational achievement was played down; the family scene, with its pastoral virtues, played up. Since then I have found similar tendencies in other groups. This would seem to hang together with the devaluation of individual success we have been discussing: children are a kind of unequivocal good in a world of changing values, and we can lavish on children the care and emotions we would now feel it egotistical to lavish on ourselves. The younger age at which people are marrying today is a further factor; having started to go steady at fourteen, they want to settle down at twenty. Whereas a generation ago a career man and career girl would have considered marriage an obstacle to their work aims, today marriage and children are in a way part of the consumption and leisure sphere, the side of life currently emphasized.   (22)

VI

Thus, children absorb some of the surplus and foundations some more of it. Especially the biggest foundation of all—the federal government. Conspicuous consumption has been socialized, and appears of necessity largely in the form of weapons, with something left over for national parks. When we speak of government spending for armaments, it is clear that the line between consumption and production is hard to draw, and the much more general point I want to make is that with the decline in conspicuous consumption—a relative rather than an absolute decline perhaps—has come a great rise in what we might call conspicuous production. (23)

As I have implied earlier, the company for which Willy Loman worked did not engage in conspicuous production—else they would have kept him on, finding a place for him in overhead. The companies that do engage in it begin by locating and designing their plants and offices for show as well as for "efficiency" in the older sense of nearness to suppliers, distributors, and other facilities. It would be interesting to know to what extent the immense tax-facilitated rebuilding of American industry since World War II has been influenced by management's desire to have a plant that looked like the *Fortune* ads of the Austin Company and other designers of low-slung, "streamlined" factories. To be sure, if such factories are good for morale, they are by definition efficient, but the Hawthorne experiments are some evidence that workers respond more to interest taken in them than to lighting, cooling, or other circumambient factors—very likely, such factories are good for executives' and directors' morale. (These experiments were made nearly a generation ago.) (24)

Conspicuous production takes a great variety of forms. If a company leads the procession in granting paid vacations or in providing some new service for employees—that may be partly conspicuous production. Many additions to overhead both constitute such production and spend time advertising it—even some incumbents of the president's chair may have that as their principal role. Officials, who would no longer be as eager as their predecessors were to buy their way into an exclusive country club, suburb, or resort, are most eager to have their companies' ads appear in the pages of *Business Week, Fortune,* or on television, whether or not their market research can wholly justify each instance of space- or time-buying. I understand that some large companies have issued manuals to their officials on how to live up to their expense accounts, and we may properly regard such manuals as successors to all the educative literature by which previous ruling groups have been taught to spend—something which, strange as it may seem to some of you, needs always to be learned. (25)

Professor Richard Hofstadter has suggested that these practices should be called conspicuous corporate consumption rather than conspicuous production. Certainly, it is as difficult to distinguish one from the other as to distinguish work from play among many of the managerial work-force. It would take a very close scrutiny of factory lay-out, for instance, to be sure what changes were the result of desires for corporate prestige rationalized as cost-cutting methods, and to know whether to allocate the costs of prestige itself to the production or the consumption side of the ledger. The aesthetics of the machines of production, factories and plants express a slightly different kind of conspicuous production. It is only when we adopt an "economizing" point of view that we can distinguish, in the activities centered around the economy, between the end of maximizing the product and the other ends, ceremonial, religious, prestige-laden, that are contextually being pursued. The conspicuousness of these other ends is the result, as Professor Martin Meyerson has pointed out to me, of our taking for granted as the sole end of work that of maximizing product—from that distorted, if traditional, perspective other ends embedded in the context of social life appear out of order, even garish. Men who in the 19th century or today seem to be pursuing wealth or efficiency as a single uncomplicated goal were certainly self-deceived as to their total gamut of motives. Nevertheless we can say, I think, that corporate consumption, in which each company goes into business as a junior welfare state, does currently rearrange our motives in a new configuration. (26)

One factor, as I have already indicated, is the increasing professionalization of management, a development which has had consequences rather different from those Brandeis or Taylor hoped for. The 18th- and 19th-century industrialist came out of a rural background or ideology: he regarded his firm as a farm, and his work-force as hired hands, often transient and easily replaced, or as a small-town business, paternalistically run. He did not think of himself as having to be an expert on human relations—that could be left to the clergy, the main professionals in his purview. Feeling, moreover, some doubt as to where he stood socially, vis-a-vis the clergy and vis-a-vis Eastern aristocrats, he built a big feudal castle of a house for himself to show everybody that he had arrived, as if to declaim that he was personally worthy by visible evidences of his net worth: if he could not outshout the clergyman and the statesman, he could at least outshine them. And his wife, lacking the cultural tutelage of aristocratic wives and excluded by patriarchal convention from any contact with the workaday world, had nothing more to occupy her than to act as his deputy in conspicuous spending, his ambassador to the dominions of culture he was too busy and too bored to bother with. (27)

Such an industrialist, when he met his competitors, frankly regarded them as such, and whatever conviviality he might show, he kept his secrets of production to himself. He met with others, that is, in terms of money,

not in terms of a specialized profession which freely exchanges its own secrets while keeping them from the lay public. Today, the communication
of industrialists and businessmen with one another is frequently quite different. Meeting as professionals, the former individuality which distinguished the American businessman is rubbed off. He seeks status in his
ability to run a smooth, attractive, and pleasant social and technological
organization. Unions obviously have done something to encourage this,
and so has government, in its tax and labor policy, but the desire of businessmen themselves to become professionals in human relations seems to
be a major element. (28)

And their wives, too, have changed. If they are college trained, it isn't
enough for them to spend their husband's income. Often they have had
jobs themselves; they may be professionals in their own right, or potential
professionals. They want to become pals and companions of their business
spouses—sleeping partners, so to speak—aware of what goes on at work, and
vicarious consumers of corporate conspicuousness, flaunting not so much
their own now-standardized fur coats but their husband's firms—a more indirect display. Both husband and wife are urban, not small-town and rural,
in their orientation; and they tend to view the factory work-force as a human collectivity in which there are roles to be played and maneuvers to
be made. The earlier 19th-century horrors of rapid urbanization, in which
human relations tended to become depersonalized and older social groupings
disintegrated, now appear to be giving way to new institutional forms
adapted to the conditions of contemporary city life. The presence of women
on this scene, in fact or in feeling, helps alter the atmosphere, introducing
a consumption mood into work relations, with its refreshing congeniality
of association as contrasted with a male society of tycoons. (29)

The divorce of corporate ownership from control and the consequent
disenfranchisement of the stockholders (plus federal tax policies) have put
responsibility for spending the corporate surplus on the executive in his
capacity as an official, for corporate savings are only to a limited extent distributed to stockholders but are increasingly retained in depreciation funds
or other concealment or reserve accounts. Business management schools
play a part in deciding what it is that the corporation should now spend
money for—whether it is for training directors, or market research, or philanthropic activity (which now supports much "pure" research)—all the
multifarious forms of conspicuous corporate consumption. (30)

In general, I think it can be said that many of the motives which were
in earlier decades built into the character structure of individuals are now
built into the institutional structure of corporate life. On the whole, I
would rather see our surplus used to allow individuals a still greater
amount of leisure, so that each of us would work, let us say, a four-hour
day, than keep us at work eight hours so that our large organizations can

generously spend the difference. And yet, in making such a judgment, I
know I must continuously keep in mind the complex and stratified nature
of the changes going on in our American life. If I had to choose between
having Lever Brothers spend the American surplus on its beautiful Park
Avenue offices and having the Happy Lomans and Glenn McCarthys spend
it, I could easily come down on the side of Lever Brothers. Corporate consumption may be, as it has often been in architecture, a pleasure in its own
right and sometimes a model for individual consumption.   (31)

John W. Gardner

(1912–   )

GARDNER *has been Secretary of Health, Education, and Welfare in the
Johnson administration since 1965 and President of the Carnegie Corpora-
tion of New York since 1955. A trained psychologist (Ph.D., University of
California, 1938), he has written two significant books:* Excellence: Can
We Be Equal and Excellent Too? *and* Self-Renewal: The Individual and
the Innovative Society.

◼ *Tyranny Without a Tyrant*

THE TYRANNY OF THE FORMULA

THE TIDES OF change that move society on to new solutions or catastrophes
run deeper than the swirling events of the day. In relation to these great
tidal movements, the trends we observe in our lifetimes are surface currents
and the crises of the morning newspaper the merest whitecaps.   (1)

One of the deep tidal currents—perhaps the most fateful—is the movement over recent centuries toward the creation of ever larger, more complex and more highly organized social groupings.   (2)

It is a trend that we must examine here because it threatens the freedom and integrity of the individual; and the capacity of society for continuous renewal depends ultimately upon the individual. He is the seedbed of change, the inventor and innovator, the critic of old ways and mapper of new paths. John Stuart Mill wrote, "A state which dwarfs its men . . . will find that with small men no great thing can be accomplished." We need only add that no *new* thing can be accomplished, no renewing thing, no revitalizing thing.   (3)

Ignorance, disease, undernourishment, political and economic subjugation are still the most powerful forces stunting individual growth. But every thoughtful man today worries about the novel and subtle restraints placed on the individual by modern large-scale organization—and fears that we may triumph over the old evils only to find ourselves enmeshed in a new and streamlined tyranny.   (4)

It is futile to hope that the movement toward more intricate and inclusive social organization will reverse itself. A modern society is—and must be—characterized by complex organization. It is not a matter of choice. We must cope as best we can with the pressures that modern large-scale organization places on the individual. These pressures have been a favorite theme of social critics and it is not necessary to describe them here. But it may be useful to clear up some of the confusions that have surrounded the subject.
                                                                             (5)

One shortcoming in current writing on this subject has been the tendency to seek a villain. An essential feature of the individual's predicament today is that there is no villain. It is not a question of one social class dominating another; nor of believers in one dogma oppressing believers in another dogma. It is not a tyrant who subjugates the individual. It is not even that tired old bogeyman, Madison Avenue. Nor that fanciful new bogeyman—The Establishment. What is oppressing the individual is the very nature of modern society.   (6)

Yet the search for a villain continues. Clearly, it fills some emotional need on the part of the searchers.   (7)

There are oppressors on the scene, of course, and we may learn something by observing them closely. We still think of the typical dictator as one who flouts the wishes of the people, but outright tyranny without concern for the appearance of popular consent is the most old-fashioned of political maneuvers today. The truly modern dictator achieves his goals *through* the people, not in spite of them. He rides their aspirations to power. He manipulates their hopes and fears and is ushered into office with their joyous shouts. He may then construct, with the consent of the people, precisely the same machinery of control that he would otherwise have had to construct over their opposition. The process may be observed in some nations today, in some communities and in some labor unions. (8)

If we understand how these things can happen, then we are in a position to understand that people can construct their own tyrannies. If one's freedom must be invaded, it is perhaps comforting to find the invasion accomplished democratically. But loss of freedom is loss of freedom.   (9)

Finally, many threats to individual freedom do not stem even remotely from the relationships of authority and subordination nor indeed from any political circumstance, but from customs, traditions and conceptions of what is "proper procedure." These can be as coercive as any tyranny. (10)

Another familiar error is to assume that the pressure on the individual may be understood as a liberal versus conservative issue or a government versus private enterprise issue. Nothing could be more misleading. Politically conservative men who saw themselves as rugged individualists created the modern corporation—a perfect example of the large-scale social organization that poses problems for the individual. Liberal-minded men who would count themselves devoted friends of freedom spearheaded the trend toward Big Government and Big Labor, both of which pose far-reaching problems for the individual.   (11)

The truth is that neither conservatives nor liberals are responsible for the hazards facing the modern individual. Neither "creeping socialism" nor "the acquisitive society" is responsible. Modern mass society has developed under various ideological climates. The techniques of large-scale organization are not the property of any ideological group. The huge urban centers characteristic of mass society have developed with equal rapidity in Japan, India, Russia and the United States.   (12)

Still another error is to assert, as many do, that the "inhuman" aspects of modern social organization are the fault of science and technology. This view has deep emotional roots and there is not much point in arguing with those who hold it. They would rather stay mad.   (13)

But the truth is that workers in the grimmest moments of modern industrialism were no more miserable than, let us say, the Egyptian slaves who built the pyramids. It is not advanced technology that causes the trouble. The root of the difficulty is an attitude of mind that has never really died out in the world, nor perhaps even diminished greatly since the days of the Pharaohs—a willingness to sacrifice human values to other objectives.   (14)

Modern technology *need not* destroy aesthetic, spiritual and social values, but it will most certainly do so unless the individuals who manage our technology are firmly committed to the preservation of such values.   (15)

The tyranny of mass society is not a matter of one man's foot on another man's neck. It is a tyranny of the formula. Mass society searches for common denominators. Sheer numbers make it impossible to take account of individual identity. Serving the mass market requires standardization.

Popular culture becomes homogenized. Even political campaigns are planned by the market researcher. (16)

The exacting requirements of a highly organized society lead to the development of ingenious and powerful management techniques—in communications, information processing, cost accounting, personnel and public relations. Such techniques are rarely designed by men who harbor conscious tyrannical purposes. But in the hands of men insensitive to the needs of the individual such techniques do all too often result in the "processing" of human beings. (17)

The pressures that produce conformity are often misunderstood. The precisely interlocked processes of a complex modern society require a high degree of predictability of individual behavior. The individual conforms because it seems like the sensible way to keep the organization running smoothly. Eccentric convictions, unpopular views, unique styles of behavior get in the way. Personnel directors look for the man who will fit in. Parents say, "You want to be popular, don't you?" The Image Managers encourage the individual to fashion himself into a smooth coin, negotiable in any market. An occasional Kierkegaard may insist that "the crowd is untruth," but the man in the street takes a more practical view. (18)

The long-run hazard for a society that needs independent and creative men and women to ensure its continued vitality is clear. The very subtlety and blandness of the process adds to the danger. (19)

Another difficulty is that the complex processes of modern society tend to force the individual into an excessively specialized role. To the extent that they do they deprive him of the wholeness, versatility and generalized competence that he should preserve at all costs. Not only does it become increasingly difficult for him to comprehend his relationship to the world about him, he has less time (or inclination) to explore this relationship as he whittles himself down to fit a slot in the intricate pattern. (20)

One of the clearest dangers in modern society is that men and women will lose the experience of participating in meaningful decisions concerning their own life and work, that they will become cogs in the machine because they *feel like* cogs in the machine. All too often today they are inert components of the group, not participating in any significant way but simply being carried along like grains of sand in a bucket. (21)

Malcolm Cowley, speaking of the Lost Generation, wrote:

> But the decay of society was psychologically equivalent to its progress: both were automatic processes that we ourselves could neither hasten nor retard. Society was something alien, which our own lives and writings could never affect; it was a sort of parlor car in which we rode, over smooth tracks, toward a destination we should never have chosen for ourselves. (22)

The disastrous consequences of such attitudes for the morale of a society are obvious. Without some grasp of the meaning of his relationship to the whole, it is not easy for the individual to retain a vivid sense of his own capacity to act as an individual, a sure sense of his own dignity and an awareness of his roles and responsibilities. He tends to accept the spectator role and to sink into passivity.   (23)

It is not easy for a modern, complex society to prevent such an outcome. The individual is fixed in a network of abstractions. Instead of working for a known boss, he is employed by a corporation. Instead of coping with a rival across the street, he copes with forces of the market. Instead of fashioning a product with his own hands, he shuffles papers, juggles figures or pushes buttons. He receives orders from people he has never met and makes recommendations without knowing those who will be affected by them. A well-known government official offered a poignant vignette of modern organizational life when he said: "What we sign we haven't written, and what we write someone else signs."   (24)

The classic criticism of the assembly line is that work has been so organized that the worker has few decisions to make and never experiences the consequences of those he does make. It is important to note that this is a consequence of the way the work has been organized and not an evil inherent in The Machine. Emotional attacks on mechanization usually miss the point. The fault is not with mechanization as such. A bucket brigade can be as frustrating as an assembly line. The fault lies in an assignment of functions that ignores the needs of the individual.   (25)

This is in some measure an inevitable consequence of large-scale modern organization. Economies of scale can be achieved by centralizing decisions, and the complex modern society has been incredibly ingenious in accomplishing such centralization. Countless schemes and devices, from prepared cake mixes to electronic computers, relieve the individual of the burden of decision. No wonder critics ask whether modern man will become a sodden, immobile consumer of predigested offerings and a mindless performer of pre-programmed tasks.   (26)

But then the individual, with some obscure instinct for his own survival, takes up a hobby in which decisions are still possible. The do-it-yourself movement deserves comment. When a manufacturer markets high-fidelity sound equipment that is designed to be sold in an unassembled state so that the customer can have the fun of assembling it, he is going counter to some of the most powerful currents of our time. Over the past century, industrial society has devoted untold ingenuity and skill to the objective of placing a foolproof, prefabricated device in the hands of a supposedly passive and moronic consumer. Now a respectable fraction of those consumers turn out to have vagrant impulses that are not served by ingenuities of prefabrication. They want to exercise their hands and minds on concrete tasks. They want to puzzle over something, shape something, contribute their sweat to something. We have hardly begun to absorb the implications of that fact. (27)

ORGANIZING FOR FREEDOM

Large-scale organization does not always diminish the individual's freedom—in some respects it enlarges it. (28)

As a result of large-scale organization modern man enjoys freedoms that he could not hope to enjoy otherwise. Out of the vast and elaborately organized medical center come findings that free the individual from illnesses that have plagued mankind for centuries. The great urban university, which strikes some critics as little more than a huge factory, places within reach of millions of low-income workers the opportunity to surmount ignorance and stretch their horizons. (29)

The man who moves from a small town to a large city experiences unaccustomed freedom. He not only escapes the stultifying web of attitudes, expectations and censorship that characterize the small town, he finds in the city more choices in every dimension—kinds of dwelling, consumer goods, entertainment, social companions, culture and work. (30)

Of course this new freedom is quickly taken for granted. When men find that their range of choice has been widened, they simply raise their aspirations with respect to freedom of choice. Instead of being grateful for new freedoms, they resent more intensely the remaining limits on their freedom. We must never forget that, while the modern world has produced grounds for complaint, it has also produced the man doing the complaining, a man who expects more than any of his forebears expected. (31)

The point was brought home to me recently when I visited an academic friend. He sat in an air-conditioned study. Behind him was a high-fidelity phonograph and record library that brought him the choicest music of three centuries. On the desk before him was the microfilm of an ancient Egyptian papyrus that he had obtained by a routine request through his university library. He described a ten-day trip he had just taken to London, Paris and Cairo to confer on recent archaeological discoveries. In short, modern technology and social organization were serving him in spectacular ways. And what was he working on at the moment? An essay for a literary journal on the undiluted evil of modern technology and large-scale organization. (32)

Some critics argue that the growth in size and complexity of organization has been accompanied by an increase in relationships of authority and subordination, but anthropologists and historians would not support this view. The spirit of hierarchy can flourish quite as fiercely in an organization consisting of one man and his secretary as it can in General Motors. Small businesses do not necessarily offer their employees a more equalitarian atmosphere than do large corporations. Small nations with a pre-modern social structure have managed to be quite as authoritarian as modern nations, generally more so. As a matter of fact, the primitive tribe or pre-industrial community has usually demanded far more profound submission of the individual to the group than has any modern society.   (33)

In short, large-scale organization is not to be condemned out of hand. That is what makes the problem difficult—and interesting. Organization serves man and rules him, increases his scope and hems him in. We must be exceedingly discriminating in weighing its benefits against possible disadvantages. And in doing so we shall discover that everything depends on the patterns of organization.   (34)

We cannot return to a simpler world. Much of contemporary social criticism is made irrelevant by its refusal to face that fact. It is true that the pressure and tumult of our society compares unfavorably with, say, the tranquillity of a village in Brittany. But the comparison does not deal with a choice that is open to us. We must live in the modern world. We cannot stem the pressure for more intricate organization of our economy, our production, our social, political and cultural life. We must master the new forms of organization or they will master us.   (35)

The most hopeful thing today is that on *some fronts* we seem to be achieving patterns of organization that avoid the stultification, rigidity and threats to freedom inherent in monolithic integrations. If this is true, it may be the most important single fact in our future.   (36)

It is possible to continue achieving economies of scale and still give attention to human needs. Too often in the past we have designed systems to meet all kinds of exacting requirements except the requirement that they contribute to the fulfillment and growth of the participants. Organizations need not be designed in such a way that they destroy human initiative. They are designed that way because we have not been willing to be as inventive about organizational matters as we have been about hardware. (37)

It is essential that in the years ahead we undertake intensive analysis of the impact of the organization on the individual. We must examine the conditions under which organization is a threat to the individual, the kinds of organizational patterns that are the greatest threat and the safeguards that can be built into organization to minimize the threat. We must discover how to design organizations and technological systems in such a way that individual talents are used to the maximum and human satisfaction and dignity preserved. We must learn to make technology serve man not only in the end product but in the doing.   (38)

Some of our social critics believe that the way to fight for freedom in a world of organization is to be, in so far as possible, a nonconforming curmudgeon. They would say, in Samuel Goldwyn's immortal phrase, "Include me out." This is not entirely to be deplored. We may see a time when we shall be grateful for individuals who are willing to shake their fists at an overorganized world. But as a strategy it has its limits. If one values freedom enough to fight for it intelligently, one will want to understand why and how certain factors in organizational life are detrimental to the individual and other factors are beneficial.   (39)

But knowledge is not enough. It never is. It could be used to enslave us as well as to liberate us. In truth, the considerable technical grasp of organization we now have has often been used in ways that are damaging to individual integrity. Knowledge will be a safe weapon *only* if it is linked to a deeply rooted conviction that organizations are made for men and not men for organizations.   (40)

The whole purpose of such knowledge is to design environments conducive to individual fulfillment. It is ridiculous that the institutions man designs for his own benefit should work to his disadvantage. We can never eliminate the conflict between man and his institutions, nor would we wish to, but we can insist that one of the aims of any organization be the development of the individuals who make it up.   (41)

We shall continue to be the querulous victims of the organizations we design to serve us until we gain a deeper understanding of organization. Just as modern ecologists use knowledge of the balance of nature to fight insect pests, using natural forces to fight natural forces, so the student of society may use a knowledge of organization to organize for freedom.   (42)

The phrase "organize for freedom" has a paradoxical sound today when to many intellectuals the very idea of organization seems hostile to individual freedom. But in fact we have been organizing for freedom for a very long time. Our legal and constitutional system is, after all, an aspect of social organization designed to protect the individual from mistreatment by others, including the social organization itself.   (43)

It is useful to remind ourselves that very few of our freedoms would exist without effort on man's part. The man in the street thinks of freedom as the natural state, and lack of freedom as the unnatural, artificial, contrived state of affairs. He imagines that freedom, like sunshine or fresh air, is always there to be had if someone isn't forcibly preventing him from enjoying it. But freedom as we now know it has been exceedingly rare in the history of mankind. It is a highly perishable product of civilization, wholly dependent on certain habits of mind widely shared, on certain institutional arrangements widely agreed upon. This is worth saying because some moderns are so enamored of the idea of individuality that they would not think

of speaking out on behalf of society. They imagine that the only effect a
society can have on the individual is a destructive one. But it is by means
of the free society that men keep themselves free. If men wish to remain
free, they had better look to the health, the vigor, the viability of their
free society—and to its capacity for renewal.   (44)

John Henry Newman

NEWMAN, *leader of the major Roman Catholic revival in Protestant
England in modern times (1833–1845), wrote persistently throughout his adult life, but three of his works continue to dominate the interests
of his readers:* The Idea of a University *(1852),* Apologia pro Vita Sua
(1864), and the Grammar of Assent *(1870). Master of one of the most serviceable prose styles of his century, he was credited by Matthew Arnold
with being his age's most urbane Englishman. He was made a Cardinal in
1879.*

■ *Literature*

A Lecture in the School of Philosophy and Letters

I

Wishing to address you, Gentlemen, at the commencement of a new session,
I tried to find a subject for discussion, which might be at once suitable to
the occasion, yet neither too large for your time, nor too minute or abstruse
for your attention. I think I see one for my purpose in the very title of
your Faculty. It is the Faculty of Philosophy and Letters. Now the question
may arise as to what is meant by "Philosophy," and what is meant by "Let-

ters." As to the other Faculties, the subject-matter which they profess is intelligible, as soon as named, and beyond all dispute. We know what Science is, what Medicine, what Law, and what Theology; but we have not so much ease in determining what is meant by Philosophy and Letters. Each department of that twofold province needs explanation: it will be sufficient, on an occasion like this, to investigate one of them. Accordingly I shall select for remark the latter of the two, and attempt to determine what we are to understand by Letters or Literature, in what Literature consists, and how it stands relatively to Science. We speak, for instance, of ancient and modern literature, the literature of the day, sacred literature, light literature; and our lectures in this place are devoted to classical literature and English literature. Are Letters, then, synonymous with books? This cannot be, or they would include in their range Philosophy, Law, and, in short, the teaching of all the other Faculties. Far from confusing these various studies, we view the works of Plato or Cicero sometimes as philosophy, sometimes as literature; on the other hand, no one would ever be tempted to speak of Euclid as literature, or of Matthiæ's Greek Grammar. Is, then, literature synonymous with composition? with books written with an attention to style? is literature fine writing? again, is it studied and artificial writing? (1)

There are excellent persons who seem to adopt this last account of Literature as their own idea of it. They depreciate it, as if it were the result of a mere art or trick of words. Professedly indeed, they are aiming at the Greek and Roman classics, but their criticisms have quite as great force against all literature as against any. I think I shall be best able to bring out what I have to say on the subject by examining the statements which they make in defence of their own view of it. They contend then (1) that fine writing, as exemplified in the Classics, is mainly a matter of conceits, fancies, and prettinesses, decked out in choice words; (2) that this is the proof of it, that the classics will not bear translating; and this is why I have said that the real attack is upon literature altogether, not the classical only; for, to speak generally, all literature, modern as well as ancient, lies under this disadvantage. This, however, they will not allow, for they maintain (3) that Holy Scripture presents a remarkable contrast to secular writings on this very point, viz., in that Scripture does easily admit of translation, though it is the most sublime and beautiful of all writings.   (2)

II

Now I will begin by stating these three positions in the words of a writer, who is cited by the estimable Catholics in question as a witness, or rather as an advocate, in their behalf, though he is far from being able in his own person to challenge the respect which is inspired by themselves.   (3)

"There are two sorts of eloquence," says this writer, "the one indeed

scarce deserves the name of it, which consists chiefly in laboured and polished periods, an over-curious and artificial arrangement of figures, tinselled over with a gaudy embellishment of words, which glitter, but convey
little or no light to the understanding. This kind of writing is for the most
part much affected and admired by the people of weak judgment and vicious taste; but it is a piece of affectation and formality the sacred writers
are utter strangers to. It is a vain and boyish eloquence; and, as it has always been esteemed below the great geniuses of all ages, so much more so
with respect to those writers who were actuated by the spirit of Infinite Wisdom, and therefore wrote with that force and majesty with which never
man writ. The other sort of eloquence is quite the reverse to this, and
which may be said to be the true characteristic of the Holy Scriptures;
where the excellence does not arise from a laboured and far-fetched elocution, but from a surprising mixture of simplicity and majesty, which is a
double character, so difficult to be united that it is seldom to be met with
in compositions merely human. We see nothing in Holy Writ of affectation
and superfluous ornament . . . Now, it is observable that the most excellent
profane authors, whether Greek or Latin, lose most of their graces whenever we find them literally translated. Homer's famed representation of
Jupiter—his cried-up description of a tempest, his relation of Neptune's
shaking the earth and opening it to its centre, his description of Pallas's
horses, with numbers of other long-since admired passages, flag, and almost
vanish away, in the vulgar Latin translation.   (4)

"Let any one but take the pains to read the common Latin interpretations of Virgil, Theocritus, or even of Pindar, and one may venture to affirm he will be able to trace out but few remains of the graces which
charmed him so much in the original. The natural conclusion from hence
is that in the classical authors the expression, the sweetness of the numbers,
occasioned by a musical placing of words, constitute a great part of their
beauties; whereas, in the sacred writings, they consist more in the greatness
of the things themselves than in the words and expressions. The ideas and
conceptions are so great and lofty in their own nature that they necessarily
appear magnificent in the most artless dress. Look but into the Bible, and
we see them shine through the most simple and literal translations. That
glorious description which Moses gives of the creation of the heavens and
the earth, which Longinus . . . was so greatly taken with, has not lost the
least whit of its intrinsic worth, and though it has undergone so many translations, yet triumphs over all, and breaks forth with as much force and
vehemence as in the original. . . . In the history of Joseph, where Joseph
makes himself known, and weeps aloud upon the neck of his dear brother
Benjamin, that all the house of Pharaoh heard him, at that instant none of
his brethren are introduced as uttering aught, either to express their present joy or palliate their former injuries to him. On all sides there imme-

diately ensues a deep and solemn silence; a silence infinitely more eloquent and expressive than anything else that could have been substituted in its place. Had Thucydides, Herodotus, Livy, or any of the celebrated classical historians, been employed in writing this history, when they came to this point they would doubtless have exhausted all their fund of eloquence in furnishing Joseph's brethren with laboured and studied harangues, which, however fine they might have been in themselves, would nevertheless have been unnatural and altogether improper on the occasion."[1]   (5)

This is eloquently written, but it contains, I consider, a mixture of truth and falsehood, which it will be my business to discriminate from each other. Far be it from me to deny the unapproachable grandeur and simplicity of Holy Scripture; but I shall maintain that the classics are, as human compositions, simple and majestic and natural too. I grant that Scripture is concerned with things, but I will not grant that classical literature is simply concerned with words. I grant that human literature is often elaborate, but I will maintain that elaborate composition is not unknown to the writers of Scripture. I grant that human literature cannot easily be translated out of the particular language to which it belongs; but it is not at all the rule that Scripture can easily be translated either—and now I address myself to my task.   (6)

III

Here, then, in the first place, I observe, Gentlemen, that Literature from the derivation of the word, implies writing, not speaking; this, however, arises from the circumstance of the copiousness, variety, and public circulation of the matters of which it consists. What is spoken cannot outrun the range of the speaker's voice, and perishes in the uttering. When words are in demand to express a long course of thought, when they have to be conveyed to the ends of the earth, or perpetuated for the benefit of posterity, they must be written down, that is, reduced to the shape of literature; still, properly speaking, the terms by which we denote this characteristic gift of man belong to its exhibition by means of the voice, not of handwriting. It addresses itself, in its primary idea, to the ear, not to the eye. We call it the power of speech, we call it language, that is, the use of the tongue; and, even when we write, we still keep in mind what was its original instrument, for we use freely such terms in our books as "saying," "speaking," "telling," "talking," "calling"; we use the terms "phraseology" and "diction"; as if we were still addressing ourselves to the ear.   (7)

Now I insist on this, because it shows that speech, and therefore literature, which is its permanent record, is essentially a personal work. It is

---

1 Sterne, Sermon xlii.

not some production or result, attained by the partnership of several persons, or by machinery, or by any natural process, but in its very idea it
proceeds, and must proceed, from some one given individual. Two persons
cannot be the authors of the sounds which strike our ear; and, as they cannot be speaking one and the same speech, neither can they be writing one
and the same lecture or discourse, which must certainly belong to some one
person or other, and is the expression of that one person's ideas and feelings—ideas and feelings personal to himself, though others may have parallel and similar ones—proper to himself, in the same sense as his voice, his
air, his countenance, his carriage, and his action, are personal. In other
words, Literature expresses, not objective truth, as it is called, but subjective; not things, but thoughts.   (8)

Now this doctrine will become clearer by considering another use of
words, which does relate to objective truth, or to things; which relates to
matters, not personal, not subjective to the individual, but which, even
were there no individual man in the whole world to know them or to talk
about them, would still exist. Such objects become the matter of Science,
and words indeed are used to express them, but such words are rather symbols than language, and however many we use, and however we may perpetuate them by writing, we never could make any kind of literature out of
them, or call them by that name. Such, for instance, would be Euclid's
Elements; they relate to truths universal and eternal; they are not mere
thoughts, but things: they exist in themselves, not by virtue of our understanding them, not in dependence upon our will, but in what is called the
nature of things, or at least on conditions external to us. The words, then,
in which they are set forth are not language, speech, literature but rather,
as I have said, symbols. And, as a proof of it, you will recollect that it is
possible, nay usual, to set forth the propositions of Euclid in algebraical
notation, which, as all would admit, has nothing to do with literature. What
is true of mathematics is true also of every study, so far forth as it is scientific; it makes use of words as the mere vehicle of things, and is thereby
withdrawn from the province of literature. Thus metaphysics, ethics, law,
political economy, chemistry, theology cease to be literature in the same degree as they are capable of a severe scientific treatment. And hence it is that
Aristotle's works, on the one hand, though at first sight literature, approach
in character, at least a great number of them, to mere science; for even
though the things which he treats of and exhibits may not always be real
and true, yet he treats them as if they were, not as if they were the thoughts
of his own mind; that is, he treats them scientifically. On the other hand,
Law or Natural History has before now been treated by an author with so
much of colouring derived from his own mind as to become a sort of literature; this is especially seen in the instance of Theology, when it takes the
shape of Pulpit Eloquence. It is seen too in historical composition, which

becomes a mere specimen of chronology, or a chronicle, when divested of the philosophy, the skill, or the party and personal feelings of the particular writer. Science, then, has to do with things, literature with thoughts; science is universal, literature is personal; science uses words merely as symbols, but literature uses language in its full compass, as including phraseology, idiom, style, composition, rhythm, eloquence, and whatever other properties are included in it. (9)

Let us then put aside the scientific use of words when we are to speak of language and literature. Literature is the personal use or exercise of language. That this is so is further proved from the fact that one author uses it so differently from another. Language itself in its very origination would seem to be traceable to individuals. Their peculiarities have given it its character. We are often able in fact to trace particular phrases or idioms to individuals; we know the history of their rise. Slang surely, as it is called, comes of and breathes of the personal. The connection between the force of words in particular languages and the habits and sentiments of the nations speaking them has often been pointed out. And, while the many use language as they find it, the man of genius uses it indeed, but subjects it withal to his own purposes, and moulds it according to his own peculiarities. The throng and succession of ideas, thoughts, feelings, imaginations, aspirations, which pass within him, the abstractions, the juxtapositions, the comparisons, the discriminations, the conceptions, which are so original in him, his views of external things, his judgments upon life, manners, and history, the exercises of his wit, of his humour, of his depth, of his sagacity, all these innumerable and incessant creations, the very pulsation and throbbing of his intellect, does he image forth, to all does he give utterance, in a corresponding language, which is as multiform as this inward mental action itself and analogous to it, the faithful expression of his intense personality, attending on his own inward world of thought as its very shadow: so that we might as well say that one man's shadow is another's as that the style of a really gifted mind can belong to any but himself. It follows him about *as* a shadow. His thought and feeling are personal, and so his language is personal. (10)

IV

Thought and speech are inseparable from each other. Matter and expression are parts of one: style is a thinking out into language. This is what I have been laying down, and this is literature; not *things*, not the verbal symbols of things; not on the other hand mere *words*; but thoughts expressed in language. Call to mind, Gentlemen, the meaning of the Greek word which expresses this special prerogative of man over the feeble intelligence of the inferior animals. It is called Logos: what does Logos mean?

it stands both for *reason* and for *speech*, and it is difficult to say which it means more properly. It means both at once: why? because really they cannot be divided, because they are in a true sense one. When we can separate light and illumination, life and motion, the convex and the concave of a curve, then will it be possible for thought to tread speech under foot, and to hope to do without it—then will it be conceivable that the vigorous and fertile intellect should renounce its own double, its instrument of expression, and the channel of its speculations and emotions.   (11)

Critics should consider this view of the subject before they lay down such canons of taste as the writer whose pages I have quoted. Such men as he is consider fine writing to be an *addition from without* to the matter treated of—a sort of ornament superinduced, or a luxury indulged in, by those who have time and inclination for such vanities. They speak as if *one* man could do the thought, and *another* the style. We read in Persian travels of the way in which young gentlemen go to work in the East, when they would engage in correspondence with those who inspire them with hope or fear. They cannot write one sentence themselves; so they betake themselves to the professional letter-writer. They confide to him the object they have in view. They have a point to gain from a superior, a favour to ask, an evil to deprecate; they have to approach a man in power, or to make court to some beautiful lady. The professional man manufactures words for them, as they are wanted, as a stationer sells them paper, or a schoolmaster might cut their pens. Thought and word are, in their conception, two things, and thus there is a division of labour. The man of thought comes to the man of words; and the man of words, duly instructed in the thought, dips the pen of desire into the ink of devotedness, and proceeds to spread it over the page of desolation. Then the nightingale of affection is heard to warble to the rose of loveliness, while the breeze of anxiety plays around the brow of expectation. This is what the Easterns are said to consider fine writing; and it seems pretty much the idea of the school of critics to whom I have been referring.   (12)

We have an instance in literary history of this very proceeding nearer home, in a great University, in the latter years of the last century. I have referred to it before now in a public lecture elsewhere[2], but it is too much in point here to be omitted. A learned Arabic scholar had to deliver a set of lectures before its doctors and professors on a historical subject in which his reading had lain. A linguist is conversant with science rather than with literature; but this gentleman felt that his lectures must not be without a style. Being of the opinion of the Orientals, with whose writings he was familiar, he determined to buy a style. He took the step of engaging a person, at a price, to turn the matter which he had got together into orna-

2 "Position of Catholics in England," pp. 101–2.

mental English. Observe, he did not wish for mere grammatical English, but for an elaborate, pretentious style. An artist was found in the person of a country curate, and the job was carried out. His lectures remain to this day, in their own place in the protracted series of annual Discourses to which they belong, distinguished amid a number of heavyish compositions by the rhetorical and ambitious diction for which he went into the market. This learned divine, indeed, and the author I have quoted, differ from each other in the estimate they respectively form of literary composition; but they agree together in this—in considering such composition a trick and a trade; they put it on a par with the gold plate and the flowers and the music of a banquet, which do not make the viands better, but the entertainment more pleasurable; as if language were the hired servant, the mere mistress of the reason, and not the lawful wife in her own house.   (13)

But can they really think that Homer, or Pindar, or Shakespeare, or Dryden, or Walter Scott were accustomed to aim at diction for its own sake, instead of being inspired with their subject, and pouring forth beautiful words because they had beautiful thoughts? This is surely too great a paradox to be borne. Rather, it is the fire within the author's breast which overflows in the torrent of his burning, irresistible eloquence; it is the poetry of his inner soul, which relieves itself in the Ode or the Elegy; and his mental attitude and bearing, the beauty of his moral countenance, the force and keenness of his logic are imaged in the tenderness, or energy, or richness of his language. Nay, according to the well-known line, "facit indignatio *versus*"; not the words alone but even the rhythm, the metre, the verse will be the contemporaneous offspring of the emotion or imagination which possesses him. "Poeta nascitur, non fit," says the proverb; and this is in numerous instances true of his poems, as well as of himself. They are born, not framed; they are a strain rather than a composition; and their perfection is the monument, not so much of his skill as of his power. And this is true of prose as well as of verse in its degree: who will not recognize in "The Vision of Mirza" a delicacy and beauty of style which is very difficult to describe, but which is felt to be in exact correspondence to the ideas of which it is the expression?   (14)

v

And, since the thoughts and reasonings of an author have, as I have said, a personal character, no wonder that his style is not only the image of his subject but of his mind. That pomp of language, that full and tuneful diction, that felicitousness in the choice and exquisiteness in the collocation of words, which to prosaic writers seems artificial, is nothing else but the mere habit and way of a lofty intellect. Aristotle, in his sketch of the magnanimous man, tells us that his voice is deep, his motions slow, and his stature commanding. In like manner, the elocution of a great intellect is great. His language expresses not only his great thoughts but his great self. Certainly he might use fewer words than he uses; but he fertilizes his simplest ideas, and germinates into a multitude of details, and prolongs the march of his sentences, and sweeps round to the full diapason of his harmony, as if κύδεϊ γαίων, rejoicing in his own vigour and richness of resource. I say, a narrow critic will call it verbiage, when really it is a sort of fullness of heart, parallel to that which makes the merry boy whistle as he walks, or the strong man, like the smith in the novel, flourish his club when there is no one to fight with.   (15)

Shakespeare furnishes us with frequent instances of this peculiarity, and all so beautiful, that it is difficult to select for quotation. For instance, in Macbeth:—

> "Canst thou not minister to a mind diseased,
> Pluck from the memory a rooted sorrow,
> Raze out the written troubles of the brain,
> And, with some sweet oblivious antidote,
> Cleanse the foul bosom of that perilous stuff,
> Which weighs upon the heart?"   (16)

Here a simple idea, by a process which belongs to the orator rather than to the poet, but still comes from the native vigour of genius, is expanded into a many-membered period.   (17)

The following from Hamlet is of the same kind:

> " 'Tis not alone my inky cloak, good mother,
> Nor customary suits of solemn black,
> Nor windy suspiration of forced breath,
> No, nor the fruitful river in the eye,
> Nor the dejected haviour of the visage,
> Together with all forms, modes, shows of grief,
> That can denote me truly."   (18)

Now, if such declamation, for declamation it is, however noble, be allowable in a poet, whose genius is so far removed from pompousness or pretence, much more is it allowable in an orator, whose very province it is to put forth words to the best advantage he can. Cicero has nothing more redundant in any part of his writings than these passages from Shakespeare. No lover then at least of Shakespeare may fairly accuse Cicero of gorgeousness of phraseology or diffuseness of style. Nor will any sound critic be tempted to do so. As a certain unaffected neatness and propriety and grace of diction may be required of any author who lays claim to be a classic, for the same reason that a certain attention to dress is expected of every gentleman, so to Cicero may be allowed the privilege of the "os magna sonatu-rum," of which the ancient critic speaks. His copious, majestic, musical flow of language, even if sometimes beyond what the subject-matter demands, is never out of keeping with the occasion or with the speaker. It is the expression of lofty sentiments in lofty sentences, the "mens magna in corpore magno." It is the development of the inner man. Cicero vividly realized the *status* of a Roman senator and statesman, and the "pride of place" of Rome, in all the grace and grandeur which attached to her; and he imbibed, and became what he admired. As the exploits of Scipio or Pompey are the expression of this greatness in deed, so the language of Cicero is the expression of it in word. And, as the acts of the Roman ruler or soldier represent to us, in a manner special to themselves, the characteristic magnanimity of the lords of the earth, so do the speeches or treatises of her accomplished orator bring it home to our imaginations as no other writing could do. Neither Livy, nor Tacitus, nor Terence, nor Seneca, nor Pliny, nor Quintilian is an adequate spokesman for the Imperial City. They write Latin; Cicero writes Roman. (19)

VI

You will say that Cicero's language is undeniably studied, but that Shakespeare's is as undeniably natural and spontaneous; and that this is what is meant when the Classics are accused of being mere artists of words. Here we are introduced to a further large question, which gives me the opportunity of anticipating a misapprehension of my meaning. I observe, then, that, not only is that lavish richness of style, which I have noticed in Shakespeare, justifiable on the principles which I have been laying down, but, what is less easy to receive, even elaborateness in composition is no mark of trick or artifice in an author. Undoubtedly the works of the Classics, particularly the Latin, *are* elaborate; they have cost a great deal of time, care, and trouble. They have had many rough copies; I grant it. I grant also that there are writers of name, ancient and modern, who really are guilty of the absurdity of making sentences, as the very end of their literary labour. Such was Isocrates; such were some of the sophists; they were set on words, to the neglect of thoughts or things; I cannot defend them. If I must give an English instance of this fault, much as I love and revere the personal character and intellectual vigour of Dr. Johnson, I cannot deny that his style often outruns the sense and the occasion, and is wanting in that simplicity which is the attribute of genius. Still, granting all this, I cannot grant, notwithstanding, that genius never need take pains, that genius may not improve by practice, that it never incurs failures, and succeeds the second time, that it never finishes off at leisure what it has thrown off in the outline at a stroke. (20)

Take the instance of the painter or the sculptor; he has a conception in his mind which he wishes to represent in the medium of his art, the Madonna and Child, or Innocence, or Fortitude, or some historical character or event. Do you mean to say he does not study his subject? does he not make sketches? does he not even call them "studies"? does he not call his workroom a *studio?* is he not ever designing, rejecting, adopting, correcting, perfecting? Are not the first attempts of Michael Angelo and Raffaelle extant, in the case of some of their most celebrated compositions? Will any one say that the Apollo Belvedere is not a conception patiently elaborated into its proper perfection? These departments of taste are, according to the received notions of the world, the very province of genius, and yet we call them *arts;* they are the "Fine Arts." Why may not that be true of literary composition which is true of painting, sculpture, architecture, and music? Why may not language be wrought as well as the clay of the modeller? why may not words be worked up as well as colours? why should not skill in diction be simply subservient and instrumental to the great prototypal ideas which are the contemplation of a Plato or a Virgil? Our greatest poet tells us:

> "The poet's eye, in a fine frenzy rolling,
> Doth glance from heaven to earth, from earth to heaven,
> And, as imagination bodies forth
> The forms of things unknown, the poet's pen
> Turns them to shapes, and gives to airy nothing
> A local habitation and a name."   (21)

Now, is it wonderful that that pen of his should sometimes be at fault for a while, that it should pause, write, erase, rewrite, amend, complete before he satisfies himself that his language has done justice to the conceptions which his mind's eye contemplated?   (22)

In this point of view, doubtless, many or most writers are elaborate; and those certainly not the least whose style is furthest removed from ornament, being simple and natural, or vehement, or severely business-like and practical. Who so energetic and manly as Demosthenes? Yet he is said to have transcribed Thucydides many times over in the formation of his style. Who so gracefully natural as Herodotus? Yet his very dialect is not his own, but chosen for the sake of the perfection of his narrative. Who exhibits such happy negligence as our own Addison? Yet artistic fastidiousness was so notorious in his instance that the report has got abroad, truly or not, that he was too late in his issue of an important state-paper, from his habit of revision and re-composition. Such great authors were working by a model which was before the eyes of their intellect, and they were labouring to say what they had to say in such a way as would most exactly and suitably express it. It is not wonderful that other authors, whose style is not simple, should be instances of a similar literary diligence. Virgil wished his *Æneid* to be burned, elaborate as is its composition, because he felt it needed more labour still, in order to make it perfect. The historian Gibbon in the last century is another instance in point. You must not suppose I am going to recommend his style for imitation, any more than his principles; but I refer to him as the example of a writer feeling the task which lay before him, feeling that he had to bring out into words for the comprehension of his readers a great and complicated scene, and wishing that those words should be adequate to his undertaking. I think he wrote the first chapter of his History three times over; it was not that he corrected or improved the first copy; but he put his first essay, and then his second, aside—he recast his matter, till he had hit the precise exhibition of it which he thought demanded by his subject.   (23)

Now in all these instances, I wish you to observe, that what I have admitted about literary workmanship differs from the doctrine which I am opposing in this—that the mere dealer in words cares little or nothing for the subject which he is embellishing, but can paint and gild anything whatever to order; whereas the artist, whom I am acknowledging, has his great or rich visions before him, and his only aim is to bring out what he thinks or what he feels in a way adequate to the thing spoken of, and appropriate to the speaker.   (24)

VII

The illustration which I have been borrowing from the Fine Arts will enable me to go a step further. I have been showing the connection of the thought with the language in literary composition; and in doing so I have exposed the unphilosophical notion that the language was an extra which could be dispensed with, and provided to order according to the demand. But I have not yet brought out what immediately follows from this, and which was the second point which I had to show, viz., that to be capable of easy translation is no test of the excellence of a composition. If I must say what I think, I should lay down, with little hesitation, that the truth was almost the reverse of this doctrine. Nor are many words required to show it. Such a doctrine, as is contained in the passage of the author whom I quoted when I began, goes upon the assumption that one language is just like another language—that every language has all the ideas, turns of thought, delicacies of expression, figures, associations, abstractions, points of view which every other language has. Now, as far as regards Science, it is true that all languages are pretty much alike for the purposes of Science; but even in this respect some are more suitable than others, which have to coin words, or to borrow them, in order to express scientific ideas. But if languages are not all equally adapted even to furnish symbols for those universal and eternal truths in which Science consists, how can they reasonably be expected to be all equally rich, equally forcible, equally musical, equally exact, equally happy in expressing the idiosyncratic peculiarities of thought of some original and fertile mind, who has availed himself of one of them? A great author takes his native language, masters it, partly throws himself into it, partly moulds and adapts it, and pours out his multitude of ideas through the variously ramified and delicately minute channels of expression which he has found or framed—does it follow that this his personal presence (as it may be called) can forthwith be transferred to every other language under the sun? Then may we reasonably maintain that Beethoven's *piano* music is not really beautiful because it cannot be played on the hurdy-gurdy? Were not this astonishing doctrine maintained by persons far superior to the writer whom I have selected for animadversion, I should find it difficult to be patient under a gratuitous extravagance. It seems that a really great author must admit of translation, and that we have a test of his excellence when he reads to advantage in a foreign language as well as in his own. Then Shakespeare *is* a genius because he cannot be translated into French. Then the multiplication-table is the most gifted of all conceivable compositions because it loses nothing by translation, and can hardly be said to belong to any one language whatever. Whereas I should rather have conceived that, in proportion as ideas are novel and recondite, they would be difficult to put into words, and that the very fact of their having insinuated themselves into one language would diminish the chance of that happy accident being repeated in another. In the language of savages you can hardly express any idea or act of the intellect at all: is the tongue of the Hottentot or Eskimos to be made the measure of the genius of Plato, Pindar, Tacitus, St. Jerome, Dante, or Cervantes?   (25)

Let us recur, I say, to the illustration of the Fine Arts. I suppose you can express ideas in painting which you cannot express in sculpture; and the more an artist is of a painter, the less he is likely to be of a sculptor. The more he commits his genius to the methods and conditions of his own art, the less he will be able to throw himself into the circumstances of another. Is the genius of Fra Angelico, of Francia, or of Raffaelle disparaged by the fact that he was able to do that in colours which no man that ever lived, which no Angel, could achieve in wood? Each of the Fine Arts has its own subject-matter; from the nature of the case you can do in one what you cannot do in another; you can do in painting what you cannot do in carving; you can do in oils what you cannot do in fresco; you can do in marble what you cannot do in ivory; you can do in wax what you cannot do in bronze. Then, I repeat, applying this to the case of languages, why should not genius be able to do in Greek what it cannot do in Latin?

and why are its Greek and Latin works defective because they will not turn into English? That genius, of which we are speaking, did not make English; it did not make all languages, present, past, and future; it did not make the laws of *any* language: why is it to be judged of by that in which it had no part, over which it has no control? (26)

VIII

And now we are naturally brought on to our third point, which is on the characteristics of Holy Scripture as compared with profane literature. Hitherto we have been concerned with the doctrine of these writers, viz., that style is an *extra*, that it is a mere artifice, and that hence it cannot be translated; now we come to their fact, viz., that Scripture has no such artificial style, and that Scripture can easily be translated. Surely their fact is as untenable as their doctrine. (27)

Scripture easy of translation! Then why have there been so few good translators? why is it that there has been such great difficulty in combining the two necessary qualities, fidelity to the original and purity in the adopted vernacular? why is it that the authorized versions of the Church are often so inferior to the original as compositions, except that the Church is bound above all things to see that the version is doctrinally correct, and in a difficult problem is obliged to put up with defects in what is of secondary importance, provided she secure what is of first? If it were so easy to transfer the beauty of the original to the copy, she would not have been content with her received version in various languages which could be named. (28)

And then in the next place, Scripture not elaborate! Scripture not ornamented in diction, and musical in cadence! Why, consider the Epistle to the Hebrews—where is there in the Classics any composition more carefully, more artificially written? Consider the book of Job—is it not a sacred drama, as artistic, as perfect, as any Greek tragedy of Sophocles or Euripides? Consider the Psalter—are there no ornaments, no rhythm, no studied cadences, no responsive members in that divinely beautiful book? And is it not hard to understand? are not the Prophets hard to understand? is not St. Paul hard to understand? Who can say that these are popular compositions? who can say that they are level at first reading with the understandings of the multitude? (29)

That there are portions indeed of the inspired volume more simple both in style and in meaning, and that these are the more sacred and sublime passages, as, for instance, parts of the Gospels, I grant at once; but this does not militate against the doctrine I have been laying down. Recollect, Gentlemen, my distinction when I began. I have said Literature is one thing, and that Science is another; that Literature has to do with ideas, and

Science with realities; that Literature is of a personal character, that Science treats of what is universal and eternal. In proportion, then, as Scripture excludes the personal colouring of its writers, and rises into the region of pure and mere inspiration, when it ceases in any sense to be the writing of man, of St. Paul or St. John, of Moses or Isaias, then it comes to belong to Science, not Literature. Then it conveys the things of heaven, unseen verities, divine manifestations, and them alone—not the ideas, the feelings, the aspirations of its human instruments, who, for all that they were inspired and infallible, did not cease to be men. St. Paul's epistles, then, I consider to be literature in a real and true sense, *as* personal, *as* rich in reflection and emotion as Demosthenes or Euripides; and, without ceasing to be revelations of objective truth, they are expressions of the subjective notwithstanding. On the other hand, portions of the Gospels, of the book of Genesis, and other passages of the Sacred Volume, are of the nature of Science. Such is the beginning of St. John's Gospel, which we read at the end of Mass. Such is the Creed. I mean, passages such as these are the mere enunciation of eternal things, without (so to say) the medium of any human mind transmitting them to us. The words used have the grandeur, the majesty, the calm, unimpassioned beauty of Science; they are in no sense Literature, they are in no sense personal; and therefore they are easy to apprehend, and easy to translate.   (30)

Did time admit I could show you parallel instances of what I am speaking of in the Classics, inferior to the inspired word in proportion as the subject-matter of the classical authors is immensely inferior to the subjects treated of in Scripture—but parallel, inasmuch as the classical author or speaker ceases for the moment to have to do with Literature, as speaking of things objectively, and rises to the serene sublimity of Science. But I should be carried too far if I began.   (31)

IX

I shall then merely sum up what I have said, and come to a conclusion. Reverting, then, to my original question, what is the meaning of Letters, as contained, Gentlemen, in the designation of your Faculty, I have answered that by Letters or Literature is meant the expression of thought in language, where by "thought" I mean the ideas, feelings, views, reasoning, and other operations of the human mind. And the Art of Letters is the method by which a speaker or writer brings out in words, worthy of his subject, and sufficient for his audience or readers, the thoughts which impress him. Literature, then, is of a personal character; it consists in the enunciations and teachings of those who have a right to speak as representatives of their kind, and in whose words their brethren find an interpretation of their own sentiments, a record of their own experience, and a suggestion for their own judgments. A great author, Gentlemen, is not one who merely has a *copia verborum*, whether in prose or verse, and can, as it were, turn on at his will any number of splendid phrases and swelling sentences; but he is one who has something to say and knows how to say it. I do not claim for him, as such, any great depth of thought, or breadth of view, or philosophy, or sagacity, or knowledge of human nature, or experience of human life, though these additional gifts he may have, and the more he has of them the greater he is; but I ascribe to him, as his characteristic gift, in a large sense the faculty of Expression. He is master of the two-fold Logos, the thought and the word, distinct but inseparable from each other. He may, if so be, elaborate his compositions, or he may pour out his improvisations, but in either case he has but one aim, which he keeps steadily before him, and is conscientious and single-minded in fulfilling. That aim is to give forth what he has within him; and from his very earnestness it comes to pass that, whatever be the splendour of his diction or the harmony of his periods, he has with him the charm of an incommunicable simplicity. Whatever be his subject, high or low, he treats it suitably and for its own sake. If he is a poet, "nil molitur *inepte*." If he is an orator, then too he speaks not only *distincte* and *splendide* but also *apte*. His page is the lucid mirror of his mind and life.

> "Quo fit, ut omnis
> Votivâ pateat veluti descripta tabellâ
> Vita senis." (32)

He writes passionately, because he feels keenly; forcibly, because he conceives vividly; he sees too clearly to be vague; he is too serious to be otiose; he can analyze his subject, and therefore he is rich; he embraces it as a whole and in its parts, and therefore he is consistent; he has a firm hold of it, and therefore he is luminous. When his imagination wells up, it overflows in ornament; when his heart is touched, it thrills along his verse. He always has the right word for the right idea, and never a word too much. If he is brief, it is because few words suffice; when he is lavish of them, still each word has its mark, and aids, not embarrasses, the vigorous march of his elocution. He expresses what all feel, but all cannot say; and his sayings pass into proverbs among his people, and his phrases become household words and idioms of their daily speech, which is tesselated with the rich fragments of his language, as we see in foreign lands the marbles of Roman grandeur worked into the walls and pavements of modern palaces. (33)

Such pre-eminently is Shakespeare among ourselves; such pre-eminently Virgil among the Latins; such in their degree are all those writers who in every nation go by the name of Classics. To particular nations they are necessarily attached from the circumstance of the variety of tongues, and the peculiarities of each; but so far they have a catholic and ecumenical character, that what they express is common to the whole race of man, and they alone are able to express it.   (34)

X

If then the power of speech is a gift as great as any that can be named, if the origin of language is by many philosophers even considered to be nothing short of divine, if by means of words the secrets of the heart are brought to light, pain of soul is relieved, hidden grief is carried off, sympathy conveyed, counsel imparted, experience recorded, and wisdom perpetuated, if by great authors the many are drawn up into unity, national character is fixed, a people speaks, the past and the future, the East and the West are brought into communication with each other, if such men are, in a word, the spokesmen and prophets of the human family—it will not answer to make light of Literature or to neglect its study; rather we may be sure that, in proportion as we master it in whatever language, and imbibe its spirit, we shall ourselves become in our own measure the ministers of like benefits to others, be they many or few, be they in the obscurer or the more distinguished walks of life—who are united to us by social ties, and are within the sphere of our personal influence.   (35)

Matthew Arnold

(1822–1880)

ARNOLD, poet, literary critic, and cultural analyst, was one of the chief men of letters in the Victorian period. Deeply influenced by Newman and himself deeply influencing Walter Pater, his critical doctrines became the principal straws to be burned by the rebellious critics of the twentieth century. Besides his poems, Arnold's chief works were Essays in Criticism *(First and Second Series, 1865 and 1888) and* Culture and Anarchy *(1869). Arnold may be said to have provided much of the vocabulary of academic criticism.*

■ *The Study of Poetry*

"THE FUTURE of poetry is immense, because in poetry, where it is worthy of its high destinies, our race, as time goes on, will find an ever surer and surer stay. There is not a creed which is not shaken, not an accredited dogma which is not shown to be questionable, not a received tradition which does not threaten to dissolve. Our religion has materialised itself in the fact, in the supposed fact; it has attached its emotion to the fact, and now the fact is failing it. But for poetry the idea is everything; the rest is a world of illusion, of divine illusion. Poetry attaches its emotion to the idea; the idea *is* the fact. The strongest part of our religion to-day is its unconscious poetry." (1)

Let me be permitted to quote these words of my own, as uttering the thought which should, in my opinion, go with us and govern us in all our study of poetry. In the present work it is the course of one great contributory stream to the world-river of poetry that we are invited to follow. We are here invited to trace the stream of English poetry. But whether we set ourselves, as here, to follow only one of the several streams that make the mighty river of poetry, or whether we seek to know them all, our governing thought should be the same. We should conceive of poetry worthily, and more highly than it has been the custom to conceive of it. We should conceive of it as capable of higher uses, and called to higher destinies, than those which in general men have assigned to it hitherto. More and more mankind will discover that we have to turn to poetry to interpret life for us, to console us, to sustain us. Without poetry, our science will appear incomplete; and most of what now passes with us for religion and philosophy will be replaced by poetry. Science, I say, will appear incomplete without it. For finely and truly does Wordsworth call poetry "the impassioned expression which is in the countenance of all science"; and what is a countenance without its expression? Again, Wordsworth finely and truly calls poetry "the breath and finer spirit of all knowledge": our religion, parading evidences such as those on which the popular mind relies now; our philosophy, pluming itself on its reasonings about causation and finite and infinite being; what are they but the shadows and dreams and false shows of knowledge? The day will come when we shall wonder at ourselves for having trusted to them, for having taken them seriously; and the more we perceive their hollowness, the more we shall prize "the breath and finer spirit of knowledge" offered to us by poetry. (2)

But if we conceive thus highly of the destinies of poetry, we must also set our standard for poetry high, since poetry, to be capable of fulfilling such high destinies, must be poetry of a high order of excellence. We must accustom ourselves to a high standard and to a strict judgment. Sainte-Beuve relates that Napoleon one day said, when somebody was spoken of in his presence as a charlatan: "Charlatan as much as you please; but where is there *not* charlatanism?"—"Yes," answers Sainte-Beuve, "in politics, in the art of governing mankind, that is perhaps true. But in the order of thought, in art, the glory, the eternal honour is that charlatanism shall find no entrance; herein lies the inviolableness of that noble portion of man's being." It is admirably said, and let us hold fast to it. In poetry, which is thought and art in one, it is the glory, the eternal honour, that charlatanism shall find no entrance; that this noble sphere be kept inviolate and inviolable. Charlatanism is for confusing or obliterating the distinctions between excellent and inferior, sound and unsound or only half-sound, true and untrue or only half-true. It is charlatanism, conscious or unconscious, whenever we confuse or obliterate these. And in poetry, more than anywhere else, it is unpermissible to confuse or obliterate them. For in poetry the distinction between excellent and inferior, sound and unsound or only half-sound, true and untrue or only half-true, is of paramount importance. It is of paramount importance because of the high destinies of poetry. In poetry, as a criticism of life under the conditions fixed for such a criticism by the laws of poetic truth and poetic beauty, the spirit of our race will find, we have said, as time goes on and as other helps fail, its consolation and stay. But the consolation and stay will be of power in proportion to the power of the criticism of life. And the criticism of life will be of power in proportion as the poetry conveying it is excellent rather than inferior, sound rather than unsound or half-sound, true rather than untrue or half-true. (3)

The best poetry is what we want; the best poetry will be found to have a power of forming, sustaining, and delighting us, as nothing else can. A clearer, deeper sense of the best in poetry, and of the strength and joy to be drawn from it, is the most precious benefit which we can gather from a poetical collection such as the present. And yet in the very nature and conduct of such a collection there is inevitably something which tends to obscure in us the consciousness of what our benefit should be, and to distract us from the pursuit of it. We should therefore steadily set it before our minds at the outset, and should compel ourselves to revert constantly to the thought of it as we proceed. (4)

Yes; constantly in reading poetry, a sense for the best, the really excellent, and of the strength and joy to be drawn from it, should be present in our minds and should govern our estimate of what we read. But this real estimate, the only true one, is liable to be superseded, if we are not watchful, by two other kinds of estimate, the historic estimate and the personal estimate, both of which are fallacious. A poet or a poem may count to us historically, they may count to us on grounds personal to ourselves, and they may count to us really. They may count to us historically. The course of development of a nation's language, thought, and poetry, is profoundly interesting; and by regarding a poet's work as a stage in this course of development we may easily bring ourselves to make it of more importance as poetry than in itself it really is, we may come to use a language of quite exaggerated praise in criticising it; in short, to over-rate it. So arises in our poetic judgments the fallacy caused by the estimate which we may call historic. Then, again, a poet or a poem may count to us on grounds personal to ourselves. Our personal affinities, likings, and circumstances, have great power to sway our estimate of this or that poet's work, and to make us attach more importance to it as poetry than in itself it really possesses, because to us it is, or has been, of high importance. Here also we over-rate the object of our interest, and apply to it a language of praise which is quite exaggerated. And thus we get the source of a second fallacy in our poetic judgments—the fallacy caused by an estimate which we may call personal.   (5)

Both fallacies are natural. It is evident how naturally the study of the history and development of a poetry may incline a man to pause over reputations and works once conspicuous but now obscure, and to quarrel with a careless public for skipping, in obedience to mere tradition and habit, from one famous name or work in its national poetry to another, ignorant of what it misses, and of the reason for keeping what it keeps, and of the whole process of growth in its poetry. The French have become diligent students of their own early poetry, which they long neglected; the study makes many of them dissatisfied with their so-called classical poetry, the court-tragedy of the seventeenth century, a poetry which Pellisson long ago reproached with its want of the true poetic stamp, with its *politesse stérile et rampante*, but which nevertheless has reigned in France as absolutely as if it had been the perfection of classical poetry indeed. The dissatisfaction is natural; yet a lively and accomplished critic, M. Charles d'Héricault, the editor of Clément Marot, goes too far when he says that "the cloud of glory playing round a classic is a mist as dangerous to the future of a literature as it is intolerable for the purposes of history." "It hinders," he goes on, "it hinders us from seeing more than one single point, the culminating and exceptional point; the summary, fictitious and arbitrary, of a thought and of a work. It substitutes a halo for a physiognomy, it puts a statue where there was once a man, and hiding from us all trace of the labour, the attempts, the weaknesses, the failures, it claims not study but veneration; it does not show us how the thing is done, it imposes upon us a model. Above all, for the historian this creation of classic personages

is inadmissible; for it withdraws the poet from his time, from his proper
life, it breaks historical relationships, it blinds criticism by conventional
admiration, and renders the investigation of literary origins unacceptable.
It gives us a human personage no longer, but a God seated immovable
amidst His perfect work, like Jupiter on Olympus; and hardly will it be
possible for the young student, to whom such work is exhibited at such a
distance from him, to believe that it did not issue ready made from that
divine head."   (6)

All this is brilliantly and tellingly said, but we must plead for a distinction. Everything depends on the reality of a poet's classic character. If he
is a dubious classic, let us sift him; if he is a false classic, let us explode
him. But if he is a real classic, if his work belongs to the class of the very
best (for this is the true and right meaning of the word *classic, classical*),
then the great thing for us is to feel and enjoy his work as deeply as ever
we can, and to appreciate the wide difference between it and all work
which has not the same high character. This is what is salutary, this is
what is formative; this is the great benefit to be got from the study of
poetry. Everything which interferes with it, which hinders it, is injurious.
True, we must read our classic with open eyes, and not with eyes blinded
with superstition; we must perceive when his work comes short, when it
drops out of the class of the very best, and we must rate it, in such cases,
at its proper value. But the use of this negative criticism is not in itself,
it is entirely in its enabling us to have a clearer sense and a deeper enjoyment of what is truly excellent. To trace the labour, the attempts, the
weaknesses, the failures of a genuine classic, to acquaint oneself with his
time and his life and his historical relationships, is mere literary dilet-
tantism unless it has that clear sense and deeper enjoyment for its end. It
may be said that the more we know about a classic the better we shall
enjoy him; and, if we lived as long as Methuselah and had all of us heads
of perfect clearness and wills of perfect steadfastness, this might be true in
fact as it is plausible in theory. But the case here is much the same as the
case with the Greek and Latin studies of our schoolboys. The elaborate
philological groundwork which we require them to lay is in theory an
admirable preparation for appreciating the Greek and Latin authors worthily. The more thoroughly we lay the groundwork, the better we shall be
able, it may be said, to enjoy the authors. True, if time were not so short,
and schoolboys' wits not so soon tired and their power of attention exhausted; only, as it is, the elaborate philological preparation goes on, but
the authors are little known and less enjoyed. So with the investigator of
"historic origins" in poetry. He ought to enjoy the true classic all the
better for his investigations; he often is distracted from the enjoyment of
the best, and with the less good he overbusies himself, and is prone to
over-rate it in proportion to the trouble which it has cost him.   (7)

The idea of tracing historic origins and historical relationships cannot be absent from a compilation like the present. And naturally the poets to be exhibited in it will be assigned to those persons for exhibition who are known to prize them highly, rather than to those who have no special inclination towards them. Moreover the very occupation with an author, and the business of exhibiting him, disposes us to affirm and amplify his importance. In the present work, therefore, we are sure of frequent temptation to adopt the historic estimate, or the personal estimate, and to forget the real estimate; which latter, nevertheless, we must employ if we are to make poetry yield us its full benefit. So high is that benefit, the benefit of clearly feeling and of deeply enjoying the really excellent, the truly classic in poetry, that we do well, I say, to set it fixedly before our minds as our object in studying poets and poetry, and to make the desire of attaining it the one principle to which, as the *Imitation* says, whatever we may read or come to know, we always return. *Cum multa legeris et cognoveris, ad unum semper oportet redire principium.* (8)

The historic estimate is likely in especial to affect our judgment and our language when we are dealing with ancient poets; the personal estimate when we are dealing with poets our contemporaries, or at any rate modern. The exaggerations due to the historic estimate are not in themselves, perhaps, of very much gravity. Their report hardly enters the general ear; probably they do not always impose even on the literary men who adopt them. But they lead to a dangerous abuse of language. So we hear Cædmon, amongst our own poets, compared to Milton. I have already noticed the enthusiasm of one accomplished French critic for "historic origins." Another eminent French critic, M. Vitet, comments upon that famous document of the early poetry of his nation, the *Chanson de Roland*. It is indeed a most interesting document. The *joculator* or *jongleur* Taillefer, who was with William the Conqueror's army at Hastings, marched before the Norman troops, so said the tradition, singing "of Charlemagne and of Roland and of Oliver, and of the vassals who died at Roncevaux"; and it is suggested that in the *Chanson de Roland* by one Turoldus or Théroulde, a poem preserved in a manuscript of the twelfth century in the Bodleian Library at Oxford, we have certainly the matter, perhaps even some of the words, of the chant which Taillefer sang. The poem has vigour and freshness; it is not without pathos. But M. Vitet is not satisfied with seeing in it a document of some poetic value, and of very high historic and linguistic value; he sees in it a grand and beautiful work, a monument of epic genius. In its general design he finds the grandiose conception, in its details he finds the constant union of simplicity with greatness, which are the marks, he truly says, of the genuine epic, and distinguish it from the artificial epic of literary ages. One thinks of Homer; this is the sort of praise which is given to Homer, and justly given. Higher praise there cannot well be, and it is the praise due to epic poetry of the highest order only, and to no other. Let us try, then, the *Chanson de Roland* at its best. Roland, mortally wounded, lays himself down under a pine-tree, with his face turned towards Spain and the enemy—

> De plusurs choses à remembrer li prist,
> De tantes teres cume li bers cunquist,
> De dulce France, des humes de sun lign,
> De Carlemagne sun seignor ki l'nurrit.[1]

That is primitive work, I repeat, with an undeniable poetic quality of its own. It deserves such praise, and such praise is sufficient for it. But now turn to Homer—

> Ὡς φάτο· τοὺς δ' ἤδη κατέχεν φυσίζοος αἶα
> ἐν Λακεδαίμονι αὖθι, φίλῃ ἐν πατρίδι γαίῃ.[2]

We are here in another world, another order of poetry altogether; here is rightly due such supreme praise as that which M. Vitet gives to the *Chanson de Roland*. If our words are to have any meaning, if our judgments are to have any solidity, we must not heap that supreme praise upon poetry of an order immeasurably inferior.   (9)

Indeed there can be no more useful help for discovering what poetry belongs to the class of the truly excellent, and can therefore do us most good, than to have always in one's mind lines and expressions of the great masters, and to apply them as a touchstone to other poetry. Of course we are not to require this other poetry to resemble them; it may be very dissimilar. But if we have any tact we shall find them, when we have lodged them well in our minds, an infallible touchstone for detecting the presence or absence of high poetic quality, and also the degree of this quality, in all other poetry which we may place beside them. Short passages, even single lines, will serve our turn quite sufficiently. Take the two lines which I have just quoted from Homer, the poet's comment on Helen's mention of her brothers;—or take his

> Ἀ δειλώ, τί σφῶϊ δόμεν Πηλῆϊ ἄνακτι
> θνητά; ὑμεις δ' ἐστὸν ἀγήρω τ' ἀθανάτω τε.
> ἢ ἵνα δυστήνοισι μετ' ἀνδράσιν ἄλγε' ἔχητον;[3]

---

1 "Then began he to call many things to remembrance,—all the lands which his valour conquered, and pleasant France, and the men of his lineage, and Charlemagne his liege lord who nourished him." —*Chanson de Roland*, iii, 939–42.

2 So said she; they long since in Earth's soft arms were reposing,
   There, in their own dear land, their fatherland, Lacedæmon.
                    Iliad, iii, 243, 244 (translated by Dr. Hawtrey).

3 Ah, unhappy pair, why gave we you to King Peleus, to a mortal? but ye are without old age, and immortal. Was it that with men born to misery ye might have sorrow?—*Iliad*, xvii, 443–45.

the address of Zeus to the horses of Peleus;—or take finally his

Καὶ σέ, γέρον, τὸ πρὶν μὲν ἀκούομεν ὄλβιον εἶναι.[4]

the words of Achilles to Priam, a suppliant before him. Take that incomparable line and a half of Dante, Ugolino's tremendous words—

Io no piangeva; sì dentro impietrai.
Piangevan elli . . .[5]

take the lovely words of Beatrice to Virgil—

Io son fatta da Dio, sua mercè, tale,
Che la vostra miseria non mi tange,
Nè fiamma d'esto incendio non m'assale . . .[6]

take the simple, but perfect, single line—

In la sua volontade è nostra pace.[7]

Take of Shakespeare a line or two of Henry the Fourth's expostulation with sleep—

Wilt thou upon the high and giddy mast
Seal up the ship-boy's eyes, and rock his brains
In cradle of the rude imperious surge . . .

and take, as well, Hamlet's dying request to Horatio—

If thou didst ever hold me in thy heart,
Absent thee from felicity awhile,
And in this harsh world draw thy breath in pain
To tell my story . . .

Take of Milton that Miltonic passage—

Darken'd so, yet shone
Above them all the archangel; but his face
Deep scars of thunder had intrench'd, and care
Sat on his faded cheek . . .

---

4 "Nay, and thou too, old man, in former days wast, as we hear, happy."—*Iliad*, xxiv, 543.
5 "I wailed not, so of stone grew I within;—*they* wailed."—*Inferno*, xxxiii, 39, 40.
6 "Of such sort hath God, thanked be His mercy, made me, that your misery toucheth me not, neither doth the flame of this fire strike me."—*Inferno*, ii, 91–93.
7 "In His will is our peace."—*Paradiso*, iii, 85.

add two such lines as—

> And courage never to submit or yield
> And what is else not to be overcome . . .

and finish with the exquisite close to the loss of Proserpine, the loss

> . . . which cost Ceres all that pain
> To seek her through the world.

These few lines, if we have tact and can use them, are enough even of themselves to keep clear and sound our judgments about poetry, to save us from fallacious estimates of it, to conduct us to a real estimate.   (10)

The specimens I have quoted differ widely from one another, but they have in common this: the possession of the very highest poetical quality. If we are thoroughly penetrated by their power, we shall find that we have acquired a sense enabling us, whatever poetry may be laid before us, to feel the degree in which a high poetical quality is present or wanting there. Critics give themselves great labour to draw out what in the abstract constitutes the characters of a high quality of poetry. It is much better simply to have recourse to concrete examples;—to take specimens of poetry of the high, the very highest quality, and to say: The characters of a high quality of poetry are what is expressed *there*. They are far better recognised by being felt in the verse of the master, than by being perused in the prose of the critic. Nevertheless if we are urgently pressed to give some critical account of them, we may safely, perhaps, venture on laying down, not indeed how and why the characters arise, but where and in what they arise. They are in the matter and substance of the poetry, and they are in its manner and style. Both of these, the substance and matter on the one hand, the style and manner on the other, have a mark, an accent, of high beauty, worth, and power. But if we are asked to define this mark and accent in the abstract, our answer must be: No, for we should thereby be darkening the question, not clearing it. The mark and accent are as given by the substance and matter of that poetry, by the style and manner of that poetry, and of all other poety which is akin to it in quality.   (11)

Only one thing we may add as to the substance and matter of poetry, guiding ourselves by Aristotle's profound observation that the superiority of poetry over history consists in its possessing a higher truth and a higher seriousness (φιλοσοφώτερον καὶ σπουδαιότερον). Let us add, therefore, to what we have said, this: that the substance and matter of the best poetry acquire their special character from possessing, in an eminent degree, truth and seriousness. We may add yet further, what is in itself evident, that to the style and manner of the best poetry their special character, their accent, is given by their diction, and, even yet more, by their movement. And though we distinguish between the two characters, the two accents, of superiority, yet they are nevertheless vitally connected one with the other. The superior character of truth and seriousness, in the matter and substance of the best poetry, is inseparable from the superiority of diction and movement marking its style and manner. The two superiorities are closely related, and are in steadfast proportion one to the other. So far as high poetic truth and seriousness are wanting to a poet's matter and substance, so far also, we may be sure, will a high poetic stamp of diction and movement be wanting to his style and manner. In proportion as this high stamp of diction and movement, again, is absent from a poet's style and manner, we shall find, also, that high poetic truth and seriousness are absent from his substance and matter. (12)

So stated, these are but dry generalities; their whole force lies in their application. And I could wish every student of poetry to make the application of them for himself. Made by himself, the application would impress itself upon his mind far more deeply than made by me. Neither will my limits allow me to make any full application of the generalities above propounded; but in the hope of bringing out, at any rate, some significance in them, and of establishing an important principle more firmly by their means, I will, in the space which remains to me, follow rapidly from the commencement the course of our English poetry with them in my view. (13)

Once more I return to the early poetry of France, with which our own poetry, in its origins, is indissolubly connected. In the twelfth and thirteenth centuries, that seed-time of all modern language and literature, the poetry of France had a clear predominance in Europe. Of the two divisions of that poetry, its productions in the *langue d'oil* and its productions in the *langue d'oc*, the poetry of the *langue d'oc*, of southern France, of the troubadours, is of importance because of its effect on Italian literature;— the first literature of modern Europe to strike the true and grand note, and to bring forth, as in Dante and Petrarch it brought forth, classics. But the predominance of French poetry in Europe, during the twelfth and thirteenth centuries, is due to its poetry of the *langue d'oil*, the poetry of northern France and of the tongue which is now the French language. In the twelfth century the bloom of this romance-poetry was earlier and stronger in England, at the court of our Anglo-Norman kings, than in France itself. But it was a bloom of French poetry; and as our native poetry formed itself, it formed itself out of this. The romance-poems which took possession of the heart and imagination of Europe in the twelfth and thirteenth centuries are French; "they are," as Southey justly says, "the pride of French literature, nor have we anything which can be placed in competition with them." Themes were supplied from all quarters; but the romance-setting which was common to them all, and which gained the ear of Europe, was French. This constituted for the French poetry, literature, and language, at the height of the Middle Age, an unchallenged predominance. The Italian Bruneto Latini, the master of Dante, wrote his *Treasure* in French because, he says, "la parleure en est plus délitable et plus *commune à toutes gens.*" In the same century, the thirteenth, the French romance-writer, Christian of Troyes, formulates the claims, in chivalry and letters, of France, his native country, as follows:

> Or vous ert par ce livre apris,
> Que Gresse ot de chevalerie
> Le premier los et de clergie;
> Puis vint chevalerie à Rome,
> Et de la clergie la some,
> Qui ore est en France venue.
> Diex doinst qu'ele i soit retenue,
> Et que li lius li abelisse
> Tant que de France n'isse
> L'onor qui s'i est arestée!

Now by this book you will learn that first Greece had the renown for chivalry and letters; then chivalry and the primacy in letters passed to Rome, and now it is come to France. God grant it may be kept there; and that the place may please it so well, that the honour which has come to make stay in France may never depart thence!   (14)

Yet it is now all gone, this French romance-poetry, of which the weight of substance and the power of style are not unfairly represented by this extract from Christian of Troyes. Only by means of the historic estimate can we persuade ourselves now to think that any of it is of poetical importance.   (15)

But in the fourteenth century there comes an Englishman nourished on this poetry, taught his trade by this poetry, getting words, rhyme, metre from this poetry; for even of that stanza which the Italians used, and which Chaucer derived immediately from the Italians, the basis and suggestion was probably given in France. Chaucer (I have already named him) fascinated his contemporaries, but so too did Christian of Troyes and Wolfram of Eschenbach. Chaucer's power of fascination, however, is enduring; his poetical importance does not need the assistance of the historic estimate; it is real. He is a genuine source of joy and strength, which is flowing still for us and will flow always. He will be read, as time goes on, far more generally than he is read now. His language is a cause of difficulty for us; but so also, and I think in quite as great a degree, is the language of Burns. In Chaucer's case, as in that of Burns, it is a difficulty to be unhesitatingly accepted and overcome.   (16)

If we ask ourselves wherein consists the immense superiority of Chaucer's poetry over the romance-poetry—why it is that in passing from this to Chaucer we suddenly feel ourselves to be in another world, we shall find that his superiority is both in the substance of his poetry and in the style of his poetry. His superiority in substance is given by his large, free, simple, clear yet kindly view of human life,—so unlike the total want, in the romance-poets, of all intelligent command of it. Chaucer has not their helplessness; he has gained the power to survey the world from a central, a truly human point of view. We have only to call to mind the Prologue to *The Canterbury Tales*. The right comment upon it is Dryden's: "It is sufficient to say, according to the proverb, that *here is God's plenty*." And again: "He is a perpetual fountain of good sense." It is by a large, free, sound representation of things, that poetry, this high criticism of life, has truth of substance; and Chaucer's poetry has truth of substance.   (17)

Of his style and manner, if we think first of the romance-poetry and then of Chaucer's divine liquidness of diction, his divine fluidity of movement, it is difficult to speak temperately. They are irresistible, and justify all the rapture with which his successors speak of his "gold dew-drops of speech." Johnson misses the point entirely when he finds fault with Dryden for ascribing to Chaucer the first refinement of our numbers, and says that Gower also can show smooth numbers and easy rhymes. The refinement of our numbers means something far more than this. A nation may have versifiers with smooth numbers and easy rhymes, and yet may have no real poetry at all. Chaucer is the father of our splendid English poetry; he is our "well of English undefiled," because by the lovely charm of his diction, the lovely charm of his movement, he makes an epoch and founds a tradition. In Spenser, Shakespeare, Milton, Keats, we can follow the tradition of the liquid diction, the fluid movement, of Chaucer; at one time it is his liquid diction of which in these poets we feel the virtue, and at another time it is his fluid movement. And the virtue is irresistible.   (18)

Bounded as is my space, I must yet find room for an example of Chaucer's virtue, as I have given examples to show the virtue of the great classics. I feel disposed to say that a single line is enough to show the charm of Chaucer's verse; that merely one line like this—

O martyr souded[8] in virginitee!

has a virtue of manner and movement such as we shall not find in all the verse of romance-poetry;—but this is saying nothing. The virtue is such as

---

8 The French *soudé;* soldered, fixed fast.

we shall not find, perhaps, in all English poetry, outside the poets whom
I have named as the special inheritors of Chaucer's tradition. A single line,
however, is too little if we have not the strain of Chaucer's verse well in
our memory; let us take a stanza. It is from *The Prioress's Tale*, the story
of the Christian child murdered in a Jewry—

> My throte is cut unto my nekke-bone
> Saidè this child, and as by way of kinde
> I should have deyd, yea, longè time agone;
> But Jesus Christ, as ye in bookès finde,
> Will that his glory last and be in minde,
> And for the worship of his mother dere
> Yet may I sing *O Alma* loud and clere.

Wordsworth has modernised this Tale, and to feel how delicate and evanescent is the charm of verse, we have only to read Wordsworth's first three
lines of this stanza after Chaucer's—

> My throat is cut unto the bone, I trow,
> Said this young child, and by the law of kind
> I should have died, yea, many hours ago.

The charm is departed. It is often said that the power of liquidness and
fluidity in Chaucer's verse was dependent upon a free, a licentious dealing
with language, such as is now impossible; upon a liberty, such as Burns too
enjoyed, of making words like *neck, bird*, into a dissyllable by adding to
them, and words like *cause, rhyme*, into a dissyllable by sounding the *e*
mute. It is true that Chaucer's fluidity is conjoined with this liberty, and
is admirably served by it; but we ought not to say that it was dependent
upon it. It was dependent upon his talent. Other poets with a like liberty
do not attain to the fluidity of Chaucer; Burns himself does not attain to
it. Poets, again, who have a talent akin to Chaucer's, such as Shakespeare
or Keats, have known how to attain to his fluidity without the like liberty.   (19)

And yet Chaucer is not one of the great classics. His poetry transcends
and effaces, easily and without effort, all the romance-poetry of Catholic
Christendom; it transcends and effaces all the English poetry contemporary
with it, it transcends and effaces all the English poetry subsequent to it
down to the age of Elizabeth. Of such avail is poetic truth of substance,
in its natural and necessary union with poetic truth of style. And yet, I
say, Chaucer is not one of the great classics. He has not their accent. What
is wanting to him is suggested by the mere mention of the name of the

first great classic of Christendom, the immortal poet who died eighty years before Chaucer,—Dante. The accent of such verse as

> In la sua volontade è nostra pace . . .

is altogether beyond Chaucer's reach; we praise him, but we feel that this accent is out of the question for him. It may be said that it was necessarily out of the reach of any poet in the England of that stage of growth. Possibly; but we are to adopt a real, not a historic, estimate of poetry. However we may account for its absence, something is wanting, then, to the poetry of Chaucer, which poetry must have before it can be placed in the glorious class of the best. And there is no doubt what that something is. It is the σπουδαιότης, the high and excellent seriousness, which Aristotle assigns as one of the grand virtues of poetry. The substance of Chaucer's poetry, his view of things and his criticism of life, has largeness, freedom, shrewdness, benignity; but it has not this high seriousness. Homer's criticism of life has it. Dante's has it, Shakespeare's has it. It is this chiefly which gives to our spirits what they can rest upon; and with the increasing demands of our modern ages upon poetry, this virtue of giving us what we can rest upon will be more and more highly esteemed. A voice from the slums of Paris, fifty or sixty years after Chaucer, the voice of poor Villon out of his life of riot and crime, has at its happy moments (as, for instance, in the last stanza of "La Belle Heaulmière"[9]) more of this important poetic virtue of seriousness than all the productions of Chaucer. But its apparition in Villon, and in men like Villon, is fitful; the greatness of the great poets, the power of their criticism of life, is that their virtue is sustained. (20)

To our praise, therefore, of Chaucer as a poet there must be this limitation; he lacks the high seriousness of the great classics, and therewith an important part of their virtue. Still, the main fact for us to bear in mind about Chaucer is his sterling value according to that real estimate which we firmly adopt for all poets. He has poetic truth of substance, though he has not high poetic seriousness, and corresponding to his truth of substance

---

[9] The name *Heaulmière* is said to be derived from a headdress (helm) worn as a mark by courtesans. In Villon's ballad, a poor old creature of this class laments her days of youth and beauty. The last stanza of the ballad runs thus—

> Ainsi le bon temps regretons
> Entre nous, pauvres vieilles sottes,
> Assises bas, à croppetons,
> Tout en ung tas comme pelottes;
> A petit feu de chenevottes
> Tost allumées, tost estainctes.
> Et jadis fusmes si mignottes!
> Ainsi en prend à maintz et maintes.

Thus amongst ourselves we regret the good time, poor silly old things, low-seated on our heels, all in a heap like so many balls; by a little fire of hemp-stalks, soon lighted, soon spent. And once we were such darlings! So fares it with many and many a one.

he has an exquisite virtue of style and manner. With him is born our real
poetry.   (21)

For my present purpose I need not dwell on our Elizabethan poetry,
or on the continuation and close of this poetry in Milton. We all of us
profess to be agreed in the estimate of this poetry; we all of us recognise it
as great poetry, our greatest, and Shakespeare and Milton as our poetical
classics. The real estimate, here, has universal currency. With the next age
of our poetry divergency and difficulty begin. An historic estimate of that
poetry has established itself; and the question is, whether it will be found
to coincide with the real estimate.   (22)

The age of Dryden, together with our whole eighteenth century which
followed it, sincerely believed itself to have produced poetical classics of
its own, and even to have made advance, in poetry, beyond all its predecessors. Dryden regards as not seriously disputable the opinion "that the
sweetness of English verse was never understood or practised by our fathers." Cowley could see nothing at all in Chaucer's poetry. Dryden heartily admired it, and, as we have seen, praised its matter admirably; but of
its exquisite manner and movement all he can find to say is that "there
is the rude sweetness of a Scotch tune in it, which is natural and pleasing,
though not perfect." Addison, wishing to praise Chaucer's numbers, compares them with Dryden's own. And all through the eighteenth century,
and down even into our own times, the stereotyped phrase of approbation
for good verse found in our early poetry has been, that it even approached
the verse of Dryden, Addison, Pope, and Johnson.   (23)

Are Dryden and Pope poetical classics? Is the historic estimate, which
represents them as such, and which has been so long established that it
cannot easily give way, the real estimate? Wordsworth and Coleridge, as is
well known, denied it; but the authority of Wordsworth and Coleridge
does not weigh much with the young generation, and there are many signs
to show that the eighteenth century and its judgments are coming into
favour again. Are the favourite poets of the eighteenth century classics?
                                                                           (24)

It is impossible within my present limits to discuss the question fully.
And what man of letters would not shrink from seeming to dispose dicta-
torially of the claims of two men who are, at any rate, such masters in
letters as Dryden and Pope; two men of such admirable talent, both of
them, and one of them, Dryden, a man, on all sides, of such energetic
and genial power? And yet, if we are to gain the full benefit from poetry,
we must have the real estimate of it. I cast about for some mode of arriving, in the present case, at such an estimate without offence. And perhaps
the best way is to begin, as it is easy to begin, with cordial praise.   (25)

When we find Chapman, the Elizabethan translator of Homer, expressing himself in his preface thus: "Though truth in her very nakedness sits

in so deep a pit, that from Gades to Aurora and Ganges few eyes can sound her, I hope yet those few here will so discover and confirm that, the date being out of her darkness in this morning of our poet, he shall now gird his temples with the sun,"—we pronounce that such a prose is intolerable. When we find Milton writing: "And long it was not after, when I was confirmed in this opinion, that he, who would not be frustrate of his hope to write well hereafter in laudable things, ought himself to be a true poem,"—we pronounce that such a prose has its own grandeur, but that it is obsolete and inconvenient. But when we find Dryden telling us: "What Virgil wrote in the vigour of his age, in plenty and at ease, I have undertaken to translate in my declining years; struggling with wants, oppressed with sickness, curbed in my genius, liable to be misconstrued in all I write,"—then we exclaim that here at last we have the true English prose, a prose such as we would all gladly use if we only knew how. Yet Dryden was Milton's contemporary.   (26)

But after the Restoration the time had come when our nation felt the imperious need of a fit prose. So, too, the time had likewise come when our nation felt the imperious need of freeing itself from the absorbing preoccupation which religion in the Puritan age had exercised. It was impossible that this freedom should be brought about without some negative excess, without some neglect and impairment of the religious life of the soul; and the spiritual history of the eighteenth century shows us that the freedom was not achieved without them. Still, the freedom was achieved; the preoccupation, an undoubtedly baneful and retarding one if it had continued, was got rid of. And as with religion amongst us at that period, so it was also with letters. A fit prose was a necessity; but it was impossible that a fit prose should establish itself amongst us without some touch of frost to the imaginative life of the soul. The needful qualities for a fit prose are regularity, uniformity, precision, balance. The men of letters, whose destiny it may be to bring their nation to the attainment of a fit prose, must of necessity, whether they work in prose or in verse, give a predominating, an almost exclusive attention to the qualities of regularity, uniformity, precision, balance. But an almost exclusive attention to these qualities involves some repression and silencing of poetry.   (27)

We are to regard Dryden as the puissant and glorious founder, Pope as the splendid high priest, of our age of prose and reason, of our excellent and indispensable eighteenth century. For the purposes of their mission and destiny their poetry, like their prose, is admirable. Do you ask me whether Dryden's verse, take it almost where you will, is not good?

> A milk-white Hind, immortal and unchanged,
> Fed on the lawns and in the forest ranged.

I answer: Admirable for the purposes of the inaugurator of an age of prose and reason. Do you ask me whether Pope's verse, take it almost where you will, is not good?

> To Hounslow Heath I point, and Banstead Down;
> Thence comes your mutton, and these chicks my own.

I answer: Admirable for the purposes of the high priest of an age of prose and reason. But do you ask me whether such verse proceeds from men with an adequate poetic criticism of life, from men whose criticism of life has a high seriousness, or even, without that high seriousness, has poetic largeness, freedom, insight, benignity? Do you ask me whether the application of ideas to life in the verse of these men, often a powerful application, no doubt, is a powerful *poetic* application? Do you ask me whether the poetry of these men has either the matter or the inseparable manner of such an adequate poetic criticism; whether it has the accent of

> Absent thee from felicity awhile . . .

or of

> And what is else not to be overcome . . .

or of

> O martyr souded in virginitee!

I answer: It has not and cannot have them; it is the poetry of the builders of an age of prose and reason. Though they may write in verse, though they may in a certain sense be masters of the art of versification, Dryden and Pope are not classics of our poetry, they are classics of our prose. (28)

Gray is our poetical classic of that literature and age; the position of Gray is singular, and demands a word of notice here. He has not the volume or the power of poets who, coming in times more favourable, have attained to an independent criticism of life. But he lived with the great poets, he lived, above all, with the Greeks, through perpetually studying and enjoying them; and he caught their poetic point of view for regarding life, caught their poetic manner. The point of view and the manner are not self-sprung in him, he caught them of others; and he had not the free and abundant use of them. But whereas Addison and Pope never had the use of them, Gray had the use of them at times. He is the scantiest and frailest of classics in our poetry, but he is a classic.   (29)

And now after Gray, we are met, as we draw towards the end of the eighteenth century, we are met by the great name of Burns. We enter now on times where the personal estimate of poets begins to be rife, and where the real estimate of them is not reached without difficulty. But in spite of the disturbing pressures of personal partiality, of national partiality, let us try to reach a real estimate of the poetry of Burns.   (30)

By his English poetry Burns in general belongs to the eighteenth century, and has little importance for us.

> Mark ruffian Violence, distain'd with crimes,
> Rousing elate in these degenerate times;
> View unsuspecting Innocence a prey,
> As guileful Fraud points out the erring way;
> While subtle Litigation's pliant tongue
> The life-blood equal sucks of Right and Wrong!

Evidently this is not the real Burns, or his name and fame would have disappeared long ago. Nor is Clarinda's love-poet, Sylvander, the real Burns either. But he tells us himself: "These English songs gravel me to death. I have not the command of the language that I have of my native tongue. In fact, I think that my ideas are more barren in English than in Scotch. I have been at 'Duncan Gray' to dress it in English, but all I can do is desperately stupid." We English turn naturally, in Burns, to the poems in our own language, because we can read them easily; but in those poems we have not the real Burns. (31)

The real Burns is of course in his Scotch poems. Let us boldly say that of much of this poetry, a poetry dealing perpetually with Scotch drink, Scotch religion, and Scotch manners, a Scotchman's estimate is apt to be personal. A Scotchman is used to this world of Scotch drink, Scotch religion, and Scotch manners; he has a tenderness for it; he meets its poet half way. In this tender mood he reads pieces like the "Holy Fair" or "Halloween." But this world of Scotch drink, Scotch religion, and Scotch manners is against the poet, not for him, when it is not a partial countryman who reads him; for in itself it is not a beautiful world, and no one can deny that it is of advantage to a poet to deal with a beautiful world. Burns's world of Scotch drink, Scotch religion, and Scotch manners, is often a harsh, a sordid, a repulsive world; even the world of his "Cotter's Saturday Night" is not a beautiful world. No doubt a poet's criticism of life may have such truth and power that it triumphs over its world and delights us. Burns may triumph over his world, often he does triumph over his world, but let us observe how and where. Burns is the first case we have had where the bias of the personal estimate tends to mislead; let us look at him closely, he can bear it. (32)

Many of his admirers will tell us that we have Burns, convivial, genuine, delightful, here—

> Leeze me on drink! it gies us mair
>   Than either school or college;
> It kindles wit, it waukens lair,
>   It pangs us fou o' knowledge.

> Be 't whisky gill or penny wheep
>   Or ony stronger potion,
> It never fails, on drinking deep,
>   To kittle up our notion
>   By night or day.

There is a great deal of that sort of thing in Burns, and it is unsatisfactory, not because it is bacchanalian poetry, but because it has not that accent of sincerity which bacchanalian poetry, to do it justice, very often has. There is something in it of bravado, something which makes us feel that we have not the man speaking to us with his real voice; something, therefore, poetically unsound.   (33)

With still more confidence will his admirers tell us that we have the genuine Burns, the great poet, when his strain asserts the independence, equality, dignity, of men, as in the famous song "For a' that and a' that"—

> A prince can mak' a belted knight,
>   A marquis, duke, and a' that;
> But an honest man's aboon his might,
>   Guid faith he mauna fa' that!
>   For a' that, and a' that,
>   Their dignities, and a' that,
>   The pith o' sense, and pride o' worth,
>   Are higher rank than a' that.

Here they find his grand, genuine touches; and still more, when this puissant genius, who so often set morality at defiance, falls moralising—

> The sacred lowe o' weel-placed love
>   Luxuriantly indulge it;
> But never tempt th' illicit rove,
>   Tho' naething should divulge it.
> I waive the quantum o' the sin,
>   The hazard o' concealing,
> But och! it hardens a' within,
>   And petrifies the feeling.

Or in a higher strain—

> Who made the heart, 'tis He alone
>   Decidedly can try us;
> He knows each chord, its various tone;
>   Each spring, its various bias.
> Then at the balance let's be mute,
>   We never can adjust it;
> What's *done* we partly may compute,
>   But know not what's resisted.

Or in a better strain yet, a strain, his admirers will say, unsurpassable—

> To make a happy fire-side clime
> To weans and wife,
> That's the true pathos and sublime
> Of human life.

There is criticism of life for you, the admirers of Burns will say to us; there is the application of ideas to life! There is, undoubtedly. The doctrine of the last-quoted lines coincides almost exactly with what was the aim and end, Xenophon tells us, of all the teaching of Socrates. And the application is a powerful one; made by a man of vigorous understanding, and (need I say?) a master of language.   (34)

But for supreme poetical success more is required than the powerful application of ideas to life; it must be an application under the conditions fixed by the laws of poetic truth and poetic beauty. Those laws fix as an essential condition, in the poet's treatment of such matters as are here in question, high seriousness;—the high seriousness which comes from absolute sincerity. The accent of high seriousness, born of absolute sincerity, is what gives to such verse as

> In la sua volontade è nostra pace . . .

to such criticism of life as Dante's, its power. Is this accent felt in the passages which I have been quoting from Burns? Surely not; surely, if our sense is quick, we must perceive that we have not in those passages a voice from the very inmost soul of the genuine Burns; he is not speaking to us from these depths, he is more or less preaching. And the compensation for admiring such passages less, from missing the perfect poetic accent in them, will be that we shall admire more the poetry where that accent is found.

No; Burns, like Chaucer, comes short of the high seriousness of the great classics, and the virtue of matter and manner which goes with that high seriousness is wanting to his work. At moments he touches it in a profound and passionate melancholy, as in those four immortal lines taken by Byron as a motto for *The Bride of Abydos*, but which have in them a depth of poetic quality such as resides in no verse of Byron's own—

> Had we never loved sae kindly,
> Had we never loved sae blindly,
> Never met, or never parted,
> We had ne'er been broken-hearted.

But a whole poem of that quality Burns cannot make; the rest, in the "Farewell to Nancy," is verbiage.   (36)

We arrive best at the real estimate of Burns, I think, by conceiving his work as having truth of matter and truth of manner, but not the accent or the poetic virtue of the highest masters. His genuine criticism of life, when the sheer poet in him speaks, is ironic; it is not—

> Thou Power Supreme, whose mighty scheme
> These woes of mine fulfil,
> Here firm I rest, they must be best
> Because they are Thy will!

It is far rather: "Whistle owre the lave o't!" Yet we may say of him as of Chaucer, that of life and the world, as they come before him, his view is large, free, shrewd, benignant,—truly poetic, therefore; and his manner of rendering what he sees is to match. But we must note, at the same time, his great difference from Chaucer. The freedom of Chaucer is heightened, in Burns, by a fiery, reckless energy; the benignity of Chaucer deepens, in Burns, into an overwhelming sense of the pathos of things;—of the pathos of human nature, the pathos, also, of non-human nature. Instead of the fluidity of Chaucer's manner, the manner of Burns has spring, bounding swiftness. Burns is by far the greater force, though he has perhaps less charm. The world of Chaucer is fairer, richer, more significant than that of Burns; but when the largeness and freedom of Burns get full sweep, as in *Tam o' Shanter,* or still more in that puissant and splendid production, *The Jolly Beggars,* his world may be what it will, his poetic genius triumphs over it. In the world of *The Jolly Beggars* there is more than hideousness and squalor, there is bestiality; yet the piece is a superb poetic success. It has a breadth, truth, and power which make the famous scene in Auerbach's Cellar, of Goethe's *Faust,* seem artificial and tame beside it, and which are only matched by Shakespeare and Aristophanes.   (37)

Here, where his largeness and freedom serve him so admirably, and also in those poems and songs where to shrewdness he adds infinite archness and wit, and to benignity infinite pathos, where his manner is flawless, and a perfect poetic whole is the result,—in things like the address to the mouse whose home he had ruined, in things like "Duncan Gray," "Tam Glen," "Whistle and I'll come to you my Lad," "Auld Lang Syne" (this list might be made much longer),—here we have the genuine Burns, of whom the real estimate must be high indeed. Not a classic, nor with the excellent σπουδαιότης of the great classics, nor with a verse rising to a criticism of life and a virtue like theirs; but a poet with thorough truth of substance and an answering truth of style, giving us a poetry sound to the core. We all of us have a leaning towards the pathetic, and may be inclined perhaps to prize Burns most for his touches of piercing, sometimes almost intolerable, pathos; for verse like—

> We twa hae paidl't i' the burn
> From mornin' sun till dine;
> But seas between us braid hae roar'd
> Sin auld lang syne . . .

where he is as lovely as he is sound. But perhaps it is by the perfection of soundness of his lighter and archer masterpieces that he is poetically most wholesome for us. For the votary misled by a personal estimate of Shelley, as so many of us have been, are, and will be,—of that beautiful spirit building his many-coloured haze of words and images

> Pinnacled dim in the intense inane—

no contact can be wholesomer than the contact with Burns at his archest and soundest. Side by side with the

> On the brink of the night and the morning
> My coursers are wont to respire,
> But the Earth has just whispered a warning
> That their flight must be swifter than fire . . .

of *Prometheus Unbound*, how salutary, how very salutary, to place this from "Tam Glen"—

> My minnie does constantly deave me
> And bids me beware o' young men;
> They flatter, she says, to deceive me;
> But wha can think sae o' Tam Glen?   (38)

But we enter on burning ground as we approach the poetry of times so near to us—poetry like that of Byron, Shelley, and Wordsworth—of which the estimates are so often not only personal, but personal with passion. For my purpose, it is enough to have taken the single case of Burns, the first poet we come to of whose work the estimate formed is evidently apt to be personal, and to have suggested how we may proceed, using the poetry of the great classics as a sort of touchstone, to correct this estimate, as we had previously corrected by the same means the historic estimate where we met with it. A collection like the present, with its succession of celebrated names and celebrated poems, offers a good opportunity to us for resolutely endeavoring to make our estimates of poetry real. I have sought

to point out a method which will help us in making them so, and to exhibit it in use so far as to put any one who likes in a way of applying
it for himself.   (39)

At any rate the end to which the method and the estimate are designed
to lead, and from leading to which, if they do lead to it, they get their
whole value,—the benefit of being able clearly to feel and deeply to enjoy
the best, the truly classic, in poetry,—is an end, let me say it once more at
parting, of supreme importance. We are often told that an era is opening in
which we are to see multitudes of a common sort of readers, and masses of
a common sort of literature; that such readers do not want and could not
relish anything better than such literature, and that to provide it is becoming a vast and profitable industry. Even if good literature entirely lost
currency with the world, it would still be abundantly worth while to continue to enjoy it by oneself. But it never will lose currency with the world,
in spite of momentary appearances; it never will lose supremacy. Currency
and supremacy are insured to it, not indeed by the world's deliberate and
conscious choice, but by something far deeper,—by the instinct of self-
preservation in humanity.   (40)

Walter Pater

(1839–1894)

*PATER does not yield to easy characterization. A retiring scholar, he yet be-
came the reluctant hero of a group of late-nineteenth-century aesthetes;
never a dogmatist, he penned one of the most considerable essays on style
in the English language and has been held up as the* locus classicus *of
stylistic impressionism. His chief works include* Studies in the History of
the Renaissance *(1873),* Marius the Epicurean, *a spiritual romance (1885),
and* Appreciations *(1889), in which this essay was included.*

◼ *Appreciations*

Style

SINCE ALL progress of mind consists for the most part in differentiation, in the resolution of an obscure and complex object into its component aspects, it is surely the stupidest of losses to confuse things which right reason has put asunder, to lose the sense of achieved distinctions, the distinction between poetry and prose, for instance, or, to speak more exactly, between the laws and characteristic excellences of verse and prose composition. On the other hand, those who have dwelt most emphatically on the distinction between prose and verse, prose and poetry, may sometimes have been tempted to limit the proper function of prose too narrowly; and this again is at least false economy, as being, in effect, the renunciation of a certain means or faculty, in a world where after all we must needs make the most of things. Critical efforts to limit art *a priori*, by anticipations regarding the natural incapacity of the material with which this or that artist works, as the sculptor with solid form, or the prose-writer with the ordinary language of men, are always liable to be discredited by the facts of artistic production; and while prose is actually found to be a coloured thing with Bacon, picturesque with Livy and Carlyle, musical with Cicero and Newman, mystical and intimate with Plato and Michelet and Sir Thomas Browne, exalted or florid, it may be, with Milton and Taylor, it will be useless to protest that it can be nothing at all, except something very tamely and narrowly confined to mainly practical ends—a kind of "good round-hand"; as useless as the protest that poetry might not touch prosaic subjects as with Wordsworth, or an abstruse matter as with Browning, or treat contemporary life nobly as with Tennyson. In subordination to one essential beauty in all good literary style, in all literature as a fine art, as there are many beauties of poetry so the beauties of prose are many, and it is the business of criticism to estimate them as such; as it is good in the criticism of verse to look for those hard, logical, and quasi-prosaic excellences which that too has, or needs. To find in the poem, amid the flowers, the allusions, the mixed perspectives, of *Lycidas* for instance, the thought, the logical structure:—how wholesome! how delightful! as to identify in prose what we call the poetry, the imaginative power, not treating it as out of place and a kind of vagrant intruder, but by way of an estimate of its rights, that is, of its achieved powers, there. (1)

Dryden, with the characteristic instinct of his age, loved to emphasise the distinction between poetry and prose, the protest against their confusion with each other, coming with somewhat diminished effect from one whose poetry was so prosaic. In truth, his sense of prosaic excellence affected his verse rather than his prose, which is not only fervid, richly figured, poetic, as we say, but vitiated, all unconsciously, by many a scanning line. Setting up correctness, that humble merit of prose, as the central literary excellence, he is really a less correct writer than he may seem, still with an imperfect mastery of the relative pronoun. It might have been foreseen that, in the rotations of mind, the province of poetry in prose would find its assertor; and, a century after Dryden, amid very different intellectual needs, and with the need therefore of great modifications in literary form, the range of the poetic force in literature was effectively enlarged by Wordsworth. The true distinction between prose and poetry he regarded as the almost technical or accidental one of the absence or presence of metrical beauty, or, say! metrical restraint; and for him the opposition came to be between verse and prose of course; but, as the essential dichotomy in this matter, between imaginative and unimaginative writing, parallel to De Quincey's distinction between "the literature of power and the literature of knowledge," in the former of which the composer gives us not fact, but his peculiar sense of fact, whether past or present.   (2)

Dismissing then, under sanction of Wordsworth, that harsher opposition of poetry to prose, as savouring in fact of the arbitrary psychology of the last century, and with it the prejudice that there can be but one only beauty of prose style, I propose here to point out certain qualities of all literature as a fine art, which, if they apply to the literature of fact, apply still more to the literature of the imaginative sense of fact, while they apply indifferently to verse and prose, so far as either is really imaginative—certain conditions of true art in both alike, which conditions may also contain in them the secret of the proper discrimination and guardianship of the peculiar excellences of either.   (3)

The line between fact and something quite different from external fact is, indeed, hard to draw. In Pascal, for instance, in the persuasive writers generally, how difficult to define the point where, from time to time, argument which, if it is to be worth anything at all, must consist of facts or groups of facts, becomes a pleading—a theorem no longer, but essentially an appeal to the reader to catch the writer's spirit, to think with him, if one can or will—an expression no longer of fact but of his sense of it, his peculiar intuition of a world, prospective, or discerned below the faulty conditions of the present, in either case changed somewhat from the actual world. In science, on the other hand, in history so far as it conforms to scientific rule, we have a literary domain where the imagination may be thought to be always an intruder. And as, in all science, the functions of literature re-

duce themselves eventually to the transcribing of fact, so all the excellences
of literary form in regard to science are reducible to various kinds of painstaking; this good quality being involved in all "skilled work" whatever, in
the drafting of an act of parliament, as in sewing. Yet here again, the
writer's sense of fact, in history especially, and in all those complex subjects
which do but lie on the borders of science, will still take the place of fact,
in various degrees. Your historian, for instance, with absolutely truthful intention, amid the multitude of facts presented to him must needs select, and
in selecting assert something of his own humour, something that comes not
of the world without but of a vision within. So Gibbon moulds his unwieldy material to a preconceived view. Livy, Tacitus, Michelet, moving
full of poignant sensibility amid the records of the past, each, after his own
sense, modifies—who can tell where and to what degree?—and becomes
something else than a transcriber; each, as he thus modifies, passing into the
domain of art proper. For just in proportion as the writer's aim, consciously or
unconsciously, comes to be the transcribing, not of the world, not of mere
fact, but of his sense of it, he becomes an artist, his work *fine* art; and good
art (as I hope ultimately to show) in proportion to the truth of his presentment of that sense; as in those humbler or plainer functions of literature also, truth—truth to bare fact, there—is the essence of such artistic
quality as they may have. Truth! there can be no merit, no craft at all,
without that. And further, all beauty is in the long run only *fineness* of
truth, or what we call expression, the finer accommodation of speech to that
vision within. (4)

—The transcript of his sense of fact rather than the fact, as being preferable, pleasanter, more beautiful to the writer himself. In literature, as in
every other product of human skill, in the moulding of a bell or a platter
for instance, wherever this sense asserts itself, wherever the producer so
modifies his work as, over and above its primary use or intention, to make
it pleasing (to himself, of course, in the first instance) there, "fine" as opposed to merely serviceable art, exists. Literary art, that is, like all art which
is in any way imitative or reproductive of fact—form, or colour, or incident—is the representation of such fact as connected with soul, of a specific
personality, in its preferences, its volition and power. (5)

Such is the matter of imaginative or artistic literature—this transcript,
not of mere fact, but of fact in its infinite variety, as modified by human
preference in all its infinitely varied forms. It will be good literary art not
because it is brilliant or sober, or rich, or impulsive, or severe, but just in
proportion as its representation of that sense, that soul-fact, is true, verse
being only one department of such literature, and imaginative prose, it may
be thought, being the special art of the modern world. That imaginative
prose should be the special and opportune art of the modern world results
from two important facts about the latter: first, the chaotic variety and

complexity of its interests, making the intellectual issue, the really master currents of the present time incalculable—a condition of mind little suscep- tible of the restraint proper to verse form, so that the most characteristic verse of the nineteenth century has been lawless verse; and secondly, an all-pervading naturalism, a curiosity about everything whatever as it really is, involving a certain humility of attitude, cognate to what must, after all, be the less ambitious form of literature. And prose thus asserting itself as the special and privileged artistic faculty of the present day, will be, how- ever critics may try to narrow its scope, as varied in its excellence as hu- manity itself reflecting on the facts of its latest experience—an instrument of many stops, meditative, observant, descriptive, eloquent, analytic, plain- tive, fervid. Its beauties will be not exclusively "pedestrian": it will exert, in due measure, all the varied charms of poetry, down to the rhythm which, as in Cicero, or Michelet, or Newman, at their best, gives its musical value to every syllable.[1]   (6)

The literary artist is of necessity a scholar, and in what he proposes to do will have in mind, first of all, the scholar and the scholarly conscience— the male conscience in this matter, as we must think it, under a system of education which still to so large an extent limits real scholarship to men. In his self-criticism, he supposes always that sort of reader who will go (full of eyes) warily, considerately, though without consideration for him, over the ground which the female conscience traverses so lightly, so amia- bly. For the material in which he works is no more a creation of his own than the sculptor's marble. Product of a myriad various minds and con- tending tongues, compact of obscure and minute association, a language has its own abundant and often recondite laws, in the habitual and sum- mary recognition of which scholarship consists. A writer, full of a matter he is before all things anxious to express, may think of those laws, the lim- itations of vocabulary, structure, and the like, as a restriction, but if a real artist will find in them an opportunity. His punctilious observance of the proprieties of his medium will diffuse through all he writes a general air of sensibility, of refined usage. *Exclusiones debitæ naturæ*—the exclusions, or rejections, which nature demands—we know how large a part these play, ac- cording to Bacon, in the science of nature. In a somewhat changed sense, we might say that the art of the scholar is summed up in the observance of those rejections demanded by the nature of his medium, the material he must use. Alive to the value of an atmosphere in which every term finds its utmost degree of expression, and with all the jealousy of a lover of

1 Mr. Saintsbury, in his *Specimens of English Prose, from Malory to Macaulay*, has succeeded in tracing, through successive English prose-writers, the tradition of that severer beauty in them, of which this admirable scholar of our literature is known to be a lover. *English Prose, from Mandeville to Thackeray*, more recently "chosen and edited" by a younger scholar, Mr. Arthur Galton, of New Col- lege, Oxford, a lover of our literature at once enthusiastic and discreet, aims at a more various illus- tration of the eloquent powers of English prose, and is a delightful companion. [Pater's note.]

words, he will resist a constant tendency on the part of the majority of those who use them to efface the distinctions of language, the facility of writers often reinforcing in this respect the work of the vulgar. He will feel the obligation not of the laws only, but of those affinities, avoidances, those mere preferences, of his language, which through the associations of literary history have become a part of its nature, prescribing the rejection of many a neology, many a license, many a gipsy phrase which might present itself as actually expressive. His appeal, again, is to the scholar, who has great experience in literature, and will show no favour to short-cuts, or hackneyed illustration, or an affectation of learning designed for the unlearned. Hence a contention, a sense of self-restraint and renunciation, having for the susceptible reader the effect of a challenge for minute consideration; the attention of the writer, in every minutest detail, being a pledge that it is worth the reader's while to be attentive too, that the writer is dealing scrupulously with his instrument, and therefore, indirectly, with the reader himself also, that he has the science of the instrument he plays on, perhaps, after all, with a freedom which in such case will be the freedom of a master. (7)

For meanwhile, braced only by those restraints, he is really vindicating his liberty in the making of a vocabulary, an entire system of composition, for himself, his own true manner; and when we speak of the manner of a true master we mean what is essential in his art. Pedantry being only the scholarship of *le cuistre*[2] (we have no English equivalent) he is no pedant, and does but show his intelligence of the rules of language in his freedoms with it, addition or expansion, which like the spontaneities of matter in a well-bred person will still further illustrate good taste.—The right vocabulary! Translators have not invariably seen how all-important that is in the work of translation, driving for the most part at idiom or construction; whereas, if the original be first-rate, one's first care should be with its elementary particles, Plato, for instance, being often reproducible by an exact following, with no variation in structure, of word after word, as the pencil follows a drawing under tracing-paper, so only each word or syllable be not of false colour, to change my illustration a little. (8)

Well! that is because any writer worth translating at all has winnowed and searched through his vocabulary, is conscious of the words he would select in systematic reading of a dictionary, and still more of the words he would reject were the dictionary other than Johnson's; and doing this with his peculiar sense of the world ever in view, in search of an instrument for the adequate expression of that, he begets a vocabulary faithful to the colouring of his own spirit, and in the strictest sense original. That living authority which language needs lies, in truth, in its scholars, who

---

2 A narrow-minded pedant.

recognising always that every language possesses a genius, a very fastidious genius, of its own, expand at once and purify its very elements, which must needs change along with the changing thoughts of living people. Ninety years ago, for instance, great mental force, certainly, was needed by Wordsworth, to break through the consecrated poetic associations of a century, and speak the language that was his, that was to become in a measure the language of the next generation. But he did it with the tact of a scholar also. English, for a quarter of a century past, has been assimilating the phraseology of pictorial art; for half a century, the phraseology of the great German metaphysical movement of eighty years ago; in part also the language of mystical theology: and none but pedants will regret a great consequent increase of its resources. For many years to come its enterprise may well lie in the naturalisation of the vocabulary of science, so only it be under the eye of a sensitive scholarship—in a liberal naturalisation of the ideas of science too, for after all the chief stimulus of good style is to possess a full, rich, complex matter to grapple with. The literary artist, therefore, will be well aware of physical science; science also attaining, in its turn, its true literary ideal. And then, as the scholar is nothing without the historic sense, he will be apt to restore not really obsolete or really worn-out words, but the finer edge of words still in use: *ascertain, communicate, discover*—words like these it has been part of our "business" to misuse. And still, as language was made for man, he will be no authority for correctness which, limiting freedom of utterance, were yet but accidents in their origin; as if one vowed not to say "*its*," which ought to have been in Shakespeare; "*his*" and "*hers*," for inanimate objects, being but a barbarous and really inexpressive survival. Yet we have known many things like this. Racy Saxon monosyllables, close to us as touch and sight, he will intermix readily with those long, savoursome, Latin words, rich in "second intention." In this late day certainly, no critical process can be conducted reasonably without eclecticism. Of such eclecticism we have a justifying example in one of the first poets of our time. How illustrative of monosyllabic effect, of sonorous Latin, of the phraseology of science, of metaphysic, of colloquialism even, are the writings of Tennyson; yet with what a fine, fastidious scholarship throughout!   (9)

A scholar writing for the scholarly, he will of course leave something to the willing intelligence of his reader. "To go preach to the first passer-by," says Montaigne, "to become tutor to the ignorance of the first I meet, is a thing I abhor"; a thing, in fact, naturally distressing to the scholar, who will therefore ever be shy of offering uncomplimentary assistance to the reader's wit. To really strenuous minds there is a pleasurable stimulus in the challenge for a continuous effort on their part, to be rewarded by securer and more intimate grasp of the author's sense. Self-restraint, a skilful economy of means, *ascêsis*, that too has a beauty of its own; and for the reader supposed there will be an æsthetic satisfaction in that frugal closeness of style which makes the most of a word, in the exaction from every sentence of a precise relief, in the just spacing out of word to thought, in the logically filled space connected always with the delightful sense of difficulty overcome. (10)

Different classes of persons, at different times, make, of course, very various demands upon literature. Still, scholars, I suppose, and not only scholars, but all disinterested lovers of books, will always look to it, as to all other fine art, for a refuge, a sort of cloistral refuge, from a certain vulgarity in the actual world. A perfect poem like *Lycidas*, a perfect fiction like *Esmond*, the perfect handling of a theory like Newman's *Idea of a University*, has for them something of the uses of a religious "retreat." Here, then, with a view to the central need of a select few, those "men of a finer thread" who have formed and maintain the literary ideal, everything, every component element, will have undergone exact trial, and, above all, there will be no uncharacteristic or tarnished or vulgar decoration, permissible ornament being for the most part structural, or necessary. As the painter in his picture, so the artist in his book, aims at the production by honourable artifice of a peculiar atmosphere. "The artist," says Schiller, "may be known rather by what he *omits*"; and in literature, too, the true artist may be best recognised by his tact of omission. For to the grave reader words too are grave; and the ornamental word, the figure, the accessory form or colour or reference, is rarely content to die to thought precisely at the right moment, but will inevitably linger awhile stirring a long "brain-wave" behind it of perhaps quite alien associations. (11)

Just there, it may be, is the detrimental tendency of the sort of scholarly attentiveness of mind I am recommending. But the true artist allows for it. He will remember that, as the very word ornament indicates what is in itself non-essential, so the "one beauty" of all literary style is of its very essence, and independent, in prose and verse alike, of all removable decoration; that it may exist in its fullest lustre, as in Flaubert's *Madame Bovary*, for instance, or in Stendhal's *Le Rouge et Le Noir*, in a composition utterly unadorned, with hardly a single suggestion of visibly beautiful things. Parallel, allusion, the allusive way generally, the flowers in the garden:— he knows the narcotic force of these upon the negligent intelligence to which any *diversion*, literally, is welcome, any vagrant intruder, because one can go wandering away with it from the immediate subject. Jealous, if he have a really quickening motive within, of all that does not hold directly to that, of the facile, the otiose, he will never depart from the strictly pedestrian process, unless he gains a ponderable something thereby. Even assured of its congruity, he will still question its serviceableness. Is it worth while, can we afford, to attend to just that, to just that figure or literary reference, just then?—Surplusage! he will dread that, as the runner on his muscles. For in truth all art does but consist in the removal of surplusage, from the last finish of the gem-engraver blowing away the last particle of invisible dust, back to the earliest divination of the finished work to be, lying somewhere, according to Michelangelo's fancy, in the rough-hewn block of stone. (12)

And what applies to figure or flower must be understood of all other accidental or removable ornaments of writing whatever; and not of specific ornament only, but of all that latent colour and imagery which language as such carries in it. A lover of words for their own sake, to whom nothing about them is unimportant, a minute and constant observer of their physiognomy, he will be on the alert not only for obviously mixed metaphors of course, but for the metaphor that is mixed in all our speech, though a rapid use may involve no cognition of it. Currently recognising the incident, the colour, the physical elements of particles in words like *absorb, consider, extract*, to take the first that occur, he will avail himself of them, as further adding to the resources of expression. The elementary particles of language will be realised as colour and light and shade through his scholarly living in the full sense of them. Still opposing the constant degradation of language by those who use it carelessly, he will not treat coloured glass as if it were clear; and while half the world is using figure unconsciously, will be fully aware not only of all that latent figurative texture in speech, but of the vague, lazy, half-formed personification—a rhetoric, depressing, and worse than nothing, because it has no really rhetorical motive—which plays so large a part there, and, as in the case of more ostentatious ornament, scrupulously exact of it, from syllable to syllable, its precise value.   (13)

So far I have been speaking of certain conditions of the literary art arising out of the medium or material in or upon which it works, the essential qualities of language and its aptitudes for contingent ornamentation, matters which define scholarship as science and good taste respectively. They are both subservient to a more intimate quality of good style: more intimate, as coming nearer to the artist himself. The otiose, the facile, surplusage: why are these abhorrent to the true literary artist, except because in literary as in all other art, structure is all-important, felt, or painfully missed, everywhere?—that architectural conception of work, which foresees the end in the beginning and never loses sight of it, and in every part is conscious of all the rest, till the last sentence does but, with undiminished vigour, unfold and justify the first—a condition of literary art, which, in contradistinction to another quality of the artist himself, to be spoken of later, I shall call the necessity of *mind* in style.   (14)

An acute philosophical writer, the late Dean Mansel[3] (a writer whose works illustrate the literary beauty there may be in closeness, and with ob-

---

3 Henry L. Mansel (1820–1871), Dean of St. Paul's and author of *Prolegomena Logica*.

vious repression or economy of a fine rhetorical gift) wrote a book, of fascinating precision in a very obscure subject, to show that all the technical laws of logic are but means of securing, in each and all of its apprehensions, the unity, the strict identity with itself, of the apprehending mind. All the laws of good writing aim at a similar unity or identity of the mind in all the processes by which the word is associated to its import. The term is right, and has its essential beauty, when it becomes, in a manner, what it signifies, as with the names of simple sensations. To give the phrase, the sentence, the structural member, the entire composition, song, or essay, a similar unity with its subject and with itself:—style is in the right way when it tends towards that. All depends upon the original unity, the vital wholeness and identity, of the initiatory apprehension or view. So much is true of all art, which therefore requires always its logic, its comprehensive reason—insight, foresight, retrospect, in simultaneous action—true, most of all, of the literary art, as being of all the arts most closely cognate to the abstract intelligence. Such logical coherency may be evidenced not merely in the lines of composition as a whole, but in the choice of a single word, while it by no means interferes with, but may even prescribe, much variety, in the building of the sentence for instance, or in the manner, argumentative, descriptive, discursive, of this or that part or member of the entire design. The blithe, crisp sentence, decisive as a child's expression of its needs, may alternate with the long-contending, victoriously intricate sentence; the sentence, born with the integrity of a single word, relieving the sort of sentence in which, if you look closely, you can see much contrivance, much adjustment, to bring a highly qualified matter into compass at one view. For the literary architecture, if it is to be rich and expressive, involves not only foresight of the end in the beginning, but also development or growth of design, in the process of execution, with many irregularities, surprises, and afterthoughts; the contingent as well as the necessary being subsumed under the unity of the whole. As truly, to the lack of such architectural design, of a single, almost visual, image, vigorously informing an entire, perhaps very intricate, composition, which shall be austere, ornate, argumentative, fanciful, yet true from first to last to that vision within, may be attributed those weaknesses of conscious or unconscious repetition of word, phrase, motive, or member of the whole matter, indicating, as Flaubert was aware, an original structure in thought not organically complete. With such foresight, the actual conclusion will most often get itself written out of hand, before, in the more obvious sense, the work is finished. With some strong and leading sense of the world, the tight hold of which secures true *composition* and not mere loose accretion, the literary artist, I suppose, goes on considerately, setting joint to joint, sustained by yet restraining the productive ardour, retracing the negligences of his first sketch, repeating his steps only that he may give the reader a sense of secure and restful progress, readjusting mere assonances even, that they may soothe the reader, or at least not interrupt him on his way; and then, somewhat before the end comes, is burdened, inspired, with his conclusion, and betimes delivered of it, leaving off, not in weariness and because he finds *himself* at an end, but in all the freshness of volition. His work now structurally complete, with all the accumulating effect of secondary shades of meaning, he finishes the whole up to the just proportion of that ante-penultimate conclusion, and all becomes expressive. The house he has built is rather a body he has informed. And so it happens, to its greater credit, that the better interest even of a narrative to be recounted, a story to be told, will often be in its second reading. And though there are instances of great writers who have been no artists, an unconscious tact sometimes directing work in which we may detect, very pleasurably, many of the effects of conscious art, yet one of the greatest pleasures of really good prose literature is in the critical tracing out of that conscious artistic structure, and the pervading sense of it as we read. Yet of poetic literature too; for, in truth, the kind of constructive intelligence here supposed is one of the forms of the imagination.   (15)

   That is the special function of mind, in style. Mind and soul:—hard to ascertain philosophically, the distinction is real enough practically, for they often interfere, are sometimes in conflict, with each other. Blake, in the last century, is an instance of preponderating soul, embarrassed, at a loss, in an era of preponderating mind. As a quality of style, at all events, soul is a fact, in certain writers—the way they have of absorbing language, of attracting it into the peculiar spirit they are of, with a subtlety which makes the actual result seem like some inexplicable inspiration. By mind, the literary artist reaches us, through static and objective indications of design in his work, legible to all. By soul, he reaches us, somewhat capriciously perhaps, one and not another, through vagrant sympathy and a kind of immediate contact. Mind we cannot choose but approve where we recognise it; soul may repel us, not because we misunderstand it. The way in which theological interests sometimes avail themselves of language is perhaps the best illustration of the force I mean to indicate generally in literature, by the word *soul*. Ardent religious persuasion may exist, may make its way, without finding any equivalent heat in language: or, again, it may enkindle words to various degrees, and when it really takes hold of them doubles its force. Religious history presents many remarkable instances in which, through no mere phrase-worship, an unconscious literary tact has, for the sensitive, laid open a privileged pathway from one to another. "The altar-fire," people say, "has touched those lips!" The Vulgate, the English Bible, the English Prayer-Book, the writings of Swedenborg, the Tracts for the Times:—there, we have instances of widely different and largely diffused phrases of religious feeling in operation as soul in style. But something of the same kind acts with similar power in certain writers of quite other than theological literature, on behalf of some wholly personal and peculiar sense of theirs. Most easily illustrated by theological literature, this quality lends to profane writers a kind of religious influence. At their best, these writers became, as we say sometimes, "prophets"; such character depending on the effect not merely of their matter, but of their matter as allied to, in "electric affinity" with, peculiar form, and working in all cases by an immediate sympathetic contact, on which account it is that it may be called soul, as opposed to mind, in style. And this too is a faculty of choosing and rejecting what is congruous or otherwise, with a drift towards unity—unity of atmosphere here, as there of design—soul securing colour (or perfume, might we say?) as mind secures form, the latter being essentially finite, the former vague or infinite, as the influence of a living person is practically infinite. There are some to whom nothing has any real interest, or real meaning, except as operative in a given person; and it is they who best appreciate the quality of soul in literary art. They seem to know a *person*, in a book, and make way by intuition: yet, although they thus enjoy the completeness of a personal information, it is still a characteristic of soul in this sense of the word, that it does but suggest what can never be uttered, not as being different from, or more obscure than, what actually gets said, but as containing that plenary substance of which there is only one phase or facet in what is there expressed.   (16)

If all high things have their martyrs, Gustave Flaubert might perhaps rank as the martyr of literary style. In his printed correspondence, a curious series of letters, written in his twenty-fifth year, records what seems to have been his one other passion—a series of letters which, with its fine casuistries, its firmly repressed anguish, its tone of harmonious grey, and the sense of disillusion in which the whole matter ends, might have been, a few slight changes supposed, one of his own fictions. Writing to Madame X. certainly he does display, by "taking thought" mainly, by constant and delicate pondering, as in his love for literature, a heart really moved, but still more, and as the pledge of that emotion, a loyalty to his work. Madame X., too, is a literary artist, and the best gifts he can send her are precepts of perfection in art, counsels for the effectual pursuit of that better love. In his love-letters it is the pains and pleasures of art he insists on, its solaces: he communicates secrets, reproves, encourages, with a view to that. Whether the lady was dissatisfied with such divided or indirect service, the reader is not enabled to see; but sees that, on Flaubert's part at least, a living person could be no rival of what was, from first to last, his leading passion, a somewhat solitary and exclusive one.

> "I must scold you," he writes, "for one thing, which shocks, scandalises me, the small concern, namely, you show for art just now. As regards glory be it so: there, I approve. But for art!—

the one thing in life that is good and real—can you compare with
it an earthly love?—prefer the adoration of a relative beauty to
the *cultus* of the true beauty? Well! I tell you the truth. That is
the one thing good in me: the one thing I have, to me estimable.
For yourself, you blend with the beautiful a heap of alien things,
the useful, the agreeable, what not?—

"The only way not to be unhappy is to shut yourself up in art,
and count everything else as nothing. Pride takes the place of all
beside when it is established on a large basis. Work! God wills it.
That, it seems to me, is clear.—

"I am reading over again the *Æneid*, certain verses of which
I repeat to myself to satiety. There are phrases there which stay
in one's head, by which I find myself beset, as with those musical
airs which are for ever returning, and cause you pain, you love
them so much. I observe that I no longer laugh much, and am no
longer depressed. I am ripe. You talk of my serenity, and envy
me. It may well surprise you. Sick, irritated, the prey a thousand
times a day of cruel pain, I continue my labour like a true work-
ing-man, who, with sleeves turned up, in the sweat of his brow,
beats away at his anvil, never troubling himself whether it rains
or blows, for hail or thunder. I was not like that formerly. The
change has taken place naturally, though my will has counted for
something in the matter.—

"Those who write in good style are sometimes accused of a
neglect of ideas, and of the moral end, as if the end of the physician were something else than healing, of the painter than painting—as if the end of art were not, before all else, the beautiful."   (17)

What, then, did Flaubert understand by beauty, in the art he pursued
with so much fervour, with so much self-command? Let us hear a sympathetic commentator:—[4]

> "Possessed of an absolute belief that there exists but one way
> of expressing one thing, one word to call it by, one adjective to
> qualify, one verb to animate it, he gave himself to superhuman
> labour for the discovery, in every phrase, of that word, that verb,
> that epithet. In this way, he believed in some mysterious har-
> mony of expression, and when a true word seemed to him to
> lack euphony still went on seeking another, with invincible pa-
> tience, certain that he had not yet got hold of the *unique* word.
> . . . A thousand preoccupations would beset him at the same mo-
> ment, always with this desperate certitude fixed in his spirit:
> Among all the expressions in the world, all forms and turns of
> expression, there is but *one*—one form, one mode—to express
> what I want to say."   (18)

4 Guy de Maupassant.

The one word for the one thing, the one thought, amid the multitude of words, terms, that might just do: the problem of style was there!—the unique word, phrase, sentence, paragraph, essay, or song, absolutely proper to the single mental presentation or vision within. In that perfect justice, over and above the many contigent and removable beauties with which beautiful style may charm us, but which it can exist without, independent of them yet dexterously availing itself of them, omnipresent in good work, in function at every point, from single epithets to the rhythm of a whole book, lay the specific, indispensable, very intellectual, beauty of literature, the possibility of which constitutes it a fine art.   (19)

One seems to detect the influence of a philosophic idea there, the idea of a natural economy, of some pre-existent adaptation, between a relative, somewhere in the world of thought, and its correlative, somewhere in the world of language—both alike, rather, somewhere in the mind of the artist, desiderative, expectant, inventive—meeting each other with the readiness of "soul and body reunited," in Blake's rapturous design; and, in fact, Flaubert was fond of giving his theory philosophical expression.—

> "There are no beautiful thoughts," he would say, "without beautiful forms, and conversely. As it is impossible to extract from a physical body the qualities which really constitute it— colour, extension, and the like—without reducing it to a hollow abstraction, in a word, without destroying it; just so it is impossible to detach the form from the idea, for the idea only exists by virtue of the form."   (20)

All the recognised flowers, the removable ornaments of literature (including harmony and ease in reading aloud, very carefully considered by him) counted certainly; for these too are part of the actual value of what one says. But still, after all, with Flaubert, the search, the unwearied research, was not for the smooth, or winsome, or forcible word, as such, as with false Ciceronians, but quite simply and honestly, for the word's adjustment to its meaning. The first condition of this must be, of course, to know yourself, to have ascertained your own sense exactly. Then, if we suppose an artist, he says to the reader,—I want you to see precisely what I see. Into the mind sensitive to "form," a flood of random sounds, colours, incidents, is ever penetrating from the world without, to become, by sympathetic selection, a part of its very structure, and, in turn, the visible vesture and expression of that other world it sees so steadily within, nay, already with a partial conformity thereto, to be refined, enlarged, corrected, at a hundred points; and it is just there, just at those doubtful points that the function of style, as tact or taste, intervenes. The unique term will come more quickly to one than another, at one time than another, according also to the kind of matter in question. Quickness and slowness, ease and closeness alike, have nothing to do with the artistic character of the true word found at last. As there is a charm of ease, so there is also a special charm in the signs of discovery, of effort and contention towards a due end, as so often with Flaubert himself—in the style which has been pliant, as only obstinate, durable metal can be, to the inherent perplexities and recusancy of a certain difficult thought.   (21)

If Flaubert had not told us, perhaps we should never have guessed how tardy and painful his own procedure really was, and after reading his confession may think that this almost endless hesitation had much to do with diseased nerves. Often, perhaps, the felicity supposed will be the product of a happier, a more exuberant nature than Flaubert's. Aggravated, certainly, by a morbid physical condition, that anxiety in "seeking the phrase," which gathered all the other small *ennuis* of a really quiet existence into a kind of battle, was connected with his lifelong contention against facile poetry, facile art—art, facile and flimsy; and what constitutes the true artist is not the slowness or quickness of the process, but the absolute success of the result. As with those labourers in the parable, the prize is independent of the mere length of the actual day's work. "You talk," he writes, odd, trying lover, to Madame X.—

> "You talk of the exclusiveness of my literary tastes. That might have enabled you to divine what kind of a person I am in the matter of love. I grow so hard to please as a literary artist, that I am driven to despair. I shall end by not writing another line."   (22)

"Happy," he cries, in a moment of discouragement at that patient labour, which for him, certainly, was the condition of a great success—

> "Happy those who have no doubts of themselves! who lengthen out, as the pen runs on, all that flows forth from their brains. As for me, I hesitate, I disappoint myself, turn round upon myself in despite: my taste is augmented in proportion as my natural vigour decreases, and I afflict my soul over some dubious word out of all proportion to the pleasure I get from a whole page of good writing. One would have to live two centuries to attain a true idea of any matter whatever. What Buffon said is a big blasphemy: genius is not long-continued patience. Still, there is some truth in the statement, and more than people think, especially as regards our own day. Art! art! art! bitter deception! phantom that glows with light, only to lead one to destruction."   (23)

Again—

> "I am growing so peevish about my writing. I am like a man
> whose ear is true but who plays falsely on the violin: his fingers
> refuse to reproduce precisely those sounds of which he has the
> inward sense. Then the tears come rolling down from the poor
> scraper's eyes and the bow falls from his hand." (24)

Coming slowly or quickly, when it comes, as it came with so much labour
of mind, but also with so much lustre, to Gustave Flaubert, this discovery of
the word will be, like all artistic success and felicity, incapable of strict
analysis: effect of an intuitive condition of mind, it must be recognised by
like intuition on the part of the reader, and a sort of immediate sense. In
every one of those masterly sentences of Flaubert there was, below all mere
contrivance, shaping and afterthought, by some happy instantaneous con-
course of the various faculties of the mind with each other, the exact apprehension of what was *needed* to carry the meaning. And that it fits with
absolute justice will be a judgment of immediate sense in the appreciative
reader. We all feel this in what may be called inspired translation. Well! all
language involves translation from inward to outward. In literature, as in
all forms of art, there are the absolute and the merely relative or accessory beauties; and precisely in that exact proportion of the term to its
purpose is the absolute beauty of style, prose or verse. All the good qualities, the beauties, of verse also, are such, only as precise expression. (25)
In the highest as in the lowliest literature, then, the one indispensable
beauty is, after all, truth:—truth to bare fact in the latter, as to some personal sense of fact, diverted somewhat from men's ordinary sense of it, in the
former; truth there as accuracy, truth here as expression, that finest and
most intimate form of truth, the *vraie vérité*. And what an eclectic principle
this really is! employing for its one sole purpose—that absolute accordance
of expression to idea—all other literary beauties and excellences whatever:
how many kinds of style it covers, explains, justifies, and at the same time
safeguards! Scott's facility, Flaubert's deeply pondered evocation of "the
phrase," are equally good art. Say what you have to say, what you have a
will to say, in the simplest, the most direct and exact manner possible,
with no surplusage:—there, is the justification of the sentence so fortunately
born, "entire, smooth, and round," that it needs no punctuation, and
also (that is the point!) of the most elaborate period, if it be right in its
elaboration. Here is the office of ornament: here also the purpose of restraint in ornament. As the exponent of truth, that austerity (the beauty, the
function, of which in literature Flaubert understood so well) becomes not
the correctness or purism of the mere scholar, but a security against the

otiose, a jealous exclusion of what does not really tell towards the pursuit of relief of life and vigour in the portraiture of one's sense. License again, the making free with rule, if it be indeed, as people fancy, a habit of genius, flinging aside or transforming all that opposes the liberty of beautiful production, will be but faith to one's own meaning. The seeming baldness of *Le Rouge et Le Noir* is nothing in itself; the wild ornament of *Les Misérables* is nothing in itself; and the restraint of Flaubert, amid a real natural opulence, only redoubled beauty—the phrase so large and so precise at the same time, hard as bronze, in service to the more perfect adaptation of words to their matter. Afterthoughts, retouchings, finish, will be of profit only so far as they too really serve to bring out the original, initiative, generative, sense in them.   (26)

In this way, according to the well-known saying, "The style is the man," complex or simple, in his individuality, his plenary sense of what he really has to say, his sense of the world; all cautions regarding style arising out of so many natural scruples as to the medium through which alone he can expose that inward sense of things, the purity of this medium, its laws or tricks of refraction: nothing is to be left there which might give conveyance to any matter save that. Style in all its varieties, reserved or opulent, terse, abundant, musical, stimulant, academic, so long as each is really characteristic or expressive, finds thus its justification, the sumptuous good taste of Cicero being as truly the man himself, and not another, justified, yet insured inalienably to him, thereby, as would have been his portrait by Raffaelle, in full consular splendour, on his ivory chair.   (27)

A relegation, you may say perhaps—a relegation of style to the subjectivity, the mere caprice, of the individual, which must soon transform it into mannerism. Not so! since there is, under the conditions supposed, for those elements of the man, for every lineament of the vision within the one word, the one acceptable word, recognisable by the sensitive, by others "who have intelligence" in the matter, as absolutely as ever anything can be in the evanescent and delicate region of human language. The style, the manner, would be the man, not in his unreasoned and really uncharacteristic caprices, involuntary or affected, but in absolutely sincere apprehension of what is most real to him. But let us hear our French guide again.—

> "Styles," says Flaubert's commentator, "*Styles,* as so many peculiar moulds, each of which bears the mark of a particular writer, who is to pour into it the whole content of his ideas, were no part of his theory. What he believed in was *Style:* that is to say, a certain absolute and unique manner of expressing a thing, in all its intensity and colour. For him the *form* was the work itself. As in living creatures, the blood, nourishing the body, determines its very contour and external aspect, just so, to his mind,

the *matter,* the basis, in a work of art, imposed, necessarily, the unique, the just expression, the measure, the rhythm—the *form* in all its characteristics." (28)

If the style be the man, in all the colour and intensity of a veritable apprehension, it will be in a real sense "impersonal." (29)

I said, thinking of books like Victor Hugo's *Les Misérables,* that prose literature was the characteristic art of the nineteenth century, as others, thinking of its triumphs since the youth of Bach, have assigned that place to music. Music and prose literature are, in one sense, the opposite terms of art; the art of literature presenting to the imagination, through the intelligence, a range of interests, as free and various as those which music presents to it through sense. And certainly the tendency of what has been here said is to bring literature too under those conditions, by conformity to which music takes rank as the typically perfect art. If music be the ideal of all art whatever, precisely because in music it is impossible to distinguish the form from the substance or matter, the subject from the expression, then, literature, by finding its specific excellence in the absolute correspondence of the term to its import, will be but fulfilling the condition of all artistic quality in things everywhere, of all good art. (30)

Good art, but not necessarily great art; the distinction between great art and good art depending immediately, as regards literature at all events, not on its form, but on the matter. Thackeray's *Esmond,* surely, is greater art than *Vanity Fair,* by the greater dignity of its interests. It is on the quality of the matter it informs or controls, its compass, its variety, its alliance to great ends, or the depth of the note of revolt, or the largeness of hope in it, that the greatness of literary art depends, as *The Divine Comedy, Paradise Lost, Les Misérables, The English Bible,* are great art. Given the conditions I have tried to explain as constituting good art;— then, if it be devoted further to the increase of men's happiness, to the redemption of the oppressed, or the enlargement of our sympathies with each other, or to such presentment of new or old truth about ourselves and our relation to the world as may ennoble and fortify us in our sojourn here, or immediately, as with Dante, to the glory of God, it will be also great art; if, over and above those qualities I summed up as mind and soul—that colour and mystic perfume, and that reasonable structure, it has something of the soul of humanity in it, and finds its logical, architectural place, in the great structure of human life. (31)

Thomas Stearns Eliot

(1888–1965)

T. S. ELIOT was one of the leading poets and critics of his generation, winning the Nobel Prize for Literature in 1948. While still at Harvard (A.B., 1910; M.A., 1911; advanced study, 1911–1914) he became disaffected with the prevailing mode of literary criticism, known as neo-humanism, and laid the principal critical foundations for the first half of the twentieth century, the so-called "new criticism." Deeply impressed with the spiritual desiccation of modern life, he established a new idiom in modern poetry and sought for poetry a new spiritual function. He was honored with degrees by many of the major universities of the West (Edinburgh, Cambridge, Oxford, London, Rome, Munich, Harvard, Yale, Princeton, Columbia, and others); and his books—poems, plays, essays—were avidly read by students of literature and culture: Collected Poems *(1936),* Collected Essays *(1932),* The Use of Poetry *(1933),* After Strange Gods *(1933),* Murder in the Cathedral *(1945),* The Family Reunion *(1939),* Four Quartets *(1943),* The Cocktail Party *(1950),* The Confidential Clerk *(1954),* On Poetry and Poets *(1957). It is a curious coincidence that Eliot was born in the year of Matthew Arnold's death (1888).*

■ *The Perfect Critic*

I

> "Eriger en lois ses impressions personnelles, c'est le grand effort d'un homme s'il est sincère."—*Lettres à 'Amazone.*

COLERIDGE was perhaps the greatest of English critics, and in a sense the last. After Coleridge we have Matthew Arnold; but Arnold—I think it will be conceded—was rather a propagandist for criticism than a critic, a popularizer rather than a creator of ideas. So long as this island remains an island (and we are no nearer the Continent than were Arnold's contemporaries) the work of Arnold will be important; it is still a bridge across the Channel, and it will always have been good sense. Since Arnold's attempt to correct his countrymen, English criticism has followed two directions. When a distinguished critic observed recently, in a newspaper article, that "poetry is the most highly organized form of intellectual activity," we were conscious that we were reading neither Coleridge nor Arnold. Not only have the words "organized" and "activity," occurring together in this phrase, that familiar vague suggestion of the scientific vocabulary which is characteristic of modern writing, but one asked questions which Coleridge and Arnold would not have permitted one to ask. How is it, for instance, that poetry is more highly organized" than astronomy, physics, or pure mathematics, which we imagine to be, in relation to the scientist who practises them, "intellectual activity" of a pretty highly organized type? "Mere strings of words," our critic continues with felicity and truth, "flung like dabs of paint across a blank canvas, may awaken surprise . . . but have no significance whatever in the history of literature." The phrases by which Arnold is best known may be inadequate, they may assemble more doubts than they dispel, but they usually have some meaning. And if a phrase like "the most highly organized form of intellectual activity" is the highest organization of thought of which contemporary criticism, in a distinguished representative, is capable, then, we conclude, modern criticism is degenerate.   (1)

The verbal disease above noticed may be reserved for diagnosis by and by. It is not a disease from which Mr. Arthur Symons (for the quotation was, of course, not from Mr. Symons) notably suffers. Mr. Symons represents the other tendency; he is a representative of what is always called "æsthetic criticism" or "impressionistic criticism." And it is this form of criticism which I propose to examine at once. Mr. Symons, the critical successor of Pater, and partly of Swinburne (I fancy that the phrase "sick or sorry" is the common property of all three), is the "impressionistic critic." He, if anyone, would be said to expose a sensitive and cultivated mind—cultivated, that is, by the accumulation of a considerable variety of impressions from all the arts and several languages—before an "object"; and his criticism, if anyone's, would be said to exhibit to us, like the plate, the faithful record of the impressions, more numerous or more refined than our own, upon a mind more sensitive than our own. A record, we observe, which is also an interpretation, a translation; for it must itself impose impressions upon us, and these impressions are as much created as transmitted by the criticism. I do not say at once that this is Mr. Symons; but it is the "impressionistic" critic, and the impressionistic critic is supposed to be Mr. Symons.   (2)

At hand is a volume which we may test.[1] Ten of these thirteen essays deal with single plays of Shakespeare, and it is therefore fair to take one of these ten as a specimen of the book:

> *Antony and Cleopatra* is the most wonderful, I think, of all Shakespeare's plays . . .

and Mr. Symons reflects that Cleopatra is the most wonderful of all women:

> The queen who ends the dynasty of the Ptolemies has been the star of poets, a malign star shedding baleful light, from Horace and Propertius down to Victor Hugo; and it is not to poets only . . .

What, we ask, is this for? as a page on Cleopatra, and on her possible origin in the dark lady of the Sonnets, unfolds itself. And we find, gradually, that this is not an essay on a work of art or a work of intellect; but that Mr. Symons is living through the play as one might live it through in the theatre; recounting, commenting:

> In her last days Cleopatra touches a certain elevation . . . she would die a thousand times, rather than live to be a mockery and a scorn in men's mouths . . . she is a woman to the last . . . so she dies . . . the play ends with a touch of grave pity . . .   (3)

Presented in this rather unfair way, torn apart like the leaves of an artichoke, the impressions of Mr. Symons come to resemble a common type of popular literary lecture, in which the stories of plays or novels are retold, the motives of the characters set forth, and the work of art therefore made easier for the beginner. But this is not Mr. Symons' reason for writing. The reason why we find a similarity between his essay and this form of education is that *Antony and Cleopatra* is a play with which we are pretty well acquainted, and of which we have, therefore, our own impressions. We can please ourselves with our own impressions of the characters and their emotions; and we do not find the impressions of another person, however sensitive, very significant. But if we can recall the time when we were ignorant of the French symbolists, and met with *The Symbolist Movement in Literature*, we remember that book as an introduction to wholly new feelings, as a revelation. After we have read Verlaine and Laforgue and Rimbaud and return to Mr. Symons' book, we may find that our own impressions dissent from his. The book has not, perhaps, a permanent value for the one reader, but it has led to results of permanent importance for him.   (4)

The question is not whether Mr. Symons' impressions are "true" or "false." So far as you can isolate the "impression," the pure feeling, it is,

---

1 *Studies in Elizabethan Drama.* By Arthur Symons.

of course, neither true nor false. The point is that you never rest at the pure feeling; you react in one of two ways, or, as I believe Mr. Symons does, in a mixture of the two ways. The moment you try to put the impressions into words, you either begin to analyse and construct, to "ériger en lois," or you begin to create something else. It is significant that Swinburne, by whose poetry Mr. Symons may at one time have been influenced, is one man in his poetry and a different man in his criticism; to this extent and in this respect only, that he is satisfying a different impulse; he is criticizing, expounding, arranging. You may say this is not the criticism of a critic, that it is emotional, not intellectual—though of this there are two opinions, but it is in the direction of analysis and construction, a beginning to "ériger en lois," and not in the direction of creation. So I infer that Swinburne found an adequate outlet for the creative impulse in his poetry; and none of it was forced back and out through his critical prose. The style of the latter is essentially a prose style; and Mr. Symons' prose is much more like Swinburne's poetry than it is like his prose. I imagine—though here one's thought is moving in almost complete darkness—that Mr. Symons is far more disturbed, far more profoundly affected, by his reading than was Swinburne, who responded rather by a violent and immediate and comprehensive burst of admiration which may have left him internally unchanged. The disturbance in Mr. Symons is almost, but not quite, to the point of creating; the reading sometimes fecundates his emotions to produce something new which is not criticism, but is not the expulsion, the ejection, the birth of creativeness. (5)

The type is not uncommon, although Mr. Symons is far superior to most of the type. Some writers are essentially of the type that reacts in excess of the stimulus, making something new out of the impressions, but suffer from a defect of vitality or an obscure obstruction which prevents nature from taking its course. Their sensibility alters the object, but never transforms it. Their reaction is that of the ordinary emotional person developed to an exceptional degree. For this ordinary emotional person, experiencing a work of art, has a mixed critical and creative reaction. It is made up of comment and opinion, and also new emotions which are vaguely applied to his own life. The sentimental person, in whom a work of art arouses all sorts of emotions which have nothing to do with that work of art whatever, but are accidents of personal association, is an incomplete artist. For in an artist these suggestions made by a work of art, which are purely personal, become fused with a multitude of other suggestions from multitudinous experience, and result in the production of a new object which is no longer purely personal, because it is a work of art itself. (6)

It would be rash to speculate, and is perhaps impossible to determine, what is unfulfilled in Mr. Symons' charming verse that overflows into his critical prose. Certainly we may say that in Swinburne's verse the circuit

of impression and expression is complete; and Swinburne was therefore
able, in his criticism, to be more a critic than Mr. Symons. This gives us an
intimation why the artist is—each within his own limitations—oftenest to be
depended upon as a critic; his criticism will be criticism, and not the satisfaction of a suppressed creative wish—which, in most other persons, is apt
to interfere fatally.   (7)

Before considering what the proper critical reaction of artistic sensibility
is, how far criticism is "feeling" and how far "thought," and what sort of
"thought" is permitted, it may be instructive to prod a little into that other
temperament, so different from Mr. Symons', which issues in generalities
such as that quoted near the beginning of this article.

II

> "L'écrivain de style abstrait est presque toujours un sentimen-
> tal, du moins un sensitif. L'écrivain artiste n'est presque jamais
> un sentimental, et très rarement un sensitif."—Le Problème du
> Style.   (8)

The statement already quoted, that "poetry is the most highly organized
form of intellectual activity," may be taken as a specimen of the abstract
style in criticism. The confused distinction which exists in most heads between "abstract" and "concrete" is due not so much to a manifest fact
of the existence of two types of mind, an abstract and a concrete, as to the
existence of another type of mind, the verbal, or philosophic. I, of course,
do not imply any general condemnation of philosophy; I am, for the moment, using the word "philosophic" to cover the unscientific ingredients of
philosophy; to cover, in fact, the greater part of the philosophic output of
the last hundred years. There are two ways in which a word may be "abstract." It may have (the word "activity," for example) a meaning which
cannot be grasped by appeal to any of the senses; its apprehension may
require a deliberate suppression of analogies of visual or muscular experience, which is none the less an effort of imagination. "Activity" will mean
for the trained scientist, if he employ the term, either nothing at all or
something still more exact than anything it suggests to us. If we are allowed
to accept certain remarks of Pascal and Mr. Bertrand Russell about mathematics, we believe that the mathematician deals with objects—which directly affect his sensibility. And during a good part of history the philosopher endeavoured to deal with objects which he believed to be of the same
exactness as the mathematician's. Finally Hegel arrived, and if not perhaps
the first, he was certainly the most prodigious exponent of emotional systematization, dealing with his emotions as if they were definite objects
which had aroused those emotions. His followers have as a rule taken for
granted that words have definite meanings, overlooking the tendency of
words to become indefinite emotions. (No one who had not witnessed the

event could imagine the conviction in the tone of Professor Eucken as he pounded the table and exclaimed *Was ist Geist? Geist ist . . .*) If verbalism were confined to professional philosophers, no harm would be done. But their corruption has extended very far. Compare a mediæval theologian or mystic, compare a seventeenth-century preacher, with any "liberal" sermon since Schleiermacher, and you will observe that words have changed their meanings. What they have lost is definite, and what they have gained is indefinite. (9)

The vast accumulations of knowledge—or at least of information—deposited by the nineteenth century have been responsible for an equally vast ignorance. When there is so much to be known, when there are so many fields of knowledge in which the same words are used with different meanings, when everyone knows a little about a great many things, it becomes increasingly difficult for anyone to know whether he knows what he is talking about or not. And when we do not know, or when we do not know enough, we tend always to substitute emotions for thoughts. The sentence so frequently quoted in this essay will serve for an example of this process as well as any, and may be profitably contrasted with the opening phrases of the *Posterior Analytics*. Not only all knowledge, but all feeling, is in perception. The inventor of poetry as the most highly organized form of intellectual activity was not engaged in perceiving when he composed this definition; he had nothing to be aware of except his own emotion about "poetry." He was, in fact, absorbed in a very different "activity" not only from that of Mr. Symons, but from that of Aristotle. (10)

Aristotle is a person who has suffered from the adherence of persons who must be regarded less as his disciples than as his sectaries. One must be firmly distrustful of accepting Aristotle in a canonical spirit; this is to lose the whole living force of him. He was primarily a man of not only remarkable but universal intelligence; and universal intelligence means that he could apply his intelligence to anything. The ordinary intelligence is good only for certain classes of objects; a brilliant man of science, if he is interested in poetry at all, may conceive grotesque judgments: like one poet because he reminds him of himself, or another because he expresses emotions which he admires; he may use art, in fact, as the outlet for the egotism which is suppressed in his own speciality. But Aristotle had none of these impure desires to satisfy; in whatever sphere of interest, he looked solely and steadfastly at the object; in his short and broken treatise he provides an eternal example—not of laws, or even of method, for there is no method except to be very intelligent, but of intelligence itself swiftly operating the analysis of sensation to the point of principle and definition. (11)

It is far less Aristotle than Horace who has been the model for criticism up to the nineteenth century. A precept, such as Horace, or Boileau gives us, is merely an unfinished analysis. It appears as a law, a rule, because it does not appear in its most general form; it is empirical. When we understand necessity, as Spinoza knew, we are free because we assent. The dogmatic critic, who lays down a rule, who affirms a value, has left his labour incomplete. Such statements may often be justifiable as a saving of time; but in matters of great importance the critic must not coerce, and he must not make judgments of worse and better. He must simply elucidate: the reader will form the correct judgment for himself.   (12)

And again, the purely "technical" critic—the critic, that is, who writes to expound some novelty or impart some lesson to practitioners of an art—can be called a critic only in a narrow sense. He may be analysing perceptions and the means for arousing perceptions, but his aim is limited and is not the disinterested exercise of intelligence. The narrowness of the aim makes easier the detection of the merit or feebleness of the work; even of these writers there are very few—so that their "criticism" is of great importance within its limits. So much suffices for Campion. Dryden is far more disinterested; he displays much free intelligence; and yet even Dryden—or any *literary* critic of the seventeenth century—is not quite a free mind, compared, for instance, with such a mind as Rochefoucauld's. There is always a tendency to legislate rather than to inquire, to revise accepted laws, even to overturn, but to reconstruct out of the same material. And the free intelligence is that which is wholly devoted to inquiry.   (13)

Coleridge, again, whose natural abilities, and some of whose performances, are probably more remarkable than those of any other modern critic, cannot be estimated as an intelligence completely free. The nature of the restraint in his case is quite different from that which limited the seventeenth-century critics, and is much more personal. Coleridge's metaphysical interest was quite genuine, and was, like most metaphysical interest, an affair of his emotions. But a literary critic should have no emotions except those immediately provoked by a work of art—and these (as I have already hinted) are, when valid, perhaps not to be called emotions at all. Coleridge is apt to take leave of the data of criticism, and arouse the suspicion that he has been diverted into a metaphysical hare-and-hounds. His end does not always appear to be the return to the work of art with improved perception and intensified, because more conscious, enjoyment; his centre of interest changes, his feelings are impure. In the derogatory sense he is more "philosophic" than Aristotle. For everything that Aristotle says illuminates the literature which is the occasion for saying it; but Coleridge only now and then. It is one more instance of the pernicious effect of emotion. (14)

Aristotle had what is called the scientific mind—a mind which, as it is rarely found among scientists except in fragments, might better be called the intelligent mind. For there is no other intelligence than this, and so far as artists and men of letters are intelligent (we may doubt whether the level of intelligence among men of letters is as high as among men of science) their intelligence is of this kind. Sainte-Beuve was a physiologist by training; but it is probable that his mind, like that of the ordinary scientific specialist, was limited in its interest, and that this was not, primarily, an interest in art. If he was a critic, there is no doubt that he was a very good one; but we may conclude that he earned some other name. Of all modern critics, perhaps Remy de Gourmont had most of the general intelligence of Aristotle. An amateur, though an excessively able amateur, in physiology, he combined to a remarkable degree sensitiveness, erudition, sense of fact and sense of history, and generalizing power.   (15)

We assume the gift of a superior sensibility. And for sensibility wide and profound reading does not mean merely a more extended pasture. There is not merely an increase of understanding, leaving the original acute impression unchanged. The new impressions modify the impressions received from the objects already known. An impression needs to be constantly refreshed by new impressions in order that it may persist at all; it needs to take its place in a system of impressions. And this system tends to become articulate in a generalized statement of literary beauty.   (16)

There are, for instance, many scattered lines and tercets in the *Divine Comedy* which are capable of transporting even a quite uninitiated reader, just sufficiently acquainted with the roots of the language to decipher the meaning, to an impression of overpowering beauty. This impression may be so deep that no subsequent study and understanding will intensify it. But at this point the impression is emotional; the reader in the ignorance which we postulate is unable to distinguish the poetry from an emotional state aroused in himself by the poetry, a state which may be merely an indulgence of his own emotions. The poetry may be an accidental stimulus. The end of the enjoyment of poetry is a pure contemplation from which all the accidents of personal emotion are removed; thus we aim to see the object as it really is and find a meaning for the words of Arnold. And without a labour which is largely a labour of the intelligence, we are unable to attain that stage of vision *amor intellectualis Dei.*   (17)

Such considerations, cast in this general form, may appear commonplaces. But I believe that it is always opportune to call attention to the torpid superstition that appreciation is one thing, and "intellectual" criticism something else. Appreciation in popular psychology is one faculty, and criticism another, an arid cleverness building theoretical scaffolds upon one's own perceptions or those of others. On the contrary, the true generalization is not something superposed upon an accumulation of perceptions; the perceptions do not, in a really appreciative mind, accumulate as a mass, but form themselves as a structure; and criticism is the statement in language of this structure; it is a development of sensibility. The bad criticism, on the other hand, is that which is nothing but an expression of emotion. And emotional people—such as stockbrokers, politicians, men of science—and a few people who pride themselves on being unemotional—detest or applaud great writers such as Spinoza or Stendhal because of their "frigidity." (18)

The writer of the present essay once committed himself to the state-

ment that "The poetic critic is criticizing poetry in order to create poetry."
He is now inclined to believe that the "historical" and the "philosophical"
critics had better be called historians and philosophers quite simply. As for
the rest, there are merely various degrees of intelligence. It is fatuous to
say that criticism is for the sake of "creation" or creation for the sake of
criticism. It is also fatuous to assume that there are ages of criticism and
ages of creativeness, as if by plunging ourselves into intellectual darkness
we were in better hopes of finding spiritual light. The two directions of
sensibility are complementary; and as sensibility is rare, unpopular, and
desirable, it is to be expected that the critic and the creative artist should
frequently be the same person.   (19)

Lionel Trilling

(1909–   )

*TRILLING, professor of English at Columbia University, has been recog-
nized as a sensitive literary and cultural critic since the publication of his
first book,* Matthew Arnold *(1939) yet the most considerable study of
the Victorian poet and essayist. His other books include* The Liberal
Imagination *(1950),* The Opposing Self *(1955),* Freud and the Crisis of
Our Culture *(1956),* A Gathering of Fugitives *(1956).*

◼ *Freud and Literature*

I

THE FREUDIAN psychology is the only systematic account of the human mind
which, in point of subtlety and complexity, of interest and tragic power, deserves to stand beside the chaotic mass of psychological insights which
literature has accumulated through the centuries. To pass from the read-

ing of a great literary work to a treatise of academic psychology is to pass from one order of perception to another, but the human nature of the Freudian psychology is exactly the stuff upon which the poet has always exercised his art. It is therefore not surprising that the psychoanalytical theory has had a great effect upon literature. Yet the relationship is reciprocal, and the effect of Freud upon literature has been no greater than the effect of literature upon Freud. When, on the occasion of the celebration of his seventieth birthday, Freud was greeted as the "discoverer of the unconscious," he corrected the speaker and disclaimed the title. "The poets and philosophers before me discovered the unconscious," he said. "What I discovered was the scientific method by which the unconscious can be studied." (1)

A lack of specific evidence prevents us from considering the particular literary "influences" upon the founder of psychoanalysis; and, besides, when we think of the men who so clearly anticipated many of Freud's own ideas—Schopenhauer and Nietzsche, for example—and then learn that he did not read their works until after he had formulated his own theories, we must see that particular influences cannot be in question here but that what we must deal with is nothing less than a whole *Zeitgeist*, a direction of thought. For psychoanalysis is one of the culminations of the Romanticist literature of the nineteenth century. If there is perhaps a contradiction in the idea of a science standing upon the shoulders of a literature which avows itself inimical to science in so many ways, the contradiction will be resolved if we remember that this literature, despite its avowals, was itself scientific in at least the sense of being passionately devoted to a research into the self. (2)

In showing the connection between Freud and this Romanticist tradition, it is difficult to know where to begin, but there might be a certain aptness in starting even back of the tradition, as far back as 1762 with Diderot's *Rameau's Nephew*. At any rate, certain men at the heart of nineteenth-century thought were agreed in finding a peculiar importance in this brilliant little work: Goethe translated it, Marx admired it, Hegel—as Marx reminded Engels in the letter which announced that he was sending the book as a gift—praised and expounded it at length, Shaw was impressed by it, and Freud himself, as we know from a quotation in his *Introductory Lectures*, read it with the pleasure of agreement. (3)

The dialogue takes place between Diderot himself and a nephew of the famous composer. The protagonist, the younger Rameau, is a despised, outcast, shameless fellow; Hegel calls him the "disintegrated consciousness" and credits him with great wit, for it is he who breaks down all the normal social values and makes new combinations with the pieces. As for Diderot, the deuteragonist, he is what Hegel calls the "honest consciousness," and Hegel considers him reasonable, decent, and dull. It is quite clear that the

author does not despise his Rameau and does not mean us to. Rameau is
lustful and greedy, arrogant yet self-abasing, perceptive yet "wrong," like
a child. Still, Diderot seems actually to be giving the fellow a kind of
superiority over himself, as though Rameau represents the elements which,
dangerous but wholly necessary, lie beneath the reasonable decorum of social life. It would perhaps be pressing too far to find in Rameau Freud's
id and in Diderot Freud's ego; yet the connection does suggest itself; and at
least we have here the perception which is to be the common characteristic
of both Freud and Romanticism, the perception of the hidden element of
human nature and of the opposition between the hidden and the visible.
We have too the bold perception of just what lies hidden: "If the little
savage [i.e., the child] were left to himself, if he preserved all his foolishness and combined the violent passions of a man of thirty with the lack of
reason of a child in the cradle, he'd wring his father's neck and go to
bed with his mother."   (4)

From the self-exposure of Rameau to Rousseau's account of his own childhood is no great step; society might ignore or reject the idea of the "immorality" which lies concealed in the beginning of the career of the "good"
man, just as it might turn away from Blake struggling to expound a psychology which would include the forces beneath the propriety of social man
in general, but the idea of the hidden thing went forward to become one
of the dominant notions of the age. The hidden element takes many forms
and it is not necessarily "dark" and "bad"; for Blake the "bad" was the
good, while for Wordsworth and Burke what was hidden and unconscious
was wisdom and power, which work in despite of the conscious intellect.
                                                                         (5)

The mind has become far less simple; the devotion to the various forms
of autobiography—itself an important fact in the tradition—provides abundant examples of the change that has taken place. Poets, making poetry by
what seems to them almost a freshly discovered faculty, find that this new
power may be conspired against by other agencies of the mind and even
deprived of its freedom; the names of Wordsworth, Coleridge, and Arnold
at once occur to us again, and Freud quotes Schiller on the danger to the
poet that lies in the merely analytical reason. And it is not only the poets
who are threatened; educated and sensitive people throughout Europe become aware of the depredations that reason might make upon the affective
life, as in the classic instance of John Stuart Mill.   (6)

We must also take into account the preoccupation—it began in the eighteenth century, or even in the seventeenth—with children, women, peasants,
and savages, whose mental life, it is felt, is less overlaid than that of the
educated adult male by the proprieties of social habit. With this preoccupation goes a concern with education and personal development, so consonant with the historical and evolutionary bias of the time. And we must

certainly note the revolution in morals which took place at the instance (we might almost say) of the *Bildungsroman,* for in the novels fathered by *Wilhelm Meister* we get the almost complete identification of author and hero and of the reader with both, and this identification almost inevitably suggests a leniency of moral judgment. The autobiographical novel has a further influence upon the moral sensibility by its exploitation of all the modulations of motive and by its hinting that we may not judge a man by any single moment in his life without taking into account the determining past and the expiating and fulfilling future. (7)

It is difficult to know how to go on, for the further we look the more literary affinities to Freud we find, and even if we limit ourselves to bibliography we can at best be incomplete. Yet we must mention the sexual revolulution that was being demanded—by Shelley, for example, by the Schlegel of *Lucinde,* by George Sand, and later and more critically by Ibsen; the belief in the sexual origin of art, badly stated by Tieck, more subtly by Schopenhauer; the investigation of sexual maladjustment by Stendhal, whose observations on erotic feeling seem to us distinctly Freudian. Again and again we see the effective, utilitarian ego being relegated to an inferior position and a plea being made on behalf of the anarchic and self-indulgent id. We find the energetic exploitation of the idea of the mind as a divisible thing, one part of which can contemplate and mock the other. It is not a far remove from this to Dostoevski's brilliant instances of ambivalent feeling. Novalis brings in the preoccupation with the death wish, and this is linked on the one hand with sleep and on the other hand with the perception of the perverse, self-destroying impulses, which in turn leads us to that fascination by the horrible which we find in Shelley, Poe, and Baudelaire. And always there is the profound interest in the dream—"Our dreams," said Gerard de Nerval, "are a second life"—and in the nature of metaphor, which reaches its climax in Rimbaud and the later Symbolists, metaphor becoming less and less communicative as it approaches the relative autonomy of the dream life. (8)

But perhaps we must stop to ask, since these are the components of the *Zeitgeist* from which Freud himself developed, whether it can be said that Freud did indeed produce a wide literary effect. What is it that Freud added that the tendency of literature itself would not have developed without him? If we were looking for a writer who showed the Freudian influence, Proust would perhaps come to mind as readily as anyone else; the very title of his novel, in French more than in English, suggests an enterprise of psychoanalysis and scarcely less so does his method—the investigation of sleep, of sexual deviation, of the way of association, the almost obsessive interest in metaphor; at these and at many other points the "influence" might be shown. Yet I believe it is true that Proust did not read Freud. Or again, exegesis of *The Waste Land* often reads remarkably like the psychoanalytic interpretation of a dream, yet we know that Eliot's methods were prepared for him not by Freud but by other poets.   (9)

Nevertheless, it is of course true that Freud's influence on literature has been very great. Much of it is so pervasive that its extent is scarcely to be determined; in one form or another, frequently in perversions or absurd simplifications, it has been infused into our life and become a component of our culture of which it is now hard to be specifically aware. In biography its first effect was sensational but not fortunate. The early Freudian biographers were for the most part Guildensterns who seemed to know the pipes but could not pluck out the heart of the mystery, and the same condemnation applies to the early Freudian critics. But in recent years, with the acclimatization of psychoanalysis and the increased sense of its refinements and complexity, criticism has derived from the Freudian system much that is of great value, most notably the license and the injunction to read the work of literature with a lively sense of its latent and ambiguous meanings, as if it were, as indeed it is, a being no less alive and contradictory than the man who created it. And this new response to the literary work has had a corrective effect upon our conception of literary biography. The literary critic or biographer who makes use of the Freudian theory is no less threatened by the dangers of theoretical systematization than he was in the early days, but he is likely to be more aware of these dangers; and I think it is true to say that now the motive of his interpretation is not that of exposing the secret shame of the writer and limiting the meaning of his work, but, on the contrary, that of finding grounds for sympathy with the writer and for increasing the possible significances of the work.   (10)

The names of the creative writers who have been more or less Freudian in tone or assumption would of course be legion. Only a relatively small number, however, have made serious use of the Freudian ideas. Freud himself seems to have thought this was as it should be: he is said to have expected very little of the works that were sent to him by writers with inscriptions of gratitude for all they had learned from him. The Surrealists have, with a certain inconsistency, depended upon Freud for the "scientific" sanction of their program. Kafka, with an apparent awareness of what he was doing, has explored the Freudian conceptions of guilt and punishment, of the dream, and of the fear of the father. Thomas Mann, whose tendency, as he himself says, was always in the direction of Freud's interests, has been most susceptible to the Freudian anthropology, finding a special charm in the theories of myths and magical practices. James Joyce, with his interest in the numerous states of receding consciousness, with his use of words as things and of words which point to more than one thing, with his pervading sense of the interrelation and interpenetration of all things, and, not least important, his treatment of familial themes, has perhaps most thoroughly and consciously exploited Freud's ideas. (11)

II

It will be clear enough how much of Freud's thought has significant affinity with the anti-rationalist element of the Romanticist tradition. But we must see with no less distinctness how much of his system is militantly rationalistic. Thomas Mann is at fault when, in his first essay on Freud, he makes it seem that the "Apollonian," the rationalistic, side of psychoanalysis is, while certainly important and wholly admirable, somehow secondary and even accidental. He gives us a Freud who is committed to the "night side" of life. Not at all: the rationalistic element of Freud is foremost; before everything else he is positivistic. If the interpreter of dreams came to medical science through Goethe, as he tells us he did, he entered not by way of the *Walpurgisnacht* but by the essay which played so important a part in the lives of so many scientists of the nineteenth century, the famous disquisition on Nature.   (12)

This correction is needed not only for accuracy but also for any understanding of Freud's attitude to art. And for that understanding we must see how intense is the passion with which Freud believes that positivistic rationalism, in its golden-age pre-Revolutionary purity, is the very form and pattern of intellectual virtue. The aim of psychoanalysis, he says, is the control of the night side of life. It is "to strengthen the ego, to make it more independent of the super-ego, to widen its field of vision, and so to extend the organization of the id." "Where id was,"—that is, where all the irrational, non-logical, pleasure-seeking dark forces were—"there shall ego be,"—that is, intelligence and control. "It is," he concludes, with a reminiscence of Faust, "reclamation work, like the draining of the Zuyder Zee." This passage is quoted by Mann when, in taking up the subject of Freud a second time, he does indeed speak of Freud's positivistic program; but even here the bias induced by Mann's artistic interest in the "night side" prevents him from giving the other aspect of Freud its due emphasis. Freud would never have accepted the role which Mann seems to give him as the legitimizer of the myth and the dark irrational ways of the mind. If Freud discovered the darkness for science he never endorsed it. On the contrary, his rationalism supports all the ideas of the Enlightenment that deny validity to myth or religion; he holds to a simple materialism, to a simple determinism, to a rather limited sort of epistemology. No great scientist of our day has thundered so articulately and so fiercely against all those who would sophisticate with metaphysics the scientific principles that were good enough for the nineteenth century. Conceptualism or pragmatism is anathema to him through the greater part of his intellectual career, and this, when we consider the nature of his own brilliant scientific methods, has surely an element of paradox in it.   (13)

From his rationalistic positivism comes much of Freud's strength and what weakness he has. The strength is the fine, clear tenacity of his positive aims, the goal of therapy, the desire to bring to men a decent measure of earthly happiness. But upon the rationalism must also be placed the blame for the often naïve scientific principles which characterize his early thought —they are later much modified—and which consist largely of claiming for his theories a perfect correspondence with an external reality, a position which, for those who admire Freud and especially for those who take seriously his views on art, is troublesome in the extreme.   (14)

Now Freud has, I believe, much to tell us about art, but whatever is suggestive in him is not likely to be found in those of his works in which he deals expressly with art itself. Freud is not insensitive to art—on the contrary—nor does he ever intend to speak of it with contempt. Indeed, he speaks of it with a real tenderness and counts it one of the true charms of the good life. Of artists, especially of writers, he speaks with admiration and even a kind of awe, though perhaps what he most appreciates in literature are specific emotional insights and observations; as we have noted, he speaks of literary men, because they have understood the part played in life by the hidden motives, as the precursors and coadjutors of his own science.   (15)

And yet eventually Freud speaks of art with what we must indeed call contempt. Art, he tells us, is a "substitute gratification," and as such is "an illusion in contrast to reality." Unlike most illusions, however, art is "almost always harmless and beneficent" for the reason that "it does not seek to be anything but an illusion. Save in the case of a few people who are, one might say, obsessed by Art, it never dares make any attack on the realm of reality." One of its chief functions is to serve as a "narcotic." It shares the characteristics of the dream, whose element of distortion Freud calls a "sort of inner dishonesty." As for the artist, he is virtually in the same category with the neurotic. "By such separation of imagination and intellectual capacity," Freud says of the hero of a novel, "he is destined to be a poet or a neurotic, and he belongs to that race of beings whose realm is not of this world."   (16)

Now there is nothing in the logic of psychoanalytical thought which requires Freud to have these opinions. But there is a great deal in the practice of the psychoanalytical therapy which makes it understandable that Freud, unprotected by an adequate philosophy, should be tempted to take the line he does. The analytical therapy deals with illusion. The patient comes to the physician to be cured, let us say, of a fear of walking in the street. The fear is real enough, there is no illusion on that score, and it produces all the physical symptoms of a more rational fear, the sweating palms, pounding heart, and shortened breath. But the patient knows that there is no cause for the fear, or rather that there is, as he says, no "real cause": there are no machine guns, man traps, or tigers in the street. The physician knows, however, that there is indeed a "real" cause for the fear, though it has nothing at all to do with what is or is not in the street; the cause is within the patient, and the process of the therapy will be to discover, by gradual steps, what this real cause is and so free the patient from its effects.   (17)

Now the patient in coming to the physician, and the physician in accepting the patient, make a tacit compact about reality; for their purpose they agree to the limited reality by which we get our living, win our loves, catch our trains and our colds. The therapy will undertake to train the patient in proper ways of coping with this reality. The patient, of course, has been dealing with this reality all along, but in the wrong way. For Freud there are two ways of dealing with external reality. One is practical, effective, positive; this is the way of the conscious self, of the ego which must be made independent of the super-ego and extend its organization over the id, and it is the right way. The antithetical way may be called, for our purpose now, the "fictional" way. Instead of doing something about, or to, external reality, the individual who uses this way does something to, or about, his affective states. The most common and "normal" example of this is daydreaming, in which we give ourselves a certain pleasure by imagining our difficulties solved or our desires gratified. Then, too, as Freud discovered, sleeping dreams are, in much more complicated ways, and even though quite unpleasant, at the service of this same "fictional" activity. And in ways yet more complicated and yet more unpleasant, the actual neurosis from which our patient suffers deals with an external reality which the mind considers still more unpleasant than the painful neurosis itself. (18)

For Freud as psychoanalytic practitioner there are, we may say, the polar extremes of reality and illusion. Reality is an honorific word, and it means what is *there;* illusion is a pejorative word, and it means a response to what is *not there.* The didactic nature of a course of psychoanalysis no doubt requires a certain firm crudeness in making the distinction; it is after all aimed not at theoretical refinement but at practical effectiveness. The polar extremes are practical reality and neurotic illusion, the latter judged by the former. This, no doubt, is as it should be; the patient is not being trained in metaphysics and epistemology.   (19)

This practical assumption is not Freud's only view of the mind in its relation to reality. Indeed what may be called the essentially Freudian view assumes that the mind, for good as well as bad, helps create its reality by selection and evaluation. In this view, reality is malleable and subject to creation; it is not static but is rather a series of situations which are dealt with in their own terms. But beside this conception of the mind stands the conception which arises from Freud's therapeutic-practical assumptions;

in this view, the mind deals with a reality which is quite fixed and static, a reality that is wholly "given" and not (to use a phrase of Dewey's) "taken." In his epistemological utterances, Freud insists on this second view, although it is not easy to see why he should do so. For the reality to which he wishes to reconcile the neurotic patient is, after all, a "taken" and not a "given" reality. It is the reality of social life and of value, conceived and maintained by the human mind and will. Love, morality, honor, esteem— these are the components of a created reality. If we are to call art an illusion then we must call most of the activities and satisfactions of the ego illusions; Freud, of course, has no desire to call them that.   (20)

What, then, is the difference between, on the one hand, the dream and the neurosis, and, on the other hand, art? That they have certain common elements is of course clear; that unconscious processes are at work in both would be denied by no poet or critic; they share too, though in different degrees, the element of fantasy. But there is a vital difference between them which Charles Lamb saw so clearly in his defense of the sanity of true genius: "The . . . poet dreams being awake. He is not possessed by his subject but he has dominion over it."   (21)

That is the whole difference: the poet is in command of his fantasy, while it is exactly the mark of the neurotic that he is possessed by his fantasy. And there is a further difference which Lamb states; speaking of the poet's relation to reality (he calls it Nature), he says, "He is beautifully loyal to that sovereign directress, even when he appears most to betray her"; the illusions of art are made to serve the purpose of a closer and truer relation with reality. Jacques Barzun, in an acute and sympathetic discussion of Freud, puts the matter well: "A good analogy between art and *dreaming* has led him to a false one between art and *sleeping*. But the difference between a work of art and a dream is precisely this, that the work of art *leads us back to the outer reality by taking account of it.*" Freud's assumption of the almost exclusively hedonistic nature and purpose of art bars him from the perception of this.   (22)

Of the distinction that must be made between the artist and the neurotic Freud is of course aware; he tells us that the artist is not like the neurotic in that he knows how to find a way back from the world of imagination and "once more get a firm foothold in reality." This however seems to mean no more than that reality is to be dealt with when the artist suspends the practice of his art; and at least once when Freud speaks of art dealing with reality he actually means the rewards that a successful artist can win. He does not deny to art its function and its usefulness; it has a therapeutic effect in releasing mental tension; it serves the cultural purpose of acting as a "substitute gratification" to reconcile men to the sacrifices they have made for culture's sake; it promotes the social sharing of highly valued emotional experiences; and it recalls men to their cultural ideals. This is not everything that some of us would find that art does, yet even this is a good deal for a "narcotic" to do. (23)

III

I started by saying that Freud's ideas could tell us something about art, but so far I have done little more than try to show that Freud's very conception of art is inadequate. Perhaps, then, the suggestiveness lies in the application of the analytic method to specific works of art or to the artist himself? I do not think so, and it is only fair to say that Freud himself was aware both of the limits and the limitations of psychoanalysis in art, even though he does not always in practice submit to the former or admit the latter. (24)

Freud has, for example, no desire to encroach upon the artist's autonomy; he does not wish us to read his monograph on Leonardo and then say of the "Madonna of the Rocks" that it is a fine example of homosexual, autoerotic painting. If he asserts that in investigation the "psychiatrist cannot yield to the author," he immediately insists that the "author cannot yield to the psychiatrist," and he warns the latter not to "coarsen everything" by using for all human manifestations the "substantially useless and awkward terms" of clinical procedure. He admits, even while asserting that the sense of beauty probably derives from sexual feeling, that psychoanalysis "has less to say about beauty than about most other things." He confesses to a theoretical indifference to the form of art and restricts himself to its content. Tone, feeling, style, and the modification that part makes upon part he does not consider. "The layman," he says, "may expect perhaps too much from analysis . . . for it must be admitted that it throws no light upon the two problems which probably interest him the most. It can do nothing toward elucidating the nature of the artistic gift, nor can it explain the means by which the artist works—artistic technique." (25)

What, then, does Freud believe that the analytical method can do? Two things: explain the "inner meanings" of the work of art and explain the temperament of the artist as man. (26)

A famous example of the method is the attempt to solve the "problem" of *Hamlet* as suggested by Freud and as carried out by Dr. Ernest Jones, his early and distinguished follower. Dr. Jones's monograph is a work of painstaking scholarship and of really masterly ingenuity. The research undertakes not only the clearing up of the mystery of Hamlet's character, but also the discovery of "the clue to much of the deeper workings of Shakespeare's mind." Part of the mystery in question is of course why Hamlet, after he had so definitely resolved to do so, did not avenge upon his hated uncle his father's death. But there is another mystery to the play—what Freud calls "the mystery of its effect," its magical appeal that draws so much interest toward it. Recalling the many failures to solve the riddle of the play's charm, he wonders if we are to be driven to the conclusion "that its magical appeal rests solely upon the impressive thoughts in it and the splendor of its language." Freud believes that we can find a source of power beyond this. (27)

We remember that Freud has told us that the meaning of a dream is its intention, and we may assume that the meaning of a drama is its intention, too. The Jones research undertakes to discover what it was that Shakespeare intended to say about Hamlet. It finds that the intention was wrapped by the author in a dreamlike obscurity because it touched so deeply both his personal life and the moral life of the world; what Shakespeare intended to say is that Hamlet cannot act because he is incapacitated by the guilt he feels at his unconscious attachment to his mother. There is, I think, nothing to be quarreled with in the statement that there is an Oedipus situation in *Hamlet;* and if psychoanalysis has indeed added a new point of interest to the play, that is to its credit.[1] And, just so, there is no reason to quarrel with Freud's conclusion when he undertakes to give us the meaning of *King Lear* by a tortuous tracing of the mythological implications of the theme of the three caskets, of the relation of the caskets to the Norns, the Fates, and the Graces, of the connection of these triadic females with Lear's daughters, of the transmogrification of the death goddess into the love goddess and the identification of Cordelia with both, all to the conclusion that the meaning of *King Lear* is to be found in the tragic refusal of an old man to "renounce love, choose death, and make friends with the necessity of dying." There is something both beautiful and suggestive in this, but it is not *the* meaning of *King Lear* any more than the Oedipus motive is *the* meaning of *Hamlet.*   (28)

It is not here a question of the validity of the evidence, though that is of course important. We must rather object to the conclusions of Freud and Dr. Jones on the ground that their proponents do not have an adequate conception of what an artistic meaning is. There is no single meaning to any work of art; this is true not merely because it is better that it should be true, that is, because it makes art a richer thing, but because historical and personal experience show it to be true. Changes in historical context and in personal mood change the meaning of a work and indicate to us that artistic understanding is not a question of fact but of value. Even if the author's intention were, as it cannot be, precisely determinable, the meaning

---

1 However, A. C. Bradley, in his discussion of Hamlet (*Shakespearean Tragedy*), states clearly the intense sexual disgust which Hamlet feels and which, for Bradley, helps account for his uncertain purpose; and Bradley was anticipated in this view by Löning. It is well known, and Dover Wilson has lately emphasized the point, that to an Elizabethan audience Hamlet's mother was not merely tasteless, as to a modern audience she seems, in hurrying to marry Claudius, but actually adulterous in marrying him at all because he was, as her brother-in-law, within the forbidden degrees.

of a work cannot lie in the author's intention alone. It must also lie in its effect. We can say of a volcanic eruption on an inhabited island that it "means terrible suffering," but if the island is uninhabited or easily evacuated it means something else. In short, the audience partly determines the meaning of the work. But although Freud sees something of this when he says that in addition to the author's intention we must take into account the mystery of *Hamlet's* effect, he nevertheless goes on to speak as if, historically, *Hamlet's* effect had been single and brought about solely by the "magical" power of the Oedipus motive to which, unconsciously, we so violently respond. Yet there was, we know, a period when *Hamlet* was relatively in eclipse, and it has always been scandalously true of the French, a people not without filial feeling, that they have been somewhat indifferent to the "magical appeal" of *Hamlet*. (29)

I do not think that anything I have said about the inadequacies of the Freudian method of interpretation limits the number of ways we can deal with a work of art. Bacon remarked that experiment may twist nature on the rack to wring out its secrets, and criticism may use any instruments upon a work of art to find its meanings. The elements of art are not limited to the world of art. They reach into life, and whatever extraneous knowledge of them we gain—for example, by research into the historical context of the work—may quicken our feelings for the work itself and even enter legitimately into those feelings. Then, too, anything we may learn about the artist himself may be enriching and legitimate. But one research into the mind of the artist is simply not practicable, however legitimate it may theoretically be. That is, the investigation of his unconscious intention as it exists apart from the work itself. Criticism understands that the artist's statement of his conscious intention, though it is sometimes useful, cannot finally determine meaning. How much less can we know from his unconscious intention considered as something apart from the whole work? Surely very little that can be called conclusive or scientific. For, as Freud himself points out, we are not in a position to question the artist; we must apply the technique of dream analysis to his symbols, but, as Freud says with some heat, those people do not understand his theory who think that a dream may be interpreted without the dreamer's free association with the multitudinous details of his dream. (30)

We have so far ignored the aspect of the method which finds the solution to the "mystery" of such a play as *Hamlet* in the temperament of Shakespeare himself and then illuminates the mystery of Shakespeare's temperament by means of the solved mystery of the play. Here it will be amusing to remember that by 1935 Freud had become converted to the theory that it was not Shakespeare of Stratford but the Earl of Oxford who wrote the plays, thus invalidating the important bit of evidence that Shakespeare's father died shortly before the composition of *Hamlet*. This is destructive enough to Dr. Jones's argument, but the evidence from which Dr. Jones draws conclusions about literature fails on grounds more relevant to literature itself. For when Dr. Jones, by means of his analysis of *Hamlet*, takes us into "the deeper workings of Shakespeare's mind," he does so with a perfect confidence that he knows what *Hamlet* is and what its relation to Shakespeare is. It is, he tells us, Shakespeare's "chief masterpiece," so far superior to all his other works that it may be placed on "an entirely separate level." And then, having established his ground on an entirely subjective literary judgment, Dr. Jones goes on to tell us that *Hamlet* "probably expresses the core of Shakespeare's philosophy and outlook as no other work of his does." That is, all the contradictory or complicating or modifying testimony of the other plays is dismissed on the basis of Dr. Jones's acceptance of the peculiar position which, he believes, *Hamlet* occupies in the Shakespeare canon. And it is upon this quite inadmissible judgment that Dr. Jones bases his argument: "It may be expected *therefore* that anything which will give us the key to the inner meaning of the play will *necessarily* give us the clue to much of the deeper workings of Shakespeare's mind." (The italics are mine.)   (31)

I should be sorry if it appeared that I am trying to say that psychoanalysis can have nothing to do with literature. I am sure that the opposite is so. For example, the whole notion of rich ambiguity in literature, of the interplay between the apparent meaning and the latent—not "hidden"—meaning, has been reinforced by the Freudian concepts, perhaps even received its first impetus from them. Of late years, the more perceptive psychoanalysts have surrendered the early pretensions of their teachers to deal "scientifically" with literature. That is all to the good, and when a study as modest and precise as Dr. Franz Alexander's essay on *Henry IV* comes along, an essay which pretends not to "solve" but only to illuminate the subject, we have something worth having. Dr. Alexander undertakes nothing more than to say that in the development of Prince Hal we see the classic struggle of the ego to come to normal adjustment, beginning with the rebellion against the father, going on to the conquest of the super-ego (Hotspur, with his rigid notions of honor and glory), then to the conquests of the *id* (Falstaff, with his anarchic self-indulgence), then to the identification with the father (the crown scene) and the assumption of mature responsibility. An analysis of this sort is not momentous and not exclusive of other meanings; perhaps it does no more than point up and formulate what we all have already seen. It has the tact to *accept* the play and does not, like Dr. Jones's study of *Hamlet*, search for a "hidden motive" and a "deeper working," which implies that there is a reality to which the play stands in the relation that a dream stands to the wish that generates it and from which it is separable; it is this reality, this "deeper working," which, according to Dr. Jones, produced the play. But *Hamlet* is not merely the product of Shakespeare's thought, it is the very instrument of his thought, and if meaning is intention, Shakespeare did not intend the Oedipus motive or anything less than *Hamlet;* if meaning is effect then it is *Hamlet* which affects us, not the Oedipus motive. *Coriolanus* also deals, and very terribly, with the Oedipus motive but the effect of the one drama is very different from the effect of the other. (32)

IV

If, then, we can accept neither Freud's conception of the place of art in life nor his application of the analytical method, what is it that he contributes to our understanding of art or to its practice? In my opinion, what he contributes outweighs his errors; it is of the greatest importance, and it lies in no specific statement that he makes about art but is, rather, implicit in his whole conception of the mind. (33)

For, of all mental systems, the Freudian psychology is the one which makes poetry indigenous to the very constitution of the mind. Indeed, the mind, as Freud sees it, is in the greater part of its tendency exactly a poetry-making organ. This puts the case too strongly, no doubt, for it seems to make the working of the unconscious mind equivalent to poetry itself, forgetting that between the unconscious mind and the finished poem there supervene the social intention and the formal control of the conscious mind. Yet the statement has at least the virtue of counterbalancing the belief, so commonly expressed or implied, that the very opposite is true, and that poetry is a kind of beneficent aberration of the mind's right course. (34)

Freud has not merely naturalized poetry; he has discovered its status as a pioneer settler, and he sees it as a method of thought. Often enough he tries to show how, as a method of thought, it is unreliable and ineffective for conquering reality; yet he himself is forced to use it in the very shaping of his own science, as when he speaks of the topography of the mind and tells us with a kind of defiant apology that the metaphors of space relationship which he is using are really most inexact since the mind is not a thing of space at all, but that there is no other way of conceiving the difficult idea except by metaphor. In the eighteenth century Vico spoke of the metaphorical, imagistic language of the early stages of culture; it was left to Freud to discover how, in a scientific age, we still feel and think in figurative formations, and to create, what psychoanalysis is, a science of tropes, of metaphor and its variants, synecdoche and metonymy. (35)

Freud showed, too, how the mind, in one of its parts, could work without logic, yet not without that directing purpose, that control of intent from which, perhaps it might be said, logic springs. For the unconscious mind works without the syntactical conjunctions which are logic's essence. It rec-

ognizes no *because,* no *therefore,* no *but;* such ideas as similarity, agreement, and community are expressed in dreams imagistically by compressing the elements into a unity. The unconscious mind in its struggle with the
conscious always turns from the general to the concrete and finds the tangible trifle more congenial than the large abstraction. Freud discovered in
the very organization of the mind those mechanisms by which art makes
its effects, such devices as the condensations of meanings and the displacement of accent.   (36)

All this is perhaps obvious enough and, though I should like to develop
it in proportion both to its importance and to the space I have given to
disagreement with Freud, I will not press it further. For there are two other
elements in Freud's thought which, in conclusion, I should like to introduce as of great weight in their bearing on art.   (37)

Of these, one is a specific idea which, in the middle of his career (1920),
Freud put forward in his essay *Beyond the Pleasure Principle.* The essay
itself is a speculative attempt to solve a perplexing problem in clinical
analysis, but its relevance to literature is inescapable, as Freud sees well
enough, even though his perception of its critical importance is not sufficiently strong to make him revise his earlier views of the nature and function of art. The idea is one which stands besides Aristotle's notion of the
catharsis, in part to supplement, in part to modify it.   (38)

Freud has come upon certain facts which are not to be reconciled with
his earlier theory of the dream. According to this theory, all dreams, even
the unpleasant ones, could be understood upon analysis to have the intention of fulfilling the dreamer's wishes. They are in the service of what Freud
calls the pleasure principle, which is opposed to the reality principle. It is,
of course, this explanation of the dream which had so largely conditioned
Freud's theory of art. But now there is thrust upon him the necessity for
reconsidering the theory of the dream, for it was found that in cases of
war neurosis—what we once called shellshock—the patient, with the utmost
anguish, recurred in his dreams to the very situation, distressing as it was,
which had precipitated his neurosis. It seemed impossible to interpret these
dreams by any assumption of a hedonistic intent. Nor did there seem to
be the usual amount of distortion in them: the patient recurred to the terrible initiatory situation with great literalness. And the same pattern of psychic behavior could be observed in the play of children; there were some
games which, far from fulfilling wishes, seemed to concentrate upon the
representation of those aspects of the child's life which were most unpleasant and threatening to his happiness.   (39)

To explain such mental activities Freud evolved a theory for which he
at first refused to claim much but to which, with the years, he attached an
increasing importance. He first makes the assumption that there is indeed
in the psychic life a repetition-compulsion which goes beyond the pleasure

principle. Such a compulsion cannot be meaningless, it must have an intent. And that intent, Freud comes to believe, is exactly and literally the developing of fear. "These dreams," he says, "are attempts at restoring control of the stimuli by developing apprehension, the pretermission of which caused the traumatic neurosis." The dream, that is, is the effort to reconstruct the bad situation in order that the failure to meet it may be recouped; in these dreams there is no obscured intent to evade but only an attempt to meet the situation, to make a new effort of control. And in the play of children it seems to be that "the child repeats even the unpleasant experiences because through his own activity he gains a far more thorough mastery of the strong impression than was possible by mere passive experience.   (40)

Freud, at this point, can scarcely help being put in mind of tragic drama; nevertheless, he does not wish to believe that this effort to come to mental grips with a situation is involved in the attraction of tragedy. He is, we might say, under the influence of the Aristotelian tragic theory which emphasizes a qualified hedonism through suffering. But the pleasure involved in tragedy is perhaps an ambiguous one; and sometimes we must feel that the famous sense of cathartic resolution is perhaps the result of glossing over terror with beautiful language rather than an evacuation of it. And sometimes the terror even bursts through the language to stand stark and isolated from the play, as does Oedipus's sightless and bleeding face. At any rate, the Aristotelian theory does not deny another function for tragedy (and for comedy, too) which is suggested by Freud's theory of the traumatic neurosis—what might be called the mithridatic function, by which tragedy is used as the homeopathic administration of pain to inure ourselves to the greater pain which life will force upon us. There is in the cathartic theory of tragedy, as it is usually understood, a conception of tragedy's function which is too negative and which inadequately suggests the sense of active mastery which tragedy can give.   (41)

In the same essay in which he sets forth the conception of the mind embracing its own pain for some vital purpose, Freud also expresses a provisional assent to the idea (earlier stated, as he reminds us, by Schopenhauer) that there is perhaps a human drive which makes of death the final and desired goal. The death instinct is a conception that is rejected by many of even the most thoroughgoing Freudian theorists (as, in his last book, Freud mildly noted); the late Otto Fenichel in his authoritative work on the neurosis argues cogently against it. Yet even if we reject the theory as not fitting the facts in any operatively useful way, we still cannot miss its grandeur, its ultimate tragic courage in acquiescence to fate. The idea of the reality principle and the idea of the death instinct form the crown of Freud's broader speculation on the life of man. Their quality of grim poetry is characteristic of Freud's system and the ideas it generates for him. (42)

And as much as anything else that Freud gives to literature, this quality of his thought is important. Although the artist is never finally determined in his work by the intellectual systems about him, he cannot avoid their influence; and it can be said of various competing systems that some hold more promise for the artist than others. When, for example, we think of the simple humanitarian optimism which, for two decades, has been so pervasive, we must see that not only has it been politically and philosophically inadequate, but also that it implies, by the smallness of its view of the varieties of human possibility, a kind of check on the creative faculties. In Freud's view of life no such limitation is implied. To be sure, certain elements of his system seem hostile to the usual notions of man's dignity. Like every great critic of human nature—and Freud is that—he finds in human pride the ultimate cause of human wretchedness, and he takes pleasure in knowing that his ideas stand with those of Copernicus and Darwin in making pride more difficult to maintain. Yet the Freudian man is, I venture to think, a creature of far more dignity and far more interest than the man which any other modern system has been able to conceive. Despite popular belief to the contrary, man, as Freud conceives him, is not to be understood by any simple formula (such as sex) but is rather an inextricable tangle of culture and biology. And not being simple, he is not simply good; he has, as Freud says somewhere, a kind of hell within him from which rise everlastingly the impulses which threaten his civilization. He has the faculty of imagining for himself more in the way of pleasure and satisfaction than he can possibly achieve. Everything that he gains he pays for in more than equal coin; compromise and the compounding with defeat constitute his best way of getting through the world. His best qualities are the result of a struggle whose outcome is tragic. Yet he is a creature of love; it is Freud's sharpest criticism of the Adlerian psychology that to aggression it gives everything and to love nothing at all.   (43)

One is always aware in reading Freud how little cynicism there is in his thought. His desire for man is only that he should be human, and to this end his science is devoted. No view of life to which the artist responds can insure the quality of his work, but the poetic qualities of Freud's own principles, which are so clearly in the line of the classic tragic realism, suggest that this is a view which does not narrow and simplify the human world for the artist but on the contrary opens and complicates it.   (44)

Cleanth Brooks

(1906–   )

BROOKS is Gray Professor of Rhetoric at Yale. In 1947 he published The Well Wrought Urn, *in which his theory of criticism was broadly applied. It became the major topic of conversation among literary academicians. He has frequently collaborated with his colleagues at Yale and fellow-Kentuckian, Robert Penn Warren, with whom he has been closely associated through most of his academic life. His other major works include* Modern Poetry and the Tradition *(1939),* Understanding Poetry *(with Warren), and* Literary Criticism: A Short History *(with W. K. Wimsatt, Jr., 1957).*

■ *Wordsworth and the Paradox*
of the Imagination

WORDSWORTH'S great "Intimations" ode has been for so long intimately connected with Wordsworth's own autobiography, and indeed, Wordsworth's poems in general have been so consistently interpreted as documents pertaining to that autobiography, that to consider one of his larger poems as an object in itself may actually seem impertinent. Yet to do so for once at least is not to condemn the usual mode of procedure and it may, in fact, have positive advantages. (1)

Wordsworth's spiritual history is admittedly important: it is just possible that it is ultimately the important thing about Wordsworth. And yet the poems are structures in their own right; and, finally, I suppose, Wordsworth's spiritual biography has come to have the importance which it has for us because he is a poet. (2)

At any rate, it may be interesting to see what happens when one considers the "Ode" as a poem, as an independent poetic structure, even to the point of forfeiting the light which his letters, his notes, and his other poems throw on difficult points. (That forfeiture, one may hasten to advise the cautious reader, need not, of course, be permanent.) But to enforce it for the moment will certainly avoid confusion between what the poem "says" and what Wordsworth in general may have meant; and it may actually surprise some readers to see how much the poem, strictly considered in its own right, manages to say, as well as precisely what it says.   (3)

If we consider the "Ode" in these terms, several observations emerge. For one thing, the poem will be seen to make more use of paradox than is commonly supposed. Of some of these paradoxes, Wordsworth himself must obviously have been aware; but he was probably not aware, the reader will conjecture, of the extent to which he was employing paradox.   (4)

The poem, furthermore, displays a rather consistent symbolism. This may be thought hardly astonishing. What may be more surprising is the fact that the symbols reveal so many ambiguities. In a few cases, this ambiguity, of which Wordsworth, again, was apparently only partially aware, breaks down into outright confusion. Yet much of the ambiguity is rich and meaningful in an Empsonian sense, and it is in terms of this ambiguity that many of the finest effects of the poem are achieved.   (5)

There are to be found in the "Ode" several varieties of irony; and some of the themes which Wordsworth treats in the poem are to be successfully related only through irony. Yet the principal defect of the "Ode" results from the fact that Wordsworth will not always accept the full consequences of some of his ironical passages.   (6)

Lastly, as may be surmised from what has already been remarked, the "Ode" for all its fine passages, is not entirely successful as a poem. Yet, we shall be able to make our best defense of it in proportion as we recognize and value its use of ambiguous symbol and paradoxical statement. Indeed, it might be maintained that, failing to do this, we shall miss much of its power as poetry and even some of its accuracy of statement.   (7)

It is tempting to interpret these propositions as proof of the fact that Wordsworth wrote the "Ode" with the "dark" side of his mind—that the poem welled up from his unconscious and that his conscious tinkering with it which was calculated to blunt and coarsen some of the finest effects was, in this case, held to a minimum. But it hardly becomes a critic who has just proposed to treat the poem strictly as a poem, apart from its reflections of Wordsworth's biography, to rush back into biographical speculation. It is far more important to see whether the generalizations proposed about the nature of the poem are really borne out by the poem itself. This is all the more true when one reflects that to propose to find in the poem ambiguities, ironies, and paradoxes will seem to many a reader an attempt to fit the poem to a Procrustean bed—in fine, the bed in which John Donne slept comfortably enough but in which a Romantic poet can hardly be supposed to find any ease.   (8)

In reading the poem, I shall emphasize the imagery primarily, and the success or relative failure with which Wordsworth meets in trying to make his images carry and develop his thought. It is only fair to myself to say that I am also interested in many other things, the metrical pattern, for example, though I shall necessarily have to omit detailed consideration of this and many other matters.   (9)

In the "Ode" the poet begins by saying that he has lost something. What is it precisely that he has lost? What does the poem itself say? It says that things uncelestial, the earth and every common sight, once seemed apparelled in celestial light. The word "apparelled" seems to me important. The light was like a garment. It could be taken off. It was not natural to the earth; it *has* been taken off. And if the celestial light is a garment, the earth must have been clad with the garment by someone (the garment motif, by the way, is to appear later with regard to the child: "trailing clouds of glory do we come").   (10)

The earth, which has had to be apparelled in the garment of light, is counterbalanced by the celestial bodies like the sun, moon, and stars of the next stanza. These are lightbearers capable of trailing clouds of glory themselves, and they clothe the earth in light of various sorts. One is tempted here to say that the poles of the basic comparison are already revealed in these first two stanzas: the common earth on which the glory has to be conferred, and the sun or moon, which confers glory. We can even anticipate the crux of the poem in these terms: has the child been clothed with light? Or does he himself clothe the world about him in light? But more of this later.   (11)

This celestial apparel, the garment of light, had, the speaker says, the glory and the freshness of a dream. A dream has an extraordinary kind of vividness often associated with strong emotional coloring. It frequently represents familiar objects, even homely ones, but with the familiarity gone and the objects endowed with strangeness. But the dream is elusive, it cannot be dissected and analyzed. (Even if Wordsworth could have been confronted with Dr. Freud, he would, we may surmise, have hardly missed seeing that Freud's brilliant accounts of dreams resemble science less than they do poems—"Odes on the Intimations of all too human humanity from unconscious recollections of early childhood.") Moreover, the phrase, taken as a whole, suggests that the glory has the unsubstantial quality of a dream. Perhaps this is to overload an otherwise innocent phrase. But I should like to point out as some warrant for this suggestion of unsubstantiality that "dream" is rhymed emphatically with "To me did *seem*," and that it is immediately followed by "It is not now as it hath been of yore." The dream quality, it seems to me, is linked definitely with the transience of the experience. Later in the poem, the dream is to be connected with "visionary gleam," is to be qualified by the adjective "fugitive," and finally is to be associated with "Those shadowy recollections." (12)

The ambiguous character of the child's vision as remembered by the man is implicit, therefore, in the first stanza of the poem. What the speaker has lost, it is suggested, is something which is fleeting, shadowy, and strange, but something which possesses a quality of insight and wholeness which no amount of other perception—least of all patient analysis—will duplicate. It is *visionary;* that is, like a vision, a revelation. But visionary perhaps also suggests something impractical, not completely real. Perhaps most interesting of all, the speaker, a little later in the "Ode," has it fade into the light of common day, which is inimical to both its freshness and its glory. The vision which has been lost is at once more intense and less intense than common daylight. (13)

The second stanza, I think, is very important in defining further the relation of the visionary gleam to the man and to the earth. Ostensibly, this second stanza simply goes on to define further the nature of the thing lost: it is not mere beauty; nature is still beautiful, but a special quality has been lost. Yet the imagery seems to me to be doing something else beneath this surface statement, and something which is very important. In contrast to the earth, we have the rainbow, the moon, the stars, and the sun —all examples of celestial light; and to these we may add the rose by the sort of extension, not too difficult to be sure, by which Cowley treats it as light in his "Hymn to Light." Wordsworth says that the rainbow and the rose are beautiful. We expect him to go on to say the same of the moon. But here, with one of the nicest touches in the poem, he reverses the pattern to say, "The moon doth with delight/Look round her when the heavens are bare." The moon is treated as if she were the speaker himself in his childhood, seeing the visionary gleam as she looks round her with joy. The poet cannot see the gleam, but he implies that the moon can see it, and suggests how she can: she sheds the gleam herself; she lights up and thus creates her world. This seems to me a hint which Wordsworth is to develop later more explicitly, that it is the child, looking round him with joy, who is at once both the source and the recipient of the vision. In this stanza even the sunshine (though as the source of common day it is to be used later in the poem as the antithesis of the visionary gleam) participates in the glory—"The sunshine is a glorious birth." The word *birth*, by the way, suggests that it is a dawn scene: it is the childhood of the sun's course, not the maturity. Like the moon, the sun joyfully creates its world. The poet is giving us here, it seems to me, some very important preparation for Stanza V, in which he is to say "Our birth is but a sleep and a forgetting:/The Soul that rises with us, our life's Star,/Hath had elsewhere its setting . . ."

Surely, it is perfectly clear here that the child, coming upon the world, trailing his clouds of glory, is like the sun or moon which brings its radiance with it, moonlight or starlight or dawn light.   (14)

I shall not try to prove here that Wordsworth consciously built up the imagery of Stanza II as preparation for Stanza V. In one sense I think the question of whether or not Wordsworth did this consciously is irrelevant. What I am certain of is this: that the lines

> *The Moon doth with delight*
> *Look round her. . . .*

strike any sensitive reader as fine to a degree which their value as decoration will not account for. Certainly it is a testimony of many readers that the famous passage "Our birth is but a sleep, etc." has registered with a special impact, with more impact than the mere "beauty" of the images will account for. The relation of both passages to the theme, and their mutual interrelations seem to me one way of accounting for their special force. (15)

This relation of both passages to the theme is so important, however, that I should like for the moment to pass over consideration of Stanzas III and IV in order to pursue further the central symbolism of light as treated in Stanza V. The basic metaphor from line sixty-seven onward has to do with the child's moving away from heaven, his home—the shades of the prison house closing about him—the youth's progress further and further from the day-spring in the east. We should, however, if the figure were worked out with thorough consistency, expect him to arrive at darkness or near darkness, the shades of the prison house having closed round the boy all but completely—the youth having traveled into some darkened and dismal west. Yet the tantalizing ambiguity in the symbol which we have noticed earlier, continues. The climax of the process is not darkness but full daylight: "At length the Man perceives it die away,/And fade into the light of common day." We have a contrast, then, between prosaic daylight and starlight or dawn light—a contrast between kinds of light, not between light and darkness. There is a further difficulty in the symbolism: the sunlight, which in Stanza II was a glorious birth, has here become the symbol for the prosaic and the common and the mortal.   (16)

I point out the ambiguities, not to convict the poet of confusion, but to praise him for his subtlety and accuracy. I suggest that the implied comparison of the child to the sun or the moon is still active here, and that Wordsworth is leaning on his earlier figure more heavily than most of his critics have pointed out, or than, perhaps, he himself realized. If the sun, at his glorious birth, lights up a world with the glory and freshness of a dream, with a light which persists even after he has begun to ascend the sky, yet the sun gradually becomes the destroyer of his earlier world and becomes

his own prisoner. Indeed it is very easy to read the whole stanza as based
on a submerged metaphor of the sun's progress: the soul is like our life's
star, the sun, which has had elsewhere its setting. It rises upon its world,
not in utter nakedness. The trailing clouds of glory suggest the sunrise. The
youth is like the sun, which, as it travels farther from the east, leaves the
glory more and more behind it, and approaches prosaic daylight. But it is
the sun itself which projects the prosaic daylight, just as the man projects
the common day which surrounds him, and upon which he now looks
without joy.   (17)

I do not insist that we have to read the stanza as a consistent parallelism
between the growing boy and the rising sun. Certainly other metaphors
intrude: that of the darkening prison house, for example. But whether or
not we bring the dominant symbolism to the surface, there is no question, I
think, that it is at work within the stanza. And it *is* a symbolism: we are not
permitted to pick up the metaphors when we please and drop them when
we please. Light plays throughout the poem, and the "Ode," one must remember, closes with another scene in which sunlight again figures promi-
nently:

> *The Clouds that gather round the setting sun*
> *Do take a sober colouring from an eye*
> *That hath kept watch o'er man's mortality. . . .*

Here, by the way, the hint that it is the child who confers the "gleam" upon
the world becomes explicit. The clouds take their sober coloring from the
eye. Even if we make "eye" refer to the sun as the eye of day, we have but
brought the basic metaphors into closer relationship. If the sun, the eye of
heaven, after it has watched over mortality, is sobered, so is the eye of the
man who has kept the same watch. The parallel between the sun and the
developing child which we noticed in Stanza V is completed.   (18)

To some readers, however, the occurrence of the word "shades" may still
render such an interpretation bizarre. But such a reader will have to prepare himself to face another even more startling ambiguity in the central
symbol. Blindness and darkness in this poem are not the easy and expected
antitheses to vision and light. The climax of man's falling away from his
source is, as we have seen, not the settling down of complete darkness, but
of common day. In Stanza IX when the poet pays his debt of gratitude to
the childhood vision he actually associates it with blindness and darkness:

> *But for those obstinate questionings*
> *Of sense and outward things,*
> *Fallings from us, vanishings;*
> *Blank misgivings. . . .*

> *But for those first affections,*
> *Those shadowy recollections,*
>   *Which, be they what they may,*
> *Are yet the fountain light of all our day,*
> *Are yet a master light of all our seeing. . . .*

The supernal light, the master-light of all our seeing, is here made to flow from the shadowy recollections. Even if we argue that "shadowy" means merely "fitful," "fugitive," we shall still find it difficult to discount some connection of the word with shades and darkness. And if we consider the changing points of view in the "Ode," we shall see that it is inevitable that light should shift into dark and dark into light. For the man who has become immersed in the hard, white light of common day, the recollections of childhood are shadowy; just as from the standpoint of the poet, such a man, preoccupied with his analysis and dissection, must appear merely blind.

(19)

As a matter of fact, I think we shall have to agree that there is method in Wordsworth's paradoxes: he is trying to state with some sensitiveness the relation between the two modes of perception, that of the analytic reason and that of the synthesizing imagination. They do have their relationships; they are both ways of seeing. The ambiguities which light and darkness take on in this poem are, therefore, not confusions, as it seems to me, but necessary paradoxes.

(20)

A further treatment of the relationship in which Wordsworth is certainly making a conscious use of paradox seems to clinch the interpretation given. I refer to the passage in which the child is addressed as

> *Thou best Philosopher, who yet dost keep*
> *Thy heritage, thou Eye among the blind,*
> *That, deaf and silent, read'st the eternal deep. . . .*
>
> *Why with such earnest pains dost thou provoke*
> *The years to bring the inevitable yoke,*
> *Thus blindly with thy blessedness at strife?*

The child who sees, does not know that he sees, and is not even aware that others are blind. Indeed, he is trying his best (or soon will try his best) to become blind like the others. Yet, in this most extravagant passage in the poem, Wordsworth keeps the balance. In the child we are dealing with the isolated fact of vision.[1] The eye, taken as an organ of sense, is naturally deaf and silent. The child cannot tell what he reads in the eternal deep, nor can he hear the poet's warning that he is actually trying to cast away his vision. If the passage seems the high point of extravagance, it is

---

[1] Cf. I. A. Richards' discussion of this passage in *Coleridge on Imagination*, pp. 133ff.

also the high point of ironic qualification. How blind is he who, possessed
of rare sight, *blindly* strives to forfeit it and become blind!   (21)

   In pursuing the implications of the light-darkness symbolism, however,
I do not mean to lose sight of the "Ode" as a rhetorical structure. To this
matter—the alternation of mood, the balance of stanza against stanza,
the metrical devices by which the poet attempts to point up these contrasts
—to this matter, I shall be able to give very little attention. But I do not
mean to desert altogether the line of development of the poem. It is high
time to turn back to Stanzas III and IV.   (22)

   With Stanza III the emphasis is shifted from sight to sound. It is a very
cunning touch. The poet has lamented the passing of a glory from the
earth. But he can, he suggests, at least *hear* the mirth of the blessed creatures for whom the earth still wears that glory. Stanza III is dominated by
sound: the birds' songs, the trumpets of the cataracts, echoes, the winds—
presumably their sound—one can't *see* them. Even the gamboling of the
lambs is associated with a strong auditory image—"As to the tabor's sound."
Hearing these sounds, the poet tries to enter into the gaiety of the season.
He asks the shepherd boy to shout, and he goes on to say in Stanza IV,

> *Ye blessed Creatures, I have heard the call*
> *Ye to each other make. . . .*

The effect is that of a blind man trying to enter the joyful dawn world. He
can bear the blessed creatures as they rejoice in the world, but he himself
is shut out from it. If one argues against this as oversubtle—and perhaps it
is—and points out that after the poet says,

> *. . . . I have heard the call*
> *Ye to each other make*

he goes on immediately to say

> *I see*
> *The heavens laugh with you in your jubilee,*

we are not left entirely without a rejoinder. One can point out that at this
point another strong auditory image intervenes again to make sound the
dominant sense, not sight. One sees a smile, but laughter is vocal. The heavens are laughing with the children. The poet does in a sense enter into the
scene; certainly he is trying very hard to enter into it. But what I notice
is that the poet seems to be straining to work up a gaiety that isn't there.
If his heart is at the children's festival, it is their festival, after all, not his.
I hasten to add that this sense of a somewhat frenetically whipped-up enthusiasm is dramatically quite appropriate. (The metrical situation of the
stanza, by the way, would seem to support the view that the strained effect

is intentional.[2]) The poet under the influence of the morning scene, feeling the winds that blow "from the fields of sleep," tries to relive the dream. He fails.   (23)

But to return to the contrast between sight and sound, the poet should be saying at the climax of his ecstasy,

> *I see, I see, with joy I see*

not,

> *I hear, I hear, with joy I hear!*

Consequently, we are not surprised that the sudden collapse of his afflatus occurs in the very next line, and occurs with the first particular object which is concretely visualized in this stanza:

> *—But there's a Tree, of many, one,*
> *A single Field which I have looked upon . . .*

The influences of the May morning will no longer work.   (24)

I have already discussed the manner in which the first two stanzas of the "Ode" charge the imagery of the famous fifth stanza. I should like to take a moment to glance at another aspect of this stanza. The poet, in "explaining" the loss of vision, says,

> *Our birth is but a sleep and a forgetting. . . .*

The connection with

> *The glory and the freshness of a dream*

of Stanza I is obvious, but I think few have noticed that the expected relation between the two is neatly reversed. Our life's star is rising: it is dawn.

---

[2] I concede that it is quite possible that Wordsworth meant to convey no sense of strain—that the rhythm of the first part of the stanza may have pleased him absolutely and been intended to seem pleasing to others. But the cluster of feminine rimes and the syncopation of the rhythm, apparently meant to connote gaiety, are actually awkward as Wordsworth uses them here.

> *My heart is át your féstivál,*
> *My head háth its córonál. . . .*

Heart and *head* are the points of contrast. Yet the accents awkwardly distinguish between them.

> *Oh évil dáy! if Í were sullen*
> *While Eárth hersélf is adórning,*
> *   This swéet Máy mórning,*
> *And the chíldren are cúlling . . .*

There may be other ways to scan the lines, but I believe that there is no way to read the lines so as to get a quick, gay rhythm. We are to read rapidly lines which are not so constructed as to allow such rapidity with grace. Whatever Wordsworth's intention, the sense of strain fits perfectly the effect which the poem as a whole demands. Unfortunately, some of the quickstep of Stanza VII—

> *A wedding or a festival,*
> *A mourning or a funeral,*

lacks this kind of justification.

We expect the poet to say that the child, in being born, is waking up, deserting sleep and the realm of dream. But instead, our birth, he says, is a sleep and a forgetting. Reality and unreality, learning and forgetting, ironically change places.   (25)

Parallel ambiguities are involved in the use of "earth." In general, earth is made to serve as a foil for the celestial light. For example, when the poet writes,

> . . . when meadow, grove, and stream,
> The earth and every common sight,

it is almost as if he had said "even the earth," and this is the implication of "While earth *herself* is adorning," in Stanza IV. Yet, logically and grammatically, we can look back and connect "earth" with "meadow, grove, and stream"—all of which are aspects of earth—just as properly as we can look forward to connect "earth" with "every common sight." The poet himself is willing at times in the poem to treat the earth as the aggregate of all the special aspects of nature, at least of terrestrial nature. This surely is the sense of such a line as

> . . . there hath passed away a glory from the earth

where the emphasis suggests some such statement as: the whole world has lost its glory.   (26)

But these somewhat contradictory aspects of the word "earth" overlay a far more fundamental paradox: in general, we think of this poem as a celebration of the influence of nature on the developing mind, and surely, to a large degree, this is true. The poem is filled with references to valleys, mountains, streams, cataracts, meadows, the sea. Yet, though these aspects are so thoroughly interwoven with the spontaneous joy of the child which the poet has himself lost, it is the earth which is responsible for the loss. Stanza VI is concerned with this paradox:

> Earth fills her lap with pleasures of her own. . . .

What are these pleasures? They would seem to be suspiciously like the pleasures which engage the children on this May morning and in which the speaker of the poem regrets that he cannot fully indulge. It is true that the next stanza of the "Ode" does emphasize the fact that the world of human affairs, as the stanza makes clear, is seized upon by the child with joy, and that this is a process which is eminently "natural":

> Fretted by sallies of his mother's kisses,
> With light upon him from his father's eyes!   (27)

Earth, "even with something of a Mother's mind," "fills her lap with pleasures."

> *Yearnings she hath in her own natural kind.*

What are these yearnings but yearnings to involve the child with herself? We can translate "in her own natural kind" as "pertaining to her," "proper to the earth"; yet there is more than a hint that "natural" means "pertaining to nature," and are not the yearnings proper to the earth, *natural* in this sense, anyway?   (28)

In trying to make the child forget the unearthly or supernatural glory, the Earth is acting out of kindness. The poet cannot find it in him to blame her. She wants the child to be at home. Here we come close upon a Wordsworthian pun, though doubtless an unpremeditated pun. In calling the Earth "the homely Nurse" there seems a flicker of this suggestion: that Earth wants the child to be at home. Yet "homely" must surely mean also "unattractive, plain." [3] She is the drudging common earth after all, homely, perhaps a little stupid, but sympathetic, and kind. Yet it is precisely this Earth which was once glorious to the poet, "Apparelled in celestial light."   (29)

This stanza, though not one of the celebrated stanzas of the poem, is one of the most finely ironical. Its structural significance too is of first importance, and has perhaps in the past been given too little weight. Two of its implications I should like to emphasize. First, the stanza definitely insists that the human soul is not merely natural. We do not of course, as Wordsworth himself suggested, have to take literally the doctrine about pre-existence; but the stanza makes it quite clear, I think, that man's soul brings an alien element into nature, a supernatural element. The child is of royal birth—"that imperial palace whence he came"—the Earth, for all her motherly affection, is only his foster-mother after all. The submerged metaphor at work here is really that of the foundling prince reared by the peasants, though the phrase, "her Inmate Man," suggests an even more sinister relation: "Inmate" can only mean inmate of the prison-house of the preceding stanza.   (30)

The second implication is this: since the Earth is really homely, the stanza underlies what has been hinted at earlier: namely, that it is the child himself who confers the radiance on the morning world upon which he looks with delight. The irony is that if the child looks long enough at that world, becomes deeply enough involved in its beauties, the celestial radiance itself disappears.   (31)

In some respects, it is a pity that Wordsworth was not content to rely

---

[3] It has been objected that "homely" in British English does not have this sense. Perhaps it does not today, but see Milton's *Comus:*

> *It is for homely features to keep home,*
> *They had their name thence. . . .*

upon this imagery to make his point and that he felt it necessary to include the weak Stanza VII. Presumably, he thought the reader required a more explicit account. Moreover, Wordsworth is obviously trying to establish his own attitude toward the child's insight. In the earlier stanzas, he has attempted to define the quality of the visionary gleam, and to account for its inevitable loss. Now he attempts to establish more definitely his attitude toward the whole experience. One finds him here, as a consequence, no longer trying to recapture the childhood joy or lamenting its loss, but withdrawing to a more objective and neutral position. The function of establishing this attitude is assigned to Stanza VII. The poet's treatment of the child here is tender, but with a hint of amused patronage in the tenderness. There is even a rather timid attempt at humor. But even if we grant Wordsworth's intention, the stanza must still be accounted very weak, and some of the lines are very flat indeed. Moreover, the amused tenderness is pretty thoroughly over-balanced by the great stanza that follows. I am not sure that the poem would not be improved if Stanza VII were omitted.   (32)

If Stanza VII patronizes the child, Stanza VIII apparently exalts him. What is the poet's attitude here? Our decision as to what it is—that is, our decision as to what the poem is actually saying here—is crucial for our interpretation of the poem as a whole. For this reason I believe that it is worth going back over some of the ground already traversed.   (33)

Coleridge, one remembers, found the paradoxes which Wordsworth uses in Stanza VIII too startling. Several years ago, in his *Coleridge on Imagination*, I. A. Richards answered Coleridge's strictures. He replies to one of Coleridge's objections as follows:

> The syntax is "faulty" only in that the reader may be required to reflect. He may have to notice that *eye* is metaphorical already for *philosopher*—that the two conjointly then have a meaning that neither would have apart. "An idea in the mind is to a Natural Law as the power of seeing is to light," said Coleridge himself. As an eye, the philosopher is free from the need to do anything but respond to the laws of his being. *Deaf* and *silent* extend the metaphor by perfectly consentaneous movements. . . . The child will not hear (cannot understand) our words; and he will tell us nothing. That which Wordsworth would derive from him he cannot give; his silence (as we take it through step after step of interpretation, up to the point at which it negates the whole *overt* implication of the rest of Wordsworth's treatment) can become the most important point in the poem. We might look to Lao Tzu to support this: "Who knows speaks not; who speaks knows not." But it is enough to quote, from Coleridge himself, "the words with which Plotinus supposes NATURE to answer a similar difficulty. 'Should anyone interrogate her, how she works, if graciously she vouchsafe to listen and speak, she will reply, it

behoves thee not to disquiet me with interrogatories, but to understand in silence even as I am silent, and work without
words' "

(34)

Before going further with Richards, however, the reader may wonder
how far Wordsworth would be prepared to accept this defense of the lines,
particularly in view of Richards' statement that the child's silence *"can
become the most important point in the poem."* *Did* it become the most
important part for Wordsworth? And regardless of how we answer that
question, *does* it become such for us? How is it that the child is an eye
among the blind?

(35)

Because he "yet [doth] keep/[His] heritage"; because he still dreams and
remembers, for all that birth is a sleep and a forgetting; because he is still
near to God, who is our home. This, I take it, is what Richards calls the
"overt implication of . . . Wordsworth's treatment." But it is not so simple
as this in Wordsworth's poem. We have seen the hints of another interpretation: the suggestion that the child is like the moon which "with de-
light/Look[s] round her," and the association of the joyous vision of the
child with the child's own joyous activity, and further, with the joyous activity of the birds and the lambs. Is the poem theistic or pantheistic? Coleridge was certainly alive to the difficulties here. He went on to question:

> . . . In what sense can the magnificent attributes, above quoted,
> be appropriated to a *child,* which would not make them equally
> suitable to a *bee,* or a *dog,* or a *field of corn;* or even to a ship,
> or to the wind and waves that propel it?

Richards' answer is forthright:

> . . . why should Wordsworth deny that, in a much less degree,
> these attributes are equally suitable to a bee, or a dog, or a field
> of corn? What else had he been saying with his

> *And let the young lambs bound*
> *As to the tabor's sound!*

> And what else is Coleridge himself to say in Appendix B of his
> *Statesman's Manual?* "Never can I look and meditate on the
> vegetable creation without a feeling similar to that with which
> we gaze at a beautiful infant. . . .

(36)

Whatever Coleridge was to say later, there can be little doubt as to what
Wordsworth's poem says. The lambs and birds are undoubtedly included,
along with the children, in the apostrophe, "Ye blessed Creatures." It will

be difficult, furthermore, to argue that the poet means to exclude the moon, the stars, and the sun. (If Wordsworth would have excluded the bee and the dog, the exclusion, we may be sure, would have been made on other grounds—not philosophical but poetic.) The matter of importance for the development of the poem is, of course, that the child is father to the man, to the man Wordsworth, for example, as the birds, the lamb, and the moon are not. But it is also a point of first importance for the poem that the child, whatever he is to develop into later, possesses the harmony and apparent joy of all these blessed creatures. It may not be amiss here to remind ourselves of Coleridge's definition of joy with which Wordsworth himself must have been familiar: ". . . a consciousness of entire and therefore well being, when the emotional and intellectual faculties are in equipoise." (37)

Consider, in this general connection, one further item from the poem itself, the last lines from the famous recovery stanza, Stanza IX:

> *Nor all that is at enmity with joy,*
> *Can utterly abolish or destroy!*
> *Hence in a season of calm weather*
> *Though inland far we be,*
> *Our Souls have sight of that immortal sea*
> *Which brought us hither,*
> *Can in a moment travel thither,*
> *And see the Children sport upon the shore,*
> *And hear the mighty waters rolling evermore.*

Wordsworth has said that the child as the best philosopher "read'st the eternal deep," and here for the first time in the poem we have the children brought into explicit juxtaposition with the deep. And how, according to the poem, are these best philosophers reading it? By sporting on the shore. They are playing with their little spades and sand-buckets along the beach on which the waves break. This is the only explicit exhibit of their "reading" which the poem gives. It seems to corroborate Richards' interpretation perfectly. (38)

In writing this, I am not trying to provoke a smile at Wordsworth's expense. Far from it. The lines are great poetry. They are great poetry because, although the sea is the sea of eternity, and the mighty waters are rolling evermore, the children are not terrified—are at home—are filled with innocent joy. The children exemplify the attitude toward eternity which the other philosopher, the mature philosopher, wins to with difficulty, if he wins to it at all. For the children are those

> *On whom these truths do rest,*
> *Which we are toiling all our lives to find.*

The passage carries with it an ironic shock—the associations of innocence and joy contrasted with the associations of grandeur and terror—but it is the kind of shock which, one is tempted to say, is almost normal in the greatest poetry.   (39)

I asked a few moments ago how the child was an "Eye among the blind." The poem seems to imply two different, and perhaps hostile, answers: because the child is from God and still is close to the source of supernal light; *and*, because the child is still close to, and like, the harmonious aspects of nature, just as are the lamb or the bee or the dog. According to the first view, the child is an eye among the blind because his soul is filled with the divine; according to the second, because he is utterly natural. Can these two views be reconciled? And are they reconciled in the poem?   (40)

Obviously, the question of whether "divine" and "natural" can be reconciled in the child depends on the senses in which we apply them to the child. What the poem is saying, I take it, is that the child, because he is close to the divine, is utterly natural—natural in the sense that he has the harmony of being, the innocence, and the joy which we associate with the harmonious forms of nature. Undoubtedly Wordsworth found a symbol of divinity in such "beauteous forms" of nature; but the poem rests on something wider than the general context of Wordsworth's poetry: throughout the entire Christian tradition, the lamb, the lilies of the field, etc., have been used as such symbols.   (41)

But we may protest further and say that such a reading of "nature" represents a selection, and a loaded selection at that, one which has been made by Wordsworth himself—that there are other accounts of nature which will yield "naturalism" which is hostile to the claims to the divine. It is profitable to raise this question, because an attempt to answer it may provide the most fundamental explanation of all for the ambiguities and paradoxes which fill the "Ode."   (42)

Richards says that from "Imagination as a 'fact of mind'" there are "two doctrines which Coleridge (and Wordsworth) at times drew from it as to a life in or behind Nature." The two doctrines he states as follows:

> 1. The mind of the poet at moments, penetrating "the film of familiarity and selfish solicitude," gains an insight into reality, reads Nature as a symbol of something behind or within Nature not ordinarily perceived. [In the "Ode," the child, untarnished by "the film of familiarity and selfish solicitude," sees nature clad in a *celestial* light.]
>
> 2. The mind of the poet creates a Nature into which his own feelings, his aspirations and apprehensions, are projected. [In the "Ode," the child projects his own joy over nature as the moon projects its light over the bare heavens.]
>
> In the first doctrine man, through Nature, is linked with something other than himself which he perceives through her. In the second, he makes of her, as with a mirror, a transformed image of his own being.   (43)

But Richards interrupts the process of determining which of these doctrines Coleridge held and which, Wordsworth, to raise two questions which he suggests have a prior status: the questions are, namely, "(1) Are these doctrines necessarily in opposition to one another? (2) What is the relation of any such doctrine to the fact of mind from which it derives?" And Richards goes on to argue:

> The Imagination projects the life of the mind not upon Nature . . . [in the sense of the whole] field of the influences from without to which we are subject, but upon a Nature that is already a projection of our sensibility. The deadest Nature that we can conceive is already a Nature of our making. It is a Nature shaped by certain of our needs, and when we "lend to it a life drawn from the human spirit" it is reshaped in accordance with our other needs. [We may interrupt Richards to use Wordsworth's own phrasing from "Tintern Abbey": ". . . all this mighty world/ Of eye, and ear,—both what they half create,/ And what perceive . . ."] But our needs do not originate in us. They come from our relations to Nature . . . [as the whole field of influences from without]. We do not create the food that we eat, or the air that we breathe, or the other people we talk to; we do create, from our relations to them, every image we have "of" them. *Image* here is a betraying and unsatisfactory word; it suggests that these images, with which all that we can know is composed, are in some way insubstantial or unreal, mere copies of actualities other than themselves—figments. But *figment* and *real* and *substantial* are themselves words with no meaning that is not drawn from our experience. To say of anything that it is a figment seems to presuppose things more real than itself; but there is nothing within our knowledge more real than these images. To say that anything is an image suggests that there is something else to which it corresponds; but here all correspondence is between images. In short, the notion of reality derives from comparison between images, and to apply it as between images and things that are not images is an illegitimate extension which makes nonsense of it.
>
> This deceiving practice is an example of that process of abstraction which makes it almost inevitable that the two doctrines . . .—the projective and the realist doctrines of the life in Nature —should be conceived as contradictory. "If projected, not real; if real, not projected," we shall say, unless we are careful to recall that the meanings of *real* and *projected* derive from the imaginative fact of mind, and that when they are thus put in opposition they are products of abstraction and are useful only for other purposes than the comprehension of the fact of mind.   (44)

This is all very well, I can hear someone say; but even if we grant that the realist and projective doctrines are not necessarily in opposition, what warrant have we for believing that *Wordsworth* believed they were not in opposition? In trying to answer this objection, I should agree that merely to point out that both realist and projective doctrines seem to *occur* in the "Ode" is not to give an answer. We can argue for the reconciliation of these doctrines only if we can find where these doctrines impinge upon each other. Where do they meet? That is to say, where is the real center of the poem? What is the poem essentially about?   (45)

The poem is about the human heart—its growth, its nature, its development. The poem finds its center in what Richards has called the "fact of imagination." Theology, ethics, education are touched upon. But the emphasis is not upon these: Wordsworth's rather awkward note in which he repudiates any notion of trying to inculcate a belief in pre-existence would support this view. The greatness of the "Ode" lies in the fact that Wordsworth is about the poet's business here, and is not trying to inculcate anything. Instead, he is trying to dramatize the changing interrelations which determine the major imagery. And it is with this theme that the poem closes. Thanks are given, not to God—at least in this poem, not to God —but to

> . . . *the human heart by which we live,*
> *Thanks to its tenderness, its joys, and fears* . . .

It is because of the nature of the human heart that the meanest flower can give, if not the joy of the celestial light, something which the poet says is not sorrow and which he implies is deeper than joy: "Thoughts that do often lie too deep for tears."   (46)

If the poem is about the synthesizing imagination, that faculty by which, as a later poet puts it,

> *Man makes a superhuman*
> *Mirror-resembling dream*

the reason for the major ambiguities is revealed. These basic ambiguities, by the way, assert themselves as the poem ends. Just before he renders thanks to the human heart, you will remember, the poet says that the clouds do not give *to*, but take *from*, the eye their sober coloring. But in the last two lines of the stanza, the flower does not take *from*, but gives *to*, the heart. We can have it either way. Indeed, the poem implies that we must have it *both* ways. And we are dealing with more than optics. What the clouds take from the eye is more than a sober coloring—the soberness is from the mind and heart. By the same token, the flower, though it gives a color—gives more, it gives thought and emotion.   (47)

It has not been my purpose to present this statement of the theme as a discovery; it is anything but that. Rather, I have tried to show how the imagery of the poem is functionally related to a theme—not vaguely and loosely related to it—and how it therefore renders that theme powerfully, and even exactly, defining and refining it. But I can make no such claim for such precision in Wordsworth's treatment of the "resolution," the recovery. In a general sense we know what Wordsworth *is* doing here: the childhood vision is only one aspect of the "primal sympathy"; this vision has been lost —is, as the earlier stanzas show, inevitably lost—but the primal sympathy remains. It is the faculty by which we live. The continuity between child and man is actually unbroken.   (48)

But I must confess that I feel the solution is asserted rather than dramatized. Undoubtedly, we can reconstruct from Wordsworth's other writings the relationship between the primal sympathy and the joy, the "High instincts" and the "soothing thoughts," but the relationship is hardly digested into poetry in the "Ode." And some of the difficulties with which we meet in the last stanzas appear to be not enriching ambiguities but distracting confusions: e.g., the years bring the philosophical mind, but the child over which the years are to pass is already the best philosopher. There is "something" that remains alive in our embers, but it is difficult for the reader to define it in relation to what has been lost. If we make a desperate effort to extend the implied metaphor—if we say that the celestial light is the flame which is beautiful but which must inevitably burn itself out— the primal sympathy is the still-glowing coal—we are forced to realize that such extension is overingenious. The metaphor was not meant to bear so much weight. With regard to this matter of imagery, it would be interesting to compare with the "Ode" several poems by Vaughan which embody a theme very closely related to that of the "Ode." And lest this remark seem to hint at an inveterate prejudice in favor of the metaphysicals, I propose another comparison: a comparison with several of Yeats's poems which deal with still another related theme: unity of being and the unifying power of the imagination. Such comparisons, I believe, would illuminate Wordsworth's difficulties and account for some of the "Ode's" defects. Yet, in closing this account of the "Ode," I want to repudiate a possible misapprehension. I do not mean to say that the general drift of the poem does not come through. It does. I do not mean that there is not much greatness in the poem. There is. But there is some vagueness—which is not the same thing as the rich multiplicity of the greatest poetry; and there are some loose ends, and there is at least one rather woeful anticlimax.   (49)

But if the type of analysis to which we have subjected the "Ode" is calculated to indicate such deficiences by demanding a great deal of the imagery, it is only fair to remind the reader that it focuses attention on the brilliance and power of the imagery, a power which is sustained almost throughout the poem, and with which Wordsworth has hardly been sufficiently credited in the past. Even the insistence on paradox does not create the defects in the "Ode"—the defects have been pointed out before—but it may help account for them. Indeed, one can argue that we can perhaps best understand the virtues and the weaknesses of the "Ode" if we see that what Wordsworth wanted to say demanded his use of paradox, that it could only be said powerfully through paradox, and if we remember in what suspicion Wordsworth held this kind of poetic strategy.   (50)

Oscar Cargill

(1898–   )

CARGILL is professor emeritus of English at New York University; for almost two decades he served as chairman of the department. Though trained in English literature of the Middle Ages, he turned his later energies to the development of studies in American literature. His years of dedication to the study of Henry James culminated in a critical work of major proportions, The Novels of Henry James *(1961).*

■ *Toward a Pluralistic Criticism*

THE FUNCTION of the critic and scholar is to make the past functional, for unless it can be used, it is deader than death itself. The only alternative is to adopt the view of Antoine Roquetin, Jean-Paul Sartre's non-hero, that the past has no existence, a thesis which does more than alienate him from bourgeoise society—it negates all continuity, all history, all culture and renders scholarship and criticism impotent. Such an assault on animal wisdom, however, compels definition, or at least description. What is the past?

Where does it begin and where does it end? Psychologists and philosophers enforce the presentness of the past by telling us that by the time our
very inadequate perceptive apparatus reports an event it is already historic, and the very notion of the present is a conventional fiction. The past is
time, or what we live in. The slippery present is that which has too much
concerned the existentialists, certainly emotionally; but a paradoxical love
of books shows how easy it would be to accept time or continuity. To
emend Descartes, from whom they really take their being, "I think, therefore I exist *in time.*" With any sense of the all-enveloping past one cannot
be a complete disaffiliate.   (1)

In literature, ostensibly, the great generation of the twenties exhibited
the fullest sort of consciousness of continuity: *Remembrance of Things
Past, Ulysses, The Waste Land, Look Homeward, Angel,* all seemed to be
documents in support of the affirmation of the ever-presence of the past.
Such, doubtless, their authors intended them to be, but was that saliently
their effect? Loneliness and alienation are themes in each of them; analogues, parallels, symbols, and metaphors from the past in each one of them
are lost in the dubious hero's swamping, dismal present. Did not they prepare the way for Camus, Sartre, Ionesco, and Duerrenmatt? Did not much
that transpired in intellectual circles, in education, prepare the way? Reverence for the past was undermined in the academies in the twenties and
thirties. Ancient history and Latin disappeared from the lower schools; today, anything resembling the orderly presentation of English and American literature in the colleges is following after. Much is said of the virtue of
studying only masterpieces, but when the *Iliad* jostles *The Divine Comedy,*
and the latter, *King Lear,* all sense of time is lost, and these masterpieces
become companion works to *Crime and Punishment* and *Death in Venice,*
if not to *Catcher in the Rye* and *Herzog.* In the ingenious presentations of
instructors who confine themselves to the work itself, that is, the work in a
modern translation, these masterpieces take on a contemporaneity scarcely
achieved by the latest novel. Virgil in *The Divine Comedy,* like Ulysses
before him, becomes a father image and Achilles, sulking in his tent, is a
symbol of onanism. But alas, when so old-fashioned a person as I makes
what he thinks is an illuminating comparison between *The Rime of the Ancient Mariner* and *The Waste Land,* he is met by blank stares—only four
persons in the class have read Coleridge's poem. It has been relegated, possibly, to a deeper past than the *Iliad.* Thus the most valuable element in
time, the sense of continuity, the sense of having a tradition, is lost for the
young.   (2)

Our appropriation of the master works of the West seems to have more
in common with the indiscriminate accumulations of the newspaper millionaire, William Randolph Hearst, than with the slow and painful assimila-
tions of Bernard Berenson. We rape from frame and setting to adorn our

own tales or to trigger a specious erudition. Unlike Hearst, however, we are very cautious not to carry away too much. This caution came from the vice of the previous age, when American literary scholarship reached a peak in the work of E. K. Rand, George Lyman Kittredge, Carleton Brown, W. W. Lawrence, Edwin Greenlaw, and others. The enormous erudition of these scholars, their supersaturation with the past, staggered and baffled younger minds until they made a liberating discovery—in the interest of frame and setting, in the interest of biography, their teachers were neglecting the work of art itself or burying it under mounds of "useless knowledge" from which it never could be excavated. The sensitive and intuitive John Livingston Lowes, author of *Convention and Revolt in Poetry*, undertook to correct the balance in *The Road to Xanadu*, but he was much too late. As early as 1920 T. S. Eliot was proclaiming that the essential critical function is "elucidation," not of the artist but of the work of art. The revolt against the *impedimenta* of scholarship went so far that it actually detached the artist from his creation. "Never trust the artist, trust the tale," declared D. H. Lawrence. The most iconoclastic position reached in this revolt is that of Marcel Proust in *Contre Sainte-Beuve*, in which Proust ridiculed all attempts to document the life of an author, asserting that quite a different ego produces the work of art from the ego which inhabits the common walks of life. A similar extremism severed the work of art from the "past" of its creation. "To appreciate a work of art," wrote Clive Bell, "we need bring with us nothing from life, no knowledge of its ideas and affairs, no familiarity with its emotions." Of the masterpiece, A. C. Bradley declared, "Its nature is not to be a part, nor a copy of the real world . . . , but a world in itself, independent, complete, autonomous."   (3)

Having separated the masterpiece from its creator and from its place in time, the new critic concentrated with great intensity upon elucidating the text itself. He found, we may infer from Cleanth Brooks, that he had to address an audience which could not read, since neglect of the masterpiece for facts about it and its author had caused the faculty of apprehension to atrophy. With John Crowe Ransom, Allen Tate, Robert Penn Warren, R. P. Blackmur, and others, Mr. Brooks set out to remedy this defect. That the method which they championed, *explication de texte*, had long been employed at the high school level in France, in the *lycée*, is no condemnation of it: very elementary beginnings had to be made. Whether "dry-as-dust" scholarship was responsible for general illiteracy or (as I think) neglect of composition (which forces attention on the text) in the lower schools is immaterial, *Americans could not read*. Even the errors made by some of the explicators only substantiate the fact. Regardless of whether or not the methods of the new critics provided a richer appreciation, it must be granted that they accomplished a major miracle—they taught some few Americans to read.   (4)

One of the announced aims of the new critic was not to interpose his own personality between the reader and the work itself. He saw that this was the equivalent, if not worse, of allowing the workaday ego of the author to interpose. The critic would deny his own ego, his hunger for recognition, for the ideal end of perfectly interpreting the text before him. Granted the human condition, however, he was utterly incapable of achieving this end. Yet it is important that we note its unearthly character, its metaphysical nature. Only a writer completely cut off from the world, only a perpetual dweller among masterpieces, only an academic—such as all new critics became—could utter such nonsense and, at least partially, believe it. For only the universities provided the proper pasturage for this kind of gamboling and, lest weeds and underbrush get in, the new critics in the main concentrated on the classics of the literature of the past, erecting stiles against current literature. F. R. Leavis, the Cambridge don who founded a magazine to scrutinize texts and kept it going for twenty years, illustrated the impossibility of a depersonalized criticism operating upon a depersonalized literature—he created a school of *obita dictarists* who ever looked anxiously to him for the Word. In the main, the new critics found that the first principles they had drawn up were narrow and stultifying and, without announcing it, they one after another abandoned them. It has been said that Cleanth Brooks is the only remaining new critic, the only one tenaciously attached to the text. The others have adopted a variety of methods: they have specialized in aesthetic structure, sociological background, morals, psychology, and myths—each, however, a champion of his own special method.   (5)

Meanwhile, although crowded into the more stony part of the pasture, and scarcely visible over the high fences, research scholars in the universities had continued to exist. Indeed, in the very years when the new criticism rocked the academies, research scholarship recorded some of its most remarkable achievements. Almost anyone can enumerate a few examples of literary scholarship that seem to be more perdurable than anything produced by the whole corps of new critics: the editing of the *Diaries* of Samuel Johnson by Edward L. McAdam, Jr., and of Thackeray's *Letters* by Gordon Ray, *The Young Shelley* by Kenneth Cameron, and the study of the mind of Walt Whitman by Gay Allen. What in the new criticism can compare with Perry Miller's investigations of Puritan culture, Thomas H. Johnson's detective work in determining the text and order of Emily Dickinson's poetry, Jay Leyda's *The Melville Log*, the editions of the letters of Pope, Keats, Coleridge, and George Eliot by George Sherburn, Hyder Rollins, Earl Griggs, and Gordon Haight, respectively, and the astonishing critical life of James Joyce by Richard Ellmann? From their labors the scholars occasionally turned aside to expose gleefully the limitations of a new criticism that depended largely on impressionism, intuition, clairvoyance, and extrasensory perception. Douglas Bush had most sport at this and delighted his colleagues. Who can forget his definition of the new criticism as "an advanced course in remedial reading"? When John Crowe Ransom wondered over Shakespeare's use of the phrase "dusty death," calling it "an odd but winning detail," Bush reminded him that the same odd but winning detail is in the Bible and *The Book of Common Prayer,* with which Shakespeare was doubtless familiar. Lillian Hornstein deflated some of the pretentiousness of Caroline Spurgeon's *Shakespeare's Imagery,* an offshoot of the new criticism, in much the same way. (6)

Though the scholars scored heavily off the critics, they themselves found the new criticism properly admonitory. Scholars wish today to be taken also for critics, and with justice they may so be regarded, for they at last have learned to emphasize the creations of the artist above his sources, background, and life, while retaining illumination from the latter. The critics, on the other hand, because they have confined their work to classics and have found the newest classics ever receding into the past, are coming more and more to respect biography and history and to take simple excursions into them. Because of their academic associations some of them undeniably have discovered it pleasing to be regarded as scholarly if not as scholars. Their choice of specialized methods applied to the all-inclusive past propels them further along the way so that a harmonizing of interests seems imminent. My present concern, however, is not to scrutinize this process but to consider the values in individual programs that might prove useful in a synthesis. (7)

Quite aware that he must work in defiance of criticism's ukase against biography, Leon Edel has become the champion of the "art of literary biography," an art which should involve a complete critical knowledge of the works of the author. Unlike the biographer of Chaucer or Shakespeare, the modern literary biographer is all but overwhelmed by his materials. "How different," Mr. Edel remarks enviously, "is the task of the critic, especially the 'new critic'! His table, in contrast to the biographer's, is uncluttered. No birth certificates, no deeds, no letters, no diaries, no excess literary baggage: only the works, to be read and re-read, pondered and analysed. . . . The literary biographer, however, must at every moment of his task be a critic. His is an act of continual and unceasing criticism." All of us who have read the first three volumes of Edel's unfinished life of Henry James realize how much he has done to restore biography to an acceptable literary standard for both criticism and scholarship, despite the fact that Henry James himself had taken many steps to defeat him, declaring at twenty-nine, before he had written his first novel, "artists, as time goes on will be likely to take alarm, empty their table-drawers and level the approaches to their privacy. The critics, psychologists and gossip mongers may then glean amid the stubble." The life of Henry James is no pinwheel accomplishment, like

Strachey's *Eminent Victorians* or Thomas Beer's *Stephen Crane,* but a substantial and enduring literary work.   (8)

Freudian literary criticism, a generic term for all types of analysis dealing with the creative psyche, has been one of the easiest methods for the
former new critics to resort to, for it contains no inherent compulsion to
abandon the text. Freud himself, equipped with a considerable knowledge
of literature and a keen sensibility, provided models for this kind of criticism. In *The Interpretation of Dreams,* for example, he suggested that Hamlet's unconscious guilt arising from his own Oedipal desires inhibited Hamlet from avenging his father. "Hamlet is able to do anything but take
vengeance upon the man who did away with his father and has taken his father's place with his mother—the man who shows him in realization the repressed desires of his own childhood. The loathing which should have
driven him to revenge is thus repressed by conscientious scruples which tell
him that he himself is no better than the murderer whom he is required to
punish." Capricious and unorthodox, D. H. Lawrence employs his own version of the method with such startling skill at times that Edmund Wilson
has declared *Studies in Classic American Literature* to be "one of the few
first-rate books to have been written on the subject." Here is Lawrence's interpretation of the close of *The Scarlet Letter:* "Right to the end Dimmesdale must have his saintly triumphs. He must preach his Election Sermon,
and win his last saintly applause. At the same time he has an almost im-
becile, epileptic impulse to defile the religious reality he exists in. In
Dimmesdale at this time lies the whole clue to Dostoevsky."   (9)

It is no response to the Freudian critic to say that an author's intention
was something other than the critic's interpretation, for the Freudian critic
may know the author's motivation better than the author himself; indeed,
once literature is confined to the couch, the Freudian speaks with an authority no other critic can assume. Yet a suspicion lingers that Mr. Leslie
Fiedler is not always right when he assumes that every pure maiden in
American fiction is but a cover for the author's animosity toward all women,
and with difficulty we repress the cry, "Physician, heal thyself." Leon Edel
properly cautions the Freudian to examine his grounds of attraction to, or
repulsion from, an author as a basis for determining his critical stances, and
this appears to be the area of real vulnerability for the Freudian. If I may
tease my truly distinguished colleague, I might observe that he has sometimes appeared to feel that he might have made a better brother, in a situation of sibling rivalry, to Henry James than did William. It is a curious fact
that both Henry and his biographer have philosopher brothers. That the
subconscious mind of an artist is the reservoir of his invention is generally
conceded. The "infamous insurance scheme" which constitutes the plot of
The Wings of the Dove I find exists in a French novel that James had read
thirty-five years earlier and possibly had forgotten. Who can say, however,
that a process of gestation was not going on in his subconscious mind? (10)

Plot parallels suggest not merely an immediate borrowing from a literary predecessor but the possibility of a remote prototype or common ancestor for similar works. This idea is basic to Sir James Frazer's great work, *The Golden Bough,* in which this Scottish anthropologist traced numerous myths back to their prehistoric and ritualistic beginnings. Carl Jung's theory that the subconscious of man is a storehouse of racial, as well as personal, history reinforced the importance of myth in creative life, and T. S. Eliot's confession that Miss Jessie Weston's *From Ritual to Romance* had influenced the creation of *The Waste Land* pointed out to the new critics a path for exploration when they found *explication de texte* too narrow a ground. Although certain British critics—F. M. Cornford, Jane Harrison, Gilbert Murray, and Andrew Lang—had dealt previously with the ritualistic background of Greek myths, it is Maud Bodkin in *Archetypal Patterns in Modern Poetry* who introduces the methods of Frazer and Jung into the study of modern literature and provides models for others to follow. Hamlet, the prime anatomical target for critical surgery in the last three hundred years, is astonishingly carved and served by Miss Bodkin. Probing the wound opened by Freud and enlarged by Ernest Jones, she accepts Hamlet as the victim of an Oedipal situation, but both Claudius and the elder Hamlet are components of the "father image," thus setting up a conflict, or "inner tension," which can only be relieved by the death of the tragic hero. The hero develops toward himself an ambivalent attitude resulting in an ego desiring self-assertion and an ego craving surrender to a greater power than itself, "the community consciousness." Thus the death of Hamlet becomes a submission or sacrifice to the tribe, like the ritual sacrifice of a king or sacred animal for the renewal of the life of the tribe. This is the significance of Hamlet's final charge to Horatio to "draw thy breath in pain,/To tell my story." Now, I find this ingenious and even fascinating, but I wonder if it is criticism. If all the great literature of the world can be reduced to a few mythological rites or archetypal patterns, do not the distinctions between works, as Professor Meyer H. Abrams contends, become less and less, and vanish? Archetypal criticism, even though it satisfies Mr. Eliot's criterion of elucidation, moves steadily away from works of art (the area of criticism) to folk superstitions (the area of the anthropologist and folklorist). (11)

Yet if tribal rites, which symbolize elemental social processes, can be shown as buried in the racial subconscious and related in even the vaguest way to the creative psyche, why does not this fact validate the use the writer makes of his economic and social background as a means of evaluating him? Surely as much of the creative act is conscious as unconscious. Surely modern society has as many rituals of which the artist is aware as tribal rites of which he is unconscious but by which he is influenced. Mr. Eliot did not get his contempt for the Jew, the Irish, and the Cockney out of Miss Weston's book, but out of his experience, out of his connection with

Lloyd's bank, his reaction to the Irish rebellion, his acquaintance with London pubs, and out of the vulgar stereotypes of his society. How is one to elucidate or scrutinize Steinbeck's *The Grapes of Wrath* with no reference to the Dust Bowl, the tractoring out of the Okies, or the labor practices of the farmers' association of California? Yet it was fully as much against sociological criticism as biographical criticism that the new criticism rebelled. Such books as Edmund Wilson's *To the Finland Station* or Granville Hicks's *The Great Tradition* seem, in retrospect, more in the nature of political tracts than works of criticism. They were, however, phenomena of the depression, and Wilson and Hicks, as well as Lionel Trilling, employing the social background of writers whom they examine, without a political *parti pris*, seem to me as able critics as America possesses. Irving Howe and Norman Podhoritz, also, with this approach, have on occasion written analyses of high merit. The lesson learned is that, while a writer's social views affect his judgment and may properly be remarked and weighed, we must ever—and without ambivalence—keep his work as an artist to the fore.   (12)

Mere elucidation must have appeared in this discussion increasingly inadequate as a definition of the function of criticism. While sticking to his contention that "poetry is not the inculcation of morals, or the direction of politics," Eliot admitted, in his Preface to the second edition of *The Sacred Wood*, that poetry did have "something to do with morals, and with religion, and even with politics," though he could not say what. Less hesitant than he, a group of writers, of whom Mr. Ivor Winters is the best known, have emphasized a moral approach to literature. In an essay called "Robert Frost, or the Spiritual Drifter as Poet" Winters declares, as a result of examining four carefully selected poems, to which "The Road Not Taken" is the key, that Frost has neither "the intelligence or energy to become a major poet." The substance of the poem is very familiar: facing the choice of divergent roads in a wood, Frost chose the least traveled one and declares his choice has "made all the difference." Winters concedes that the poet has described a comprehensible predicament—"his poem is good as far as it goes, [but] . . . it does not go far enough, it is incomplete, and it puts on the reader a burden of critical intelligence which ought to be borne by the poet." This is a just stricture, so far as this particular poem is concerned, and more or less just in regard to the companion pieces. But the selective process through which Winters condemns Frost has been somehow characteristic of moral criticism: the human limitation, whatever it is, looms larger than the general conduct of the man. Frost is no spiritual drifter in "The Black Cottage," "New Hampshire," "To a Thinker," or dozens of other poems. If "poetry is the record of the best and happiest moments," as Shelley thought, "of the best and happiest minds," it is essentially ethical, for who can imagine a superior mind finding delight in the discomfort of others? Since literature ceased providing, in the early years of our century, examples of superior conduct, as in Tom Tulliver, Henry Esmond, Captain McWhirr, and Max Gottlieb, and confined itself to the lot of the underprivileged and the outcast, its motivation has been empathy. Empathy by its very nature is ethical—it assumes redemptive power in a situation. The business of the critic is then, so far as it is ethical, to determine the quality of the empathy. Is it bathetic? Is it directed toward worthless objects? Does the author lower himself or degrade society to raise his object? So many of the answers lie in psychology and sociology that a critic, giving appreciative attention, needs to be very sure of his training before he does so; nevertheless, this is an area for fair employment of his sensibilities, and at the moment his emphasis in criticism is most needed and rarest. (13)

The chief defect, however, of an approach to literature through only one method is the presumption that, if pursued with the utmost efficiency, it should extract all the values of a work of art. Yet if art in any sense mirrors life, it mirrors a complexity unyielding to a monist approach. I cannot go so far as Mr. Eliot and assert a poem means whatever it means to a reader, for this might reduce it to having no meaning at all, but I am willing to concede to a masterpiece many powers of ever renewing the delight it gives. Ours is a pluralistic universe, to borrow a phrase from William James, a universe without stability, its order ever threatened by disorder, a universe of contingency and change. In so far as the work of art mirrors that universe it must partake somewhat of its pluralism, even of its transiency. "Values are as unstable as the forms of clouds," John Dewey tells us. "Cultivated taste alone is capable of prolonged appreciation of the same object; and it is capable of it because it has been trained to a discriminating procedure which constantly uncovers in the object new meanings to be perceived and enjoyed." Forgotten and recovered meanings are also capable of producing delight. The instability of the very language in which a poem is written is at once a defect and a virtue: original meanings decay but the language takes on new meanings conveying new pleasures. Yet as compared with life itself, it has a relative kind of transient fixity, a retarded instability of meaning. These are the qualities that attract the reader away from the uncertainty of life to art. It is the relative "permanence" of art that solicits continuous attention fully as much as its other values. The obligation of the critic is to approach the work of art with every faculty, with every technique, with every method he can command, for he must know not only what the poem probably meant to its creator but also what it probably means to several different kinds of readers in his own generation if he is to communicate his appreciation and delight to them. In a word, he must have the keenest sense of time to deal with the pluralistic values of any given work of art; he must himself be a pluralist, athletically able to keep receding values in view, willing to embrace new values as they come on, in order to dispense in acceptable language an appreciation appropriate to the sensibilities of the youngest of his generation as the purest form of judgment. His role, if properly understood, is neither that of ambassador of the old nor ambassador of the new, for each is a partisan, but of liaison officer between the two. It is the role of both scholar and critic.   (14)

Institute for Propaganda Analysis

*THE INSTITUTE FOR PROPAGANDA ANALYSIS, INC. was announced in October, 1937—*Propaganda Analysis: A Monthly Letter to Help the Intelligent Citizen Detect and Analyze Propaganda. *The monthly letter was "circulated privately to educators and students, publishers and journalists, business men and trade unionists, ministers and welfare workers, and to all who desire periodic, objective appraisals of today's propagandas, their sources and the channels through which they flow: newspapers, magazines, radio stations, motion pictures, labor and business groups, patriotic societies, farm organizations, schools, churches, political parties." The following article constituted the substance of the second number of the publication.*

■ *How to Detect Propaganda*

WE ARE FOOLED by propaganda chiefly because we don't recognize it when we see it. It may be fun to be fooled but, as the cigarette ads used to say, it is more fun to know. We can more easily recognize propaganda when we see it if we are familiar with the seven common propaganda devices. These are:

1. The Name Calling Device
2. The Glittering Generalities Device
3. The Transfer Device

Why are we fooled by these devices? Because they appeal to our emotions rather than to our reason. They make us believe and do something we would not believe or do if we thought about it calmly, dispassionately. In examining these devices, note that they work most effectively at those times when we are too lazy to think for ourselves; also, they tie into emotions which sway us to be "for" or "against" nations, races, religions, ideals, economic and political policies and practices, and so on through automobiles, cigarettes, radios, toothpastes, presidents, and wars. With our emotions stirred, it may be fun to be fooled by these propaganda devices, but it is more fun and infinitely more to our own interests to know how they work.   (2)

Lincoln must have had in mind citizens who could balance their emotions with intelligence when he made his remark: ". . . but you can't fool all of the people all of the time."   (3)

Name Calling

"Name Calling" is a device to make us form a judgment without examining the evidence on which it should be based. Here the propagandist appeals to our hate and fear. He does this by giving "bad names" to those individuals, groups, nations, races, policies, practices, beliefs, and ideals which he would have us condemn and reject. For centuries the name "heretic" was bad. Thousands were oppressed, tortured, or put to death as heretics. Anybody who dissented from popular or group belief or practice was in danger of being called a heretic. In the light of today's knowledge, some heresies were bad and some were good. Many of the pioneers of modern science were called heretics; witness the cases of Copernicus, Galileo, Bruno. (See "A History of the Warfare of Science with Theology," Andrew Dickson White, D. Appleton & Co.) Today's bad names include: Fascist, demagogue, dictator, Red, financial oligarchy, Communist, muckraker, alien, outside agitator, economic royalist, Utopian, rabble-rouser, trouble-maker, Tory, Constitution wrecker.   (4)

"Al" Smith called Roosevelt a Communist by implication when he said in his Liberty League speech, "There can be only one capital, Washington or Moscow." When "Al" Smith was running for the presidency many called him a tool of the Pope, saying in effect, "We must choose between Washington and Rome." That implied that Mr. Smith, if elected President, would take his orders from the Pope. Recently, Mr. Justice Hugo Black has been associated with a bad name, Ku Klux Klan. In these cases some propagandists have tried to make us form judgments without examining essential evidence and implications. "Al Smith is a Catholic. He must never be President." "Roosevelt is a Red. Defeat his program." "Hugo Black is or was a Klansman. Take him out of the Supreme Court."   (5)

Use of "bad names" without presentation of their essential meaning, without all their pertinent implications, comprises perhaps the most common of all propaganda devices. Those who want to *maintain* the status quo apply bad names to those who would change it. For example, the Hearst press applies bad names to Communists and Socialists. Those who want to *change* the status quo apply bad names to those who would maintain it. For example, the Daily Worker and the American Guardian apply bad names to conservative Republicans and Democrats.   (6)

Glittering Generalities

"Glittering Generalities" is a device by which the propagandist identifies his program with virtue by use of "virtue words." Here he appeals to our emotions of love, generosity, and brotherhood. He uses words like truth, freedom, honor, liberty, social justice, public service, the right to work, loyalty, progress, democracy, the American way, Constitution defender. These words suggest shining ideals. All persons of good will believe in these ideals. Hence the propagandist, by identifying his individual group, nation, race, policy, practice, or belief with such ideals, seeks to win us to his cause. As Name Calling is a device to make us form a judgment to *reject and condemn*, without examining the evidence, Glittering Generalities is a device to make us *accept and approve*, without examining the evidence. (7)

For example, use of the phrases, "the right to work" and "social justice" may be a device to make us accept programs for meeting the labor-capital problem which, if we examined them critically, we would not accept at all.   (8)

In the Name Calling and the Glittering Generalities devices, words are used to stir up our emotions and to befog our thinking. In one device "bad words" are used to make us mad; in the other "good words" are used to make us glad. (See "The Tyranny of Words," by Stuart Chase, in *Harpers Magazine* for November, 1937.)   (9)

The propagandist is most effective in use of these devices when his words make us create devils to fight or gods to adore. By his use of the "bad words," we personify as a "devil" some nation, race, group, individual, policy, practice, or ideal; we are made fighting mad to destroy it. By use of "good words," we personify as a god-like idol some nation, race, group, etc. Words which are "bad" to some are "good" to others, or may be made so. Thus, to some the New Deal is "a prophecy of social salvation" while to others it is "an omen of social disaster."   (10)

From consideration of names, "bad" and "good," we pass to institutions and symbols, also "bad" and "good." We see these in the next device. (11)

Transfer

"Transfer" is a device by which the propagandist carries over the authority, sanction, and prestige of something we respect and revere to something he would have us accept. For example, most of us respect and revere our church and our nation. If the propagandist succeeds in getting church or nation to approve a campaign in behalf of some program, he thereby transfers its authority, sanction, and prestige to that program. Thus we may accept something which otherwise we might reject.   (12)

In the Transfer device symbols are constantly used. The cross represents the Christian Church. The flag represents the nation. Cartoons like Uncle Sam represent a consensus of public opinion. Those symbols stir emotions. At their very sight, with the speed of light, is aroused the whole complex of feelings we have with respect to church or nation. A cartoonist by having Uncle Sam disapprove a budget for unemployment relief would have us feel that the whole United States disapproves relief costs. By drawing an Uncle Sam who approves the same budget, the cartoonist would have us feel that the American people approve it. Thus, the Transfer device is used both for and against causes and ideas.   (13)

Testimonial

The "Testimonial" is a device to make us accept anything from a patent medicine or a cigarette to a program of national policy. In this device the propagandist makes use of testimonials. "When I feel tired, I smoke a Camel and get the grandest 'lift'." "We believe the John Lewis plan of labor organization is splendid; C.I.O. should be supported." This device works in reverse also; counter-testimonials may be employed. Seldom are these used against commercial products like patent medicines and cigarettes, but they are constantly employed in social, economic, and political issues. "We believe that the John Lewis plan of labor organization is bad; C.I.O. should not be supported."   (14)

Plain Folks

"Plain Folks" is a device used by politicians, labor leaders, business men, and even by ministers and educators to win our confidence by appearing to be people like ourselves—"just plain folks among the neighbors." In election years especially do candidates show their devotion to little children and the common, homey things of life. They have front porch campaigns. For the newspaper men they raid the kitchen cupboard, finding there some

of the good wife's apple pie. They go to country picnics; they attend service at the old frame church; they pitch hay and go fishing; they show
their belief in home and mother. In short, they would win our votes by
showing that they're just as common as the rest of us—"just plain folks,"—
and, therefore, wise and good. Business men often are "plain folks" with the
factory hands. Even distillers use the device. "It's our family's whiskey,
neighbor; and neighbor, it's your price."   (15)

Card Stacking

"Card Stacking" is a device in which the propagandist employs all the
arts of deception to win our support for himself, his group, nation, race,
policy, practice, belief or ideal. He stacks the cards against the truth. He
uses under-emphasis and over-emphasis to dodge issues and evade facts.
He resorts to lies, censorship, and distortion. He omits facts. He offers false
testimony. He creates a smoke-screen of clamor by raising a new issue
when he wants an embarrassing matter forgotten. He draws a red herring
across the trail to confuse and divert those in quest of facts he does not
want revealed. He makes the unreal appear real and the real appear unreal.
He lets half-truth masquerade as truth. By the Card Stacking device, a
mediocre candidate, through the "build-up," is made to appear an intellectual titan; an ordinary prize fighter a probable world champion; a worthless patent medicine a beneficent cure. By means of this device propagandists would convince us that a ruthless war of aggression is a crusade for
righteousness. Some member nations of the Non-Intervention Committee
send their troops to intervene in Spain. Card Stacking employs sham, hypocrisy, effrontery.   (16)

The Band Wagon

The "Band Wagon" is a device to make us follow the crowd, to accept
the propagandist's program en masse. Here his theme is: "Everybody's doing it." His techniques range from those of medicine show to dramatic
spectacle. He hires a hall, fills a great stadium, marches a million men in
parade. He employs symbols, colors, music, movement, all the dramatic
arts. He appeals to the desire, common to most of us, to "follow the crowd."
Because he wants us to "follow the crowd" in masses, he directs his appeal
to groups held together by common ties of nationality, religion, race, environment, sex, vocation. Thus propagandists campaigning for or against a
program will appeal to us as Catholics, Protestants, or Jews; as members
of the Nordic race or as Negroes; as farmers or as school teachers; as housewives or as miners. All the artifices of flattery are used to harness the fears
and hatreds, prejudices and biases, convictions and ideals common to the

group; thus emotion is made to push and pull the group on to the Band Wagon. In newspaper articles and in the spoken word this device is also found. "Don't throw your vote away. Vote for our candidate. He's sure to win." Nearly every candidate wins in every election—before the votes are in.

(17)

Propaganda and Emotion

Observe that in all these devices our emotion is the stuff with which propagandists work. Without it they are helpless; with it, harnessing it to their purposes, they can make us glow with pride or burn with hatred, they can make us zealots in behalf of the program they espouse. As we said in our first letter, propaganda as generally understood is expression of opinion or action by individuals or groups with reference to predetermined ends. Without the appeal to our emotion—to our fears and to our courage, to our selfishness and unselfishness, to our loves and to our hates—propagandists would influence few opinions and few actions.   (18)

To say this is not to condemn emotion, an essential part of life, or to assert that all predetermined ends of propagandists are "bad." What we mean is that the intelligent citizen does not want propagandists to utilize his emotions, even to the attainment of "good" ends, without knowing what is going on. He does not want to be "used" in the attainment of ends he may later consider "bad." He does not want to be gullible. He does not want to be fooled. He does not want to be duped, even in a "good" cause. He wants to know the facts and among these is included the fact of the utilization of his emotions.   (19)

For better understanding of the relationship between propaganda and emotion see Ch. 1 of *Folkways* by William Graham Sumner (Ginn and Company). This shows why most of us tend to feel, believe, and act in traditional patterns. See also *Mind in the Making* by James Harvey Robinson (Harper Bros.). This reveals the nature of the mind and suggests how to analyze propaganda appealing to traditional thought patterns.   (20)

Keeping in mind the seven common propaganda devices, turn to today's newspapers and almost immediately you can spot examples of them all. At election time or during any campaign, Plain Folks and Band Wagon are common. Card Stacking is hardest to detect because it is adroitly executed or because we lack the information necessary to nail the lie. A little practice with the daily newspapers in detecting these propaganda devices soon enables us to detect them elsewhere—in radio, news-reel, books, magazines, and in expressions of labor unions, business groups, churches, schools, political parties.   (21)

Samuel T. Williamson

(1891–1962)

WILLIAMSON throughout his long career (1916–1962) brought a salty New England realism to the volatile world of journalism and a "down-Eastern philosophy" from the rock-bound coast of Maine to the arena of American politics. He joined the New York Times *upon graduation from Harvard and except for two periods (1916–1918, as a soldier; 1933–1938, as first editor of* Newsweek*) continued to be identified with it: as a staff member, as White House correspondent, as an assistant Sunday editor, and as a free-lance contributor to the Magazine section.*

■ *How to Write Like a Social Scientist*

DURING MY YEARS as an editor, I have seen probably hundreds of job applicants who were either just out of college or in their senior years. All wanted "to write." Many brought letters from their teachers. But I do not recall one letter announcing that its bearer could write what he wished to say with clarity and directness, with economy of words, and with pleasing variety of sentence structure.   (1)

Most of these young men and women could not write plain English. Apparently their noses had not been rubbed in the drudgery of putting one simple, well-chosen word behind the other. If this was true of teachers' pets, what about the rest? What about those going into business and industry? Or those going into professions? What about those who remain at college—first for a Master of Arts degree, then an instructorship combined with work for a Ph.D., then perhaps an assistant professorship, next a full professorship and finally, as an academic crown of laurel, appointment as head of a department or as dean of a faculty?   (2)

Certainly, faculty members of a front-rank university should be better able to express themselves than those they teach. Assume that those in the English department have this ability: Can the same be said of the social scientists—economists, sociologists, and authorities on government? We need today as we never needed so urgently before all the understanding they can give us of problems of earning a living, caring for our fellows, and governing ourselves. Too many of them, I find, can't write as well as their students. (3)

I am still convalescing from over-exposure some time ago to products of the academic mind. One of the foundations engaged me to edit the manuscripts of a socio-economic research report designed for the thoughtful citizen as well as for the specialist. My expectations were not high—no deathless prose, merely a sturdy, no-nonsense report of explorers into the wilderness of statistics and half-known fact. I knew from experience that economic necessity compels many a professional writer to be a cream-skimmer and a gatherer of easily obtainable material; for unless his publisher will stand the extra cost, he cannot afford the exhaustive investigation which endowed research makes possible. Although I did not expect fine writing from a trained, professional researcher, I did assume that a careful fact-finder would write carefully. (4)

And so, anticipating no literary treat, I plunged into the forest of words of my first manuscript. My weapons were a sturdy eraser and several batteries of sharpened pencils. My armor was a thesaurus. And if I should become lost, a near-by public library was a landmark, and the *Encyclopedia of Social Sciences* on its references shelves was an ever-ready guide. (5)

Instead of big trees, I found underbrush. Cutting through involved, lumbering sentences was bad enough, but the real chore was removal of the burdocks of excess verbiage which clung to the manuscript. Nothing was big or large; in my author's lexicon, it was "substantial." When he meant "much," he wrote "to a substantially high degree." If some event took place in the early 1920's, he put it "in the early part of the decade of the twenties." And instead of "that depends," my author wrote, "any answer to this question must bear in mind certain peculiar characteristics of the industry." (6)

So it went for 30,000 words. The pile of verbal burdocks grew—sometimes twelve words from a twenty-word sentence. The shortened version of 20,000 words was perhaps no more thrilling than the original report; but it was terser and crisper. It took less time to read and it could be understood quicker. That was all I could do. As S. S. McClure once said to me, "An editor can improve a manuscript, but he cannot put in what isn't there." (7)

I did not know the author I was editing; after what I did to his copy, it may be just as well that we have not met. Aside from his cat-chasing-its-own-tail verbosity, he was a competent enough workman. Apparently he is well thought of. He has his doctorate, he is a trained researcher and a pupil of an eminent professor. He has held a number of fellowships and he has performed competently several jobs of economic research. But, after this long academic preparation for what was to be a life work, it is a mystery why so little attention was given to acquiring use of simple English.   (8)

Later, when I encountered other manuscripts, I found I had been too hard on this promising Ph.D. Tone-deaf as he was to words, his report was a lighthouse of clarity among the chapters turned in by his so-called academic betters. These brethren—and sister'n—who contributed the remainder of the foundation's study were professors and assistant professors in our foremost colleges and universities. The names of one or two are occasionally in newspaper headlines. All of them had, as the professorial term has it, "published."   (9)

Anyone who edits copy, regardless of whether it is good or bad, discovers in a manuscript certain pet phrases, little quirks of style and other individual traits of its author. But in the series I edited, all twenty reports read alike. Their words would be found in any English dictionary, grammar was beyond criticism, but long passages in these reports demanded not editing but actual translation. For hours at a time, I floundered in brier patches like this: "In eliminating wage changes due to purely transitory conditions, collective bargaining has eliminated one of the important causes of industrial conflict, for changes under such conditions are almost always followed by a reaction when normal conditions appear." (10)

I am not picking on my little group of social scientists. They are merely members of a caste; they are so used to taking in each other's literary washing that it has become a habit for them to clothe their thoughts in the same smothering verbal garments. Nor are they any worse than most of their colleagues, for example:

> In the long run, developments in transportation, housing, optimum size of plant, etc., might tend to induce an industrial and demographic pattern similar to the one that consciousness of vulnerability would dictate. Such a tendency might be advanced by public persuasion and governmental inducement, and advanced more effectively if the causes of urbanization had been carefully studied.   (11)

Such pedantic Choctaw may be all right as a sort of code language or shorthand of social science to circulate among initiates, but its perpetrators have no right to impose it on others. The tragedy is that its users appear to be under the impression that it is good English usage.   (12)

Father, forgive them; for they know not what they do! There once was a time when everyday folk spoke one language, and learned men wrote another. It was called the Dark Ages. The world is in such a state that we may return to the Dark Ages if we do not acquire wisdom. If social scientists have answers to our problems yet feel under no obligation to make themselves understood, then we laymen must learn their language. This may take some practice, but practice should become perfect by following six simple rules of the guild of social science writers. Examples which I give are sound and well tested; they come from manuscripts I edited.   (13)

RULE 1. *Never use a short word when you can think of a long one.* Never say "now" but "currently." It is not "soon" but "presently." You did not have "enough" but a "sufficiency." Never do you come to the "end" but to the "termination." This rule is basic.   (14)

RULE 2. *Never use one word when you can use two or more.* Eschew "probably." Write, "it is improbable," and raise this to "it is not improbable." Then you'll be able to parlay "probably" into "available evidence would tend to indicate that it is not unreasonable to suppose."   (15)

RULE 3. *Put one-syllable thought into polysyllabic terms.* Instead of observing that a work force might be bigger and better, write, "In addition to quantitative enlargement, it is not improbable that there is need also for qualitative improvement in the personnel of the service." If you have discovered that musicians out of practice can't hold jobs, report that "the fact of rapid deterioration of musical skill when not in use soon converts the employed into the unemployable." Resist the impulse to say that much men's clothing is machine made. Put it thus: "Nearly all operations in the industry lend themselves to performance by machine, and all grades of men's clothing sold in significant quantity involve a very substantial amount of machine work."   (16)

RULE 4. *Put the obvious in terms of the unintelligible.* When you write that "the product of the activity of janitors is expended in the identical locality in which that activity takes place," your lay reader is in for a time of it. After an hour's puzzlement, he may conclude that janitors' sweepings are thrown on the town dump. See what you can do with this: "Each article sent to the cleaner is handled separately." You become a member of the guild in good standing if you put it like this: "Within the cleaning plant proper the business of the industry involves several well-defined processes, which, from the economic point of view, may be characterized simply by saying that most of them require separate handling of each individual garment or piece of material to be cleaned."   (17)

RULE 5. *Announce what you are going to say before you say it.* This pitcher's wind-up technique before hurling towards—not at—home plate has two varieties. First is the quick wind-up: "In the following sections the policies of the administration will be considered." Then you become strong enough for the contortionist wind-up: "Perhaps more important, therefore, than the question of what standards are in a particular case, there are the questions of the extent of observance of these standards and the methods of their enforcement." Also, you can play with reversing Rule 5 and *say what you have said after you have said it.*   (18)

RULE 6. *Defend your style as "scientific."* Look down on—not up to— clear, simple English. Sneer at it as "popular." Scorn it as "journalistic." Explain your failure to put more mental sweat into your writing on the ground that "the social scientists who want to be scientific believe that we can have scientific description of human behavior and trustworthy predictions in the scientific sense only as we build adequate taxonomic systems for observable phenomena and symbolic systems for the manipulation of ideal and abstract entities."   (19)

For this explanation I am indebted to Lyman Bryson in an *SRL* article (Oct. 13, 1945) "Writers: Enemies of Social Science." Standing on ground considerably of his own choosing, Mr. Bryson argued against judging social science writing by literary standards.   (20)

Social scientists are not criticized because they are not literary artists. The trouble with social science does not lie in its special vocabulary. Those words are doubtless chosen with great care. The trouble is that too few social scientists take enough care with words outside their special vocabularies.   (21)

It is not too much to expect that teachers should be more competent in the art of explanation than those they teach. Teachers of social sciences diligently try to acquire knowledge; too few of them exert themselves enough to impart it intelligently.   (22)

Too long has this been excused as "the academic mind." It should be called by what it is: intellectual laziness and grubby-mindedness.   (23)

George Orwell

(1903–1950)

ORWELL (pen name of Eric Blair), English novelist, essayist, and critic, was a colorful gentleman-radical: he served with the Imperial Police in Burma, lived as a vagabond in Paris and London, and fought on the Republican side in the Spanish Civil War. His most popular novels are Animal Farm (1945) and 1984 (1949), penetrating satires of the totalitarianism of the extreme Right and the extreme Left.

◼ *Politics and the English Language*

MOST PEOPLE who bother with the matter at all would admit that the English language is in a bad way, but it is generally assumed that we cannot by conscious action do anything about it. Our civilization is decadent and our language—so the argument runs—must inevitably share in the general collapse. It follows that any struggle against the abuse of language is a sentimental archaism, like preferring candles to electric light or hansom cabs to aeroplanes. Underneath this lies the half-conscious belief that language is a natural growth and not an instrument which we shape for our own purposes.   (1)

Now, it is clear that the decline of a language must ultimately have political and economic causes: it is not due simply to the bad influence of this or that individual writer. But an effect can become a cause, reinforcing the original cause and producing the same effect in an intensified form, and so on indefinitely. A man may take to drink because he feels himself to be a failure, and then fail all the more completely because he drinks.

It is rather the same thing that is happening to the English language. It becomes ugly and inaccurate because our thoughts are foolish, but the slovenliness of our language makes it easier for us to have foolish thoughts. The point is that the process is reversible. Modern English, especially written English, is full of bad habits which spread by imitation and which can be avoided if one is willing to take the necessary trouble. If one gets rid of these habits one can think more clearly, and to think clearly is a necessary first step toward political regeneration: so that the fight against bad English is not frivolous and is not the exclusive concern of professional writers. I will come back to this presently, and I hope that by that time the meaning of what I have said here will have become clearer. Meanwhile, here are five specimens of the English language as it is now habitually written. (2)

These five passages have not been picked out because they are especially bad—I could have quoted far worse if I had chosen—but because they illustrate various of the mental vices from which we now suffer. They are a little below the average, but are fairly representative samples. I number them so that I can refer back to them when necessary:

(1) I am not, indeed, sure whether it is not true to say that the Milton who once seemed not unlike a seventeenth-century Shelley had not become, out of an experience ever more bitter in each year, more alien [*sic*] to the founder of that Jesuit sect which nothing could induce him to tolerate.

Professor Harold Laski
(Essay in *Freedom of Expression*)

(2) Above all, we cannot play ducks and drakes with a native battery of idioms which prescribes such egregious collocations of vocables as the Basic *put up with* for *tolerate* or *put at a loss* for *bewilder*.

Professor Lancelot Hogben (*Interglossa*)

(3) On the one side we have the free personality: by definition it is not neurotic, for it has neither conflict nor dream. Its desires, such as they are, are transparent, for they are just what institutional approval keeps in the forefront of consciousness; another institutional pattern would alter their number and intensity; there is little in them that is natural, irreducible, or culturally dangerous. But *on the other side,* the social bond itself is nothing but the mutual reflection of these self-secure integrities. Recall the definition of love. Is not this the very picture of a small academic? Where is there a place in this hall of mirrors for either personality or fraternity?

Essay on psychology in *Politics* (New York)

(4) All the "best people" from the gentlemen's clubs, and all the frantic fascist captains, united in common hatred of Socialism and bestial horror of the rising tide of the mass revolutionary movement, have turned to acts of provocation, to foul incendiarism, to medieval legends of poisoned wells, to legalize their own destruction of proletarian organizations, and rouse the agitated petty-bourgeoisie to chauvinistic fervor on behalf of the fight against the revolutionary way out of the crisis.

Communist pamphlet

(5) If a new spirit *is* to be infused into this old country, there is one thorny and contentious reform which must be tackled, and that is the humanization and galvanization of the B.B.C. Timidity here will bespeak canker and atrophy of the soul. The heart of Britain may be sound and of strong beat, for instance, but the British lion's roar at present is like that of Bottom in Shakespeare's *Midsummer Night's Dream*—as gentle as any sucking dove. A virile new Britain cannot continue indefinitely to be traduced in the eyes or rather ears, of the world by the effete languors of Langham Place, brazenly masquerading as "standard English." When the Voice of Britain is heard at nine o'clock, better far and infinitely less ludicrous to hear aitches honestly dropped than the present priggish, inflated, inhibited, school-ma'amish arch braying of blameless bashful mewing maidens!

Letter in Tribune   (3)

Each of these passages has faults of its own, but, quite apart from avoidable ugliness, two qualities are common to all of them. The first is staleness of imagery; the other is lack of precision. The writer either has a meaning and cannot express it, or he inadvertently says something else, or he is almost indifferent as to whether his words mean anything or not. This mixture of vagueness and sheer incompetence is the most marked characteristic of modern English prose, and especially of any kind of political writing. As soon as certain topics are raised, the concrete melts into the abstract and no one seems able to think of turns of speech that are not hackneyed: prose consists less and less of *words* chosen for the sake of their meaning, and more and more of *phrases* tacked together like the sections of a prefabricated henhouse. I list below, with notes and examples, various of the tricks by means of which the work of prose-construction is habitually dodged.   (4)

Dying metaphors. A newly invented metaphor assists thought by evoking a visual image, while on the other hand a metaphor which is technically "dead" (e.g. *iron resolution*) has in effect reverted to being an ordinary word and can generally be used without loss of vividness. But in between these two classes there is a huge dump of worn-out metaphors which have lost all evocative power and are merely used because they save people the trouble of inventing phrases for themselves. Examples are: *Ring the changes on, take up the cudgels for, toe the line, ride roughshod over, stand shoulder to shoulder with, play into the hands of, no axe to grind, grist to the mill, fishing in troubled waters, on the order of the day, Achilles' heel, swan song, hotbed.* Many of these are used without knowledge of their meaning (what is a "rift," for instance?), and incompatible metaphors are frequently mixed, a sure sign that the writer is not interested in what he is saying. Some metaphors now current have been twisted out of their original meaning without those who use them even being aware of the fact. For example, *toe the line* is sometimes written *tow the line.* Another example is *the hammer and the anvil,* now always used with the implication that the anvil gets the worst of it. In real life it is always the anvil that breaks the hammer, never the other way about: a writer who stopped to think what he was saying would be aware of this, and would avoid perverting the original phrase.   (5)

Operators or *verbal false limbs.* These save the trouble of picking out appropriate verbs and nouns, and at the same time pad each sentence with extra syllables which give it an appearance of symmetry. Characteristic phrases are *render inoperative, militate against, make contact with, be subjected to, give rise to, give grounds for, have the effect of, play a leading part (role) in, make itself felt, take effect, exhibit a tendency to, serve the purpose of, etc., etc.* The keynote is the elimination of simple verbs. Instead of being a single word, such as *break, stop, spoil, mend, kill,* a verb becomes a *phrase,* made up of a noun or adjective tacked on to some general-purpose verb such as *prove, serve, form, play, render.* In addition, the passive voice is wherever possible used in preference to the active, and noun constructions are used instead of gerunds (*by examination of* instead of *by examining*). The range of verbs is further cut down by means of the *-ize* and *de-* formations, and the banal statements are given an appearance of profundity by means of the *not un-* formation. Simple conjunctions and prepositions are replaced by such phrases as *with respect to, having regard to, the fact that, by dint of, in view of, in the interests of, on the hypothesis that;* and the ends of sentences are saved by anticlimax by such resounding commonplaces as *greatly to be desired, cannot be left out of account, a development to be expected in the near future, deserving of serious consideration, brought to a satisfactory conclusion,* and so on and so forth.   (6)

Pretentious diction. Words like *phenomenon, element, individual* (as noun), *objective, categorical, effective, virtual, basic, primary, promote, con-*

stitute, exhibit, exploit, utilize, eliminate, liquidate, are used to dress up simple statement and give an air of scientific impartiality to biased judgments. Adjectives like *epoch-making, epic, historic, unforgettable, triumphant, age-old, inevitable, inexorable, veritable,* are used to dignify the sordid processes of international politics, while writing that aims at glorifying war usually takes on an archaic color, its characteristic words being: *realm, throne, chariot, mailed fist, trident, sword, shield, buckler, banner, jackboot, clarion.* Foreign words and expressions such as *cul de sac, ancien régime, deus ex machina, mutatis mutandis, status quo, gleichschaltung, weltanschauung,* are used to give an air of culture and elegance. Except for the useful abbreviations *i.e., e.g.,* and *etc.,* there is no real need for any of the hundreds of foreign phrases now current in English. Bad writers, and especially scientific, political, and sociological writers, are nearly always haunted by the notion that Latin or Greek words are grander than Saxon ones, and unnecessary words like *expedite, ameliorate, predict, extraneous, deracinated, clandestine, subaqueous,* and hundreds of others constantly gain ground from their Anglo-Saxon opposite numbers.[1] The jargon peculiar to Marxist writing (*hyena, hangman, cannibal, petty bourgeois, these gentry, lackey, flunkey, mad dog, White Guard,* etc.) consists largely of words and phrases translated from Russian, German, or French; but the normal way of coining a new word is to use a Latin or Greek root with the appropriate affix and, where necessary, the size formation. It is often easier to make up words of this kind (*deregionalize, impermissible, extramarital, nonfragmentary* and so forth) than to think up the English words that will cover one's meaning. The result, in general, is an increase in slovenliness and vagueness. (7)

Meaningless words. In certain kinds of writing, particularly in art criticism and literary criticism, it is normal to come across long passages which are almost completely lacking in meaning.[2] Words like *romantic, plastic, values, human, dead, sentimental, natural, vitality,* as used in art criticism, are strictly meaningless, in the sense that they not only do not point to any discoverable object, but are hardly ever expected to do so by the reader. When one critic writes, "The outstanding feature of Mr. X's work is its living quality," while another writes, "The immediately striking thing about Mr. X's work is its peculiar deadness," the reader accepts this as a simple difference of opinion. If words like *black* and *white* were involved,

---

1 An interesting illustration of this is the way in which the English flower names which were in use till very recently are being ousted by Greek ones, *snapdragon* becoming *antirrhinum, forget-me-not* becoming *myosotis,* etc. It is hard to see any practical reason for this change of fashion: it is probably due to an instinctive turning away from the more homely word and a vague feeling that the Greek word is scientific.

2 Example: "Comfort's catholicity of perception and image, strangely Whitmanesque in range, almost the exact opposite in aesthetic compulsion, continues to evoke that trembling atmospheric accumulative hinting at a cruel, an inexorably serene timelessness. . . . Wrey Gardiner scores by aiming at simple bull's-eyes with precision. Only they are not so simple, and through this contented sadness runs more than the surface bittersweet of resignation." (*Poetry Quarterly.*)

instead of the jargon words *dead* and *living,* he would see at once that language was being used in an improper way. Many political words are similarly abused. The word *Fascism* has now no meaning except in so far as it signifies "something not desirable." The words *democracy, socialism, freedom, patriotic, realistic, justice,* have each of them several different meanings which cannot be reconciled with one another. In the case of a word like *democracy,* not only is there no agreed definition, but the attempt to make one is resisted from all sides. It is almost universally felt that when we call a country democratic we are praising it: consequently the defenders of every kind of régime claim that it is a democracy, and fear that they might have to stop using the word if it were tied down to any one meaning. Words of this kind are often used in a consciously dishonest way. That is, the person who uses them has his own private definition, but allows his hearer to think he means something quite different. Statements like *Marshal Pétain was a true patriot, The Soviet press is the freest in the world, The Catholic Church is opposed to persecution,* are almost always made with intent to deceive. Other words used in variable meanings, in most cases more or less dishonestly, are: *class, totalitarian, science, progressive, reactionary, bourgeois, equality.* (8)

Now that I have made this catalogue of swindles and perversions, let me give another example of the kind of writing that they lead to. This time it must of its nature be an imaginary one. I am going to translate a passage of good English into modern English of the worst sort. Here is a well-known verse from *Ecclesiastes:*

> I returned and saw under the sun, that the race is not to the swift, nor the battle to the strong, neither yet bread to the wise, nor yet riches to men of understanding, nor yet favour to men of skill; but time and chance happeneth to them all. (9)

Here it is in modern English:

> Objective considerations of contemporary phenomena compels the conclusion that success or failure in competitive activities exhibits no tendency to be commensurate with innate capacity, but that a considerable element of the unpredictable must invariably be taken into account. (10)

This is a parody, but not a very gross one. Exhibit (3), above, for instance, contains several patches of the same kind of English. It will be seen that I have not made a full translation. The beginning and ending of the sentence follow the original meaning fairly closely, but in the middle the concrete illustrations—race, battle, bread—dissolve into the vague phrase "success or failure in competitive activities." This had to be so, because no modern writer of the kind I am discussing—no one capable of using phrases

like "objective consideration of contemporary phenomena"—would ever tab-
ulate his thoughts in that precise and detailed way. The whole tendency of
modern prose is away from concreteness. Now analyze these two sentences
a little more closely. The first contains forty-nine words but only sixty syllables, and all its words are those of everyday life. The second contains
thirty-eight words of ninety syllables: eighteen of its words are from Latin
roots, and one from Greek. The first sentence contains six vivid images, and
only one phrase ("time and chance") that could be called vague. The second
contains not a single fresh, arresting phrase, and in spite of its ninety syllables it gives only a shortened version of the meaning contained in the first.
Yet without a doubt it is the second kind of sentence that is gaining ground
in modern English. I do not want to exaggerate. This kind of writing is not
yet universal, and outcrops of simplicity will occur here and there in the
worst-written page. Still, if you or I were told to write a few lines on the
uncertainty of human fortunes, we should probably come much nearer to
my imaginary sentence than to the one from *Ecclesiastes.*   (11)

As I have tried to show, modern writing at its worst does not consist
in picking out words for the sake of their meaning and inventing images
in order to make the meaning clearer. It consists in gumming together long
strips of words which have already been set in order by someone else,
and making the results presentable by sheer humbug. The attraction of
this way of writing is that it is easy. It is easier—even quicker, once you
have the habit—to say *In my opinion it is not an unjustifiable assumption
that* than to say *I think.* If you use ready-made phrases, you not only don't
have to hunt about for words; you also don't have to bother with the
rhythms of your sentences, since these phrases are generally so arranged as
to be more or less euphonious. When you are composing in a hurry—when
you are dictating to a stenographer, for instance, or making a public speech
—it is natural to fall into a pretentious, Latinized style. Tags like *a consideration which we should do well to bear in mind* or *a conclusion to which
all of us would readily assent* will save many a sentence from coming down
with a bump. By using stale metaphors, similes, and idioms, you save
much mental effort, at the cost of leaving your meaning vague, not only
for your reader but for yourself. This is the significance of mixed metaphors. The sole aim of a metaphor is to call up a visual image. When these
images clash—as in *The Fascist octopus has sung its swan song, the jackboot is thrown into the melting pot*—it can be taken as certain that the
writer is not seeing a mental image of the objects he is naming; in other
words he is not really thinking. Look again at the examples I gave at the
beginning of this essay. Professor Laski (1) uses five negatives in fifty-
three words. One of these is superfluous, making nonsense of the whole
passage, and in addition there is the slip—*alien* for akin—making further nonsense, and several avoidable pieces of clumsiness which increase the gen-

eral vagueness. Professor Hogben (2) plays ducks and drakes with a battery which is able to write prescriptions, and, while disapproving of the
everyday phrase *put up with,* is unwilling to look *egregious* up in the
dictionary and see what it means; (3), if one takes an uncharitable attitude towards it, is simply meaningless: probably one could work out its
intended meaning by reading the whole of the article in which it occurs.
In (4), the writer knows more or less what he wants to say, but an accumulation of stale phrases chokes him like tea leaves blocking a sink. In (5),
words and meaning have almost parted company. People who write in this
manner usually have a general emotional meaning—they dislike one thing
and want to express solidarity with another—but they are not interested in
the detail of what they are saying. A scrupulous writer, in every sentence
that he writes, will ask himself at least four questions, thus: What am I
trying to say? What words will express it? What image or idiom will make
it clearer? Is this image fresh enough to have an effect? And he will probably ask himself two more: Could I put it more shortly? Have I said anything that is avoidably ugly? But you are not obliged to go to all this trouble. You can shirk it by simply throwing your mind open and letting the
ready-made phrases come crowding in. They will construct your sentences
for you—even think your thoughts for you, to a certain extent—and at need
they will perform the important service of partially concealing your meaning even from yourself. It is at this point that the special connection between politics and the debasement of language becomes clear.   (12)

In our time it is broadly true that political writing is bad writing. Where
it is not true, it will generally be found that the writer is some kind of
rebel, expressing his private opinions and not a "party line." Orthodoxy, of
whatever color, seems to demand a lifeless, imitative style. The political dialects to be found in pamphlets, leading articles, manifestoes, White Papers
and the speeches of undersecretaries do, of course, vary from party to
party, but they are all alike in that one almost never finds in them a fresh,
vivid, home-made turn of speech. When one watches some tired hack on
the platform mechanically repeating the familiar phrases—*bestial atroci-
ties, iron heel, bloodstained tyranny, free peoples of the world, stand
shoulder to shoulder*—one often has a curious feeling that one is not watching a live human being but some kind of dummy: a feeling which suddenly
becomes stronger at moments when the light catches the speaker's spectacles and turns them into blank discs which seem to have no eyes behind
them. And this is not altogether fanciful. A speaker who uses that kind of
phraseology has gone some distance toward turning himself into a machine.
The appropriate noises are coming out of his larynx, but his brain is not
involved as it would be if he were choosing his words for himself. If the
speech he is making is one that he is accustomed to make over and over
again, he may be almost unconscious of what he is saying, as one is when

one utters the responses in church. And this reduced state of consciousness, if not indispensable, is at any rate favorable to political conformity. (13)

In our time, political speech and writing are largely the defense of the indefensible. Things like the continuance of British rule in India, the Russian purges and deportations, the dropping of the atom bombs on Japan, can indeed be defended, but only by arguments which are too brutal for most people to face, and which do not square with the professed aims of political parties. Thus political language has to consist largely of euphemism, question-begging and sheer cloudy vagueness. Defenseless villages are bombarded from the air, the inhabitants driven out into the countryside, the cattle machine-gunned, the huts set on fire with incendiary bullets: this is called *pacification*. Millions of peasants are robbed of their farms and sent trudging along the roads with no more than they can carry: this is called *transfer of population* or *rectification of frontiers*. People are imprisoned for years without trial, or shot in the back of the neck or sent to die of scurvy in Arctic lumber camps: this is called *elimination of unreliable elements*. Such phraseology is needed if one wants to name things without calling up mental pictures of them. Consider for instance some comfortable English professor defending Russian totalitarianism. He cannot say outright, "I believe in killing off your opponents when you can get good results by doing so." Probably, therefore, he will say something like this: (14)

"While freely conceding that the Soviet régime exhibits certain features which the humanitarian may be inclined to deplore, we must, I think, agree that a certain curtailment of the right to political opposition is an unavoidable concomitant of transitional periods, and that the rigors which the Russian people have been called upon to undergo have been amply justified in the sphere of concrete achievement." (15)

The inflated style is itself a kind of euphemism. A mass of Latin words falls upon the facts like soft snow, blurring the outlines and covering up all the details. The great enemy of clear language is insincerity. When there is a gap between one's real and one's declared aims, one turns as it were instinctively to long words and exhausted idioms, like a cuttlefish squirting out ink. In our age there is no such thing as "keeping out of politics." All issues are political issues, and politics itself is a mass of lies, evasions, folly, hatred, and schizophrenia. When the general atmosphere is bad, language must suffer. I should expect to find—this is a guess which I have not sufficient knowledge to verify—that the German, Russian and Italian languages have all deteriorated in the last ten or fifteen years, as a result of dictatorship. (16)

But if thought corrupts language, language can also corrupt thought. A bad usage can spread by tradition and imitation, even among people who should and do know better. The debased language that I have been discussing is in some ways very convenient. Phrases like *a not unjustifiable assumption, leaves much to be desired, would serve no good purpose, a consideration which we should do well to bear in mind*, are a continuous temptation, a packet of aspirins always at one's elbow. Look back through this essay, and for certain you will find that I have again and again committed the very faults I am protesting against. By this morning's post I have received a pamphlet dealing with conditions in Germany. The author tells me that he "felt impelled" to write it. I open it at random, and here is almost the first sentence that I see: "[The Allies] have an opportunity not only of achieving a radical transformation of Germany's social and political structure in such a way as to avoid a nationalistic reaction in Germany itself, but at the same time of laying the foundations of a co-operative and unified Europe." You see, he "feels impelled" to write—feels, presumably, that he has something new to say—and yet his words, like cavalry horses answering the bugle, group themselves automatically into the familiar dreary pattern. This invasion of one's mind by ready-made phrases (*lay the foundations, achieve a radical transformation*) can only be prevented if one is constantly on guard against them, and every such phrase anaesthetizes a portion of one's brain.   (17)

I said earlier that the decadence of our language is probably curable. Those who deny this would argue, if they produced an argument at all, that language merely reflects existing social conditions, and that we cannot influence its development by any direct tinkering with words and constructions. So far as the general tone or spirit of a language goes, this may be true, but it is not true in detail. Silly words and expressions have often disappeared, not through any evolutionary process but owing to the conscious action of a minority. Two recent examples were *explore every avenue* and *leave no stone unturned*, which were killed by the jeers of a few journalists. There is a long list of flyblown metaphors which could similarly be got rid of if enough people would interest themselves in the job; and it should also be possible to laugh the *not un-* formation out of existence,[3] to reduce the amount of Latin and Greek in the average sentence, to drive out foreign phrases and strayed scientific words, and, in general, to make pretentiousness unfashionable. But all these are minor points. The defense of the English language implies more than this, and perhaps it is best to start by saying what it does *not* imply.   (18)

To begin with it has nothing to do with archaism, with the salvaging of obsolete words and turns of speech, or with the setting up of a "standard English" which must never be departed from. On the contrary, it is especially concerned with the scrapping of every word or idiom which has outworn its usefulness. It has nothing to do with correct grammar and syntax,

---

3 One can cure oneself of the *not un-* formation by memorizing this sentence: *A not unblack dog was chasing a not unsmall rabbit across a not ungreen field.*

which are of no importance so long as one makes one's meaning clear, or with the avoidance of Americanisms, or with having what is called a "good prose style." On the other hand it is not concerned with fake simplicity and the attempt to make written English colloquial. Nor does it even imply in every case preferring the Saxon word to the Latin one, though it does imply using the fewest and shortest words that will cover one's meaning. What is above all needed is to let the meaning choose the word, and not the other way about. In prose, the worst thing one can do with words is to surrender to them. When you think of a concrete object, you think wordlessly, and then, if you want to describe the thing you have been visualizing you probably hunt about till you find the exact words that seem to fit it. When you think of something abstract you are more inclined to use words from the start, and unless you make a conscious effort to prevent it, the existing dialect will come rushing in and do the job for you, at the expense of blurring or even changing your meaning. Probably it is better to put off using words as long as possible and get one's meaning as clear as one can through pictures or sensations. Afterward one can choose—not simply *accept*—the phrases that will best cover the meaning, and then switch round and decide what impression one's words are likely to make on another person. This last effort of the mind cuts out all stale or mixed images, all prefabricated phrases, needless repetitions, and humbug and vagueness generally. But one can often be in doubt about the effect of a word or a phrase, and one needs rules that one can rely on when instinct fails. I think the following rules will cover most cases:

(i) Never use a metaphor, simile, or other figure of speech which you are used to seeing in print.

(ii) Never use a long word where a short one will do.

(iii) If it is possible to cut a word out, always cut it out.

(iv) Never use the passive where you can use the active.

(v) Never use a foreign phrase, a scientific word, or a jargon word if you can think of an everyday English equivalent.

(vi) Break any of these rules sooner than say anything outright barbarous.

These rules sound elementary, and so they are, but they demand a deep change of attitude in anyone who has grown used to writing in the style now fashionable. One could keep all of them and still write bad English, but one could not write the kind of stuff that I quoted in those five specimens at the beginning of this article.   (19)

I have not here been considering the literary use of language, but merely language as an instrument for expressing and not for concealing or preventing thought. Stuart Chase and others have come near to claiming that all abstract words are meaningless, and have used this as a pretext for advocating a kind of political quietism. Since you don't know what Fascism is, how can you struggle against Fascism? One need not swallow such absurdities as this, but one ought to recognize that the present political chaos is connected with the decay of language, and that one can probably bring about some improvement by starting at the verbal end. If you simplify your English, you are freed from the worst follies of orthodoxy. You cannot speak any of the necessary dialects, and when you make a stupid remark its stupidity will be obvious, even to yourself. Political language—and with variations this is true of all political parties, from Conservatives to Anarchists—is designed to make lies sound truthful and murder respectable, and to give an appearance of solidity to pure wind. One cannot change this all in a moment, but one can at least change one's own habits, and from time to time one can even, if one jeers loudly enough, send some worn-out and useless phrase—some *jackboot, Achilles' heel, hotbed, melting pot, acid test, veritable inferno,* or other lump of verbal refuse —into the dustbin where it belongs. (20)

John Illo

(1926–)

ILLO was credited as follows in the issue of the Columbia University Forum *in which this essay appeared: "John Illo teaches English at Monmouth College and received his M.A. degree from Columbia University in 1955. His critical essays have appeared in several literary journals. This is his second contribution to* The Forum."

■ *The Rhetoric of Malcolm X*

IN A NATION of images without substances, of rehearsed emotions, in a politic of consensus where platitude replaces belief or belief is fashioned by consensus, genuine rhetoric, like authentic prose, must be rare. For rhetoric, like any verbal art, is correlative with the pristine idea of reason and justice which, if it decays with the growth of every state and jurisprudence, now has developed into an unreason that aggressively claims the allegiance of the national mind.   (1)

Jurisprudence is the prudent justification of an absurd society, of institutionalized inequity and internal contradiction. Law, and juridical logic, and grammar conspire to frustrate the original idea of a just and good society, in which all men may freely become the best that they may be. Rhetoric, like the Shelleyan poetic, returns us to primal intelligence, to the golden idea and the godly nature whose mirror is unspoiled reason. The critical and reformist function of rhetoric, apparent in processes like irony and paradox, is perceptible in the whole range of tropes and syntactic and tonal devices. Repetitions and transposals of syntax recall the emphases of nature, before civil logic; and metaphor recalls the true relations, resemblances, predications, that we have been trained to forget. Love is not a fixation but a fire, for it consumes and cleanses; and man is not a rational animal so essentially as he is dust and breath, crumbling, evanescent, and mysterious because moved invisibly.   (2)

To use schemes, figures, tropes, in a plan or plot that corresponds with the broad proceeding of the juridically logical mind, is to make an oration. Within the grammatical frame of his society, the orator, using the language of primordial reason and symbol, restores to his audience the ideas that have been obscured by imposed categories that may correspond to institution but not to reality. Rhetoric, Aristotle taught, is analogous to logic because enthymeme is related to syllogism; but, more significantly, rhetoric is related to logic as logic is related to reality. And rhetoric is also related to poetry, as Cicero observed, his prosaic Roman mind reducing poetry to ornamented language, as the lyric mind of Plato had reduced rhetoric to "cookery." Cicero and Aristotle were each half right. Rhetoric is in fact poeticized logic, logic revised by the creative and critical imagination recalling original ideas. Rhetoric, the art that could grow only in a *polis* and a system of judicature, is the art that restores the primitive value of the mystical word and the human voice. With a matured craft and a legalist's acuteness, orators contrive the free language of childlike reason, innocently reproving the unnatural and perverse, which institution, custom, law, and policy ask us to accept as the way of the world.   (3)

And so great orators, when great, have spoken for absolute justice and reason as they perceived it, in defiance of their governments or societies; accusing tyrants, protesting vicious state policies that seduced the general will, execrating the deformation of popular morality. We think of an Isaiah prophesying against the corruption of ancestral religion, of a Demosthenes against Philip, a Cicero against Antony, a Burke against a colonial war, a Garrison against slavery. At the summit of their art they recalled the language of primal intelligence and passion in defense of elemental truth; and their symbols and transposed syntax, though deliberated, were no more spurious or obtrusive than in poetry. But unlike the pure poet, the orator always holds near enough to the juridical logic, grammar, and semantic of the institution to be able to attack the institution. He never yields his reformist responsibility for the private vision that may be illusive, and may be incommunicable. The orator unlinks the mind-forged manacles, but refashions them into an armor for the innocent intelligence, the naked right.

(4)

Lesser oratory, venal, hypocritical, in defense of the indefensible, is patently factitious, its free language a cosmetic, a youthful roseate complexion arranged on an old, shrewd and degenerate visage, as in the forced prosopopoeias of Cicero appealing for a criminal Milo, or in the tediously predictable alliterated triads of Everett McKinley Dirksen. Bad morals usually produce bad rhetoric, and such is the dureful weight of institutions and their parties that *rhetoric* had been pejorated, generally, into *bad rhetoric*. Even Henry Steele Commager can regard oratory like Senator Long's as "eloquent but shameless," attributes ideally exclusive. The swelling anaphoras of a Southern Congressman are not eloquent but ludicrous, raising irrepressible images of toads and swine. Little else but bad rhetoric is possible to those within the establishment, so far from original reason, so committed to the apologetics of unreason. And those outside are conditioned by established styles, or are graceless, or are misdirected in eccentric contrariety. The poetry of Bob Dylan veers in its metaphoric texture between the more lyrical ads and the *Daily News* editorials; the new left sniffles and stumbles into the unwitting anacolutha of *uh* and *you-know;* the old left tends to rant and cant, persuasive only to the persuaded. There are clear teachers like Allen Krebs and Staughton Lynd, but as good teachers they are probably not orators.   (5)

The achievement of Malcolm X, then, though inevitable, seems marvelous. Someone had to rise and speak the fearful reality, to throw the light of reason into the hallucinatory world of the capitalist and biracial society that thinks itself egalitarian, that thinks itself humanitarian and pacific. But it was unexpected that the speaking should be done with such power and precision by a russet-haired field Negro translated from conventional thief to zealot and at the end nearly to Marxist and humanist.   (6)

For the rhetoric of the American black outsider in this age has seldom been promising; this is not the century of Toussaint L'Ouverture or the nation of Frederick Douglass. The charismatic strength of Father Divine, or of Elijah Muhammad, did not derive from rhetoric. The language of one was hypnotically abstruse, if not perfectly unintelligible, related not to oratory or to religion but to New Thought. The oratory of the other is diffuse and halting, unornamented, solecistic, provincial, its development over-deliberate, its elocution low-keyed though rising to an affecting earnestness. Robert Williams has force but not majesty or art. Men like James Baldwin and Le Roi Jones are primarily writers, and each is deficient in the verbal and vocal size and action required in oratory, which is neither writing nor talking. The young Negro radicals are beyond criticism, the gloomy product not so much of the ghetto as of TV and the American high school. The Nobel Laureate and the Harlem Congressman have different oratorical talents, but neither is an outsider. (7)

The rhetoric of Malcolm X was in the perennial traditions of the art, but appropriate to his audiences and purpose—perennial because appropriate. A Harlem rally is not the Senate of the Roman Republic, but Cicero would have approved Malcolm's discourses as *accommodatus, aptus, congruens,* suitable to his circumstances and subject. His exordia were properly brief, familiar, sometimes acidly realistic (". . . brothers and sisters, friends and enemies: I just can't believe everyone in here is a friend and I don't want to leave anybody out."), and he moved to his proposition within the first minute, for his audience needed relevant ideas and theses, not dignity and amplitude. His perorations were similarly succinct, sometimes entirely absorbed into the confirmations. His personal apologiae, negative or self-depreciatory, contrary to those of a Cicero or a Burke, assured his hearers that he was on the outside, like them: "I'm not a politician, not even a student of politics; in fact, I'm not a student of much of anything. I'm not a Democrat, I'm not a Republican, and I don't even consider myself an American," an ironic gradation or augmentative climax that was, in the world of Malcolm and his people, really a kind of declination or reversed climax. (8)

His narration and confirmation were densely analytical, but perspicuous because of their familiar diction and analogies, and their catechetical repetitions: "And to show you what his [Tshombe's] thinking is—a hired killer —what's the first thing he did? He hired more killers. He went out and got the mercenaries from South Africa. And what is a mercenary? A hired killer. That's all a mercenary is. The anti-Castro Cuban pilots, what are they? Mercenaries, hired killers. Who hired them? The United States. Who hired the killers from South Africa? The United States; they just used Tshombe to do it." (9)

Instruction was the usual purpose of Malcolm's oratory; he was primarily a teacher, his oratory of the demonstrative kind, and his speeches filled with significant matter. It was the substantive fullness and penetration, the honesty and closeness to reality of Malcolm's matter that imparted much of the force to his oratory. (10)

A representative political speech in the United States is empty of content. What did President Kennedy's Inaugural Address contain that a commencement address does not? Indeed, the Inaugural displayed the meaning-

less chiasmus, the fatuous or sentimental metaphor, the callow hyper-
baton of a valedictory. President Johnson's speeches on foreign affairs vitiate
reason and intelligence as his foreign policy violates international morality: temporarily not to attack a neutral nation is a positive beneficence that
should evoke gratitude and concessions, and one is ready to negotiate with
any party under any conditions except the party and conditions that are
relevant. But such is the tradition of vacant and meaningless political oratory in America, and such the profusion of the universally accepted and
discredited rhetoric of advertising, that the public nods and acquiesces, not
believes. We expect truth and substance not in open oration, but in secret
conference or in caucus, "on the inside"—where we can't hear it. We assume
that rhetoric is a futile and deceptive or self-deceived art, because rhetoric should persuade through rational conviction, but business and government are ruled by power and interest. And perhaps Congressional or
party oratory is a facade, the votes having been decided not by analogies
and metonymies but by the Dow-Jones averages.   (11)

Yet the people, closer to reason than their legislators, may still be moved
by rhetoric, and popular oratory may still be a political force. We wonder
how a crowd in Havana can listen to the Premier for three hours. A revolution needs people, and to explain a revolution needs time, and three hours
is little enough. To explain a self-maintaining American polity and economy
while evading its real problems needs very little time, and three hours of
Hubert Humphrey would be unconscionable.   (12)

Malcolm's speeches, if not so complex, not so informed or copious as
those of an accomplished revolutionary, were not vacuous. The man whose
secondary education began painstakingly and privately in the Norfolk Prison Colony was able to analyze for his people their immediate burden, its
maintenance in a system of domestic power and its relation to colonialism,
more acutely than the white and black Ph.D's with whom he debated. A
man about whose life it is difficult not to sentimentalize was seldom sentimental in his oratory, and though he simplified he did not platitudinize.
                                                                (13)

Malcolm's simplifications, sometimes dangerous, though commonplace in
popular oratory and less sophistic than those in establishment rhetoric, derived from the simplicity of his central message: that colored people have
been oppressed by white people whenever white people have been able
to oppress them, that because immediate justice is not likely ("Give it to us
yesterday, and that's not fast enough"), the safest thing for all is to separate, that the liberty to "sit down next to white folks—on the toilet" is
not adequate recompense for the past 400 years. Like Robert Owen or John
Brown or William Lloyd Garrison, Malcolm spent the good years of his
life asserting one idea and its myriad implications and its involved strategies in a society in which the black is often a noncitizen even *de jure*. And

because what he said was as intelligible and obvious as a lynching, his rhetorical content was not embarrassed by the tergiversations, the sophisms, the labored evasions, the empty grandiloquence of American political oratory.   (14)

The American press attributed the preaching of violence to a man who was no political activist, who moved in the arena of words and ideas, and who usually described a condition of violence rather than urged a justifiably violent response. The *New York Times* obituary editorial, magisterially obtuse, was representative. At worst, Malcolm X, like St. Alphonsus Liguori, taught the ethic of self-defense. *Méchant animal!* The weakness of Malcolm, in fact, and of Elijah Muhammad, is that they were not activists; unlike Martin Luther King, neither had a "movement," for neither went anywhere. Malcolm's success in enlarging the Nation of Islam from 400 to 40,000 and in drawing "well-wishers" by the hundreds of thousands was from the ideas and the words, not from an appeal to action, and not from an appeal to license: the call to moral responsibility and the perpetual Lent of the Muslims repelled most Negroes as it would repel most whites.   (15)

But Malcolm's essential content was so simple and elemental, his arguments, like Thoreau's, so unanswerable, that the American press, even when not covertly racist, could not understand him, accustomed as it is to the settled contradictions of civil logic in a biracial country.   (16)

What answer is there to the accusations that in a large part of America, a century after the 14th Amendment, some kinds of murderers cannot be punished by law, that the law is the murderer? Is it an answer that we must tolerate injustice so that we may enjoy justice? Contemning such deformed logic, and adhering to obvious moral truths, Malcolm, like the Bogalusa Deacons, had little difficulty in understanding and explaining to his audiences the Thomistic conception of law better than the Attorney General of the United States understands it. Malcolm was always disconcerted when the powers that be and their exponents refused to recognize the legality of humanity. His strongest vocal emphases were on words like law and right: "They don't use *law*," he exclaimed of the United States Government, which, he asserted, directed the Central Congolese Government, and the lawfulness of the Eastern Government was more valid, he thought, because it was of its own people.   (17)

Justice and equity and emancipation, not violence, not hatred, not retribution, and not the theology of the Muslims were the central matter of Malcolm's oratory, though that theology was useful as a repudiation of American white Christianity. He had entered the stream of sane and moral social teaching before his parting from Elijah Muhammad, and was deepening his knowledge and expression of it at the moment of the death he expected each day "Ερχεται νυξ.   (18)

If his theses were terrible, it was because they were asserted without compromise or palliation, and because the institutional reality they challenged was terrible. How else to indicate reality and truth if not by direct challenge? Indirection is not workable, for the state has stolen irony; satire is futile, its only resource to repeat the language of the Administration. To say that the American tradition beckons us onward to the work of peace in Vietnam, or that they who reject peace overtures are great servants of peace, is to speak not ironically but authoritatively. The critical efficacy even of absurd literature is threatened by real reductions toward the absurd and beyond, and when usable, absurd statement cannot be at once terse, clear, complex, and unequivocal. The only useful attack is directness, which, opposed to outrage, is outraged and, to apologists of outrage, outrageous. (19)

Malcolm's challenge soon implied anticolonialism, in which was implied anticapitalism. Not a doctrinal Marxist when he died, Malcolm had begun to learn a relation between racism and capitalism during his first African journey, and a relation between socialism and national liberation. Rising above the ethical limitations of many civil rights leaders, he rejected a black symbiosis in the warfare state. The black housewife may collect Green Stamps or dividends, the black paterfamilias may possess an Impala and a hi-fi, the black student an unimpeachable graduate degree and a professorship, but what moral black or white could be happy in the world of color TV and Metrecal and napalm? If a rising Negro class could be contented by such hopes and acquirements, if it yearned for the glittering felicities of the American dream, for the Eden of Life and Ebony, Malcolm had finer longings, and so his following was small: his vision was more intense, more forbidding than that of King or Wilkins or Farmer. They preached integrated Americanism; Malcolm taught separation for goodness, the co-existence of morally contrary cultures in a geographic unit, in "America." (20)

Because the black had been always alien in America, had been always taught to hate himself in America ("We hated our heads . . . the shape of our nose . . . the color of our skin. . . ."), he now had the freedom to despise, not embrace, a society that had grown alien to humanity, and whose profound alienation had been intimated for the black first in slavery, then in racism. Separation promised not the means to make a black image of Beverly Hills or Westchester, but the liberty to build a new Jerusalem. How might such an evangel be grasped by a social worker or a Baptist minister? (21)

Malcolm's earlier expressions of racism, sometimes augmented or distorted in the misreporting, were a means or an error that receded after his Islamic-African pilgrimage, qualified into renouncement. Their white counterparts have been the political hardware of thousands of local American statesmen and scores of United States Congressmen, and how many have not outgrown them, are legislators because of them? An American President can admit to prior racism with little embarrassment, with becoming repentance. (22)

It is the growth and maturing that matter, and Malcolm's ideological journey, truncated after beginning late, was leftward, enlightened, and opening toward humanitarianism and unsentimental fraternalism, contrary to that of some British lords and some Yale graduates, contrary to that of the young American Marxists of the 1930s, now darkening into polarized anticommunism. There were no saner, more honest and perspicuous analyses of the racial problem than Malcolm's last speeches and statements, beside which the pronouncements of most administrations and civic officials are calculated nonsense. Only from the outside can some truths be told. (23)

In the rhetoric of Malcolm X, as in all genuine rhetoric, figures correspond to the critical imagination restoring the original idea and to the conscience protesting the desecration of the idea. Tropes and schemes of syntax are departures from literal meaning, *abusiones*, "abuses" of a grammar and semantic that have themselves grown into abuses of original reason. As Shelley saw, the abusion, or trope, like revolutionism, destroys conventional definitions to restore original wholeness and reality. Rhetoric, like revolution, is "a way of redefining reality." (24)

The frequent repetitions in Malcolm's rhetoric, like those of Cicero or St. Paul, are communications of the passion that is not satisfied by single statement, but that beats through the pulses. Good rhetorical repetition is viscerally didactic. (25)

But it is an especially dangerous device, its potential of fraudulence proportionate to its elemental power to persuade. It may reinforce truths, it may add stones to build great lies. The anaphoras of Administration rhetoric lead successive clauses each further from reality. Abstractions in repetitions, like the "peace" and "freedom" of the Presidential addresses, are usually doubtful, because ambiguous and inaccessible to testing. War may very well be peace, and slavery freedom, if the predications are repeated often enough. (26)

The substantives and verbs in Malcolm's repetitions were usually concrete, exposing themselves to empirical judgment:

> As long as the white man sent you to Korea, you bled. He sent you to Germany, you bled. He sent you to the South Pacific to fight the Japanese, you bled. You bleed for white people, but when it comes to seeing your own church being bombed and little black girls murdered, you haven't got any blood. You bleed when the white man says bleed; you bite when the white man says bite; and you bark when the white man says bark. (27)

Malcolm here began with epistrophe for reinforcement of a repeated reality, combined it with anaphora to shift focus to "the man," moved to epanastrophe in the third and fourth sentences, in which "the man" and the black man share the repeating emphasis, and to epanadiplosis in the fourth for a doubled emphasis on *bleed*, while a tolling alliteration of labials and liquids instructs the outer ear, while asyndeton accelerates a tautness and indignation, and while the fullness of emotion evokes a pathetic-sardonic syllepsis on *blood*.   (28)

His rhetorical questions and percunctations with repetition, here anaphora and epistrophe, have the urgency of a Massillon convincing a noble audience of the probability of their damnation:

> *Why should white people be running all the stores in our community? Why should white people be running the banks of our community? Why should the economy of our community be in the hands of the white man? Why?*   (29)

The orator may redirect as well as repeat his syntactic units. Malcolm used chiasmus, or crossing of antithetic sets, not deceptively, not to confound realities, but to explore the calculated fantasies of the American press, to untangle the crossing of image and reality:

> *. . . you end up hating your friends and loving your enemies . . . The press is so powerful in its image-making role, it can make a criminal look like he's the victim and make the victim look like he's the criminal. . . . If you aren't careful, the newspapers will have you hating the people who are being oppressed and loving the people who are doing the oppressing.*   (30)

Malcolm was attracted to chiasmus as an economy in dialectic. In the Oxford Union Society debate of December 1964, he explicated and defended Senator Goldwater's chiasmus of *extremism* and *moderation*, converting the memorable assault upon radical reform into an apology for black militancy.   (31)

As the strict clausal scheme may be varied to represent emotional thought, strict demonstration may be relieved by paradox and analogy. Paradox, here climactic and with repetitions, writes itself into any narrative of American Negro history since 1863:

> *How can you thank a man for giving you what's already yours? How then can you thank him for giving you only part of what's already yours?*   (32)

With an analogy Malcolm dismissed Roy Wilkins' quaver that though the black may be a second-class American, he is yet an American, with his little part of the affluent dream:

> *I'm not going to sit at your table and watch you eat, with nothing on my plate, and call myself a diner. Sitting at the table doesn't make you a diner, unless you eat some of what's on that plate. Being here in America doesn't make you an American. Being born here in America doesn't make you an American.* (33)

We see a black man with half the income of a white, and think of other hungers, and the analogy works as symbol and image, like Bacon's winding stair to great place or Demosthenes' Athenian boxer defending himself from multiple blows. (34)

Metaphor and metonymy are the symbolic image condensed and made freer from customary logic than the more explicit analogy. Like repetitions and analogies they may be recognizably fraudulent, for symbolic language is not dissociated from truth. We must know or imagine the referent before we can judge and be moved by the symbol. When an American President now says, "The door of peace must be kept wide open for all who wish to avoid the scourge of war, but the door of aggression must be closed and bolted if man himself is to survive," he is disquieting tame, weary metaphors, long since grown insipid and moribund, into a defiance of meaning, and the very antithesis emphasizes the inanity of the ghostwritten rhetoric in a linguistic culture that has not finally adopted Newspeak. If the figures are initially suspect because of the designed, limitless ambiguity and abstractness of the referents, they are contemptible when related to the realities they profess to clarify. Such metaphor is not the discovery of truth but its concealment. "When I can't talk sense," said the eighteenth-century Irish orator, John Curran, "I talk metaphor." (35)

The metaphors of Malcolm X, sometimes ethnically conventional, sometimes original, sometimes inevitable ("I don't see an American dream. I see an American nightmare."), were rarely ambiguous in the abstract member, and were often concrete in both, lending themselves to the touch of common experience. They were infrequent, less frequent than in the elevated tradition of Pitt and Burke and Webster. Malcolm's oratory resembled rather that of the self-educated reformer Cobden in its simple, unornamented vigor, in its reduction to essential questions, in its analytic directness and clarity. In Malcolm's oratory as in Cobden's, metaphor was exceptional in a pattern of exposition by argumentation in abstract and literal diction. (36)

And because Malcolm wished to demonstrate rather than suggest, he preferred the more fully ratiocinative structure, the analogy, to the more condensed and poetic metaphor: he had wished to be not a poet but a lawyer when his elementary school English teacher advised him to turn to carpentry. So also, Malcolm composed in the larger grammatical unit, the paragraph, which corresponds to analogy, rather than in the sentence, which corresponds to metaphor. In answering questions he often prefaced his extended expositions with the request not for one more word or one more sentence, but for "one more paragraph"—and a paragraph indeed was what he usually produced, extemporaneous and complete with counter-thesis, thesis, devolpment, synthesis and summary.   (37)

The metaphors and metonymies, restricted in number, often suggested truth, like the analogies, by fusing image and symbol, as in poetry: Blake's little black thing amid the snow is sensuously and spiritually black, the snow sensuously and spiritually white. Malcolm used the same deliberate indetermination of perception in the image by which he characterized white immigrants in America:

> *Everything that came out of Europe, every blue-eyed thing is*
> *already an American.*

Synecdoche and tmesis combine to refocus on generic essentials for a black audience.   (38)

In quick answer to an immoderating Stan Bernard and an uncivil Gordon Hall, and trying to defend the thesis that the Muslims were a force in the Negro movement though numerically insignificant, Malcolm compared them with the Mau Mau, then condensed an implicit analogy to a metaphor and, with characteristically temerarious simplification, expanded and explicated the metaphor into analogy:

> *The Mau Mau was also a minority, a microscopic minority,*
> *but it was the Mau Mau who not only brought independence to*
> *Kenya, but— . . . but it brought it—that wick. The powder keg is*
> *always larger than the wick. . . . It's the wick that you touch that*
> *sets the powder off.*   (39)

By a folk metonymy in one pronoun, more convincing than the usual rhetorical patriotic genealogies, Malcolm enlarged to their real dimension the time and space of the Negro's misfortune:

> *many of us probably passed through [Zanzibar] on our way to*
> *America 400 years ago.*   (40)

The identification of Malcolm with his audience, not merely through the plural pronoun, was so thorough that he effected the desired harmony or union in which the speaker can disregard his audience as an object and speak his own passion and reason, when between himself and his hearers there is no spiritual division. The great orator does not play upon his audience as upon a musical instrument; his verbal structures are artful but urged from within. (41)

Malcolm's composition and elocution were remarkable in their assimilative variety. Before the mixed or white audiences, as at college forums, the composition was more abstract and literal, austerely figured, grammatically pure, and the elocution sharper, somewhat rapid and high-pitched, near his speaking voice, enunciated precisely but not mimetic or overarticulated. Before the great black audiences Malcolm adopted a tone and ornament that were his and his audience's but that he relinquished before the white or the academic. The composition of the black speeches was rich in ethnic figuration and humor, in paronomasia, alliteration, and rhyme (the novocained patient, blood running down his jaw, suffers "peacefully"; if you are a true revolutionary "You don't do any singing, you're too busy swinging"; the Negroes who crave acceptance in white America "aren't asking for any nation—they're trying to crawl back on the plantation.") The elocution of this, Malcolm's grand style, was deeper, slower, falling into a tonal weighting and meiosis, wider in its range of pitch, dynamics, emphasis. (42)

Always exhibiting a force of moral reason, never hectic or mainly emotional, Malcolm changed from *homo afer* to *homo europaeus* as the ambience and occasion required. In the mosques he employed the heavy vocal power of impassioned Negro discourse; in academic dialogue and rebuttal his voice sometimes resembled that of Adlai Stevenson in its east-north-central nasality, and in its hurried, thoughtful pauses, its wry humor, its rational rather than emotional emphases. (43)

It is understandable that he was correct, intelligible, lucid, rational, for few public orators in our time have been as free as Malcolm from the need to betray their own intelligence. John Kennedy, who in January pledged a quest for peace and a revulsion from colonialism, in one week of the following April repudiated the Cuban invasion he was then assisting, in another week of the same April pugnaciously justified the intervention, and, having been rebuked by reality, reproached reality with a dialectic from the Mad Tea-Party. His audience was appropriate: American newspaper editors. Later, waving a flag in the Orange Bowl, he would promise the émigré landlords warfare and their restored rents with melodramatic and puerile metonymy. Adlai Stevenson, who twice had talked sense to the American people, denied his government's aggression in Cuba with juridical solemnity, with the noble anaphoras, the poignant metaphors, the sensitive ironies of the campaign speeches, and, fatally drawn to display *expertise*, derisively censured the oratory of Raul Roa. His indignant exposure of revolutionaries was submerged in the laughter of the black galleries of the world; he indulged himself, during the Congo debates, in the pointless metonymies of Independence Day addresses; and his recurrent denunciations of colonialism were freaks of unintended irony. (44)

"Who would not weep, if Atticus were he?" (45)

Malcolm, more fortunate than these, was not ordained by history to be the spokesman or the apologist of violence and unthinkable power, and so was not forced to violate reason. In his last years he was in the great tradition of rational and moral speech, consanguineous with Isaiah, with Demosthenes and Cicero, with Paine and Henry, Lincoln and Douglass, as they were allied to the primitive idea of goodness. He was not an emotionalist or a demagogue, but an orator who combined familiarity with passion, with compelling ideas and analytic clarity, and with sober force of utterance, and with a sense, now usually deficient except when depraved, of rhetoric as an art and a genre. (46)

His feeling for the art was probably the benefit of his old-fashioned verbal and literary education in prison. As the rhetoric of Frederick Douglass, then a young slave, originated in his readings of Sheridan's oratory, so Malcolm's alma mater, he said, was "books." The methodical longhand copying of thousands of logical definitions, his nightly labor with the dictionary in prison, left an impress of precision in diction and syntax, later tested and hardened in hostile debate. As he learned the science and the habits of grammar, Malcolm learned the unfamiliar subtleties of the art of rhetoric within a few years. As late as 1961 he prevailed in debate more by conviction than by linguistic accuracy, and the solecisms were embarrassing to his literate admirers and probably to himself, as were the parochial pronunciations, atavistic traces of which could be heard very rarely in the last year ("influence"). But this sense of rhetoric derived also from his perception of the ideas that antedate rhetoric and that inform all moral language. His teaching, because elemental and unsophisticated in its morality, was more sane, more philosophic than the wisdom of many an academician who, detached from the facts of human pain, has the institutionalized intelligence to devise a morality to fit his institution, who can make policy his morality: Arthur Schlesinger, Jr., can regard the genocidal war in Vietnam as "an experiment, . . . something you have to try." (47)

In his maturity, Malcolm was always aware of the centrally ethical and honest enough not to elude it, and so he soon outgrew what was doctrinally grotesque in the Nation of Islam (what native American religious movement is without such grotesqueness?). But he retained the religious commitment and the wholesome ascesis of the Muslims, and thus was helped in the exhausting work of the last years, the weeks of eighteen-hour days. A mixed seed fell in good soil. (48)

He emerged from dope, prostitution, burglary, prison, and a fanciful sectarianism to enter a perennial humanist art, to achieve a brilliant facility in oratory and debate, in less time than many of us consume in ambling through graduate school. His developing accomplishment in the last year was, as a *New York Times* reporter exclaimed but could not write, "incredible." The Oxford Union Society, venerable, perceptive, and disinterested because un-American, adjudged him among the best of living orators after his debate there three months before his death, a pleasant triumph ignored by the American press. Though he may be diluted, or obliterated, or forgotten by the established civil rights movement, which is built into the consensus, Malcolm was for all time an artist and thinker. In the full Aristotelean meaning he was a rhetorician, who, to be such, knew more than rhetoric: ethics, logic, grammar, psychology, law, history, politics; and his best speeches might be texts for students of that comprehensive science and art.   (49)

His controlled art, his tone of pride without arrogance, have followers if not a school, in his own Muslim Mosque and among the Nation of Islam, audible in the rational and disdainful replies of Norman 3X in the murder trial. But Malcolm is distinct rhetorically from his admirers among the surly school of Negro speakers, the oratorical equivalent of *Liberator*, who have little to offer their mixed auditory but insolence and commonplaces in broken and frenetic, in monotonous or ill-accented language. And he was remote from the misanthropic and negativist among the alienated. Malcolm, a religionist, could not be "bitter," or descend to scatology in expressing moral outrage. The laughter or chuckling, in his several oratorical styles, was, in motive and in sound, not embittered, or malicious, or frustrated, but apodictic; it was the laughter of assured rectitude, and amusement at the radical unreason of the opposition. For not he but the established structures were the opposition, dissentient to godly reason and justice, which were the authority for his teaching. Hearing Malcolm was an experience not morbid or frightening, but joyous, as Mark Van Doren said of reading *Hamlet*. Though the drama and the man were tragic, in each the confident and varied movement of language and moral ideas told us something superb about our humanity. Malcolm combined magnificence and ethnic familiarity to demonstrate what he asserted: the potential majesty of the black man even in America, a majesty idiosyncratic but related to all human greatness. And so his last ten years tell us that a man can be more fully human serving a belief, even if to serve it requires that he borrow from the society that his service and belief affront. If he and his people illustrate that the grand primal ideas and their grand expression can be spoiled for men by institutions, the whole work and life of Malcolm X declare that the good man, if he has the soul to resist the state and its courts and senates, can restore the ideal world of art and justice.
                                                                                             (50)

Marshall McLuhan

(1911–   )

MCLUHAN, recently appointed Albert Schweitzer Professor of the Humanities at Fordham University, is certainly the most luminous student of communications media on the contemporary scene and, for some, the most illuminating. From his first-published literary essays in traditional academic journals, he was recognized as a little shocking and more than a little original. In 1964, he climaxed a life-time of interest in communications and more than a decade of intense study of our "mechanical bride" with the publication of Understanding Media; The Extensions of Man. *This bombshell was followed by another in 1967,* The Medium is the Message: An Inventory of Effects, *in which he adapted the best-known proposition from* Understanding Media *("the medium is the message") to his intention "to draw attention to the fact that a medium is not something neutral—it does something to people. It takes hold of them. It rubs them off, it massages them, it bumps them around." Professor McLuhan holds the Ph.D. degree in English literature from Cambridge University.*

◼ *Television*
The Timid Giant

PERHAPS THE most familiar and pathetic effect of the TV image is the posture of children in the early grades. Since TV, children—regardless of eye condition—average about six and a half inches from the printed page. Our children are striving to carry over to the printed page the all-involving sensory mandate of the TV image. With perfect psycho-mimetic skill, they carry out the commands of the TV image. They pore, they probe, they slow down and involve themselves in depth. This is what they had learned to do in the cool iconography of the comic-book medium. TV carried the process much further. Suddenly they are transferred to the hot print medium with its uniform patterns and fast lineal movement. Pointlessly they strive to read print in depth. They bring to print all their senses, and print rejects them. Print asks for the isolated and stripped-down visual faculty, not for the unified sensorium. (1)

The Mackworth head-camera, when worn by children watching TV, has revealed that their eyes follow, not the actions, but the reactions. The eyes scarcely deviate from the faces of the actors, even during scenes of violence. This head-camera shows by projection both the scene and the eye movement simultaneously. Such extraordinary behavior is another indication of the very cool and involving character of this medium. (2)

On the Jack Paar show for March 8, 1963, Richard Nixon was Paared down and remade into a suitable TV image. It turns out that Mr. Nixon is both a pianist and a composer. With sure tact for the character of the TV medium, Jack Paar brought out this *pianoforte* side of Mr. Nixon, with excellent effect. Instead of the slick, glib, legal Nixon, we saw the doggedly creative and modest performer. A few timely touches like this would have quite altered the result of the Kennedy-Nixon campaign. TV is a medium that rejects the sharp personality and favors the presentation of processes rather than of products. (3)

The adaptation of TV to processes, rather than to the neatly packaged products, explains the frustration many people experience with this medium in its political uses. An article by Edith Efron in *TV Guide* (May 18–24, 1963) labeled TV "The Timid Giant," because it is unsuited to hot issues and sharply defined controversial topics: "Despite official freedom from censorship, a self-imposed silence renders network documentaries almost mute on many great issues of the day." As a cool medium TV has, some feel, introduced a kind of *rigor mortis* into the body politic. It is the extraordinary degree of audience participation in the TV medium that explains its failure to tackle hot issues. Howard K. Smith observed: "The networks are delighted if you go into a controversy in a country 14,000 miles away. They don't want real controversy, real dissent, at home." For people conditioned to the hot newspaper medium, which is concerned with the clash of *views*, rather than involvement in *depth* in a situation, the TV behavior is inexplicable. (4)

Such a hot news item that concerns TV directly was headlined "It finally happened—a British film with English subtitles to explain the dialects." The film in question is the British comedy "Sparrows Don't Sing." A glossary of Yorkshire, Cockney, and other slang phrases has been printed for the customers so that they can figure out just what the subtitles mean. Sub subtitles are as handy an indicator of the depth of effects of TV as the new "rugged" styles in feminine attire. One of the most extraordinary developments since TV in England has been the upsurge of regional dialects. A regional brogue or "burr" is the vocal equivalent of gaiter stockings. Such brogues undergo continual erosion from literacy. Their sudden prominence in England in areas in which previously one had heard only standard English is one of the most significant cultural events of our time. Even in the classrooms of Oxford and Cambridge, the local dialects are heard again. The undergraduates of those universities no longer strive to achieve a uniform speech. Dialectal speech since TV has been found to provide a social bond in depth, not possible with the artificial "standard English" that began only a century ago. (5)

An article on Perry Como bills him as "Low-pressure king of a high-pressure realm." The success of any TV performer depends on his achieving a low-pressure style of presentation, although getting his act on the air may require much high-pressure organization. Castro may be a case in point. According to Tad Szulc's story on "Cuban Television's One-man Show" *(The Eighth Art)*, "in his seemingly improvised 'as-I-go-along' style he can evolve politics and govern his country—right on camera." Now, Tad Szulc is under the illusion that TV is a hot medium, and suggests that in the Congo "television might have helped Lumumba to incite the masses to even greater turmoil and bloodshed." But he is quite wrong. Radio is the medium for frenzy, and it has been the major means of hotting up the tribal blood of Africa, India, and China, alike. TV has cooled Cuba down, as it is cooling down America. What the Cubans are getting by TV is the experience of being directly engaged in the making of political decisions. Castro presents himself as a teacher, and as Szulc says, "manages to blend political guidance and education with propaganda so skillfully that it is often difficult to tell where one begins and the other ends." Exactly the same mix is used in entertainment in Europe and America alike. Seen outside the United States, any American movie looks like subtle political propaganda. Acceptable entertainment has to flatter and exploit the cultural and political assumptions of the land of its origin. These unspoken presuppositions also serve to blind people to the most obvious facts about a new medium like TV. (6)

In a group of simulcasts of several media done in Toronto a few years back, TV did a strange flip. Four randomized groups of university students were given the same information at the same time about the structure of preliterate languages. One group received it via radio, one from TV, one by lecture, and one read it. For all but the reader group, the information was passed along in straight verbal flow by the same speaker without discussion or questions or use of blackboard. Each group had half an hour of exposure to the material. Each was asked to fill in the same quiz afterward. It was quite a surprise to the experimenters when the students performed better with TV-channeled information and with radio than they did with lecture and print—and the TV group stood *well* above the radio group. Since nothing had been done to give special stress to any of these four media, the experiment was repeated with other randomized groups. This time each medium was allowed full opportunity to do its stuff. For radio and TV, the material was dramatized with many auditory and visual features. The lecturer took full advantage of the blackboard and class discussion. The printed form was embellished with an imaginative use of typography and page layout to stress each point in the lecture. All of these media had been stepped up to high intensity for this repeat of the original performance. Television and radio once again showed results high above lecture and print. Unexpectedly to the testers, however, radio now stood significantly above television. It was a long time before the obvious reason declared itself, namely that TV is a cool, participant medium. When hotted up by dramatization and stingers, it performs less well because there is less opportunity for participation. Radio is a hot medium. When given additional intensity, it performs better. It doesn't invite the same degree of participation in its users. Radio will serve as background-sound or as noise-level control, as when the ingenious teenager employs it as a means of privacy. TV will not work as background. It engages you. You have to be *with it*. (The phrase has gained acceptance since TV.) (7)

A great many things will not work since the arrival of TV. Not only the movies, but the national magazines as well, have been hit very hard by this new medium. Even the comic books have declined greatly. Before TV, there had been much concern about why Johnny couldn't read. Since TV, Johnny has acquired an entirely new set of perceptions. He is not at all the same. Otto Preminger, director of *Anatomy of a Murder* and other hits, dates a great change in movie making and viewing from the very first year of general TV programming. "In 1951," he wrote, "I started a fight to get the release in motion-picture theaters of *The Moon Is Blue* after the production code approval was refused. It was a small fight and I won it." (*Toronto Daily Star*, October 19, 1963) (8)

He went on to say, "The very fact that it was the word 'virgin' that was objected to in *The Moon Is Blue* is today laughable, almost incredible." Otto Preminger considers that American movies have advanced toward maturity owing to the influence of TV. The cool TV medium promotes depth structures in art and entertainment alike, and creates audience involvement in depth as well. Since nearly all our technologies and entertainment since Gutenberg have been not cool, but hot; and not deep, but fragmentary; not producer-oriented, but consumer-oriented, there is scarcely a single area of established relationships, from home and church to school and market, that has not been profoundly disturbed in its pattern and texture. (9)

The psychic and social disturbance created by the TV image, and not the TV programming, occasions daily comment in the press. Raymond Burr, who plays Perry Mason, spoke to the National Association of Municipal Judges, reminding them that, "Without our laymen's understanding and acceptance, the laws which you apply and the courts in which you preside cannot continue to exist." What Mr. Burr omitted to observe was that the Perry Mason TV program, in which he plays the lead, is typical of that intensely participational kind of TV experience that has altered our relation to the laws and the courts.   (10)

The mode of the TV image has nothing in common with film or photo, except that it offers also a nonverbal *gestalt* or posture of forms. With TV, the viewer is the screen. He is bombarded with light impulses that James Joyce called the "Charge of the Light Brigade" that imbues his "soulskin with sobconscious inklings." The TV image is visually low in data. The TV image is not a *still* shot. It is not photo in any sense, but a ceaselessly forming contour of things limned by the scanning-finger. The resulting plastic contour appears by light *through*, not light *on*, and the image so formed has the quality of sculpture and icon, rather than of picture. The TV image offers some three million dots per second to the receiver. From these he accepts only a few dozen each instant, from which to make an image.   (11)

The film image offers many more millions of data per second, and the viewer does not have to make the same drastic reduction of items to form his impression. He tends instead to accept the full image as a package deal. In contrast, the viewer of the TV mosaic, with technical control of the image, unconsciously reconfigures the dots into an abstract work of art on the pattern of a Seurat or Rouault. If anybody were to ask whether all this would change if technology stepped up the character of the TV image to movie data level, one could only counter by inquiring, "Could we alter a cartoon by adding details of perspective and light and shade?" The answer is "Yes," only it would then no longer be a cartoon. Nor would "improved" TV be television. The TV image is *now* a mosaic mesh of light and dark spots which a movie shot never is, even when the quality of the movie image is very poor.   (12)

As in any other mosaic, the third dimension is alien to TV, but it can be superimposed. In TV the illusion of the third dimension is provided slightly by the stage sets in the studio; but the TV image itself is a flat two-dimensional mosaic. Most of the three-dimensional illusion is a carryover of habitual viewing of film and photo. For the TV camera does not have a built-in angle of vision like the movie camera. Eastman Kodak now has a two-dimensional camera that can match the flat effects of the TV camera. Yet it is hard for literate people, with their habit of fixed points of view and three-dimensional vision, to understand the properties of two-dimensional vision. If it had been easy for them, they would have had no difficulties with abstract art, General Motors would not have made a mess of motorcar design, and the picture magazine would not be having difficulties now with the relationship between features and ads. The TV image requires each instant that we "close" the spaces in the mesh by a convulsive sensuous participation that is profoundly kinetic and tactile, because tactility is the interplay of the senses, rather than the isolated contact of skin and object.   (13)

To contrast it with the film shot, many directors refer to the TV image as one of "low definition," in the sense that it offers little detail and a low degree of information, much like the cartoon. A TV close-up provides only as much information as a small section of a long-shot on the movie screen. For lack of observing so central an aspect of the TV image, the critics of program "content" have talked nonsense about "TV violence." The spokesmen of censorious views are typically semiliterate book-oriented individuals who have no competence in the grammars of newspaper, or radio, or of film, but who look askew and askance at all nonbook media. The simplest question about any psychic aspect, even of the book medium, throws these people into a panic of uncertainty. Vehemence of projection of a single isolated attitude they mistake for moral vigilance. Once these censors became aware that in all cases "the medium is the message" or the basic source of effects, they would turn to suppression of media as such, instead of seeking "content" control. Their current assumption that content or programming is the factor that influences outlook and action is derived from the book medium, with its sharp cleavage between form and content.
                                                                              (14)

Is it not strange that TV should have been as revolutionary a medium in America in the 1950s as radio in Europe in the 1930s? Radio, the medium that resuscitated the tribal and kinship webs of the European mind in the 1920s and 1930s, had no such effect in England or America. There, the erosion of tribal bonds by means of literacy and its industrial extensions had gone so far that our radio did not achieve any notable tribal reactions. Yet ten years of TV have Europeanized even the United States, as witness its changed feelings for space and personal relations. There is new sensitivity to the dance, plastic arts, and architecture, as well as the demand for the small car, the paperback, sculptural hairdos and molded dress effects—to say nothing of a new concern for complex effects in cuisine and in the use of wines. Notwithstanding, it would be misleading to say that TV will retribalize England and America. The action of radio on the world of resonant speech and memory was hysterical. But TV has certainly made England and America vulnerable to radio where previously they had immunity to a great degree. For good or ill, the TV image has exerted a unifying synesthetic force on the sense-life of these intensely literate populations, such

as they have lacked for centuries. It is wise to withhold all value judgments when studying these media matters, since their effects are not
capable of being isolated.   (15)

Synesthesia, or unified sense and imaginative life, had long seemed an
unattainable dream to Western poets, painters, and artists in general.
They had looked with sorrow and dismay on the fragmented and impoverished imaginative life of Western literate man in the eighteenth century
and later. Such was the message of Blake and Pater, Yeats and D. H. Lawrence, and a host of other great figures. They were not prepared to have
their dreams realized in everyday life by the esthetic action of radio and
television. Yet these massive extensions of our central nervous systems have
enveloped Western man in a daily session of synesthesia. The Western
way of life attained centuries since by the rigorous separation and specialization of the senses, with the visual sense atop the hierarchy, is not able
to withstand the radio and TV waves that wash about the great visual
structure of abstract Individual Man. Those who, from political motives,
would now add their force to the anti-individual action of our electric technology are puny subliminal automatons aping the patterns of the prevailing electric pressures. A century ago they would, with equal somnambu-
lism, have faced in the opposite direction. German Romantic poets and
philosophers had been chanting in tribal chorus for a return to the dark unconscious for over a century before radio and Hitler made such a return
difficult to avoid. What is to be thought of people who wish such a return
to preliterate ways, when they have no inkling of how the civilized visual
way was never substituted for tribal auditory magic?   (16)

At this hour, when Americans are discovering new passions for skin-
diving and the wraparound space of small cars, thanks to the indomitable
tactile promptings of the TV image, the same image is inspiring many English people with race feelings of tribal exclusiveness. Whereas highly literate
Westerners have always idealized the condition of integration of races, it
has been their literate culture that made impossible real uniformity among
races. Literate man naturally dreams of visual solutions to the problems of
human differences. At the end of the nineteenth century, this kind of
dream suggested similar dress and education for both men and women.
The failure of the sex-integration programs has provided the theme of much
of the literature and psychoanalysis of the twentieth century. Race integration, undertaken on the basis of visual uniformity, is an extension of
the same cultural strategy of literate man, for whom differences always
seem to need eradication, both in sex and in race, and in space and in
time. Electronic man, by becoming ever more deeply involved in the ac-
tualities of the human condition, cannot accept the literate cultural strategy.
The Negro will reject a plan of visual uniformity as definitely as women
did earlier, and for the same reasons. Women found that they had been

robbed of their distinctive roles and turned into fragmented citizens in "a man's world." The entire approach to these problems in terms of uniformity and social homogenization is a final pressure of the mechanical and industrial technology. Without moralizing, it can be said that the electric age, by involving all men deeply in one another, will come to reject such mechanical solutions. It is more difficult to provide uniqueness and diversity than it is to impose the uniform patterns of mass education; but it is such uniqueness and diversity that can be fostered under electric conditions as never before. (17)

Temporarily, all preliterate groups in the world have begun to feel the explosive and aggressive energies that are released by the onset of the new literacy and mechanization. These explosions come just at a time when the new electric technology combines to make us share them on a global scale. (18)

The effect of TV, as the most recent and spectacular electric extension of our central nervous system, is hard to grasp for various reasons. Since it has affected the totality of our lives, personal and social and political, it would be quite unrealistic to attempt a "systematic" or visual presentation of such influence. Instead, it is more feasible to "present" TV as a complex *gestalt* of data gathered almost at random. (19)

The TV image is of low intensity or definition, and, therefore, unlike film, it does not afford detailed information about objects. The difference is akin to that between the old manuscripts and the printed word. Print gave intensity and uniform precision, where before there had been a diffuse texture. Print brought in the taste for exact measurement and repeatability that we now associate with science and mathematics. (20)

The TV producer will point out that speech on television must not have the careful precision necessary in the theater. The TV actor does not have to project either his voice or himself. Likewise, TV acting is so extremely intimate, because of the peculiar involvement of the viewer with the completion or "closing" of the TV image, that the actor must achieve a great degree of spontaneous casualness that would be irrelevant in movie and lost on stage. For the audience participates in the inner life of the TV actor as fully as in the outer life of the movie star. Technically, TV tends to be a close-up medium. The close-up that in the movie is used for shock is, on TV, a quite casual thing. And whereas a glossy photo the size of the TV screen would show a dozen faces in adequate detail, a dozen faces on the TV screen are only a blur. (21)

The peculiar character of the TV image in its relation to the actor causes such familiar reactions as our not being able to recognize in real life a person whom we see every week on TV. Not many of us are as alert as the kindergartner who said to Garry Moore, "How did you get off TV?" Newscasters and actors alike report the frequency with which they are approached by people who feel they've met them before. Joanne Woodward in an interview was asked what was the difference between being a movie star and a TV actress. She replied: "When I was in the movies I heard people say, 'There goes Joanne Woodward.' Now they say, 'There goes somebody I think I know.'"   (22)

The owner of a Hollywood hotel in an area where many movie and TV actors reside reported that tourists had switched their allegiance to TV stars. Moreover, most TV stars are men, that is, "cool characters," while most movie stars are women, since they can be presented as "hot" characters. Men and women movie stars alike, along with the entire star system, have tended to dwindle into a more moderate status since TV. The movie is a hot, high-definition medium. Perhaps the most interesting observation of the hotel proprietor was that the tourists wanted to *see* Perry Mason and Wyatt Earp. They did not want to see Raymond Burr and Hugh O'Brian. The old movie-fan tourists had wanted to see their favorites as they were in *real* life, not as they were in their film roles. The fans of the cool TV medium want to see their star in *role*, whereas the movie fans want the *real thing*.   (23)

A similar reversal of attitudes occurred with the printed book. There was little interest in the private lives of authors under manuscript or scribal culture. Today the comic strip is close to the preprint woodcut and manuscript form of expression. Walt Kelly's *Pogo* looks very much indeed like a gothic page. Yet in spite of great public interest in the comic-strip form, there is as little curiosity about the private lives of these artists as about the lives of popular-song writers. With print, the private life became of the utmost concern to readers. Print is a hot medium. It projects the author at the public as the movie did. The manuscript is a cool medium that does not project the author, so much as involve the reader. So with TV. The viewer is involved and participant. The *role* of the TV star, in this way, seems more fascinating than his private life. It is thus that the student of media, like the psychiatrist, gets more data from his informants than they themselves have perceived. Everybody experiences far more than he understands. Yet it is experience, rather than understanding, that influences behavior, especially in collective matters of media and technology, where the individual is almost inevitably unaware of their effect upon him.   (24)

Some may find it paradoxical that a cool medium like TV should be so much more compressed and condensed than a hot medium like film. But it is well known that a half minute of television is equal to three minutes of stage or vaudeville. The same is true of manuscript in contrast to print. The "cool" manuscript tended toward compressed forms of statement, aphoristic and allegorical. The "hot" print medium expanded expression in the direction of simplification and the "spelling-out" of meanings. Print speeded up and "exploded" the compressed script into simpler fragments.   (25)

A cool medium, whether the spoken word or the manuscript or TV, leaves much more for the listener or user to do than a hot medium. If the medium is of high definition, participation is low. If the medium is of low intensity, the participation is high. Perhaps this is why lovers mumble so.   (26)

Because the low definition of TV insures a high degree of audience involvement, the most effective programs are those that present situations which consist of some process to be completed. Thus, to use TV to teach poetry would permit the teacher to concentrate on the poetic process of actual *making*, as it pertained to a particular poem. The book form is quite unsuited to this type of involved presentation. The same salience of process of do-it-yourself-ness and depth involvement in the TV image extends to the art of the TV actor. Under TV conditions, he must be alert to improvise and to embellish every phrase and verbal resonance with details of gesture and posture, sustaining that intimacy with the viewer which is not possible on the massive movie screen or on the stage.   (27)

There is the alleged remark of a the Nigerian who, after seeing a TV western, said delightedly, "I did not realize you valued human life so little in the West." Offsetting this remark is the behavior of our children in watching TV westerns. When equipped with the new experimental head-cameras that follow their eye movements while watching the image, children keep their eyes on the faces of the TV actors. Even during physical violence their eyes remain concentrated on the facial *reactions*, rather than on the eruptive *action*. Guns, knives, fists, all are ignored in preference for the facial expression. TV is not so much an action, as a re-action, medium.   (28)

The yen of the TV medium for themes of process and complex reactions has enabled the documentary type of film to come to the fore. The movie *can* handle process superbly, but the movie viewer is more disposed to be a passive consumer of actions, rather than a participant in reactions. The movie western, like the movie documentary, has always been a lowly form. With TV, the western acquired new importance, since its theme is always: "Let's make a town." The audience participates in the shaping and processing of a community from meager and unpromising components. Moreover, the TV image takes kindly to the varied and rough textures of Western saddles, clothes, hides, and shoddy match-wood bars and hotel lobbies. The movie camera, by contrast, is at home in the slick chrome world of the night club and the luxury spots of a metropolis. Moreover, the contrasting camera preferences of the movies in the Twenties and Thirties, and of TV in the Fifties and Sixties spread to the entire population. In ten years the new tastes of America in clothes, in food, in housing, in entertainment, and in vehicles express the new pattern of interrelation of forms and do-it-yourself involvement fostered by the TV image.   (29)

It is no accident that such major movie stars as Rita Hayworth, Liz Taylor, and Marilyn Monroe ran into troubled waters in the new TV age. They ran into an age that questioned all the "hot" media values of the pre-TV consumer days. The TV image challenges the values of fame as much as the values of consumer goods. "Fame to me," said Marilyn Monroe, "certainly is only a temporary and a partial happiness. Fame is not really for a daily diet, that's not what fulfills you. . . . I think that when you are famous every weakness is exaggerated. This industry should behave to its stars like a mother whose child has just run out in front of a car. But instead of clasping the child to them they start punishing the child."   (30)

The movie community is now getting clobbered by TV, and lashes out at anybody in its bewildered petulance. These words of the great movie puppet who wed Mr. Baseball and Mr. Broadway are surely a portent. If many of the rich and successful figures in America were to question publicly the absolute value of money and success as means to happiness and human welfare, they would offer no more shattering a precedent than Marilyn Monroe. For nearly fifty years, Hollywood had offered "the fallen woman" a way to the top and a way to the hearts of all. Suddenly the love-goddess emits a horrible cry, screams that eating people is wrong, and utters denunciations of the whole way of life. This is exactly the mood of the suburban beatniks. They reject a fragmented and specialist consumer life for anything that offers humble involvement and deep commitment. It is the same mood that recently turned girls from specialist careers to early marriage and big families. They switch from jobs to roles.   (31)

The same new preference for depth participation has also prompted in the young a strong drive toward religious experience with rich liturgical overtones. The liturgical revival of the radio and TV age affects even the most austere Protestant sects. Choral chant and rich vestments have appeared in every quarter. The ecumenical movement is synonymous with electric technology.   (32)

Just as TV, the mosaic mesh, does not foster perspective in art, it does not foster lineality in living. Since TV, the assembly line has disappeared from industry. Staff and line structures have dissolved in management. Gone are the stag line, the party line, the receiving line, and the pencil line from the backs of nylons.   (33)

With TV came the end of bloc voting in politics, a form of specialism and fragmentation that won't work since TV. Instead of the voting bloc, we have the icon, the inclusive image. Instead of a political viewpoint or platform, the inclusive political posture or stance. Instead of the product, the process. In periods of new and rapid growth there is a blurring of outlines. In the TV image we have the supremacy of the blurred outline, itself the maximal incentive to growth and new "closure" or completion, especially for a consumer culture long related to the sharp visual values that had become separated from the other senses. So great is the change in American lives, resulting from the loss of loyalty to the consumer package in entertainment and commerce, that every enterprise, from Madison Avenue and General Motors to Hollywood and General Foods, has been shaken thoroughly and forced to seek new strategies of action. What electric implosion or contraction has done inter-personally and inter-nationally, the TV image does intra-personally or intra-sensuously. (34)

It is not hard to explain this sensuous revolution to painters and sculptors, for they have been striving, ever since Cézanne abandoned perspective illusion in favor of structure in painting, to bring about the very change that TV has now effected on a fantastic scale. TV is the Bauhaus program of design and living, or the Montessori educational strategy, given total technological extension and commercial sponsorship. The aggressive lunge of artistic strategy for the remaking of Western man has, *via* TV, become a vulgar sprawl and an overwhelming splurge in American life. (35)

It would be impossible to exaggerate the degree to which this image has disposed America to European modes of sense and sensibility. America is now Europeanizing as furiously as Europe is Americanizing. Europe, during the Second War, developed much of the industrial technology needed for its first mass consumer phase. It was, on the other hand, the First War that had readied America for the same consumer "take-off." It took the electronic *implosion* to dissolve the nationalist diversity of a splintered Europe, and to do for it what the industrial *explosion* had done for America. The industrial explosion that accompanies the fragmenting expansion of literacy and industry was able to exert little unifying effect in the European world with its numerous tongues and cultures. The Napoleonic thrust had utilized the combined force of the new literacy and early industrialism. But Napoleon had had a less homogenized set of materials to work with than even the Russians have today. The homogenizing power of the literate process had gone further in America by 1800 than anywhere in Europe. From the first, America took to heart the print technology for its educational, industrial, and political life; and it was rewarded by an unprecedented pool of standardized workers and consumers, such as no culture had ever had before. That our cultural historians have been oblivious of the homogenizing power of typography, and of the irresistible strength of homogenized populations, is no credit to them. Political scientists have been quite unaware of the effects of media anywhere at any time, simply because nobody has been willing to study the personal and social effects of media apart from their "content." (36)

America long ago achieved its Common Market by mechanical and literate homogenization of social organization. Europe is now getting a unity under the electric auspices of compression and interrelation. Just how much homogenization via literacy is needed to make an effective producer-consumer group in the postmechanical age, in the age of automation, nobody has ever asked. For it has never been fully recognized that the role of literacy in shaping an industrial economy is basic and archetypal. Literacy is indispensable for habits of uniformity at all times and places. Above all, it is needed for the workability of price systems and markets. This factor has been ignored exactly as TV is now being ignored, for TV fosters many preferences that are quite at variance with literate uniformity and repeatability. It has sent Americans questing for every sort of oddment and quaintness in objects from out of their storied past. Many Americans will now spare no pains or expense to get to taste some new wine or food. The uniform and repeatable now must yield to the uniquely askew, a fact that is increasingly the despair and confusion of our entire standardized economy.   (37)

The power of the TV mosaic to transform American innocence into depth sophistication, independently of "content," is not mysterious if looked at directly. This mosaic TV image had already been adumbrated in the popular press that grew up with the telegraph. The commercial use of the telegraph began in 1844 in America, and earlier in England. The electric principle and its implications received much attention in Shelley's poetry. Artistic rule-of-thumb usually anticipates the science and technology in these matters by a full generation or more. The meaning of the telegraph mosaic in its *journalistic* manifestations was not lost to the mind of Edgar Allan Poe. He used it to establish two startlingly new inventions, the symbolist poem and the detective story. Both of these forms require do-it-yourself participation on the part of the reader. By offering an incomplete image or process, Poe *involved* his readers in the creative process in a way that Baudelaire, Valéry, T. S. Eliot, and many others have admired and followed. Poe had grasped at once the electric dynamic as one of public participation in creativity. Nevertheless, even today the homogenized consumer complains when asked to participate in creating or completing an abstract poem or painting or structure of any kind. Yet Poe knew even then that participation in depth followed at once from the telegraph mosaic. The more lineal and literal-minded of the literary brahmins "just couldn't see it." They still can't see it. They prefer not to participate in the creative process. They have accommodated themselves to the completed packages, in prose and verse and in the plastic arts. It is these people who must confront, in every classroom in the land, students who have accommodated themselves to the tactile and nonpictorial modes of symbolist and mythic structures, thanks to the TV image.   (38)

Life magazine for August 10, 1962, had a feature on how "Too Many Subteens Grow Up Too Soon and Too Fast." There was no observation of the fact that similar speed of growth and precociousness have always been the norm in tribal cultures and in nonliterate societies. England and America fostered the institution of prolonged adolescence by the negation of the tactile participation that is sex. In this, there was no conscious strategy, but rather a general acceptance of the consequences of prime stress on the printed word and visual values as a means of organizing personal and social life. This stress led to triumphs of industrial production and political conformity that were their own sufficient warrant. (39)

Respectability, or the ability to sustain visual inspection of one's life, became dominant. No European country allowed print such precedence. Visually, Europe has always been shoddy in American eyes. American women, on the other hand, who have never been equaled in any culture for visual turnout, have always seemed abstract, mechanical dolls to Europeans. Tactility is a supreme value in European life. For that reason, on the Continent there is no adolescence, but only the leap from childhood to adult ways. Such is now the American state since TV, and this state of evasion of adolescence will continue. The introspective life of long, long thoughts and distant goals, to be pursued in lines of Siberian railroad kind, cannot coexist with the mosaic form of the TV image that commands immediate participation in *depth* and admits of no delays. The mandates of that image are so various yet so consistent that even to mention them is to describe the revolution of the past decade. (40)

The phenomenon of the paperback, the book in "cool" version, can head this list of TV mandates, because the TV transformation of book culture into something else is manifested at that point. Europeans have had paperbacks from the first. From the beginnings of the automobile, they have preferred the wraparound space of the small car. The pictorial value of "enclosed space" for book, car, or house has never appealed to them. The paperback, especially in its highbrow form, was tried in America in the 1920s and thirties and forties. It was not, however, until 1953 that it suddenly became acceptable. No publisher really knows why. Not only is the paperback a tactile, rather than a visual, package; it can be as readily concerned with profound matters as with froth. The American since TV has lost his inhibitions and his innocence about depth culture. The paperback reader has discovered that he can enjoy Aristotle or Confucius by simply slowing down. The old literate habit of racing ahead on uniform lines of print yielded suddenly to depth reading. Reading in depth is, of course, not proper to the printed word as such. Depth probing of words and language is a normal feature of oral and manuscript cultures, rather than of print. Europeans have always felt that the English and Americans lacked depth in their culture. Since radio, and especially since TV, English and American literary critics have exceeded the performance of any European in depth and subtlety. The beatnik reaching out for Zen is only carrying the mandate of the TV mosaic out into the world of words and perception.

The paperback itself has become a vast mosaic world in depth, expressive of the changed sense-life of Americans, for whom depth experience in words, as in physics, has become entirely acceptable, and even sought after.   (41)

Just where to begin to examine the transformation of American attitudes since TV is a most arbitrary affair, as can be seen in a change so great as the abrupt decline of baseball. The removal of the Brooklyn Dodgers to Los Angeles was a portent in itself. Baseball moved West in an attempt to retain an audience after TV struck. The characteristic mode of the baseball game is that it features one-thing-at-a-time. It is a lineal, expansive game which, like golf, is perfectly adapted to the outlook of an individualist and inner-directed society. Timing and waiting are of the essence, with the entire field in suspense waiting upon the performance of a single player. By contrast, football, basketball, and ice hockey are games in which many events occur simultaneously, with the entire team involved at the same time. With the advent of TV, such isolation of the individual performance as occurs in baseball became unacceptable. Interest in baseball declined, and its stars, quite as much as movie stars, found that fame had some very cramping dimensions. Baseball had been, like the movies, a hot medium featuring individual virtuosity and stellar performers. The real ball fan is a store of statistical information about previous explosions of batters and pitchers in numerous games. Nothing could indicate more clearly the peculiar satisfaction provided by a game that belonged to the industrial metropolis of ceaselessly exploding populations, stocks and bonds, and production and sales records. Baseball belonged to the age of the first onset of the hot press and the movie medium. It will always remain a symbol of the era of the hot mommas, jazz babies, of sheiks and shebas, of vamps and gold-diggers and the fast buck. Baseball, in a word, is a hot game that got cooled off in the new TV climate, as did most of the hot politicians and hot issues of the earlier decades.   (42)

There is no cooler medium or hotter issue at present than the small car. It is like a badly wired woofer in a hi-fi circuit that produces a tremendous flutter in the bottom. The small European car, like the European paperback and the European belle, for that matter, was no visual package job. Visually, the entire batch of European cars are so poor an affair that it is obvious their makers never thought of them as something to look at. They are something to put on, like pants or a pullover. Theirs is the kind of space sought by the skin-diver, the water-skier, and the dinghy sailor. In an immediate tactile sense, this new space is akin to that to which the picture-window fad had catered. In terms of "view," the picture window never made any sense. In terms of an attempt to discover a new dimension in the out-of-doors by pretending to be a goldfish, the picture window does make sense. So do the frantic efforts to roughen up the indoor walls and textures as if they were the outside of the house. Exactly the same impulse sends the indoor spaces and furniture out into the patios in an attempt to experience the outside as inside. The TV viewer is in just that role at all times. He is submarine. He is bombarded by atoms that reveal the outside as inside in an endless adventure amidst blurred images and mysterious contours. (43)

However, the American car had been fashioned in accordance with the *visual* mandates of the typographic and the movie images. The American car was an enclosed space, not a tactile space. And an enclosed space is one in which all spatial qualities have been reduced to visual terms. So in the American car, as the French observed decades ago, "one is not on the road, one is in the car." By contrast, the European car aims to drag you alone the road and to provide a great deal of vibration for the bottom. Brigitte Bardot got into the news when it was discovered that she liked to drive barefoot in order to get the maximal vibration. Even English cars, weak on visual appearance as they are, have been guilty of advertising that "at sixty miles an hour all you can hear is the ticking of the clock." That would be a very poor ad, indeed, for a TV generation that has to be *with* everything and has to *dig* things in order to get at them. So avid is the TV viewer for rich tactile effects that he could be counted on to revert to skis. The wheel, so far as he is concerned, lacks the requisite abrasiveness. (44)

Clothes in this first TV decade repeat the same story as vehicles. The revolution was heralded by bobby-soxers who dumped the whole cargo of visual effects for a set of tactile ones so extreme as to create a dead level of flat-footed dead-panism. Part of the cool dimension of TV is the cool, deadpan mug that came in with the teenager. Adolescence, in the age of hot media, of radio and movie, and of the ancient book, had been a time of fresh, eager, and expressive countenances. No elder statesman or senior executive of the 1940s would have ventured to wear so dead and sculptural a pan as the child of the TV age. The dances that came in with TV were to match—all the way to the Twist, which is merely a form of very unanimated dialogue, the gestures and grimaces of which indicate involvement in depth, but "nothing to say." (45)

Clothing and styling in the past decade have gone so tactile and sculptural that they present a sort of exaggerated evidence of the new qualities of the TV mosaic. The TV extension of our nerves in hirsute pattern possesses the power to evoke a flood of related imagery in clothing, hairdo, walk, and gesture. (46)

All this adds up to the compressional implosion—the return to nonspecialized forms of clothes and spaces, the seeking of multi-uses for rooms and things and objects, in a single word—the iconic. In music and poetry and painting, the tactile implosion means the insistence on qualities that are close to casual speech. Thus Schönberg and Stravinsky and Carl Orff and Bartok, far from being advanced seekers of esoteric effects, seem now to have brought music very close to the condition of ordinary human speech. It is this colloquial rhythm that once seemed so unmelodious about their work. Anyone who listens to the medieval works of Perotinus or Dufay will find them very close to Stravinsky and Bartok. The great explosion of the Renaissance that split musical instruments off from song and speech and gave them specialist functions is now being played backward in our age of electronic implosion.   (47)

One of the most vivid examples of the tactile quality of the TV image occurs in medical experience. In closed-circuit instruction in surgery, medical students from the first reported a strange effect—that they seemed not to be watching an operation, but performing it. They felt that they were holding the scalpel. Thus the TV image, in fostering a passion for depth involvement in every aspect of experience, creates an obsession with bodily welfare. The sudden emergence of the TV medico and the hospital ward as a program to rival the western is perfectly natural. It would be possible to list a dozen untried kinds of programs that would prove immediately popular for the same reasons. Tom Dooley and his epic of Medicare for the backward society was a natural outgrowth of the first TV decade.   (48)

Now that we have considered the subliminal force of the TV image in a redundant scattering of samples, the question would seem to arise: "What possible *immunity* can there be from the subliminal operation of a new medium like television?" People have long supposed that bulldog opacity, backed by firm disapproval, is adequate enough protection against any new experience. It is the theme of this piece that not even the most lucid understanding of the peculiar force of a medium can head off the ordinary "closure" of the senses that causes us to conform to the pattern of experience presented. The utmost purity of mind is no defense against bacteria, though the confreres of Louis Pasteur tossed him out of the medical profession for his base allegations about the invisible operation of bacteria. To resist TV, therefore, one must acquire the antidote of related media like print.   (49)

It is an especially touchy area that presents itself with the question: "What has been the effect of TV on our political life?" Here, at least, great traditions of critical awareness and vigilance testify to the safeguards we have posted against the dastardly uses of power.   (50)

When Theodore White's *The Making of the President: 1960* is opened at the section on "The Television Debates," the TV student will experience dismay. White offers statistics on the number of sets in American homes and the number of hours of daily use of these sets, but not one clue as to the nature of the TV image or its effects on candidates or viewers. White considers the "content" of the debates and the deportment of the debaters, but it never occurs to him to ask why TV would inevitably be a disaster for a sharp intense image like Nixon's, and a boon for the blurry, shaggy texture of Kennedy.   (51)

At the end of the debates, Philip Deane of the London *Observer* explained my idea of the coming TV impact on the election to the *Toronto Globe and Mail* under the headline of "The Sheriff and the Lawyer," October 15, 1960. It was that TV would prove so entirely in Kennedy's favor that he would win the election. Without TV, Nixon had it made. Deane, toward the end of his article, wrote:

> Now the press has tended to say that Mr. Nixon has been gaining in the last two debates and that he was bad in the first. Professor McLuhan thinks that Mr. Nixon has been sounding progressively more definite; regardless of the value of the Vice-President's views and principles, he has been defending them with too much flourish for the TV medium. Mr. Kennedy's rather sharp responses have been a mistake, but he still presents an image closer to the TV hero, Professor McLuhan says—something like the shy young Sheriff—while Mr. Nixon with his very dark eyes that tend to stare, with his slicker circumlocution, has resembled more the railway lawyer who signs leases that are not in the interests of the folks in the little town.
>
> In fact, by counterattacking and by claiming for himself, as he does in the TV debates, the same goals as the Democrats have, Mr. Nixon may be helping his opponent by blurring the Kennedy image, by confusing what exactly it is that Mr. Kennedy wants to change.
>
> Mr. Kennedy is thus not handicapped by clear-cut issues; he is visually a less well-defined image, and appears more nonchalant. He seems less anxious to sell himself than does Mr. Nixon. So far, then, Professor McLuhan gives Mr. Kennedy the lead without underestimating Mr. Nixon's formidable appeal to the vast conservative forces of the United States.   (52)

Another way of explaining the acceptable, as opposed to the unacceptable, TV personality is to say that anybody whose *appearance* strongly declares his role and status in life is wrong for TV. Anybody who looks as if he might be a teacher, a doctor, a businessman, or any of a dozen other things all at the same time is right for TV. When the person presented *looks* classifiable, as Nixon did, the TV viewer has nothing to fill in. He feels uncomfortable with his TV image. He says uneasily, "There's something about the guy that isn't right." The viewer feels exactly the same about an exceedingly pretty girl on TV, or about any of the intense "high definition" images and messages from the sponsors. It is not accidental that advertising has become a vast new source of comic effects since the ad-

vent of TV. Mr. Khrushchev is a very filled-in or completed image that
appears on TV as a comic cartoon. In wirephoto and on TV, Mr. Khrushchev is a jovial comic, an entirely disarming presence. Likewise, precisely
the formula that recommends anybody for a movie role disqualifies that
same person for TV acceptance. For the hot movie medium needs people
who look very definitely a *type* of some kind. The cool TV medium cannot abide the typical because it leaves the viewer frustrated of his job of
"closure" or completion of image. President Kennedy did not look like a
rich man or like a politician. He could have been anything from a grocer
or a professor to a football coach. He was not too precise or too ready of
speech in such a way as to spoil his pleasantly tweedy blur of countenance
and outline. He went from palace to log cabin, from wealth to the White
House, in a pattern of TV reversal and upset.   (53)

The same components will be found in any popular TV figure. Ed Sullivan, "the great stone face," as he was known from the first, has the much
needed harshness of texture and general sculptural quality demanded for
serious regard on TV. Jack Paar is quite otherwise—neither shaggy nor
sculptural. But on the other hand, his presence is entirely acceptable on TV
because of his utterly cool and casual verbal agility. The Jack Paar show
revealed the inherent need of TV for spontaneous chat and dialogue. Jack
discovered how to extend the TV mosaic image into the entire format of
his show, seemingly snaffling up just anybody from anywhere at the drop
of a hat. In fact, however, he understood very well how to create a mosaic
from other media, from the world of journalism and politics, books,
Broadway, and the arts in general, until he became a formidable rival to
the press mosaic itself. As Amos and Andy had lowered church attendance
on Sunday evenings in the old days of radio, so Jack Paar certainly cut
nightclub patronage with his late show.   (54)

How about Educational Television? When the three-year-old sits watching the President's press conference with Dad and Grandad, that illustrates
the serious educational role of TV. If we ask what is the relation of TV
to the learning process, the answer is surely that the TV image, by its
stress on participation, dialogue, and depth, has brought to America new
demand for crash-programming in education. Whether there ever will be
TV in every classroom is a small matter. The revolution has already taken
place at home. TV has changed our sense-lives and our mental processes.
It has created a taste for all experience *in depth* that affects language teaching as much as car styles. Since TV, nobody is happy with a mere book
knowledge of French or English poetry. The unanimous cry now is, "Let's
talk French," and "Let the bard be *heard*." And oddly enough, with the
demand for depth, goes the demand for crash-programming. Not only
deeper, but further, into all knowledge has become the normal popular demand since TV. Perhaps enough has been said about the nature of the TV

image to explain why this should be. How could it possibly pervade our lives any more than it does? Mere classroom use could not extend its influence. Of course, in the classroom its role compels a reshuffling of subjects, and approaches to subjects. Merely to put the present classroom on TV would be like putting movies on TV. The result would be a hybrid that is neither. The right approach is to ask, "What can TV do that the classroom cannot do for French, or for physics?" The answer is: "TV can illustrate the interplay of process and the growth of forms of all kinds as nothing else can." (55)

The other side of the story concerns the fact that, in the visually organized educational and social world, the TV child is an underprivileged cripple. An oblique indication of this startling reversal has been given by William Golding's *Lord of the Flies*. On the one hand, it is very flattering for hordes of docile children to be told that, once out of the sight of their governesses, the seething savage passions within them would boil over and sweep away pram and playpen, alike. On the other hand, Mr. Golding's little pastoral parable does have some meaning in terms of the psychic changes in the TV child. This matter is so important for any future strategy of culture or politics that it demands a headline prominence, and capsulated summary: (56)

WHY THE TV CHILD CANNOT SEE AHEAD

The plunge into depth experience via the TV image can only be explained in terms of the differences between visual and mosaic space. Ability to discriminate between these radically different forms is quite rare in our Western world. It has been pointed out that, in the country of the blind, the one-eyed man is not king. He is taken to be an hallucinated lunatic. In a highly visual culture, it is as difficult to communicate the nonvisual properties of spatial forms as to explain visuality to the blind. In the ABC of Relativity Bertrand Russell began by explaining that there is nothing difficult about Einstein's ideas, but that they do call for total reorganization of our imaginative lives. It is precisely this imaginative reorganization that has occurred via the TV image. (57)

The ordinary inability to discriminate between the photographic and the TV image is not merely a crippling factor in the learning process today; it is symptomatic of an age-old failure in Western culture. The literate man, accustomed to an environment in which the visual sense is extended everywhere as a principle of organization, sometimes supposes that the mosaic world of primitive art, or even the world of Byzantine art, represents a mere difference in degree, a sort of failure to bring their visual portrayals up to the level of full visual effectiveness. Nothing could be further from the truth. This, in fact, is a misconception that has impaired understanding between East and West for many centuries. Today it impairs relations between colored and white societies.   (58)

Most technology produces an amplification that is quite explicit in its separation of the senses. Radio is an extension of the aural, high-fidelity photography of the visual. But TV is, above all, an extension of the sense of touch, which involves maximal interplay of all the senses. For Western man, however, the all-embracing extension had occurred by means of phonetic writing, which is a technology for extending the sense of sight. All nonphonetic forms of writing are, by contrast, artistic modes that retain much variety of sensuous orchestration. Phonetic writing, alone, has the power of separating and fragmenting the senses and of sloughing off the semantic complexities. The TV image reverses this literate process of analytic fragmentation of sensory life.   (59)

The visual stress on continuity, uniformity, and connectedness, as it derives from literacy, confronts us with the great technological means of implementing continuity and lineality by fragmented repetition. The ancient world found this means in the brick, whether for wall or road. The repetitive, uniform brick, indispensable agent of road and wall, of cities and empires, is an extension, via letters, of the visual sense. *The brick wall is not a mosaic form,* and neither is the mosaic form a visual structure. The mosaic can be *seen* as dancing can, but is not *structured* visually; nor is it an extension of the visual power. For the mosaic is not uniform, continuous, or repetitive. It is discontinuous, skew, and nonlineal, like the tactual TV image. To the sense of touch, all things are sudden, counter, original, spare, strange. The "Pied Beauty" of G. M. Hopkins is a catalogue of the notes of the sense of touch. The poem is a manifesto of the nonvisual, and like Cézanne or Seurat, or Rouault it provides an indispensable approach to understanding TV. The nonvisual mosaic structures of modern art, like those of modern physics and electric-information patterns, permit little detachment. The mosaic form of the TV image demands participation and involvement in depth of the whole being, as does the sense of touch. Literacy, in contrast, had, by extending the visual power to the uniform organization of time and space, psychically and socially, conferred the power of detachment and noninvolvement.   (60)

The visual sense when extended by phonetic literacy fosters the analytic habit of perceiving the single facet in the life of forms. The visual power enables us to isolate the single incident in time and space, as in representational art. In visual representation of a person or an object, a single phase or moment or aspect is separated from the multitude of known and felt phases, moments and aspects of the person or object. By contrast, iconographic art uses the eye as we use our hand in seeking to create an inclusive image, made up of many moments, phases, and aspects of the person or thing. Thus the iconic mode is not visual representation, nor the specialization of visual stress as defined by viewing from a single position. The tactual mode of perceiving is sudden but not specialist. It is total, synesthetic, involving all the senses. Pervaded by the mosaic TV image, the TV child encounters the world in a spirit antithetic to literacy.   (61)

The TV image, that is to say, even more than the icon, is an extension of the sense of touch. Where it encounters a literate culture, it necessarily thickens the sense-mix, transforming fragmented and specialist extensions into a seamless web of experience. Such transformation is, of course, a "disaster" for a literate, specialist culture. It blurs many cherished attitudes and procedures. It dims the efficacy of the basic pedagogic techniques, and the relevance of the curriculum. If for no other reason, it would be well to understand the dynamic life of these forms as they intrude upon us and upon one another. TV makes for myopia.   (62)

The young people who have experienced a decade of TV have naturally imbibed an urge toward involvement in depth that makes all the remote visualized goals of usual culture seem not only unreal but irrelevant, and not only irrelevant but anemic. It is the total involvement in all-inclusive *nowness* that occurs in young lives via TV's mosaic image. This change of attitude has nothing to do with programming in any way, and would be the same if the programs consisted entirely of the highest cultural content. The change in attitude by means of relating themselves to the mosaic TV image would occur in any event. It is, of course, our job not only to understand this change but to exploit it for its pedagogical richness. The TV child expects involvement and doesn't want a specialist *job* in the future. He does want a *role* and a deep commitment to his society. Unbridled and misunderstood, this richly human need can manifest itself in the distorted forms portrayed in *West Side Story*.   (63)

The TV child cannot see ahead because he wants involvement, and he cannot accept a fragmentary and merely visualized goal or destiny in learning or in life.   (64)

MURDER BY TELEVISION

Jack Ruby shot Lee Oswald while tightly surrounded by guards who were paralyzed by television cameras. The fascinating and involving power of television scarcely needed this additional proof of its peculiar operation upon human perceptions. The Kennedy assassination gave people an immediate sense of the television power to create depth involvement, on the one hand, and a numbing effect as deep as grief, itself, on the other hand. Most people were amazed at the depth of meaning which the event communicated to them. Many more were surprised by the coolness and calm of the mass reaction. The same event, handled by press or radio (in the absence of television), would have provided a totally different experience. The national "lid" would have "blown off." Excitement would have been enormously greater and depth participation in a common awareness very much less.   (65)

As explained earlier, Kennedy was an excellent TV image. He had used the medium with the same effectiveness that Roosevelt had learned to achieve by radio. With TV, Kennedy found it natural to involve the nation in the office of the Presidency, both as an operation and as an image. TV reaches out for the corporate attributes of office. Potentially, it can transform the Presidency into a monarchic dynasty. A merely elective Presidency scarcely affords the depth of dedication and commitment demanded by the TV form. Even teachers on TV seem to be endowed by the student audiences with a charismatic or mystic character that much exceeds the feelings developed in the classroom or lecture hall. In the course of many studies of audience reactions to TV teaching, there recurs this puzzling fact. The viewers feel that the teacher has a dimension almost of sacredness. This feeling does not have its basis in concepts or ideas, but seems to creep in uninvited and unexplained. It baffles both the students and the analysts of their reactions. Surely, there could be no more telling touch to tip us off to the character of TV. This is not so much a visual as a tactual-auditory medium that involves all of our senses in depth interplay. For people long accustomed to the merely visual experience of the typographic and photographic varieties, it would seem to be the *synesthesia*, or tactual depth of TV experience, that dislocates them from their usual attitudes of passivity and detachment.   (66)

The banal and ritual remark of the conventionally literate, that TV presents an experience for passive viewers, is wide of the mark. TV is above all a medium that demands a creatively participant response. The guards who failed to protect Lee Oswald were not passive. They were so involved by the mere sight of the TV cameras that they lost their sense of their merely practical and specialist task.   (67)

Perhaps it was the Kennedy funeral that most strongly impressed the audience with the power of TV to invest an occasion with the character of corporate participation. No national event except in sports has ever had such coverage or such an audience. It revealed the unrivaled power of TV to achieve the involvement of the audience in a complex *process*. The funeral as a corporate process caused even the image of sport to pale and dwindle into puny proportions. The Kennedy funeral, in short, manifested the power of TV to involve an entire population in a ritual process. By comparison, press, movie and even radio are mere packaging devices for consumers.   (68)

Most of all, the Kennedy event provides an opportunity for noting a paradoxical feature of the "cool" TV medium. It involves us in moving depth, but it does not excite, agitate or arouse. Presumably, this is a feature of all depth experience.   (69)

Jacques Barzun

(1907–   )

BARZUN was until recently Dean of the Faculties and Provost at Columbia University, where he has been continuously since his undergraduate days (B.A., 1927). The breadth of his interests in cultural history is indicated by some representative titles from among his books: Teacher in America *(1945),* Music in American Life *(1956),* The House of Intellect *(1959),* Science: The Glorious Entertainment *(1964).*

■ *Conversation, Manners, and the Home*

IN PRIVATE LIFE the counterpart of public debate is conversation. The word sounds old-fashioned and its meaning is blurred, because in the years since conversation was given a name and made an ideal, its nature has changed as much as that of public debate—and for the same reasons. Yet whether we use the word to mean all forms of verbal exchange or, more narrowly, the sociable sifting of opinion for pleasure, conversation is the testing ground of manners. This is so because manners are minor morals which facilitate the relations of men, chiefly through words. When those verbal relations are deliberately staged, for no other purpose than pleasure, men find themselves engaged in an intellectual exercise that is one of the delights of life. Manners, therefore, are not solely a clue to the deeper moral assumptions of an age, they are also a strong or weak guardian of Intellect at its most exposed. (1)

Conversation being difficult, the reality of it has always been inferior to the ideal. We can nevertheless deduce almost as much from the ideal—or the lack of it—as from the audible reality. The reader will have noticed that I did not speak of sociable conversation as the *exchange*, but as the *sifting* of opinion. The 'exchange' view is a nearly correct description of modern practice: A delivers an opinion while B thinks of the one he will inject as soon as he decently can. It is an exchange in the same sense that we 'exchange' greetings: we offer a formula and are offered another, but generally go off with our own.   (2)

In this rudimentary game Intellect plays a small role. It contents itself with finding words adequate to the belief or impression of the moment, while navigating a passable course among other ideas suspected of being afloat in the vicinity. The genuine exercise or true conversation sifts opinion, that is, tries to develop tenable positions by alternate statements, objections, modifications, examples, arguments, distinctions, expressed with the aid of the rhetorical arts—irony, exaggeration, and the rest—properly muted to the size and privateness of the scene.   (3)

In modern life this discovery of opinion by conversing is supposed to have more than pleasurable uses. We are addicted to 'panels' and 'forums' and 'round tables' on given topics. When broadcast, such performances are supposed to interest, and even instruct, millions of listeners and viewers, also in living rooms. That these conversations in public most often fail is a proof of the lack of conversational skill among the educated. After one such failure on a national network, an introspective member of the group, a psychiatrist, tried to state the causes, for the use of program directors. He blamed the latter as well as the speakers: 'Every one . . . did a bad job. Our inept efforts at discussion reminded me of a lot of falling-down drunks trying to shake hands.' He then listed the requisites of success: 'not a group of yes-men, but of men who are on a par in their knowledge of the field . . . so that they can communicate without such purely verbal confusions as clouded our interchange. I will say flatly that unless any panel . . . is given lots of prebroadcast time for free discussion, and repeatedly, the group cannot be expected to talk effectively in front of the camera. . . . An unrehearsed poly-disciplinary group lack a common language. . . . We had assembled for an hour and a half before the broadcast, but failed to take advantage even of that meager time. This was because after about ten minutes of groping talk, further discussion was halted lest we become stale. . . . Similarly, during the conduct of the discussion, just as we would begin to join issue around some problem, our moderator would abruptly change the topic. . . . Everybody on the panel felt increasingly frustrated and the audience was confused and unenlightened.'   (4)

Most participants in public conversations would agree with the critic and would welcome one or two hours of warming up. But in a practiced conversationalist a prolonged rehearsal would kill interest and spontaneity before the broadcast. The director's fear of staleness was therefore justified;

his error was to suppose that his experts—lecturers and writers though they were—were conversationalists. Our use of panels and other discussion groups offers a curious instance of a social form that does not produce its adepts. The cause must lie in the existence of a stronger contrary force.* In a discussion of 'Political Communication and Social Structure in the United States,' Mr. David Riesman makes clear that the eliciting of opinion, notably by interviewers, is universally considered the very opposite of conversation. That name is reserved for 'chit-chat about health, personal relations, the job.' (5)

A German writer, noting recently that in the title of the latest edition of Brockhaus, the term 'Konversations-lexicon' has been dropped, attributes the general decay of conversation to the lack of an idle class, or more simply, of leisure. But leisure is increasing, and enough time, surely is spent by persons with a college degree in 'exchanging' ideas, on social as well as on public occasions. It cannot be our material circumstances alone that hamper us, but rather our manners, that is to say, at bottom, our emotions. (6)

For the starting point of conversation is contradiction, and this democratic manners do not tolerate. Contradiction implies that one or another of the conversing group must be wrong, and under modern manners, as I said earlier without trying to explain it, peculiar feelings cling to error. Perhaps science has made small accuracy sacred to all, though everybody thinks that to be caught in a mistake is necessary to prove that one is human. Or again it may be that business and industry lead us to overestimate the interest of facts, about which contradiction is foolish. I think it more likely that the fear of being wrong which prohibits contradiction has in view, not error as an intellectual mishap, but the punishment that follows a breach of group unity. If your hostess says that the latest play by Mr. Kentucky Jones is very fine, and you contradict her, no matter how sweetly, one of you will have the majority in opposition. And this, regardless of who is the odd man out, nobody will enjoy. The reasoning goes: you are one against several = you are wrong = you are a fool. In some companies, the series of inferences would run: perverse = showing off = a snob; and the rejection would be no less complete. (7)

In either form, the syllogism is bound to be hard to refute when the first premise of a society is that the voice of the people, ascertained by majority vote, is the voice of God. All the great men since Socrates may have asserted the contrary, but their assertion was evidently self-serving. Virtue in modern politics is against the solitary dissident. It is assumed

---

* The program called "Conversation" and led by Mr. Clifton Fadiman was, it is true, generally successful as conversation. It received several awards and a good deal of written approval. But it did not commend itself very long to NBC, nor to any advertising sponsors, for whom monologue has an obvious advantage.

that he too wants the backing of a majority, and having gained it will enjoy power. This is never allowable in a populist culture. Even in the Soviet Union the 'cult of personality' has been denounced, which is comic but indicative.   (8)

By confining conversation to facts or to the exchange of bland opinions, trouble is avoided. This is elementary self-protection in a system where the absence of fixed place and privilege puts one at the mercy of the group. When we quote what Tocqueville said: 'I know of no country in which there is so little independence of mind and real freedom of discussion as in America,' we must not ascribe wholly to timidity what is in part sensible self-restraint. Even in the great days of militant liberalism it was decreed that politics and religion should be excluded from general conversation. This is a tribute to the power of words, in that people take them as the signs of instant action, of treason, rape, sacrilege. One does not know whether to wonder more at the imagination of the listener who is so readily hurt and alarmed, or at the skill of the speaker who over a cup of tea can with a few phrases produce flushed faces and the grim ardor of a militia defending hearth and home. However it comes about, the motive of curiosity about ideas, the play of mind, is not accounted a social possibility. But subversion is.   (9)

That is why full democracy has simply extended the no-politics-or-religion rule to any strong opinion. Yeats, moving in circles full of intellectuals and full of ideas, could yet long for the conversation of a *society*, for gaiety of mind and the fantasy that prepares matured convictions, for the kind of agreement that comes with, and not instead of, the free play of Intellect. What he found and what we have is the political judgment of dissidence carried into the living room and using the threat of mild or harsh ostracism to prevent even the shadow of conflict.   (10)

In putting first the political, I do not mean to overlook other impeding emotions. Good conversation, like any game, calls for equals in strength. But in a social system where movement is easy and frequent, one meets mostly strangers, whose equality other than legal and abstract has to be presumed. To safeguard that presumption, democratic manners prevent a jousting in which somebody might appear stronger, brighter, quicker, or richer of mind. This is not to say that democratic society is without snobbery. But like our public opinion, our accepted snobbery seldom ventures outside the tangible. It relies on differences that are not subject to dispute, such as disinfected wealth or descent from a famous historical event. Otherwise, the assumption of social equality indispensable to our life is preserved by blinking or suppressing all signs of the contrary.   (11)

This description may suggest that underneath its amiability the democratic group hides ugly sentiments. This is rarely true. Whatever his unconscious fear of Intellect, the democrat's conscious desire is philanthropic;

he wants love to prevail; he wants to add friends to friends and find them friends to one another, as in Euclid; he wants, above all, that everything and everybody should be agreeable, by which he means interchangeable, indistinguishable—like a prefabricated part—until the taste for human encounters is purified and uplifted from the social to the gregarious. The highest merit and pleasure is to love people, to want to be with people, to be 'good with people.'   (12)

Only a churlish man could profess insensibility to so much warmth and such regal indifference to the marks, precisely, of difference. For the true-born democrat, origin, education, and intellect matter no more than clothes, speech, and deportment. He no longer sees them, or he feels remorse when the thought of them breaks through his proper manners to his conscious mind.   (13)

The philanthropic motive thus generates its atmosphere and chooses its goals. The hope being to found unity on a simple similarity among men, the search is for essences. Not externals, depths. The taste for psychologizing takes it for granted that depths are more real than surfaces, and since depths will be shown only to the face of love, each person seeks out the other's heart. No longer does anyone think or say of a new acquaintance: 'I disliked him, but we had a fine conversation.' Rather, we guard against this discrepancy by prefacing the slightest reference to disagreement with: 'Please understand, I'm very fond of Ted, but I think he's wrong about transplanting irises.' Face to face, we say: 'I entirely agree with you, but—' This means, surely, that knowing the weakness of our intellects, we confess that we might disagree unreasonably, out of dislike. So strong is the belief that to differ is to endanger the budding love of new friends, that the word 'candid' has become synonymous with critical: 'I was candid with him. I told him—' As everybody knows, the desire for personal rapport knows no bounds or season; it is just as passionate in the committee meeting as in the living room. Indeed, who can now tell the two places apart by manners or subjects of discourse? On the occasions called sociable, the sought-for communion untroubled by ideas—that is, the discovery of the stranger's essence—brings forth the ultimate praise: 'She's a real person,' 'I found him very real.'   (14)

To reach that reality quickly, the preliminaries must be reduced to a minimum—hence the supreme duty of informality, the casual style. Its contrary, politeness, would be sniffed at as 'formal manners,' rebuked as 'aloofness' and 'reserve,' or condemned as 'superiority.' This is one more reason to bar Intellect, which incurs all these disapprovals: it has and is form, and it is superior to nonintellect as any skill is to the corresponding incapacity. Aware of the burden, some possessors of Intellect try to mask or apologize for it. They exhibit a rough, boisterous simplicity, or they belittle mind, disclaim it, and patronize by turns. In this self-consciousness begins that shuffling which is the characteristic manner produced by our manners. (15)

Shuffling is what one cannot help doing when one is pulled by contrary feelings or chaotic perceptions, and unwilling or unable to make any prevail. To occupy this position might be mistaken for the self-awareness I call an attribute of Intellect. But there is a distinction between the shuffling of the self-conscious and the act of choice of the self-aware. The conventions that informality condemns were invented to facilitate this choice until it becomes second nature. To the lack of such habits under the reign of casualness can be attributed the painful extremes of tact and rudeness that characterize the modern scene.   (16)

To be sure, the rudeness exists only from the point of view of Intellect. Its opponents find natural the use of conversation for quick intimacy through probing and diagnosis. They scarcely attend to what you say in their eagerness to discern what you are. Their antennas and instincts are at work and not—as is soon plain—their ears and their reason. This accounts for the incoherence of the panel discussion and for the difficulty of maintaining general conversation among six or eight people. They break up into tête-à-têtes for mutual auscultation. Odd little indelicacies follow: people do not hesitate to ascertain your circumstances in full detail. They expect the same interviewing in return, to which they say: 'That's a good question.' You are evidently a bright, engaging specimen; they are noting down points. They remark: 'You said something just now that interested me'; i.e., the rest was useless for my purpose. No one thinks it improper to *personalize* in this way, but would deem it stiff and artificial to address himself to a theme that, like an object in the midst of the conversing group, stood at a distance from each participant.   (17)

It being accepted practice to start conversation by asking people what they do, one hears what is uppermost in their minds, and one is not always pleased. The lawyer's or the doctor's case, the businessman's or housewife's worry, can be as trying in talk as in reality. But it is wrong to conclude that shop talk is boring and should be ruled out. People seldom object when the shop is their own—the men on one side 'exchanging' stock-market rumors and opinions; the women on the other comparing children, schools, and clothes. These concerns being the stuff of life may be talked about in society, provided the speaker keeps his distance from them and *makes* something of his facts or views. He must, that is, mix the raw material of experience with some thought that gives a handle to further thought, to disagreement, to speculation—Yeats's 'phantasy.' Any subject—a lost button—then becomes matter for conversation and a source of delight.
                                                                        (18)

Achieving this calls for effort and a practice we now lack. Even if the personal view of sociability did not bar impersonal Intellect, the exercise

would prove too taxing for minds atrophied on the side of reasoning, helpless to judge what is fitting. Sometimes in a gathering an idea does emerge
in spite of everybody, stopping all other talk. One then sees how unprepared for this virgin birth intelligent people can be. They have thought the
thought but never reflected on it. They are forced to improvise; but their
span of attention hardly takes in one or two modifiers, and their faculty
of inference stumbles over every fallacy. Try, for example, to advance the
proposition discussed here, that for true sociability being agreeable is not
enough: five indignant voices will exclaim, 'So you like disagreeable people!' A nicely articulated idea, neither conventional nor perverse, nor
charged with ulterior motive, seems an unknown species *in society*—for
every educated person must frequently meet one in his reading. In society,
it may be surmised, everyone is made more delicate, fine-grained, and impres-
sionable by the presence of others; and since impressions strike at random
and exclude their rivals, each person is engulfed in the confusion of the
senses, hence self-conscious rather than self-aware, oppressed by surfeit of
personality, his own and others'.   (19)

At other times, a vestige of the desire to not merely report but comment
on life will produce the accepted substitutes for conversation—the anecdote of the raconteur and the quasi-lecture of the expert. Both may be,
like any other thing, good or bad of their kind, but at their best they still
are not conversation, even though either may be so much preferred by intellectual people to the usual small-talk-in-depth that they always invite a
known 'entertainer' for the evening. Whatever the burden of his monologue, his presence implies the other guests' known inadequacy—especially
if his words purport to inform or instruct. For conversation—as must be
said of most good things in this infatuated age—is the antithesis of education. Before conversation begins, the participants must be finished and polished persons; what must be 'real' about them is the possession of their
intellectual resources. They must know their own minds and have taken
care to furnish them, deliberately, with tenable ideas—Yeats's 'matured convictions.' With opposing views they must deal briskly, lightly, and in evident pleasure—Yeats's gaiety of mind. The result is a spectacle the beauty
of which is the subject of a famous passage in James's *Psychology:*   (20)

'When two minds of a high order, interested in kindred subjects, come
together, their conversation is chiefly remarkable for the summariness of its
allusions and the rapidity of its transitions. Before one of them is half
through a sentence, the other knows his meaning and replies. Such genial
play with such massive materials, such an easy flashing of light over far
perspectives, such careless indifference to the dust and apparatus that ordinarily surround a subject and seem to pertain to its essence, make these
conversations seem true feasts for gods to a listener who is educated enough
to follow them at all. . . .   (21)

'But we need not go as far as the ways of genius. Ordinary social intercourse will do. There the charm of conversation is in direct proportion to
the possibility of abridgment and elision and in inverse ratio to the need
of explicit statement . . . some persons have a real mania for completeness,
they must express every step. They are the most intolerable of companions,
and although their mental energy must in its way be great, they always
strike us as weak and second-rate. In short, the essence of plebeianism,
that which separates vulgarity from aristocracy, is perhaps less a defect
than an excess, the constant need to animadvert upon matters which for
the aristocratic temperament do not exist.'   (22)

If James is right in his terms as well as in his description, it is not
surprising that democratic manners spoil conversation and make it the
last resort of the socially marooned. But where he says 'aristocratic' he
might more aptly say 'patrician,' for he is thinking of the nineteenth-
century blend of lordly and upper bourgeois manners, and not of politics
and the prerogatives of class. The aboriginal aristocrat is certainly not a
causeur, much less an intellect; he is a fighter, not a reasoner. It was the
high middle class that historically wedded knowledge and elegance, reasoning and *politesse*. This compromise excluded pedantry, on one side,
and arrogance on the other, while retaining a pleasurable echo of both conflict and learning. From which it follows that the problem of manners for
democratic societies—supposing that modern men and women desired conversation—would be to add the democrat's good will and brotherliness to
the earlier ingredients without upsetting their balance within the ideal. (23)

To do this, and find again a place for Intellect, the democratic heart
would have to be purged of some of its other feelings. For, as James
goes on to show: '. . . the gentleman ignores considerations relative to
conduct, sordid suspicions, fears, calculations, etc., which the vulgarian is
fated to entertain; . . . he is silent where the vulgarian talks; . . . he gives
nothing but results where the vulgarian is profuse of reasons; . . . he does
not explain or apologize; . . . he uses one sentence instead of twenty; . . . in
a word, there is an amount of *interstitial* thinking, so to call it, which it is
quite impossible to get him to perform, but which is nearly all that the
vulgarian mind performs at all. All this suppression of the secondary leaves
the field *clear*—for higher flights should they choose to come.'   (24)

These observations, made when class lines were not yet effaced, bring
us back to the expedient of shuffling in our manners and its hindrance to
free intellectual movement. Shuffling is not an individual fault, but an
accepted solution to a general problem. Thus in the common round of
committee meetings, it is necessary to differ, but also impossible. Manners
therefore decree that one shall say: 'I may be all wrong, but—'; 'You'll
correct me if I'm wrong'; 'I'm only thinking aloud'; 'It looks that way from

where I sit—'; 'It's only a crazy notion that crossed my mind.' The lexicon
of pussyfooting is familiar. On its title page should appear the motto:
'Never say, "I think," which is obsolete; always say, "I feel," as in, "I feel
that the Treasurer has been dipping into the till"; then if you are wrong,
you haven't said anything.' Though the shuffling vocabulary is all hypocrisy,
it is a routine hypocrisy concealing a desperate wish to placate. Torn
between the fear of error and the fear of being thought inhuman, hating
to be misunderstood and hating even worse to be misliked, we verbally cast
off self-confidence and throw ourselves on the mercy of the court, saying
'frankly' before every sentence and giving warning when we are going
to be 'candid.'   (25)

The dominant feeling confronting its mate in these encounters is vanity
and not pride. Vanity is a static thing. It puts its faith in what it has
and is easily wounded. Pride is active, and satisfied only with what it can
do, hence accustomed not to feel small stings. The distinction, though not
absolute, is highly suggestive. True, men have always been vain and the
proud have not all died out. But if under democracy the effort to placate
has eclipsed the art of pleasing, it is because democratic life exposes tender
vanity more widely, and because increased numbers multiply the claimants
to placation, that is, to being kept in good humor. Formerly, the crux of the
art of pleasing was to 'shine,' which meant to flatter others' pride by a
visible effort of mind, charm, wit—in short, by a gift of something more
valuable than plain unvarnished self. Nowadays we coax rather than flatter
and we do it by whittling down the self so as to spare vanity the smallest
hurt. To shine would be egotistical, one must merely glow. This is of
especial importance in the practical relations of life, or as we say, in public
relations. Just as contradiction is taboo within doors, to avoid division, so
any 'stern opinion'* is ruled out abroad, in deference to a vague self-
interest: everybody senses that in the free agitation of so many human
molecules anyone may become another's customer, relative, employer, employee, or 'opposite number.' One must guard against disaffection by being
always smooth, lubricated, ready to talk and even to lunch. This is neither
politeness nor servility but public relations.   (26)

The native critics of Western culture blame commercialism for this
mind-destroying habit, as if trade by itself produced the wormlike stance.
They fail to see that it is popular government which has made accountability universal and thus caused everybody to be forever 'selling himself'
to everybody else. It is not commercial greed or any clear advantage that
moves one government official to butter up another in a distant bureau: he

---

* I borrow this useful phrase from a sketch of the life and character of the great American athlete,
Rafer Johnson: 'Johnson never says anything controversial, has no stern opinions about anything, and
is not generally regarded as "good copy" by track reporters. Yet everybody likes him. . . . A lot of
kids,' adds the university coach, 'are shy and look away when they're talking to you. Not Rafer. He is
literate.' *New York Times*, July 29, 1958.

is moved by the you-never-know which a society of unsure equals engenders. And to his mild apprehension, mixed with genuine fellow-feeling, the other responds. This mutual tenderness is the wellspring of all our philanthropies. Conversely, in a society that had little free movement but fixed ranks and set forms, the most rapacious merchant could go through life without fawning and would not dare sell himself or anything else during social intercourse. He might represent as fitly as anyone the human dignity we talk about so much, seeing it so little.   (27)

To generalize, the main cause of our distress as social beings, a distress all the greater for being obscure, lies in the democratic rule of Everything for All. Distinction, discrimination, by which the intellect divides and reduces its burdens, mean for us only invidious distinction and unjust discrimination. We resist exclusions and accordingly do not even exclude ourselves but remain perpetually in competition with all our fellow men; we never give up, a priori, any of our pretensions, in consequence of which there is nothing to relieve us of being continually our own shock absorbers.   (28)

Meanwhile, this obsession with public relations injures Intellect by taking precedence over all other motives and interests—simplicity, independence, acquired rank and repute, and the force or fantasy of talent itself. The surrender is by no means a purely American weakness, or one affecting only the captive intellectuals of Madison Avenue. The world over, the demands of every profession now come second to the need of perpetual self-justification. To take a foreign example that is especially vivid by its contrast of then and now, consider the English stationmaster. Traditionally, he has been a man of strong character and quick intelligence, whose responsibilities, far heavier than those of his American counterpart, could only be shouldered after a long apprenticeship. Until recently, his dignity was signalized by the wearing of a top hat, dark clothes including pin-striped trousers, and often some decoration in the buttonhole. A modern 'profile' confirms the fact that 'of all railway functionaries the stationmaster is the most impressive,' and goes on to detail his nerve-racking generalship. Then comes the modern conclusion: 'But perhaps the most important qualification for the job is being able to get on with people—both his own staff and the public. The pleasantries exchanged with passengers on the platform, the views he expresses as a member of the Newbury Chamber of Commerce, his weekly visit to the cattle market to discuss the day's traffic with the local farmers, play a vital part in keeping British Railways in touch with its customers.'   (29)

In the accompanying illustration, the stationmaster new style wears a sack suit and cap. As his technical duties have yielded first place to public relations, he has become informal, casual, 'human.' But the rational necessity for this is worth noting: the public must not be allowed to forget so inconspicuous an institution as the railways; must be made to love them *via* the stationmaster and his pleasantries. Which suggests that if man ever conquers space, a competent staff will be needed to keep the public favorably reminded of the existence of the sun and moon. (30)

The extent to which the difficulties inherent in framing a code of democratic manners have been aggravated by the spread of literary emotions is still imperfectly appreciated. This is true even though modern art has portrayed the shuffler in all his poses, and proved again and again that the maze of his feelings is superior to the rectilinear intellect. From the many fictional models everyone has learned that 'the other' to whom all manners are directed is, like oneself, sensitive and a psychologizer. He is watchful, anxious, and vain where patrician pride would scorn 'sordid suspicions, fears, and calculations.' What ensues among the educated is a game of forestalling and reassurance by self-depreciation, which is shuffling intellectualized. Its manifestations are so familiar that we cease noticing how they destroy good sense—as, for instance, in this circular from a research institute: 'Despite some difficulties undoubtedly traceable to the recession (the term has possibly been replaced by another, equally inadequate and confusing word by the time these lines reach you). . . .' Or again, in a column about books: 'We are not the one to tell you about the virtues of one dictionary as against another. We hardly know anything about them and we have never quite believed in them. They disquiet us. . . . Nevertheless . . .' (31)

What is the double play here? A does not want us to think he believes the recession is an entity or an excuse, while he actually does what he deprecates. B does not want us to think he is a highbrow familiar with dictionaries, or that he is about to say what in fact he does say after his 'Nevertheless.' This wanting to and not wanting to seem to, because one knows how others will gloat or blame or laugh, has been exquisitely described by a distinguished essayist and writer of short stories who is a connoisseur in self-consciousness. He tells of going into a bookstore in Athens to buy the supposedly dirty book, Nabokov's *Lolita:* 'I . . . held it in my hands . . . while a lady clerk, very clean and genteel, stood smirking beside me. . . . Perhaps I only imagined it, but she seemed so clearly to condescend to me, so unmistakably to consider it beneath her station to engage in such transactions (she had to make a living, of course, and she did not hold it against me *personally*) that I left finally without buying the book. (32)

'If I could only have said or done something to make it clear that I was not just another provincial American professor on a moral toot (after all, I was precisely a provincial American professor), but a reader who has relished for a long time Nabokov's oblique, unidiomatic war on our culture, and who—it would not really have been the point, even if I could have said it. Either way, it is a trap.'   (33)

The description is ironic, of course—what statement these days is not?— but modern irony includes literalism, and we can take this *marivaudage*, this dizzying interplay of 'insights' (plus irony), as the formula of the suspicions, fears, and calculations that make up sophisticated shuffling. In reason, all these formulas and episodes are indefensible. Simple reflection says to the researcher: use the word that everyone uses or find a better, only come to the point; and to the critic: in a column about books why hesitate to speak of dictionaries? Do it, we expect it; only, forget yourself and omit apologies. As for the professor and the lady clerk, their tangled emotions would require a revolution to dissever.   (34)

But in tracing the trouble to its source, reflection picks out of the recital the reference to the novelist Nabokov's 'oblique war on our culture.' For the phrase gives a clue to the tortuous relation between the shuffling manners of democracy and the modern artist's oblique thrust at society. Where have intellectuals learned, together with their anti-intellectualism, these diffident gestures of the spirit? The answer is: in the novel. The novel from its beginnings in *Don Quixote* and *Tom Jones* has persistently made war on two things—our culture and the heroic.* Unlike tragedy voluminous and explicit, the novel, depicting life with cruel educational intent, has been the textbook of increasingly plain manners, a manual of resentful self-consciousness. Again unlike tragedy, in which everyone is in the right, the novel is a melodrama in which everyone is in the wrong. The novel knows no magnanimity or logic and makes the most trivial traits indicative. The inflection of a voice, the angle at which a head is carried, the coarse hairs that grow on the back of a hand—at some time or other, every physical accident has served a novelist to characterize the victim or the instrument of a moral lesson. Two centuries of geniuses have shown us that every moral attitude betrays an immoral urge, every virtue its complementary vice, every institution the evil it is meant to restrict. No wonder modern man has grown suspicious of himself and others, devious, ironic.   (35)

And now our scientific determinism reinforces the novelist's habit of reading back from sign to soul. Owing to this psychological license, the same manners which ignore birth, position, speech, and deportment, fasten on a man's complexion and habitus with the avowed endeavor to 'see what makes him tick.' The upshot is to reduce ticking to near-inaudibility. Everyone muffles his soul for fear he shall be deemed one who thinks well of himself, a seeker after power.   (36)

---

*We speak indeed of the 'hero of a novel' and continue to regard Don Quixote, Tom Jones, Julien Sorel, Pierre Bezuhov, and Dmitri Karamazov as figures larger than life. But their careers and that of their equals show chiefly their weakness even as they imply the wrongness of society. The ultimate models of this joint inadequacy are Flaubert's Frédéric Moreau and Joyce's Bloom. Only Scott and his disciple Balzac attempted to portray heroic heroes.

But evasion is useless: the novelist's point of fire is never still and there is no pleasing him. He will blame his puppets for not being or doing something which, if they attempted it, he would brand as affectation and would kill with ridicule. This double standard the intellectual part of society learns from him and so acquires the knack of captiousness: nothing, no one, is ever quite good enough. Better to carp at all who stand up in public than turn magnanimous and overlook inevitable flaws, for skepticism is a better guard against power than admiration. This temper affects the judgment of lives, including one's own. Biography, which has borrowed from the novel the guerrilla technique, derides ambition as pretentious and absurd, though it also blames thinkers and doers for not having converted the world and made it perfect. From these failures, miscalled 'tragedies,' the reader learns the futility of taking risks, and studies to be small.   (37)

Behind these literary lessons lies the fear of power, to which I have often referred. Why is this fear so pervasive as to seem obvious wisdom? One reason is that, historically, democracy has followed the libertarian ideal, which asserted itself slowly and painfully at the expense of monarchical and aristocratic power. The long struggle has left us the tradition that power as such is evil; power is something that need not be and that no good man would want, for whoever seeks evil must be evil. Since the world cannot subsist without some visible concentrations of power, the *world* is evil. And it follows that the acts and attitudes suggestive of powerlessness constitute the definition of virtue. The effusions of philanthropy, the self-abnegation of science, the unworldliness of art, seem the models of the good life. Like the history of liberty, the history of art is used as a Golden Legend full of pious examples. The naughty world, triumphant over genius, proves the artist a martyr, not a doer, and hence superior to the power that destroys him.   (38)

The increasing zeal for art thus re-enforces the hatred of power, quite as if artistic geniuses were not in fact the embodiment of ruthless power, fanatically bent on exercising sway outside art as well as within it. The truth is that when great artists go under, it is not as slaughtered lambs but as the vanquished in the struggle for power. Yet even when a modern critic perceives this, the moral drawn from it is that art must renounce the struggle 'in the court of kings' and search for its rightful place 'in the castle of God.' Though Western art as a whole teaches no such lesson, modern artists have not resisted, but abetted, our century's obsession about power, often with a lack of humor which will divert posterity. Not until our time, as Diana Trilling pointed out, had anyone enacted Mozart's Don Juan as a victim of his impulses, innocent of the lust for power, simply a dilettante carried away, presumably, by the possibilities of public relations.   (39)

This other-worldliness of our day necessarily fears and shuns Intellect. Discipline is too close to power, logic too far from philanthropy. Rather, the relaxed will associated with art and with its many surrogates called 'creative' appears as the only goal for the intelligent. Men no longer speak of careers, they disavow ambition; they are rebels without a cause. Formerly, the goal of a rebel was to destroy in order to *do*. On his way, he would bend the least possible under pressure, he schooled himself to yield without losing integrity. But for this kind of success one must be an integer to start with. A man can resist, a little more each day, along a self-set course, until he masters his soul, his work, perhaps his age. Though often beaten, his intellect and his conscience help keep each other clear. But the dis-integrated, dis-intellected intellectual of today, whether simon-pure bohemian or turned commercial in his own despite, fights sullenly and shuffles his way out of any possible exercise of power. His excuse to himself rests on the postulate that unless he can set the whole world right, he can do nothing. And thus the doctrine of a universal, unconquerable evil feeds itself.   (40)

Abdicating power generates the taste for organized inaction and the pursuit of pseudo-work: I refer to redundant talk, broody sittings of committees and proliferating plans and reports fore and aft of nonexisting accomplishments. It is not exaggerating to say that ritual gathering has by now become a polite form of debauch. I have before me a pressing request to attend one of these consultations without fee: 'Our meetings so far have been so stimulating that I can't imagine you would be bored. We're full of ideas and anxious to bring to these ideas the best . . . the most. . . . Could you come to lunch [with six others] at which time you could give us some invaluable . . . which should . . . most serious consideration?'   (41)

In these conferrings, of course, anything resembling direct assertion and the maintenance of intellectual order is forbidden by the manners and vocabulary of good-fellowship, and this insures at once the orgiastic effect and its prolongation. But we are left with a puzzling fact. Some of the participants in meetings of this sort feel penitent. Why have they come? It is of course part of the ritual to protest against the waste of time, but some few mean what they say. Why do they not decline? I would not impute to them the desire of the guilty to corrupt others. Rather, they give in as the drunkard does when urged by his cronies: he does not want to be pointed at. That the haunter of committee rooms has forgotten the strain of genuine intellectual work is evidenced by his long loose reports. His endurance is reserved for 'work-type' activities—telephoning, dictating, scheduling, and lunching creatively. He and his kind are caught in a tight web of these obligations, which must be discharged day by day under pain of chaos and reprisals. The executive aim becomes the subduing of 'arrears,' whereby all are overoccupied and underworked.   (42)

Critics who observe this entrapment of the able generally ascribe it to 'organization' and the authority of the group, which are in turn attributed to the inertia of the 'mass man' and the strength of his unanimous desires.* This view implies that it is the weight of the characterless millions which oppresses a stoutly resisting intellectual class of individualists, after robbing each of the dignity and pleasure of work in solitude. But the behavior of intellectuals in living rooms, editorial rooms, and committee rooms does not support that generalization.† True, intellectuals often think of themselves as individualists, because of their dislike of concerted action; but this lack of cohesiveness is not necessarily the mark of a self-aware, self-confident individual. It may be, rather, the disease of a bewildered group-seeker. It is noticeable that in circles where one would expect quick responses to common difficulties—say, in educational or medical administration—'individualistic' diversity in words is enormous. But this often expresses little more than a stubborn whimsicality of impression and utterance. (43)

Again, nothing is more common than to attend a forum or conference on social or artistic 'problems' and to hear, after a few hours of guarded meandering, a growing majority declare that a consensus is impossible. The next remark is that this is another symptom of the contemporary chaos. Soon, a ghostly yearning for the thirteenth century is seen to emerge from the wainscoting. Despair seems the only tenable conclusion. The truth is that the twenty or thirty gentlemen who are thus ready to give back their tickets are extraordinarily alike in outlook, as they are also in training and temperament. They have once more said the familiar things that enlivened many another three-day conference. But the repeated failure to join issue, the perverse wish to remain misunderstood and put upon, and the decay of certain intellectual powers, including the faculty of analogy, have left them unskilled in the art of concurring. They cannot translate what they hear into what they think; they jib at incidentals and misconceive the main points. They are reminded of the wrong instances and they humor themselves in the nursing of abstract grudges. In a word, they lack the high purposeful of intellectual passion. (44

Yet they are not free of self-distrust, and since this is with them a habit rather than a judgment, it helps to create the ill-success they regularly meet. From that self-imprisonment they then choose a vicarious rescue: they idealize youth. If this is Intellect at work, they say, if reason and discussion produce only this irritable shadow-boxing, then let us have the prattle of

---

*E.g., most recently by Mr. Aldous Huxley in an interview with Mike Wallace, published by the Fund for the Republic in the series *Survival and Freedom*, No. 4, p. 12.

† An uncommon sociological study tells us that villager and townsman form their image of themselves after the models which come to them from large-scale journalism and broadcasting. If so, the influence is not up from the mass but down from the articulate, who transmit, with their own anti-heroism, the next-to-latest conceptions of high art and literature. *Small Town in Mass Society* by A. J. Vidich and J. Bensman, Princeton University Press, 1958, 101–105.

babes. With this added cause for resignation goes the hope that youth will bring to the conduct of life an energy that manners have sapped in their elders. We saw an expression of that despair and that hope in *The Family of Man*. One is reminded that the earliest dithyrambs on youth as saviors occurred in Germany in the 1880's, when Langbehn and others, who were waging an oblique war on their culture, were demanding 'an age of art' and, soon afterward, 'a youth movement for adults.' Their love of innocence and art was hatred for the present that neglected them and a vengeful appeal to the future. In our century, the worshipers of innocence have similarly laid on the future the task of repairing all their mistakes. But forgetting that innocence petted and prolonged can only make dupes and cynics, they have produced conditions in which strength other than physical cannot grow. The notion that 'free growth' and 'integrity' in the young requires the absence of formal manners—no thanks and no subordination, no regard for time or fitness, no patience with difficulty or distate, no feelings of reverence or pride, and in many 'excellent' households, no respect for objects and no constraint of cleanliness—that anarchical notion seems curious only till we see it as a first step in liberation from power and its attendant responsibility. Those who are reared in this permissive atmosphere seem embarrassed by, almost afraid of, human respect. They try hard to earn the opposite by affecting a slovenliness of dress and a lack of reliability which are so *outré* as to prove casualness a branch of study. That this pose is not merely to shock the public appears from the fact that the young unshaven, half-shod, intellectual beachcomber does not exhibit himself differently to his best—I mean, his only—girl. The behavior at least shows thoroughness: having nothing, claiming nothing, he knows nothing can be required or reproved. What is odd is the expectation that such a mode of life should produce individuals, that is, persons distinguishable from one another. (45)

Even when the pose is only a passing phase in the adolescent intellectual, its drawback is that it allows but two lines of retreat: anger and resignation. The ego is hemmed in and cannot disport itself. It swings dissatisfied between antagonism and conformity, out of which one can fashion but few objects of delight: one imagines with difficulty a life's work wholly devoted to expressing rage or listlessness. What is left for private or social purposes is a kind of moral vagrant, who projects upon his surroundings the menace of his own indiscipline. I can think of a case in point, that of an intelligent young man of twenty-five, with all the makings of a good painter. He works at his art, but by dint of brooding about his aims and talents he has concluded that 'to be himself' he must show rudeness and hostility to all who approach him, including the teacher he has himself chosen. His easygoing parents are to him as Oriental despots. They have promised to support him in his artistic career if he will go to college—a sinister attempt to clamp him in a mold and turn him into a 'square.' Their evident goodness barely shackles his hostility, which he turns on others with a virulence close to delinquency.   (46)

Delinquency itself is usually thought to be a mirror image of 'the dreadful world in which we live.' But the truth of the explanation depends on which dreadful world is meant, public or domestic. The delinquents from suburban families* who seem to want risk and a barrier to push against, find it only in the rival gang or the police, now that the paternal power, which is youth's proper and useful antagonist, has abdicated.† The young also are underworked and deprived of the outlet that intellectual effort and polemic with peers offer to aggressive energy.   (47)

Everywhere, the void left by the suppression of mind and ambition is filled by improvised generalship and conflict. Battle is joined, more or less openly, whenever a group of children invade a public vehicle. It lurks in the notorious behavior of undergraduates at a certain college where, it is said, guest lecturers are systematically heckled while the faculty looks on helplessly. And it was unmistakable in recent events at a large university, where an undergraduate grievance growing out of restrictions on receiving girls in dormitories was made clear by throwing eggs at the president and dean, the rebel leader being the son of a faculty member. This is not animal spirits or the traditional prank: it an oblique war on our culture in order to find out whether there are not, somewhere, some angry old men. And intellectually speaking, it is the effort to replace a torturing self-consciousness by a self-aware reason for living.   (48)

For in the straight wars against culture, those waged from strength and not weakness, the fount of power is Intellect. By it, the enemy is singled out from the rest and the strategy devised. When the war is over, it is deemed just or unjust by its intellectual rightness. Nowadays, on the contrary, it is assumed that all attacks on culture are equal in virtue, and that attacking society, because it is society, is the one aim and test of genius.‡ The young therefore enlist and fight, without asking of the ugly world they have inherited whether anybody ever received it fresh, perfect, and beautiful. Their intellect does not stretch so far as to criticize, with whatever *furor adolescentium;* it condemns, vaguely yet vehemently, as one would expect from the sentimental education they have received. Just

---

* The United Nations report on juvenile delinquency notes that in the United States this type of crime 'thrives in communities and families where standards of living are relatively high.' *New York Times,* August 3, 1958.

† A California psychiatrist, Dr. Milton Wexler, detects the virtue of energy in the "horror of juvenile delinquency,' and prefers it, as I do, to 'apathy, tranquilizers, and inspirational psychologies.' *New York Times,* May 19, 1958.

‡ The assumption is well expressed in a comment on Samuel Beckett who, according to Mr. Rexroth, 'is so significant, or so great, because he has said the final word to date [*sic*] in the long indictment of industrial and commercial civilization. . . . Now this is not only the main stream of what the squares call Western European culture, by which they mean the culture of the capitalist era: it is really all the stream there is.' *The Nation,* April 14, 1956.

so did the unfortunate Smerdyakov, whom his half-brother Ivan Karamazov, a thorough intellectual, had tried to awaken: (49)

'He had encouraged him to talk to him, although he had always wondered at a certain incoherence, or rather restlessness in his mind, and could not understand what it was that so continually and insistently worked upon the brain of "the contemplative." They discussed philosophical questions . . . but Ivan soon saw that . . . Smerdyakov . . . was looking for something altogether different. In one way or another, he began to betray a boundless vanity, and a wounded vanity, too. . . . There was in fact something surprising in the illogicality and incoherence of some of his desires, accidentally betrayed and always vaguely expressed.'   (50)

It would be foolish to imagine that a whole generation could be composed of Smerdyakovs. The young in this country or elsewhere do not all make up for raw manners and lax discipline by truculence, much less delinquency. The 'abolitionism' of our leading prophets under thirty is indicative of only one, and the most arid, tendency. The majority of college graduates with some pretensions to education deal otherwise with their innocence and the horrors they are asked to contemplate. Many conceive themselves as modestly contributing, through some organization, to the general good. Practical philanthropy gives them, perhaps for the first time, ideas linked by purpose, and a guarantee besides: it must be good to do good—though often they suffer intervals of bewilderment and are beset by problems that only intellect could solve. For example, some forty graduates of an Eastern woman's college, now living in a Western city, not long ago addressed to their alma mater a piteous but not untypical request. They wanted help, undefined, to get themselves established as young wives in a new community, so that they might in turn help their college in some way, through meetings, teas, lectures, publicity—anything desired. They wanted (in their own words) someone to inspire them and co-ordinate their efforts, to 'indoctrinate' them.   (51)

The college of course publishes the usual illustrated bulletin, which is full of applicable suggestions, and provides a traveling representative to aid local clubs. This person found the young wives 'eager to work though they did not know how or for what.' Now comes the oddest part of the story. The traveling delegate's recommendation was that not only the forty lost sheep, but many others throughout the land, should periodically be brought back to the college 'to renew contact and inspiration, help them in their lives and make them feel part of the group . . . . I speak,' added the reporter, 'from a feeling of osmosis.'   (52)

Obvious points could be made about the apparent uselessness of the written word and a college training, and about the hidden costs of higher education, but what concerns manners is the acute self-consciousness which paralyzed the group and created this 'problem.' The desire for special ministrations viewed as 'help,' the need to be directed, the urge to hold meetings without object, the longing to come home to the sheltering herd—these are the unexpected fruits of 'free, individual growth,' coupled with the cult of informality and the refusal of power. It can hardly be coincidence that, shortly before, these young wives were among the undergraduates for whom recitations and laboratories could not be scheduled on Monday mornings or Friday afternoons, because they would be cut, and who had to be subjected to biweekly room inspections to maintain in the dormitories the semblance of civilized life. (53)

Bewildered or sullen or defiant, the young who are wise enough to conclude that meetings are no substitute for careers, nor publicity for power, gravitate toward the last institution that promises rest from evil and uncertainty—the self-centered family. Having started an exclusive courtship in childhood, John marries Jane as soon as practicable, for only she means peace, goodness, and truth—that is, until little Jonathans come to share the exclusive virtue and interest of John and Jane. The self-centered family competes with study, politics, and social life, and makes them show cause why they should interfere with individualism à deux. To put it another way, this latest substitute for status and privilege gains strength by domesticating everything—love, study, pleasure, ambition, liberality, and the broken remnants of intellectual curiosity and conversation. By reducing all these to its appetite, the self-centered family is a small fortress against the monsters outside—the huge institutions, the anonymous mass, the agitated world. The self-centered family is not an institution, it is a cocoon. Warm and small, it matches the other reductions of size and scope we are witnessing: the tiny house, the tiny car, the tiny stature of humanity on the bluish window through which, cozily, in the dark, the family views some of the strange events outside.* (54)

What I have been describing does not of course imply the physical isolation of the young family, nor does it contradict their elders' gregariousness or their own. Rather, it shows in another setting the social quest which we defined at the outset as the search for essences. The search occurs between families in an attempt to reproduce the intimacy of the home, the warmth (rather than the affection) brought into our lives by (as we say) our *personal* friends. They are known by their ability to be no different at home and in company, and their easy, informal behavior is the model for strangers who want to join the circle. We know what they must do. They must divest themselves of their last names, as would the men of their coats and ties on a hot day and the women of their shoes at almost any time. And they must have a sense of humor. (55)

---

* Life imitates art: when Mr. Cyril Connolly made his witty remark about anxious man's desire for 'a womb with a view,' television had not become the fulfillment of that wish.

For since we decline to meet as minds or characters, and cannot boast
a multitude of pals, we need humor to provide a moral holiday. Con-
straints dissolve and something like self-assertiveness can sally forth when
cloaked in humor. This is why humor is so overused in our meetings
and greetings. The term humor, indeed, is here a courtesy title, for most
of the laughter and the words that arouse it are mechanical and we are
not amused. At home or in the course of business, the jokes express self-
depreciation or make fun of the routine duties and accidents of life, loudly
burying our false shames. After everyone is seated and holds a glass, the
laughs and grins (as in newspaper photography) shield our vacuity and
make plain that the danger of falling into a Roman *gravitas* is permanently
at bay.   (56)

At times, too, one suspects that the forms of this humorless humor stand
for the lost forms of the drama of intellect in true conversation. This is
noticeable in everyone's heavy irony and in the special, noisy overemphasis
affected by women to pass off triviality or dullness: the abnormal drawl,
the contorted features, the limbs and torso acting out some unfathomable
anecdote of dustpan and brush, give us a glimpse of the abyss and reconcile us to the large, anonymous cocktail party which, for all its toll on the
five senses, often serves moral decency like a curtain.   (57)

That it is impossible to talk or hear at a cocktail party does not lower
much the amount of successful 'exchange of ideas' in a society. A more
potent influence is the state of the language. The erosion of the mother
tongue will occupy us on a later page. Here it is enough to point to the
fact that our manners do not favor highly organized speech. The desire to
be inconspicuous, that is, to take on the color of one's surroundings, encourages the use of vogue words and phrases, which, being for the most
part inexpressive, have to be helped out by grimaces, interjections, and test
borings into the listener's receptivity. All this augments agitation and decreases attention which, even among the articulate, is strained by the
great number of professional jargons and ready-made conversations—the
cant of political, psychological, and artistic coteries. The upshot is that
where these groups mix and also where they remain apart, there is no
society.   (58)

One can readily understand why such groups might prefer separateness. Intuitive and self-conscious, they too seek a family in which to exchange warmth and share anxieties. Comfort takes precedence of curiosity,
the comfort of quaking by the same hearthstone. How often do they not
say of the passing event, 'It is frightening!' But each group finds a different
cause for the fright that unites them, and the last virtue displayed or desired is equanimity. It would seem even more arrogant than lacking in
sensitiveness, a breach of the equality based on common suffering, and
hence a sign of superiority. To this it might of course be answered that the

implied claim is not against others but against oneself, and that those who claim nothing of themselves have nothing to give. (59)

But to continue on this theme would be to propose new, unheard-of manners, which is beyond my present purpose. It only remains to point out that it is the manners of the powerless, and not outside forces, that bring about the invasions of our privacy. If we must all suffer, agree, worry, partake, in unison, under pain of reproof, then the world is no longer a stage peopled by distinguishable actors, and the living room vanishes with the individual—there is only a tribe milling under a tent. To this image, some reply that the modern world being full of concentration camps it is absurd to hope anywhere for individualism and privacy. But the intellect is not deceived by this fallacious argument from horror: the fact that under necessity some detestable thing happens is no reason why it has to be everywhere reproduced and accepted. (60)

The fallacy is more consequential than it looks, for it is generally the same 'thoughtful' propounder of the concentration camp analogy who at other times indicts 'our culture' for violating the dignity of man. But how does he resist encroachment on his own privacy and dignity from day to day? We have had no statistical survey on this point, but an incident for which I can vouch throws light on the question. One of the world's leading photographers concludes his session with a sitter by requesting a favor: will the sitter jump for him? The artist explains by bringing out a stack of photographs of the world's leading notables taken in the act of jumping. Fists clenched, faces taut, feet off the ground, they are on view—prime ministers and presidential candidates, noted jurists and princes of the royal blood, lady novelists and Nobel Prize winners. If an unprepossessing rictus casts a doubt on their identity, the photographer dispels the doubt in the course of his running commentary on what the photograph reveals of the jumper's character. This one is a coward; that other, jumping with his wife and looking at her, is obviously ruled by her; the next is a pompous fool, and so on. *Now* will you jump for me? According to the artist himself, only two of his subjects have refused. Each time he asked for their reasons. Whether both mentioned the supreme informality of the pose, the impudent overdose of candor, or the rancid flavor of amateur psychologizing, the photographer is too offended to remember. (61)

Lewis Mumford

(1895–   )

For a brief statement of facts about the author, see the headnote preceding his essay "The Suburban Way of Life."

■ *Architecture as Symbol*

"THE PROBLEMS OF bettering life and its environment are not separate ones, as political and other mechanically educated minds constantly think, and as religious ones have also too much come to believe. Nor is it, as politicians especially think—now with mistaken hope, or again with unnecessary discouragement—a matter of moving great numbers and masses before anything can be done. It is not a matter of area and wealth. It is at bottom an experimental problem, that of starting a re-adaptation." These words of Geddes and Branford have been verified during the last twenty years. In the housing of families and the building of communities a re-adaptation has started; and against the very grain of capitalist finance, over active protest and passive sabotage and dull indifference, the housing movement has continued to grow.   (1)

The symbol of this new adaptation is a common architectural form, and new types of communal layout. So far these growths have been sporadic: they have taken place, for the most part, on the outskirts of great cities, London, Amsterdam, Paris, Berlin, Wien; and they still bear some of the defects of their origin. But the movement toward better housing, not for isolated fortunate individuals, but for a whole community, is one that has been going on for a century; and it has now reached a point where the positive results have awakened desire and emulation. In this approaching transformation of our cities lies the justification of Patrick Geddes's prophetic words, in 1905, in describing the transition from the paleotechnic to the neo-technic phase of modern industry: "As the former period may be characterized by the predominance of the relatively unskilled workman and the skilled, so this next incipient age by the development of the chief workman proper, the literal *architektos* or architect; and by his companion, the rustic improver, gardener, and forester, farmer, irrigator, and their correspondingly evolved types of civil engineer."   (2)

In the transformation of the environment, architecture has a peculiar part to play. This arises not merely because buildings constitute such a large part of man's daily surroundings; but because architecture reflects and focuses such a wide variety of social facts: the character and resources of the natural environment, the state of the industrial arts and the empirical tradition and experimental knowledge that go into their application, the processes of social organization and association, and the beliefs and world-outlooks of a whole society. In an age of social disintegration and unrelated specialism, like the passing one, architecture loses most of its essential character: in an age of synthesis and construction, it steps forward once more as the essential commanding art.   (3)

And precisely because architectural form crystallizes, becomes visible, is subject to the test of constant use, it endows with special significance the impulses and ideas that shape it: it externalizes the living beliefs, and in doing so, reveals latent relationships. With the help of his orderly accurate plans, the architect brings together a multitude of crafts, skills, and arts, creating in the act of building that species of intelligent co-operation which we seek on a wider scale in society: the very notion of planning owes more to this art than to any other, except perhaps the co-ordinate art of the engineer.   (4)

The architect confronts human needs and desires with the obdurate facts of site, materials, space, costs: in turn, he molds the environment closer to the human dream. And in a social sense, architecture is more advanced than any purely mechanical technique because good building has always embodied, as an essential element in both design and operation, the understanding and expression of organic human purposes. In the state of building at any period one may discover, in legible script, the complicated processes and changes that are taking place within civilization itself. In a period of integration, such as we are now again on the brink of, architecture becomes a guide to order in every other department of activity.   (5)

Architecturally speaking, the nineteenth century was a period of disintegration. Buildings outwardly without roots in their landscape or affiliations with their society appeared in the midst of the growing cities. Such buildings were the work of individual architects, responsible only for their individual building: producing work that was bound to be swallowed up in the disorderly urban mass produced by the speculative builder, the ground landlord, and the industrial corporation, operating solely under the principles of laissez-faire. This original architectural Babel became more confused as foreign travel and wide archaeological research combined with a lack of creative impulse to encourage either dead imitation or a feeble eclecticism.   (6)

Originally the architects of the Renascence had turned to the dead for inspiration: as if the breath of life could come from the tomb. No one could doubt the improvements in farming that followed when Columella's treatise on farming began to influence progressive agricultural practice. No one could doubt the stimulus to mechanical invention that arose from the reprinting of Hero of Alexandria's experiments with the steam engine. But there was a vast difference between such experimental selection and lifeless imitation; in architecture, after Brunelleschi, what was taken over was not the process, capable of modification and complete alteration as new needs arose, but the external form: the dead stereotype of another culture. Note how post-sixteenth century architecture, instead of organizing the banked window further as a constructional form, relapsed into the more primitive system of the hole left gaping in the solid masonry wall: a loss both in terms of technical facility and livability; for the overhead glare of the tall rectangular window in turn resulted in a need for curtains to cut off some of the irritating light, while the entering in the lower part of the window was optically useless.   (7)

This period from the sixteenth century to the twentieth witnesses the fatal lack of connection between architecture and the dominant social sources of order. The proof that architecture in the social sense was dead lies in the series of dusty revivals that took place. People sought, in Roman forms, Greek forms, neo-gothic forms, finally in Romanesque and even Byzantine forms, some quick and easy route to a real society and a living culture: lacking the soil and the plants that could produce a beautiful efflorescence, they fashioned for themselves paper flowers. As drawn on paper, or photographed, who could tell the difference between the living and the dead? Unconsciously seeking the bread of social life, the architect offered decorated stones: empty symbols of a non-existent society. Meanwhile, the germs of a living order existed alike in building, in technics, and in the culture of the landscape; but the confused minds and irresolute purposes of the directing classes did not find it easy to accept these beginnings. The common Victorian justification for the new industrial buildings was not that they were good art, but that a progressive industrial civilization had no need for art.   (8)

Viewed on the surface, the battle of the styles that was carried on between the early baroque architects and the traditional medieval builder, or between the neo-classicists of the nineteenth century and the neo-medievalists, was trivial; for both schools were united in this respect: they had lost their connections with a common social milieu. Meanwhile society itself was losing all sense of a common order: its forms were capricious because its values were uncertain and it had yielded to a belief in purely quantitative achievement: fine architecture had become a matter of size and expense, while common building, divorced from human standards, became cheap, niggardly, cramped.   (9)

As if to add an ironic touch to this social disorganization, the field was marked out roughly between the two great schools. After the opening of the nineteenth century, the classic style claimed the government offices, the courts of justice, the police stations, the banks, the art museums; while the gothic style claimed the school, the university, the town hall, the church, the natural history museum. There would, of course, be occasional compromises and modifications in this program. Survivals that stubbornly refused to acknowledge their death, mistaking mumification for vitality, combined with mutations that shrank from the struggles of birth—such was architecture during most of the nineteenth century in those reaches of the community where it still had any significance. Even the most penetrating of critics was confused: Ruskin had the courage to admire the Ashmolean Museum at Oxford.   (10)

Yet, from the beginning of the nineteenth century on, a succession of thinkers and planners appeared who knew that a more fundamental attack must be made on the whole problem of form. With those who went into form from the standpoint of community planning, beginning with Robert Owen, I have dealt elsewhere. Here we are concerned with the architects who realized that society itself was the main source of architectural form, and that only in terms of living functions could living form be created. There were many forerunners in this movement: but perhaps the most important figure of all was William Morris; for Morris, with Philip Webb, created the famous Red House in 1851, where Morris was to spend the early part of his married life. Here an attempt was made to discard ornamental tags and go back to essentials: honest materials, well-wrought: plain brick walls: a roof of heavy slates: every detail as straightforward and sensible as in a seventeenth century English farmhouse.   (11)

Heretofore architectural monuments had alone been the center of appreciation and the accepted source of style: the Pantheon, the Maison Carrée, the palace of Diocletian at Spalato, the Cathedral of Strasbourg, St. Mark's in Venice. These monumental buildings, crystallizations of a whole social order, were mistakenly seized as starting points for architectural design. In the middle of the nineteenth century this error had been carried so far that little cottages cowered behind massive Greek pediments, and the student of architecture began his apprenticeship with a study of the decorative elements in classic monumental forms; while he had so little training in matter-of-fact design that he would leave his atelier, proud of his skill in handling pencil or brush, and ignorant of the first motions in handling a trowel or a plumb-line; capable of designing a Hall of Justice but without the capacity to design an honest dog-kennel, to say nothing of a human dwelling.   (12)

By making the dwelling house a *point of departure* for the new movement in architecture, William Morris symbolically achieved a genuine revolution. The doctrines he laid down with respect to its design were fundamental ones: implicit in them, as he himself realized in his development as a revolutionary socialist, was the conception of a new social order, oriented not toward mechanization and profits, but toward humanization, welfare, and service. Little though Morris liked the machine—little though he had *reason* to like it in its defective early manifestations—he had achieved an attitude toward form and society that was capable of utilizing and directing the real advances that were being made in the organization of men and materials and the impersonal forces of nature. If the factory was the nucleus of the paleotechnic community, the house was to become the nucleus of the biotechnic age: his instincts here served him well.   (13)

"Believe me," William Morris wrote, "if we want art to begin at home, as it must, we must clear our houses of troublesome superfluities that are forever in our way; conventional comforts that are no real comforts, and do but make work for servants and doctors; if you want the golden rule that will fit everybody, this is it: have nothing in your house that you do not know to be useful or believe to be beautiful." This clearing away of the historic debris, this stripping to the skin, was the first essential mark of the new architecture, as it was, in effect, for the new view of life and cosmic relations that was introduced by the systematic sciences. In building: the open window, the blank wall, the unlittered floor: nothing for show and nothing that cannot be shown.   (14)

The next great impulse toward coherent form came from the American master builder, H. H. Richardson. Starting work after the American Civil War, Richardson at first used the current eclectic symbols, and finally established a reputation for himself by his bold handling of monumental forms: so far, an obstacle to genuine achievement. But as Richardson entered more deeply into the problems of his age, and became familiar with its social and economic forces, he turned to the design of an office building, a warehouse, a railroad station, a public library: he found himself on new ground. Richardson discarded, step by step, the archaic touches and the hampering symbols: he worked with the fundamental forms of masonry, organizing the elements solely with a view to the practical and visual expression of the function to be encompassed: he carried the lesson Webb and Morris had worked out in the dwelling house into every aspect of building. Though it was only in his latest buildings that Richardson finally came face to face with the possibility of new form, organically based on the technical resources and social principles of the new society, he achieved a sort of preliminary integration in terms of masonry. He proved that the ugliness of utilitarian forms had not been due to their origins nor their uses but to the inferior quality of mind applied to their development. Organically conceived, a railroad station had no less capacity for beauty than a medieval fortress or a bridge; and a dwelling house in wood might be better related to human needs than a costly palace.   (15)

Richardson's work was confirmed at a later period in Europe by the advances of kindred architects: Berlage's handsome bourse in Amsterdam is a parallel example of great force and merit; and Richardson laid the foundation for the work of another group of architects, Adler and Sullivan, and Frank Lloyd Wright in Chicago, who carried the theme farther. Sullivan's task was to formulate, in social terms, the order that was implicit in Richardson's last work: he took up, perhaps unconsciously, perhaps quite independently, the rule laid down by the American sculptor, Horatio Greenough—form follows function. And Sullivan sought, on this basis, to create an architecture in which the fundamental principles formulated for one type of building would hold for other types—a rule so broad that it would admit of no exceptions. Such a rule must have its foundations, not only in the architect's mind, but in the political institutions, the working order, the social attitudes of his community. To formulate it in fact, and to translate it from fantasy to concrete reality, the architect needs the active co-operation of his contemporaries; and no one had better reason than Sullivan to appreciate the failure of energies and the paralysis of imagination that follows when the architect is either at odds with his community, or is forced to degrade his best energies in order to conform to the limitations of his clients. Taken together, Sullivan's buildings do not have that unity his doctrine demands.   (16)

It remained for Frank Lloyd Wright, working again in the same medium as Morris, the dwelling house, to effect a synthesis of nature, the machine, and human activities and purposes. Wright increased the size of the window opening and restored the horizontal window bank, which had been lost, except for a sporadic revival or two, since the seventeenth century. By altering the layout of the house and keeping it low, and close to the soil of the prairie, he made a fundamental change in the relation of the house and the land, and introduced the garden almost into the heart of the living room. Outside and inside became aspects of a single unity, as in the human organism: the house-in-nature, nature-in-the-house. Although Wright showed special gifts in using natural materials and in adapting his designs to the local landscape, he used, likewise with masterly facility, the modern constructional methods and the new utilities provided by the machine: he treated the machine as a collaborating agent of human purpose, not merely as the cheapener of costs and the purveyor of spurious imitations that it had been during the formative period of Morris's thought. (17)

In his respect for the soil, the site, the climate, the environing region, Wright was in advance, not merely of his eclectic contemporaries, but of those metropolitanized interpreters of the "modern" who followed almost a generation later: his "prairie architecture," like his later "desert architecture," was true regional form. Wright, indeed, depolarized regionalism from its connection with the historic and the archaic: he oriented it toward the living present, which contains both the past and the future; and he brought together in his new building forms the special and the universal, the local and the worldwide. It is not by accident that Wright's prairie architecture took deepest hold in Holland, a country not without geographic parallels to the prairie and Great Lakes areas, though built to a different scale. He created, not a mechanical form to be copied, as the clichés of the classicist were copied in the eighteenth century, and those of Le Corbusier during the last decade: he created an organic form, to be adapted and modified, precisely because the principles upon which it was based were universal. (18)

Wright's architecture was therefore, to an unusual degree, a prophetic synthesis: a microcosm of the new biotechnic economy. This synthesis antedated in its individual forms the best work done on similar lines in Europe: antedated it by a generation. Unfortunately, Wright's early work had the weakness of being conceived in response to demand within the communal pattern of the romantic suburb: an individual free-standing house for the well-to-do bourgeois family. Except for one abortive, over-ingenious effort at group housing, which accepted far too high a level of density, Wright did not pass on to the more fundamental problem of communal integration until he developed, during the present decade, the plans and models and projects of Broadacre City. That failure to incorporate the communal into the personal was perhaps responsible for the small extent of his influence in the actual housing movement, even after 1920. (19)

All these architects were, in effect, the representatives of a society that had not yet appeared. Their contributions were like delicate seedlings, carefully nurtured, and well-grown in March, before the blanket of snow has lifted from the garden where they are to be transplanted: often they died before the weather had taken a favorable change or the season had advanced sufficiently. The best of their buildings even when they were brought into the open were lost in weedy patches of speculative enterprise and industrial disorder: deprived even of their main esthetic effect through the lack of a background built on the same principles. Thus Wright's magnificent Larkin Administration Building rises like some enigmatic temple in the midst of a black industrial desert—contradicting but not suppressing the ugliness and disorder around it. (20)

These architects, then, share a place with the romantic poets, like Blake and Whitman, who wrote for a non-existent democracy, and with romantic individualists in all the other arts who were attempting to embody in their own personalities and in their own work something that could not be brought into secure existence without the political and social co-operation of a sympathetic community. In the main, these romantics were prophets of life: but of a life and order to come. What the artist created was but a sample, a small working model, which must be thrown as it were into mass production before the existence of the new pattern could be guaranteed and its full meaning for society realized. (21)

In almost every country, similar innovators appeared and the first assays toward new form were made. Voysey, Mackintosh, Baillie-Scott, Lutyens, Unwin, and Parker in England: Van de Velde in Belgium: Wagner, Hoffmann, and Loos in Austria: Behrens, Poelzig, Schumacher in Germany, Berlage in Holland, Tony Garnier and the Perrets in France. And in each country, with the possible exception of America, the new movement in life first registered itself in the arts and crafts, in printing, in textiles, in pottery, in furniture, before it became generalized and socialized as architectural and communal form. Being more closely connected with machine technics than the inherited handicrafts of building, it was perhaps natural that these subordinate departments of design should be influenced first. Perhaps another reason lies in the fact that the most fundamental change involved at first was a change in attitude and interest: a refocusing of the social objectives. The desire for sunlight and open air appeared symbolically in the painting of the impressionists more than a generation before it became widespread in the community: almost two generations before it was embodied formally in architecture. Does not the mind tend to project in a more facile medium, that which responds quickest to the artist's impression, what can be embodied only through long painful processes of trial and error, and co-operative discipline, in the structure of the community? One has reason to respect such symbols—except when they are treated as fetiches and accepted as subsitutes for the life which they postulate. (22)

From the eighties onward there was no lack of vigorous and intelligently conceived individual buildings; but at first the esthetic conception prevailed over the more comprehensive social conception, which includes the esthetic as but one of its ingredients. One sees the danger of a purely esthetic formulation of the problem in the rise of the new style toward the end of the nineteenth century: the style called Art Nouveau in France and Jugendstil in Germany. The two main technical examples of this form were embodied in printing and in jewelry; and in the latter department, indeed, one is conscious of the benign influence of woman, never wholly at ease in the power-world of the machine, turning instinctively to the symbols of life: flowers and fruit and her own naked body. L'Art Nouveau was an early attempt to incorporate biological symbolism in the arts. In architecture, it disdained straight lines and rigid geometric surfaces: it cultivated wavy lines, lines of growth and free movement: the designer turned electroliers into sprays of metallic flowers, and a simple balustrade railing into a descending foam of metallic waves. The first marks of this type of floral ornament were to be found in the old iron bridges, and before its expression in the furniture of Bing at the Paris Fair of 1900 it had left its marks on the base of the Eiffel Tower.   (23)

In the actual handling of its materials, chiefly metal and glass, l'Art Nouveau showed many examples of brilliant architectural design, some of which was more decisively functional than that of later schools which paid greater verbal respect to the principle of function. What was weak in l'Art Nouveau was in fact not its constructive execution but its formal symbolism: its reliance upon extraneous ornament for an expression of its purposes. It was indeed high time that the living was expressed in architecture: this precisely was a necessary mark of the new biotechnic age that was dawning, an age effectively distinguished by the radical contributions of scientists like Pasteur in bio-chemistry, Geddes in bio-sociology, and artists like Rodin—if one may conclude the verbal parallel—in bio-sculpture.   (24)

But "living" in architecture means in adequate relation to life. It does not mean an imitation in stone or metal of the external appearance of organic form: houses with mushroom roofs or rooms shaped like the corolla of a flower. It was not flowered wallpaper that was needed in the modern house, but space and sunlight and temperature conditions under which living plants could grow: not pliant and moving lines in the furniture, but furniture that responded adequately to the anatomical form and physiological needs of the body: chairs that furthered good posture and gave repose, beds that favored sexual intercourse and permitted deep slumber. In short: a physical environment that responded sensitively to the vital and personal needs of the occupants.   (25)

Symbolically, the Art Nouveau architects were right in exhibiting and glorifying life: practically, they were mistaken, because in their art they exerted most of their zeal to provide only a formal counterfeit: mere ornamental forms. The problem for the new age was to create a new type of living environment: to enable people to live in cities without losing the fellowship of nature, and to group together for the sake of specialized social activities without losing the means of good health and the decent nurture of children. None of these needs could be satisfied by mere ornament, no matter how whimsically imaginative, or how vitally fluent that ornament might be. Architecture required structural forms which were organically at one with life: flexible, adaptable, renewable.   (26)

For this reason the reaction against l'Art Nouveau in Europe, which took shape in the cubist movement in painting, and in the constructivist movement in architecture, pointed form once more in the right direction. (The movement had never really taken hold in America, and Wright's early work needed no such admonition.) Contrary to l'Art Nouveau, the symbolism of cubism was mistaken: it glorified the machine as an unmitigated benefactor of mankind, in strange innocence of all the social horrors that had accompanied capitalist exploitation; it placed an excessive emphasis upon formal geometrical shapes, particularly the rectangle and the cube which do not characterize real machines; and it proposed to turn the dwelling house into a machine, without explaining why mechanism should exercise such a one-sided control over life. But cubism was the necessary corrective of the dogma of the wavy line which, in pursuing the external forms of life, forgot the objective conditions: the form of a bowl, as conditioned by the potter's wheel: the form of a room, as conditioned by the economic placement of beams, posts, windows.   (27)

Instead of disguising the forms of modern construction under a load of decoration, the cubists sought to dramatize them. The cubists went out of their way to use concrete, to exhibit cantilever construction, to raise the house above the ground on steel columns. And instead of seeking to display the egoistic touch of the individual architect, they sought after an anonymous method of design and a collective formula. Structurally speaking cubism performed an important work of purification: it divorced itself from capitalist canons of reputability and expense, and it cleared the ground for a fresh start. In its keen appreciation of the products of the machine (led by artists like Marcel Duchamp), it pointed toward more conspicuous efforts to achieve clean forms within other branches of industry than architecture.   (28)

Although cubism had at the beginning a certain bias against living forms, the fact is that the machine itself is a product and an instrument of life: the more perfect it becomes, the more it simulates the automatisms and self-regulating devices of real organisms and the more finely it mimics the eye, the ear, the voice, the memory. In the attempt to use the machine adequately and create a more universal order, the collective interests of cubism inevitably led toward the formulation, in modern terms, of a theory of the city.   (29)

Under the leadership of Le Corbusier the cubists ceased to concern themselves alone with the isolated architectural product: they passed on to the urban environment as a whole, and sought to place the entire process of building and re-building on a fresh foundation.   (30)

Le Corbusier himself began with the stale nineteenth century notion of the city so often explored in the time-romances of Mr. H. G. Wells: *la ville mécanique*. His early schemes explore a series of blind alleys: the skyscraper city, the traffic city, finally the grotesque combination of the two in a curving viaduct whose supports were to be filled with apartment

houses. But by a steady process of reformulation he has drawn closer to the
biotechnic notion of *la ville radieuse:* a marked ideological improvement,
and his plan for Nemours is one of the best rational layouts that has yet
appeared. Thus life re-enters the picture, not in the form of extraneous
ornament, but in the demand for air, sunlight, gardens, parks, playgrounds,
recreation fields, and all the various forms of social equipment that are
necessary for the stimulating life of the city: informal places of meeting
and relaxation, like the café, and formal places of purposive education,
like the museum and the university. In the orientation of architecture toward life and the processes of life the architect began with the decoration of the house: he ends with the city.   (31)

In their attempt actively to incorporate the machine into architecture
the cubists were sometimes misled by a static and external conception of
the machine; but unconsciously they were recognizing the direct tribute
that the mechanical arts owed to improvements that were first made in the
culture of living things, particularly in horticulture. The first evolved pattern of the new architecture appeared in the glass hothouse: the Crystal
Palace in London was but the monumental embodiment of this mutation.
Just as the Crystal Palace was the work of an engineer in the service of
horticulture, so, by reverse process, the new system of ferro-concrete construction was the invention of the gardener, Monnier, seeking to build more
efficient bird baths and fountain basins for his gardens.   (32)

*The new improvements in domestic heating, too, were originally the
conception of gardeners.* One of the first persons to suggest steam heating
was Sir Hugh Platt, who had the notion of conveying heat from a steam
boiler on a kitchen stove through pipes to growing plants in order to
keep them at a temperate heat, no matter what the conditions of the weather
outside. In 1745 Platt's suggestion was improved by Sir William Cook, who
published a diagram for heating all the rooms in the house from the kitchen
fire. The full importance of these inventions was grasped for the first time
by Paxton himself. In a letter to the Illustrated London News (July 5,
1851) he sketched out the design of a Crystal Sanitorium: not merely
to give patients the benefit of extra oxygen from the growing plants, but
for the sake of sunlight and room wherein to exercise in all weather. To
make this possible, he suggested the installation of apparatus to provide
filtered and heated air: the first proposal for complete air-conditioning—not
as a mere remedy against baneful gases, as in mines or in the British House
of Parliament, but as a positive aid to health.   (33)

Thus the new methods of construction, the new materials, and the new
means of regulating the air of a building in order to adapt it more perfectly
to the needs of living occupants *came directly from the biotechnics of gardening.* These changes were to prove more important to human welfare
than the symbolic incorporation of floral shapes by means of carved ornaments and curved trusses.   (34)

Taken together, modern form, modern architecture, modern communities are prophetic emergents of a biotechnic society: a society whose productive system and consumptive demands will be directed toward the maximum possible nurture, under even more adequate material conditions, of the human group, and the maximum possible culture of the human personality. What has so far been accomplished is but a taste of the more thoroughgoing order that is to come. So far, architecture and community planning have aided experimentally in the clarification of this order: but further re-valuations of doctrine and belief, further accretions of positive knowledge, will in turn alter profoundly the new communities we are in process of building. Throughout the world, a consensus is gradually being established among men of good will and effective competence.   (35)

H. W. Janson

(1913–   )

JANSON is Professor of Fine Arts at New York University and Chairman of the Department of Fine Arts in the University's Washington Square College of Arts and Science. For several years editor of the Art Bulletin, *official organ of the College Art Association, Dr. Janson has written several distinguished scholarly works:* Apes and Ape Lore in the Middle Ages and the Renaissance, The Sculpture of Donatello, Key Monuments of the History of Art, *and* History of Art, *the most widely used textbook in general art history in America today.*

■ *The Artist and His Public*

"WHY IS THIS supposed to be art?" How often have we heard this question asked—or asked it ourselves, perhaps—in front of one of the strange, disquieting works that we are likely to find nowadays in museums or art exhibitions. There usually is an undertone of exasperation, for the question implies that *we* don't think we are looking at a work of art, but that the experts—the critics, museum curators, art historians—must suppose it to be one, why else would they put it on public display? Clearly, their standards are very different from ours; we are at a loss to understand them and we wish they'd give us a few simple, clear-cut rules to go by. Then maybe we would learn to like what we see, we would know "why it is art." But the experts do not post exact rules, and the layman is apt to fall back upon his final line of defense: "Well, I don't know anything about art but I know what I like."   (1)

It is a formidable roadblock, this stock phrase, in the path of understanding between expert and layman. Until not so very long ago, there was no great need for the two to communicate with each other; the general public had little voice in matters of art and therefore could not challenge the judgment of the expert few. Today both sides are aware of the barrier between them (the barrier itself is nothing new, although it may be greater now than at certain times in the past) and of the need to level it. Let us begin, then, by examining the roadblock and the various unspoken assumptions that buttress it. The most fateful among them, it seems to me, is the belief that there are, or ought to be, exact rules by which we can tell art from what is not art, and that, on the basis of these rules, we can then grade any given work according to its merits. Deciding what is art and evaluating a work of art are separate problems; if we had an absolute method for distinguishing art from non-art, this method would not necessarily enable us to measure quality. People have long been in the habit of compounding the two problems into one; quite often when they ask, "Why is it art?" they mean, "Why is it *good* art?" Yet, all systems for rating art so far proposed fall short of being completely satisfactory; we tend to agree with their authors only if they like the same things we do. If we do not share their taste, their system seems like a strait jacket to us. This brings us to another, more basic difficulty. In order to have any rating scale at all, we must be willing to assume that there are fixed, timeless values in art, that the true worth of a given work is a stable thing, independent of time and circumstance. Perhaps such values exist; we cannot be sure that they do not. We do know, however, that opinions about works of art keep changing, not only today but throughout the known course of history. Even the greatest classics have had their ups and downs, and the history of taste—which is part of the history of art—is a continuous process of discarding established values and rediscovering neglected ones. It would seem, therefore, that absolute qualities in art elude us, that we cannot escape viewing works of art in the context of time and circumstance, whether past or present. How indeed could it be otherwise, so long as art is still being created all around us, opening our eyes almost daily to new experiences and thus forcing us to adjust our sights, Perhaps, in the distant future, men will cease to produce works of art. It is not inconceivable, after all, that mankind may some day "outgrow" its need for art. When that happens, the history of art will have come to an end, and our descendants will then be in a better position to work out an enduring scale of artistic values—if the problem still interests them. Until that time, we had better admit that it is impossible to measure the merits of works of art as a scientist measures distances.   (2)

But if we must give up any hope of a trustworthy rating scale for artistic quality, can we not at least expect to find a reliable, objective way to tell art from non-art? Unfortunately, even this rather more modest goal proves so difficult as to be almost beyond our powers. Defining art is about as troublesome as defining a human being. Plato, it is said, tried to solve the latter problem by calling man "a featherless biped," whereupon Diogenes introduced a plucked rooster as "Plato's Man." Generalizations about art are, on the whole, equally easy to disprove. Even the most elementary statements turn out to have their pitfalls. Let us test, for instance, the simple claim that a work of art must be made by man, rather than by nature. This definition at least eliminates the confusion of treating as works of art phenomena such as flowers, sea shells, or sunsets. It is a far from sufficient definition, to be sure, since man makes many things other than works of art. Still, it might serve as a starting point. Our difficulties begin as soon as we ask, "What do we mean by making?" If, in order to simplify our problem, we concentrate on the visual arts, we might say that a work of art must be a tangible thing shaped by human hands. Now let us look at the striking *Bull's Head* by Picasso (fig. 1), which consists of nothing but the seat and handlebars of an old bicycle. How meaningful is our formula here? Of course the materials used by Picasso are man-made, but it would be absurd to insist that Picasso must share the credit with the manufacturer, since the seat and handlebars in themselves are not works of art. While we feel a certain jolt when we first recognize the ingredients of this visual pun, we also sense that it was a stroke of genius to put them together in this unique way, and we cannot very well deny that it is a work of art. Yet the handiwork—the mounting of the seat on the handlebars—is ridiculously simple. What is far from simple is the leap of the imagination by which Picasso recognized a bull's head in these unlikely objects; that, we feel, only he could have done. Clearly, then, we must be careful not to confuse the making of a work of art with manual skill or craftsmanship. Some works of art may demand a great deal of technical discipline; others do not. And even the most painstaking piece of craft does not deserve to be called a work of art unless it involves a leap of the imagination. But if this is true, are we not forced to conclude that the real making of the *Bull's Head* took place in the artist's mind? No, that is not so, either. Suppose that, instead of actually putting the two pieces together and showing them to us, Picasso merely told us, "You know, today I saw a bicycle seat and handlebars that looked just like a bull's head to me." Then there would be no work of art and his remark would not even strike us as an interesting bit of conversation. Moreover, Picasso himself would not feel the satisfaction of having created something on the basis of his leap of the imagination alone. Once he had conceived his visual pun, he could never be sure that it would really work unless he put it into effect.   (3)

Thus the artist's hands, however modest the task they may have to perform, play an essential part in the creative process. Our *Bull's Head* is, of course, an ideally simple case, involving only one leap of the imagination and a single manual act in response to it—once the seat had been properly placed on the handlebars, the job was done. Ordinarily, artists do not work with ready-made parts but with materials that have little or no shape of their own; the creative process consists of a long series of leaps of the imagination and the artist's attempts to give them form by shaping the material accordingly. The hand tries to carry out the commands of the imagination and hopefully puts down a brush stroke, but the result may not be quite what had been expected, partly because all matter resists the human will, partly because the image in the artist's mind is constantly shifting and changing, so that the commands of the imagination cannot be very precise. In fact, the mental image begins to come into focus only as the artist "draws the line somewhere." That line then becomes part—the only fixed part—of the image; the rest of the image, as yet unborn, remains fluid. And each time the artist adds another line, a new leap of the imagination is needed to incorporate that line into his ever-growing mental image. If the line cannot be incorporated, he discards it and puts down a new one. In this way, by a constant flow of impulses back and forth between his mind and the partly shaped material before him, he gradually defines more and more of the image, until at last all of it has been given visible form. Needless to say, artistic creation is too subtle and intimate an experience to permit an exact step-by-step description; only the artist himself can observe it fully, but he is so absorbed by it that he has great difficulty explaining it to us. Still, our metaphor of birth comes closer to the truth than would a description of the process in terms of a transfer or projection of the image from the artist's mind, for the making of a work of art is both joyous and painful, replete with surprises, and in no sense mechanical. We have, moreover, ample testimony that the artist himself tends to look upon his creation as a living thing. Thus, Michelangelo, who has described the anguish and glory of the artist's experience more eloquently than anyone else, speaks of his "liberating the figure from the marble that imprisons it." We may translate this, I think, to mean that he started the process of carving a statue by trying to visualize a figure in the rough, rectilinear block as it came to him from the quarry. (At times he may even have done so while the marble was still part of the living rock;

we know that he liked to go to the quarries and pick out his material on the spot.) It seems fair to assume that at first he did not see the figure any more clearly than one can see an unborn child inside the womb, but we may believe he could see isolated "signs of life" within the marble—a knee or an elbow pressing against the surface. In order to get a firmer grip on this dimly felt, fluid image, he was in the habit of making numerous drawings, and sometimes small models in wax or clay, before he dared to assault the "marble prison" itself, for that, he knew, was the final contest between him and his material. Once he started carving, every stroke of the chisel would commit him more and more to a specific conception of the figure hidden in the block, and the marble would permit him to free the figure whole only if his guess as to its shape was correct. Sometimes he did not guess well enough—the stone refused to give up some essential part of its prisoner, and Michelangelo, defeated, left the work unfinished, as he did with his *St. Matthew* (figs. 2, 3), whose every gesture seems to record the vain struggle for liberation. Looking at the side view of the block (fig. 3), we may get some inkling of Michelangelo's difficulties here. But could he not have finished the statue in *some* fashion? Surely there is enough material left for that. Well, he probably could have, but perhaps not in the way he wanted, and in that case the defeat would have been even more stinging.

(4)

Clearly, then, the making of a work of art has little in common with what we ordinarily mean by "making." It is a strange and risky business in which the maker never quite knows what he is making until he has actually made it; or, to put it another way, it is a game of find-and-seek in which the seeker is not sure what he is looking for until he has found it. (In the *Bull's Head*, it is the bold "finding" that impresses us most, in the *St. Matthew*, the strenuous "seeking.") To the non-artist, it seems hard to believe that this uncertainty, this need-to-take-a-chance, should be the essence of the artist's work. For we all tend to think of "making" in terms of the craftsman or manufacturer who knows exactly what he wants to produce from the very outset, picks the tools best fitted to his task, and is sure of what he is doing at every step. Such "making" is a two-phase affair: first the craftsman makes a plan, then he acts on it. And because he—or his customer—has made all the important decisions in advance, he has to worry only about means, rather than ends, while he carries out his plan. There is thus little risk, but also little adventure, in his handiwork, which as a consequence tends to become routine. It may even be replaced by the mechanical labor of a machine. No machine, on the other hand, can replace the artist, for with him conception and execution go hand in hand and are so completely interdependent that he cannot separate the one from the other. Whereas the craftsman only attempts what he knows to be possible, the artist is always driven to attempt the impossible—or at least the improbable or unimaginable. Who, after all, would have imagined that a bull's head was hidden in the seat and handlebars of a bicycle until Picasso discovered it for us; did he not, almost literally, "make a silk purse out of a sow's ear"? No wonder the artist's way of working is so resistant to any set rules, while the craftsman's encourages standardization and regularity. We acknowledge this difference when we speak of the artist as *creating* instead of merely *making* something, although the word is being done to death by overuse nowadays, when every child and every lipstick manufacturer is labeled "creative." (5)

Needless to say, there have always been many more craftsmen than artists among us, since our need for the familiar and expected far exceeds our capacity to absorb the original but often deeply unsettling experiences we get from works of art. The urge to penetrate unknown realms, to achieve something original, may be felt by every one of us now and then; to that extent, we can all fancy ourselves potential artists—mute inglorious Miltons. What sets the real artist apart is not so much the desire to *seek*, but that mysterious ability to *find* which we call talent. We also speak of it as a "gift," implying that it is a sort of present from some higher power; or as "genius," a term which originally meant that a higher power—a kind of "good demon"—inhabits the artist's body and acts through him. All we can really say about talent is that it must not be confused with aptitude. Aptitude is what the craftsman needs; it means a better-than-average knack for doing something that any ordinary person can do. An aptitude is fairly constant and specific; it can be measured with some success by means of tests which permit us to predict future performance. Creative talent, on the other hand, seems utterly unpredictable; we can spot it only on the basis of *past* performance. And even past performance is not enough to assure us that a given artist will continue to produce on the same level: some artists reach a creative peak quite early in their careers and then "go dry," while others, after a slow and unpromising start, may achieve astonishingly original work in middle or even later. (6)

Originality, then, is what distinguishes art from craft. We may say, therefore, that it is the yardstick of artistic greatness or importance. Unfortunately, it is also very hard to define; the usual synonyms—uniqueness, novelty, freshness—do not help us very much, and the dictionaries tell us only that an original work must not be a copy, reproduction, imitation, or translation. What they fail to point out is that originality is always relative: there is no such thing as a completely original work of art. Thus, if we want to rate works of art on an "originality scale," our problem does not lie in deciding whether or not a given work is original (the obvious copies and reproductions are for the most part easy enough to eliminate) but in establishing just exactly *how* original it is. To do that is not impossible. However, the difficulties besetting our task are so great that we cannot hope for more than tentative and incomplete answers. Which does not mean, of course, that we should not try; quite the contrary. For whatever the outcome of our labors in any particular case, we shall certainly learn a great deal about works of art in the process.   (7)

Let us look at a few of the baffling questions that come up when we investigate the problem of originality. The *Thorn Puller*, or *Spinario* (fig. 4), has long been one of the most renowned pieces of ancient bronze sculpture and enjoys considerable fame as a work of art even today—except among classical archaeologists who have studied it with care. They will point out that the head, which is cast separately and is of slightly different metal, does not match the rest: the planes of the face are far more severe than the soft, swelling forms of the body; and the hair, instead of falling forward, behaves as if the head were held upright. The head, therefore, must have been designed for another figure, probably a standing one, of the fifth century B.C., but the body could not have been conceived until more than a hundred years later. As soon as we become aware of this, our attitude toward the *Spinario* changes sharply: we no longer see it as a single, harmonious unit but as a somewhat incongruous combination of two ready-made pieces. And since the pieces are separate—though fragmentary—works of art in their own right (unlike the separate pieces, which are not works of art in themselves, in Picasso's *Bull's Head*), they cannot grow together into a new whole that is more than the sum of its parts. Obviously, this graft is not much of a creative achievement. Hence we find it hard to believe that the very able artist who modeled the body should have been willing to countenance such a "marriage of convenience." The combination must be of a later date, presumably Roman rather than Greek. Perhaps the present head was substituted when the original head was damaged by accident? But are the head and body really authentic Greek fragments of the fifth and fourth century B.C., or could they be Roman copies or adaptations of such pieces? These questions may be settled eventually by comparison with other ancient bronzes of less uncertain origin, but even then the degree of artistic originality of the *Spinario* is likely to remain a highly problematic matter.   (8)

A straightforward copy can usually be recognized as such on internal evidence alone. If the copyist is merely a conscientious craftsman, rather than an artist, he will produce a work of craft; the execution will strike us as pedestrian and thus out of tune with the conception of the work. There are also likely to be small slip-ups and mistakes that can be spotted in much the same way as misprints in a text. But what if one great artist copies another? The drawing, *Battle of Sea Gods*, by Albrecht Dürer (fig. 5) is a case in point. An experienced eye will not only recognize it as a copy (because, while the "handwriting" is Dürer's, the design as a whole has a flavor distinctively different from that of the master's other output at that time), it will also be able to identify the source: the original must have been some work by Andrea Mantegna, a somewhat older Italian painter with a powerful artistic personality of his own. Dürer's drawing, of course, does not permit us to say with assurance what kind of work by Mantegna served as its model—it might have been a drawing, a painting, a print, possibly even a relief—or how faithful a copy it is. Yet it would be instructive to find this out, in order for us to gain a better insight into the character of our drawing. The next step, therefore, is to check through the known works of Mantegna; if the same composition does not occur among them, we will have learned nothing new about the drawing but we may have added something to our knowledge of Mantegna, for in that event the Dürer drawing would be a valuable record of an otherwise unknown—and thus presumably lost—composition by the older master. It so happens that Dürer's model, a Mantegna engraving, has survived (fig. 6). As we compare the two, we are surprised to see that the drawing, although it follows Mantegna's design detail for detail, somehow retains the quality of an independent work of art as well. How can we resolve this paradox? Perhaps we may put it this way: in using the engraving as his model, Dürer did not really copy it in the accepted sense of that word, since he did not try to achieve the effect of a duplicate. He drew purely for his own instruction, which is to say that he looked at the engraving the way he would look at something in nature, transcribing it very accurately yet with his own inimitable rhythm of line. In other words, he was not in the least constrained or intimidated by the fact that his model, in this instance, was another work of art. Once we understand this, it becomes clear to us that Dürer's drawing *represents* (it does not *copy*) the engraving in the same way that other drawings represent a landscape or a living person, and that its artistic originality does not suffer thereby. Dürer here gives us a highly original view of Mantegna, a view that is uniquely Dürer's.   (9)

A relationship as close as this between two works of art is not as rare as one might think. Ordinarily, though, the link is less obvious. Edouard Manet's famous painting, *Luncheon on the Grass* (fig. 7), seemed so revolutionary a work when first exhibited almost a century ago that it caused a scandal in part because the artist had dared to show an undressed young woman next to two fashionably clothed men. In real life such a party might indeed get raided by the police, and people assumed that Manet had intended to represent an actual event. Not until many years later did an art historian discover the source of these figures: a group of classical deities from an engraving after Raphael (fig. 9). The relationship, so striking once it has been pointed out to us, had escaped attention, for Manet did not *copy* or *represent* the Raphael composition—he merely *borrowed* its main outlines while translating the figures into modern terms. Had his contemporaries known of this, the *Luncheon* would have seemed a rather less disreputable kind of outing to them, since now the hallowed shade of Raphael could be seen to hover nearby as a sort of chaperon. (Perhaps the artist meant to tease the conservative public, hoping that after the initial shock had passed, somebody would recognize the well-hidden quotation behind his "scandalous" group.) For us, the main effect of the comparison is to make the cool, formal quality of Manet's figures even more conspicuous. But does it decrease our respect for his originality? True, he is "indebted" to Raphael; yet his way of bringing the forgotten old composition back to life is in itself so original and creative that he may be said to have more than repaid his debt. As a matter of fact, Raphael's figures are just as "derivative" as Manet's; they stem from still older sources which lead us back to ancient Roman art and beyond (compare the relief of *River Gods*, fig. 8).   (10)

Thus Manet, Raphael, and the Roman river gods form three links in a chain of relationships that arises somewhere out of the dim and distant past and continues into the future—for the *Luncheon on the Grass* has in turn served as a source of more recent works of art (fig. 10). Nor is this an exceptional case. All works of art anywhere—yes, even such works as Picasso's *Bull's Head*—are part of similar chains that link them to their predecessors. If it is true that "no man is an island," the same can be said of works of art. The sum total of these chains makes a web in which every work of art occupies its own specific place, and which we call *tradition*. Without tradition—the word means "that which has been handed down to us"—no originality would be possible; it provides, as it were, the firm platform from which the artist makes his leap of the imagination. The place where he lands will then become part of the web and serve as a point of departure for further leaps. And for us, too, the web of tradition is equally essential. Whether we are aware of it or not, tradition is the framework within which we inevitably form our opinions of works of art and assess their degree of originality. Let us not forget, however, that such assessments must always remain incomplete and subject to revision. For in order to arrive at a definitive view, we should not only need to know *all* the different chains of relationships that pass through a given work of art, we should be able to survey the entire length of every chain. And that we can never hope to achieve.   (11)

If originality is what distinguishes art from craft, tradition serves as the common meeting ground of the two. Every budding artist starts out on the level of craft, by imitating other works of art. In this way, he gradually absorbs the artistic tradition of his time and place until he has gained a firm footing in it. But only the truly gifted ever leave that stage of traditional competence and become creators in their own right. No one, after all, can be taught how to create; he can only be taught how to go through the motions of creating. If he has talent, he will eventually achieve the real thing. What the apprentice or art student learns are skills and techniques—established ways of drawing, painting, carving, designing; established ways of *seeing*. And if he senses that his gifts are too modest for painting, sculpture, or architecture, he is likely to turn to one of the countless special fields known collectively as "applied art." There he can be fruitfully active on a more limited scale: he may become an illustrator, typographer, or interior decorator; he may design textile patterns, chinaware, furniture, clothing, or advertisements. All these pursuits stand somewhere between "pure" art and "mere" craft. They provide some scope for originality to their more ambitious practitioners, but the flow of creative endeavor is hemmed in by such factors as the cost and availability of materials or manufacturing processes, accepted notions of what is useful, fitting, or desirable; for the applied arts are more deeply enmeshed in our everyday lives and thus cater to a far wider public than do painting and sculpture. Their purpose, as the name suggests, is to beautify the useful—an important and honorable one, no doubt, but of a lesser order than that of art pure-and-simple. Nevertheless, we often find it difficult to maintain this distinction. Medieval painting, for instance, is to a large extent "applied," in the sense that it embellishes surfaces which serve another, practical purpose as well—walls, book pages, windows, furniture. The same may be said of much ancient and medieval sculpture. Greek vases, although technically pottery, are sometimes decorated by artists of very impressive ability. And in architecture the distinction breaks down altogether, since the design of every building, from country cottage to cathedral, reflects external limitations imposed upon it by the site, by cost factors, materials, technique, and by the practical purpose of the structure. (The only "pure" architecture is imaginary architecture.) Thus architecture is, almost by definition, an applied art, but it is also a major art (as against the others, which are often called the "minor arts").   (12)

It is now time to return to our troubled layman and his assumptions about art. He may be willing to grant, on the basis of our discussion so far, that art is indeed a complex and in many ways mysterious human activity about which even the experts can hope to offer only tentative and partial conclusions; but he is also likely to take this as confirming his own belief that "I don't know anything about art." Are there really people who know nothing about art? If we except small children and the victims of severe mental illness or deficiency, our answer must be no, for we cannot help knowing *something* about it, just as we all know something about politics and economics no matter how indifferent we may be to the issues of the day. Art is so much a part of the fabric of human living that we encounter it all the time, even if our contacts with it are limited to magazine covers, advertising posters, war memorials, and the buildings where we live, work, and worship. Much of this art, to be sure, is pretty shoddy

1. Pablo Picasso. *Bull's Head.* 1943. Handlebars and seat of a bicycle. Galerie Louise Leiris, Paris

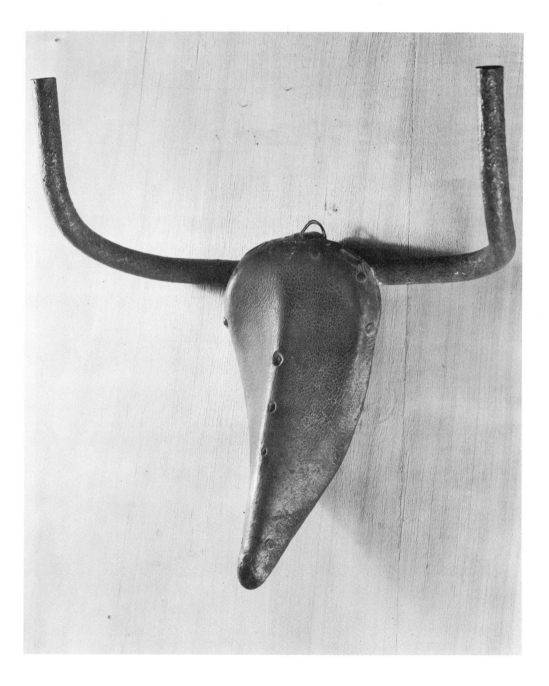

2, 3. MICHELANGELO. *St. Matthew*. 1506. Marble, height 8′ 11″. Academy, Florence

4. *Thorn Puller* (Spinario). Bronze, height 28¾″. Capitoline Museums, Rome

5. ALBRECHT DÜRER. *Battle of Sea Gods.* 1494. Pen drawing, 11⅞ x 15″. Albertina, Vienna

6. ANDREA MANTEGNA. *Battle of Sea Gods.* c. 1493. Engraving 11⅜ x 15⅞″. The Metropolitan Museum of Art, New York (Rogers Fund, 1920)

7. EDOUARD MANET. *Luncheon on the Grass (Le Déjeuner sur l'Herbe).* 1863. Oil on canvas, 7′ x 8′ 10″. The Louvre, Paris

8. *River Gods* (detail of a Roman sarcophagus). 3rd century A.D. Villa Medici, Rome

9. Marcantonio Raimondi, after Raphael. *The Judgment of Paris* (detail) c. 1520. Engraving

10. PABLO PICASSO with sketches after Manet's *Luncheon on the Grass.* 1954

—art at third- and fourth-hand, worn out by endless repetition, representing the lowest common denominator of popular taste. Still, it is art of a sort; and since it is the only art most people ever experience, it molds their ideas on art in general. When they say, "I know what I like," they really mean, "I like what I know (and I reject whatever fails to match the things I am familiar with)"; such likes are not in truth theirs at all, for they have been imposed upon them by habit and circumstance, without any personal choice. To like what we know and to distrust what we do not know is an age-old human trait. We always tend to think of the past as "the good old days," while the future seems fraught with danger. But why should so many of us cherish the illusion of having made a personal choice in art when in actual fact we have not? I suspect there is another unspoken assumption here, which goes something like this: "Since art is such an 'unruly' subject that even the experts keep disagreeing with each other, my opinion is as good as theirs—it's all a matter of subjective preference. In fact, my opinion may be *better* than theirs, because as a layman I react to art in a direct, straightforward fashion, without having my view obstructed by a lot of complicated theories. There must be something wrong with a work of art if it takes an expert to appreciate it." (13)

Behind these mistaken conclusions we find a true and important premise —that works of art exist in order to be liked rather than to be debated. The artist does not create merely for his own satisfaction, but wants his work approved by others. In fact, the hope for approval is what makes him want to create in the first place, and the creative process is not completed until the work has found an audience. Here we have another paradox: the birth of a work of art is an intensely private experience (so much so that many artists can work only when completely alone and refuse to show their unfinished pieces to anyone), yet it must, as a final step, be shared by the public, in order for the birth to be successful. Perhaps we can resolve the paradox once we understand what the artist means by "public." He is concerned not with *the* public as a statistical entity but with his particular public, his audience; quality rather than quantity is what matters to him. At a minimum, this audience need consist of no more than one or two people whose opinion he values. If he can win them over by his work, he feels encouraged to go on; without them, he despairs of his calling. There have been some very great artists who had only such a minimum audience. They hardly ever sold any of their work or had an opportunity to display it in public, but they continued to create because of the moral support of a few faithful friends. These, of course, are rare cases. Ordinarily, artists also need patrons who will purchase their work, thus combining moral and financial support; from the artist's point of view, patrons are always "audience" rather than "customers." There is a vital difference between these last two terms. A customer buys the products of craftsmanship, he knows from previous experience what he will get and that he is going to like it—why else should he have established the custom of returning to the same source of supply? We think of him as "regular" and "satisfied." An audience, in contrast, merits such adjectives as critical, fickle, receptive, enthusiastic; it is uncommitted, free to accept or reject, so that anything placed before it is on trial—nobody knows in advance how the work will be received. Hence there is an emotional tension between artist and audience that has no counterpart in the relationship of craftsman and customer. It is this very tension, this sense of uncertainty and challenge, that the artist needs. He must feel that his work is able to overcome the resistance of the audience, otherwise he cannot be sure that what he has brought forth is a genuine creation, a work of art in fact as well as in intention. The more ambitious and original his work, the greater the tension, and the more triumphant his sense of release after the response of the audience has shown him that his leap of the imagination is successful. On a tiny scale we all have a similar experience when we happen to think up a joke: we have an irresistible urge to tell it to someone, for we can't be sure that it really *is* a joke until we find out whether it strikes others as funny, too. This analogy should not be pressed too far, but it does suggest why artists need an audience to "complete" their work.   (14)

The audience whose approval looms so large in the artist's mind is a limited and special one, not the general public: the merits of the artist's work can never be determined by a popularity contest. The size and composition of this primary audience vary a good deal with time and circumstance; its members may be other artists as well as patrons, friends, critics, and interested bystanders. The one qualification they all have in common is an informed love of works of art—an attitude at once discriminating and enthusiastic that lends particular weight to their judgments. They are, in a word, *experts*, people whose authority rests on experience rather than theoretical knowledge. And because experience, even within a limited field, varies from one individual to the other, it is only natural that they should at times disagree among themselves. Such disagreement often stimulates new insights; far from invalidating the experts' role, it shows, rather, how passionately they care about their subject, whether this be the art of their own time or of the past.   (15)

The active minority which we have termed the artist's primary audience draws its recruits from a much larger and more passive secondary audience, whose contact with works of art is less direct and continuous. This group, in turn, shades over into the vast numbers of those who believe they "don't know anything about art," the laymen pure-and-simple. What distinguishes the layman, as we have seen before, is not that he actually *is* pure and simple but that he likes to think of himself as being so. In reality, there is no sharp break, no difference in kind, between him and the expert, only a difference in degree. The road to expertness invites anyone with an open mind and a capacity to absorb new experiences. As we travel on it, as our understanding grows, we shall find ourselves liking a great many more things than we had thought possible at the start, yet at the same time we shall gradually acquire the courage of our own convictions, until—if we travel far enough—we know how to make a meaningful individual choice among works of art. By then, we shall have joined the active minority that participates directly in shaping the course of art in our time. And we shall be able to say, with some justice, that we know what we like.   (16)

Van Wyck Brooks

(1886–   )

VAN WYCK BROOKS has long been recognized as one of America's leading biographers, critics, and cultural historians. His major series, an effort at a "history of the writer in America," includes, among other volumes, The Flowering of New England *(1936, winner of the Pulitzer prize),* New England's Indian Summer *(1940), and* The Confident Years *(1952). He has also written significant individual works on Mark Twain, Henry James, and Melville and Whitman. He has analyzed particularly the influence of the Puritan tradition on the aesthetic life of America.*

■ *The Flowering of New England*

CONCLUSION

THE CIVIL WAR brought to a head, however inconclusively, a phase of American culture that later times described as the New England "renaissance." This movement of mind continued in the generation that followed, and many of the writers who embodied it long outlived the war. Some of them produced their best work, or work, at least, equal to their best, during

this later period. But all had given their measure before the war, and several
had disappeared before it. That they stood for some collective impulse,
exceptional in the history of the national mind, no one questioned then or
questioned later.   (1)

This movement of mind in New England followed the typical pattern
of the "culture-cycle," as Spengler convincingly described it. Setting aside
the question of scale, one finds in it the same succession of phases that once
finds in the great culture-cycles,—for Spengler, in this, at least, made a
case that is so suggestive as to seem conclusive. Here we have a homogeneous people, living close to the soil, intensely religious, unconscious,
unexpressed in art and letters, with a strong sense of home and fatherland.
One of its towns becomes a "culture-city," for Boston, with Cambridge and
Concord considered as suburbs, answers to this name, which Spengler accords to Florence, Bruges and Weimar, as no other town has ever answered
in either of the Americas. There is a springtime feeling in the air, a joyous
sense of awakening, a free creativeness, an unconscious pride, expressed
in the founding of institutions, intellectual, humanitarian, artistic, and—at
first a little timid, cold and shy—the mind begins to shape into myths and
stories the dreams of the pre-urban countryside. There is a moment of
equipoise, a widespread flowering of the imagination in which the thoughts
and feelings of the people, with all their faiths and hopes, find expression.
The culture-city dominates the country, but only as its accepted vent and
mouthpiece. Then gradually the mind, detached from the soil, grows more
and more self-conscious. Contradictions arise within it, and worldlier arts
supplant the large, free, ingenuous forms through which the poetic mind
has taken shape. What formerly grew from the soil begins to be planned,
and the Hawthornes yield to the Henry Jameses. Over-intelligent, fragile,
cautious and doubtful, the soul of the culture-city loses the self-confidence
and joy that have marked its early development,—it is filled with a presentiment of the end; and the culture-city itself surrenders to the world-
city,—Boston surrenders to New York,—which stands for cosmopolitan de-
racination. What has once been vital becomes provincial; and the sense that
one belongs to a dying race dominates and poisons the creative mind.   (2)

Not to press a formula too far, is not this the story of New England, as
the New England mind has confessed it, from the days of Channing and
Webster to those of Barrett Wendell and Henry Adams? In religion, the
springtime faith of Channing, with its feeling of a world to create and
redeem, yielded to the conception of religion as hygiene in the valetudinarian Mrs. Eddy. In politics, the robust and confident Webster gave place
to the querulous Henry Cabot Lodge. The scholars and historians lost themselves among their documents; and the cheerful, unconscious, generous note
of the essayists and poets of the eighteen-fifties made way for the analytical and the precious. No doubt, the New England mind exaggerated its

own decline and decay. But that it had passed through a cycle and some such cycle as Spengler pictured,—this grew more and more apparent.   (3)

"Men are free," said D. H. Lawrence, "when they are in a living home-land, not when they are straying and breaking away. Men are free when they are obeying some deep, inward voice of religious belief. Obeying from within. Men are free when they belong to a living, organic, believing com-munity, active in fulfilling some unfulfilled, perhaps unrealized purpose." This was the case with the New England authors, in the epoch of the building of the nation. Perhaps it was never more truly the case with any group of authors, all question of intensity aside. They were as com-pletely of their people as any authors of the oldest nations; and they saw, if not themselves,—for they were not self-conscious,—at least their profes-sion as having a Promethean role to play. They were teachers, educators and bringers of light, with a deep and affectionate feeling of obligation towards the young republic their fathers had brought into being. That New England was appointed to guide the nation, to civilize it and humanize it, none of them ever doubted, a motive that was evident in all their writings, from Emerson's early addresses to the table-talk of Holmes, from Long-fellow's *Hiawatha*, in which an Indian myth conveys the poet's notion of his role, to the prophecies of *Uncle Tom's Cabin*. Sometimes they sug-gested Miss Ophelia reforming Dinah's kitchen; but there was so little of the condescending, so much of the humble and fraternal, in their state of mind and point of view, and they threw so many ideas into circulation and wrote so sincerely and so well that they came to be accepted as fathers and sages.   (4)

What was the cause of this transfiguration? The breadth of their con-scious horizon, the healthy objectivity of their minds, their absorption in large preoccupations, historical, political, religious, together with a literary feeling, a blend of the traditional and the local, that gave the local wider currency while it brought the traditional home to men's business and bosoms. They filled the New England scene with associations and set it, as it were, in three dimensions, creating the visible foreground it had never possessed. They helped to make their countrypeople conscious of the great world-movements of thought and feeling in which they played parts side by side with the intellectual leaders of the older countries. In their scholar-ship, their social thought, their moral passion, their artistic feeling, they spoke for the universal republic of letters, giving their own province a form and body in the consciousness of the world. Moreover, there was something in their temper that made them seem friends of the human spirit. They stood for good faith and fair play and all that was generous and hopeful in the life of their time. The hold they gained and kept over the nation possessed an extra-literary sanction, as if they were voices of the national ethos. If they found themselves "done up in spices, like so many

Pharaohs," as Dr. Holmes remarked in later years, it was because they
were looked upon as classics,—

> In whom is plainest taught, and easiest learnt,
> What makes a nation happy, and keeps it so.   (5)

This process of canonization went hand in hand with the spread of New
England culture over the country. As the New England strain died out in
the West, with the second and third generations of the pioneers and the
growth of a native point of view, the reputations of the New England
authors had to face another test. They encountered an increasing neglect
and indifference, and even a widespread hostility. This was partly due to
the reaction against the romantic authors in every country; but it was
inevitable that the West should have turned against New England. In
order to establish its independence, it was obliged to do so, as the East
had turned against the mother-country. Of the popular writers, Longfel-
low, Whittier, Holmes, something seemed destined to survive in the general
mind of the nation, when the life of all the regions, taken together, formed
a final synthesis; but much of their work was ephemeral, and most of it
was so bound up with regional modes of feeling and local traditions that
it could only endure in the regional mind. For the rest, there are two
kinds of classics, the popular and the esoteric, those that yield their meaning at the first encounter and those that one has to discover by effort
and insight, the classics of the intellectual surface and the classics of the
spiritual depths. The popular New England authors, whom every child
could understand, remained as classics indeed, but mainly for children;
while the handful of esoteric authors,—Hawthorne, with his cloudy symbols,
whom one could only see through a glass, darkly, Thoreau, who "listened
behind him for his wit," and Emerson, who, in life, never gave a direct
answer and said that one should speak in parables,—came more and
more into their own. Ironically enough, it was Boston and Cambridge that
grew to seem provincial, while the local and even parochial Concord mind,
which had always been universal, proved to be also national. Whatever
doubts the country at large felt regarding the other New England authors,
Hawthorne, Thoreau and Emerson were clearly of the main stream, with
Emily Dickinson, Whitman, Poe and Melville.   (6)

Thoreau died in 1862. He had caught cold from overexposure while
counting the rings of some trees on a snowy day and had fought for a
year and a half with tuberculosis. He had outlived his juvenile-braggart
phase and had grown more and more to seem the sage, whose life and
opinions might have appeared in the pages of Diogenes Laertius. In an

effort to regain his health, he had journeyed to Minnesota and had made friends with some of the Indians there. Then, knowing that nothing could save him, he had settled down among his papers, with an Indian's indifference to the future, completing some of his lists of birds and flowers and finishing *The Maine Woods*. No more walks to Bateman's Pond, to Becky Stow's swamp or Nine-Acre Corner. But he said he enjoyed existence as well as ever. His thoughts had entertained him all his life, never so much as at present. Fields, the second editor of *The Atlantic*, had asked him for some of his essays, and he spent his last months revising these.   (7)

His friends could hardly imagine Concord without him. Solitude peered out from the dells and wood-roads, and the bobolinks seemed to sing a minor strain. One had thought of Henry Thoreau as a part of nature, destined to be transformed perhaps at last into a mossy rock or a leaf-strewn spring. At least, he was like the hourglass apple-shrub of which he had written in his journal. By the end of October, when the leaves had fallen, one saw the wild yellow fruit growing, which the cows could not reach over the thorny hedge. It was so with the rude, neglected genius of the Concord woods and meadows. He had suffered many a check at first, browsed upon by fate, springing up in a rocky pasture, the nursery of other creatures there, and had grown up scraggy and thorny, not like the sleek orchard-trees whose forces had all been husbanded. When, at first, within this rind and hedge, the man shot up, one saw the thorny scrub of his youth about him; but, as he grew, the thorns disappeared, and he bore golden crops of Porters and Baldwins, apples whose fame was destined to spread through all orchards for generations, when the thrifty orchard-trees that had been his rivals had long since ceased to bear their engrafted fruit. It was true that Thoreau's fame was slow in growing. Emerson and Ellery Channing brought out his posthumous books,—he had published only two during his lifetime; and Emerson collected his poems and letters. But only his friends could imagine why anyone should wish to see his journal. Emerson was convinced that, if it was published, it would soon produce in New England a "plentiful crop of naturalists." This proved to be true a generation later. When volumes of selections from the journal appeared, a school of lesser Thoreaus sprang up at once;[1] and

> The happy man who was content
> With his own town, his continent,

became a teacher of wisdom, even in Asia.   (8)

[1] Thoreau's manuscript journal consisted of thirty-nine blankbooks of all shapes and sizes, packed in a strong wooden box built by himself. It was bequeathed by Sophia Thoreau to H. G. O. Blake, who brought out four volumes of selections, 1881–1892. The complete journal was edited by Bradford Torrey and published in fourteen volumes, 1906.

Two years after Thoreau, Hawthorne faded out of the Concord picture. He had come home from Italy and England just before the outbreak of the war and had taken up his life again at Wayside, the house he had bought from Alcott, where a man was said to have lived who believed he was never to die. Hawthorne built a tower over the house, a reminiscence of the Italian villa in which he had stayed in Florence. There he had his study, reached by a trap-door, with a standing desk fastened to the wall. With England still fresh in his mind, he composed from his note-books the beautifully rounded chapters of *Our Old Home*, a book that was somewhat unhappily named; but a sudden change seemed to have come upon him with his return to America, a blight as of winter, a deadly estrangement even from his own imagination. Had he been too old to be transplanted, so that he could never take root again? He made a few half-hearted efforts to gather up the threads of his former life. He appeared at the Saturday Club for a few of the dinners; but even Alcott and Emerson seldom saw him. Once, at Emerson's house, he picked up some photographs of Concord, the common, the court-house and the Mill-dam, which he passed in his walks every day, and asked what the pictures represented. The sight of a friend or a stranger approaching his house drove him up the hill into the woods. Along the top of the ridge, among the pines, between the huckleberry and sweetfern bushes, he walked to and fro, brooding over the novel he could not finish. He fancied that the grass and the little shrubs shrank away as he passed them because there was something in his broodings that was alien to nature. Seventy-five years later, one could still trace the path that Hawthorne's footsteps wore on the tree-covered ridge.   (9)

He had wasted away and the glow in his eyes had vanished; and, hard as he tried to write, pulling down the blinds and locking his door, he could not bring his mind into focus. The novel became two novels, and the two became four. He could not fix upon a single setting: Salem, Concord, England, Wayside and Smithall's Hall drifted in confusion through his mind, their outlines melting into one another. Even his theme eluded him. Was it the unpardonable sin, the "ancestral footstep," the man who believed he was never to die? He made four beginnings, constantly changing his perspective, until he could scarcely bear to touch his blurred and meaningless manuscripts. A few of the scenes took form, with all his old perfection, with the sculptural repose of his earlier writing and a touch of the Gothic imagination that seemed to connect America with the Middle Ages. But life shook before his eyes, like the picture on the surface of a pond when a stone has disturbed its tranquil mirror. His mind had grown like Melville's in *Pierre*, groping in a fog for the firm conceptions that turned to vapour as he tried to grasp them. Then, one day in 1864, the news reached Concord from Plymouth, New Hampshire, that he had died in his sleep at the village inn. For years, he had been in the habit, while idly scribbling, of writing the number 64, which had, he felt, some fatal meaning for him. He had not disappeared, like Septimius Felton, crushed by the failure of his dream, but he had wandered away with as little purpose, knowing perhaps that he would not return.   (10)

The Alcotts had settled in Orchard House, next door to Hawthorne's. Alcott had rebuilt it, leaving the old beams and rafters, making arched alcoves of the ovens and ash-holes; and, over the chimney-piece in Alcott's study, Ellery Channing's lines were inscribed,—

> The hills were reared, the valleys scooped in vain,
> If Learning's altars vanish from the plain.

Alcott had been made superintendent of the public schools in Concord. His vindication had come late, and one could only think what he might have accomplished if he had had this chance when he was younger. Louisa had begun to write the stories that were to carry his name around the world. Meanwhile, now that Thoreau was gone, Emerson was the master of the Concord revels. He liked to pile the children into the haycart, which they had bedecked with flowers and mosses, and carry them off for a swim and a picnic at Walden.   (11)

Emerson was travelling, on his lecture-tours, further and further westward. He was still an impossible puzzle in the popular mind, even a national joke, a byword of the country paragraphers. No matter, there were always a few of his hearers for whom all mythology spoke in his voice, the Indian gods and the gods of the North, who felt that the beautiful and the good must also be the true, if only because Emerson had said so. He seemed to have made his own all the victories of genius, which he invited one to share, he who had never doubted the riches of nature, the gifts of the future, the wealth of the mind. Whatever one's occupation was, mechanics, law, the ministry, he broke the spell of one's routine, relating one's craft and task to the laws of the world: one felt how one's life was intertwined with the whole chain of being. He spoke for magnanimity and the power of thought. In *The Conduct of Life* he had met the objections of those who found his optimism too facile. He had fully recognized the existence of evil, the brutal and barbarous elements in the core of the world, the habits of snake and spider in human beings, the snap of the tiger, the crackle of the bones of his prey in the coils of the anaconda. Even as men rose in culture, fate continued to follow them, as Vishnu followed Maya through all her ascending changes. While their checks and limitations became finer and finer, the ring of necessity still remained perched at the top. But fate had its lord, limitation its limits. It was dif-

ferent seen from above and seen from below. For, if fate was immense, so
was power. Man was a stupendous antagonism, and as long as he thought,
he was free. It was true, there was nothing more disgusting than the crowing
about liberty by slaves, as most men were, and the flippant mistaking for
freedom of some statute right to vote by those who had never dared to think or
act; yet men had the power to look not at fate but the other way. The practical view was the other. Well had the oracle said, "Look not on Nature, for
her name is fatal!" as Hafiz described the phrase on the gate of heaven,
"Woe unto him who suffers himself to be betrayed by Fate!" Instead of
cringing to facts, one could use and command them. Every jet of chaos
that threatened extermination, one could convert by intellect into wholesome force. The water drowned ship and sailor. But, if one learned to swim
and trimmed one's bark, one clove the water with it, and the waves were
obliged to carry it, like their own foam, a plume and a power.   (12)

Thus Emerson spoke to the active forces waiting in his hearers, eager
for the word that would set them free. For himself, he found that the
more he spent the more he had to spend, the more he communicated the
results of his thinking the more new thoughts he had. His zest and curiosity grew with the years; and, for all the discomforts of his lecture-tours,
he liked to get away from the Eastern sea-board, where the American current was so superficial. He learned the resources of the country, going to
school to the prairies. He had no fear of the future, he did not distrust
the rough, wild, incalculable road America would have to travel to find
itself. As between the civil and the forcible, he had always leaned, in his
sympathies, to the latter. The Hoosiers and the Badgers of the West, the
hard heads of Oregon and Utah, the rough-riders and legislators in shirtsleeves, let them drive as they might. Better than to quote English standards
and miss the sovereignty of power. Out of pirates and berserkers the English
race had sprung, and no strong nation could ever develop without its own
strong, wild will; and the power of the buffalo-hunters, bullying the peace-
able and the loyal, would bring its own antidote at last. For liberty in all
its wildness bred iron conscience; the instinct of the people was right in
the end, and natures with great impulses had great resources and could be
trusted to return from far.   (13)

There, in the West, he thought, lay nature sleeping, too much by half
for man in the picture, with its rank vegetation of swamps and forests,
steeped in dews and rains. In this great sloven continent, in its high Alle-
ghany pastures, in the sea-wide, sea-skirted prairie, the great mother still
slept and murmured. Man had as yet made little impression upon it. But
there, where stars and woods and hills abounded, with all things still
untried, could one not foresee a social state more excellent than history had
recorded, one that turned its back on musket-worship and lived by the law
of love and justice? Let men but know that every day is doomsday, and

let them look within, in the populous, all-loving solititude which they left for the tattle of towns; for there *he* lurked and hid, he who was reality, joy and power. So Emerson felt, in the streets of New York, or at Concord, as he strolled through grove and glen. Others, as they saw him, tall and slender, leaving the village behind him, might have said to themselves, with the Swedish poet, "The last skald walks over the meadows."   (14)

Malcolm Cowley

(1898–   )

COWLEY is a free-lance writer and literary arbiter who has from time to time held visiting professorships, most frequently at Stanford University. For fifteen years, he was associate editor of The New Republic, *and more recently he has edited selections from the works of major American authors of this century—Hemingway, Faulkner, Whitman, F. Scott Fitzgerald, and so forth. His years as a student in France have resulted in numerous translations of the works of French authors.*

■ *The Greenwich Village Idea*

In those days when division after division was landing in Hoboken and marching up Fifth Avenue in full battle equipment, when Americans were fighting the Bolshies in Siberia and guarding the Rhine—in those still belligerent days that followed the Armistice there was a private war between Greenwich Village and the *Saturday Evening Post.*   (1)

Other magazines fought in the same cause, but the *Post* was persistent and powerful enough to be regarded as chief of the aggressor nations. It published stories about the Villagers, editorials and articles against them,

grave or flippant serials dealing with their customs in a mood of disparagement or alarm, humorous pieces done to order by its staff writers, cartoons
in which the Villagers were depicted as long-haired men and short-haired
women with ridiculous bone-rimmed spectacles—in all, a long campaign of
invective beginning before the steel strike or the Palmer Raids and continuing through the jazz era, the boom and the depression. The burden of
it was always the same: that the Village was the haunt of affectation; that
it was inhabited by fools and fakers; that the fakers hid Moscow heresies
under the disguise of cubism and free verse; that the fools would eventually be cured of their folly: they would forget this funny business about
art and return to domesticity in South Bend, Indiana, and sell motorcars,
and in the evenings sit with slippered feet while their children romped
about them in paper caps made from the advertising pages of the *Saturday
Evening Post*. The Village was dying, had died already, smelled to high
heaven and Philadelphia. . . .   (2)

The Villagers did not answer this attack directly: instead they carried on
a campaign of their own against the culture of which the *Post* seemed to
be the final expression. They performed autopsies, they wrote obituaries of
civilization in the United States, they shook the standardized dust of the
country from their feet. Here, apparently, was a symbolic struggle: on the
one side, the great megaphone of middle-class America; on the other, the
American disciples of art and artistic living. Here, in its latest incarnation,
was the eternal warfare of bohemian against bourgeois, poet against propriety—Villon and the Bishop of Orléans, Keats and the quarterly reviewers,
Rodolphe, Mimi and the landlord. But perhaps, if we review the history
of the struggle, we shall find that the issue was other than it seemed, and
the enmity less ancient.   (3)

Alexander Pope, two centuries before, had taken the side of property
and propriety in a similar campaign against the slums of art. When writing
The Dunciad and the *Epistle to Dr. Arbuthnot*, he lumped together all
his enemies—stingy patrons, homosexual peers, hair-splitting pedants; but
he reserved his best-considered insults for the garret dwellers of Grub
Street, the dramatists whose lives were spent dodging the bailiff, the epic
poets "lulled by a zephyr through the broken pane." These he accused of
slander, dullness, theft, bootlicking, ingratitude, every outrage to man and
the Muses; almost the only charge he did not press home against them was
that of affectation. They were not play-acting their poverty. The thread-
bare Miltons of his day were rarely the children of prosperous parents;
they could not go home to Nottingham or Bristol and earn a comfortable
living by selling hackney coaches; if they "turned a Persian tale for half a
crown," it was usually because they had no other means of earning half a
crown and so keeping themselves out of debtors' prison. And the substance

of Pope's attack against them is simply that they were poor, that they belonged to a class beneath his own, without inherited wealth, that they did not keep a gentleman's establishment, or possess a gentleman's easy manners, or the magnanimity of a gentleman sure of tomorrow's dinner:

> Yet then did Gildon draw his venal quill;
> I wish'd the man a dinner, and sate still.
> Yet then did Dennis rave in furious fret;
> I never answer'd, I was not in debt.   (4)

Pope was a far wittier poet than any of his adversaries, but the forces he brought against them were not those of wit or poetry alone: behind him, massed in reserve, was all the prejudice of eighteenth-century gentlefolk against intruders into the polite world of letters. He was fighting a literary class war, and one that left deep wounds. To many a poor scribbler it meant the difference between starvation and the roast of mutton he lovingly appraised in a bake-shop window and promised himself to devour if his patron sent him a guinea: after *The Dunciad*, patrons closed their purses. Pope had inflicted a defeat on Grub Street but—the distinction is important—he had left bohemia untouched, for the simple reason that Queen Anne's and King George's London had no bohemia to defeat. (5)

Grub Street is as old as the trade of letters—in Alexandria, in Rome, it was already a crowded quarter; bohemia is younger than the Romantic movement. Grub Street develops in the metropolis of any country or culture as soon as men are able to earn a precarious living with pen or pencil; bohemia is a revolt against certain features of industrial capitalism and can exist only in a capitalist society. Grub Street is a way of life unwillingly followed by the intellectual proletariat; bohemia attracts its citizens from all economic classes: there are not a few bohemian millionaires, but they are expected to imitate the customs of penniless artists. Bohemia is Grub Street romanticized, doctrinalized and rendered self-conscious; it is Grub Street on parade.   (6)

It originated in France, not England, and the approximate date of its birth was 1830: thus, it followed the rise of French industry after the Napoleonic Wars. The French Romantic poets complained of feeling oppressed—perhaps it was, as Musset believed, the fault of that great Emperor whose shadow fell across their childhood; perhaps it was Science, or the Industrial Revolution, or merely the money-grubbing, the stuffy morals and stupid politics of the people about them; in any case they had to escape from middle-class society. Some of them became revolutionists; others took refuge in pure art; but most of them demanded a real world of present satisfactions, in which they could cherish aristocratic ideals while living among carpenters and grisettes. The first bohemians, the first inhabitants of that world, were the friends of Théophile Gautier and Gérard de Nerval, young men of good family, bucks and dandies with money enough to indulge their moods; but the legend of it was spread abroad, some twenty years later, by a poor hack named Henry Murger, the son of a German immigrant to Paris.   (7)

Having abandoned all hopes of a formal education when he left primary school, and feeling no desire to follow his father's trade of tailor, Murger began to write mediocre verse and paint incredible pictures, meanwhile supporting himself by his wits. Soon he joined a group that called itself the Water Drinkers because it could rarely afford another beverage. A dozen young men with little talent and extravagant ambitions, they lived in hovels or in lofts over a cow stable, worked under the lash of hunger, and wasted their few francs in modest debauchery. One winter they had a stove for the first time: it was a hole cut in the floor, through which the animal heat of the stable rose into their chamber. They suffered from the occupational diseases of poor artists—consumption, syphilis, pneumonia—all of them aggravated by undernourishment. Joseph Desbrosses died in the winter of 1844; he was an able sculptor, possibly the one genius of the group. His funeral was the third in six weeks among the Water Drinkers, and they emptied their pockets to buy a wooden cross for the grave. When the last sod clumped down, the gravediggers stood waiting for their tip. There was not a sou in the party.   (8)

"That's all right," said the gravediggers generously, recognizing the mourners. "It will be for the next time."   (9)

Spring came and their feelings rose with the mercury. One evening when his friends were making war maps in water color, Murger began unexpectedly to tell them stories. They listened, chuckled and roared for two good hours, till somebody advised him, seriously between gales of laughter, to abandon poetry for fiction. A little later he followed this advice, writing about the life of his friends, the only life he knew. Personally he hated this existence on the cold fringes of starvation and planned to escape from it as soon as he could, but for the public he tried to render it attractive.   (10)

In *Scènes de la Vie de Bohème*, he succeeded beyond his ambition. He succeeded not only in writing a popular book, one that was translated into twenty languages, successfully dramatized, candied into an opera, one that enabled its author to live in bourgeois comfort, but also in changing an image in the public mind. Grub Street, where dinnerless Gildon drew his venal quill, contemptible Grub Street, the haunt of apprentices and failures and Henry Murger, was transformed into glamorous bohemia. The unwilling expedient became a permanent way of life, became a cult with rituals and costumes, a doctrine adhered to not only by artists, young and old, rich and poor, but also in later years by designers, stylists, trade-paper sub-editors, interior decorators, wolves, fairies, millionaire patrons of art, sadists, nyphomaniacs, bridge sharks, anarchists, women living on alimony, tired reformers, educational cranks, economists, hopheads, dipsomaniac playwrights, nudists, restaurant keepers, stockbrokers and dentists craving self-expression.   (11)

Even during Murger's lifetime, the bohemian cult was spreading from France into other European countries. Having occupied a whole section of Paris—three sections, in fact, for it moved from the Boul' Mich' to Montmartre and thence to Montparnasse—it founded new colonies in Munich, Berlin, London, St. Petersburg. In the late 1850s it reached New York, where it established headquarters in Charlie Pfaff's lager-beer saloon under the sidewalk of lower Broadway. Again in 1894 the "Trilby" craze spawned forth dozens of bohemian groups and magazines; in New York a writer explained that the true bohemia may exist at millionaires' tables; in Philadelphia young married couples south of Market Street would encourage their guests: "Don't stand on ceremony; you know we are thorough bohemians." All over the Western world, bohemia was carrying on a long warfare with conventional society, but year by year it was making more converts from the ranks of the enemy.   (12)

When the American magazines launched their counteroffensive, in 1919, a curious phenomenon was to be observed. The New York bohemians, the Greenwich Villagers, came from exactly the same social class as the readers of the *Saturday Evening Post*. Their political opinions were vague and by no means dangerous to Ford Motors or General Electric: the war had destroyed their belief in political action. They were trying to get ahead, and the proletariat be damned. Their economic standards were those of the small American businessman.   (13)

The art-shop era was just beginning. Having fled from Dubuque and Denver to escape the stultifying effects of a civilization ruled by business, many of the Villagers had already entered business for themselves, and many more were about to enter it. They would open tea shops, antique shops, book shops, yes, and bridge parlors, dance halls, night clubs and real-estate offices. By hiring shop assistants, they would become the exploiters of labor. If successful, they tried to expand their one restaurant into a chain of restaurants, all with a delightfully free and intimate atmosphere, but run on the best principles of business accounting. Some of them leased houses, remodeled them into studio apartments, and raised the rents three or four hundred per cent to their new tenants. Others clung faithfully to their profession of painting or writing, rose in it slowly, and at last had their stories or illustrations accepted by *Collier's* or the *Saturday Evening Post*. There were occasions, I believe, when Greenwich Village writers were editorially encouraged to write stories making fun of the Village, and some of them were glad to follow the suggestion. Of course they complained, when slightly tipsy, that they were killing themselves—but how else could maintain their standard of living? What they meant was that they could not live like *Vanity Fair* readers without writing for the *Saturday Evening Post*.   (14)

And so it was that many of them lived during the prosperous decade that followed. If the book succeeded or if they got a fat advertising contract, they bought houses in Connecticut, preferably not too far from the Sound. They hired butlers; they sent their children to St. Somebody's; they collected highboys, lowboys, tester beds; they joined the local Hunt and rode in red coats across New England stone fences and through wine-red sumacs in pursuit of a bag of imported aniseed. In the midst of these new pleasures they continued to bewail the standardization of American life, while the magazines continued their polemic against Greenwich Village. You came to suspect that some of the Villagers themselves, even those who remained below Fourteenth Street, were not indignant at a publicity that brought tourists to the Pirates' Den and customers to Ye Olde Curiowe Shoppe and increased the value of the land in which a few of them had begun to speculate. The whole thing seemed like a sham battle. Yet beneath it was a real conflict of ideas and one that would soon be mirrored in the customs of a whole country.   (15)

Greenwich Village was not only a place, a mood, a way of life: like all bohemias, it was also a doctrine. Since the days of Gautier and Murger, this doctrine had remained the same in spirit, but it had changed in several details. By 1920, it had become a system of ideas that could roughly be summarized as follows: (16)

1. The idea of salvation by the child.—Each of us at birth has special potentialities which are slowly crushed and destroyed by a standardized society and mechanical methods of teaching. If a new educational system can be introduced, one by which children are encouraged to develop their own personalities, to blossom freely like flowers, then the world will be saved by this new, free generation.   (17)

2. The idea of self-expression.—Each man's, each woman's, purpose in life is to express himself, to realize his full individuality through creative work and beautiful living in beautiful surroundings.   (18)

3. The idea of paganism.—The body is a temple in which there is nothing unclean, a shrine to be adorned for the ritual of love.   (19)

4. The idea of living for the moment.—It is stupid to pile up treasures that we can enjoy only in old age, when we have lost the capacity for enjoyment. Better to seize the moment as it comes, to dwell in it intensely, even at the cost of future suffering. Better to live extravagantly, gather June rosebuds, "burn my candle at both ends. . . . It gives a lovely light."   (20)

5. The idea of liberty.—Every law, convention or rule of art that prevents self-expression or the full enjoyment of the moment should be shattered and abolished. Puritanism is the great enemy. The crusade against puritanism is the only crusade with which free individuals are justified in allying themselves.   (21)

6. The idea of female equality.—Women should be the economic and moral equals of men. They should have the same pay, the same working conditions, the same opportunity for drinking, smoking, taking or dismissing lovers.   (22)

7. The idea of psychological adjustment.—We are unhappy because we are maladjusted, and maladjusted because we are repressed. If our individual repressions can be removed—by confessing them to a Freudian psychologist—then we can adjust ourselves to any situation, and be happy in it. (But Freudianism is only one method of adjustment. What is wrong with us may be our glands, and by a slight operation, or merely by taking a daily dose of thyroid, we may alter our whole personalities. Again, we may adjust ourselves by some such psycho-physical discipline as was taught by Gurdjieff. The implication of all these methods is the same—that the environment itself need not be altered. That explains why most radicals who became converted to psychoanalysis or glands or Gurdjieff[1] gradually abandoned their political radicalism.)   (23)

8. The idea of changing place.—"They do things better in Europe." England and Germany have the wisdom of old cultures; the Latin peoples have admirably preserved their pagan heritage. By expatriating himself, by living in Paris, Capri or the South of France, the artist can break the puritan shackles, drink, live freely and be wholly creative.   (24)

All these, from the standpoint of the business-Christian ethic then represented by the *Saturday Evening Post*, were corrupt ideas. This older ethic is familiar to most people, but one feature of it has not been sufficiently emphasized. Substantially, it was a *production* ethic. The great virtues it taught were industry, foresight, thrift and personal initiative. The workman should be industrious in order to produce more for his employer; he should look ahead to the future; he should save money in order to become a capitalist himself; then he should exercise personal initiative and found new factories where other workmen would toil industriously, and save, and become capitalists in their turn.   (25)

During the process many people would suffer privations: most workers would live meagerly and wrack their bodies with labor; even the employers would deny themselves luxuries that they could easily purchase, choosing instead to put back the money into their business; but after all, our bodies

---

1 George Ivanovich Gurdjieff, a Russian living in France, had worked out a system of practical mysticism based largely on Yoga. His chief disciple was A. E. Orage, the editor of the *New English Weekly*. In the spring of 1924, when Orage was in New York, he gained a great many converts, chiefly among older members of the Greenwich Village set.

were not to be pampered; they were temporary dwelling places, and we should be rewarded in Heaven for our self-denial. On earth, our duty was to accumulate more wealth and produce more goods, the ultimate use of which was no subject for worry. They would somehow be absorbed, by new markets opened in the West, or overseas in new countries, or by the increased purchasing power of workmen who had saved and bettered their position.   (26)

That was the ethic of a young capitalism, and it worked admirably, so long as the territory and population of the country were expanding faster than its industrial plant. But after the war the situation changed. Our industries had grown enormously to satisfy a demand that suddenly ceased. To keep the factory wheels turning, a new domestic market had to be created. Industry and thrift were no longer adequate. There must be a new ethic that encouraged people to buy, a *consumption* ethic.   (27)

It happened that many of the Greenwich Village ideas proved useful in the altered situation. Thus, *self-expression* and *paganism* encouraged a demand for all sorts of products—modern furniture, beach pajamas, cosmetics, colored bathrooms with toilet paper to match. *Living for the moment* meant buying an automobile, radio or house, using it now and paying for it tomorrow. *Female equality* was capable of doubling the consumption of products—cigarettes, for example—that had formerly been used by men alone. Even *changing place* would help to stimulate business in the country from which the artist was being expatriated. The exiles of art were also trade missionaries: involuntarily they increased the foreign demand for fountain pens, silk stockings, grapefruit and portable typewriters. They drew after them an invading army of tourists, thus swelling the profits of steamship lines and travel agencies. Everything fitted into the business picture.   (28)

I don't mean to say that Greenwich Village was the source of the revolution in morals that affected all our lives in the decade after the war, and neither do I mean that big business deliberately plotted to render the nation extravagant, pleasure worshiping and reckless of tomorrow.   (29)

The new moral standards arose from conditions that had nothing to do with the Village. They were, as a matter of fact, not really new. Always, even in the great age of the Puritans, there had been currents of licentiousness that were favored by the immoderate American climate and held in check only by hellfire preaching and the hardships of settling a new country. Old Boston, Providence, rural Connecticut, all had their underworlds. The reason puritanism became so strong in America was perhaps that it had to be strong in order to checkmate its enemies. But it was already weakening as the country grew richer in the twenty years before the war; and the war itself was the puritan crisis and defeat.   (30)

All standards were relaxed in the stormy-sultry wartime atmosphere. It wasn't only the boys of my age, those serving in the army, who were transformed by events: their sisters and younger brothers were affected in a different fashion. With their fathers away, perhaps, and their mothers making bandages or tea-dancing with lonely officers, it was possible for boys and girls to do what they pleased. For the first time they could go to dances unchaperoned, drive the family car and park it by the roadside while they made love, and come home after midnight, a little tipsy, with nobody to reproach them in the hallway. They took advantage of these stolen liberties —indeed, one might say that the revolution in morals began as a middle-class children's revolt.   (31)

But everything conspired to further it. Prohibition came and surrounded the new customs with illicit glamour; prosperity made it possible to practice them; Freudian psychology provided a philosophical justification and made it unfashionable to be repressed; still later the sex magazines and the movies, even the pulpit, would advertise a revolution that had taken place silently and triumphed without a struggle. In all this Greenwich Village had no part. The revolution would have occurred if the Village had never existed, but—the point is important—it would not have followed the same course. The Village, older in revolt, gave form to the movement, created its fashions, and supplied the writers and illustrators who would render them popular. As for American business, though it laid no plots in advance, it was quick enough to use the situation, to exploit the new markets for cigarettes and cosmetics, and to realize that, in advertising pages and movie palaces, sex appeal was now the surest appeal.   (32)

The Greenwich Village standards, with the help of business, had spread through the country. Young women east and west had bobbed their hair, let it grow and bobbed it again; they had passed through the period when corsets were checked in the cloakroom at dances and the period when corsets were not worn. They were not very self-conscious when they talked about taking a lover; and the conversations ran from mother fixations to birth control while they smoked cigarettes between the courses of luncheons eaten in black-and-orange tea shops just like those in the Village. People of forty had been affected by the younger generation: they spent too much money, drank too much gin, made love to one another's wives and talked about their neuroses. Houses were furnished to look like studios. Stenographers went on parties, following the example of the boss and his girl friend and her husband. The "party," conceived as a gathering together of men and women to drink gin cocktails, flirt, dance to the phonograph or radio and gossip about their absent friends, had in fact become one of the most popular American institutions; nobody stopped to think how short its history had been in this country. It developed out of the "orgies" celebrated by the French 1830 Romantics, but it was introduced into this country by Greenwich Villagers—before being adopted by salesmen from Kokomo and the younger country-club set in Kansas City. (33)

Wherever one turned the Greenwich Village ideas were making their way: even the *Saturday Evening Post* was feeling their influence. Long before Repeal, it began to wobble on Prohibition. It allowed drinking, petting and unfaithfulness to be mentioned in the stories it published; its illustrations showed women smoking. Its advertising columns admitted one after another of the strictly pagan products—cosmetics, toilet tissues, cigarettes—yet still it continued to thunder against Greenwich Village and bohemian immorality. It even nourished the illusion that its long campaign had been successful. On more than one occasion it announced that the Village was dead and buried: "The sad truth is," it said in the autumn of 1931, "that the Village was a flop." Perhaps it was true that the Village was moribund—of that we can't be sure, for creeds and ways of life among artists are hard to kill. If, however, the Village was really dying, it was dying of success. It was dying because it became so popular that too many people insisted on living there. It was dying because women smoked cigarettes on the streets of the Bronx, drank gin cocktails in Omaha and had perfectly swell parties in Seattle and Middletown—in other words, because American business and the whole of middle-class America had been going Greenwich Village. (34)

Ralph Waldo Emerson

(1803–1882)

EMERSON, more than any other writer, translated English Romanticism, German Idealism, and Swedenborgian mysticism into the American consciousness. He was one of the major forces in nineteenth-century American thought and literature—teaching (or preaching) a series of philosophical corollaries based on his faith in individualism, self-reliance, the spiritual nature of reality, and the existence and importance of a unifying Over-Soul. See Van Wyck Brooks' treatment of Emerson in "Conclusion."

◼ *The American Scholar*

AN ORATION DELIVERED BEFORE THE PHI BETA KAPPA
SOCIETY, AT CAMBRIDGE, AUGUST 31, 1837

MR. PRESIDENT AND GENTLEMEN:—I greet you on the re-commencement of our literary year. Our anniversary is one of hope, and, perhaps, not enough of labor. We do not meet for games of strength or skill, for the recitation of histories, tragedies, and odes, like the ancient Greeks; for parliaments of love and poesy, like the Troubadours; nor for the advancement of science, like our cotemporaries in the British and European capitals. Thus far, our holiday has been simply a friendly sign of the survival of the love of letters amongst a people too busy to give to letters any more. As such, it is precious as the sign of an indestructible instinct. Perhaps the time is already come, when it ought to be, and will be, something else; when the sluggard intellect of this continent will look from under its iron lids, and fill the postponed expectation of the world with something better than the exertions of mechanical skill. Our day of dependence, our long apprenticeship to the learning of other lands, draws to a close. The millions, that around us are rushing into life, cannot always be fed on the sere remains of foreign harvests. Events, actions arise, that must be sung, that will sing themselves. Who can doubt, that poetry will revive and lead in a new age, as the star in the constellation Harp, which now flames in our zenith, astronomers announce, shall one day be the pole-star for a thousand years? (1)

In this hope, I accept the topic which not only usage, but the nature of our association, seem to prescribe to this day,—the AMERICAN SCHOLAR. Year by year, we come up hither to read one more chapter of his biography. Let us inquire what light new days and events have thrown on his character, and his hopes. (2)

It is one of those fables, which, out of an unknown antiquity, convey an unlooked-for wisdom, that the gods, in the beginning, divided Man into men, that he might be more helpful to himself; just as the hand was divided into fingers, the better to answer its end. (3)

The old fable covers a doctrine ever new and sublime; that there is One Man,—present to all particular men only partially, or through one faculty; and that you must take the whole society to find the whole man. Man is not a farmer, or a professor, or an engineer, but he is all. Man is priest, and scholar, and statesman, and producer, and soldier. In the *divided* or social state, these functions are parcelled out to individuals, each of whom aims to do his stint of the joint work, whilst each other performs his. The fable implies, that the individual, to possess himself, must sometimes return from his own labor to embrace all the other laborers. But unfortunately, this original unit, this fountain of power, has been so distributed to multitudes, has been so minutely subdivided and peddled out, that it is spilled into drops, and cannot be gathered. The state of society is one in which the members have suffered amputation from the trunk, and strut about so many walking monsters,—a good finger, a neck, a stomach, an elbow, but never a man. (4)

Man is thus metamorphosed into a thing, into many things. The planter, who is Man sent out into the field to gather food, is seldom cheered by any idea of the true dignity of his ministry. He sees his bushel and his cart, and nothing beyond, and sinks into the farmer, instead of Man on the farm. The tradesman scarcely ever gives an ideal worth to his work, but is ridden by the routine of his craft, and the soul is subject to dollars. The priest becomes a form; the attorney, a statute-book; the mechanic, a machine; the sailor, a rope of a ship. (5)

In this distribution of functions, the scholar is the delegated intellect. In the right state, he is, *Man Thinking*. In the degenerate state, when the victim of society, he tends to become a mere thinker, or, still worse, the parrot of other men's thinking. (6)

In this view of him, as Man Thinking, the theory of his office is contained. Him nature solicits with all her placid, all her monitory pictures; him the past instructs; him the future invites. Is not, indeed, every man a student, and do not all things exist for the student's behoof? And, finally, is not the true scholar the only true master? But the old oracle said, "All things have two handles: beware of the wrong one." In life, too often, the scholar errs with mankind and forfeits his privilege. Let us see him in his school, and consider him in reference to the main influences he receives. (7)

I. The first in time and the first in importance of the influences upon the mind is that of nature. Every day, the sun; and, after sunset, night and her stars. Ever the winds blow; ever the grass grows. Every day, men and women, conversing, beholding and beholden. The scholar is he of all men whom this spectacle most engages. He must settle its value in his mind. What is nature to him? There is never a beginning, there is never an end, to the inexplicable continuity of this web of God, but always circular power returning into itself. Therein it resembles his own spirit, whose beginning, whose ending, he never can find,—so entire, so boundless. Far, too, as her splendors shine, system on system shooting like rays, upward, downward, without centre without circumference,—in the mass and in the particle, nature hastens to render account of herself to the mind. Classification begins. To the young mind, every thing is individual, stands by itself. By and by, it finds how to join two things, and see in them one nature; then three, then three thousand; and so, tyrannized over by its own unifying instinct, it goes on tying things together, diminishing anomalies, discovering roots running under ground, whereby contrary and remote things cohere, and flower out from one stem. It presently learns, that, since the dawn of history, there has been a constant accumulation and classifying of facts. But what is classification but the perceiving that these objects are not chaotic, and are not foreign, but have a law which is also a law of the human mind? The astronomer discovers that geometry, a pure abstraction of the human mind, is the measure of planetary motion. The chemist finds proportions and intelligible method throughout matter; and science is nothing but the finding of analogy, identity, in the most remote parts. The ambitious soul sits down before each refractory fact; one after another, reduces all strange constitutions, all new powers, to their class and their law, and goes on for ever to animate the last fibre of organization, the outskirts of nature, by insight. (8)

Thus to him, to this school-boy under the bending dome of day, is suggested, that he and it proceed from one root; one is leaf and one is flower; relation, sympathy, stirring in every vein. And what is that Root? Is not that the soul of his soul?—A thought too bold,—a dream too wild. Yet when this spiritual light shall have revealed the law of more earthly natures,— when he has learned to worship the soul, and to see that the natural philosophy that now is, is only the first gropings of its gigantic hand, he shall look forward to an ever expanding knowledge as to a becoming creator. He shall see, that nature is the opposite of the soul, answering to it part for part. One is seal, and one is print. Its beauty is the beauty of his own mind. Its laws are the laws of his own mind. Nature then becomes to him the measure of his attainments. So much of nature as he is ignorant of, so much of his own mind does he not yet possess. And, in fine, the ancient precept, "Know thyself," and the modern precept, "Study nature," become at last one maxim. (9)

II. The next great influence into the spirit of the scholar, is, the mind of the Past,—in whatever form, whether of literature, of art, of institutions, that mind is inscribed. Books are the best type of the influence of the past, and perhaps we shall get at the truth,—learn the amount of this influence more conveniently,—by considering their value alone. (10)

The theory of books is noble. The scholar of the first age received into him the world around; brooded thereon; gave it the new arrangement of his own mind, and uttered it again. It came into him, life; it went out from him, truth. It came to him, short-lived actions; it went out from him, immortal thoughts. It came to him, business; it went from him, poetry. It was dead fact; now, it is quick thought. It can stand, and it can go. It now endures, it now flies, it now inspires. Precisely in proportion to the depth of mind from which it issued, so high does it soar, so long does it sing.   (11)

Or, I might say, it depends on how far the process had gone, of transmuting life into truth. In proportion to the completeness of the distillation, so will the purity and imperishableness of the product be. But none is quite perfect. As no air-pump can by any means make a perfect vacuum, so neither can any artist entirely exclude the conventional, the local, the perishable from his book, or write a book of pure thought, that shall be as efficient, in all respects, to a remote posterity, as to cotemporaries, or rather to the second age. Each age, it is found, must write its own books; or rather, each generation for the next succeeding. The books of an older period will not fit this.   (12)

Yet hence arises a grave mischief. The sacredness which attaches to the act of creation,—the act of thought,—is transferred to the record. The poet chanting, was felt to be a divine man: henceforth the chant is divine also. The writer was a just and wise spirit: henceforward it is settled, the book is perfect; as love of the hero corrupts into worship of his statue. Instantly, the book becomes noxious: the guide is a tyrant. The sluggish and perverted mind of the multitude, slow to open to the incursions of Reason, having once received this book, stands upon it, and makes an outcry, if it is disparaged. Colleges are built on it. Books are written on it by thinkers, not by Man Thinking; by men of talent, that is, who start wrong, who set out from accepted dogmas, not from their own sight of principles. Meek young men grow up in libraries, believing it their duty to accept the views, which Cicero, which Locke, which Bacon, have given, forgetful that Cicero, Locke, and Bacon were only young men in libraries, when they wrote these books.   (13)

Hence, instead of Man Thinking, we have the bookworm. Hence, the book-learned class, who value books, as such; not as related to nature and the human constitution, but as making a sort of Third Estate with the world and the soul. Hence, the restorers of readings, the emendators, the bibliomaniacs of all degrees.   (14)

Books are the best of things, well used; abused, among the worst. What is the right use? What is the one end, which all means go to effect? They are for nothing but to inspire. I had better never see a book, than to be warped by its attraction clean out of my own orbit, and made a satellite instead of a system. The one thing in the world, of value, is the active soul. This every man is entitled to; this every man contains within him, although, in almost all men, obstructed, and as yet unborn. The soul active sees absolute truth; and utters truth, or creates. In this action, it is genius; not the privilege of here and there a favorite, but the sound estate of every man. In its essence, it is progressive. The book, the college, the school of art, the institution of any kind, stop with some past utterance of genius. This is good, say they,—let us hold by this. They pin me down. They look backward and not forward. But genius looks forward: the eyes of man are set in his forehead, not in his hindhead: man hopes: genius creates. Whatever talents may be, if the man create not, the pure efflux of the Deity is not his;—cinders and smoke there may be, but not yet flame. There are creative manners, there are creative actions, and creative words; manners, actions, words, that is, indicative of no custom or authority, but springing spontaneous from the mind's own sense of good and fair. (15)

On the other part, instead of being its own seer, let it receive from another mind its truth, though it were in torrents of light, without periods of solitude, inquest, and self-recovery, and a fatal disservice is done. Genius is always sufficiently the enemy of genius by over influence. The literature of every nation bear me witness. The English dramatic poets have Shakspearized now for two hundred years. (16)

Undoubtedly there is a right way of reading, so it be sternly subordinated. Man Thinking must not be subdued by his instruments. Books are for the scholar's idle times. When he can read God directly, the hour is too precious to be wasted in other men's transcripts of their readings. But when the intervals of darkness come, as come they must,—when the sun is hid, and the stars withdraw their shining,—we repair to the lamps which were kindled by their ray, to guide our steps to the East again, where the dawn is. We hear, that we may speak. The Arabian proverb says, "A fig tree, looking on a fig tree, becometh fruitful." (17)

It is remarkable, the character of the pleasure we derive from the best books. They impress us with the conviction, that one nature wrote and the same reads. We read the verses of one of the great English poets, of Chaucer, of Marvell, of Dryden, with the most modern joy,—with a pleasure, I mean, which is in great part caused by the abstraction of all *time* from their verses. There is some awe mixed with the joy of our surprise, when this poet, who lived in some past world, two or three hundred years ago, says that which lies close to my own soul, that which I also had wellnigh thought and said. But for the evidence thence afforded to the philosophical doctrine of the identity of all minds, we should suppose some preëstablished harmony, some foresight of souls that were to be, and some preparation of stores for their future wants, like the fact observed in insects, who lay up food before death for the young grub they shall never see. (18)

I would not be hurried by any love of system, by any exaggeration of instincts, to underrate the Book. We all know, that, as the human body can be nourished on any food, though it were boiled grass and the broth of shoes, so the human mind can be fed by any knowledge. And great and heroic men have existed, who had almost no other information than by the printed page. I only would say, that it needs a strong head to bear that diet. One must be an inventor to read well. As the proverb says, "He that would bring home the wealth of the Indies, must carry out the wealth of the Indies." There is then creative reading as well as creative writing. When the mind is braced by labor and invention, the page of whatever book we read becomes luminous with manifold allusion. Every sentence is doubly significant, and the sense of our author is as broad as the world. We then see, what is always true, that, as the seer's hour of vision is short and rare among heavy days and months, so is its record, perchance, the least part of his volume. The discerning will read, in his Plato or Shakspeare, only that least part,—only the authentic utterances of the oracle;—all the rest he rejects, were it never so many times Plato's and Shakspeare's. (19)

Of course, there is a portion of reading quite indispensable to a wise man. History and exact science he must learn by laborious reading. Colleges, in like manner, have their indispensable office,—to teach elements. But they can only highly serve us, when they aim not to drill, but to create; when they gather from far every ray of various genius to their hospitable halls, and, by the concentrated fires, set the hearts of their youth on flame. Thought and knowledge are natures in which apparatus and pretension avail nothing. Gowns, and pecuniary foundations, though of towns of gold, can never countervail the least sentence or syllable of wit. Forget this, and our American colleges will recede in their public importance, whilst they grow richer every year. (20)

III. There goes in the world a notion, that the scholar should be a recluse, a valetudinarian,—as unfit for any handiwork or public labor, as a penknife for an axe. The so-called "practical men" sneer at speculative men, as if, because they speculate or *see*, they could do nothing. I have heard it said that the clergy,—who are always, more universally than any other class, the scholars of their day,—are addressed as women; that the rough, spontaneous conversation of men they do not hear, but only a mincing and diluted speech. They are often virtually disfranchised; and, indeed, there are advocates for their celibacy. As far as this is true of the studious classes, it is not just and wise. Action is with the scholar subordinate, but it is essential. Without it, he is not yet man. Without it, thought can never ripen into truth. Whilst the world hangs before the eye as a cloud of beauty, we cannot even see its beauty. Inaction is cowardice, but there can be no scholar without the heroic mind. The preamble of thought, the transition through which it passes from the unconscious to the conscious, is action. Only so much do I know, as I have lived. Instantly we know whose words are loaded with life, and whose not. (21)

The world,—this shadow of the soul, or *other me*, lies wide around. Its attractions are the keys which unlock my thoughts and make me acquainted with myself. I run eagerly into this resounding tumult. I grasp the hands of those next me, and take my place in the ring to suffer and to work, taught by an instinct, that so shall the dumb abyss be vocal with speech. I pierce its order; I dissipate its fear; I dispose of it within the circuit of my expanding life. So much only of life as I know by experience, so much of the wilderness have I vanquished and planted, or so far have I extended my being, my dominion. I do not see how any man can afford, for the sake of his nerves and his nap, to spare any action in which he can partake. It is pearls and rubies to his discourse. Drudgery, calamity, exasperation, want, are instructors in eloquence and wisdom. The true scholar grudges every opportunity of action past by, as a loss of power.

(22)

It is the raw material out of which the intellect moulds her splendid products. A strange process too, this, by which experience is converted into thought, as a mulberry leaf is converted into satin. The manufacture goes forward at all hours.

(23)

The actions and events of our childhood and youth, are now matters of calmest observation. They lie like fair pictures in the air. Not so with our recent actions,—with the business which we now have in hand. On this we are quite unable to speculate. Our affections as yet circulate through it. We no more feel or know it, than we feel the feet, or the hand, or the brain of our body. The new deed is yet a part of life,—remains for a time immersed in our unconscious life. In some contemplative hour, it detaches itself from the life like a ripe fruit, to become a thought of the mind. Instantly, it is raised, transfigured; the corruptible has put on incorruption. Henceforth it is an object of beauty, however base its origin and neighborhood. Observe, too, the impossibility of antedating this act. In its grub state, it cannot fly, it cannot shine, it is a dull grub. But suddenly, without observation, the selfsame thing unfurls beautiful wings, and is an angel of wisdom. So is there no fact, no event, in our private history, which shall not, sooner or later, lose its adhesive, inert form, and astonish us by soaring from our body into the empyrean. Cradle and infancy, school and playground, the fear of boys, and dogs, and ferules, the love of little maids and berries, and many another fact that once filled the whole sky, are gone already; friend and relative, profession and party, town and country, nation and world, must also soar and sing.

(24)

Of course, he who has put forth his total strength in fit actions, has the richest return of wisdom. I will not shut myself out of this globe of action, and transplant an oak into a flower-pot, there to hunger and pine; nor trust the revenue of some single faculty, and exhaust one vein of thought, much like those Savoyards, who, getting their livelihood by carving shepherds, shepherdesses, and smoking Dutchmen, for all Europe, went out one day to the mountain to find stock, and discovered that they had whittled up the last of their pine trees. Authors we have, in numbers, who have written out their vein, and who, moved by a commendable prudence, sail for Greece or Palestine, follow the trapper into the prairie, or ramble round Algiers, to replenish their merchantable stock. (25)

If it were only for a vocabulary, the scholar would be covetous of action. Life is our dictionary. Years are well spent in country labors; in town,—in the insight into trades and manufactures; in frank intercourse with many men and women; in science; in art; to the one end of mastering in all their facts a language by which to illustrate and embody our perceptions. I learn immediately from any speaker how much he has already lived, through the poverty or the splendor of his speech. Life lies behind us as the quarry from whence we get tiles and cope-stones for the masonry of to-day. This is the way to learn grammar. Colleges and books only copy the language which the field and the workyard made. (26)

But the final value of action, like that of books, and better than books, is, that it is a resource. That great principle of Undulation in nature, that shows itself in the inspiring and expiring of the breath; in desire and satiety; in the ebb and flow of the sea; in day and night; in heat and cold; and as yet more deeply ingrained in every atom and every fluid, is known to us under the name of Polarity,—these "fits of easy transmission and reflection," as Newton called them, are the law of nature because they are the law of spirit. (27)

The mind now thinks; now acts; and each fit reproduces the other. When the artist has exhausted his materials, when the fancy no longer paints, when thoughts are no longer apprehended, and books are a weariness,—he has always the resource *to live*. Character is higher than intellect. Thinking is the function. Living is the functionary. The stream retreats to its source. A great soul will be strong to live, as well as strong to think. Does he lack organ or medium to impart his truths? He can still fall back on this elemental force of living them. This is a total act. Thinking is a partial act. Let the grandeur of justice shine in his affairs. Let the beauty of affection cheer his lowly roof. Those "far from fame," who dwell and act with him, will feel the force of his constitution in the doings and passages of the day better than it can be measured by any public and designed display. Time shall teach him, that the scholar loses no hour which the man lives. Herein he unfolds the sacred germ of his instinct, screened from influence. What is lost in seemliness is gained in strength. Not out of those, on whom systems of education have exhausted their culture, comes the helpful giant to destroy the old or to build the new, but out of unhandselled savage nature, out of terrible Druids and Berserkirs, come at last Alfred and Shakspeare. (28)

I hear therefore with joy whatever is beginning to be said of the dignity and necessity of labor to every citizen. There is virtue yet in the hoe and the spade, for learned as well as for unlearned hands. And labor is everywhere welcome; always we are invited to work; only be this limitation observed, that a man shall not for the sake of wider activity sacrifice any opinion to the popular judgments and modes of action. (29)

I have now spoken of the education of the scholar by nature, by books, and by action. It remains to say somewhat of his duties. (30)

They are such as become Man Thinking. They may all be comprised in self-trust. The office of the scholar is to cheer, to raise, and to guide men by showing them facts amidst appearances. He plies the slow, unhonored, and unpaid task of observation. Flamsteed and Herschel, in their glazed observatories, may catalogue the stars with the praise of all men, and, the results being splendid and useful, honor is sure. But he, in his private observatory, cataloguing obscure and nebulous stars of the human mind, which as yet no man has thought of as such,—watching days and months, sometimes, for a few facts; correcting still his old records;—must relinquish display and immediate fame. In the long period of his preparation, he must betray often an ignorance and shiftlessness in popular arts, incurring the disdain of the able who shoulder him aside. Long he must stammer in his speech; often forego the living for the dead. Worse yet, he must accept,—how often? poverty and solitude. For the ease and pleasure of treading the old road, accepting the fashions, the education, the religion of society, he takes the cross of making his own, and, of course, the self-accusation, the faint heart, the frequent uncertainty and loss of time, which are the nettles and tangling vines in the way of the self-relying and self-directed; and the state of virtual hostility in which he seems to stand to society, and especially to educated society. For all this loss and scorn, what offset? He is to find consolation in exercising the highest functions of human nature. He is one, who raises himself from private considerations, and breathes and lives on public and illustrious thoughts. He is the world's eye. He is the world's heart. He is to resist the vulgar prosperity that retrogrades ever to barbarism, by preserving and communicating heroic sentiments, noble biographies, melodious verse, and the conclusions of history. Whatsoever oracles the human heart, in all emergencies, in all solemn hours, has uttered as its commentary on the world of actions,—these he shall receive and impart. And whatsoever new verdict Reason from her inviolable seat pronounces on the passing men and events of to-day,—this he shall hear and promulgate. (31)

These being his functions, it becomes him to feel all confidence in himself, and to defer never to the popular cry. He and he only knows the world. The world of any moment is the merest appearance. Some great decorum, some fetish of a government, some ephemeral trade, or war, or man, is cried up by half mankind and cried down by the other half, as if all depended on this particular up or down. The odds are that the whole question is not worth the poorest thought which the scholar has lost in listening to the controversy. Let him not quit his belief that a popgun is a popgun, though the ancient and honorable of the earth affirm it to be the crack of doom. In silence, in steadiness, in severe abstraction, let him hold by himself; add observation to observation, patient of neglect, patient of reproach; and bide his own time,—happy enough, if he can satisfy himself alone, that this day he has seen something truly. Success treads on every right step. For the instinct is sure, that prompts him to tell his brother what he thinks. He then learns, that in going down into the secrets of his own mind, he has descended into the secrets of all minds. He learns that he who has mastered any law in his private thoughts, is master to that extent of all men whose language he speaks, and of all into whose language his own can be translated. The poet, in utter solitude remembering his spontaneous thoughts and recording them, is found to have recorded that, which men in crowded cities find true for them also. The orator distrusts at first the fitness of his frank confessions,—his want of knowledge of the persons he addresses,—until he finds that he is the complement of his hearers;—that they drink his words because he fulfils for them their own nature; the deeper he dives into his privatest, secretest presentiment, to his wonder he finds, this is the most acceptable, most public, and universally true. The people delight in it; the better part of every man feels, This is my music; this is myself.   (32)

In self-trust, all the virtues are comprehended. Free should the scholar be,—free and brave. Free even to the definition of freedom, "without any hindrance that does not arise out of his own constitution." Brave; for fear is a thing, which a scholar by his very function puts behind him. Fear always springs from ignorance. It is a shame to him if his tranquillity, amid dangerous times, arise from the presumption, that, like children and women, his is a protected class; or if he seek a temporary peace by the diversion of his thoughts from politics or vexed questions, hiding his head like an ostrich in the flowering bushes, peeping into microscopes, and turning rhymes, as a boy whistles to keep his courage up. So is the danger a danger still; so is the fear worse. Manlike let him turn and face it. Let him look into its eye and search its nature, inspect its origin,—see the whelping of this lion,—which lies no great way back; he will then find in himself a perfect comprehension of its nature and extent; he will have made his hands meet on the other side, and can henceforth defy it, and pass on superior. The world is his, who can see through its pretension. What deafness, what stone-blind custom, what overgrown error you behold, is there only by sufferance,—by your sufferance. See it to be a lie, and you have already dealt it its mortal blow.   (33)

Yes, we are the cowed,—we the trustless. It is a mischievous notion that

we are come late into nature; that the world was finished a long time ago.
As the world was plastic and fluid in the hands of God, so it is ever to so
much of his attributes as we bring to it. To ignorance and sin, it is flint.
They adapt themselves to it as they may; but in proportion as a man
has any thing in him divine, the firmament flows before him and takes his
signet and form. Not he is great who can alter matter, but he who can
alter my state of mind. They are the kings of the world who give the
color of their present thought to all nature and all art, and persuade men
by the cheerful serenity of their carrying the matter, that this thing which
they do, is the apple which the ages have desired to pluck, now at last
ripe, and inviting nations to the harvest. The great man makes the great
thing. Wherever Macdonald sits, there is the head of the table. Linnæus
makes botany the most alluring of studies, and wins it from the farmer
and the herb-woman; Davy, chemistry; and Cuvier, fossils. The day is
always his, who works in it with serenity and great aims. The unstable estimates of men crowd to him whose mind is filled with a truth, as the
heaped waves of the Atlantic follow the moon.   (34)

For this self-trust, the reason is deeper than can be fathomed,—darker
than can be enlightened. I might not carry with me the feeling of my
audience in stating my own belief. But I have already shown the ground
of my hope, in adverting to the doctrine that man is one. I believe man
has been wronged; he has wronged himself. He has almost lost the light,
that can lead him back to his prerogatives. Men are become of no account. Men in history, men in the world of to-day are bugs, are spawn,
and are called "the mass" and "the herd." In a century, in a millennium,
one or two men; that is to say,—one or two approximations to the right
state of every man. All the rest behold in the hero or the poet their own
green and crude being,—ripened; yes, and are content to be less, so *that*
may attain to its full stature. What a testimony,—full of grandeur, full of
pity, is borne to the demands of his own nature, by the poor clansman,
the poor partisan, who rejoices in the glory of his chief. The poor and
the low find some amends to their immense moral capacity, for their acquiescence in a political and social inferiority. They are content to be
brushed like flies from the path of a great person, so that justice shall be
done by him to that common nature which it is the dearest desire of all
to see enlarged and glorified. They sun themselves in the great man's light,
and feel it to be their own element. They cast the dignity of man from
their downtrod selves upon the shoulders of a hero, and will perish to add
one drop of blood to make that great heart beat, those giant sinews combat
and conquer. He lives for us, and we live in him.   (35)

Men such as they are, very naturally seek money or power; and power
because it is as good as money,—the "spoils," so called, "of office." And why
not? for they aspire to the highest, and this, in their sleepwalking, they

dream is highest. Wake them, and they shall quit the false good, and leap
to the true, and leave governments to clerks and desks. This revolution is to be
wrought by the gradual domestication of the idea of Culture. The main enterprise of the world for splendor, for extent, is the upbuilding of a man. Here
are the materials strown along the ground. The private life of one man shall be
a more illustrious monarchy,—more formidable to its enemy, more sweet
and serene in its influence to its friend, than any kingdom in history. For a
man, rightly viewed, comprehendeth the particular natures of all men. Each
philosopher, each bard, each actor, has only done for me, as by a delegate,
what one day I can do for myself. The books which once we valued more
than the apple of the eye, we have quite exhausted. What is that but
saying, that we have come up with the point of view which the universal
mind took through the eyes of one scribe; we have been that man, and
have passed on. First, one; then, another; we drain all cisterns, and, wax-
ing greater by all these supplies, we crave a better and more abundant
food. The man has never lived that can feed us ever. The human mind
cannot be enshrined in a person, who shall set a barrier on any one side to
this unbounded, unboundable empire. It is one central fire, which, flaming
now out of the lips of Etna, lightens the capes of Sicily; and, now out of
the throat of Vesuvius, illuminates the towers and vineyards of Naples. It
is one light which beams out of a thousand stars. It is one soul which
animates all men.   (36)

But I have dwelt perhaps tediously upon this abstraction of the Scholar.
I ought not to delay longer to add what I have to say, of nearer reference
to the time and to this country.   (37)

Historically, there is thought to be a difference in the ideas which predominate over successive epochs, and there are data for marking the genius
of the Classic, of the Romantic, and now of the Reflective or Philosophical
age. With the views I have intimated of the oneness or the identity of the
mind through all individuals, I do not much dwell on these differences.
In fact, I believe each individual passes through all three. The boy is a
Greek; the youth, romantic; the adult, reflective. I deny not, however, that
a revolution in the leading idea may be distinctly enough traced.   (38)

Our age is bewailed as the age of Introversion. Must that needs be
evil? We, it seems, are critical; we are embarrassed with second thoughts;
we cannot enjoy any thing for hankering to know whereof the pleasure consists; we are lined with eyes; we see with our feet; the time is infected with
Hamlet's unhappiness,—

"Sicklied o'er with the pale cast of thought."

Is it so bad then? Sight is the last thing to be pitied. Would we be blind?
Do we fear lest we should out-see nature and God, and drink truth dry?

I look upon the discontent of the literary class, as a mere announcement of the fact, that they find themselves not in the state of mind of their fathers, and regret the coming state as untried; as a boy dreads the water before he has learned that he can swim. If there is any period one would desire to be born in,—is it not the age of Revolution; when the old and the new stand side by side, and admit of being compared; when the energies of all men are searched by fear and by hope; when the historic glories of the old, can be compensated by the rich possibilities of the new era? This time, like all times, is a very good one, if we but know what to do with it.   (39)

I read with joy some of the auspicious signs of the coming days, as they glimmer already through poetry and art, through philosophy and science, through church and state.   (40)

One of these signs is the fact, that the same movement which effected the elevation of what was called the lowest class in the state, assumed in literature a very marked and as benign an aspect. Instead of the sublime and beautiful; the near, the low, the common, was explored and poetized. That, which had been negligently trodden under foot by those who were harnessing and provisioning themselves for long journeys into far countries, is suddenly found to be richer than all foreign parts. The literature of the poor, the feelings of the child, the philosophy of the street, the meanings of household life, are the topics of the time. It is a great stride. It is a sign,— is it not? of new vigor, when the extremities are made active, when currents of warm life run into the hands and the feet. I ask not for the great, the remote, the romantic; what is doing in Italy or Arabia; what is Greek art, or Provençal minstrelsy; I embrace the common, I explore and sit at the feet of the familiar, the low. Give me insight into to-day, and you may have the antique and future worlds. What would we really know the meaning of? The meal in the firkin; the milk in the pan; the ballad in the street; the news of the boat; the glance of the eye; the form and the gait of the body;—show me the ultimate reason of these matters; show me the sublime presence of the highest spiritual cause lurking, as always it does lurk, in these suburbs and extremities of nature; let me see every trifle bristling with the polarity that ranges it instantly on an eternal law; and the shop, the plough, and the leger, referred to the like cause by which light undulates and poets sing;—and the world lies no longer a dull miscellany and lumber-room, but has form and order; there is no trifle; there is no puzzle; but one design unites and animates the farthest pinnacle and the lowest trench.   (41)

This idea has inspired the genius of Goldsmith, Burns, Cowper, and, in a newer time, of Goethe, Wordsworth, and Carlyle. This idea they have differently followed and with various success. In contrast with their writing, the style of Pope, of Johnson, of Gibbon, looks cold and pedantic. This writing is blood-warm. Man is surprised to find that things near are not less beautiful and wondrous than things remote. The near explains the far. The drop is a small ocean. A man is related to all nature. This perception of the worth of the vulgar is fruitful in discoveries. Goethe, in this very thing the most modern of the moderns, has shown us, as none ever did, the genius of the ancients.   (42)

There is one man of genius, who has done much for this philosophy of life, whose literary value has never yet been rightly estimated;—I mean Emanuel Swedenborg. The most imaginative of men, yet writing with the precision of a mathematician, he endeavored to engraft a purely philosophical Ethics on the popular Christianity of his time. Such an attempt, of course, must have difficulty, which no genius could surmount. But he saw and showed the connection between nature and the affections of the soul. He pierced the emblematic or spiritual character of the visible, audible, tangible world. Especially did his shade-loving muse hover over and interpret the lower parts of nature; he showed the mysterious bond that allies moral evil to the foul material forms, and has given in epical parables a theory of insanity, of beasts, of unclean and fearful things.   (43)

Another sign of our times, also marked by an analogous political movement, is, the new importance given to the single person. Every thing that tends to insulate the individual,—to surround him with barriers of natural respect, so that each man shall feel the world is his, and man shall treat with man as a sovereign state with a sovereign state;—tends to true union as well as greatness. "I learned," said the melancholy Pestalozzi, "that no man in God's wide earth is either willing or able to help any other man." Help must come from the bosom alone. The scholar is that man who must take up into himself all the ability of the time, all the contributions of the past, all the hopes of the future. He must be an university of knowledges. If there be one lesson more than another, which should pierce his ear, it is, The world is nothing, the man is all; in yourself is the law of all nature, and you know not yet how a globule of sap ascends; in yourself slumbers the whole of Reason; it is for you to know all, it is for you to dare all. Mr. President and Gentlemen, this confidence in the unsearched might of man belongs, by all motives, by all prophecy, by all preparation, to the American Scholar. We have listened too long to the courtly muses of Europe. The spirit of the American freeman is already suspected to be timid, imitative, tame. Public and private avarice make the air we breathe thick and fat. The scholar is decent, indolent, complaisant. See already the tragic consequences. The mind of this country, taught to aim at low objects, eats upon itself. There is no work for any but the decorous and the complaisant. Young men of the fairest promise, who begin life upon our shores, inflated by the mountain winds, shined upon by all the stars of God, find the earth below not in unison with these,—but are hindered from action by the disgust which the principles on which business is managed inspire, and turn drudges, or die of disgust,—some of them suicides. What is the remedy? They did not yet see, and thousands of young men as hopeful now crowding to the barriers for the career, do not yet see, that, if the single man plant himself indomitably on his instincts, and there abide, the huge world will come round to him. Patience,—patience;—with the shades of all the good and great for company; and for solace, the perspective of your own infinite life; and for work, the study and the communication of principles, the making those instincts prevalent, the conversion of the world. Is it not the chief disgrace in the world, not to be an unit;—not to be reckoned one character;—not to yield that peculiar fruit which each man was created to bear, but to be reckoned in the gross, in the hundred, or the thousand, of the party, the section, to which we belong; and our opinion predicted geographically, as the north, or the south? Not so, brothers and friends,—please God, ours shall not be so. We will walk on our own feet; we will work with our own hands; we will speak our own minds. The study of letters shall be no longer a name for pity, for doubt, and for sensual indulgence. The dread of man and the love of man shall be a wall of defence and a wreath of joy around all. A nation of men will for the first time exist, because each believes himself inspired by the Divine Soul which also inspires all men. (44)

Arthur Bestor

(1908–   )

BESTOR is a professor of history at the University of Washington in Seattle. In the early fifties, while at the University of Illinois, he provoked national controversy by his critical analyses of liberal arts education: Educational Wastelands *(1953) and* The Restoration of Learning *(with others, 1955).*

◾ *The College of* Liberal *Arts and Sciences*

THE FOUR-YEAR liberal-arts college is a distinctive feature of the English and the American educational systems, and it has made a distinctive contribution to the public life of Great Britain and the United States. The nature of the liberal-arts college ought to be better understood than it is, for we are in danger of losing a uniquely precious part of our educational heritage through sheer inattention to its essential characteristics. (1)

To compare the educational systems of different countries accurately is an exceedingly difficult task, and to offer generalizations concerning their theoretical (let alone their actual) structure is a rash proceeding. Nevertheless, such a generalization must be hazarded here. The actual standards and performance of the educational systems of other countries need not be examined at this time. Our present concern is with the theoretical relationship between secondary and higher education, or, more accurately, the way in which responsibility for secondary and higher education is theoretically apportioned among institutions of different levels. And, for purposes of this discussion, we are interested only in the student who proceeds through all the levels. (2)

Secondary education, for such a student, is conceived of in all countries as rigorous training in the fundamentals of the various fields of learning—languages, sciences, mathematics, history, and the rest. Secondary-school instruction differs from higher education (in the theory of most systems) in that it is carried out methodically, in a pattern of courses that are largely prescribed, with relatively little expectation that the student will engage in independent, wide-ranging investigations of his own. At the opposite pole is the educational scheme of the Continental university, and of those portions of English and American universities which are not embraced within the undergraduate college. University work, in this sense, is highly specialized. It is concerned with training for research or for one of the learned professions. Independent reading and original investigation are generally more important than course work. Students are largely on their own. The schoolmaster is gone, and in his place is the professor, interested not in what the student does day by day, but in the results he can demonstrate at the end of his academic career through examinations and a written thesis. (3)

Here are two diametrically opposed educational procedures. On the Continent of Europe the student proceeds directly from the first to the second. Secondary education (in the *Gymnasium* or *lycée*) is more prolonged than with us; university work is from the beginning more independent and more specialized. The undergraduate college of England and America is interpolated, as it were, into this scheme. It is a transitional institution, in the sense that it partakes of the qualities of both the secondary school and the university, and it covers the years that on the Continent are divided between the two.   (4)

But the liberal-arts college is a great deal more than a mere transitional institution. It has a unique character of its own. And its distinctive features have had much to do, I am convinced, with producing among the educated classes of the United States (as also of England) the kind of mutual understanding that underlies our success in maintaining national unity and harmony in the midst of social and political changes as drastic as those that have rent the societies of Continental Europe apart.   (5)

What characteristics of the liberal-arts college can justify such a sweeping assertion? To put the matter simply, the liberal-arts college permits students to complete their fundamental intellectual training in an atmosphere of greater freedom than the secondary school can allow. And in the liberal-arts college, students move gradually toward specialization, mingling the while and exchanging ideas with comrades whose intellectual paths are beginning to diverge. A sense of sharing in a common intellectual life is produced by the liberal-arts college as it is not produced by any institution in the Continental educational system.   (6)

The secondary school, of course, provides a unity of background, but this is an enforced and even regimented unity. When freedom of choice is suddenly granted, in the Continental university, the sense of unity in intellectual life disappears in the pursuit of intensively specialized scholarly and professional training. Under this system, unity is associated with intellectual immaturity; mature intellectual life is compartmentalized, divided, self-consciously specialized. The English and American conception is different. As students approach intellectual maturity, the methodical preceptorial methods of the schoolroom are gradually relaxed, and a study of the fundamental intellectual disciplines is continued under conditions of freedom and individual responsibility that approximate those of the university. A free exchange of ideas among fellow students, at the level of intellectual maturity, increases and is encouraged. And as these students progress toward greater specialization, they explore among themselves the interrelations between their various fields, thus cultivating the habit of discussion and mutual understanding. They are preparing themselves for the kind of public life in which a fundamental unity of purpose and principle underlies even the most striking differences, thus permitting honest compromise. The liberal-arts college exemplifies, and prepares for the realization of, the motto inscribed upon our Great Seal: *E pluribus unum.*   (7)

Theory of course is very imperfectly carried out in practice. The contrasts I have made are admittedly too sharp, and the generalizations too sweeping. Nevertheless they help to make clear, I believe, the features of liberal education which we need to safeguard and strengthen in our colleges, if these are to serve, as they have served in the past, as the bulwarks of enlightened, harmonious, democratic public life.   (8)

The ideal of the college of liberal arts and sciences is to raise up a body of men and women who understand in common the fundamentals of intellectual life in its various branches, and who are able to apply to their own problems not one, but a choice of powerful intellectual techniques over which they have achieved some measure of disciplined control. The crucial problem is how to encourage young men and women to range freely over the various fields of knowledge and yet to maintain that unified comprehension which will enable them to understand and co-operate in one another's intellectual pursuits.   (9)

The kind of unity we require in intellectual life is the kind that comes when educated men are able to command several, not merely one, of the distinctive ways of thinking that are central in the modern world. There is no genuine unity of intellectual life if men have merely learned the same sets of facts from so-called "subject-matter" fields. There is merely a specious unity if men have been taught to think in their respective disciplines alone and have been offered merely a smattering of information *about* other ways of thinking. And there is only a narrow and shackled unity if one way of thinking has been exalted above all others and made the *sine qua non* of education.[1]   (10)

Men need to know a fair number of the crucial ways of thinking upon which modern intellectual life is based. This implies that the truly distinctive ways of thinking are reasonably limited in number, and that there is a recognizable hierarchy of importance among them. The implications of this must be squarely faced. Educational reform must begin with a courageous assertion that all the various subjects and disciplines in the curriculum are *not* of equal value. Some disciplines are fundamental, in the sense that they represent essential ways of thinking, which can be generalized and applied to a wide range of intellectual problems. Other disciplines, though equal in intellectual potency, are somewhat less central to the purposes of liberal education, either because they can be studied only after the fundamental disciplines are mastered, or because they represent highly specialized intellectual techniques, restricted in their range of applicability.

---

1 Despite its many strong points, the so-called "great books" program seems to me at fault in this respect. It tends to emphasize dialectical argument at the expense of all those intellectual processes that call upon men to sift multifarious evidence and draw conclusions from it.

Other courses in the modern curriculum do not represent disciplines at all, but offer professional preparation, or training in mechanical skills, or helpful hints on vocational and personal matters. Still other courses, alas, offer nothing at all, save collections of more or less interesting facts, opinions, or fallacies.   (11)

When we have the courage to specify which disciplines belong in the first category—that is, which ones are truly fundamental—then, and only then, can we begin to restore intellectual unity to the curricula of our schools and colleges. The decision may not be as difficult as it seems, for we are talking about disciplines, or ways of thinking, not about "subject-matter" fields. The basically different ways of thinking are few compared with the number of factual areas within which they can be applied. The method of controlled experimentation, for example, is one sort of disciplined thinking, and it underlies several different physical sciences. Mathematics is another distinctive way of thinking, historical investigation is a third, philosophical criticism a fourth. One can go on, but one cannot go on far without exhausting the ways of thinking that are genuinely fundamental, that are clearly distinctive, and that are susceptible of being introduced at the elementary- or high-school level and carried forward systematically in college. All choices have something of the arbitrary about them, but a decision that certain disciplines are fundamental and others not can be made on reasonable and judicious grounds.   (12)

Once these premises are accepted—and not merely accepted, but believed with the kind of conviction that will lead to action—then some plan for genuinely liberal education appropriate to the mid-twentieth century becomes possible. Such a plan must provide for specialization. It must also establish standards and prerequisites that will permit an orderly progress from introductory to advanced work. It must consider the nature of the courses that are best adapted to the instruction of the non-specialist. It must develop a philosophy for guiding the student in his quest for intellectual breadth. And it must set up a final test for achievement in terms of knowledge and skill acquired, not of credits accumulated. These various points will be taken up in order in the remainder of this essay.   (13)

Intellectual training is so laborious and time-consuming that it tends to become specialized education in *a* discipline rather than liberal education in *the* disciplines. Given the complexity of modern knowledge, a high degree of specialization is an escapable thing. In point of fact genuine specialization is not in itself an evil. It is false specialization that we need to fear and avoid.   (14)

One kind of false specialization is exemplified by the man who imagines that he will be able to solve important problems by using only one set of mental tools. No intellectual activity is ever so specialized that it involves only a single way of thinking. If a specialist is to solve new problems in his own field he must be prepared to draw upon ways of thinking that have never yet been applied to the problem. The greater his achievement as a specialist, the broader must be his fund of general knowledge and the wider his acquaintance with other ways of thinking. Specialization that is false because of its narrowness is also self-defeating. Genuine specialization always involves the careful study of related fields.   (15)

A second type of false specialization in intellectual life is more insidious. It arises from the failure to discriminate between an intellectual discipline defined as a way of thinking and a field of study defined in some other way—defined, say, as the body of practical information connected with some specified vocation. Now, vocational training is perfectly compatible with liberal education, but it is not the same thing. The *liberal* part of the training for any profession or trade is the part devoted to the scientific and scholarly disciplines that underlie the profession or trade. The *vocational* or *professional* aspect of the training is something added to liberal education. It should not be reckoned a *part* of liberal education at all.   (16)

A man's vocational or professional training is necessarily specialized. The liberal education upon which it is based need not be, but if it is, the specialization that is considered part of his liberal education can only be in one of the intellectual disciplines. There is no place in genuinely liberal education for a major in journalism, or home economics, or pedagogy, even though courses in these vocational subjects may be taken as supplements to a program in liberal education.   (17)

Because both specialization and the quest for intellectual breadth are recognized aims of the liberal-arts college, a problem arises over the proper grading of courses. In his special field an upperclassman or a graduate student will be pursuing advanced courses, but at the same time he may be receiving his first introduction to some other field. American colleges customarily assign different sets of numbers to courses of different levels. This is entirely reasonable. But they usually take another step, the logic of which is utterly specious. Thinking to uphold standards, they are apt to forbid a graduate student or even an upperclassman to enroll for full credit in a course the number of which indicates that it is on the introductory level. This is absurd. Where, may one ask, should a student be introduced to a new subject if not in an introductory course?   (18)

The consequence of this mechanical way of treating advanced credit is that the student enrolls in an advanced course without knowing anything of the fundamental processes of thought involved. An advanced student in history may need to commence the study of economics as a supporting discipline, but he is likely to find that to secure full credit he must enroll in an advanced course in the subject, though he has never mastered the introductory material. Not one student does so, but scores, and the instructor is forced to adjust his teaching to the situation. He cannot assume that his students possess a common fund of knowledge in the field or a command of certain clearly defined intellectual skills of a specialized nature. The supposedly advanced course becomes partly an introductory one. The compromise is unsatisfactory to all concerned. Thoroughly prepared students do not advance in disciplined thinking as far or as fast as they should, and new students are not initiated into disciplined thinking as systematically or as thoroughly as they ought to be. (19)

If the introductory course is a really rigorous one, there is no reason why it should not be elected for full credit by upperclassmen and graduate students. Only in this way can advanced courses become and remain truly advanced ones, and a rational system of prerequisites be maintained. The difference between an introductory course and an advanced one has almost nothing to do with the chronological age of the student or his academic status. No one can vault lightly over the difficulties involved in learning the elements of an intellectual discipline merely because he happens to be a senior or a graduate student. He may learn a little faster, it is true, but he does not learn differently. In particular, he cannot skip essential steps in a process of thought. Knowledge, after all, *is* cumulative, and intellectual processes do advance through clearly defined stages of increasing complexity. (20)

Once the difference between introductory and advanced courses is firmly established, we can deal more intelligently with the harder question of the kind of course that a student should be offered in a discipline outside the field of his special interest and effort. What, for example, does a student majoring in the discipline of history need to know of mathematical reasoning, of scientific investigation, of philosophical criticism, of literary expression, of æsthetic comprehension? The answer is that he needs to know the things represented by the nouns or gerunds in the phrases above—that is to say, the nature of reasoning, investigation, criticism, expression, and comprehension, as these appear in their various special forms. He does not need to know all the different lines of inquiry pursued in a given field, but he needs to know its particular way of thinking well enough to grasp its special power and applicability. (21)

Liberal education is training in thinking. It is not the mere communication of facts. What every student—specialist or nonspecialist—should gain from a course is command, even if only limited command, of the processes of thought employed in the discipline he is studying. Far less than the specialist does the student from another field need to fix in his mind a multitude of facts already discovered and verified. These facts and formulas may be necessary parts of the equipment that a specialist requires for further work in the field; hence to him they are important in themselves. To a non-specialist, however, the facts and formulas are significant as examples, as the fruits of successful inquiry, as tests of the validity of some process of reasoning. Few are so important that they must be remembered for their own sakes.   (22)

To have solved a quadratic equation is the vital thing if one wishes to grasp the nature of algebraic reasoning. Whether to memorize the general formula of solution depends entirely on one's future use for it. Similarly, to have weighed historical evidence in order to reach a conclusion and to have explored the problems of historical causality are the crucial matters. The number of specific historical facts that the student remembers is of secondary importance. Actually a student will remember a great many facts without special effort if he has really entered into the process of investigation which produced them. His score on a factual test is thus an indirect, not a direct, measure of what he has learned. It can be a fairly reliable test (if not abused by the get-rich-quick technique of factual "cramming"), because the student who has thought a lot will remember a lot, and the student who remembers nothing has probably never thought at all. Memory and disciplined thinking do go hand in hand, but we must never forget that it is the latter that really counts.   (23)

So far as "general" education is concerned, these considerations lead to a conclusion the opposite of the one ordinarily accepted. The course for the non-specialist should emphasize theoretical reasoning to an even greater extent than the course for the specialist. The latter needs to know —and hence should be drilled to remember—facts, conclusions, and formulas for which the non-specialist has little use once he has grasped the reasoning involved. In practice, colleges and universities have acted upon a contrary premise. Courses originally planned for specialists have been adapted for general students by eliminating or reducing the discussion of methodology and theory, and crowding in as much purely factual information as possible. Such courses advance neither intellectual discipline nor mutual understanding among educated men.   (24)

If this reasoning is correct, the proper introduction to each of the great areas of knowledge is a rigorous course, emphasizing intellectual processes, in one of the fundamental disciplines lying within the area. In certain fields it may be desirable to create for the non-specialist a course somewhat different in structure and emphasis from that offered to the future specialist. In the sciences, for example, it is possible that a study of crucial principles in the historical order of their discovery (as President Conant has suggested) might be more effective for the non-specialist than the study of them in the systematic order in which they need to be known by the man who is to do research in the field. Two courses, equally rigorous and equally thorough in their use of laboratory techniques, are a possibility here. Needless to say, when alternative courses are offered, there ought never to be a qualitative difference between them. Every course must discipline the mind of every student who enrolls in it. In actual fact, however, separate courses in most fields are quite unnecessary. The typical introductory course in college would serve the needs of both specialists and non-specialists more effectively if it were reorganized in such a way as to pay *more* attention than at present to methodology, to rigorous thinking, and to abstract theory. If, however, classes for non-specialists seem necessary, the instructors in charge should eschew the encyclopedic approach, should select with care the topics that exemplify basic methodological and theoretical questions, and should concentrate upon making perfectly clear the kinds of thinking involved.[2]   (25)

Courses alone, even though properly organized for the non-specialist, will not guarantee breadth of intellectual understanding. A plan of study outside the field of specialization is needed. And American colleges are only gradually emerging from an era of complete planlessness. The free-elective system has long since proved a faulty answer to the questions raised for education by the increasing complexity of modern knowledge. It did not solve the problem of integrating the new disciplines into an ordered structure of learning; it simply dodged the problem. Under the free-elective system, two programs of study might contain no element whatever in common. Worse than that, the very mechanics of the free-elective system put all subjects on a par with one another, and tended even to treat advanced courses as if they were quantitatively equivalent to elementary ones. It fostered the belief that a man acquires a liberal education by adding so many hours in one classroom to so many hours in another until he has served his time in full.   (26)

American colleges have begun to put behind them the follies of the free-elective system. But at best they have usually done no more than apply palliatives to the evil. A college may force the student to make his choices in such a way that each of the broad areas of knowledge is represented somewhere and in some fashion among the array of courses he offers for the degree. Or the college may institute omnibus courses designed to "survey" each of these broad areas for the student, usually in his freshman or sophomore year. Or it may seek in some other mechanical way to produce unity by adding together disunities.   (27)

It must do a great deal more than this if it is really to restore among liberally educated men a sense of participating in and comprehending the varied ways of thinking that belong to modern intellectual life. To devise an adequate scheme for that part of liberal education which aims to give a student breadth of understanding is far more difficult than to devise a

---

2 The principles I have in mind are admirably exemplified by the series of *Select Problems in Historical Interpretation* prepared for use in undergraduate courses by various members of the Department of History at Yale, and by the proposals for scientific instruction embodied in James B. Conant's *On Understanding Science.*

scheme for that part which aims at intensive, specialized knowledge. The difficulties are not insurmountable, however, provided we make clear to ourselves exactly what we are after. We have failed, I think, to do this, and we have masked our confusions under vague and undefined terms like "general education."   (28)

The last-mentioned phrase has gained widespread currency in the United States since the end of World War II, thanks largely, I suppose, to the prestige of the Harvard report on *General Education in a Free Society* (1945). In that document, as I read its arguments, "general education" was simply a synonym for "liberal education." The report dealt with education in the basic intellectual disciplines, and it proposed various means for introducing students more effectively than before to a wider range of such disciplines. There was nothing anti-intellectual in its recommendations, but the term "general education," which was unfortunately chosen to describe them, was sufficiently ambiguous to be applied elsewhere to almost any kind of pseudo-educational program. On many campuses university administrators announced that they were following in the footsteps of Harvard, and proceeded to set up rambling, catch-all courses, geared to the meager abilities of the marginal student. In teacher-training institutions the professional educationists seized upon the term with glee and promptly introduced into the curriculum college versions of "life-adjustment" training. At one state teachers' college that I visited, a faculty member asked me in all seriousness whether a course in general education was not the proper place to teach good table manners to college students. Since "general education" has come to signify, in so many institutions, complete educational inanity, we ought to abandon the term forthwith and restore the traditional phrase "liberal education," which, despite frequent misuse, has never suffered such utter degradation as the new one.   (29)

To get back to first principles, liberal education involves three distinct kinds of intellectual training. It aims to give a student thorough, and hence creative, command of one discipline. It undertakes, in addition, to give him control over the basic and related intellectual skills that are necessary to successful work in his field of specialization. Finally, it seeks to give him breadth of intellectual understanding.   (30)

The last two of these objectives are not very clearly differentiated in most college programs. They need to be, if we are to deal effectively with the problems involved. For the sake of clarity, I should like to avail myself, in the paragraphs that follow, of a more or less arbitrary terminology. The term "major" will be given its usual meaning, the discipline in which a student specializes. The term "supporting fields" will be used to describe the work a student needs to do in the disciplines that are closely related to his "major." And the term "minor" will be used to describe the work outside the "major" and the "supporting fields"—the work, that is, which is designed to produce breadth of comprehension. This special usage needs to be borne in mind, for at present the term "minor" is used sometimes for the work in what I call the "supporting fields," and sometimes for that which I too call the "minor." (31)

The fields that are necessary to "support" sound specialization include both the basic intellectual disciplines of general applicability, and the specialized disciplines that fall within the same general area as the "major." An adequately trained chemist, for example, requires knowledge of mathematics (one of the disciplines of general applicability) and also of physics (one of the related specialized disciplines). Similarly a well-trained historian requires knowledge of foreign languages and also of economics. For the most part the training in the disciplines of general applicability ought to be completed in the secondary school, and rigorous college entrance examinations should take care of the matter. Once minimum standards in English grammar and composition, in mathematics, and in foreign languages (at least one, and preferably two) are assured for college matriculation, the further requirements in these disciplines should be established in terms of the actual demands of each major field. Likewise, a rational plan of study in the related "supporting" disciplines needs to be worked out for each field of specialization. These requirements, it should be noted, are in the interests of sound specialization. They do not, by themselves, completely solve the problem of securing breadth of intellectual understanding. (32)

The latter problem, indeed, is the most difficult of any that can arise in liberal education. Present-day attempts to solve it have proved, in my judgment, quite unsatisfactory. The existing "distribution" requirements of most colleges—that is, the requirements that specify work in a number of different areas—are at once too impatient, too mechanical, too ambitious, and yet too distrustful. They are too impatient because they do not take into account the time required to achieve a mature grasp of a subject. They are too mechanical because they do not go beyond scattering a student's effort. They are too ambitious because they expect an undergraduate to range over more fields than he is really capable of assimilating. And they are too distrustful because they assume no ability on the part of an individual to enlarge his range of intellectual powers through his own efforts. (33)

It takes time to acquire a usable command of any intellectual discipline. This seems to me the most neglected fact in American educational thinking. Psychologists and physiologists make use of a concept that is relevant here. A stimulus must reach a certain intensity before it can produce a response. This critical point is called the *threshold*. Below the critical point the stimulus might as well not exist so far as any observable reaction is concerned. There is, it seems to me, such a critical point or threshold in intellectual training. The study of a foreign language, for example, if pursued for only a single school year, does not bring the knowledge of the language up to the threshold where it produces the desired response in the student—namely, a sense of being at home in the language. American colleges usually proceed on the theory that at least two college years of language study are necessary to reach this threshold. I believe, incidentally, that this figure is too low, but the important fact is that a threshold is tacitly recognized in the learning of a foreign language. My conviction is that such a critical point or threshold exists for every intellectual discipline, and that to disregard it is to doom any educational program to futility.   (34)

Unless we bring a student's command of a discipline beyond the threshold, we give him nothing that he can use for ordinary working purposes. We leave him bewildered and uncomprehending. Instead of opening a door for him, we may actually slam it shut. In the early stages of learning a new discipline, the student is mainly impressed with how much there is to be known and how unfamiliar and hence difficult the processes of reasoning are. Only when he reaches the threshold does he acquire pleasure and confidence as the reward of his labors. If we cut him off before he reaches the critical point, we frustrate the process of learning. The student carries his discouragement away with him, and usually convinces himself that he could never have mastered the discipline sufficiently well to make it a part of his own thinking. Thereafter he makes no real effort to understand it.
(35)

As a psychological compensation he is apt to convert what is actually self-distrust into active distaste for the discipline that he feels has betrayed him. If he becomes a teacher he communicates this feeling to his students, and they go through life with blind spots for certain disciplines, most of which are simply the consequence of bad teaching. The distaste of many students for mathematics, I firmly believe (and many mathematicians with me), is a measure of the number of elementary- and secondary-school teachers who are frightened of the subject because they have never been required to bring their command of it up to the threshold of genuine comprehension. And the neglect of foreign languages—one of the gravest weaknesses of our educational system—seems to me the result of a vicious circle, originating in the shame that most American teachers (including a great number of university scholars) feel, but suppress, concerning their own linguistic inadequacies.   (36)

This situation must be corrected in the elementary and secondary schools which are, with devastating success, killing off every budding intellectual interest by refusing to carry forward any disciplined study to the point where the student passes the threshold into confidence and enjoyment. In the college we must avoid the same mistake when we try to counter the evils of overspecialization. If we send a student into a multitude of courses without making sure that his knowledge of each discipline reaches the all-important critical point, we run the risk of producing not breadth but an almost neurotic narrowness of mind.   (37)

In my judgment, the college should approach the problem of producing intellectual breadth in a quite different way from the one it has customarily followed. I have already pointed out that the distinctively different ways of thinking are limited in number. There is another fact to be noted. For any given discipline there is another in which the processes of thought are of an almost opposite character. The discipline of chemistry, for example, is at an opposite pole from the discipline of literary criticism. The process of inductive generalization in history stands in the sharpest possible contrast with the process of deductive reasoning characteristic of mathematics. The college of liberal arts and sciences, I suggest, should recognize this fact and make it the principal basis of its efforts to encourage a wide-ranging comprehension on the part of students.   (38)

To be specific, I propose that the college should require each student to offer (besides his "major" and his work in its "supporting fields") a "minor" in some discipline that is as remote as possible, in its way of thinking, from the one to which his principal efforts are devoted. A physicist, for example, should choose his minor from one of the humanities; an economist from one of the biological sciences. Such a minor would not be a mere collection of courses, but a systematic program of study, which would bring the student well beyond the threshold of genuine understanding. Other plans, admittedly, disperse a student's efforts more widely, but dispersed effort is no virtue in an educational program. Dispersed effort is usually halfhearted effort. One virtue of such a minor as I have described would be that it would guarantee that all a student's work—outside his own field as well as in it—would be equally serious, equally rigorous, and equally productive of demonstrable intellectual power.   (39)

Would not such a program provide the essential basis for the intellectual breadth we are really seeking, and for the mutual understanding among educated men which we so desperately need? The danger in specialization is that a man will fail to recognize that there are cogent ways of thinking markedly different from those he customarily employs. This realization can be brought home to him by giving him a thorough grasp of one such divergent way of thinking. This experience should teach him, if he is a truly thoughtful man, that every disciplined field has its rationale and its reason for existence. It should teach him that no field is beyond his grasp, if only he will devote the requisite effort to understanding it. The arrogance that arises from narrow specialization will dissolve, and real unity of intellectual life will emerge. The liberally educated man will overcome the barriers that now keep specialists from fruitful conversation and collaboration. The liberally educated teacher (and all teachers should be such) will be able to explain to students of divergent temperament the processes of thinking in his own field because he will be able to relate them to processes of thinking in fields of remote and opposite character.   (40)

If the college aims to give a student true breadth of understanding, it should abandon the hopeless task of acquainting him with every one of the disciplines. Instead it should bring the student's efforts to a focus, first of all upon his own discipline with its related fields, then upon some discipline far beyond the normal horizon of his specialty. We cannot (to change the metaphor) enable him to conquer the whole world of learning in one undergraduate career. We can, however, assist him to win a foothold on two different continents. Thereafter we ought to be content to trust him, as an educated man, to plant his banner in whatever province he wishes and win control of it by his own efforts.   (41)

In the last analysis, moreover, the synthesis of knowledge must be the student's own achievement. Only the things that he can bring together in his own mind has he really learned. Only the intellectual skills that he can co-ordinate for his own purposes has he really mastered. It is the responsibility of the college not only to offer the courses that might produce such intellectual powers, but also to satisfy itself that the student has in fact acquired them. The degree should be awarded only when the college is so satisfied. Indispensable to a sound college program of liberal arts is a comprehensive examination at the end. This should test the student's command not only of his own discipline, but also, if possible, of the "supporting" fields that are a necessary part of fruitful specialization. Many colleges require such examinations; every college worthy of recognition should require them.   (42)

A way should also be found to examine the student's command of the field remote from his own that he has elected to study, lest the work there be considered by him a mere accumulation of credit hours. A comprehensive examination in this minor field of concentration, administered perhaps at the end of the sophomore or junior year, should form part of the pattern of the college which strives for genuine breadth and balance in its program. And if the work in the minor field is validated by an examination, then the field itself can safely be set up, if desired, on an interdisciplinary basis.   (43)

Liberal education—in both its specialized and its generalized aspects— can be placed on a sound basis only if we restore to the college curriculum as a whole the intellectual vitality that has so largely departed from it in recent years. We are not producing men and women with a general and liberal education by requiring students to elect specified fragments of a curriculum that has been pulverized into unrelated three-semester-hour courses, and in which the distinction between elementary and advanced work has been forgotten. We are not producing them by adding more "survey" courses. We shall not produce them until we go back to first principles and create a college curriculum which, as a whole and in its interrelated parts, provides ordered and progressive training in the various forms of disciplined thought. When we do this we shall at last train up specialists who are scholars and scientists in the highest sense, and citizens who are truly educated men. Liberal education will then become a reality, because it will introduce all men alike into that world of disciplined thought where scholars and reflective citizens meet on common ground.   (44)

Robert Maynard Hutchins

(1899–   )

HUTCHINS commanded the attention of American educators during his tenure as chief executive officer of the University of Chicago (1929–1951), having been appointed president at the age of thirty. A brilliant orator and controversialist, he struck his habitual posture in No Friendly Voice (1936). After a brief period (1951–1954) as associate director of the Ford Foundation, he became director of the Fund for the Republic (since 1954). His analyses and recommendations continue to provoke lively discussion.

◼ *The Higher Learning*

I

THE MOST characteristic feature of the modern world is bewilderment. It has become the fashion to be bewildered. Anybody who says he knows anything or understands anything is at once suspected of affectation or falsehood. Consistency has become a vice and opportunism a virtue. We do not know where we are going, or why; and we have almost given up the attempt to find out.   (1)

This is an extraordinary situation. Certainly we have more facts about the world, about ourselves, and the relations among ourselves than were available to any of our ancestors. We console ourselves with the delusion that the world is much more complicated than the one our ancestors inhabited. It does not seem possible that its complexity has increased at anywhere near the same rate as our knowledge of facts about it. If, as Descartes led us to believe, the soul's good is the domination of the physical universe, our souls have achieved a very high degree of good indeed. If, as we have been convinced since the Renaissance, the advance of the race is in direct proportion to the volume of information it possesses, we should by now have reached every imaginable human goal. We have more information, more means of getting more information, and more means of distributing information than at any time in history. Every citizen is equipped with information, useful and useless, sufficient to deck out a Cartesian paradise. And yet we are bewildered. (2)

For three hundred years we have cherished a faith in the beneficent influences of facts. As Hilaire Belloc's doggerel puts it:

> The path of life, men said, is hard and rough
> Only because we do not know enough.
> When science has discovered something more,
> We shall be happier than we were before. (3)

Our faith in facts grew with every succeeding century, until it became the dominant force in our society. It excluded every other interest and determined every procedure. Let us get the facts, we said, serene in the confidence that, if we did, all our problems would be solved. We got them. Our problems are insoluble still. (4)

Since we have confused science with information, ideas with facts, and knowledge with miscellaneous data, and since information, facts, and data have not lived up to our high hopes of them, we are witnessing today a revulsion against science, ideas, and knowledge. The anti-intellectualism of the nineteenth century was bad enough. A new and worse brand is now arising. We are in despair because the keys which were to open the gates of heaven have let us into a larger but more oppressive prison-house. We thought those keys were science and the free intelligence of man. They have failed us. To what can we now appeal? One answer comes in the undiluted animalism of the last works of D. H. Lawrence, in the emotionalism of demagogues, in Hitler's scream: "We think with our blood." Man, satisfied that he has weighed reason and found it wanting, turns now to passion. He attempts to cease to be a rational animal, and endeavors to become merely animal. In this attempt he is destined to be unsuccessful. It is his reason which tells him he is bewildered. (5)

My thesis is that in modern times we have seldom tried reason at all, but something we mistook for it; that our bewilderment results in large part from this mistake; and that our salvation lies not in the rejection of the intellect but in a return to it. Let me say at once that in urging a return to the intellect I do not urge a return to that vicious intellectualism whose leading exponent is Descartes. He turned his back to the world and its past, and there by his German stove in a heavy woolen bathrobe thought himself into a mathematical universe which was to be understood by measurement alone. His thinking produced a reaction in succeeding generations which led at the last to a denial of the intellectual powers of mankind. (6)

Let me say, too, that in advocating a return to reason I do not advocate abandonment of our interest in facts. I proclaim the value of observation and experiment. I would proclaim, also, the value of rational thought and would suggest that without it facts may prove worthless, trivial, and irrelevant. In the words of a great contemporary, "The flame remains feeble on which piles of green wood are flung." During the nineteenth century and since, we have been flinging piles of green wood on the fire and have almost succeeded in putting it out. Now we can hardly see through the smoke. (7)

Our program has amounted to a denial of the nature of man. Tested a priori, such denial results in self-contradiction; tested by its consequences, it has been found unsuccessful. It has led us to devote ourselves to measuring and counting the phenomena which passed before our eyes. It has diverted us from the task of understanding them. Modern empirical science, which in origin was the application of mathematics to experience by means of measurement and experiment, has come in recent exposition to be considered exclusively an affair of experiment and measurement. Contemporary physical and biological research inherited the analytical procedures which, combined with observation, constitute a science; and to a great extent the heritage has been fruitful. But contemporary physical and biological scientists have also inherited the nineteenth century's anti-intellectual account of empirical science, which placed primary emphasis upon the accumulation of observed facts. The practice of contemporary scientists is thus paradoxically better than what they preach about the nature and ideals of science. In this paradox we have a source of our bewilderment. And, unfortunately, other disciplines, the social studies and the humanities, have been more influenced by the precepts of the natural scientists than by their practices. They, too, even in the fine arts, have decided they must be scientific and have thought they could achieve this aim merely by accumulating facts. So we have lots of "gadgets" in the natural sciences and lots of information in the other fields of knowledge. The gadgeteers and the data-collectors, masquerading as scientists, have threatened to become the supreme chieftains of the scholarly world. (8)

Now, a university should be a center of rational thought. Certainly it is more than a storehouse of rapidly aging facts. It should be the stronghold of those who insist on the exercise of reason, who will not be moved by passion or buried by blizzards of data. The gaze of a university should be turned toward ideas. By the light of ideas it may promote understanding of the nature of the world and of man. Its object is always understanding. In the faith that the intellect of men may yet preserve him, it seeks to emphasize, develop, and protect his intellectual powers. Facts and data it will obtain to assist in formulating and to illustrate the principles it establishes, as Galileo used experiments to assist and exemplify his analysis, not as a substitute for it. Rational thought is the only basis of education and research. Whether we know it or not, it has been responsible for our scientific successes; its absence has been responsible for our bewilderment. A university is the place of all places to grapple with those fundamental principles which rational thought seeks to establish.   (9)

A university so organized and so conducted might stand unmoved by public clamor; it might be an island in a sea of turmoil; it might be a rallying-point of all honest and upright men. It might show us the social order we should desire, and help us keep it when it was achieved. A university may make these contributions not by having its professors politicians on the one hand or hermits on the other. Both extremes are equally disastrous. The university must find better and better means of communicating the ideas which it is its duty to foster and develop. A university without these means of communication will die, or at least will not be fruitful. Its ideas are not intellectual playthings, but forces which will drive the world. A university must be intelligible as well as intelligent.   (10)

If we look at the modern American university, we have some difficulty in seeing that it is uniformly either one. It sometimes seems to approximate a kindergarten at one end and a clutter of specialists at the other. The specialists are frequently bent on collecting more and more information rather than grappling with fundamentals. So much is already known, so much is being discovered, so many new fields are opening up, that this approach requires more courses, more hours, more laboratories, and more departments. And the process has carried with it surprising losses in general intelligibility. Since the subject matter is intelligible only in terms of the volume of known facts which must be familiar to the scholar, universities have broken down into smaller and smaller compartments. And yet Whitehead may have been right when he said, not long ago, that "the increasing departmentalization of universities has trivialized the intellect of professors."   (11)

Nor do we seem always to grapple with fundamentals when we come to education as distinguished from research. The system has been to pour facts into the student with splendid disregard of the certainty that he will forget them, that they may not be facts by the time he graduates, and that he won't know what to do with them if they are. It is a system based on the false notion that education is a substitute for experience, and that therefore little imitation experiences should be handed out day by day until the student is able to stand the shock of a real experience when he meets one. Yet we know that it is impossible to imitate experience in the classroom and that the kind of experience we might reconstruct there would not be the kind the student will meet when he leaves us.   (12)

To tell a law student that the law is what the courts will do, and have him reach his conclusions on this point by counting up what they have done, is to forego rational analysis, to deny the necessity of principles, and to prevent the exercise of the intellect. To remit a business student to cases representing what business used to do, not only provides little intellectual experience but also little practical experience, for the cases of the past might be a positive disservice in solving the problems of the present. To turn the divinity student away from the great intellectual tradition of the church and teach him how to organize a party in the parish house is neither to prepare him for the ministry nor to contribute to its improvement. To instruct a medical student in the mechanics of his trade and to fill him full of the recollection of particular instances may result in a competent craftsman, but hardly in a product of which a university may be proud. If professional schools are to rise above the level of vocational training, they must restore ideas to their place in the educational scheme.   (13)

The three worst words in education are "character," "personality," and "facts." Facts are the core of an anti-intellectual curriculum. Personality is the qualification we look for in an anti-intellectual teacher. Character is what we expect to produce in the student by the combination of a teacher of personality and a curriculum of facts. How this result can emerge from the mixture of these elements is a mystery to me. Apparently we insist on personality in the teacher because we cannot insist on intellect; we are anti-intellectual. We talk of character as the end of education because an anti-intellectual world will not accept intelligence as its proper aim. Certainly since the *Meno* of Plato, we have had little reason to suppose that we could teach character directly. Courses in elementary, intermediate, and advanced character will fail of their object. The moral virtues are formed by lifelong habit; a university education contributes to them, but it is not its primary purpose to supply them. A university education must chiefly be directed to inculcating the intellectual virtues, and these are the product of rigorous intellectual effort. Such effort is the indispensable constituent of a university course of study.   (14)

We see, then, that an anti-intellectual university involves a contradiction in terms. Unless we are to deny forever the essential nature of man, unless we are to remain content with our bewilderment, we must strive somehow to make the university once again the home of the intellect. I repeat: a university is the place of all places to grapple with those fundamental principles which may be established by rational thought. A university course of study, therefore, will be concerned first of all not with current events, for they do not remain current, but with the recognition, application, and discussion of ideas. These ideas may chiefly be discovered in the books of those who clarified and developed them. These books are, I suggest, at once more interesting and more important than the textbooks which, consumed at the rate of ten pages a day, now constitute our almost exclusive diet from the grades to the Ph.D. To aid in his understanding of ideas the student should be trained in those intellectual techniques which have been developed for the purpose of stating and comprehending fundamental principles. Armed with these, he may at length be able to effect transformations and combinations in any subject matter.   (15)

Such a course of study would involve in the fine arts, for example, more aesthetics and far less biographical and factual material. In the physical sciences and in experimental biology it would require more attention to the nature of measurement and its relation to the formulation of a science, and far fewer of the countless isolated measurements and exercises now performed in the laboratory. Here I am referring, of course, to the laboratory as an educational institution, not to the laboratory method as a method of research. In so far as biology deals with evolution, a university course of study would diminish the emphasis now given to innumerable details about innumerable organisms and place it on the comprehension of the general scheme of evolution as a theory of history. And in all that study which appears in every department and which is called "history," a university would endeavor to transmit to the student, not a confused list of places, dates, and names, but some understanding of the nature and schemes of history, through which alone its multitudinous facts become intelligible. By some such course of study the university might pass on the tremendous intellectual heritage of the race.   (16)

The scholars in a university which is trying to grapple with fundamentals will, I suggest, devote themselves first of all to the rational analysis of the principles of each subject matter. They will seek to establish general propositions under which the facts they gather may be subsumed. I repeat: they would not cease to gather facts, but would know what facts to look for, what they wanted them for, and what to do with them after they got them. They would not confine themselves to rational analysis and ignore the latest bulletin of the Department of Commerce. But they would understand that without analysis current data remain a meaningless tangle of minute facts. They would realize that without some means of ordering and comprehending their material they would sink deeper and deeper beneath the weight of the information they possessed, as the legal scholar has long since sunk beneath the countless decisions and statutes rained down upon him every year.   (17)

Since the multiplicity and overlapping of specialties are caused by the superficiality of our analysis, and since grappling with fundamentals should show us what our subject matters are, the ordering of our concrete material by rational means should show us, too, the absurdity of many intellectual barriers that now divide us. We might see again the connections of ideas, and thus of subject matters. We might recapture the grand scheme of the intellect and the unity of thought. Once the three "departments" of the European university, and the only ones, were medicine, theology, and law. These three fields were so studied as to deal with the same propositions and facts, but with different ultimate references. Each one thus penetrated the whole of contemporary thought and was penetrated by the other two. The scholar and student laboring in one of these fields never lost consciousness of the rest. Thus, wherever he was working he remained aware of the individual, living in society, and under God. To this formal organization of a university we cannot and should not return. But it may suggest to us some consequences of believing that the result of general education should be clear and distinct ideas; the end of university training, some notion of humanity and its destiny; and the aim of scholarship, the revelation of the possibilities of the highest powers of mankind.   (18)

II

I HAVE affirmed that the object of a university is to emphasize, develop, and protect the intellectual powers of mankind. Scholarship and teaching must be tested by their contribution to this intellectual end. I have attempted to show that facts are not science and that the collection of facts will not make a science; that scientific research, therefore, cannot consist of the accumulation of data alone; that the anti-intellectual account of science given by scientists has produced unfortunate effects on the work of other disciplines which wished to be scientific; and that our anti-intellectual scheme of education, resulting in large part from this anti-intellectual account, was misconceived and incapable of accomplishing the objects set for it by its sponsors. At the same time I have proclaimed the value of observation and experiment. Nor have I suggested that ideas are revealed. All ideas come from experience. Propositions, however, do not. Propositions are relations between ideas, and science consists of propositions. As Whitehead has said in speaking of the world which is the goal of scientific thought, "My contention is that this world is a world of ideas, and that its internal relations are relations between abstract concepts. . . ." I have insisted upon the logical priority of rational analysis, not its psychological priority. The psychology of scientists and the time order in which they do things—their behavior, in short—is something I have never ventured to discuss. I have been talking about how a science, which must be distinguished from the isolated activities of individual scientists, is constructed. I repeat: I am concerned with the logic of science, not with the psychology of scientists. Without proposing that we discontinue anything we are doing, I have proposed a shift in emphasis and attitude. Our emphasis and our attitude should be intellectual. If they are, we may then discover whether all the things we are doing are equally significant.   (19)

These ideas were not original with me. If they were, they might be discredited merely by pointing out that fact. I offer you instead Bertrand Russell: "Many people," he says, "have a passionate hatred of abstraction, chiefly, I think, because of its intellectual difficulty, but as they do not wish to give this reason they invent all sorts of others that sound grand. . . . Those who argue in this way are, in fact, concerned with matters quite other than those that concern science. . . ." "The power of using abstractions," says Russell, "is the essence of the intellect, and with every increase in abstraction the intellectual triumphs of science are enhanced."   (20)

Perhaps you prefer Jevons: "Hundreds of investigators," he says, "may be constantly engaged in experimental inquiry; they may compile numberless books full of scientific facts, and endless tables of numerical results; but . . . they can never by such work alone rise to new and great discoveries. . . . Francis Bacon spread abroad the notion that to advance science we must begin by accumulating facts, and then draw from them, by a process of digestion, successive laws of higher and higher generality. . . . His notion of scientific method was a kind of scientific bookkeeping. Facts were to be indiscriminately gathered from every source, and posted in a ledger, from which would emerge in time a balance of truth. . . . It is difficult to imagine a less likely way of arriving at great discoveries. The greater the array of facts the less is the probability that they will by any routine system of classification disclose the laws of nature they embody. . . ." "Newton's comprehension of logical method," says Jevons, "was perfect; no hypothesis was entertained unless it was definite in conditions and admitted of unquestionable deductive reasoning, and the value of each hypothesis was entirely decided by the comparison of its consequences with facts. . . ." "Francis Bacon," Jevons says, "held that science should be founded on experience, but he mistook the true method of using experience, and in attempting to apply his method, ludicrously failed. Newton did not less found his method on experience, but he seized the true method of treating it, and applied it with a power and success never since equalled. It is a great mistake to say that modern science is the result of the Baconian philosophy; it is the Newtonian philosophy and the Newtonian method which have led to all the great triumphs of physical science. . . ."   (21)

Perhaps you prefer Poincaré: "Can we not be content," he asks, "with just the bare experiment? No, that is impossible; it would be to mistake utterly the true nature of science. . . . Science is built up with facts, as a house is built up with stones. But a collection of facts is no more a science than a heap of stones is a house." (22)

Or listen to Claude Bernard: "The experimental method cannot give new and fruitful ideas to men who have none; it can serve only to guide the ideas of men who have them, to direct their ideas and to develop them so as to get the best possible results. . . . As only what has been sown in the ground will ever grow in it, so nothing will be developed by the experimental method except the ideas submitted to it. The method itself gives birth to nothing." (23)

You may say that all this is perfectly obvious; that everybody knows it; that you don't know anybody that is merely gathering facts for the sake of gathering them; that I am simply setting up a straw man in order to knock him down again. I agree that research in the natural sciences proceeds, for the most part, in accordance with the principles which I am advocating. Physics, for example, is an excellent empirical science. The reason for this is not necessarily that all physicists have a clear understanding of what they are doing. It is rather because of the intellectual heritage of the science. This has resulted in turn from the intellectual endowments of such men as Galileo and Newton. It is not necessary for physicists to understand the nature of science, because the techniques of experimental and theoretical work in physics are so explicit and so well established that they cannot escape them. In the law, the humanities, and the social sciences, however, scholars have received no such inheritance. If they are to be scientific, they must understand what science is. From Francis Bacon on, many people have advised them that it consists merely in accumulating data. Some of them have taken this advice seriously and have concluded that their scientific attainments would be measured by the number of items of fact which they had written on cards. I know some of them have done it; I have done it myself. (24)

You may deny that natural scientists even think or talk as though science were the accumulation of data. For answer I refer you to what they teach. We have in every university in America the interesting spectacle of pure scientists teaching in ways which cannot be reconciled with the way they work. They offend as much as, or more than, the rest of us in filling their students full of facts, in putting them through countless little measurements, in multiplying their courses, in insisting they must have more of the student's time so that they can give him more information, and in dividing up their subjects into smaller and smaller bits. Contrast the amount of information which the student in science has when he enters the medical school here and in Europe. Here I am sure the student knows many more facts than some of the older professors. In Europe his information will probably not be a third of that of his American contemporary; but he will have something else: he will have ideas, and he will have that understanding of the relation of ideas which John Locke thought was all that knowledge could be.   (25)

As for the rest of us, we have taught our students in harmony with the worst American tradition. We have assumed that they could learn nothing except in the classroom or from textbooks. The reading periods at Harvard and Yale are ridiculous because they show how little time those universities feel should be devoted to thought. Courses get longer and longer. There are more and more of them. The number of hours in the classroom is the measure of the labors of both teacher and student. And the hours in the classroom are devoted to the exposition of detail.   (26)

And yet the words of Whitehead are apposite: ". . . the university course," he says, "is the great period of generalization. The spirit of generalization should dominate a university. At the university [the student] should start from general ideas and study their application to concrete cases. A well-planned university course is a wide sweep of generality. I do not mean to say that it should be abstract in the sense of divorce from concrete fact, but that concrete fact should be studied as illustrating the scope of general ideas. . . . Whatever be the detail with which you cram your student, the chance of his meeting in after-life exactly that detail is almost infinitesimal; and if he does meet it, he will probably have forgotten what you taught him about it. . . . The function of a university is to enable you to shed details in favor of principles."   (27)

An anti-intellectual attitude toward education reduces the curriculum to the exposition of detail. There are no principles. The world is a flux of events. We cannot hope to understand it. All we can do is watch it. This is the conclusion of the leading anti-intellectuals of our time. Since the fact that certain things went by us once is no guaranty that they will go by again, there is really not much use in watching them, except that we may be able to discover certain patterns of behavior which will enable us to tell sometimes what is going to happen next. In this view our object, in so far as we have one, is prediction and control, the exploitation of the universe.
                                                                           (28)

I may point out that this anti-intellectualism will mean the end of pure science and of education. The driving power behind science has not been merely the desire to master nature; it has been the desire to understand it. If we cannot understand it, we may as well abandon pure science and betake ourselves to engineering. If we cannot understand it, we can give our students nothing but evanescent facts selected on the basis of the kind of experiences we think they will have when they graduate. The multitude of facts, as well as their evanescence, and the tremendous number of possible experiences mean that education in this view is a hopeless task. If we want to give our students experiences, we should go out of business. The place to get experiences is in life. (29)

Nor can education in this view include any contact with the intellectual inheritance of the race. So to anti-intellectuals, rational values are worthless; they are based on the past. They cannot be valid for the future, because man and his world are changing. A curriculum of current events, without reference to the intellectual and artistic tradition that has come down to us from antiquity, is the only possible course of study which anti-intellectualism affords. (30)

Anti-intellectualism dooms pure science; it dooms any kind of education that is more than training in technical skill. It must be a foreboding of this doom which accounts for the sense of inferiority which we find widespread among academic people. Those who have it feel that business and politics are the really important things in the world, far more important than education and research. Certainly they are right if research is merely the collection of facts, and education is committing them to memory. Neither process is significant and neither will long be supported by a hard-pressed people. But if research is understanding and education is understanding and what the world needs is understanding, then education and research are what the world needs. They become at once the most significant of all possible undertakings. They offer the only hope of salvation, the hope held out to us by the intellect of man. (31)

It was such considerations as these that induced John Dewey in 1930 to clarify his views—a clarification, unfortunately, which has escaped the notice of some of his followers. Mr. C. I. Lewis had written that "Professor Dewey seems to view such abstractionism in science as a defect—something unnecessary, but always regrettable." Mr. Dewey replied: "I fear that on occasion I may so have written as to give this impression. I am glad therefore to have the opportunity of saying that this is not my actual position. Abstraction is the heart of thought; there is no other way . . . to control and enrich concrete experience except through an intermediate flight of thought with conceptions, relata, abstractions. . . . I wish to agree also with Mr. Lewis that the need of the social sciences at present is precisely such abstractions as will get their unwieldy elephants into box-cars that will move on rails arrived at by other abstractions. What is to be regretted is, to my mind, the tendency of many inquirers in the field of human affairs to be over-awed by the abstractions of the physical sciences and hence to fail to develop the conceptions or abstractions appropriate to their own subject-matter." This statement of Dewey is a recognition that ideas are the essential elements in the development of a science, and is a repudiation of the anti-intellectual position. (32)

The anti-intellectual position must be repudiated if a university is to achieve its ends. Its buildings may be splendid, its endowment adequate, and its faculty notable; it may have achieved unity, liberty, and clarity in its organization. Its mechanics may be perfect. It is nothing without an abiding faith in the intellect of man. Without such faith its efforts are blind and groping, and will at length expire. The university is the home of the intellect; it is its natural and perhaps its only home. Teaching and scholarship will be fruitful in such measure as the university realizes its intellectual aims. Such realization will be fruitful not merely in the higher learning. It may create an atmosphere congenial to philosophy and the arts, to moral and social theory, to the imaginative reaches of science, and to the noblest aspirations of mankind. And it may at last bring order, enlightenment, and understanding to a bewildered world.   (33)

Peter F. Drucker

(1909–   )

DRUCKER, professor of management at New York University since 1950, has been a consultant to major American corporations for more than a quarter of a century. Widely honored, he has been awarded numerous gold medals in his field and has received honorary doctorates from several American universities and from Nikon University in Tokyo. His special interest in the relationship of industry to society is reflected in his numerous books—for example, The Future of Industrial Man *(1941),* The New Society *(1950),* Power and Democracy in America *(1962).*

■ *The Educational Revolution*

AN ABUNDANT and increasing supply of highly educated people has become the absolute prerequisite of social and economic development in our world. It is rapidly becoming a condition of national survival. What matters is not that there are so many more individuals around who have been exposed to long years of formal schooling—though this is quite recent. The essential new fact is that a developed society and economy are less than fully effective if anyone is educated to less than the limit of his potential. The uneducated man is fast becoming an economic liability and unproductive. Society must be an "educated society" today—to progress, to grow, even to survive. (1)

A sudden, sharp change has occurred in the meaning and impact of knowledge for society. Because we now can organize men of high skill and knowledge for joint work through the exercise of responsible judgment, the highly educated man has become the central resource of today's society, the supply of such men the true measure of its economic, its military and even its political potential. (2)

This is a complete reversal of man's history within the last fifty years or so. Until the twentieth century no society could afford more than a handful of educated people; for throughout the ages to be educated meant to be unproductive. (3)

> A man who is now chief executive of one of America's largest businesses did not dare admit when applying for his first job, in 1916, that he had an advanced degree in economics. "I told the man who hired me that I had been a railroad clerk since I was 14," he says, "otherwise I would have been turned down as too educated for a job in business." Even in the late twenties, when I myself started, commercial firms in England or on the Continent still hesitated before hiring anyone as a junior clerk who had finished secondary school. (4)

It has always been axiomatic that the man of even a little education would forsake the hoe and the potter's wheel and would stop working with his hands. After all our word "school"—and its equivalent in all European languages—derives from a Greek word meaning "leisure." (5)

To support more educated people than the barest minimum required gross exploitation of the "producers," if not strict rules to keep them at work and away from education. The short burst of education in the Athens of Pericles rested on a great expansion of slavery, the intellectual and artistic splendor of the Italian Renaissance on a sharp debasement of the economic and social position of peasant and artisan. (6)

Idealists tried to break this "iron law" by combining manual work and education—the tradition goes back to the Rule of St. Benedict with its mixture of farmwork and study. It found its best expression in the mid-nineteenth century in Emerson's New England farmer who supposedly read Homer in the original Greek while guiding a plow. But this, of course, never worked. The Benedictines—imperiling their salvation to the lasting benefit of mankind—very soon left farming to villains and serfs and concentrated on study. Long before Emerson's death those New England farmers who cared for the plow had left both Homer and New England for the rich soils of the Midwest, while those few who had cared for Homer had left farming altogether to become lawyers, preachers, teachers or politicians. The "iron law" was indeed inescapable as long as manual labor was the really productive labor.   (7)

Thomas Jefferson believed in higher education and in equality as much as any American. He considered the founding of the University of Virginia and the authorship of the Declaration of Independence, rather than the Presidency, his greatest achievements. Yet in his educational master plan he proposed to limit access to higher education to a handful of geniuses. It was obvious that only a few could be spared from manual labor.   (8)

Today the dearth of educated people in the formerly colonial areas appears such a handicap as by itself to be adequate condemnation of colonialism and proof of the "wickedness" of the imperialists. But education did not come first in the scale of social needs even fifty years ago; flood control and land boundaries, equitable taxation and improved agriculture, railroads and incorruptible magistrates, all ranked much higher. If the colonial powers were then criticized on the score of education, it was for forcing it on too many, for destroying thereby the native culture, and for creating an unemployable, overeducated proletariat. The educated person was then still a luxury rather than a necessity, and education a preparation for dignified leisure rather than for productive work.   (9)

In my own childhood forty years ago, schools still assumed that education was for "nonwork." They preached that the educated man should not despise the honest worker as schools had preached since the days of Seneca in the first century.   (10)

The Scale of the Explosion

Thirty years ago only one out of every eight Americans at work had been to high school. Today four out of every five of the young people of high school age in the United States attend high school. Twenty years hence, when today's middle-aged will have retired, practically every working American will be a high school graduate. We have already passed the half-way mark.   (11)

Even greater has been the jump in college and university attendance. Thirty years ago it was still an almost negligible 4 per cent or less of the appropriate age group. Today the figure is around 35 per cent for the nation; this takes in groups such as the Southern Negro or the Southern "poor white," for whom going to college is still all but unknown. In the metropolitan areas of the country—even in such predominantly working-class cities as Detroit—the figure is nearly 50 per cent. It will, barring catastrophe, be that high for the nation as a whole in another fifteen years. By then two out of every three young Americans in the metropolitan areas will, regardless almost of income, race or sex, be exposed to higher education. (12)

In the American work force of thirty years ago there were at most three college graduates for every hundred men and women at work. There are eighteen today; the figure will be thirty-five, twenty years hence—even if, contrary to all expectations, going to college becomes no more general than it is already among the two thirds of our people who live in metropolitan areas. (13)

On top of all this, adult education is booming. Fifty years ago only those adults went back to school who had been unable to get a formal education as children. Adult education was for the educationally underprivileged—the immigrant from Southern Europe who wanted to learn English or the man who had gone to work at age fourteen and wanted to improve himself. In England adult education was the "Workers Educational Alliance" or the "Home University Library," both offering standard school subjects to workers and clerks. The German *Volkshochschule* served the same purpose. (14)

Adult education during the last fifteen years has been growing faster in this country than college enrollment. And now increasingly it means advanced education for the already highly educated. It is almost routine for the experienced and successful physician to go back to school for advanced training every two or three years. Refresher courses are increasingly demanded of our teachers. Some fifty universities—in addition to a dozen large companies and professional management associations—offer advanced management courses to successful men in the middle and upper ranks of business, who usually already have college if not advanced degrees. Yet before World War II, only two such programs existed, both new, and both struggling to get students. (15)

The educational revolution has been even more explosive in Soviet Russia. Thirty years ago basic literacy was confined to a small minority—had probably fallen even below the low standards of czarist Russia. The educational push hardly began until the mid-thirties. Today, because of Russia's larger population, the proportion of young people in secondary or higher education is still quite a bit lower than in this country, but the absolute numbers are fast approaching ours. (16)

In the total population of the Soviet Union educated people must still be a small group. Few if any of the top people in the Soviet Union have had more than elementary formal schooling; certainly of those over forty in the Soviet Union, even high school graduates are still only a tiny fraction. But in Russia, too, it has become evident that education is the capital resource of a modern, industrial society. We know now that the Russian achievement does not rest on the Communist tenets of "socialist ownership of productive resources," the "dictatorship of the proletariat," "collectivization of agriculture" or "national planning." Every one of them has been as much an impediment as a help, a source of weakness fully as much as a source of strength. The achievement rests squarely upon the tremendous concentration of resources, time and effort on producing an educated society.   (17)

The two outstanding success stories among small nations, Switzerland and Mexico, have nothing in common save extraordinary educational development. Switzerland is the one European country where secondary education, in the last thirty years, has become almost universal. Mexico is the only country in the world that, since the mid-thirties, has spent no money on defense but has instead made education the first charge on its national income. And is it entirely coincidence that the major countries in the Free World that have found the going the roughest since World War II, Great Britain and France, are also the countries in which the educational revolution has advanced the least, in which the supply of educated people, though of high quality, is today still not much larger proportionately than it was in 1930 or even in 1913? In England the supply may well be smaller considering the steady emigration of so many of the highly educated young people.   (18)

We are undergoing the educational revolution because the work of knowledge is no longer unproductive in terms of goods and services. In the new organization it becomes the specifically productive work. The man who works exclusively or primarily with his hands is the one who is increasingly unproductive. Productive work in today's society and economy is work that applies vision, knowledge and concepts—work that is based on the mind rather than on the hand.   (19)

There will therefore be no permanent oversupply of educated people. On the contrary, the more there are, the greater should be the demand for them. Educated people are the "capital" of a developed society. The immediate impact of, say, using physicians instead of barbers is to uncover needs, opportunities and areas of ignorance, leading to the need both for more physicians and for more medical and biological research. The same process can be seen in every other field—and with particular force in the economic field of production and distribution. Every engineer, every chemist, every accountant, every market analyst immediately creates the opportunity and the need for more men who can apply knowledge and concepts, both in his own field and all around it.   (20)

This may sound obvious. But it is so new that it is not yet recognized. Our accountants, for instance, still base their terms and measurements on the eighteenth-century tenet that manual labor creates all value. They still call it "productive labor"; the work of men of knowledge is "nonproductive labor" or "overhead," a term reeking of moral disapproval. When economists talk of "capital" they rarely include "knowledge." Yet this is the only real capital today. The devolpment of educated people is the most important capital formation, their number, quality and utilization the most meaningful index of the wealth-producing capacity of a country. (21)

The Impact on Society

What is today called "automation," that is the rapid substitution of work by knowledge and concept for work by human hands, is a first impact of the educated society. It is a moot question whether the essence of automation lies in specific machinery and technical ideas or whether it lies rather in basic concepts about the nature of work. (22)

But there can be little doubt that the driving force in automation is the fact that people who have been exposed to formal schooling for twelve or sixteen years have expectations in respect to work and jobs which manual work, no matter how well paid, does not fulfill. They increasingly demand jobs in which they can apply knowledge, concepts and system. They increasingly refuse to accept jobs in which they cannot apply what they have learned, namely, to work with their minds. They may be satisfied with a job of little skill—and there are a good many semiskilled knowledge jobs—but they expect work that draws on mental rather than manual faculties. (23)

In the United States, where most of the young people in the metropolitan areas go at least to high school, the assembly line is already obsolete. The labor necessary to run it is becoming scarce. Young people with a high school education do not want to work as human machine tools. Moreover, to use people with that degree of education for the semiskilled and unskilled manual jobs of the assembly line would be a gross waste of valuable, expensive and scarce resources. (24)

Tomorrow everybody—or practically everybody—will have had the education of the upper class of yesterday, and will expect equivalent opportunities. Yet only a small minority can get ahead no matter what work they choose. This is why we face the problem of making every kind of job meaningful and capable of satisfying an educated man. This is why the new organization must create an effective relationship of function, rank, rewards and responsibility, not only for its professionals but for all those employed in knowledge jobs. (25)

How new these expectations are is shown in the field of personnel management. Only forty years old—it began in World War I—the discipline is already outdated in its concepts and its assumptions. Its principles, its rules, its practices and procedures all represent a distillation of experience with unskilled or semiskilled machine workers, largely from the metalwork-

ing industries. Today the majority of the personnel employed even in manufacturing industries are no longer of this kind, are rather people doing
knowledge work, however unskilled. How far our personnel management
theories really applied even to yesterday's machine workers is an open
question. For managing tomorrow's employees, the products of the educated
society, they are likely to be quite inadequate.   (26)

The educational revolution has had an equal impact on the world economy. Educational capacity, as much as natural resources or industrial
plants, is becoming a crucial factor in international trade, economic development and economic competition. Educational development, above all,
has become a central problem of the poor countries.   (27)

Many of these underdeveloped countries spend today a larger proportion of their national income on education than does the United States.
Yet where we complain that one fifth of our young people still do not
finish high school, many of these countries can barely keep one fifth of
their young people in elementary school. They cannot finance the cost of
a literate society, let alone that of an educated society.   (28)

This educational inequality is a serious international and interracial
problem. Its inevitable result is to make inequality greater, to make the
rich richer and the poor poorer. Even greater is the danger that it will
push poor, underdeveloped countries into the totalitarian camp; for a totalitarian tyranny, so it appears to them, can raise enough money for the
rapid development of education even in the poorest. (This is a delusion.
Practically all the poor underdeveloped countries are much poorer than
Russia was in 1917 and much further behind in education. They are unlikely therefore to repeat her performance in education even by faithfully
copying every Russian tenet and action. But this may be found out only
when it is too late.)   (29)

Here, it would seem, is a highly promising area for international aid
and co-operation. There is need—and opportunity—for financial aid to help
the underdeveloped countries pay for the rapid expansion of education.
There is need for systematic co-operative effort in training and developing
people, especially future teachers. There is need—and opportunity—to help
think through the purposes, the structure and the methods of education needed in those countries. Above all there is need for the developed
countries, and especially for the United States, to accept a national policy
of assisting underdeveloped countries in building education.   (30)

The Educational Competition

"The Battle of Waterloo," it is said, "was won on the playing fields of
Eton." Perhaps; but no one asserts that it was won in Eton's classrooms.

"The Prussian schoolmaster," another saying goes, "defeated France in the War of 1870 that created imperial Germany." But long ago this was exposed as empty boast; the credit belongs to the German railway and the German armaments designers. (31)

With the launching of Russia's Sputnik, however, the old pleasantry became a grim fact. The higher education of a country controls its military, its technological and its econmic potential. In an age of superpowers and absolute weapons, higher education may indeed be the only area in which a country can still be ahead, can still gain decisive advantage. (32)

The greatest impact of the educational revolution is therefore on international power and politics. It has made the supply of highly educated people a decisive factor in the competition between powers—for leadership and perhaps even for survival. (33)

The conclusion from this is as simple as it is new: Educational developmental becomes a priority of national policy. (34)

International leadership is not a matter of power alone. It is as much a matter of policy. Power can never substitute for policy. But purposeful, principled, courageous policy is a potent substitute for power, has again and again given leadership to a weaker rather than to a stronger nation. (35)

Concern for the quantity of educated people is therefore not enough for a national policy in this age of the educational revolution. Numbers of engineers and scientists, of language students and physicians, are not very meaningful in themselves. It is not even enough that national policy aim at the largest possible supply of highly schooled people. It is not enough, in other words, that the graduates know their engineering, their science, their law, languages or medicine. National policy is only possible if these are also highly *educated* people—that is, people who can formulate, understand and support purposeful, principled, courageous policies. (36)

This leads us back to education. And indeed the greatest impact of the educational revolution is on education itself. It raises basic questions about the values, the purposes, the structure and the tools of education. On the one hand, education has become the central capital investment, the highly educated people the central productive resource in such society. On the other hand, education, while "higher" and perhaps "highest," can no longer be limited to an elite, but must be general education. (37)

Jerome S. Bruner

(1915–   )

BRUNER *is professor of psychology at Harvard and director of the Center for Cognitive Studies. His special field of research is the nature of perception, learning, thinking, as affected by motives, personality. His major works include* The Process of Education *(1960),* A Study of Thinking *(with others, 1956), and* Processes of Cognitive Growth *(1965).*

■ *Motives for Learning*

IN ASSESSING what might be done to improve the state of the curricular art, we are inevitably drawn into discussion of the nature of motives for learning and the objectives one might expect to attain in educating youth. Obviously, matters of such enormous scope can be considered only briefly here. Yet certain issues seem to be particularly in need of closer scrutiny in relation to the designing of curricula.

In planning a curriculum, one properly distinguishes between the long-run objective one hopes to achieve and certain short-run steps that get one toward that objective. Those of a practical turn of mind are likely to say that little is served by stating long-term objectives unless one can propose short-run methods for their achievement. More idealistic critics may too readily dismiss short-run educational goals on the grounds that they cannot see where they lead. We are inclined to take a middle ground. While one benefits from clarity about the ends of education, it is often true that we may discover or rediscover new ultimate objectives in the process of trying to reach more modest goals. Something of this order seems to have occurred in recent efforts to improve school curricula.   (2)

The efforts of the past decade began with the modest intention of doing a better job of teaching physics or mathematics or some other subject. The impulse that led a group of highly competent physicists, for example, to join together in this effort was the sense of how great a gap had developed between physics as known by the physicist and physics as taught in school, a gap of particular importance because of revolutionary advances in science and the crisis in national security. But as the effort broadened, as scholars and scientists from other disciplines entered the field, a broader objective began to emerge. It is clear that there is in American education today a new emphasis upon the pursuit of excellence. There appear to be several things implied by the pursuit of excellence that have relevance not only to what we teach, but to how we teach and how we arouse the interest of our students.   (3)

The view has already been expressed that the pursuit of excellence must not be limited to the gifted student. But the idea that teaching should be aimed at the average student in order to provide something for everybody is an equally inadequate formula. The quest, it seems to many of us, is to devise materials that will challenge the superior student while not destroying the confidence and will-to-learn of those who are less fortunate. We have no illusions about the difficulty of such a course, yet it is the only one open to us if we are to pursue excellence and at the same time honor the diversity of talents we must educate. Much has already been said about the importance of preparing curricula adequate to this end, of educating teachers, of using all available teaching aids. These are steps toward the achievement of excellence. Another essential step has to do with motivation.   (4)

Arnold Bennett remarked that the French sacrifice the girl to the woman; the English, the woman to the girl. How do we fare? It has been said of the American high school that its emphasis on the "peer" culture negates some of the adult aims of education. The claim is debatable, but the issue is a real one, as such commentators on the social setting of American secondary education as James Coleman and David Riesman have pointed out. One need only examine the advertisements directed to the teen-age set to sense the central role of social life and "the sociables." Studies of American high school culture point particularly to the higher value placed on social popularity than upon academic achievement. Yet the 1960 *Report on Admissions Policy* prepared by a Committee of the Harvard Faculty under the chairmanship of Professor Franklin Ford indicates that Harvard students enrolled from public high schools carry away more honors than students of like aptitude enrolled from the great independent preparatory schools of the Eastern seaboard. It may well be that the high school students in the Harvard group are the outstanding ones in their schools, but, even at that, it would certainly indicate that at the very least

American high schools are not ruining these students for later outstanding work.   (5)

Granting, then, that the situation is not as black as some would have us believe nor yet as good as some would like to hope, what can be said about motives for learning in our schools? What results from emphasis upon units of curriculum, upon grades and promotion, upon rote examinations, and the rest, with respect to the continuity and deepening of school learning?   (6)

Somewhere between apathy and wild excitement, there is an optimum level of aroused attention that is ideal for classroom activity. What is that level? Frenzied activity fostered by the competitive project may leave no pause for reflection, for evaluation, for generalization, while excessive orderliness, with each student waiting passively for his turn, produces boredom and ultimate apathy. There is a day-to-day problem here of great significance. Short-run arousal of interest is not the same as the long-term establishment of interest in the broader sense. Films, audio-visual aids, and other such devices may have the short-run effect of catching attention. In the long run, they may produce a passive person waiting for some sort of curtain to go up to arouse him. We do not know. Perhaps anything that holds the child's attention is justified on the ground that eventually the child will develop a taste for more self-controlled attention—a point on which there is no evidence. The issue is particularly relevant in an entertainment-oriented, mass-communication culture where passivity and "spectatorship" are dangers. Perhaps it is in the technique of arousing attention in school that first steps can be taken to establish that active autonomy of attention that is the antithesis of the spectator's passivity.   (7)

There will always be, perhaps, mixed motives for learning among schoolchildren. There are parents and teachers to be pleased, one's contemporaries to be dealt with, one's sense of mastery to be developed. At the same time, interests are developing, the world opens up. Schoolwork is only a part of the quickened life of the growing child. To different children it means different things. To some it is the road to parental approbation; to others it is an intrusion on the social world of contemporaries, and is to be handled by the minimum effort that will "get by." The culture of the school may be anti-intellectual or quite the opposite. And within this complex picture there is the subtle attraction of the subjects in school that a child finds interesting. One can spell out the details of the picture, but in the main they are familiar enough. How, within this context, do we arouse the child's interest in the world of ideas?   (8)

Several tentative recommendations have already been made in the spirit of suggesting needed research. Principal among these were increasing the inherent interest of materials taught, giving the student a sense of discovery, translating what we have to say into the thought forms appropriate to the child, and so on. What this amounts to is developing in the child an interest in what he is learning, and with it an appropriate set of attitudes and values about intellectual activity generally. Surely we shall not by presently conceivable reforms create a nation of devoted intellectuals, nor is it apparent that this should be the major guiding aim of our schools. Rather, if teaching is done well and what we teach is worth learning, there are forces at work in our contemporary society that will provide the external prod that will get children more involved in the process of learning than they have been in the past. (9)

Our cultural climate has not been marked traditionally by a deep appreciation of intellectual values. We have as a people always expressed a great faith in education. There are many reasons for this—the absence of an aristocracy, the pragmatic demands inherent in a frontier society, and so on —but these need not concern us here. Education has been conceived as a means to better the lot of our children rather than our own lot; it is almost a universal belief that children should have a better educational opportunity than their parents. Yet for all our reverence for education, we have paid little enough attention to its content: a vague reference to the "three R's" has seemed sufficient. We have been a country in which doing has been taken as the mark of effectiveness in thinking, and, perhaps more than any other major Western power, we have conceived of the gap between theory and practice as a yawning one. Insofar as we have idealized the thinker, it has been in the form of celebrating arcane wizardry as in the case of Einstein, who was presumably incomprehensible but brilliant, or of rewarding the practical accomplishments that have followed from thought. Thomas Edison was our conception of the American scientist as engineer. The writer, the poet, the theorist, and the savant have not been folk figures in America, have not stimulated legends. (10)

Today, many Americans have become conscious, not just of the practical virtues of education, but of its content and quality—what it is and what it might be. Several factors are contributing to this trend. We are moving into a new era of scientific technology, a second industrial revolution, perhaps more drastic than the first one of over a century ago. Control systems, automation, new sources of power, new space to explore—all of these have livened interest in the nature of our schools and what our young people are learning in them. Unquestionably, there has also been a surge of awareness born of our sense of imperiled national security. The Soviet Union's conquests in space, its capability of producing not only powerful weapons but also an effective industrial society, have shaken American complacency to a degree that, looking back, would have seemed inconceivable a decade ago. And, finally, part of the growing interest in education comes from the fact that the American population now contains a very high proportion of college graduates. We also have the good fortune to be wealthy. The proportion of young people graduating from college today is higher than the proportion graduating from high school forty years ago. All of these factors have stimulated a renewal of interest in education that is making itself felt among students and parents alike.   (11)

There is much discussion about how to give our schools a more serious intellectual tone, about the relative emphasis on athletics, popularity, and social life on the one hand and on scholarly application on the other. There is an effort afoot throughout the nation to redress what has clearly been an imbalance. Admiration for and interest in scholarship is likely to increase faster than expected. There are even some amusing sidelights in which the old symbols are being poured into new bottles—as in certain high schools where the coveted athlete's "letter" is being given as well to students who make distinguished grade averages. But there is another problem, more remote in time, that may eventually prove more serious and for which planning can now be effectively undertaken.   (12)

It is highly probable that certain changes in our educational system will occur in the years ahead, given the demands placed upon it by the community. The first is that there will be an increasing demand for the teaching of science, technology, and supporting subjects. Jobs will be abundant in the newer technical industries. The decentralized American school system has always responded to the opportunities available in American industry and will respond again. It is very difficult to tell on the basis of population statistics and of extrapolations of economic developments when the supply and demand for such technical specialists will meet. At the present time we are far from it. Some estimates suggest that within twenty years, as a combined result of the increased training of engineers and the postwar baby crop now reaching college age, the first part of this demand will be taken up. What will occur after that will depend upon a host of factors, not the least of which will be the speed and thoroughness with which American industry absorbs the new scientific technology available to it.   (13)

A second almost inevitable consequence of the national security crisis is that there will be a quickened flow of federal funds in support of education at the state and local levels. The present National Defense Education Act is only a beginning. A likely, though scarcely inevitable, consequence of federal aid is that there may be a reduction in the disparity in quality that now exists among local school systems. The lower limit of teachers' salaries is likely to increase faster than the upper limit, and better school facilities everywhere will be available as a result of present and proposed legislation on school construction.   (14)

Both of these trends—increasing emphasis on technological progress and federal aid in the interest of coping with the competitive crisis that America must face as a world power—are likely to lead to one result that has questionable consequences for American education and American life unless change is planned well in advance. Let us not be so involved in present efforts to improve the intellectual level of American schools that we overlook preparations for dealing with our success in doing so. The peril of success under the conditions sketched is the growth of what has been called "meritocracy." Partly out of the inertia of present practice and partly in response to the challenge of the new developments described earlier, there will be a strong tendency to move the able student ahead faster and particularly to move him ahead if he shows early promise in technical or scientific fields. Planned carefully, such acceleration can be good for the student and for the nation. A meritocracy, however, implies a system of competition in which students are moved ahead and given further opportunities on the basis of their achievement, with position in later life increasingly and irreversibly determined by earlier school records. Not only later educational opportunities but subsequent job opportunities become increasingly fixed by earlier school performance. The late bloomer, the early rebel, the child from an educationally indifferent home—all of them, in a full-scale meritocracy, become victims of an often senseless irreversibility of decision.

(15)

A meritocracy is likely to have several undesirable effects on the climate in which education occurs, though with advance planning we may be able to control them. One consequence may be an overemphasis upon examination performance. C. P. Snow's Rede Lecture of 1959 (*The Two Cultures and the Scientific Revolutions*, Cambridge, 1959) contains these comments (pp. 19–20) on the Cambridge Mathematical Tripos. They might well give us pause: "For over a hundred years, the nature of the Tripos had been crystallizing. The Competition for the top places had got fiercer, and careers hung on them. In most colleges, certainly in my own, if one managed to come out as a Senior or Second Wrangler, one was elected a Fellow out of hand. A whole apparatus of coaching had grown up. Men of the quality of Hardy, Littlewood, Russell, Eddington, Jeans, Keynes, went in for two or three years' training for an examination that was intensely competitive and intensely difficult. Most people in Cambridge were very proud of it, with a similar pride to that which almost anyone in England always has for our existing educational institutions, whatever they happen to be. . . . In every respect but one, the old Mathematical Tripos seemed perfect. The one exception, however, appeared to some to be rather important. It was simply—so the young creative mathematicians, such as Hardy and Littlewood, kept saying—that the training had no intellectual merit at all. They went a little further, and said that the Tripos had killed serious mathematics in England stone dead for a hundred years." It is, to be sure, highly unlikely that anything approaching the fierceness of the Mathematical Tripos would develop in the United States, and certainly not at the level of our high schools and primary schools. But caricatured extremes help quicken understanding. If it should become the case that certain highly desirable jobs are assured to winners of National Merit Scholarships, then we may be quite sure that it will not be long before teaching and learning reflect the importance of such scholarships. If, further, the principal scholarships and prizes come increasingly to be awarded for merit in the sciences and mathematics, then we may also expect, and this is another danger we face, that there will be a devaluation of other forms of scholarly enterprise. Literature, history, and the arts will, under such circumstances, likely become the prerogative of a group whose family values rather than school values provide the principal support for the pursuit of these topics. Good teachers in the nonscientific subjects will be harder to recruit, harder to attract into teaching. Motives for learning in these fields will become feebler. One exaggerates, to be sure, but these are all possible contingencies that should be guarded against.   (16)

Perhaps it would not be amiss at this point in our educational history to consider the forms of countervailing activity that might prevent such an eventual outcome. We can ill afford an alienated group of literary intellectuals who feel that advances in science, which they may fail to understand out of a sense of being shunned by the system of rewards for technical and scientific achievement, betoken the destruction of traditional culture. It is certainly plain that at the very least there will have to be energy devoted to improving curricula and teaching in the humanities and social sciences comparable to what is now being devoted to science and mathematics. Future legislative provisions for federal and state aid to education might well include specific titles concerned with such problems, and it is none too early to consider, before appropriate legislative committees, the nature and extent of such support.   (17)

Emphasis on competitive performance in the scientific subjects can, of course, be converted to useful ends through imaginativeness and flexibility in the construction of examinations. An examination can also foster thoughtfulness. Special counseling will be necessary in what is almost certain to be a more competitive school system than we ever have known before in America. It will be needed not only for the student who is moving ahead rapidly but more especially for the student—and he represents an important segment of our younger population—who is not the fast, early, and steady producer.   (18)

But remedies such as better examinations and counseling do not provide the major answer. If the dangers of meritocracy and competitiveness, the risks of an overemphasis on science and technology, and the devaluation of humanistic learning are to be dealt with, we shall have to maintain and nurture a vigorous pluralism in America. The theatre, the arts, music, and the humanities as presented in our schools and colleges will need the fullest support.   (19)

To sum up the matter, motives for learning must be kept from going passive in an age of spectatorship, they must be based as much as possible upon the arousal of interest in what there is to be learned, and they must be kept broad and diverse in expression. The danger signs of meritocracy and a new form of competitiveness are already in evidence. Already it is possible to see where advance planning can help. Such planning and the research to support it should be given high priority.   (20)

Margaret Mead

(1901–   )

MARGARET MEAD has been a working anthropologist since she entered graduate school at Columbia University in 1923. She has done field work in Samoa, the Admiralty Islands, New Guinea, Bali, and elsewhere. She has been with the American Museum of Natural History since 1926, the curator of ethnology since 1964. Her dozens of books range from Coming of Age in Samoa *(1928) to* American Women *(1965). She is still wholly dedicated to the development of anthropological studies in American universities.*

■ *The Education of the Samoan Child*

BIRTHDAYS ARE of little account in Samoa. But for the birth itself of the baby of high rank, a great feast will be held, and much property given away. The first baby must always be born in the mother's village and if she has gone to live in the village of her husband, she must go home for the occasion. For several months before the birth of the child the father's relatives have brought gifts of food to the prospective mother, while the mother's female relatives have been busy making pure white bark cloth for baby clothes and weaving dozens of tiny pandanus mats which form the layette. The expectant mother goes home laden with food gifts and when she returns to her husband's family, her family provide her with the exact equivalent in mats and bark cloth as a gift to them. At the birth itself the father's mother or sister must be present to care for the new-born baby while the midwife and the relatives of the mother care for her. There is no privacy about a birth. Convention dictates that the mother should neither writhe, nor cry out, nor inveigh against the presence of twenty or thirty people in the house who sit up all night if need be, laughing, joking, and playing games. The midwife cuts the cord with a fresh bamboo knife and then all wait eagerly for the cord to fall off, the signal for a feast. If the baby is a girl, the cord is buried under a paper mulberry tree (the tree from which bark cloth is made) to ensure her growing up to be industrious at household tasks; for a boy it is thrown into the sea that he may be a skilled fisherman, or planted under a taro plant to give him industry in farming. Then the visitors go home, the mother rises and goes about her daily tasks, and the new baby ceases to be of much interest to any one. The day, the month in which it was born, is forgotten. Its first steps or first word are remarked without exuberant comment, without ceremony. It has lost all ceremonial importance and will not regain it again until after puberty; in most Samoan villages a girl will be ceremonially ignored until she is married. And even the mother remembers only that Losa is older than Tupu, and that her sister's little boy, Fale, is younger than her brother's child, Vigo. Relative age is of great importance, for the elder may always command the younger—until the positions of adult life upset the arrangement—but actual age may well be forgotten.　　　(1)

Babies are always nursed, and in the few cases where the mother's milk fails her, a wet nurse is sought among the kinsfolk. From the first week they are also given other food, papaya, cocoanut milk, sugar-cane juice; the food is either masticated by the mother and then put into the baby's mouth on her finger, or if it is liquid, a piece of bark cloth is dipped into it and the child allowed to suck it, as shepherds feed orphaned lambs. The babies are nursed whenever they cry and there is no attempt at regularlity. Unless a woman expects another child, she will nurse a baby until it is two or three years old, as the simplest device for pacifying its crying. Babies sleep with their mothers as long as they are at the breast; after weaning they are usually handed over to the care of some younger girl in the household. They are bathed frequently with the juice of a wild orange and rubbed with cocoanut oil until their skins glisten.　　　(2)

The chief nurse-maid is usually a child of six or seven who is not strong enough to lift a baby over six months old, but who can carry the child straddling the left hip, or on the small of the back. A child of six or seven months of age will assume this straddling position naturally when it is picked up. Their diminutive nurses do not encourage children to walk, as babies who can walk about are more complicated charges. They walk before they talk, but it is impossible to give the age of walking with any exactness, though I saw two babies walk whom I knew to be only nine months old, and my impression is that the average age is about a year. The life on the floor, for all activities within a Samoan house are conducted on the floor, encourages crawling, and children under three or four years of age optionally crawl or walk.   (3)

From birth until the age of four or five a child's education is exceedingly simple. They must be housebroken, a matter made more difficult by an habitual indifference to the activities of very small children. They must learn to sit or crawl within the house and never to stand upright unless it is absolutely necessary; never to address an adult in a standing position; to stay out of the sun; not to tangle the strands of the weaver; not to scatter the cut-up cocoanut which is spread out to dry; to keep their scant loin cloths at least nominally fastened to their persons; to treat fire and knives with proper caution; not to touch the kava bowl, or the kava cup; and, if the father is a chief, not to crawl on his bed-place when he is by. These are really simply a series of avoidances, enforced by occasional cuffings and a deal of exasperated shouting and ineffectual conversation.   (4)

The weight of the punishment usually falls upon the next oldest child, who learns to shout, "Come out of the sun," before she has fully appreciated the necessity of doing so herself. By the time Samoan girls and boys have reached sixteen or seventeen years of age these perpetual admonitions to the younger ones have become an inseparable part of their conversation, a monotonous, irritated undercurrent to all their comments. I have known them to intersperse their remarks every two or three minutes with, "Keep still," "Sit still," "Keep your mouths shut," "Stop that noise," uttered quite mechanically although all of the little ones present may have been behaving as quietly as a row of intimidated mice. On the whole, this last requirement of silence is continually mentioned and never enforced. The little nurses are more interested in peace than in forming the characters of their small charges and when a child begins to howl, it is simply dragged out of earshot of its elders. No mother will ever exert herself to discipline a younger child if an older one can be made responsible.   (5)

If small families of parents and children prevailed in Samoa, this system would result in making half of the population solicitous and self-sacrificing and the other half tyrannous and self-indulgent. But just as a child is getting old enough so that its wilfulness is becoming unbearable, a younger one is saddled upon it, and the whole process is repeated again, each child being disciplined and socialised through responsibility for a still younger one.   (6)

This fear of the disagreeable consequences resulting from a child's cry-

ing, is so firmly fixed in the minds of the older children that long after
there is any need for it, they succumb to some little tyrant's threat of making a scene, and five-year-olds bully their way into expeditions on which
they will have to be carried, into weaving parties where they will tangle
the strands, and cook-houses where they will tear up the cooking leaves or
get thoroughly smudged with the soot and have to be washed—all because
an older boy or girl has become so accustomed to yielding any point to
stop an outcry.   (7)

This method of giving in, coaxing, bribing, diverting the infant disturb-
ers is only pursued within the household or the relationship group, where
there are duly constituted elders in authority to punish the older children
who can't keep the babies still. Towards a neighbour's children or in a
crowd the half-grown girls and boys and even the adults vent their full
irritation upon the heads of troublesome children. If a crowd of children
are near enough, pressing in curiously to watch some spectacle at which
they are not wanted, they are soundly lashed with palm leaves, or dispersed with a shower of small stones, of which the house floor always furnishes a ready supply. This treatment does not seem actually to improve
the children's behaviour, but merely to make them cling even closer to their
frightened and indulgent little guardians. It may be surmised that stoning
the children from next door provides a most necessary outlet for those
who have spent so many weary hours placating their own young relatives.
And even these bursts of anger are nine-tenths gesture. No one who throws
the stones actually means to hit a child, but the children know that if they
repeat their intrusions too often, by the laws of chance some of the flying
bits of coral will land in their faces. Even Samoan dogs have learned to
estimate the proportion of gesture that there is in a Samoan's "get out
of the house." They simply stalk out between one set of posts and with
equal dignity and all casualness stalk in at the next opening.   (8)

By the time a child is six or seven she has all the essential avoidances
well enough by heart to be trusted with the care of a younger child. And
she also develops a number of simple techniques. She learns to weave firm
square balls from palm leaves, to make pin-wheels of palm leaves or frangi-
pani blossoms, to climb a cocoanut tree by walking up the trunk on flexible
little feet, to break open a cocoanut with one firm well-directed blow of a
knife as long as she is tall, to play a number of group games and sing the
songs which go with them, to tidy the house by picking up the litter on
the stony floor, to bring water from the sea, to spread out the copra to
dry and to help gather it in when rain threatens, to roll the pandanus
leaves for weaving, to go to a neighbouring house and bring back a
lighted fagot for the chief's pipe or the cook-house fire, and to exercise
tact in begging slight favours from relatives.   (9)

But in the case of the little girls all of these tasks are merely supplementary to the main business of baby-tending. Very small boys also have some care of the younger children, but at eight or nine years of age they are usually relieved of it. Whatever rough edges have not been smoothed off by this responsibility for younger children are worn off by their contact with older boys. For little boys are admitted to interesting and important activities only so long as their behaviour is circumspect and helpful. Where small girls are brusquely pushed aside, small boys will be patiently tolerated and they become adept at making themselves useful. The four or five little boys who all wish to assist at the important business of helping a grown youth lasso reef eels, organise themselves into a highly efficient working team; one boy holds the bait, another holds an extra lasso, others poke eagerly about in holes in the reef looking for prey, while still another tucks the captured eels into his *lavalava*. The small girls, burdened with heavy babies or the care of little staggerers who are too small to adventure on the reef, discouraged by the hostility of the small boys and the scorn of the older ones, have little opportunity for learning the more adventurous forms of work and play. So while the little boys first undergo the chastening effects of baby-tending and then have many opportunities to learn effective co-operation under the supervision of older boys, the girls' education is less comprehensive. They have a high standard of individual responsibility but the community provides them with no lessons in co-operation with one another. This is particularly apparent in the activities of young people; the boys organise quickly; the girls waste hours in bickering, innocent of any technique for quick and efficient co-operation.   (10)

And as the woman who goes fishing can only get away by turning the babies over to the little girls of the household, the little girls cannot accompany their aunts and mothers. So they learn even the simple processes of reef fishing much later than do the boys. They are kept at the baby-tending, errand-running stage until they are old enough and robust enough to work on the plantations and carry foodstuffs down to the village.   (11)

A girl is given these more strenuous tasks near the age of puberty, but it is purely a question of her physical size and ability to take responsibility, rather than of her physical maturity. Before this time she has occasionally accompanied the older members of the family to the plantations if they were willing to take the babies along also. But once there, while her brothers and cousins are collecting cocoanuts and roving happily about in the bush, she has again to chase and shepherd and pacify the ubiquitous babies.   (12)

As soon as the girls are strong enough to carry heavy loads, it pays the family to shift the responsibility for the little children to the younger girls and the adolescent girls are released from baby-tending. It may be said with some justice that the worst period of their lives is over. Never again will they be so incessantly at the beck and call of their elders, never again so tyrannised over by two-year-old tyrants. All the irritating, detailed routine of

housekeeping, which in our civilisation is accused of warping the souls and
souring the tempers of grown women, is here performed by children under
fourteen years of age. A fire or a pipe to be kindled, a call for a drink, a
lamp to be lit, the baby's cry, the errand of the capricious adult—these
haunt them from morning until night. With the introduction of several
months a year of government schools these children are being taken out of
their homes for most of the day. This brings about a complete disorganisa-
tion of the native households which have no precedents for a manner of
life where mothers have to stay at home and take care of their children
and adults have to perform small routine tasks and run errands.   (13)

Before their release from baby-tending the little girls have a very limited knowledge of any of the more complicated techniques. Some of them
can do the simpler work in preparing food for cooking, such as skinning bananas, grating cocoanuts, or scraping taro. A few of them can weave the
simple carrying basket. But now they must learn to weave all their own
baskets for carrying supplies; learn to select taro leaves of the right age for
cooking, to dig only mature taro. In the cook-house they learn to make *palu-
sami*, to grate the cocoanut meat, season it with hot stones, mix it with sea
water and strain out the husks, pour this milky mixture into a properly made
little container of taro leaves from which the aromatic stem has been
scorched off, wrap these in a breadfruit leaf and fasten the stem tightly to
make a durable cooking jacket. They must learn to lace a large fish into a
palm leaf, or roll a bundle of small fish in a breadfruit leaf; to select the
right kind of leaves for stuffing a pig, to judge when the food in the oven
of small heated stones is thoroughly baked. Theoretically the bulk of the
cooking is done by the boys and where a girl has to do the heavier work, it
is a matter for comment: "Poor Losa, there are no boys in her house and
always she must make the oven." But the girls always help and often do a
great part of the work.   (14)

Once they are regarded as individuals who can devote a long period of
time to some consecutive activity, girls are sent on long fishing expeditions.
They learn to weave fish baskets, to gather and arrange the bundles of
fagots used in torch-light fishing, to tickle a devil fish until it comes out of
its hole and climbs obediently upon the waiting stick, appropriately dubbed
a "come hither stick"; to string the great rose-coloured jellyfish, *lole*, a name
which Samoan children give to candy also, on a long string of hibiscus bark,
tipped with a palm leaf rib for a needle; to know good fish from bad fish,
fish that are in season from fish which are dangerous at some particular time
of the year; and never to take two octopuses, found paired on a rock, lest
bad luck come upon the witless fisher.   (15)

Before this time their knowledge of plants and trees is mainly a play
one, the pandanus provides them with seeds for necklaces, the palm tree
with leaves to weave balls; the banana tree gives leaves for umbrellas and

half a leaf to shred into a stringy "choker"; cocoanut shells cut in half, with cinet strings attached, make a species of stilt; the blossoms of the *Pua* tree can be sewed into beautiful necklaces. Now they must learn to recognise these trees and plants for more serious purposes; they must learn when the pandanus leaves are ready for the cutting and how to cut the long leaves with one sure quick stroke; they must distinguish between the three kinds of pandanus used for different grades of mats. The pretty orange seeds which made such attractive and also edible necklaces must now be gathered as paint brushes for ornamenting bark cloth. Banana leaves are gathered to protect the woven platters, to wrap up puddings for the oven, to bank the steaming oven full of food. Banana bark must be stripped at just the right point to yield the even, pliant, black strips, needed to ornament mats and baskets. Bananas themselves must be distinguished as to those which are ripe for burying, or the golden curved banana ready for eating, or bananas ready to be sun-dried for making fruit-cake rolls. Hibiscus bark can no longer be torn off at random to give a raffia-like string for a handful of shells; long journeys must be made inland to select bark of the right quality for use in weaving.   (16)

In the house the girl's principal task is to learn to weave. She has to master several different techniques. First, she learns to weave palm branches where the central rib of the leaf serves as a rim to her basket or an edge to her mat and where the leaflets are already arranged for weaving. From palm leaves she first learns to weave a carrying basket, made of half a leaf, by plaiting the leaflets together and curving the rib into a rim. Then she learns to weave the Venetian blinds which hang between the house posts, by laying one-half leaf upon another and plaiting the leaflets together. More difficult are the floor mats, woven of four great palm leaves, and the food platters with their intricate designs. There are also fans to make, simple two-strand weaves which she learns to make quite well, more elaborate twined ones which are the prerogative of older and more skilled weavers. Usually some older woman in the household trains a girl to weave and sees to it that she makes at least one of each kind of article, but she is only called upon to produce in quantity the simpler things, like the Venetian blinds. From the pandanus she learns to weave the common floor mats, one or two types of the more elaborate bed mats, and then, when she is thirteen or fourteen, she begins her first fine mat. The fine mat represents the high point of Samoan weaving virtuosity. Woven of the finest quality of pandanus which has been soaked and baked and scraped to a golden whiteness and paper-like thinness, of strands a sixteenth of an inch in width, these mats take a year or two years to weave and are as soft and pliable as linen. They form the unit of value, and must always be included in the dowry of the bride. Girls seldom finish a fine mat until they are nineteen or twenty, but the mat has been started, and, wrapped up in a coarser one, it rests among the rafters, a testimony to the girl's industry and manual skill. She learns the rudiments of bark cloth making; she can select and cut the paper mulberry wands, peel off the bark, beat it after it has been scraped by more expert hands. The patterning of the cloth with a pattern board or by free hand drawing is left for the more experienced adult.   (17)

Throughout this more or less systematic period of education, the girls maintain a very nice balance between a reputation for the necessary minimum of knowledge and a virtuosity which would make too heavy demands. A girl's chances of marriage are badly damaged if it gets about the village that she is lazy and inept in domestic tasks. But after these first stages have been completed the girl marks time technically for three or four years. She does the routine weaving, especially of the Venetian blinds and carrying baskets. She helps with the plantation work and the cooking, she weaves a very little on her fine mat. But she thrusts virtuosity away from her as she thrusts away every other sort of responsibility with the invariable comment, "Laititi a'u" ("I am but young"). All of her interest is expended on clandestine sex adventures, and she is content to do routine tasks as, to a certain extent, her brother is also.   (18)

But the seventeen-year-old boy is not left passively to his own devices. He has learned the rudiments of fishing, he can take a dug-out canoe over the reef safely, or manage the stern paddle in a bonito boat. He can plant taro or transplant cocoanut, husk cocoanuts on a stake and cut the meat out with one deft quick turn of the knife. Now at seventeen or eighteen he is thrust into the *Aumaga*, the society of the young men and the older men without titles, the group that is called, not in euphuism but in sober fact, "the strength of the village." Here he is badgered into efficiency by rivalry, precept and example. The older chiefs who supervise the activities of the *Aumaga* gaze equally sternly upon any backslidings and upon any undue precocity. The prestige of his group is ever being called into account by the *Aumaga* of the neighbouring villages. His fellows ridicule and persecute the boy who fails to appear when any group activity is on foot, whether work for the village on the plantations, or fishing, or cooking for the chiefs, or play in the form of a ceremonial call upon some visiting maiden. Furthermore, the youth is given much more stimulus to learn and also a greater variety of occupations are open to him. There is no specialisation among women, except in medicine and mid-wifery, both the prerogatives of very old women who teach their arts to their middle-aged daughters and nieces. The only other vocation is that of the wife of an official orator, and no girl will prepare herself for his one type of marriage which demands special knowledge, for she has no guarantee that she will marry a man of this class.
                          (19)

For the boy it is different. He hopes that some day he will hold a *matai* name, a name which will make him a member of the *Fono*, the assembly of headmen, which will give him a right to drink kava with chiefs, to work with chiefs rather than with the young men, to sit inside the house, even though his new title is only of "between the posts" rank, and not of enough importance to give him a right to a post for his back. But very seldom is he absolutely assured of getting such a name. Each family holds several of these titles which they confer upon the most promising youths in the whole family connection. He has many rivals. They also are in the *Aumaga*. He must always pit himself against them in the group activities. There are also several types of activities in one of which he must specialise. He must become a house-builder, a fisherman, an orator or a wood carver. Proficiency in some technique must set him off a little from his fellows. Fishing prowess means immediate rewards in the shape of food gifts to offer to his sweetheart; without such gifts his advances will be scorned. Skill in house-building means wealth and status, for a young man who is a skilled carpenter must be treated as courteously as a chief and addressed with the chief's language, the elaborate set of honorific words used to people of rank. And with this goes the continual demand that he should not be too efficient, too outstanding, too precocious. He must never excel his fellows by more than a little. He must neither arouse their hatred nor the disapproval of his elders who are far readier to encourage and excuse the laggard than to condone precocity. And at the same time he shares his sister's reluctance to accept responsibility, and if he should excel gently, not too obviously, he has good chances of being made a chief. If he is sufficiently talented, the *Fono* itself may deliberate, search out a vacant title to confer upon him and call him in that he may sit with the old men and learn wisdom. And yet so well recognised is the unwillingness of the young men to respond to this honour, that the provision is always made, "And if the young man runs away, then never shall he be made a chief, but always he must sit outside the house with the young men, preparing and serving the food of the *matais* with whom he may not sit in the *Fono*." Still more pertinent are the chances of his relationship group bestowing a *matai* name upon the gifted young man. And a *matai* he wishes to be, some day, some far-off day when his limbs have lost a little of their suppleness and his heart the love of fun and of dancing. As one chief of twenty-seven told me: "I have been a chief only four years and look, my hair is grey, although in Samoa grey hair comes very slowly, not in youth, as it comes to the white man. But always, I must act as if I were old. I must walk gravely and with a measured step. I may not dance except upon most solemn occasions, neither may I play games with the young men. Old men of sixty are my companions and watch my every word, lest I make a mistake. Thirty-one people live in my household. For them I must plan, I must find them food and clothing, settle their disputes, arrange their marriages. There is no one in my whole family who dares to scold me or even to address me familiarly by my first name. It is hard to be so young and yet to be a chief." And the old men shake their heads and agree that it is unseemly for one to be a chief so young. (20)

The operation of natural ambition is further vitiated by the fact that the young man who is made a *matai* will not be the greatest among his former associates, but the youngest and greenest member of the *Fono*. And no longer may he associate familiarly with his old companions; a *matai* must associate only with *matais*, must work beside them in the bush and sit and talk quietly with them in the evening. (21)

And so the boy is faced by a far more difficult dilemma than the girl. He dislikes responsibility, but he wishes to excel in his group; skill will hasten the day when he is made a chief, yet he receives censure and ridicule if he slackens his efforts; but he will be scolded if he proceeds too rapidly; yet if he would win a sweetheart, he must have prestige among his fellows. And conversely, his social prestige is increased by his amorous exploits. (22)

So while the girl rests upon her "pass" proficiency, the boy is spurred to greater efforts. A boy is shy of a girl who does not have these proofs of efficiency and is known to be stupid and unskilled; he is afraid he may come to want to marry her. Marrying a girl without proficiency would be a most imprudent step and involve an endless amount of wrangling with his family. So the girl who is notoriously inept must take her lovers from among the casual, the jaded, and the married who are no longer afraid that their senses will betray them into an imprudent marriage. (23)

But the seventeen-year-old girl does not wish to marry—not yet. It is better to live as a girl with no responsibility, and a rich variety of emotional experience. This is the best period of her life. There are as many beneath her whom she may bully as there are others above her to tyrannise over her. What she loses in prestige, she gains in freedom. She has very little baby-tending to do. Her eyes do not ache from weaving nor does her back break from bending all day over the tapa board. The long expeditions after fish and food and weaving materials give ample opportunities for rendezvous. Proficiency would mean more work, more confining work, and earlier marriage, and marriage is the inevitable to be deferred as long as possible. (24)

Ruth Benedict

(1887–1948)

RUTH BENEDICT was a member of the group of bright young scholars who were attracted to the study of anthropology at Columbia University in the early 1920's. She was appointed to the rank of full professor at Columbia in the year of her death. Her book Patterns of Culture *has introduced more general readers to some of the conclusions of anthropological study than any other book ever published in America.*

■ *The Diversity of Cultures*

A CHIEF of the Digger Indians, as the Californians call them, talked to me a great deal about the ways of his people in the old days. He was a Christian and a leader among his people in the planting of peaches and apricots on irrigated land, but when he talked of the shamans who had transformed themselves into bears before his eyes in the bear dance, his hands trembled and his voice broke with excitement. It was an incomparable thing, the power his people had had in the old days. He liked best to talk of the desert foods they had eaten. He brought each uprooted plant lovingly and with an unfailing sense of its importance. In those days his people had eaten 'the health of the desert,' he said, and knew nothing of the insides of tin cans and the things for sale at butcher shops. It was such innovations that had degraded them in these latter days. (1)

One day, without transition, Ramon broke in upon his descriptions of grinding mesquite and preparing acorn soup. 'In the beginning,' he said, 'God gave to every people a cup, a cup of clay, and from this cup they drank their life.' I do not know whether the figure occurred in some traditional ritual of his people that I never found, or whether it was his own imagery. It is hard to imagine that he had heard it from the whites he had known at Banning; they were not given to discussing the ethos of different peoples. At any rate, in the mind of this humble Indian the figure of speech was clear and full of meaning. 'They all dipped in the water,' he continued, 'but their cups were different. Our cup is broken now. It has passed away.'   (2)

Our cup is broken. Those things that had given significance to the life of his people, the domestic rituals of eating, the obligations of the economic system, the succession of ceremonials in the villages, possession in the bear dance, their standards of right and wrong—these were gone, and with them the shape and meaning of their life. The old man was still vigorous and a leader in relationships with the whites. He did not mean that there was any question of the extinction of the people. But he had in mind the loss of something that had value equal to that of life itself, the whole fabric of his people's standards and beliefs. There were other cups of living left, and they held perhaps the same water, but the loss was irreparable. It was no matter of tinkering with an addition here, lopping off something there. The modelling had been fundamental, it was somehow all of a piece. It had been their own.   (3)

Ramon had had personal experience of the matter of which he spoke. He straddled two cultures whose values and ways of thought were incommensurable. It is a hard fate. In Western civilization our experiences have been different. We are bred to one cosmopolitan culture, and our social sciences, our psychology, and our theology persistently ignore the truth expressed in Ramon's figure.   (4)

The course of life and the pressure of environment, not to speak of the fertility of human imagination, provide an incredible number of possible leads, all of which, it appears, may serve a society to live by. There are the schemes of ownership, with the social hierarchy that may be associated with possessions; there are material things and their elaborate technology; there are all the facets of sex life, parenthood and post-parenthood; there are the guilds or cults which may give structure to the society; there is economic exchange; there are the gods and supernatural sanctions. Each one of these and many more may be followed out with a cultural and ceremonial elaboration which monopolizes the cultural energy and leaves small surplus for the building of other traits. Aspects of life that seem to us most important have been passed over with small regard by peoples whose culture, oriented in another direction, has been far from poor. Or the same trait may be so greatly elaborated that we reckon it as fantastic.   (5)

It is in cultural life as it is in speech; selection is the prime necessity. The numbers of sounds that can be produced by our vocal cords and our oral and nasal cavities are practically unlimited. The three or four dozen of the English language are a selection which coincides not even with those of such closely related dialects as German and French. The total that are used in different languages of the world no one has even dared to estimate. But each language must make its selection and abide by it on pain of not being intelligible at all. A language that used even a few hundreds of the possible—and actually recorded—phonetic elements could not be used for communication. On the other hand a great deal of our misunderstanding of languages unrelated to our own has arisen from our attempts to refer alien phonetic systems back to ours as a point of reference. We recognize only one *k*. If other people have five *k* sounds placed in different positions in the throat and mouth, distinctions of vocabulary and of syntax that depend on these differences are impossible to us until we master them. We have a *d* and an *n*. They may have an intermediate sound which, if we fail to identify it, we write now *d* and now *n*, introducing distinctions which do not exist. The elementary prerequisite of linguistic analysis is a consciousness of these incredibly numerous available sounds from which each language makes its own selections.   (6)

In culture too we must imagine a great arc on which are ranged the possible interests provided either by the human age-cycle or by the environment or by man's various activities. A culture that capitalized even a considerable proportion of these would be as unintelligible as a language that used all the clicks, all the glottal stops, all the labials, dentals, sibilants, and gutturals from voiceless to voiced and from oral to nasal. Its identity as a culture depends upon the selection of some segments of this arc. Every human society everywhere has made such selection in its cultural institutions. Each from the point of view of another ignores fundamentals and exploits irrelevancies. One culture hardly recognizes monetary values; another has made them fundamental in every field of behaviour. In one society technology is unbelievably slighted even in those aspects of life which seem necessary to ensure survival; in another, equally simple, technological achievements are complex and fitted with admirable nicety to the situation. One builds an enormous cultural superstructure upon adolescence, one upon death, one upon after-life.   (7)

The case of adolescence is particularly interesting, because it is in the limelight in our own civilization and because we have plentiful information from other cultures. In our own civilization a whole library of psychological studies has emphasized the inevitable unrest of the period of puberty. It is in our tradition a physiological state as definitely characterized by domestic explosions and rebellion as typhoid is marked by fever. There is no question of the facts. They are common in America. The question is rather of their inevitability.   (8)

The most casual survey of the ways in which different societies have handled adolescence makes one fact inescapable: even in those cultures which have made most of the trait, the age upon which they focus their attention varies over a great range of years. At the outset, therefore, it is clear that the so-called puberty institutions are a misnomer if we continue to think of biological puberty. The puberty they recognize is social, and the ceremonies are a recognition in some fashion or other of the child's new status of adulthood. This investiture with new occupations and obligations is in consequence as various and as culturally conditioned as the occupations and obligations themselves. If the sole honourable duty of manhood is conceived to be deeds of war, the investiture of the warrior is later and of a different sort from that in a society where adulthood gives chiefly the privilege of dancing in a representation of masked gods. In order to understand puberty institutions, we do not most need analyses of the necessary nature of *rites de passage;* we need rather to know what is identified in different cultures with the beginning of adulthood and their methods of admitting to the new status. Not biological puberty, but what adulthood means in that culture conditions the puberty ceremony.   (9)

Adulthood in central North America means warfare. Honour in it is the great goal of all men. The constantly recurring theme of the youth's coming-of-age, as also of preparation for the warpath at any age is a magic ritual for success in war. They torture not one another, but themselves: they cut strips of skin from their arms and legs, they strike off their fingers, they drag heavy weights pinned to their chest or leg muscles. Their reward is enhanced prowess in deeds of warfare.   (10)

In Australia, on the other hand, adulthood means participation in an exclusively male cult whose fundamental trait is the exclusion of women. Any woman is put to death if she so much as hears the sound of the bull-roarer at the ceremonies, and she must never know of the rites. Puberty ceremonies are elaborate and symbolic repudiations of the bonds with the female sex; the men are symbolically made self-sufficient and the wholly responsible element of the community. To attain this end they use drastic sexual rites and bestow supernatural guaranties.   (11)

The clear physiological facts of adolescence, therefore, are first socially interpreted even where they are stressed. But a survey of puberty institutions makes clear a further fact: puberty is physiologically a different matter in the life-cycle of the male and the female. If cultural emphasis followed the physiological emphasis, girls' ceremonies would be more marked than boys'; but it is not so. The ceremonies emphasize a social fact: the adult prerogatives of men are more far-reaching in every culture than women's, and consequently, as in the above instances, it is more common for societies to take note of this period in boys than in girls.   (12)

Girls' and boys' puberty, however, may be socially celebrated in the same tribe in identical ways. Where, as in the interior of British Columbia, adolescent rites are a magical training for all occupations, girls are included on the same terms as boys. Boys roll stones down mountains and beat them to the bottom to be swift of foot, or throw gambling-sticks to be lucky in gambling; girls carry water from distant springs, or drop stones down inside their dresses that their children may be born as easily as the pebble drops to the ground.   (13)

In such a tribe as the Nandi of the lake region of East Africa, also, girls and boys share an even-handed puberty rite, though, because of the man's dominant rôle in the culture, his boyhood training period is more stressed than the woman's. Here adolescent rites are an ordeal inflicted by those already admitted to adult status upon those they are now forced to admit. They require of them the most complete stoicism in the face of ingenious tortures associated with circumcision. The rites for the two sexes are separate, but they follow the same pattern. In both the novices wear for the ceremony the clothing of their sweethearts. During the operation their faces are watched for any twinge of pain, and the reward of bravery is given with great rejoicing by the lover, who runs forward to receive back some of his adornments. For both the girl and the boy the rites mark their *entrée* into a new sex status: the boy is now a warrior and may take a sweetheart, the girl is marriageable. The adolescent tests are for both a pre-marital ordeal in which the palm is awarded by their lovers.   (14)

Puberty rites may also be built upon the facts of girls' puberty and admit of no extension to boys. One of the most naïve of these is the institution of the fatting-house for girls in central Africa. In the region where feminine beauty is all but identified with obesity, the girl at puberty is segregated, sometimes for years, fed with sweet and fatty foods, allowed no activity, and her body rubbed assiduously with oils. She is taught during this time her future duties, and her seclusion ends with a parade of her corpulence that is followed by her marriage to her proud bridegroom. It is not regarded as necessary for the man to achieve pulchritude before marriage in a similar fashion.   (15)

The usual ideas around which girls' puberty institutions are centered, and which are not readily extended to boys', are those concerned with menstruation. The uncleanness of the menstruating woman is a very widespread idea, and in a few regions first menstruation has been made the focus of all the associated attitudes. Puberty rites in these cases are of a thoroughly different character from any of which we have spoken. Among the Carrier Indians of British Columbia, the fear and horror of a girl's puberty was at its height. Her three or four years of seclusion was called 'the burying alive,' and she lived for all that time alone in the wilderness, in a hut of branches far from all beaten trails. She was a threat to any person who might so much as catch a glimpse of her, and her mere footstep defiled a path or a river. She was covered with a great headdress of tanned skin that shrouded her face and breasts and fell to the ground behind. Her arms and legs were loaded with sinew bands to protect her from the evil spirit

with which she was filled. She was herself in danger and she was a source
of danger to everybody else.   (16)

Girls' puberty ceremonies built upon ideas associated with the menses
are readily convertible into what is, from the point of view of the individual
concerned, exactly opposite behaviour. There are always two possible
aspects to the sacred: it may be a source of peril or it may be a source of
blessing. In some tribes the first menses of girls are a potent supernatural
blessing. Among the Apaches I have seen the priests themselves pass on
their knees before the row of solemn little girls to receive from them the
blessing of their touch. All the babies and the old people come also of
necessity to have illness removed from them. The adolescent girls are not
segregated as sources of danger, but court is paid to them as to direct
sources of supernatural blessing. Since the ideas that underlie puberty rites
for girls, both among the Carrier and among the Apache, are founded on
beliefs concerning menstruation, they are not extended to boys, and boys'
puberty is marked instead, and lightly, with simple tests and proofs of
manhood.   (17)

The adolescent behaviour, therefore, even of girls was not dictated by
some physiological characteristic of the period itself, but rather by marital
or magic requirements socially connected with it. These beliefs made adolescence in one tribe serenely religious and beneficent, and in another so dangerously unclean that the child had to cry out in warning that others might
avoid her in the woods. The adolescence of girls may equally, as we have
seen, be a theme which a culture does not institutionalize. Even where, as
in most of Australia, boys' adolescence is given elaborate treatment, it may
be that the rites are an induction into the status of manhood and male
participation in tribal matters, and female adolescence passes without any
kind of formal recognition.   (18)

These facts, however, still leave the fundamental question unanswered.
Do not all cultures have to cope with the natural turbulence of this period,
even though it may not be given institutional expression? Dr. Mead has
studied this question in Samoa. There the girl's life passes through well-
marked periods. Her first years out of baby-hood are passed in small neighbourhood gangs of age mates from which the little boys are strictly excluded. The corner of the village to which she belongs is all-important,
and the little boys are traditional enemies. She has one duty, that of
baby-tending, but she takes the baby with her rather than stay home to
mind it, and her play is not seriously hampered. A couple of years before
puberty, when she grows strong enough to have more difficult tasks required of her and old enough to learn more skilled techniques, the little
girls' play group in which she grew up ceases to exist. She assumes woman's
dress and must contribute to the work of the household. It is an uninteresting period of life to her and quite without turmoil. Puberty brings no
change at all.   (19)

A few years after she has come of age, she will begin the pleasant years of casual and irresponsible love affairs that she will prolong as far as possible into the period when marriage is already considered fitting. Puberty itself is marked by no social recognition, no change of attitude or of expectancy. Her pre-adolescent shyness is supposed to remain unchanged for a couple of years. The girl's life in Samoa is blocked out by other considerations than those of physiological sex maturity, and puberty falls in a particularly unstressed and peaceful period during which no adolescent conflicts manifest themselves. Adolescence, therefore, may not only be culturally passed over without ceremonial; it may also be without importance in the emotional life of the child and in the attitude of the village toward her. (20)

Warfare is another social theme that may or may not be used in any culture. Where war is made much of, it may be with contrasting objectives, with contrasting organization in relation to the state, and with contrasting sanctions. War may be, as it was among the Aztecs, a way of getting captives for the religious sacrifices. Since the Spaniards fought to kill, according to Aztec standards they broke the rules of the game. The Aztecs fell back in dismay and Cortez walked as victor into the capital. (21)

There are even quainter notions, from our standpoint, associated with warfare in different parts of the world. For our purposes it is sufficient to notice those regions where organized resort to mutual slaughter never occurs between social groups. Only our familiarity with war makes it intelligible that a state of warfare should alternate with a state of peace in one tribe's dealings with another. The idea is quite common over the world, of course. But on the one hand it is impossible for certain peoples to conceive the possibility of a state of peace, which in their notion would be equivalent to admitting enemy tribes to the category of human beings, which by definition they are not even though the excluded tribe may be of their own race and culture. (22)

On the other hand, it may be just as impossible for a people to conceive of the possibility of a state of war. Rasmussen tells of the blankness with which the Eskimo met his exposition of our custom. Eskimos very well understand the act of killing a man. If he is in your way, you cast up your estimate of your own strength, and if you are ready to take it upon yourself, you kill him. If you are strong, there is no social retribution. But the idea of an Eskimo village going out against another Eskimo village in battle array or a tribe against a tribe, or even of another village being fair game in ambush warfare, is alien to them. All killing comes under one head, and is not separated, as ours is, into categories, the one meritorious, the other a capital offence. (23)

I myself tried to talk of warfare to the Mission Indian of California, but it was impossible. Their misunderstanding of warfare was abysmal. They did not have the basis in their own culture upon which the idea could

exist, and their attempts to reason it out reduced the great wars to which
we are able to dedicate ourselves with moral fervour to the level of alley
brawls. They did not happen to have a cultural pattern that distinguished
between them.   (24)

War is, we have been forced to admit even in the face of its huge place
in our own civilization, an asocial trait. In the chaos following the World
War all the wartime arguments that expounded its fostering of courage, of
altruism, of spiritual values, give out a false and offensive ring. War in our
own civilization is as good an illustration as one can take of the destructive
lengths to which the development of a culturally selected trait may go. If
we justify war, it is because all peoples always justify the traits of which
they find themselves possessed, not because war will bear an objective
examination of its merits.   (25)

Warfare is not an isolated case. From every part of the world and from
all levels of cultural complexity it is possible to illustrate the overweening
and finally often the asocial elaboration of a cultural trait. Those cases are
clearest where, as in dietary or mating regulations, for example, traditional
usage runs counter to biological drives. Social organization, in anthropology,
has a quite specialized meaning owing to the unanimity of all human societies in stressing relationship groups within which marriage is forbidden.
No known people regard all women as possible mates. This is not in an
effort, as is so often supposed, to prevent inbreeding in our sense, for over
great parts of the world it is an own cousin, often the daughter of one's
mother's brother, who is the predestined spouse. The relatives to whom
the prohibition refers differ utterly among different peoples, but all human
societies are alike in placing a restriction. No human idea has received
more constant and complex elaboration in culture than this of incest. The
incest groups are often the most important functioning units of the tribe,
and the duties of every individual in relation to any other are defined by
their relative positions in these groups. These groups function as units in
religious ceremonials and in cycles of economic exchange, and it is impossible to exaggerate the importance of the rôle they have played in social
history.   (26)

Some areas handle the incest tabu with moderation. In spite of the
restrictions there may be a considerable number of women available for a
man to marry. In others the group that is tabu has been extended by a
social fiction to include vast numbers of individuals who have no traceable
ancestors in common, and choice of a mate is in consequence excessively
limited. This social fiction receives unequivocal expression in the terms of
relationship which are used. Instead of distinguishing lineal from collateral kin as we do in the distinction between father and uncle, brother
and cousin, one term means literally 'man of my father's group (relationship, locality, etc.) of his generation,' not distinguishing between direct

and collateral lines, but making other distinctions that are foreign to us. Certain tribes of eastern Australia use an extreme form of this so-called classificatory kinship system. Those whom they call brothers and sisters are all those of their generation with whom they recognize any relationship. There is no cousin category or anything that corresponds to it; all relatives of one's own generation are one's brothers and sisters.   (27)

This manner of reckoning relationship is not uncommon in the world, but Australia has in addition an unparalleled horror of sister marriage and an unparalleled development of exogamous restrictions. So the Kurnai, with their extreme classificatory relationship system, feel the Australian horror of sex relationship with all their 'sisters,' that is, women of their own generation who are in any way related to them. Besides this, the Kurnai have strict locality rules in the choice of a mate. Sometimes two localities, out of the fifteen or sixteen of which the tribe is composed, must exchange women, and can have no mates in any other group. Sometimes there is a group of two or three localities that may exchange with two or three others. Still further, as in all Australia, the old men are a privileged group, and their prerogatives extend to marrying the young and attractive girls. The consequence of these rules is, of course, that in all the local group which must by absolute prescription furnish a young man with his wife, there is no girl who is not touched by one of these tabus. Either she is one of those who through relationship with his mother is his 'sister,' or she is already bargained for by an old man, or for some lesser reason she is forbidden to him.   (28)

That does not bring the Kurnai to reformulate their exogamous rules. They insist upon them with every show of violence. Therefore, the only way they are usually able to marry is by flying violently in the face of the regulations. They elope. As soon as the village knows that an elopement has occurred, it sets out in pursuit, and if the couple are caught the two are killed. It does not matter that possibly all of the pursuers were married by elopement in the same fashion. Moral indignation runs high. There is, however, an island traditionally recognized as a safe haven, and if the couple can reach it and remain away till the birth of a child, they are received again with blows, it is true, but they may defend themselves. After they have run the gauntlet and been given their drubbing, they take up the status of married people in the tribe.   (29)

The Kurnai meet their cultural dilemma typically enough. They have extended and complicated a particular aspect of behaviour until it is a social liability. They must either modify it, or get by with a subterfuge. And they use the subterfuge. They avoid extinction, and they maintain their ethics without acknowledged revision. This manner of dealing with the *mores* has lost nothing in the progress of civilization. The older generation of our own civilization similarly maintained monogamy and supported prostitution, and the panegyrics of monogamy were never so fervent as in the great days of the red-light districts. Societies have always justified favourite traditional forms. When these traits get out of hand and some form of supplementary behaviour is called in, lip service is given as readily to the traditional form as if the supplementary behaviour did not exist. (30)

Such a bird's-eye survey of human cultural forms makes clear several common misconceptions. In the first place, the institutions that human cultures build up upon the hints presented by the environment or by man's physical necessities do not keep as close to the original impulse as we easily imagine. These hints are, in reality, mere rough sketches, a list of bare facts. They are pin-point potentialities, and the elaboration that takes place around them is dictated by many alien considerations. Warfare is not the expression of the instinct of pugnacity. Man's pugnacity is so small a hint in the human equipment that it may not be given any expression in inter-tribal relations. When it is institutionalized, the form it takes follows other grooves of thought than those implied in the original impulse. Pugnacity is no more than the touch to the ball of custom, a touch also that may be withheld.   (31)

Such a view of cultural processes calls for a recasting of many of our current arguments upholding our traditional institutions. These arguments are usually based on the impossibility of man's functioning without these particular traditional forms. Even very special traits come in for this kind of validation, such as the particular form of economic drive that arises under our particular system of property ownership. This is a remarkably special motivation and there are evidences that even in our generation it is being strongly modified. At any rate, we do not have to confuse the issue by discussing it as if it were a matter of biological survival values. Self-support is a motive our civilization has capitalized. If our economic structure changes so that this motive is no longer so potent a drive as it was in the era of the great frontier and expanding industrialism, there are many other motives that would be appropriate to a changed economic organization. Every culture, every era, exploits some few out of a great number of possibilities. Changes may be very disquieting, and involve great losses, but this is due to the difficulty of change itself, not to the fact that our age and country has hit upon the one possible motivation under which human life can be conducted. Change, we must remember, with all its difficulties, is inescapable. Our fears over even very minor shifts in custom are usually quite beside the point. Civilizations might change far more radically than any human authority has ever had the will or the imagination to change them, and still be completely workable. The minor changes that occasion so much denunciation today, such as the increase of divorce, the growing secularization in our cities, the prevalence of the petting party, and many more, could be taken up quite readily into a slightly different pattern of culture. Becoming traditional, they would be given the same richness of content, the same importance and value, that the older patterns had in other generations.   (32)

The truth of the matter is rather that the possible human institutions and motives are legion, on every plane of cultural simplicity or complexity, and that wisdom consists in a greatly increased tolerance toward their divergencies. No man can thoroughly participate in any culture unless he has been brought up and has lived according to its forms, but he can grant to other cultures the same significance to their participants which he recognizes in his own.   (33)

II

The diversity of culture results not only from the ease with which societies elaborate or reject possible aspects of existence. It is due even more to a complex interweaving of cultural traits. The final form of any traditional institution, as we have just said, goes far beyond the original human impulse. In great measure this final form depends upon the way in which the trait has merged with other traits from different fields of experience.
                                                                        (34)

A widespread trait may be saturated with religious beliefs among one people and function as an important aspect of their religion. In another area it may be wholly a matter of economic transfer and be therefore an aspect of their monetary arrangements. The possibilities are endless and the adjustments are often bizarre. The nature of the trait will be quite different in the different areas according to the elements with which it has combined.   (35)

It is important to make this process clear to ourselves because otherwise we fall easily into the temptation to generalize into a sociological law the results of a local merging of traits, or we assume their union to be a universal phenomenon. The great period of European plastic art was religiously motivated. Art pictured and made common property the religious scenes and dogmas which were fundamental in the outlook of that period. Modern European æsthetics would have been quite different if mediæval art had been purely decorative and had not made common cause with religion.
                                                                        (36)

As a matter of history great developments in art have often been remarkably separate from religious motivation and use. Art may be kept definitely apart from religion even where both are highly developed. In the pueblos of the Southwest of the United States, art-forms in pottery and textiles command the respect of the artist in any culture, but their sacred bowls carried by the priests or set out on the altars are shoddy and the decorations crude and unstylized. Museums have been known to throw out

Southwest religious objects because they were so far below the traditional standard of workmanship. 'We have to put a frog there,' the Zuñi
Indians say, meaning that the religious exigencies eliminate any need of
artistry. This separation between art and religion is not a unique trait of the
Pueblos. Tribes of South America and of Siberia make the same distinction,
though they motivate it in various ways. They do not use their artistic skill
in the service of religion. Instead, therefore, of finding the sources of art
in a locally important subject matter, religion, as older critics of art have
sometimes done, we need rather to explore the extent to which these two
can mutually interpenetrate, and the consequences of such merging for
both art and religion.   (37)

The interpenetration of different fields of experience, and the consequent modification of both of them, can be shown from all phases of
existence: economics, sex relations, folklore, material culture, and religion.
The process can be illustrated in one of the widespread religious traits of
the North American Indians. Up and down the continent, in every culture
area except that of the pueblos of the Southwest, supernatural power was
obtained in a dream or vision. Success in life, according to their beliefs,
was due to personal contact with the supernatural. Each man's vision gave
him power for his lifetime, and in some tribes he was constantly renewing
his personal relationship with the spirits by seeking further visions. Whatever he saw, an animal or a star, a plant or a supernatural being, adopted
him as a personal protégé, and he could call upon him in need. He had
duties to perform for his visionary patron, gifts to give him and obligations of all kinds. In return the spirit gave him the specific powers he promised him in his vision.   (38)

In every great region of North America this guardian spirit complex
took different form according to the other traits of the culture with which
it was most closely associated. In the plateaus of British Columbia it
merged with the adolescent ceremonies we have just spoken of. Both boys
and girls, among these tribes, went out into the mountains at adolescence
for a magic training. Puberty ceremonies have a wide distribution up and
down the Pacific Coast, and over most of this region they are quite distinct
from the guardian spirit practices. But in British Columbia they were
merged. The climax of the magic adolescent training for boys was the
acquisition of a guardian spirit who by its gifts dictated the lifetime profession of the young man. He became a warrior, a shaman, a hunter, or a
gambler according to the supernatural visitant. Girls also received guardian
spirits representing their domestic duties. So strongly is the guardian spirit
experience among these peoples moulded by its association with the ceremonial of adolescence that anthropologists who know this region have
argued that the entire vision complex of the American Indians had its
origin in puberty rites. But the two are not genetically connected. They are

locally merged, and in the merging both traits have taken special and
characteristic forms.   (39)

In other parts of the continent, the guardian spirit is not sought at
puberty, nor by all the youths of the tribe. Consequently the complex
has in these cultures no kind of relationship with puberty rites even when
any such exist. On the southern plains it is adult men who must acquire
mystic sanctions. The vision complex merged with a trait very different
from puberty rites. The Osage are organized in kinship groups in which
descent is traced through the father and disregards the mother's line. These
clan groups have a common inheritance of supernatural blessing. The legend of each clan tells how its ancestor sought a vision, and was blessed by
the animal whose name the clan has inherited. The ancestor of the mussel
clan sought seven times, with the tears running down his face, a supernatural blessing. At last he met the mussel and spoke to it, saying:

> O grandfather,
> The little ones have nothing of which to make their bodies.

Thereupon the mussel answered him:

> You say the little ones have nothing of which to make their
>   bodies.
> Let the little ones make of me their bodies.
> When the little ones make of me their bodies,
> They shall always live to see old age.
> Behold the wrinkles upon my skin [shell]
> Which I have made to be the means of reaching old age.
> When the little ones make of me their bodies
> They shall always live to see the signs of old age upon their skins.
> The seven bends of the river [of life]
> I pass successfully.
> And in my travels the gods themselves have not the power to see
>   the trail that I make.
> When the little ones make of me their bodies
> No one, not even the gods, shall be able to see the trail they
>   make.   (40)

Among these people all the familiar elements of the vision quest are
present, but it was attained by a first ancestor of the clan, and its blessings
are inherited by a blood-relationship group.   (41)

This situation among the Osage presents one of the fullest pictures in
the world of totemism, that close mingling of social organization and of
religious veneration for the ancestor. Totemism is described from all parts
of the world, and anthropologists have argued that the clan totem originated in the 'personal totem,' or guardian spirit. But the situation is exactly

analogous to that of the plateaus of British Columbia where the vision quest merged with the adolescent rites, only that here it has merged with hereditary privileges of the clan. So strong has this new association become that a vision is no longer thought to give a man power automatically. The blessings of the vision are attained only by inheritance, and among the Osage long chants have grown up describing the ancestor's encounters, and detailing the blessings which his descendants may claim in consequence.   (42)

In both these cases it is not only the vision complex which receives a different character in different regions as it merges with puberty rites or clan organization. The adolescence ceremonies and the social organization are equally coloured by the interweaving of the vision quest. The interaction is mutual. The vision complex, the puberty rites, the clan organization, and many other traits that enter also into close relationship with the vision, are strands which are braided in many combinations. The consequences of the different combinations that result from this intermingling of traits cannot be exaggerated. In both the regions of which we have just spoken, both where the religious experience was merged with puberty rites and where it was merged with clan organization, as a natural corollary of the associated practices all individuals of the tribe could receive power from the vision for success in any undertaking. Achievement in any occupation was credited to the individual's claim upon a vision experience. A successful gambler or a successful hunter drew his power from it just as a successful shaman did. According to their dogma all avenues of advancement were closed to those who had failed to obtain a supernatural patron. (43)

In California, however, the vision was the professional warrant of the shaman. It marked him as a person apart. It was just in this region, therefore, that the most aberrant aspects of this experience were developed. The vision was no longer a slight hallucination for which the stage could be set by fasting and torture and isolation. It was a trance experience which overtook the exceptionally unstable members of the community and especially the women. Among the Shasta it was the convention that only women were so blessed. The required experience was definitely cataleptic and came upon the novice after a preliminary dreaming had prepared the way. She fell senseless and rigid to the ground. When she came to herself, blood oozed from her mouth. All the ceremonies by which for years after she validated her call to be a shaman were further demonstrations of her liability to cataleptic seizures and were regarded as the cure by which her life was saved. In tribes like the Shasta not only the vision experience had changed its character to a violent seizure which differentiated religious practitioners from all others, but the character of the shamans was equally modified by the nature of the trance experience. They were definitely the

unstable members of the community. In this region contests between shamans took the form of dancing each other down, that is, of seeing which
one could withstand longest in a dance the cataleptic seizure which would
inevitably overtake them. Both the vision experience and shamanism had
been profoundly affected by the close relationship into which they had
entered. The merging of the two traits, no less than the merging of the
vision experience and puberty rites or clan organization, had drastically
modified both fields of behaviour. (44)

In the same way in our own civilization the separateness of the church
and of the marriage sanction is historically clear, yet the religious sacra-
ment of wedlock for centuries dictated developments both in sex behaviour
and in the church. The peculiar character of marriage during those centuries was due to the merging of two essentially unrelated cultural traits.
On the other hand, marriage has often been the means by which wealth
was traditionally transferred. In cultures where this is true, the close association of marriage with economic transfer may quite obliterate the fact
that marriage is fundamentally a matter of sexual and child-rearing adjustments. Marriage in each case must be understood in relation to other
traits to which it has become assimilated, and we should not run into the
mistake of thinking that 'marriage' can be understood in the two cases by
the same set of ideas. We must allow for the different components which
have been built up into the resulting trait. (45)

We greatly need the ability to analyze traits of our own cultural heritage into their several parts. Our discussions of the social order would gain
in clarity if we learned to understand in this way the complexity of even
our simplest behaviour. Racial differences and prestige prerogatives have
so merged among Anglo-Saxon peoples that we fail to separate biological racial matters from our most socially conditioned prejudices. Even
among nations as nearly related to the Anglo-Saxons as the Latin peoples,
such prejudices take different forms, so that, in Spanish-colonized countries
and in British colonies racial differences have not the same social significance. Christianity and the position of women, similarly, are historically
interrelated traits, and they have at different times interacted very differently. The present high position of women in Christian countries is no more
a 'result' of Christianity than was Origen's coupling of woman with the
deadly temptations. These interpenetrations of traits occur and disappear,
and the history of culture is in considerable degree a history of their nature
and fates and associations. But the genetic connection we so easily
see in a complex trait and our horror at any disturbance of its interrelation-
ships is largely illusory. The diversity of the possible combinations is endless, and adequate social orders can be built indiscriminately upon a great
variety of these foundations. (46)

Ralph Linton

(1893–1953)

*LINTON was a conspicuous pioneer in the early codification of anthropology
as a formal social science. His academic career was spent largely at the
University of Wisconsin; at Columbia University, where he was chairman
of the department; and at Yale, where he was Sterling Professor of Anthropology. He did extensive field work in archaeology and in ethnology
throughout the midwestern states, as well as in Guatemala, the Marquesas
Islands, Polynesia, Madagascar, and South Africa. His major works include*
The Study of Man, an Introduction *(1936)*, Acculturation in Seven American Indian Tribes *(1940), and* Cultural Background of Personality *(1945)*.

◼ *Race*

IT IS NATURAL that man should be intensely interested in the physical
characteristics of his own species, but the very strength of this interest is
likely to lead to a certain loss of perspective. The study of human varieties, i.e., races, is really a branch of zoölogy. Man is subject to exactly
the same biological laws as other mammals and owes his present variations
to the same evolutionary processes. If we are to understand the origins of
race and evaluate the importance of racial differences correctly, we must
try to forget that we are dealing with men and study our own species as
objectively as we would study any other. That so many students of physical
anthropology have failed to do this seems to be due mainly to historic
causes. This science seems to have had more difficulty in breaking with its
past than has any other of the natural sciences.   (1)
    Physical anthropology took shape as a distinct science during the later
eighteenth and early nineteenth centuries. It grew out of a combination of

anatomy and the systematic zoölogy of the period, and its early efforts were directed entirely toward the establishment of classifications of human varieties and the development of techniques of observation which would make more accurate classifications possible. In its inception it was a purely descriptive science only incidentally interested in the problem of racial origins and the dynamics of human variation. Although these problems could not be completely ignored, it disposed of them in summary fashion. Unfortunately, the early guesses on these points became dogmas which still have a strong influence on the thought of many workers in this field.

(2)

The first physical anthropologists were handicapped by a scarcity of material from outside Europe and by ignorance of the principles of heredity and a lack of any adequate techniques for distinguishing between pure and mixed strains. The material which they did have indicated the existence of a great number of human varieties, and these varieties offered such irregular combinations of physical traits that it was extremely difficult to find any satisfactory classification for them. A classification based on any one trait, such as head form, would be totally out of agreement with one based on some other trait such as skin color or hair texture. At this time the principles of evolution were just beginning to be enunciated but were not yet generally accepted. The first physical anthropologists still believed that every species and variety was the result of a separate act of creation and was therefore fixed and unchangeable. However, it strained even their credulity to believe that all the human varieties they were forced to recognize had been created separately. The phenomenon of race mixture, which could be observed wherever different human varieties came into even casual contact, offered a convenient way out. They were able to solve their problems of origin and classification simultaneously by setting up a small series of ideal types, each characterized by a particular combination of physical traits, and assuming that all varieties which did not conform to these ideal types were a result of hybridization. (3)

Each of these ideal types corresponded to an actual variety of man, but the selection of a particular variety as constituting a basic type depended entirely upon the judgment of the observer. However, this fact was conveniently forgotten as soon as the type hypothesis had come to be accepted. Although there has never been the slightest proof that any one of these ideal types was actually ancestral to any other human variety, it has become heresy to question the idea. To do so strikes at the very foundation of those classifications in which the science is still primarily interested. Even when the idea of separate creations had to be abandoned, the concept of primary types survived. It was assumed that these types had been evolved from different subhuman species or, at the very least, had become differentiated at the very dawn of our species development. (4)

It is plain that the whole problem of racial origins and relationships needs to be reviewed in the light of modern biological knowledge. In attempting to do this we can ignore the question of classification for the present. Although classifications have a profound effect upon our thinking, they are always imposed from without and have no functional relationship to the material which they arrange. In the first place, all existing human varieties are members of a single species by the most elementary of biological tests. They all produce fertile hybrids on crossing. Moreover, these hybrids appear to be, if anything, more fertile than the parent strains and at least equally vigorous. The results of crossing human varieties appear to be identical with those obtained from crossing strains within any plant or animal species after these strains have become fixed by inbreeding. In view of this, it seems highly improbable that any of the human varieties derive from different sub-human species.   (5)

Even without the hybridization test, the evidence that all human beings belong to a single species is overwhelming. The physical differences between various human varieties look large to us because we are so close to them, just as the physical differences between individuals whom we know seem much more marked than the differences between strangers. Actually, the differences between even the most diverse human varieties are not very great, and all of them lie in secondary characteristics. Man has his color phases, as have many other mammalian species, his large and small varieties, and a wide range of minor variations in such matters as hair texture, shape of the skull, and limb proportions. However, his skeletal structure, organs, and musculature are practically the same in all varieties, and the differences which do exist are so slight that they can be detected only by experts. An equally intensive study of any other mammalian species of fairly wide range would reveal almost as much variation and in many cases a good deal more. Thus the widest range of variation in our species is much less than that in the black bears and only about one-half that in a single species of South American spider monkeys. When we come to domestic animals, the range is several times as great. There are no differences between human varieties which even remotely approach those between a pug and a greyhound or even between a Hereford and an old-style Texas longhorn. Since man is a domestic animal and has the widest range of any mammalian species, the striking thing about him is not that he has developed different varieties but that these varieties are not more widely different than they are.   (6)

How the present human varieties have come into existence is a problem which is by no means solved, but our present knowledge of evolutionary process makes it possible to guess with a fair degree of probability. Even our first ancestors were probably equipped with tools and fire, making it possible for them to exist in many different environments, while they certainly had no non-portable property which might tie them to a single locality. Every species has a tendency to breed up to the available food supply, which, for gregarious animals, is fixed by the territory which the herd, moving as a whole, can cover. It seems highly probable that the first men, like all modern men, were gregarious. When the human band became too large for its territory, it split in two and one part moved into new territory. This process can still be observed among peoples at the hunting stage. As long as there was plenty of unexploited territory available this process of population increase and band fission must have gone on rapidly, and it is not impossible that our species had occupied most of the habitable portions of the Old World within a few thousand years of its emergence. (7)

The social horizon of uncivilized groups is always very limited. They know only the members of their own band and possibly those of the bands whose territory immediately adjoins theirs. They are often on hostile terms even with these close neighbors. The result of this is fairly close and continuous inbreeding. Although all tribes forbid marriage between relatives in certain degrees, all the members of a small tribe marrying within itself will come in a few generations to have very much the same heredity. Thus in such a group as the Cape York Eskimo, who probably never numbered more than 500 individuals and who had been completely inbred for at least 300 years, the whole tribe had become a single family line. From the genetic point of view it would make little difference whether a man married his first cousin or the least-related individual whom he could find. Such a condition is especially favorable to the fixation of mutations. A physical variation of any sort, if hereditary, will soon become a part of the heredity of every individual in the group and have a double chance of appearing in the offspring of any marriage. The whole tribe is really one large family, genetically speaking, and all its members soon come to show a family resemblance. (8)

If we are correct in our belief that all existing men belong to a single species, early man must have been a generalized form with potentialities for evolving into all the varieties which we know at present. It further seems probable that this generalized form spread widely and rapidly and that within a few thousand years of its appearance small bands of individuals of this type were scattered over most of the Old World. These bands would find themselves in many different environments, and the physical peculiarities which were advantageous in one of these might be of no importance or actually deleterious in another. Moreover, due to the relative isolation of these bands and their habit of inbreeding, any mutation which was favorable or at least not injurious under the particular circumstances would have the best possible chance of spreading to all the members of the group. It seems quite possible to account for all the known

variations in our species on this basis without invoking the theory of a
small number of originally distinct varieties. (9)

We know that environment has a selective effect on physical variations
after they appear. It ensures to individuals who vary in certain directions
a better chance of survival and therefore of passing on such variations to
later generations, while it decreases the chances of survival for those who
vary in other directions. This is the well-known principle of natural selection. Whether environment also has a positive effect in producing variations or even encouraging variation in a particular direction remains to be
proved. It seems quite possible that it does, although the mechanics involved are still completely unknown. Thus a study of plants shows that
certain species show a great increase in the number of mutants produced
when they are introduced into a new environment, this tendency decreasing
with the length of residence. We also know that even in man settlement in
a new environment may result in changes in physical type which are not
arrived at by the selective process. Thus Dr. Boas's studies of emigrants
in America have shown that even in the first generation there is a slight
change in head form which certainly cannot be accounted for on the selective theory. Children of long-headed groups are, on the average, shorter-
headed than their own parents, and the tendency increases in direct ratio
to the length of time the parents had been in America when the children
were born. Conversely, the children of short-headed groups tend to be
longer-headed than their parents, with the same ratio between degree of
change and length of residence. It certainly looks as though the American
environment was working in some non-selective fashion toward the production of an intermediate head form, but we cannot even conjecture the
how or why of this. (10)

While we cannot exclude the possibility that the settlement of the
ancestral, generalized human type in various environments may have
stimulated variation and even directed it in certain lines, we know so little
of the processes involved that it is safest to leave this out of the discussion.
The processes of natural selection are much better understood, but it must
be remembered that the influence of environment is, in this case, negative.
It cuts off certain variations from among the wide range of those brought
to it by the processes of mutation, but there are many others which are
neither advantageous nor disadvantageous. Thus it is hard to see how curly
hair gives its possessor either a better or a worse chance for survival than
straight hair, unless there happen to be certain social factors present in the
situation. The establishment of such variations of neutral value must be
due to genetic factors of dominance and recession. Even with these, it is
difficult to see how such neutral traits could ever be completely bred out
of a strain. (11)

It is a curious fact that of all the variations which have become fixed in particular human groups only those connected with skin color seem to have any significance with regard to natural environment. It has been recognized since classical times that in the Old World dark-skinned people occupy tropical regions and light-skinned ones temperate to cold regions. The possible explanation for this has only recently been discovered. It seems to lie in differences not of heat but of light intensity. The actinic rays of the sun are beneficial to man's system in small quantities, harmful in large ones. Skin pigment seems to act as a ray filter, its efficiency in this respect being correlated with its depth of color.   (12)

Let us suppose that two divisions of the same strain settled one in Somaliland and the other beside the Baltic and that both had, in the beginning, medium brown skin color. The Somaliland group would be exposed to intense sunlight. Individuals who varied toward lighter pigmentation would get more actinic rays than were good for them. Like modern Europeans living in the tropics they would be subject to nervous disorders, and females of this type would show a higher percentage of disorders of the reproductive system than females of darker skin color. Although by no means all of these lighter individuals would die young, those who survived would be at a certain disadvantage and less likely to perpetuate their type than individuals who varied toward the dark end of the scale. In the course of time the norm for skin color for the group would move over toward the dark end and might, with the aid of favorable mutations, become very dark indeed.   (13)

The group which settled beside the Baltic would be faced by a totally different light situation. This region lies far north to begin with, and the amount of light is further decreased by a great deal of fog and cloudy weather. Individuals whose skin color varied in the direction of heavy pigment would not get enough actinic rays into their systems. Unless they ate raw fish, like the Eskimo, and thus obtained the vitamin which these rays help to produce, they would be very likely to suffer from rickets. Even individuals of a medium shade would have the same difficulty, but those who were lightest, especially partial albinos, would have little or none of it. The absence of pigmentation would make it possible for their systems to get the full benefit of the scanty sun. Rickets is rarely a fatal disease, but it deforms the bones, and women who have suffered from it in childhood frequently have malformations of the pelvis which make childbearing difficult or impossible. In due course of time the norm for pigmentation for the group would shift toward the light end of the scale and might, with the aid of occasional semi-albino mutations, become as light as that of the modern Nordic.   (14)

It is easy to see how a human group living in a particular environment might, in course of time, reach the optimum condition with regard to skin color, but this is only one of many variable traits which have assumed fairly constant form in particular human strains. We cannot say positively that such traits are unconnected with biological survival, since they may reflect some deep-seated condition which is favorable to the survival of the particular group. Thus to cite a purely hypothetical case, the kinky hair of the Negro does not in itself give its possessors any advantage for life in the tropics, but it may be one of several things all of which result from a particular balance of endocrine secretions. Some of the invisible results of this condition might be highly important to survival. It might, for example, give the individuals who had it a high degree of immunity to malaria. If so, those who had this condition, outwardly manifested in kinky hair, would have a better chance of reproducing themselves than those who lacked it, and, in time, kinky hair would become the normal form for the group. The example just cited is purely imaginary, and we have no proof that any linkages of this sort actually exist, but at least the matter would repay study. It seems certain that there is some connection between physical type and the ductless glands. To cite only one example, failure of thyroid secretions will produce many Mongoloid characteristics in persons of pure European stock. These glands, in turn, have a profound influence on the life processes of the individual and even on his personality. It is quite possible that a hormone balance which would be favorable in one environment might be unfavorable in another.   (15)

We have then, as possible causes for the present diversity of human types, the tendency toward variation which is common to all mammalian species, the operation of natural selection in each of the varying environments in which human groups live, and the favorable conditions for the fixation of variations present in small, continually inbreeding groups. However, there is another factor in the situation the importance of which must not be overlooked. This is the matter of social selection arising from the group's preference for a particular physical type. This type of selection sometimes assumes a direct and vigorous form. Thus among the Tanala, in Madagascar, there are two groups which differ markedly in skin color although they seem to be much alike in their other physical characteristics and are nearly identical in culture and language. These groups are known by terms which may be translated as the Red clan and the Black clan. Normal members of the Red clan are a very light brown, the pigmentation being slight enough to show a blush. Normal members of the Black clan are a deep brown, as dark as the average American Negro. If one may judge from superficial observations, these two groups represent the limits of the range of skin color present for the tribe as a whole, although the average for the tribe would be nearer the dark end of the scale. If a dark child of unquestioned clan parentage is born into the Red clan it is believed that it will grow up to be either a sorcerer, a thief, a person guilty of incest, or a leper. It is therefore put to death. The Black clan holds exactly the same belief with regard to light children and disposes of them in the same summary fashion. Since nearly all marriages are still made within the clan, this type of social selection could hardly fail to affect the physical type of the group. Variants in the socially undesired direction would be eliminated generation after generation, while even if they were allowed to grow up they would find themselves at a disadvantage and have less opportunity to reproduce their type. (16)

It has often been urged by those who question the importance of social selection as a mechanism for fixing a particular physical type that all members of a primitive community normally marry and beget children. This is perfectly true, but they do not all marry the same people. Quite as among ourselves, the ablest or richest men take what are, by tribal standards, the prettiest girls. There may be some exceptions to this in societies which give their members no choice in matings, but such societies are rare. In general, ugly women have to content themselves with inferior men. Even at the simplest hunting level the children of a good hunter have more and better food and therewith a better chance of survival than those of poor hunters. Conversely, the handsome man has a better chance of perpetuating his type than the ugly one. Even if he lacks the qualities which make for a desirable husband, he will be in demand as a lover. Social selection of this sort works more slowly than the direct elimination practiced by the Tanala clans, but its cumulative effects must be considerable. (17)

Of course the direction taken by social selection will depend upon cultural factors. Standards of beauty vary profoundly from one group to another and even, in sophisticated societies, from one period to another. Many persons still in middle age have witnessed the full bloom of feminine curves, their attempted elimination, and their gradual return to favor. Such short-time changes can have no permanent effect on the physical type of a group, but admiration for the black that shines or for ample hips or for heavy whiskers, if maintained for a thousand years, might very well shift the norm for the entire group toward the goal of physical perfection which it has set for itself. (18)

Hitherto our discussion has dealt only with the factors affecting the evolution of divergent varieties from older and more generalized ones. However, there is another aspect of the problem. Human varieties have an incurable tendency to mix wherever and whenever they are brought into contact with each other. Whether new varieties may arise as a result of such hybridization is still an open question. First-generation hybrids between two pure-bred human varieties tend to be fairly uniform in type, but when these hybrids are interbred the offspring appear to be highly variable with throwbacks to both the pure ancestral types and all sorts of intermediate forms. It seems quite possible that, through a combination of natural and social selection, such inbred hybrid groups might in time develop a new stable type, since animal-breeders are able to attain the same end by careful selection and line breeding. However, the process must be a slow one, and the actual production of a new human variety from a hybrid group has never been observed. Herskovitz finds evidence that something of the sort is occurring among the American Negroes, who represent a very complex mixture of various Negro, European, and American Indian breeds, but the process of fixation of the new type is still incomplete.

(19)

Throughout the history of our species two forces have constantly been at work. On the one hand the combined factors of variation, selection, and fixation of traits by inbreeding have worked steadily toward the production of a greater and greater number of human varieties. On the other hand, the ease with which human strains can and do cross has worked to blur the outlines of these varieties and to produce multitudes of individuals of mixed heredity and variable physical type. The first of these forces was dominant during the early period of man's existence. The second became increasingly important as time passed and has risen to a crescendo with the elimination of space and the breakdown of old local groupings which are characteristic of modern civilization.   (20)

The early history of our species probably witnessed its fairly rapid dispersal over the Old World and the development of a large number of local varieties. Some of these varieties were no doubt more vigorous and more intelligent than others, which made it possible for them to increase and to occupy additional territory at the expense of their less able neighbors. However, if we admit that the processes of variation and of fixation of new types have gone on continuously, as the study of all other mammalian species seems to indicate, no single human variety could have established itself over a very wide area without undergoing local modifications. As soon as a group of individuals of any given variety established themselves in an environment markedly different from that in which this variety had been developed, the evolution of a new variety would begin. The possible forms which this new variety might assume would be limited not only by the new environment but also by the potentialities for variation inherent in the parent variety. Thus members of a pure-bred blond strain could hardly develop into a new brunette variety. Pigmentation is a genetically dominant factor in heredity and, once eliminated from a strain, apparently cannot be reassumed. However, such an original blond strain might retain potentialities for variation in other physical characteristics such as head form and might give rise, in different environments, to both round-headed blond varieties and long-headed blond varieties. In other words, the spread of certain able varieties and the elimination of less able ones would not, in the long run, lead to the establishment of a uniform physical type over a wide area. It would simply lead to the development of a series of new varieties.   (21)

To complicate the situation still more, any movement of members of a particular variety into territory which had previously been occupied by another variety accelerated the process of hybridization. Even in the lowest stages of culture wars between groups rarely end in the complete extermination or expulsion of the vanquished. The more attractive women are taken as concubines by the victors, and through them some of the heredity of the vanquished passes into the conquering group. In the higher stages of culture, when agriculture, manufactures, and trade have been developed, it becomes more profitable to settle among and exploit the vanquished than to exterminate them. This results in close and continuous contact between conquerors and conquered and a rapid and extensive mixture of the two strains. Although hybrids produced under these conditions may be at a social disadvantage, they have at least as good a chance of survival as pure-bred members of the conquered group and by interbreeding with them spread the blood of the conquerors downward in ever-widening circles. (22)

Even the conquerors cannot maintain their purity of blood under these conditions. Although history affords numerous examples of conscious attempts to do this, all of these attempts have failed. The conquerors may be able to guard their women successfully, limiting crosses to those arising from relations between their men and conquered women, but as soon as any crossing begins the purity of their type is doomed. Certain of the offspring of the hybrids will throw back toward the type of their aristocratic relatives, and such individuals can usually worm their way into the aristocratic group. The "passing" of Negroes in our own society would be a case in point. Such individuals carry the heredity of both groups, and through their intermarriage with the aristocrats more and more of the heredity of the conquered is introduced into the ruling group, until finally the physical distinction between the two types disappears. (23)

It has been said that the only group which would have any chance of maintaining absolute purity of blood would be one all of whose women were too hideous to attract the men of any other tribe and all of whose men were too cowardly to steal the women of any other tribe. To this might be added inhabitants of islands never visited after the original settlement. However, primitive groups, with their narrow geographic ranges and limited contacts, have a much better chance of retaining relative purity of blood than have civilized ones. Any conditions which bring individuals of different varieties into more frequent contact will increase the number of hybrids. Every civilized group of which we have record has been a hybrid group, a fact which disposes effectively of the theory that hybrid peoples are inferior to pure-bred ones. (24)

Attitudes toward hybridization have varied profoundly in different societies and at different periods, but there seems to be no biological justification for any strong feeling either for or against it. It is true that the purest human strains now extant are to be found among culturally backward groups and that all civilized peoples are predominantly of hybrid composition, but this does not indicate that hybrids are intrinsically superior. The same contacts which stimulate the development of civilization stimulate the production of hybrids, so that both conditions owe their presence to a common cause. Conversely, the fact that hybrid populations are quite capable of perpetuating and adding to the cultural equipment which they have received from their pure-bred ancestors shows that they are at least equal to these in ability. The social connotations of hybridization may be important in particular situations, but the biological and cultural connotations appear to be negligible. In the long run it causes more grief to the students who are trying to classify human varieties than to any one else.   (25)

It seems slightly ludicrous that the main exponents of the theory of the superiority of pure strains should be inhabitants of Europe, one of the most thoroughly hybridized regions in the world. It is improbable that there is a single European alive to-day who does not have at least one hybrid among his ancestors, while most Europeans are the result of a long series of crossings. Tribes have marched and countermarched across the face of this continent since before the dawn of history, and the ancestry of most of the present population is not even pure white. The Huns, a yellow tribe from far eastern Asia, raided almost to the Atlantic and, after their defeat, dissolved into the European population. Other Asiatic tribes such as the Avars and Magyars settled large areas in eastern Europe, interbreeding with the earlier inhabitants until they disappeared as a distinct physical type. The Romans brought in Negro slaves while, in later times, the Mohammedan conquerors of Spain and Sicily had more than a tinge of black blood. Lastly, there have been several varieties of whites in Europe since before the close of the Old Stone Age. Although numerous books have been written on the origins, characteristics, and interrelations of these varieties, hardly two eminent authorities will agree exactly as to what these have been, and there is even some disagreement as to number of varieties which can be recognized. It seems that the only thing we can be perfectly sure of is that every variety wandered, underwent local modifications, and crossed with other varieties whenever the opportunity arose. The result of all this has been an extreme mixture of heredity in Europe and a perfect hodgepodge of varying physical types.   (26)

Even when the characteristics of one of the original white varieties can be determined with a fair degree of probability, it by no means follows that individuals who show these characteristics will breed true. Members of mixed groups have a strong tendency to throw back toward the original varieties which have gone into the mixture. In spite of their physical type, such throwbacks carry and transmit a mixed heredity. To resurrect any of the original European varieties in pure form would require several generations of careful selective breeding with the elimination in each generation of all individuals who did not conform to the desired type. This presents practical difficulties insurmountable even by a totalitarian state. (27)

European physical types have been studied more intensively than those of any other region, but it seems certain that similar conditions of extreme mixture exist in all regions of dense population and advanced culture. The situation which confronts physical anthropologists in their attempts to determine original human varieties and to classify them is therefore extremely complex. Their work has also been hampered by a lack of agreement on terminology and by the very loose usage of certain terms, particularly *race*. This has been applied indiscriminately to classificatory units ranging all the way from small and presumably closely inbred groups whose members show a very high degree of physical uniformity to huge divisions of mankind within which the differences are actually more numerous than the similarities. (28)

It must be clearly understood at the outset of any attempt to classify human varieties that such classifications rest entirely upon observable physical characteristics. Although similarities in the characteristics of various human groups may imply genetic relationships and more or less remote common origins, these relationships cannot be proved. All classifications rest upon the presence of a number of characteristics, and the greater part of these are, unfortunately, of a sort which cannot be ascertained from skeletal material alone. Skeletons provide no clue to their former owners' skin color, hair texture, or eye, nose, and lip form, all of these being items currently used as a basis for racial classifications. There is no human group whose ancestry is known for even five generations in the exact terms necessary for racial determinations. In fact, there is not even a family line for which we have satisfactory information over this brief period. Most genealogies are simply lists of names, and even the family portrait gallery fails to yield information on many important points. All that we can do is to classify human varieties as we find them to-day. Any conclusions as to their relationships which may be based on these classifications are merely conjectures with varying degrees of probability. (29)

The term *race* has been used so loosely that it seems wisest to substitute for it a series of three terms: *breed, race,* and *stock.* Even this terminology is too limited for a really accurate classification, but one that was exact enough to meet all conditions would be so complex that it would lose much of its utility. Under this terminology, a *breed* is a group of individuals all of whom vary about a particular norm with respect to each of their physical characteristics. This usage corresponds exactly to the usage of the same term when applied to domestic animals, say Scotch terriers. (30)

It is almost impossible to find any human group which constitutes a pure breed, but the condition is approached in certain primitive tribes living in relative isolation. It seems fairly certain that such breeds are estab-

lished by long-continued inbreeding with the elimination of extreme variants, although absolute proof of this is lacking. Even in the most isolated
human groups there are some individuals who fall outside the normal
range of variation for the group as a whole with regard to certain of their
characteristics. This may be due either to remote crosses with other breeds
or to individual mutations. In either case such atypical persons can be
eliminated from the study by statistical methods. If there are a number of
them all of whom vary from the norm in very much the same way, this is
usually considered an indication of an earlier crossing with some other
breed.   (31)

After such individuals have been eliminated, the investigator proceeds
to establish the norms for the group with regard to each of a series of
physical characteristics. Those most commonly employed are head form,
including the face; color of the skin, hair, and eyes; form of the features;
hair texture; amount of body hair and beard; and stature. Any number of
additional characteristics can be taken into consideration, but those just
named are the most easily ascertainable, and most of them can be recorded in exact terms. If we take the adult males or females of the group,
we will find that although no two of them are identical with respect to any
one of these characteristics, say stature, the bulk of them will cluster about
a particular point in the total range of variation. Thus the whole series of
adult males may range in height from five feet six inches to six feet, but
there will be few individuals at the two extremes and more as we move
toward the center, with the largest number falling around five feet nine
inches. Five feet nine inches would then be considered the norm with regard to this particular trait. A combination of the norms for all the traits
observed will give the ideal physical type for the breed. This bears
somewhat the same relation to the members of the breed as a whole that
the ideal type for the Scotch terrier at a dog-show bears to the dogs actually
exhibited. No individual, whether animal or human, is ever a perfect example of the ideal type for his breed, but this type represents what the completely average individual would be.   (32)

By the use of statistical methods applied to large series of individuals
it is possible to distinguish such breeds even in fairly mixed populations
and from this to deduce, with a fair degree of probability, what were the
original pure strains which went to their making. The same methods make
it possible to determine whether a group which appears to be intermediate
between two known breeds is a distinct, pure-bred strain or a hybrid one.
Of course this does not eliminate the possibility that such an intermediate
breed may have come into existence through an ancient hybridization with
the subsequent development and fixation of a new physical type, but this
does not lessen the value of the method for classificatory purposes.   (33)

Only a small part of the world's population has been studied by this method, but the results indicate that there are, or have been, hundreds of human breeds scattered over the earth. It also seems probable that these units are in a constant state of flux, new breeds coming into existence wherever a small group of individuals settle in relative isolation and inter-marry among themselves for several generations. Conversely old breeds are constantly being eliminated through mixture or failure in the struggle for survival. A classification of mankind by breeds would thus represent the situation only at a particular point in human history. It would be invalid even ten generations before this point or after it. (34)

The next larger classificatory unit in our system is the *race*. This consists of a number of breeds whose ideal types have a series of characteristics in common. In establishing such races it is impossible to use the same exact methods applied to the establishment of breeds. In the study of breeds the group of individuals to be considered is clearly outlined, while the racial groupings have no such well-defined boundaries. If we take any one physi-cal characteristic and study its variations throughout the whole range of human breeds, we will find that certain of these breeds are closely simi-lar with regard to it, others somewhat similar, and still others markedly different. However, the relative position of any breed with regard to one trait will be different from its relative position with regard to another. Thus a classification of breeds which is based on head form may be quite at variance with one based on some other trait, such as skin color. Two breeds which have much the same head form may have markedly different pig-mentation or vice versa. (35)

Racial classifications are, therefore, based upon the presence of similari-ties with respect to a selected series of physical traits. The content of any group within the classification depends both upon the traits selected and upon the degree of similarity which the investigator considers significant. Although there are certain breeds whose resemblances are so close and numerous that their assignment to a single racial grouping is never ques-tioned, there are many others which lie on the border lines of such group-ings with their resemblances rather equally divided. Where such breeds will be placed in the racial classification depends, in the last analysis, on the judgment of the investigator. To cite a single example, there is in eastern Europe a breed of large but stockily built blonds with medium to round heads and broad faces. In pigmentation this breed resembles the charac-teristics used to determine membership in the Nordic racial group, in head and face form it resembles the Alpine group, while in bodily build and stature it is intermediate between the two, leaning a little toward the Nordic side. Whether this breed is to be classed with the Nordic or with the Alpine race depends upon which of these resemblances are judged to be more significant. (36)

The real point of all this is that, while breeds are genuine biological entities, races, as we have chosen to use the term, are creations of the investigator and creations with regard to which all the creators are by no means in agreement. The same thing holds in even greater degree for the third and largest division of our classification, the stocks. *Stocks* are groups of races, the content of any stock being established by the same techniques as those used for establishing racial classifications. The only difference is that a still smaller series of traits are taken into consideration and the limits of the group are correspondingly extended. The difficulties encountered in arranging races into stocks are much the same as those connected with the assignment of breeds to races. Here again, there are races which lie on the border line between stocks and whose assignment to one or another stock will always be open to question. Thus in northeast Africa there is a race which is like the Negro stock in its skin color and, to a lesser degree, in its hair form, but which lies closer to whites than it does to Negroes with respect to its head form and especially its features. Where it shall be placed in the classification depends, in the last analysis, on the judgment of the investigator.   (37)

The difficulty of classifying the varieties of mankind resulted in a tendency to increase the number of races and stocks until the system became so complex and unwieldy that it broke down of its own weight. At the present time the tendency is to classify the whole of mankind under three stocks, with a recognition that there are certain races and breeds which it is impossible to place. These stocks are the Caucasic, or white, the Negroid, or black, and the Mongoloid, or yellow. The Caucasic stock as a whole is characterized by high, thin noses, medium lips, slight prognathism (i.e., projection of the face), straight eyes, wavy to curly hair and considerable body hair and beard. In all other respects it is variable, including tall and short, long- and round-headed, and both blond and very dark-skinned groups. Although we are accustomed to think of Caucasians as white, some of the breeds in this stock are darker than the average American Negro.   (38)

Within the Caucasic stock at least five races are commonly distinguished. The much advertised Nordic race, which centers in northern Europe, has the general characteristics of the stock plus long heads, tall stature, and blond pigmentation. The Alpine race, strongest in central Europe, has the general characteristics plus round heads, medium to short stature with a strong, stocky build, and medium pigmentation with brown hair and eyes. The Mediterranean race, centering in southern Europe, has the general characteristics plus long heads, medium to short stature with a light build, and rather dark pigmentation with dark brown to black hair and eyes and a tendency toward quite curly hair. In southeastern Europe and the Near East there is another race, the Armenoid, which is characterized by dark pigmentation, short, high heads, and a curious facial type. The nose is large and forms a continuous line with the somewhat sloping fore-head. An idealization of this type may be seen in Greek statues. Lastly, in India, the Hindi race combines most of the characteristics of the Mediter-raneans with taller stature and a much deeper skin color which becomes almost black in certain breeds. (39)

The Negroid stock as a whole is characterized by flat noses, thick lips, considerable prognathism, straight eyes, kinky hair, very dark pigmentation, and a tendency toward long-headedness, although it includes a few me-dium- to short-headed breeds. It is more variable than any other stock with regard to stature, including both the tallest and the shortest of the human breeds. Its racial composition has never been adequately worked out, but at least five races can be distinguished tentatively. The Nilotic Negroes are distinguished by extremely tall, thin build and a relative ab-sence of body hair and beard. The Forest Negroes are shorter and more powerfully built, with a fairly heavy development of body hair and beard and exaggeratedly negroid features. It was from this group that the ances-tors of most of the American Negroes were drawn. In the dense forests of Central Africa there is a third racial group, the Pigmies. These are much like the Forest Negroes except for their extremely short stature, which rarely reaches five feet even in adult males, and their somewhat shorter heads. (40)

There are two other races which are usually classed with the Negroid stock although their habitat lies far from the rest. The Negritoes or black dwarfs have a broken distribution throughout far southeastern Asia and the neighboring islands. They are almost as short as the African pigmies but have a much lighter build and a tendency toward round-headedness, with little or no body hair and beard. The Oceanic Negroes are found in New Guinea and the neighboring islands. They present the stock charac-teristics, but it is extremely difficult to characterize them as a race. The region is one of numerous highly localized breeds and of extensive mix-ture with other stocks. (41)

In South Africa there is still another race, the Bushmen-Hottentots, which defies assignment to any of the stocks. These people are short, lightly built, with Negroid noses and lips and extremely kinky hair, but they have light yellow skins and slant eyes. Largely because of their geographical position they are frequently classed as an extreme variant of the Negro stock. Some of the breeds within this race have the further peculiarity of steatopygia, the storing-up of masses of fat in the buttocks, but this is not characteristic of the race as a whole. (42)

The Mongoloid stock is the most difficult of all to define, since it has not only been very incompletely studied but has also been used as a catch-all for races and stocks which clearly were not Negroid but which the Cau-casian scholars were unwilling to admit to their own select company. In general, this stock is characterized by medium dark skin color, ranging from the copper-brown of the American Indian to the light yellow of the North Chinese, straight, lank hair, and sparse body hair and beard. Its members are variable in all other respects. Even the slant eye, frequently mentioned as characteristic of this stock, is of only sporadic occurrence among American Indians. The stock really falls into two divisions, the Old World Mongoloids and the New World ones, i.e., the Indians. The Old World division includes at least two well-marked races and probably a much greater number. The North Chinese race is tall, round-headed, with light yellow skins, small, straight noses, thin lips, and slant eyes. The Malay race, which centers in southeastern Asia, is short, with rather variable head form and features and with medium brown skin color. In northeastern Asia there is still another race or group of races which resembles the American Indian. (43)

The American Indians might almost be classified as constituting a distinct stock. They have developed into many different breeds, most of which have the common factors of copper-brown skin color and straight hair while showing extreme variation in other respects. Thus the shortest and longest undeformed skulls known to us come from different Indian breeds. Even skin color and hair texture are somewhat variable. There are certain light, yellowish breeds in South America, and wavy to moderately curly hair occurs sporadically in both continents. No satisfactory racial classification for these various breeds has so far been developed.   (44)

In northern Japan and the neighboring island of Sakhalin there is a small racial group, the Ainu, who are of doubtful status. These people are short, stocky, with medium heads, brown hair, and gray or green eyes, somewhat wavy hair texture and abundant body hair and beard, and dusky white skins with a slightly brownish cast. Their eyes are usually straight, but the general cast of their features is more Mongoloid than European. They appear to be one of those border-line groups who show relationships with two stocks in about equal measure, but they have been very tentatively classed with the Caucasians. Throughout the farther islands of the Pacific we have still another race, the Polynesian, which is of even more doubtful status. This race shows a fairly equal proportion of Caucasic and Mongoloid traits with a few not very pronounced Negroid characteristics. This region is one of numerous and widely scattered islands, particularly well adapted to the development of a multiplicity of breeds, and some of these breeds apparently differ as much from each other as they do from particular breeds assigned to the Caucasic or Mongoloid stocks. (45)

There is one other race which defies classification under the standard three-fold grouping and which is, at the same time, of especial interest to anthropologists. This is the Australians. The ancestors of this group seem to have entered their continent in very ancient times and to have had little contact with the outside world afterward. The present members of this race seem to have more in common with certain extinct breeds of man than with any existing breed, and it seems possible that they are only slightly modified descendants of the ancient generalized human type from which all the later breeds and races were evolved. The Australians are characterized by long heads with retreating foreheads, very massive ridges over the eyes, short, wide noses, moderately full lips, very marked prognathism, abundant body hair and beard, wavy hair texture, and medium to dark brown pigmentation. They show vague resemblances to all the stocks in one respect or another, but all these are outweighed by their primitive characteristics. (46)

While the classification which has just been given is a convenient tool for the arrangement of descriptive material, the only units within it which are functionally significant are the breeds. These are genuine biological entities, groups characterized by close physical resemblances and common heredity. Races and stocks, on the other hand, are abstractions. This becomes much clearer when we study the distribution of breeds and their resemblances to each other. Except in regions where there have been extensive recent movements of population, it will usually be found that each breed resembles its immediate neighbors in most respects and more remote breeds in a decreasing number of respects. Even the most markedly different breeds are connected by a graded series of other and intermediate ones. Breeds seem to grade into each other very much as environments grade into each other, both showing gradual but cumulative changes as we move out from any given point. This is exactly the situation which we would expect to find in a species which had spread widely and then differentiated into a series of local varieties. At the same time, it is extremely difficult to account for it on the theory of a small series of originally distinct types unless we assume that the bulk of all existing breeds are a result of hybridization. (47)

The difficulties of the hybridization theory have already been pointed out. If new breeds can be produced in this way, at least it requires a long and drastic process of selection. For the present this theory can neither be proved nor disproved, and until the matter has been settled we must reserve judgment on the assumption that all human varieties have been derived from a few widely different ancestral types. In particular, we must be cautious of all historic reconstructions which are based on the assumption that all the breeds assigned to any one stock have a common ancestry other than that presumably common to all members of our species. To cite one example, it has been generally assumed that the Oceanic Negroes and the Negritoes must share a common origin with the Africa Negroes, and various migration theories have been advanced to account for their presence so far from the other members of the stock. Actually, the environment in which we find them is much like that of tropical Africa, and it seems quite possible that the same ancient generalized human type, if it established itself in both localities, might undergo a parallel evolution. Again, the Caucasic traits which we find in Ainu and Polynesians do not necessarily indicate that these groups have had any historic connection with our own ancestors. The Ainu environment, in particular, was much like that of some parts of Europe. It is safer, for the present, to consider all racial and stock classifications as tools for descriptive study and to avoid building theories of any sort upon them.   (48)

Adolf Hitler

(1889–1945)

HITLER, German Nazi and Fuehrer of the Third Reich, was chief precipitator of World War II. He became Chancellor in 1933 and complete dictator, by plebiscite, in 1934. A popular orator and shrewd political tactician, he was publicly dedicated to avenging Germany's post-World War I degradation and to re-establishing the grandeur of "the Aryan race," the original Indo-European race from which the Nazis claimed the Germans to be direct descendants. Mein Kampf was dictated to Rudolf Hess while the two were in prison.

■ *Nation and Race*

THERE ARE some truths which are so obvious that for this very reason they are not seen or at least not recognized by ordinary people. They sometimes pass by such truisms as though blind and are most astonished when someone suddenly discovers what everyone really ought to know. Columbus's eggs lie around by the hundreds of thousands, but Columbuses are met with less frequently.   (1)

Thus men without exception wander about in the garden of Nature; they imagine that they know practically everything and yet with few exceptions pass blindly by one of the most patent principles of Nature's rule: the inner segregation of the species of all living beings on this earth.
(2)

Even the most superficial observation shows that Nature's restricted form of propagation and increase is an almost rigid basic law of all the innumerable forms of expression of her vital urge. Every animal mates only with a member of the same species. The titmouse seeks the titmouse, the finch the finch, the stork the stork, the field mouse the field mouse, the dormouse the dormouse, the wolf the she-wolf, etc.
(3)

Only unusual circumstances can change this, primarily the compulsion of captivity or any other cause that makes it impossible to mate within the same species. But then Nature begins to resist this with all possible means, and her most visible protest consists either in refusing further capacity for propagation to bastards or in limiting the fertility of later offspring; in most cases, however, she takes away the power of resistance to disease or hostile attacks.
(4)

This is only too natural.
(5)

Any crossing of two beings not at exactly the same level produces a medium between the level of the two parents. This means: the offspring will probably stand higher than the racially lower parent, but not as high as the higher one. Consequently, it will later succumb in the struggle against the higher level. Such mating is contrary to the will of Nature for a higher breeding of all life. The precondition for this does not lie in associating superior and inferior, but in the total victory of the former. The stronger must dominate and not blend with the weaker, thus sacrificing his own greatness. Only the born weakling can view this as cruel, but he after all is only a weak and limited man; for if this law did not prevail, any conceivable higher development of organic living beings would be unthinkable.
(6)

The consequence of this racial purity,[1] universally valid in Nature, is not only the sharp outward delimitation of the various races, but their uniform character in themselves. The fox is always a fox, the goose a goose, the tiger a tiger, etc., and the difference can lie at most in the varying measure of force, strength, intelligence, dexterity, endurance, etc., of the individual specimens. But you will never find a fox who in his inner attitude might, for example, show humanitarian tendencies toward geese, as similarly there is no cat with a friendly inclination toward mice.
(7)

Therefore, here, too, the struggle among themselves arises less from inner aversion than from hunger and love. In both cases, Nature looks on

---

[1] Second edition inserts 'urge toward' before 'racial purity.'

calmly, with satisfaction, in fact. In the struggle for daily bread all those who are weak and sickly or less determined succumb, while the struggle of the males for the female grants the right or opportunity to propagate only to the healthiest. And struggle is always a means for improving a species' health and power of resistance and, therefore, a cause of its higher development.   (8)

If the process were different, all further and higher development would cease and the opposite would occur. For, since the inferior always predominates numerically over the best, if both had the same possibility of preserving life and propagating, the inferior would multiply so much more rapidly that in the end the best would inevitably be driven into the background, unless a correction of this state of affairs were undertaken. Nature does just this by subjecting the weaker part to such severe living conditions that by them alone the number is limited, and by not permitting the remainder to increase promiscuously, but making a new and ruthless choice according to strength and health.   (9)

No more than Nature desires the mating of weaker with stronger individuals, even less does she desire the blending of a higher with a lower race, since, if she did, her whole work of higher breeding, over perhaps hundreds of thousands of years, might be ruined with one blow.   (10)

Historical experience offers countless proofs of this. It shows with terrifying clarity that in every mingling of Aryan blood with that of lower peoples the result was the end of the cultured people. North America, whose population consists in by far the largest part of Germanic elements who mixed but little with the lower colored peoples, shows a different humanity and culture from Central and South America, where the predominantly Latin immigrants often mixed with the aborigines on a large scale. By this one example, we can clearly and distinctly recognize the effect of racial mixture. The Germanic inhabitant of the American continent, who has remained racially pure and unmixed, rose to be master of the continent; he will remain the master as long as he does not fall a victim to defilement of the blood.   (11)

The result of all racial crossing is therefore in brief always the following:

(a) Lowering of the level of the higher race;

(b) Physical and intellectual regression and hence the beginning of a slowly but surely progressing sickness.   (12)

To bring about such a development is, then, nothing else but to sin against the will of the eternal creator.   (13)

And as a sin this act is rewarded.   (14)

When man attempts to rebel against the iron logic of Nature, he comes into struggle with the principles to which he himself owes his existence as a man. And this attack[2] must lead to his own doom.   (15)

---

2 Second edition: 'so his action against Nature' instead of 'this attack.'

Here, of course, we encounter the objection of the modern pacifist, as truly Jewish in its effrontery as it is stupid! 'Man's rôle is to overcome Nature!' (16)

Millions thoughtlessly parrot this Jewish nonsense and end up by really imagining that they themselves represent a kind of conqueror of Nature; though in this they dispose of no other weapon than an idea, and at that such a miserable one, that if it were true no world at all would be conceivable. (17)

But quite aside from the fact that man has never yet conquered Nature in anything, but at most has caught hold of and tried to lift one or another corner of her immense gigantic veil of eternal riddles and secrets, that in reality he invents nothing but only discovers everything, that he does not dominate Nature, but has only risen on the basis of his knowledge of various laws and secrets of Nature to be lord over those other living creatures who lack this knowledge—quite aside from all this, an idea cannot overcome the preconditions for the development and being of humanity, since the idea itself depends only on man. Without human beings there is no human idea in this world, therefore, the idea as such is always conditioned by the presence of human beings and hence of all the laws which created the precondition for their existence. (18)

And not only that! Certain ideas are even tied up with certain men. This applies most of all to those ideas whose content originates, not in an exact scientific truth, but in the world of emotion, or, as it is so beautifully and clearly expressed today, reflects an 'inner experience.' All these ideas, which have nothing to do with cold logic as such, but represent only pure expressions of feeling, ethical conceptions, etc., are chained to the existence of men, to whose intellectual imagination and creative power they owe their existence. Precisely in this case the preservation of these definite races and men is the precondition for the existence of these ideas. Anyone, for example, who really desired the victory of the pacifistic idea in this world with all his heart would have to fight with all the means at his disposal for the conquest of the world by the Germans; for, if the opposite should occur, the last pacifist would die out with the last German, since the rest of the world has never fallen so deeply as our own people, unfortunately, has for this nonsense so contrary to Nature and reason. Then, if we were serious, whether we liked it or not, we would have to wage wars in order to arrive at pacifism. This and nothing else was what Wilson, the American world savior, intended, or so at least our German visionaries believed— and thereby his purpose was fulfilled. (19)

In actual fact the pacifistic-humane idea is perfectly all right perhaps when the highest type of man has previously conquered and subjected the world to an extent that makes him the sole ruler of this earth. Then this idea lacks the power of producing evil effects in exact proportion as its practical application becomes rare and finally impossible. Therefore, first struggle and then we shall see what can be done.[3] Otherwise mankind has passed the high point of its development and the end is not the domination of any ethical idea but barbarism and consequently chaos. At this point someone or other may laugh, but this planet once moved through the ether for millions of years without human beings and it can do so again some day if men forget that they owe their higher existence, not to the ideas of a few crazy ideologists, but to the knowledge and ruthless application of Nature's stern and rigid laws.   (20)

Everything we admire on this earth today—science and art, technology and inventions—is only the creative product of a few peoples and originally perhaps of *one* race. On them depends the existence of this whole culture. If they perish, the beauty of this earth will sink into the grave with them.   (21)

However much the soil, for example, can influence men, the result of the influence will always be different depending on the races in question. The low fertility of a living space may spur the one race to the highest achievements; in others it will only be the cause of bitterest poverty and final undernourishment with all its consequences. The inner nature of peoples is always determining for the manner in which outward influences will be effective. What leads the one to starvation trains the other to hard work.   (22)

All great cultures of the past perished only because the originally creative race died out from blood poisoning.   (23)

The ultimate cause of such a decline was their forgetting that all culture depends on men and not conversely; hence that to preserve a certain culture the man who creates it must be preserved. This preservation is bound up with the rigid law of necessity and the right to victory of the best and stronger in this world.[4]   (24)

Those who want to live, let them fight, and those who do not want to fight in this world of eternal struggle do not deserve to live.   (25)

Even if this were hard—that is how it is! Assuredly, however, by far the harder fate is that which strikes the man who thinks he can overcome Nature, but in the last analysis only mocks her. Distress, misfortune, and diseases are her answer.   (26)

The man who misjudges and disregards the racial laws actually forfeits the happiness that seems destined to be his. He thwarts the triumphal march of the best race and hence also the precondition for all human progress, and remains, in consequence, burdened with all the sensibility of man, in the animal realm of helpless misery.[5]   (27)

---

3 Second edition: 'struggle and then perhaps pacifism.'
4 Second edition omits: 'in the world.'
5 *'und verbleibt in der Folge dann, belastet mit der Empfindlichkeit des Menschen, im Bereich des hilflosen Jammers der Tiere.'* Second edition has: *'Er begibt sich in der Folge, belastet mit der Empfindlichkeit des Menschen, ins Bereich des hilflosen Tieres.'* This would read: 'In consequence, burdened with all the sensibility of man, he moves into the realm of the helpless beast.'

It is idle to argue which race or races were the original representative of human culture and hence the real founders of all that we sum up under the word 'humanity.' It is simpler to raise this question with regard to the present, and here an easy, clear answer results. All the human culture, all the results of art, science, and technology that we see before us today, are almost exclusively the creative product of the Aryan. This very fact admits of the not unfounded inference that he alone was the founder of all higher humanity, therefore representing the prototype of all that we understand by the word 'man.' He is the Prometheus of mankind from whose bright forehead the divine spark of genius has sprung at all times, forever kindling anew that fire of knowledge which illumined the night of silent mysteries and thus caused man to climb the path to mastery over the other beings of this earth. Exclude him—and perhaps after a few thousand years darkness will again descend on the earth, human culture will pass, and the world turn to a desert.   (28)

If we were to divide mankind into three groups, the founders of culture, the bearers of culture, the destroyers of culture, only the Aryan could be considered as the representative of the first group. From him originate the foundations and walls of all human creation, and only the outward form and color are determined by the changing traits of character of the various peoples. He provides the mightiest building stones and plans for all human progress and only the execution corresponds to the nature of the varying men and races. In a few decades, for example, the entire east of Asia will possess a culture whose ultimate foundation will be Hellenic spirit and Germanic technology, just as much as in Europe. Only the *outward* form— in part at least—will bear the features of Asiatic character. It is not true, as some people think, that Japan adds European technology to its culture; no, European science and technology are trimmed with Japanese characteristics. The foundation of actual life is no longer the special Japanese culture, although it determines the color of life—because outwardly, in consequence of its inner difference, it is more conspicuous to the European—but the gigantic scientific-technical achievements of Europe and America; that is, of Aryan peoples. Only on the basis of these achievements can the Orient follow general human progress. They furnish the basis of the struggle for daily bread, create weapons and implements for it, and only the outward form is gradually adapted to Japanese character.   (29)

If beginning today all further Aryan influence on Japan should stop, assuming that Europe and America should perish, Japan's present rise in science and technology might continue for a short time; but even in a few years the well would dry up, the Japanese special character would gain, but the present culture would freeze and sink back into the slumber from which it was awakened seven decades ago by the wave of Aryan culture. Therefore, just as the present Japanese development owes its life to Aryan origin, long ago in the gray past foreign influence and foreign spirit awakened the Japanese culture of that time. The best proof of this is furnished by the fact of its subsequent sclerosis and total petrifaction. This can occur in a people only when the original creative racial nucleus has been lost, or if the external influence which furnished the impetus and the material for the first development in the cultural field was later lacking. But if it is established that a people receives the most essential basic materials of its culture from foreign races, that it assimilates and adapts them, and that then, if further external influence is lacking, it rigidifies again and again, such a race may be designated as *'culture-bearing,'* but never as *'culture-creating.'* An examination of the various peoples from this standpoint points to the fact that practically none of them were originally *culture-founding*, but almost always *culture-bearing*.   (30)

Approximately the following picture of their development always results: (31)

Aryan races—often absurdly small numerically—subject foreign peoples, and then, stimulated by the special living conditions of the new territory (fertility, climatic conditions, etc.) and assisted by the multitude of lower-type beings standing at their disposal as helpers, develop the intellectual and organizational capacities dormant within them. Often in a few millenniums or even centuries they create cultures which originally bear all the inner characteristics of their nature, adapted to the above-indicated special qualities of the soil and subjected beings. In the end, however, the conquerors transgress against the principle of blood purity, to which they had first adhered; they begin to mix with the subjugated inhabitants and thus end their own existence; for the fall of man in paradise has always been followed by his expulsion.   (32)

After a thousand years and more, the last visible trace of the former master people is often seen in the lighter skin color which its blood left behind in the subjugated race, and in a petrified culture which it had originally created. For, once the actual and spiritual conqueror lost himself in the blood of the subjected people, the fuel for the torch of human progress was lost! Just as, through the blood of the former masters, the color preserved a feeble gleam in their memory, likewise the night of cultural life is gently illumined by the remaining creations of the former light-bringers. They shine through all the returned barbarism and too often inspire the thoughtless observer of the moment with the opinion that he beholds the picture of the present people before him, whereas he is only gazing into the mirror of the past.   (33)

It is then possible that such a people will a second time, or even more often in the course of its history, come into contact with the race of those who once brought it culture, and the memory of former encounters will not necessarily be present. Unconsciously the remnant of the former master blood will turn toward the new arrival, and what was first possible only by compulsion can now succeed through the people's own will. A new cultural wave makes its entrance and continues until those who have brought it are again submerged in the blood of foreign peoples. (34)

It will be the task of a future cultural and world history to carry on researches in this light and not to stifle in the rendition of external facts, as is so often, unfortunately, the case with our present historical science. (35)

This mere sketch of the development of 'culture-bearing' nations gives a picture of the growth, of the activity, and—the decline—of the true culture-founders of this earth, the Aryans themselves. (36)

As in daily life the so-called genius requires a special cause, indeed, often a positive impetus, to make him shine, likewise the genius-race in the life of peoples. In the monotony of everyday life even significant men often seem insignificant, hardly rising above the average of their environment; as soon, however, as they are approached by a situation in which others lose hope or go astray, the genius rises manifestly from the inconspicuous average child, not seldom to the amazement of all those who had hitherto seen him in the pettiness of bourgeois life—and that is why the prophet seldom has any honor in his own country. Nowhere have we better occasion to observe this than in war. From apparently harmless children, in difficult hours when others lose hope, suddenly heroes shoot up with death-defying determination and an icy cool presence of mind.[6] If this hour of trial had not come, hardly anyone would ever have guessed that a young hero was hidden in this beardless boy. It nearly always takes some stimulus to bring the genius on the scene. The hammer-stroke of Fate which throws one man to the ground suddenly strikes steel in another, and when the shell of everyday life is broken, the previously hidden kernel lies open before the eyes of the astonished world. The world then resists and does not want to believe that the type which is apparently identical with it is suddenly a very different being; a process which is repeated with every eminent son of man. (37)

Though an inventor, for example, establishes his fame only on the day of his invention, it is a mistake to thing that genius as such entered into the man only at this hour—the spark of genius exists in the brain of the truly creative man from the hour of his birth. True genius is always inborn and never cultivated, let alone learned. (38)

As already emphasized, this applies not only to the individual man but also to the race. Creatively active peoples always have a fundamenal creative gift, even if it should not be recognizable to the eyes of superficial observers. Here, too, outward recognition is possible only in consequence of accomplished deeds, since the rest of the world is not capable of recognizing genius in itself, but sees only its visible manifestations in the form

6 'eisige Kühle der Uberlegung.'

of inventions, discoveries, buildings, pictures, etc.; here again it often takes a long time before the world can fight its way through to this knowledge. Just as in the life of the outstanding individual, genius or extraordinary ability strives for practical realization only when spurred on by special occasions, likewise in the life of nations the creative forces and capacities which are present can often be exploited only when definite preconditions invite.   (39)

We see this most distinctly in connection with the race which has been and is the bearer of human cultural development—the Aryans. As soon as Fate leads them toward special conditions, their latent abilities begin to develop in a more and more rapid sequence and to mold themselves into tangible forms. The cultures which they found in such cases are nearly always decisively determined by the existing soil, the given climate, and— the subjected people. This last item, to be sure, is almost the most decisive. The more primitive the technical foundations for a cultural activity, the more necessary is the presence of human helpers who, organizationally assembled and employed, must replace the force of the machine. Without this possibility of using lower human beings, the Aryan would never have been able to take his first steps toward his future culture; just as without the help of various suitable beasts which he knew how to tame, he would not have arrived at a technology which is now gradually permitting him to do without these beasts. The saying, 'The Moor has worked off his debt, the Moor can go,'[7] unfortunately has only too deep a meaning. For thousands of years the horse had to serve man and help him lay the foundations of a development which now, in consequence of the motor car, is making the horse superfluous. In a few years his activity will have ceased, but without his previous collaboration man might have had a hard time getting where he is today.   (40)

Thus, for the formation of higher cultures the existence of lower human types was one of the most essential preconditions, since they alone were able to compensate for the lack of technical aids without which a higher development is not conceivable. It is certain that the first culture of humanity was based less on the tamed animal than on the use of lower human beings.   (41)

Only after the enslavement of subjected races did the same fate strike beasts, and not the other way around, as some people would like to think. For first the conquered warrior drew the plow—and only after him the horse. Only pacifistic fools can regard this as a sign of human depravity, failing to realize that this development had to take place in order to reach the point where today these sky-pilots could force their drivel on the world.

(42)

---

7 Schiller. *Die Verschwörung des Fiesko*, Act III, Scene 4, spoken by the Moor. It properly reads: *'Der Moor hat seine Arbeit getan,'* etc. (The Moor has done his work), but is often quoted in the altered version with *'Schuldigkeit'* in place of *'Arbeit.'*

The progress of humanity is like climbing an endless ladder; it is impossible to climb higher without first taking the lower steps. Thus, the Aryan had to take the road to which reality directed him and not the one that would appeal to the imagination of a modern pacifist. The road of reality is hard and difficult, but in the end it leads where our friend would like to bring humanity by dreaming, but unfortunately removes more than bringing it closer. (43)

Hence it is no accident that the first cultures arose in places where the Aryan, in his encounters with lower peoples, subjugated them and bent them to his will. They then became the first technical instrument in the service of a developing culture. (44)

Thus, the road which the Aryan had to take was clearly marked out. As a conqueror he subjected the lower beings and regulated their practical activity under his command, according to his will and for his aims. But in directing them to a useful, though arduous activity, he not only spared the life of those he subjected; perhaps he gave them a fate that was better than their previous so-called 'freedoms.' As long as he ruthlessly upheld the master attitude, not only did he really remain master, but also the preserver and increaser of culture. For culture was based exclusively on his abilities and hence on his actual survival. As soon as the subjected people began to raise themselves up and probably approached the conqueror in language, the sharp dividing wall between master and servant fell. The Aryan gave up the purity of his blood and, therefore, lost his sojourn in the paradise which he had made for himself. He became submerged in the racial mixture, and gradually, more and more, lost his cultural capacity, until at last, not only mentally but also physically, he began to resemble the subjected aborigines more than his own ancestors. For a time he could live on the existing cultural benefits, but then petrifaction set in and he fell a prey to oblivion. (45)

Thus cultures and empires collapsed to make place for new formations. (46)

Blood mixture and the resultant drop in the racial level is the sole cause of the dying out of old cultures; for men do not perish as a result of lost wars, but by the loss of that force of resistance which is contained only in pure blood. (47)

All who are not of good race in this world are chaff. (48)

And all occurrences in world history are only the expression of the races' instinct of self-preservation, in the good or bad sense. (49)

Karl Marx
(1818–1883)

Friedrich Engels
(1820–1895)

MARX was a German socialist who, with Friedrich Engels, formulated the principles of dialectical materialism, or economic determinism. Their joint document, The Communist Manifesto, *appeared in 1848. In 1864, Marx organized the First Internationale, an association of European socialists, and in 1867 he published the first volume of his classic work,* Das Kapital.

ENGELS, who met Marx in Paris in 1844, completed the work from Marx's notes after his death.

■ *The Communist Manifesto*

A SPECTRE IS haunting Europe, the spectre of Communism. All the powers of old Europe have entered into a holy alliance to exorcise this spectre; Pope and Czar, Metternich and Guizot, French Radicals and German police-spies. (1)

Where is the party in opposition that has not been decried as communistic by its opponents in power? Where is the Opposition that has not hurled back the branding reproach of Communism, against the more advanced opposition parties, as well as against its reactionary adversaries? (2)

Two things result from this fact:

1. Communism is already acknowledged by all European powers to be itself a power.

2. It is high time that Communists should openly, in the face of the whole world, publish their views, their aims, their tendencies, and meet this nursery tale of the spectre of Communism with a manifesto of the party itself. (3)

To this end, Communists of various nationalities have assembled in London, and sketched the following manifesto, to be published in the English, French, German, Italian, Flemish, and Danish languages.   (4)

I. Bourgeois and Proletarians

The history of all hitherto existing society is the history of class struggles.   (5)

Freeman and slave, patrician and plebeian, lord and serf, guild-master and journeyman, in a word, oppressor and oppressed, stood in constant opposition to one another, carried on an uninterrupted, now hidden, now open fight, a fight that each time ended either in a revolutionary reconstitution of society at large, or in the common ruin of the contending classes.   (6)

In the earlier epochs of history, we find almost every where a complicated arrangement of society into various orders, a manifold gradation of social rank. In ancient Rome we have patricians, knights, plebeians, slaves; in the Middle Ages, feudal lords, vassals, guild-masters, journeymen, apprentices, serfs; in almost all of these classes, again, subordinate gradations.   (7)

The modern bourgeois society that has sprouted from the ruins of feudal society has not done away with class antagonisms. It has but established new classes, new conditions of oppression, new forms of struggle in place of the old ones.   (8)

Our epoch, the epoch of the bourgeoisie, possesses, however, this distinctive feature; it has simplified the class antagonisms. Society as a whole is more and more splitting up into two great hostile camps, into two great classes directly facing each other: Bourgeoisie and Proletariat.   (9)

From the serfs of the Middle Ages sprang the chartered burghers of the earliest towns. From these burgesses the first elements of the bourgeoisie were developed.   (10)

The discovery of America, the rounding of the Cape, opened up fresh ground for the rising bourgeoisie. The East-Indian and Chinese markets, the colonization of America, trade with the colonies, the increase in the means of exchange and in commodities generally, gave to commerce, to navigation, to industry, an impulse never before known, and thereby, to the revolutionary element in the tottering feudal society, a rapid development.   (11)

The feudal system of industry, in which industrial production was monopolized by closed guilds, now no longer sufficed for the growing wants of the new markets. The manufacturing system took its place. The guild-masters were pushed on one side by the manufacturing middle-class; divi-

sion of labor between the different corporate guilds vanished in the face
of division of labor in each single workshop. Meantime the markets kept
ever growing, the demand, ever rising. Even manufacture no longer sufficed.
Thereupon steam and machinery revolutionized industrial production. The
place of manufacture was now taken by the giant, modern industry, the
place of the industrial middle-class, by industrial millionaires, the leaders
of whole industrial armies, the modern bourgeois.   (12)

Modern industry has established the world-market, for which the discovery of America paved the way. This market has given an immense development to commerce, to navigation, to communication by land. This
development has, in its turn, reacted on the extension of industry; and in
proportion as industry, commerce, navigation, railways extended, in the
same proportion the bourgeoisie developed, increased its capital, and
pushed into the background every class handed down from the Middle
Ages. We see, therefore, how the modern bourgeoisie is itself the product of
a long course of development, of a series of revolutions in the modes of
production and of exchange.   (13)

Each step in the development of the bourgeoisie was accompanied by
a corresponding political advance of that class. An oppressed class under
the sway of the feudal nobility, it became an armed and self-governing
association in the mediaeval commune; here independent urban republic
(as in Italy and Germany), there taxable "third estate" of the monarchy
(as in France); afterwards, in the period of manufacture proper, serving
either the semi-feudal or the absolute monarchy as a counterpoise against
the nobility, and, in fact, cornerstone of the great monarchies in general,
the bourgeoisie has at last, since the establishment of Modern Industry
and of the world-market, conquered for itself, in the modern representative
State, exclusive political sway. The executive of the modern State is but a
committee for managing the common affairs of the whole bourgeoisie.   (14)

The bourgeoisie has played a most revolutionary role in history.   (15)

The bourgeoisie, wherever it has got the upper hand, has put an end
to all feudal, patriarchal, idyllic relations. It has pitilessly torn asunder the
motley feudal ties that bound man to his "natural superiors," and has left
remaining no other bond between man and man than naked self-interest,
than callous "cash payment". It has drowned the most heavenly ecstacies
of religious fervor, of chivalrous enthusiasm, of philistine sentimentalism,
in the icy water of egotistical calculation. It has resolved personal worth
into exchange value, and in place of the numberless indefeasible chartered
freedoms, has set up that single, unconscionable freedom, Free Trade. In
one word, for exploitation, veiled by religious and political illusions, it
has substituted naked, shameless, direct, brutal exploitation.   (16)

The bourgeoisie has stripped of its halo every occupation hitherto honored and looked up to with reverent awe. It has converted the physician, the lawyer, the priest, the poet, the man of science, into its paid wage-laborers. (17)

The bourgeoisie has torn away from the family its sentimental veil, and has reduced the family relation to a mere money relation. (18)

The bourgeoisie has disclosed how it came to pass that the brutal display of vigor in the Middle Ages, which Reactionists so much admire, found its fitting complement in the most slothful indolence. It has been the first to show what man's activity can bring about. It has accomplished wonders far surpassing Egyptian pyramids, Roman aqueducts, and Gothic cathedrals; it has conducted expeditions that put in the shade all former migrations of nations and crusades. (19)

The bourgeoisie cannot exist without constantly revolutionizing the instruments of production, and thereby the relations of production, and with them the whole relations of society. Conservation of the old modes of production in unaltered form was, on the contrary, the first condition of existence for all earlier industrial classes. Constant revolutionizing of production, uninterrupted disturbance of all social conditions, everlasting uncertainty and agitation distinguish the bourgeois epoch from all earlier ones. All fixed, fast-frozen relations, with their train of ancient and venerable prejudices and opinions, are swept away, all new-formed ones become antiquated before they can ossify. All that is solid melts into air, all that is holy is profaned, and man is at last compelled to face with sober senses his real conditions of life, and his relations with his kind. The need of a constantly expanding market for its products chases the bourgeoisie over the whole surface of the globe. It must nestle everywhere, settle everywhere, establish connections everywhere. (20)

The bourgeoisie has through its exploitation of the world-market given a cosmopolitan character to production and consumption in every country. To the great chagrin of Reactionists, it has drawn from under the feet of industry the national ground on which it stood. All old-established national industries have been destroyed or are daily being destroyed. They are dislodged by new industries, whose introduction becomes a life and death question for all civilized nations, by industries that no longer work up indigenous raw material, but raw material drawn from the remotest zones; industries whose products are consumed, not only at home, but in every quarter of the globe. In place of the old wants, satisfied by the production of the country, we find new wants, requiring for their satisfaction the products of distant lands and climes. In place of the old local and national seclusion and self-sufficiency, we have intercourse in every direction, universal interdependence of nations. And as in material, so also in intellectual production. The intellectual creations of individual nations become common property. National one-sidedness and narrow-mindedness become more and more impossible, and from the numerous national and local literatures there arises a world literature.   (21)

The bourgeoisie, by the rapid improvement of all instruments of production, by the immensely facilitated means of communication, draws all, even the most barbarian, nations into civilization. The cheap prices of its commodities are the heavy artillery with which it batters down all Chinese walls, with which it forces the barbarians' intensely obstinate hatred of foreigners to capitulate. It compels all nations, on pain of extinction, to adopt the bourgeois mode of production; it compels them to introduce what it calls civilization into their midst, i.e., to become bourgeois themselves. In a word, it creates a world after its own image.   (22)

The bourgeoisie has subjected the country to the rule of the towns. It has created enormous cities, has greatly increased the urban population as compared with the rural, and has thus rescued a considerable part of the population from the idiocy of rural life. Just as it has made the country dependent on the towns, so it has made barbarian and semi-barbarian countries dependent on the civilized ones, nations of peasants on nations of bourgeois, the East on the West.   (23)

The bourgeoisie keeps more and more doing away with the scattered state of the population, of the means of production, and of property. It has agglomerated population, centralized means of production, and has concentrated property in a few hands. The necessary consequence of this was political centralization. Independent, or but loosely connected provinces, with separate interests, laws, systems of taxation, and governments, became lumped together in one nation, with one government, one code of laws, one national class-interest, one frontier, and one customs tariff.   (24)

The bourgeoisie, during its rule of scarce one hundred years, has created more massive and more colossal productive forces than have all preceding generations together. Subjection of Nature's forces to man, machinery, application of chemistry to industry and agriculture, steam-navigation, railways, electric telegraphs, clearing of whole continents for cultivation, canalization of rivers, whole populations conjured out of the ground. What earlier century had even a presentiment that such productive forces slumbered in the lap of social labor?   (25)

We see then: the means of production and of exchange on whose foundation the bourgeoisie built itself up were generated in feudal society. At a certain stage in the development of these means of production and of exchange, the conditions under which feudal society produced and exchanged, the feudal organization of agriculture and manufacturing industry, in one word, the feudal relations of property became no longer compatible with the already developed productive forces; they became so many fetters. They had to burst asunder; they were burst asunder.   (26)

Into their places stepped free competition, accompanied by a social and political constitution adapted to it, and by the economical and political sway of the bourgeois class. (27)

A similar movement is going on before our own eyes. Modern bourgeois society with its relations of production, of exchange and of property, a society that has conjured up such gigantic means of production and of exchange, is like the sorcerer, who is no longer able to control the powers of the nether world whom he has called up by his spells. For many a decade past the history of industry and commerce is but the history of the revolt of modern productive forces against modern conditions of production, against the property relations that are the conditions for the existence of the bourgeoisie and of its rule. It is enough to mention the commercial crises that by their periodical return put on its trial, each time more threateningly, the existence of the entire bourgeois society. In these crises a great part not only of the existing products but also of the previously created productive forces are periodically destroyed. In these crises there breaks out an epidemic that, in all earlier epochs, would have seemed an absurdity, the epidemic of overproduction. Society suddenly finds itself put back into a state of momentary barbarism; it appears as if a famine, a universal war of devastation had cut off the supply of every means of subsistence; industry and commerce seem to be destroyed; and why? Because there is too much civilization, too much means of subsistence, too much industry, too much commerce. The productive forces at the disposal of society no longer tend to further the development of the conditions of bourgeois property; on the contrary, they have become too powerful for these conditions, by which they are fettered, and so soon as they overcome these fetters, they bring disorder into the whole of bourgeois society, endanger the existence of bourgeois property. The conditions of bourgeois society are too narrow to comprise the wealth created by them. And how does the bourgeoisie get over these crises? On the one hand by enforced destruction of a mass of productive forces; on the other, by the conquest of new markets, and by the more thorough exploitation of the old ones. That is to say, by paving the way for more extensive and more destructive crises, and by diminishing the means whereby crises are prevented. (28)

The weapons with which the bourgeoisie felled feudalism to the ground are now turned against the bourgeoisie itself. (29)

But not only has the bourgeoisie forged the weapons that bring death to itself; it has also called into existence the men who are to wield those weapons, the modern working-class, the proletarians. (30)

In proportion as the bourgeoisie, i.e., capital, is developed, in the same proportion is the proletariat, the modern working-class, developed, a class of laborers, who live only so long as they find work, and who find work only

so long as their labor increases capital. These laborers, who must sell themselves piecemeal, are a commodity, like every other article of commerce,
and are consequently exposed to all the vicissitudes of competition, to all
the fluctuations of the market.   (31)

Owing to the extensive use of machinery and to division of labor, the
work of the proletarians has lost all individual character, and, consequently,
all charm for the workman. He becomes an appendage of the machine,
and it is only the most simple, most monotonous, and most easily acquired
knack that is required of him. Hence, the cost of production of a workman
is restricted, almost entirely, to the means of subsistence that he requires
for his maintenance, and for the propagation of his race. But the price
of a commodity, and also of labor, is equal to its cost of production. In
proportion, therefore, as the repulsiveness of the work increases, the wage
decreases. Nay more, in proportion as the use of machinery and division
of labor increases, in the same proportion the burden of toil also increases,
whether by prolongation of the working hours, by increase of the work
enacted in a given time, or by increased speed of the machinery, etc.   (32)

Modern industry has converted the little workshop of the patriarchal
master into the great factory of the industrial capitalist. Masses of laborers, crowded into the factory, are organized like soldiers. As privates of
the industrial army they are placed under the command of a perfect hierarchy of officers and sergeants. Not only are they the slaves of the bourgeois class, and of the bourgeois State, they are daily and hourly enslaved
by the machine, by the overlooker, and, above all, by the individual bourgeois manufacturer himself. The more openly this despotism proclaims
gain to be its end and aim, the more petty, the more hateful and the more
embittering it is.   (33)

The less the skill and exertion or strength implied in manual labor, in
other words, the more modern industry becomes developed, the more is
the labor of men superseded by that of women. Differences of age and sex
have no longer any distinctive social validity for the working class. All are
instruments of labor, more or less expensive to use, according to their age
and sex.   (34)

No sooner is the exploitation of the laborer by the manufacturer, so
far at an end, that he receives his wages in cash, than he is set upon by the
other portions of the bourgeoisie, the landlord, the shopkeeper, the pawn-
broker, etc.   (35)

The lower strata of the Middle class, the small tradespeople, shopkeepers, and retired tradesmen generally, the handicraftsmen and peasants, all
these sink gradually into the proletariat, partly because their diminutive
capital does not suffice for the scale on which Modern Industry is carried
on, and is swamped in the competition with the large capitalists, partly
because their specialized skill is rendered worthless by new methods of

production. Thus the proletariat is recruited from all classes of the population. (36)

The proletariat goes through various stages of development. With its birth begins its struggle with the bourgeoisie. At first the contest is carried on by individual laborers, then by the workpeople of a factory, then by the operatives of one trade, in one locality, against the individual bourgeois who directly exploits them. They direct their attacks not against the bourgeois conditions of production, but against the instruments of production themselves; they destroy imported wares that compete with their labor, they smash to pieces machinery, they set factories ablaze, they seek to restore by force the vanished status of the workman of the Middle Ages. (37)

At this stage the laborers still form an incoherent mass scattered over the whole country, and broken up by their mutual competition. If anywhere they unite to form more compact bodies, this is not yet the consequence of their own active union, but of the union of the bourgeoisie, which class, in order to attain its own political ends, is compelled to set the whole proletariat in motion, and is moreover yet, for a time, able to do so. At this stage, therefore, the proletarians do not fight their enemies, but the enemies of their enemies, the remnants of absolute monarchy, the landowners, the non-industrial bourgeois, the petty bourgeoisie. Thus the whole historical movement is concentrated in the hands of the bourgeoisie; every victory so obtained is a victory for the bourgeoisie. (38)

But with the development of industry the proletariat not only increases in number, it becomes concentrated in greater masses, its strength grows, and it feels that strength more. The various interests and conditions of life within the ranks of the proletariat are more and more equalized, in proportion as machinery obliterates all distinctions of labor, and nearly everywhere reduces wages to the same low level. The growing competition among the bourgeois, and the resulting commercial crises, make the wages of the workers ever more fluctuating. The unceasing improvement of machinery, ever more rapidly developing, makes their livelihood more and more precarious; the collisions between individual workmen and individual bourgeois take more and more the character of collisions between two classes. Thereupon the workers begin to form combinations (Trades' Unions) against the bourgeois; they club together in order to keep up the rate of wages; they found permanent associations in order to make provision beforehand for these occasional revolts. Here and there the contest breaks out into riots. Now and then the workers are victorious, but only for a time. The real fruit of their battles lies, not in the immediate result, but in the ever expanding union of the workers. This union is helped on by the improved means of communication that are created by modern industry, and that place the workers of different localities in contact with one another. It was just this contact that was needed to centralize the numerous local struggles, all of the same character, into one national struggle between classes. But every class struggle is a political struggle. And that union, to attain which the burghers of the Middle Ages, with their miserable highways, required centuries, the modern proletarians, thanks to railways, achieve in a few years.   (39)

This organization of the proletarians into a class, and consequently into a political party, is continually being upset again by the competition between the workers themselves. But it ever rises up again, stronger, firmer, mightier. It compels legislative recognition of particular interests of the workers by taking advantage of the divisions among the bourgeoisie itself. Thus the ten-hour bill in England was carried.   (40)

Altogether collisions between the classes of the old society further, in many ways, the course of development of the proletariat. The bourgeoisie finds itself involved in a constant battle. At first with the aristocracy; later on with those portions of the bourgeoisie itself, whose interests have become antagonistic to the progress of industry; at all times, with the bourgeoisie of foreign countries. In all these battles it sees itself compelled to appeal to the proletariat, to ask for its help, and thus to drag it into the political arena. The bourgeoisie itself, therefore, supplies the proletariat with its own elements of political and general education, in other words, it furnishes the proletariat with weapons for fighting the bourgeoisie. (41)

Further, as we have already seen, entire sections of the ruling classes are, by the advance of industry, precipitated into the proletariat, or are at least threatened in their conditions of existence. These also supply the proletariat with fresh elements of enlightenment and progress.   (42)

Finally, in times when the class-struggle nears the decisive hour, the process of dissolution going on within the ruling class, in fact, within the whole range of old society, assumes such a violent, glaring character, that a small section of the ruling class cuts itself adrift, and joins the revolutionary class, the class that holds the future in its hands. Just as, therefore, at an earlier period, a section of the nobility went over to the bourgeoisie, so now a portion of the bourgeoisie goes over to the proletariat, and in particular, a portion of the bourgeois ideologists, who have raised themselves to the level of comprehending theoretically the historical movements as a whole.   (43)

Of all the classes that stand face to face with the bourgeoisie today, the proletariat alone is a really revolutionary class. The other classes decay and finally disappear in the face of modern industry; the proletariat is its special and essential product.   (44)

The lower middle-class, the small manufacturer, the shopkeeper, the artisan, the peasant, all these fight against the bourgeoisie, to save from extinction their existence as fractions of the middle class. They are, therefore, not revolutionary, but conservative. Nay more, they are reactionary, for they try to roll back the wheel of history. If by chance they are revolutionary, they are so, only in view of their impending transfer into the proletariat; they thus defend not their present, but their future interests, they desert their own standpoint to place themselves at that of the proletariat. (45)

The "dangerous class," the social scum, that passively rotting mass thrown off by the lowest layers of old society, may, here and there, be swept into the movement by a proletarian revolution; its conditions of life, however, prepare it far more for the part of a bribed tool of reactionary intrigue. (46)

In the conditions of the proletariat, those of old society at large are already virtually swamped. The proletarian is without property; his relation to his wife and children has no longer anything in common with the bourgeois family relations; modern industrial labor, modern subjection to capital, the same in England as in France, in America as in Germany, has stripped him of every trace of national character. Law, morality, religion, are to him so many bourgeois prejudices, behind which lurk in ambush just as many bourgeois interests. All the preceding classes that got the upper hand sought to fortify their already acquired status by subjecting society at large to their conditions of appropriation. The proletarians cannot become masters of the productive forces of society, except by abolishing their own previous mode of appropriation, and thereby also every other previous mode of appropriation. They have nothing of their own to secure and to fortify; their mission is to destroy all previous securities for, and insurances of, individual property. (47)

All previous historical movements were movements of minorities, or in the interest of minorities. The proletarian movement is the self-conscious, independent movement of the immense majority, in the interest of the immense majority. The proletariat, the lowest stratum of our present society, cannot stir, cannot raise itself up, without the whole superincumbent strata of official society being sprung into the air. (48)

Though not in substance, yet in form, the struggle of the proletariat with the bourgeoisie is at first a national struggle. The proletariat of each country must first of all settle matters with its bourgeoisie. In depicting the most general phases of the development of the proletariat, we traced the more or less veiled civil war, raging within existing society, up to the point where that war breaks out into open revolution, and where the violent overthrow of the bourgeoisie, lays the foundation for the sway of the proletariat. (49)

Hitherto, every form of society has been based, as we have already seen, on the antagonism of oppressing and oppressed classes. But in order to oppress a class, certain conditions must be assured to it under which it can, at least, continue its slavish existence. The serf, in the period of serf-dom, raised himself to membership in the commune, just as the petty bour-geois, under the yoke of feudal absolutism, managed to develop into a bour-geois. The modern laborer, on the contrary, instead of rising with the prog-ress of industry, sinks deeper and deeper below the conditions of existence of his own class. He becomes a pauper, and pauperism develops more rapidly than population and wealth. And here it becomes evident that the bourgeoisie is unfit any longer to be the ruling class in society, and to impose its conditions of existence upon society, as an overriding law. It is unfit to rule, because it is incompetent to assure an existence to its slave within his slavery, because it cannot help letting him sink into such a state that it has to feed him. Society can no longer live under this bourgeoisie, in other words, its existence is no longer compatible with society. The essen-tial condition for the existence, and for the sway of the bourgeois class, is the formation and augmentation of capital; the condition for capital is wage-labor. Wage-labor rests exclusively on competition between the la-borers. The advance of industry, whose involuntary promoter is the bour-geoisie, replaces the isolation of the laborers, due to competition, by their involuntary combination, due to association. The development of Modern Industry therefore cuts from under its feet the very foundation on which the bourgeoisie produces and appropriates products. What the bourgeoisie therefore produces, above all, are its own grave-diggers. Its fall and the victory of the proletariat are equally inevitable.   (50)

II. Proletarians and Communists

In what relation do the Communists stand to the proletarians as a whole?   (51)

The Communists do not form a separate party opposed to other work-ing-class parties.   (52)

They have no interests separate and apart from those of the proletariat as a whole.   (53)

They do not set up any sectarian principles of their own, by which to shape and mould the proletarian movement.   (54)

The Communists are distinguished from the other working-class par-ties by this only: 1. In the national struggles of the proletarians of the different countries they point out and bring to the front the common interests of the entire proletariat independently of all nationality. 2. In the various stages of development which the struggle of the working class against the bourgeoisie has to pass through, they always and everywhere represent the interests of the movement as a whole.   (55)

The Communists, therefore, are on the one hand practically the most advanced and resolute section of the working-class parties of every country, that section which pushes forward all others; on the other hand, theoretically, they have over the great mass of the proletariat the advantage of clearly understanding the line of march, the conditions, and the ultimate general results of the proletarian movement.   (56)

The immediate aim of the Communists is the same as that of all the other proletarian parties; formation of the proletariat into a class, overthrow of the bourgeois supremacy, conquest of political power by the proletariat.   (57)

The theoretical conclusions of the Communists are in no way based on ideas or principles that have been invented, or discovered, by this or that would-be universal reformer.   (58)

They merely express, in general terms, actual relations springing from an existing class struggle, from an historical movement going on under our very eyes. The abolition of existing property relations is not at all a distinctive feature of Communism. All property relations in the past have continually been subject to historical change consequent upon the change in historical conditions.   (59)

The French Revolution, for example, abolished feudal property in favor of bourgeois property.   (60)

The distinguishing feature of Communism is not the abolition of property generally, but the abolition of bourgeois property. But modern bourgeois private property is the final and most complete expression of the system of producing and appropriating products, that is based on class antagonism, on the exploitation of the many by the few.   (61)

In this sense, the theory of the Communists may be summed up in the single sentence: Abolition of private property.   (62)

We Communists have been reproached with the desire of abolishing the right of personally acquiring property as the fruit of a man's own labor, which property is alleged to be the groundwork of all personal freedom, activity, and independence. Hard-won, self-acquired, self-earned property! Do you mean the property of the petty artisan and of the small peasant, a form of property that preceded the bourgeois form? There is no need to abolish that; the development of industry has to a great extent already destroyed it, and is still destroying it, daily.   (63)

Or do you mean modern bourgeois private property?   (64)

But does wage-labor create any property for the laborer? Not a bit. It creates capital, i.e., that kind of property which exploits wage-labor, and which cannot increase except upon condition of getting a new supply of wage-labor for fresh exploitation. Property, in its present form, is based on the antagonism of capital and wage-labor. Let us examine both sides of this antagonism.   (65)

To be a capitalist is to have not only a purely personal but a social status in production. Capital is a collective product, and only by the united action of many members, nay, in the last resort, only by the united action of all members of society, can it be set in motion.   (66)

Capital is therefore not a personal, it is a social power.   (67)

When, therefore, capital is converted into common property, into the property of all members of society, personal property is not thereby transformed into social property. It is only the social character of the property that has changed. It loses its class character.   (68)

Let us now take wage-labor.   (69)

The average price of wage-labor is the minimum wage, i.e., that quantum of the means of subsistence which is absolutely requisite to keep the laborer in bare existence as a laborer. What, therefore, the wage-laborer appropriates by means of his labor, merely suffices to prolong and reproduce a bare existence. We by no means intend to abolish this personal appropriation of the products of labor, an appropriation that is made for the maintenance and reproduction of human life, and that leaves no surplus wherewith to command the labor of others. All that we want to do away with is the miserable character of this appropriation, under which the laborer lives merely to increase capital, and is allowed to live only in so far as the interest of the ruling class requires it.   (70)

In bourgeois society, living labor is but a means to increase accumulated labor. In Communist society, accumulated labor is but a means to widen, to enrich, to promote the existence of the laborer.   (71)

In bourgeois society, therefore, the past dominates the present; in Communist society, the present dominates the past. In bourgeois society capital is independent and has individuality, while the living person is dependent and has no individuality.   (72)

And the abolition of this state of things is called by the bourgeois, abolition of individuality and freedom! And rightly so. The abolition of bourgeois individuality, bourgeois independence, and bourgeois freedom is undoubtedly aimed at.   (73)

By freedom is meant, under the present bourgeois conditions of production, free trade, free selling and buying.   (74)

But if selling and buying disappears, free selling and buying disappears also. This talk about free selling and buying, and all the other "brave words" of our bourgeoisie about freedom in general, have a meaning, if any, only in contrast with restricted selling and buying, with the fettered traders of the Middle Ages, but have no meaning when opposed to the Communist abolition of buying and selling, of the bourgeois conditions of production, and of the bourgeoisie itself.   (75)

You are horrified at our intending to do away with private property. But in your existing society, private property is already done away with for nine-tenths of the population; its existence for the few is solely due to its non-existence in the hands of those nine-tenths. You reproach us, therefore, with intending to do away with a form of property, the necessary condition for whose existence is the non-existence of any property for the immense majority of society. In a word, you reproach us with intending to do away with your property. Precisely so; that is just what we intend. (76)

From the moment when labor can no longer be converted into capital, money, or rent, into a social power capable of being monopolized, i.e., from the moment when individual property can no longer be transformed into bourgeois property, into capital, from that moment, you say, individuality vanishes. You must, therefore, confess that by "individual" you mean no other person than the bourgeois, than the middle-class owner of property. This person must, indeed, be swept out of the way, and made impossible. (77)

Communism deprives no man of the power to appropriate the products of society; all that it does is to deprive him of the power to subjugate the labor of others by means of such appropriation. (78)

It has been objected, that upon the abolition of private property all work will cease, and universal laziness will overtake us. (79)

According to this, bourgeois society ought long ago to have gone to the dogs through sheer idleness; for those of its members who work, acquire nothing, and those who acquire anything, do not work. The whole of this objection is but another expression of the tautology: there can no longer be any wage-labor when there is no longer any capital. (80)

All objections urged against the Communistic mode of producing and appropriating material products, have, in the same way, been urged against the Communistic modes of producing and appropriating intellectual products. Just as, to the bourgeois, the disappearance of class property is the disappearance of production itself, so the disappearance of class culture is to him identical with the disappearance of all culture. (81)

That culture, the loss of which he laments, is, for the enormous majority, a mere training to act as a machine. (82)

But don't wrangle with us so long as you apply, to our intended abolition of bourgeois property, the standard of your bourgeois notions of freedom, culture, law, etc. Your very ideas are but the outgrowth of the conditions of your bourgeois production and bourgeois property, just as your jurisprudence is but the will of your class made into a law for all, a will, whose essential character and direction are determined by the economic conditions of existence of your class. (83)

The selfish misconception that induces you to transform into eternal laws of nature and of reason, the social forms springing from your present mode of production and form of property, historical relations that rise and disappear in the progress of production, this misconception you share with every ruling class that has preceded you. What you see clearly in the case of ancient property, what you admit in the case of feudal property, you are of course forbidden to admit in the case of your own bourgeois form of property.   (84)

Abolition of the family! Even the most radical flare up at this infamous proposal of the Communists.   (85)

On what foundation is the present family, the bourgeois family, based? On capital, on private gain. In its completely developed form this family exists only among the bourgeoisie. But this state of things finds its complement in the practical absence of the family among the proletarians, and in public prostitution.   (86)

The bourgeois family will vanish as a matter of course when its complement vanishes, and both will vanish with the vanishing of capital.   (87)

Do you charge us with wanting to stop the exploitation of children by their parents? To this crime we plead guilty.   (88)

But, you will say, we destroy the most hallowed of relations, when we replace home education by social. And your education! Is not that also social, and determined by the social conditions under which you educate, by the intervention, direct or indirect, of society by means of school, etc.? The Communists have not invented the intervention of society in education; they do but seek to alter the character of that intervention, and to rescue education from the influence of the ruling class.   (89)

The bourgeois clap-trap about the family and education, about the hallowed co-relation of parent and child, becomes all the more disgusting, the more, by the action of Modern Industry, all family ties among the proletarians are torn asunder, and their children transformed into simple articles of commerce and instruments of labor.   (90)

But you Communists would introduce community of women, screams the whole bourgeoisie in chorus. The bourgeois sees in his wife a mere instrument of production. He hears that the instruments of production are to be exploited in common, and, naturally, can come to no other conclusion than that the lot of being common to all will likewise fall to the women.
                                                                     (91)

He has not even a suspicion that the real point aimed at is to do away with the status of women as the mere instruments of production in society. For the rest, nothing is more ridiculous than the virtuous indignation of our bourgeois at the community of women which, they pretend, is to be openly and officially established by the Communists. The Communists have no need to introduce community of women; it has existed almost from time immemorial.   (92)

Our bourgeois, not content with having the wives and daughters of their proletarians at their disposal, not to speak of the common prostitutes, take the greatest pleasure in seducing each others' wives. Bourgeois marriage is in reality a system of wives in common and thus, at the most, what the Communists might possibly be reproached with, is that they desire to introduce, in substitution for a hypocritically concealed, an openly legalized community of women. For the rest, it is self-evident that the abolition of the present system of production must bring with it the abolition of the community of women springing from that system, i.e., of prostitution both public and private.   (93)

The Communists are further reproached with desiring to abolish countries and nationalities.   (94)

The working men have no country. We cannot take from them what they have not got. Since the proletariat must first of all acquire political supremacy, must rise to be the leading class of the nation, must constitute itself the nation, it is, so far, itself national, though not in the bourgeois sense of the word.   (95)

The national differences and antagonisms between peoples are daily more and more vanishing, owing to the development of the bourgeoisie, to freedom of commerce, to the world-market, to uniformity in the mode of production and in the conditions of life corresponding thereto.   (96)

The supremacy of the proletariat will cause them to vanish still faster. United action, of the leading civilized countries at least, is one of the first conditions for the emancipation of the proletariat.   (97)

In proportion as the exploitation of one individual by another is put an end to, the exploitation of one nation by another will also be put an end to. In proportion as the antagonism between classes within the nation vanishes, the hostility of one nation to another will come to an end.   (98)

The charges against Communism made from a religious, a philosophical, and generally, from an ideological standpoint, are not deserving of serious examination.   (99)

Does it require deep intuition to comprehend that man's ideas, views, and conceptions, in one word, man's consciousness, changes with every change in the conditions of his material existence, in his social relations and in his social life?   (100)

What else does the history of ideas prove, than that intellectual production changes in character in proportion as material production is changed? The ruling ideas of each age have ever been the ideas of its ruling class.
                                                    (101)

When people speak of ideas that revolutionize society, they do but express the fact, that within the old society, the elements of a new one have been created, and that the dissolution of the old ideas keeps even pace with the dissolution of the old conditions of existence.   (102)

When the ancient world was in its last throes, the ancient religions were overcome by Christianity. When Christian ideas succumbed in the 18th century to rationalist ideas, feudal society fought its death battle with the then revolutionary bourgeoisie. The ideas of religious liberty and freedom of conscience, merely gave expression to the sway of free competition within the domain of knowledge. "Undoubtedly," it will be said, "religious, moral, philosophical and juridical ideas have been modified in the course of historical development. But religion, morality, philosophy, political science, and law, constantly survived this change."   (103)

"There are, besides, eternal truths, such as Freedom, Justice, etc., that are common to all states of society. But Communism abolishes eternal truths, it abolishes all religion, and all morality, instead of constituting them on a new basis; it therefore acts in contradiction to all past historical experience."   (104)

What does this accusation reduce itself to? The history of all past society has consisted in the development of class antagonisms, antagonisms that assumed different forms at different epochs.   (105)

But whatever form they may have taken, one fact is common to all past ages, viz., the exploitation of one part of society by the other. No wonder, then, that the social consciousness of past ages, despite all the multiplicity and variety it displays, moves within certain common forms, or general ideas, which cannot completely vanish except with the total disappearance of class antagonisms.   (106)

The Communist revolution is the most radical rupture with traditional property relations; no wonder its development involves the most radical rupture with the traditional ideas of all of the bourgeoisie. But let us have done with the bourgeois objections to Communism.   (107)

We have seen above, that the first step in the revolution by the working class, is to raise the proletariat to the position of ruling class, to win the battle of democracy.   (108)

The proletariat will use its political supremacy to wrest, by degrees, all capital from the bourgeoisie, to centralize all instruments of production in the hands of the State, i.e., of the proletariat organized as the ruling class, and to increase the total of productive forces as rapidly as possible.
                                                              (109)

Of course, in the beginning, this cannot be effected except by means of despotic inroads on the rights of property, and on the conditions of bourgeois production; by means of measures, therefore, which appear economically insufficient and untenable, but which, in the course of the movement, outstrip themselves, necessitate further inroads upon the old social order, and are unavoidable as a means of entirely revolutionizing the mode of production.   (110)

These measures will of course be different in different countries. (111)

Nevertheless in the most advanced countries the following will be found pretty generally applicable:

1. Abolition of property in land and application of all rents of land to public purposes.

2. A heavy progressive or graduated income tax.

3. Abolition of all right of inheritance.

4. Confiscation of property of emigrants and rebels.

5. Centralization of credit in the hands of the State, by means of a national bank with State capital and an exclusive monopoly.

6. Centralization of the means of communication and transport in the hands of the State.

7. Extension of factories and instruments of production owned by the State; the bringing into cultivation of waste lands, and the improvement of the soil generally in accordance with a common plan.

8. Equal liability of all to labor. Establishment of industrial armies, especially for agriculture.

9. Combination of agriculture with manufacturing industries; gradual abolition of the distinction between town and country, by a more equable distribution of population over the country.

10. Free education for all children in public schools. Abolition of children's factory labor in its present form. Combination of education with industrial production, etc., etc.   (112)

When, in the course of development, class distinctions have disappeared, and all production has been concentrated in the hands of a vast association of the whole nation, the public power will lose its political character. Political power, properly so called, is merely the organized power of one class for oppressing another. If the proletariat during its contest with the bourgeoisie is compelled, by the force of circumstances, to organize itself as a class, if, by means of a revolution, it makes itself the ruling class, and, as such, sweeps away by force the old conditions of production, then it will, along with these conditions, have swept away the conditions for the existence of class antagonisms, and of classes generally, and will thereby have abolished its own supremacy as a class.   (113)

In place of the old bourgeois society, with its classes and class antagonisms, we shall have an association, in which the free development of each is the condition for the free development of all.   (114)

III. Socialist and Communist Literature

1. Reactionary Socialism

a. Feudal Socialism

Owing to their historical position, it became the vocation of the aristocracies of France and England to write pamphlets against modern bourgeois society. In the French revolution of July, 1830, and in the English

reform agitation, these aristocracies again succumbed to the hateful up-
start. Thenceforth, a serious political contest was altogether out of the
question. A literary battle alone remained possible. But even in the domain
of literature the old cries of the restoration period had become impossible.
(115)

In order to arouse sympathy, the aristocracy were obliged to lose sight,
apparently, of their own interests, and to formulate their indictment against
the bourgeoisie in the interest of the exploited working class alone. Thus
the aristocracy took their revenge by singing lampoons on their new master,
and whispering in his ears sinister prophecies of coming catastrophe. (116)

In this way arose feudal socialism; half lamentation, half lampoon; half
echo of the past, half menace of the future; at times, by its bitter, witty,
and incisive criticism, striking the bourgeoisie to the very hearts' core, but
always ludicrous in its effect, through total incapacity to comprehend the
march of modern history.   (117)

The aristocracy, in order to rally the people to them, waved the proletarian alms-bag in front for a banner. But the people, so often as it joined
them, saw on their hindquarters the old feudal coats of arms, and deserted
with loud and irreverent laughter.   (118)

One section of the French Legitimists, and "Young England," exhibited
this spectacle.   (119)

In pointing out that their mode of exploitation was different to that of
the bourgeoisie, the feudalists forget that they exploited under circumstances and conditions that were quite different, and that are now antiquated. In showing that, under their rule, the modern proletariat never
existed, they forget that the modern bourgeoisie is the necessary offspring
of their own form of society.   (120)

For the rest, so little do they conceal the reactionary character of their
criticism, that their chief accusation against the bourgeoisie amounts to
this, that under the bourgeois regime a class is being developed, which is
destined to cut up root and branch the old order of society.   (121)

What they upbraid the bourgeoisie with is not so much that it creates a
proletariat, as that it creates a revolutionary proletariat.   (122)

In political practice, therefore, they join in all coercive measures against
the working-class; and in ordinary life, despite their high falutin phrases,
they stoop to pick up the golden apples dropped from the tree of industry,
and to barter truth, love, and honor for traffic in wool, beetroot-sugar and
potato spirit.   (123)

As the parson has ever gone hand in hand with the landlord, so has
Clerical Socialism gone along with Feudal Socialism.   (124)

Nothing is easier than to give Christian asceticism a Socialist tinge. Has
not Christianity declaimed against private property, against marriage,
against the State? Has it not preached in the place of these charity and

poverty, celibacy, and mortification of the flesh, monastic life and Mother Church? Christian Socialism is but the Holy Water with which the priest consecrates the heart-burnings of the aristocrat.   (125)

b. Petty Bourgeois Socialism

The feudal aristocracy was not the only class that was ruined by the bourgeoisie, not the only class whose conditions of existence pined and perished in the atmosphere of modern bourgeois society. The medieval burgesses and the small peasant bourgeoisie, were the precursors of the modern bourgeoisie. In those countries which are but little developed, industrially and commercially, these two classes still vegetate side by side with the rising bourgeoisie. In countries where modern civilization has become fully developed, a new class of petty bourgeois has been formed, fluctuating between proletariat and bourgeoisie, and ever renewing itself as a supplementary part of bourgeois society. The individual members of this class, however, are being constantly hurled down into the proletariat by the action of competition, and, as modern industry develops, they even see the moment approaching when they will completely disappear as an independent section of modern society, to be replaced, in manufactures, agriculture and commerce, by overlookers, bailiffs and shopmen.   (126)

In countries like France, where the peasants constitute far more than half of the population, it was natural that writers who sided with the proletariat against the bourgeoisie, should use, in their criticism of the bourgeoisie regime, the standard of the peasant and petty bourgeois, and from the standpoint of these intermediate classes should take up the cudgels for the working-class. Thus arose petty bourgeois Socialism. Sismondi was the head of this school, not only in France, but also in England.   (127)

This school of Socialism dissected with great acuteness the contradictions in the conditions of modern production. It laid bare the hypocritical apologies of economists. It proved, incontrovertibly, the disastrous effects of machinery and division of labor; the concentration of capital and land in a few hands; overproduction and crises; it pointed out the inevitable ruin of the petty bourgeois and peasant, the misery of the proletariat, the anarchy in production, the crying inequalities in the distribution of wealth, the industrial war of extermination between nations, the dissolution of old moral bonds, of the old family relations, of the old nationalities.   (128)

In its positive aims, however, this form of Socialism aspires either to restoring the old means of production and of exchange, and with them the old property relations, and the old society, or to cramping the modern means of production and of exchange, within the framework of the old property relations that have been, and were bound to be, exploded by those means. In either case, it is both reactionary and Utopian.   (129)

Its last words are: corporate guilds for manufacture; patriarchal relations in agriculture.   (130)

Ultimately, when stubborn historical facts had dispersed all intoxicating
effects of self-deception, this form of Socialism ended in a miserable fit of
the blues.   (131)

German or "True" Socialism

The Socialist and Communist literature of France, a literature that originated under the pressure of a bourgeoisie in power, and that was the
expression of the struggle against this power, was introduced into Germany
at a time when the bourgeoisie, in that country, had just begun its contest
with feudal absolutism.   (132)

German philosophers, would-be philosophers, and beaux esprits, eagerly
seized on this literature, only forgetting this, that when these writings
emigrated from France into Germany, French social conditions had not emigrated along with them. In contact with German social conditions, this
French literature lost all its immediate practical significance, and assumed
a purely literary aspect. Thus, to the German philosophers of the eighteenth
century, the demands of the first French Revolution were nothing more
than the demands of "Practical Reason" in general, and the utterance of the
will of the revolutionary French bourgeoisie signified in their eyes the laws
of pure Will, of Will as it was bound to be, of true human Will generally.
                                                                   (133)

The work of the German literati consisted solely in bringing the new
French ideas into harmony with their ancient philosophical conscience, or
rather in annexing the French ideas without deserting their own philosophic point of view.   (134)

This annexation took place in the same way in which a foreign language
is appropriated, by translation. It is well known how the monks wrote silly
lives of Catholic saints over the manuscripts on which the classical works
of ancient heathendom had been written. The German literati reversed this
process with the profane French literature. They wrote their philosophical
nonsense beneath the French original. For instance, beneath the French
criticism of the economic functions of money, they wrote, "Alienation of
Humanity," and beneath the French criticism of the bourgeois State they
wrote, "Dethronement of the Category of the General," and so forth. (135)

The introduction of these philosophical phrases at the back of the
French historical criticisms they dubbed "Philosophy of Action," "True
Socialism," "German Science of Socialism," "Philosophical Foundation of
Socialism," and so on.   (136)

The French Socialist and Communist literature was thus completely
emasculated. And, since it ceased in the hands of the German to express the

struggle of one class with the other, he felt conscious of having overcome "French one-sidedness" and of representing, not true requirements, but the requirements of Truth, not the interests of the proletariat, but the interests of Human Nature, of Man in general, who belongs to no class, has no reality, who exists only in the realm of philosophical phantasy. This German Socialism, which took its schoolboy task so seriously and solemnly and extolled its poor stock-in-trade in such mountebank fashion, meanwhile gradually lost its pedantic innocence.   (137)

The fight of the German, and, especially, of the Prussian bourgeoisie, against feudal aristocracy and absolute monarchy, in other words, the liberal movement, became more earnest.   (138)

By this, the long-wished-for opportunity was offered to "True Socialism" of confronting the political movement with the socialist demands of hurling the traditional anathemas against liberalism, against representative government, against bourgeois competition, bourgeois freedom of the press, bourgeois legislation, bourgeois liberty and equality, and of preaching to the masses that they had nothing to gain and everything to lose by this bourgeois movement. German Socialism forgot, in the nick of time, that the French criticism, whose silly echo it was, presupposed the existence of modern bourgeois society, with its corresponding economic conditions of existence, and the political constitution adapted thereto, the very things whose attainment was the object of the pending struggle in Germany. (139)

To the absolute governments, with their following of parsons, professors, country squires and officials, it served as more than a welcome scarecrow against the threatening bourgeoisie.   (140)

It was a sweet finish after the bitter pills of floggings and bullets, with which these same governments, just at that time, dosed the German working-class risings.   (141)

While this True Socialism thus served the governments as a weapon for fighting the German bourgeoisie, it at the same time directly represented a reactionary interest, the interest of the German Philistines. In Germany the petty bourgeois class, a relic of the sixteenth century, and since then constantly cropping up again under various forms, is the real social basis of the existing state of things.   (142)

To preserve this class is to preserve the existing state of things in Germany. The industrial and political supremacy of the bourgeoisie threatens it with certain destruction; on the one hand from the concentration of capital; on the other from the rise of a revolutionary proletariat. True Socialism appeared to kill these two birds with one stone. It spread like an epidemic.   (143)

The robe of speculative cobwebs, embroidered with flowers of rhetoric, steeped in the dew of sickly sentiment, this transcendental robe in which the German Socialists wrapped their sorry eternal truths, all skin and bone, served wonderfully to increase the sale of their goods amongst such a public.   (144)

And on its part, German Socialism recognized more and more its own calling as the bombastic representative of the petty bourgeois Philistine.
(145)

It proclaimed the German nation to be the model nation, and the German petty Philistine to be the typical man. To every villainous meanness of this model man it gave a hidden, higher, socialistic interpretation, the exact contrary of its true character. It went to the extreme length of directly opposing the "brutally destructive" tendency of Communism, and of proclaiming its supreme and impartial contempt of all class struggles. With very few exceptions, all the so-called Socialist and Communist publications that now (1847) circulate in Germany belong to the domain of this foul and enervating literature.   (146)

2. Conservative or Bourgeois Socialism

A part of the bourgeoisie is desirous of redressing social grievances in order to secure the continued existence of bourgeois society.   (147)

To this section belong economists, philanthropists, humanitarians, improvers of the condition of the work class, organizers of charity, members of societies for the prevention of cruelty to animals, temperance fanatics, hole and corner reformers of every imaginable kind. This form of Socialism has, moreover, been worked out into complete systems.   (148)

We may cite Proudhon's "Philosophie de la Misere" as an example of this form.   (149)

The socialistic bourgeois want all the advantages of modern social conditions without the struggles and dangers necessarily resulting therefrom. They desire the existing state of society minus its revolutionary and disintegrating elements. They wish for a bourgeoisie without a proletariat. The bourgeoisie naturally conceives the world in which it is supreme to be the best; and bourgeois Socialism develops this comfortable conception into various more or less complete systems. In requiring the proletariat to carry out such a system, and thereby to march straightway into the social New Jerusalem, it but requires in reality, that the proletariat should remain within the bounds of existing society, but should cast away all its hateful ideas about the bourgeoisie. A second and more practical, but less systematic, form of this Socialism sought to depreciate every revolutionary movement in the eyes of the working class, by showing that no mere political reform, but only a change in the material conditions of existence, in economical relations, could be of any advantage to them. By changes in the material conditions of existence, this form of Socialism, however, by no means understands abolition of the bourgeois relations of production, an

abolition that can be effected only by a revolution, but administrative reforms, based on the continued existence of these relations; reforms, therefore, that in no respect affect the relations between capital and labor, but,
at the best, lessen the cost and simplify the administrative work of bourgeois
government. (150)

Bourgeois Socialism attains adequate expression, when, and only when,
it becomes a mere figure of speech. (151)

Free trade: for the benefit of the working class. Protective duties: for
the benefit of the working class. Prison Reform: for the benefit of the
working class. These are the last words and the only seriously meant words
of bourgeois Socialism. (152)

It is summed up in the phrase: the bourgeois are bourgeois for the
benefit of the working class. (153)

3. Critical-Utopian Socialism and Communism

We do not here refer to that literature which in every great modern
revolution has always given voice to the demands of the proletariat, such as
the writings of Babeuf and others. (154)

The first direct attempts of the proletariat to attain its own ends were
made in time of universal excitment when feudal society was being overthrown. These attempts necessarily failed, owing to the then undeveloped
state of the proletariat, as well as to the absence of the economic conditions
for its emancipation, conditions that had yet to be produced, and could be
produced by the impending bourgeois epoch alone. The revolutionary literature that accompanied these first movements of the proletariat had necessarily a reactionary character. It inculcated universal asceticism and social leveling in its crudest form. (155)

The Socialist and Communist systems properly so-called, those of St.
Simon, Fourier, Owen, and others, spring to existence in the early undeveloped period described above, of the struggle between proletariat and
bourgeoisie (see I. Bourgeoisie and Proletariat). The founders of these systems see, indeed, the class antagonisms, as well as the action of the decom-
posing elements in the prevailing form of society. But the proletariat, as yet
in its infancy, offers to them the spectacle of a class without any historical
initiative or any independent political movement. Since the development
of class antagonism keeps even pace with the development of industry, the
economic situation, as they find it, does not as yet offer to them the
material conditions for the emancipation of the proletariat. They therefore
search after a new social science, after new social laws, that are to create
these conditions. (156)

Historical action is to yield to their personal inventive action; historically
created conditions of emancipation to fantastic ones; and the gradual,

spontaneous class organization of the proletariat to an organization of society specially contrived by these inventors. Future history resolves itself, in their eyes, into the propaganda and the practical carrying out of their social plans.   (157)

In the formation of their plans they are conscious of caring chiefly for the interests of the working class, as being the most suffering class. Only from the point of view of being the most suffering class does the proletariat exist for them.   (158)

The undeveloped state of the class struggle, as well as their own surroundings, cause Socialists of this kind to consider themselves far superior to all class antagonisms. They want to improve the condition of every member of society, even that of the most favored. Hence, they habitually appeal to society at large, without distinction of class; nay, by preference, to the ruling class. For how can people, when once they understand their system, fail to see in it the best possible plan of the best state of society? Hence, they reject all political and especially all revolutionary action; they wish to attain their ends by peaceful means, and endeavor by small experiments, necessarily doomed to failure, and by the force of example to pave their way for the new social Gospel. Such fantastic pictures of future society, painted at a time when the proletariat is still in a very undeveloped state and has but a fantastic conception of its own position, correspond with the first instinctive yearnings of that class for a general reconstruction of society.   (159)

But these Socialist and Communist publications contain also a critical element. They attack every principle of existing society. Hence they are full of the most valuable materials for the enlightenment of the working class. The practical measures proposed in them, such as the abolition of the distinction between town and country, of the family, of the carrying on of industries for the account of private individuals, and of the wage system, the proclamation of social harmony, the conversion of the functions of the State into a mere superintendence of production, all these proposals point solely to the disappearance of class antagonisms which were, at that time, only just cropping up, and which, in these publications, are recognized under their earliest, indistinct and undefined forms only. These proposals therefore are of a purely Utopian character.   (160)

The significance of Critical-Utopian Socialism and Communism bears an inverse relation to historcial development. In proportion as the modern class struggle develops and takes definite shape, this fantastic standing apart from the contest, these fantastic attacks on it lose all practical value and all theoretical justification. Therefore, although the originators of these systems were, in many respects, revolutionary, their disciples have, in every case, formed mere reactionary sects. They hold fast by the original views of their masters, in opposition to the progressive historical development of the proletariat. They endeavor, therefore, and that consistently, to deaden the class struggle and to reconcile the class antagonisms. They still dream of experimental realization of their social Utopias, of founding isolated "phalansteres", of establishing "Home Colonies", of setting up a "Little Icaria", duodecimo editions of the New Jerusalem, and to realize all these castles in the air, they are compelled to appeal to the feelings and purses of the bourgeois. By degrees they sink into the category of the reactionary conservative Socialists depicted above, differing from these only by more systematic pedantry, and by their fanatical and superstitious belief in the miraculous effects of their social science. (161)

They, therefore, violently oppose all political action on the part of the working class; such action, according to them, can only result from blind unbelief in the new Gospel. (162)

The Owenites in England, and the Fourierists in France, respectively, oppose the Chartists and the "Reformistes". (163)

IV. Position of the Communists in
Relation to the Various
Existing Opposition Parties

Section II has made clear the relations of the Communists to existing working-class parties, such as the Chartists in England and the Agrarian Reformers in America. (164)

The Communists are constantly fighting for the attainment of the immediate aims for the enforcement of the interests of the working class; but in the movement of the present, they also represent and take care of the future of that movement. In France the Communists ally themselves with the Social-Democrats against the conservative and radical bourgeoisie, reserving, however, the right to take up a critical position in regard to phrases and illusions traditionally handed down from the great Revolution. (165)

In Switzerland they support the Radicals without losing sight of the fact that this party consists of antagonistic elements, partly of Democratic Socialists, in the French sense, partly of radical bourgeois. (166)

In Poland they support the party that insists on an agrarian revolution, as the prime condition for national emancipation, that party which fomented the insurrection at Cracow in 1846. (167)

In Germany they fight with the bourgeoisie whenever it acts in a revolutionary way, against the absolute monarchy, the feudal squirearchy, and the petty bourgeoisie. (168)

But they never cease, for a single instant, to instill into the working class the clearest possible recognition of the hostile antagonism between

bourgeoisie and proletariat, in order that the German workers may straight-way use, as so many weapons against the bourgeoisie, the social and politi-cal conditions that the bourgeoisie must necessarily introduce along with its supremacy, and in order that, after the fall of the reactionary classes in Germany, the fight against the bourgeoisie itself may immediately begin.
(169)

The Communists turn their attention chiefly to Germany, because that country is on the eve of a bourgeois revolution that is bound to be carried out under more advanced conditions of European civilization and with a more developed proletariat than existed in England in the seventeenth, and in France in the eighteenth century, and because the bourgeois revolu-tion in Germany will be but the prelude to an immediately following prole-tarian revolution. In short, the Communists everywhere support every rev-olutionary movement against the existing social and political order of things.   (170)

In all these movements they bring to the front, as the leading question in each, the property question, no matter what its degree of development at that time.   (171)

Finally, they labor everywhere for the union and agreement of the democratic parties of all countries. The Communists disdain to conceal their views and aims. They openly declare that their ends can be attained only by the forcible overthrow of all existing social conditions. Let the ruling classes tremble at a Communistic revolution. The proletarians have nothing to lose but their chains. They have a world to win.   (172)

Working men of all countries, unite!   (173)

Mao Tse-Tung

(1893–   )

MAO TSE-TUNG has been active in China's political and ideological af-fairs for almost half a century and is now known, if allowed the ritualistic phrase, as "the grand old man" of Communist China. He took part in the founding of the Communist Party in China in 1921 and from the first served on its Central Committee. After the defeat of Kuomintang in 1949, he be-came Chairman of the Central People's Government of the People's Repub-lic of China. A poet and a persistent ideologist, he has published several volumes of Selected Writings *and numerous pamphlets.*

■ *Methods of Thinking and Methods of Work*

THE HISTORY OF mankind is one of continuous development from the realm of necessity to the realm of freedom. This process is never-ending. In any society in which classes exist class struggle will never end. In classless society the struggle between the new and the old and between truth and falsehood will never end. In the fields of the struggle for production and scientific experiment, mankind makes constant progress and nature under-goes constant change; they never remain at the same level. Therefore, man has constantly to sum up experience and go on discovering, inventing, creating and advancing. Ideas of stagnation, pessimism, inertia and com-placency are all wrong. They are wrong because they agree neither with the historical facts of social development over the past million years, nor with the historical facts of nature so far known to us (*i.e.,* nature as re-vealed in the history of celestial bodies, the earth, life, and other natural phenomena). (1)

> Quoted in "Premier Chou En-lai's Report on the Work of the Government to the First Session of the Third National People's Congress of the People's Republic of China" (December 21–22, (1964).

Natural science is one of man's weapons in his fight for freedom. For the purpose of attaining freedom in society, man must use social science to understand and change society and carry out social revolution. For the purpose of attaining freedom in the world of nature, man must use natural science to understand, conquer and change nature and thus attain freedom from nature. (2)

> Speech at the inaugural meeting of the Natural Science Research Society of the Border Region (February 5, 1940).

The Marxist philosophy of dialectical materialism has two outstanding characteristics. One is its class nature: it openly avows that dialectical materialism is in the service of the proletariat. The other is its practicality: it emphasizes the dependence of theory on practice, emphasizes that theory is based on practice and in turn serves practice.   (3)

"On Practice" (July 1937), *Selected Works*, Vol. I, p. 297.

Marxist philosophy holds that the most important problem does not lie in understanding the laws of the objective world and thus being able to explain it, but in applying the knowledge of these laws actively to change the world.   (4)

Ibid., p. 304.

Where do correct ideas come from? Do they drop from the skies? No. Are they innate in the mind? No. They come from social practice, and from it alone; they come from three kinds of social practice, the struggle for production, the class struggle and scientific experiment.   (5)

Where Do Correct Ideas Come from? (May 1963), 1st pocket ed., p. 1.

It is man's social being that determines his thinking. Once the correct ideas characteristic of the advanced class are grasped by the masses, these ideas turn into a material force which changes society and changes the world.   (6)

Ibid.

In their social practice, men engage in various kinds of struggle and gain rich experience, both from their successes and from their failures. Countless phenomena of the objective external world are reflected in a man's brain through his five sense organs—the organs of sight, hearing, smell, taste and touch. At first, knowledge is perceptual. The leap to conceptual knowledge, *i.e.*, to ideas, occurs when sufficient perceptual knowledge is accumulated. This is one process in cognition. It is the first stage in the whole process of cognition, the stage leading from objective matter to subjective consciousness, from existence to ideas. Whether or not one's consciousness or ideas (including theories, policies, plans or measures) do correctly reflect the laws of the objective external world is not yet proved at this stage, in which it is not yet possible to ascertain whether they are correct or not. Then comes the second stage in the process of cognition, the stage leading from consciousness back to matter, from ideas back to existence, in which the knowledge gained in the first stage is applied in social practice to ascertain whether the theories, policies, plans or measures meet with the anticipated success. Generally speaking, those that succeed are correct and those that fail are incorrect, and this is especially true of man's struggle with nature. In social struggle, the forces representing the advanced class sometimes suffer defeat not because their ideas are incorrect but because, in the balance of forces engaged in struggle, they are not as powerful for the time being as the forces of reaction; they are therefore temporarily defeated, but they are bound to triumph sooner or later. Man's knowledge makes another leap through the test of practice. This leap is more important than the previous one. For it is this leap alone that can prove the correctness or incorrectness of the first leap in cognition, *i.e.*, of the ideas, theories, policies, plans or measures formulated in the course of reflecting the objective external world. There is no other way of testing truth.   (7)

   Ibid., pp. 1–3.

   Often, correct knowledge can be arrived at only after many repetitions of the process leading from matter to consciousness and then back to matter, that is, leading from practice to knowledge and then back to practice. Such is the Marxist theory of knowledge, the dialectical materialist theory of knowledge.   (8)

   Ibid., p. 3.

   Whoever wants to know a thing has no way of doing so except by coming into contact with it, that is, by living (practicing) in its environment. . . . If you want knowledge, you must take part in the practice of changing reality. If you want to know the taste of a pear, you must change the pear by eating it yourself. . . . If you want to know the theory and methods of revolution, you must take part in revolution. All genuine knowledge originates in direct experience.   (9)

   "On Practice" (July 1937), *Selected Works*, Vol. I, pp. 299–300.

Knowledge begins with practice, and theoretical knowledge which is acquired through practice must then return to practice. The active function of knowledge manifests itself not only in the active leap from perceptual to rational knowledge, but—and this is more important—it must manifest itself in the leap from rational knowledge to revolutionary practice.   (10)

Ibid., p. 304.

It is well known that when you do anything, unless you understand its actual circumstances, its nature and its relations to other things, you will not know the laws governing it, or know how to do it, or be able to do it well.   (11)

"Problems of Strategy in China's Revolutionary War" (December 1936), Selected Works, Vol. I, p. 179.

If a man wants to succeed in his work, that is, to achieve the anticipated results, he must bring his ideas into correspondence with the laws of the objective external world; if they do not correspond, he will fail in his practice. After he fails, he draws his lessons, corrects his ideas to make them correspond to the laws of the external world, and can thus turn failure into success; this is what is meant by "failure is the mother of success" and "a fall into the pit, a gain in your wit."   (12)

"On Practice" (July 1937), Selected Works, Vol. I, pp. 296–97.

We are Marxists, and Marxism teaches that in our approach to a problem we should start from objective facts, not from abstract definitions, and that we should derive our guiding principles, policies and measures from an analysis of these facts.   (13)

"Talks at the Yenan Forum on Literature and Art" (May 1942), Selected Works, Vol. III, p. 74.

The most fundamental method of work which all Communists must firmly bear in mind is to determine our working policies according to actual conditions. When we study the causes of the mistakes we have made, we find that they all arose because we departed from the actual situation at a given time and place and were subjective in determining our working policies. (14)

> "Speech at a Conference of Cadres in the Shansi-Suiyuan Liberated Area" (April 1, 1948), *Selected Works*, Vol. IV, pp. 229–30.

Idealism and metaphysics are the easiest things in the world, because people can talk as much nonsense as they like without basing it on objective reality or having it tested against reality. Materialism and dialectics, on the other hand, need effort. They must be based on and tested by objective reality. Unless one makes the effort, one is liable to slip into idealism and metaphysics. (15)

> Introductory note to "Material on the Hu Feng Counter-Revolutionary Clique" (May 1955).

When we look at a thing, we must examine its essence and treat its appearance merely as an usher at the threshold, and once we cross the threshold, we must grasp the essence of the thing; this is the only reliable and scientific method of analysis. (16)

> "A Single Spark Can Start a Prairie Fire" (January 5, 1930), *Selected Works*, Vol. I, p. 119.

The fundamental cause of the development of a thing is not external but internal; it lies in the contradictoriness within the thing. This internal contradiction exists in every single thing, hence its motion and development. Contradictoriness within a thing is the fundamental cause of its development, while its interrelations and interactions with other things are secondary causes. (17)

> "On Contradiction" (August 1937), *Selected Works*, Vol. I, p. 313.

It [materialist dialectics] holds that external causes are the condition of change and internal causes are the basis of change, and that external causes become operative through internal causes. In a suitable temperature an egg changes into a chicken, but no temperature can change a stone into a chicken, because each has a different basis. (18)

> *Ibid.*, p. 314.

Marxist philosophy holds that the law of the unity of opposites is the fundamental law of the universe. This law operates universally, whether in the natural world, in human society, or in man's thinking. Between the opposites in a contradiction there is at once unity and struggle, and it is this that impels things to move and change. Contradictions exist everywhere, but they differ in accordance with the different nature of different things. In any given phenomenon or thing, the unity of opposites is conditional, temporary and transitory, and hence relative, whereas the struggle of opposites is absolute. (19)

> *On the Correct Handling of Contradictions Among the People* (February 27, 1957), 1st pocket ed., p. 18.

The analytical method is dialectical. By analysis, we mean analysing the contradictions in things. And sound analysis is impossible without intimate knowledge of life and without real understanding of the pertinent contradictions. (20)

> *Speech at the Chinese Communist Party's National Conference on Propaganda Work* (March 12, 1957), 1st pocket ed., p. 20.

Concrete analysis of concrete conditions, Lenin said, is "the most essential thing in Marxism, the living soul of Marxism." Lacking an analytical approach, many of our comrades do not want to go deeply into complex matters, to analyse and study them over and over again, but like to draw simple conclusions which are either absolutely affirmative or absolutely negative. . . . From now on we should remedy this state of affairs. (21)

> "Our Study and the Current Situation" (April 12, 1944), *Selected Works*, Vol. III, p. 165.

The way these comrades look at problems is wrong. They do not look at the essential or main aspects but emphasize the non-essential or minor ones. It should be pointed out that these non-essential or minor aspects must not be overlooked and must be dealt with one by one. But they should not be taken as the essential or main aspects, or we will lose our bearings. (22)

> *On the Question of Agricultural Co-operation* (July 31, 1955), 3rd ed., pp. 17–18.

In this world, things are complicated and are decided by many factors. We should look at problems from different aspects, not from just one. (23)

> "On the Chungking Negotiations" (October 17, 1945), *Selected Works*, Vol. IV, p. 54.

Only those who are subjective, one-sided and superficial in their approach to problems will smugly issue orders or directives the moment they arrive on the scene, without considering the circumstances, without viewing things in their totality (their history and their present state as a whole) and without getting to the essence of things (their nature and the internal relations between one thing and another). Such people are bound to trip and fall. (24)

> "On Practice" (July 1937), *Selected Works*, Vol. I, p. 302.

In studying a problem, we must shun subjectivity, one-sidedness and superficiality. To be subjective means not to look at problems objectively, that is, not to use the materialist viewpoint in looking at problems. I have discussed this in my essay "On Practice." To be one-sided means not to look at problems all-sidedly. . . . Or it may be called seeing the part but not the whole, seeing the trees but not the forest. That way it is impossible to find the method for resolving a contradiction, it is impossible to accomplish the tasks of the revolution, to carry out assignments well or to develop inner-Party ideological struggle correctly. When Sun Wu Tzu said in discussing military science, "Know the enemy and know yourself, and you can fight a hundred battles with no danger of defeat," he was referring to the two sides in a battle. Wei Cheng of the Tang Dynasty also understood the error of one-sidedness when he said, "Listen to both sides and you will be enlightened, heed only one side and you will be benighted." But our comrades often look at problems one-sidedly, and so they often run into snags. . . . Lenin said:

> . . . in order really to know an object we must embrace, study, all its sides, all connections and "mediations." We shall never achieve this completely, but the demand for all-sidedness is a safeguard against mistakes and rigidity.

We should remember his words. To be superficial means to consider neither the characteristics of a contradiction in its totality nor the characteristics of each of its aspects: it means to deny the necessity for probing deeply into a thing and minutely studying the characteristics of its contradiction, but instead merely to look from afar and, after glimpsing the rough outline, immediately to try to resolve the contradiction (to answer a question, settle a dispute, handle work, or direct a military operation). This way of doing things is bound to lead to trouble. . . . To be one-sided and superficial is at the same time to be subjective. For all objective things are actually interconnected and are governed by inner laws, but, instead of undertaking the task of reflecting things as they really are, some people only look at things one-sidedly or superficially and know neither their interconnections nor their inner laws, and so their method is subjectivist. (25)

"On Contradiction" (August 1937), *Selected Works*, Vol. I, pp. 323–24.

One-sidedness means thinking in terms of absolutes, that is, a metaphysical approach to problems. In the appraisal of our work, it is one-sided to regard everything either as all positive or as all negative. . . . To regard everything as positive is to see only the good and not the bad, and to tolerate only praise and no criticism. To talk as though our work is good in every respect is at variance with the facts. It is not true that everything is good; there are still shortcomings and mistakes. But neither is it true that everything is bad, and that, too, is at variance with the facts. Here analysis is necessary. To negate everything is to think, without having made any analysis, that nothing has been done well and that the great work of socialist construction, the great struggle in which hundreds of millions of people are participating, is a complete mess with nothing in it worth commending. Although there is a difference between the many people who hold such views and those who are hostile to the socialist system, these views are very mistaken and harmful and can only dishearten people. It is wrong to appraise our work either from the viewpoint that everything is positive, or from the viewpoint that everything is negative. (26)

Speech at the Chinese Communist Party's National Conference on Propaganda Work (March 12, 1957), 1st pocket ed., pp. 16–17.

In approaching a problem a Marxist should see the whole as well as the parts. A frog in a well says, "The sky is no bigger than the mouth of the well." That is untrue, for the sky is not just the size of the mouth of the well.

If it said, "A part of the sky is the size of the mouth of a well," that would be true, for it tallies with the facts. (27)

> "On Tactics Against Japanese Imperialism" (December 27, 1935), *Selected Works*, Vol. I, p. 159.

We must learn to look at problems all-sidedly, seeing the reverse as well as the obverse side of things. In given conditions, a bad thing can lead to good results and a good thing to bad results. (28)

> *On the Correct Handling of Contradictions Among the People* (February 27, 1957), 1st pocket ed., pp. 66–67.

While we recognize that in the general development of history the material determines the mental and social being determines social consciousness, we also—and indeed must—recognize the reaction of mental on material things, of social consciousness on social being and of the superstructure on the economic base. This does not go against materialism; on the contrary, it avoids mechanical materialism and firmly upholds dialectical materialism. (29)

> "On Contradiction" (August 1937), *Selected Works*, Vol. I, p. 336.

In seeking victory, those who direct a war cannot overstep the limitations imposed by the objective conditions; within these limitations, however, they can and must play a dynamic role in striving for victory. The stage of action for commanders in a war must be built upon objective possibilities, but on that stage they can direct the performance of many a drama, full of sound and colour, power and grandeur. (30)

> "On Protracted War" (May 1938), *Selected Works*, Vol. II, p. 152.

People must adapt their thinking to the changed conditions. Of course no one should go off into wild flights of fancy, or make plans of action unwarranted by the objective situation, or stretch for the impossible. The problem today, however, is that Rightist conservative thinking is still causing mischief in many spheres and preventing the work in these spheres from keeping pace with the development of the objective situation. The present problem is that many people consider it impossible to accomplish things which could be accomplished if they exerted themselves. (31)

> Preface to *The Socialist Upsurge in China's Countryside* (December 27, 1955), Chinese ed., Vol. I.

We should always use our brains and think everything over carefully. A common saying goes, "Knit your brows and you will hit upon a stratagem." In other words, much thinking yields wisdom. In order to get rid of the blindness which exists to a serious extent in our Party, we must encourage our comrades to think, to learn the method of analysis and to cultivate the habit of analysis. (32)

> "Our Study and the Current Situation" (April 12, 1944), *Selected Works*, Vol. III, pp. 174–75.

If in any process there are a number of contradictions, one of them must be the principal contradiction playing the leading and decisive role, while the rest occupy a secondary and subordinate position. Therefore, in studying any complex process in which there are two or more contradictions, we must devote every effort to finding its principal contradiction. Once this principal contradiction is grasped, all problems can be readily solved. (33)

> "On Contradiction" (August 1937), *Selected Works*, Vol. I, p. 332.

Of the two contradictory aspects, one must be principal and the other secondary. The principal aspect is the one playing the leading role in the contradiction. The nature of a thing is determined mainly by the principal aspect of a contradiction, the aspect which has gained the dominant position. (34)

But this situation is not static; the principal and the non-principal aspects of a contradiction transform themselves into each other and the nature of the thing changes accordingly. (35)

> *Ibid.*, p. 333.

It is not enough to set tasks, we must also solve the problem of the methods for carrying them out. If our task is to cross a river, we cannot cross it without a bridge or a boat. Unless the bridge or boat problem is solved, it is idle to speak of crossing the river. Unless the problem of method is solved, talk about the task is useless.   (36)

> "Be Concerned with the Well-Being of the Masses, Pay Attention to Methods of Work" (January 27, 1934), *Selected Works*, Vol. I, p. 150.

In any task, if no general and widespread call is issued, the broad masses cannot be mobilized for action. But if persons in leading positions confine themselves to a general call—if they do not personally, in some of the organizations, go deeply and concretely into the work called for, make a break-through at some single point, gain experience and use this experience for guiding other units—then they will have no way of testing the correctness or of enriching the content of their general call, and there is the danger that nothing may come of it.   (37)

> "Some Questions Concerning Methods of Leadership" (June 1, 1943), *Selected Works*, Vol. III, p. 117.

No one in a leading position is competent to give general guidance to all the units unless he derives concrete experience from particular individuals and events in particular subordinate units. This method must be promoted everywhere so that leading cadres at all levels learn to apply it.   (38)

> *Ibid.*, p. 118.

In any given place, there cannot be a number of central tasks at the same time. At any one time there can be only one central task, supplemented by other tasks of a second or third order of importance. Consequently, the person with over-all responsibility in the locality must take into account the history and circumstances of the struggle there and put the different tasks in their proper order; he should not act upon each instruction as it comes from the higher organization without any planning of his own, and thereby create a multitude of "central tasks" and a state of confusion and disorder. Nor should a higher organization simultaneously assign many tasks to a lower organization without indicating their relative importance and urgency or without specifying which is central, for that will lead to confusion in the steps to be taken by the lower organizations in their work and thus no definite results will be achieved. It is part of the art of leadership to take the whole situation into account and plan accordingly

in the light of the historical conditions and existing circumstances of each
locality, decide correctly on the centre of gravity and the sequence of the
work for each period, steadfastly carry through the decision, and make sure
that definite results are achieved.   (39)

   Ibid., p. 121.

   It [a regional or sub-regional bureau of the Central Committee of the
Party] should constantly have a grip on the progress of the work, exchange
experience and correct mistakes; it should not wait several months, half a
year or a year before holding summing-up meetings for a general check-up
and a general correction of mistakes. Waiting leads to great loss, while
correcting mistakes as soon as they occur reduces loss.   (40)

   "On the Policy Concerning Industry and Commerce" (February
   27, 1948), *Selected Works*, Vol. IV, p. 204.

   Don't wait until problems pile up and cause a lot of trouble before
trying to solve them. Leaders must march ahead of the movement, not lag
behind it.   (41)

   Introductory note to "Contract on a Seasonal Basis" (1955),
   The Socialist Upsurge in China's Countryside, Chinese ed., Vol.
   III.

   What we need is an enthusiastic but calm state of mind and intense but
orderly work.   (42)

   "Problems of Strategy in China's Revolutionary War" (December 1936), *Selected Works*, Vol. I, p. 211.

Pope John XXIII

(1881–1963)

POPE JOHN XXIII was the 262nd Supreme Pontiff of the Roman Catholic Church (1958–1963). He was born Angelo Giuseppi Roncalli, one of thirteen children of a sharecropper who tilled the land in the Po Valley. For a quarter of a century he served the Church as a diplomat—in Bulgaria, Greece, Turkey, France, and elsewhere. He was an accomplished linguist and an industrious biographer-historian: his five-volume history of the life and times of St. Charles Borromea appeared between 1936 and 1952. He was known as a liberal Pope and a warm human being. He convened the Second Vatican Council of the Church in 1962, credited with having precipitated the "ecumenical spirit" of reason and modernization prevalent in our time.

■ *Relations Between Individuals and the Public Authorities Within a Single State*

Necessity and divine origin of authority

HUMAN SOCIETY can be neither well-ordered nor prosperous unless it has some people invested with legitimate authority to preserve its institutions and to devote themselves as far as is necessary to work and care for the good of all. These, however, derive their authority from God, as St. Paul teaches in the words, *Authority comes from God alone.* These words of St.

Paul are explained thus by St. John Chrysostom: *What are you saying?* *Is every ruler appointed by God? I do not say that,* he replies, *for I am not dealing now with individual rulers, but with authority itself. What I say is, that it is the divine wisdom and not mere chance, that had ordained that there should be government, that some should command and others obey.* Moreover, since God made men social by nature, and since no society can hold together unless some one be over all, directing all to strive earnestly for the common good, every civilized community must have a ruling authority, and this authority, no less than society itself, has its source in nature, and has, consequently, God for its author.   (1)

But authority is not to be thought of as a force lacking all control. Indeed, since it is the power to command according to right reason, authority must derive its obligatory force from the moral order, which in turn has God for its first source and final end. Wherefore Our Predecessor of happy memory, Pius XII, said: *That same absolute order of beings and their ends which presents man as an autonomous person, that is, as the subject of inviolable duties and rights, and as at once the basis of society and the purpose for which it exists, also includes the state as a necessary society invested with the authority without which it could not come into being or live . . . And since this absolute order, as we learn from sound reason, especially from the Christian faith, can have no origin save in a personal God Who is our Creator, it follows that the dignity of the State's authority is due to its sharing to some extent in the authority of God Himself.*   (2)

Where the civil authority uses as its only or its chief means either threats and fear of punishment or promises of rewards, it cannot effectively move men to promote the common good of all. Even if it did so move them, this would be altogether opposed to their dignity as men, endowed with reason and free will. As authority is chiefly concerned with moral force, it follows that civil authority must appeal primarily to the conscience of individual citizens, that is, to each one's duty to collaborate readily for the common good of all. Since by nature all men are equal in human dignity, it follows that no one may be coerced to perform inferior acts. That is in the power of God alone, Who sees and judges the hidden designs of men's hearts. Those therefore who have authority in the State may oblige men in conscience only if their authority is intrinsically related with the authority of God and shares in it.   (3)

By this principle the dignity of the citizens is protected. When, in fact, men obey their rulers, it is not at all as men that they obey them, but through their obedience it is God, the provident Creator of all things, Whom they reverence, since He has decreed that men's dealings with one another should be regulated by an order which He Himself has established. Moreover, in showing this due reverence to God, men not only do not debase themselves but rather perfect and ennoble themselves. For *to serve God is to rule.* (4)

Since the right to command is required by the moral order and has its source in God, it follows that, if civil authorities legislate for or allow any-thing that is contrary to that order and therefore contrary to the will of God, neither the laws made nor the authorizations granted can be binding on the consciences of the citizens, since *God has more right to be obeyed than men.* Otherwise, authority breaks down completely and results in shameful abuse. As St. Thomas Aquinas teaches: *Human law has the true nature of law only in so far as it corresponds to right reason, and there-fore is derived from the eternal law. In so far as it falls short of right reason, a law is said to be a wicked law; and so, lacking the true nature of law, it is rather a kind of violence.* (5)

It must not be concluded, however, because authority comes from God, that therefore men have no right to choose those who are to rule the state, to decide the form of government, and to determine both the way in which authority is to be exercised and its limits. It is thus clear that the doctrine which We have set forth is fully consonant with any truly democratic regime. (6)

*Attainment of the common good
is the purpose of the public authority*

Individual citizens and intermediate groups are obliged to make their specific contributions to the common welfare. One of the chief conse-quences of this is that they must bring their own interests into harmony with the needs of the community, and must dispose of their goods and their services as civil authorities have prescribed, in accord with the norms of justice, in due form, and within the limits of their competence. This they must do by means of formally perfect actions, the content of which must be morally good, or at least capable of being directed towards good. (7)

Indeed since the whole reason for the existence of civil authorities is the realization of the common good, it is clearly necessary that, in pursuing this objective, they should respect its essential elements, and at the same time conform their laws to the needs of a given historical situation. (8)

Essentials of the common good

Assuredly, the ethnic characteristics of the various human groups are to be respected as constituent elements of the common good, but these values and characteristics by no means exhaust the content of the common good. For the common good is intimately bound up with human nature. It can never exist fully and completely unless, its intimate nature and realiza-tion being what they are, the human person is taken into account. (9)

In the second place, the very nature of the common good requires that all members of the political community be entitled to share in it, although in different ways according to each one's tasks, merits and circumstances. For this reason, every civil authority must take pains to promote the common good of all, without preference for any single citizen or civic group. As Our Predecessor of immortal memory, Leo XIII, has said: *The civil power must not serve the advantage of any one individual, or of some few persons, inasmuch as it was established for the common good of all.* Considerations of justice and equity, however, can at times demand that those involved in civil government give more attention to the less fortunate members of the community, since they are less able to defend their rights and to assert their legitimate claims.   (10)

In this context, We judge that attention should be called to the fact that the common good touches the whole man, the needs both of his body and of his soul. Hence it follows that the civil authorities must undertake to effect the common good by ways and means that are proper to them; that is, while respecting the hierarchy of values, they should promote simultaneously both the material and the spiritual welfare of the citizens.   (11)

These principles are clearly contained in the doctrine stated in Our Encyclical, *Mater et Magistra,* where We emphasized that the common good of all *embraces the sum total of those conditions of social living whereby men are enabled to achieve their own integral perfection more fully and more easily.*   (12)

Men, however, composed as they are of bodies and immortal souls, can never in this mortal life succeed in satisfying all their needs or in attaining perfect happiness. Therefore all efforts made to promote the common good, far from endangering the eternal salvation of men, ought rather to serve to promote it.   (13)

Responsibilities of the public authority,
and rights and duties of individuals

It is agreed that in our time the common good is chiefly guaranteed when personal rights and duties are maintained. The chief concern of civil authorities must therefore be to ensure that these rights are acknowledged, respected, coordinated with other rights, defended and promoted, so that in this way each one may more easily carry out his duties. For *to safeguard the inviolable rights of the human person, and to facilitate the fulfillment of his duties, should be the essential office of every public authority.*   (14)

This means that, if any government does not acknowledge the rights of man or violates them, it not only fails in its duty, but its orders completely lack juridical force.   (15)

*Reconciliation and protection of rights
and duties of individuals*

One of the fundamental duties of civil authorities, therefore, is to coordinate social relations in such fashion that the exercise of one man's rights does not threaten others in the exercise of their own rights nor hinder them in the fulfillment of their duties. Finally, the rights of all should be effectively safeguarded and, if they have been violated, completely restored.

(16)

Duty of promoting the rights of individuals

It is also demanded by the common good that civil authorities make earnest efforts to bring about a situation in which individual citizens can easily exercise their rights and fulfill their duties as well. For experience has taught us that, unless these authorities take suitable action with regard to economic, political and cultural matters, inequalities between the citizens tend to become more and more widespread, especially in the modern world, and as a result human rights are rendered totally ineffective, and the fulfillment of duties is compromised.   (17)

It is therefore necessary that the administration give wholehearted and careful attention to the social as well as to the economic progress of the citizens, and to the development, in keeping with the development of the productive system, of such essential services as the building of roads, transportation, communications, water supply, housing, public health, education, facilitation of the practice of religion, and recreational facilities. It is necessary also that governments make efforts to see that insurance systems are made available to the citizens, so that, in case of misfortune or increased family responsibilities, no person will be without the necessary means to maintain a decent standard of living. The government should make similarly effective efforts to see that those who are able to work can find employment in keeping with their aptitudes, and that each worker receives a wage in keeping with the laws of justice and equity. It should be equally the concern of civil authorities to ensure that workers be allowed their proper responsibility in the work undertaken in industrial organization, and to facilitate the establishment of intermediate groups which will make social life richer and more effective. Finally, it should be possible for all the citizens to share as far as they are able in their country's cultural advantages.   (18)

*Harmonious relation between
public authority's two forms of intervention*

The common good requires that civil authorities maintain a careful balance between coordinating and protecting the rights of the citizens, on the one hand, and promoting them, on the other. It should not happen that certain individuals or social groups derive special advantage from the fact that their rights have received preferential protection. Nor should it happen that governments in seeking to protect these rights, become obstacles to their full expression and free use. *For this principle must always be retained: that State activity in the economic field, no matter what its breadth or depth may be, ought not to be exercised in such a way as to curtail an individual's freedom of personal initiative. Rather it should work to expand that freedom as much as possible by the effective protection of the essential personal rights of each and every individual.* (19)

The same principle should inspire the various steps which governments take in order to make it possible for the citizens more easily to exercise their rights and fulfill their duties in every sector of social life. (20)

Structure and operation of the public authority

It is impossible to determine, once and for all, what is the most suitable form of government, or how civil authorities can most effectively fulfill their respective functions, i.e., the legislative, judicial and executive functions of the State. In determining the structure and operation of government which a State is to have, great weight has to be given to the historical background and circumstances of given political Communities, circumstances which will vary at different times and in different places. We consider, however, that it is in keeping with the innate demands of human nature that the State should take a form which embodies the three-fold division of powers corresponding to the three principal functions of public authority. In that type of State, not only the official functions of government but also the mutual relations between citizens and public officials are set down according to law, which in itself affords protection to the citizens both in the enjoyment of their rights and in the fulfillment of their duties. (21)

If, however, this political and juridical structure is to produce the advantages which may be expected of it, public officials must strive to meet the problems which arise in a way that conforms both to the complexities of the situation and the proper exercise of their function. This requires that, in constantly changing conditions, legislators never forget the norms of morality, or constitutional provisions, or the objective requirements of the common good. Moreover, executive authorities must coordinate the activities of society with discretion, with a full knowledge of the law and after a careful consideration of circumstances, and the courts must administer justice impartially and without being influenced by favoritism or pressure. The good order of society also demands that individual citizens and intermediate organizations should be effectively protected by law whenever they have rights to be exercised or obligations to be fulfilled. This protection should be granted to citizens both in their dealings with each other and in their relations with government agencies.   (22)

Law and conscience

It is unquestionable that a legal structure in conformity with the moral order and corresponding to the level of development of the political Community is of great advantage to achievement of the common good.   (23)

And yet, social life in the modern world is so varied, complex and dynamic that even a juridical structure which has been prudently and thoughtfully established is always inadequate for the needs of society. (24)

It is also true that the relations of the citizens with each other, of citizens and intermediate groups with public authorities, and finally of the public authorities with one another, are often so complex and so sensitive that they cannot be regulated by flexible legal provisions. Such a situation therefore demands that the civil authorities have clear ideas about the nature and extent of their official duties if they wish to maintain the existing juridical structure in its basic elements and principles, and at the same time meet the exigencies of social life, adapting their legislation to the changing social scene and solving new problems .They must be men of great equilibrium and integrity, competent and courageous enough to see at once what the situation requires and to take necessary action quickly and effectively.
                                                                    (25)

Citizens' participation in public life

It is in keeping with their dignity as persons that human beings should take an active part in government, although the manner in which they share in it will depend on the level of development of the political Community to which they belong.   (26)

Men will find new and extensive advantages in the fact that they are allowed to participate in government. In this situation, those who administer the government come into frequent contact with the citizens, and it is thus easier for them to learn what is really needed for the common good. The fact too that ministers of government hold office only for a limited time keeps them from growing stale and allows for their replacement in accordance with the demands of social progress.   (27)

Characteristics of the present day

In modern times, where there is question of organizing political Communities juridically, there is observable first of all the tendency to write in concise and limpid phraseology a charter of fundamental human rights, which is, as often as not, inserted in the State Constitutions, or is an integral part of them.   (28)

Secondly, there is also an inclination to determine, by the compilation of a document called the *Constitution*, the procedures through which the governing powers are to be created, along with their mutual relations, the spheres of their competence, the forms and systems they are obliged to follow in the performance of their office.   (29)

The relations between the government and the governed are then set forth in terms of rights and duties; and it is clearly laid down that the paramount task assigned to government officials is that of recognizing, respecting, reconciling, protecting and promoting the rights and duties of citizens.   (30)

It is, of course, impossible to accept the theory which professes to find the original and single source of civic rights and duties, of the binding force of the Constitution, and of a government's right to command, in the mere will of human beings, individually or collectively.   (31)

The tendencies to which We have referred, however, do clearly show that the men of our time have become increasingly conscious of their dignity as human persons. This awareness prompts them to claim a share in the public administration of their country, while it also accounts for the demand that their own inalienable and inviolable rights be protected by law. It also requires that government officials be chosen in conformity with constitutional procedures, and perform their specific functions within the limits of law.   (32)

R. H. Tawney

(1880–1962)

TAWNEY, British historian, wrote a classic study of the relationship between Protestantism and economic development in the sixteenth and seventeenth centuries: Religion and the Rise of Capitalism *(1926).*

◼ *Rights and Functions*

A FUNCTION may be defined as an activity which embodies and expresses the idea of social purpose. The essence of it is that the agent does not perform it merely for personal gain or to gratify himself, but recognizes that he is responsible for its discharge to some higher authority. The purpose of industry is obvious. It is to supply man with things which are necessary, useful or beautiful, and thus to bring life to body or spirit. In so far as it is governed by this end, it is among the most important of human activities. In so far as it is diverted from it, it may be harmless, amusing, or even exhilarating to those who carry it on, but it possesses no more social significance than the orderly business of ants and bees, the strutting of peacocks, or the struggles of carnivorous animals over carrion.   (1)

Men have normally appreciated this fact, however unwilling or unable they may have been to act upon it; and therefore from time to time, in so far as they have been able to control the forces of violence and greed, they have adopted various expedients for emphasizing the social quality of economic activity. It is not easy, however, to emphasize it effectively, because to do so requires a constant effort of will, against which egotistical instincts are in rebellion, and because, if that will is to prevail, it must be embodied in some social and political organization, which may itself become so arbitrary, tyrannical and corrupt as to thwart the performance of function instead of promoting it. When this process of degeneration has gone far, as in most European countries it had by the middle of the eighteenth century, the indispensable thing is to break the dead organization up and to clear the ground. In the course of doing so, the individual is emancipated and his rights are enlarged; but the idea of social purpose is discredited by the discredit justly attaching to the obsolete order in which it is embodied.   (2)

It is not surprising, therefore, that in the new industrial societies which arose on the ruins of the old régime the dominant note should have been the insistence upon individual rights, irrespective of any social purpose to which their exercise contributed. The economic expansion which concentrated population on the coal-measures was, in essence, an immense movement of colonization drifting from the south and east to the north and west; and it was natural that in those regions of England, as in the American settlements, the characteristic philosophy should be that of the pioneer

and the mining camp. The change of social quality was profound. But in
England, at least, it was gradual, and the "industrial revolution," though
catastrophic in its effects, was only the visible climax of generations of
subtle moral change. The rise of modern economic relations, which may be
dated in England from the latter half of the seventeenth century, was coincident with the growth of a political theory which replaced the conception
of purpose by that of mechanism. During a treat part of history men
had found the significance of their social order in its relation to the universal purposes of religion. It stood as one rung in a ladder which stretched
from hell to Paradise, and the classes who composed it were the hands, the
feet, the head of a corporate body which was itself a microcosm imperfectly
reflecting a larger universe. When the Reformation made the Church a
department of the secular government, it undermined the already enfeebled
spiritual forces which had erected that sublime, but too much elaborated,
synthesis. But its influence remained for nearly a century after the roots
which fed it had been severed. It was the atmosphere into which men were
born, and from which, however practical, or even Machiavellian, they could
not easily disengage their spirits. Nor was it inconvenient for the new state-
craft to see the weight of a traditional religious sanction added to its own
concern in the subordination of all classes and interests to the common
end, of which it conceived itself, and during the greater part of the sixteenth century was commonly conceived, to be the guardian. The lines
of the social structure were no longer supposed to reproduce in miniature
the plan of a universal order. But common habits, common traditions and
beliefs, common pressure from above gave them a unity of direction, which
restrained the forces of individual variation and lateral expansion; and the
center towards which they converged, formerly a Church possessing some
of the characteristics of a State, was now a State that had clothed itself
with many of the attributes of a Church.   (3)

The difference between the England of Shakespeare, still visited by the
ghosts of the Middle Ages, and the England which merged in 1700 from
the fierce polemics of the last two generations, was a difference of social
and political theory even more than of constitutional and political arrangements. Not only the facts, but the minds which appraised them, were
profoundly modified. The essence of the change was the disappearance of
the idea that social institutions and economic activities were related to
common ends, which gave them their significance and which served as
their criterion. In the eighteenth century both the State and the Church had
abdicated that part of the sphere which had consisted in the maintenance
of a common body of social ethics; what was left of it was repression of a
class, not the discipline of a nation. Opinion ceased to regard social institutions and economic activity as amenable, like personal conduct, to moral
criteria, because it was no longer influenced by the spectacle of institutions

which, arbitrary, capricious, and often corrupt in their practical operation, had been the outward symbol and expression of the subordination of
life to purposes transcending private interests. That part of government
which had been concerned with social administration, if it did not end,
became at least obsolescent. For such democracy as had existed in the Middle Ages was dead, and the democracy of the Revolution was not yet born,
so that government passed into the lethargic hands of classes who wielded
the power of the State in the interests of an irresponsible aristocracy. And
the Church was even more remote from the daily life of mankind than the
State. Philanthropy abounded; but religion, once the greatest social force,
had become a thing as private and individual as the estate of the squire or
the working clothes of the laborer. There were special dispensations and
occasional interventions, like the acts of a monarch who reprieved a criminal or signed an order for his execution. But what was familiar, and human
and lovable—what was Christian in Christianity had largely disappeared.
God had been thrust into the frigid altitudes of infinite space. There was a
limited monarchy in Heaven, as well as upon earth. Providence was the
spectator of the curious machine which it had constructed and set in
motion, but the operation of which it was neither able nor willing to control.
Like the occasional intervention of the Crown in the proceedings of Parliament, its wisdom was revealed in the infrequency of its interference. (4)

The natural consequence of the abdication of authorities which had
stood, however imperfectly, for a common purpose in social organization,
was the gradual disappearance from social thought of the idea of purpose
itself. Its place in the eighteenth century was taken by the idea of mechanism. The conception of men as united to each other, and of all mankind
as united to God, by mutual obligations arising from their relation to a
common end, which vaguely conceived and imperfectly realized, had been
the keystone holding together the social fabric, ceased to be impressed upon
men's minds, when Church and State withdrew from the center of
social life to its circumference. What remained when the keystone of the
arch was removed, was private rights and private interests, the materials of a society rather than a society itself. These rights and interests were
the natural order which had been distorted by the ambitions of kings and
priests, and which emerged when the artificial super-structure disappeared,
because they were the creation, not of man, but of Nature herself. They
had been regarded in the past as relative to some public end, whether
religion or national welfare. Henceforward they were thought to be absolute and indefeasible, and to stand by their own virtue. They were the
ultimate political and social reality; and since they were the ultimate reality, they were not subordinate to other aspects of society, but other aspects
of society were subordinate to them.   (5)

The State could not encroach upon these rights, for the State existed for their maintenance. They determined the relation of classes, for the most obvious and fundamental of all rights was property—property absolute and unconditioned—and those who possessed it were regarded as the natural governors of those who did not. Society arose from their exercise, through the contracts of individual with individual. It fulfilled its object in so far as, by maintaining contractual freedom, it secured full scope for their unfettered exercise. It failed in so far as, like the French monarchy, it overrode them by the use of an arbitrary authority. Thus conceived, society assumed something of the appearance of a great joint-stock company, in which political power and the receipt of dividends were justly assigned to those who held the most numerous shares. The currents of social activity did not converge upon common ends, but were dispersed through a multitude of channels, created by the private interests of the individuals who composed society. But in their very variety and spontaneity, in the very absence of any attempt to relate them to a larger purpose than that of the individual, lay the best security of its attainment. There is a mysticism of reason as well as of emotion, and the eighteenth century found, in the beneficence of natural instincts, a substitute for the God whom it had expelled from contact with society, and did not hesitate to identify them.

> "Thus God and nature planned the general frame
> And bade self-love and social be the same."   (6)

The result of such ideas in the world of practice was a society which was ruled by law, not by the caprice of Governments, but which recognized no moral limitation on the pursuit by individuals of their economic self-interest. In the world of thought, it was a political philosophy which made rights the foundation of the social order, and which considered the discharge of obligations, when it considered it at all, as emerging by an inevitable process from their free exercise. The first famous exponent of this philosophy was Locke, in whom the dominant conception is the indefeasibility of private rights, not the pre-ordained harmony between private rights and public welfare. In the great French writers who prepared the way for the Revolution, while believing that they were the servants of an enlightened absolutism, there is an almost equal emphasis upon the sanctity of rights and upon the infallibility of the alchemy by which the pursuit of private ends is transmuted into the attainment of public good. Though their writings reveal the influence of the conception of society as a self-adjusting mechanism, which afterwards became the most characteristic note of the English individualism, what the French Revolution burned into the mind of Europe was the former not the latter. In England the idea of right had been negative and defensive, a barrier to the encroachment of Governments. The French leapt to the attack from trenches which the English had been content to defend, and in France the idea became affirmative and militant, not a weapon of defense, but a principle of social organization. The attempt to refound society upon rights, and rights springing not from musty charters, but from the very nature of man himself, was at once the triumph and the limitation of the Revolution. It gave it the enthusiasm and infectious power of religion. (7)

What happened in England might seem at first sight to have been precisely the reverse. English practical men, whose thoughts were pitched in a lower key, were a little shocked by the pomp and brilliance of that tremendous creed. They had scanty sympathy with the absolute affirmations of France. What captured their imagination was not the right to liberty, which made no appeal to their commercial instincts, but the expediency of liberty, which did; and when the Revolution had revealed the explosive power of the idea of natural right, they sought some less menacing formula. It had been offered them first by Adam Smith and his precursors, who showed how the mechanism of economic life converted," "as with an invisible hand," the exercise of individual rights into the instrument of public good. Bentham, who despised metaphysical subtleties, and thought the Declaration of the Rights of Man as absurd as any other dogmatic religion, completed the new orientation by supplying the final criterion of political institutions in the principle of Utility. Henceforward emphasis was transferred from the right of the individual to exercise his freedom as he pleased to the expediency of an undisturbed exercise of freedom to society. (8)

The change is significant. It is the difference between the universal and equal citizenship of France, with its five million peasant proprietors, and the organized inequality of England established solidly upon class traditions and class institutions; the descent from hope to resignation, from the fire and passion of an age of illimitable vistas to the monotonous beat of the factory engine, from Turgot and Condorcet to the melancholy mathematical creed of Bentham and Ricardo and James Mill. Mankind has, at least, this superiority over its philosophers, that great movements spring from the heart and embody a faith, not the nice adjustments of the hedonistic calculus. So in the name of the rights of property France abolished in three years a great mass of property rights which, under the old régime, had robbed the peasant of part of the produce of his labor, and the social transformation survived a whole world of political changes. In England the glad tidings of democracy were broken too discreetly to reach the ears of the hind in the furrow or the shepherd on the hill; there were political changes without a social transformation. The doctrine of Utility, though trenchant in the sphere of politics, involved no considerable interference with the fundamentals of the social fabric. Its exponents were principally concerned with the removal of political abuses and legal anomalies. They attacked sinecures and pensions and the criminal code and the procedure of the law courts. But they touched only the surface of social institutions. They thought it a monstrous injustice that the citizen should pay one-tenth of his income in taxation to an idle Government, but quite reasonable that he should pay one-fifth of it in rent to an idle landlord.   (9)

The difference, nevertheless, was one of emphasis and expression, not of principle. It mattered very little in practice whether private property and unfettered economic freedom were stated, as in France, to be natural rights, or whether, as in England, they were merely assumed once for all to be expedient. In either case they were taken for granted as the fundamentals upon which social organization was to be based, and about which no further argument was admissible. Though Bentham argued that rights were derived from utility, not from nature, he did not push his analysis so far as to argue that any particular right was relative to any particular function, and thus endorsed indiscriminately rights which were not accompanied by service as well as rights which were. While eschewing, in short, the phraseology of natural rights, the English Utilitarians retained something not unlike the substance of them. For they assumed that private property in land, and the private ownership of capital, were natural institutions, and gave them, indeed, a new lease of life, by proving to their own satisfaction that social well-being must result from their continued exercise. Their negative was as important as their positive teaching. It was a conductor which diverted the lightning. Behind their political theory, behind the practical conduct, which, as always, continues to express theory long after it has been discredited in the world of thought, lay the acceptance of absolute rights to property and to economic freedom as the unquestioned center of social organization.   (10)

The result of that attitude was momentous. The motive and inspiration of the Liberal Movement of the eighteenth century had been the attack on Privilege. But the creed which had exorcised the specter of agrarian feudalism haunting village and *château* in France was impotent to disarm the new ogre of industrialism which was stretching its limbs in the north of England. When, shorn of its splendors and illusions, liberalism triumphed in England in 1832, it carried without criticism into the new world of capitalist industry categories of private property and freedom of contract which had been forged in the simpler economic environment of the pre-industrial era. In England these categories are being bent and twisted till they are no longer recognizable, and will, in time, be made harmless. In America, where necessity compelled the crystallization of principles in a constitution, they have the rigidity of an iron jacket. The magnificent formulæ in which a society of farmers and master craftsmen enshrined its philosophy of freedom are in danger of becoming fetters used by an Anglo-Saxon business aristocracy to bind insurgent movements on the part of an immigrant and semi-servile proletariat.   (11)

Walter Lippmann

(1899–   )

LIPPMANN has, from his early years as associate editor of the New Republic, *been identified with liberalism of mind and politics. At one time
associated with the* New York Herald-Tribune, *he has contributed to many
newspapers and to the national magazines* (Atlantic, Harper's, Life). *A
Pulitzer prize winner (1962), his books span more than half a century, from*
A Preface to Politics *(1913), published three years after his graduation from*
Harvard, *to* Western Unity and the Common Market *(1962).*

◼ *The Pursuit of Liberty*

I. A Human Affirmation

OF THE DEVELOPMENT of liberty we have seen only the beginnings: the
emancipation even of Englishmen, let alone mankind, was not completed
in 1859 when Mill wrote his *Essay on Liberty.* At best the foundation for
the advancement of liberty had been laid in a few countries. But the
advance itself has no visible end. Always there will remain to be liquidated
subtler privileges and immunities; always there will remain to be checked
the refinements of violence, fraud, intrigue, and conspiracy by which men
bedevil themselves and their fellows. The ideal of a society in which all
are equally free of all arbitrary coercion is a receding goal. From each new
plateau in the ascent higher levels become visible.   (1)

   If we scrutinize the progress of human emancipation, it appears to consist largely in a series of restraints upon the exercise of power by men over
men. The organized liberty of mankind is established by laws and usages
which seek to limit coercive authority, traditional prerogatives, vested rights,
and all manner of predatory, violent, fraudulent dealing among men.   (2)

But though in practice the organization of liberty is achieved largely by restraints and denials, these bounds have been set upon arbitrary power by men who had to be free, by men who would rather have been dead than submit to it any longer. Now men have not staked their fortunes and their lives simply because it was irrational that their kings and their lords and masters should have so much power: the pursuit of liberty has not been inspired by a pedantic, a doctrinaire, an ideological predilection. Men have rebelled against arbitrary power because they collided with it in their work and in the enjoyment of their faculties. So while the constitutional means to liberty are in the main a series of negatives raised against the powerful, the pursuit of liberty is a great affirmation inspired by the positive energies of the human race.   (3)

Once we have discerned the character of these energies, we cannot but recognize that they are inexhaustible and irresistible. By virtue of these energies mankind will, because it must, seek its happiness, not by submitting to providential authority but by organizing its liberty. Those energies we must affirm once more as we call upon men to resist and overcome the great reaction of our times.   (4)

II. The Will to Be Free

When the Inquisitors summoned Galileo before them, they told him he must not find that the earth revolves around the sun. Galileo had been observing the heavens through a telescope: he had become convinced that the evidence warranted his conclusion. But the Inquisitors did not look through the telescope. They knew all about astronomy from reading the Bible. So against Galileo's telescope the Inquisitors employed another instrument: the rack. And by the rack, which could inflict pain on the astronomer's body, they undertook to cure the astronomer of his scientific error. Thus they prohibited the exploration of the heavens by the exercise of their physical power.   (5)

But the rack is not an instrument for exploring the heavens. A concentration camp is not a political seminar. Burning men at the stake is not a mode of religious revelation. Firing squads are not commissions for observing and analyzing the economic situation. Censorship is not testimony and argument. As regards the intrinsic issues, these exercises of power are nothing but senseless interference, sheer brute irrelevance like the incursion of a herd of wild asses. What Galileo needed was the criticism of other astronomers: what he suffered was the meddling of powerful ignoramuses. Galileo was unfree to be an astronomer because these ignoramuses insisted on weighting the scales with the terror of prisons, torture chambers, and the stake; but he had to take his astronomy from men who had never studied it.   (6)

The movement which drives human life forward is exemplified by Galileo's impulse to explore the heavens. The forces which hold mankind back, pinned to the ignorance they happen to be in, are exemplified by the Inquisitors insisting that the preponderant force and not the preponderant evidence shall determine whether the sun is the center of our solar system. Thus we may think of the creative, the productive, and the adaptive energies of mankind as struggling to release themselves from the entanglements and perversions, the exploitation and the smothering, the parasitism and the obfuscation and the discouragement of aggressive, acquisitive, dogmatic, and arbitrary impulses. Men are moved to plant, but the seeds bear fruit with difficulty, so rank are the weeds which choke them. The cutting back of the weeds, the clearing of little spaces in which good things can grow, has been the task of human emancipation. Its method is to restrain arbitrariness. But its object is to disengage the human spirit in order that it may flourish. (7)

Thus liberalism, which in its moral essence is a challenge to all arbitrariness, to all who would use the rack rather than the telescope, is not itself the substantive principle of the good life. The substantive principle is in Galileo's curiosity and his genius: in fostering and protecting curiosity and genius, liberalism is the guardian principle of the good life. It stakes its hopes upon the human spirit released from and purged of all arbitrariness. It does not say what such a spirit can or will or ought to make of men's lives. For men have never yet known but a little of such freedom. And they cannot hope to imagine what they have never yet known. But they have known enough of freedom to know that the arbitrary power of men over men is parasitical, that it perverts, that it sterilizes and corrupts. (8)

Though liberalism has often been identified with indifference, inaction, and nonresistance, it should now be evident that this is mere confusion. A doctrine which is opposed to all arbitrariness must mean the determination to resist arbitrariness, to check it, to cut it down, to crush it, wherever and whenever it appears. It cannot mean, for example, that in the seventeenth century the King was under God and the law, but that in the nineteenth century the owners of property were not, that in the twentieth century majorities, pluralities, mobs, or dictators are not, under God and the law. For liberalism all arbitrary power is evil. It matters not what are the titles or the pretensions or the promises of arbitrary power. It must be resisted and brought under control. (9)

So liberalism is not quietism and weak government. That is the corruption of liberalism. In its vigorous periods liberalism has always meant rebellion against oppression and a determination to police aggression and acquisitiveness. Liberalism, therefore, is not the doctrine of laissez-faire, let her rip, and the devil take the hindmost. It does not envisage the demobilization of the police, the repeal of the laws, the disestablishment of legislatures and courts. On the contrary, the effective liberals have always been concerned with the development of the law, with the definition of rights and duties, with the organizing of constitutions, with the absorption of all power to coerce in the hands of duly constituted authorities, with the liquidation or regulation of all kinds of private and petty powers within the community. For the liberal, as distinguished from the anarchist, holds that mere unrestraint does not give the freedom of a voluntary society, that unrestraint merely inaugurates a competitive struggle in which the ruthless will exploit the rest. He insists that the promise of a voluntary life can be realized only as the law is strong enough to restrain aggressors at home and abroad.   (10)

But in the liberal view the reward for restraining the aggressor is that the creative and productive faculties can then begin to work. Suppose that Galileo had been able to study the heavens without having at any time to consider whether he would be punished for his conclusions. Suppose that he had needed only to argue with the theologians and to debate with other astronomers. Suppose that his opponents and his critics had been unable to invoke the threats of prison and the rack, or even of ostracism and the muttering of the mob. Suppose that his relations with his contemporaries had been purged of all the irrelevance of arbitrary power, that he had felt that if he was wrong his only punishment would be the knowledge that he had been wrong. Suppose that those who opposed him could have thrown into the scales only the immaterial weight of tradition, experience, observation, and dialectic. Is there any question that in such a community Galileo's faculties would have been enhanced, that others would have been encouraged to use theirs, that immense energy devoted to the coercive enforcement of a particular dogma would have been available in the search for the truest cosmology?   (11)

The essence of the matter is that arbitrariness is a disturbing intrusion in the creative life of mankind. It may be a mere annoyance, like the buzzing of a fly around the nose of a philosopher; or it may be like a great catastrophe, say an earthquake, which stops his work by bringing down the house around his ears. We can appreciate the real energy of freedom if we think of men, working, studying, collaborating, but beset by conquerors, exploiters, adventurers—by men who do not work, but appropriate the work of others; who do not produce, but take tolls; who do not invent, but impose prejudices; who do not create, but coerce those who do. The pursuit of liberty is the affirmation of those who produce the really good things of life.   (12)

When a Galileo is coerced by a more powerful but a more ignorant inquisitor, his scientific genius is arbitrarily leveled down to the obscurantism of his masters. It is only by freeing him from the bondage of authority that his superiority as an observer and thinker can be exercised. In our time there are governments which enforce an official culture by exile, proscription, the axe, firing squads, castor oil, and imprisonment in concentration camps: they are using arbitrary force to reduce scholars and artists, and in fact the whole population, to the cultural level of the dominant politicians. The opinion of unqualified men is artificially, by the mere arbitrary intervention of the police, made to prevail over the opinion of men who are specially gifted and have labored to qualify themselves. (13)

The same kind of obscurantism results from the exercise of all privileges. The man who has built himself a castle above the highway in order that he may exact a toll from the merchants on their way to market acquires wealth not by producing it but by seizing it. His predatory incursions arbitrarily yield the returns which would otherwise go to invention, industry, and thrift. But for his castle and his armed hands he would be poorer than the passing merchant whom he despoils: because he is more powerful but is unrestrained, he reaps a greater reward from highway robbery than other men can make by producing wealth. Thus the ideal of equal rights for all and special privileges for none is inseparable from the pursuit of liberty. A free society is one in which inequalities in the condition of men, in their rewards, and in their social status do not arise out of extrinsic and artificial causes—out of the physical power to coerce, out of legal privilege, out of special prerogative, or out of fraud, sharp practice, necessitous bargaining. (14)

This is no forcible leveling of men to a uniform condition of life. That is the tyrant's way. The libertarian does not demand that all the runners in the race must keep in step and finish together; he asks that they start from scratch and that none shall be permitted to elbow his rival off the track. Then the winner will be the best runner. The winner will not be the competitor who wangled a handicap from the judges, or obtained an advantage which had nothing to do with his ability to run the race. Manifestly, the liberal conception of equality does not promise to make all men equal in riches, influence, honor, and wisdom. On the contrary, its promise is that as the extrinsic inequalities imposed by prerogative and privilege are reduced, the intrinsic superiorities will assert themselves. (15)

This, I believe, is the insight at the heart of the liberal conception of society. I am only too well aware of how imperfectly I have understood it, how imprecisely I have been able to put it into words. But I think it is not misleading to say that some such dim but pregnant apprehension as this has been hammered out on the anvil of long experience, that it is no abstract and a priori speculation arrived at in the eighteenth century and declared to mankind by William Ewart Gladstone, but that it is much older, has its roots in centuries of confused struggle with all manner of censorship and inquisition, prerogative and privilege. (16)

In those struggles men gradually perceived that they must disengage creative and productive labor and the friendly adaptability of men to one another from the exactions and interferences of the predatory, acquisitive, parasitic, prejudicial, domineering, and irrational elements of human life. This is the "obvious and simple system of natural liberty"[1] which the classic liberals discerned. Though their history was wrong when they adopted the naïve belief that this natural order prevailed in the childhood of the race, though they greatly underestimated the length and the complexity of the struggle, their insight was true and their hearts were in the right place. (17)

We must not deny the prophet because he speaks in parables and ephemeral myths: the classic liberals arrived at a profound and enduring insight into the difference between the real and the factitious in human affairs. They were on the side of Galileo because by protecting Galileo the knowledge of astronomy is advanced. They knew that to find truth is to add to the real values of human existence. They were against the Inquisitors because they knew that astronomy cannot be advanced by imprisoning astronomers, or by compelling them to obtain a license from the secret police and the minister of propaganda.   (18)

The ultimate concern of the liberal is with the enhancement of real values by men who actually observe, reason, meditate, invent, dig, construct —seeking to arrange the world to satisfy human demands. To this end the laws, constitutions, bills of rights, courts, and social philosophies are but the means which allow creative labor to proceed without arbitrary interference.   (19)

Thus the challenge to oppression arises from the productive energies of men. The movement toward human emancipation is the rebellion of those who plant and till, dig and make, invent and construct, explore and understand; they cannot work and reap their rewards until they have subdued those who exploit and throttle and dominate their productive labors. Men withdrawn into an ivory tower can be indifferent to oppression and can come to terms with it; but those who must earn their living in the sweat of their brows cannot be indifferent, nor those who have the instinct of workmanship, or are curious and must understand the world and their destiny in it.   (20)

Among them the liberators have found their followers—among rebellious slaves, serfs demanding land and peace, merchants crying out against the robber barons, small men resisting the monopolists, industrial workers demanding recognition and status and equality of bargaining power, among artists and men of science and educators and parents crying out against the conscription of all they have created.   (21)

Their impulse to create has been their impulse to be free. And as they create it becomes more and more necessary that they should be free. For as men work, and perfect their work by invention and skill, they lift themselves out of the primitive condition in which they lead a meagre and self-sufficing existence. The improvement of their skill, the development of their

---

1 Adam Smith, *The Wealth of Nations*, Bk. IV, Ch. 9.

special aptitudes, the use of their particular opportunities, result in the specialization of their labor. Because they do the work they are able to do, they are no longer self-sufficing and must live by the exchange of their products. They enter into the economy of the division of labor.   (22)

The division of labor was not invented by economists; it was not invented by the inventors of machinery and steam railroads. The division of labor in an exchange economy is implied in the very essence of productive labor itself. In order that Galileo might study the heavens it was not sufficient that the Inquisitors should let him alone; it was necessary that someone else should grow the food he ate and make the clothes he wore and grind the lenses through which he observed the heavens. He had to be liberated not only from the oppression of arbitrary authority but from the sterile drudgery of a self-sufficient existence. And because by the division of labor he was liberated from the drudgery, he was able to be an astronomer who necessarily rebelled against authority.   (23)

Thus the connection between liberty and the industrial revolution is organic. The impulse to create and the impulse to be free are cumulative: each is to the other both cause and effect. Because men wish to work they insist on freedom from arbitrary interference; because they are free, they work by a division of labor which requires the freedom of certain and equal rights.   (24)

This is the reason why all the conceptions which constitute the testament of liberty have been evolved in great societies that have lived by extensive and complicated commerce. They come to us from the Græco-Roman society, from the merchant cities of the Renaissance, from western Europe, from England, France, the Netherlands, and Italy, from the peoples who first emerged from self-sufficiency and had to establish a common law in which their transactions could be secure. It is no accident that it was the Athenians, living by commerce, rather than the Spartans living by exploitation and war, who conceived the good life; or that the Romans who traded all over the known world should have understood the necessity for law; or that the nation of shopkeepers was the mother of parliaments; or that Yankee traders in Boston fomented the American Revolution and the abolition of slavery. For among a people living by a primitive undifferentiated economy under routine and in isolation, the necessity for constitutional liberty does not exist and can scarcely be conceived.   (25)

III. On Designing a New Society

This truth our contemporary authoritarians, whether of the left or of the right, have failed to grasp. They look upon the great sprawling complex of transactions by which mankind lives; seeing that these transactions are in large part still unregulated by law, and that therefore there is much confusion and injustice, they have turned their backs upon the task of regulation by law and have beguiled themselves with the notion that they can plan this economy systematically and administer it rationally. The exact contrary is the truth. The modern economy is perhaps the least systematic of any that has ever existed. It is world-wide, formless, vast, complicated, and, owing to technological progress, in constant change. For that reason it is incapable of being conceived as a system, or of being replaced by another system, or of being managed as an administrative unit.   (26)

The hankering for schemes and systems and comprehensive organization is the wistfulness of an immature philosophy which has not come to terms with reality, no less when the conservators of vested interests would stabilize the modern economy in statu quo by protective laws and monopolistic schemes than when the revolutionist makes blueprints of a world composed of planned national economies "coördinated" by a world-planning authority. Neither takes any more account of reality than if he were studying landscape architecture with a view to making a formal garden out of the Brazilian jungle.   (27)

For the greater the society, the higher and more variable the standards of life, the more diversified the energies of its people for invention, enterprise, and adaptation, the more certain it is that the social order cannot be planned ex cathedra or governed by administrative command. We live in such an immensely diversified civilization that the only intelligible criterion which political thinkers can entertain in regard to it, the only feasible goal which statesmen can set themselves in governing it, is to reconcile the conflicts which spring from this diversity. They cannot hope to comprehend it as a system. For it is not a system. They cannot hope to plan and direct it. For it is not an organization. They can hope only to dispense lawful justice among individuals and associations where their interests conflict, to mitigate the violence of conflict and competition by seeking to make lawful justice more and more equitable.   (28)

It requires much virtue to do that well. There must be a strong desire to be just. There must be a growing capacity to be just. There must be discernment and sympathy in estimating the particular claims of divergent interests. There must be moral standards which discourage the quest of privilege and the exercise of arbitrary power. There must be resolution and valor to resist oppression and tyranny. There must be patience and tolerance and kindness in hearing claims, in argument, in negotiation, and in reconciliation.   (29)

But these are human virtues; though they are high, they are within the attainable limits of human nature as we know it. They actually exist. Men do have these virtues, all but the most hopelessly degenerate, in some degree. We know that they can be increased. When we talk about them we are talking about virtues that have affected the course of actual history, about virtues that some men have practiced more than other men, and no man sufficiently, but enough men in great enough degree to have given mankind here and there and for varying periods of time the intimations of a Good Society.   (30)

But the virtues that are required for the overhead administration of a civilization are superhuman; they are attributes of Providence and not of mortal men. It is true that there have been benevolent despots and that for a little while in a particular place they have made possible a better life than their subjects were able to achieve without the rule of a firm and authoritative guardian. And no doubt it is still true that a community which does not have the essential discipline of liberty can choose only among alternative disciplines by authority. But if a community must have such a guardian, then it must resign itself to living a simple regimented existence, must entertain no hopes of the high and diversified standard of life which the division of labor and modern technology make possible. For despots cannot be found who could plan, organize, and direct a complex economy.
                              (31)

To do that would require a comprehensive understanding of the life and the labor and the purposes of hundreds of millions of persons, the gift of prophesying their behavior and omnipotence to control it. These faculties no man has ever possessed. When in theorizing we unwittingly postulate such faculties, we are resting our hopes on a conception of human nature which has no warrant whatever in any actual experience. The collectivist planners are not talking about the human race but about some other breed conceived in their dreams. They postulate qualities of intelligence and of virtue so unlike those which men possess that it would be just as intelligible to make plans for a society in which human beings were born equipped to fly like the angels, to feed on the fragrance of the summer breezes, and endowed with all possible knowledge.   (32)

Thus while the liberal philosophy is concerned with the reform of the laws in order to adapt them to the changing needs and standards of the dynamic economy, while the agenda of reform are long and varied, no one must look to liberalism for a harmonious scheme of social reconstruction. The Good Society has no architectural design. There are no blueprints. There is no mold in which human life is to be shaped. Indeed, to expect the blueprint of such a mold is a mode of thinking against which the liberal temper is a constant protest.   (33)

To design a personal plan for a new society is a pleasant form of madness; it is in imagination to play at being God and Cæsar to the human race. Any such plan must implicitly assume that the visionary or someone else might find the power, or might persuade the masses to give him the power, to shape society to the plan; all such general plans of social reconstruction are merely the rationalization of the will to power. For that reason they are the subjective beginnings of fanaticism and tyranny. In these utopias the best is the enemy of the good, the heart's desire betrays the interests of man. To think in terms of a new scheme for a whole society is to use the idiom of authority, to approach affairs from the underlying premise that they can be shaped and directed by an overhead control, that social relations can be fabricated according to a master plan drawn up by a supreme architect.   (34)

The supreme architect, who begins as a visionary, becomes a fanatic, and ends as a despot. For no one can be the supreme architect of society without employing a supreme despot to execute the design. So if men are to seek freedom from the arbitrary dominion of men over men, they must not entertain fantasies of the future in which they play at being the dictators of civilization. It is the bad habit of an undisciplined imagination. The descent from fantasy to fanaticism is easy. Real dictators raised to power by the fanatics who adore them are only too likely to adopt the fantasy to justify their lust for power.   (35)

On the other hand, reasonable and civilized people who would like to make the best of the situation before them, but have no ambition for, or expectation of, the power to reshape a whole society, get no help from these architectural designs. The blueprint, be it as grandiose a work of genius as Plato's *Republic*, cannot hope to fit the specific situation. No a priori reasoning can anticipate the precise formulæ which will reconcile the infinitely varied interests of men. The reconciliation has to be achieved by the treatment of specific issues and the solution will appear only after the claims and the evidence have been examined and fairly judged. Thus in Plato's great scheme each man was assigned his station and his duties; any architectural plan is necessarily based on the same presumption. But Plato's scheme worked only in Plato's imagination, never in the real world. No such scheme can ever work in the real world. For the scheme implies that men will remain content in the station which the visionary has assigned to them. To formulate such plans is not to design a society for real men. It is to re-create men to fit the design. For in real life men rest content in their station only if their interests have been successfully reconciled: failing that, they do not fit the design until they have been dosed with castor oil, put in concentration camps, or exiled to Siberia.   (36)

That is why the testament of liberty does not contain the project of a new social order. It adumbrates a way of life in which men seek to reconcile their interests by perfecting the rules of justice. No scheme which promises to obliterate the differences of interest can be deduced from it, no architectural design of society in which all human problems have been resolved. There is no plan of the future: there is, on the contrary, the conviction that the future must have the shape that human energies, purged in so far as possible of arbitrariness, will give it. Compared with the elegant and harmonious schemes which are propounded by the theoretical advocates of capitalism, communism, fascism, it must seem intellectually unsatisfying, and I can well imagine that many will feel about the liberal society as Emma Darwin felt when she wrote about the *Descent of Man*, "I think it will be very interesting, but that I shall dislike it very much as again putting God further off."[2]   (37)

But though it must seem an insufficient ideal both to those who wish to exercise authority and to those who feel the need of leaning upon authority, it is the only practicable ideal of government in the Great Society. When huge masses of men have become dependent upon one another through the division of labor in countless, infinitely complex transactions, their activities cannot be planned and directed by public officials.   (38)

Thus it is true that the liberal state is not to be conceived as an earthly providence administering civilization. That is the essence of the matter. To the liberal mind the notion that men can authoritatively plan and impose a good life upon a great society is ignorant, impertinent, and pretentious. It can be entertained only by men who do not realize the infinite variety of human purposes, who do not appreciate the potentialities of human effort, or by men who do not choose to respect them.   (39)

The liberal state is to be conceived as the protector of equal rights by dispensing justice among individuals. It seeks to protect men against arbitrariness, not arbitrarily to direct them. Its ideal is a fraternal association among free and equal men. To the initiative of individuals, secure in their rights and accountable to others who have equal rights, liberalism entrusts the shaping of the human destiny. It offers no encouragement to those who dream of what they could make of the world if they possessed supreme power. In the testament of liberty these ambitions have been assessed: the record of all the Cæsars from Alexander to Adolf is visible. The world has known many societies in which each man had his station, his duties, and his ordained destiny, and the record shows that it is beyond the understanding of men to know all human needs, to appreciate all human possibilities, to imagine all human ends, to shape all human relations.   (40)

Yet if the ambitions of liberalism are more modest than those of authority, its promise is greater. It relies upon the development of the latent faculties of all men, shaped by their free transactions with one another. Liberalism commits the destiny of civilization, not to a few finite politicians here and there, but to the whole genius of mankind. This is a grander vision than that of those who would be Cæsar and would set themselves up as little tin gods over men. It is a hope engendered in the human heart during the long ages in which the slowly emerging impulses of civilization, beset by barbarism, have struggled to be free.   (41)

---

[2] Cited in Donald Culross Peattie's *Green Laurels*, p. 323.

Lyman Bryson

(1888–1959)

BRYSON was, until his retirement in 1953, professor of education at Teachers College, Columbia University. He had begun his career as a newspaper man in Omaha, and he later returned to communications media as director of the CBS program "Invitation to Learning." He held several honorary doctorates (Occidental, Moravian, Drexel, Columbia) and was the author of several books: Communications of Ideas *(1948),* Science and Freedom *(1947),* The Next America *(1952),* The Drive Toward Reason *(1954).*

◼ *On Deceiving the Public for the Public Good*

THIS BOLDLY stated question, "Should a leader deceive the public for the public good?" is not likely to get less important as time goes on, for leaders do not get less powerful or less ambitious and the means of deceiving the people increases. We have made political leaders more than ever dependent on the suffrage of their followers, but we have put mechanical messengers into their hands by which they can coerce public consent. The growth of an industrial culture has tended also to enlarge constantly the units of organization in which men work, and also the collectives in which they think and communicate with each other and act together. The great collectives take over more and more of our lives, in their economic and political aspects especially, and make it more and more difficult for us to see the relations between what we do and any general principles of truth or rightness. The leader is tempted by the tools of manipulation. Is it ever wise for him to use them? (1)

We ought first to ask ourselves the more general question: What are leaders for? Why do we need leaders in a free country? I would answer that the leader's function is to help to determine, in any crisis, which of our possible selves will act. We are all multiple: our personalities are bundles of possible responses, each with the accent of our own peculiar self, but still all widely differing from each other. If we could always be counted on, each one of us, always to act in the same way, no matter how we are challenged, life and politics would be much simpler. It would also be dull and uninteresting: our unpredictability is part of our human charm. The leader is an embodied suggestion, and the combinations of causes and chances that determine the leader who will catch our attention and our support at any time, are the causal chain of history.   (2)

We might suppose, for an example, that the people of a tragically unhappy country like Germany could have followed a more calm and righteous leader than Hitler, and that they had all reacted to the pressure of the situation in the same way. In that case there might never have been a world conflict. We know that the Germans were confused, as well as hurt. Some of them, as we know from the investigations of Theodore Abel and other sociologists, tried to retreat into a fantasy of martyrdom. To them the world was not only tragic; it was unjust. They could blame anyone but themselves for what had happened. Others took refuge in crime, as if to say, "Since all the foundations of our state have been destroyed, we'll get what we can for ourselves out of the wreck." Others were willing to begin the hard work of reconstruction. And among the possibilities was the idea of reasserting the greatness of the German people and the German state. It was possible to believe that Germany was still one of the strong and aggressive factors in the world. All these possible ways of reacting existed among the German people, and many of them existed side by side within the personalities of every individual German. Each man or woman was more or less capable of making any one of these responses to trouble, and the one the great mass took was what was suggested by the most persuasive leadership.   (3)

What did Hitler actually do? He called out the aggressive self that was latent in practically every normal German and made it the dominant active self. He made most of them as aggressive as they were individually capable of being. More than that, he called out and got into positions of power all the Germans who were even more than normally aggressive, and the nation was put in a generally aggressive and dangerous posture. Great crises make for great instability of selves, or of character, and Germany's crisis was catastrophic. The result was an enormous overdevelopment of a normal human trait, socially organized and expressed. This, in generally less damaging ways, sometimes to our great good, is the function of the

leader. He cannot make us over; he can make us be our best or our
worst within our range.   (4)

A free country, which is our ideal and our partial accomplishment, has
the same need for leaders of the right kind as any other. But before we
conclude this discussion we have to ask ourselves another question of general principle. What is the purpose of political life and active citizenship in
a free country? I believe that the purpose of sharing in the political thought
of my country, and of my own community as a part of it, is not ultimately
the solution of political problems. Freedom for men to think and learn and
act on their acquired wisdom is, I believe, more likely to get good solutions
for political problems than any other system; our record would prove that.
But even if there were a better way of getting the merely correct technical,
or practical—shall we say, the material answers?—to a political problem, I
would still hold fast to democracy and to decision by the people. Our
ultimate judgment on a social or a political system should not be based,
solely, on the criterion of practical success. It is based on the evidence of
growth in the people. Sometimes free men make mistakes; they must be
allowed that privilege. If they learn the lessons of politics and conduct
from making mistakes, the principle of democracy is fulfilled. Whether or
not there are other areas of living, outside the political, in which this principle cannot be followed, is another question. We shall stick to politics. (5)

I can turn to Germany again for an example to make the point. Several
years ago a small group of German women who were then holding political
office at home were brought over here for some lessons in American ideas
of democracy. Asked to help in that project, I chose to meet them after they
had made their journeys and observations. I wanted to hear their questions,
after they knew what America looked like. In the conversation we had, one
of the most intelligent of the nine women struggled to understand the essential relation in a democracy between freedom and authority, political freedom and technical authority. She told of being in a city where the administration of municipal affairs was entrusted to a city manager. He was
appointed because of his professional competence and experience. He was
an excellent person and it was evident that he would know the right answers to most practical questions. And yet—this disturbed her deeply—the
members of the city council, who were not elected for professional competence, had final authority to overrule his decisions. Even his right decisions!
she said.   (6)

My answer was that the principle of democracy would always make it
necessary for the directly elected representatives of the people to have the
final word. Even when they were wrong? Even when, by any technical
judgment, they were wrong. And I insisted that she would not understand
democracy until she could see why that had to be so. I tried to explain to
her that she was still thinking of political action as having no purpose other

than to solve political problems, and that if this principle, which was ultimately not democratic but authoritarian, was followed in any country, the rule of the people would eventually be ended. The purpose of political action and the opportunity of free political life is for the people ultimately to determine their own destiny, and—after they have had the chance to learn—even to make their own mistakes. The great end they are serving is the development of their country through the development of themselves, not by authoritative interventions, no matter how competent or benevolent. It is not true that tyrants can never be benevolent. The trouble is that they go on being tyrants, and under tyranny individual men dry up for lack of spiritual exercise.   (7)

We too often forget that it means something real and important, and perhaps greatly daring, to say that the purpose of a democratic society is to make great persons, that the end is the development of the person by experience and not the technical answers to civic problems. In fact, political experience has been and still is, and probably will always be, one of the greatest of the educational factors in any person's life; it cannot count for much unless it includes free decisions and a chance to learn from the consequences. We have to decide for ourselves in the light of what we can learn of the facts, and then learn the great lessons from the results of our choice. Both collective organization and authority can interfere with this purpose and defeat us. Unless we learn from politics, then politics is not worth our time. Decisions should be made for the good of the state, but the ultimate value of all political decisions is the experience of bearing part of the responsibility of making them.   (8)

The leader, then, is a person who helps us to choose, and if he is a great leader he helps us also to learn. He cannot do his work for us, if this is what we demand of him, in any society where the closed theories of freedom prevail. Through the long course of political and social debate in Western history there have been two ideas of freedom, and this is not the place to question the sincerity of those who take the ancient line that we, in America, have learned to reject. The closed theory of freedom, as it is advocated vigorously in all totalitarian countries, is that men have a right to know an official doctrine which is always called the truth. But it implies also that they have a right to know nothing but this official doctrine, and that the state or some other authoritative group of men, acting in the name of the doctrine embodied in some institution, have the right to interfere in their experience and keep them from knowing anything contrary to it. It implies that authority, which in considering our problem, means the men in power, knows what the truth is, and will keep all citizens of the state from any contamination with any other opinion. This is called "freedom" in totalitarian countries, and its defenders can look for support to a long line of teachers in our Western tradition. The other theory, the open theory, which has an equally numerous body of teachers behind it and is the dominant ideal of freedom for which we have fought for centuries, and which we have attempted to embody in our American political institutions, is that men must seek truth by free choice and consequence. They must have the freedom to make mistakes, because freedom is given for the ultimate purpose of democratic political life which is individual growth.   (9)

These are all preliminary considerations which must be taken into account, I think, before we can answer our question: which is, if you have forgotten, "Should a leader deceive the public for the public good?" But we still have to answer another prior question: "What kind of society do we want?" There seems to be good evidence in history and in our own times that only those societies that believe their own political slogans and in the myths of their national virtue can build successful empires. By this, I mean, of course, that nations which dominate others must first put themselves under spiritual domination.   (10)

This is not the same thing as to say that we should lose our democracy if we set out to run the world; I do not believe that the problem is best put in those terms. Certainly other nations in the remote past and in approximately modern times have built empires and still remained democracies. Britain is the best example; Britain built her empire and her own democracy through the same period. But it is still true that nations which set out more or less deliberately to dominate other nations must be ruled by men who pronounce some political slogans that are not to be questioned, and if the people have even a healthy skepticism toward the goals of empire or the myths of their country's unspecked virtue, the will to power is fatally weakened.   (11)

We need only look at the difference between the attitude of the Greeks, who brilliantly failed at empire, and the attitude of the Romans who brilliantly succeeded. It is not now a question of their degrees of democracy at home, although we might have stopped to notice that Rome also built her empire while building her civil law and the civil rights of her people. The point is to mark the difference between a magnificently endowed but skeptical people like the Greeks, and a very different people, the Romans, who learned how to conquer. We can be quite sure, I think, that most of the Romans who brought their own version of the classical civilization to the Western world and gave the Mediterranean basin several centuries of magnificent peace, really believed that Roman ideas and Roman slogans were not only best but were not to be examined. The Greeks in their most insolent moments never seemed able quite to believe that their imperial depredations were for the good of subjected peoples. When the Romans began their career as a mean tribe with great ideas, in the little group of hills in the center of Italy, when they conquered and took more and more of their neighbors into the Roman state, they believed not only that it was good for the Romans but also good for the slaves and the conquered who might, of course, end up by being taken into citizenship but who were, in the meantime, to be made over in the Roman image. They believed their slogans and took over the Western world.   (12)

It helps to have the slogans and the political myths founded on facts, but the crucial point is that they are believed. Today we can study the British and find them much like the Romans in their early brutal innocence and faith, like them also perhaps in the late phase, their present refinement, their discovery that social welfare at home is more important than carrying the white man's burden, perhaps that the white man's burden can be best carried at home, their period of the Antonines. We can, if necessary, save them from the next stage of being overcome by barbarians. But when they were powerful, they were extraordinary for efficiency as rulers and for self-confidence. They believed their own stuff. The French, on the other hand, like the Greeks, have long since been skeptical and weak imperialists. The principle holds.   (13)

We do not know how much of our own destiny is ever in our own hands. This is a philosophic, not a practical, question we are dealing with and we can assume for ourselves the power of national choice. We do not need to destroy our own freedoms to save us from destroying the freedoms of others; that ironic crime has often been committed, to keep freedom at home and conquer abroad. Witness Britain and India. The cost of empire lies not in our political freedoms, but in the adjacent area of our freedom to know and to learn by free informed experience. To lead us into building an empire, provided it is possible to us in material terms, our leaders have got to convince us and keep us convinced that all slogans of imperialism are true, that we are destined because of our virtue as well as our strength to subdue the world for its own sake, to spread the unquestioned doctrines of our own political and economic commonplaces, to repeat again the sorry old pattern of dominion.   (14)

The purpose of empire building, however, is not the building of great citizens; it is the building of a great state. Great states are built by leaders who lead their people into sacrifice for dreams of power and glory, who lead them to believe that some kinds of doctrinally prescribed freedom may be good for them but that weaker peoples must be led. Great men and women are built by leaders who lead them into sacrifice for the right freely to seek the truth.   (15)

It has to be made quite clear, I believe, that a love of free inquiry and other higher virtues will not destroy the power of a great nation, nor make it helpless against attack, by force or by insidious ideas. It is altogether likely that, in modern circumstances, an open freedom of thought will make a country materially strong, as well as strong in spirit. There is as yet no evidence whatever that totalitarian countries, which suppress skepticism and honest deviation in the name of doctrine, or officially pronounced "truth," can either build or manage a really great industrial system which depends in the long run on the freedom of skill and invention. Neither Britain nor Germany nor the United States created a great industrial state by totalitarian management. Russia has not yet proved that it can succeed industrially after thirty-three years of effort. Our point, however, lies elsewhere. What we are saying is that great citizens can be built only when leaders will dare to let them use their own minds, when the state helps us to knowledge of alternative choices, conserving for us the essential democratic experience, which is to seek the truth by our own efforts, to know it as far as it can be known, to act on it freely, and to learn freely from free action. We can be strong and we can be free. If we want to dominate others and shove our doctrines down the throats of weaker peoples, then our leaders will have to deal often in lies in order to blind us to the true picture of our behavior.   (16)

This question, then, can be put in Kantian terms. We can follow Immanuel Kant's distinction: we can take men as means or as ends. It is as simple and as difficult as that. If men are to be used as means, if human beings are to be treated by their leaders as means to an end—and I am specifying nothing whatever as to the quality or character of that end, even the realization of national power, or the greatness of an institution, the realization of an ideal, or the sacrifice of the present to the future—if men are to be taken as means to an end, then it is inevitable that leaders will at certain times deceive them for the public good. But if we accept Kant's ethical principle and believe that men should never be used as means but always as ends in themselves, if their experience is the purpose of political life, then the leader, by interfering with the people's experience of free inquiry, no matter how bitter their discoveries may be, is defeating democracy.   (17)

The distinction is easy but to make it work is difficult, because a leader, even within my definition, is always also a teacher. Part of his job in every situation and on any scale of operation, social or political or intellectual, is to enlarge constantly the range of thought and the range of possible choices in the minds of his followers. A leader who believes in our kind of democracy, which we practice with considerable success, although we often get mixed up in trying to define it, will say, "My duty is also the duty of a teacher, to increase men's freedom by enlarging their knowledge." The biggest dimension of freedom is the dimension of knowing. As we have to repeat, over and over in these days of deliberate obfuscation and innocent confusions, the choice you never can make is the choice you never heard of. Ignorance is not only a chain on your mind, it is also a chain that binds your will.   (18)

Any kind of so-called freedom that protects men against making mistakes cannot be what we are talking about, because you cannot protect men from error except by protecting them against knowledge. Any government or institution or leader that sets out to protect men from making mistakes must act on the assumption that there is an ultimate truth that can be stated as final closed doctrine—and here I am still speaking of political and social truths because religious truth may present other problems— not only that there is an ultimate truth but that it can be exactly stated and that they can state it better than anyone else. It implies that this doctrine is of a kind that cannot maintain itself by its own character in the open market of ideas, and that it cannot do its work for men unless they are forcibly prevented from ever hearing anything else.   (19)

This is the principle, explicitly stated in their own documents, followed by the present Russian government. The Russians argue in international committees: "We have freedom of information in Russia because all agencies of information are in the hands of the government and therefore they cannot fall into the hands of anyone who would deceive the people." In spite of the fact that such a statement seems to us either naive or cynical, as it does not admit the ever present danger that the government might be the agency that was out to fool the people, we must take it, I think, as sincere. It is in the minds of sincere persons that it can really do the most damage. We need not really fear very much those who are cynical enough to realize that they are using suppression of knowledge to keep themselves in power and laugh with each other behind closed conference doors. Institutions founded on cynicism have a way of disintegrating. It is possible, of course, for men in the Kremlin to think this is a joke, although I doubt even that. It is absolutely necessary, if Russia is to last very long as a totalitarian state, that the rank and file of the bureaucracy, the little leaders, believe in what they are doing.   (20)

No, the most dangerous tyrant is the one who has succumbed to the ultimate corruption of power and believes in his own benevolence. He can believe that he is helping the people, that he is doing us good by keeping us from knowing anything but the official doctrine whatever it may be. He will in all honesty and zeal keep us from learning by our own choice. (21)

You may be thinking that we do not learn much from experience and that making a mistake is not a step that leads always to wisdom. This is true enough; if we learned from our mistakes and never repeated them, the world would not be so full of defeated and frustrated people. But, however much we may fail to learn from experience, it is quite certain that there are many things we cannot learn from anything else. They cannot be handed down to us, nor handed out, and if there is any new truth in the world it will not be discovered by men who are protected from error. (22)

So we come back again to the leader. His chief work is to help us make a choice. He can lead us to take great spiritual risks and be great citizens.

Or, he can play safe, stick to the doctrine, and let us drift into the fallacies of power. In that case, we may possibly win an empire but we are almost certain to lose our own souls. I am making a clear contrast here, between greatness in nations and greatness in men, meaning power and domination on the one hand, and the expansion of the soul by the search for truth, on the other. These are different ideals, and it often happens in the practical affairs of men that nations attain to mixtures and combinations of the ideals that are held by various members of their national group. By my own preference among the definitions of freedom, I should have to say that I should prefer a nation in which there was a generous variety of different goals, on all levels of political opinion, except in those matters that would endanger freedom itself. And I do not believe that all the overt national actions of a national group will always serve the same ideal. What we are seeking is the answer to a question that proposes a choice between two kinds of effort and two kinds of demand to be made on our leaders, knowing that the results will be mixed. The true spirit of freedom and power are not antithetical, any more than righteousness and prosperity are antitheses. But the man who seeks prosperity above righteousness will probably lose both, and the nation that seeks power above truth will have the same double disaster.   (23)

The alternative that we are not quite willing to state in realistic terms can be put this way: Do we want our leaders to decide what shall be our national fate without letting us in on their secret, and then manipulate our ignorance to achieve what they think we ought to have, without our knowing what are the other choices? It might be said that a little license to a ruler is not a mandate for tyranny. The difficulty is that if we give willingly to a leader the right to deceive us, we give over to him also the right and the chance to decide when and whenever the deceit shall be practiced. It is certain that the fates of nations are mixed, evil with good, and we may seek virtue even while we have a concern for material power. But which value is to be sacrificed to the other? It is the habit of knowing what value is to be held to, even at the cost of the others, that gives us our national morality.   (24)

In the present crisis in American life, it is important to look closely at one assumption, an almost unconscious assumption that gets into much discussion of our possible future power and influence. It is taken for granted and it is false. The notion, which you will meet in all kinds of writing and talk and political polemics, is that we can justify our material power, even a career of material domination, by the cultural achievements that our power makes possible. I mean, of course, cultural achievements by ourselves, great art and thought and science and philosophy, the great expression of our own ideals. And the notion is false because, in spite of the commonplaces of the textbooks and careless historians, great cultural achievements have not been inevitably, or even generally, concurrent with great material power, and certainly are not the results of it.   (25)

This is a thesis that shocks certain kinds of commonplace minds because the fallacy is so comforting. It may be selfish of us to spread over the world, by the means of bayonets and bombs. But we bring civilization and much more; we express our own greatness for the good of later generations in imperishable art and thought. Look at Periclean Greece, and Elizabethan England and France under Louis XIV and the others. Well, I ask you really to look at them. This is no place for a thoroughgoing analysis of the relations, at these times, of the factors of power and cultural productiveness, but I am saying as boldly as I know how that the idea that nations grow great materially and then, and as a result, show greatness in art and thought and in letters, is a fallacy, unhistorical, and untrue.   (26)

If the fate of any nation displayed before our contemporary eyes were needed to set up the truth of the relation between material power and cultural achievement, it could well be found in Germany. Between Bismarck and Hitler, Germany dominated Europe and made two bids toward world hegemony that terrified and exhausted the rest of Europe. Out of that time, whose names will be remembered with anything but infamy? A few scientists, a few men of art and letters. But at the turn of the century a hundred years before that, when Germany was only a name for a culture scattered among petty quarreling states, and there was no material power anywhere in her national organizations, German culture produced Lessing, Herder, Goethe, Schiller, Kant, Hegel, Schopenhauer, Mozart, Beethoven— you can think of many others. The same kind of parallel can be shown in the material confusions and degradations of nineteenth century France when her art and science blazed with glory. On this point, two modern social philosophers, Kroeber and Sorokin, have collected the evidence and the conclusion is inescapable.   (27)

This is dwelt on because the fallacy is old, comforting, deepseated and frequently expressed as a rule of history. We can delude ourselves into thinking that for us to turn back from a career of domination, from taking over the world with our gasoline and steel and precarious uranium, would be to forego the great chance to be a great nation and leave a heritage of greatness for the use and admiration of others. Persons and nations are, in moral questions, faced with like decisions. If we look back at the records of the men and women to whom we owe greatness in thought, greatness in artistry, greatness in spirit, we see that almost never were they persons who had power in their own time. Material power and spiritual greatness are almost irrelevant in the lives of men. They are also irrelevant in the history of nations. A man or a country may have either material power or cultural greatness with or without the other. But neither one of them is the cause or the result of the other.   (28)

We are in a critical period and we have a choice to make among ideals. Whether or not we are in fact allowed to choose our course may be a debatable question, because we are deep in change and we can neither see clearly, nor control completely, the forces that we ride. We may want to be great in the material sense, dominant, imperialistic, oppressive, and also to do great things with our minds and spirits. But if we seek to gain the city, in the Biblical phrase, we may all too easily lose our own souls, without realizing that it is no better for a nation than it is for a man to want power at too great a cost, or to be unaware of what is paid for it.   (29)

We have said that this price is not our freedom at home. There is an evident paradox here. If we can have an empire without giving up our freedom as citizens of our home country, how are we paying for empire by giving up freedom of thought? The examples already given of Rome and Britain, where domestic citizenship got to be more equitable and free during much of the time when the empire was being conquered, ought to indicate an answer. And it seems to me certain that, in Britain in the nineteenth century, the citizen of Birmingham or Aberdeen, busy with his own political and business affairs, did not know what his government was doing in Burma or the Sudan. He believed in the imperial myth and was willing to support it, the myth that his government was bringing benevolent civilization to recalcitrant "niggers" the world over, and when his leaders lied to him as they consistently did, he believed them and was willing, when needed, to die for empire.   (30)

If we can choose for our country, if there is still time, what do we want, power in the commonplace imperial sense? Or shall we be a people who want to advance freedom for all peoples, who want to live in the bracing air of freedom of thought at home and be—not the slaves or the beneficiaries of another great empire—but great persons in our own right? (31)

Such a choice, on such a scale as we could make it, has not been made before. If it is possible for us, it will be because we have the institutions, the leaders, and the faiths. And, in fact, I believe that we owe great respect to the national leaders whom we have had in my generation. No one of them, I think, has been a supremely great man in power of mind. They have not been great inventors of values or teachers to the nation. They have been mostly normal and ordinary men, except for courage and political skill. But we cannot find among them anyone who tried consistently to make the American people believe what he thought was a lie. The "golden" lies of Plato's guardians have not ruled us.   (32)

We might have had, beginning with Theodore Roosevelt, the kind of leader who would manipulate the sources of public information and the sources of agencies of public opinion, as we saw done in Germany, and as is now being done in many other places. In our country the net of public communication is very wide and very difficult to manage from a central point, but it is also pervasive and influential. A persistent plan to deceive us might have succeeded. If that had been done, it is conceivable that our policies, especially in foreign relations, might have been less vacillating as well as less democratically criticized, and we might have been a mightier power. Having more honest leaders we have been less successfully aggressive than others, and against aggression we have fought back only at the last moment with great cost to ourselves. We have not been the big masterful nation that we sometimes think we ought to be. But if, as a nation, we had been more masterful, our people in this generation would be much less fully aware of what has been going on and would have been less challenged by a painfully real knowledge of the issues. In that case, we might have been a greater nation of lesser persons.   (33)

Our question then, "Should a leader deceive the public for the public good?" is not a simple question of good or evil. It is a real choice in political action. Shall we, on the one hand, follow the example of the nations that can set forth uncomplicated simple myths about themselves and their destiny in the world, and believe them, and go on to conquest? Shall we have our own version of the slogan, "Take up the white man's burden"? We, too, can have our imperial adventure, and there are leaders already in training to take us in hand with the right slogans and comforting reassuring myths about our destiny, if we are ready to respond.   (34)

But if we want above all things the wisdom and knowledge of free experience, the high privilege of searching for truth by our own powers, we had better give up campaigns against the liberties of others and also— this is harder to do—all campaigns to save other nations from their own errors. We can declare our own faiths and our own gospels, of course, but not with sanctions. Nations that encourage their citizens to be openminded, skeptical, questioning, free, are not good candidates for hegemony. But they have something else. They have a democracy of the spirit and the mind, and what they achieve may really be for the good of others, as well as for themselves.   (35)

Sidney Hook

(1902–   )

HOOK, professor of philosophy at New York University, was a student of John Dewey's and continues to be his disciple. He has been a Guggenheim Fellow and a Fellow of the Center for Advanced Studies in the Behavioral Sciences at Stanford. In the late 'forties and early 'fifties, he was at the center of the controversy over the communist threat; in the mid-'sixties he has given much attention to restlessness on the college campus. His books include Education for the Modern Man *(1946),* Political Power and Personal Freedom *(1959), and* The Paradoxes of Freedom *(1962).*

◼ *The Conflict of Freedoms*

ALTHOUGH the theme of this article bears on issues that have become extremely topical in the United States, it has a general significance for all free societies in which the freedoms guaranteed by law are sometimes used to provoke violence, and even to destroy the political system which makes these freedoms possible. The question whether freedom has limits becomes acute in times of social ferment, especially when all embattled interests claim to be fighting on behalf of freedom.   (1)

Whether all current senses of the term 'freedom' or 'liberty' are compatible with each other is questionable. They certainly are not logically derivable from each other. For example, those who speak of 'freedom of the will,' whether to affirm it or deny it, are not saying anything relevant about political freedom. Two individuals who agree that man's will is determined by antecedent causes may still differ about the desirability of political freedom. Conversely they may agree about political freedom and differ about the meaning and/or validity of freedom of the will.   (2)

By 'political freedom' we usually mean the power of a people to determine the nature of the government under which it lives and who its rulers should be. It is a specific form of freedom whose root conception is the absence of coercion or restraint by others on the effective expression of desire. A free government is not necessarily a good government although those who support it believe that it is better than any other government feasible at the time. Those who in principle are opposed to a free government like Plato believe that most human beings are too stupid or vicious to be entrusted with the power of self-government. This is also assumed by those who support the dictatorship of a minority political party. In rare moments of honesty they admit it. Thus Kadar, the Communist leader, after the suppression of the Hungarian Revolution, asserted: 'The task of the leaders is not to put into effect the wishes and will of the masses . . . The task is to realize and accomplish their interests. Why do I differentiate between the will and interests of the masses? In the recent past we have encountered the phenomena of workers acting *against* their interest.' (Speech of May 11, 1957.) (3)

Political freedom is obviously a matter of degree but in the most consistent use of the term 'free', a government is called free when a legally recognized opposition exists and is permitted to function, thus making it possible for a minority peacefully to become a majority. It is therefore integral to the conception of political freedom that the processes by which political consent is won must be free, that, in other words, freedom of speech, press, assembly and association, the cluster of freedoms of the Bill of Rights, must have legal sanction. (4)

Are there any limits to such freedoms? This is a perennial question which arises whenever in the storm and stress of political strife disorder on a local or national scale becomes rampant. A very influential segment of American judicial opinion, headed by Mr. Justice Black, holds that in a politically free society, as defined above, the freedoms of the Bill of Rights are absolute, and that they cannot be abridged without unconstitutionally breaching the law of the land. This view is usually contrasted with the position defended by Justice Felix Frankfurter and Judge Learned Hand who interpret these freedoms as 'admonitions' to legislative bodies what to avoid. What is really at issue is whether the freedoms of the Bill of Rights should be interpreted as categorical rules to which no exceptions should be made or as, in Jefferson's words, 'general rules to which there may be proper exceptions.' (5)

That any specific freedom can be deemed inviolable independently of its consequence on other specific freedoms, as well as of its consequences on the health and welfare of the community, seems on the face of it quite unplausible. Three large and rather obvious considerations are usually overlooked by those who hold the absolutist position. (6)

The first is the tendency to use the term 'freedom' as a slogan and to transfer the emotive, historical associations of the term in one of its specific normative uses, to the analysis of the meaning of freedom. Because in the past, demands for freedom have often been demands for liberation from restraints and coercions condemned on moral grounds, freedom defined as the power of action without let or hindrance from others has been regarded as always and intrinsically desirable. Freedom *tout court* is proclaimed good. The absurdity of this view is sometimes concealed by a distinction drawn between 'real' or 'true' freedom and 'apparent' freedom. This has led some philosophers to say of true or real freedom that 'it is and cannot but be freedom for the good'. Analogously, when Communists oppose in the name of the real interests of the workers, the workers' wishes or will, and claim that this furthers their real freedom, they confuse two different things. It is as if one were to define money not merely as a medium of exchange but as a medium of exchange for the purchase of good things.
(7)

If we ask what 'true' freedom and 'apparent' freedom have in common, we find that it is no more than the power to effect one's desire. Once we realize this, then it becomes clear that no one approves of freedom as such, for that would mean that one approved of anybody having the power to do anything he pleased, that one approved of any voluntary action. Since what some people please to do may be highly unpleasant, even if it is short of cutting our throat, no one can soberly say that he approves of *all* freedoms. By making a fetish of the abstraction, freedom, a consequence of the disregard of specific context, politics corrupts common usage or the ordinary sense of the word. *Common usage* recognizes that freedom is voluntary, uncoerced action; *Common sense* recognizes that unless we know the character of the action, we cannot say whether the freedom to do it is good or bad, whether it should be encouraged and defended or curbed. Those who talk about freedom as an absolute value tend to forget this. (8)

A second consideration is even more obvious. Not only is it psychologically impossible to approve of all freedoms, it is also logically impossible. A demand for a specific freedom entails a demand that the freedom of others to interfere with or frustrate that freedom be prevented or abridged. Freedom of Negroes in the South to vote is possible only if the freedom of action of those who in the past prevented them from voting is curbed. My freedom to own property requires that your freedom to deprive me of it be forbidden. A man who claims to believe in tolerance to a point of tolerance of those who are actively intolerant does not know what he believes. To be tolerant requires that one be intolerant of the actively intolerant. (9)

The third consideration is the most important of all. The specific freedoms of which we approve sometimes conflict. We find that on many occasions we are committed to incompatible freedoms. Just as the moral situation is best defined not in terms of a conflict between good and bad, right and wrong—there is no genuine conflict in such situations since we know what should be done—but between good and good, right and right, good and right, so it is in a situation of political or legal conflict. Every enumeration of rights in a Bill of Rights expresses a potential conflict among them. Freedom of speech or press may conflict with a man's right to a fair trial or with his right to privacy or his right to earn his livelihood. Freedom to own property in the instruments of social production, under certain conditions, may conflict with a man's right to work. In some countries those who own the only available arable land and can therefore deny access to it by others may affect their very right to life. The balancing of freedoms and rights against each other in the light of the public interest is the heart of the democratic political process. Some rights at some point to some degree must always give way. (10)

Under the circumstances how can anyone hold that there can be more than one absolute or unqualified valid right? Who can guarantee that two allegedly absolute rights will not conflict? In the world of time and human affairs no 'consistency proof' is possible. (11)

Despite these considerations, Mr. Justice Black has written: 'It is my belief that there *are* "absolutes" in our Bill of Rights, and that they were put there on purpose by men who knew what words meant and meant their prohibitions to be "absolute".' I leave the historical issue aside. Elsewhere I have sought to show that those who drew up the Bill of Rights were too intelligent to believe any such thing. (12)

The untenability of Justice Black's position can be established by pointing to the fact that in defense of his position he is compelled to hold that no publicity can ever seriously interfere with a man's right to a fair trial— an outrageous disregard of fact. He also asserts that the freedom of an individual falsely to shout 'Fire!' in a crowded theatre—the paradigm case of speech which is not constitutionally privileged—is punishable 'not because of what he shouted but because he shouted'. Presumably if he had whispered or maliciously flashed the word on a screen he would be in the clear. The punishment in this case, according to Justice Black, is for violating the right of private property. But suppose it took place on public property or what was shouted was true? At any rate even on Justice Black's bizarre reading of the paradigm case, we have a clear conflict between the freedom of speech and the freedom to own property. Both cannot be absolute. How far Justice Black's absolutism extends with respect to speech is evident in his contention that there should be no laws against libel and defamation no matter what the damaging consequences of such speech are. (13)

There are some who have sought to defend absolutism with respect to speech by making a distinction between 'private speech' and 'public speech'. The first is the realm of ordinary affairs, and it is admitted that here speech cannot always be privileged. The second is the realm of public affairs. Since a free society is one in which the electorate must have the right to hear all points of view on public issues, not only to make informed judgment but to insure that the government rests on freely given consent, there must be no restrictions whatsoever on the expression of opinion. No matter what 'the clear and present danger' of speech about any matter of public policy may be, it is absolutely privileged.   (14)

There is sometimes, to be sure, an obvious difficulty in clearly differentiating between speech about private affairs and speech about public affairs, but the distinction is recognized in law if not always in morals. Thus one may say a great many harsh and untrue things with impunity about a figure in public life which would be actionable if said of a private person. It is undoubtedly true that in any free society a great deal of latitude must be enjoyed in the advocacy of policy and in the discussion of public affairs. This is the rule. But it does not follow in the least that if speech goes beyond advocacy to the incitement of violence or illegal action, it is privileged. Such speech may be proscribed, it may be legally punishable because the presupposition of the free society whose general rule is freedom of speech is that the consequences of such speech will permit the settlement of issues by free discussion and not by force and violence. One may advocate the repeal of the Conscription Law or oppose the ban on racial segregation, but one may not urge conscripts to refuse to serve or to desert, or incite a crowd to riot or to lynch. Incitement is a form of speech. The themes and issues about which crowds are usually incited fall within the sphere of public affairs. In certain situations, as anyone knows who has studied the riots that have recently broken out in many American cities, words may be considered as a phase of the mob action, as the proximate causes that have triggered off widespread violence. Lynch law is a form of social action that invariably grows out of the words of agitators discussing a public issue. That is why it sounds so strange to read in one of Justice Black's opinions: 'I believe that the First Amendment forbids Congress to punish people for talking about public affairs *whether or not such discussion incites to action, legal or illegal.*' (My italics.) No free society could long endure if incitements to illegal actions were legally privileged. Morally if an action is wrong, it is morally wrong to incite its performance.   (15)

The freedoms or rights in the Bill of Rights are not absolute but *strategic*. By that I mean that in a free society they are essential to the eliciting of freely given consent and therefore must be furthered at the cost of nonstrategic rights when a conflict develops. That is why as a rule they must be upheld even in difficult and trying circumstances. Sometimes, however, when there is a clear and present, not to speak of an overwhelming, danger to public order or of substantual harm to social interests of overriding importance, we may have to abridge one or another strategic freedom or right for a limited time, in a limited place. The preservation of the entire complex of strategic freedoms may sometimes depend upon the abridgment of one of them.   (16)

The chief arguments against this position are two. The above reason may function as a 'rationalization' to prevent full and fair discussion of public policy, as a means of stifling the expression of dissent. Secondly, once we begin to abridge any strategic freedom or right, we establish a dangerous precedent, and find ourselves on 'a slippery slope' headed for the abyss of totalitarianism.   (17)

That a 'reason' may sometimes turn out to be a rationalization is true. But this holds just as much for 'bad' reasons as for 'good'. In free societies when the principle of 'the clear and present danger' is illegitimately invoked to limit the freedom of speech or assembly, it is more often out of a false assessment of the consequences of permitting it than because of fear of dissent. Dissent in a free society can find multiple forms of expression. Nonetheless it is true that a free society can permit a considerable amount of disorder before it gets out of hand. The problem lies in educating law enforcement officers and agencies to an appreciation of the importance of the freedom to dissent, and of realistically appraising the dangers of mob action. The harm done to a free society by curbing a racialist, white or black, inciting a crowd is much less than the harm of a race riot. Agitators can find other opportunities to air grievances and advocate nostrums but the horrible consequences of a race riot are irrevocable.   (18)

The objection that once any strategic freedom is abridged there is no stopping short of the destruction of all our freedoms has very little validity. This attitude would make exceptions to any rule impermissible. Every policy would have to be formulated in terms of all or none. To the question: 'Where will you stop?', whenever it is proposed to abridge some specific freedom, our answer must be: 'where our intelligence and sense of proportion tells us to stop, where the situation is sufficiently changed in consequence of our action to permit the expression of this freedom without imperilling equally or more desirable freedoms'. Because a thing is good, it is not good without limits. If a non-eliminable poison like fluoride is added to water to reduce the incidence of caries, it does not mean that we will not stop short of adding potassium cyanide. Yet this argument in uncritical form has been used again and again to obstruct progressive legislation. Recently when Congress adopted legislation outlawing discrimination and segregation in places of public accommodation, the argument was heard: 'Once you deny the freedom of a man to hire whom he pleases, to sell or cater to whom he pleases, to rent to whom he pleases, where will you stop? Before long you will deny him the right to choose his friends as he pleases, even to marry whom he pleases.'   (19)

Behind the conflicts of freedoms lie conflicts of interests. The possibility of their peaceful resolution depends upon the existence of social institutions and practices which enable them to be shared. There may be a shared interest in living peacefully together despite the existence of some interests that cannot be shared. If we cannot live and help live we can live and let live. But it takes two to keep the peace. At any rate, whatever freedoms we establish have a price in other freedoms. This is not so much a paradox as a character of the human condition in every area. The more we are aware of it, the more intelligent is our choice, the fewer the occasions for our regret. This is an important commonplace—a commonplace because the absolutism it opposes is absurd and dangerous; important because in our world today there are many individuals and groups committed to the absurd and the dangerous.   (20)

Charles Frankel

(1917–   )

FRANKEL, professor of philosophy at Columbia University, has concerned himself deeply and continuously with questions of personal rights, professional ethics, and public responsibilities. He has held named lectureships at several colleges, from Bennington College to the University of Dublin, and has been awarded fellowships by the Guggenheim Foundation, the Fulbright Commission, and the Carnegie Corporation. His major works include The Case for Modern Man *(1956),* The Democratic Prospect *(1962), and* The Love of Anxiety and Other Essays *(1965).*

◼ *Ideals and Idols of Democracy*

FIRST AND FOREMOST, "democracy is a political term." It is a name for a particular set of conditions under which the right to coerce others is acquired and held. To be sure, there are many definitions of democracy, as many as there are men with causes they want to coat with legitimacy. Democracy is defined as rule by law, as a society that makes the individual central, as government by the people, as government for the people. Many conceive it as a great process of turning history around, a lifting of the masses from their ancient condition. And there is a point to most of these definitions. By and large, democracy works towards such ends, though not unfailingly. But to try to pin down the meaning of democracy by talking about these products of democracy is like defining the game of bridge in terms of brainwork and pleasant evenings. The one incontrovertible sign of a democracy is the way in which it makes the sticky decisions that are the business of politics. In its primary meaning, democracy is a system in which men acquire the right to govern through a system of free and open competition for votes, and in which they make their decisions while under the pressure of outside groups whose right to put them under pressure they must protect. (1)

Yet politics is only machinery. Elections, parties, political bosses, and pressure groups are the unmistakable signs of the existence of democracy, but they have obviously not been the reasons why democracy has excited men. Something else, a change in the character of their experience at a deeper and more intimate level, has been what democracy has seemed to promise them. It is traditional to speak of the ideals that are presupposed by a political system—a habit of thought at once flattering and misleading, since it suggests that men know what they are about when they commit themselves to a political system. It is more appropriate to judge a system by the character of the ideals and expectations it encourages men to hold, and by the degree to which it fulfills these expectations. It is time for us to turn, therefore, from the framework of democracy to the aspirations that give it its reason for being. What is all the shooting about? What is the democratic system an attempt to accomplish? (2)

To ask these questions is to begin to find out why so many devoted partisans of the successful democracy we enjoy in the United States today are nevertheless disoriented and disturbed. For the democratic system depends on a population that has certain expectations, and encourages them to have these expectations. And changes of geological proportions in the social terrain on which we move have challenged these expectations. (3)

THE DEMOCRATIC BIAS

The way to begin, I think, is not with abstract ideals but with something simpler and more fundamental—a state of feeling and sentiment, an emotional posture. Beneath democratic ideals there is an elementary bias, an attitude that belongs to men who, without taking thought or giving reasons, look at the world in a certain way. (4)

Our everyday use of the word "democratic" suggests what this attitude is. A man with democratic feelings habitually judges his fellows without regard to their rank or status. He looks on them as members of a single moral community in which all possess the same fundamental rights and obligations. He is suspicious of the sweeping social distinctions that place men in separate boxes. But he is also suspicious of universal formulas that place all men in the same box. He looks skeptically on any effort to define the good life for everyone. The ideal democrat is egalitarian not because he thinks all men are the same, but because he doubts, when the chips are down, that there is any single comprehensive standard of human excellence by which all men can be measured and compared. He is ready to assign all men the same rights without insisting that they all live by the same rights. (5)

Democratic cultures, therefore, are normally the scene for a kind of moral drama, a recurrent contest between Babbitts and Bohemians, conformists and freebooters. There is a tension within them between gregariousness and a respect for privacy, between hostility towards the man who sets himself apart and admiration for achievement. Thirty years ago moral criticism in the United States was principally directed against unchecked individualism, particularly in the economic sphere. Today criticism is directed against a sentimental egalitarianism that denies the differences between individuals. By and large, indeed, there are two democratic traditions, not one. The Continental democratic tradition has in the main stressed the equality and fraternity of men—the falseness and injustice of class distinctions and racial barriers, the essential identity of all individuals as possessors of the same fundamental rights. The Anglo-Saxon tradition, in contrast, has stressed liberty—the intrinsic value of freedom of choice, the irreducible diversity of persons, temperaments, and talents for which a just society must find room. But the quarrel between these two traditions is a family quarrel. The belief that men are members of the same moral community and the belief that each man has his own singular good to pursue both represent the effort to escape the gravitational pull of a simple and stubborn human inclination—suspicion of the outsider, hostility towards the man who is different. (6)

Far from being the expression of an aboriginal human preference, a democratic moral outlook is an instrument and symptom of the breakdown of the traditional moral codes which have divided men into members of the tribe and strangers, believers and unbelievers, U's and non-U's. Although democracy has been said to rest on the doctrine of natural rights, it is an acquired taste. The democratic outlook occurs only to those who have learned to look upon the existing line between men as conventions, who want to redraw these lines, who think they may have some business on the other side of any line. And it is the attitude of men who have learned to take human diversity in stride, and who think that the man who sets himself up as a watchman over his neighbors is precisely the man who bears watching.   (7)

These are the twin attitudes—the belief in a moral community, the regard for individual difference and privacy—that generate the characteristic ideals of democracy. And there are many ways of describing these ideals. But if we examine the sources of our present anxieties, if we try to bring together the experiences that have led us to suspect that the democratic image and democratic realities do not fit together, certain central themes emerge. Political democracy may be conceived as an instrument for the construction of a civilization in which four ideals are pursued.   (8)

THE CONSENT OF THE GOVERNED

The first is the ideal of the consent of the governed. If the lines between men are to be softened, then the most irritating and dangerous line of all— that between those who command and those who obey—has to be redrawn. It cannot be erased, but it has to be made emotionally and morally digestible. And this can be done, so democratic theory has held, only if government rests on the consent of the governed.   (9)

Yet the phrase "the consent of the governed" is not an easy one to unravel. If those who are governed always consented to the decisions of their rulers, there would be no need for government, for police and taxes and penal sanctions. And no actual government, after all, can be absolutely even-handed in the way it conducts its business. The beginning of political education might be said to lie in the recognition that there is no such thing as an entirely equitable law. Ordinances against walking on the grass fall more heavily on dog-owners than on those who keep goldfish for pets, and rules against smoking in elevators ask smokers to sacrifice themselves while allowing nonsmokers to enjoy the benefits without cost. Even the recognition of everybody's right to free speech creates difficulties, after all, for the man who treasures silence. With the best will in the world, government is inevitably a process that takes more from some and gives more to others. And democratic government is simply one technique for determining who the winners and who the losers in the political fray will be. "Government by consent" cannot be interpreted to mean that those who are governed necessarily agree with what their rulers decide to do. Nor can it mean that "the majority" agrees. For in a democracy the minority, too, is presumably governed by its consent.   (10)

But to speak of majorities and minorities and the inevitability of disagreements is to suggest what "government by consent" expresses. It expresses the hope for a society in which ordinary people can influence the actions their leaders take. This means that they can exercise some control over who their leaders will be. And it also means that they are required to obey only after having been actively consulted by those who issue the orders. Coercion is implicit in all forms of government, but democracy nevertheless promises a peculiar prize to the individual citizen. It promises him that he will be present, personally or through a representative, when decisions that concern him are made, and that he will have instruments at his disposal that will give his presence some force.   (11)

The inside story, the experienced substance, of government by consent is told, therefore, when we describe the distribution of power and opportunity in a society, when we look at the internal structure of the groups that take part in the political competition and at the people they represent and the powers they command. The ideal of government by consent, to be fully effective, demands a society in which individuals who want to do something about their condition can find the allies, money, and talent to help them. It requires a social system which places weapons at the disposal of the ordinary citizen that force his rulers to deal with him as a party to a bargain and not as a passive instrument of their own purposes. The promise of government by consent does not imply that the individual will ever inhabit a social order in which all gradations of power and prestige have been abolished and everyone enjoys precisely the same amount of influence and authority. But it is a promise whose fulfillment requires much more than just one vote to every man or legal guarantees of personal freedom.
(12)

Accordingly, if significant sections of the community are unorganized, or if their opinions and interests are not brought insistently to the attention of the decision-makers, government by consent is absent to that extent. Similarly, if those who are attempting to press their opinions and interests have no powers to reward or punish those who make the decisions, their consent becomes gratuitous. Again, if there is a sizable imbalance of power between contending groups, then the settlement that is reached is an imposed settlement and not a free bargain. And if individuals cannot make their voices heard in the groups that claim to represent them, then they are not active participants in the processes by which the decisions that affect them are reached. "Government by consent," in short, is a function of underlying social arrangements.   (13)

But if this is true, then one reason for our present uneasiness becomes plain. The fundamental social arrangements in which government by consent has traditionally been embodied have undergone a radical alteration. The ideal of government by consent defines one major area in which we are in trouble.   (14)

THE IDEAL OF AN OPEN SOCIETY

Closely connected to the ideal of government by consent is the ideal of an open society. "Democracy" designates at least this much—a social order that deliberately protects men and agencies whose function it is to criticize what exists and to indicate other possibilities. The ideal of the open society proposes that men live under arrangements all of which are open to question. It holds that loyalty should be given to a social order precisely because it permits this process of criticism to take place. It insists that the process should be public and that everyone is in principle qualified to take part in it. And finally, it assumes that criticism and judgment are the preludes to corrective action.   (15)

To want an open society is thus to reject the classic view that men ought to expect a radical disparity between their hopes and the facts. There is a quality of impatience in a democratic culture. It eats away at any interest its members may have in consolation prizes. And in a community in which the ideal of an open society is widely accepted, those who have power or special knowledge must respond to a new imperative in human affairs. They have to provide those who do not have as much power or knowledge with information about what they are doing; worse, they have to appear to listen when their audience reports its reactions. In an open society, messages flow in two directions—from followers to leaders as well as from leaders to followers.   (16)

Even more than the ideal of government by consent, such an ideal presupposes social arrangements which cannot be secured simply by guarantees of freedom of speech and thought. These are essential but not sufficient. For communication is a complicated process. It depends not only on having something to say and knowing how to say it, but on being able to find an audience, and one that can do something about the message it receives. Freedom of speech serves a useful purpose even if it does nothing more than give men the chance to release their feelings by sending sounds out into the air. But the ideal of an open society encourages men to expect that freedom of speech will have other uses as well. In order for it to have these other uses, however, access to the instruments of communication has to be open, audiences have to be available that are organized and have powers of action, and the various participants in the discussion have to know the things they ought to know in order to speak intelligently and usefully. A bill of rights, therefore, provides only the supporting skeleton for an open society. The practical conditions for making such a society work lie outside the area of legal formalities.   (17)

And this is why the ideal of an open society is now not simply a promise but a provocation to cynicism. For the structure of the communications industry, the character of the groups that take part in the public debate, and the very nature of the issues that must now be debated do not fit our traditional assumptions. To say that what we now possess is an open society is not false. But it is a statement that requires a certain exercise of the imagination.   (18)

INDIVIDUAL AUTONOMY

The ideals of government by consent and of an open society bring us to another ideal—the one that is at the center of the democratic vision of human possibility. This is the ideal of individual autonomy.   (19)

One way to understand the emotional and moral impact of democracy is to see that it encourages great numbers of men to hold an expectation which only a life of privilege has bred in the past. Like the members of hereditary aristocracies in other days, a contemporary citizen of the United States is likely to grow up with the feeling that he counts just because he is who he is. And if his family is respectable and his skin not too heavily pigmented, he will probably feel that he is entitled to lead a life that he has chosen and made for himself. This, to coin a fresh and youthful phrase, is "the American dream." And pushed far enough, it is also the American fantasy. Scott Fitzgerald drew the picture of the pluperfect American in the great Gatsby—the man who interpreted the American ideal of the self-made man so simply and literally that he made himself up, inventing his past, writing his own ticket of admission to the great world, and creating a personality for himself as he would create a character in a romance. (20)

But this pipe dream, this fantasy of self-creation, of perfect control over one's own nature and the conditions of one's life, does not prove that democratic ideals are immoderate and adolescent in their essence. Every social order produces its own special form of mad dream. Medieval society existed to make the journey of the soul to God more possible, but it was forced to organize monasteries in order to tame and socialize the extremists who took this promise too simply and literally. There is a kind of extremism proper to every society. The source of the Gatsby fantasy lies in the special sort of promise that a democratic culture makes to its members. It promises them that they will have personal autonomy—that they will be able to make uncoerced choices in terms of standards they choose for themselves. That no man can be free to adopt any standards he chooses is evident. But the presumed point of democracy, the consequence which those who have believed in it have claimed that it has, is that it gives its citizens the chance, more generously than any other system, to find themselves and their own talents and tastes, and, within reason, to seek their own ideals.   (21)

Yet not only the extremists, the moral purists and the morally insatiable, are doubtful today that democracy has this consequence. The realistic and the modest are also disturbed. Personal autonomy, so far as most men are concerned, seems to have been moved to the fringes of contemporary life. The packaged arrangements that are offered for our work and play; the massive industries that exist to manufacture opinion and engineer consent; the interventions of the State; the growth of technology and bureaucracy; the complexities of organization and regulation; the sheer pressure of our existence together in a crowded society—if the dim view of our future that now prevails has any substance, all these have weakened the ideal of personal autonomy and left the conditions in which it thrives in disarray. If the moral vision of liberal democracy is to be renewed, the prospects of individual autonomy on the contemporary scene have to be re-examined.   (22)

THE IDEAL OF RESPONSIBLE GOVERNMENT

Finally, there is a fundamental ideal in democracy which does not belong to democracy alone, but to all efforts to connect politics with the life of reason. What is it that the Greek meant, Mr. Kitto has asked, when he called himself "free" and the barbarian a "slave"? "Politically it meant not necessarily that he governed himself—because oftener than not he didn't—but that however his polity was governed it respected his rights. State affairs were public affairs, not the private concern of a despot. He was ruled by Law, a known Law which respected justice. . . . Arbitrary government offended the Greek in his very soul." To avoid arbitrary government, to live under laws that have reasons behind them that reasonable men can accept—this is not all there is to the idea of democracy. But it is the hope that allies democratic politics to other enterprises of liberal civilization. One large element in what men have meant by "freedom" is not the absence of external restraints on their behavior, but simply the chance to live under restraints they find intelligible rather than senseless and demeaning.   (23)

Liberal democracy has given a specific interpretation to this ideal of rational government. Rational government has meant, above all, responsible government. A responsible government, like a responsible man, is one that knows its limits. It conducts its affairs in accordance with the rule of law and with respect for the fundamental rights of individuals. Secondly, it is responsive government—government that is alert to the legitimate wants and potentialities of those it governs. And finally, it is a government that must respond satisfactorily when it is asked to account for its decisions. By responsible government liberal democracy has not meant simply government by responsible men. It has meant a government embedded in a certain sort of social structure, a government that is accountable to a larger society. (24)

This is the basic ideal that justifies the curious organization of liberal societies. They are "dual societies," societies deliberately arranged to be at conflict with themselves. In all societies there are groups outside the official government—clans, businesses, clubs, cliques, and gangs—that lay down rules which control the behavior of men; and these groups, in all societies, possess sanctions like excommunication, expulsion, economic penalties, or the withdrawal of privileges, by which they enforce obedience to their rules. But in a liberal society these private governments do not exist through the weakness or indifference of the State. They exist as a matter of policy. They are conceived as checks against arbitrary government by the State, instruments that compel those who alone have the legal authority to use force to think twice before they resort to force. The existence of such private governments, indeed, is not only a condition for responsible government by the State. It is the source of one of liberal democracy's outstanding problems. For these private governments are also governments, possessing coercive powers, and powers sanctioned and supported by the State. If they exist to control the State and to keep it accountable, they, too, need to be controlled and held accountable.   (25)

And this seems to be the difficulty. Despite the persistence of elections, an independent judiciary, and all the institutions of free social inquiry and criticism that characterize liberal democracy, the process of holding the public and private governments that rule us to some effective system of accountability seems to have become increasingly complicated and uncertain.   (26)

SETTING WORDS ARIGHT

Before we can turn to examine the problems that now beset these ideals, we have to look carefully at some of the words we use to describe the democratic political method. For we shall have to deal with these problems democratically; and our discontents, indeed, are the consequences of what we think to be democratic standards. Yet there are easy but confusing misconceptions which lead us to diagnose our ailments improperly and sometimes to confuse symptoms of democratic health with symptoms of disease. There is good reason for many of our present discontents; but some of them are the products of our own unexamined and faulty ideas about democracy. Let us pass a number of them in review as a first step in putting our political ideas in order.   (27)

Begin with the most obvious mistake of all. It is the notion that government by consent, participation by the governed in the making of public decisions, means referenda, plebiscites, direct appeal to the people at every turn—in brief, a kind of giant and continuing town meeting. The idea has deep roots in the Western tradition. It is an inheritance from the theory and practice of democracy in the Greek city-state and the Puritan congregations of the seventeenth century. And it is a conception that is implicit in much that Rousseau, the prophet of popular sovereignty, had to say about the nature of political freedom. But it is plain, once the idea is made explicit, that the model of a town meeting is inapplicable to the processes by which the government of a modern nation-state can or should carry on its business. It expresses the hope, and the still realistic hope, that between the State and the individual, and between the large organization and the individual, there will be smaller, more manageable associations which the individual can join, and which will offer him the experience of face-to-face cooperation in dealing with immediate problems. But when this hope is inflated many times over, when it is applied to a modern nation-state as a whole, it overlooks the sheer size of modern societies, the fact of factions, the need for professional leadership, and the advantages that are bound to accrue to the specialist who can give the political business his full-time attention.   (28)

Yet despite the quixotic character of this ideal, it is invoked more often than we think. It is not invoked to say what should be done, but it is tacitly invoked to condemn what is done. Thus, some serious critics of the American scene have offered the fact that there was no general public debate before the atom bomb was dropped on Hiroshima as evidence that democracy in the United States is more advertised than real. But such criticism does more than skirt the question whether a popular referendum —and, necessarily, a secret referendum—in the middle of a war was possible. It overlooks the implications of the fact that there was widespread discussion after the decision. It treats as a lapse from democracy the legal fact that those who made the decision had the Constitutional responsibility to do so, and were prohibited from passing this responsibility on to others. And not least, it appears to rest on the cheerful assumption that the decision of the electorate would have been more gentle and humane than the decision that was actually made. It is an undeniable fact that our existing system assigns extraordinary power to a relatively small number of men. But the fact is not surprising. It is true of all large societies and of most small ones. To condemn this state of affairs as a distortion of democracy is to wash out all important distinctions in a bath of indignation. It is to employ a concept of democracy that could have no possible applicability. A man may complain if he thinks the wrong people have great power. But some people are going to have such power.   (29)

More plausible notions than that of the town meeting, however, are also capable of causing misformulations of the issues. The apparently simple idea of "majority rule," for example, is full of pitfalls which become noticeable only after the idea has been held in the air for a moment and examined. The majority of those who vote surely do determine who wins. But that majority is not a cohesive social group that persists once the election is over. It is an abstraction, a creation of the electoral procedure itself.

Once the vote is counted, it is replaced by more palpable entities like
political parties, businesses, unions, and the inevitable individuals who take
it upon themselves to speak for "the majority." And if the idea of a majority is elusive, the idea of majority rule is doubly so. For an electoral majority registers no single definite opinion on any question but that of the
candidate who is preferred. And even this preference is governed by the
alternatives presented. "The people's choice" need not be the man most
preferred. He may only be less dispreferred than his opponent. In between
elections, furthermore, the decisions made in a democracy are also influenced by the advice of administrative officers, the pressures of different
groups, the necessities for compromise, the interpreted information about
"public opinion" that comes to the decision-makers, and the simple and
not-so-simple play of events. No political leader can say what his policy
will be with regard to questions that no one has foreseen at the time of the
election; and he cannot stop and turn to the electorate for its judgment
when such questions arise.   (30)

This is not to say that elections have no influence over events. The announced programs of contending parties have more to do with the decisions
a government makes than the cynics say. At the very least they tell the
electorate where the candidate would like them to think his heart lies, and
sometimes they tell the candidate, too. In the end "majority rule" has a
meaning, but it is metaphorical rather than strictly literal. It describes a
society in which the fact that there are elections exerts a general climatic
influence on the decision-making process, requiring those who make the
decisions to keep themselves aware of the reactions of ordinary citizens. It
points to the fact that while decisions in a democracy may be made behind
closed doors, there is always someone pounding at the doors. "Majority rule"
is in this sense an arithmetical figure of speech describing a government
that can be discussed, investigated, and scolded. And most important of
all, "majority rule" points to a fundamental characteristic of democracy.
Democracy is not exclusive rule by any minority.   (31)

In the American democratic system most of the organized groups in the
community are able to make themselves heard in the elaborate process by
which the decisions of government are finally made. The statement has to
be read as it is written. It is the organized groups, not the unorganized
ones, that make themselves heard; they make themselves heard mainly
through their leaders; and we can only be reasonably sure that they make
themselves heard, and not that what they say necessarily makes a difference.
Still, such a process is one of extended competition among different
interests, no one of which has a clearly secure position in the forefront, and
every one of which has to fight for the approval of the bystander.   (32)

"Majority rule," in short, expresses the democratic attempt to give ordinary people a large measure of control over their leaders. It speaks for the

effort to organize a society in such a way that it will not be dominated by any single center of power. And it describes the historical direction in which democratic governments, with slips and falls, but steadily over the long run, have come to serve the interests of ever larger sections of the nations they rule. But, strictly speaking, the phrase "majority rule" is a misnomer when applied to the democratic process. The proper phrase, as Robert Dahl has suggested, is rule by minorities. For every interest is in the minority when set against all the other interests with which it competes. It is cant, therefore, to condemn the victory of any interest in a democracy simply because it is a minority interest. There is no other kind.   (33)

This examination of what we can mean when we speak of "majority rule" leads us to an even more crucial idea in the lexicon of democracy—"representative government." The classic idea of representative government, and the idea that still forms our image of what democracy is or should be, is that of an electorate which chooses representatives who carry the popular will into effect. It is not an idea that stands up to scrutiny, and it causes unnecessary and debilitating anxieties and complaints when it is not scrutinized.
(34)

The first of the difficulties with the conventional belief that a democratic government exists simply to carry the views of the electorate into practice is that it rests on the concept of a "popular will." In large modern societies, political parties, the media of communication, voluntary organizations, and government itself act to define the questions to which the electorate addresses itself; they propose the alternatives between which the electorate makes its choice; they give the "popular will" its preoccupations, organization, and principal modes of expression. To assert under such conditions that "the people," or a majority of the people, have wholly self-engendered and precise demands to make on their leaders is to venture into the occult. And a second and even more serious difficulty with the theory that government should simply do what the citizens say is that it rests on an ideal that is clearly unrealistic—the ideal of the omnicompetent citizen, the man with a formed and informed opinion on all major issues.   (35)

The ideal is unrealistic not only because it demands a degree of omniscience which no citizen can have. It is also unrealistic because it overlooks a fact about human psychology. Few arguments are more difficult or dubious than those about the rationality or irrationality of the so-called "common man." But it is unnecessary to enter into such arguments. Imagine that all voters are reasonable and disciplined and have the necessary facts at their easy disposal. The views they hold about matters that are remote are formed under conditions that are significantly different just the same. For while the principle is not ironclad, a certain state of mind is generally a prerequisite to responsible judgment.   (36)

Normally, the individual making the judgment has to feel that the question under consideration is his personal business and that he will pay a personal price for giving the wrong answer. And this is the attitude that is bound to be attenuated in a contemporary polity. The housewife who has to decide whether the corner grocer is honest is under some compulsion to make a judgment that rests on more than a platitude about the honesty or dishonesty of all grocers. And besides, she has the inestimable advantage of being able to observe the grocer's behavior directly. These fundamental conditions do not hold in the relation of a contemporary citizen to his government. He may be concerned and informed, he may recognize the bearing that public issues have on his everyday life, but his identification with the issues is still mainly vicarious rather than direct.   (37)

This does not mean that education and public spirit have no bearing on the success of a democracy. It makes them more important, not less. If men are to make intelligent judgments about their leaders, they need a general understanding of the main drift of the issues, they need to have some shrewdness about the people they listen to, and they need to be able to tell the difference between sense and nonsense. And if democracy is unworkable, it is because the electorate cannot be counted on to have even these qualities. But the recognition of the difference between the two kinds of space in which men's minds move allows us to fix our sights more modestly and intelligently, and less discouragingly, on the proper objectives of democratic education and public spirit. Democratic government does not require an all-knowing electorate any more than any other system of government does. The theory of democracy that demands such an assumption is in error. Democratic government is simply a system in which the authority to govern is acquired through competition for the people's votes. The function of the electorate is to choose and remove a government. It is the function of the government to govern.   (38)

Nor is this a state of affairs that ought to be mourned. In the best of all possible worlds the ordinary citizen, we may hope, would still have his own work to do, and his own intimate and absorbing sphere of private experience and responsibility. The image of a society in which all men are wholly devoted to the great public business is worse than utopian. It is disagreeable.   (39)

But to point out that representative government means nothing more nor less than government chosen by free elections is not to finish the story. For the concept of a "free election" carries a whole baggage of notions with it. The liberal democratic tradition can be justly criticized for having frequently entertained an abstract and legalistic conception of representative government. Elections do not become free elections simply because legal safeguards may surround the exercise of the franchise. To speak of "representative government" is to presuppose the existence of appropriate

social conditions as well. The distinction between a state of affairs in which an electorate is presented with actual alternatives and one in which it is only given the chance to acclaim the powers that be is fundamental. No reflections on the sociological conditions for free elections can erase that distinction. "Representative government," nevertheless, always refers to a relative state of affairs. Even mature liberal democracies never perfectly fulfill all the conditions that make government a representative process.
(40)

In estimating the degree to which elections are free and government is representative, the education, composition, and social circumstances of the electorate have to be taken into account. Will voters suffer ostracism if they support a particular slate? Is there an alternative in which a large number of them are vitally interested, but which has been excluded from the alternatives on which they vote? Has relevant information been systematically withheld from the electorate, or does any single agency monopolize all the important channels of information? Have representatives of all significant groups had a chance to formulate the issues under debate? The failure to raise such questions has been responsible for the fetishistic application of the principle of free elections to societies where the conditions for such elections are not present. It partly explains why the gospel of free elections has had less resonance in many parts of the world than liberal democrats habitually assume that it will.   (41)

For the conditions that make elections free and government representative include a cultural climate that is relatively open and tolerant; an electorate that understands the purpose of voting; broad participation in the organization of the election and in the formulation of party programs; a press that gives expression to enough crosscurrents of opinion to put any single interpretation of the facts under pressure to defend itself; and not least, a reasonably broad and balanced distribution of powers in the community, so that all important groups have a chance to get into the act. Indeed, the most important condition of representative government lies outside elections and the official representative institutions of democratic society. The decisive representative institutions of democracy are unofficial.
(42)

They are the political blocs and the pressure groups; it is these that carry most of the democratic mail. Representative government is of course a matter of elections, competitive party politics, public discussion, and civil liberties. But these are thin and precarious without the existence of social groups that make it probable that those who are going to be affected by a social decision will be seriously and honestly consulted by those who make the decision. That aspect of democracy which most regularly troubles its partisans—the open struggle among special interests—is precisely what marks democracy as a system resting on the consent of the governed. The politics of pressure groups is the essential feature of the politics of democracy. The only alternative to the politics of pressure groups is government that rules over isolated and rootless individuals who have no groups other than the government to protect them, and no autonomous social power of their own. (43)

That is why a democratic system of government cannot promise what most other systems promise. It cannot promise to do away with the dirty business of politics and to melt all men together in love of God, country, or historical necessity. Politics is a democracy's official business, and not, as in other systems, an unofficial and hidden business. The basic instrument of the democratic citizen is the organized group with enough power and influence to command the attention of those who make the decisions. The basic instruments of democratic government are the bargain and the compromise. And the one unmistakable goal of all democratic governments, when they arrange their bargains and compromises, is to win the next election. (44)

This is the context in which every discussion of planning and of the development of consistent policy in a democracy must be placed. It does not make planning or consistent policy impossible. But it gives the formation of plans and policies a quality of responsiveness—or, if one prefers, of opportunism—which is not so likely to be present in systems that do not have to worry about elections. To ask the living to sacrifice themselves for their grandchildren is easier in a dictatorship than in a democracy. And since it is not easy, in a world of accelerating changes, to predict the condition or desires of our grandchildren, this democratic state of affairs has some manifest virtues. (45)

But it is for this reason too that democratic politics requires ideas. Unless men have some coherent conceptions of their existing condition, unless they can imagine the long direction in which they would like to move, the politics of the bargain, the politics of equilibrium, can be a deadly affairs—unfocused, uninspired, and for all its realism, unrealistic. It can settle down, not simply very close to the center, but to a dead center, quarreling over issues that are ghosts of the past and tinkering with problems that lie at the fringes of the questions that have to be faced. With reservations, that is the picture of American politics at present, at any rate so far as domestic politics are concerned. Were it not for the Russians, we could not be sure that we would have a purpose in life. (46)

No doubt we can get rid of some misconceptions about democracy and, when we do, some of our discontents may be removed. But these are not the major reasons for our unmistakable dissatisfaction with things as they are. At bottom, our present uneasiness, our curiously embarrassed prosperity, is the consequence of the unfulfilled demands which democratic civilization itself has set in motion. The ideals of government by consent, of an open society, of individual autonomy, of responsible government, have become problems rather than promises, sources of disillusion rather than aspirations. For the social conditions on which they lean seem to have been subverted. Each of these ideals defines a major area in which image does not fit reality. (47)

Gunnar Myrdal

(1898–   )

MYRDAL is a professor of international economics at the University of Stockholm and has been continuously active in public affairs in Sweden (a member of the Swedish Senate, for a time Minister of Commerce). He has been widely recognized as an international authority on the relationships between the economic, social, and fiscal policies of governments. An American Dilemma: The Negro Problem and Modern Democracy (1944) was the result of a study sponsored by the Carnegie Corporation of which Professor Myrdal was director (1938–1942).

▣ *A Methodological Note on Valuations and Beliefs*

1.   THE MECHANISM OF RATIONALIZATION

PEOPLE HAVE ideas about how reality actually is, or was, and they have ideas about how it ought to be, or ought to have been. The former we call *"beliefs."* The latter we call *"valuations."* A person's beliefs, that is, his knowledge, can be objectively judged to be true or false and more or less complete. His valuations—that a social situation or relation is, or was, "just," "right," "fair," "desirable," or the opposite, in some degree of intensity or other—cannot be judged by such objective standards as science provides. In their *"opinions"* people express both their beliefs and their valuations. Usually people do not distinguish between what they think they know and what they like or dislike.   (1)

There is a close psychological interrelation between the two types of ideas. In our civilization people want to be rational and objective in their beliefs. We have faith in science and are, in principle, prepared to change our beliefs according to its results. People also want to have "reasons" for the valuations they hold, and they usually express only those valuations for which they think they have "reasons." To serve as opinions, specific valuations are selected, are formulated in words and are motivated by acceptable "reasons." With the help of certain beliefs about reality, valuations are posited as parts of a general value order from which they are taken to be logical inferences. This value hierarchy has a simple or elaborate architecture, depending mainly upon the cultural level of a person. But independently of this, most persons want to present to their fellows—and to themselves—a trimmed and polished sphere of valuations, where honesty, logic, and consistency rule. For reasons which we shall discuss, most people's advertised opinions are, however, actually illogical and contain conflicting valuations abridged by skewed beliefs about social reality. In addition, they indicate very inadequately the behavior which can be expected, and they usually misrepresent its actual motivation.   (2)

The basic difficulty in the attempt to present a logical order of valuations is, of course, that those valuations actually are conflicting. When studying the way in which the valuations clash, and the personal and social results brought about by the conflicts, we shall, moreover, have to observe that the valuations simply cannot be treated as if they existed on the same plane. They refer to different levels of the moral personality. The moral precepts contained in the respective valuations correspond to different degrees of generality of moral judgment. Some valuations concern human beings in general; others concern Negroes or women or foreigners; still others concern a particular group of Negroes or an individual Negro. Some valuations have general and eternal validity; others have validity only for certain situations. In the Western culture people assume, as an abstract proposition, that the more general and timeless valuations are morally higher. We can, therefore, see that the motivation of valuations, already referred to, generally follows the pattern of trying to present the more specific valuations as inferences from the more general.   (3)

In the course of actual day-to-day living a person will be found to focus attention on the valuations of one particular plane of his moral personality and leave in the shadow, for the time being, the other planes with their often contradicting valuations. Most of the time the selection of this focus of evaluation is plainly opportunistic. The expressed valuations and beliefs brought forward as motives for specific action or inaction are selected in relation to the expediencies of the occasion. They are the "good" reasons rather than the "true" reasons; in short, they are "rationalizations."   (4)

The whole "sphere of valuations"—by which we mean the entire aggregate of a person's numerous and conflicting valuations, as well as their expressions in thought, speech, and behavior—is thus never present in conscious apperception. Some parts of it may even be constantly suppressed from awareness. But it would be a gross mistake to believe that the valuations temporarily kept in the shadow of subjective inattention—and the deeper-seated psychic inclinations and loyalties represented by them—are permanently silenced. Most of them rise to consciousness now and then as the focus of apperception changes in reaction to the flow of experiences and impulses. Even when submerged, they are not without influence on actual behavior. They ordinarily bend behavior somewhat in their direction; the reason for suppressing them from conscious attention is that, if obeyed, they would affect behavior even more. In this treatise, therefore, behavior is conceived of as being typically the outcome of a moral compromise of heterogeneous valuations, operating on various planes of generality and rising in varying degrees and at different occasions to the level of consciousness. To assume the existence of homogeneous "attitudes" behind behavior would violate the facts, as we must well know from everyday introspection and from observation and reflection. It tends to conceal the moral conflicts which are the ultimate object of our study.   (5)

The individual or the group whose behavior we are studying, moreover, does not act in moral isolation. He is not left alone to manage his rationalizations as he pleases, without interference from outside. His valuations will, instead, be questioned and disputed. Democracy is a "government by discussion," and so, in fact, are other forms of government, though to a lesser degree. Moral discussion goes on in all groups from the intimate family circle to the international conference table. Modern means of intellectual communication have increased the volume and the intensity of such moral interrelations.   (6)

When discussion takes the form of moral criticism by one person or group of another, it is not that the one claims to have certain valuations that the other does not have. It is rather an appeal to valuations which the other keeps in the shadow of inattention, but which are assumed, nevertheless, to be actually held in common. This assumption, that those with opposing opinions have valuations in common, is ordinarily correct. Cultural unity in America consists in the fact that most Americans have most valuations in common, though they are differently arranged and bear different intensity coefficients for different individuals and groups. This makes discussion possible and secures an understanding of, and a response to, criticism.   (7)

In this process of moral criticism which men make upon each other, the valuations on the higher and more general planes—referring to *all* human beings and *not* to specific small groups—are regularly invoked by one party or the other, simply because they are held in common among all groups in society, and also because of the supreme prestige they are traditionally awarded. By this democratic process of open discussion there is started a tendency which constantly forces a larger and larger part of the valuation sphere into conscious attention. More is made conscious than any single person or group would on his own initiative find it advantageous to bring forward at the particular moment. In passing, we might be allowed to remark that this effect—and in addition our common trust that the more general valuations actually represent a "higher" morality—is the principal reason why we, who are convinced democrats, hold that public discussion is purifying and that democracy itself provides a moral education of the people.   (8)

When thus even the momentarily inopportune valuations are brought to attention, an element of indecision and complication is inserted. A need will be felt by the person or group, whose inconsistencies in valuations are publicly exposed, to find a means of reconciling the inconsistencies. This can be accomplished by adjusting one of the conflicting pairs of valuations. If the valuation to be modified is on the less general plane, a greater moral harmony in the larger group is brought about. Specific attitudes and forms of behavior are then reconciled to the more general moral principles. If, on the other hand, an attempt is made to change or reinterpret valuations which are more general in scope and most of the time consciously shared with all other groups in society, the deviant group will see its moral conflict with other groups becoming increasingly explicit (that is, if the other groups are not themselves prepared to change their general valuations toward a moral compromise). This process might go on until discussion no longer becomes feasible. In the extreme case such a moral isolation, if the dissenting group is powerful enough, may break the peace and order of society and plunge a nation into civil war.   (9)

In the short-run day-to-day conflicts, usually no abrupt changes of valuations will occur. The need for reconciling conflicting valuations brought into the open through public discussion will, for the time being, only result in quasi-logical constructions. In the very nature of things, these constructions must be fantastic, as they represent an attempt to reconcile the illogicalities by logical reasoning.   (10)

The temptation will be strong to deny the very existence of a valuation conflict. This will sometimes bring in its wake grossly distorted notions about social reality. There is a sort of social ignorance which is most adequately explained as an attempt to avoid the twinges of conscience. It is, for instance, an experience of every social scientist, who has been working on problems of social policy and has taken some interest in people's reactions, that the strongest psychic resistance is aroused when an attempt is made to teach the better situated classes in a society about actual lower class standards of living and what causes them. This particular type of moral escapism works, sometimes with extraordinary effectiveness, in the American Negro problem.   (11)

The feeling of need for logical consistency within the hierarchy of moral valuations—and the embarrassed and sometimes distressed feeling that the moral order is shaky—is, in its modern intensity, a rather new phenomenon. With less mobility, less intellectual communication, and less public discussion, there was in previous generations less exposure of one another's valuation conflicts. The leeway for false beliefs, which makes rationalizations of valuations more perfect for their purpose, was also greater in an age when science was less developed and education less extensive. These historical differentials can be observed today within our own society among the different social layers with varying degrees of education and communication with the larger society, stretching all the way from the tradition-bound, inarticulate, quasi-folk-societies in isolated backward regions to the intellectuals of the cultural centers. When one moves from the former groups to the latter, the sphere of moral valuations becomes less rigid, more ambiguous and also more translucent. At the same time, the more general valuations increasingly gain power over the ones bound to traditional peculiarities of regions, classes, or other smaller groups. One of the surest generalizations is that society, in its entirety, is rapidly moving in the direction of the more general valuations. The speed stands in some relation to, and can be gauged by, geographical mobility, the development of intellectual communication, the decrease of illiteracy and the funds spent on education.   (12)

During this process of growing intellectualization, people's awareness of inconsistencies in their own spheres of valuations tends to be enhanced. At the same time—if moral cynicism does not spread, a possibility which we shall consider presently—they are increasingly reconditioned to demand consistency in their own valuations and, particularly, in those of other people. They learn to recognize and to avoid the use of illogicalities and misconceptions of social reality for overcoming the incongruities in their valuations. The impatient humanitarian might find this process exasperatingly slow, and the results meager. The perspective of decades and generations, however—providing moral catastrophes do not interrupt the growth process —yields a more optimistic impression.   (13)

We have already hinted at the fact that valuations are seldom overtly expressed except when they emerge in the course of a person's attempts to formulate his beliefs concerning the facts and their implication in relation to some section of social reality. Beliefs concerning the facts are the very building stones for the logical hierarchies of valuations into which a person tries to shape his opinions. When the valuations are conflicting, as they normally are, beliefs serve the rationalization function of bridging illogicalities. The beliefs are thus not only determined by available scientific knowledge in society and the efficacy of the means of its communication to various population groups but are regularly "biased," by which we mean that they are systematically twisted in the one direction which fits them best for purposes of rationalization.   (14)

There are in the Negro problem whole systems of popular beliefs concerning the Negro and his relations to the larger society which are crudely false and can only be understood in this light. These "popular theories," or ideologies, are themselves important data in our study, as they represent strategic social facts in the practical and political problems of race relations. A legitimate task of education is to attempt to correct popular beliefs by subjecting them to rigorous examination in the light of the factual evidence. This educational objective must be achieved in the face of the psychic resistance mobilized by the people who feel an urgent need to retain their biased beliefs in order to justify their way of life.   (15)

If this educational effort meets with success, the illogicalities involving valuations become exposed to the people who hold them. They are then pressed to change their valuations to some degree or other. For if popular beliefs depend upon valuations, as we have shown, the valuations also depend upon the beliefs in our civilization bent upon rationalism. When supporting beliefs are drawn away, people will have to readjust their value hierarchies and, eventually, their behavior. As the more general norms in our culture are given supreme moral sanction, this means—if we assume that this "valuation of the valuations" is upheld, and moral cynicism counteracted—that the valuations on a more specific level (often called "prejudices") will yield to them. This is the reason, and the only reason, why we generally assume that improved knowledge will make for "better" citizens. Facts by themselves do not improve anything.   (16)

There is a question of terminology which should be touched upon, as it is not without importance for our scheme of thinking. The term "value" has, in its prevalent usage, a loose meaning. When tightened it is generally taken to refer to the object of valuations, rather than to the valuations themselves. Unfortunately it has a connotation of something solid and homogeneous while our hypothesis is that the valuations are conflicting. We shall avoid using the term "value." The term "attitude" has the same connotation of solidity. Too, it is often used to denote beliefs as well as valuations. When used in this article "attitude" should be understood as simply a convenient synonym for valuation.[1]   (17)

---

[1] This paragraph will, perhaps, explain why the author has not been able to avoid the term "valuation" though knowing well that it is not widely used in America. The term has been used, however, by John Dewey in several of his works, by Charles H. Cooley in his *Social Process* (1918), by Robert M. MacIver in his *Social Causation* (1942), and probably by others.

2. THEORETICAL CRITIQUE OF THE CONCEPT "MORES"

We must voice our grave skepticism toward the simple explanatory scheme concerning the role of valuations in social life typified by William Graham Summer's concepts, "folkways" and "mores." [2] Since his time these concepts—or one of their several synonyms—have been widely used by social scientists and have, in particular, determined the approach to the Negro problem. The formula will be found to be invoked with some regularity whenever an author expresses his attitude that changes will be slow, or, more particularly, that nothing practical can be done about a matter. It is closely related to a bias in social science against induced changes, and especially against all attempts to intervene in the social process by legislation. The concept of mores actually implies a whole social theory and an entire *laissez-faire* ("do-nothing") metaphysics, and is so utilized.   (18)

Leaving aside for the present the political connotations of Sumner's construction, and focusing our interest only on its usefulness as a scientific tool, our main criticism is the following: By stowing the commonly held valuations into the system of mores, conceived of as a homogeneous, unproblematic, fairly static,[3] social entity, the investigator is likely to underestimate the actual difference between individuals and groups and the actual fluctuations and changes in time. He is also likely to lose sight entirely of the important facts, that even within a single individual valuations are operative on different planes of generality, that they are typically conflicting, and that behavior is regularly the outcome of a moral compromise.   (19)

It might be that Sumner's construction contains a valid generalization and offers a useful methodological tool for studying primitive cultures and isolated, stationary folk-communities under the spell of magic and sacred tradition. It might even be that the most convenient definition of such a folk-culture is the applicability of the theory of folkways and mores. The theory is, however, crude and misleading when applied to a modern Western society in process of rapid industrialization, moving in swift trends rippled by indeterminate cyclical waves: a society characterized by national and international mobility, by unceasing changes and differentiations of all valuations and institutions, by spreading intellectualization, by widening intellectual communication and secularization, by ever more daring discussion even of fundamentals and intimacies, and by a consequent virtually universal expectation of change and a firm belief in progress. If Sumner's construction is applied to such a society, except as a contrast

---

2 William Graham Sumner, *Folkways* (1911, first edition 1906).

3 Summer recognized a "strain toward consistency" within the mores because of conflicting principles, but his main emphasis—and the same is true when the concept is used by contemporary writers—is always upon stability, inertia, and resistance against induced change.

conception to mark off some remaining backward cultural isolates which
are merely dragged along and do not themselves contain the active factors
of social dynamics, it is likely to conceal more than to expose. It conceals
what is most important in our society: the changes, the conflicts, the absence of static equilibria, the liability in all relations even when they are
temporarily, though perhaps for decades, held at a standstill. The valuation
spheres, in such a society as the American, more nearly resemble pow-
der-magazines than they do Sumner's concept of mores.   (20)

3. Valuation Dynamics

In our view, changes in valuations—of the type known as "revolutions,"
"mutations," or "explosions"—are likely to occur continuously in modern
society. "Stability," or rather lack of change, when it reigns, is the thing
which requires explanation. Individual persons in modern society are in
the same sort of labile equilibrium as the molecules of explosives. Their
valuations are inconsistent, and they are constantly reminded of the inconsistency. Occasionally the moral personalities of individuals burst, and a
modification and rearrangement of the valuations in the direction of a
more stable equilibrium is accomplished.   (21)

Since similar influences work upon all individuals in the society, the
cumulative results include continuous changes of "public opinion." Such
changes are "intentional," in a sense, and part of a democratic development.
The trend of opinions and changes in institutions in a democracy—the
"reforms"—usually have their core in the cumulation of such valuation explosions in the minds of people. When the inconsistency between people's
valuations is large and has effectively been exposed, the change might occasionally be sudden and quite big, and we speak then of a social revolution. But the more evolutionary social changes, if they are dissected into
their elements, are not very different except in magnitude.   (22)

The history of every nation and of every community, in fact, of every
group, is, in one sense, the record of the successive waves of such opinion
explosions. Even societies have their catharses and, like individuals, they
have them almost all the time. It is the weakness, not only of the static
and fatalistic traditions in social science attached to the great names of
Marx and Sumner, but of our common tendency to look for explanations in
terms only of natural forces and material trends, that we blind ourselves
to the dynamics of opinion as it develops from day to day; or, in any case,
we become inclined to deal with human opinions more as the result of
social change than as part of the cause of it.   (23)

By stressing that opinions are not passive elements in the social process,
we have, of course, not meant to make them altogether independent of
material forces. The very fact that opinions to an extent are opportunistic

implies that they will change as a result of every other change in social environment. Changes in the technique of production, of communication and of consumption force individual and group revaluations. But so, also, does spread of knowledge, as well as moral discussion and political propaganda. Ideas have a momentum of their own; they are partly primary causes in the social process; or rather, they are integral factors in an interdependent system of causation.   (24)

In an opinion catharsis—of an individual or a group—a new, temporary, and labile equilibrium of conflicting valuations is established. The direction in a normal and peaceful process of popular education is toward decreasing inconsistency. We said that ordinarily the new balance gives greater weight to the more general valuations. But our reason for the conclusion was that those valuations were generally agreed to be morally "higher" and have supreme social sanction, and we added the reservation that our conclusion assumes that moral cynicism does not spread. If moral cynicism should spread, however—that is, if people become willing to throw aside even their most cherished general valuations, such as their faith in democratic liberty, equality, and Christian brotherhood—the situation permits almost any type of reconstruction. Instead of a rebirth of democracy and Christianity such that those terms acquire new personal meanings for every individual, there may be a revulsion to fascism and pagan gods.   (25)

When a sudden and great opinion catharsis occurs in society, customs and social trends seem to the participants to be suspended or radically changed, as they actually are to a certain extent. In this sense history is undecided; it can take several courses. Ideological forces take on a greater importance. Leaders—whom we call either "statesmen," "thinkers" and "prophets" or "demagogues" and "charlatans," depending upon our valuation of their aims and means—capture the attention of the masses and manage to steer the upheaval in one direction or the other. On a smaller scale the same occurs in every group at all times, and the "leaders" are legion; in a sense we are all "leaders." In the explanation of this type of process, where ideological factors, together with all other factors, are active forces within an interdependent system of causation, the materialistic conception of history breaks down. Indeed, any mechanical philosophy of human dynamics is inadequate—except when looking backward, because in looking backwards, *any* development can be organized into *any* scheme, if it is general enough.   (26)

Before leaving the subject of social dynamics, we must qualify our remarks to recognize the existence of social statics. By stressing the instability of valuations we do not deny that there is an enormous amount of resistance to change. There *is* a great deal of practically mechanistic causation in human life, almost completely divorced from valuations. People do strive to keep their valuation conflicts under control. They want to keep them off their minds, and they are trained to overlook them. Conventions, stereotypes, and convenient blind spots in knowledge about social reality do succeed in preserving a relative peace in people's conscience. Even more important, perhaps, is the fact that there are only a few hours a day free from the business of living, and that there are so many "pleasant" things to do during these few hours. Most people, most of the time, live a routine life from day to day and do not worry too much. If it could be measured, the amount of both simple and opportune ignorance and unconcernedness about social affairs would undoubtedly be greater than the amount of knowledge and concern.   (27)

But to stress these things is not to invalidate the dynamic theory we have presented. Modern people *do* have conflicting valuations, and the spread of knowledge and the increase of interrelations *are* more and more exposing them. Changes in the material environment also keep minds from becoming settled. If we call the relative absence of change in modern society "stability," we must recognize that it is not such as is envisaged in the theory of the folksways and mores. There is *instability* at bottom, a *balancing of forces in conflict with each other*, and there is continuously the possibility of rapid, and even induced, change, the direction of which is not altogether predetermined by trends and natural forces.   (28)

Alfred North Whitehead

(1861–1947)

WHITEHEAD was educated at Cambridge University and taught philosophy at Harvard University from 1924 to 1936. A mathematician and keen student of science, he was an early voyager in the sea of "the two cultures." His important works include Science and the Modern World *(1925),* Religion in the Making *(1926),* Symbolism *(1927), and* Process and Reality *(1929).*

◼ *The Origins of Modern Science*

THE PROGRESS of civilisation is not wholly a uniform drift towards better things. It may perhaps wear this aspect if we map it on a scale which is large enough. But such broad views obscure the details on which rests our whole understanding of the process. New epochs emerge with comparative suddenness, if we have regard to the scores of thousands of years throughout which the complete history extends. Secluded races suddenly take their places in the main stream of events: technological discoveries transform the mechanism of human life: a primitive art quickly flowers into full satisfaction of some aesthetic craving: great religions in their crusading youth spread through the nations the peace of Heaven and the sword of the Lord. (1)

The sixteenth century of our era saw the disruption of Western Christianity and the rise of modern science. It was an age of ferment. Nothing was settled, though much was opened—new worlds and new ideas. In science, Copernicus and Vesalius may be chosen as representative figures:

they typify the new cosmology and the scientific emphasis on direct observation. Giordano Bruno was the martyr; though the cause for which he suffered was not that of science, but that of free imaginative speculation. His death in the year 1600 ushered in the first century of modern science in the strict sense of the term. In his execution there was an unconscious symbolism: for the subsequent tone of scientific thought has contained distrust of his type of general speculativeness. The Reformation, for all its importance, may be considered as a domestic affair of the European races. Even the Christianity of the East viewed it with profound disengagement. Furthermore, such disruptions are no new phenomena in the history of Christianity or of other religions. When we project this great revolution upon the whole history of the Christian Church, we cannot look upon it as introducing a new principle into human life. For good or for evil, it was a great transformation of religion; but it was not the coming of religion. It did not itself claim to be so. Reformers maintained that they were only restoring what had been forgotten.   (2)

It is quite otherwise with the rise of modern science. In every way it contrasts with the contemporary religious movement. The Reformation was a popular uprising, and for a century and a half drenched Europe in blood. The beginnings of the scientific movement were confined to a minority among the intellectual élite. In a generation which saw the Thirty Years' War and remembered Alva in the Netherlands, the worst that happened to men of science was that Galileo suffered an honourable detention and a mild reproof, before dying peacefully in his bed. The way in which the persecution of Galileo has been remembered is a tribute to the quiet commencement of the most intimate change in outlook which the human race had yet encountered. Since a babe was born in a manger, it may be doubted whether so great a thing has happened with so little stir.   (3)

The thesis which these lectures will illustrate is that this quiet growth of science has practically recoloured our mentality so that modes of thought which in former times were exceptional are now broadly spread through the educated world. This new colouring of ways of thought had been proceeding slowly for many ages in the European peoples. At last it issued in the rapid development of science; and has thereby strengthened itself by its most obvious application. The new mentality is more important even than the new science and the new technology. It has altered the metaphysical presuppositions and the imaginative contents of our minds; so that now the old stimuli provoke a new response. Perhaps my metaphor of a new colour is too strong. What I mean is just that slightest change of tone which yet makes all the difference. This is exactly illustrated by a sentence from a published letter of that adorable genius, William James. When he was finishing his great treatise on the *Principles of Psychology*, he wrote to his brother Henry James, 'I have to forge every sentence in the teeth of irreducible and stubborn facts.' (4)

This new tinge to modern minds is a vehement and passionate interest in the relation of general principles to irreducible and stubborn facts. All the world over and at all times there have been practical men, absorbed in 'irreducible and stubborn facts': all the world over and at all times there have been men of philosophic temperament who have been absorbed in the weaving of general principles. It is this union of passionate interest in the detailed facts with equal devotion to abstract generalisation which forms the novelty in our present society. Previously it had appeared sporadically and as if by chance. This balance of mind has now become part of the tradition which infects cultivated thought. It is the salt which keeps life sweet. The main business of universities is to transmit this tradition as a widespread inheritance from generation to generation. (5)

Another contrast which singles out science from among the European movements of the sixteenth and seventeenth centuries is its universality. Modern science was born in Europe, but its home is the whole world. In the last two centuries there has been a long and confused impact of Western modes upon the civilisation of Asia. The wise men of the East have been puzzling, and are puzzling, as to what may be the regulative secret of life which can be passed from West to East without the wanton destruction of their own inheritance which they so rightly prize. More and more it is becoming evident that what the West can most readily give to the East is its science and its scientific outlook. This is transferable from country to country, and from race to race, wherever there is a rational society. (6)

In this course of lectures I shall not discuss the details of scientific discovery. My theme is the energising of a state of mind in the modern world, its broad generalisations, and its impact upon other spiritual forces. There are two ways of reading history, forwards and backwards. In the history of thought, we require both methods. A climate of opinion—to use the happy phrase of a seventeenth century writer—requires for its understanding the consideration of its antecedents and its issues. Accordingly in this lecture I shall consider some of the antecedents of our modern approach to the investigation of nature. (7)

In the first place, there can be no living science unless there is a widespread instinctive conviction in the existence of an *Order of Things*, and, in particular, of an *Order of Nature*. I have used the word *instinctive* advisedly. It does not matter what men say in words, so long as their activities are controlled by settled instincts. The words may ultimately destroy the instincts. But until this has occurred, words do not count. This remark is important in respect to the history of scientific thought. For we shall find

that since the time of Hume, the fashionable scientific philosophy has been
such as to deny the rationality of science. This conclusion lies upon the
surface of Hume's philosophy. Take, for example, the following passage
from Section IV of his *Inquiry Concerning Human Understanding:*

> 'In a word, then, every effect is a distinct event from its cause. It
> could not, therefore, be discovered in the cause; and the first in-
> vention or conception of it, *a priori*, must be entirely arbitrary.'

If the cause in itself discloses no information as to the effect, so that the
first invention of it must be *entirely* arbitrary, it follows at once that science
is impossible, except in the sense of establishing *entirely arbitrary* connections which are not warranted by anything intrinsic to the natures either
of causes or effects. Some variant of Hume's philosophy has generally
prevailed among men of science. But scientific faith has risen to the occasion, and has tacitly removed the philosophic mountain.   (8)

In view of this strange contradiction in scientific thought, it is of the
first importance to consider the antecedents of a faith which is impervious
to the demand for a consistent rationality. We have therefore to trace the
rise of the instinctive faith that there is an Order of Nature which can be
traced in every detained occurrence.   (9)

Of course we all share in this faith, and we therefore believe that the
reason for the faith is our apprehension of its truth. But the formation of
a general idea—such as the idea of the Order of Nature—and the grasp of
its importance, and the observation of its exemplification in a variety of
occasions are by no means the necessary consequences of the truth of the
idea in question. Familiar things happen, and mankind does not bother
about them. It requires a very unusual mind to undertake the analysis of
the obvious. Accordingly I wish to consider the stages in which this analysis
became explicit, and finally became unalterably impressed upon the educated minds of Western Europe.   (10)

Obviously, the main recurrences of life are too insistent to escape the
notice of the least rational of humans; and even before the dawn of rationality, they have impressed themselves upon the instincts of animals. It is
unnecessary to labour the point, that in broad outline certain general states
of nature recur, and that our very natures have adapted themselves to such
repetitions.   (11)

But there is a complementary fact which is equally true and equally
obvious:—nothing ever really recurs in exact detail. No two days are identical, no two winters. What has gone, has gone forever. Accordingly the
practical philosophy of mankind has been to expect the broad recurrences,
and to accept the details as emanating from the inscrutable womb of

things beyond the ken of rationality. Men expected the sun to rise, but the wind bloweth where it listeth.   (12)

Certainly from the classical Greek civilisation onwards there have been men, and indeed groups of men, who have placed themselves beyond this acceptance of an ultimate irrationality. Such men have endeavoured to explain all phenomena as the outcome of an order of things which extends to every detail. Geniuses such as Aristotle, or Archimedes, or Roger Bacon, must have been endowed with the full scientific mentality, which instinctively holds that all things great and small are conceivable as exemplifications of general principles which reign throughout the natural order.   (13)

But until the close of the Middle Ages the general educated public did not feel that intimate conviction, and that detailed interest, in such an idea, so as to lead to an unceasing supply of men, with ability and opportunity adequate to maintain a coördinated search for the discovery of these hypothetical principles. Either people were doubtful about the existence of such principles, or were doubtful about any success in finding them, or took no interest in thinking about them, or were oblivious to their practical importance when found. For whatever reason, search was languid, if we have regard to the opportunities of a high civilisation and the length of time concerned. Why did the pace suddenly quicken in the sixteenth and seventeenth centuries? At the close of the Middle Ages a new mentality discloses itself. Invention stimulated thought, thought quickened physical speculation, Greek manuscripts disclosed what the ancients had discovered. Finally although in the year 1500 Europe knew less than Archimedes who died in the year 212 B. C., yet in the year 1700, Newton's *Principia* had been written and the world was well started on the modern epoch.   (14)

There have been great civilisations in which the peculiar balance of mind required for science has only fitfully appeared and has produced the feeblest result. For example, the more we know of Chinese art, of Chinese literature, and of the Chinese philosophy of life, the more we admire the heights to which that civilisation attained. For thousands of years, there have been in China acute and learned men patiently devoting their lives to study. Having regard to the span of time, and to the population concerned, China forms the largest volume of civilisation which the world has seen. There is no reason to doubt the intrinsic capacity of individual Chinamen for the pursuit of science. And yet Chinese science is practically negligible. There is no reason to believe that China if left to itself would have ever produced any progress in science. The same may be said of India. Furthermore, if the Persians had enslaved the Greeks, there is no definite ground for belief that science would have flourished in Europe. The Romans showed no particular originality in that line. Even as it was, the

Greeks, though they founded the movement, did not sustain it with the concentrated interest which modern Europe has shown. I am not alluding to the last few generations of the European peoples on both sides of the ocean; I mean the smaller Europe of the Reformation period, distracted as it was with wars and religious disputes. Consider the world of the eastern Mediterranean, from Sicily to western Asia, during the period of about 1400 years from the death of Archimedes [in 212   B. C.] to the irruption of the Tartars. There were wars and revolutions and large changes of religion: but nothing much worse than the wars of the sixteenth and seventeenth centuries throughout Europe. There was a great and wealthy civilisation, Pagan, Christian, Mahometan. In that period a great deal was added to science. But on the whole the progress was slow and wavering; and, except in mathematics, the men of the Renaissance practically started from the position which Archimedes had reached. There had been some progress in medicine and some progress in astronomy. But the total advance was very little compared to the marvellous success of the seventeenth century. For example, compare the progress of scientific knowledge from the year 1560, just before the births of Galileo and of Kepler, up to the year 1700, when Newton was in the height of his fame, with the progress in the ancient period, already mentioned, exactly ten times as long.   (15)

Nevertheless, Greece was the mother of Europe; and it is to Greece that we must look in order to find the origin of our modern ideas. We all know that on the eastern shores of the Mediterranean there was a very flourishing school of Ionian philosophers, deeply interested in theories concerning nature. Their ideas have been transmitted to us, enriched by the genius of Plato and Aristotle. But, with the exception of Aristotle, and it is a large exception, this school of thought had not attained to the complete scientific mentality. In some ways, it was better. The Greek genius was philosophical, lucid and logical. The men of this group were primarily asking philosophical questions. What is the substratum of nature? Is it fire, or earth, or water, or some combination of any two, or of all three? Or is it a mere flux, not reducible to some static material? Mathematics interested them mightily. They invented its generality, analysed its premises, and made notable discoveries of theorems by a rigid adherence to deductive reasoning. Their minds were infected with an eager generality. They demanded clear, bold ideas, and strict reasoning from them. All this was excellent; it was genius; it was ideal preparatory work. But it was not science as we understand it. The patience of minute observation was not nearly so prominent. Their genius was not so apt for the state of imaginative muddled suspense which precedes successful inductive generalisation. They were lucid thinkers and bold reasoners.   (16)

Of course there were exceptions, and at the very top: for example, Aristotle and Archimedes. Also for patient observation, there were the astronomers. There was a mathematical lucidity about the stars, and a fascination about the small numerable band of run-a-way planets. (17)

Every philosophy is tinged with the colouring of some secret imaginative background, which never emerges explicitly into its trains of reasoning. The Greek view of nature, at least that cosmology transmitted from them to later ages, was essentially dramatic. It is not necessarily wrong for this reason: but it was overwhelmingly dramatic. It thus conceived nature as articulated in the way of a work of dramatic art, for the exemplification of general ideas converging to an end. Nature was differentiated so as to provide its proper end for each thing. There was the centre of the universe as the end of motion for those things which are heavy, and the celestial spheres as the end of motion for those things whose natures lead them upwards. The celestial spheres were for things which are impassible and ingenerable, the lower regions for things passible and generable. Nature was a drama in which each thing played its part. (18)

I do not say that this is a view to which Aristotle would have subscribed without severe reservations, in fact without the sort of reservations which we ourselves would make. But it was the view which subsequent Greek thought extracted from Aristotle and passed on to the Middle Ages. The effect of such an imaginative setting for nature was to damp down the historical spirit. For it was the end which seemed illuminating, so why bother about the beginning? The Reformation and the scientific movement were two aspects of the historical revolt which was the dominant intellectual movement of the later Renaissance. The appeal to the origins of Christianity, and Francis Bacon's appeal to efficient causes as against final causes, were two sides of one movement of thought. Also for this reason Galileo and his adversaries were at hopeless cross purposes, as can be seen from his *Dialogues on the Two Systems of the World*. (19)

Galileo keeps harping on how things happen, whereas his adversaries had a complete theory as to why things happen. Unfortunately the two theories did not bring out the same results. Galileo insists upon 'irreducible and stubborn facts,' and Simplicius, his opponent, brings forward reasons, completely satisfactory, at least to himself. It is a great mistake to conceive this historical revolt as an appeal to reason. On the contrary, it was through and through an anti-intellectualist movement. It was the return to the contemplation of brute fact; and it was based on a recoil from the inflexible rationality of medieval thought. In making this statement I am merely summarising what at the time the adherents of the old régime themselves asserted. For example, in the fourth book of Father Paul Sarpi's *History of the Council of Trent*, you will find that in the year 1551 the Papal Legates who presided over the Council ordered: 'That the Divines ought to confirm their opinions with the holy Scripture, Traditions of the Apos-

tles, sacred and approved Councils, and by the Constitutions and Authorities of the holy Fathers; that they ought to use brevity, and avoid superfluous and unprofitable questions, and perverse contentions. . . . This order
did not please the Italian Divines; who said it was a novity, and a con-
demning of School-Divinity, which, in all difficulties, *useth reason,* and
because it was not lawful [*i.e.,* by this decree] to treat as St. Thomas
[Aquinas], St. Bonaventure, and other famous men did.'   (20)

It is impossible not to feel sympathy with these Italian divines, maintaining the lost cause of unbridled rationalism. They were deserted on all
hands. The Protestants were in full revolt against them. The Papacy failed
to support them, and the Bishops of the Council could not even understand
them. For a few sentences below the foregoing quotation, we read: 'Though
many complained here-of [*i.e.,* of the Decree], yet it prevailed but little,
because generally the Fathers [*i.e.,* the Bishops] desired to hear men speak
with intelligible terms, not abstrusely, as in the matter of justification, and
others already handled.'   (21)

Poor belated medievalists! When they used reason they were not even
intelligible to the ruling powers of their epoch. It will take centuries before
stubborn facts are reducible by reason, and meanwhile the pendulum
swings slowly and heavily to the extreme of the historical method.   (22)

Forty-three years after the Italian divines had written this memorial,
Richard Hooker in his famous *Laws of Ecclesiastical Polity* makes exactly
the same complaint of his Puritan adversaries.[1] Hooker's balanced thought
—from which the appellation 'The Judicious Hooker' is derived—and his
diffuse style, which is the vehicle of such thought, make his writings singularly unfit for the process of summarising by a short, pointed quotation.
But, in the section referred to, he reproaches his opponents with *Their
Disparagement of Reason;* and in support of his own position definitely
refers to 'The greatest amongst the school-divines' by which designation I
presume that he refers to St. Thomas Aquinas.   (23)

Hooker's *Ecclesiastical Polity* was published just before Sarpi's *Council of
Trent.* Accordingly there was complete independence between the two
works. But both the Italian divines of 1551, and Hooker at the end of that
century testify to the anti-rationalist trend of thought at that epoch, and in
this respect contrast their own age with the epoch of scholasticism.   (24)

This reaction was undoubtedly a very necessary corrective to the un-
guarded rationalism of the Middle Ages. But reactions run to extremes.
Accordingly, although one outcome of this reaction was the birth of modern
science, yet we must remember that science thereby inherited the bias of
thought to which it owes its origin.   (25)

The effect of Greek dramatic literature was many-sided so far as con-

---

1 *Cf.* Book III, Section viii.

cerns the various ways in which it indirectly affected medieval thought. The pilgrim fathers of the scientific imagination as it exists today are the great tragedians of ancient Athens, Aeschylus, Sophocles, Euripides. Their vision of fate, remorseless and indifferent, urging a tragic incident to its inevitable issue, is the vision possessed by science. Fate in Greek Tragedy becomes the order of nature in modern thought. The absorbing interest in the particular heroic incidents, as an example and a verification of the workings of fate, reappears in our epoch as concentration of interest on the crucial experiments. It was my good fortune to be present at the meeting of the Royal Society in London when the Astronomer Royal for England announced that the photographic plates of the famous eclipse, as measured by his colleagues in Greenwich Observatory, had verified the prediction of Einstein that rays of light are bent as they pass in the neighborhood of the sun. The whole atmosphere of tense interest was exactly that of the Greek drama: we were the chorus commenting on the decree of destiny as disclosed in the development of a supreme incident. There was dramatic quality in the very staging:—the traditional ceremonial, and in the background the picture of Newton to remind us that the greatest of scientific generalisations was now, after more than two centuries, to receive its first modification. Nor was the personal interest wanting: a great adventure in thought had at length come safe to shore. (26)

Let me here remind you that the essence of dramatic tragedy is not unhappiness. It resides in the solemnity of the remorseless working of things. This inevitableness of destiny can only be illustrated in terms of human life by incidents which in fact involve unhappiness. For it is only by them that the futility of escape can be made evident in the drama. This remorseless inevitableness is what pervades scientific thought. The laws of physics are the decrees of fate. (27)

The conception of the moral order in the Greek plays was certainly not a discovery of the dramatists. It must have passed into the literary tradition from the general serious opinion of the times. But in finding this magnificent expression, it thereby deepened the stream of thought from which it arose. The spectacle of a moral order was impressed upon the imagination of classical civilisation. (28)

The time came when that great society decayed, and Europe passed into the Middle Ages. The direct influence of Greek literature vanished. But the concept of the moral order and of the order of nature had enshrined itself in the Stoic philosophy. For example, Lecky in his *History of European Morals* tells us 'Seneca maintains that the Divinity has determined all things by an inexorable law of destiny, which He has decreed, but which He Himself obeys.' But the most effective way in which the Stoics influenced the mentality of the Middle Ages was by the diffused sense of order which arose from Roman law. Again to quote Lecky, 'The Roman legislation was in a twofold manner the child of philosophy. It was in the first place formed upon the philosophical model, for, instead of being a mere empirical system adjusted to the existing requirements of society, it laid down abstract principles of right to which it endeavoured to conform; and, in the next place, these principles were borrowed directly from Stoicism.' In spite of the actual anarchy throughout large regions in Europe after the collapse of the Empire, the sense of legal order always haunted the racial memories of the Imperial populations. Also the Western Church was always there as a living embodiment of the traditions of Imperial rule.

(29)

It is important to notice that this legal impress upon medieval civilisation was not in the form of a few wise precepts which should permeate conduct. It was the conception of a definite articulated system which defines the legality of the detailed structure of social organism, and of the detailed way in which it should function. There was nothing vague. It was not a question of admirable maxims, but of definite procedure to put things right and to keep them there. The Middle Ages formed one long training of the intellect of Western Europe in the sense of order. There may have been some deficiency in respect to practice. But the idea never for a moment lost its grip. It was preëminently an epoch of orderly thought, rationalist through and through. The very anarchy quickened the sense for coherent system; just as the modern anarchy of Europe has stimulated the intellectual vision of a League of Nations.

(30)

But for science something more is wanted than a general sense of the order in things. It needs but a sentence to point out how the habit of definite exact thought was implanted in the European mind by the long dominance of scholastic logic and scholastic divinity. The habit remained after the philosophy had been repudiated, the priceless habit of looking for an exact point and of sticking to it when found. Galileo owes more to Aristotle than appears on the surface of his *Dialogues:* he owes to him his clear head and his analytic mind.

(31)

I do not think, however, that I have even yet brought out the greatest contribution of medievalism to the formation of the scientific movement. I mean the inexpugnable belief that every detailed occurrence can be correlated with its antecedents in a perfectly definite manner, exemplifying general principles. Without this belief the incredible labours of scientists would be without hope. It is this instinctive conviction, vividly poised before the imagination, which is the motive power of research:—that there is a secret, a secret which can be unveiled. How has this conviction been so vividly implanted on the European mind?

(32)

When we compare this tone of thought in Europe with the attitude of other civilisations when left to themselves, there seems but one source for its origin. It must come from the medieval insistence on the rationality of God, conceived as with the personal energy of Jehovah and with the rationality of a Greek philosopher. Every detail was supervised and ordered: the search into nature could only result in the vindication of the faith in rationality. Remember that I am not talking of the explicit beliefs of a few individuals. What I mean is the impress on the European mind arising from the unquestioned faith of centuries. By this I mean the instinctive tone of thought and not a mere creed of words. (33)

In Asia, the conceptions of God were of a being who was either too arbitrary or too impersonal for such ideas to have much effect on instinctive habits of mind. Any definite occurrence might be due to the fiat of an irrational despot, or might issue from some impersonal, inscrutable origin of things. There was not the same confidence as in the intelligible rationality of a personal being. I am not arguing that the European trust in the scrutability of nature was logically justified even by its own theology. My only point is to understand how it arose. My explanation is that the faith in the possibility of science, generated antecedently to the development of modern scientific theory, is an unconscious derivative from medieval theology. (34)

But science is not merely the outcome of instinctive faith. It also requires an active interest in the simple occurrences of life for their own sake. (35)

This qualification 'for their own sake' is important. The first phase of the Middle Ages was an age of symbolism. It was an age of vast ideas, and of primitive technique. There was little to be done with nature, except to coin a hard living from it. But there were realms of thought to be explored, realms of philosophy and realms of theology. Primitive art could symbolise those ideas which filled all thoughtful minds. The first phase of medieval art has a haunting charm beyond compare: its own intrinsic quality is enhanced by the fact that its message, which stretched beyond art's own self-justification of aesthetic achievement, was the symbolism of things lying behind nature itself. In this symbolic phase, medieval art energised in nature as its medium, but pointed to another world. (36)

In order to understand the contrast between these early Middle Ages and the atmosphere required by the scientific mentality, we should compare the sixth century in Italy with the sixteenth century. In both centuries the Italian genius was laying the foundations of a new epoch. The history of the three centuries preceding the earlier period, despite the promise for the future introduced by the rise of Christianity, is overwhelmingly infected by the sense of the decline of civilisation. In each generation something has been lost. As we read the records, we are haunted by the shadow of the coming barbarism. There are great men, with fine achievements in action or in thought. But their total effect is merely for some short time to arrest the general decline. In the sixth century we are, so far as Italy is concerned, at the lowest point of the curve. But in that century every action is laying the foundation for the tremendous rise of the new European civilisation. In the background the Byzantine Empire, under Justinian, in three ways determined the character of the early Middle Ages in Western Europe. In the first place, its armies, under Belisarius and Narses, cleared Italy from the Gothic domination. In this way, the stage was freed for the exercise of the old Italian genius for creating organisations which shall be protective of ideals of cultural activity. It is impossible not to sympathise with the Goths: yet there can be no doubt but that a thousand years of the Papacy were infinitely more valuable for Europe than any effects derivable from a well-established Gothic kingdom of Italy.   (37)

In the second place, the codification of the Roman law established the ideal of legality which dominated the sociological thought of Europe in the succeeding centuries. Law is both an engine for government, and a condition restraining government. The canon law of the Church, and the civil law of the State, owe to Justinian's lawyers their influence on the development of Europe. They established in the Western mind the ideal that an authority should be at once lawful, and law-enforcing, and should in itself exhibit a rationally adjusted system of organisation. The sixth century in Italy gave the initial exhibition of the way in which the impress of these ideas was fostered by contact with the Byzantine Empire.   (38)

Thirdly, in the non-political spheres of art and learning Constantinople exhibited a standard of realised achievement which, partly by the impulse to direct imitation, and partly by the indirect inspiration arising from the mere knowledge that such things existed, acted as a perpetual spur to Western culture. The wisdom of the Byzantines, as it stood in the imagination of the first phase of medieval mentality, and the wisdom of the Egyptians as it stood in the imagination of the early Greeks, played analogous rôles. Probably the actual knowledge of these respective wisdoms was, in either case, about as much as was good for the recipients. They knew enough to know the sort of standards which are attainable, and not enough to be fettered by static and traditional ways of thought. Accordingly, in both cases men went ahead on their own and did better. No account of the rise of the European scientific mentality can omit some notice of this influence of the Byzantine civilisation in the background. In the sixth century there is a crisis in the history of the relations between the Byzantines and the West; and this crisis is to be contrasted with the influence of Greek literature on European thought in the fifteenth and sixteenth centuries. The two outstanding men, who in the Italy of the sixth century laid the foundations of the future, were St. Benedict and Gregory the Great. By reference to them, we can at once see how absolutely in ruins was the approach to the scientific mentality which had been attained by the Greeks. We are at the zero point of scientific temperature. But the lifework of Gregory and of Benedict contributed elements to the reconstruction of Europe which secured that this reconstruction, when it arrived, should include a more effective scientific mentality than that of the ancient world. The Greeks were over-theoretical. For them science was an offshoot of philosophy. Gregory and Benedict were practical men, with an eye for the importance of ordinary things; and they combined this practical temperament with their religious and cultural activities. In particular, we owe it to St. Benedict that the monasteries were the homes of practical agriculturalists, as well as of saints and of artists and men of learning. The alliance of science with technology, by which learning is kept in contact with irreducible and stubborn facts, owes much to the practical bent of the early Benedictines. Modern science derives from Rome as well as from Greece, and this Roman strain explains its gain in an energy of thought kept closely in contact with the world of facts. (39)

But the influence of this contact between the monasteries and the facts of nature showed itself first in art. The rise of Naturalism in the later Middle Ages was the entry into the European mind of the final ingredient necessary for the rise of science. It was the rise of interest in natural objects and in natural occurrences, for their own sakes. The natural foliage of a district was sculptured in out-of-the-way spots of the later buildings, merely as exhibiting delight in those familiar objects. The whole atmosphere of every art exhibited a direct joy in the apprehension of the things which lie around us. The craftsmen who executed the late medieval decorative sculpture, Giotto, Chaucer, Wordsworth, Walt Whitman, and, at the present day, the New England poet Robert Frost, are all akin to each other in this respect. The simple immediate facts are the topics of interest, and these reappear in the thought of science as the 'irreducible stubborn facts.' (40)

The mind of Europe was now prepared for its new venture of thought. It is unnecessary to tell in detail the various incidents which marked the rise of science: the growth of wealth and leisure; the expansion of universities; the invention of printing; the taking of Constantinople; Copernicus; Vasco da Gama; Columbus; the telescope. The soil, the climate, the seeds, were there, and the forest grew. Science has never shaken off the impress of its origin in the historical revolt of the later Renaissance. It has remained predominantly an anti-rationalistic movement, based upon a naïve faith. What reasoning it has wanted, has been borrowed from mathematics which is a surviving relic of Greek rationalism, following the deductive method. Science repudiates philosophy. In other words, it has never cared to justify its faith or to explain its meanings; and has remained blandly indifferent to its refutation by Hume. (41)

Of course the historical revolt was fully justified. It was wanted. It was more than wanted: it was an absolute necessity for healthy progress. The world required centuries of contemplation of irreducible and stubborn facts. It is difficult for men to do more than one thing at a time, and that was the sort of thing they had to do after the rationalistic orgy of the Middle Ages. It was a very sensible reaction; but it was not a protest on behalf of reason.   (42)

There is, however, a Nemesis which waits upon those who deliberately avoid avenues of knowledge. Oliver Cromwell's cry echoes down the ages, 'My brethren, by the bowels of Christ I beseech you, bethink you that you may be mistaken.'   (43)

The progress of science has now reached a turning point. The stable foundations of physics have broken up: also for the first time physiology is asserting itself as an effective body of knowledge, as distinct from a scrap-heap. The old foundations of scientific thought are becoming unintelligible. Time, space, matter, material, ether, electricity, mechanism, organism, configuration, structure, pattern, function, all require reinterpretation. What is the sense of talking about a mechanical explanation when you do not know what you mean by mechanics?   (44)

The truth is that science started its modern career by taking over ideas derived from the weakest side of the philosophies of Aristotle's successors. In some respects it was a happy choice. It enabled the knowledge of the seventeenth century to be formularised so far as physics and chemistry were concerned with a completeness which has lasted to the present time. But the progress of biology and psychology has probably been checked by the uncritical assumption of half-truths. If science is not to degenerate into a medley of *ad hoc* hypotheses, it must become philosophical and must enter upon a thorough criticism of its own foundations.   (45)

In the succeeding lectures of this course, I shall trace the successes and the failures of the particular conceptions of cosmology with which the European intellect has clothed itself in the last three centuries. General climates of opinion persist for periods of about two to three generations, that is to say, for periods of sixty to a hundred years. There are also shorter waves of thought, which play on the surface of the tidal movement. We shall find, therefore, transformations in the European outlook, slowly modifying the successive centuries. There persists, however, throughout the whole period the fixed scientific cosmology which presupposes the ultimate fact of an irreducible brute matter, or material, spread throughout space in a flux of configurations. In itself such a material is senseless, valueless, purposeless. It just does what it does do, following a fixed routine imposed by external relations which do not spring from the nature of its being. It is this assumption that I call 'scientific materialism.' Also it is an assumption which I shall challenge as being entirely unsuited to the scientific situation at which we have now arrived. It is not wrong, if properly construed. If we confine ourselves to certain types of facts, abstracted from the complete circumstances in which they occur, the materialistic assumption expresses these facts to perfection. But when we pass beyond the abstraction, either by more subtle employment of our senses, or by the request for meanings and for coherence of thoughts, the scheme breaks down at once. The narrow efficiency of the scheme was the very cause of its supreme methodological success. For it directed attention to just those groups of facts which, in the state of knowledge then existing, required investigation. (46)

The success of the scheme has adversely affected the various currents of European thought. The historical revolt was anti-rationalistic, because the rationalism of the scholastics required a sharp correction by contact with brute fact. But the revival of philosophy in the hands of Descartes and his successors was entirely coloured in its development by the acceptance of the scientific cosmology at its face value. The success of their ultimate ideas confirmed scientists in their refusal to modify them as the result of an enquiry into their rationality. Every philosophy was bound in some way or other to swallow them whole. Also the example of science affected other regions of thought. The historical revolt has thus been exaggerated into the exclusion of philosophy from its proper rôle of harmonising the various abstractions of methodological thought. Thought is abstract; and the intolerant use of abstractions is the major vice of the intellect. This vice is not wholly corrected by the recurrence to concrete experience. For after all, you need only attend to those aspects of your concrete experience which lie within some limited scheme. There are two methods for the purification of ideas. One of them is dispassionate observation by means of the bodily senses. But observation is selection. Accordingly, it is difficult to transcend a scheme of abstraction whose success is sufficiently wide. The other method is by comparing the various schemes of abstraction which are well founded in our various types of experience. This comparison takes the form of satisfying the demands of the Italian scholastic divines whom Paul Sarpi mentioned. They asked that *reason* should be used. Faith in reason is the trust that the ultimate natures of things lie together in a harmony which excludes mere arbitrariness. It is the faith that at the base of things we shall not find mere arbitrary mystery. The faith in the order of nature which has made possible the growth of science is a particular example of a deeper faith. This faith cannot be justified by any inductive generalisation. It springs from direct inspection of the nature of things as disclosed in our own immediate present experience. There is no parting from your own shadow. To experience this faith is to know that in being ourselves we are more than ourselves: to know that our exeprience, dim and fragmentary as it is, yet sounds the utmost depths of reality: to know that detached details merely in order to be themselves demand that they should find themselves in a system of things: to know that this system includes the harmony of logical rationality, and the harmony of aesthetic achievement: to know that, while the harmony of logic lies upon the universe as an iron necessity, the aesthetic harmony stands before it as a living ideal moulding the general flux in its broken progress towards finer, subtler issues. (47)

John Dewey

(1859–1952)

DEWEY succeeded to the leadership of philosophical pragmatism in Amer-
ica after the death of William James. Dewey himself dubbed his philosophy
as "instrumentalism," built on experience as the only reality and knowl-
edge as functional rather than theoretical. He was the "father" of the move-
ment in primary and secondary education called "Progressive," which was
widespread in the 1930's and 1940's. His major works include Democracy
and Education *(1916),* The Quest for Certainty *(1929),* Logic, The Theory
of Inquiry *(1938).*

■ *Science and Free Culture*

It is no longer possible to hold the simple faith of the Enlightenment that
assured advance of science will produce free institutions by dispelling
ignorance and superstition:—the sources of human servitude and the pillars
of oppressive government. The progress of natural science has been even
more rapid and extensive than could have been anticipated. But its technological application in mass production and distribution of goods has
required concentration of capital; it has resulted in business corporations
possessed of extensive legal rights and immunities; and, as is a commonplace, has created a vast and intricate set of new problems. It has put at the
disposal of dictators means of controlling opinion and sentiment of a potency which reduces to a mere shadow all previous agencies at the command of despotic rulers. For negative censorship it has substituted means
of propaganda of ideas and alleged information on a scale that reaches
every individual, reiterated day after day by every organ of publicity and
communication, old and new. In consequence, for practically the first time

in human history, totalitarian states exist claiming to rest upon the active consent of the governed. While despotic governments are as old as political history, this particular phenomenon is as startlingly unexpected as it is powerful. (1)

One of the earlier arguments for democracy is countered in the most disturbing way. Before the industrial revolution had made much headway it was a commonplace that oppressive governments had the support of only a relatively small class. Republican government, it was assumed, would have the broad support of the masses, so that the "people" who, as Rousseau expressed it, had been nothing would become everything. We are now told the contrary. Democracy is said to be but a numerical contrivance, resting upon shifting combinations of individuals who happen at a given time to make up a majority of voters. We are told that the moral consensus which exists only when there is unity of beliefs and aims, is conspicuously lacking in democracies, and is of the very essence of totalitarian states. The claim stands side by side with that of Marxist communists who say that since their views are inherently scientific, false opinions have no legitimate standing as against the authority of The Truth. But in a way the Fascist claim goes deeper since it pretends to extend below merely intellectual loyalties, to which science appeals, and lay hold of fundamental emotions and impulses. (2)

There is an argument about science which so far has found comparatively little response in democratic countries, but which nevertheless puts a problem so basic that it will receive more and more attention as time goes by. It is said that the principles of laissez-faire individualism have governed the conduct of scientific inquiry; that the tastes and preferences of individual investigators have been allowed to regulate its course to such an extent that present intellectual confusion and moral chaos of the world exists because of tacit connivance of science with uncontrolled individualistic activity in industry. (3)

The position is so extreme and goes so contrary to all we had come to believe that it is easily passed over as an aberration. But the view, because of its extreme character, may be taken to point to a genuine issue: just what are the social consequences of science? Are they not so important, because of technological applications, that the social interest is paramount over intellectual interest? Can the type of social control of industry urged by socialists be carried through without some kind of public regulation of the scientific investigations that are the source of the inventions determining the course of industry? And might not such regulation throttle the freedom of science? Those who say that the social effect of inventions (which exist only because of the findings of scientific inquiry) is so unsettling that the least which can be done is to declare a moratorium on science express the same problem with more moderation. (4)

The claim is made in Russia that the direction taken by science has in the last hundred and fifty years been so determined by the interest of the dominant economic class, that science has been upon the whole an organ of bourgeois democracy:—not so consciously perhaps as in the case of government, the police and the army, but yet in substantial effect. Since it is impossible to draw any fixed line between the physical and the social sciences, and since the latter—both with respect to investigation and teaching—must be regulated in the interest of the politics of the new social order, it is impossible to allow the physical sciences to go their way apart without political regulation. Nazi Germany decrees what is scientific truth in anthropology regarding race, and Moscow determines that Mendelism is scientifically false, and dictates the course to be pursued by Genetics. Both countries look askance at the theory of Relativity, although on different grounds. Quite aside, however, from special cases, a general atmosphere of control of opinion cannot exist without reacting in pretty fundamental ways upon every form of intellectual activity—art too as well as science.   (5)

Even if we hold that extreme views are so extreme as to be distorted caricatures, there remains an actual problem. Can society, especially a democratic society, exist without a basic consensus and community of beliefs? If it cannot, can the required community be achieved without regulation of scientific pursuits exercised by a public authority in behalf of social unity?   (6)

In this connection the accusation of irresponsibility as to social consequences is brought against scientific men, and it is in this context that the underlying issue takes shape. It is argued (and some who take the position are themselves scientists) that the main directions of physical science during the past hundred years, increasingly so in the last half century, have been set, indirectly and directly, by the requirements of industry carried on for private profit. Consideration of the *problems* which have not received attention in comparison with those which have absorbed expenditure of intellectual energies will, it is said, prove the proposition.   (7)

Direct control has been exercised for the most part by governments. They have subsidized the kind of investigations that promise increased national power, either by promoting manufacturing and commerce as against other national states, or by fostering researches that strengthen military prowess. Indirect control has been exercised in subtler ways. The place of industry is so central in modern life that quite apart from questions handed directly over to scientific laboratories by industrial enterprises, it is psychologically impossible for men engaged in scientific research not to be most sensitive and most responsive to the *type* of problems presented in practical effort to control natural energies;—which in the concrete means manufacturing and distributing goods. Moreover, a kind of positive halo surrounds scientific endeavors. For it has been held, not without grounds, that general social—or at least national—welfare is thereby promoted. Germany led other countries in physical research; and it was in Germany that scientific advances could be shown to have contributed most directly to national strength and prestige. It was thus possible for some intellectual observers, not particularly naïve, to hold up German universities as models to follow in our own country. (8)

It is not implied that personal economic interest has played any important part in directing the researches of individual scientists. The contrary is notoriously the rule. But attention and interest are not freely ranging searchlights that can be directed at all parts of the natural universe with equal ease. They operate within certain channels, and the general state of culture determines what and where the channels are. The "climate of opinion" decides the direction taken by scientific activity as truly as physical climate decides what agricultural pursuits can be carried on. Social imagination comes to have a certain tone and color; intellectual immunity in one direction and intellectual sensitivity in other directions are the result. It has even been said, and with a good deal of evidence in its support, that the prevailing mechanistic creed of science during the nineteenth century was an indirect product of the importance assumed by the machine in industrial production, so that now, when machine-production is giving way to power-production, basic scientific "concepts" are also changing. (9)

I referred above to the role of nationalism in deciding the direction taken by science. The striking instance is of course the organization of scientific men for aid to a nation in time of war. The instance brings to a head tendencies that are going on in less overt and more unconscious ways pretty much all the time, even in times of nominal peace. Increase of the scope of governmental activities in all industrialized countries, going on for some years at an accelerated pace, has reinforced the alliance between national interest and scientific inquiry. It is certainly arguable that when the choice at hand is between regulation of science by private economic interests and by nationalist interest, the latter should have preference. It may be inferred that the open control of science exercised in totalitarian states is but a culmination of tendencies that have been going on in more or less covert ways for some time—from which it follows that the problem presented extends beyond the borders of those particular states. (10)

Strangely enough, at first sight, the demand for direct social control of scientific inquiries and conclusions is unwittingly reinforced by an attitude quite commonly taken by scientific men themselves. For it is commonly said and commonly believed that science is completely neutral and indifferent as to the ends and values which move men to act: that at most it only provides more efficient means for realization of ends that are and must be due to wants and desires completely independent of science. It is at this point that the present climate of opinion differs so widely from that which marked the optimistic faith of the Enlightenment; the faith that human science and freedom would advance hand in hand to usher in an era of indefinite human perfectibility. (11)

That the popular esteem of science is largely due to the aid it has given to men for attainment of things they wanted independently of what they had learned from science is doubtless true. Russell has stated in a vivid way the sort of thing that has enabled science to displace beliefs that had previously been held: "The world ceased to believe that Joshua caused the sun to stand still, because Copernican astronomy was useful in navigation; it abandoned Aristotle's physics, because Galileo's theory of falling bodies made it possible to calculate the trajectory of a cannonball. It rejected the theory of the flood because geology is useful in mining and so on."* That the quotation expresses the sort of thing that gave the conclusions of the new science prestige and following at a time when it badly needed some outside aid in getting a hearing can hardly be doubted. As illustrative material it is especially impressive because of the enormous authority enjoyed by the doctrines of Aristotle and of the Church. If even in the case where all the advantage was on the side of old doctrines, the demonstrated serviceability of science gave it the victory, we can easily judge the enhancement of the esteem in which science was held in matters where it had no such powerful foe to contend with. (12)

Quite apart from the antagonism to science displayed by entrenched institutional interests that had previously obtained a monopoly over beliefs in, say, astronomy, geology and some fields of history, history proves the existence of so much indifference on the part of mankind to the quality of its beliefs and such lethargy towards methods that disturb old beliefs, that we should be glad that the new science has had such powerful adventitious aid. But it leaves untouched the question as to whether scientific knowledge has power to modify the ends which men prize and strive to attain. Is it proved that the findings of science—the best authenticated knowledge we have—add only to our power to realize desires already in existence? Or is this view derived from some previous theory about the constitution of human nature? Can it be true that desires and knowledge exist in separate non-communicating compartments? Do the facts which can undoubtedly be cited as evidence, such as the use of scientific knowledge indifferently to heal disease and prolong human life and to provide the instruments for wholesale destruction of life, really prove the case? Or are they specially selected cases that support a doctrine that originated on other grounds than the evidence of facts? Is there such a complete separation of human ends from human beliefs as the theory assumes? (13)

* Bertrand Russell, *Power*, p. 138.

The shock given old ideas by the idea that knowledge is incapable of modifying the quality of desires (and hence cannot affect the formation of ends and purposes) is not of course in itself a ground for denying it is sound. It may be that the old view is totally false. Nevertheless, the point is worth discussion. We do not have to refer to the theory of Plato that knowledge, or what passes as knowledge, is the sole final determinant of men's ideas of the Good and hence of their actions. Nor is it needful to refer to Bacon's vision of the organization of scientific knowledge as the prospective foundation of future social policies directed exclusively to the advance of human well-being. The simple fact is that all the deliberately liberal and progressive movements of modern times have based themselves on the idea that action is determined by ideas, up to the time when Hume said that reason was and should be the "slave of the passions"; or, in contemporary language, of the emotions and desires. Hume's voice was a lonely one when he uttered the remark. The idea is now echoed and re-echoed from almost every quarter. The classic economic school made wants the prime motors of human action, reducing reason to a power of calculating the means best fitted to satisfy the wants. The first effect of biology upon psychology was to emphasize the primacy of appetites and instincts. Psychiatrists have enforced the same conclusion by showing that intellectual disturbances originate in emotional maladjustments, and by exhibiting the extent of dictation of belief by desire.   (14)

It is one thing, however, to recognize that earlier theories neglected the importance of emotions and habits as determinants of conduct and exaggerated that of ideas and reason. It is quite another thing to hold that ideas (especially those warranted by competent inquiry) and emotions (with needs and desires) exist in separate compartments so that no interaction between them exists. When the view is as baldly stated it strikes one as highly improbable that there can be any such complete separation in the constitution of human nature. And while the idea must be accepted if the evidence points that way, no matter into what plight human affairs are forever plunged, the implications of the doctrine of complete separation of desire and knowledge must be noted. The assumption that desires are rigidly fixed is not one on its face consistent with the history of man's progress from savagery through barbarism to even the present defective state of civilization. If knowledge, even of the most authenticated kind, cannot influence desires and aims, if it cannot determine what is of value and what is not, the future outlook as to formation of desires is depressing. Denial that they can be influenced by knowledge points emphatically to the non-rational and anti-rational forces that will form them. One alternative to the power of ideas is habit or custom, and then when the rule of sheer habit breaks down—as it has done at the present time—all that is left is competition on the part of various bodies and interests to decide which shall come out ahead in a struggle, carried on by intimidation, coercion, bribery, and all sorts of propaganda, to shape the desires which shall predominantly control the ends of human action. The prospect is a black one. It leads one to consider the possibility that Bacon, Locke, and the leaders of the Enlightenment—typified by the act of Condorcet, writing, while imprisoned and waiting for death, about the role of science in the future liberation of mankind—were after all quite aware of the actual influence of appetite, habit, and blind desire upon action, but were engaged in holding up another and better way as the alternative to follow in the future.   (15)

That the course they anticipated has not come to fruition is obvious without argument. Bacon's action in using his own knowledge as a servant of the Crown in strengthening Great Britain in a military way against other nations now seems more prophetic of what has happened than what he put down in words. The power over Nature which he expected to follow the advance of science has come to pass. But in contradiction to his expectations, it has been largely used to increase, instead of reduce, the power of Man over Man. Shall we conclude that the early prophets were totally and intrinsically wrong? Or shall we conclude that they immensely underestimated the obduracy of institutions and customs antedating the appearance of science on the scene in shaping desires in their image? Have events after all but accentuated the problem of discovering the means by which authenticated beliefs shall influence desires, the formation of ends, and thereby the course of events? Is it possible to admit the power of propaganda to shape ends and deny that of science?   (16)

Looked at from one angle, the question brings us back to our fundamental issue: the relation of culture and human nature. For the fact which is decisive in answering the question whether verified knowledge is or is not capable of shaping desires and ends (as well as means) is whether the desires that are effective in settling the course of action are innate and fixed, or are themselves the product of a certain culture. If the latter is the case, the practical issue reduces itself to this: Is it possible for the scientific attitude to become such a weighty and widespread constituent of culture that, through the medium of culture, it may shape human desires and purposes?   (17)

To state the question is a long way from ability to answer it. But it is something to have the issue before us in its actual instead of in its factitious form. The issue ceases to be the indeterminate one of the relation of knowledge and desires in the native psychological constitution of man—indeterminate, among other reasons, because it is disputable whether there is any such thing as the latter apart from native biological constitution. It becomes the determinate one of the institution of the kind of culture in which scientific method and scientific conclusions are integrally incorporated.   (18)

The problem stated in this way puts in a different light the esteem gained by science because of its serviceability. That there are individuals here and there who have been influenced to esteem science because of some obvious contribution to satisfaction of their merely personal desires may well be a fact. That there are groups similarly influenced must be admitted. But the reasons why men have been willing to accept conclusions derived from science in lieu of older ideas are not exclusively or even mainly those of direct personal and class benefit. Improvements in navigation and mining have become part of the state of culture. It is in this capacity they have tended to displace beliefs that were congenial to an earlier state of culture. By and large the same thing is true of the application of physics and chemistry in more effective satisfaction of wants and in creation of new wants. While their application to produce increased efficiency in carrying on war has doubtlessly recommended those sciences to persons like rulers and generals, who otherwise would have been indifferent, the mass of persons have been moved to an attitude of favorable esteem by what has happened in the arts of peace. The decisive factor would seem to be whether the arts of war or of peace are to be in the future the ones that will control culture, a question that involves the need of discovering why war is such an important constituent of present culture.   (19)

I should be on controversial ground if I held up as evidence the belief that the technologies, which are the practical correlates of scientific theories, have now reached a point in which they can be used to create an era of abundance instead of the deficit-economies that existed before natural science developed, and that with an era of abundance and security the causes of conflict would be reduced. It may be mentioned as a hypothetical illustration. The kind of serviceability which is capable of generating high esteem for science *may* possibly be serviceability for general and shared, or "social," welfare. If the economic regime were so changed that the resources of science were employed to maintain security for all, the present view about the limitation of science might fade away. I imagine there are not many who will deny that esteem for science, even when placed upon the ground of serviceability alone, is produced at least in part by an admixture of general with private serviceability. If there is a skeptic let him consider the contribution made by science both actually and still more potentially to agriculture, and the social consequences of the change in production of foods and raw materials, thereby effected.   (20)

The other side of the ledger is marked by such a debit entry as the following from the English chemist Soddy: "So far the pearls of science have been cast before swine, who have given us in return millionaires and slums, armaments and the desolation of war." The contrast is real. If its existence seems to support the doctrine that science only supplies means for more efficient execution of already existing desires and purposes, it is because it points to the division which exists in our culture. The war that mobilizes science for wholesale destruction mobilizes it, also, for support of life and for healing the wounded. The desires and ends involved proceed not from native and naked human nature but from modifications it has undergone in interaction with a complex of cultural factors of which science is indeed one, but one which produces social consequences only as it is affected by economic and political traditions and customs formed before its rise.   (21)

For in any case, the influence of science on both means and ends is not exercised directly upon individuals but indirectly through incorporation within culture. In this function and capacity it is that scientific beliefs have replaced earlier unscientific beliefs. The position stated at its worst is that science operates as a part of folklore, not just as science. Even when put in this way, attention is invited to differences in folklore and to differences of the consequences that are produced by different folklores. And when it is admitted that the folklore may be one of aggressive nationalism, where the consequences of science as part of the prevailing folklore is war of the present destructive scope, we at least have the advantage of clear knowledge as to the location of the problem.   (22)

We have been considering science as a body of conclusions. We have ignored science in its equality of an attitude embodied in habitual will to employ certain methods of observation, reflection, and test rather than others. When we look at science from this point of view, the significance of science as a constituent of culture takes on a new color. The great body of scientific inquirers would deny with indignation that they are actuated in *their* esteem for science by its material serviceability. If they use words sanctioned by long tradition, they say they are moved by love of the truth. If they use contemporary phraseology, less grandiloquent in sound but of equivalent meaning, they say they are moved by a controlling interest in inquiry, in discovery, in following where the evidence of discovered facts points. Above all they say that this kind of interest excludes interest in reaching any conclusion not warranted by evidence, no matter how personally congenial it may be.   (23)

In short, it is a fact that a certain group of men, perhaps relatively not very numerous, have a "disinterested" interest in scientific inquiry. This interest has developed a morale having its own distinctive features. Some of its obvious elements are willingness to hold belief in suspense, ability to doubt until evidence is obtained; willingness to go where evidence points instead of putting first a personally preferred conclusion; ability to hold ideas in solution and use them as hypotheses to be tested instead of as dogmas to be asserted; and (possibly the most distinctive of all) enjoyment of new fields for inquiry and of new problems. (24)

Every one of these traits goes contrary to some human impulse that is naturally strong. Uncertainty is disagreeable to most persons; suspense is so hard to endure that assured expectation of an unfortunate outcome is usually preferred to a long-continued state of doubt. "Wishful thinking" is a comparatively modern phrase; but men upon the whole have usually believed what they wanted to believe, except as very convincing evidence made it impossible. Apart from a scientific attitude, guesses, with persons left to themselves, tend to become opinions and opinions dogmas. To hold theories and principles in solution, awaiting confirmation, goes contrary to the grain. Even today questioning a statement made by a person is often taken by him as a reflection upon his integrity, and is resented. For many millennia opposition to views widely held in a community was intolerable. It called down the wrath of the deities who are in charge of the group. Fear of the unknown, fear of change and novelty, tended, at all times before the rise of scientific attitude, to drive men into rigidity of beliefs and habits; they entered upon unaccustomed lines of behavior—even in matters of minor moment—with qualms which exacted rites of expiation. Exceptions to accepted rules have either been ignored or systematically explained away when they were too conspicuous to ignore. Baconian idols of the tribe, the cave, the theater, and den have caused men to rush to conclusions, and then to use all their powers to defend from criticism and change the conclusions arrived at. The connection of common law with custom and its resistance to change are familiar facts. Even religious beliefs and rites which were at first more or less heretical deviations harden into modes of action it is impious to question, after once they have become part of the habits of a group. (25)

If I mention such familiar considerations it is in part to suggest that we may well be grateful that science has had undeniable social serviceability, and that to some extent and in some places strong obstructions to adoption of changed beliefs have been overcome. But the chief reason for calling attention to them is the proof they furnish that in some persons and to some degree science has already created a new morale—which is equivalent to the creation of new desires and new ends. The existence of the scientific attitude and spirit, even upon a limited scale, is proof that science is capable of developing a distinctive type of disposition and purpose: a type that goes far beyond provision of more effective means for realizing desires which exist independently of any effect of science. (26)

It is not becoming, to put it moderately, for those who are themselves animated by the scientific morale to assert that other persons are incapable of coming into possession of it and being moved by it. (27)

Such an attitude is saved from being professional snobbery only when it

is the result of sheer thoughtlessness. When one and the same representative of the intellectual class denounces any view that attaches inherent
importance to the consequences of science, claiming the view is false to the
spirit of science—and also holds that it is impossible for science to do anything to affect desires and ends, the inconsistency demands explanation.
(28)

A situation in which the fundamental dispositions and ends of a few
are influenced by science while that of most persons and most groups is
not so influenced proves that the issue is cultural. The difference sets a
social problem: what are the causes for the existence of this great gap, especially since it has such serious consequences? If it is possible for persons to
have their beliefs formed on the ground of evidence, procured by systematic and competent inquiry, nothing can be more disastrous socially
than that the great majority of persons should have them formed by habit,
accidents of circumstance, propaganda, personal and class bias. The existence, even on a relatively narrow scale, of a morale of fairmindedness,
intellectual integrity, of will to subordinate personal preference to ascertained facts and to share with others what is found out, instead of using it
for personal gain, is a challenge of the most searching kind. Why don't a
great many more persons have this attitude?   (29)

The answer given to this challenge is bound up with the fate of democracy. The spread of literacy, the immense extension of the influence of the
press in books, newspapers, periodicals, make the issue peculiarly urgent
for a democracy. The very agencies that a century and a half ago were
looked upon as those that were sure to advance the cause of democratic
freedom, are those which now make it possible to create pseudo-public
opinion and to undermine democracy from within. Callousness due to
continuous reiteration may produce a certain immunity to the grosser
kinds of propaganda. But in the long run negative measures afford no
assurance. While it would be absurd to believe it desirable or possible for
every one to become a scientist when science is defined from the side of
subject matter, the future of democracy is allied with spread of the scientific attitude. It is the sole guarantee against wholesale misleading by propaganda. More important still, it is the only assurance of the possibility of a
public opinion intelligent enough to meet present social problems.   (30)

To become aware of the problem is a condition of taking steps toward
its solution. The problem is in part economic. The nature of control of the
means of publicity enters directly; sheer financial control is not a favorable
sign. The democratic belief in free speech, free press and free assembly is
one of the things that exposes democratic institutions to attack. For representatives of totalitarian states, who are the first to deny such freedom
when they are in power, shrewdly employ it in a democratic country to
destroy the foundations of democracy. Backed with the necessary financial

means, they are capable of carrying on a work of continuous sapping and mining. More dangerous, perhaps, in the end is the fact that all economic conditions tending toward centralization and concentration of the means of production and distribution affect the public press, whether individuals so desire or not. The causes which require large corporate capital to carry on modern business, naturally influence the publishing business.   (31)

The problem is also an educative one. A book instead of a paragraph could be given to this aspect of the topic. That the schools have mostly been given to imparting information ready-made, along with teaching the tools of literacy, cannot be denied. The methods used in acquiring such information are not those which develop skill in inquiry and in test of opinions. On the contrary, they are positively hostile to it. They tend to dull native curiosity, and to load powers of observation and experimentation with such a mass of unrelated material that they do not operate as effectively as they do in many an illiterate person. The problem of the common schools in a democracy has reached only its first stage when they are provided for everybody. Until what shall be taught and how it is taught is settled upon the basis of formation of the scientific attitude, the so-called educational work of schools is a dangerously hit-or-miss affair as far as democracy is concerned.   (32)

The problem—as was suggested earlier—is also one of art. It is difficult to write briefly on this aspect of the question without giving rise to false impressions. For of late there has been an active campaign, carried on in the name of the social function of art, for using the arts, the plastic arts as well as literature, in propaganda for special views which are dogmatically asserted to be socially necessary. In consequence, any reference to the topic may seem to have a flavor of commendation of something of the same kind, only exercised by way of a counter-campaign in behalf of democratic ideas. The point is different. It is a reminder that ideas are effective not as bare ideas but as they have imaginative content and emotional appeal. I have alluded to the extensive reaction that has set in against the earlier over-simplified rationalism. The reaction tended to go to an opposite extreme. In emphasizing the role of wants, impulse, habit, and emotion, it often denied any efficacy whatever to ideas, to intelligence. The problem is that of effecting the union of ideas and knowledge with the non-rational factors in the human make-up. Art is the name given to all the agencies by which this union is effected.   (33)

The problem is also a moral and religious one. That religions have operated most effectively in alliance with the fine arts was indicated earlier. Yet the historic influence of religions has often been to magnify doctrines that are not subject to critical inquiry and test. Their cumulative effect in producing habits of mind at odds with the attitudes required for maintenance of democracy is probably much greater than is usually recognized.

Shrewd observers have said that one factor in the relatively easy victory
of totalitarianism in Germany was the void left by decay of former theological beliefs. Those who had lost one external authority upon which they had
depended were ready to turn to another one which was closer and more
tangible.   (34)

To say that the issue is a moral one is to say that in the end it comes
back to personal choice and action. From one point of view everything
which has been said is a laboring of the commonplace that democratic
government is a function of public opinion and public sentiment. But identification of its formation in the democratic direction with democratic
extension of the scientific morale till it is part of the ordinary equipment of
the ordinary individual indicates the issue is a moral one. It is individual
persons who need to have this attitude substituted for pride and prejudice,
for class and personal interest, for beliefs made dear by custom and early
emotional associations. It is only by the choice and the active endeavor
of many individuals that this result can be effected.   (35)

A former president of the United States once made a political stir by
saying that "Public office is a public trust." The saying was a truism although one that needed emphasis. That possession of knowledge and
special skill in intellectual methods is a public trust has not become a
truism even in words. Scientific morale has developed in some persons to a
point where it is a matter of course that what is found out is communicated
to other persons who are also engaged in specialized research. But it has
not developed to the point where wider responsibility for communication is
acknowledged. Circumstances which have attended the historic growth of
modern science explain why this is so, although they do not justify its
continuance. Internal and external circumstances have brought about a
social seclusion of science which from a certain standpoint is analogous to
an earlier monastic seclusion.   (36)

The external circumstance was the opposition scientific men had to
overcome before it was possible for them to carry on their work free from
dictation or persecution. The internal circumstance was in part the need for
extreme specialization of inquiries which necessarily accompanied the novelty of the new method; in part, it was a self-protective policy for maintaining the purity of a new, still immature and struggling attitude from
contamination that proceeded from taking sides in practical affairs. This
attitude had the blessing of the old and ingrained tradition of the "purity"
of science as an exclusively theoretical subject; a subject aloof from practice, since reason and theory were so high above practice, which was,
according to tradition, only material and utilitarian. The danger of loss of
the impartiality of the scientific spirit through affiliation with some partisan
and partial interest seemed to give significance to the established tradition
about "purity," which, like traditional feminine chastity, needed all kinds of

external safeguards to hedge it about. The need is not that scientific men become crusaders in special practical causes. Just as the problem with art is to unite the inherent integrity of the artist with imaginative and emotional appeal of ideas, so the present need is recognition by scientific men of social responsibility for contagious diffusion of the scientific attitude: a task not to be accomplished without abandoning once for all the belief that science is set apart from all other social interests as if possessed of a peculiar holiness.   (37)

Extension of the qualities that make up the scientific attitude is quite a different matter than dissemination of the results of physics, chemistry, biology and astronomy, valuable as the latter may be. The difference is the reason why the issue is a moral one. The question of whether science is capable of influencing the formation of ends for which men strive or is limited to increasing power of realizing those which are formed independently of it is the question whether science has intrinsic moral potentiality. Historically, the position that science is devoid of moral quality has been held by theologians and their metaphysical allies. For the position points unmistakably to the necessity for recourse to some other source of moral guidance. That a similar position is now taken in the name of science is either a sign of a confusion that permeates all aspects of culture, or is an omen of ill for democracy. If control of conduct amounts to conflict of desires with no possibility of determination of desire and purpose by scientifically warranted beliefs, then the practical alternative is competition and conflict between unintelligent forces for control of desire. The conclusion is so extreme as to suggest that denial in the name of science of the existence of any such things as moral facts may mark a transitional stage thoughtlessly taken to be final. It is quite true that science cannot affect moral values, ends, rules, principles as these were once thought of and believed in, namely, prior to the rise of science. But to say that there are no such things as moral facts because desires control formation and valuation of ends is in truth but to point to desires and interests as themselves moral facts requiring control by intelligence equipped with knowledge. Science through its physical technological consequences is now determining the relations which human beings, severally and in groups, sustain to one another. If it is incapable of developing moral techniques which will also determine these relations, the split in modern culture goes so deep that not only democracy but all civilized values are doomed. Such at least is the problem. A culture which permits science to destroy traditional values but which distrusts its power to create new ones is a culture which is destroying itself. War is a symptom as well as a cause of the inner division.   (38)

Sir Arthur Stanley Eddington

(1882–1944)

A. S. EDDINGTON was a professor of astronomy at Cambridge University from 1913 on. His reputation was many-dimensional, stemming principally from three qualities: he carried further than any predecessor the theoretical investigation of the interior of stars; he was among the first, along with Bertrand Russell and Alfred North Whitehead, to appreciate the significance of Albert Einstein's theories of relativity; he belonged to that honored British tradition of scientists who considered it important to interpret scientific developments for the layman. The Expanding Universe is a notable result of such an effort.

◼ *Man's Place in the Universe*

THE SIDEREAL UNIVERSE. The largest telescopes reveal about a thousand million stars. Each increase in telescopic power adds to the number and we can scarcely set a limit to the multitude that must exist. Nevertheless there are signs of exhaustion, and it is clear that the distribution which surrounds us does not exist uniformly through infinite space. At first an increase in light-grasp by one magnitude brings into view three times as many stars; but the factor diminishes so that at the limit of faintness reached by the giant telescopes a gain of one magnitude multiplies the number of stars seen by only 1·8, and the ratio at that stage is rapidly decreasing. It is as though we were approaching a limit at which increase of power will not bring into view very many additional stars.   (1)

Attempts have been made to find the whole number of stars by a risky extrapolation of these counts, and totals ranging from 3,000 to 30,000 millions are sometimes quoted. But the difficulty is that the part of the stellar universe which we mainly survey is a local condensation or star-cloud forming part of a much greater system. In certain directions in the sky our telescopes penetrate to the limits of the system, but in other directions the extent is too great for us to fathom. The Milky Way, which on a dark night forms a gleaming belt round the sky, shows the direction in which there lie stars behind stars until vision fails. This great flattened distribution is called the Galactic System. It forms a disk of thickness small compared to its areal extent. It is partly broken up into subordinate condensations, which are probably coiled in spiral form like the spiral nebulae which are observed in great numbers in the heavens. The centre of the galactic system lies somewhere in the direction of the constellation Sagittarius; it is hidden from us not only by great distance but also to some extent by tracts of obscuring matter (dark nebulosity) which cuts off the light of the stars behind.   (2)

We must distinguish then between our local star-cloud and the great galactic system of which it is a part. Mainly (but not exclusively) the star-counts relate to the local star-cloud, and it is this which the largest telescopes are beginning to exhaust. It too has a flattened form—flattened nearly in the same plane as the galactic system. If the galactic system is compared to a disk, the local star-cloud may be compared to a bun, its thickness being about one-third of its lateral extension. Its size is such that light takes at least 2,000 years to cross from one side to the other; this measurement is necessarily rough because it relates to a vague condensation which is probably not sharply separated from other contiguous condensations. The extent of the whole spiral is of the order 100,000 light-years. It can scarcely be doubted that the flattened form of the system is due to rapid rotation, and indeed there is direct evidence of strong rotational velocity; but it is one of the unexplained mysteries of evolution that nearly all celestial bodies have come to be endowed with fast rotation. (3)

Amid this great population the sun is a humble unit. It is a very ordinary star about midway in the scale of brilliancy. We know of stars which give at least 10,000 times the light of the sun; we know also of stars which give 1/10,000 of its light. But those of inferior light greatly outnumber those of superior light. In mass, in surface temperature, in bulk, the sun belongs to a very common class of stars; its speed of motion is near the average; it shows none of the more conspicuous phenomena such as variability which excite the attention of astronomers. In the community of stars the sun corresponds to a respectable middle-class citizen. It happens to be quite near the centre of the local star-cloud; but this apparently favoured position is discounted by the fact that the star-cloud itself is placed very eccentrically in relation to the galactic system, being in fact near the confines of it. We cannot claim to be at the hub of the universe.   (4)

The contemplation of the galaxy impresses us with the insignificance of our own little world; but we have to go still lower in the valley of humiliation. The galactic system is one among a million or more spiral nebulae. There seems now to be no doubt that, as has long been suspected, the spiral nebulae are 'island universes' detached from our own. They too are great systems of stars—or systems in the process of developing into stars—built on the same disk-like plan. We see some of them edgeways and can appreciate the flatness of the disk; others are broadside on and show the arrangement of the condensations in the form of a double spiral. Many show the effects of dark nebulosity breaking into the regularity and blotting out the starlight. In a few of the nearest spirals it is possible to detect the brightest of the stars individually; variable stars and novae (or 'new stars') are observed as in our own system. From the apparent magnitudes of the stars of recognizable character (especially the Cepheid variables) it is possible to judge the distance. The nearest spiral nebula is 850,000 light-years away.   (5)

From the small amount of data yet collected it would seem that our own nebula or galactic system is exceptionally large; it is even suggested that if the spiral nebulae are 'islands' the galactic system is a 'continent.' But we can scarcely venture to claim premier rank without much stronger evidence. At all events these other universes are aggregations of the order of 100 million stars.   (6)

Again the question raises itself, How far does this distribution extend? Not the stars this time but universes stretch one behind the other beyond sight. Does this distribution too come to an end? It may be that imagination must take another leap, envisaging supersystems which surpass the spiral nebulae as the spiral nebulae surpass the stars. But there is one feeble gleam of evidence that perhaps this time the summit of the hierarchy has been reached, and that the system of the spirals is actually the whole world. As has already been explained the modern view is that space is finite—finite though unbounded. In such a space light which has travelled an appreciable part of the way 'round the world' is slowed down in its vibrations, with the result that all spectral lines are displaced towards the red. Ordinarily we interpret such a red displacement as signifying receding velocity in the line of sight. Now it is a striking fact that a great majority of the spirals which have been measured show large receding velocities often exceeding 1,000 kilometres per second. There are only two serious exceptions, and these are the largest spirals which must be nearer to us than most of the others. On ordinary grounds it would be difficult to explain why these other universes should hurry away from us so fast and so unanimously. Why should they shun us like a plague? But the phenomenon is intelligible if what has really been observed is the slowing down of vibrations consequent on the light from these objects having travelled an appreciable part of the way round the world. On that theory the radius of space is of the order twenty times the average distance of the nebulae observed, or say 100 million light-years.

That leaves room for a few million spirals; but there is nothing beyond. There is no beyond—in spherical space 'beyond' brings us back towards the earth from the opposite direction.[1]   (7)

THE SCALE OF TIME. The corridor of time stretches back through the past. We can have no conception how it all began. But at some stage we imagine the void to have been filled with matter rarefied beyond the most tenuous nebula. The atoms sparsely strewn move hither and thither in formless disorder.

> Behold the throne
> Of Chaos and his dark pavilion spread
> Wide on the wasteful deep.

Then slowly the power of gravitation is felt. Centres of condensation begin to establish themselves and draw in other matter. The first partitions are the star-systems such as our galactic system; sub-condensations separate the star-clouds or clusters; these divide again to give the stars.   (8)

Evolution has not reached the same development in all parts. We observe nebulae and clusters in different stages of advance. Some stars are still highly diffuse; others are concentrated like the sun with density greater than water; others, still more advanced, have shrunk to unimaginable density. But no doubt can be entertained that the genesis of the stars is a single process of evolution which has passed and is passing over a primordial distribution. Formerly it was freely speculated that the birth of a star was an individual event like the birth of an animal. From time to time two long extinct stars would collide and be turned into vapour by the energy of the collision; condensation would follow and life as a luminous body would begin all over again. We can scarcely affirm that this will never occur and that the sun is not destined to have a second or third innings; but it is clear from the various relations traced among the stars that the present stage of existence of the sidereal universe is the *first innings*. Groups of stars are found which move across the sky with common proper motion; these must have had a single origin and cannot have been formed by casual collisions. Another abandoned speculation is that lucid stars may be the exception, and that there may exist thousands of dead stars for every one that is seen shining. There are ways of estimating the total mass in interstellar space by its gravitational effect on the average speed of the stars; it is found that the lucid stars account for something approaching the total mass admissible and the amount left over for dark stars is very limited. (9)

---

1 A very much larger radius of space (10^{11} light-years) has recently been proposed by Hubble; but the basis of his calculation, though concerned with spiral nebulae, is different and to my mind unacceptable. It rests on an earlier theory of closed space proposed by Einstein which has generally been regarded as superseded. The theory given above (due to W. de Sitter) is, of course, very speculative, but it is the only clue we possess as to the dimensions of space.

Biologists and geologists carry back the history of the earth some thousand million years. Physical evidence based on the rate of transmutation of radioactive substances seems to leave no escape from the conclusion that the older (Archaean) rocks in the earth's crust were laid down 1,200 million years ago. The sun must have been burning still longer, living (we now think) on its own matter which dissolves bit by bit into radiation. According to the theoretical time-scale, which seems best supported by astronomical evidence, the beginning of the sun as a luminous star must be dated five billion ($5 \cdot 10^{12}$) years ago. The theory which assigns this date cannot be trusted confidently, but it seems a reasonably safe conclusion that the sun's age does not exceed this limit. The future is not so restricted and the sun may continue as a star of increasing feebleness for 50 or 500 billion years. The theory of sub-atomic energy has prolonged the life of a star from millions to billions of years, and we may speculate on processes of rejuvenescence which might prolong the existence of the sidereal universe from billions to trillions of years. But unless we can circumvent the second law of thermodynamics—which is as much as to say unless we can find cause for time to run backwards—the ultimate decay draws surely nearer and the world will at the last come to a state of uniform changelessness. (10)

Does this prodigality of matter, of space, of time, find its culmination in Man? (11)

PLURALITY OF WORLDS. I will here put together the present astronomical evidence as to the habitability of other worlds. The popular idea that an answer to this question is one of the main aims of the study of celestial objects is rather disconcerting to the astronomer. Anything that he has to contribute is of the nature of fragmentary hints picked up in the course of investigations with more practicable and commonplace purposes. Nevertheless, the mind is irresistibly drawn to play with the thought that somewhere in the universe there may be other beings 'a little lower than the angels' whom Man may regard as his equals—or perhaps his superiors. (12)

It is idle to guess the forms that life might take in conditions differing from those of our planet. If I have rightly understood the view of palaeontologists, mammalian life is the third terrestrial dynasty—Nature's third attempt to evolve an order of life sufficiently flexible to changing conditions and fitted to dominate the earth. Minor details in the balance of circumstances must greatly affect the possibility of life and the type of organism destined to prevail. Some critical branch-point in the course of evolution must be negotiated before life can rise to the level of consciousness. All this is remote from the astronomer's line of study. To avoid endless conjecture I shall assume that the required conditions of habitability are not unlike those on the earth, and that if such conditions obtain life will automatically make its appearance. (13)

We survey first the planets of the solar system; of these only Venus and

Mars seem at all eligible. Venus, so far as we know, would be well adapted for life similar to ours. It is about the same size as the earth, nearer the sun but probably not warmer, and it possesses an atmosphere of satisfactory density. Spectroscopic observation has unexpectedly failed to give any indication of oxygen in the upper atmosphere and thus suggests a doubt as to whether free oxygen exists on the planet; but at present we hesitate to draw so definite an inference. If transplanted to Venus we might perhaps continue to live without much derangement of habit—except that I personally would have to find a new profession, since Venus is not a good place for astronomers. It is completely covered with cloud or mist. For this reason no definite surface markings can be made out, and it is still uncertain how fast it rotates on its axis and in which direction the axis lies. One curious theory may be mentioned though it should perhaps not be taken too seriously. It is thought by some that the great cavity occupied by the Pacific Ocean is a scar left by the moon when it was first disrupted from the earth. Evidently this cavity fulfills an important function in draining away superfluous water, and if it were filled up practically all the continental area would be submerged. Thus indirectly the existence of dry land is bound up with the existence of the moon. But Venus has no moon, and since it seems to be similar to the earth in other respects, it may perhaps be inferred that it is a world which is all ocean—where fishes are supreme. The suggestion at any rate serves to remind us that the destinies of organic life may be determined by what are at first sight irrelevant accidents. (14)

The sun is an ordinary star and the earth is an ordinary planet, but the moon is not an ordinary satellite. No other known satellite is anything like so large in proportion to the planet which it attends. The moon contains about $\frac{1}{80}$ part of the mass of the earth, which seems a small ratio; but it is abnormally great compared with other satellites. The next highest ratio is found in the system of Saturn whose largest satellite Titan has 1/4,000 of the planet's mass. Very special circumstances must have occurred in the history of the earth to have led to the breaking away of so unusual a fraction of the mass. The explanation proposed by Sir George Darwin, which is still regarded as most probable, is that a resonance in period occurred between the solar tides and the natural free period of vibration of the globe of the earth. The tidal deformation of the earth thus grew to large amplitude, ending in a cataclysm which separated the great lump of material that formed the moon. Other planets escaped this dangerous coincidence of period, and their satellites separated by more normal development. If ever I meet a being who has lived in another world, I shall feel very humble in most respects, but I expect to be able to boast a little about the moon. (15)

Mars is the only planet whose solid surface can be seen and studied; and it tempts us to consider the possibility of life in more detail. Its smaller size leads to considerably different conditions; but the two essentials, air and water, are both present though scanty. The Martian atmosphere is thinner than our own but it is perhaps adequate. It has been proved to contain oxygen. There is no ocean; the surface markings represent, not sea and land, but red desert and darker ground which is perhaps moist and fertile. A conspicuous feature is the white cap covering the pole which is clearly a deposit of snow; it must be quite shallow since it melts away completely in the summer. Photographs show from time to time indubitable clouds which blot out temporarily large areas of surface detail; clear weather, however, is more usual. The air, if cloudless, is slightly hazy. W. H. Wright has shown this very convincingly by comparing photographs taken with light of different wave-lengths. Light of short wave-length is much scattered by haze and accordingly the ordinary photographs are disappointingly blurry. Much sharper surface-detail is shown when visual yellow light is employed (a yellow screen being commonly used to adapt visual telescopes for photography); being of longer wave-length the visual rays penetrate the haze more easily.[2] Still clearer detail is obtained by photographing with the long infra-red waves.   (16)

Great attention has lately been paid to the determination of the temperature of the surface of Mars; it is possible to find this by direct measurement of the heat radiated to us from different parts of the surface. The results, though in many respects informative, are scarcely accurate and accordant enough to give a definite idea of the climatology. Naturally the temperature varies a great deal between day and night and in different latitudes; but on the average the conditions are decidedly chilly. Even at the equator the temperature falls below freezing-point at sunset. If we accepted the present determinations as definitive we should have some doubt as to whether life could endure the conditions.   (17)

In one of Huxley's Essays there occurs the passage: 'Until human life is longer and the duties of the present press less heavily I do not think that wise men will occupy themselves with Jovian or Martian natural history.' To-day it would seem that Martian natural history is not altogether beyond the limits of serious science. At least the surface of Mars shows a seasonal change such as we might well imagine the forest-clad earth would show to an outside onlooker. This seasonal change of appearance is very conspicuous to the attentive observer. As the spring in one hemisphere advances (I mean, of course, the Martian spring), the darker areas, which are at first few and faint, extend and deepen in contrast. The same regions darken year after year at nearly the same date in the Martian calendar. It may be that there is an inorganic explanation; the spring rains moisten the surface and change its colour. But it is perhaps unlikely that there is enough

---

[2] It seems to have been a fortunate circumstance that the pioneers of Martian photography had no suitable photographic telescopes and had to adapt visual telescopes—thus employing visual (yellow) light which, as it turned out, was essential for good results.

rain to bring about this change as a direct effect. It is easier to believe that we are witnessing the annual awakening of vegetation so familiar on our own planet.   (18)

The existence of oxygen in the Martian atmosphere supplies another argument in support of the existence of vegetable life. Oxygen combines freely with many elements, and the rocks in the earth's crust are thirsty for oxygen. They would in course of time bring about its complete disappearance from the air, were it not that the vegetation extracts it from the soil and sets it free again. If oxygen in the terrestrial atmosphere is maintained in this way, it would seem reasonable to assume that vegetable life is required to play the same part on Mars. Taking this in conjunction with the evidence of the seasonal changes of appearance, a rather strong case for the existence of vegetation seems to have been made out.   (19)

If vegetable life must be admitted, can we exclude animal life? I have come to the end of the astronomical data and can take no responsibility for anything further that you may infer. It is true that the late Prof. Lowell argued that certain more or less straight markings on the planet represent an artificial irrigation system and are the signs of an advanced civilization; but this theory has not, I think, won much support. In justice to the author of this speculation it should be said that his own work and that of his observatory have made a magnificent contribution to our knowledge of Mars; but few would follow him all the way on the more picturesque side of his conclusions.[3] Finally we may stress one point. Mars has every appearance of being a planet long past its prime; and it is in any case improbable that two planets differing so much as Mars and the Earth would be in the zenith of biological development contemporaneously.   (20)

FORMATION OF PLANETARY SYSTEMS. If the planets of the solar system should fail us, there remain some thousands of millions of stars which we have been accustomed to regard as suns ruling attendant systems of planets. It has seemed a presumption, bordering almost on impiety, to deny to them life of the same order of creation as ourselves. It would indeed be rash to assume that nowhere else in the universe has Nature repeated the strange experiment which she has performed on the earth. But there are considerations which must hold us back from populating the universe too liberally.   (21)

On examining the stars with a telescope we are surprised to find how many of those which appear single points to the eye are actually two stars close together. When the telescope fails to separate them the spectroscope often reveals two stars in orbital revolution round each other. At least one

---

[3] Mars is not seen under favourable conditions except from low latitudes and high altitudes. Astronomers who have not these advantages are reluctant to form a decided opinion on the many controversial points that have arisen.

star in three is double—a pair of self-luminous globes both comparable in dimensions with the sun. The single supreme sun is accordingly not the only product of evolution; not much less frequently the development has taken another turn and resulted in two suns closely associated. We may probably rule out the possibility of planets in double stars. Not only is there a difficulty in ascribing to them permanent orbits under the more complicated field of gravitation, but a cause for the formation of planets seems to be lacking. The star has satisfied its impulse to fission in another manner; it has divided into two nearly equal portions instead of throwing off a succession of tiny fragments.   (22)

The most obvious cause of division is excessive rotation. As the gaseous globe contracts it spins faster and faster until a time may come when it can no longer hold together, and some kind of relief must be found. According to the nebular hypothesis of Laplace the sun gained relief by throwing off successively rings of matter which have formed the planets. But were it not for this one instance of a planetary system which is known to us, we should have concluded from the thousands of double stars in the sky that the common consequence of excessive rotation is to divide the star into two bodies of equal rank.   (23)

It might still be held that the ejection of a planetary system and the fission into a double star are alternative solutions of the problem arising from excessive rotation, the star taking one course or the other according to circumstances. We know of myriads of double stars and of only one planetary system; but in any case it is beyond our power to detect other planetary systems if they exist. We can only appeal to the results of theoretical study of rotating masses of gas; the work presents many complications and the results may not be final; but the researches of Sir J. H. Jeans lead to the conclusion that rotational break-up produces a double star and never a system of planets. The solar system is not the typical product of development of a star; it is not even a common variety of development; it is a freak.   (24)

By elimination of alternatives it appears that a configuration resembling the solar system would only be formed if at a certain stage of condensation an unusual accident had occurred. According to Jeans the accident was the close approach of another star casually pursuing its way through space. This star must have passed within a distance not far outside the orbit of Neptune; it must not have passed too rapidly, but have slowly overtaken or been overtaken by the sun. By tidal distortion it raised big protuberances on the sun, and caused it to spurt out filaments of matter which have condensed to form the planets. That was more than a thousand million years ago. The intruding star has since gone on its way and mingled with the others; its legacy of a system of planets remains, including a globe habitable by man.   (25)

Even in the long life of a star encounters of this kind must be extremely rare. The density of distribution of stars in space has been compared to that of twenty tennis balls roaming the whole interior of the earth. The accident that gave birth to the solar system may be compared to the casual approach of two of these balls within a few yards of one another. The data are too vague to give any definite estimate of the odds against this occurrence, but I should judge that perhaps not one in a hundred millions of stars can have undergone this experience in the right stage and conditions to result in the formation of a system of planets.   (26)

However doubtful this conclusion as to the rarity of solar systems may be, it is a useful corrective to the view too facilely adopted which looks upon every star as a likely minister to life. We know the prodigality of Nature. How many acorns are scattered for one that grows to an oak? And need she be more careful of her stars than of her acorns? If indeed she has no grander aim than to provide a home for her greatest experiment, Man, it would be just like her methods to scatter a million stars whereof one might haply achieve her purpose.   (27)

The number of possible abodes of life severely restricted in this way at the outset may no doubt be winnowed down further. On our house-hunting expedition we shall find it necessary to reject many apparently eligible mansions on points of detail. Trivial circumstances may decide whether organic forms originate at all; further conditions may decide whether life ascends to a complexity like ours or remains in a lower form. I presume, however, that at the end of the weeding out there will be left a few rival earths dotted here and there about the universe.   (28)

A further point arises if we have especially in mind contemporaneous life. The time during which man has been on the earth is extremely small compared with the age of the earth or of the sun. There is no obvious physical reason why, having once arrived, man should not continue to populate the earth for another ten billion years or so; but—well, can you contemplate it? Assuming that the stage of highly developed life is a very small fraction of the inorganic history of the star, the rival earths are in general places where conscious life has already vanished or is yet to come. I do not think that the whole purpose of the Creation has been staked on the one planet where we live; and in the long run we cannot deem ourselves the only race that has been or will be gifted with the mystery of consciousness. But I feel inclined to claim that *at the present time* our race is supreme; and not one of the profusion of stars in their myriad clusters looks down on scenes comparable to those which are passing beneath the rays of the sun.   (29)

Isaac Asimov

(1920–   )

ASIMOV was credited as follows by the editorial staff of Harper's Magazine *when they prepared this article for publication:* "Isaac Asimov, who is
associate professor of biochemistry at the Boston University Medical School,
is famous as a writer of scientific popularizations, with 78 books to his
credit. The most recent is "The Universe" (Walker, 1966); the next—"Is Anyone There?"— includes this article and will be published in June by Doubleday."

◼ *Over the Edge of the Universe*

IT ISN'T OFTEN that a scientist can make the front pages by giving up a
theory, but Fred Hoyle, the English astronomer, managed to do so in the
fall of 1965. He gave up on "continuous creation" because of objects fifty
billion trillion miles away in space and ten billion years ago in time.   (1)

It was necessary to go that far from the here and now to settle the most
grandiose clash of theories in all the history of science. Those theories involve nothing less than the birth (or non-birth) and death (or non-death)
of the universe. The dispute began a half-century ago, when astronomers
still knew very little about the universe outside our own Milky Way galaxy
—a lens-shaped conglomeration of 130 billion stars 100,000 light-years
across (a light-year is roughly six trillion miles in length). Here and there
in the sky one could glimpse small patches of cloudy light which, some
astronomers suspected even then, might be other conglomerations of stars,
other galaxies. These might be millions of light-years away.   (2)

The light from these galaxies, or from any glowing heavenly object, can
be gathered by means of telescopes, then spread out into a faint rainbow
(or "spectrum") crossed by a number of dark lines. Each dark line is pro-

duced by a particular chemical element and has a particular place in the spectrum, *if* the light source is stationary with respect to the earth. If the light source is receding from us, those lines would all be shifted toward the red end of the spectrum; the greater the velocity of recession, the greater the extent of this "red-shift." If the light source is approaching us, the lines would shift toward the opposite, or violet, end of the spectrum in a "violet-shift." (3)

In 1912, the American astronomer, Vesto Melvin Slipher, began to collect light from the various galaxies in order to measure the nature and extent of the shift of the dark lines. He fully expected to find that roughly half would show a red-shift and half a violet-shift; that half were receding from us and half approaching us. (4)

That proved not to be the case. To Slipher's surprise, only a few of the very nearest galaxies showed a violet-shift. The others all showed a red-shift. By 1917, he had found two galaxies which were approaching us, and thirteen that were receding. What's more, the size of the red-shift was unusually great. Individual stars within our own galaxy showed red-shifts that indicated recessions of less than a hundred miles a second, but Slipher was detecting galactic recessions of up to 400 miles a second, judging by the amount of the red-shift. (5)

Another American astronomer, Milton La Salle Humason, began exposing photographic film, night after night, to the light of very faint galaxies, allowing the feeble rays to accumulate to the point where a detectable spectrum would be imprinted upon the film. In this way he could measure the motions of particularly distant galaxies. *All* the faint galaxies showed a red-shift, with never an exception. And the fainter (and, presumably, more distant) they were, the greater the red-shift. By 1936, he was clocking velocities of recession of 25,000 miles per second, better than one-eighth the speed of light. (6)

In the late 1920s, the American astronomer, Edwin Powell Hubble, had generalized this phenomenon, evolving what is now called "Hubble's Law." This states that the distant galaxies recede from us at a rate proportional to their distance from us. According to present notions, this steadily increasing velocity of recession reaches a value equal to the velocity of light at a distance of about 13 billion light-years from the earth. If a galaxy recedes from us at the velocity of light, the light it emits in our direction can never reach us. This means that nothing we do, no instrument we can possibly use, can detect that galaxy. We could not see its light, receive subatomic particles from it, or even detect its gravitational field. (7)

The distance of 13 billion light-years represents, then, the edge of the "observable universe." Whether or not there is anything farther is of no moment, for nothing farther can impinge on us or affect us in any way.

Our universe, then, is a gigantic sphere of space, pockmarked with galaxies, with ourselves at the center and with its edge 13 billion light-years away in every direction.   (8)

WHEN THE EGG EXPLODED

It seems odd that we should happen to be at the center of the universe and that the galaxies should all be racing away from us. What is so special about *us*? The answer is: Nothing, of course. If there seems to be something special, it can only be an illusion.   (9)

Einstein's general theory of relativity, advanced in 1916, can be made to fit the view that the universe is expanding. As it expands, the galaxies within it find themselves scattered through a constantly enlarging volume of space. Each one finds itself farther and farther from its neighbors. In such a universe, it would seem to an observer on *any* galaxy that all the other galaxies were receding from him (except for one or two very near ones that might be part of a common cluster). What's more, it would seem to an observer on *any* galaxy in an expanding universe, that other galaxies receded at a rate proportional to distance. Indeed, the general appearance of the universe would remain the same regardless of the position in space from which it is viewed. This is called the "cosmological principle"— "cosmology" being the branch of science that studies the general properties of the universe as a whole.   (10)

This expansion may simply be an intrinsic property of space, but in 1927 a Belgian astronomer, Georges Edouard Lemaître, advanced a physical explanation. The universe might be expanding because it was showing the effects of a colossal explosion that had taken place billions of years before. Originally, Lemaître suggested, all the matter of the universe had been collected into one solid, very dense mass of material. This "cosmic egg" exploded in the vastest imaginable cataclysm and broke into pieces that eventually evolved into the present arrangement of galaxies. The galaxies are still separating from each other following that original explosion and thus create what seems to be an expanding universe.   (11)

Others have taken up this view since 1927 and have worked out its consequences in great detail. Perhaps the most vocal proponent of this "big bang" theory (as it is popularly called) is the Russian-American physicist, George Gamow. This theory envisages a universe that changes drastically with time. At first (about 10 to 15 billion years ago, astronomers now estimate) the universe was just a globe of superdense matter. Then it became an exploding mass of very hot fragments, very close together. With time, the fragments cooled off, spread apart, evolved into stars and galaxies, and continued to spread apart. Now the fragments are millions of light-years apart and as time goes on they will become even farther apart.   (12)

THE RIDDLE OF TIME

The "big bang" theory with its necessary view of a universe that changed with time, did not satisfy all astronomers. To three of them in England—Hermann Bondi, Thomas Gold, and Fred Hoyle—it seemed, in 1948, that the cosmological principle (by which the universe was assumed to appear generally the same to all observers) was incomplete if it referred only to observers at different places in space. They extended the notion to observers at different moments in time and called the result the "perfect cosmological principle." By this extended view, the universe as a whole did not change with time, but remained essentially the same in appearance throughout the eons. (13)

But the universe *was* expanding, they admitted. The galaxies *were* drawing farther apart. To save their extended principle, Bondi, Gold, and Hoyle suggested that as the universe expanded, and as the galaxies moved farther apart, new matter was being continually created everywhere at a rate so slow as to be indetectable by our most delicate instruments. By the time two galaxies had doubled the distance between themselves as a result of the expansion of space, enough matter had been created between them, even at this exceedingly slow rate, to conglomerate into a new galaxy. (14)

In this way, although the universe expanded forever, the distances between neighboring galaxies remained always the same, for new galaxies formed within the sphere of the observable universe as fast as old ones moved outward beyond its limits. The appearance of the universe as a whole remained the same then through all the eternal past and into all the eternal future. (15)

Each view—the "big bang" and "continuous creation"—has its separate beauty and each has its proponents, led by George Gamow and Fred Hoyle, respectively. Even among nonastronomers, emotional attachments were formed. Some people found themselves attracted to the colossal super-spectacle of a huge "let-there-be-light" explosion, while others found an austere glory in the thought of a universe without beginning and without ending, a universe that changed continually and yet remained always in the same place. (16)

But which theory, if either, is correct? Is there no way to choose between them? The choice might be easy if only astronomers had a time machine. All one would have to do would be to get into the time machine and move ten billion years into the past (or into the future) and take a quick look at the universe. If it looks just about the same as today, then the "big bang" cannot be right and "continuous creation" will seem plausible. If, on the other hand, the universe looks radically different from what it is today, then "continuous creation" can't be right and "big bang" will hold the field. (17)

COLLIDING GALAXIES

Oddly enough, astronomers *do* have a time machine, after a fashion. Light (or any other form of radiation) cannot travel faster than 186,282 miles per second. This is fast, on the terrestrial scale, but it is a mere creep in the universe as a whole. Light from the most distant galaxies we can see takes a billion years or more to reach us. This means that when we look at the very distant galaxies we are seeing the universe as it was a billion years ago or more.   (18)

All we have to decide, then, is whether what we see far, far away is essentially the same as what we see in our own neighborhood. If the very distant galaxies are just like the nearer ones and show no change, then we can forget about the "big bang" (which postulates change). If the very distant galaxies are quite different from those in our own neighborhood, indicating a clear change with time, we can forget about "continuous creation" (which postulates no change).   (19)

But it is very difficult to see things at the billion-light-year mark and beyond. All we can make out, at best, seem to be tiny patches of foggy light. If there are significant differences in the fine structure of those distant galaxies as compared to our own, we are almost bound to miss them. In order for a difference to be detectable across billions of light-years of space, it would have to be a huge and very general difference. Through 1950, nothing of the sort had been detected.   (20)

In the meantime, however, a new kind of tool had been developed for peering into the ultimate depths of space. It had its origins in the work of an American radio engineer, Karl Jansky, who was engaged in 1931 in the nonastronomic problem of countering the disruptive effects of static in radio communication. There was one source of static which he could not at first pin down and which, he finally decided, had to come from outer space.   (21)

His announcement made no splash at the time. For one thing, it seemed interesting but impractical. The radio waves from outer space were very short, and devices for detecting feeble beams of such radiation had not yet been developed. Radar apparatus, however, involved the detection of just such radiation, and by the time World War II was over the effort to make radar practical had resulted in new abilities to deal with short-wave radio from outer space. In this way radio astronomy was born and huge receiving devices (radio telescopes) were turned on the heavens.   (22)

Radio waves were detected from the sun and from a few cloudy objects which seem to have been the remnants of stars that had once exploded in a ferocious manner. Radio waves were even detected from the central core of our own galaxy, a core that is hidden from sight (as far as ordinary light is concerned) by the existence between it and the earth of vast clouds of light-absorbing dust.   (23)

By 1950, over a thousand separate sources of radio-wave emissions had been marked out in the sky, but only a very few of them had been pinned down to something visible. The trouble was that even short radio waves are much longer than ordinary light waves; and the longer the waves, the fuzzier the "vision." Trying to find the exact source of a faint beam of radio waves was rather like trying to spot the exact source of a light beam viewed through frosted glass. All you see is a smear of radiation.   (24)

Nevertheless, a particularly powerful source of radio-wave radiation (called "Cygnus A") had, with patience and perseverance, been boxed down to a very small area by 1951. Within that area, the German-American astronomer, Walter Baade, noted a peculiarly shaped galaxy. On closer study, it seemed to be not one, but two galaxies; the two being in collision. The source of that particular beam of radio waves apparently was a pair of colliding galaxies 700 million light-years away. For the first time, it became clear that radio waves could be detected at enormous distances. Indeed, radio galaxies which emitted radio waves as powerfully as Cygnus A did could be easily detected at distances so vast that their light would be indetectable by even our most powerful ordinary telescopes. The knowledge that radio telescopes could reach back in time over an unprecedented number of eons opened up exciting possibilities for astronomers. It might be that virtually all the radio wave sources were far-distant galaxies which emitted radio waves in enormous concentration because they were colliding or exploding or undergoing some other huge catastrophe. To be sure only a very small percentage of galaxies were likely to be involved in such catastrophes. But the universe contains many billions of galaxies and a few thousand could be "radio galaxies."   (25)

It seemed reasonable to suppose that the feebler the radio-wave source, the more distant the galaxy it represented. In that case, it would be possible to count the number of such sources at various distances. If the "continuous creation" theory is correct, then the universe is always generally the same throughout time and there ought to be the same number of catastrophes taking place at all times. In that case, the number of radio sources for a given volume of space ought to remain at a steady value with increasing distance. If, on the other hand, the "big bang" theory is correct, the youthful universe one detects at great distances must have been much hotter and more crowded than our present universe. In such a youthful universe catastrophes might reasonably be expected to be more common than in our own. Therefore, the number of radio sources for a given volume of space ought to increase with distance.   (26)

In the mid-1950s, the English astronomer, Martin Ryle, undertook a careful count of the radio sources and announced that the number of sources did, indeed, increase with distance as the "big bang" theory required. Ryle's work was not completely convincing, however. It rested upon the detection and measurement of very faint radio sources and even slight errors, which might easily have occurred, would suffice to wipe out completely the trend upon which Ryle had based his conclusion. The backers of "continuous creation" grimly clung, therefore, to their own view of the universe.   (27)

NEW KNOWLEDGE—NEW MYSTERIES

As astronomers continued to pin down radio-wave sources into narrower areas, several in particular attracted attention. These seemed to be so small that it was possible they might be individual stars rather than galaxies. If so, they could be quite close and Ryle's assumption that all radio sources were distant galaxies would be upset and with it his conclusion. "Continuous creation" would then gain a new lease on life.   (28)

Among the compact radio sources were several known as 3C48, 3C147, 3C196, 3C273, and 3C286. The "3C" is short for "Third Cambridge Catalogue of Radio Stars," a listing compiled by Ryle and his group, while the remaining numbers represent the placing of the source on that list. An intense effort was made to detect the stars that might be giving rise to these 3C sources. In America, Allan Sandage was carefully searching the suspected areas with the 200-inch telescope at Mount Palomar, ready to pounce on any suspicious-looking star. In Australia, Cyril Hazard kept his radio telescope focused on 3C273, while the moon bore down in its direction. As the moon moved in front of 3C273, the radio-wave beam was cut off. At the instant of cutoff, the edge of the moon was cutting across the exact location of the source.   (29)

By 1960, the stars had been found. They were not new discoveries at all; they had been recorded on previous photographic sweeps of the sky but had always been taken to be nothing more than faint members of our own galaxy. A new painstaking investigation, spurred by their unusual radio-wave emission, now showed, however, that they were not ordinary stars after all. Faint clouds of matter seemed to hover about a couple of them, and 3C273 showed signs of a tiny jet of something or other emerging from it.   (30)

What's more, their spectra, when obtained by two American astronomers, Jesse L. Greenstein and the Dutch-born Maarten Schmidt, proved to be most peculiar. The few lines that were present were in locations that couldn't be identified with any known element. It was a most puzzling mystery and was abandoned for a time. In 1963, Schmidt returned to the spectrum of 3C273. Six lines were present and it suddenly occurred to him that four of these were spaced in such a way as to resemble a well-known series of lines that should be in a far different part of the spectrum. In order for these four lines to be in the place they were actually observed, they would have had to have undergone a red-shift of unprecedented size. Could that be?   (31)

He turned to the other spectra. If he allowed very large red-shifts, he could identify every single one of the lines involved. Within the next two or three years, a concentrated search of the skies uncovered about forty of these objects altogether. The spectra of more than half were obtained and all showed enormous red-shifts. One, in fact, is receding at a record velocity of 150,000 miles per second and is estimated to be about eight billion light-years away (fifty billion trillion miles.) (32)

Such red-shifts would mean that these apparent "stars" are very distant, for according to the expanding-universe theory, a large red-shift is always associated with huge distances. In fact, these queer objects had to be farther away than any other known body in the universe. At such distances, what looked like stars certainly could not be stars. No ordinary star could possibly be seen at such huge distances. The objects were therefore called "quasi-stellar" ("star-like") radio sources, and quasi-stellar soon came to be shortened to "quasar." (33)

The quasars are a rich source of puzzlement for astronomers. If the red-shift is interpreted in the light of the expanding universe and if the quasars are indeed billions of light-years away, then they have unusual properties indeed. To appear as bright as they do at such enormous distances, they must be glowing with the luminosity of ten to a hundred galaxies. And yet there are many reasons for supposing that they are not very large in size. They may be only one to ten light-years in diameter rather than the 100,000-light-year span of an ordinary galaxy. (34)

What kind of body can it be that has its substance crowded into so tiny a fraction of a galactic volume and yet blazes with the light of dozens of galaxies? There are almost as many theories as there are astronomers—but as far as the fate of the "continuous creation" view of the universe is concerned, the theories don't matter. The mere fact that quasars exist might be enough. (35)

The key point is that there are many quasars far away and no quasars within a billion light-years of ourselves. This means that there were many quasars in the long-gone youthful universe and none now. The number of quasars (which may be the source of all or almost all the radio wave beams studied by Ryle) may increase with distance and, therefore, with the youthfulness of the universe. This means that we have detected one important change in the universe with advancing time—the number of quasars diminishes. That is enough to eliminate "continuous creation." (36)

It is enough, that is, *if*, indeed, the quasars are far, far distant objects. The belief that they are rests on the assumption that the gigantic red-shift they display is part of the expansion of the universe. But what if it isn't? (37)

Suppose that quasars are small portions of nearby galaxies, hurled outward by core-sized explosions. Examples of "exploding galaxies" have indeed been detected in recent years and astronomers are now carefully tracking down galaxies which for one reason or other—odd shapes, wisps of fogginess, signs of internal convulsion—look unusual. A few quasars have been detected not far from such "peculiar galaxies."   (38)

Is this coincidence? Do the quasars happen to be in the same line of sight as the peculiar galaxies? Or were they cast outward with monstrous velocities from those galaxies as a result of explosions involving millions of stars? If so, the quasars might not all be unusually far away from us, after all. Some might be close, some far, and their distribution might not force us to give up the "continuous creation" theory.   (39)

This is possible, but there are arguments against it. Suppose that quasars are objects hurled out of galaxies with such force as to be traveling at large fractions of the speed of light. Some of them would indeed be hurled away from us and would show a gigantic red-shift that would be misleading if it were interpreted as representing a recession caused by the general expansion of the universe rather than by a special explosion of a galaxy. A roughly equal number would, however, be hurled toward us and would be approaching us at large fractions of the speed of light. They would then show a gigantic violet-shift.   (40)

Then, too, some would be hurled neither toward us nor away from us, but more or less across our line of sight in a sideways direction. Such quasars would show only a small (if any) red-shift or violet-shift, but, considering how close they might be and how rapidly they might be moving, they would alter their positions in the sky by a slight but measurable amount over the couple of years they have been observed.   (41)

The fact is, however, that no quasars have been found that show a violet-shift, and none that alter position. Only red-shifts have been observed—gigantic red-shifts. To suppose that comparatively nearby explosions have cast out quasars in such a way as to produce red-shifts only is to ask too much of coincidence. So the weight of the evidence is in favor of the great distance of the quasars and against the "continuous creation" theory. That is why Fred Hoyle gave up.   (42)

WHAT ABOUT MAN'S FATE?

The elimination of "continuous creation" does not necessarily mean the establishment of the "big bang." Suppose there is some third possibility that is as yet unsuggested. To strengthen the "big bang" theory it would be useful to consider some phenomenon that the "big bang" theory could predict, some phenomenon that could then actually be observed.   (43)

Suppose, for instance, that the universe *did* begin as an incredibly dense cosmic egg that exploded. At the moment of explosion, it must have been tremendously hot—possibly as hot as 10 billion degrees Centigrade (which is equivalent to 18 billion degrees Fahrenheit.) Then if our instruments could penetrate far enough, to nearly the very edge of the observable universe, they might reach far enough back in time to catch a whiff of the radiation that accompanied the "big bang." At temperatures of billions of degrees, the radiation would be in the form of very energetic X-rays. However, the expanding universe would be carrying that source of X-rays away from us at nearly the speed of light. This incredible speed of recession would have the effect of vastly weakening the energy of the radiation; weakening it to the point where it would reach us in the form of radio waves with a certain group of properties. Through the 1960s, estimates of what those properties might be were advanced.   (44)

Then, early in 1966, a weak background of radio-wave radiation was detected in the skies; radiation that would just fit the type to be expected of the "big bang." This has been verified and it looks very much as though we have not only eliminated "continuous creation" but have actually detected the "big bang." If so, then we have lost something. In facing our own individual deaths, it was possible after all, even for those who lacked faith in an afterlife, to find consolation. Life itself would still go on. In a "continuous creation" universe, it was even possible to conceive of mankind as moving, when necessary, from an old galaxy to a young one and existing eventually through all infinity and for all eternity. It is a colossal, godlike vision, that might almost make individual death a matter of no consequence.   (45)

In the "big bang" scheme of things, however, our particular universe has a beginning—and an ending, too. Either it spreads out ever more thinly while *all* the galaxies grow old and the individual stars die, one by one. Or it reaches some maximum extent and then begins to collapse once more, returning after many eons to a momentary existence as a cosmic egg.
                    (46)

In either case, mankind, as we know it, must cease to exist and the dream of godhood must end. Death has now been rediscovered and Homo sapiens, as a species, like men as individuals, must learn to face the inevitable end.   (47)

—Or, if the universe oscillates, and if the cosmic egg is re-formed every hundred billion years or so, to explode once more; then, perhaps, in each of an infinite number of successive universes, a man-like intelligence (or a vast number of them) arises to wonder about the beginning and end of it all.   (48)

Rachel Carson

(1907–1964)

*RACHEL CARSON, scientist and writer, commanded both scientific and literary attention. Her books—*The Sea Around Us *(1951),* The Edge of the Sea *(1956), and* The Silent Spring *(1962)—excited wide popular interest. The last provoked much controversy.*

■ *And No Birds Sing*

OVER INCREASINGLY large areas of the United States, spring now comes unheralded by the return of the birds, and the early mornings are strangely silent where once they were filled with the beauty of bird song. This sudden silencing of the song of birds, this obliteration of the color and beauty and interest they lend to our world have come about swiftly, insidiously, and unnoticed by those whose communities are as yet unaffected. (1)

From the town of Hinsdale, Illinois, a housewife wrote in despair to one of the world's leading ornithologists, Robert Cushman Murphy, Curator Emeritus of Birds at the American Museum of Natural History.

> Here in our village the elm trees have been sprayed for several years [she wrote in 1958]. When we moved here six years ago, there was a wealth of bird life; I put up a feeder and had a steady stream of cardinals, chickadees, downies and nuthatches all winter, and the cardinals and chickadees brought their young ones in the summer.
>
> After several years of DDT spray, the town is almost devoid of robins and starlings; chickadees have not been on my shelf for

two years, and this year the cardinals are gone too; the nesting population in the neighborhood seems to consist of one dove pair and perhaps one catbird family.

It is hard to explain to the children that the birds have been killed off, when they have learned in school that a Federal law protects the birds from killing or capture. "Will they ever come back?" they ask, and I do not have the answer. The elms are still dying, and so are the birds. *Is* anything being done? *Can* anything be done? Can *I* do anything? (2)

A year after the federal government had launched a massive spraying program against the fire ant, an Alabama woman wrote: "Our place has been a veritable bird sanctuary for over half a century. Last July we all remarked, 'There are more birds than ever.' Then, suddenly, in the second week of August, they all disappeared. I was accustomed to rising early to care for my favorite mare that had a young filly. There was not a sound of the song of a bird. It was eerie, terrifying. What was man doing to our perfect and beautiful world? Finally, five months later a blue jay appeared and a wren." (3)

The autumn months to which she referred brought other somber reports from the deep South, where in Mississippi, Louisiana, and Alabama the *Field Notes* published quarterly by the National Audubon Society and the United States Fish and Wildlife Service noted the striking phenomenon of "blank spots weirdly empty of virtually *all* bird life." The *Field Notes* are a compilation of the reports of seasoned observers who have spent many years afield in their particular areas and have unparalleled knowledge of the normal bird life of the region. One such observer reported that in driving about southern Mississippi that fall she saw "no land birds at all for long distances." Another in Baton Rouge reported that the contents of her feeders had lain untouched "for weeks on end," while fruiting shrubs in her yard, that ordinarily would be stripped clean by that time, still were laden with berries. Still another reported that his picture window, "which often used to frame a scene splashed with the red of 40 or 50 cardinals and crowded with other species, seldom permitted a view of as many as a bird or two at a time." Professor Maurice Brooks of the University of West Virginia, an authority on the birds of the Appalachian region, reported that the West Virginia bird population had undergone "an incredible reduction." (4)

One story might serve as the tragic symbol of the fate of the birds—a fate that has already overtaken some species, and that threatens all. It is the story of the robin, the bird known to everyone. To millions of Americans, the season's first robin means that the grip of winter is broken. Its coming is an event reported in newspapers and told eagerly at the breakfast table.

And as the number of migrants grows and the first mists of green appear in the woodlands, thousands of people listen for the first dawn chorus of the robins throbbing in the early morning light. But now all is changed, and not even the return of the birds may be taken for granted.   (5)

The survival of the robin, and indeed of many other species as well, seems fatefully linked with the American elm, a tree that is part of the history of thousands of towns from the Atlantic to the Rockies, gracing their streets and their village squares and college campuses with majestic archways of green. Now the elms are stricken with a disease that afflicts them throughout their range, a disease so serious that many experts believe all efforts to save the elms will in the end be futile. It would be tragic to lose the elms, but it would be doubly tragic if, in vain efforts to save them, we plunge vast segments of our bird populations into the night of extinction. Yet this is precisely what is threatened.   (6)

The so-called Dutch elm disease entered the United States from Europe about 1930 in elm burl logs imported for the veneer industry. It is a fungus disease; the organism invades the water-conducting vessels of the tree, spreads by spores carried in the flow of sap, and by its poisonous secretions as well as by mechanical clogging causes the branches to wilt and the tree to die. The disease is spread from diseased to healthy trees by elm bark beetles. The galleries which the insects have tunneled out under the bark of dead trees become contaminated with spores of the invading fungus, and the spores adhere to the insect body and are carried wherever the beetle flies. Efforts to control the fungus disease of the elms have been directed largely toward control of the carrier insect. In community after community, especially throughout the strongholds of the American elm, the Midwest and New England, intensive spraying has become a routine procedure.   (7)

What this spraying could mean to bird life, and especially to the robin, was first made clear by the work of two ornithologists at Michigan State University, Professor George Wallace and one of his graduate students, John Mehner. When Mr. Mehner began work for the doctorate in 1954, he chose a research project that had to do with robin populations. This was quite by chance, for at that time no one suspected that the robins were in danger. But even as he undertook the work, events occurred that were to change its character and indeed to deprive him of his material.   (8)

Spraying for Dutch elm disease began in a small way on the university campus in 1954. The following year the city of East Lansing (where the university is located) joined in, spraying on the campus was expanded, and, with local programs for gypsy moth and mosquito control also under way, the rain of chemicals increased to a downpour.   (9)

During 1954, the year of the first light spraying, all seemed well. The following spring the migrating robins began to return to the campus as usual. Like the bluebells in Tomlinson's haunting essay "The Lost Wood," they were "expecting no evil" as they reoccupied their familiar territories. But soon it became evident that something was wrong. Dead and dying robins began to appear on the campus. Few birds were seen in their normal foraging activities or assembling in their usual roosts. Few nests were built; few young appeared. The pattern was repeated with monotonous regularity in succeeding springs. The sprayed area had become a lethal trap in which each wave of migrating robins would be eliminated in about a week. Then new arrivals would come in, only to add to the numbers of doomed birds seen on the campus in the agonized tremors that precede death. (10)

"The campus is serving as a graveyard for most of the robins that attempt to take up residence in the spring," said Dr. Wallace. But why? At first he suspected some disease of the nervous system, but soon it became evident that "in spite of the assurances of the insecticide people that their sprays were 'harmless to birds' the robins were really dying of insecticidal poisoning; they exhibited the well-known symptoms of loss of balance, followed by tremors, convulsions, and death." (11)

Several facts suggested that the robins were being poisoned, not so much by direct contact with the insecticides as indirectly, by eating earthworms. Campus earthworms had been fed inadvertently to crayfish in a research project and all the crayfish had promptly died. A snake kept in a laboratory cage had gone into violent tremors after being fed such worms. And earthworms are the principal food of robins in the spring. (12)

A key piece in the jigsaw puzzle of the doomed robins was soon to be supplied by Dr. Roy Barker of the Illinois Natural History Survey at Urbana. Dr. Barker's work, published in 1958, traced the intricate cycle of events by which the robins' fate is linked to the elm trees by way of the earthworms. The trees are sprayed in the spring (usually at the rate of 2 to 5 pounds of DDT per 50-foot tree, which may be the equivalent of as much as 23 *pounds per acre* where elms are numerous) and often again in July, at about half this concentration. Powerful sprayers direct a stream of poison to all parts of the tallest trees, killing directly not only the target organism, the bark beetle, but other insects, including pollinating species and predatory spiders and beetles. The poison forms a tenacious film over the leaves and bark. Rains do not wash it away. In the autumn the leaves fall to the ground, accumulate in sodden layers, and begin the slow process of becoming one with the soil. In this they are aided by the toil of the earthworms, who feed in the leaf litter, for elm leaves are among their favorite foods. In feeding on the leaves the worms also swallow the insecticide, accumulating and concentrating it in their bodies. Dr. Barker found deposits of DDT throughout the digestive tracts of the worms, their blood vessels, nerves, and body wall. Undoubtedly some of the earthworms themselves succumb, but others survive to become "biological magnifiers" of the poison. In the spring the robins return to provide another link in the cycle. As few as 11 large earthworms can transfer a lethal dose of DDT to a robin. And 11 worms form a small part of a day's rations to a bird that eats 10 to 12 earthworms in as many minutes.   (13)

Not all robins receive a lethal dose, but another consequence may lead to the extinction of their kind as surely as fatal poisoning. The shadow of sterility lies over all the bird studies and indeed lengthens to include all living things within its potential range. There are now only two or three dozen robins to be found each spring on the entire 185-acre campus of Michigan State University, compared with a conservatively estimated 370 adults in this area before spraying. In 1954 every robin nest under observation by Mehner produced young. Toward the end of June, 1957, when at least 370 young birds (the normal replacement of the adult population) would have been foraging over the campus in the years before spraying began, Mehner could find *only one young robin.* A year later Dr. Wallace was to report: "At no time during the spring or summer [of 1958] did I see a fledgling robin anywhere on the main campus, and so far I have failed to find anyone else who has seen one there."   (14)

Part of this failure to produce young is due, of course, to the fact that one or more of a pair of robins dies before the nesting cycle is completed. But Wallace has significant records which point to something more sinister —the actual destruction of the birds' capacity to reproduce. He has, for example, "records of robins and other birds building nests but laying no eggs, and others laying eggs and incubating them but not hatching them. We have one record of a robin that sat on its eggs faithfully for 21 days and they did not hatch. The normal incubation period is 13 days . . . Our analyses are showing high concentrations of DDT in the testes and ovaries of breeding birds," he told a congressional committee in 1960. "Ten males had amounts ranging from 30 to 109 parts per million in the testes, and two females had 151 and 211 parts per million respectively in the egg follicles in their ovaries."   (15)

Soon studies in other areas began to develop findings equally dismal. Professor Joseph Hickey and his students at the University of Wisconsin, after careful comparative studies of sprayed and unsprayed areas, reported the robin mortality to be at least 86 to 88 per cent. The Cranbrook Institute of Science at Bloomfield Hills, Michigan, in an effort to assess the extent of bird loss caused by the spraying of the elms, asked in 1956 that all birds thought to be victims of DDT poisoning be turned in to the institute for examination. The request had a response beyond all expectations. Within a few weeks the deep-freeze facilities of the institute were taxed to capacity, so that other specimens had to be refused. By 1959 a thousand poisoned birds from this single community had been turned in or reported. Although the robin was the chief victim (one woman calling the institute reported 12 robins lying dead on her lawn as she spoke), 63 different species were included among the specimens examined at the institute. (16)

The robins, then, are only one part of the chain of devastation linked to the spraying of the elms, even as the elm program is only one of the multitudinous spray programs that cover our land with poisons. Heavy mortality has occurred among about 90 species of birds, including those most familiar to suburbanites and amateur naturalists. The populations of nesting birds in general have declined as much as 90 per cent in some of the sprayed towns. As we shall see, all the various types of birds are affected—ground feeders, treetop feeders, bark feeders, predators. (17)

It is only reasonable to suppose that all birds and mammals heavily dependent on earthworms or other soil organisms for food are threatened by the robins' fate. Some 45 species of birds include earthworms in their diet. Among them is the woodcock, a species that winters in southern areas recently heavily sprayed with heptachlor. Two significant discoveries have now been made about the woodcock. Production of young birds on the New Brunswick breeding grounds is definitely reduced, and adult birds that have been analyzed contain large residues of DDT and heptachlor. (18)

Already there are disturbing records of heavy mortality among more than 20 other species of ground-feeding birds whose food—worms, ants, grubs, or other soil organisms—has been poisoned. These include three of the thrushes whose songs are among the most exquisite of bird voices, the olive-backed, the wood, and the hermit. And the sparrows that flit through the shrubby understory of the woodlands and forage with rustling sounds amid the fallen leaves—the song sparrow and the white-throat—these, too, have been found among the victims of the elm sprays. (19)

Mammals, also, may easily be involved in the cycle, directly or indirectly. Earthworms are important among the various foods of the raccoon, and are eaten in the spring and fall by opossums. Such subterranean tunnelers as shrews and moles capture them in some numbers, and then perhaps pass on the poison to predators such as screech owls and barn owls. Several dying screech owls were picked up in Wisconsin following heavy rains in spring, perhaps poisoned by feeding on earthworms. Hawks and owls have been found in convulsions—great horned owls, screech owls, red-shouldered hawks, sparrow hawks, marsh hawks. These may be cases of secondary poisoning, caused by eating birds or mice that have accumulated insecticides in their livers or other organs. (20)

Nor is it only the creatures that forage on the ground or those who prey on them that are endangered by the foliar spraying of the elms. All of the treetop feeders, the birds that glean their insect food from the leaves, have disappeared from heavily sprayed areas, among them those woodland sprites the kinglets, both ruby-crowned and golden-crowned, the tiny gnatcatchers, and many of the warblers, whose migrating hordes flow through the trees in spring in a multicolored tide of life. In 1956, a late spring delayed spraying so that it coincided with the arrival of an exceptionally heavy wave of warbler migration. Nearly all species of warblers present in the area were represented in the heavy kill that followed. In Whitefish Bay, Wisconsin, at least a thousand myrtle warblers could be seen in migration during former years; in 1958, after the spraying of the elms, observers could find only two. So, with additions from other communities, the list grows, and the warblers killed by the spray include those that most charm and fascinate all who are aware of them: the black-and-white, the yellow, the magnolia, and the Cape May; the ovenbird, whose call throbs in the Maytime woods; the Blackburnian, whose wings are touched with flame; the chestnut-sided, the Canadian, and the black-throated green. These treetop feeders are affected either directly by eating poisoned insects or indirectly by a shortage of food.   (21)

The loss of food has also struck hard at the swallows that cruise the skies, straining out the aerial insects as herring strain the plankton of the sea. A Wisconsin naturalist reported: "Swallows have been hard hit. Everyone complains of how few they have seen compared to four or five years ago. Our sky overhead was full of them only four years ago. Now we seldom see any . . . This could be both lack of insects because of spray, or poisoned insects."   (22)

Of other birds this same observer wrote: "Another striking loss is the phoebe. Flycatchers are scarce everywhere but the early hardy common phoebe is no more. I've seen one this spring and only one last spring. Other birders in Wisconsin make the same complaint. I have had five or six pair of cardinals in the past, none now. Wrens, robins, catbirds and screech owls have nested each year in our garden. There are none now. Summer mornings are without bird song. Only pest birds, pigeons, starlings and English sparrows remain. It is tragic and I can't bear it."   (23)

The dormant sprays applied to the elms in the fall, sending the poison into every little crevice in the bark, are probably responsible for the severe reduction observed in the number of chickadees, nuthatches, titmice, woodpeckers, and brown creepers. During the winter of 1957–58, Dr. Wallace saw no chickadees or nuthatches at his home feeding station for the first time in many years. Three nuthatches he found later provided a sorry little step-by-step lesson in cause and effect: one was feeding on an elm, another was found dying of typical DDT symptoms, the third was dead. The dying nuthatch was later found to have 226 parts per million of DDT in its tissues.   (24)

The feeding habits of all these birds not only make them especially vulnerable to insect sprays but also make their loss a deplorable one for economic as well as less tangible reasons. The summer food of the white-breasted nuthatch and the brown creeper, for example, includes the eggs, larvae, and adults of a very large number of insects injurious to trees. About three quarters of the food of the chickadee is animal, including all stages of the life cycle of many insects. The chickadee's method of feeding is described in Bent's monumental *Life Histories* of North American birds: "As the flock moves along each bird examines minutely bark, twigs, and branches, searching for tiny bits of food (spiders' eggs, cocoons, or other dormant insect life)."   (25)

Various scientific studies have established the critical role of birds in insect control in various situations. Thus, woodpeckers are the primary control of the Engelmann spruce beetle, reducing its populations from 45 to 98 per cent and are important in the control of the codling moth in apple orchards. Chickadees and other winter-resident birds can protect orchards against the cankerworm.   (26)

But what happens in nature is not allowed to happen in the modern, chemical-drenched world, where spraying destroys not only the insects but their principal enemy, the birds. When later there is a resurgence of the insect population, as almost always happens, the birds are not there to keep their numbers in check. As the Curator of Birds at the Milwaukee Public Museum, Owen J. Gromme, wrote to the Milwaukee *Journal:* "The greatest enemy of insect life is other predatory insects, birds, and some small mammals, but DDT kills indiscriminately, including nature's own safeguards or policemen . . . In the name of progress are we to become victims of our own diabolical means of insect control to provide temporary comfort, only to lose out to destroying insects later on? By what means will we control new pests, which will attack remaining tree species after the elms are gone, when nature's safeguards (the birds) have been wiped out by poison?"   (27)

Mr. Gromme reported that calls and letters about dead and dying birds had been increasing steadily during the years since spraying began in Wisconsin. Questioning always revealed that spraying or fogging had been done in the area where the birds were dying.   (28)

Mr. Gromme's experience has been shared by ornithologists and conservationists at most of the research centers of the Midwest such as the Cranbrook Institute in Michigan, the Illinois Natural History Survey, and the University of Wisconsin. A glance at the Letters-from-Readers column of newspapers almost anywhere that spraying is being done makes clear the fact that citizens are not only becoming aroused and indignant but that often they show a keener understanding of the dangers and inconsistencies of spraying than do the officials who order it done. "I am dreading the days to come soon now when many beautiful birds will be dying in our back yard," wrote a Milwaukee woman. "This is a pitiful, heartbreaking experience . . . It is, moreover, frustrating and exasperating, for it evidently does not serve the purpose this slaughter was intended to serve . . . Taking a long look, can you save trees without also saving birds? Do they not, in the economy of nature, save each other? Isn't it possible to help the balance of nature without destroying it?" (29)

The idea that the elms, majestic shade trees though they are, are not "sacred cows" and do not justify an "open end" campaign of destruction against all other forms of life is expressed in other letters. "I have always loved our elm trees which seemed like trademarks on our landscape," wrote another Wisconsin woman. "But there are many kinds of trees . . . We must save our birds, too. Can anyone imagine anything so cheerless and dreary as a springtime without a robin's song?" (30)

To the public the choice may easily appear to be one of stark black-or-white simplicity: Shall we have birds or shall we have elms? But it is not as simple as that, and by one of the ironies that abound throughout the field of chemical control we may very well end by having neither if we continue on our present, well-traveled road. Spraying is killing the birds but it is not saving the elms. The illusion that salvation of the elms lies at the end of a spray nozzle is a dangerous will-o'-the-wisp that is leading one community after another into a morass of heavy expenditures, without producing lasting results. Greenwich, Connecticut, sprayed regularly for ten years. Then a drought year brought conditions especially favorable to the beetle and the mortality of elms went up 1000 per cent. In Urbana, Illinois, where the University of Illinois is located, Dutch elm disease first appeared in 1951. Spraying was undertaken in 1953. By 1959, in spite of six years' spraying, the university campus had lost 86 per cent of its elms, half of them victims of Dutch elm disease. (31)

In Toledo, Ohio, a similar experience caused the Superintendent of Forestry, Joseph A. Sweeney, to take a realistic look at the results of spraying. Spraying was begun there in 1953 and continued through 1959. Meanwhile, however, Mr. Sweeney had noticed that a city-wide infestation of the cottony maple scale was worse after the spraying recommended by "the books and the authorities" than it had been before. He decided to review the results of spraying for Dutch elm disease for himself. His findings shocked him. In the city of Toledo, he found, "the only areas under any control were the areas where we used some promptness in removing the diseased or brood trees. Where we depended on spraying the disease was out of control. In the country where nothing has been done the disease has not spread as fast as it has in the city. This indicates that spraying destroys any natural enemies. (32)

"We are abandoning spraying for the Dutch elm disease. This has brought me into conflict with the people who back any recommendations by the United States Department of Agriculture but I have the facts and will stick with them." (33)

It is difficult to understand why these midwestern towns, to which the elm disease spread only rather recently, have so unquestioningly embarked on ambitious and expensive spraying programs, apparently without waiting to inquire into the experience of other areas that have had longer acquaintance with the problem. New York State, for example, has certainly had the longest history of continuous experience with Dutch elm disease, for it was via the Port of New York that diseased elm wood is thought to have entered the United States about 1930. And New York State today has a most impressive record of containing and suppressing the disease. Yet it has not relied upon spraying. In fact, its agricultural extension service does not recommend spraying as a community method of control.   (34)

How, then, has New York achieved its fine record? From the early years of the battle for the elms to the present time, it has relied upon rigorous sanitation, or the prompt removal and destruction of all diseased or infected wood. In the beginning some of the results were disappointing, but this was because it was not at first understood that not only diseased trees but all elm wood in which the beetles might breed must be destroyed. Infected elm wood, after being cut and stored for firewood, will release a crop of fungus-carrying beetles unless burned before spring. It is the adult beetles, emerging from hibernation to feed in late April and May, that transmit Dutch elm disease. New York entomologists have learned by experience what kinds of beetle-breeding material have real importance in the spread of the disease. By concentrating on this dangerous material, it has been possible not only to get good results, but to keep the cost of the sanitation program within reasonable limits. By 1950 the incidence of Dutch elm disease in New York City had been reduced to $\frac{2}{10}$ of 1 per cent of the city's 55,000 elms. A sanitation program was launched in Westchester County in 1942. During the next 14 years the average annual loss of elms was only $\frac{2}{10}$ of 1 per cent a year. Buffalo, with 185,000 elms, has an excellent record of containing the disease by sanitation, with recent annual losses amounting to only $\frac{3}{10}$ of 1 per cent. In other words, at this rate of loss it would take about 300 years to eliminate Buffalo's elms.   (35)

What has happened in Syracuse is especially impressive. There no effective program was in operation before 1957. Between 1951 and 1956 Syracuse lost nearly 3000 elms. Then, under the direction of Howard C. Miller of the New York State University College of Forestry, an intensive drive was made to remove all diseased elm trees and all possible sources of beetle-breeding elm wood. The rate of loss is now well below 1 per cent a year.   (36)

The economy of the sanitation method is stressed by New York experts in Dutch elm disease control. "In most cases the actual expense is small compared with the probable saving," says J. G. Matthysse of the New York

State College of Agriculture. "If it is a case of a dead or broken limb, the limb would have to be removed eventually, as a precaution against possible property damage or personal injury. If it is a fuel-wood pile, the wood can be used before spring, the bark can be peeled from the wood, or the wood can be stored in a dry place. In the case of dying or dead elm trees, the expense of prompt removal to prevent Dutch elm disease spread is usually no greater than would be necessary later, for most dead trees in urban regions must be removed eventually."   (37)

The situation with regard to Dutch elm disease is therefore not entirely hopeless provided informed and intelligent measures are taken. While it cannot be eradicated by any means now known, once it has become established in a community, it can be suppressed and contained within reasonable bounds by sanitation, and without the use of methods that are not only futile but involve tragic destruction of bird life. Other possibilities lie within the field of forest genetics, where experiments offer hope of developing a hybrid elm resistant to Dutch elm disease. The European elm is highly resistant, and many of them have been planted in Washington, D.C. Even during a period when a high percentage of the city's elms were affected, no cases of Dutch elm disease were found among these trees.   (38)

Replanting through an immediate tree nursery and forestry program is being urged in communities that are losing large numbers of elms. This is important, and although such programs might well include the resistant European elms, they should aim at a variety of species so that no future epidemic could deprive a community of its trees. The key to a healthy plant or animal community lies in what the British ecologist Charles Elton calls "the conservation of variety." What is happening now is in large part a result of the biological unsophistication of past generations. Even a generation ago no one knew that to fill large areas with a single species of tree was to invite disaster. And so whole towns lined their streets and dotted their parks with elms, and today the elms die and so do the birds.   (39)

Like the robin, another American bird seems to be on the verge of extinction. This is the national symbol, the eagle. Its populations have dwindled alarmingly within the past decade. The facts suggest that something is at work in the eagle's environment which has virtually destroyed its ability to reproduce. What this may be is not yet definitely known, but there is some evidence that insecticides are responsible.   (40)

The most intensively studied eagles in North America have been those nesting along a stretch of coast from Tampa to Fort Myers on the western coast of Florida. There a retired banker from Winnipeg, Charles Broley, achieved ornithological fame by banding more than 1000 young bald eagles during the years 1939–49. (Only 166 eagles had been banded in all the earlier history of birdbanding.) Mr. Broley banded eagles as young birds

during the winter months before they had left their nests. Later recoveries
of banded birds showed that these Florida-born eagles range northward
along the coast into Canada as far as Prince Edward Island, although they
had previously been considered nonmigratory. In the fall they return to
the South, their migration being observed at such famous vantage points
as Hawk Mountain in eastern Pennsylvania. (41)

During the early years of his banding, Mr. Broley used to find 125
active nests a year on the stretch of coast he had chosen for his work. The
number of young banded each year was about 150. In 1947 the production
of young birds began to decline. Some nests contained no eggs; others contained eggs that failed to hatch. Between 1952 and 1957, about 80 per cent
of the nests failed to produce young. In the last year of this period only 43
nests were occupied. Seven of them produced young (8 eaglets); 23 contained eggs that failed to hatch; 13 were used merely as feeding stations by
adult eagles and contained no eggs. In 1958 Mr. Broley ranged over 100
miles of coast before finding and banding one eaglet. Adult eagles, which
had been seen at 43 nests in 1957, were so scarce that he observed them at
only 10 nests. (42)

Although Mr. Broley's death in 1959 terminated this valuable series of
uninterrupted observations, reports by the Florida Audubon Society, as
well as from New Jersey and Pennsylvania, confirm the trend that may
well make it necessary for us to find a new national emblem. The reports
of Maurice Broun, curator of the Hawk Mountain Sanctuary, are especially significant. Hawk Mountain is a picturesque mountaintop in southeastern Pennsylvania, where the easternmost ridges of the Appalachians
form a last barrier to the westerly winds before dropping away toward the
coastal plain. Winds striking the mountains are deflected upward so that
on many autumn days there is a continuous updraft on which the broad-
winged hawks and eagles ride without effort, covering many miles of
their southward migration in a day. At Hawk Mountain the ridges converge and so do the aerial highways. The result is that from a widespread
territory to the north birds pass through this traffic bottleneck. (43)

In his more than a score of years as custodian of the sanctuary there,
Maurice Broun has observed and actually tabulated more hawks and
eagles than any other American. The peak of the bald eagle migration
comes in late August and early September. These are assumed to be Florida
birds, returning to home territory after a summer in the North. (Later in
the fall and early winter a few larger eagles drift through. These are
thought to belong to a northern race, bound for an unknown wintering
ground.) During the first years after the sanctuary was established, from
1935 to 1939, 40 per cent of the eagles observed were yearlings, easily identified by their uniformly dark plumage. But in recent years these immature birds have become a rarity. Between 1955 and 1959, they made up only

20 per cent of the total count, and in one year (1957) there was only one young eagle for every 32 adults.   (44)

Observations at Hawk Mountain are in line with findings elsewhere. One such report comes from Elton Fawks, an official of the Natural Resources Council of Illinois. Eagles—probably northern nesters—winter along the Mississippi and Illinois Rivers. In 1958 Mr. Fawks reported that a recent count of 59 eagles had included only one immature bird. Similar indications of the dying out of the race come from the world's only sanctuary for eagles alone, Mount Johnson Island in the Susquehanna River. The island, although only 8 miles above Conowingo Dam and about half a mile out from the Lancaster County shore, retains its primitive wildness. Since 1934 its single eagle nest has been under observation by Professor Herbert H. Beck, an ornithologist of Lancaster and custodian of the sanctuary. Between 1935 and 1947 use of the nest was regular and uniformly successful. Since 1947, although the adults have occupied the nest and there is evidence of egg laying, no young eagles have been produced.
(45)

On Mount Johnson Island as well as in Florida, then, the same situation prevails—there is some occupancy of nests by adults, some production of eggs, but few or no young birds. In seeking an explanation, only one appears to fit all the facts. This is that the reproductive capacity of the birds has been so lowered by some environmental agent that there are now almost no annual additions of young to maintain the race.   (46)

Exactly this sort of situation has been produced artificially in other birds by various experimenters, notably Dr. James DeWitt of the United States Fish and Wildlife Service. Dr. DeWitt's now classic experiments on the effect of a series of insecticides on quail and pheasants have established the fact that exposure to DDT or related chemicals, even when doing no observable harm to the parent birds, may seriously affect reproduction. The way the effect is exerted may vary, but the end result is always the same. For example, quail into whose diet DDT was introduced throughout the breeding season survived and even produced normal numbers of fertile eggs. But few of the eggs hatched. "Many embryos appeared to develop normally during the early stages of incubation, but died during the hatching period," Dr. DeWitt said. Of those that did hatch, more than half died within 5 days. In other tests in which both pheasants and quail were the subjects, the adults produced no eggs whatever if they had been fed insecticide-contaminated diets throughout the year. And at the University of California, Dr. Robert Rudd and Dr. Richard Genelly reported similar findings. When pheasants received dieldrin in their diets, "egg production was markedly lowered and chick survival was poor." According to these authors, the delayed but lethal effect on the young birds follows from

storage of dieldrin in the yolk of the egg, from which it is gradually
assimilated during incubation and after hatching.   (47)

This suggestion is strongly supported by recent studies by Dr. Wallace
and a graduate student, Richard F. Bernard, who found high concentrations of DDT in robins on the Michigan State University campus. They
found the poison in all of the testes of male robins examined, in developing egg follicles, in the ovaries of females, in completed but unlaid eggs,
in the oviducts, in unhatched eggs from deserted nests, in embryos within
the eggs, and in a newly hatched, dead nestling.   (48)

These important studies establish the fact that the insecticidal poison
affects a generation once removed from initial contact with it. Storage of
poison in the egg, in the yolk material that nourishes the developing em-
bryo, is a virtual death warrant and explains why so many of DeWitt's
birds died in the egg or a few days after hatching.   (49)

Laboratory application of these studies to eagles presents difficulties
that are nearly insuperable, but field studies are now under way in Florida,
New Jersey, and elsewhere in the hope of acquiring definite evidence as
to what has caused the apparent sterility of much of the eagle population.
Meanwhile, the available circumstantial evidence points to insecticides. In
localities where fish are abundant they make up a large part of the eagle's
diet (about 65 per cent in Alaska; about 52 per cent in the Chesapeake Bay
area). Almost unquestionably the eagles so long studied by Mr. Broley
were predominantly fish eaters. Since 1945 this particular coastal area has
been subjected to repeated sprayings with DDT dissolved in fuel oil. The
principal target of the aerial spraying was the salt-marsh mosquito, which
inhabits the marshes and coastal areas that are typical foraging areas for
the eagles. Fishes and crabs were killed in enormous numbers. Laboratory
analyses of their tissues revealed high concentrations of DDT—as much as
46 parts per million. Like the grebes of Clear Lake, which accumulated
heavy concentrations of insecticide residues from eating the fish of the
lake, the eagles have almost certainly been storing up the DDT in the
tissues of their bodies. And like the grebes, the pheasants, the quail, and
the robins, they are less and less able to produce young and to preserve
the continuity of their race.   (50)

From all over the world come echoes of the peril that faces birds in our
modern world. The reports differ in detail, but always repeat the theme of
death to wildlife in the wake of pesticides. Such are the stories of hundreds
of small birds and partridges dying in France after vine stumps were
treated with an arsenic-containing herbicide, or of partridge shoots in
Belgium, once famous for the numbers of their birds, denuded of partridges after the spraying of nearby farmlands.   (51)

In England the major problem seems to be a specialized one, linked with the growing practice of treating seed with insecticides before sowing. Seed treatment is not a wholly new thing, but in earlier years the chemicals principally used were fungicides. No effects on birds seem to have been noticed. Then about 1956 there was a change to dual-purpose treatment; in addition to a fungicide, dieldrin, aldrin, or heptachlor was added to combat soil insects. Thereupon the situation changed for the worse. (52)

In the spring of 1960 a deluge of reports of dead birds reached British wildlife authorities, including the British Trust for Ornithology, the Royal Society for the Protection of Birds, and the Game Birds Association. "The place is like a battlefield," a landowner in Norfolk wrote. "My keeper has found innumerable corpses, including masses of small birds—Chaffinches, Greenfinches, Linnets, Hedge Sparrows, also House Sparrows . . . the destruction of wild life is quite pitiful." A gamekeeper wrote: "My Partridges have been wiped out with the dressed corn, also some Pheasants and all other birds, hundreds of birds have been killed. . . . As a lifelong gamekeeper it has been a distressing experience for me. It is bad to see pairs of Partridges that have died together."   (53)

In a joint report, the British Trust for Ornithology and the Royal Society for the Protection of Birds described some 67 kills of birds—a far from complete listing of the destruction that took place in the spring of 1960. Of these 67, 59 were caused by seed dressings, 8 by toxic sprays. (54)

A new wave of poisoning set in the following year. The death of 600 birds on a single estate in Norfolk was reported to the House of Lords, and 100 pheasants died on a farm in North Essex. It soon became evident that more counties were involved than in 1960 (34 compared with 23). Lincolnshire, heavily agricultural, seemed to have suffered most, with reports of 10,000 birds dead. But destruction involved all of agricultural England, from Angus in the north to Cornwall in the south, from Anglesey in the west to Norfolk in the east.   (55)

In the spring of 1961 concern reached such a peak that a special committee of the House of Commons made an investigation of the matter, taking testimony from farmers, landowners, and representatives of the Ministry of Agriculture and of various governmental and nongovernmental agencies concerned with wildlife.   (56)

"Pigeons are suddenly dropping out of the sky dead," said one witness. "You can drive a hundred or two hundred miles outside London and not see a single kestrel," reported another. "There has been no parallel in the present century, or at any time so far as I am aware, [this is] the biggest risk to wildlife and game that ever occurred in the country," officials of the Nature Conservancy testified.   (57)

Facilities for chemical analysis of the victims were most inadequate to the task, with only two chemists in the country able to make the tests (one the government chemist, the other in the employ of the Royal Society for the Protection of Birds). Witnesses described huge bonfires on which the bodies of the birds were burned. But efforts were made to have carcasses collected for examination, and of the birds analyzed, all but one contained pesticide residues. The single exception was a snipe, which is not a seed-eating bird. (58)

Along with the birds, foxes also may have been affected, probably indirectly by eating poisoned mice or birds. England, plagued by rabbits, sorely needs the fox as a predator. But between November 1959 and April 1960 at least 1300 foxes died. Deaths were heaviest in the same counties from which sparrow hawks, kestrels, and other birds of prey virtually disappeared, suggesting that the poison was spreading through the food chain, reaching out from the seed eaters to the furred and feathered carnivores. The actions of the moribund foxes were those of animals poisoned by chlorinated hydrocarbon insecticides. They were seen wandering in circles, dazed and half blind, before dying in convulsions. (59)

The hearings convinced the committee that the threat to wildlife was "most alarming"; it accordingly recommended to the House of Commons that "the Minister of Agriculture and the Secretary of State for Scotland should secure the immediate prohibition for the use as seed dressings of compounds containing dieldrin, aldrin, or heptachlor, or chemicals of comparable toxicity." The committee also recommended more adequate controls to ensure that chemicals were adequately tested under field as well as laboratory conditions before being put on the market. This, it is worth emphasizing, is one of the great blank spots in pesticide research everywhere. Manufacturers' tests on the common laboratory animals—rats, dogs, guinea pigs—include no wild species, no birds as a rule, no fishes, and are conducted under controlled and artificial conditions. Their application to wildlife in the field is anything but precise. (60)

England is by no means alone in its problem of protecting birds from treated seeds. Here in the United States the problem has been most troublesome in the rice-growing areas of California and the South. For a number of years California rice growers have been treating seed with DDT as protection against tadpole shrimp and scavenger beetles which sometimes damage seedling rice. California sportsmen have enjoyed excellent hunting because of the concentrations of waterfowl and pheasants in the rice fields. But for the past decade persistent reports of bird losses, especially among pheasants, ducks, and blackbirds, have come from the rice-growing counties. "Pheasant sickness" became a well-known phenomenon: birds "seek water, become paralyzed, and are found on the ditch banks and rice checks quivering," according to one observer. The "sickness" comes in the spring, at the time the rice fields are seeded. The concentration of DDT used is many times the amount that will kill an adult pheasant. (61)

The passage of a few years and the development of even more poisonous insecticides served to increase the hazard from treated seed. Aldrin,
which is 100 times as toxic as DDT to pheasants, is now widely used as a
seed coating. In the rice fields of eastern Texas, this practice has seriously
reduced the populations of the fulvous tree duck, a tawny-colored, goose-
like duck of the Gulf Coast. Indeed, there is some reason to think that the
rice growers, having found a way to reduce the populations of blackbirds,
are using the insecticide for a dual purpose, with disastrous effects on
several bird species of the rice fields.

As the habit of killing grows—the resort to "eradicating" any creature
that may annoy or inconvenience us—birds are more and more finding
themselves a direct target of poisons rather than an incidental one. There
is a growing trend toward aerial applications of such deadly poisons as
parathion to "control" concentrations of birds distasteful to farmers. The
Fish and Wildlife Service has found it necessary to express serious concern
over this trend, pointing out that "parathion treated areas constitute a
potential hazard to humans, domestic animals, and wildlife." In southern
Indiana, for example, a group of farmers went together in the summer
of 1959 to engage a spray plane to treat an area of river bottomland with
parathion. The area was a favored roosting site for thousands of blackbirds
that were feeding in nearby cornfields. The problem could have been
solved easily by a slight change in agricultural practice—a shift to a variety
of corn with deep-set ears not accessible to the birds—but the farmers had
been persuaded of the merits of killing by poison, and so they sent in the
planes on their mission of death.   (63)

The results probably gratified the farmers, for the casualty list included
some 65,000 red-winged blackbirds and starlings. What other wildlife deaths
may have gone unnoticed and unrecorded is not known. Parathion is not
a specific for blackbirds: it is a universal killer. But such rabbits or rac-
coons or opossums as may have roamed those bottomlands and perhaps
never visited the farmers' cornfields were doomed by a judge and jury
who neither knew of their existence nor cared.   (64)

And what of human beings? In California orchards sprayed with this
same parathion, workers handling foliage that had been treated *a month*
earlier collapsed and went into shock, and escaped death only through
skilled medical attention. Does Indiana still raise any boys who roam
through woods or fields and might even explore the margins of a river? If
so, who guarded the poisoned area to keep out any who might wander in,
in misguided search for unspoiled nature? Who kept vigilant watch to tell
the innocent stroller that the fields he was about to enter were deadly—all
their vegetation coated with a lethal film? Yet at so fearful a risk the
farmers, with none to hinder them, waged their needless war on blackbirds.
                                                                          (65)

In each of these situations, one turns away to ponder the question: Who has made the decision that sets in motion these chains of poisonings, this ever-widening wave of death that spreads out, like ripples when a pebble is dropped into a still pond? Who has placed in one pan of the scales the leaves that might have been eaten by the beetles and in the other the piti-ful heaps of many-hued feathers, the lifeless remains of the birds that fell before the unselective bludgeon of insecticidal poisons? Who has decided— who has the *right* to decide—for the countless legions of people who were not consulted that the supreme value is a world without insects, even though it be also a sterile world ungraced by the curving wing of a bird in flight? The decision is that of the authoritarian temporarily entrusted with power; he has made it during a moment of inattention by millions to whom beauty and the ordered world of nature still have a meaning that is deep and imperative.   (66)

Sigmund Freud

(1856–1939)

FREUD hardly needs an introduction to a generation of movie-goers in a psychoanalytically oriented world. Known as "the inventor of psychoanaly-sis," he called scientific attention to the influence of the unconscious on the conscious mind, to the conflicts of contending inner forces, and to the in-fluence on mental development of the child's semi-consciousness of sex.

◼ *Repression*

ONE OF THE vicissitudes an instinctual impulse may undergo is to meet with resistances the aim of which is to make the impulse inoperative. Un-der certain conditions, which we shall presently investigate more closely, the impulse then passes into the state of *repression*. If it were a question of the operation of an external stimulus, obviously flight would be the appropriate remedy; with an instinct, flight is of no avail, for the ego cannot escape from itself. Later on, rejection based on judgment (*condemnation*) will be found to be a good weapon against the impulse. Repression is a preliminary phase of condemnation, something between flight and condemnation; it is a concept which could not have been formulated before the time of psycho-analytic research. (1)

It is not easy in theory to deduce the possibility of such a thing as repression. Why should an instinctual impulse suffer such a fate? For this to happen, obviously a necessary condition must be that attainment of its aim by the instinct should produce "pain" instead of pleasure. But we cannot well imagine such a contingency. There are no such instincts; satisfaction of an instinct is always pleasurable. We should have to assume certain peculiar circumstances, some sort of process which changes the pleasure of satisfaction into "pain." (2)

In order the better to define repression we may discuss some other situations in which instincts are concerned. It may happen that an external stimulus becomes internal, for example, by eating into and destroying a bodily organ, so that a new source of constant excitation and increase of tension is formed. The stimulus thereby acquires a far-reaching similarity to an instinct. We know that a case of this sort is experienced by us as *physical pain*. The aim of this pseudo-instinct, however, is simply the cessation of the change in the organ and of the pain accompanying it. There is no other direct pleasure to be attained by cessation of the pain. Further, pain is imperative; the only things which can subdue it are the effect of some toxic agent in removing it and the influence of some mental distraction. (3)

The case of physical pain is too obscure to help us much in our purpose. Let us suppose that an instinctual stimulus such as hunger remains unsatisfied. It then becomes imperative and can be allayed by nothing but the appropriate action for satisfying it; it keeps up a constant tension of need. Anything like a repression seems in this case to be utterly out of the question. (4)

So repression is certainly not an essential result of the tension produced by lack of satifaction of an impulse being raised to an unbearable degree. The weapons of defence of which the organism avails itself to guard against that situation must be discussed in another connection. (5)

Let us instead confine ourselves to the clinical experience we meet with in the practice of psycho-analysis. We then see that the satisfaction of an instinct under repression is quite possible; further, that in every instance such a satisfaction is pleasurable in itself, but is irreconcilable with other claims and purposes; it therefore causes pleasure in one part of the mind and "pain" in another. We see then that it is a condition of repression that the element of avoiding "pain" shall have acquired more strength than the pleasure of gratification. Psycho-analytic experience of the transference neuroses, moreover, forces us to the conclusion that repression is not a defence-mechanism present from the very beginning, and that it cannot occur until a sharp distinction has been established between what is conscious and what is unconscious: that *the essence of repression lies simply in the function of rejecting and keeping something out of consciousness.* This conception of repression would be supplemented by assuming that, before the mental organization reaches this phase, the other vicissitudes which may befall instincts, e.g., reversal into the opposite or turning round upon the subject, deal with the task of mastering the instinctual impulses. (6)

It seems to us now that, in view of the very great extent to which repression and the unconscious are correlated, we must defer probing more deeply into the nature of repression until we have learnt more about the structure of the various institutions in the mind—and about what differentiates consciousness from the unconscious. Till we have done this, all we can do is to put together in purely descriptive fashion some characteristics of repression noted in clinical practice, even though we run the risk of having to repeat unchanged much that has been said elsewhere. (7)

Now we have reason for assuming *a primal repression,* a first phase of repression, which consists in a denial of entry into consciousness to the mental (ideational) presentation of the instinct. This is accompanied by a *fixation;* the ideational presentation in question persists unaltered from then onwards, and the instinct remains attached to it. This is due to certain properties of unconscious processes of which we shall speak later. (8)

The second phase of repression, *repression proper,* concerns mental derivatives of the repressed instinct-presentation, or such trains of thought as, originating elsewhere, have come into associative connection with it. On account of this association, these ideas experience the same fate as that which underwent primal repression. Repression proper, therefore, is actually an after-expulsion. Moreover, it is a mistake to emphasize only the rejection which operates from the side of consciousness upon what is to be repressed. We have to consider just as much the attraction exercised by what was originally repressed upon everything with which it can establish a connection. Probably the tendency to repression would fail of its purpose if these forces did not co-operate, if there were not something previously repressed ready to assimilate that which is rejected from consciousness. (9)

Under the influence of study of the psycho-neuroses, which brings before us the important effects of repression, we are inclined to overestimate their psychological content and to forget too readily that repression does not hinder the instinct-presentation from continuing to exist in the unconscious and from organizing itself further, putting forth derivatives and instituting connections. Really, repression interferes only with the relation of the instinct-presentation to one system of the mind, namely, to consciousness. (10)

Psycho-analysis is able to show us something else which is important for understanding the effects of repression in the psycho-neuroses. It shows us, for instance, that the instinct-presentation develops in a more unchecked and luxuriant fashion if it is withdrawn by repression from conscious influence. It ramifies like a fungus, so to speak, in the dark, and takes on extreme forms of expression, which when translated and revealed to the neurotic are bound not merely to seem alien to him, but to terrify him by the way in which they reflect an extraordinary and dangerous strength of instinct. This illusory strength of instinct is the result of an uninhibited development of it in phantasy and of the damming-up consequent on lack of real satisfaction. The fact that this last result is bound up with repression points the direction in which we have to look for the true significance of the latter. (11)

In reverting to the contrary aspect, however, let us state definitely that it is not even correct to suppose that repression withholds from consciousness all the derivatives of what was primally repressed. If these derivatives are sufficiently far removed from the repressed instinct-presentation, whether owing to the process of distortion or by reason of the number of intermediate associations, they have free access to consciousness. It is as though the resistance of consciousness against them was in inverse proportion to their remoteness from what was originally repressed. During the practice of the psycho-analytic method, we continually require the patient to produce such derivatives of what has been repressed as, in consequence either of their remoteness or of distortion, can pass the censorship of consciousness. Indeed, the associations which we require him to give, while refraining from any consciously directed train of thought or any criticism, and from which we reconstruct a conscious interpretation of the repressed instinct-presentation, are precisely derivatives of this kind. We then observe that the patient can go on spinning a whole chain of such associations, till he is brought up in the midst of them against some thought-formation, the relation of which to what is repressed acts so intensely that he is compelled to repeat his attempt at repression. Neurotic symptoms, too, must have fulfilled the condition referred to, for they are derivatives of the repressed, which has finally by means of these formations wrested from consciousness the right of way previously denied it. (12)

We can lay down no general rule concerning the degree of distortion and remoteness necessary before the resistance of consciousness is abrogated. In this matter a delicate balancing takes place, the play of which is hidden from us; its mode of operation, however, leads us to infer that it is a question of a definite degree of intensity in the cathexis of the unconscious—beyond which it would break through for satisfaction. Repression acts, therefore, in a *highly specific* manner in each instance; every single derivative of the repressed may have its peculiar fate—a little more or a little less distortion alters the whole issue. In this connection, it becomes comprehensible that those objects to which men give their preference, that is, their ideals, originate in the same perceptions and experiences as those objects of which they have most abhorrence, and that the two originally differed from one another only by slight modifications. Indeed, as we found in the origin of the fetish, it is possible for the original instinct-presentation to be split into two, one part undergoing repression, while the remainder, just on account of its intimate association with the other, undergoes idealization. (13)

The same result as ensues from an increase or a decrease in the degree of distortion may also be achieved at the other end of the apparatus, so to speak, by a modification in the conditions producing pleasure and "pain." Special devices have been evolved, with the object of bringing about such changes in the play of mental forces that what usually gives rise to "pain" may on this occasion result in pleasure, and whenever such a device comes into operation the repression of an instinct-presentation that is ordinarily repudiated is abrogated. The only one of these devices which has till now been studied in any detail is that of joking. Generally the lifting of the repression is only transitory; the repression is immediately reestablished. (14)

Observations of this sort, however, suffice to draw our attention to some further characteristics of repression. Not only is it, as we have just explained, *variable* and *specific*, but it is also exceedingly *mobile*. The process of repression is not to be regarded as something which takes place once for all, the results of which are permanent, as when some living thing has been killed and from that time onward is dead; on the contrary, repression demands a constant expenditure of energy, and if this were discontinued the success of the repression would be jeopardized, so that a fresh act of repression would be necessary. We may imagine that what is repressed exercises a continuous straining in the direction of consciousness, so that the balance has to be kept by means of a steady counter-pressure. A constant expenditure of energy, therefore, is entailed in maintaining a repression, and economically its abrogation denotes a saving. The mobility of the repression, incidentally, finds expression also in the mental characteristics of the condition of sleep, which alone renders dream-formation possible. With a return to waking life, the repressive cathexes which have been called in are once more put forth. (15)

Finally, we must not forget that after all we have said very little about an instinctual impulse when we state it to be repressed. Without prejudice to the repression, such an impulse may find itself in widely different conditions; it may be inactive, i.e., cathected with only a low degree of mental energy, or its degree of cathexis (and consequently its capacity for activity) may vary. True, its activity will not result in a direct abrogation of the repression, but it will certainly set in motion all the processes which terminate in a breaking through into consciousness by circuitous routes. With unrepressed derivatives of the unconscious, the fate of a particular idea is often decided by the degree of its activity or cathexis. It is an everyday occurrence that such a derivative can remain unrepressed so long as it represents only a small amount of energy, although its content is of such a nature as to give rise to a conflict with conscious control. But the quantitative factor is manifestly decisive for this conflict; as soon as an idea which is fundamentally offensive exceeds a certain degree of strength, the conflict takes on actuality, and it is precisely activation of the idea that leads to its repression. So that, where repression is concerned, an increase in energic cathexis operates in the same way as an approach to the unconscious, while a decrease in that energy operates like distance from the unconscious or like distortion. We understand that the repressing tendencies can find a substitute for repression in a weakening or lessening of whatever is distasteful to them.   (16)

In our discussion hitherto we have dealt with the repression of an instinct-presentation, and by that we understood an idea or group of ideas which is cathected with a definite amount of the mental energy (libido, interest) pertaining to an instinct. Now clinical observation forces us further to dissect something that hitherto we have conceived of as a single entity, for it shows us that beside the idea there is something else, another presentation of the instinct to be considered, and that this other element undergoes a repression which may be quite different from that of the idea. We have adopted the term *charge of affect* for this other element in the mental presentation; it represents that part of the instinct which has become detached from the idea, and finds proportionate expression, according to its quantity, in processes which become observable to perception as affects. From this point on, in describing a case of repression, we must follow up the fate of the idea which undergoes repression separately from that of the instinctual energy attached to the idea.   (17)

We should be glad enough to be able to give some general account of the outcome of both of these, and when we have taken our bearings a little we shall actually be able to do so. In general, repression of the ideational presentation of an instinct can surely only have the effect of causing it to vanish from consciousness, if it had previously been in consciousness, or of holding it back, if it is about to enter it. The difference, after all, is not important; it amounts to much the same thing as the difference between ordering an undesirable guest out of my drawing-room or out of my front hall, and refusing to let him cross my threshold once I have recognized

him.[1] The fate of the quantitative factor in the instinct-presentation may be one of three, as we see by a cursory survey of the observations made through psycho-analysis: either the instinct is altogether suppressed, so that no trace of it is found, or it appears in the guise of an affect of a particular qualitative tone, or it is transformed into anxiety. With the two last possibilities we are obliged to focus our attention upon the *transformation* into *affects*, and especially into *anxiety*, of the mental energy belonging to the *instincts*, this being a new possible vicissitude undergone by an instinct.
(18)

We recall the fact that the motive and purpose of repression was simply the avoidance of "pain." It follows that the fate of the charge of affect belonging to the presentation is far more important than that of the ideational content of it and is decisive for the opinion we form of the process of repression. If a repression does not succeed in preventing feelings of "pain" or anxiety from arising, we may say that it has failed, even though it may have achieved its aim as far as the ideational element is concerned. Naturally, the case of unsuccessful repression will have more claim on our interest than that of repression which is eventually successful; the latter will, for the most part, elude our study.   (19)

We now wish to gain some insight into the mechanism of the process of repression, and especially we want to know whether it has a single mechanism only, or more than one, and whether perhaps each of the psychoneuroses may be distinguished by a characteristic repression-mechanism peculiar to itself. At the outset of this inquiry, however, we encounter complications. The mechanism of a repression becomes accessible to us only when we deduce it from its final results. If we confine our observations to the results of its effect on the ideational part of the instinct-presentation, we discover that as a rule repression creates a *substitute-formation*. What, then, is the mechanism of such a substitute-formation, or must we distinguish several mechanisms here also? Further, we know that repression leaves *symptoms* in its train. May we then regard substitute-formation and symptom-formation as coincident processes, and, if this is on the whole possible, does the mechanism of substitute-formation coincide with that of repression? So far as we know at present, it seems probable that the two are widely divergent, that it is not the repression itself which produces substitute-formations and symptoms, but that these latter constitute indications of a *return of the repressed* and owe their existence to quite other processes. It would also seem advisable to examine the mechanisms of substitute- and symptom-formation before those of repression.   (20)

---

1 This metaphor, applicable to the process of repression, may also be extended to include one of the characteristics of repression mentioned earlier. I need only add that I have to place a sentinel to keep constant guard over the door which I have forbidden this guest to pass, lest he should burst it open (see above).

Obviously there is no ground here for speculation to explore: on the contrary, the solution of the problem must be found by careful analysis of the results of repression observable in the individual neuroses. I must, however, suggest that we should postpone this task, too, until we have formed reliable conceptions of the relation of consciousness to the unconscious. Only, in order that the present discussion may not be quite unfruitful, I will anticipate by saying: (1) that the mechanism of repression does not in fact coincide with the mechanism or mechanisms of substitute-formation, (2) that there are many different mechanisms of substitute-formation, and (3) that the different mechanisms of repression have at least this one thing in common: *a withdrawal of energic cathexis* (or of *libido*, if it is a question of sexual instincts).   (21)

Further, confining myself to the three best-known forms of psycho-neurosis, I will show by means of some examples how the conceptions here introduced find application to the study of repression. From *anxiety-hysteria*, I will choose an instance which has been subjected to thorough analysis—that of an animal-phobia. The instinctual impulse subjected to repression here is a libidinal attitude towards the father, coupled with dread of him. After repression, this impulse vanishes out of consciousness: the father does not appear in consciousness as an object for the libido. As a substitute for him we find in a corresponding situation some animal which is more or less suited to be an object of dread. The substitute-formation of the ideational element has established itself by way of a displacement along the line of a series of associated ideas which is determined in some particular way. The quantitative element has not vanished, but has been transformed into anxiety. The result is a fear of a wolf, instead of a claim for love from the father. Of course the categories here employed are not enough to supply a complete explanation even of the simplest case of psycho-neurosis: there are always other points of view to be taken into account.   (22)

Such a repression as that which takes place in an animal-phobia must be described as radically unsuccessful. All that it has done is to remove the idea and set another in its place; it has not succeeded at all in its aim of avoiding "pain." On this account, too, the work of the neurosis, far from ceasing, proceeds into a *second movement*, so to speak, which is designed to attain its immediate and more important aim. There follows an attempt at flight, the formation of the *phobia proper*—a number of things have to be *avoided* in order to prevent an outbreak of anxiety. A more particular investigation would enable us to understand the mechanism by which the phobia achieves its aim.   (23)

We are led to quite another view of the process of repression when we consider the picture of a true *conversion-hysteria*. Here the salient point is that it is possible to bring about a total disappearance of the charge of affect. The patient then displays towards his symptoms what Charcot called *"la belle indifférence des hystériques."* At other times, this suppression is not so completely successful: a part of the sensation of distress attaches to the symptoms themselves, or it has proved impossible entirely to prevent outbreaks of anxiety, and this in its turn sets the mechanism of phobia-formation working. The ideational content of the instinct-presentation is completely withdrawn from consciousness; as a substitute-formation—and concurrently, as a symptom—we have an excessive innervation (in typical cases, a somatic innervation), sometimes of a sensory, sometimes of a motor character, either as an excitation or as an inhibition. The area of over-innervation proves on closer observation to belong to the repressed in-stinct-presentation itself, and, as if by a process of *condensation,* to have absorbed the whole cathexis. Of course, these remarks do not cover the whole mechanism of a conversion-hysteria; the element of *regression* espe-cially, which will be appraised in another connection, has to be taken into account. (24)

In so far as it is rendered possible only by means of extensive substitute-formations, the repression which takes place in hysteria may be pro-nounced entirely unsuccessful; with reference to mastering the charge of affect however, which is the real task of repression, it generally betokens a complete success. Again, in conversion-hysteria the process of repression terminates with the formation of the symptom and does not, as in anxiety-hysteria, need to proceed to a *second-movement*—or, strictly speaking, an unlimited number of *movements.* (25)

A totally different aspect of repression is shown in the third affection to which we are referring for purposes of this comparison: in the *obses-sional neurosis.* Here we are at first in doubt what it is that we have to regard as the repressed instinct-presentation—a libidinal or a hostile trend. This uncertainty arises because the obsessional neurosis rests on the prem-ise of a regression by means of which a sadistic trend has been substituted for a tender one. It is this hostile impulse against a loved person which has undergone repression. The effect at an early phase of the work of repres-sion is quite different from that produced later. At first the repression is completely successful, the ideational content is rejected, and the affect made to disappear. As a substitute-formation, there arises an alteration in the ego, an increased sensitiveness of conscience, which can hardly be called a symptom. Substitute- and symptom-formation do not coincide here. Here, too, we learn something about the mechanism of repression. Repression, as it invariably does, has brought about a withdrawal of libido, but for this purpose it has made use of a *reaction-formation,* by intensify-ing an antithesis. So here the substitute-formation has the same mechanism as the repression and at bottom coincides with it, while yet chronologically, as well as in its content, it is distinct from the symptom-formation. It is very probable that the whole process is made possible by the ambivalent relation into which the sadistic impulse destined for repression has been introduced. (26)

But the repression, at first successful, does not hold; in the further course of things its failure becomes increasingly obvious. The ambivalence which has allowed repression to come into being by means of reaction-formation also constitutes the point at which the repressed succeeds in breaking through again. The vanished affect is transformed, without any diminution, into dread of the community, pangs of conscience, or self-reproaches; the rejected idea is replaced by a *displacement-substitute*, often by displacement on to something utterly trivial or indifferent. For the most part, there is an unmistakable tendency to complete reestablishment of the repressed idea. Failure of repression of the quantitative factor brings into play, by means of various taboos and prohibitions, the same mechanism of flight as we have seen at work in the formation of hysterical phobias. The rejection of the idea from consciousness is, however, obstinately maintained, because it ensures abstention from action, preclusion of the motor expression of an impulse. So the final form of the work of repression in the obsessional neurosis is a sterile and never-ending struggle. (27)

The short series of comparisons which have been presented here may easily convince us that more comprehensive investigations are necessary before we can hope to understand thoroughly the processes connected with repression and the formation of neurotic symptoms. The extraordinary intricacy of all the factors to be taken into consideration leaves us only one way open by which to present them. We must select first one and then another point of view, and follow it up through the material at our disposal, as long as application of it seems to prove fruitful. Each separate point so treated will be incomplete in itself and there cannot fail to be obscurities where we touch upon material not previously dealt with; but we may hope that the final synthesis of them all will lead to a good understanding of the subject. (28)

Sir Julian Huxley

(1887–   )

SIR JULIAN HUXLEY, *English biologist and author, has written or collaborated in the authorship of more than forty books since 1911, from* The Individual in the Animal Kingdom *(1911) to* Darwin and His World *(1965). His persistent interest in all aspects of evolutionary theory is seen in the following titles:* Evolution, the Modern Synthesis *(1942),* Evolutionary Ethics *(1943),* Evolution and Ethics *(1947),* Evolution in Action *(1953),* The Story of Evolution *(1959.)*

◼ *Science and God:*
The Naturalistic Approach

GODS ARE AMONG the empirical facts of cultural history. Like other empirical facts, they can be investigated by the method of science—dispassionate observation and analysis, leading to the formulation of hypotheses which can then be tested by further observation and analysis, followed by synthesis and the framing of broad interpretative concepts.   (1)

Thanks to the labours of social anthropologists, historians, archæologists, and students of comparative religion, the facts about gods are now so abundant that their comparative and evolutionary study can readily be pursued, while the progress of the natural and social sciences and in particular of psychology has made it possible to attempt a radical analysis of their nature, functions and effects. Theology was once called the Queen of the Sciences; but that was in an age when the word *science* was equated (as it still is on the continent of Europe) with the whole of organised learning. In the restricted modern English sense of the term, theology has been, as my grandfather T. H. Huxley said, only a pseudo-science. But if the scientific method were applied to its subject-matter, it could become a true science. As sub-sciences of such a truly scientific theology, we might envisage Comparative Theomorphology, Divine in addition to Animal and Plant Physiology, Psychodivinity, and Evolutionary Theobiology.   (2)

There are, it seems to me, three possible ways of envisaging and defining the nature of gods. In briefest terms, the first is that gods have real independent existence as personal but supernatural beings able to control or influence the natural world. The second is that gods are personalised representations, created by human minds, of the forces affecting human destiny. And the third, which is in a sense a compromise between the other two, is that they are more or less adequate attempts by man to describe or denote a single eternal suprapersonal and supernatural Being with a real existence behind or above nature.   (3)

Before going further, I had better amplify these statements a little. By *personal beings,* I mean beings endowed with the higher attributes of human personalities—knowing, feeling, and willing—integrated in an organised and enduring unity of consciousness: by *suprapersonal,* I intend a being with a nature akin to human personality, but beyond our limited human understanding: and by *personalised representation* I mean an attempt to describe or interpret natural phenomena with an objective existence, in terms of action by hypothetical personal beings in or behind phenomena—in psychological terms, the projection of the idea of supernatural personality into our experience of nature and our ideas about destiny.   (4)

There are of course other types of attempted definition of gods. For the consistent materialist and the fanatical rationalist, gods are pure fictions, not only without any real existence, but without any basis or background in fact, invented by priests and rulers to keep ordinary people in intellectual and moral subjection. This is, to me, itself a fiction as gross as the one it pretends to demolish, an error as childish as the semantic error of taking the existence of the word God as evidence of His real existence.   (5)

Then there are the attempts of theologians to evade the dilemmas in which they are landed by the acceptance of an all-wise, all-good and all-powerful God as ruler of a world in which chaos and ignorance, suffering, strife and evil are such regrettably prominent features. Some take refuge in the thesis that God is beyond human comprehension, and that we must therefore accept the apparent contradiction resignedly without attempting to understand. This is a counsel of despair and an abrogation of man's intelligence and mental powers. If the universe is ruled by a god, it must be our business to try to understand his policy: if there is a divine design for the world, a prime task of religion must be to discover and interpret it. If such understanding and discovery is intrinsically impossible, then belief in god is a poor basis for religion or for conduct.   (6)

Then there are the attempts to redefine god so as to fit in with historical and scientific knowledge. We are told that god is the Absolute, whatever that may mean; or 'a power, not ourselves, that makes for righteousness'; without specifying the nature of that power; or a general spiritual force behind phenomena; or the everlasting ground of being; etcetera. However, to assert, like some idealist philosophers, that the ground of all reality is wholly spiritual, and then, after christening this hypothetical ground the Absolute, to pretend that it is a new and better version of the god built up by religion out of quite other aspects of reality, is intellectually unjustified. Such a god is only a dummy divinity, a theatrical *deus ex machina* dropped on to the religious stage through the trapdoor of metaphysics.   (7)

And for theologians to claim that god is 'in reality' some abstract entity or depersonalised spiritual principle, while in practice their churches inculcate belief in a personal divinity who rules and judges, who demands worship and submission, who is capable of anger and forgiveness—that is plain intellectual dishonesty.   (8)

Let me return to the three possible ways of envisaging the nature of gods. In the light of our present knowledge I maintain that only the second is tenable—that gods are creations of man, personalised representations of the forces of destiny, with their unity projected into them by human thought and imagination.   (9)

In parentheses I should say that I do *not* mean only our present knowledge in the field of natural science, but also our knowledge in the fields of history, prehistory, and cultural anthropology, of human psychology and of comparative religion.   (10)

This general statement on the nature of gods can be profitably reformulated and spelled out somewhat as follows. History shows an increasingly successful extension of the naturalistic approach to more and more fields of experience, coupled with a progressive failure and restriction of supernaturalist interpretation. The time has now come for a naturalistic approach to theology. In the light of this approach, gods appear as interpretative concepts or hypotheses. They are hypotheses aiming at fuller comprehension of the facts of human destiny, in the same way that scientific hypotheses aim at fuller comprehension of the facts of nature.[1] They are theoretical constructions of the human mind, in the same way as are

---

1 For an interesting philosophical discussion of the problem see Professor John Wisdom's essay on Gods in his *Philosophy and Psychoanalysis*. He rightly points out that statements about God are often statements about real phenomena, in the shape of experiences, but he does not come to grips with the view that the term *God* itself involves a hypothesis or assumption.

scientific theories and concepts: and, like scientific theories and laws, they are based on experience and observable facts.   (11)

God hypotheses are part of a more general theory, the daimonic theory as it is usefully called, according to which supernatural spiritual beings, good, bad, or indifferent, and of very different degrees of importance, play a part in the affairs of the cosmos.[2]   (12)

The analogy between theology and natural science deserves a little further exploration. In the history of natural science the absolutist approach, involving *a priori*, dogmatic or purely rationalistic methods, has been gradually given up in favour of scientific naturalism—the progressive method of observation and hypothesis, followed by the checking of hypothesis by fresh observation.   (13)

As every schoolboy knows, many hypotheses and theories and so-called laws of nature have been abandoned or superseded in the light of new factual knowledge. Thus for centuries astronomical theory was subordinated to the *a priori* principle that perfection reigned in celestial affairs and that accordingly, since the circle was the perfect form, the heavenly bodies must move in circles. This led to the impossible complications of Ptolemaic astronomy, which fell like a house of cards when Kepler showed that elliptical orbits provided a simpler and more adequate explanation of the observed facts.   (14)

Again, the classical theory (which might better be described as a scientific myth) of the Four Elements—Earth, Air, Fire and Water—held the field for centuries, and it was possible by ingenious manipulation to fit a great many facts into its theoretical framework. But eventually this became impossible—the framework proved to be not merely inadequate but downright wrong; and the atomic theory, which is still in process of development, took its place. Similarly in biology, Darwin's work necessitated the immediate abandonment of the theory of creation in favour of evolution; and the Lamarckian theory of evolution by the inheritance of acquired characters has been dropped because it no longer fits the facts.   (15)

Gods, like scientific hypotheses, are attempts to understand the cosmos and explain or at least interpret the facts of experience. But they differ from modern scientific hypotheses in various ways. For one thing, they are still largely dogmatic or *a priori*, deriving from authority or feeling or intuition instead of from constant checking and rechecking against fact. As a consequence, they no longer fit the facts; but in so far as they are formulated in absolutist terms, they cannot afford to die and be reborn in new guise. Authoritarian dogmas and revelations resemble the Struldbrugs of *Gulliver's Travels* in being condemned to an uncomfortable survival

---

2 See Professor Ralph Turner's discussion of 'the Daimonic Universe' in his *The Great Cultural Traditions*, vols. 1 and 2 (McGraw-Hill, New York, 1941).

long after their original vigour and significance has been exhausted. Luckily, however, they differ from Struldbrugs in not being immortal. They *can* die—though usually their death is belated, so that they have kept their youthful competitors in the world of ideas out of their rightful place for far too long.   (16)

Gods differ even more radically from the hypotheses of science in being created by primitive and prescientific methods of thinking. They are thus unscientific in essence, and in the long run anti-scientific in their effects. Gods are among the products of what Ernst Cassirer in his notable three-volume study, *The Philosophy of Symbolic Forms,*[3] calls mythical thought, which is basically non-rational: it fails to exclude feeling and fantasy from its judgments, and does not operate according to the laws of logic or by utilising scientific method.   (17)

Mythical thought in Cassirer's sense includes three rather different modes of thinking and of framing its ideas and symbols. The most primitive, and the one which appears to operate inevitably in the earliest stages of individual life, I would call the magic mode. For magic thinking, the world is basically a reservoir of magic power. It works as a system of interacting magic influences, some diffused, some concentrated in particular external objects or processes, some intrinsic in man and operating through verbal symbols and ritual actions. Magic thinking apparently grows out of the infantile phase that Freud has characterised as that of the omnipotence of thought. The early infantile world is a world of feeling and emotion, of the satisfaction and frustration of desires. The infant speedily discovers that he can often obtain satisfactions by expressing his emotions; such expression is of necessity to some extent symbolic, an external symbol to others of the internal reality. That reality is a reality of emotion, intense and without compromise. Emotional thinking operates by the primitive all-or-nothing methods of animal instinct: the personality is wholly possessed by one emotion—and then of a sudden it is not possessed at all. The expression of his emotions is the infant's only method of communication with the world outside himself. Only after learning to speak does he acquire the capacity for rational thought and the communication of non-emotional experience.   (18)

It seems clear that the idea of magic influence originates from this pre-rational phase of individual mental life, but is later enlarged by primitive society to cover the workings of nature as a whole.   (19)

Whatever its actual origin, it is clear that the magic mode of thinking operates by extending the idea of immanent power, emotionally and morally charged, from man's primal experience of it within himself to the universe around him. Magic is an interpretation of destiny in terms of per-

---

3 Yale University Press, New Haven.

vading spiritual—or rather, non-material—influences or forces, making for enjoyment or misery, good or evil, fruition or frustration, and capable of being humanly controlled by appropriate methods.   (20)

Magic thought is a coherent and self-consistent system. It is also delightfully elastic. Whenever magic methods fail to secure the desired control of events, an excuse is always ready to hand—the ritual was not properly executed, the spells not quite right, the occasion not propitious, another magician was making more powerful magic. . . .   (21)

The second mode of organising mythical thought may be called the projective, in which personality is projected into the external world. (22)

After the primary infantile phase in which the baby lives in a world of his own emotions, the next step in experience is the awareness of personality—first other people's, beginning with the mother's, and later his own. Personal beings are recognised, and are found to influence the world of desires and emotions by their control of events. The natural and apparently inevitable consequence is for the child to personalise events and objects which arouse emotion and favour or frustrate his desires.   (23)

Lewis Mumford, in his admirable book *The Conduct of Life,*[4] has stressed the fact, too often neglected by the intellectualism of logicians and philosophers and the materialist 'scientism' of empirical scientists and practical technicians, that the infant's early world is a world of feelings and people, in which objects are not separately distinguished, but are apprehended only as part of an emotional experience. This being so, it is inevitable that primitive thinking should operate in terms of emotional powers and personal agents.   (24)

Only later, with the aid of words as mental tools, can the child categorise experience in terms of things and ideas, and start thinking objectively and intellectually. And even then, objects and events often remain charged with the emotional forces and projected personalities of earlier modes of thought. Indeed language itself is primitively charged with such emotional and personal significance: the progress of human science and learning has been bound up with the development of appropriate language, more objective and more rational. Mathematics, of course, represents the fullest expression of such emotionally uncommitted language, while the arts have concentrated on emotionally charged and often non-verbal symbolism.   (25)

In any case, the projection of personality into external things and events provides the basis on which the daimonic phase of early human thinking was organised. Projective thought peopled the universe with demons, spirits, devils, ghosts and gods. And under the outer pressure of accumulated experience and the inner pressure of man's exercise of logical

4 Harcourt, Brace, New York, 1951.

reasoning, these cultural entities proceeded to evolve in fantastic multiplicity. (26)

The third mode of mythical thought may be specifically called the mythological, which sets out to give theoretical explanations of phenomena, especially explanations of their origins, whenever factual knowledge is insufficient. To do this, it requires language and must wait on reason applied to experience; and so, like the later creation of gods by projective thinking, it can only operate when, with the aid of speech, the infant has become a child. (27)

Just as magic becomes intertwined with daimonic thinking, so gods are frequently involved in mythology: the three modes of mythical thought, though apparently successive in origin, remain entangled for much of history. Sometimes, indeed, as with culture-heroes, mythology makes a novel use of the god-hypothesis as part of its explanation. All mythical thought is purposely interpretative, and attempts to confer significance on reality. The trouble is that, since it always starts from incomplete knowledge and almost always from false premises, its significances are usually wrong, distorted or misleading. (29)

In passing, it should be noted that elements of the mythical modes of thinking may survive in naturalistic and scientific thought. Hypostasised 'forces' and 'principles' are de-emotionalised refinements of personalised thinking; and cosmological speculations like that of continuous creation are myths dressed up in scientific guise and expressed in the naturalistic mode. (29)

I have spoken of the origin of gods: it remains now to consider the fascinating subject of their subsequent evolution. (30)

In biological evolution, we find many different types, characterised by different plans of organisation (for instance insect *versus* vertebrate, or mammal *versus* reptile). Every successful type evolves into a large group, characterised by a rapid increase in numbers and in variety of sub-types. During its evolution, it shows gradual trends towards improvement—sometimes improvement in general organisation, sometimes in this or that specialised efficiency. In the great majority of cases, these trends eventually become stabilised. In plain language, they come to an end, and the type (if it does not die out) continues indefinitely on the same level of organisation or specialisation: it has exhausted its inherent possibilities of major improvement. (31)

Further, every type of course finds itself in competition with other evolving types: and such competition may modify the course of its evolution, restrict its improvement, reduce its numbers and variety, and sometimes even lead to its virtual or total extinction. And large-scale biological progress occurs through the replacement of one successful or dominant type by another, as in the classical example of the replacement of the coldblooded reptiles by the warm-blooded mammals and birds as the dominant type of land animals at the close of the Mesozoic about sixty million years ago.   (32)

Gods are not organisms, but they are organised cultural entities: like other cultural entities, they can and do evolve, and in a way which shows many points of resemblance (though also of difference) to the biological evolution of organisms. Substantially, they are organisations of human thought which seek to represent, canalise, and give a comprehensible interpretation of the forces affecting human destiny: formally, they are organised in the guise of personal beings.   (33)

The forces affecting human destiny that underlie the construction of gods are immensely various. They include the elemental forces of nature and its catastrophes, from earthquake to pestilence; the phenomena of growth and reproduction, plant, animal and human; the emotional forces aroused by the terrifying and the mysterious, and by the sense of sacredness experienced at the crises of human life, like birth and death, puberty and marriage; authority, of father and family, of priest and king, of law and church, of city, tribe and society at large; the power of conscience, of ideals, of the forces of light struggling with the forces of darkness; the power of all compulsions, whether external or internal.   (34)

In his religions, man starts with variety and gradually organises it into some sort of a unity. In certain stages, every society has multiform gods, often of different degrees of importance, representing different special bits of destiny and its forces. Particular objects or places may be deified; or separate aspects of nature like sea, sun, or storm; or different aspects of human natures as in the later Greek pantheon; the city may be represented by a god as in ancient Mesopotamia, or the tribe as in early Judaism, or the household as in ancient Rome; human individuals may be deified or divinised, whether for their mythical exploits like hero-gods, or by traditional virtue of their office like the Egyptian Pharaohs, or deliberately like Roman Emperors, or in their rôle as saviours like Jesus or the Buddha. There is, in fact, as in biological evolution, a proliferation of specialised variety.[5]   (35)

Improvement of the type also takes place. In the first place, gods are transferred from the natural to the supernatural world, from the material to the non-material or spiritual. It is no longer the tree or the rock, the animal or the image which is worshipped, but the spiritual being behind the object or above the phenomena. At the same time, gods are spiritualised: in their make-up, less emphasis is laid on the crude forces of physical

---

5 Homer Smith's *Man and his Gods* (Little, Brown, Boston, 1952) gives a vivid picture of the evolution of gods during human history.

nature and life, more on the human ideals of justice and truth, benevolence and wise but firm authority, compassion and love. The conflict between the unimproved and the improved type of god is familiarly exemplified by the struggle of the Hebrew prophets against 'idolatry'. (36)

This also illustrates another kind of improvement—the trend from variety towards unity or at least some degree of unification. A first approach may be made by erecting one god in a pantheon to the position of chief ruler, as occurred with Zeus in Greek religion; or by divinising a human ruler as symbolising the unity of a vast empire over and above the variety of other gods and cults which it contains, as with the Roman Emperors. (37)

A further radical step may take place by the conversion of a tribal god into a universal deity, as in Judaism. Or the universality and singularity of the deity may be proclaimed from the outset, as with Islam. Or finally the difficulty of embodying all attributes of divinity in a single person may be met by that brilliant device of Christian theology, triunity—the tripartite unity of the Trinity. (38)

During cultural as during biological evolution, there is a struggle for existence between ideas and belief. There is not only a struggle between gods, but gods in general come into competition with other cultural entities which are seeking to interpret a similar range of phenomena, and so compete for the same area of ideological territory. The most important of these competitors are scientific concepts concerning various aspects of man's destiny, beginning with the world of physical nature in which that destiny is cast, and gradually invading the field of human nature. (39)

The so-called 'conflict between religion and science' results from, or indeed is constituted by, this competition. In broadest terms, the competition is between two dominant types of cultural entity—the god hypothesis, organised on the basis of mythical thinking, and the naturalistic hypothesis, organised on the basis of scientific method. (40)

As a matter of historical fact, the results of this competition have been to expel gods from positions of effective control, from direct operative contact with more and more aspects of nature, to push them into an ever further remoteness behind or beyond phenomena. Newton showed that gods did not control the movements of the planets: Laplace in a famous aphorism affirmed that astronomy had no need of the god hypothesis: Darwin and Pasteur between them did the same for biology: and in our own century the rise of scientific psychology and the extension of historical knowledge have removed gods to a position where they are no longer of value in interpreting human behaviour and cannot be supposed to control human history or interfere with human affairs. Today, God can no longer be considered as the controller of the universe in any but a Pickwickian

sense. The god hypothesis is no longer of any pragmatic value for the interpretation or comprehension of nature, and indeed often stands in the way
of better and truer interpretation. Operationally, God is beginning to resemble not a ruler, but the last fading smile of a cosmic Cheshire Cat.
(41)

There has been other competition too—from the progressive seculari-
sation of the sacred. Many areas of life once unquestioningly recognised as
God's domain, many activities originally regarded as pertaining solely to
the service or worship of gods, have now been secularised. In ancient
Mesopotamia, economic affairs were a province of the god of the city, and
astronomy was practised only by his ministers. Government was originally
a divine prerogative: the Pharaohs of Egypt ruled as gods, and the Divine
Right of Kings survived into modern times. Drama was first liberated from
religion in classical Greece, and Sunday still belongs almost entirely to
God in parts of Scotland. For the Jews, morals were the edict of Jehovah.
Only in high civilisations does art become emancipated from religious or
pseudo-religious domination. The Bible was for long regarded as the Word
of God: we all know how this notion of divine revelation has impeded
the growth of knowledge.[6]   (42)

This secular competition has also modified the evolution of gods during history. The relations with social activities have become progressively
restricted. Today, gods are no longer spearheads of history, as they were in
early Islam or in the Spanish conquest of the New World; they no longer
operate in international politics as the Christian god did in the medieval
days of the Holy Roman Empire; they no longer enforce opinion and doctrine by war or punishment, torture or death as in the Albigensian Crusade or the early days of the Inquisition or in Calvin's theocracy, nor are
they effective in inciting large-scale persecutions, as against witches; they
no longer have much say in laying down the curriculum of universities, or
in dictating how citizens shall spend their time on Sundays; they no longer
dictate economic behaviour, as for instance by prohibiting the lending of
money at interest in medieval Christendom.   (43)

There are of course local exceptions, such as the Scottish sabbath I have
already mentioned, or the invoking of God to justify *apartheid* in South
Africa; and sex has not yet been secularised, at least in respect of marriage,
divorce, and birth control, for Roman Catholics. But by and large, in the

---

6 The grave results of authoritarianism based on the arrogant assumption of possessing the sole
and absolute religious truth are well documented by Paul Blanshard in his trilogy, *American Freedom
and Catholic Power; Communism, Democracy and Catholic Power;* and *The Irish and Catholic Power;*
while the alarming effects of idolising a sacred book are shown in Marley Cole's study of *Jehovah's
Witnesses* (1956).
Eric Fromm, in his brilliant book *Escape from Freedom*, has pointed out how human timidity and the
desire for reassurance at all costs have inhibited the rational approach and encouraged the growth of
authoritarian systems of belief which claim to have all the answers.

Western world and in various other countries too, they have been forced out of public affairs and everyday activities, and their dominions have been in large measure taken over by the secular arm: their functions are now largely confined to providing individual salvation and assurance and—what is clearly of the greatest importance—awareness of a reality transcending customary limitations of time and space, more embracing than the nation, more enduring than any present organisation, larger than humanity.　　　　　　　　　　　　　　　　　　　　　　　(44)

But though their direct social and political functions have been diminished, they still continue to exert a powerful indirect influence on affairs. If men think about their destiny in terms of the god hypothesis it is impossible to avoid certain conclusions and practical consequences: belief in gods inevitably influences human conduct and the course of history. Among innumerable examples I may point to the rise of the Egyptian priesthood to powerful land-ownership; the weakness of the Aztec empire; the discouragement of many branches of science by the Church; and in our own day the effect of the Roman Catholic view of God on divorce, education, and population, or the attempts to impose a Koranic constitution on Islamic countries. T. D. Kendrick's admirable little book *The Lisbon Earthquake* gives a particular example of the practical effects of a theological as opposed to a scientific hypothesis of the causation of natural disasters.　　　　　　　　　　　　　　　　　　　　　　　　　(45)

The last major feature of biological evolution is progress by replacement of old by new dominant types of organism. This too is paralleled in cultural evolution. In the ideological field, as we have seen, cultural entities and systems concerned with destiny are of three main types—the magic, the divine, theistic or daimonic, and the naturalistic, the first organised on the magic hypothesis of pervading non-material power and magic influence, the second on the god hypothesis of supernatural beings, the third on the scientific hypothesis of comprehensible natural forces. (46)

Some time in prehistory gods replaced magic as the dominant type of belief-system, though magical concepts continued to play a considerable but increasingly subordinate rôle. The naturalistic type of belief-system made a premature appearance in the classical Greek world: but its organisation was then inadequate to compete with the god-system, and after a limited and primitive flowering, it went through a long period of repression and subordination. Only when it achieved an adequate plan of organisation, with the conscious formulation of scientific method in the seventeenth century, did it begin to play any significant rôle on the stage of cultural evolution. But from that time on, its rise was assured.　　　　(47)

There is a striking parallel with the biological evolution of a new dominant group such as the mammals. The earliest mammals appeared in the Triassic. But they were only proto-mammals, which had not achieved fully mammalian organisation. As a result they remained small and unimportant for the best part of a hundred million years. It was not until the reptiles had become stabilised and perhaps over-specialised, and the mammalian organisation at the same time radically improved, and after a world-wide climatic revolution had removed many competitors, that the mammals began their rapid rise to dominance.   (48)

Cultural evolution, however, is never identical with biological. Evolving biological entities are separate organic types. A single original organic type can produce a group by branching into a number of distinct sub-types, the ramifications remaining separate down to the level of species. A dominant group is one in which this process of diversification has produced a large variety of sub-types and a very large number of species: it is a biological entity defined on the one hand by the common ancestry of all its separate members, and on the other by its evolutionary success.   (49)

In cultural evolution, however, convergence and fusion are increasingly superposed on divergence and separation. Originally separate cultural elements may diffuse from one culture to another, ideas and practices arising in one segment of cultural life may invade other segments. Accordingly any cultural entity or system dealing with a major social function, like law or religion or education, is bound to be in some sort a synthesis, containing elements from other systems and other cultures.   (50)

For the materialistic and scientific approach, there is no such thing as religion in the abstract, only a number of actual religions. And all actual religions are organs of man in society for dealing with the problem of destiny on the one hand and the sense of the sacred on the other. If you like to combine the two, you can say that religion attempts to deal with the problem of destiny considered in the light of our sense of its essential sacredness and inevitable mystery.   (51)

Destiny confronts us in particular events of our individual lives—sickness, falling in love, bereavement, death, good or ill fortune. It is involved in the ordering of our personal existence on earth and the great question-mark of our continuance after death. In national guise, it confronts us through war, or hardship, or social evil that makes us ashamed. Finally, destiny extends beyond the nation to humanity at large; and beyond humanity to all of nature. Destiny confronts us in our ideals and our shortcomings, our aspirations and our sins, in our questioning thoughts about what is most comprehensive and most enduring, and about all that remains unknown. Perhaps most embracingly, destiny is apprehended in the confrontation of actuality with unrealised possibility, of our sense of guilt with our sense of sacredness, of our imperfections with our possible perfectibility.   (52)

The time is ripe for the dethronement of gods from their dominant position in our interpretation of destiny, in favour of a naturalistic type of belief-system. The supernatural is being swept out of the universe in the flood of new knowledge of what is natural. It will soon be as impossible for an intelligent, educated man or woman to believe in a god as it is now to believe that the earth is flat, that flies can be spontaneously generated, that disease is a divine punishment, or that death is always due to witch-craft. Gods will doubtless survive, sometimes under the protection of vested interests, or in the shelter of lazy minds, or as puppets used by politicians, or as refuges for unhappy and ignorant souls: but the god type will have ceased to be dominant in man's ideological evolution.   (53)

However, this will not happen unless the emerging naturalistic type of belief is fully adequate to its task: and that task is the formidable one of interpreting and canalising human destiny. Thus the short-lived Goddess of Reason of the French Revolution was a non-viable hybrid between the naturalistic and the god type of belief.   (54)

Already some non-theistic belief-systems have emerged to dominate large sections of humanity. The two most obvious are Nazism in Germany and Marxist Communism in Russia. Nazism was inherently self-destructive because of its claim to world domination by a small group. It was also grotesquely incorrect and limited as an interpretation of destiny, analogous to some of the primitive products of the theistic type, such as deified beasts, bloodthirsty tribal deities, or revengeful divine tyrants.   (55)

Marxist Communism is much better organised and more competent, but its purely materialist basis has limited its efficacy. It has tried to deny the reality of spiritual values. But they exist, and the Communists have had to accept the consequences of their ideological error, and grudgingly throw the churches open to the multitudes seeking the spiritual values which had been excluded from the system.   (56)

Before an adequate naturalistic belief-system can develop, scientific method must have been applied in all the fields contributing to human destiny: otherwise the system will be incomplete and will merely provide one of the premature syntheses that Gardner Murphy[7] rightly stigmatises as standing in the way of fuller comprehension. To be adequate, it must include scientific knowledge about cultural as well as cosmic and biological evolution, about human nature and social nature as well as about physical and organic nature, about values and gods, rituals and techniques, practical moralities and religious ideals as well as about atoms and cells, moons and suns, weather and disease-germs.   (57)

Only when scientific knowledge is organised in a way relevant to our

[7] *Proceedings of the Columbia Bicentennial*, 1954.

ideas about destiny can we speak of a naturalistic belief-system; and only
when the scientific knowledge concerns all aspects of destiny will the belief-
system begin to be adequate.   (58)

> I will not cease from mental fight,
>   Nor shall my sword sleep in my hand,
> Till we have built Jerusalem
>   In England's green and pleasant land.
>   —WILLIAM BLAKE.

> We cannot kindle when we will
>   The fire that in the heart resides,
> The spirit bloweth and is still,
>   In mystery the soul abides.
> But tasks in hours of insight willed
> May be through hours of gloom fulfilled.
>   —MATTHEW ARNOLD, *Morality.*

> But at my back I always hear
> Time's wingèd chariot hurrying near;
> And yonder all before us lie
> Deserts of vast eternity. . . .
> . . . Let us roll all our strength and all
> Our sweetness up into one ball,
> And tear our pleasures with rough strife
> Through the iron gates of life.
>   —ANDREW MARVELL, *To his coy mistress.*

> . . . Not for these I raise
>   The song of thanks and praise;
> But for those obstinate questionings
> Of sense and outward things,
>   Fallings from us, vanishings;
>   Blank misgivings of a Creature
> Moving about in worlds not realised,
> High instincts before which our mortal Nature
> Did tremble like a guilty thing surprised.
>   —WILLIAM WORDSWORTH,
>   *Ode on Intimations of Immortality.*   (59)

Bertrand Russell

(1872–   )

RUSSELL, Third Earl Russell, winner of the Nobel Prize for Literature and mathematician and philosopher extraordinary, has been a prolific commentator on a wide variety of subjects for more than seventy years, as a select few of his multitude of titles will quickly show: German Social Democracy *(1896),* Principles of Mathematics *(1903),* Principles of Social Reconstruction *(1917),* The ABC of Atoms *(1923),* The ABC of Relativity *(1926),* Education and the Social Order *(1932),* Power: A New Social Analysis *(1938),* History of Western Philosophy *(1946),* The Impact of Science upon Society *(1952),* Has Man a Future? *(1961),* Unarmed Victory *(1963). Lord Russell has been conspicuous in growing peace movements in recent years, and his eminence has attracted a great deal of journalistic comment. Perhaps Alan Wood's biography keynotes Russell's mood:* Bertrand Russell: The Passionate Sceptic *(1957).*

■ *A Free Man's Worship*

To DR. FAUSTUS in his study Mephistopheles told the history of the Creation, saying,

> The endless praises of the choirs of angels had begun to grow wearisome; for, after all, did he not deserve their praise? Had he not given them endless joy? Would it not be more amusing to obtain undeserved praise, to be worshiped by beings whom he tortured? He smiled inwardly, and resolved that the great drama should be performed.
>
> For countless ages the hot nebula whirled aimlessly through space. At length it began to take shape, the central mass threw

off planets, the planets cooled, boiling seas and burning mountains heaved and tossed, from black masses of cloud hot sheets
of rain deluged the barely solid crust. And now the first germ of
life grew in the depths of the ocean and developed rapidly in the
fructifying warmth into vast forest trees, huge ferns springing
from the damp mold, sea monsters breeding, fighting, devouring,
and passing away. And from the monsters, as the play unfolded
itself, Man was born, with the power of thought, the knowledge
of good and evil, and the cruel thirst for worship. And Man saw
that all is passing in this mad, monstrous world, that all is struggling to snatch, at any cost, a few brief moments of life before
Death's inexorable decree. And Man said, "There is a hidden
purpose, could we but fathom it, and the purpose is good; for
we must reverence something, and in the visible world there is
nothing worthy of reverence." And Man stood aside from the
struggle, resolving that God intended harmony to come out of
chaos by human efforts. And when he followed the instincts
which God had transmitted to him from his ancestry of beasts of
prey, he called it Sin, and asked God to forgive him. But he
doubted whether he could be justly forgiven, until he invented a
divine Plan by which God's wrath was to have been appeased.
And seeing the present was bad, he made it yet worse, that
thereby the future might be better. And he gave God thanks for
the strength that enabled him to forgo even the joys that were
possible. And God smiled; and when he saw that Man had become perfect in renunciation and worship, he sent another sun
through the sky, which crashed into Man's sun; and all returned
again to nebula.   (1)

"Yes," he murmured, "it was a good play; I will have it performed
again."   (2)

Such, in outline, but even more purposeless, more void of meaning,
is the world which science presents for our belief. Amid such a world, if
anywhere, our ideals henceforward must find a home. That man is the
product of causes which had no prevision of the end they were achieving;
that his origin, his growth, his hopes and fears, his loves and his beliefs,
are but the outcome of accidental collocations of atoms; that no fire, no
heroism, no intensity of thought and feeling, can preserve an individual
life beyond the grave; that all the labors of the ages, all the devotion, all
the inspiration, all the noonday brightness of human genius, are destined
to extinction in the vast death of the solar system, and that the whole
temple of man's achievement must inevitably be buried beneath the debris
of a universe in ruins—all these things, if not quite beyond dispute, are yet
so nearly certain that no philosophy which rejects them can hope to

stand. Only within the scaffolding of these truths, only on the firm foundation of unyielding despair, can the soul's habitation henceforth be safely
built. (3)

How, in such an alien and inhuman world, can so powerless a creature
as man preserve his aspirations untarnished? A strange mystery it is that
nature, omnipotent but blind, in the revolutions of her secular hurryings
through the abysses of space, has brought forth at last a child, subject still
to her power, but gifted with sight, with knowledge of good and evil, with
the capacity of judging all the works of his unthinking mother. In spite of
death, the mark and seal of the parental control, man is yet free, during
his brief years, to examine, to criticize, to know, and in imagination to
create. To him alone, in the world with which he is acquainted, this freedom belongs; and in this lies his superiority to the resistless forces that
control his outward life. (4)

The savage, like ourselves, feels the oppression of his impotence before
the powers of nature; but having in himself nothing that he respects more
than power, he is willing to prostrate himself before his gods, without
inquiring whether they are worthy of his worship. Pathetic and very terrible
is the long history of cruelty and torture, of degradation and human sacrifice, endured in the hope of placating the jealous gods: surely, the trembling
believer thinks, when what is most precious has been freely given, their
lust for blood must be appeased, and more will not be required. The
religion of Moloch—as such creeds may be generically called—is in essence
the cringing submission of the slave, who dare not, even in his heart, allow
the thought that his master deserves no adulation. Since the independence
of ideals is not yet acknowledged, power may be freely worshiped and
receive an unlimited respect, despite its wanton infliction of pain. (5)

But gradually, as morality grows bolder, the claim of the ideal world
begins to be felt; and worship, if it is not to cease, must be given to gods
of another kind than those created by the savage. Some, though they feel
the demands of the ideal, will still consciously reject them, still urging that
naked power is worthy of worship. Such is the attitude inculcated in
God's answer to Job out of the whirlwind: the divine power and knowledge
are paraded, but of the divine goodness there is no hint. Such also is the
attitude of those who, in our own day, base their morality upon the struggle for survival, maintaining that the survivors are necessarily the fittest.
But others, not content with an answer so repugnant to the moral sense,
will adopt the position which we have become accustomed to regard as
specially religious, maintaining that, in some hidden manner, the world
of fact is really harmonious with the world of ideals. Thus man created
God, all-powerful and all-good, the mystic unity of what is and what
should be. (6)

But the world of fact, after all, is not good; and, in submitting our judgment to it, there is an element of slavishness from which our thoughts must be purged. For in all things it is well to exalt the dignity of man, by freeing him as far as possible from the tyranny of nonhuman power. When we have realized that power is largely bad, that man, with his knowledge of good and evil, is but a helpless atom in a world which has no such knowledge, the choice is again presented to us: Shall we worship force, or shall we worship goodness? Shall our God exist and be evil, or shall he be recognized as the creation of our own conscience?   (7)

The answer to this question is very momentous and affects profoundly our whole morality. The worship of force, to which Carlyle and Nietzsche and the creed of militarism have accustomed us, is the result of failure to maintain our own ideals against a hostile universe: it is itself a prostrate submission to evil, a sacrifice of our best to Moloch. If strength indeed is to be respected, let us respect rather the strength of those who refuse that false "recognition of facts" which fails to recognize that facts are often bad. Let us admit that, in the world we know, there are many things that would be better otherwise, and that the ideals to which we do and must adhere are not realized in the realm of matter. Let us preserve our respect for truth, for beauty, for the ideal of perfection which life does not permit us to attain, though none of these things meet with the approval of the unconscious universe. If power is bad, as it seems to be, let us reject it from our hearts. In this lies man's true freedom: in determination to worship only the God created by our own love of the good, to respect only the heaven which inspires the insight of our best moments. In action, in desire, we must submit perpetually to the tyranny of outside forces; but in thought, in aspiration, we are free, free from our fellow men, free from the petty planet on which our bodies impotently crawl, free even, while we live, from the tyranny of death. Let us learn, then, that energy of faith which enables us to live constantly in the vision of the good; and let us descend, in action, into the world of fact, with that vision always before us.
                                (8)

When first the opposition of fact and ideal grows fully visible, a spirit of fiery revolt, of fierce hatred of the gods, seems necessary to the assertion of freedom. To defy with Promethean constancy a hostile universe, to keep its evil always in view, always actively hated, to refuse no pain that the malice of power can invent, appears to be the duty of all who will not bow before the inevitable. But indignation is still a bondage, for it compels our thoughts to be occupied with an evil world; and in the fierceness of desire from which rebellion springs there is a kind of self-assertion which it is necessary for the wise to overcome. Indignation is a submission of our thoughts but not of our desires; the Stoic freedom in which wisdom consists is found in the submission of our desires but not of our thoughts. From the submission of our desires springs the virtue of resignation; from the freedom of our thoughts springs the whole world of art and philosophy, and the vision of beauty by which, at last, we half reconquer the reluctant world. But the vision of beauty is possible only to unfettered contemplation, to thoughts not weighted by the load of eager wishes; and thus freedom comes only to those who no longer ask of life that it shall yield them any of those personal goods that are subject to the mutations of time.   (9)

Although the necessity of renunciation is evidence of the existence of evil, yet Christianity, in preaching it, has shown a wisdom exceeding that of the Promethean philosophy of rebellion. It must be admitted that, of the things we desire, some, though they prove impossible, are yet real goods; others, however, as ardently longed for, do not form part of a fully purified ideal. The belief that what must be renounced is bad, though sometimes false, is far less often false than untamed passion supposes; and the creed of religion, by providing a reason for proving that it is never false, has been the means of purifying our hopes by the discovery of many austere truths.
(10)

But there is in resignation a further good element: even real goods, when they are unattainable, ought not to be fretfully desired. To every man comes, sooner or later, the great renunciation. For the young, there is nothing unattainable; a good thing desired with the whole force of a passionate will, and yet impossible, is to them not credible. Yet, by death, by illness, by poverty, or by the voice of duty, we must learn, each one of us, that the world was not made for us, and that, however beautiful may be the things we crave, Fate may nevertheless forbid them. It is the part of courage, when misfortune comes, to bear without repining the ruin of our hopes, to turn away our thoughts from vain regrets. This degree of submission to power is not only just and right: it is the very gate of wisdom.   (11)

But passive renunciation is not the whole of wisdom; for not by renunciation alone can we build a temple for the worship of our own ideals. Haunting foreshadowings of the temple appear in the realm of imagination, in music, in architecture, in the untroubled kingdom of reason, and in the golden sunset magic of lyrics, where beauty shines and glows, remote from the touch of sorrow, remote from the fear of change, remote from the failures and disenchantments of the world of fact. In the contemplation of these things the vision of heaven will shape itself in our hearts, giving at once a touchstone to judge the world about us and an inspiration by which to fashion to our needs whatever is not incapable of serving as a stone in the sacred temple.   (12)

Except for those rare spirits that are born without sin, there is a cavern of darkness to be traversed before that temple can be entered. The gate of the cavern is despair, and its floor is paved with the gravestones of abandoned hopes. There self must die; there the eagerness, the greed of untamed desire, must be slain, for only so can the soul be freed from the empire of Fate. But out of the cavern, the Gate of Renunciation leads again to the daylight of wisdom, by whose radiance a new insight, a new joy, a new tenderness, shine forth to gladden the pilgrim's heart.   (13)

When, without the bitterness of impotent rebellion, we have learned both to resign ourselves to the outward rule of Fate and to recognize that the nonhuman world is unworthy of our worship, it becomes possible at last so to transform and refashion the unconscious universe, so to transmute it in the crucible of imagination, that a new image of shining gold replaces the old idol of clay. In all the multiform facts of the world—in the visual shapes of trees and mountains and clouds, in the events of the life of man, even in the very omnipotence of death—the insight of creative idealism can find the reflection of a beauty which its own thoughts first made. In this way mind asserts its subtle mastery over the thoughtless forces of nature. The more evil the material with which it deals, the more thwarting to untrained desire, the greater is its achievement in inducing the reluctant rock to yield up its hidden treasures, the prouder its victory in compelling the opposing forces to swell the pageant of its triumph. Of all the arts, tragedy is the proudest, the most triumphant: for it builds its shining citadel in the very center of the enemy's country, on the very summit of his highest mountain; from its impregnable watchtowers, his camps and arsenals, his columns and forts, are all revealed; within its walls the free life continues, while the legions of death and pain and despair, and all the servile captains of tyrant Fate, afford the burghers of that dauntless city new spectacles of beauty. Happy those sacred ramparts, thrice happy the dwellers on that all-seeing eminence. Honor to those brave warriors who, through countless ages of warfare, have preserved for us the priceless heritage of liberty and have kept undefiled by sacrilegious invaders the home of the unsubdued.   (14)

But the beauty of tragedy does but make visible a quality which, in more or less obvious shapes, is present always and everywhere in life. In the spectacle of death, in the endurance of intolerable pain, and in the irrevocableness of a vanished past, there is a sacredness, an overpowering awe, a feeling of the vastness, the depth, the inexhaustible mystery of existence, in which, as by some strange marriage of pain, the sufferer is bound to the world by bonds of sorrow. In these moments of insight, we lose all eagerness of temporary desire, all struggling and striving for petty ends, all care for the little trivial things that, to a superficial view, make up the common life of day by day; we see, surrounding the narrow raft illumined by the flickering light of human comradeship, the dark ocean on whose rolling waves we toss for a brief hour; from the great night without, a chill blast breaks in upon our refuge; all the loneliness of humanity and hostile forces is concentrated upon the individual soul, which must struggle alone, with what of courage it can command, against the whole weight of a universe that cares nothing for its hopes and fears. Victory, in this struggle with the powers of darkness, is the true baptism into the glorious company of heroes, the true initiation into the overmastering beauty of human existence. From that awful encounter of the soul with the outer world, renunciation, wisdom, and charity are born; and with their birth a new life begins. To take into the inmost shrine of the soul the irresistible forces whose puppets we seem to be—death and change, the irrevocableness of the past, and the powerlessness of man before the blind hurry of the universe from vanity to vanity—to feel these things and know them is to conquer them. (15)

This is the reason why the past has such magical power. The beauty of its motionless and silent pictures is like the enchanted purity of late autumn, when the leaves, though one breath would make them fall, still glow against the sky in golden glory. The past does not change or strive; like Duncan, after life's fitful fever it sleeps well; what was eager and grasping, what was petty and transitory, has faded away; the things that were beautiful and eternal shine out of it like stars in the night. Its beauty, to a soul not worthy of it, is unendurable; but to a soul which has conquered Fate it is the key of religion. (16)

The life of man, viewed outwardly, is but a small thing in comparison with the forces of nature. The slave is doomed to worship Time and Fate and Death, because they are greater than anything he finds in himself, and because all his thoughts are of things which they devour. But, great as they are, to think of them greatly, to feel their passionless splendor, is greater still. And such thought makes us free men; we no longer bow before the inevitable in Oriental subjection, but we absorb it and make it a part of ourselves. To abandon the struggle for private happiness, to expel all eagerness of temporary desire, to burn with passion for eternal things— this is emancipation, and this is the free man's worship. And this liberation is effected by contemplation of Fate; for Fate itself is subdued by the mind which leaves nothing to be purged by the purifying fire of time. (17)

United with his fellow men by the strongest of all ties, the tie of a common doom, the free man finds that a new vision is with him always, shedding over every daily task the light of love. The life of man is a long march through the night, surrounded by invisible foes, tortured by weariness and pain, toward a goal that few can hope to reach, and where none may tarry long. One by one, as they march, our comrades vanish from our sight, seized by the silent orders of omnipotent death. Very brief is the time in which we can help them, in which their happiness or misery is decided. Be it ours to shed sunshine on their path, to lighten their sorrows by the balm of sympathy, to give them the pure joy of a never-tiring affection, to strengthen failing courage, to instill faith in hours of despair. Let us not weigh in grudging scales their merits and demerits, but let us think only of their need—of the sorrows, the difficulties, perhaps the blindnesses, that make the misery of their lives; let us remember that they are fellow sufferers in the same darkness, actors in the same tragedy with ourselves. And so, when their day is over, when their good and their evil have become eternal by the immortality of the past, be it ours to feel that, where they suffered, where they failed, no deed of ours was the cause; but wherever a spark of the divine fire kindled in their hearts, we were ready with encouragement, with sympathy, with brave words in which high courage glowed. (18)

Brief and powerless is man's life; on him and all his race the slow, sure doom falls pitiless and dark. Blind to good and evil, reckless of destruction, omnipotent matter rolls on its relentless way; for man, condemned today to lose his dearest, tomorrow himself to pass through the gate of darkness, it remains only to cherish, ere yet the blow falls, the lofty thoughts that ennoble his little day; disdaining the coward terrors of the slave of Fate, to worship at the shrine that his own hands have built; undismayed by the empire of chance, to preserve a mind free from the wanton tyranny that rules his outward life; proudly defiant of the irresistible forces that tolerate, for a moment, his knowledge and his condemnation, to sustain alone, a weary but unyielding Atlas, the world that his own ideals have fashioned despite the tramping march of unconscious power. (19)

Alan Wilson Watts

(1915–   )

WATTS *has in recent years devoted himself to independent writing and lecturing. Before that, he had been professor of comparative philosophy and dean at the American Academy of Asian Studies, University of the Pacific. He has held several distinguished research fellowships (Harvard, the Bollingen Foundation, and so forth) and has been appointed guest lecturer at many universities, including Harvard, Yale, Cambridge, Cornell, Chicago, Hawaii, and Zurich. Representative titles include* The Legacy of Asia *and Western Man (1937),* Myth and Ritual in Christianity *(1953),*

The Way of Liberation in Zen Buddhism *(1955),* The Joyous Cosmology *(1962), and* Beyond Theology *(1964). His most persistent specialization has been in "the way of Zen."*

■ *"Sitting Quietly, Doing Nothing"*

IN BOTH LIFE and art the cultures of the Far East appreciate nothing more highly than spontaneity or naturalness (*tzu-jan*). This is the unmistakable tone of sincerity marking the action which is not studied and contrived. For a man rings like a cracked bell when he thinks and acts with a split mind—one part standing aside to interfere with the other, to control, to condemn, or to admire. But the mind, or the true nature of man cannot actually be split. According to a *Zenrin* poem, it is

> *Like a sword that cuts, but cannot cut itself;*
> *Like an eye that sees, but cannot see itself.*

The illusion of the split comes from the mind's attempt to be both itself and its idea of itself, from a fatal confusion of fact with symbol. To make an end of the illusion, the mind must stop trying to act upon itself, upon its stream of experiences, from the standpoint of the idea of itself which we call the ego. This is expressed in another *Zenrin* poem as

> *Sitting quietly, doing nothing,*
> *Spring comes, and the grass grows by itself.*   (1)

This "by itself" is the mind's and the world's natural way of action, as when the eyes see by themselves, and the ears hear by themselves, and the mouth opens by itself without having to be forced apart by the fingers. As the *Zenrin* says again:

> *The blue mountains are of themselves blue mountains;*
> *The white clouds are of themselves white clouds.*

In its stress upon naturalness, Zen is obviously the inheritor of Taoism, and its view of spontaneous action as "marvelous activity" (*miao-yung*) is precisely what the Taoists meant by the word *te*—"virtue" with an overtone of magical power. But neither in Taoism nor in Zen does it have anything to do with magic in the merely sensational sense of performing superhuman "miracles." The "magical" or "marvelous" quality of spontaneous action is, on the contrary, that it is perfectly human, and yet shows no sign of being contrived.$^{\bullet}$ (2)

Such a quality is peculiarly subtle (another meaning of *miao*), and extremely hard to put into words. The story is told of a Zen monk who wept upon hearing of the death of a close relative. When one of his fellow students objected that it was most unseemly for a monk to show such personal attachment he replied, "Don't be stupid! I'm weeping because I want to weep." The great Hakuin was deeply disturbed in his early study of Zen when he came across the story of the master Yen-t'ou, who was said to have screamed at the top of his voice when murdered by a robber.[1] Yet this doubt was dissolved at the moment of his *satori*, and in Zen circles his own death is felt to have been especially admirable for its display of human emotion. On the other hand, the abbot Kwaisen and his monks allowed themselves to be burned alive by the soldiers of Oda Nobunaga, sitting calmly in the posture of meditation. Such contradictory "naturalness" seems most mysterious, but perhaps the clue lies in the saying of Yün-men: "In walking, just walk. In sitting, just sit. Above all, don't wobble." For the essential quality of naturalness is the sincerity of the undivided mind which does not dither between alternatives. So when Yen-t'ou screamed, it was such a scream that it was heard for miles around.   (3)

But it would be quite wrong to suppose that this natural sincerity comes about by observing such a platitude as "Whatsoever thy hand findeth to do, do it with all they might." When Yen-t'ou screamed, he was not screaming *in order* to be natural, nor did he first make up his mind to scream and then implement the decision with the full energy of his will. There is a total contradiction in planned naturalness and intentional sincerity. This is to overlay, not to discover, the "original mind." Thus to try to be natural is an affectation. To try not to try to be natural is also an affectation. As a *Zenrin* poem says:

> *You cannot get it by taking thought;*
> *You cannot seek it by not taking thought.*

But this absurdly complex and frustrating predicament arises from a simple and elementary mistake in the use of the mind. When this is understood, there is no paradox and no difficulty. Obviously, the mistake arises in the attempt to split the mind against itself, but to understand this clearly we have to enter more deeply into the "cybernetics" of the mind, the basic pattern of its self-correcting action.   (4)

It is, of course, part of the very genius of the human mind that it can, as

---

1 *Ch'uan Teng Lu*, 26.

it were, stand aside from life and reflect upon it, that it can be aware of its own existence, and that it can criticize its own processes. For the mind has something resembling a "feed-back" system. This is a term used in communications engineering for one of the basic principles of "automation," of enabling machines to control themselves. Feed-back enables a machine to be informed of the effects of its own action in such a way as to be able to correct its action. Perhaps the most familiar example is the electrical thermostat which regulates the heating of a house. By setting an upper and a lower limit of desired temperature, a thermometer is so connected that it will switch the furnace on when the lower limit is reached, and off when the upper limit is reached. The temperature of the house is thus kept within the desired limits. The thermostat provides the furnace with a kind of sensitive organ—an extremely rudimentary analogy of human self-consciousness.[2] (5)

The proper adjustment of a feed-back system is always a complex mechanical problem. For the original machine, say, the furnace, is adjusted by the feed-back system, but this system in turn needs adjustment. Therefore to make a mechanical system more and more automatic will require the use of a series of feed-back systems—a second to correct the first, a third to correct the second, and so on. But there are obvious limits to such a series, for beyond a certain point the mechanism will be "frustrated" by its own complexity. For example, it might take so long for the information to pass through the series of control systems that it would arrive at the original machine too late to be useful. Similarly, when human beings think too carefully and minutely about an action to be taken, they cannot make up their minds in time to act. In other words, one cannot correct one's means of self-correction indefinitely. There must soon be a source of information at the end of the line which is the final authority. Failure to trust its authority will make it impossible to act, and the system will be paralyzed. (6)

The system can be paralyzed in yet another way. Every feed-back system needs a margin of "lag" or error. If we try to make a thermostat absolutely accurate—that is, if we bring the upper and lower limits of temperature very close together in an attempt to hold the temperature at a constant 70 degrees—the whole system will break down. For to the extent that the upper and lower limits coincide, the signals for switching off and switching on will coincide! If 70 degrees is both the lower and upper limit the "go"

2 I do not wish to press the analogy between the human mind and servo-mechanisms to the point of saying that the mind-body is "nothing but" an extremely complicated mechanical automaton. I only want to go so far as to show that feed-back involves some problems which are similar to the problems of self-consciousness and self-control in man. Otherwise, mechanism and organism seem to me to be different in principle—that is, in their actual functioning—since the one is made and the other grown. The fact that no one can translate some organic processes into mechanical terms no more implies that organism is mechanism than the translation of commerce into arithmetical terms implies that commerce *is* arithmetic.

sign will also be the "stop" sign; "yes" will imply "no" and "no" will imply "yes." Whereupon the mechanism will start "trembling," going on and off, on and off, until it shakes itself to pieces. The system is too sensitive and shows symptoms which are startlingly like human anxiety. For when a human being is so self-conscious, so self-controlled that he cannot let go of himself, he dithers or wobbles between opposites. This is precisely what is meant in Zen by going round and round on "the wheel of birth-and-death," for the Buddhist *samsara* is the prototype of all vicious circles.[3]   (7)

Now human life consists primarily and originally in action—in living in the concrete world of "suchness." But we have the power to control action by reflection, that is, by thinking, by comparing the actual world with memories or "reflections." Memories are organized in terms of more or less abstract images—words, signs, simplified shapes, and other symbols which can be reviewed very rapidly one after another. From such memories, reflections, and symbols the mind constructs its idea of itself. This corresponds to the thermostat—the source of information about its own past action by which the system corrects itself. The mind-body must, of course, trust that information in order to act, for paralysis will soon result from trying to remember whether we have remembered everything accurately.   (8)

But to keep up the supply of information in the memory, the mind-body must continue to act "on its own." It must not cling too closely to its own record. There must be a "lag" or distance between the source of information and the source of action. This does *not* mean that the source of action must hesitate before it accepts the information. It means that it must not identify itself with the source of information. We saw that when the furnace responds too closely to the thermostat, it cannot go ahead without also trying to stop, or stop without also trying to go ahead. This is just what happens to the human being, to the mind, when the desire for certainty and security prompts identification between the mind and its own image of itself. It cannot let go of itself. It feels that it should not do what it is doing, and that it should do what it is not doing. It feels that it should not be what it is, and be what it isn't. Furthermore, the effort to remain always "good" or "happy" is like trying to hold the thermostat to a constant 70 degrees by making the lower limit the same as the upper.   (9)

The identification of the mind with its own image is, therefore, paralyzing because the image is fixed—it is past and finished. But it is a fixed image of oneself in motion! To cling to it is thus to be in constant contradiction and conflict. Hence Yün-men's saying, "In walking, just walk. In sitting, just sit. Above all, don't wobble." In other words, the mind cannot act with-

<hr>

[3] See the fascinating discussion of analogies between mechanical and logical contradictions and the psychoneuroses by Gregory Bateson in Reusch and Bateson, *Communication: the Social Matrix of Psychiatry*, esp. Chap. 8. (Norton; New York, 1950.)

out giving up the impossible attempt to control itself beyond a certain point. It must let go of itself both in the sense of trusting its own memory and reflection, and in the sense of acting spontaneously, on its own into the unknown. (10)

This is why Zen often seems to take the side of action as against reflection, and why it describes itself as "no-mind" (*wu-hsin*) or "no-thought" (*wu-nien*), and why the masters demonstrate Zen by giving instantaneous and unpremeditated answers to questions. When Yün-men was asked for the ultimate secret of Buddhism, he replied, "Dumpling!" In the words of the Japanese master Takuan:

> When a monk asks, "What is the Buddha?" the master may raise his fist; when he is asked, "What is the ultimate idea of Buddhism?" he may exclaim even before the questioner finishes his sentence, "A blossoming branch of the plum," or "The cypress-tree in the court-yard." The point is that the answering mind does not "stop" anywhere, but responds straightway without giving any thought to the felicity of an answer.[4]

This is allowing the mind to act on its own. (11)

But reflection is also action, and Yün-men might also have said, "In acting, just act. In thinking, just think. Above all, don't wobble." In other words, if one is going to reflect, just reflect—but do not reflect about reflecting. Yet Zen would agree that reflection about reflection is also action—provided that in doing it we do just that, and do not tend to drift off into the infinite regression of trying always to stand above or outside the level upon which we are acting. Thus Zen is also a liberation from the dualism of thought and action, for it thinks as it acts—with the same quality of abandon, commitment, or faith. The attitude of *wu-hsin* is by no means an anti-intellectualist exclusion of thinking. *Wu-hsin is* action on any level whatsoever, physical or psychic, without trying *at the same moment* to observe and check the action from outside. This attempt to act and think about the action simultaneously is precisely the identification of the mind with its idea of itself. It involves the same contradiction as the statement which states something about itself—"This statement is false." (12)

The same is true of the relationship between feeling and action. For feeling blocks action, and blocks itself as a form of action, when it gets caught in this same tendency to observe or feel itself indefinitely—as when, in the midst of enjoying myself, I examine myself to see if I am getting the utmost out of the occasion. Not content with tasting the food, I am also trying to taste my tongue. Not content with feeling happy, I want to feel myself feeling happy—so as to be sure not to miss anything. (13)

4 In Suzuki (7), p. 80.

Whether trusting our memories or trusting the mind to act on its own, it comes to the same thing: ultimately we must act and think, live and die, from a source beyond all "our" knowledge and control. But this source is ourselves, and when we see that, it no longer stands over against us as a threatening object. No amount of care and hesitancy, no amount of intro- spection and searching of our motives, can make any ultimate difference to the fact that the mind is

Like an eye that sees, but cannot see itself.

In the end, the only alternative to a shuddering paralysis is to leap into action regardless of the consequences. Action in this spirit may be right or wrong with respect to conventional standards. But our decisions upon the conventional level must be supported by the conviction that whatever we do, and whatever "happens" to us, is ultimately "right." In other words, we must enter into it without "second thought," without *arrière-pensée* of regret, hesitancy, doubt, or self-recrimination. Thus when Yün-men was asked, "What is the Tao?" he answered simply, "Walk on! (*ch'ü*)." (14)

But to act "without second thought," without double-mindedness, is by no means a mere precept for our imitation. For we cannot realize this kind of action until it is clear beyond any shadow of doubt that it is actually impossible to do anything else. In the words of Huang-po:

> Men are afraid to forget their own minds, fearing to fall through the void with nothing on to which they can cling. They do not know that the void is not really the void but the real realm of the Dharma. . . . It cannot be looked for or sought, comprehended by wisdom or knowledge, explained in words, contacted mate- rially (i.e., objectively) or reached by meritorious achieve- ment. [5]   (15)

Now this impossibility of "grasping the mind with the mind" is, when realized, the non-action (*wu-wei*), the "sitting quietly, doing nothing" whereby "spring comes, and the grass grows by itself." There is no neces- sity for the mind to try to let go of itself, or to try not to try. This introduces further artificialities. Yet, as a matter of psychological strategy, there is no need for trying to avoid artificialities. In the doctrine of the Japanese master Bankei (1622–1693) the mind which cannot grasp itself is called the "Unborn" (*fusho*), the mind which does not arise or appear in the realm of symbolic knowledge.

> A layman asked, "I appreciate very much your instruction about the Unborn, but by force of habit second thoughts [*nien*] keep

_____
[5] In Chu Ch'an (1), p. 29.

tending to arise, and being confused by them it is difficult to be in perfect accord with the Unborn. How am I to trust in it entirely?"

Bankei said, "If you make an attempt to stop the second thoughts which arise, then the mind which does the stopping and the mind which is stopped become divided, and there is no occasion for peace of mind. So it is best for you simply to believe that originally there is no (possibility of control by) second thoughts. Yet because of karmic affinity, through what you see and what you hear these thoughts arise and vanish temporarily, but are without substance."

"Brushing off thoughts which arise is just like washing off blood with blood. We remain impure because of being washed with blood, even when the blood that was first there has gone— and if we continue in this way the impurity never departs. This is from ignorance of the mind's unborn, unvanishing, and unconfused nature. If we take second thought for an effective reality, we keep going on and on around the wheel of birth-and-death. You should realize that such thought is just a temporary mental construction, and not try to hold or to reject it. Let it alone just as it occurs and just as it ceases. It is like an image reflected in a mirror. The mirror is clear and reflects anything which comes before it, and yet no image sticks in the mirror. The Buddha mind (i.e., the real, unborn mind) is ten thousand times more clear than a mirror, and more inexpressibly marvelous. In its light all such thoughts vanish without trace. If you put your faith in this way of understanding, however strongly such thoughts may arise, they do no harm." [6]

This is also the doctrine of Huang-po, who says again:

If it is held that there is something to be realized or attained apart from mind, and, thereupon, mind is used to seek it, (that implies) failure to understand that mind and the object of its search are one. Mind cannot be used to seek something from mind for, even after the passage of millions of kalpas, the day of success would never come.[7]   (16)

One must not forget the social context of Zen. It is primarily a way of liberation for those who have mastered the disciplines of social convention, of the conditioning of the individual by the group. Zen is a medicine for the ill effects of this conditioning, for the mental paralysis and anxiety which come from excessive self-consciousness. It must be seen against the

[6] Bankei's *Daiho Shogen Kokushi Hogo.* Japanese text edited by Furata and Suzuki. (Tokyo, 1943.) Translation read to the author by Professor Hasegawa.
[7] In Chu Ch'an (1), p. 24.

background of societies regulated by the principles of Confucianism, with their heavy stress on propriety and punctilious ritual. In Japan, too, it must be seen in relation to the rigid schooling required in the training of the *samurai* caste, and the emotional strain to which the *samurai* were exposed in times of constant warfare. As a medicine for these conditions, it does not seek to overthrow the conventions themselves, but, on the contrary, takes them for granted—as is easily seen in such manifestations of Zen as the *cha-no-yu* or "tea ceremony" of Japan. Therefore Zen might be a very dangerous medicine in a social context where convention is weak, or, at the other extreme, where there is a spirit of open revolt against convention ready to exploit Zen for destructive purposes.   (17)

With this in mind, we can observe the freedom and naturalness of Zen without loss of perspective. Social conditioning fosters the identification of the mind with a fixed idea of itself as the means of self-control, and as a result man thinks of himself as "I"—the ego. Thereupon the mental center of gravity shifts from the spontaneous or original mind to the ego image. Once this has happened, the very center of our psychic life is identified with the self-controlling mechanism. It then becomes almost impossible to see how "I" can let go of "myself," for I am precisely my habitual effort to hold on to myself. I find myself totally incapable of any mental action which is not intentional, affected, and insincere. Therefore anything I do to give myself up, to let go, will be a disguised form of the habitual effort to hold on. I cannot be intentionally unintentional or purposely spontaneous. As soon as it becomes important for me to be spontaneous, the intention to be so is strengthened; I cannot get rid of it, and yet it is the one thing that stands in the way of its own fulfillment. It is as if someone had given me some medicine with the warning that it will not work if I think of a monkey while taking it.   (18)

While I am remembering to forget the monkey, I am in a "double-bind" situation where "to do" is "not to do," and vice versa. "Yes" implies "no," and "go" implies "stop." At this point Zen comes to me and asks, "If you cannot help remembering the monkey, are you doing it on purpose?" In other words, do I have an intention for being intentional, a purpose for being purposive? Suddenly I realize that my very intending is spontaneous, or that my controlling self—the ego—arises from my uncontrolled or natural self. At this moment all the machinations of the ego come to nought; it is annihilated in its own trap. I see that it is actually impossible not to be spontaneous. For what I cannot help doing I am doing spontaneously, but if I am at the same time trying to control it, I interpret it as a compulsion. As a Zen master said, "Nothing is left to you at this moment but to have a good laugh."   (19)

In this moment the whole quality of consciousness is changed, and I feel myself in a new world in which, however, it is obvious that I have always been living. As soon as I recognize that my voluntary and purposeful action happens spontaneously "by itself," just like breathing, hearing, and feeling, I am no longer caught in the contradiction of trying to be spontaneous. There is no real contradiction, since "trying" is "spontaneity." Seeing this, the compulsive, blocked, and "tied-up" feeling vanishes. It is just as if I had been absorbed in a tug-of-war between my two hands, and had forgotten that both were mine. No block to spontaneity remains when the trying is seen to be needless. As we saw, the discovery that both the voluntary and involuntary aspects of the mind are alike spontaneous makes an immediate end of the fixed dualism between the mind and the world, the knower and the known. The new world in which I find myself has an extraordinary transparency or freedom from barriers, making it seem that I have somehow become the empty space in which everything is happening. (20)

Here, then, is the point of the oft-repeated assertion that "all beings are in *nirvana* from the very beginning," that "all dualism is falsely imagined," that "the ordinary mind is the Tao" and that there is therefore no meaning in trying to get into accord with it. In the words of the *Cheng-tao Ke:*

> *Like the empty sky it has no boundaries,*
> *Yet it is right in this place, ever profound and clear.*
> *When you seek to know it, you cannot see it.*
> *You cannot take hold of it,*
> *But you cannot lose it.*
> *In not being able to get it, you get it.*
> *When you are silent, it speaks;*
> *When you speak, it is silent.*
> *The great gate is wide open to bestow alms,*
> *And no crowd is blocking the way.*

It was through seeing this that, in the moment of his *satori*, Hakuin cried out, "How wondrous! How wondrous! There is no birth-and-death from which one has to escape nor is there any supreme knowledge after which one has to strive!"[8] Or in the words of Hsiang-yen:

> *At one stroke I forgot all my knowledge!*
> *There's no use for artificial discipline,*
> *For, move as I will, I manifest the ancient Way.*[9]

Paradoxically, nothing is more artificial than the notion of artificiality. Try as one may, it is as impossible to go against the spontaneous Tao as to live in some other time than now, or some other place than here. When a

---

[8] *Orategama*, in Suzuki (1), vol. 1, p. 239.
[9] *Wu-teng Hui-yüan*, 9.

monk asked Bankei what he thought of disciplining oneself to attain *satori,* the master said, "*Satori* stands in contrast to confusion. Since each person is the substance of Buddha, (in reality) there is not one point of confusion. What, then, is one going to achieve by *satori?*"[10]   (21)

Seeing, then, that there is no possibility of departing from the Tao, one is like Hsüan-chüeh's "easygoing" man who

> *Neither avoids false thoughts nor seeks the true,*
> *For ignorance is in reality the Buddha nature,*
> *And this illusory, changeful, empty body is the Dharmakaya.*[11]

One stops trying to be spontaneous by seeing that it is unnecessary to try, and then and there it can happen. The Zen masters often bring out this state by the device of evading a question and then, as the questioner turns to go, calling him suddenly by name. As he naturally replies, "Yes?" the master exclaims, "There it is!"   (22)

To the Western reader it may seem that all this is a kind of pantheism, an attempt to wipe out conflicts by asserting that "everything is God." But from the standpoint of Zen, this is a long way short of true naturalness since it involves the use of the artificial concept—"everything is God" or "every-thing is the Tao." Zen annihilates this concept by showing that it is as un-necessary as every other. One does not realize the spontaneous life by depending on the repetition of thoughts or affirmations. One realizes it by seeing that no such devices are necessary. Zen describes all means and meth-ods for realizing the Tao as "legs on a snake"—utterly irrelevant attach-ments.   (23)

To the logician it will of course seem that the point at which we have arrived is pure nonsense—as, in a way, it is. From the Buddhist point of view, reality itself has no meaning since it is not a sign, pointing to some-thing beyond itself. To arrive at reality—at "suchness"—is to go beyond *karma,* beyond consequential action, and to enter a life which is completely aimless. Yet to Zen and Taoism alike this is the very life of the universe, which is complete at every moment and does not need to justify itself by aiming at something beyond. In the words of a *Zenrin* poem:

> *If you don't believe, just look at September, look at October!*
> *The yellow leaves falling, falling, to fill both mountain and river.*

To see this is to be like the two friends of whom another *Zenrin* poem says:

> *Meeting, they laugh and laugh—*
> *The forest grove, the many fallen leaves!*

---

[10] *Bankei Kokushi Seppo.* Read to the author by Professor Hasegawa.
[11] *Cheng-tao Ke,* 1.

To the Taoist mentality, the aimless, empty life does not suggest anything depressing. On the contrary, it suggests the freedom of clouds and mountain streams, wandering nowhere, of flowers in impenetrable canyons, beautiful for no one to see, and of the ocean surf forever washing the sand, to no end.   (24)

Furthermore, the Zen experience is more of a conclusion than a premise. It is never to be used as the first step in a line of ethical or metaphysical reasoning, since conclusions draw to it rather than from it. Like the Beatific Vision of Christianity, it is a "which than which there is no whicher"—the true end of man—not a thing to be used for some other end. Philosophers do not easily recognize that there is a point where thinking— like boiling an egg—must come to a stop. To try to formulate the Zen experience as a proposition—"everything is the Tao"—and then to analyze it and draw conclusions from it is to miss it completely. Like the Crucifixion, it is "to the Jews [the moralists] a stumblingblock and to the Greeks [the logicians] foolishness." To say that "everything is the Tao" almost gets the point, but just at the moment of getting it, the words crumble into nonsense. For we are here at a limit at which words break down because they always imply a meaning beyond themselves—and here there is no meaning beyond.   (25)

Zen does not make the mistake of using the experience "all things are of one Suchness" as the premise for an ethic of universal brotherhood. On the contrary, Yüan-wu says:

> If you are a real man, you may by all means drive off with the
> farmer's ox, or grab the food from a starving man.[12]

This is only to say that Zen lies beyond the ethical standpoint, whose sanctions must be found, not in reality itself, but in the mutual agreement of human beings. When we attempt to universalize or absolutize it, the ethical standpoint makes it impossible to exist, for we cannot live for a day without destroying the life of some other creature.   (26)

If Zen is regarded as having the same function as a religion in the West, we shall naturally want to find some logical connection between its central experience and the improvement of human relations. But this is actually putting the cart before the horse. The point is rather that some such experience or way of life as this is the object of improved human relations. In the culture of the Far East the problems of human relations are the sphere of Confucianism rather than Zen, but since the Sung dynasty (959–1278) Zen has consistently fostered Confucianism and was the main source of the introduction of its principles into Japan. It saw their importance for creating the type of cultural matrix in which Zen could flourish without

12 Comment on *Pi-yen Lu*, 3.

coming into conflict with social order, because the Confucian ethic is admittedly human and relative, not divine and absolute.   (27)

Although profoundly "inconsequential," the Zen experience has consequences in the sense that it may be applied in any direction, to any conceivable human activity, and that wherever it is so applied it lends an unmistakable quality to the work. The characteristic notes of the spontaneous life are *mo chih ch'u* or "going ahead without hesitation," and *wu-shih*, lack of affectation or simplicity.   (28)

While the Zen experience does not imply any specific course of action, since it has no purpose, no motivation, it turns unhesitatingly to anything that presents itself to be done. *Mo chih ch'u* is the mind functioning without blocks, without "wobbling" between alternatives, and much of Zen training consists in confronting the student with dilemmas which he is expected to handle without stopping to deliberate and "choose." The response to the situation must follow with the immediacy of sound issuing from the hands when they are clapped, or sparks from a flint when struck. The student unaccustomed to this type of response will at first be confused, but as he gains faith in his "original" or spontaneous mind he will not only respond with ease, but the responses themselves will acquire a startling appropriateness. This is something like the professional comedian's gift of unprepared wit which is equal to any situation.   (29)

The master may begin a conversation with the student by asking a series of very ordinary questions about trivial matters, to which the student responds with perfect spontaneity. But suddenly he will say, "When the bathwater flows down the drain, does it turn clockwise or counter-clockwise?" As the student stops at the unexpectedness of the question, and perhaps tries to remember which way it goes, the master shouts, "Don't think! Act! This way—" and whirls his hand in the air. Or, perhaps less helpfully, he may say, "So far you've answered my questions quite naturally and easily, but where's your difficulty now?"   (30)

The student, likewise, is free to challenge the master, and one can imagine that in the days when Zen training was less formal the members of Zen communities must have had enormous fun laying traps for each other. To some extent this type of relationship still exists, despite the great solemnity of the *sanzen* interview in which the *koan* is given and answered. The late Kozuki Roshi was entertaining two American monks at tea when he casually asked, "And what do you gentlemen know about Zen?" One of the monks flung his closed fan straight at the master's face. All in the same instant the master inclined his head slightly to one side, the fan shot straight through the paper *shoji* behind him, and he burst into a ripple of laughter.   (31)

Suzuki has translated a long letter from the Zen master Takuan on the relationship of Zen to the art of fencing, and this is certainly the best literary source of what Zen means by *mo chih ch'u,* by "going straight ahead without stopping."[13] Both Takuan and Bankei stressed the fact that the "original" or "unborn" mind is constantly working miracles even in the most ordinary person. Even though a tree has innumerable leaves, the mind takes them in all at once without being "stopped" by any one of them. Explaining this to a visiting monk, Bankei said, "To prove that your mind is the Buddha mind, notice how all that I say here goes into you without missing a single thing, even though I don't try to push it into you."[14] When heckled by an aggressive Nichiren monk who kept insisting that he couldn't understand a word, Bankei asked him to come closer. The monk stepped forward. "Closer still," said Bankei. The monk came forward again. "How well," said Bankei, "you understand me!"[15] In other words, our natural organism performs the most marvelously complex activities without the least hesitation or deliberation. Conscious thought is itself founded upon its whole system of spontaneous functioning, for which reason there is really no alternative to trusting oneself completely to its working. Oneself *is* its working.   (32)

Zen is not merely a cult of impulsive action. The point of *mo chih ch'u* is not to eliminate reflective thought but to eliminate "blocking" in both action and thought, so that the response of the mind is always like a ball in a mountain stream—"one thought after another without hesitation." There is something similar to this in the psychoanalytic practice of free association, employed as a technique to get rid of obstacles to the free flow of thought from the "unconscious." For there is a tendency to confuse "blocking"—a purely obstructive mechanism—with thinking out an answer, but the difference between the two is easily noticed in such a purely "thinking out" process as adding a column of figures. Many people find that at certain combinations of numbers, such as 8 and 5 or 7 and 6, a feeling of resistance comes up which halts the process. Because it is always annoying and disconcerting, one tends also to block at blocking, so that the state turns into the kind of wobbling dither characteristic of the snarled feedback system. The simplest cure is to feel free to block, so that one does not block at blocking. When one feels free to block, the blocking automatically eliminates itself. It is like riding a bicycle. When one starts falling to the left, one does not resist the fall (i.e., the block) by turning to the right. One turns the wheel to the left—and the balance is restored. The principle here is, of course, the same as getting out of the contradiction of "trying to be spontaneous" through accepting the "trying" as "spontaneous," through not resisting the block.   (33)

"Blocking" is perhaps the best translation of the Zen term *nien* as it oc-

---

13 Suzuki (7), pp. 73–87. Excerpts from this letter also appear in Suzuki (1), vol. 3, pp. 318–19.
14 *Bankei Kokushi Seppo.* Read to the author by Professor Hasegawa.
15 In Suzuki (10), p. 123.

curs in the phrase *wu-nien,* "no-thought" or, better, "no second thought."
Takuan points out that this is the real meaning of "attachment" in Buddhism, as when it is said that a Buddha is free from worldly atttachments.
It does not mean that he is a "stone Buddha" with no feelings, no emotions,
and no sensations of hunger or pain. It means that he does not block at
anything. Thus it is typical of Zen that its style of action has the strongest
feeling of commitment, of "follow-through." It enters into everything whole-
heartedly and freely without having to keep an eye on itself. It does not
confuse spirituality with thinking about God while one is peeling potatoes.
Zen spirituality is just to peel the potatoes. In the words of Lin-chi:

> When it's time to get dressed, put on your clothes. When you
> must walk, then walk. When you must sit, then sit. Don't have a
> single thought in your mind about seeking for Buddhahood. . . .
> You talk about being perfectly disciplined in your six senses and
> in all your actions, but in my view all this is making *karma.* To
> seek the Buddha (nature) and to seek the Dharma is at once to
> make *karma* which leads to the hells. To seek (to be) Bodhisatt-
> vas is also making *karma,* and likewise studying the *sutras* and
> commentaries. Buddhas and Patriarchs are people without such
> artificialities. . . . It is said everywhere that there is a Tao which
> must be cultivated and a Dharma which must be realized. What
> Dharma do you say must be realized, and what Tao cultivated?
> What do you lack in the way you are functioning right now?
> What will you add to where you are?[16]

As another *Zenrin* poem says:

> There's nothing equal to wearing clothes and eating food.
> Outside this there are neither Buddhas nor Patriarchs.   (34)

This is the quality of *wu-shih,* of naturalness without any contrivances
or means for being natural, such as thoughts of Zen, of the Tao, or of the
Buddha. One does not exclude such thoughts; they simply fall away when
seen to be unnecessary. "He does not linger where the Buddha is, and
where there is no Buddha he passes right on."[17]

For as the *Zenrin* says again:

> To be conscious of the original mind, the original nature—
> Just this is the great disease of Zen!

---

[16] *Lin-chi Lu* in *Ku-tsun-hsü Yü-lu,* 1. 4. 6, 11–12, 12.
[17] *Shih Niu T'u,* 8.

As "the fish swims in the water but is unmindful of the water, the bird flies in the wind but knows not of the wind," so the true life of Zen has no need to "raise waves when no wind is blowing," to drag in religion or spirituality as something over and above life itself. This is why the sage Fa-yung received no more offerings of flowers from the birds after he had had his interview with the Fourth Patriarch, for his holiness no longer "stood out like a sore thumb." Of such a man the *Zenrin* says:

> *Entering the forest he moves not the grass;*
> *Entering the water he makes not a ripple.*

No one notices him because he does not notice himself. (35)

It is often said that to be clinging to oneself is like having a thorn in the skin, and that Buddhism is a second thorn to extract the first. When it is out, both thorns are thrown away. But in the moment when Buddhism, when philosophy or religion, becomes another way of clinging to oneself through seeking a spiritual security, the two thorns become one—and how is it to be taken out? This, as Bankei said, is "wiping off blood with blood." Therefore in Zen there is neither self nor Buddha to which one can cling, no good to gain and no evil to be avoided, no thoughts to be eradicated and no mind to be purified, no body to perish and no soul to be saved. At one blow this entire framework of abstractions is shattered to fragments. As the *Zenrin* says:

> *To save life it must be destroyed.*
> *When utterly destroyed, one dwells for the first time in peace.*
>
> *One word settles heaven and earth;*
> *One sword levels the whole world.*

Of this "one sword" Lin-chi said:

> If a man cultivates the Tao, the Tao will not work—on all sides
> evil conditions will head up competitively. But when the sword
> of wisdom [*prajna*] comes out there's not one thing left.[18] (36)

The "sword of *prajna*" which cuts away abstraction is that "direct pointing" whereby Zen avoids the entanglements of religiosity and goes straight to the heart. Thus when the Governor of Lang asked Yao-shan, "What is the Tao?" the master pointed upwards to the sky and downwards to a water jug beside him. Asked for an explanation, he replied: "A cloud in the sky and water in the jug." (37)

---

18 In *Ku-tsun-hsü Yü-lu*, 1. 4. 13.

C. S. Lewis

(1898–1963)

C. S. LEWIS was known to the gentleman reader principally by The Screwtape Letters *(1942), a popular work on Christian moral and theological problems, and to the scholar principally by* The Allegory of Love *(1936), a study of medieval courtly tradition. He also wrote Christian allegories of good and evil in the form of interplanetary fantasies.*

◼ *The Abolition of Man*

It came burning hot into my mind, whatever he said and however he flattered, when he got me home to his house, he would sell me for a slave.

BUNYAN

'MAN'S CONQUEST OF NATURE' is an expression often used to describe the progress of applied science. 'Man has Nature whacked' said someone to a friend of mine not long ago. In their context the words had a certain tragic beauty, for the speaker was dying of tuberculosis. 'No matter,' he said, 'I know I'm one of the casualties. Of course there are casualties on the winning as well as on the losing side. But that doesn't alter the fact that it is winning.' I have chosen this story as my point of departure in order to make it clear that I do not wish to disparage all that is really beneficial in the process described as 'Man's conquest,' much less all the real devotion and self-sacrifice that has gone to make it possible. But having done so I must proceed to analyse this conception a little more closely. In what sense is Man the possessor of increasing power over Nature?   (1)

Let us consider three typical examples: the aeroplane, the wireless, and the contraceptive. In a civilized community, in peace-time, anyone who can pay for them may use these things. But it cannot strictly be said that when he does so he is exercising his own proper or individual power over Nature. If I pay you to carry me, I am not therefore myself a strong man. Any or all of the three things I have mentioned can be withheld from some men by other men—by those who sell, or those who allow the sale, or those who own the sources of production, or those who make the goods. What we call Man's power is, in reality, a power possessed by some men which they may, or may not, allow other men to profit by. Again, as regards the powers manifested in the aeroplane or the wireless, Man is as much the patient or subject as the possessor, since he is the target both for bombs and for propaganda. And as regards contraceptives, there is a paradoxical, negative sense in which all possible future generations are the patients or subjects of a power wielded by those already alive. By contraception simply, they are denied existence; by contraception used as a means of selective breeding, they are, without their concurring voice, made to be what one generation, for its own reasons, may choose to prefer. From this point of view, what we call Man's power over Nature turns out to be a power exercised by some men over other men with Nature as its instrument.   (2)

It is, of course, a commonplace to complain that men have hitherto used badly, and against their fellows, the powers that science has given them. But that is not the point I am trying to make. I am not speaking of particular corruptions and abuses which an increase of moral virtue would cure: I am considering what the thing called 'Man's power over Nature' must always and essentially be. No doubt, the picture could be modified by public ownership of raw materials and factories and public control of scientific research. But unless we have a world state this will still mean the power of one nation over others. And even within the world state or the nation it will mean (in principle) the power of majorities over minorities, and (in the concrete) of a government over the people. And all long-term exercises of power, especially in breeding, must mean the power of earlier generations over later ones.   (3)

The latter point is not always sufficiently emphasized, because those who write on social matters have not yet learned to imitate the physicists by always including Time among the dimensions. In order to understand fully what Man's power over Nature, and therefore the power of some men over other men, really means, we must picture the race extended in time from the date of its emergence to that of its extinction. Each generation exercises power over its successors: and each, in so far as it modifies the environment bequeathed to it and rebels against tradition, resists and limits the power of its predecessors. This modifies the picture which is sometimes painted of a progressive emancipation from tradition and a progressive control of natural processes resulting in a continual increase of human power. In reality, of course, if any one age really attains, by eugenics and scientific education, the power to make its descendants what it pleases, all men who live after it are the patients of that power. They are weaker, not stronger: for though we may have put wonderful machines in their hands we have pre-ordained how they are to use them. And if, as is almost certain, the age which had thus attained maximum power over posterity were also the age most emancipated from tradition, it would be engaged in reducing the power of its predecessors almost as drastically as that of its successors. And we must also remember that, quite apart from this, the later a generation comes—the nearer it lives to that date at which the species becomes extinct—the less power it will have in the forward direction, because its subjects will be so few. There is therefore no question of a power vested in the race as a whole steadily growing as long as the race survives. The last men, far from being the heirs of power, will be of all men most subject to the dead hand of the great planners and conditioners and will themselves exercise least power upon the future. The real picture is that of one dominant age—let us suppose the hundredth century A.D.—which resists all previous ages most successfully and dominates all subsequent ages most irresistibly, and thus is the real master of the human species. But even within this master generation (itself an infinitesimal minority of the species) the power will be exercised by a minority smaller still. Man's conquest of Nature, if the dreams of some scientific planners are realized, means the rule of a few hundreds of men over billions upon billions of men. There neither is nor can be any simple increase of power on Man's side. Each new power won *by* man is a power *over* man as well. Each advance leaves him weaker as well as stronger. In every victory, besides being the general who triumphs, he is also the prisoner who follows the triumphal car. (4)

I am not yet considering whether the total result of such ambivalent victories is a good thing or a bad. I am only making clear what Man's conquest of Nature really means and especially that final stage in the conquest, which, perhaps, is not far off. The final stage is come when Man by eugenics, by pre-natal conditioning, and by an education and propaganda based on a perfect applied psychology, has obtained full control over himself. *Human* nature will be the last part of Nature to surrender to Man. The battle will then be won. We shall have 'taken the thread of life out of the hand of Clotho' and be henceforth free to make our species whatever we wish it to be. The battle will indeed be won. But who, precisely, will have won it? (5)

For the power of Man to make himself what he pleases means, as we have seen, the power of some men to make other men what *they* please. In all ages, no doubt, nurture and instruction have, in some sense, attempted to exercise this power. But the situation to which we must look forward will be novel in two respects. In the first place, the power will be enormously increased. Hitherto the plans of educationalists have achieved very little of what they attempted and indeed, when we read them—how Plato would have every infant 'a bastard nursed in a bureau,' and Elyot would have the boy see no men before the age of seven and, after that, no women,[1] and how Locke wants children to have leaky shoes and no turn for poetry[2]—we may well thank the beneficent obstinacy of real mothers, real nurses, and (above all) real children for preserving the human race in such sanity as it still possesses. But the man-moulders of the new age will be armed with the powers of an omnicompetent state and an irresistible scientific technique: we shall get at last a race of conditioners who really can cut out all posterity in what shape they please. The second difference is even more important. In the older systems both the kind of man the teachers wished to produce and their motives for producing him were prescribed by the *Tao*—a norm to which the teachers themselves were subject and from which they claimed no liberty to depart. They did not cut men to some pattern they had chosen. They handed on what they had received: they initiated the young neophyte into the mystery of humanity which over-arched him and them alike. It was but old birds teaching young birds to fly. This will be changed. Values are now mere natural phenomena. Judgements of value are to be produced in the pupil as part of the conditioning. Whatever *Tao* there is will be the product, not the motive, of education. The conditioners have been emancipated from all that. It is one more part of Nature which they have conquered. The ultimate springs of human action are no longer, for them, something given. They have surrendered—like electricity: it is the function of the Conditioners to control, not to obey them. They know how to *produce* conscience and decide what kind of conscience they will produce. They themselves are outside, above. For we are assuming the last stage of Man's struggle with Nature. The final victory has been won. Human nature has been conquered—and, of course, has conquered, in whatever sense those words may now bear. (6)

The Conditioners, then, are to choose what kind of artificial *Tao* they will, for their own good reasons, produce in the Human race. They are the motivators, the creators of motives. But how are they going to be motivated themselves? For a time, perhaps, by survivals, within their own minds, of the old 'natural' *Tao*. Thus at first they may look upon themselves as

---

1 *The Boke Named the Governour*, 1. iv: 'Al men except physicians only shulde be exclude and kepte out of the norisery.' 1. vi: 'After that a childe is come to seuen yeres of age . . . the most sure counsaile is to withdrawe him from all company of women.'

2 *Some Thoughts concerning Education*, § 7: 'I will also advise his *Feet to be wash'd* every Day in cold Water, and to have his Shoes so thin that they might leak and *let in Water*, whenever he comes near it.' § 174: 'If he have a poetick vein, 'tis to me the strangest thing in the World that the Father should desire or suffer it to be cherished or improved. Methinks the Parents should labour to have it stifled and suppressed as much as may be.' Yet Locke is one of our most sensible writers on education.

servants and guardians of humanity and conceive that they have a 'duty' to do it 'good.' But it is only by confusion that they can remain in this state. They recognize the concept of duty as the result of certain processes which they can now control. Their victory has consisted precisely in emerging from the state in which they were acted upon by those processes to the state in which they use them as tools. One of the things they now have to decide is whether they will, or will not, so condition the rest of us that we can go on having the old idea of duty and the old reactions to it. How can duty help them to decide that? Duty itself is up for trial: it cannot also be the judge. And 'good' fares no better. They know quite well how to produce a dozen different conceptions of good in us. The question is which, if any, they should produce. No conception of good can help them to decide. It is absurd to fix on one of the things they are comparing and make it the standard of comparison.   (7)

To some it will appear that I am inventing a factitious difficulty for my Conditioners. Other, more simple-minded, critics may ask 'Why should you suppose they will be such bad men?' But I am not supposing them to be bad men. They are, rather, not men (in the old sense) at all. They are, if you like, men who have sacrificed their own share in traditional humanity in order to devote themselves to the task of deciding what 'Humanity' shall henceforth mean. 'Good' and 'bad,' applied to them, are words without content: for it is from them that the content of these words is henceforward to be derived. Nor is their difficulty factitious. We might suppose that it was possible to say 'After all, most of us want more or less the same things— food and drink and sexual intercourse, amusement, art, science, and the longest possible life for individuals and for the species. Let them simply say, This is what we happen to like, and go on to condition men in the way most likely to produce it. Where's the trouble?' But this will not answer. In the first place, it is false that we all really like the same things. But even if we did, what motive is to impel the Conditioners to scorn delights and live laborious days in order that we, and posterity, may have what we like? Their duty? But that is only the *Tao*, which they may decide to impose on us, but which cannot be valid for them. If they accept it, then they are no longer the makers of conscience but still its subjects, and their final conquest over Nature has not really happened. The preservation of the species? But why should the species be preserved? One of the questions before them is whether this feeling for posterity (they know well how it is produced) shall be continued or not. However far they go back, or down, they can find no ground to stand on. Every motive they try to act on becomes at once a *petitio*. It is not that they are bad men. They are not men at all. Stepping outside the *Tao*, they have stepped into the void. Nor are their subjects necessarily unhappy men. They are not men at all: they are artifacts. Man's final conquest has proved to be the abolition of Man. (8)

Yet the Conditioners will act. When I said just now that all motives fail them, I should have said all motives except one. All motives that claim any validity other than that of their felt emotional weight at a given moment have failed them. Everything except the *sic volo, sic jubeo* has been explained away. But what never claimed objectivity cannot be destroyed by subjectivism. The impulse to scratch when I itch or to pull to pieces when I am inquisitive is immune from the solvent which is fatal to my justice, or honour, or care for posterity. When all that says 'it is good' has been debunked, what says 'I want' remains. It cannot be exploded or 'seen through' because it never had any pretensions. The Conditioners, therefore, must come to be motivated simply by their own pleasure. I am not here speaking of the corrupting influence of power nor expressing the fear that under it our Conditioners will degenerate. The very words *corrupt* and *degenerate* imply a doctrine of value and are therefore meaningless in this context. My point is that those who stand outside all judgements of value cannot have any ground for preferring one of their own impulses to another except the emotional strength of that impulse. We may legitimately hope that among the impulses which arise in minds thus emptied of all 'rational' or 'spiritual' motives, some will be benevolent. I am very doubtful myself whether the benevolent impulses, stripped of that preference and encouragement which the *Tao* teaches us to give them and left to their merely natural strength and frequency as psychological events, will have much influence. I am very doubtful whether history shows us one example of a man who, having stepped outside traditional morality and attained power, has used that power benevolently. I am inclined to think that the Conditioners will hate the conditioned. Though regarding as an illusion the artificial conscience which they produce in us their subjects, they will yet perceive that it creates in us an illusion of meaning for our lives which compares favourably with the futility of their own: and they will envy us as eunuchs envy men. But I do not insist on this, for it is mere conjecture. What is not conjecture is that our hope even of a 'conditioned' happiness rests on what is ordinarily called 'chance'—the chance that benevolent impulses may on the whole predominate in our Conditioners. For without the judgement 'Benevolence is good'—that is, without re-entering the *Tao*—they can have no ground for promoting or stabilizing their benevolent impulses rather than any others. By the logic of their position they must just take their impulses as they come, from chance. And Chance here means Nature. It is from heredity, digestion, the weather, and the association of ideas, that the motives of the Conditioners will spring. Their extreme rationalism, by 'seeing through' all 'rational' motives, leaves them creatures of wholly irrational behaviour. If you will not obey the *Tao*, or else commit suicide, obedience to impulse (and therefore, in the long run, to mere 'nature') is the only course left open.   (9)

At the moment, then, of Man's victory over Nature, we find the whole human race subjected to some individual men, and those individuals subjected to that in themselves which is purely 'natural'—to their irrational impulses. Nature, untrammelled by values, rules the Conditioners and, through them, all humanity. Man's conquest of Nature turns out, in the moment of its consummation, to be Nature's conquest of Man. Every victory we seemed to win has led us, step by step, to this conclusion. All Nature's apparent reverses have been but tactical withdrawals. We thought we were beating her back when she was luring us on. What looked to us like hands held up in surrender was really the opening of arms to enfold us forever. If the fully planned and conditioned world (with its *Tao* a mere product of the planning) comes into existence, Nature will be troubled no more by the restive species that rose in revolt against her so many millions of years ago, will be vexed no longer by its chatter of truth and mercy and beauty and happiness. *Ferum victorem cepit:* and if the eugenics are efficient enough there will be no second revolt, but all snug beneath the Conditioners, and the Conditioners beneath her, till the moon falls or the sun grows cold.   (10)

My point may be clearer to some if it is put in a different form. Nature is a word of varying meanings, which can best be understood if we consider its various opposites. The Natural is the opposite of the Artificial, the Civil, the Human, the Spiritual, and the Supernatural. The Artificial does not now concern us. If we take the rest of the list of opposites, however, I think we can get a rough idea of what men have meant by Nature and what it is they oppose to her. Nature seems to be the spatial and temporal, as distinct from what is less fully so or not so at all. She seems to be the world of quantity, as against the world of quality: of objects as against consciousness: of the bound, as against the wholly or partially autonomous: of that which knows no values as against that which both has and perceives value: of efficient causes (or, in some modern systems, of no causality at all) as against final causes. Now I take it that when we understand a thing analytically and then dominate and use it for our own convenience we reduce it to the level of 'Nature' in the sense that we suspend our judgements of value about it, ignore its final cause (if any), and treat it in terms of quantity. This repression of elements in what would otherwise be our total reaction to it is sometimes very noticeable and even painful: something has to be overcome before we can cut up a dead man or a live animal in a dissecting room. These objects *resist* the movement of the mind whereby we thrust them into the world of mere Nature. But in other instances too, a similar price is exacted for our analytical knowledge and manipulative power, even if we have ceased to count it. We do not look at trees either as Dryads or as beautiful objects while we cut them into beams: the first man who did so may have felt the price keenly, and the bleeding trees in Virgil and Spenser may be far-off echoes of that primeval sense of impiety. The stars lost their divinity as astronomy developed, and the Dying God has no place in chemical agriculture. To many, no doubt, this process is simply the gradual discovery that the real world is different from what we expected, and the old opposition to Galileo or to 'bodysnatchers' is simply obscurantism. But that is not the whole story. It is not the greatest of modern scientists who feel most sure that the object, stripped of its qualitative properties and reduced to mere quantity, is wholly real. Little scientists, and little unscientific followers of science, may think so. The great minds know very well that the object, so treated, is an artificial abstraction, that something of its reality has been lost.   (11)

From this point of view the conquest of Nature appears in a new light. We reduce things to mere Nature *in order that* we may 'conquer' them. We are always conquering Nature, because 'Nature' is the name for what we have, to some extent, conquered. The price of conquest is to treat a thing as mere Nature. Every conquest over Nature increases her domain. The stars do not become Nature till we can weigh and measure them: the soul does not become Nature till we can psycho-analyse her. The wresting of powers *from* Nature is also the surrendering of things *to* Nature. As long as this process stops short of the final stage we may well hold that the gain outweighs the loss. But as soon as we take the final step of reducing our own species to the level of mere Nature, the whole process is stultified, for this time the being who stood to gain and the being who has been sacrificed are one and the same. This is one of the many instances where to carry a principle to what seems its logical conclusion produces absurdity. It is like the famous Irishman who found that a certain kind of stove reduced his fuel bill by half and thence concluded that two stoves of the same kind would enable him to warm his house with no fuel at all. It is the magician's bargain: give up our soul, get power in return. But once our souls, that is, our selves, have been given up, the power thus conferred will not belong to us. We shall in fact be the slaves and puppets of that to which we have given our souls. It is in Man's power to treat himself as a mere 'natural object' and his own judgements of value as raw material for scientific manipulation to alter at will. The objection to his doing so does not lie in the fact that this point of view (like one's first day in a dissecting room) is painful and shocking till we grow used to it. The pain and the shock are at most a warning and a symptom. The real objection is that if man chooses to treat himself as raw material, raw material he will be: not raw material to be manipulated, as he fondly imagined, by himself, but by mere appetite, that is, mere Nature, in the person of his dehumanized Conditioners. (12)

We have been trying, like Lear, to have it both ways: to lay down our human prerogative and yet at the same time to retain it. It is impossible. Either we are rational spirit obliged forever to obey the absolute values of the *Tao*, or else we are mere nature to be kneaded and cut into new shapes for the pleasures of masters who must, by hypothesis, have no motive but their own 'natural' impulses. Only the *Tao* provides a common human law of action which can over-arch rulers and ruled alike. A dogmatic belief in objective value is necessary to the very idea of a rule which is not tyranny or an obedience which is not slavery.   (13)

I am not here thinking solely, perhaps not even chiefly, of those who are our public enemies at the moment. The process which, if not checked, will abolish Man, goes on apace among Communists and Democrats no less than among Fascists. The methods may (at first) differ in brutality. But many a mild-eyed scientist in pince-nez, many a popular dramatist, many an amateur philosopher in our midst, means in the long run just the same as the Nazi rulers of Germany. Traditional values are to be 'debunked' and mankind to be cut out into some fresh shape at the will (which must, by hypothesis, be an arbitrary will) of some few lucky people in one lucky generation which has learned how to do it. The belief that we can invent 'ideologies' at pleasure, and the consequent treatment of mankind as mere ὕλη, specimens, preparations, begins to affect our very language. Once we killed bad men: now we liquidate unsocial elements. Virtue has become *integration* and diligence *dynamism,* and boys likely to be worthy of a commission are 'potential officer material.' Most wonderful of all, the virtues of thrift and temperance, and even of ordinary intelligence, are *sales-resistance.*   (14)

The true significance of what is going on has been concealed by the use of the abstraction Man. Not that the word Man is necessarily a pure abstraction. In the *Tao* itself, as long as we remain within it, we find the concrete reality in which to participate is to be truly human: the real common will and common reason of humanity, alive, and growing like a tree, and branching out, as the situation varies, into ever new beauties and dignities of application. While we speak from within the *Tao* we can speak of Man having power over himself in a sense truly analogous to an individual's self-control. But the moment we step outside and regard the *Tao* as a mere subjective product, this possibility has disappeared. What is now common to all men is a mere abstract universal, an H.C.F., and Man's conquest of himself means simply the rule of the Conditioners over the conditioned human material, the world of post-humanity which, some knowingly and some unknowingly, nearly all men in all nations are at present labouring to produce.   (15)

Nothing I can say will prevent some people from describing this lecture as an attack on science. I deny the charge, of course: and real Natural Philosophers (there are some now alive) will perceive that in defending value I defend *inter alia* the value of knowledge, which must die like every other when its roots in the *Tao* are cut. But I can go further than that. I even suggest that from Science herself the cure might come. I have described as a 'magician's bargain' that process whereby man surrenders object after object, and finally himself, to Nature in return for power. And I meant what I said. The fact that the scientist has succeeded where the magician failed has put such a wide contrast between them in popular thought that the real story of the birth of Science is misunderstood. You will even find people who write about the sixteenth century as if Magic were a medieval survival and Science the new thing that came in to sweep it away. Those who have studied the period know better. There was very little magic in the Middle Ages: the sixteenth and seventeenth centuries are the high noon of magic. The serious magical endeavour and the serious scientific endeavour are twins: one was sickly and died, the other strong and throve. But they were twins. They were born of the same impulse. I allow that some (certainly not all) of the early scientists were actuated by a pure love of knowledge. But if we consider the temper of that age as a whole we can discern the impulse of which I speak. There is something which unites magic and applied science while separating both from the 'wisdom' of earlier ages. For the wise men of old the cardinal problem had been how to conform the soul to reality, and the solution had been knowledge, self-discipline, and virtue. For magic and applied science alike the problem is how to subdue reality to the wishes of men: the solution is a technique; and both, in the practice of this technique, are ready to do things hitherto regarded as disgusting and impious—such as digging up and mutilating the dead. If we compare the chief trumpeter of the new era (Bacon) with Marlowe's Faustus, the similarity is striking. You will read in some critics that Faustus has a thirst for knowledge. In reality, he hardly mentions it. It is not truth he wants from his devils, but gold and guns and girls. 'All things that move between the quiet poles shall be at his command' and 'a sound magician is a mighty god.' [3] In the same spirit Bacon condemns those who value knowledge as an end in itself: this, for him, is to use as a mistress for pleasure what ought to be a spouse for fruit. [4] The true object is to extend Man's power to the performance of all things possible. He rejects magic because it does not work, [5] but his goal is that of the magician. In Paracelsus the characters of magician and scientist are combined. No doubt those who really founded modern science were usually those whose love of truth exceeded their love of power; in every mixed movement the efficacy comes from the good elements not from the bad. But the presence of the bad elements is not irrelevant to the direction the

---

[3] *Dr. Faustus*, 77–90.

[4] *Advancement of Learning*, Bk. I (p. 60 in Ellis and Spedding, 1905; p. 35 in Everyman Edn.).

[5] *Filum Labyrinthi*, i.

efficacy takes. It might be going too far to say that the modern scientific movement was tainted from its birth: but I think it would be true to say that it was born in an unhealthy neighbourhood and at an inauspicious hour. Its triumphs may have been too rapid and purchased at too high a price: reconsideration, and something like repentance, may be required. (16)

Is it, then, possible to imagine a new Natural Philosophy, continually conscious that the 'natural object' produced by analysis and abstraction is not reality but only a view, and always correcting the abstraction? I hardly know what I am asking for. I hear rumours that Goethe's approach to nature deserves fuller consideration—that even Dr. Steiner may have seen something that orthodox researchers have missed. The regenerate science which I have in mind would not do even to minerals and vegetables what modern science threatens to do to man himself. When it explained, it would not explain away. When it spoke of the parts it would remember the whole. While studying the *It* it would not lose what Martin Buber calls the *Thou*-situation. The analogy between the *Tao* of Man and the instincts of an animal species would mean for it new light cast on the unknown thing, Instinct, by the only known reality of conscience and not a reduction of conscience to the category of Instinct. Its followers would not be free with the words *only* and *merely*. In a word, it would conquer Nature without being at the same time conquered by her and buy knowledge at a lower cost than that of life. (17)

Perhaps I am asking impossibilities. Perhaps, in the nature of things, analytical understanding must always be a basilisk which kills what it sees and only sees by killing. But if the scientists themselves cannot arrest this process before it reaches the common Reason and kills that too, then someone else must arrest it. What I most fear is the reply that I am 'only one more' obscurantist, that this barrier, like all previous barriers set up against the advance of science, can be safely passed. Such a reply springs from the fatal serialism of the modern imagination—the image of infinite unilinear progression which so haunts our minds. Because we have to use numbers so much we tend to think of every process as if it must be like the numeral series, where every step, to all eternity, is the same kind of step as the one before. I implore you to remember the Irishman and his two stoves. There are progressions in which the last step is *sui generis*—incommensurable with the others—and in which to go the whole way is to undo all the labour of your previous journey. To reduce the *Tao* to a mere natural product is a step of that kind. Up to that point, the kind of explanation which explains things away may give us something, though at a heavy cost. But you cannot go on 'explaining away' forever: you will find that you have explained explanation itself away. You cannot go on 'seeing through' things forever. The whole point of seeing through something is to see something through it. It is good that the window should be transparent, because the street or garden beyond it is opaque. How if you saw through the garden too? It is no use trying to 'see through' first principles. If you see through everything, then everything is transparent. But a wholly transparent world is an invisible world. To 'see through' all things is the same as not to see.

(18)

Jacques Maritain

(1882–   )

MARITAIN, professor emeritus at Princeton University since 1953, has been generally recognized as the leading Thomist of our day and a pioneering critic of Bergsonism. He wrote voluminously for well over half a century and has written almost a book a year since his retirement. His intellectual interests in recent years are reflected in the following selected titles: Man and the State *(1950),* Approaches to God *(1954),* The Degrees of Knowledge *(1959),* The Responsibility of the Artist *(1960),* Moral Philosophy *(1964).*

■ *The Crisis of Modern Humanism*

THE WORD "HUMANISM" lends itself to many different interpretations, each of them depending, in turn, upon the notion one has of the nature of man. It might prove advisable, then, to furnish a definition here at the outset. Even though such a definition as this can itself be developed in many different directions, in order to leave all further discussion open, let us say simply that humanism tends essentially to render man more truly human and to manifest his original greatness by enabling him to partake of everything in nature and in history capable of enriching him. It requires both that man develop the latent tendencies he possesses, his creative powers and the life of reason, and that he work to transform into instruments of his liberty the forces of the physical universe. Obviously, we cannot delete from the humanistic tradition the wisdom of ancient Greece, which, in its own terms, sought to attain "that which is better than reason, being the principle itself of reason." From this, one should take warning never to define humanism in such a way as to exclude from it all that is ordained to the supra-human and as to forswear all considerations of transcendence.   (1)

If we take our point of view from the concrete logic of the events of history, we see that in the practical order of human life and action—not in the order of pure philosophic speculation—many positions tenable in theory (rightly or wrongly) are quickly swept away because after a short while they appear to be *unlivable* in practice—not necessarily for a given individual, but for the common consciousness.   (2)

Here we have a glimpse into the nature of the great defect of classical humanism, the brand of humanism which, since the Renaissance, has occupied the last three centuries. This defect, it seems to me, lies not so much in that which is affirmed in this sort of humanism, as in that which consists of negation, denial, and separation; it lies in what one might call an *anthropocentric*[1] concept of man and culture. One might add that the error involved boils down to affirming human nature as closed in upon itself or absolutely self-sufficient.   (3)

In the place of an *open* human nature and of an *open* reason, which are the only true nature and the only true reason, man claims to possess a nature and a reason isolated in themselves and *shut up* in themselves, each of them exclusive of whatever is not itself. Instead of a human and rational development in continuance of the Gospel, man has sought this development from pure reason *as a substitute* for the Gospel. And for human life, for the concrete movement of history, this means real and very serious amputations. Prayer, evangelical virtues, supra-rational truths, sense of sin and of grace and of the Gospel's beatitudes, the necessity for self-sacrifice and ascetic discipline, for contemplation, for the means of the Cross— all this has been either stuck between parentheses or finally denied. In the concrete realm of human life, reason has become divorced from the supra-rational.   (4)

Reason isolates itself also from all that is irrational in man or else denies it, always acting on the fallacy that whatever is "irrational" in the sense of not being reducible to reason is, by this very fact, "irrational" in the sense of being anti-rational, or incompatible with reason. On the one hand, the proper life of the universe of will is disregarded. And whatever

---

[1] I realize that this term is not particularly felicitous; I use it for want of a better term to express a concept which shuts man up in himself and separates him from Nature, Grace and God.

is non-rational even in the world of knowledge is also overlooked. Then, too, the whole universe of the infra-rational, of instincts, of obscure tendencies, and of the unconscious, with all its malicious and even demonic, as well as fertile, implications is also put in parentheses or chastely forgotten.   (5)

Thus we witness the gradual formation of the man of the bourgeois pharisaism in whom the nineteenth century long believed, and whom Marx, Nietzsche and Freud were to glory in unmasking. And indeed they did unmask him, but not without disfiguring man himself in the process.
                                                                     (6)

At the same time, tremendous promises were made to mankind from the time of Descartes on. Automatically the progress of man's enlightenment was to produce a full happiness of leisure and rest, an earthly beatitude.   (7)

Well, *all this simply did not work:* the unfolding of the story—of history —has shown it clearly enough. After having put aside God in order to become self-sufficient, man loses his soul; he seeks himself in vain, turning the universe upside down in his effort to find himself again. He finds only masks, and, behind those masks, death.   (8)

And then there follows the spectacle which we are now witnessing, the *irrationalist* tidal wave. It is the awakening of a tragic opposition between life and intellect. This opposition had begun with Luther, had continued on with Rousseau. Later, however, it happened that certain phenomena of symbiosis, which I have not the time to analyze here, were produced, intermingling irrationalist and rationalist trends.   (9)

Today this opposition has cropped up again and sometimes appears in the meanest forms, for example under the form of racism or under the highly simplified form given it by those who cry "Death to intelligence." I shall return to this in a moment.   (10)

It also finds noble—and very noble—forms of expression in such thinkers, for instance, as Nietzsche, or even Kierkegaard, Karl Barth,[2] and Chestov. It is through the love of that which is the most free and most highly spiritual that these men undertake to defend man against reason. Even if the path which they follow is erroneous, it would be extremely unjust of us to confuse it with that of the servile enemies of reason, who are their foe as well as ours. Still, even here, with whatever intelligence one attacks the value of intelligence, and with whatever generosity one tries to save human values, this position definitely gives rise to what might be called a *counter-humanism.*   (11)

---

2 As a matter of fact, the splendid attitude of Karl Barth during the present war, and the progress of his doctrine about the temporal order, are proof that the "counter-humanism" of his theology is now balanced by more humanistic conceptions.

In the concrete existence and the effective evolution of societies, the trouble with all forms of noble or lofty counter-humanism is that inevitably men end by substituting for them the meanest forms. In the end, Nietzsche gives way to Mr. Rosenberg.   (12)

It would appear here that reason has been imperiled through worship of reason, that humanism has been endangered by anthropocentric humanism, a humanism that fell short of the mark. Terrible voices are raised in man, crying, "Enough prevaricating optimism, enough illusory morality! Enough murderous idealism, idealism which denies evil and misfortune and which deprives us of the means of struggling against them. Let us return to the great spiritual fecundity of the abyss, of the absurd, and of the ethics of despair!" Poor Nietzsche! The really terrible voice, the fatal voice is not that of Nietzsche. It is the voice of that base and mediocre multitude, the very baseness, the mediocrity and the disgrace of which seem indeed to be apocalyptic signs; of that multitude which hurls out to the four corners of space, under the form of the cult of race and blood or under the form of the cult of war, the gospel of the hatred of reason. (13)

When love and sanctity fail to transfigure the condition of mankind or to change slaves into sons of God, the Law claims many victims. Nietzsche could not endure the sight of the lame and halt of Christianity: even more than Goethe, he revolted against the Cross. He dreamt of a dionysiac superman—who was to remain only a figment of the imagination. Dionysius?—The newspapers and the radio bring us news of him each morning. They have shown us how he leads his dance through the concentration camps, through the new ghettos where millions of Jews and political suspects are condemned to lingering death, through the disemboweled cities of China and Spain, and now through a Europe delivered up to murder and starvation, oppression and enslavement, through a world set ablaze by war. Nietzsche did not grasp that man has no choice except between two roads: the road to Calvary and the road to the slaughterhouse. The irrationalist tidal wave is in reality the tragic catastrophe of rationalist humanism. It reacts against the type of humanism characterized by a reason closed upon itself, but in so doing it subjects man to the influence of forces from below, it shuts off still further communications from above and alienates man from the spirit which liberates; it walls the creature up in the abyss of animal vitality.   (14)

On the other hand there is the spectacle of a continuance, an aggravation and exasperation of anthropocentric humanism in the direction in which is had pointed from the very start, the direction of rationalistic hopes, constituted no longer in mere speculative religion, but in a lived religion.   (15)

This sums up all the consequences of the principle that *man alone, and by himself alone, works out his salvation.*   (16)

The pure case which we are facing here is Marxism. While turning Hegelianism upside down, Marx nevertheless remained a rationalist to the point of averring that the proper movement of matter is a *dialectical* movement. In this Marxist materialism, it is not irrational instinct or biological mysticism but reason itself which decapitates reason.   (17)

Man alone, it is claimed, man alone and by himself alone, achieves his destiny and works out his salvation. It follows that this destiny is merely and exclusively *temporal* and this salvation is of course achieved *without God,* since man is truly alone and acts by himself alone, only if God does not exist. It is achieved even *against God,* since it is achieved against everything in man and in human society which bears a likeness to God; that is to say, a likeness to what they would call alienation or heteronomy. This salvation requires the organization of the human race into one body the supreme destiny of which is not to see God but to gain sovereign domination of history. It is a position which still styles itself humanistic, but which is radically atheistic, and which, by that very fact, actually destroys the humanism which it professes in theory. The manner in which the revolutionary materialistic dialectic has imposed itself in Russia is enough to edify us on this score. Whatever may have been the achievements of Soviet Russia—more powerful indeed than the world previously believed—Communism itself, as a doctrine and a way of life, is situated in the lines of development of rationalistic humanism, but as a spiritual catastrophe thereof.   (18)

Finally there is a position as far removed from anthropocentric humanism as it is from anti-humanist irrationalism. It is the Christian humanist position, according to which the misfortune of classical humanism did not consist in having been humanism, but in having been anthropocentric; did not consist in having trusted reason, but in having isolated reason and caused it to dry up at its well-springs; did not consist in the quest for liberty but in the trend toward the illusory myth of the City of the *individual set up as a selfish god,* instead of toward the ideal of the City of *the human person considered as the image of God.*   (19)

In short, according to this point of view, the modern world has pursued good things down wrong pathways. It has thus compromised the very pursuit of the authentic human values, which we must now save by the acknowledgment of a more profound truth and by a substantial recasting of humanism.   (20)

A new humanism must assume again and lift up into a purified atmosphere all the work of the classical period. It must remake anthropology. It must discover the rehabilitation and the "dignification" of the creature not in a species of isolation, thus enclosing the creature within itself, but in an opening up of the creature to the universe of the divine and the supra-rational. And as a matter of fact such a task implies a work of sanctification of the profane and the temporal. It means the discovery of a more profound and real sense of the dignity of the human person. As a consequence, man would rediscover himself in God rediscovered, and would direct social work toward an heroic ideal of fraternal love conceived, not as a spontaneous return of sentiment to some illusory primitive state, but as a difficult and painful conquest of the spirit, as a work of grace and virtue. Such a humanism, which considers man in the integrality of his natural and supernatural being and which sets no *a priori* limits to the descent of the divine into man, could be termed the *humanism of the Incarnation.* (21)

In the perspectives of this integral humanism, there must be no conflict between the vertical movement toward eternal life (begun and existing here and now) and the horizontal movement through which are revealed progressively the substance and the creative forces of man in history. Nor can there be mutual exclusion of the one by the other, for these two directions must be pursued simultaneously. And the latter, the horizontal movement of historical progression, cannot be achieved well or prevented from turning to the destruction of man unless it be vitally joined to the former, the vertical movement toward eternal life; for this horizontal movement, while it has its proper and properly temporal aims, and tends by itself to better the condition of man here below, nevertheless prepares the way, within human history, for the Kingdom of God, which, for each individual person and for all humanity, is something beyond history. (22)

Arnold J. Toynbee

(1889–   )

TOYNBEE, professor emeritus of international history at the University of London, has been publishing books for more than fifty years: in 1915 he published two books, Nationality and War *and* The New Europe; *in 1965 he published two books,* Between Niger and Nile *and* Hannibal's Legacy. *Between 1934 and 1960, he published his ambitious* A Study of History *in twelve volumes.*

◼ *Christianity and Civilization*

As I was re-reading my notes for this essay during the last few days, there floated into my mind the picture of a scene which was transacted in the capital of a great empire about fourteen hundred years ago, when that capital was full of war—not a war on a front but a war in the rear, a war of turmoil and street fighting. The emperor of that empire was holding council to decide whether he should carry on the struggle or whether he should take ship and sail away to safety. At the crown council his wife, the empress, was present and spoke, and she said: 'You, Justinian, can sail away if you like; the ship is at the quay and the sea is still open; but I am going to stay and see it out, because καλὸν ἐντάφιον ἡ βασιλεία: "Empire is a fine winding sheet."' I thought of this passage and my colleague, Professor Baynes, found it for me; and, as I thought of it, and also thought of the day and the circumstances in which I was writing, I decided to emend it; and I emended it to κάλλιον ἐντάφιον ἡ βασιλεία τοῦ Θεοῦ: 'a finer winding-sheet is the Kingdom of God'—a finer because that is a winding-sheet from which there is a resurrection. Now that paraphrase of a famous phrase of Greek comes, I venture to think, rather near to the three Latin words which are the motto of the University of Oxford; and, if we believe in these three words *Dominus Illuminatio Mea* and can live up to them, we can look forward without dismay to any future that may be coming to us. The material future is very little in our power. Storms might come which might lay low that noble and beloved building and leave not one stone upon another. But, if the truth about this university and about our-selves is told in those three Latin words, then we know for certain that, though the stones may fall, the light by which we live will not go out. (1)

Now let me come by a very easy transition to what is my subject in this essay—the relation between Christianity and civilization. This is a ques-tion which has always been at issue since the foundation of the Christian Church, and of course there have been a number of alternative views on it.
(2)

One of the oldest and most persistent views is that Christianity was the destroyer of the civilization within whose framework it grew up. That was, I suppose, the view of the Emperor Marcus, as far as he was aware of the presence of Christianity in his world. It was most emphatically and vio-lently the view of his successor the Emperor Julian, and it was also the view of the English historian Gibbon, who recorded the decline and fall of the Roman Empire long after the event. In the last chapter of Gibbon's history there is one sentence in which he sums up the theme of the whole work. Looking back, he says: 'I have described the triumph of barbarism and religion.' And, to understand his meaning, you have to turn from the middle of Chapter LXXI to the opening passage of Chapter I, that extraordinarily majestic description of the Roman Empire at peace in the age of the Antonines, in the second century after Christ. He starts you there, and at the end of the long story he says 'I have described the triumph of barbarism and religion,' meaning that it was Christianity as well as barbarism which overthrew the civilization for which the Antonines stood.   (3)

One hesitates to question Gibbon's authority, but I believe there is a fallacy in this view which vitiates the whole of it. Gibbon assumes that the Graeco-Roman civilization stood at its height in the age of the Antonines and that in tracing its decline from that moment he is tracing that decline from the beginning. Evidently, if you take that view, Christianity rises as the empire sinks, and the rise of Christianity is the fall of civilization. I think Gibbon's initial error lies in supposing that the ancient civilization of the Graeco-Roman world began to decline in the second century after Christ and that the age of the Antonines was that civilization's highest point. I think it really began to decline in the fifth century before Christ. It died not by murder, but by suicide; and that act of suicide was committed before the fifth century B.C. was out. It was not even the philosophies which preceded Christianity that were responsible for the death of the ancient Graeco-Roman civilization. The philosophies arose because the civic life of that civilization had already destroyed itself by turning itself into an idol to which men paid an exorbitant worship. And the rise of the philosophies, and the subsequent rise of the religions out of which Christianity emerged as the final successor of them all, was something that happened after the Graeco-Roman civilization had already put itself to death. The rise of the philosophies, and *a fortiori* that of the religions, was not a cause; it was a consequence.   (4)

When Gibbon in that opening passage of his work looks at the Roman Empire in the age of the Antonines, he does not say explicitly—but I am sure this was in his mind—that he is also thinking of himself as standing on another peak of civilization and looking back towards that distant peak in the past across a broad trough of barbarism in between. Gibbon thought to himself: 'On the morrow of the death of the Emperor Marcus the Roman Empire went into decline. All the values that I, Gibbon, and my kind care for began then to be degraded. Religion and barbarism began to triumph. This lamentable state of affairs continued to prevail for hundreds and hundreds of years; and then, a few generations before my time, no longer ago than the close of the seventeenth century, a rational civilization began to emerge again.' From his peak in the eighteenth century Gibbon looks back to the Antonine peak in the second century, and that view— which is, I think, implicit in Gibbon's work—has been put very clearly and sharply by a writer of the twentieth century, from whom I propose to quote a passage somewhat at length because it is, so to speak, the formal antithesis of the thesis which I want to maintain.

> Greek and Roman society was built on the conception of the subordination of the individual to the community, of the citizen to the state; it set the safety of the commonwealth, as the supreme aim of conduct, above the safety of the individual whether in this world or in a world to come. Trained from infancy in this unselfish ideal, the citizens devoted their lives to the public service and were ready to lay them down for the common good; or, if they shrank from the supreme sacrifice, it never occurred to them that they acted otherwise than basely in preferring their personal existence to the interests of their country. All this was changed by the spread of Oriental religions which inculcated the communion of the soul with God and its eternal salvation as the only objects worth living for, objects in comparison with which the prosperity and even the existence of the state sank into insignificance. The inevitable result of this selfish and immoral doctrine was to withdraw the devotee more and more from the public service, to concentrate his thoughts on his own spiritual emotions, and to breed in him a contempt for the present life which he regarded merely as a probation for a better and an eternal. The saint and the recluse, disdainful of earth and rapt in ecstatic contemplation of heaven, became in popular opinion the highest ideal of humanity, displacing the old ideal of the patriot and hero who, forgetful of self, lives and is ready to die for the good of his country. The earthly city seemed poor and contemptible to men whose eyes beheld the City of God coming in the clouds of heaven. Thus the centre of gravity, so to say, was shifted from the present to a future life, and, however much the other world may have gained, there can be little doubt that this one lost heavily by the change. A general disintegration of the body politic set in. The ties of the state and the family were loosened: the structure of society tended to resolve itself into its individual elements and thereby to relapse into barbarism; for civilization is only possible through the active co-operation of the citizens and their willingness to subordinate their private interests to the common good. Men refused to defend their country and even to continue their kind. In their anxiety to save their own souls and the souls of others, they were content to leave the material world, which they identified with the principle of evil, to perish around them. This obsession lasted for a thou-

> sand years. The revival of Roman law, of the Aristotelian philo-
> sophy, of ancient art and literature at the close of the Middle
> Ages, marked the return of Europe to native ideals of life and
> conduct, to saner, manlier views of the world. The long halt in
> the march of civilization was over. The tide of Oriental invasion
> had turned at last. It is ebbing still.   (5)

It is ebbing indeed! And one might speculate about what the author of this passage, which was first published in 1906, would now write if he were revising his work for a fourth edition today. Many reading this article are, of course, familiar with the passage. I have not yet mentioned the author's name; but, for those who do not know it already, I would say that it is not Alfred Rosenberg; it is Sir James Frazer.[1] I wonder what that gentle scholar thinks of the latest form in which Europe's return 'to native ideals of life and conduct' is manifesting itself.   (6)

Now you will have seen that the most interesting thesis in that passage of Frazer's is the contention that trying to save one's soul is something contrary to, and incompatible with, trying to do one's duty to one's neighbour. I am going, in the course of this essay, to challenge that thesis; at the moment I merely want to point out that Frazer is at the same time putting Gibbon's thesis and stating it in explicit terms; and on this point I would give Frazer the answer that I have already ventured to give to Gibbon: that Christianity was not the destroyer of the ancient Greek civilization, because that civilization had decayed from inherent defects of its own before Christianity arose. But I would agree with Frazer, and would ask you to agree with me, that the tide of Christianity has been ebbing and that our post-Christian Western secular civilization that has emerged is a civilization of the same order as the pre-Christian Graeco-Roman civilization. This observation opens up a second possible view of the relation between Christianity and civilization—not the same view as that held in common by Gibbon and Frazer, not the view that Christianity has been the destroyer of civilization, but an alternative view in which Christianity appears in the role of civilization's humble servant.   (7)

According to this second possible view, Christianity is, as it were, the egg, grub, and chrysalis between butterfly and butterfly. Christianity is a transitional thing which bridges the gap between one civilization and another, and I confess that I myself held this rather patronizing view for many years. On this view you look at the historical function of the Christian Church in terms of the process of the reproduction of civilizations. Civilization is a species of being which seeks to reproduce itself, and Christianity has had a useful but a subordinate role in bringing two new secular

---

[1] Frazer, Sir J. G.: *The Golden Bough*, Part IV: 'Adonis, Attis, Osiris,' vol. I, pp. 300–301 (third edition, London 1914, Macmillan, preface dated January, 1914).

civilizations to birth after the death of their predecessor. You find the ancient Graeco-Roman civilization in decline from the close of the second century after Christ onwards. And then after an interval you find—perhaps as early as the ninth century in Byzantium, and as early as the thirteenth century in the West in the person of the *Stupor Mundi* Frederick II —a new secular civilization arising out of the ruins of its Graeco-Roman predecessor. And you look at the role of Christianity in the interval and conclude that Christianity is a kind of chrysalis which has held and preserved the hidden germs of life until these have been able to break out again into a new growth of secular civilization. That is an alternative view to the theory of Christianity being the destroyer of the ancient Graeco-Roman civilization; and, if one looks abroad through the history of civilizations, one can see other cases which seem to conform to the same pattern.

(8)

Take the other higher religions which are still living on in the world of today side by side with Christianity: Islam, Hinduism, and the Mahayana form of Buddhism which now prevails in the Far East. You can see the role of Islam as a chrysalis between the ancient civilization of Israel and Iran and the modern Islamic civilization of the Near and Middle East. Hinduism, again, seems to bridge a gap in the history of civilization in India between the modern Hindu culture and the ancient culture of the Aryas; and Buddhism, likewise, seems to play the same part as a mediator between the modern history of the Far East and the history of ancient China. In that picture the Christian Church would be simply one of a series of churches whose function is to serve as chrysalises to provide for the reproduction of civilizations and thus to preserve that secular species of society.

(9)

Now I think there is perhaps a chrysalis-like element in the constitution of the Christian Church—an institutional element that I am going to deal with later—which may have quite a different purpose from that of assisting in the reproduction of civilizations. But, before we accept at all an account of the place and role of Christianity and of the other living higher religions in social history which represents these religions as being mere instruments for assisting in the process of the reproduction of civilizations, let us go on testing the hypothesis by examining whether, in every instance of the parent-and-child relation between civilizations, we find a chrysalis-church intervening between the parent civilization and the daughter civilization. If you look at the histories of the ancient civilizations of South-Western Asia and Egypt, you find there a rudimentary higher religion in the form of the worship of a god and a related goddess. I call it rudimentary because, in the worship of Tammuz and Ishtar, of Adonis and Astarte, of Attis and Cybele, of Osiris and Isis, you are very close to the nature-worship of the Earth and her fruits; and I think that, here again, you can see that this rudimentary higher religion, in each of its different variants, has in every case played the historical role of filling a gap where there was a break in the continuity of secular civilization.   (10)

If, however, we complete our survey, we shall find that this apparent 'law' does not always hold good. Christianity intervenes in this way between our own civilization and the Graeco-Roman one. Go back behind the Graeco-Roman one and you find a Minoan civilization behind that. But between the Minoan and the Graeco-Roman you do not find any higher religion corresponding to Christianity. Again, if you go back behind the ancient civilization of Aryan India, you find vestiges of a still more ancient pre-Aryan civilization in the Indus Valley which have only been excavated within the last twenty years, but here again you do not seem to find any higher religion intervening between the two. And, if you pass from the Old World to the New and look at the civilization of the Mayas in Central America, which, again, has had daughter civilizations born from it, you do not find, here either, in the intervening period, any trace at all of any higher religion or church of the same species as Christianity or Islam or Hinduism or Mahayanian Buddhism; nor again is there any evidence of any such chrysalis bridging the transition from primitive societies to the earliest known civilizations—to what we might call the first generation of civilizations; and so, when we complete our view of the whole field of civilizations, as we have now done in a very summary way, we find that the relation between higher religions and civilizations seems to differ according to the generation of the civilization with which we are dealing. We seem to find no higher religion at all between primitive societies and civilizations of the first generation, and between civilizations of the first and those of the second generation either none or only rudiments. It is between civilizations of the second and those of the third generation that the intervention of a higher religion seems to be the rule, and here only.   (11)

If there is anything in this analysis of the relation between civilizations and higher religions, this suggests a third possible view of that relation which would be the exact inverse of the second view which I have just put before you. On that second view, religion is subsidiary to the reproduction of secular civilizations, and the inverse of that would be that the successive rises and falls of civilizations may be subsidiary to the growth of religion.   (12)

The breakdowns and disintegration of civilization might be stepping-stones to higher things on the religious plane. After all, one of the deepest spiritual laws that we know is the law that is proclaimed by Aeschylus in the two words πάθει μάθος—'it is through suffering that learning comes' —and in the New Testament in the verse 'whom the Lord loveth, He chasteneth; and scourgeth every son whom He receiveth.' If you apply that to the rise of the higher religions which has culminated in the flowering of Christianity, you might say that in the mythical passions of Tammuz and Adonis and Attis and Osiris the Passion of Christ was foreshadowed, and that the Passion of Christ was the culminating and crowning experience of the sufferings of human souls in successive failures in the enterprise of secular civilization. The Christian Church itself arose out of the spiritual travail which was a consequence of the breakdown of the Graeco-Roman civilization. Again, the Christian Church has Jewish and Zoroastrian roots, and those roots sprang from an earlier breakdown, the breakdown of a Syrian civilization which was a sister to the Graeco-Roman. The kingdoms of Israel and Judah were two of the many states of this ancient Syrian world; and it was the premature and permanent overthrow of these worldly commonwealths and the extinction of all the political hopes which had been bound up with their existence as independent polities that brought the religion of Judaism to birth and evoked the highest expression of its spirit in the elegy of the Suffering Servant, which is appended in the Bible to the book of the prophet Isaiah. Judaism, likewise, has a Mosaic root which in its turn sprang from the withering of the second crop of the ancient Egyptian civilization. I do not know whether Moses and Abraham are historical characters, but I think it can be taken as certain that they represent historical stages of religious experience, and Moses' forefather and forerunner Abraham received his enlightenment and his promise at the dissolution, in the nineteenth or eighteenth century before Christ, of the ancient civilization of Sumer and Akkad—the earliest case, known to us, of a civilization going to ruin. These men of sorrows were precursors of Christ; and the sufferings through which they won their enlightenment were Stations of the Cross in anticipation of the Crucifixion. That is, no doubt, a very old idea, but it is also an ever new one. (13)

If religion is a chariot, it looks as if the wheels on which it mounts towards Heaven may be the periodic downfalls of civilizations on Earth. It looks as if the movement of civilizations may be cyclic and recurrent, while the movement of religion may be on a single continuous upward line. The continuous upward movement of religion may be served and promoted by the cyclic movement of civilizations round the cycle of birth, death, birth. (14)

If we accept this conclusion, it opens up what may seem a rather startling view of history. If civilizations are the handmaids of religion and if the Graeco-Roman civilization served as a good handmaid to Christianity by bringing it to birth before that civilization finally went to pieces, then the civilizations of the third generation may be vain repetitions of the Gentiles. If, so far from its being the historical function of higher religions to minister, as chrysalises, to the cyclic process of the reproduction of civilizations, it is the historical function of civilizations to serve, by their downfalls, as stepping-stones to a progressive process of the revelation of always deeper religious insight, and the gift of ever more grace to act on this insight, then the societies of the species called civilizations will have fulfilled their function when once they have brought a mature higher religion to birth; and, on this showing, our own Western post-Christian secular civilization might at best be a superfluous repetition of the pre-Christian Graeco-Roman one, and at worst a pernicious back-sliding from the path of spiritual progress. In our Western world of today, the worship of Leviathan—the self-worship of the tribe—is a religion to which all of us pay some measure of allegiance; and this tribal religion is, of course, sheer idolatry. Communism, which is another of our latter-day religions, is, I think, a leaf taken from the book of Christianity—a leaf torn out and misread. Democracy is another leaf from the book of Christianity, which has also, I fear, been torn out and, while perhaps not misread, has certainly been half emptied of meaning by being divorced from its Christian context and secularized; and we have obviously, for a number of generations past, been living on spiritual capital, I mean clinging to Christian practice without possessing the Christian belief—and practice unsupported by belief is a wasting asset, as we have suddenly discovered, to our dismay, in this generation.   (15)

If this self-criticism is just, then we must revise the whole of our present conception of modern history; and if we can make the effort of will and imagination to think this ingrained and familiar conception away, we shall arrive at a very different picture of the historical retrospect. Our present view of modern history focuses attention on the rise of our modern Western secular civilization as the latest great new event in the world. As we follow that rise, from the first premonition of it in the genius of Frederick II Hohenstaufen, through the Renaissance to the eruption of democracy and science and modern scientific technique, we think of all this as being the great new event in the world which demands our attention and commands our admiration. If we can bring ourselves to think of it, instead, as one of the vain repetitions of the Gentiles—an almost meaningless repetition of something that the Greeks and Romans did before us and did supremely well—then the greatest new event in the history of mankind will be seen to be a very different one. The greatest new event will then not be the monotonous rise of yet another secular civilization out of the bosom of the Christian Church in the course of these latter centuries; it will still be the Crucifixion and its spiritual consequences. There is one curious result of our immense modern scientific discoveries which is, I think, often overlooked. On the vastly changed time-scale which our astronomers and geologists have opened up to us, the beginning of the Christian era is an extremely recent date; on a time-scale in which nineteen hundred years are no more than the twinkling of an eye, the beginning of the Christian era is only yesterday. It is only on the old-fashioned time-scale, on which the creation of the world and the beginning of life on the planet were reckoned to have taken place not more than six thousand years ago, that a span of nineteen hundred years seems a long period of time and the beginning of the Christian era therefore seems a far-off event. In fact it is a very recent event—perhaps the most recent significant event in history—and that brings us to a consideration of the prospects of Christianity in the future history of mankind on Earth. (16)

On this view of the history of religion and of the civilizations, it has not been the historical function of the Christian Church just to serve as a chrysalis between the Graeco-Roman civilization and its daughter civilizations in Byzantium and the West; and, supposing that these two civilizations, which are descended from the ancient Graeco-Roman one, turn out to be no more than vain repetitions of their parent, then there will be no reason to suppose that Christianity itself will be superseded by some distinct, separate, and different higher religion which will serve as a chrysalis between the death of the present Western civilization and the birth of its children. On the theory that religion is subservient to civilization, you would expect some new higher religion to come into existence on each occasion, in order to serve the purpose of tiding over the gap between one civilization and another. If the truth is the other way round—if it is civilization that is the means and religion that is the end—then, once again, a civilization may break down and break up, but the replacement of one higher religion by another will not be a necessary consequence. So far from that, if our secular Western civilization perishes, Christianity may be expected not only to endure but to grow in wisdom and stature as the result of a fresh experience of secular catastrophe. (17)

There is one unprecedented feature of our own post-Christian secular civilization which, in spite of being a rather superficial feature, has a certain importance in this connection. In the course of its expansion our modern Western secular civilization has become literally world-wide and has drawn into its net all other surviving civilizations as well as primitive societies. At its first appearance, Christianity was provided by the Graeco-Roman civilization with a universal state, in the shape of the Roman Empire with its policed roads and shipping routes, as an aid to the spread of Christianity round the shores of the Mediterranean. Our modern Western secular civilization in its turn may serve its historical purpose by providing Christianity with a completely world-wide repetition of the Roman Empire to spread over. We have not quite arrived at our Roman Empire yet, though the victor in this war may be the founder of it. But, long before a world is unified politically, it is unified economically and in other material ways; and the unification of our present world has long since opened the way for St. Paul, who once travelled from the Orontes to the Tiber under the aegis of the *Pax Romana,* to travel on from the Tiber to the Mississippi and from the Mississippi to the Yangtse; while Clement's and Origen's work of infusing Greek philosophy into Christianity at Alexandria might be emulated in some city of the Far East by the infusion of Chinese philosophy into Christianity. This intellectual feat has indeed been partly performed already. One of the greatest of modern missionaries and modern scholars, Matteo Ricci, who was both a Jesuit father and a Chinese literatus, set his hand to that task before the end of the sixteenth century of the Christian era. It is even possible that as, under the Roman Empire, Christianity drew out of and inherited from the other Oriental religions the heart of what was best in them, so the present religions of India and the form of Buddhism that is practised today in the Far East may contribute new elements to be grafted onto Christianity in days to come. And then one may look forward to what may happen when Caesar's empire decays—for Caesar's empire always does decay after a run of a few hundred years. What may happen is that Christianity may be left as the spiritual heir of all the other higher religions, from the post-Sumerian rudiment of one in the worship of Tammuz and Ishtar down to those that in A.D. 1948 are still living separate lives side by side with Christianity, and of all the philosophies from Ikhnaton's to Hegel's; while the Christian Church as an institution may be left as the social heir of all the other churches and all the civilizations.   (18)

That side of the picture brings one to another question which is both always old and always new—the question of the relation of the Christian Church to the Kingdom of Heaven. We seem to see a series of different kinds of society succeeding one another in this world. As the primitive species of societies has given place to a second species known as the civilizations within the brief period of the last six thousand years, so this second species of local and ephemeral societies may perhaps give place in its turn to a third species embodied in a single world-wide and enduring representative in the shape of the Christian Church. If we can look forward to that, we shall have to ask ourselves this question: Supposing that this were to happen, would it mean that the Kingdom of Heaven would then have been established on Earth?   (19)

I think this question is a very pertinent one in our day, because some kind of earthly paradise is the goal of most of the current secular ideologies. To my mind the answer is emphatically 'No,' for several reasons which I shall now do my best to put before you.   (20)

One very obvious and well-known reason lies in the nature of society and in the nature of man. Society is, after all, only the common ground between the fields of action of a number of personalities, and human personality, at any rate as we know it in this world, has an innate capacity for evil as well as for good. If these two statements are true, as I believe them to be, then in any society on Earth, unless and until human nature itself undergoes a moral mutation which would make an essential change in its character, the possibility of evil, as well as of good, will be born into the world afresh with every child and will never be wholly ruled out as long as that child remains alive. This is as much as to say that the replacement of a multiplicity of civilizations by a universal church would not have purged human nature of original sin; and this leads to another consideration: so long as original sin remains an element in human nature, Caesar will always have work to do, and there will still be Caesar's things to be rendered to Caesar, as well as God's to God, in this world. Human society on Earth will not be able wholly to dispense with institutions of which the sanction is not purely the individual's active will to make them work, but is partly habit and partly even force. These imperfect institutions will have to be administered by a secular power which might be subordinated to religious authority but would not thereby be eliminated. And even if Caesar were not merely subordinated but were wholly eliminated by the Church, something of him would still survive in the constitution of his supplanter; for the institutional element has historically, up to date, been dominant in the life of the Church herself in her traditional Catholic form, which, on the long historical view, is the form in which one has to look at her. (21)

In this Catholic form of the Church, I see two fundamental institutions, the Sacrifice of the Mass and the Hierarchy, which are indissolubly welded together by the fact that the priest, by definition, is the person with the power to perform the rite. If, in speaking of the Mass, one may speak, without offence, with the tongues of the historian and the anthropologist, then, using this language, one may describe the Sacrifice of the Mass as the mature form of a most ancient religious rite of which the rudiments can be traced back to the worship of the fertility of the Earth and her fruits by the earliest tillers of the soil. (I am speaking here merely of the mundane origin of the rite.) As for the Hierarchy of the Church in its traditional form, this, as one knows, is modelled on a more recent and less awe-inspiring yet nevertheless most potent institution, the imperial civil service of the Roman Empire. The Church in its traditional form thus stands forth armed with the spear of the Mass, the shield of the Hierarchy, and the helmet of the Papacy; and perhaps the subconscious purpose—or the divine intention, if you prefer that language—of this heavy panoply of institutions in which the Church has clad herself is the very practical one of outlasting the toughest of the secular institutions of this world, including all the civilizations. If we survey all the institutions of which we have knowledge in the present and in the past, I think that the institutions created, or adopted and adapted, by Christianity are the toughest and the most enduring of any that we know and are therefore the most likely to last—and outlast all the rest. The history of Protestantism would seem to indicate that the Protestant act of casting off this armour four hundred years ago was premature; but that would not necessarily mean that this step would always be a mistake; and, however that may be, the institutional element in the traditional Catholic form of the Church Militant on Earth, even if it proves to be an invaluable and indispensable means of survival, is all the same a mundane feature which makes the Church Militant's life different from that of the Kingdom of Heaven, in which they neither marry nor are given in marriage but are as the angels of God, and in which each individual soul catches the spirit of God from direct communion with Him— 'like light caught from a leaping flame,' as Plato puts it in his Seventh Letter. Thus, even if the Church had won a fully world-wide allegiance and had entered into the inheritance of the last of the civilizations and of all the other higher religions, the Church on Earth would not be a perfect embodiment here on Earth of the Kingdom of Heaven. The Church on Earth would still have sin and sorrow to contend with as well as to profit by as a means of grace on the principle of $\pi\acute{a}\vartheta\epsilon\iota\ \mu\acute{a}\vartheta o\varsigma$, and she would still have to wear for a long time to come a panoply of institutions to give her the massive social solidity that she needs in the mundane struggle for survival, but this at the inevitable price of spiritually weighing her down. On this showing, the victorious Church Militant on Earth will be a province of the Kingdom of God, but a province in which the citizens of the heavenly commonwealth have to live and breathe and labour in an atmosphere that is not their native element.   (22)

The position in which the Church would then find herself is well conveyed in Plato's conceit, in the *Phaedo*, of the true surface of the Earth. We live, Plato suggests, in a large but local hollow, and what we take to be the air is really a sediment of fog. If one day we could make our way to the upper levels of the surface of the Earth, we should there breathe the pure ether and should see the light of the Sun and stars direct; and then we should realize how dim and blurred had been our vision down in the hollow, where we see the heavenly bodies, through the murky atmosphere in which we breathe, as imperfectly as the fishes see them through the water in which they swim. This Platonic conceit is a good simile for the life of the Church Militant on Earth; but the truth cannot be put better than it has been by Saint Augustine.

> It is written of Cain that he founded a commonwealth; but Abel—true to the type of the pilgrim and sojourner that he was— did not do the like. For the Commonwealth of the Saints is not of this world, though it does give birth to citizens here in whose persons it performs its pilgrimage until the time of its kingdom shall come—the time when it will gather them all together.[2]   (23)

---

2 Saint Augustine: *De Civitate Dei*, Book xv, chap. i.

This brings me in conclusion to the last of the topics on which I am going to touch, that of the relation between Christianity and progress. (24)

If it is true, as I think it is, that the Church on Earth will never be a perfect embodiment of the Kingdom of Heaven, in what sense can we say the words of the Lord's Prayer: 'Thy Kingdom come, Thy will be done in Earth as it is in Heaven'? Have we been right, after all, in coming to the conclusion that—in contrast to the cyclic movement of the rises and falls of civilizations—the history of religion on Earth is a movement in a single continuous upward line? What are the matters in which there has been, in historical times, a continuous religious advance? And have we any reason to think that this advance will continue without end? Even if the species of societies called civilizations does give way to a historically younger and perhaps spiritually higher species embodied in a single world-wide and enduring representative in the shape of the Christian Church, may there not come a time when the tug of war between Christianity and original sin will settle down to a static balance of spiritual forces? (25)

Let me put forward one or two considerations in reply to these questions. (26)

In the first place, religious progress means spiritual progress, and spirit means personality. Therefore religious progress must take place in the spiritual lives of personalities—it must show itself in their rising to a spiritually higher state and achieving a spiritually finer activity. (27)

Now, in assuming that this individual progress is what spiritual progress means, are we after all admitting Frazer's thesis that the higher religions are essentially and incurably anti-social? Does a shift of human interest and energy from trying to create the values aimed at in the civilizations to trying to create the values aimed at in the higher religions mean that the values for which the civilizations stand are bound to suffer? Are spiritual and social values antithetical and inimical to each other? Is it true that the fabric of civilization is undermined if the salvation of the individual soul is taken as being the supreme aim of life? (28)

Frazer answers these questions in the affirmative. If his answer were right it would mean that human life was a tragedy without a catharsis. But I personally believe that Frazer's answer is not right, because I think it is based on a fundamental misconception of what the nature of souls or personalities is. Personalities are inconceivable except as agents of spiritual activity; and the only conceivable scope for spiritual activity lies in relations between spirit and spirit. It is because spirit implies spiritual relations that Christian theology has completed the Jewish doctrine of the Unity of God with the Christian doctrine of the Trinity. The doctrine of the Trinity is the theological way of expressing the revelation that God is a spirit; the doctrine of the Redemption is the theological way of expressing the revelation that God is Love. If man has been created in the likeness of God, and if the true end of man is to make this likeness ever more and more like, then Aristotle's saying that 'man is a social animal' applies to man's highest potentiality and aim—that of trying to get into ever closer communion with God. Seeking God is itself a social act. And if God's love has gone into action in this world in the Redemption of mankind by Christ, then man's efforts to make himself liker to God must include efforts to follow Christ's example in sacrificing himself for the redemption of his fellow men. Seeking and following God in this way, that is God's way, is the only true way for a human soul on Earth to seek salvation. The antithesis between trying to save one's own soul by seeking and following God and trying to do one's duty to one's neighbour is therefore wholly false. The two activities are indissoluble. The human soul that is truly seeking to save itself is as fully social a being as the ant-like Spartan or the bee-like Communist. Only, the Christian soul on Earth is a member of a very different society from Sparta or Leviathan. He is a citizen of the Kingdom of God, and therefore his paramount and all-embracing aim is to attain the highest degree of communion with, and likeness to, God Himself; his relations with his fellow men are consequences of, and corollaries to, his relations with God; and his way of loving his neighbour as himself will be to try to help his neighbour to win what he is seeking for himself —that is, to come into closer communion with God and to become more godlike. (29)

If this is a soul's recognized aim for itself and for its fellow souls in the Christian Church Militant on Earth, then it is obvious that under a Christian dispensation God's will *will* be done in Earth as it is in Heaven to an immeasurably greater degree than in a secular mundane society. It is also evident that, in the Church Militant on Earth, the good social aims of the mundane societies will incidentally be achieved very much more successfully than they ever have been or can be achieved in a mundane society which aims at these objects direct, and at nothing higher. In other words, the spiritual progress of individual souls in this life will in fact bring with it much more social progress than could be attained in any other way. It is a paradoxical but profoundly true and important principle of life that the most likely way to reach a goal is to be aiming not at that goal itself but at some more ambitious goal beyond it. This is the meaning of the fable in the Old Testament of Solomon's Choice and of the saying in the New Testament about losing one's life and saving it. (30)

Therefore, while the replacement of the mundane civilizations by the world-wide and enduring reign of the Church Militant on Earth would certainly produce what today would seem a miraculous improvement in those mundane social conditions which the civilizations have been seeking to improve during the last six thousand years, the aim, and test, of progress under a truly Christian dispensation on Earth would not lie in the field of mundane social life; the field would be the spiritual life of individual souls in their passages through this earthly life from birth into this world to death out of it. (31)

But if spiritual progress in time in this world means progress achieved by individual human souls during their passages through this world to the other world, in what sense can there be any spiritual progress over a time-span far longer than that of individual lives on Earth, and running into thousands of years, such as that of the historical development of the higher religions from the rise of Tammuz-worship and the generation of Abraham to the Christian era? (32)

I have already confessed my own adherence to the traditional Christian view that there is no reason to expect any change in unredeemed human nature while human life on Earth goes on. Till this Earth ceases to be physically habitable by man, we may expect that the endowments of individual human beings with original sin and with natural goodness will be about the same, on the average, as they always have been as far as our knowledge goes. The most primitive societies known to us in the life or by report provide examples of as great natural goodness as, and no lesser wickedness than, the highest civilizations or religious societies that have yet come into existence. There has been no perceptible variation in the average sample of human nature in the past; there is no ground, in the evidence afforded by History, to expect any great variation in the future either for better or for worse. (33)

The matter in which there might be spiritual progress in time on a time-span extending over many successive generations of life on Earth is not the unregenerate nature of man, but the opportunity open to souls, by way of the learning that comes through suffering, for getting into closer communion with God, and becoming less unlike Him, during their passage through this world. (34)

What Christ, with the Prophets before Him and the Saints after Him, has bequeathed to the Church, and what the Church, by virtue of having been fashioned into an incomparably effective institution, succeeds in accumulating, preserving, and communicating to successive generations of Christians, is a growing fund of illumination and of grace—meaning by 'illumination' the discovery or revelation or revealed discovery of the true nature of God and the true end of man here and hereafter, and by 'grace,' the will or inspiration or inspired will to aim at getting into closer communion with God and becoming less unlike Him. In this matter of increasing spiritual opportunity for souls in their passages through life on Earth, there is assuredly an inexhaustible possibility of progress in this world. (35)

Is the spiritual opportunity given by Christianity, or by one or other of the higher religions that have been forerunners of Christianity and have partially anticipated Christianity's gifts of illumination and grace to men on Earth, an indispensable condition for salvation—meaning by 'salvation' the spiritual effect on a soul of feeling after God and finding Him in its passage through life on Earth?   (36)

If this were so, then the innumerable generations of men who never had the chance of receiving the illumination and grace conveyed by Christianity and the other higher religions would have been born and have died without a chance of the salvation which is the true end of man and the true purpose of life on Earth. This might be conceivable, though still repugnant, if we believed that the true purpose of life on Earth was not the preparation of souls for another life, but the establishment of the best possible human society in this world, which in the Christian belief is not the true purpose, though it is an almost certain by-product of a pursuit of the true purpose. If progress is taken as being the social progress of Leviathan and not the spiritual progress of individual souls, then it would perhaps be conceivable that, for the gain and glory of the body social, innumerable earlier generations should have been doomed to live a lower social life in order that a higher social life might eventually be lived by successors who had entered into their labours. This would be conceivable on the hypothesis that individual human souls existed for the sake of society, and not for their own sakes or for God's. But this belief is not only repugnant but it is also inconceivable when we are dealing with the history of religion, where the progress of individual souls through this world towards God, and not the progress of society in this world, is the end on which the supreme value is set. We cannot believe that the historically incontestable fact that illumination and grace have been imparted to men on Earth in successive instalments, beginning quite recently in the history of the human race on Earth, and even then coming gradually in the course of generations, can have entailed the consequence that the vast majority of souls born into the world up to date, who have had no share in this spiritual opportunity, have, as a result, been spiritually lost. We must believe that the possibilities, provided by God, of learning through suffering in this world have always afforded a sufficient means of salvation to every soul that has made the best of the spiritual opportunity offered to it here, however small that opportunity may have been.   (37)

But, if men on Earth have not had to wait for the advent of the higher religions, culminating in Christianity, in order to qualify, in their life on Earth, for eventually attaining, after death, the state of eternal felicity in the other world, then what difference has the advent on Earth of the higher religions, and of Christianity itself, really made? The difference, I should say, is this, that, under the Christian dispensation, a soul which does make the best of its spiritual opportunities will, in qualifying for salvation, be advancing farther towards communion with God and towards likeness to God under the conditions of life on Earth, before death, than has been possible for souls that have not been illuminated, during their pilgrimage on Earth, by the light of the higher religions. A pagan soul, no less than a Christian soul, has ultimate salvation within its reach; but a soul which has been offered, and has opened itself to, the illumination and the grace that Christianity conveys, will, while still in this world, be more brightly irradiated with the light of the other world than a pagan soul that has won salvation by making the best, in this world, of the narrower opportunity here open to it. The Christian soul can attain, while still on Earth, a greater measure of man's greatest good than can be attained by any pagan soul in this earthly stage of its existence.   (38)

Thus the historical progress of religion in this world, as represented by the rise of the higher religions and by their culmination in Christianity, may, and almost certainly will, bring with it, incidentally, an immeasurable improvement in the conditions of human social life on Earth; but its direct effect and its deliberate aim and its true test is the opportunity which it brings to individual souls for spiritual progress in this world during the passage from birth to death. It is this individual spiritual progress in this world for which we pray when we say 'Thy will be done in Earth as it is in Heaven.' It is for the salvation that is open to all men of good will— pagan as well as Christian, primitive as well as civilized—who make the most of their spiritual opportunities on Earth, however narrow these opportunities may be, that we pray when we say 'Thy Kingdom come.'   (39)

Reinhold Niebuhr

(1892–   )

NIEBUHR has been recognized as one of the principal critical theologians for well over a quarter of a century. He took his degree of Doctor of Divinity from the Eden Theological Seminary, St. Louis, Missouri, in 1930. Since 1936 he has received numerous honorary doctorates from colleges and universities, including Grinnell College, Glasgow University, Harvard, and New York University. His several books include, besides Moral Man and Immoral Society *(1932),* The Nature and Destiny of Man *(1941) and* Structure of Nations and Empires *(1963).*

■ *The Conflict Between Individual and Social Morality*

A REALISTIC analysis of the problems of human society reveals a constant and seemingly irreconcilable conflict between the needs of society and the imperatives of a sensitive conscience. This conflict, which could be most briefly defined as the conflict between ethics and politics, is made inevitable by the double focus of the moral life. One focus is in the inner life of the individual, and the other in the necessities of man's social life. From the perspective of society the highest moral ideal is justice. From the perspective of the individual the highest ideal is unselfishness. Society must strive for justice even if it is forced to use means, such as self-assertion, resistance, coercion and perhaps resentment, which cannot gain the moral sanction of the most sensitive moral spirit. The individual must strive to realise his life by losing and finding himself in something greater than himself.   (1)

These two moral perspectives are not mutually exclusive and the contradiction between them is not absolute. But neither are they easily harmonised. The highest moral insights and achievements of the individual conscience are both relevant and necessary to the life of society. The most perfect justice cannot be established if the moral imagination of the individual does not seek to comprehend the needs and interests of his fellows. Nor can any non-rational instrument of justice be used without great peril to society, if it is not brought under the control of moral goodwill. Any justice which is only justice soon degenerates into something less than justice. It must be saved by something which is more than justice. The realistic wisdom of the statesman is reduced to foolishness if it is not under the influence of the foolishness of the moral seer. The latter's idealism results in political futility and sometimes in moral confusion, if it is not brought into commerce and communication with the realities of man's collective life. This necessity and possibility of fusing moral and political insights does not, however, completely eliminate certain irreconcilable elements in the two types of morality, internal and external, individual and social. These elements make for constant confusion but they also add to the richness of human life.   (2)

From the internal perspective the most moral act is one which is actuated by disinterested motives. The external observer may find good in selfishness. He may value it as natural to the constitution of human nature and as necessary to society. But from the viewpoint of the author of an action, unselfishness must remain the criterion of the highest morality. For only the agent of an action knows to what degree self-seeking corrupts his socially approved actions. Society, on the other hand, makes justice rather than unselfishness its highest moral ideal. Its aim must be to seek equality of opportunity for all life. If this equality and justice cannot be achieved without the assertion of interest against interest, and without restraint upon the self-assertion of those who infringe upon the rights of their neighbors, then society is compelled to sanction self-assertion and restraint. It may even be forced to sanction social conflict and violence.   (3)

Historically the internal perspective has usually been cultivated by religion. For religion proceeds from profound introspection and naturally makes good motives the criteria of good conduct. It may define good motives either in terms of love or of duty, but the emphasis is upon the inner springs of action. Rationalised forms of religion usually choose duty rather than love as the expression of highest virtue (as in Kantian and Stoic morality), because it seems more virtuous to them to bring all impulse under the dominion of reason than to give any impulses, even altruistic ones, moral pre-eminence. The social viewpoint stands in sharpest contrast to religious morality when it views the behavior of collective rather than individual man, and when it deals with the necessities of political life. Political morality, in other words, is in the most uncompromising antithesis to religious morality.   (4)

Rational morality usually holds an intermediary position between the two. Sometimes it tries to do justice to the inner moral necessities of the human spirit rather than to the needs of society. If it emphasises the former it may develop an ethic of duty rather than the religious ethic of disinterestedness. But usually rationalism in morals tends to some kind of utilitarianism. It views human conduct from the social perspective and finds its ultimate standards in some general good and total social harmony. From that viewpoint it gives moral sanction to egoistic as well as to altruistic impulses, justifying them because they are natural to human nature and necessary to society. It asks only that egoism be reasonably expressed. Upon that subject Aristotle said the final as well as the first authoritative word. Reason, according to his theory, establishes control over all the impulses, egoistic and altruistic, and justifies them both if excesses are avoided and the golden mean is observed.   (5)

The social justification for self-assertion is given a typical expression by the Earl of Shaftesbury, who believed that the highest morality represented a harmony between "self-affections" and "natural affections." "If," said Shaftesbury, "a creature be self-neglectful and insensible to danger, or if he want such a degree of passion of any kind, as is useful to preserve,

sustain and defend himself, this must certainly be esteemed vicious in regard of the end and design of nature."[1]   (6)

It is interesting that a rational morality which gives egoism equality of
moral standing with altruism, provided both are reasonably expressed and
observe the "law of measure," should again and again find difficulty in
coming to terms with the natural moral preference which all unreflective
moral thought gives to altruism. Thus Bishop Butler begins his moral
theorising by making conscience the balancing force between "self-love"
and "benevolence." But gradually conscience gives such a preference to
benevolence that it becomes practically identified with it. Butler is therefore forced to draw in reason (originally identified with conscience) as a
force higher than conscience to establish harmony between self-love and
conscience.[2]   (7)

The utilitarian attempt to harmonise the inner and outer perspectives
of morality is inevitable and, within limits, possible. It avoids the excesses,
absurdities and perils into which both religious and political morality
may fall. By placing a larger measure of moral approval upon egoistic impulses than does religious morality and by disapproving coercion, conflict
and violence more unqualifiedly than politically oriented morality, it manages to resolve the conflict between them. But it is not as realistic as either.
It easily assumes a premature identity between self-interest and social
interest and establishes a spurious harmony between egoism and altruism.
With Bishop Butler most utilitarian rationalists in morals believe "that
though benevolence and self-love are different . . . yet they are so perfectly
coincident that the greatest satisfaction to ourselves depends upon having
benevolence in due degree, and that self-love is one chief security of our
right behavior to society."[3] Rationalism in morals therefore insists on less
inner restraint upon self-assertion than does religion, and believes less
social restraint to be necessary than political realism demands.   (8)

The dangers of religion's inner restraint upon self-assertion, and of its
effort to achieve complete disinterestedness, are that such a policy easily
becomes morbid, and that it may make for injustice by encouraging and
permitting undue self-assertion in others. Its value lies in its check upon
egoistic impulses, always more powerful than altruistic ones. If the moral
enterprise is begun with the complacent assumption that selfish and
social impulses are nicely balanced and equally justified, even a minimum
equilibrium between them becomes impossible.   (9)

The more the moral problem is shifted from the relations of individuals to the relations of groups and collectives, the more the preponderance

---

1 Third Earl of Shaftesbury, *An Inquiry Concerning Virtue or Merit*, Bk. II, Part I, sec. III.
2 *Cf.* Joseph Butler, *Fifteen Sermons on Human Nature*.
3 Butler, *op. cit.*, Sermon I.

of the egoistic impulses over the social ones is established. It is therefore revealed that no inner checks are powerful enough to bring them under complete control. Social control must consequently be attempted; and it cannot be established without social conflict. The moral perils attending such a political strategy are diametrically opposite to the perils of religious morality. The latter tend to perpetuate injustice by discouraging self-assertion against the inordinate claims of others. The former justify not only self-assertion but the use of non-rational power in reinforcing claims. They may therefore substitute new forms of injustice for old ones and enthrone a new tyranny on the throne of the old. A rational compromise between these two types of restraint easily leads to a premature complacency toward self-assertion. It is therefore better for society to suffer the uneasy harmony between the two types of restraint than to run the danger of inadequate checks upon egoistic impulses. Tolstoi and Lenin both present perils to the life of society; but they are probably no more dangerous than the compromises with human selfishness effected by modern disciples of Aristotle.   (10)

If we contemplate the conflict between religious and political morality it may be well to recall that the religious ideal in its purest form has nothing to do with the problem of social justice. It makes disinterestedness an absolute ideal without reference to social consequences. It justifies the ideal in terms of the integrity and beauty of the human spirit. While religion may involve itself in absurdities in the effort to achieve the ideal by purely internal discipline, and while it may run the peril of deleterious social consequences, it does do justice to inner needs of the human spirit. The veneration in which a Tolstoi, a St. Francis, a crucified Christ, and the saints of all the ages have been held, proves that, in the inner sanctuary of their souls, selfish men know that they ought not be selfish, and venerate what they feel they ought to be and cannot be.   (11)

Pure religious idealism does not concern itself with the social problem. It does not give itself to the illusion that material and mundane advantages can be gained by the refusal to assert your claims to them. It may believe, as Jesus did, that self-realisation is the inevitable consequence of self-abnegation. But this self-realisation is not attained on the level of physical life or mundane advantages. It is achieved in spiritual terms, such as the martyr's immortality and the Saviour's exaltation in the hearts of his disciples. Jesus did not counsel his disciples to forgive seventy times seven in order that they might convert their enemies or make them more favorably disposed. He counselled it as an effort to approximate complete moral perfection, the perfection of God. He did not ask his followers to go the second mile in the hope that those who had impressed them into service would relent and give them freedom. He did not say that the enemy ought to be loved so that he would cease to be an enemy. He did not dwell upon the social consequences of these moral actions, because he viewed them from an inner and a transcendent perspective.   (12)

Nothing is clearer than that a pure religious idealism must issue in a policy of non-resistance which makes no claims to be socially efficacious. It submits to any demands, however unjust, and yields to any claims, however inordinate, rather than assert self-interest against another. "You will meekly bear," declared Epictetus, "for you will say on every occasion 'It seemed so to him.'" This type of moral idealism leads either to asceticism, as in the case of Francis and other Catholic saints, or at least to the complete disavowal of any political responsibility, as in the case of Protestant sects practicing consistent non-resistance, as, for instance, the Anabaptists, Mennonites, Dunkers and Doukhobors. The Quakers assumed political responsibilities, but they were never consistent non-resisters. They disavowed violence but not resistance.   (13)

While social consequences are not considered in such a moral strategy, it would be shortsighted to deny that it may result in redemptive social consequences, at least within the area of individual and personal relationships. Forgiveness may not always prompt the wrongdoer to repentance; but yet it may. Loving the enemy may not soften the enemy's heart; but there are possibilities that it will. Refusal to assert your own interests against another may not shame him into unselfishness; but on occasion it has done so. Love and benevolence may not lead to complete mutuality; but it does have that tendency, particularly within the area of intimate relationships. Human life would, in fact, be intolerable if justice could be established in all relationships only by self-assertion and counter-assertion, or only by a shrewd calculation of claims and counter-claims. The fact is that love, disinterestedness and benevolence do have a strong social and utilitarian value, and the place they hold in the hierarchy of virtues is really established by that value, though religion may view them finally from an inner or transcendent perspective. "The social virtues," declares David Hume, "are never regarded without their beneficial tendencies nor viewed as barren and unfruitful. The happiness of mankind, the order of society, the harmony of families, the mutual support of friends, are always considered as a result of their gentle dominion over the breasts of men."[4] The utilitarian and social emphasis is a little too absolute in the words of Hume, but it is true within limits. Even the teachings of Jesus reveal a prudential strain in which the wholesome social consequences of generous attitudes are emphasised. "With what measure you mete, it shall be measured to you again." The paradox of the moral life consists in this: that the highest mutuality is achieved where mutual advantages are not consciously sought as the fruit of love. For love is purest where it desires no

---

4 David Hume, *An Enquiry Concerning the Principles of Morals*, Part 2, sec. II.

returns for itself; and it is most potent where it is purest. Complete mutuality, with its advantages to each party to the relationship, is therefore most perfectly realised where it is not intended, but love is poured out without seeking returns. That is how the madness of religious morality, with its trans-social ideal, becomes the wisdom which achieves wholesome social consequences. For the same reason a purely prudential morality must be satisfied with something less than the best.   (14)

Where human relations are intimate (and love is fully effective only in intimate and personal relations), the way of love may be the only way to justice. Where rights and interests are closely interwoven, it is impossible to engage in a shrewd and prudent calculation of comparative rights. Where lives are closely intertwined, happiness is destroyed if it is not shared. Justice by assertion and counter-assertion therefore becomes impossible. The friction involved in the process destroys mutual happiness. Justice by a careful calculation of competing rights is equally difficult, if not impossible. Interests and rights are too mutual to allow for their precise definition in individual terms. The very effort to do so is a proof of the destruction of the spirit of mutuality by which alone intimate relations may be adjusted. The spirit of mutuality can be maintained only by a passion which does not estimate the personal advantages which are derived from mutuality too carefully. Love must strive for something purer than justice if it would attain justice. Egoistic impulses are so much more powerful than altruistic ones that if the latter are not given stronger than ordinary support, the justice which even good men design is partial to those who design it.   (15)

This social validity of a moral ideal which transcends social considerations in its purest heights is progressively weakened as it is applied to more and more intricate, indirect and collective human relations. It is not only unthinkable that a group should be able to attain a sufficiently consistent unselfish attitude toward other groups to give it a very potent redemptive power, but it is improbable that any competing group would have the imagination to appreciate the moral calibre of the achievement. Furthermore a high type of unselfishness, even if it brings ultimate rewards, demands immediate sacrifices. An individual may sacrifice his own interests, either without hope of reward or in the hope of an ultimate compensation. But how is an individual, who is responsible for the interests of his group, to justify the sacrifice of interests other than his own? "It follows," declares Hugh Cecil, "that all that department of morality which requires an individual to sacrifice his interests to others, everything which falls under the heading of unselfishness, is inappropriate to the action of a state. No one has a right to be unselfish with other people's interests."[5]
                    (16)

5 Hugh Cecil, *Conservatism*, p. 182.

This judgment is not sufficiently qualified. A wise statesman is hardly justified in insisting on the interests of his group when they are obviously in unjust relation to the total interests of the community of mankind. Nor is he wrong in sacrificing immediate advantages for the sake of higher mutual advantages. His unwillingness to do this is precisely what makes nations so imprudent in holding to immediate advantages and losing ultimate values of mutuality. Nevertheless it is obvious that fewer risks can be taken with community interests than with individual interests. The inability to take risks naturally results in a benevolence in which selfish advantages must be quite apparent, and in which therefore the moral and redemptive quality is lost.   (17)

Every effort to transfer a pure morality of disinterestedness to group relations has resulted in failure. The Negroes of America have practiced it quite consistently since the Civil War. They did not rise against their masters during the war and remained remarkably loyal to them. Their social attitudes since that time, until a very recent date, have been compounded of genuine religious virtues of forgiveness and forbearance, and a certain social inertia which was derived not from religious virtue but from racial weakness. Yet they did not soften the hearts of their oppressors by their social policy.   (18)

During the early triumphs of fascism in Italy the socialist leaders suddenly adopted pacifist principles. One of the socialist papers counselled the workers to meet the terror of fascism with the following strategy: "(1) Create a void around fascism. (2) Do not provoke; suffer any provocation with serenity. (3) To win, be better than your adversary. (4) Do not use the weapons of your enemy. Do not follow in his footsteps. (5) Remember that the blood of guerrilla warfare falls upon those who shed it. (6) Remember that in a struggle between brothers those are victors who conquer themselves. (7) Be convinced that it is better to suffer wrong than to commit it. (8) Don't be impatient. Impatience is extremely egoistical; it is instinct; it is yielding to one's ego urge. (9) Do not forget that socialism wins the more when it suffers, because it was born in pain and lives on its hopes. (10) Listen to the mind and to the heart which advises you that the working people should be nearer to sacrifice than to vengeance."[6] A nobler decalogue of virtues could hardly have been prescribed. But the Italian socialists were annihilated by the fascists, their organisations destroyed, and the rights of the workers subordinated to a state which is governed by their enemies. The workers may live "on their hopes," but there is no prospect of realising their hopes under the present regime by practicing the pure moral principles which the socialistic journal advocated. Some of them are not incompatible with the use of coercion against their foes. But inasfar

---

6 Quoted by Max Nomad, *Rebels and Renegades*, p. 294.

as they exclude coercive means they are ineffectual before the brutal will-to-power of fascism.   (19)

The effort to apply the doctrines of Tolstoi to the political situation of Russia had a very similar effect. Tolstoi and his disciples felt that the Russian peasants would have the best opportunity for victory over their oppressors if they did not become stained with the guilt of the same violence which the czarist regime used against them. The peasants were to return good for evil, and win their battles by non-resistance. Unlike the policies of Gandhi, the political programme of Tolstoi remained altogether unrealistic. No effort was made to relate the religious ideal of love to the political necessity of coercion. Its total effect was therefore socially and politically deleterious. It helped to destroy a rising protest against political and economic oppression and to confirm the Russian in his pessimistic passivity. The excesses of the terrorists seemed to give point to the Tolstoian opposition to violence and resistance. But the terrorists and the pacifists finally ended in the same futility. And their common futility seemed to justify the pessimism which saw no escape from the traditional injustices of the Russian political and economic system. The real fact was that both sprang from a romantic middle-class or aristocratic idealism, too individualistic in each instance to achieve political effectiveness. The terrorists were diseased idealists, so morbidly oppressed by the guilt of violence resting upon their class that they imagined it possible to atone for that guilt by deliberately incurring guilt in championing the oppressed. Their ideas were ethical and, to a degree, religious, though they regarded themselves as irreligious. The political effectiveness of their violence was a secondary consideration. The Tolstoian pacifists attempted the solution of the social problem by diametrically opposite policies. But, in common with the terrorists, their attitudes sprang from the conscience of disquieted individuals. Neither of them understood the realities of political life because neither had an appreciation for the significant characteristics of collective behavior. The romantic terrorists failed to relate their isolated acts of terror to any consistent political plan. The pacifists, on the other hand, erroneously attributed political potency to pure non-resistance. (20)

Whenever religious idealism brings forth its purest fruits and places the strongest check upon selfish desire it results in policies which, from the political perspective, are quite impossible. There is, in other words, no possibility of harmonising the two strategists designed to bring the strongest inner and the most effective social restraint upon egoistic impulse. It would therefore seem better to accept a frank dualism in morals than to attempt a harmony between the two methods which threatens the effectiveness of both. Such a dualism would have two aspects. It would make a distinction between the moral judgments applied to the self and to others; and it would distinguish between what we expect of individuals and of groups. The first distinction is obvious and is explicitly or implicitly accepted whenever the moral problem is taken seriously. To disapprove your own selfishness more severely than the egoism of others is a necessary discipline if the natural complacency toward the self and severity in the judgment of others is to be corrected. Such a course is, furthermore, demanded by the logic of the whole moral situation. One can view the actions of others only from an external perspective; and from that perspective the social justification of self-assertion becomes inevitable. Only the actions of the self can be viewed from the internal perspective; and from that viewpoint all egoism must be morally disapproved. If such disapproval should occasionally destroy self-assertion to such a degree as to invite the aggression of others, the instances will be insignificant in comparison with the number of cases in which the moral disapproval of egoism merely tends to reduce the inordinate self-assertion of the average man. Even in those few cases in which egoism is reduced by religious discipline to such proportions that it invites injustice in an immediate situation, it will have social usefulness in glorifying the moral principle and setting an example for future generations.   (21)

The distinction between individual and group morality is a sharper and more perplexing one. The moral obtuseness of human collectives makes a morality of pure disinterestedness impossible. There is not enough imagination in any social group to render it amenable to the influence of pure love. Nor is there a possibility of persuading any social group to make a venture in pure love, except, as in the case of the Russian peasants, the recently liberated Negroes and other similar groups, a morally dubious social inertia should be compounded with the ideal. The selfishness of human communities must be regarded as an inevitability. Where it is inordinate it can be checked only by competing assertions of interest; and these can be effective only if coercive methods are added to moral and rational persuasion. Moral factors may qualify, but they will not eliminate, the resulting social contest and conflict. Moral goodwill may seek to relate the peculiar interests of the group to the ideal of a total and final harmony of all life. It may thereby qualify the self-assertion of the privileged, and support the interests of the disinherited, but it will never be so impartial as to persuade any group to subject its interests completely to an inclusive social ideal. The spirit of love may preserve a certain degree of appreciation for the common weaknesses and common aspirations which bind men together above the areas of social conflict. But again it cannot prevent the conflict. It may avail itself of instruments of restraint and coercion, through which a measure of trust in the moral capacities of an opponent may be expressed and the expansion rather than contraction of those capacities is encouraged. But it cannot hide the moral distrust expressed by the very use of the instruments of coercion. To some degree the conflict between the purest individual morality and an adequate political policy must therefore remain. (22)

The needs of an adequate political strategy do not obviate the necessity of cultivating the strictest individual moral discipline and the most uncompromising idealism. Individuals, even when involved in their communities, will always have the opportunity of loyalty to the highest canons of personal morality. Sometimes, when their group is obviously bent upon evil, they may have to express their individual ideals by disassociating themselves from their group. Such a policy may easily lead to political irresponsibility, as in the case of the more extreme sects of non-resisters. But it may also be socially useful. Religiously inspired pacifists who protest against the violence of their state in the name of a sensitive individual conscience may never lame the will-to-power of a state as much as a class-conscious labor group. But if their numbers grew to large proportions, they might affect the policy of the government. It is possible, too, that their example may encourage similar non-conformity among individuals in the enemy nation and thus mitigate the impact of the conflict without weakening the comparative strength of their own community. (23)

The ideals of a high individual morality are just as necessary when loyalty to the group is maintained and its general course in relation to other groups is approved. There are possibilities for individual unselfishness, even when the group is asserting its interests and rights against other communities. The interests of the individual are related to those of the group, and he may therefore seek advantages for himself when he seeks them for his group. But this indirect egoism is comparatively insignificant beside the possibilities of expressing or disciplining his egotism in relation to his group. If he is a leader in the group, it is necessary to restrain his ambitions. A leadership, free of self-seeking, improves the morale of the whole group. The leaders of disinherited groups, even when they are avowed economic determinists and scorn the language of personal idealism, are frequently actuated by high moral ideals. If they sought their own personal advantage they could gain it more easily by using their abilities to rise from their group to a more privileged one. The temptation to do this among the abler members of disinherited groups is precisely what has retarded the progress of their class or race. (24)

The progress of the Negro race, for instance, is retarded by the inclination of many able and educated Negroes to strive for identification and assimilation with the more privileged white race and to minimise their relation to a subject race as much as possible. The American Labor Movement has failed to develop its full power for the same reason. Under the influence of American individualism, able labor men have been more ambitious to rise into the class of owners and their agents than to solidify the laboring class in its struggle for freedom. There is, furthermore, always the possibility that an intelligent member of a social group will begin his career in unselfish devotion to the interests of his community, only to be tempted by the personal prizes to be gained, either within the group or by shifting his loyalty to a more privileged group. The interests of individuals are, in other words, never exactly identical with those of their communities. The possibility and necessity of individual moral discipline is therefore never absent, no matter what importance the social struggle between various human communities achieves. Nor can any community achieve unity and harmony within its life, if the sentiments of goodwill and attitudes of mutuality are not cultivated. No political realism which emphasises the inevitability and necessity of a social struggle, can absolve individuals of the obligation to check their own egoism, to comprehend the interests of others and thus to enlarge the areas of co-operation.   (25)

Whether the co-operative and moral aspects of human life, or the necessities of the social struggle, gain the largest significance, depends upon time and circumstance. There are periods of social stability, when the general equilibrium of social forces is taken for granted, and men give themselves to the task of making life more beautiful and tender within the limits of the established social system. The Middle Ages were such a period. While they took injustices for granted, such as would affront the conscience of our day, it cannot be denied that they elaborated amenities, urbanities and delicate refinements of life and art which must make our age seem, in comparison, like the recrudescence of barbarism.   (26)

Our age is, for good or ill, immersed in the social problem. A technological civilisation makes stability impossible. It changes the circumstances of life too rapidly to incline any one to a reverent acceptance of an ancestral order. Its rapid developments and its almost daily changes in the physical circumstances of life destroy the physical symbols of stability and therefore make for restlessness, even if these movements were not in a direction which imperil the whole human enterprise. But the tendencies of an industrial era are in a definite direction. They tend to aggravate the injustices from which men have perennially suffered; and they tend to unite the whole of humanity in a system of economic interdependence. They make us more conscious of the relations of human communities to each other, than of the relations of individuals within their communities. They obsess us therefore with the brutal aspects of man's collective behavior. They, furthermore, cumulate the evil consequences of these brutalities so rapidly that we feel under a tremendous urgency to solve our social problem before it is too late. As a generation we are therefore bound to feel harassed as well as disillusioned.   (27)

In such a situation all the highest ideals and tenderest emotions which men have felt all through the ages, when they became fully conscious of their heritage and possible destiny as human beings, will seem from our

perspective to be something of a luxury. They will be under a moral disadvantage, because they appear as a luxury which only those are able to
indulge who are comfortable enough to be comparatively oblivious to the
desperate character of our contemporary social situation. We live in an age
in which personal moral idealism is easily accused of hypocrisy and frequently deserves it. It is an age in which honesty is possible only when it
skirts the edges of cynicism. All this is rather tragic. For what the individual conscience feels when it lifts itself above the world of nature and the
system of collective relationships in which the human spirit remains under
the power of nature, is not a luxury but a necessity of the soul. Yet there
is beauty in our tragedy. We are, at least, rid of some of our illusions. We
can no longer buy the highest satisfactions of the individual life at the
expense of social injustice. We cannot build our individual ladders to
heaven and leave the total human enterprise unredeemed of its excesses
and corruptions.   (28)

In the task of that redemption the most effective agents will be men
who have substituted some new illusions for the abandoned ones. The
most important of these illusions is that the collective life of mankind
can achieve perfect justice. It is a very valuable illusion for the moment;
for justice cannot be approximated if the hope of its perfect realization
does not generate a sublime madness in the soul. Nothing but such madness will do battle with malignant power and "spiritual wickedness in
high places." The illusion is dangerous because it encourages terrible
fanaticisms. It must therefore be brought under the control of reason. One
can only hope that reason will not destroy it before its work is done.   (29)

Paul Tillich

(1886–1965)

*TILLICH was born in Prussia, educated in the major German universi-
ties, and naturalized as an American citizen in 1940. He held numerous
professorships, the last being the John Nuveen Professorship of Theology
at the University of Chicago, and was honored with doctorates by universities throughout the world. He wrote profusely and with compelling rele-*

vance, his major work being Systematic Theology *(3 vols., 1951–1963).*
He characterized the ends for which he strove as follows: "I have tried to
make the Christian message relevant for the people of our time."

◼ *Man and History*

A HISTORY AND HISTORICAL CONSCIOUSNESS.—A semantic consideration may
help us to discover a particular quality of history. The well-known fact
that the Greek word *historia* means primarily inquiry, information, report,
and only secondarily the events inquired about and reported is a case in
point. It shows that for those who originally used the word "history" the
subjective side preceded the objective side. Historical consciousness, according to this view, "precedes" historical happenings. Of course, historical
consciousness does not precede in temporal succession the happenings of
which it is conscious. But it transforms mere happenings into historical
events, and in this sense it "precedes" them. Strictly speaking, one should
say that the same situation produces both the historical occurrences and
the awareness of them as historical events.   (1)

Historical consciousness expresses itself in a tradition, i.e., in a set of
memories which are delivered from one generation to the other. Tradition
is not a casual collection of remembered events but the recollection of those
events which have gained significance for the bearers and receivers of the
tradition. The significance which an occurrence has for a tradition-conscious
group determines whether it will be considered as a historical event.   (2)

It is natural that the influence of the historical consciousness on the
historical account should mold the tradition in accordance with the active
needs for the historical group in which the tradition is alive. Consequently
the ideal of pure, unbiased historical research appears at a rather late stage
in the development of the writing of history. It is preceded by combinations
of myth and history, by legends and sagas, by epic poetry. In all these
cases, occurrences are elevated to historical significance, but the way in
which it is done transforms the occurrences into symbols of the life of a
historical group. Tradition unites historical reports with symbolic interpretations. It does not report "naked facts," which itself is a questionable concept; but it does bring to mind significant events through a symbolic transformation of the facts. This does not mean that the factual side is mere
invention. Even the epic form in which tradition is expressed has historical
roots, however hidden they may be, and saga and legend reveal their

historical origins rather obviously. But in all these forms of tradition it is virtually impossible to separate the historical occurrence from its symbolic interpretation. In every living tradition the historical is seen in the light of the symbolic, and historical research can disentangle this amalgamation only in terms of higher or lower probability. For the way in which historical events are experienced is determined by their valuation in terms of significance, which implies that in their original receptions the records are partly dependent on their symbolic element. The biblical records are classical examples of this situation. (3)

But one must ask whether the scholarly approach to historical facts is not also dependent on concealed symbols of interpretation. It seems this cannot be denied. There are several points in every historical statement of an intentionally detached character which show the influence of a symbolic vision. The choice of occurrences which are to be established as facts is the most important. Since in every moment of time at every point of space an inexhaustible number of occurrences takes place, the choice of the object of historical inquiry is dependent on the valuation of its importance for the establishment of the life of a historical group. In this respect history is dependent on historical consciousness. But this is not the only point in which this is the case. Every piece of historiography evaluates the weight of concurring influences on a person or a group and on their actions. This is one cause of the endless differences in historical presentations of the same factual material. Another cause, which is less obvious but even more decisive, is the context of the active life of the group in which the historian works, for he participates in the life of his group, sharing its memories and traditions. Out of this factor questions arise to which the presentation of the facts gives the answer. Nobody writes history on a "place above all places." Such a claim would be no less utopian than the claim that perfect social conditions are just approaching. All history-writing is dependent both on actual occurrences and on their reception by a concrete historical consciousness. There is no history without factual occurrences, and there is no history without the reception and interpretation of factual occurrences by historical consciousness. (4)

These considerations do not conflict with the demands of the methods of historical research; the scientific criteria used by historical scholarship are as definite, obligatory and objective as those in any other realm of inquiry. But precisely in and through the act of applying them the influence of the historical consciousness becomes effective—though unintentionally in the case of honest historical work. (5)

Another implication of the subject-object character of history must be mentioned. Through the interpretative element of all history, the answer to the question of the meaning of history has an indirect, mediated impact on a historical presentation. One cannot escape the destiny of belonging to a tradition in which the answer to the question of the meaning of life in all its dimensions, including the historical, is given in symbols which influence every encounter with reality. There can be no doubt that even the most objective scholar, if he is existentially determined by the Christian tradition, interprets historical events in the light of this tradition, however unconscious and indirect its influence may be.   (6)

b) The historical dimension in the light of human history.—Human history, as the semantic study of the implications of the term *historia* has shown, is always a union of objective and subjective elements. An "event" is a syndrome (i.e., a running-together) of facts and interpretation. If we now turn from the semantic of the material discussion, we find that same double structure in all occurrences which deserve the name "historical event."   (7)

The horizontal direction under the dimension of the spirit has the character of intention and purpose. In a historical event, human purposes are the decisive, though not the exclusive, factor. Given institutions and natural conditions are other factors, but only the presence of actions with a purpose makes an event historical. Particular purposes may or may not be actualized, or they may lead to something not intended (according to the principle of the "heterogony of purposes"); but the decisive thing is that they are a determining factor in historical events. Processes in which no purpose is intended are not historical.   (8)

Man, in so far as he sets and pursues purposes, is free. He transcends the given situation, leaving the real for the sake of the possible. He is not bound to the situation in which he finds himself, and it is just this self-transcendence that is the first and basic quality of freedom. Therefore, no historical situation determines any other historical situation completely. The transition from one situation to another is in part determined by man's centered reaction, by his freedom. According to the polarity of freedom and destiny, such self-transcendence is not absolute; it comes out of the totality of elements of past and present, but within these limits it is able to produce something qualitatively new.   (9)

Therefore, the third characteristic of human history is the production of the new. In spite of all abstract similarities of past and future events, every concrete event is unique and in its totality incomparable. This assertion, however, needs qualification. It is not only human history in which the new is produced. The dynamics of nature create the new by producing individuality in the smallest parts as well as in the largest composites of nature and also by producing new species in the evolutionary process and new constellations of matter in the extensions and contractions of the universe. But there is a qualitative difference between these forms of the new and the new in history proper. The latter is essentially related to meanings or values. Both terms can be adequate if correctly defined. Most philosophies of history in the last one hundred years have spoken of history as the realm in which values are actualized. The difficulty of this terminology is the necessity of introducing a criterion which distinguishes arbitrary values from objective values. Arbitrary values, unlike objective values, are not subject to such norms as truth, expressiveness, justice, humanity, holiness. The bearers of objective valuations are personalities and communities. If we call such valuations "absolute" (where by "absolute" we mean that their validity is independent of the valuating subject), it is possible to describe the creation of the new in human history as the creation of new actualizations of value *in* centered personalities. However, if one is hesitant about the term "value," an alternative is "meaning." Life in meanings is life determined by the functions of the spirit and the norms and principles controlling them. The word "meaning," of course, is not unambiguous. But the merely logical use of the term ("a word has a meaning") is transcended if one speaks of "life in meanings." If the term "meaning" is used in this sense, one should describe the production of the new in history as the production of new and unique embodiments of meaning. My preference for this latter terminology is based partly on the rejection of the anti-ontological value theory and partly on the importance of terms like "the meaning of life" for the philosophy of religion. A phrase like "the value of life" has neither the depth nor the breadth of "the meaning of life."   (10)

The fourth characteristic of history proper is the significant uniqueness of a historical event. The unique, novel quality of all processes of life is shared by the historical processes. But the unique event has significance only in history. To signify something means to point beyond one's self to that which is signified—to represent something. A historical personality is historical because it represents larger events, which themselves represent the human situation, which itself represents the meaning of being as such. Personalities, communities, events, and situations are significant when more is embodied in them than a transitory occurrence within the universal process of becoming. These occurrences, of which innumerable ones come and go in every second of time, are not historical in the proper sense, but a combination of them may assume historical significance if it represents a human potentiality in a unique, incomparable way. History describes the sequence of such potentialities but with a decisive qualification: it describes them as they appear under the conditions of existence and within the ambiguities of life. Without the revelation of human potentialities (generally speaking, potentialities of life), historical accounts would not report significant events. Without the unique embodiment of these potentialities, they would not appear in history; they would remain pure essences. Yet they are both significant, because they are above history, and unique, because they are within history. There is, however, another reason for the significance of unique historical events: the significance of the historical process as a whole. Whether there is such a thing as "world history" or not, the historical processes within historical mankind have an inner aim. They go ahead in a definite direction, they run toward a fulfilment, whether they reach it or not. A historical event is significant in so far as it represents a moment within the historical movement toward the end. Thus, historical events are significant for three reasons: they represent essential human potentialities, they show these potentialities actualized in a unique way, and they represent moments in the development toward the aim of history —in which way the aim itself is symbolized.   (11)

The four characteristics of human history (to be connected with purpose, to be influenced by freedom, to create the new in terms of meaning, to be significant in a universal, particular, and teleological sense lead to the distinction between human history and the historical dimension in general. The distinctions are implicit in the four characteristics of human history and can also be shown from the other side, i.e., from the dimension of the historical in the realms of life other than human history. If we take as examples the life of higher animals, the evolution of species, and the development of the astronomical universe, we observe first of all that in none of these examples are purpose and freedom effective. Purposes, e.g., in the higher animals, do not transcend the satisfaction of their immediate needs; the animals do not transcend their natural bondage. Nor is there any particular intention operating in the evolution of the species or in the movements of the universe. The question becomes more complicated when we ask whether there is absolute meaning and significant uniqueness in these realms of life, e.g., whether the genesis of a new species in the animal realm has meaning comparable to the rise of a new empire or a new artistic style in human history. Obviously, the new species is unique, but the question is whether it is significantly unique in the sense of an embodiment of absolute meaning. Again we must answer negatively: there is no absolute meaning and there is no significant uniqueness where the dimension of the spirit is not actual. The uniqueness of a species or of a particular exemplar within a species is real but not ultimately significant, whereas the act in which a person establishes himself as a person, a cultural creation with its inexhaustible meaning, and a religious experience in which ultimate meaning breaks through preliminary meanings are infinitely significant. These assertions are based on the fact that life under the dimension of the spirit is able to experience ultimacy and to produce embodiments and symbols of the ultimate. If there were absolute meaning in a tree or a new animal species or a new galaxy of stars, this meaning could be understood by men, for meaning is experienced by man. This factor in human existence has led to the doctrine of the infinite value of every human soul. Although such a doctrine is not directly biblical, it is implied in the promises and threats pronounced by all biblical writers: "heaven" and "hell" are symbols of ultimate meaning and unconditional significance. But no such threat or promise is made about other than human life. (12)

Nevertheless, there is no realm of life in which the historical dimension is not present and actualized in an anticipatory way. Even in the inorganic, and certainly in the organic, realm, there is *telos* (inner aim) which is quasi-historical, even though it is not a part of history proper. This is also true of the genesis of species and the development of the universe; they are analogues to history, but they are not history proper. The analogy appears in the spontaneity in nature, in the new produced by the progress in biological evolution, in the uniqueness of cosmic constellations. But it remains analogy. Freedom and absolute meaning are lacking. The historical dimension in life universal is analogous to life in history proper, but it is not history itself. In life universal the dimension of spirit is actualized only in anticipation. There are analogies between life under the biological dimension and life under the dimension of the spirit, but the biological is not spirit. Therefore, history remains an anticipated, but unactualized, dimension in all realms except that of human history. (13)

c) Prehistory and posthistory.—The development from anticipated to actual history can be described as the stage of prehistorical man. He is already man in some respects, but he is not yet historical man. For if that being which eventually will produce history is called "man," he must have the freedom to set purposes, he must have language and universals, however limited these may be, and he must also have artistic and cognitive possibilities and a sense of the holy. If he had all this he would already be historical in a way in which not other being in nature is historical, but the historical potentiality in him would only be in transition from possibility to reality. It would be, metaphorically speaking, the state of "awakening" humanity. There is no way of verifying such a state; yet it can be postulated as the basis for the later development of man, and it can be used as a critical weapon against unrealistic ideas about the early state of mankind which attribute to prehistorical man either too much or too little. Too much is attributed to him if he is endowed with all kinds of perfections which anticipate either later developments or even a state of fulfilment. Examples of this are theological interpretations of the paradise myth which attribute to Adam the perfection of the Christ and the secular interpretations of the original state of mankind which attribute to the "noble savage" the perfections of the humanist ideal of man. (14)

On the other hand, too little is attributed to prehistorical man if he is considered as a beast without at least the possibility of universals and, consequently, of language. If this were true, there would be no prehistorical man, and historical man would be a "creation out of nothing." But all empirical evidence stands against such an assumption. Prehistorical man is that organic being which is predisposed to actualize the dimensions of

spirit and history and which in his development drives toward their actualization. There is no identifiable moment when animal self-awareness
becomes human spirit and when human spirit enters the historical dimension. The transition from one dimension to the other is hidden, although the
result of this transition is obvious when it appears. We do not know when
the first spark of historical consciousness dawned in the human race, but we
do recognize expressions of this consciousness. We can distinguish historical
from prehistorical man though we do not know the moment of transition
from one to the other because of the mixture of slow transformation and
sudden leap in all evolutionary processes. If evolution proceeded only by
leaps, one could identify the result of each leap. If evolution proceeded only
by a slow transformation, no radical change could be noticed at all. But
evolutionary processes combine both the leap and the slow change, and
therefore, although one can distinguish the results, one cannot fix the moments in which they appear. The darkness which veils prehistorical mankind is not a matter of preliminary scholarly failure but rather of the indefi-
niteness of all evolutionary processes with respect to the appearance of the
new. Historical man is new, but he is prepared for and anticipated by
prehistorical man, and the point of transition from the one to the other is
essentially indefinite.   (15)

A similar consideration must be brought to bear upon the idea of posthistory. The question is whether one must anticipate a stage of the evolutionary process in which historical mankind, though not as human race,
comes to an end. The significance of this question lies in its relation to
utopian ideas with respect to the future of mankind. The last stage of
historical man has been identified with the final stage of fulfilment—with
the Kingdom of God actualized on earth. But the "last" in the temporal
sense is not the "final" in the eschatological sense. It is not by chance that
the New Testament and Jesus resisted the attempt to put the symbols of the
end into a chronological frame. Not even Jesus knows when the end will
come; it is independent of the historical-posthistorical development of mankind, although the mode of "future" is used in its symbolic description. This
leaves the future of historical mankind open for possibilities derived from
present experience. For example, it is not impossible that the self-destructive power of mankind will prevail and bring historical mankind to an end.
It is also possible that mankind will lose not its potential freedom of transcending the given—this would make of him something no longer man—but
the dissatisfaction with the given and consequently the drive toward the
new. The character of the human race in this state would be similar to
what Nietzsche has described as the "last man" who "knows everything"
and is not interested in anything; it would be the state of "blessed animals."
The negative utopias of our century, such as Brave New World, anticipate
—rightly or wrongly—such a stage of evolution. A third possibility is a con-

tinuation of the dynamic drive of the human race toward unforeseeable actualizations of man's potentialities, up to the gradual or sudden disappearance of the biological and physical conditions for the continuation of historical mankind. These and perhaps other chances of posthistorical mankind must be envisaged and liberated from any entanglement with the symbols of the "end of history" in their eschatological sense.   (16)

d) *The bearers of history: communities, personalities, mankind.*—Man actualizes himself as a person in the encounter with other persons within a community. The process of self-integration under the dimension of the spirit actualizes both the personality and the community. . . .   (17)

History-bearing groups are characterized by their ability to act in a centered way. They must have a centered power which is able to keep the individuals who belong to it united and which is able to preserve its power in the encounter with similar power groups. In order to fulfil the first condition a history-bearing group must have a central, law-giving, administering, and enforcing authority. In order to fulfil the second condition a history-bearing group must have tools to keep itself in power in the encounter with other powers. Both conditions are fulfilled in what is called, in modern terminology, a "state," and in this sense history is the history of states. But this statement needs several qualifications. First, one must point to the fact that the term "state" is much younger than the statelike organizations of large families, clans, tribes, cities, and nations, in which the two conditions of being bearers of history were previously fulfilled. Second, one must emphasize that historical influence can be exercised in many ways by economical, cultural, or religious groups and movements that work within a state or that cut across many states. Still, their historical effect is conditioned by the existence of the organized internal and external power of history-bearing groups. The fact that in many countries even the periods of artistic style are named for emperors or sequences of emperors indicates the basic character of political organization for all historical existence. (18)

The history-bearing group was described as a centered group with internal and external power. This, however, does not mean that the political power in both directions is a mechanism independent of the life of the group. In every power structure *eros* relations underly the organizational form. Power through administering and enforcing the law, or power through imposing law by conquest, presupposes a central power group whose authority is acknowledged at least silently; otherwise it would not have the support necessary for enforcement and conquest. A withdrawal of such silent acknowledgment by the supporters of a power structure undercuts it. The support is based on an experience of belonging, a form of communal *eros* which does not exclude struggles for power within the supporting group but which unites it against other groups. This is obvious in all statelike organizations from the family up to the nation. Blood relations, language, traditions, and memories create many forms of *eros* which make the power structure possible. Preservation by enforcement and increase by conquest follow, but do not produce, the historical power of a group. The element of compulsion in every historical power structure is not its foundation but an unavoidable condition of its existence. It is at the same time the cause of its destruction if the *eros* relations disappear or are completely replaced by force.   (19)

One way among others in which the *eros* relations that underly a power structure express themselves is in the legal principles that determine the laws and their administration by the ruling center. The legal system of a history-bearing group is derived neither from an abstract concept of justice nor from the will to power of the ruling center. Both factors contribute to the concrete structure of justice. They also can destroy it if one of them prevails, for neither of them is the basis of a statelike structure. The basis of every legal system is the *eros* relations of the group in which they appear.   (20)

It is, however, not only the power of the group in terms of enforceable internal unity and external security but also the aim toward which it strives which makes it a history-bearing group. History runs in a horizontal direction, and the groups which give it this direction are determined by an aim toward which they strive and a destiny they try to fulfill. One could call this the "vocational consciousness" of a history-bearing group. It differs from group to group not only in character but also in the degree of consciousness and of motivating power. But vocational feeling has been present since the earliest times of historical mankind. Its most conspicuous expression is perhaps the call to Abraham in which the vocational consciousness of Israel finds its symbolic expression; and we find analogous forms in China, in Egypt, and in Babylon. The vocational consciousness of Greece was expressed in the distinction between Greeks and barbarians, that of Rome was based on the superiority of the Roman law, that of medieval Germany on the symbol of the Holy Roman Empire of German nationality, that of Italy on the "rebirth" of civilization in the Renaissance, that of Spain on the idea of the Catholic unity of the world, that of France on its leadership in intellectual culture, that of England on the task of subjecting all peoples to a Christian humanism, that of Russia on the salvation of the West through the traditions of the Greek church or through the Marxist prophecy, that of the United States on the belief in a new beginning in which the curses of the Old World are overcome and the democratic missionary task fulfilled. Where the vocational consciousness has vanished or was never fully developed, as in nineteenth-century Germany and Italy and smaller states with artificial boundaries, the element of power becomes predominant either in an aggressive or in a merely defensive sense. But even in these cases, as the recent examples of Germany and Italy show, the need for a vocational self-understanding is so strong that the absurdities of Nazi-racism were accepted because they filled a vacuum.   (21)

The fact of a vocational consciousness shows that the content of history is the life of the history-bearing group in all dimensions. No dimension of life is excluded from the living memory of the group, but there are differences in choice. The political realm is always predominant because it is constitutive of historical existence. Within this frame, social, economic, cultural, and religious developments have an equal right to consideration. In some periods, more—and in other periods, less—emphasis can be given any one of them. Certainly, the history of man's cultural functions is not confined to any concrete history-bearing group, not even the largest. But if the cultural or religious historian crosses the political boundaries he is aware that this is an abstraction from actual life, and he does not forget that the *political* unities, whether large or small, remain the conditions of all cultural life. The primacy of political history cannot be disregarded, either for the sake of an independent intellectual history demanded by idealistic historians or for the sake of a determining economic history demanded by materialistic historians. History itself has refuted the demands of the latter whenever they seemed to be near fulfilment, as in Zionist Israel or Communist Russia. It is significant that the symbol in which the Bible expresses the meaning of history is political: "Kingdom of God," and not "Life of the Spirit" or "economic abundance." The element of centeredness which characterizes the political realm makes it an adequate symbol for the ultimate aim of history.   (22)

This leads to the question of whether one could call mankind, rather than particular human groups, the bearer of history. For the limited character of groups necessarily seems to disrupt the unity which is intended in the symbol "Kingdom of God." But the form of this question prejudices the answer; the aim of history does not lie in history. There is no united mankind within history. It certainly did not exist in the past; nor can it exist in the future because a politically united mankind, though imaginable, would be a diagonal between convergent and divergent vectors. Its political unity would be the framework for a disunity that is the consequence of human freedom with its dynamic that surpasses everything given. The situation would be different only if the unity of mankind were the end of history and the frame for the posthistorical stage in which man's aroused freedom would have come to rest. This would be the state of "animal blessedness." As long as there is history, a "united mankind" is the frame for a "disunited mankind." Only in posthistory could the disunity disappear, but such a stage would not be the Kingdom of God, for the Kingdom of God is not "animal blessedness."   (23)

Historical groups are communities of individuals. They are not entities alongside or above the individuals of whom they are constituted; they are products of the social function of these individuals. The social function produces a structure which gains a partial independence from the individuals (as is the case in all other functions), but this independence does not produce a new reality, with a center of willing and acting. It is not "the community" that wills and acts; it is individuals in their social quality and through their representatives who make communal actions possible by making centeredness possible. The "deception of personifying the group" should be revealed and denounced, especially to point out tyrannical abuses of this deception. So we must ask again: In what sense is the individual a bearer of history? In spite of the criticism of any attempt to personalize the group, the answer must be that the individual is a bearer of history only in relation to a history-bearing group. His individual life process is not history, and therefore biography is not history. But it can become significant either as the story of somebody who actively and symbolically represents a history-bearing group (Caesar, Lincoln) or as an individual who represents the average situation within a group (*the* peasant, *the* bourgeois). The relation to the group of historically significant individuals is especially obvious in persons who have left the community to go into seclusion in the "desert" or into "exile." In so far as they are historically significant, they remain related to the group from which they come and to which they might return, or they establish a relation with the new group which they enter and in which they may become historically significant. But as mere individuals they have no historical significance. History is the history of groups.   (24)

This, however, does not answer the question: Who determines the historical processes, "great" individuals or mass movements? The question in this form is unanswerable because no empirical evidence can be found to support the one or the other point of view. The question is also misleading. The adjective "great," in history, is attributed to persons who are great as leaders in the movements of history-bearing groups. The term "great" in this sense implies the relation to masses. Individuals who have had potential historical greatness but have never reached actualization are not called great, because the potentiality to greatness can be tested only by its actualization. Concretely speaking, one would have to say that no one can achieve historical greatness who is not received by history-bearing groups. On the other hand, the movements of the masses would never occur without the productive power of individuals in whom the potentialities and actual trends of the many become conscious and formulated. The question of whether individuals or "masses" determine history must be replaced by an exact description of their interplay.   (25)

Martin Buber

(1878–1965)

BUBER, Israeli theologian, was a professor of the science of religion at the University of Frankfurt until 1933 and afterwards professor of social philosophy at the Hebrew University. His books in translation include Moses *(1946),* Eclipse of God *(1952),* Hasidism and Modern Man *(1958), and* The Origin and Meaning of Hasidism *(1960).*

■ *Postscript*

I

WHEN I DRAFTED the first sketch of this article (more than forty years ago), I was impelled by an inward necessity. A vision which had come to me again and again since my youth, and which had been clouded over again and again, had now reached steady clarity. This clarity was so manifestly suprapersonal in its nature that I at once knew I had to bear witness to it. Some time after I had received the right word as well, and could write the book again in its final form,[1] it became apparent that while there was need of some additions these had to be in their own place and in independent form. In this way there arose some shorter writings,[2] which clarified the vision by means of examples, or explained it in face of objections, or criticised views to which it indeed owed important points but upon which my most essential concern had not dawned in its central significance—namely, the close

---

1 It appeared in German in 1923, in English in 1937.
2 *Zwiesprache,* 1932; *Die Frage an den Einzelnen,* 1936; *Rede über das Erzieherische,* 1926; *Das Problem des Menschen,* first edition in Hebrew, 1942, German in the volume *Dialogisches Leben,* 1947, individual edition, 1948. English editions appeared in one volume, *Between Man and Man,* 1947.

connexion of the relation to God with the relation to one's fellow-man. Later there were added some references to anthropological foundations[3] and to sociological consequences.[4] Nevertheless it has turned out that by no means everything has been sufficiently clarified. Again and again readers have turned to me to ask about the meaning of this and that. For a long time I answered each individually, but I gradually realised that I was not able to do justice to the demand laid upon me; besides, I must not limit the dialogical relationship to those readers who make up their minds to speak: perhaps there are many among the silent who deserve special consideration. So I have had to set about giving a public answer, first of all to some essential questions which are bound together by their meaning.   (1)

II

The first question may be formulated with some precision as follows: If— as the book says—we can stand in the *I-Thou* relationship not merely with other men, but also with beings and things which come to meet us in nature, what is it that makes the real difference between the two relationships? Or, more closely, if the *I-Thou* relationship requires a mutual action which in fact embraces both the *I* and the *Thou*, how may the relation to something in nature be understood as such a relationship? More precisely still, if we are to assume that we are granted a kind of mutuality by beings and things in nature as well, which we meet as our *Thou*, what is then the character of this reciprocity and what justification have we for using this fundamental concept in order to describe it?   (2)

Clearly there is no unified answer to this question. Instead of grasping nature as a whole, in our customary fashion, we must here consider its different fields separately.   (3)

Man once "tamed" animals, and he is still capable of this singular achievement. He draws animals into his atmosphere and moves them to accept him, the stranger, in an elemental way, and to respond to him. He wins from them an often astonishing active response to his approach, to his addressing them, and moreover a response which in general is stronger and directer in proportion as his attitude is a genuine saying of *Thou*. Animals, like children, are not seldom able to see through any hypocritical tenderness. But even outside the sphere of taming a similar contact between men and animals sometimes takes place—with men who have in the depths of their being a potential partnership with animals, not predomi-

---

[3] *Urdistanz und Beziehung*, 1951, "Distance and Relation," *Psychiatry*, Vol. XX, No. 2 (May 1957), pp. 97–104. To be included in Martin Buber, *We: Studies in Philosophical Anthropology*.

[4] "Elemente des Zwischenmenschlichen," in the volume *Die Schriften über das dialogische Prinzip*, 1954, "Elements of the Interhuman," *Psychiatry*, Vol. XX, No. 2 (May 1957), pp. 105–113. To be included in Martin Buber, *We: Studies in Philosophical Anthropology*.

nantly persons of "animal" nature, but rather those whose very nature is
spiritual. (4)

An animal is not, like man, twofold: the twofold nature of the primary
words *I–Thou* and *I–It* is strange to it, even though it can turn to another
being as well as consider objects. Nevertheless we should like to say that
there is here a latent twofoldness. That is why we may call this sphere, in
respect of our saying of *Thou* out towards the creature, the threshold of
mutuality. (5)

It is quite different with those spheres of nature where the spontaneity
we share with the animals is lacking. It is part of our concept of a plant
that it cannot react to our action towards it: it cannot "respond." Yet this
does not mean that here we are given simply no reciprocity at all. The deed
or attitude of an individual being is certainly not to be found here, but there
is a reciprocity of the being itself, a reciprocity which is nothing but being
in its course (*seiend*). That living wholeness and unity of the tree, which
denies itself to the sharpest glance of the mere investigator and discloses
itself to the glance of one who says *Thou*, is there when he, the sayer of
Thou, is there: it is he who vouchsafes to the tree that it manifest this unity
and wholeness; and now the tree which is in being manifests them. Our
habits of thought make it difficult for us to see that here, awakened by our
attitude, something lights up and approaches us from the course of being.
In the sphere we are talking of we have to do justice, in complete can-
dour, to the reality which discloses itself to us. I should like to describe this
large sphere, stretching from stones to stars, as that of the pre-threshold or
preliminal, i.e. the stage before the threshold. (6)

III

Now the question arises concerning the sphere which in the same imagery may be termed the sphere above the threshold, the superliminal, i.e.
the sphere of the lintel which is over the door: the sphere of the spirit. (7)

Here too a division must be made between two fields, which goes
deeper, however, than the division in nature. It is the division between on
the one hand what of spirit has already entered the world and can be
perceived in it by means of our senses, and on the other hand what of spirit
has not yet entered the world but is ready to do so, and becomes present
to us. This division is based on the fact that I can as it were point out to
you, my reader, the structure of the spirit which has already entered the
world; but I cannot point out the other. I can refer you to the structures of
the spirit which are "to hand," in the world that is common to us, no less
than a thing or a being of nature, as to something accessible to you in reality
or in potentiality. But I cannot refer to that which has not yet entered the
world. If I am asked where then the mutuality is to be found here, in this

boundary region, then all I can do is indicate indirectly certain events in man's life, which can scarcely be described, which experience spirit as meeting; and in the end, when indirect indication is not enough, there is nothing for me but to appeal, my reader, to the witness of your own mysteries—buried, perhaps, but still attainable.   (8)

Let us return, then, to the first realm, that of what is "to hand." Here we can adduce examples.   (9)

Let the questioner make present to himself one of the traditional sayings of a master who died thousands of years ago; and let him attempt, as well as he can, to take and receive the saying with his ears, that is, as though spoken by the speaker in his presence, even spoken to him. To do this he must turn with his whole being to the speaker (who is not to hand) of the saying (which is to hand). This means that he must adopt towards him who is both dead and living the attitude which I call the saying of *Thou*. If he succeeds (and of course his will and his effort are not adequate for this, but he can undertake it again and again), he will hear a voice, perhaps only indistinctly at first, which is identical with the voice he hears coming to him from other genuine sayings of the same master. Now he will no longer be able to do what he could do so long as he treated the saying as an object—that is, he will not be able to separate out of the saying any content or rhythm: but he receives only the indivisible wholeness of something spoken.   (10)

But this is still bound to a person, to what a person may have at any time to say in his words. What I mean is not limited to the continued influence of any personal life in words. Therefore I must complete my description with another example to which no personal quality clings. I choose, as always, an example which has powerful memories for some people: this time the Doric pillar, wherever it appears to a man who is ready and able to turn to it. Out of a church wall in Syracuse, in which it had once been immured, it first came to encounter me: mysterious primal mass represented in such simple form that there was nothing individual to look at, nothing individual to enjoy. All that could be done was what I did: took my stand, stood fast, in face of this structure of spirit, this mass penetrated and given body by the mind and hand of man. Does the concept of mutuality vanish here? It only plunges back into the dark, or it is transformed into a concrete content which coldly declines to assume conceptual form, but is bright and reliable.   (11)

From this point we may look over into that other realm, the realm of what is "not to hand," of contact with "spiritual being," of the *arising* of word and form.   (12)

Spirit become word, spirit become form—in some degree or other everyone who has been touched by the Spirit and did not shut himself to it, knows about the basic fact of the situation—that this does not germinate and grow in man's world without being sown, but arises from this world's meetings with the other. Not meetings with Platonic ideas—of which I have no direct knowledge at all and which I am not in a position to understand as what is in course of being (*Seiendes*); but meetings with the Spirit which blows around us and in us. Again and again I am reminded of the strange confession of Nietzsche when he described the event of "inspiration" as taking but not asking who gives. Even if we do not ask we should "thank." (13)

He who knows the breath of the Spirit trespasses if he desires to get power over the Spirit or to ascertain its nature and qualities. But he is also disloyal when he ascribes the gift to himself. (14)

IV

Let us look afresh at what is said here of meetings with what is of nature and what is of spirit, and let us look at them together. (15)

May we then—it may now be asked—speak of "response" or "address," which come from outside everything to which, in our consideration of the orders of being, we adjudge spontaneity and consciousness, as of something that happens in the world of man in which we live, just in this way—as a response or an address? Has what is here described any other validity than that of a "personifying" metaphor? Is there not a danger here of a problematic "mysticism," blurring the boundaries which are drawn, and which must be drawn, by all rational knowledge? (16)

The clear and firm structure of the *I–Thou* relationship, familiar to everyone with a candid heart and the courage to pledge it, has not a mystical nature. From time to time we must come out of our habits of thought in order to understand it; but we do not have to leave the primal norms which determine human thinking about reality. As in the realm of nature, so in the realm of spirit—the spirit which lives on in word and work, and the spirit which wishes to become word and work: what is effected upon us may be understood as something effected by the ongoing course of being (*Seiendes*). (17)

V

In the next question we are no longer concerned with the threshold, the preliminal and the superliminal of mutuality, but with mutuality itself as the door into our existence. (18)

The question is, how is it with the *I–Thou* relationship between men? Is it always entirely reciprocal? Can it always be, may it always be? Is it not—like everything human—delivered up to limitation by our insufficiency, and also placed under limitation by the inner laws of our life together? (19)

The first of these two hindrances is well enough known. From your own glance, day by day, into the eyes which look out in estrangement of your "neighbour" who nevertheless does need you, to the melancholy of holy men who time and again vainly offered the great gift—everything tells you that full mutuality is not inherent in men's life together. It is a grace, for which one must always be ready and which one never gains as an assured possession.   (20)

Yet there are some *I–Thou* relationships which in their nature may not unfold to full mutuality if they are to persist in that nature.   (21)

Elsewhere[5] I have characterized the relationship of the genuine educator to his pupil as being a relationship of this kind. In order to help the realisation of the best potentialities in the pupil's life, the teacher must really *mean* him as the definite person he is in his potentiality and his actuality; more precisely, he must not know him as a mere sum of qualities, strivings and inhibitions, he must be aware of him as a whole being and affirm him in this wholeness. But he can only do this if he meets him again and again as his partner in a bipolar situation. And in order that his effect upon him may be a unified and significant one he must also live this situation, again and again, in all its moments not merely from his own end but also from that of his partner: he must practise the kind of realisation which I call inclusion (*Umfassung*).   (22)

But however much depends upon his awakening the *I–Thou* relationship in the pupil as well—and however much depends upon the pupil, too, meaning and affirming him as the particular person he is—the special educative relation could not persist if the pupil for his part practised "inclusion," that is, if he lived the teacher's part in the common situation. Whether the *I–Thou* relationship now comes to an end or assumes the quite different character of a friendship, it is plain that the specifically educative relation as such is denied full mutuality.   (23)

Another no less illuminating example of the normative limitation of mutuality is presented to us in the relation between a genuine psychotherapist and his patient. If he is satisfied to "analyse" him, i.e. to bring to light unknown factors from his microcosm, and to set to some conscious work in life the energies which have been transformed by such an emergence, then he may be successful in some repair work. At best he may help a soul which is diffused and poor in structure to collect and order itself to some extent. But the real matter, the regeneration of an atrophied personal centre, will not be achieved. This can only be done by one who grasps the buried latent unity of the suffering soul with the great glance of the doctor: and this can only be attained in the person-to-person attitude of a partner, not by the consideration and examination of an object. In order

5 "Education," section III of *Between Man and Man.*

that he may coherently further the liberation and actualisation of that unity in a new accord of the person with the world, the psychotherapist, like the educator, must stand again and again not merely at his own pole in the bipolar relation, but also with the strength of present realisation at the other pole, and experience the effect of his own action. But again, the specific "healing" relation would come to an end the moment the patient thought of, and succeeded in, practising "inclusion" and experiencing the event from the doctor's pole as well. Healing, like educating, is only possible to the one who lives over against the other, and yet is detached.[6]   (24)

The most emphatic example of normative limitation of mutuality could be provided by the pastor with a cure of souls, for in this instance an "inclusion" coming from the other side would attack the sacral authenticity of the commission.   (25)

Every *I–Thou* relationship, within a relation which is specified as a purposive working of one part upon the other, persists in virtue of a mutuality which is forbidden to be full.   (26)

VI

In this context only one question more must be discussed, but it must be discussed since it is incomparably the most important of all.   (27)

The question is, how can the eternal *Thou* in the relation be at once exclusive and inclusive? How can the *Thou*–relationship of man to God, which is conditioned by an unconditioned turning to him, diverted by nothing, nevertheless include all other *I–Thou* relations of this man, and bring them as it were to God?   (28)

Note that the question is not about God, but about our relation to him. And yet in order to be able to answer I must speak of him. For our relation to him is as above contradictions as it is, because he is as above contradictions as he is.   (29)

Of course we speak only of what God is in his relation to a man. And even that is only to be expressed in paradox; more precisely, by the paradoxical use of a concept; more precisely still, by the paradoxical combination of a substantive concept with an adjective which contradicts its normal content. The assertion of this contradiction must yield to the insight that the indispensable description of the object by this concept can be justified only in this way. The content of the concept is revolutionised, transformed, and extended—but this is indeed what we experience with every concept which we take out of immanence—compelled by the reality of faith—and use with reference to the working of transcendence.   (30)

---

6 Cf. Martin Buber, *Pointing the Way: Collected Essays*, ed. and tr. by Maurice Friedman (New York: Harpers, 1957), "Healing Through Meeting," pp. 93–97. See also Martin Buber, "Guilt and Guilt Feelings," tr. by M. Friedman, *Psychiatry, ibid.*

The description of God as a Person is indispensable for everyone who like myself means by "God" not a principle (although mystics like Eckhart sometimes identify him with "Being") and like myself means by "God" not an idea (although philosophers like Plato at times could hold that he was this): but who rather means by "God," as I do, him who—whatever else he may be—enters into a direct relation with us men in creative, revealing and redeeming acts, and thus makes it possible for us to enter into a direct relation with him. This ground and meaning of our existence constitutes a mutuality, arising again and again, such as can subsist only between persons. The concept of personal being is indeed completely incapable of declaring what God's essential being is, but it is both permitted and necessary to say that God is *also* a Person. If as an exception I wished to translate what is meant by this into philosophical language, that of Spinoza, I should have to say that of God's infinitely many attributes we men do not know two, as Spinoza thinks, but three: to spiritual being (in which is to be found the source of what we call spirit) and to natural being (which presents itself in what is known to us as nature) would be added the attribute of personal being. From this attribute would stem my and all men's being as person, as from those other attributes would stem my and all men's being as spirit and being as nature. And only this third attribute of personal being would be given to us to be known direct in its quality as an attribute. (31)

But now the contradiction appears in the appeal to the familiar content of the concept person. This says that it is indeed the property of a person that its independence should consist in itself, but that it is limited in its total being by the plurality of other independent entities; and this can of course not be true of God. This contradiction is countered by the paradoxical description of God as the absolute Person, i.e. the Person who cannot be limited. It is as the absolute Person that God enters into direct relation with us. The contradiction yields to deeper insight.   (32)

As a Person God gives personal life, he makes us as persons become capable of meeting with him and with one another. But no limitation can come upon him as the absolute Person, either from us or from our relations with one another; in fact we can dedicate to him not merely our persons but also our relations to one another. The man who turns to him therefore need not turn away from any other *I–Thou* relation; but he properly brings them to him, and lets them be fulfilled "in the face of God."   (33)

One must, however, take care not to understand this conversation with God—the conversation of which I have to speak in this book and in almost all the works which followed—as something happening solely alongside or above the everyday. God's speech to men penetrates what happens in the life of each one of us, and all that happens in the world around us, biographical and historical, and makes it for you and me into instruction, message, demand. Happening upon happening, situation upon situation, are enabled and empowered by the personal speech of God to demand of the human person that he take his stand and make his decision. Often enough we think there is nothing to hear, but long before we have ourselves put wax in our ears. (34)

The existence of mutuality between God and man cannot be proved, just as God's existence cannot be proved. Yet he who dares to speak of it, bears witness, and calls to witness him to whom he speaks—whether that witness is now or in the future. (35)

Jerusalem, October 1957

Translated by Ronald Gregor Smith
Glasgow, November 1957

NARRATIVE, INCLUDING DESCRIPTION

Factual Narrative

Mark Twain

(1835–1910)

MARK TWAIN (Samuel Langhorne Clemens) is known to every American schoolboy as the author of The Adventures of Tom Sawyer *(1876) and* The Adventures of Huckleberry Finn *(1884). The eclipse of the last twenty years of his life seems unimportant after these high-water marks of American folk literature. The* Autobiography *(A. B. Paine, 1924) recreates factual events from the author's life which he had later translated into fiction.*

◼ *The Farm of My Uncle John's*

IT WAS A heavenly place for a boy, that farm of my uncle John's. The house was a double log one, with a spacious floor (roofed in) connecting it with the kitchen. In the summer the table was set in the middle of that shady and breezy floor, and the sumptuous meals—well, it makes me cry to think of them. Fried chicken, roast pig; wild and tame turkeys, ducks, and geese; venison just killed; squirrels, rabbits, pheasants, partridges, prairie-chickens; biscuits, hot batter cakes, hot buckwheat cakes, hot "wheat bread," hot rolls, hot corn pone; fresh corn boiled on the ear, succotash, butter-beans, string-beans, tomatoes, peas, Irish potatoes, sweet potatoes; buttermilk, sweet milk, "clabber"; watermelons, muskmelons, cantaloupes—all fresh from the garden; apple pie, peach pie, pumpkin pie, apple dumplings, peach cobbler—I can't remember the rest. The way that the things were cooked was perhaps the main splendor—particularly a certain few of the dishes. For instance, the corn bread, the hot biscuits and wheat bread, and the fried chicken. These things have never been properly cooked in the North—in fact, no one there is able to learn the art, so far as my experience goes. The North thinks it knows how to make corn bread, but this is mere superstition. Perhaps no bread in the world is quite so good as Southern corn bread, and perhaps no bread in the world is quite so bad as the Northern imitation of it. The North seldom tries to fry chicken, and this is well; the art cannot be learned north of the line of Mason and Dixon, nor anywhere in Europe. This is not hearsay; it is experience that is speaking. In Europe it is imagined that the custom of serving various kinds of bread blazing hot is "American," but that is too broad a spread; it is custom in the South, but is much less than that in the North. In the North and in Europe hot bread is considered unhealthy. This is probably another fussy superstition, like the European superstition that ice-water is unhealthy. Europe does not need ice-water and does not drink it; and yet, notwithstanding this, its word for it is better than ours, because it describes it, whereas ours doesn't. Europe calls it "iced" water. Our word describes water made from melted ice—a drink which has a characterless taste and which we have but little acquaintance with.   (1)

It seems a pity that the world should throw away so many good things merely because they are unwholesome. I doubt if God has given us any refreshment which, taken in moderation, is unwholesome, except microbes. Yet there are people who strictly deprive themselves of each and every eatable, drinkable, and smokable which has in any way acquired a shady reputation. They pay this price for health. And health is all they get for it. How strange it is! It is like paying out your whole fortune for a cow that has gone dry.   (2)

The farmhouse stood in the middle of a very large yard, and the yard was fenced on three sides with rails and on the rear side with high palings; against these stood the smoke-house; beyond the palings was the orchard; beyond the orchard were the negro quarters and the tobacco fields. The front yard was entered over a stile made of sawed-off logs of graduated heights; I do not remember any gate. In a corner of the front yard were a dozen lofty hickory trees and a dozen black walnuts, and in the nutting season riches were to be gathered there.   (3)

Down a piece, abreast the house, stood a little log cabin against the rail fence; and there the woody hill fell sharply away, past the barns, the corn-crib, the stables, and the tobacco-curing house, to a limpid brook which sang along over its gravelly bed and curved and frisked in and out and here and there and yonder in the deep shade of overhanging foliage and vines—a divine place for wading, and it had swimming pools, too, which were forbidden to us and therefore much frequented by us. For we were little Christian children and had early been taught the value of forbidden fruit. . . .
                                                                        (4)

I can see the farm yet, with perfect clearness. I can see all its belongings, all its details; the family room of the house, with a "trundle" bed in one corner and a spinning-wheel in another—a wheel whose rising and falling wail, heard from a distance, was the mournfulest of all sounds to me, and made me homesick and low spirited, and filled my atmosphere with the wandering spirits of the dead; the vast fireplace, piled high, on winter nights, with flaming hickory logs from whose ends a sugary sap bubbled out, but did not go to waste, for we scraped it off and ate it; the lazy cat spread out on the rough hearthstones; the drowsy dogs braced against the jambs and blinking; my aunt in one chimney corner, knitting; my uncle in the other, smoking his corn-cob pipe; the slick and carpetless oak floor faintly mirroring the dancing flame tongues and freckled with black indentations where fire coals had popped out and died a leisurely death; half a dozen children romping in the background twilight; "split"-bottomed chairs here and there, some with rockers; a cradle—out of service, but waiting, with confidence; in the early cold mornings a snuggle of children, in shirts and chemises, occupying the hearthstone and procrastinating—they could not bear to leave that comfortable place and go out on the wind-swept floor space between the house and kitchen where the general tin basin stood, and wash. (5)

Along outside of the front fence ran the country road, dusty in the summertime, and a good place for snakes—they liked to lie in it and sun themselves; when they were rattlesnakes or puff adders, we killed them; when they were black snakes, or racers, or belonged to the fabled "hoop" breed, we fled, without shame; when they were "house snakes," or "garters," we carried them home and put them in Aunt Patsy's work basket for a surprise; for she was prejudiced against snakes, and always when she took the basket in her lap and they began to climb out of it it disordered her mind. She never could seem to get used to them; her opportunities went for nothing. And she was always cold toward bats, too, and could not bear them; and yet I think a bat is as friendly a bird as there is. My mother was Aunt Patsy's sister and had the same wild superstitions. A bat is beautifully soft and silky; I do not know any creature that is pleasanter to the touch or is more grateful for caressings, if offered in the right spirit. I know all about these coleoptera, because our great cave, three miles below Hannibal, was multitudinously stocked with them, and often I brought them home to amuse my mother with. It was easy to manage if it was a school day, because then I had ostensibly been to school and hadn't any bats. She was not a suspicious person, but full of trust and confidence; and when I said, "There's something in my coat pocket for you," she would put her hand in. But she always took it out again, herself; I didn't have to tell her. It was remarkable, the way she couldn't learn to like private bats. The more experience she had, the more she could not change her views. (6)

I think she was never in the cave in her life; but everybody else went there. Many excursion parties came from considerable distances up and down the river to visit the cave. It was miles in extent and was a tangled wilderness of narrow and lofty clefts and passages. It was an easy place to get lost in; anybody could do it—including the bats. I got lost in it myself, along with a lady, and our last candle burned down to almost nothing before we glimpsed the search party's lights winding about in the distance. (7)

"Injun Joe," the half-breed, got lost in there once, and would have starved to death if the bats had run short. But there was no chance of that; there were myriads of them. He told me all his story. In the book called *Tom Sawyer* I starved him entirely to death in the cave, but that was in the interest of art; it never happened. "General" Gaines, who was our first town drunkard before Jimmy Finn got the place, was lost in there for a space of a week, and finally pushed his handkerchief out of a hole in a hilltop near Saverton, several miles down the river from the cave's mouth, and somebody saw it and dug him out. There is nothing the matter with his statistics except the handkerchief. I knew him for years and he hadn't any. But it could have been his nose. That would attract attention. (8)

The cave was an uncanny place, for it contained a corpse—the corpse of a young girl of fourteen. It was in a glass cylinder inclosed in a copper one which was suspended from a rail which bridged a narrow passage. The body was preserved in alcohol, and it was said that loafers and rowdies used to drag it up by the hair and look at the dead face. The girl was the daughter of a St. Louis surgeon of extraordinary ability and wide celebrity. He was an eccentric man and did many strange things. He put the poor thing in that forlorn place himself. (9)

Beyond the road where the snakes sunned themselves was a dense young thicket, and through it a dim-lighted path led a quarter of a mile; then out of the dimness one emerged abruptly upon a level great prairie which was covered with wild strawberry plants, vividly starred with prairie pinks, and walled in on all sides by forests. The strawberries were fragrant and fine, and in the season we were generally there in the crisp freshness of the early morning, while the dew beads still sparkled upon the grass and the woods were ringing with the first songs of the birds. (10)

Down the forest slopes to the left were the swings. They were made of bark stripped from hickory saplings. When they became dry they were dangerous. They usually broke when a child was forty feet in the air, and this was why so many bones had to be mended every year. I had no ill luck myself, but none of my cousins escaped. There were eight of them, and at one time and another they broke fourteen arms among them. But it cost next to nothing, for the doctor worked by the year—twenty-five dollars for the whole family. I remember two of the Florida doctors, Chowning and Meredith. They not only tended an entire family for twenty-five dollars a year, but furnished the medicines themselves. Good measure, too. Only the largest persons could hold a whole dose. Castor oil was the principal beverage. The dose was half a dipperful, with half a dipperful of New Orleans molasses added to help it down and make it taste good, which it never did. The next standby was calomel; the next, rhubarb; and the next, jalap. Then they bled the patient, and put mustard plasters on him. It was a dreadful system, and yet the death rate was not heavy. The calomel was nearly sure to salivate the patient and cost him some of his teeth. There were no dentists. When teeth became touched with decay or were otherwise ailing, the doctor knew of but one thing to do—he fetched his tongs and dragged them out. If the jaw remained, it was not his fault. Doctors were not called in cases of ordinary illness; the family grandmother attended to those. Every old woman was a doctor, and gathered her own medicines in the woods, and knew how to compound doses that would stir the vitals of a cast-iron dog. And then there was the "Indian doctor"; a grave savage, remnant of his tribe, deeply read in the mysteries of nature and the secret properties of herbs; and most backwoodsmen had high faith in his powers and could tell of wonderful cures achieved by him. In Mauritius, away off yonder in the solitudes of the Indian Ocean, there is a person who answers to our Indian doctor of the old times. He is a negro, and has had no teaching as a doctor, yet there is one disease which he is master of and can cure and the doctors can't. They send for him when they have a case. It is a child's disease of a strange and deadly sort, and the negro cures it with a herb medicine which he makes, himself, from a prescription which has come down to him from his father and grandfather. He will not let anyone see it. He keeps the secret of its components to himself, and it is feared that he will die without divulging it; then there will be consternation in Mauritius. I was told these things by the people there, in 1896.   (11)

We had the "faith doctor," too, in those early days—a woman. Her specialty was toothache. She was a farmer's old wife and lived five miles from Hannibal. She would lay her hand on the patient's jaw and say, "Believe!" and the cure was prompt. Mrs. Utterback. I remember her very well. Twice I rode out there behind my mother, horseback, and saw the cure performed. My mother was the patient.   (12)

Doctor Meredith removed to Hannibal, by and by, and was our family physician there, and saved my life several times. Still, he was a good man and meant well. Let it go.   (13)

I was always told that I was a sickly and precarious and tiresome and uncertain child, and lived mainly on allopathic medicines during the first seven years of my life. I asked my mother about this, in her old age—she was in her eighty-eighth year—and said: (14)

"I suppose that during all that time you were uneasy about me?"   (15)

"Yes, the whole time."   (16)

"Afraid I wouldn't live?"   (17)

After a reflective pause—ostensibly to think out the facts—"No—afraid
you would."   (18)

The country schoolhouse was three miles from my uncle's farm. It stood
in a clearing in the woods and would hold about twenty-five boys and girls.
We attended the school with more or less regularity once or twice a week,
in summer, walking to it in the cool of the morning by the forest paths, and
back in the gloaming at the end of the day. All the pupils brought their dinners in baskets—corn dodger, buttermilk, and other good things—and sat in
the shade of the trees at noon and ate them. It is the part of my education
which I look back upon with the most satisfaction. My first visit to the
school was when I was seven. A strapping girl of fifteen, in the customary
sunbonnet and calico dress, asked me if I "used tobacco"—meaning did I
chew it. I said no. It roused her scorn. She reported me to all the crowd, and
said: (19)

"Here is a boy seven years old who can't chew tobacco."   (20)

By the looks and comments which this produced I realized that I was a
degraded object, and was cruelly ashamed of myself. I determined to reform. But I only made myself sick; I was not able to learn to chew tobacco.
I learned to smoke fairly well, but that did not conciliate anybody and I remained a poor thing, and characterless. I longed to be respected, but I never
was able to rise. Children have but little charity for one another's defects.
                                                                                 (21)

As I have said, I spent some part of every year at the farm until I was
twelve or thirteen years old. The life which I led there with my cousins was
full of charm, and so is the memory of it yet. I can call back the solemn
twilight and mystery of the deep woods, the earthy smells, the faint odors
of the wild flowers, the sheen of rain-washed foliage, the rattling clatter
of drops when the wind shook the trees, the far-off hammering of woodpeckers and the muffled drumming of wood pheasants in the remoteness of
the forest, the snapshot glimpses of disturbed wild creatures scurrying
through the grass—I can call it all back and make it as real as it ever was,
and as blessed. I can call back the prairie, and its loneliness and peace,
and a vast hawk hanging motionless in the sky, with his wings spread wide
and the blue of the vault showing through the fringe of their end feathers.
I can see the woods in their autumn dress, the oaks purple, the hickories
washed with gold, the maples and the sumachs luminous with crimson fires,
and I can hear the rustle made by the fallen leaves as we plowed through
them. I can see the blue clusters of wild grapes hanging among the foliage
of the saplings, and I remember the taste of them and the smell. I know
how the wild blackberries looked, and how they tasted, and the same with
the pawpaws, the hazelnuts, and the persimmons; and I can feel the thumping rain, upon my head, of hickory nuts and walnuts when we were out in

the frosty dawn to scramble for them with the pigs, and the gusts of wind loosed them and sent them down. I know the stain of blackberries, and how pretty it is, and I know the stain of walnut hulls, and how little it minds soap and water, also what grudged experience it had of either of them. I know the taste of maple sap, and when to gather it, and how to arrange the troughs and the delivery tubes, and how to boil down the juice, and how to hook the sugar after it is made, also how much better hooked sugar tastes than any that is honestly come by, let bigots say what they will. I know how a prize watermelon looks when it is sunning its fat rotundity among pumpkin vines and "simblins"; I know how to tell when it is ripe without "plugging" it; I know how inviting it looks when it is cooling itself in a tub of water under the bed, waiting; I know how it looks when it lies on the table in the sheltered great floor space between house and kitchen, and the children gathered for the sacrifice and their mouths watering; I know the crackling sound it makes when the carving knife enters its end, and I can see the split fly along in front of the blade as the knife cleaves its way to the other end; I can see its halves fall apart and display the rich red meat and the black seeds, and the heart standing up, a luxury fit for the elect; I know how a boy looks behind a yard-long slice of that melon, and I know how he feels; for I have been there. I know the taste of the watermelon which has been honestly come by, and I know the taste of the watermelon which has been acquired by art. Both taste good, but the experienced know which tastes best. I know the look of green apples and peaches and pears on the trees, and I know how entertaining they are when they are inside of a person. I know how ripe ones look when they are piled in pyramids under the trees, and how pretty they are and how vivid their colors. I know how a frozen apple looks, in a barrel down cellar in the wintertime, and how hard it is to bite, and how the frost makes the teeth ache, and yet how good it is, notwithstanding. I know the disposition of elderly people to select the specked apples for the children, and I once knew ways to beat the game. I know the look of an apple that is roasting and sizzling on a hearth on a winter's evening, and I know the comfort that comes of eating it hot, along with some sugar and a drench of cream. I know the delicate art and mystery of so cracking hickory nuts and walnuts on a flatiron with a hammer that the kernels will be delivered whole, and I know how the nuts, taken in conjunction with winter apples, cider, and doughnuts, make old people's old tales and old jokes sound fresh and crisp and enchanting, and juggle an evening away before you know what went with the time. I know the look of Uncle Dan'l's kitchen as it was on the privileged nights, when I was a child, and I can see the white and black children grouped on the hearth, with the firelight playing on their faces and the shadows flickering upon the walls, clear back toward the cavernous gloom of the rear, and I can hear Uncle Dan'l telling the immortal tales which Uncle Remus Harris was to gather into his book and charm the world with, by and by; and I can feel again the creepy joy which quivered through me when the time for the ghost story was reached—and the sense of regret, too, which came over me, for it was always the last story of the evening and there was nothing between it and the unwelcome bed.   (22)

I can remember the bare wooden stairway in my uncle's house, and the turn to the left above the landing, and the rafters and the slanting roof over my bed, and the squares of moonlight on the floor, and the white cold world of snow outside, seen through the curtainless window. I can remember the howling of the wind and the quaking of the house on stormy nights, and how snug and cozy one felt, under the blankets, listening; and how the powdery snow used to sift in, around the sashes, and lie in little ridges on the floor and make the place look chilly in the morning and curb the wild desire to get up—in case there was any. I can remember how very dark that room was, in the dark of the moon, and how packed it was with ghostly stillness when one woke up by accident away in the night, and forgotten sins came flocking out of the secret chambers of the memory and wanted a hearing; and how ill chosen the time seemed for this kind of business; and how dismal was the hoo-hooing of the owl and the wailing of the wolf, sent mourning by on the night wind.   (23)

I remember the raging of the rain on that roof, summer nights, and how pleasant it was to lie and listen to it, and enjoy the white splendor of the lightning and the majestic booming and crashing of the thunder. It was a very satisfactory room, and there was a lightning rod which was reachable from the window, an adorable and skittish thing to climb up and down, summer nights, when there were duties on hand of a sort to make privacy desirable.   (24)

I remember the 'coon and 'possum hunts, nights, with the negroes, and the long marches through the black gloom of the woods, and the excitement which fired everybody when the distant bay of an experienced dog announced that the game was treed; then the wild scramblings and stumblings through briers and bushes and over roots to get to the spot; then the lighting of a fire and the felling of the tree, the joyful frenzy of the dogs and the negroes, and the weird picture it all made in the red glare—I remember it all well, and the delight that everyone got out of it, except the 'coon.   (25)

I remember the pigeon seasons, when the birds would come in millions and cover the trees and by their weight break down the branches. They were clubbed to death with sticks; guns were not necessary and were not used. I remember the squirrel hunts, and prairie-chicken hunts, and wild-turkey hunts, and all that; and how we turned out, mornings, while it was still dark, to go on these expeditions, and how chilly and dismal it was, and how often I regretted that I was well enough to go. A toot on a tin horn brought twice as many dogs as were needed, and in their happiness they raced and scampered about, and knocked small people down, and made no end of unnecessary noise. At the word, they vanished away toward the woods, and we drifted silently after them in the melancholy gloom. But presently the gray dawn stole over the world, the birds piped up, then the sun rose and poured light and comfort all around, everything was fresh and dewy and fragrant, and life was a boon again. After three hours of tramping we arrived back wholesomely tired, overladen with game, very hungry, and just in time for breakfast.   (26)

Alfred Kazin

(1915–   )

KAZIN is a distinguished member of the faculty at the State University of New York at Stonybrook. A creative writer who has done significant critical research, he has devoted his energies largely but not exclusively to American studies: F. Scott Fitzgerald, Herman Melville, Theodore Dreiser, Emerson. He has received Guggenheim fellowships twice and has held professional posts at the University of Minnesota, Smith College, Amherst, Harvard, and New York University. He has been a steady contributor to newspapers and magazines (The New Republic, Fortune, and so forth), and has written several books, including On Native Grounds (1942), A Walker in the City (1951), and The Inmost Leaf (1955).

■ *School Days at Brownsville*

ALL MY EARLY life lies open to my eye within five city blocks. When I passed the school, I went sick with all my old fear of it. With its standard New York public school brown brick courtyard shut in on three sides of the square and the pretentious battlements overlooking that cockpit in which I can still smell the fiery sheen of the rubber ball, it looks like a factory over which has been imposed the façade of a castle. It gave me the shivers to stand up in that courtyard again; I felt as if I had been mustered back into the service of those Friday morning "tests" that were the terror of my childhood. (1)

It was never learning I associated with that school: only the necessity to succeed, to get ahead of the others in the daily struggle to "make a good impression" on our teachers, who grimly, wearily, and often with ill-concealed distaste watched against our relapsing into the natural savagery they expected of Brownsville boys. The white, cool, thinly ruled record book sat over us from their desks all day long, and had remorselessly entered into it each day—in blue ink if we had passed, in red ink if we had not—our attendance, our conduct, our "effort," our merits and demerits; and to the last possible decimal point in calculation, our standing in an unending series of "tests"—surprise tests, daily tests, weekly tests, formal midterm tests, final tests. They never stopped trying to dig out of us whatever small morsel of fact we had managed to get down the night before. We had to prove that we were really alert, ready for anything, always in the race. That white thinly ruled record book figured in my mind as the judgment seat; the very thinness and remote blue lightness of its lines instantly showed its cold authority over me; so much space had been left on each page, columns and columns in which to note down everything about us, implacably and forever. As it lay there on a teacher's desk, I stared at it all day long with such fear and anxious propriety that I had no trouble believing that God, too, did nothing but keep such record books, and that on the final day He would face me with an account in Hebrew letters whose phonetic dots and dashes looked strangely like decimal points counting up my every sinful thought on earth. (2)

All teachers were to be respected like gods, and God Himself was the greatest of all school superintendents. Long after I had ceased to believe that our teachers could see with the back of their heads, it was still understood, by me, that they knew everything. They were the delegates of all visible and invisible power on earth—of the mothers who waited on the stoops every day after three for us to bring home tales of our daily triumphs; of the glacially remote Anglo-Saxon principal, whose very name was King; of the incalculably important Superintendent of Schools who would someday rubberstamp his name to the bottom of our diplomas in grim acknowledgment that we had, at last, given satisfaction to him, to the Board of Superintendents, and to our benefactor the City of New York—and so up and up, to the government of the United States and to the great Lord Jehovah Himself. My belief in teachers' unlimited wisdom and power rested not so much on what I saw in them—how impatient most of them looked, how wary—but on our abysmal humility, at least in those of us who were "good" boys, who proved by our ready compliance and "manners" that we wanted to get on. The road to a professional future would be shown us only as we pleased *them. Make a good impression the first day of the term, and they'll help you out. Make a bad impression, and you might as well cut your throat.* This was the first article of school folklore, whispered around the classroom the opening day of each term. You made the "good impression" by sitting firmly at your wooden desk, hands clasped; by silence for the greatest part of the live-long day; by standing up obsequiously when it was so expected of you; by sitting down noiselessly when you had answered a question; by "speaking nicely," which meant reproducing their painfully exact enunciation; by "showing manners," or an ecstatic submissiveness in all things; by outrageous flattery; by bringing little gifts at Christmas, on their birthdays, and at the end of the term—the well-known significance of these gifts being that they came not from us, but from our parents, whose eagerness in this matter showed a high level of social consideration, and thus raised our standing in turn.   (3)

It was not just our quickness and memory that were always being tested. Above all, in that word I could never hear without automatically see-ing it raised before me in gold-plated letters, it was our *character.* I always felt anxious when I heard the word pronounced. Satisfactory as my "char-acter" was, on the whole, except when I stayed too long in the playground reading; outrageously satisfactory, as I can see now, the very sound of the word as our teachers coldly gave it out from the end of their teeth, with a solemn weight on each dark syllable, immediately struck my heart cold with fear—they could not believe I really had it. Character was never something you had; it had to be trained in you, like a technique. I was never very clear about it. On our side *character* meant demonstrative obedience; but teachers already had it—how else could they have become teachers? They had it; the aloof Anglo-Saxon principal whom we remotely saw only on ceremonial occasions in the assembly was positively encased in it; it glit-tered off his bald head in spokes of triumphant light; the President of the United States had the greatest conceivable amount of it. Character be-longed to great adults. Yet we were constantly being driven onto it; it was the great threshold we had to cross. *Alfred Kazin, having shown proficiency in his course of studies and having displayed satisfactory marks of charac-ter . . .* Thus someday the hallowed diploma, passport to my further ad-vancement in high school. But there—I could already feel it in my bones— they would put me through even more doubting tests of character; and after that, if I should be good enough and bright enough, there would be still more. *Character* was a bitter thing, racked with my endless striving to please. The school—from every last stone in the courtyard to the battlements frowning down at me from the walls—was only the stage for a trial. I felt that the very atmosphere of learning that surrounded us was fake—that every lesson, every book, every approving smile was only a pretext for the constant probing and watching of me, that there was not a secret in me that would not be decimally measured into that white record book. All week long I lived for the blessed sound of the dismissal gong at three o'clock on Friday afternoon.   (4)

I was awed by this system, I believed in it, I respected its force. The alternative was "going bad." The school was notoriously the toughest in our tough neighborhood, and the dangers of "going bad" were constantly impressed upon me at home and in school in dark whispers of the "reform school" and in examples of boys who had been picked up for petty thievery, rape, or flinging a heavy inkwell straight into a teacher's face. Behind any failure in school yawned the great abyss of a criminal career. Every refractory attitude doomed you with the sound "Sing Sing." Anything less than absolute perfection in school always suggested to my mind that I might fall out of the daily race, be kept back in the working class forever, or— dared I think of it?—fall into the criminal class itself.   (5)

I worked on a hairline between triumph and catastrophe. Why the odds should always have felt so narrow I understood only when I realized how little my parents thought of their own lives. It was not for myself alone that I was expected to shine, but for them—to redeem the constant anxiety of their existence. I was the first American child, their offering to the strange new God; I was to be the monument of their liberation from the shame of being—what they were. And that there was shame in this was a fact that everyone seemed to believe as a matter of course. It was in the gleeful discounting of themselves—what do we know?—with which our parents greeted every fresh victory in our savage competition for "high averages," for prizes, for a few condescending words of official praise from the principal at assembly. It was in the sickening invocation of "Americanism"—the word itself accusing us of everything we apparently were not. Our families and teachers seemed tacitly agreed that we were somehow to be a little ashamed of what we were. Yet it was always hard to say why this should be so. It was certainly not—in Brownsville!—because we were Jews, or simply because we spoke another language at home, or were absent on our holy days. It was rather that a "refined," "correct," "nice" English was required of us at school that we did not naturally speak, and that our teachers could never be quite sure we would keep. This English was peculiarly the ladder of advancement. Every future young lawyer was known by it. Even the Communists and Socialists on Pitkin Avenue spoke it. It was bright and clean and polished. We were expected to show it off like a new pair of shoes. When the teacher sharply called a question out, then your name, you were expected to leap up, face the class, and eject those new words fluently off the tongue.   (6)

There was my secret ordeal: I could never say anything except in the most roundabout way; I was a stammerer. Although I knew all those new words from my private reading—I read walking in the street, to and from the Children's Library on Stone Avenue; on the fire escape and the roof; at every meal when they would let me; read even when I dressed in the morning, propping my book up against the drawers of the bureau as I pulled on my long black stockings—I could never seem to get the easiest words out with the right dispatch, and would often miserably signal from my desk that I did not know the answer rather than get up to stumble and fall and crash on every word. If, angry at always being put down as lazy or stupid, I did get up to speak, the black wooden floor would roll away under my feet, the teacher would frown at me in amazement, and in unbearable loneliness I would hear behind me the groans and laughter: *tuh-tuh-tuh-tuh.*   (7)

The word was my agony. The word that for others was so effortless and so neutral, so unburdened, so simple, so exact, I had first to meditate in advance, to see if I could make it, like a plumber fitting together odd lengths and shapes of pipe. I was always preparing words I could speak, storing them away, choosing between them. And often, when the word did come from my mouth in its great and terrible birth, quailing and bleeding as if forced through a thornbush, I would not be able to look the others in the face, and would walk out in the silence, the infinitely echoing silence behind my back, to say it all cleanly back to myself as I walked in the streets. Only when I was alone in the open air, pacing the roof with pebbles in my mouth, as I had read Demosthenes had done to cure himself of stammering; or in the street, where all words seemed to flow from the length of my stride and the color of the houses as I remembered the perfect tranquillity of a phrase in Beethoven's *Romance in F* I could sing back to myself as I walked—only then was it possible for me to speak without the infinite premeditations and strangled silences I toiled through whenever I got up at school to respond with the expected, the exact answer.   (8)

It troubled me that I could speak in the fullness of my own voice only when I was alone on the streets, walking about. There was something unnatural about it; unbearably isolated. I was not like the others! I was not like the others! At midday, every freshly shocking Monday noon, they sent me away to a speech clinic in a school in East New York, where I sat in a circle of lispers and cleft palates and foreign accents holding a mirror before my lips and rolling difficult sounds over and over. To be sent there in the full light of the opening week, when everyone else was at school or going about his business, made me feel as if I had been expelled from the great normal body of humanity. I would gobble down my lunch on my way to the speech clinic and rush back to the school in time to make up for the classes I had lost. One day, one unforgettable dread day, I stopped to catch my breath on a corner of Sutter Avenue, near the wholesale fruit markets, where an old drugstore rose up over a great flight of steps. In the window were dusty urns of colored water floating off iron chains; cardboard placards advertising hairnets, Ex-Lax; a great illustrated medical chart headed THE HUMAN FACTORY, which showed the exact course a mouthful of food follows as it falls from chamber to chamber of the body. I hadn't meant to stop there at all, only to catch my breath; but I so hated the speech clinic that I thought I would delay my arrival for a few minutes by eating my lunch on the steps. When I took the sandwich out of my bag, two bitterly hard pieces of hard salami slipped out of my hand and fell through a grate onto a hill of dust below the steps. I remember how sickeningly vivid an odd thread of hair looked on the salami, as if my lunch were turning stiff with death. The factory whistles called their short, sharp blasts stark through the middle of noon, beating at me where I sat outside the city's magnetic circle. I had never known, I knew instantly I would never in my heart again submit to, such wild passive despair as I felt at that moment, sitting on the steps before THE HUMAN FACTORY, where little robots gathered and shoveled the food from chamber to chamber of the body. They had put me out into the streets, I thought to myself; with their mirrors and their everlasting pulling at me to imitate their effortless bright speech and their stupefaction that a boy could stammer and stumble on every other English word he carried in his head, they had put me out into the streets, had left me high and dry on the steps of that drugstore staring at the remains of my lunch turning black and grimy in the dust.   (9)

In the great cool assembly hall, dominated by the gold sign above the stage KNOWLEDGE IS POWER, the windowsills were lined with Dutch bulbs, each wedged into a mound of pebbles massed in a stone dish. Above them hung a giant photograph of Theodore Roosevelt. Whenever I walked in to see the empty assembly hall for myself, the shiny waxed floor of the stage dangled in the middle of the air like a crescent. On one side was a great silk American flag, the staff crowned by a gilt eagle. Across the dry rattling of varnish-smelling empty seats bowing to the American flag, I saw in the play of the sun on those pebbles wildly sudden images of peace. *There* was the other land, crowned by the severe and questioning face of Theodore Roosevelt, his eyes above the curiously endearing straw-dry mustache, behind the pince-nez glittering with light, staring and staring me through as if he were uncertain whether he fully approved of me.   (10)

The light pouring through window after window in that great empty varnished assembly hall seemed to me the most wonderful thing I had ever seen. It was that thorough varnished cleanness that was of the new land, that light dancing off the glasses of Theodore Roosevelt, those green and white roots of the still raw onion-brown bulbs delicately flaring up from the hill of pebbles into which they were wedged. The pebbles moved me in themselves, there were so many of them. They rose up around the bulbs in delicately strong masses of colored stone, and as the sun fell between them, each pebble shone in its own light. Looking across the great rows of empty seats to those pebbles lining the windowsills, I could still smell summer from some long veranda surrounded by trees. On that veranda sat the family and friends of Theodore Roosevelt. I knew the name: Oyster Bay. Because of that picture, I had read *The Boy's Life of Theodore Roosevelt;* knew he had walked New York streets night after night as Police Commissioner, unafraid of the Tenderloin gangsters; had looked into *Theodore Roosevelt's Letters to His Children*, pretending that those hilarious drawings on almost every page were for me. *There* was America, I thought, the real America, *his* America, where from behind the glass on the wall of our assembly hall he watched over us to make sure we did right, thought right, lived right. (11)

"Up, boys! Up San Juan Hill!" I still hear our roguish old civics teacher, a little white-haired Irishman who was supposed to have been with Teddy in Cuba, driving us through our Friday morning tests with these shouts and cries. He called them "Army Navy" tests, to make us feel big, and dividing the class between Army and Navy, got us to compete with each other for a coveted blue star. Civics was city government, state government, federal government; each government had functions; you had to get them out fast in order to win for the Army or the Navy. Sometimes this required filling in three or four words, line by line, down one side of the grimly official yellow foolscap that was brought out for tests. (In the tense silence just before the test began, he looked at us sharply, the watch in his hand ticking as violently as the sound of my heart, and on command, fifty boys simultaneously folded their yellow test paper and evened the fold with their thumbnails in a single dry sigh down the middle of the paper.) At other times it meant true-or-false tests; then he stood behind us to make sure we did not signal the right answers to each other in the usual way—for true, nodding your head; for false, holding your nose. You could hear his voice barking from the rear. "*Come on now, you Army boys! On your toes like West Point cadets! All ready now? Get set! Go! Three powers of the legislative branch? The judiciary? The executive? The subject of the fifteenth amendment? The capital of Wyoming? Come on, Navy! Shoot those landlubbers down! Give 'em a blast from your big guns right through the middle! The third article of the Bill of Rights? The thirteenth amendment? The sixteenth? True or false, Philadelphia is the capital of Pennsylvania. Up and at 'em Navy! Mow them down! COME ON!!!*" Our "average" was calculated each week, and the boys who scored 90 per cent or over were rewarded by seeing *their own names* lettered on the great blue chart over the blackboard. Each time I entered that room for a test, I looked for my name on the blue chart as if the sight of it would decide my happiness for all time. (12)

Down we go, down the school corridors of the past smelling of chalk, lysol out of the open toilets, and girl sweat. The staircases were a gray stone I saw nowhere else in the school, and they were shut in on both sides by some thick unreflecting glass on which were pasted travel posters inviting us to spend the summer in the Black Forest. Those staircases created a spell in me that I had found my way to some distant, cool, neutral passageway deep in the body of the school. There, enclosed within the thick, green boughs of a classic summer in Germany, I could still smell the tense probing chalk smells from every classroom, the tickling high surgical odor of lysol from the open toilets, could still hear that continuous babble, babble of water dripping into the bowls. Sex was instantly connected in my mind with the cruel openness of those toilets, and in the never-ending sound of the bowls being flushed I could detect, as I did in the maddeningly elusive fragrance of cologne brought into the classroom by Mrs. B., the imminence of something severe, frightening, obscene. Sex, as they said in the "Coney Island" dives outside the school, was like going to the toilet; there was a great contempt in this that made me think of the wet rings left by our sneakers as we ran down the gray stone steps after school.   (13)

Outside the women teachers' washroom on the third floor, the tough guys would wait for the possible appearance of Mrs. B., whose large goiterous eyes seemed to bulge wearily with mischief, who always looked tired and cynical, and who wore thin chiffon dresses that affected us much more than she seemed to realize. Mrs. B. often went about the corridors in the company of a trim little teacher of mathematics who was a head shorter than she and had a mustache. Her chiffon dresses billowed around him like a sail; she seemed to have him in tow. It was understood by us as a matter of course that she wore those dresses to inflame us; that she *was* tired and cynical, from much practice in obscene lovemaking; that she was a "bad one" like the young Polish blondes from East New York I occasionally saw in the "Coney Island" dives sitting on someone's lap and smoking a cigarette. How wonderful and unbelievable it was to find this in a teacher; to realize that the two of them, after we had left the school, probably met to rub up against each other in the faculty toilet. Sex was a grim test where sooner or later you would have to prove yourself doing things to women. In the smell of chalk and sweat and the unending smirky babble of the water as it came to me on the staircase through my summer's dream of old Germany, I could feel myself being called to still another duty—to conquer Mrs. B., to rise to the challenge she had whispered to us in her slyness. I had seen pictures of it on the block—they were always passing them around between handball games—the man's face furious, ecstatic with lewdness as he proudly looked down at himself; the woman sniggering as she teased him with droplets from the contraceptive someone had just shown me in the gutter—its crushed, filmy slyness the very sign of the forbidden.   (14)

They had never said anything about this at home, and I thought I knew why. Sex was the opposite of books, of pictures, of music, of the open air, even of kindness. They would not let you have both. Something always lingered to the sound of those toilets to test you. In and out of the class-room they were always testing you. *Come on, Army! Come on, Navy!* As I stood up in that school courtyard and smelled again the familiar sweat, heard again the unending babble from the open toilets, I suddenly re-membered how sure I had always been that even my failures in there would be entered in a white, thinly ruled, official record book.   (15)

Sherwood Anderson

(1876–1941)

ANDERSON devoted his literary career to the analysis of the frustrations and sterile lives of white Americans. His best known book, and the one that first brought him national attention, Winesburg, Ohio *(1919), contains a preface ("The Book of the Grotesque") which gives a clue to his outlook: "It was the truths that made the people grotesque . . . The moment one of the people took one of the truths to himself, called it his truth, and tried to live his life by it, he became a grotesque and the truth he embraced became falsehood." Other identifying titles are* The Triumph of the Egg *(1921),* Dark Laughter *(1925), and* Death in the Woods *(1933).*

◼ *Discovery of a Father*

YOU HEAR IT said that fathers want their sons to be what they feel they cannot themselves be, but I tell you it also works the other way. A boy wants something very special from his father. I know that as a small boy I wanted my father to be a certain thing he was not. I wanted him to be a proud,

silent, dignified father. When I was with other boys and he passed along the
street, I wanted to feel a flow of pride. "There he is. That is my father." (1)

But he wasn't such a one. He couldn't be. It seemed to me then that
he was always showing off. Let's say someone in our town had got up a
show. They were always doing it. The druggist would be in it, the shoe-
store clerk, the horse doctor, and a lot of women and girls. My father would
manage to get the chief comedy part. It was, let's say, a Civil War play
and he was a comic Irish soldier. He had to do the most absurd things.
They thought he was funny, but I didn't.   (2)

I thought he was terrible. I didn't see how mother could stand it. She
even laughed with the others. Maybe I would have laughed if it hadn't
been my father.   (3)

Or there was a parade, the Fourth of July or Decoration Day. He'd be
in that, too, right at the front of it, as Grand Marshal or something, on a
white horse hired from a livery stable.   (4)

He couldn't ride for shucks. He fell off the horse and everyone hooted
with laughter, but he didn't care. He even seemed to like it. I remember
once when he had done something ridiculous, and right out on Main Street,
too. I was with some other boys and they were laughing and shouting at
him and he was shouting back and having as good a time as they were.
I ran down an alley back of some stores and there in the Presbyterian
Church sheds I had a good long cry.   (5)

Or I would be in bed at night and father would come home a little lit
up and bring some men with him. He was a man who was never alone.
Before he went broke, running a harness shop, there were always a lot of
men loafing in the shop. He went broke, of course, because he gave too much
credit. He couldn't refuse it and I thought he was a fool. I had got to
hating him.   (6)

There'd be men I didn't think would want to be fooling around with
him. There might even be the superintendent of our schools and a quiet
man who ran the hardware store. Once I remember there was a white-
haired man who was a cashier of the bank. It was a wonder to me
they'd want to be seen with such a windbag. That's what I thought he was.
I know now what it was that attracted them. It was because life in our
town, as in all small towns, was at times pretty dull and he livened it up.
He made them laugh. He could tell stories. He'd even get them to singing. (7)

If they didn't come to our house they'd go off, say at night, to where
there was a grassy place by a creek. They'd cook food there and drink beer
and sit about listening to his stories.   (8)

He was always telling stories about himself. He'd say this or that wonderful thing had happened to him. It might be something that made him
look like a fool. He didn't care.   (9)

If an Irishman came to our house, right away father would say he was

Irish. He'd tell what county in Ireland he was born in. He'd tell things that happened there when he was a boy. He'd make it seem so real that, if I hadn't known he was born in southern Ohio, I'd have believed him myself.   (10)

If it was a Scotchman the same thing happened. He'd get a burr into his speech. Or he was a German or a Swede. He'd be anything the other man was. I think they all knew he was lying, but they seemed to like him just the same. As a boy that was what I couldn't understand.   (11)

And there was mother. How could she stand it? I wanted to ask but never did. She was not the kind you asked such questions.   (12)

I'd be upstairs in my bed, in my room above the porch, and father would be telling some of his tales. A lot of father's stories were about the Civil War. To hear him tell it he'd been in about every battle. He'd known Grant, Sherman, Sheridan and I don't know how many others. He'd been particularly intimate with General Grant so that when Grant went East to take charge of all the armies, he took father along.   (13)

"I was an orderly at headquarters and Sim Grant said to me, 'Irve,' he said, "I'm going to take you along with me.'"   (14)

It seems he and Grant used to slip off sometimes and have a quiet drink together. That's what my father said. He'd tell about the day Lee surrendered and how, when the great moment came, they couldn't find Grant.   (15)

"You know," my father said, "about General Grant's book, his memoirs. You've read of how he said he had a headache and how, when he got word that Lee was ready to call it quits, he was suddenly and miraculously cured.
(16)

"Huh," said father. "He was in the woods with me.   (17)

"I was in there with my back against a tree. I was pretty well corned. I had got hold of a bottle of pretty good stuff.   (18)

"They were looking for Grant. He had got off his horse and come into the woods. He found me. He was covered with mud.   (19)

"I had the bottle in my hand. What'd I care? The war was over. I knew we had them licked."   (20)

My father said that he was the one who told Grant about Lee. An orderly riding by had told him, because the orderly knew how thick he was with Grant. Grant was embarrassed.   (21)

"But, Irve, look at me. I'm all covered with mud," he said to father.   (22)

And then, my father said, he and Grant decided to have a drink together. They took a couple of shots and then, because he didn't want Grant to show up potted before the immaculate Lee, he smashed the bottle against the tree.   (23)

"Sim Grant's dead now and I wouldn't want it to get out on him," my father said.   (24)

That's just one of the kind of things he'd tell. Of course the men knew he was lying, but they seemed to like it just the same. (25)

When we got broke, down and out, do you think he ever brought anything home? Not he. If there wasn't anything to eat in the house, he'd go off visiting around at farmhouses. They all wanted him. Sometimes he'd stay away for weeks, mother working to keep us fed, and then home he'd come bringing, let's say, a ham. He'd got it from some farmer friend. He'd slap it on the table in the kitchen. "You bet I'm going to see that my kids have something to eat," he'd say, and mother would just stand smiling at him. She'd never say a word about all the weeks and months he'd been away, not leaving us a cent for food. Once I heard her speaking to a woman in our street. Maybe the woman had dared to sympathize with her. "Oh," she said, "it's all right. He isn't ever dull like most of the men in this street. Life is never dull when my man is about." (26)

But often I was filled with bitterness, and sometimes I wished he wasn't my father. I'd even invent another man as my father. To protect my mother I'd make up stories of a secret marriage that for some strange reason never got known. As though some man, say the president of a railroad company or maybe a Congressman, had married my mother, thinking his wife was dead and then it turned out she wasn't. (27)

So they had to hush it up but I got born just the same. I wasn't really the son of my father. Somewhere in the world there was a very dignified, quite wonderful man who was really my father. I even made myself half believe these fancies. (28)

And then there came a certain night. He'd been off somewhere for two or three weeks. He found me alone in the house, reading by the kitchen table. (29)

It had been raining and he was very wet. He sat and looked at me for a long time, not saying a word. I was startled, for there was on his face the saddest look I had ever seen. He sat for a time, his clothes dripping. Then he got up. (30)

"Come on with me," he said. (31)

I got up and went with him out of the house. I was filled with wonder but I wasn't afraid. We went along a dirt road that led down into a valley, about a mile out of town, where there was a pond. We walked in silence. The man who was always talking had stopped his talking. (32)

I didn't know what was up and had the queer feeling that I was with a stranger. I don't know whether my father intended it so. I don't think he did. (33)

The pond was quite large. It was still raining hard and there were flashes of lightning followed by thunder. We were on a grassy bank at the pond's edge when my father spoke, and in the darkness and rain his voice sounded strange. (34)

"Take off your clothes," he said. Still filled with wonder, I began to undress. There was a flash of lightning and I saw that he was already naked. (35)

Naked, we went into the pond. Taking my hand he pulled me in. It may be that I was too frightened, too full of a feeling of strangeness, to speak. Before that night my father had never seemed to pay any attention to me. (36)

"And what is he up to now?" I kept asking myself. I did not swim very well, but he put my hand on his shoulder and struck out into the darkness. (37)

He was a man with big shoulders, a powerful swimmer. In the darkness I could feel the movement of his muscles. We swam to the far edge of the pond and then back to where we had left our clothes. The rain continued and the wind blew. Sometimes my father swam on his back and when he did he took my hand in his large powerful one and moved it over so that it rested always on his shoulder. Sometimes there would be a flash of lightning and I could see his face quite clearly. (38)

It was as it was earlier, in the kitchen, a face filled with sadness. There would be the momentary glimpse of his face and then again the darkness, the wind and the rain. In me there was a feeling I had never known before. (39)

It was a feeling of closeness. It was something strange. It was as though there were only we two in the world. It was as though I had been jerked suddenly out of myself, out of my world of the schoolboy, out of a world in which I was ashamed of my father. (40)

He had become blood of my blood; he the strong swimmer and I the boy clinging to him in the darkness. We swam in silence and in silence we dressed in our wet clothes, and went home. (41)

There was a lamp lighted in the kitchen and when we came in, the water dripping from us, there was my mother. She smiled at us. I remember that she called us "boys." (42)

"What have you boys been up to?" she asked, but my father did not answer. As he had begun the evening's experience with me in silence, so he ended it. He turned and looked at me. Then he went, I thought, with a new and strange dignity out of the room. (43)

I climbed the stairs to my own room, undressed in the darkness and got into bed. I couldn't sleep and did not want to sleep. For the first time I knew that I was the son of my father. He was a story teller as I was to be. It may be that I even laughed a little softly there in the darkness. If I did, I laughed knowing that I would never again be wanting another father. (44)

James Agee

(1909–1955)

AGEE was a gifted writer who failed to find the completely adequate vehicle for the exposure of his talents. His best known work was A Death in the Family *(1957); otherwise, he served on the staffs of* Fortune, Time, *and the* Nation *and wrote, variously, commentary, dialogue, and adaptations for the films (* The Quiet One, Face to Face, The African Queen*) and for television (the life of Abraham Lincoln for the Ford Foundation's "Omnibus" program). He also published a youthful volume of verse,* Permit Me Voyage *(1934), and a short novel,* The Morning Watch *(1951).*

■ *A Letter to Father Flye*

[Cambridge, Mass.]
November 19th, 1930

DEAR FATHER FLYE:

Last summer, and more this fall, I've thought of you often, and wished I could see you, and intended to write you. Until now I haven't even begun and lost a letter to you—as I did several times last spring. I'd like to make this a long letter, and a good one; but as is usual these days I feel fairly tongue-tied the minute I have a sheet of paper before me. If I could see you for any decent length of time, I'd without effort say what here I can't write. But I haven't seen you or even written you in a very long time—and would like if possible to give some sort of account of myself in the interim. That's a difficult job for me, and I don't know just how to go about it.   (1)

I suppose the two chief things that have happened to me, and that after a fashion include the others, have to do with what I want to do with my life, and with the nasty process of growing up, or developing, or whatever it may best be called.   (2)

So far as I can tell, I definitely want to write—probably poetry in the main. At any rate, nothing else holds me in the same way. As you know, I had two other interests just as strong a few years ago—music and directing movies of my own authorship. These have slowly been killed off, partly by brute and voluntary force on my part, chiefly by the overcrowding of my wish to write. Each of them occasionally flares up; last spring I was all but ready to quit college and bum to California and trust to luck for the rest. And more often, I feel I'd give anything to have forgotten everything but music, because I want so to compose. I really think I could have done it—possibly better than writing. I suppose a native inertia has as much to do with my keeping on with writing instead, as has an instinct (which I over-credit) for knowing that writing is my one even moderate talent. (3)

Up to 6 or 8 months ago, I took this with only sporadic seriousness. But as I read more and wrote somewhat more carefully, it took hold of me more. Last spring I finished a fairly longish poem that finally finished the business. For one thing, I worked harder on it than ever before. And, when it was finished, various people thought it was very good, and encouraged me a good deal. I don't know what I think of the poem itself—but I'm from now on committed to writing with a horrible definiteness. (4)

In fact it amounts to a rather unhealthy obsession. I'm thinking about it every waking minute, in one way or another; and my head is spinning and often—as now—dull with the continuous overwork. The sad part of it —but necessary—is that, most of the time, I'm absorbed in no tangible subject that can be thought through and put aside. The thing I'm trying hardest to do is, to decide what I want to write, and in exactly what way. After a fashion, I know, but it will take a lot more time before I'm able to do it. The great trouble is, I'm terribly anxious to do as well as I possibly can. It sounds conceited; whether it is or not: I'd do anything on earth to become a really great writer. That's as sincere a thing as I've ever said. Do you see, though, where it leads me? In the first place I have no faith to speak of in my native ability to become more than a very minor writer. My intellectual pelvic girdle simply is not Miltonically wide. So, I have, pretty much, to keep same on a stretcher, or more properly a rack, day and night. I've got to make my mind as broad and deep and rich as possible, as quick and fluent as possible; abnormally sympathetic and yet perfectly balanced. At the same time, I've got to strengthen those segments of my talent which are naturally weak; and must work out for myself a way of expressing what I want to write. You see, I should like to parallel, foolish as it sounds, what Shakespeare did. That is, in general—to write primarily about people —giving their emotions and dramas the expression that, because of its beauty and power, will be most likely to last. But—worse than that: I'd like, in a sense, to combine what Chekhov did with what Shakespeare did —that is, to move from the dim, rather eventless beauty of C. to huge geometric plots such as Lear. And to make this transition without its seeming ridiculous. And to do the whole so that it flows naturally, and yet, so that the whole—words, emotion, characters, situation, etc.—has a discernible symmetry and a very definite *musical* quality—inaccurately speaking—I want to *write symphonies*. That is, character introduced quietly (as are themes in a symphony, say) will recur in new lights, with new verbal orchestration, will work into counterpoint and get a sort of monstrous grinding beauty—and so on. By now you probably see what I mean at least as well as I do.   (5)

Well—this can't be done to best advantage in a novel. Prose holds you down from the possibility of such music. And put into poetic drama, it would certainly be stillborn or worse; besides, much of what I want to get can't well be expressed in dialogue. It's got to be narrative poetry, but of a sort that so far as I know has never been tried. In the sort I've read, the medium is too stiff to allow you to get exactly a finely shaded atmosphere, for instance—in brief, to get the effects that *can* be got in a short story or novel. I've thought of inventing a sort of amphibious style—prose that would run into poetry when the occasion demanded poetic expression. That may be the solution; but I don't entirely like the idea. What I want to do is, to devise a poetic diction that will cover the whole range of events as perfectly and evenly as skin covers every organ, vital as well as trivial, of the human body. And this style can't, of course, be incongruous, no matter what I'm writing about. For instance, I'm quite determined to include comedy in it—of a sort that would demand realistic slangy dialogue and description.   (6)

That leads to another thing—the use of words in general. I'm very anxious not to fall into archaism or "literary" diction. I want my vocabulary to have a very large range, but the words *must* be alive.   (7)

Well, that's one thing that keeps me busy: you can see what it leads to. For instance, what sort of characters to use? I want them to be of the present day—at least superficially. Well, present-day characters are obviously good for novels, but not so obviously material for high poetry. Further, just how shall they speak? At the climaxes they certainly can't speak realistically: and in the calmer stretches it would be just as silly for them to speak idealized blank verse.   (8)

Life is too short to try to go further into details about this. But it's part of what serves to keep me busy; and unhappy. The whole thing still seems just within the bounds of possible achievement; but highly improbable. There are too many other things crowding in to ruin it: the whole course of everyday life. And yet, of course, it's absolutely necessary for me to live as easily and calmly and fully as I can; and to be and feel human rather than coldblooded about the whole thing. It's only too easy, I find, to be "Human." I care as much as I ever did about other people's feelings, and worry much more when I hurt them. Of course I should be and am thankful for this, but it certainly helps complicate matters. For one thing, with most of my best friends, I feel rather dumb. I don't like to be unhappy or introspective to any noticeable extent in their presence; the result is that I'm pretty dull. Also, most of them are graduated or otherwise removed from the neighborhood, so that I'm pretty awfully lonely a good deal of the time. I'm too preoccupied with the whole business sketched in above to give my courses constant or thorough attention; I don't do much actual work; yet I feel exhausted most of the time. There are a few ways of relaxing, to a certain extent; I like to walk—especially at night; but frequently am too tired. I love to listen to music; but that involves being parasitic around music stores, or cutting classes to get rush seat at Friday symphony. At times, I like to play the piano. Just now, I'm cracked about it, having got a lovely thing by Cesar Franck: Prelude, Fugue and Variation. I played it for three hours tonight. I've been to half-a-dozen movies, one play, and three concerts. Once a week or so Franklin Miner comes in from the suburbs and we take a walk and eat together. I see a young tutor named Ted Spencer when I can . . .   (9)

I've got to stop, and get to bed soon. This isn't as full a letter as I'd like to have written, but I'm deadly tired. I hope you'll write soon—and I shall, too. Will you tell me about any further plans for your school? And about yourself and Mrs. Flye? I wish I could see you both again. Are you by any chance coming north this Christmas? Maybe I could see you then. I hope you are.   (10)

Much love to you both,   (11)

Rufus.

Thomas Merton

(1915–   )

MERTON, now known as Father Louis, is a Trappist monk at the Abbey of Our Lady of Gethsemani, Trappist, Kentucky. He was born in France and educated in England and the United States, taking his B.A. and M.A.

degrees from Columbia University. His autobiography, Seven Story Mountain, *was the literary sensation of 1948–1949. He is the author of more than two dozen volumes of prose and poetry.*

◼ *God's Will at Columbia*

Now I COME to speak of the real part Columbia seems to have been destined to play in my life in the providential designs of God. Poor Columbia! It was founded by sincere Protestants as a college predominantly religious. The only thing that remains of that is the university motto: *In lumine tuo videbimus lumen*—one of the deepest and most beautiful lines of the psalms. "In Thy light, we shall see light." It is, precisely, about grace. It is a line that might serve as the foundation stone of all Christian and Scholastic learning, and which simply has nothing whatever to do with the standards of education at modern Columbia. It might profitably be changed to *In lumine Randall videbimus Dewey.*   (1)

Yet, strangely enough, it was on this big factory of a campus that the Holy Ghost was waiting to show me the light, in His own light. And one of the chief means He used, and through which He operated, was human friendship.   (2)

God has willed that we should all depend on one another for our salvation, and all strive together for our own mutual good and our own common salvation. Scripture teaches us that this is especially true in the supernatural order, in the doctrine of the Mystical Body of Christ, which flows necessarily from Christian teaching on grace.   (3)

"You are the body of Christ and members one of another. . . . And the eye cannot say to the hand: I need not thy help: nor again the head to the feet, I have no need of you. . . . And if one member suffer anything, all the members suffer with it; and if one member glory all the others rejoice with it."   (4)

So now is the time to tell a thing that I could not realize then, but which has become very clear to me: that God brought me and a half a dozen others together at Columbia, and made us friends, in such a way that our friendship would work powerfully to rescue us from the confusion and the misery in which we had come to find ourselves, partly through our own fault, and partly through a complex set of circumstances which might be grouped together under the heading of the "modern world," "modern society." But the qualification "modern" is unnecessary and perhaps unfair. The traditional Gospel term, "the world," will do well enough.   (5)

All our salvation begins on the level of common and natural and ordinary things. (That is why the whole economy of the Sacraments, for instance, rests, in its material element, upon plain and ordinary things like bread and wine and water and salt and oil) And so it was with me. Books and ideas and poems and stories, pictures and music, buildings, cities, places, philosophies were to be the materials on which grace would work. But these things are themselves not enough. The more fundamental instinct of fear for my own preservation came in, in a minor sort of a way, in this strange, half-imaginary sickness which nobody could diagnose completely.   (6)

The coming war, and all the uncertainties and confusions and fears that followed necessarily from that, and all the rest of the violence and injustice that were in the world, had a very important part to play. All these things were bound together and fused and vitalized and prepared for the action of grace, both in my own soul and in the souls of at least one or two of my friends, merely by our friendship and association together. And it fermented in our sharing of our own ideas and miseries and headaches and perplexities and fears and difficulties and desires and hangovers and all the rest.   (7)

I have already mentioned Mark Van Doren. It would not be exactly true to say that he was a kind of nucleus around whom this concretion of friends formed itself: that would not be accurate. Not all of us took his courses, and those who did, did not do so all at the same time. And yet nevertheless our common respect for Mark's sanity and wisdom did much to make us aware of how much we ourselves had in common.   (8)

Perhaps it was for me, personally, more than for the others, that Mark's course worked in this way. I am thinking of one particular incident.   (9)

It was the fall of 1936, just at the beginning of the new school year—on one of those first, bright, crazy days when everybody is full of ambition. It was the beginning of the year in which Pop was going to die and my own resistance would cave in under the load of pleasures and ambitions I was too weak to carry: the year in which I would be all the time getting dizzy, and in which I learned to fear the Long Island railroad as if it were some kind of a monster, and to shrink from New York as if it were the wide-open mouth of some burning Aztec god.   (10)

That day, I did not foresee any of this. My veins were still bursting with the materialistic and political enthusiasms with which I had first come to Columbia and, indeed, in line with their general direction, I had signed up for courses that were more or less sociological and economic and historical. In the obscurity of the strange, half-conscious semi-conversion that had attended my retreat from Cambridge, I had tended more and more to be suspicious of literature, poetry—the things towards which my nature drew me—on the grounds that they might lead to a sort of futile estheticism, a philosophy of "escape."   (11)

This had not involved me in any depreciation of people like Mark. However, it had just seemed more important to me that I should take some history course, rather than anything that was still left of his for me to take. (12)

So now I was climbing one of the crowded stairways in Hamilton Hall to the room where I thought this history course was to be given. I looked into the room. The second row was filled with the unbrushed heads of those who every day at noon sat in the *Jester* editorial offices and threw paper airplanes around the room or drew pictures on the walls.   (13)

Taller than them all, and more serious, with a long face, like a horse, and a great mane of black hair on top of it, Bob Lax meditated on some incomprehensible woe, and waited for someone to come in and begin to talk to them. It was when I had taken off my coat and put down my load of books that I found out that this was not the class I was supposed to be taking, but Van Doren's course on Shakespeare.   (14)

So I got up to go out. But when I got to the door I turned around again and went back and sat down where I had been, and stayed there. Later I went and changed everything with the registrar, so I remained in that class for the rest of the year.   (15)

It was the best course I ever had at college. And it did me the most good, in many different ways. It was the only place where I ever heard anything really sensible said about any of the things that were really fundamental—life, death, time, love, sorrow, fear, wisdom, suffering, eternity. A course in literature should never be a course in economics or philosophy or sociology or psychology: and I have explained how it was one of Mark's great virtues that he did not make it so. Nevertheless, the material of literature and especially of drama is chiefly human acts—that is, free acts, moral acts. And, as a matter of fact, literature, drama, poetry, make certain statements about these acts that can be made in no other way. That is precisely why you will miss all the deepest meaning of Shakespeare, Dante, and the rest if you reduce their vital and creative statements about life and men to the dry, matter-of-fact terms of history, or ethics, or some other science. They belong to a different order.   (16)

Nevertheless, the great power of something like *Hamlet, Coriolanus,* or the *Purgatorio* or Donne's *Holy Sonnets* lies precisely in the fact that they are a kind of commentary on ethics and psychology and even metaphysics, even theology. Or, sometimes, it is the other way 'round, and those sciences can serve as a commentary on these other realities, which we call plays, poems.   (17)

All that year we were, in fact, talking about the deepest springs of human desire and hope and fear; we were considering all the most important realities, not indeed in terms of something alien to Shakespeare and to poetry, but precisely in his own terms, with occasional intuitions of another order. And, as I have said, Mark's balanced and sensitive and clear way of seeing things, at once simple and yet capable of subtlety, being fundamentally scholastic, though not necessarily and explicitly Christian, presented these things in ways that made them live within us, and with a life that was healthy and permanent and productive. This class was one of the few things that could persuade me to get on the train and go to Columbia at all. It was, that year, my only health, until I came across and read the Gilson book. (18)

It was this year, too, that I began to discover who Bob Lax was, and that in him was a combination of Mark's clarity and my confusion and misery—and a lot more besides that was his own. (19)

To name Robert Lax in another way, he was a kind of combination of Hamlet and Elias. A potential prophet, but without rage. A king, but a Jew too. A mind full of tremendous and subtle intuitions, and every day he found less and less to say about them, and resigned himself to being inarticulate. In his hesitations, though without embarrassment or nervousness at all, he would often curl his long legs all around a chair, in seven different ways, while he was trying to find a word with which to begin. He talked best sitting on the floor. (20)

And the secret of his constant solidity I think has always been a kind of natural, instinctive spirituality, a kind of inborn direction to the living God. Lax has always been afraid he was in a blind alley, and half aware that, after all, it might not be a blind alley, but God, infinity. (21)

He had a mind naturally disposed, from the very cradle, to a kind of affinity for Job and St. John of the Cross. And I now know that he was born so much of a contemplative that he will probably never be able to find out how much. (22)

To sum it up, even the people who have always thought he was "too impractical" have always tended to venerate him—in the way people who value material security unconsciously venerate people who do not fear insecurity. (23)

In those days one of the things we had most in common, although perhaps we did not talk about it so much, was the abyss that walked around in front of our feet everywhere we went, and kept making us dizzy and afraid of trains and high buildings. For some reason, Lax developed an implicit trust in all my notions about what was good and bad for mental and physical health, perhaps because I was always very definite in my likes and dislikes. I am afraid it did not do him too much good, though. For even though I had my imaginary abyss, which broadened immeasurably and became ten times dizzier when I had a hangover, my ideas often tended to some particular place where we would hear this particular band and drink this special drink until the place folded up at four o'clock in the morning. (24)

The months passed by, and most of the time I sat in Douglaston, drawing cartoons for the paper-cup business, and trying to do all the other things I was supposed to do. In the summer, Lax went to Europe, and I continued to sit in Douglaston, writing a long stupid novel about a college football player who got mixed up in a lot of strikes in a textile mill.   (25)

I did not graduate that June, although I nominally belonged to that year's class: I had still one or two courses to take, on account of having entered Columbia in February. In the fall of 1937 I went back to school, then, with my mind a lot freer, since I was not burdened with any more of those ugly and useless jobs on the fourth floor. I could write and do the drawings I felt like doing for *Jester*.   (26)

I began to talk more to Lax and to Ed Rice who was now drawing better and funnier pictures than anybody else for the magazine. For the first time I saw Sy Freedgood, who was full of a fierce and complex intellectuality which he sometimes liked to present in the guise of a rather suspicious suavity. He was in love with a far more technical vocabulary than any of the rest of us possessed, and was working at something in the philosophy graduate school. Seymour used consciously to affect a whole set of different kinds of duplicity, of which he was proud, and he had carried the *mendacium jocosum* or "humorous lie" to its utmost extension and frequency. You could sometimes gauge the falsity of his answers by their promptitude: the quicker the falser. The reason for this was, probably, that he was thinking of something else, something very abstruse and far from the sphere of your question, and he could not be bothered to bring his mind all that way back, to think up the real answer.   (27)

For Lax and myself and Gibney there was no inconvenience about this, for two reasons. Since Seymour generally gave his false answers only to practical questions of fact, their falsity did not matter: we were all too impractical. Besides his false answers were generally more interesting than the truth. Finally, since we knew they were false anyway, we had the habit of seeing all his statements, in the common factual order by a kind of double standard, instituting a comparison between what he had said and the probable truth, and this cast many interesting and ironical lights upon life as a whole.   (28)

In his house at Long Beach, where his whole family lived in a state of turmoil and confusion, there was a large, stupid police dog that got in everybody's way with his bowed head and slapped-down ears and amiable, guilty look. The first time I saw the dog, I asked: "What's his name?" (29)

"Prince," said Seymour, out of the corner of his mouth.   (30)

It was a name to which the beast responded gladly. I guess he responded to any name, didn't care what you called him, so flattered was he to be called at all, being as he knew an extremely stupid dog.   (31)

So I was out on the boardwalk with the dog, shouting: "Hey, Prince; hey, Prince!"   (32)

Seymour's wife, Helen, came along and heard me shouting all this and said nothing, imagining, no doubt, that it was some way I had of making fun of the brute. Later, Seymour or someone told me that "Prince" wasn't the dog's name, but they told me in such a way that I got the idea that his name was really "Rex." So for some time after that I called him: "Hey, Rex; hey, Rex!" Several months later, after many visits to the house, I finally learned that the dog was called nothing like Prince nor Rex, but "Bunky." (33)

Moral theologians say that the *mendacium jocosum* in itself does not exceed a venial sin. (34)

Seymour and Lax were rooming together in one of the dormitories, for Bob Gibney, with whom Lax had roomed the year before, had now graduated, and was sitting in Port Washington with much the same dispositions with which I had been sitting in Douglaston, facing a not too dissimilar blank wall, the end of his own blind-alley. He occasionally came in to town to see Dona Eaton who had a place on 112th Street, but no job, and was more cheerful about her own quandary than the rest of us, because the worst that could happen to her was that she would at last run completely out of money and have to go home to Panama. (35)

Gibney was not what you would call pious. In fact, he had an attitude that would be commonly called impious, only I believe God understood well enough that his violence and sarcasms covered a sense of deep metaphysical dismay—an anguish that was real, though not humble enough to be of much use to his soul. What was materially impiety in him was directed more against common ideas and notions which he saw or considered to be totally inadequate, and maybe it subjectively represented a kind of oblique zeal for the purity of God, this rebellion against the commonplace and trite, against mediocrity, religiosity. (36)

During the year that had passed, I suppose it must have been in the spring of 1937, both Gibney and Lax and Bob Gerdy had all been talking about becoming Catholics. Bob Gerdy was a very smart sophomore with the face of a child and a lot of curly hair on top of it, who took life seriously, and had discovered courses on Scholastic Philosophy in the graduate school, and had taken one of them. (37)

Gibney was interested in Scholastic Philosophy in much the same way as James Joyce was—he respected its intellectuality, particularly that of the Thomists, but there was not enough that was affective about his interest to bring about any kind of a conversion. (38)

For the three or four years that I knew Gibney, he was always holding out for some kind of a "sign," some kind of a sensible and tangible interior jolt from God, to get him started, some mystical experience or other. And while he waited and waited for this to come along, he did all the things that normally exclude and nullify the action of grace. So in those days, none of them became Catholics. (39)

The most serious of them all, in this matter, was Lax: he was the one that had been born with the deepest sense of Who God was. But he would not make a move without the others.   (40)

And then there was myself. Having read *The Spirit of Medieval Philosophy* and having discovered that the Catholic conception of God was something tremendously solid, I had not progressed one step beyond this recognition, except that one day I had gone and looked up St. Bernard's *De Diligendo Deo* in the catalogue of the University Library. It was one of the books Gilson had frequently mentioned: but when I found that there was no good copy of it, except in Latin, I did not take it out.   (41)

Now it was November 1937. One day, Lax and I were riding downtown on one of those busses you caught at the corner of 110th Street and Broadway. We had skirted the southern edge of Harlem, passing along the top of Central Park, and the dirty lake full of rowboats. Now we were going down Fifth Avenue, under the trees. Lax was telling me about a book he had been reading, which was Aldous Huxley's *Ends and Means*. He told me about it in a way that made me want to read it too.   (42)

So I went to Scribner's bookstore and bought it, and read it, and wrote an article about it, and gave the article to Barry Ulanov who was editor of *Review* by that time. He accepted the article with a big Greek smile and printed it. The smile was on account of the conversion it represented, I mean the conversion in me, as well as in Huxley, although one of the points I tried to make was that perhaps Huxley's conversion should not have been taken as so much of a surprise.   (43)

Huxley had been one of my favorite novelists in the days when I had been sixteen and seventeen and had built up a strange, ignorant philosophy of pleasure based on all the stories I was reading. And now everybody was talking about the way Huxley had changed. The chatter was all the more pleasant because of Huxley's agnostic old grandfather—and his biologist brother. Now the man was preaching mysticism.   (44)

Huxley was too sharp and intelligent and had too much sense of humor to take any of the missteps that usually make such conversions look ridiculous and oafish. You could not laugh at him, very well—at least not for any one concrete blunder. This was not one of those Oxford Group conversions, complete with a public confession.   (45)

On the contrary, he had read widely and deeply and intelligently in all kinds of Christian and Oriental mystical literature, and had come out with the astonishing truth that all this, far from being a mixture of dreams and magic and charlatanism, was very real and very serious.   (46)

Not only was there such a thing as a supernatural order, but as a matter of concrete experience, it was accessible, very close at hand, an extremely near, an immediate and most necessary source of moral vitality, and one

which could be reached most simply, most readily by prayer, faith, detachment, love. (47)

The point of his title was this: we cannot use evil means to attain a good
end. Huxley's chief argument was that we were using the means that precisely made good ends impossible to attain: war, violence, reprisals, rapac-
ity. And he traced our impossibility to use the proper means to the fact that
men were immersed in the material and animal urges of an element in their
nature which was blind and crude and unspiritual. (48)

The main problem is to fight our way free from subjection to this more
or less inferior element, and to reassert the dominance of our mind and
will: to vindicate for these faculties, for the spirit as a whole, the freedom
of action which it must necessarily have if we are to live like anything but
wild beasts, tearing each other to pieces. And the big conclusion from all
this was: we must practice prayer and asceticism. (49)

Asceticism! The very thought of such a thing was a complete revolution
in my mind. The word had so far stood for a kind of weird and ugly per-
version of nature, the masochism of men who had gone crazy in a warped
and unjust society. What an idea! To deny the desires of one's flesh, and
even to practice certain disciplines that punished and mortified those desires: until this day, these things had never succeeded in giving me anything but gooseflesh. But of course Huxley did not stress the physical angle
of mortification and asceticism—and that was right, in so far as he was more
interested in striking to the very heart of the matter, and showing the
ultimate positive principle underlying the need for detachment. (50)

He showed that this negation was not something absolute, sought for its
own sake: but that it was a freeing, a vindication of our real selves, a liberation of the spirit from limits and bonds that were intolerable, suicidal—
from a servitude to flesh that must ultimately destroy our whole nature and
society and the world as well. (51)

Not only that, once the spirit was freed, and returned to its own element, it was not alone there: it could find the absolute and perfect Spirit,
God. It could enter into union with Him: and what is more, this union was
not something vague and metaphorical, but it was a matter of real experience. What that experience amounted to, according to Huxley, might or
might not have been the nirvana of the Buddhists, which is the ultimate
negation of all experience and all reality whatever: but anyway, somewhere along the line, he quoted proofs that it was and could be a real and
positive experience. (52)

The speculative side of the book—its strongest—was full, no doubt, of
strange doctrines by reason of its very eclecticism. And the practical element, which was weak, inspired no confidence, especially when he tried to
talk about a concrete social program. Huxley seemed not to be at home

with the Christian term "Love" which sounded extraordinarily vague in his contexts—and which must nevertheless be the heart and life of all true mysticism. But out of it all I took these two big concepts of a supernatural, spiritual order, and the possibility of real, experimental contact with God.   (53)

Huxley was thought, by some people, to be on the point of entering the Church, but *Ends and Means* was written by a man who was not at ease with Catholicism. He quoted St. John of the Cross and St. Teresa of Avila indiscriminately with less orthodox Christian writers like Meister Eckhart: and on the whole he preferred the Orient. It seems to me that in discarding his family's tradition of materialism he had followed the old Protestant groove back into the heresies that make the material creation evil of itself, although I do not remember enough about him to accuse him of formally holding such a thing. Nevertheless, that would account for his sympathy for Buddhism, and for the nihilistic character which he preferred to give to his mysticism and even to his ethics. This also made him suspicious, as the Albigensians had been, and for the same reason, of the Sacraments and Liturgical life of the Church, and also of doctrines like the Incarnation.   (54)

With all that I was not concerned. My hatred of war and my own personal misery in my particular situation and the general crisis of the world made me accept with my whole heart this revelation of the need for a spiritual life, an interior life, including some kind of mortification. I was content to accept the latter truth purely as a matter of theory: or at least, to apply it most vociferously to one passion which was not strong in myself, and did not need to be mortified: that of anger, hatred, while neglecting the ones that really needed to be checked, like gluttony and lust.   (55)

But the most important effect of the book on me was to make me start ransacking the university library for books on Oriental mysticism.   (56)

I remember those winter days, at the end of 1937 and the beginning of 1938, peaceful days when I sat in the big living room at Douglaston, with the pale sun coming in the window by the piano, where one of my father's water-colors of Bermuda hung on the wall.   (57)

The house was very quiet, with Pop and Bonnemaman gone from it, and John Paul away trying to pass his courses at Cornell. I sat for hours, with the big quarto volumes of the Jesuit Father Wieger's French translations of hundreds of strange Oriental texts.   (58)

I have forgotten the titles, even the authors, and I never understood a word of what they said in the first place. I had the habit of reading fast, without stopping, or stopping only rarely to take a note, and all these mysteries would require a great deal of thought, even were a man who knew something about them to puzzle them out. And I was completely unfamiliar with anything of the kind. Consequently, the strange great jumble of myths and theories and moral aphorisms and elaborate parables made little or no real impression on my mind, except that I put the books down with the impression that mysticism was something very esoteric and complicated, and that we were all inside some huge Being in whom we were involved and out of whom we evolved, and the thing to do was to involve ourselves back in to him again by a system of elaborate disciplines subject more or less to the control of our own will. The Absolute Being was an infinite, timeless, peaceful, impersonal Nothing. (59)

The only practical thing I got out of it was a system for going to sleep, at night, when you couldn't sleep. You lay flat in bed, without a pillow, your arms at your sides and your legs straight out, and relaxed all your muscles, and you said to yourself: (60)

"Now I have no feet, now I have no feet . . . no feet . . . no legs . . . no knees." (61)

Sometimes it really worked: you did manage to make it feel as if your feet and legs and the rest of your body had changed into air and vanished away. The only section with which it almost never worked was my head: and if I had not fallen asleep before I got that far, when I tried to wipe out my head, instantly chest and stomach and legs and feet all came back to life with a most exasperating reality and I did not get to sleep for hours. Usually, however, I managed to get to sleep quite quickly by this trick. I suppose it was a variety of auto-suggestion, a kind of hypnotism, or else simply muscular relaxation, with the help of a little work on the part of an active fancy. (62)

Ultimately, I suppose all Oriental mysticism can be reduced to techniques that do the same thing, but in a far more subtle and advanced fashion: and if that is true, it is not mysticism at all. It remains purely in the natural order. That does not make it evil, *per se*, according to Christian standards: but it does not make it good, in relation to the supernatural. It is simply more or less useless, except when it is mixed up with elements that are strictly diabolical: and then of course these dreams and annihilations are designed to wipe out all vital moral activity, while leaving the personality in control of some nefarious principle, either of his own, or from outside himself. (63)

It was with all this in my mind that I went and received my diploma of Bachelor of Arts from one of the windows in the Registrar's office, and immediately afterwards put my name down for some courses in the Graduate School of English. (64)

The experience of the last year, with the sudden collapse of all my physical energy and the diminution of the brash vigor of my worldly ambitions, had meant that I had turned in terror from the idea of anything so active and uncertain as the newspaper business. This registration in the graduate school represented the first remote step of a retreat from the fight for money and fame, from the active and worldly life of conflict and competition. If anything, I would now be a teacher, and live the rest of my life in the relative peace of a college campus, reading and writing books. (65)

That the influence of the Huxley book had not, by any means, lifted me bodily out of the natural order overnight is evident from the fact that I decided to specialize in eighteenth century English Literature, and to choose my subject for a Master of Arts Thesis from somewhere in that century. As a matter of fact, I had already half decided upon a subject, by the time the last pile of dirty snow had melted from the borders of South Field. It was an unknown novelist of the second half of the eighteenth century called Richard Graves. The most important thing he wrote was a novel called the *Spiritual Quixote,* which was in the Fielding tradition, a satire on the more excited kind of Methodists and other sects of religious enthusiasts in England at that time. (66)

I was to work under Professor Tyndall, and this would have been just his kind of a subject. He was an agnostic and rationalist who took a deep and amused interest in all the strange perversions of the religious instinct that our world has seen in the last five hundred years. He was just finishing a book on D. H. Lawrence which discussed, not too kindly, Lawrence's attempt to build up a synthetic, home-made religion of his own out of all the semi-pagan spiritual jetsam that came his way. All Lawrence's friends were very much annoyed by it when it was published. I remember that in that year one of Tyndall's favorite topics of conversation was the miracles of Mother Cabrini, who had just been beatified. He was amused by these, too, because, as for all rationalists, it was for him an article of faith that miracles cannot happen. (67)

I remember with what indecision I went on into the spring, trying to settle the problem of a subject with finality. Yet the thing worked itself out quite suddenly: so suddenly that I do not remember what brought it about. One day I came running down out of the Carpenter Library, and passed along the wire fences by the tennis courts, in the sun, with my mind made up that there was only one possible man in the eighteenth century for me to work on: the one poet who had least to do with his age, and was most in opposition to everything it stood for. (68)

I had just had in my hands the small, neatly printed Nonesuch Press edition of the *Poems of William Blake,* and I now knew what my thesis would probably be. It would take in his poems and some aspect of his religious ideas. (69)

In the Columbia bookstore I bought the same edition of Blake, on credit. (I paid for it two years later.) It had a blue cover, and I suppose it is now hidden somewhere in our monastery library, the part to which nobody has access. And that is all right. I think the ordinary Trappist would be only

dangerously bewildered by the "Prophetic Books," and those who still might be able to profit by Blake, have a lot of other things to read that are still better. For my own part, I no longer need him. He has done his work for me: and he did it very thoroughly. I hope that I will see him in heaven.
(70)

But oh, what a thing it was to live in contact with the genius and the holiness of William Blake that year, that summer, writing the thesis! I had some beginning of an appreciation of his greatness above the other men of his time in England: but from this distance, from the hill where I now stand, looking back I can really appreciate his stature.   (71)

To assimilate him to the men of the ending eighteenth century would be absurd. I will not do it: all those conceited and wordy and stuffy little characters! As for the other romantics: how feeble and hysterical their inspirations seem next to the tremendously genuine and spiritual fire of William Blake. Even Coleridge, in the rare moments when his imagination struck the pitch of true creativeness, was still only an artist, an imaginer, not a seer; a maker, but not a prophet.   (72)

Perhaps all the great romantics were capable of putting words together more sensibly than Blake, and yet he, with all his mistakes of spelling, turned out the greater poet, because his was the deeper and more solid inspiration. He wrote better poetry when he was twelve than Shelley wrote in his whole life. And it was because at twelve he had already seen, I think, Elias, standing under a tree in the fields south of London.   (73)

It was Blake's problem to try and adjust himself to a society that understood neither him nor his kind of faith and love. More than once, smug and inferior minds conceived it to be their duty to take this man Blake in hand and direct and form him, to try and canalize what they recognized as "talent" in some kind of a conventional channel. And always this meant the cold and heartless disparagement of all that was vital and real to him in art and in faith. There were years of all kinds of petty persecution, from many different quarters, until finally Blake parted from his would-be patrons, and gave up all hope of an alliance with a world that thought he was crazy, and went his own way.   (74)

It was when he did this, and settled down as an engraver for good, that the Prophetic Books were no longer necessary. In the latter part of his life, having discovered Dante, he came in contact, through him, with Catholicism, which he described as the only religion that really taught the love of God, and his last years were relatively full of peace. He never seems to have felt any desire to hunt out a priest in the England where Catholicism was still practically outlawed: but he died with a blazing face and great songs of joy bursting from his heart.   (75)

As Blake worked himself into my system, I became more and more conscious of the necessity of a vital faith, and the total unreality and unsubstantiality of the dead, selfish rationalism which had been freezing my mind and will for the last seven years. By the time the summer was over, I was to become conscious of the fact that the only way to live was to live in a world that was charged with the presence and reality of God.   (76)

To say that, is to say a great deal: and I don't want to say it in a way that conveys more than the truth. I will have to limit the statement by saying that it was still, for me, more an intellectual realization than anything else: and it had not yet struck down into the roots of my will. The life of the soul is not knowledge, it is love, since love is the act of the supreme faculty, the will, by which man is formally united to the final end of all his strivings—by which man becomes one with God.   (77)

Carl Sandburg

(1878–1967)

SANDBURG began to win literary prizes in 1914; in 1950 he received the Pulitzer Prize for poetry; and in 1959 he addressed a joint session of Congress on the 150th anniversary of the birth of Abraham Lincoln. He was an indefatigable and unpretentious poet and student of the life of Abraham Lincoln—the symbolic voice of midwestern America.

■ *The Boyhood of Lincoln*

DURING THE YEAR 1817, little Abe Lincoln, eight years old, going on nine, had an ax put in his hands and helped his father cut down trees and notch logs for the corners of their new cabin, forty yards from the pole-shed where the family was cooking, eating, and sleeping.   (1)

Wild turkey, ruffed grouse, partridge, coon, rabbit, were to be had for the shooting of them. Before each shot Tom Lincoln took a rifle-ball out of a bag and held the ball in his left hand; then with his right hand holding the gunpowder horn he pulled the stopper with his teeth, slipped the powder into the barrel, followed with the ball; then he rammed the charge down the barrel with a hickory ramrod held in both hands, looked to his trigger, flint, and feather in the touch-hole—and he was ready to shoot—to kill for the home skillet. (2)

Having loaded his rifle just that way several thousand times in his life, he could do it in the dark or with his eyes shut. Once Abe took the gun as a flock of wild turkeys came toward the new log cabin, and, standing inside, shot through a crack and killed one of the big birds; and after that, somehow, he never felt like pulling the trigger on game-birds. A mile from the cabin was a salt lick where deer came; there the boy could have easily shot the animals, as they stood rubbing their tongues along the salty slabs or tasting of saltish ooze. His father did the shooting; the deer killed gave them meat for Nancy's skillet; and the skins were tanned, cut, and stitched into shirts, trousers, mitts, moccasins. They wore buckskin; their valley was called the Buckhorn Valley. (3)

After months the cabin stood up, four walls fitted together with a roof, a one-room house eighteen feet square, for a family to live in. A stick chimney plastered with clay ran up outside. The floor was packed and smoothed dirt. A log-fire lighted the inside; no windows were cut in the walls. For a door there was a hole cut to stoop through. Bedsteads were cleated to the corners of the cabin; pegs stuck in the side of a wall made a ladder for young Abe to climb up in a loft to sleep on a hump of dry leaves; rain and snow came through chinks of the roof onto his bearskin cover. A table and three-legged stools had the top sides smoothed with an ax, and the bark-side under, in the style called "puncheon." (4)

A few days of this year in which the cabin was building, Nancy told Abe to wash his face and hands extra clean; she combed his hair, held his face between her two hands, smacked him a kiss on the mouth, and sent him to school—nine miles and back—Abe and Sally hand in hand hiking eighteen miles a day. Tom Lincoln used to say Abe was going to have "a real eddication," explaining, "You air a-goin' to larn readin', writin', and cipherin'." (5)

He learned to spell words he didn't know the meaning of, spelling the words before he used them in sentences. In a list of "words of eight syllables accented upon the sixth," was the word "incomprehensibility." He learned that first, and then such sentences as "Is he to go in?" and "Ann can spin flax." (6)

Some neighbors said, "It's a pore make-out of a school," and Tom complained it was a waste of time to send the children nine miles just to sit with a lot of other children and read out loud all day in a "blab" school. But Nancy, as she cleaned Abe's ears in corners where he forgot to clean them, and as she combed out the tangles in his coarse, sandy black hair,

used to say, "Abe, you go to school now, and larn all you kin." And he
kissed her and said, "Yes, Mammy," and started with his sister on the nine-
mile walk through timberland where bear, deer, coon, and wildcats ran
wild.   (7)

Fall time came with its early frost and they were moved into the new
cabin, when horses and a wagon came breaking into the clearing one
day. It was Tom and Betsy Sparrow and their seventeen-year-old boy, Dennis Hanks, who had come from Hodgenville, Kentucky, to cook and sleep
in the pole-shed of the Lincoln family till they could locate land and settle.
Hardly a year had passed, however, when both Tom and Betsy Sparrow
were taken down with the "milk sick," beginning with a whitish coat on the
tongue. Both died and were buried in October on a little hill in a clearing
in the timbers near by.   (8)

Soon after, there came to Nancy Hanks Lincoln that white coating of the
tongue; her vitals burned; the tongue turned brownish; her feet and hands
grew cold and colder, her pulse slow and slower. She knew she was dying,
called for her children, and spoke to them her last choking words. Sarah
and Abe leaned over the bed. A bony hand of the struggling mother went
out, putting its fingers into the boy's sandy black hair; her fluttering gut-
tural words seemed to say he must grow up and be good to his sister and
father.   (9)

So, on a bed of poles cleated to the corner of the cabin, the body of
Nancy Hanks Lincoln lay, looking tired . . . tired . . . with a peace settling in
the pinched corners of the sweet, weary mouth, silence slowly etching away
the lines of pain and hunger drawn around the gray eyes where now the
eyelids closed down in the fine pathos of unbroken rest, a sleep without
interruption settling about the form of the stooped and wasted shoulder-
bones, looking to the children who tiptoed in, stood still, cried their tears
of want and longing, whispered "Mammy, Mammy," and heard only their
own whispers answering, looking to these little ones of her brood as though
new secrets had come to her in place of the old secrets given up with the
breath of life.   (10)

And Tom Lincoln took a log left over from the building of the cabin,
and he and Dennis Hanks whipsawed the log into planks, planed the planks
smooth, and made them of a measure for a box to bury the dead wife and
mother in. Little Abe, with a jackknife, whittled pine-wood pegs. And then,
while Dennis and Abe held the planks, Tom bored holes and stuck the
whittled pegs through the bored holes. This was the coffin, and they carried
it the next day to the same little timber clearing near by, where a few
weeks before they had buried Tom and Betsy Sparrow. It was in the way
of the deer-run leading to the saltish water; light feet and shy hoofs ran
over those early winter graves.   (11)

So the woman, Nancy Hanks, died, thirty-six years old, a pioneer sacrifice, with memories of monotonous, endless everyday chores, of mystic Bible verses read over and over for their promises, and with memories of blue wistful hills and a summer when the crab-apple blossoms flamed white and she carried a boy-child into the world.   (12)

She had looked out on fields of blue-blossoming flax and hummed "Hey, Betty Martin, tiptoe, tiptoe"; she had sung "Greenland's Icy Mountains" and seen the early frost leaf its crystals on the stalks of buttonweed and redbud; she had sung:

> You may bury me in the east,
> You may bury me in the west,
> And we'll all rise together in that morning.   (13)

Some weeks later, when David Elkin, elder of the Methodist church, was in that neighborhood, he was called on to speak over the grave of Nancy Hanks. He had been acquainted with her in Kentucky, and to the Lincoln family and a few neighbors he spoke of good things she had done, sweet ways she had of living her life in this Vale of Tears, and her faith in another life yonder past the River Jordan.   (14)

The "milk sick" took more people in that neighborhood the same year, and Tom Lincoln whipsawed planks for more coffins. One settler lost four milch cows and eleven calves. The nearest doctor for people or cattle was thirty-five miles away. The wilderness is careless.   (15)

Lonesome and dark months came for Abe and Sarah. Worst of all were the weeks after their father went away, promising to come back.   (16)

Elizabethtown, Kentucky, was the place Tom Lincoln headed for. As he footed it through the woods and across the Ohio River, he was saying over to himself a speech—the words he would say to Sarah Bush Johnston, down in Elizabethtown. Her husband had died a few years before, and she was now in Tom's thoughts.   (17)

He went straight to the house where she was living in Elizabethtown, and, speaking to her as "Miss Johnston," he argued: "I have no wife and you no husband. I came a-purpose to marry you. I knowed you from a gal and you knowed me from a boy. I've no time to lose; and if you're willin' let it be done straight off."   (18)

Her answer was, "I got debts." She gave him a list of the debts; he paid them; a license was issued; and they were married on December 2, 1819.
                                                                      (19)

He could write his name; she couldn't write hers. Trying to explain why the two of them took up with each other so quickly, Dennis Hanks at a later time said, "Tom had a kind o' way with women, an' maybe it was somethin' she took comfort in to have a man that didn't drink an' cuss none."   (20)

Little Abe and Sarah, living in the lonesome cabin on Little Pigeon Creek, Indiana, got a nice surprise one morning when four horses and a wagon came into their clearing, and their father jumped off, then Sarah Bush Lincoln, the new wife and mother, then John, Sarah, and Matilda Johnston, Sarah Bush's three children by her first husband. Next off the wagon came a feather mattress, feather pillows, a black walnut bureau, a large clothes-chest, a table, chairs, pots and skillets, knives, forks, spoons. (21)

Abe ran his fingers over the slick wood of the bureau, pushed his fist into the feather pillows, sat in the new chairs, and wondered to himself, because this was the first time he had touched such fine things, such soft slick things. (22)

"Here's your new mammy," his father told Abe as the boy looked up at a strong, large-boned, rosy woman, with a kindly face and eyes, with a steady voice, steady ways. The cheekbones of her face stood out and she had a strong jaw-bone; she was warm and friendly for Abe's little hands to touch, right from the beginning. As one of her big hands held his head against her skirt he felt like a cold chick warming under the soft feathers of a big wing. She took the corn-husks Abe had been sleeping on, piled them in the yard and said they would be good for a pig-pen later on; and Abe sunk his head and bones that night in a feather pillow and a feather mattress. (23)

Ten years pass with that cabin on Little Pigeon Creek for a home, and that farm and neighborhood the soil for growth. There the boy Abe grows to be the young man, Abraham Lincoln. (24)

Ten years pass and the roots of a tree spread out finding water to carry up to branches and leaves that are in the sun; the trunk thickens, the forked limbs shine wider in the sun, they pray with their leaves in the rain and the whining wind; the tree arrives, the mystery of its coming, spreading, growing, a secret not even known to the tree itself; it stands with its arms stretched to the corners the four winds come from, with its murmured testimony, "We are here, we arrived, our roots are in the earth of these years," and beyond that short declaration, it speaks nothing of the decrees, fates, accidents, destinies, that made it an apparition of its particular moment. (25)

Abe Lincoln grows up. His father talks about the waste of time in "eddication"; it is enough "to larn readin', writin', cipherin'"; but the stanch, yearning stepmother, Sarah Bush Lincoln, comes between the boy and the father. And the father listens to the stepmother and lets her have her way. (26)

When he was eleven years old, Abe Lincoln's young body began to change. The juices and glands began to make a long, tall boy out of him. As the months and years went by, he noticed his lean wrists getting longer his legs too, and he was now looking over the heads of other boys. Men said, "Land o' Goshen, that boy air a-growin'!" (27)

As he took on more length, they said he was shooting up into the air like green corn in the summer of a good corn-year. So he grew. When he reached seventeen years of age, and they measured him, he was six feet, nearly four inches, high, from the bottoms of his moccasins to the top of his skull. (28)

These were years he was handling the ax. Except in spring plowing-time and the fall fodder-pulling, he was handling the ax nearly all the time. The insides of his hands took on callus thick as leather. He cleared openings in the timber, cut logs and puncheons, split firewood, built pig-pens. (29)

He learned how to measure with his eye the half-circle swing of the ax so as to nick out the deepest possible chip from off a tree-trunk. The trick of swaying his body easily on the hips so as to throw the heaviest possible weight into the blow of the ax—he learned that. (30)

On winter mornings he wiped the frost from the ax-handle, sniffed sparkles of air into his lungs, and beat a steady cleaving of blows into a big tree —till it fell—and he sat on the main log and ate his noon dinner of corn bread and fried salt pork—and joked with the gray squirrels that frisked and peeped at him from high forks of near-by walnut trees. (31)

He learned how to make his ax flash and bite into a sugarmaple or a sycamore. The outside and the inside look of black walnut and black oak, hickory and jack oak, elm and white oak, sassafras, dogwood, grapevines, sumac—he came on their secrets. He could guess close to the time of the year, to the week of the month, by the way the leaves and branches of trees looked. He sniffed the seasons. (32)

Often he worked alone in the timbers, all day long with only the sound of his own ax, or his own voice speaking to himself, or the crackling and swaying of branches in the wind, and the cries and whirs of animals, of brown and silver-gray squirrels, of partridges, hawks, crows, turkeys, sparrows, and the occasional wildcats. (33)

The tricks and whimsies of the sky, how to read clear skies and cloudy weather, the creeping vines of ivy and wild grape, the recurrence of dogwood blossoms in spring, the ways of snow, rain, drizzle, sleet, the visitors of sky and weather coming and going hour by hour—he tried to read their secrets, he tried to be friendly with their mystery. (34)

So he grew, to become hard, tough, wiry. The muscle on his bones and the cords, tendons, cross-weaves of fiber, and nerve centres, these became instruments to obey his wishes. He found with other men he could lift his own end of a log—and more too. One of the neighbors said he was strong as three men. Another said, "He can sink an ax deeper into wood than any man I ever saw." And another, "If you heard him fellin' trees in a clearin,' you would say there was three men at work by the way the trees fell." (35)

He was more than a tough, long, rawboned boy. He amazed men with his man's lifting power. He put his shoulders under a new-built corncrib one day and walked away with it to where the farmer wanted it. Four men, ready with poles to put under it and carry it, didn't need their poles. He played the same trick with a chicken house; at the new, growing town of Gentryville near by, they said the chicken house weighed six hundred pounds, and only a big boy with a hard backbone could get under it and walk away with it.   (36)

A blacksmith shop, a grocery, and a store had started up on the cross-roads of the Gentry farm. And one night after Abe had been helping thresh wheat on Dave Turnham's place, he went with Dennis Hanks, John Johnston, and some other boys to Gentryville where the farm-hands sat around with John Baldwin, the blacksmith, and Jones, the storekeeper, passed the whisky jug, told stories, and talked politics and religion and gossip. Going home late that night, they saw something in a mud puddle alongside the road. They stepped over to see whether it was a man or a hog. It was a man—drunk—snoring—sleeping off his drunk—on a frosty night outdoors in a cold wind.   (37)

They shook him by the shoulders, doubled his knees to his stomach, but he went on sleeping, snoring. The cold wind was getting colder. The other boys said they were going home, and they went away leaving Abe alone with the snoring sleeper in the mud puddle. Abe stepped into the mud, reached arms around the man, slung him over his shoulders, carried him to Dennis Hanks's cabin, built a fire, rubbed him warm and left him sleeping off the whisky.   (38)

And the man afterward said Abe saved his life. He told John Hanks, "It was mighty clever of Abe to tote me to a warm fire that night."   (39)

So he grew, living in that Pigeon Creek cabin for a home, sleeping in the loft, climbing up at night to a bed just under the roof, where sometimes the snow and the rain drove through the cracks, eating sometimes at a table where the family had only one thing to eat—potatoes. Once at the table, when there were only potatoes, his father spoke a blessing to the Lord for potatoes; the boy murmured, "Those are mighty poor blessings." And Abe made jokes once when company came and Sally Bush Lincoln brought out raw potatoes, gave the visitors a knife apiece, and they all peeled raw potatoes, and talked about the crops, politics, religion, gossip.   (40)

Days when they had only potatoes to eat didn't come often. Other days in the year they had "yaller-legged chicken" with gravy, and corn dodgers with shortening, and berries and honey. They tasted of bear meat, deer, coon, quail, grouse, prairie turkey, catfish, bass, perch.   (41)

Abe knew the sleep that comes after long hours of work outdoors, the feeling of simple food changing into blood and muscle as he worked in those young years clearing timberland for pasture and corn crops, cutting loose the brush, piling it and burning it, splitting rails, pulling the crosscut saw and the whipsaw, driving the shovel-plow, harrowing, planting, hoeing, pulling fodder, milking cows, churning butter, helping neighbors at house-raisings, log-rollings, corn-huskings. (42)

He found he was fast, strong, and keen when he went against other boys in sports. On farms where he worked, he held his own at scuffling, knocking off hats, wrestling. The time came when around Gentryville and Spencer County he was known as the best "rassler" of all, the champion. In jumping, foot-racing, throwing the maul, pitching the crowbar, he carried away the decisions against the lads of his own age always, and usually won against those older than himself. (43)

He earned his board, clothes, and lodgings, sometimes working for a neighbor farmer. He watched his father, while helping make cabinets, coffins, cupboards, window frames, doors. Hammers, saws, pegs, cleats, he understood first-hand, also the scythe and the cradle for cutting hay and grain, the corn-cutter's knife, the leather piece to protect the hand while shucking corn, and the horse, the dog, the cow, the ox, the hog. He could skin and cure the hides of coon and deer. He lifted the slippery two-hundred-pound hog carcass, head down, holding the hind hocks up for others of the gang to hook, and swung the animal clear of the ground. He learned where to stick a hog in the under side of the neck so as to bleed it to death, how to split it in two, and carve out the chops, the parts for sausage grinding, for hams, for "cracklings." (44)

Farmers called him to butcher for them at thirty-one cents a day, this when he was sixteen and seventeen years old. He could "knock a beef in the head," swing a maul and hit a cow between the eyes, skin the hide, halve and quarter it, carve out the tallow, the steaks, kidneys, liver. (45)

And the hiding-places of fresh spring water under the earth crust had to be in his thoughts; he helped at well-digging; the wells Tom Lincoln dug went dry one year after another; neighbors said Tom was always digging a well and had his land "honey-combed"; and the boy, Abe, ran the errands and held the tools for the well-digging. (46)

When he was eighteen years old, he could take an ax at the end of the handle and hold it out in a straight horizontal line, easy and steady—he had strong shoulder muscles and steady wrists early in life. He walked thirty-four miles in one day, just on an errand, to please himself, to hear a lawyer make a speech. He could tell his body to do almost impossible things, and the body obeyed. (47)

Growing from boy to man, he was alone a good deal of the time. Days came often when he was by himself all the time except at breakfast and supper hours in the cabin home. In some years more of his time was spent in loneliness than in the company of other people. It happened, too, that this loneliness he knew was not like that of people in cities who can look from a window on streets where faces pass and repass. It was the wilderness loneliness he became acquainted with, solved, filtered through body, eye, and brain, held communion with in his ears, in the temples of his forehead, in the works of his beating heart.   (48)

He lived with trees, with the bush wet with shining raindrops, with the burning bush of autumn, with the lone wild duck riding a north wind and crying down on a line north to south, the faces of open sky and weather, the ax which is an individual one-man instrument, these he had for companions, books, friends, talkers, chums of his endless changing soliloquies.
(49)

His moccasin feet in the winter-time knew the white spaces of snow-drifts piled in whimsical shapes against timber slopes or blown in levels across the fields of last year's cut corn stalks; in the summer-time his bare feet toughened in the gravel of green streams while he laughed back to the chatter of bluejays in the red-haw trees or while he kept his eyes ready in the slough quack-grass for the cow-snake, the rattler, the copperhead. (50)

He rested between spells of work in the springtime when the upward push of the coming out of the new grass can be heard, and in autumn weeks when the rustle of a single falling leaf lets go a whisper that a listening ear can catch.   (51)

He found his life thrown in ways where there was a certain chance for a certain growth. And so he grew. Silence found him; he met silence. In the making of him as he was, the element of silence was immense.   (52)

George Orwell

(1903–1950)

For a brief statement of facts about the author, see the headnote preceding his essay "Politics and the English Language."

■ *Marrakech*

As THE CORPSE went past the flies left the restaurant table in a cloud and rushed after it, but they came back a few minutes later.   (1)

The little crowd of mourners—all men and boys, no women—threaded their way across the market-place between the piles of pomegranates and the taxis and the camels, wailing a short chant over and over again. What really appeals to the flies is that the corpses here are never put into coffins, they are merely wrapped in a piece of rag and carried on a rough wooden bier on the shoulders of four friends. When the friends get to the burying-ground they hack an oblong hole a foot or two deep, dump the body in it and fling over it a little of the dried-up, lumpy earth, which is like broken brick. No gravestone, no name, no identifying mark of any kind. The burying-ground is merely a huge waste of hummocky earth, like a derelict building-lot. After a month or two no one can even be certain where his own relatives are buried.   (2)

When you walk through a town like this—two hundred thousand inhabitants, of whom at least twenty thousand own literally nothing except the rags they stand up in—when you see how the people live, and still more how easily they die, it is always difficult to believe that you are walking among human beings. All colonial empires are in reality founded upon that fact. The people have brown faces—besides, there are so many of them! Are they really the same flesh as yourself? Do they even have names? Or are they merely a kind of undifferentiated brown stuff, about as individual as bees or coral insects? They rise out of the earth, they sweat and starve for a few years, and then they sink back into the nameless mounds of the grave-yard and nobody notices that they are gone. And even the graves them-selves soon fade back into the soil. Sometimes, out for a walk, as you break your way through the prickly pear, you notice that it is rather bumpy under-foot, and only a certain regularity in the bumps tells you that you are walking over skeletons. (3)

I was feeding one of the gazelles in the public gardens. (4)

Gazelles are almost the only animals that look good to eat when they are still alive, in fact, one can hardly look at their hindquarters without thinking of mint sauce. The gazelle I was feeding seemed to know that this thought was in my mind, for though it took the piece of bread I was holding out it obviously did not like me. It nibbled rapidly at the bread, then lowered its head and tried to butt me, then took another nibble and then butted again. Probably its idea was that if it could drive me away the bread would some-how remain hanging in mid-air. (5)

An Arab navvy working on the path nearby lowered his heavy hoe and sidled slowly towards us. He looked from the gazelle to the bread and from the bread to the gazelle, with a sort of quiet amazement, as though he had never seen anything quite like this before. Finally he said shyly in French: (6)

"I could eat some of that bread." (7)

I tore off a piece and he stowed it gratefully in some secret place under his rags. This man is an employee of the Municipality. (8)

When you go through the Jewish quarters you gather some idea of what the medieval ghettoes were probably like. Under their Moorish rulers the Jews were only allowed to own land in certain restricted areas, and after centuries of this kind of treatment they have ceased to bother about over-crowding. Many of the streets are a good deal less than six feet wide, the houses are completely windowless, and sore-eyed children cluster every-where in unbelievable numbers, like clouds of flies. Down the centre of the street there is generally running a little river of urine. (9)

In the bazaar huge families of Jews, all dressed in the long black robe and little black skull-cap, are working in dark fly-infested booths that look like caves. A carpenter sits crosslegged at a prehistoric lathe, turning chair-legs at lightning speed. He works the lathe with a bow in his right hand and guides the chisel with his left foot, and thanks to a lifetime of sitting in this position his left leg is warped out of shape. At his side his grandson, aged six, is already starting on the simpler parts of the job. (10)

I was just passing the coppersmiths' booths when somebody noticed that I was lighting a cigarette. Instantly, from the dark holes all round, there was a frenzied rush of Jews, many of them old grandfathers with flowing grey beards, all clamouring for a cigarette. Even a blind man somewhere at the back of one of the booths heard a rumour of cigarettes and came crawling out, groping in the air with his hand. In about a minute I had used up the whole packet. None of these people, I suppose, works less than twelve hours a day, and every one of them looks on a cigarette as a more or less impossible luxury. (11)

As the Jews live in self-contained communities they follow the same trades as the Arabs, except for agriculture. Fruit-sellers, potters, silversmiths, blacksmiths, butchers, leatherworkers, tailors, water-carriers, beggars, porters—whichever way you look you see nothing but Jews. As a matter of fact there are thirteen thousand of them, all living in the space of a few acres. A good job Hitler wasn't here. Perhaps he was on his way, however. You hear the usual dark rumours about the Jews, not only from the Arabs but from the poorer Europeans. (12)

"Yes, mon vieux, they took my job away from me and gave it to a Jew. The Jews! They're the real rulers of this country, you know. They've got all the money. They control the banks, finance—everything." (13)

"But," I said, "isn't a fact that the average Jew is a labourer working for about a penny an hour?" (14)

"Ah, that's only for show! They're all moneylenders really. They're cunning, the Jews." (15)

In just the same way, a couple of hundred years ago, poor old women used to be burned for witchcraft when they could not even work enough magic to get themselves a square meal. (16)

All people who work with their hands are partly invisible, and the more important the work they do, the less visible they are. Still, a white skin is always fairly conspicuous. In northern Europe, when you see a labourer ploughing a field, you probably give him a second glance. In a hot country, anywhere south of Gibraltar or east of Suez, the chances are that you don't even see him. I have noticed this again and again. In a tropical landscape one's eye takes in everything except the human beings. It takes in the dried-up soil, the prickly pear, the palm tree and the distant mountain, but it always misses the peasant hoeing at his patch. He is the same colour as the earth, and a great deal less interesting to look at. (17)

It is only because of this that the starved countries of Asia and Africa are accepted as tourist resorts. No one would think of running cheap trips to the Distressed Areas. But where the human beings have brown skins their poverty is simply not noticed. What does Morocco mean to a Frenchman? An orange-grove or a job in Government service. Or to an Englishman? Camels, castles, palm trees, Foreign Legionnaires, brass trays, and bandits. One could probably live there for years without noticing that for nine-tenths of the people the reality of life is an endless, back-breaking struggle to wring a little food out of an eroded soil. (18)

Most of Morocco is so desolate that no wild animal bigger than a hare can live on it. Huge areas which were once covered with forest have turned into a treeless waste where the soil is exactly like broken-up brick. Nevertheless a good deal of it is cultivated, with frightful labour. Everything is done by hand. Long lines of women, bent double like inverted capital L's, work their way slowly across the fields, tearing up the prickly weeds with their hands, and the peasant gathering lucerne for fodder pulls it up stalk by stalk instead of reaping it, thus saving an inch or two on each stalk. The plough is a wretched wooden thing, so frail that one can easily carry it on one's shoulder, and fitted underneath with a rough iron spike which stirs the soil to a depth of about four inches. This is as much as the strength of the animals is equal to. It is usual to plough with a cow and a donkey yoked together. Two donkeys would not be quite strong enough, but on the other hand two cows would cost a little more to feed. The peasants possess no harrows, they merely plough the soil several times over in different directions, finally leaving it in rough furrows, after which the whole field has to be shaped with hoes into small oblong patches to conserve water. Except for a day or two after the rare rainstorms there is never enough water. Along the edges of the fields channels are hacked out to a depth of thirty or forty feet to get at the tiny trickles which run through the subsoil.
(19)

Every afternoon a file of very old women passes down the road outside my house, each carrying a load of firewood. All of them are mummified with age and the sun, and all of them are tiny. It seems to be generally the case in primitive communities that the women, when they get beyond a certain age, shrink to the size of children. One day a poor old creature who could not have been more than four feet tall crept past me under a vast load of wood. I stopped her and put a five-sou piece (a little more than a farthing) into her hand. She answered with a shrill wail, almost a scream, which was partly gratitude but mainly surprise. I suppose that from her point of view, by taking any notice of her, I seemed almost to be violating a law of nature. She accepted her status as an old woman, that is to say as a beast of burden. When a family is travelling it is quite usual to see a father and a grown-up son riding ahead on donkeys, and an old woman following on foot, carrying the baggage. (20)

But what is strange about these people is their invisibility. For several weeks, always at about the same time of day, the file of old women had hobbled past the house with their firewood, and though they had registered themselves on my eyeballs I cannot truly say that I had seen them. Firewood was passing—that was how I saw it. It was only that one day I happened to be walking behind them, and the curious up-and-down motion of a load of wood drew my attention to the human being beneath it. Then for the first time I noticed the poor old earth-coloured bodies, bodies reduced to bones and leathery skin, bent double under the crushing weight. Yet I suppose I had not been five minutes on Moroccan soil before I noticed the overloading of the donkeys and was infuriated by it. There is no question that the donkeys are damnably treated. The Moroccan donkey is hardly bigger than a St. Bernard dog, it carries a load which in the British Army would be considered too much for a fifteen-hands mule, and very often its pack-saddle is not taken off its back for weeks together. But what is peculiarly pitiful is that it is the most willing creature on earth, it follows its master like a dog and does not need either bridle or halter. After a dozen years of devoted work it suddenly drops dead, whereupon its master tips it into the ditch and the village dogs have torn its guts out before it is cold. (21)

This kind of thing makes one's blood boil, whereas—on the whole—the plight of the human beings does not. I am not commenting, merely pointing to a fact. People with brown skins are next door to invisible. Anyone can be sorry for the donkey with its galled back, but it is generally owing to some kind of accident if one even notices the old woman under her load of sticks. (22)

As the storks flew northward the Negroes were marching southward—a long, dusty column, infantry, screw-gun batteries, and then more infantry, four or five thousand men in all, winding up the road with a clumping of boots and a clatter of iron wheels. (23)

They were Senegalese, the blackest Negroes in Africa, so black that sometimes it is difficult to see whereabouts on their necks the hair begins. Their splendid bodies were hidden in reach-me-down khaki uniforms, their feet squashed into boots that looked like blocks of wood, and every tin hat seemed to be a couple of sizes too small. It was very hot and the men had marched a long way. They slumped under the weight of their packs and the curiously sensitive black faces were glistening with sweat. (24)

As they went past a tall, very young Negro turned and caught my eye. But the look he gave me was not in the least the kind of look you might expect. Not hostile, not contemptuous, not sullen, not even inquisitive. It was the shy, wide-eyes Negro look, which actually is a look of profound respect. I saw how it was. This wretched boy, who is a French citizen and has therefore been dragged from the forest to scrub floors and catch syphilis in garrison towns, actually has feelings of reverence before a white skin. He has been taught that the white race are his masters, and he still believes it. (25)

But there is one thought which every white man (and in this connection it doesn't matter twopence if he calls himself a socialist) thinks when he sees a black army marching past. "How much longer can we go on kidding these people? How long before they turn their guns in the other direction?" (26)

It was curious, really. Every white man there had this thought stowed somewhere or other in his mind. I had it, so had the other onlookers, so had the officers on their sweating chargers and the white N.C.O.'s marching in the ranks. It was a kind of secret which we all knew and were too clever to tell; only the Negroes didn't know it. And really it was like watching a flock of cattle to see the long column, a mile or two miles of armed men, flowing peacefully up the road, while the great white birds drifted over them in the opposite direction, glittering like scraps of paper.   (27)

Robert Penn Warren

(1905–   )

WARREN, poet, novelist, critic, and professor of English, has twice won the Pulitzer prize—for fiction, 1947, and for poetry, 1958—and has received the National Book Award (1958). His principal work of fiction is All the King's Men. *He has been a member of the Yale University faculty since 1950.*

◾ *Segregation*

JUST LISTENING to talk as it comes is best, but sometimes it doesn't come, or the man says, "You ask me some questions," and so, bit by bit, a certain pattern of questions emerges, the old obvious questions, I suppose—the questions people respond to or flinch from.   (1)

What are the white man's reasons for segregation?   (2)

The man I am talking to is a yellow man, about forty years old, shortish, rather fat, with a very smooth, faintly Mongolian face, eyes very shrewd but ready to smile. When the smile really comes, there is a gold tooth showing, to become, in that gold face, part of the sincerity of the smile. His arms seem somewhat short, and as he sits very erect in a straight chair, he folds his hands over his stomach. He gives the impression of a man very much at home in himself, at peace in himself, in his dignity, in his own pleasant, smooth-skinned plumpness, in some sustaining humorousness of things. He owns a small business, a shoe shop with a few employees.   (3)

"What does the white man do it for?" he rephrases the question. He pauses, and you can see he is thinking, studying on it, his smooth, yellow face compressing a little. All at once the face relaxes, a sort of humorous ripple, humorous but serious too, in a sort of wry way, before the face settles to its blandness. "You know," he says, "you know, years and years I look at some white feller, and I caint never figure him out. You go long with him, years and years, and all of a sudden he does something. I caint figure out what makes him do the way he does. It is like a mystery, you might say. I have studied on it."   (4)

Another Negro, a very black man, small-built and intense, leans forward in his chair. He says it is money, so the white man can have cheap labor, can make the money. He is a bookish man, has been to a Negro college, and though he has never been out of the South, his speech surprises me the way my native ear used to be surprised by the speech of a Negro born and raised, say, in Akron, Ohio. I make some fleeting, tentative association of his speech, his education, his economic interpretation of things; then let the notion slide.   (5)

"Yeah, yeah," the yellow man is saying, agreeing, "but—" He stops, shakes his head.   (6)

"But what?" I ask.   (7)

He hesitates, and I see the thumbs of the hands lightly clasped across his belly begin to move, ever so slowly, round and round each other. "All right," he says, "I might as well say it to you."   (8)

"Say what?"   (9)

"Mongrelization," he says, "that's what a white man will say. You ask him and he'll say that. He wants to head it off, he says. But—" He grins, the skin crinkles around his eyes, the grin shows the gold tooth. "But," he says, "look at my face. It wasn't any black man hung it on me."   (10)

The other man doesn't seem to think this is funny. "Yes," he says, "yes, they claim they don't want mongrelization. But who has done it? They claim Negroes are dirty, diseased, that that's why they want segregation. But they have Negro nurses for their children, they have Negro cooks. They claim Negroes are ignorant. But they won't associate with the smartest and best educated Negro. They claim—" And his voice goes on, winding up the bitter catalogue of paradoxes. I know them all. They are not new.   (11)

The smooth-faced, yellow man is listening. But he is thinking, too, the yellow blandness of his face creaming ever so little with his slow, humorous intentness. I ask him what he is thinking.   (12)

He grins, with philosophic ruefulness. "I was just studying on it," he says. "It's all true, what Mr. Elmo here says. But there must be something behind it all. Something he don't ever say, that white feller. Maybe—" He pauses, hunting for the formulation. "Maybe it's just pridefulness," he says, "him being white."   (13)

Later, I am talking with the hill-man organizer, the one with the handsome wife who asks me where I live now, and he is telling me why he wants segregation. "The Court," he says, "hit caint take no stick and mix folks up like you swivel and swull eggs broke in a bowl. Naw," he says, "you got to raise 'em up, the niggers, not bring the white folks down to nigger level." He illustrates with his pudgy, strong hands in the air before him, one up, one down, changing levels. He watches the hands, with fascination, as though he has just learned to do a complicated trick.   (14)

How would you raise the level? I ask.   (15)

"Give 'em good schools and things, yeah. But"—and he warms to the topic, leaning at me—"I'd 'bolish common law marriage. I'd put 'em in jail fer hit, and make 'em learn morals. Now a nigger don't know how to treat no wife, not even a nigger wife. He whup her and beat her and maybe carve on her jaw with a pocketknife. When he ought to trick and pet her, and set her on his knee like a white man does his wife."   (16)

Then I talk with a Negro grade-school teacher, in the country, in Tennessee. She is a mulatto woman, middle-aged, with a handsome aquiline face, rather Indian-looking. She is sitting in her tiny, pridefully clean house, with a prideful bookcase of books beyond her, talking with slow and detached tones. I know what her story has been, years of domestic service, a painfully acquired education, marriage to a professional man, no children ("It was a cross to bear, but maybe that's why I love 'em so and like to teach 'em not my own").   (17)

I ask her why white people want to keep segregation.   (18)

"You ought to see the school house I teach in," she says, and pauses, and her lips curl sardonically, "set in the mud and hogs can come under it, and the privies set back in the mud. And see some of the children that come there, out of homes with nothing, worse than the school house, no sanitation or cleanness, with disease and dirt and no manners. You wouldn't blame a white person for not wanting the white child set down beside them." Then with a slow movement of the shoulders, again the curl of the lips: "Why didn't the Federal Government give us money ten years ago for our school? To get ready, to raise us up a little to integrate. It would have made it easier. But now—"   (19)

But now? I ask.   (20)

"You got to try to be fair," she says.   (21)

I am talking with an official of one of the segregation outfits, late at night, in his house, in a fringe subdivision, in a small living room with red velvet drapes at the one window, a TV set, new, on a table, a plastic or plaster bas-relief of a fox hunter hung on the wall, in color, the hunting coat very red and arrogant. My host is seventy-five years old, bald except for a fringe of gray hair, sallow-skinned, very clean and scrubbed-looking, white shirt but no tie, a knife-edge crease to his hard-finish gray trousers. He smokes cigarettes, one after another, with nervous, stained fingers.   (22)

He was born in North Kentucky, romantically remembers the tobacco night riders ("Yeah, it was tight, nobody talked tobacco much, you might get shot"), remembers the Civil War veterans ("even the GAR's") sitting round, talking to the kids ("Yeah, they talked their war, they had something to remember and be proud of, not like these veterans we got nowadays, nothing to be proud of"), started out to be a lawyer ("But Blackstone got too dry, but history now, that's different, you always get something out of it to think about"), but wound up doing lots of things, finally, for years, a fraternal organizer.   (23)

Yes, he is definitely a pro, and when he talks of Gerald L. K. Smith he bursts out, eyes a-gleam: "Lord, that man's mailing list would be worth a million dollars!" He is not the rabble-rouser, the crusader, but the persuader, the debater, the man who gives the reasons. He is, in fact, a very American type, the old-fashioned, self-made, back-country intellectual—the type that finds apotheosis in Mark Twain and Abraham Lincoln. If he is neither of them, if he says "gondorea" and "enviro-mental" and "ethnolology," if something went wrong, if nothing ever came out quite right for him along the long way, you can still sense the old, unappeased hungers, the old drives of a nameless ambition. And he is sadly contemptuous of his organizers, who "aren't up to it," who "just aren't posted on history and ethnolology," who just haven't got "the old gray matter."   (24)

I ask him why the white man wants segregation.   (25)

"He'll say one thing and another," he says, "he knows in his bones it ain't right to have mixing. But you got to give him the reasons, explain it to him. It is the ethnolology of it you got to give. You got to explain how no *Negroes*"—he pronounces it with the elaborate polemical correctness, but not for polemics, just to set himself off intellectually, I suppose, from the people who might say *nigger*—"explain how no Negroes ever created a civilization. They are parasites. They haven't got the stuff up here." And he taps his forehead. "And explain how there is just two races, white and black, and—"
(26)

"What about the Bible," I ask, "doesn't the Bible say three?"   (27)

"Yes, but you know, between you and me, I don't reckon you have to take much stock in the Bible in this business. I don't take much stock in Darwin in some ways, either. He is too environmental, he don't think enough about the blood. Yes, sir, I'll tell you, it's hard to come by good books on ethnolology these days. Got a good one from California the other day, though. But just one copy. Been out of print a long time. But like I was saying, the point is there's just two races, black and white, and the rest of them is a kind of mixing. You always get a mess when the mixing starts. Take India. They are a pure white people like you and me, and they had a pretty good civilization, too. Till they got to shipping on a little Negro blood. It don't take much to do the damage. Look at 'em now."   (28)

That is his argument. It is much the same argument given me by another official of another segregation group, whom I sit with a week later in another state, a lawyer, forty-five or -six, of strong middle height, sandy blond, hands strong with pale hairs and square-cut, scrubbed-looking nails. He is cagey at first, then suddenly warm, in an expanding, sincere, appealing way. He really wants to explain himself, wants to be regarded as an honest man, wants to be liked. I do like him, as he tells about himself, how he had gone to college, the hard way I gather, had prepared to be a teacher of history in high school, had given that up, had tried business in one way or another, had given that up, had studied law. "You ought to know my politics, too," he says. He was New Deal till the Court-packing plan. "That disgusted me," he says, and you believe him. Then he was for Willkie, then for Dewey, then Dixiecrat, then for Eisenhower. (I remember another lawyer, hired by another group: "Hell, all Southerners are Republicans at heart, conservative, and just don't know they're Republican.")   (29)

But Eisenhower doesn't satisfy my friend now. "We'll elect our own President. Our organization isn't just Southern. We're going national. Plenty of people in Chicago and other places feel like we do. And afraid of a big central government, too. We'll elect our own President and see how Chief Justice Warren's decision comes out."   (30)

I ask if the main point is the matter of States Rights, of local integrity.   (31)

"Yes, in a way," he says, "but you got to fight on something you can rouse people up about, on segregation. There's the constitutional argument, but your basic feeling, that's what you've got to trust—what you feel, not your reasons for it. But we've got argument, reasons."   (32)

He hesitates, thumps the desk top in a quick tattoo of his strong, scrubbed-looking fingers (he isn't a nervous man in the ordinary sense, but there are these sudden bursts), twists himself in his chair, then abruptly leans forward, jerks a drawer open (literally jerks it), and thrusts an envelope at me. "Heck, you might as well see it," he says.   (33)

I look at it. The stuff is not new. I have seen it before, elsewhere. It was used in the last gubernatorial campaign in Tennessee, it was used in the march on the Capitol at Nashville a few weeks ago. There are the handbills showing "Harlem Negro and White Wife," lying abed, showing "Crooner Roy Hamilton & Teenage Fans," who are white girls, showing a school yard in Baltimore with Negro and white children, "the new look in education." On the back of one of the handbills is a crudely drawn valentine-like heart, in it the head of a white woman who (with feelings not indicated by the artist) is about to be kissed by a black man of the most primitive physiognomy. On the heart two vultures perch. Beneath it is the caption: "The Kiss of Death."   (34)

Below are the "reasons": "While Russia makes laws to protect her own race she continues to prod us to accept 14,000,000 Negroes as social equals and we are doing everything possible to please her. . . . Segregation is the law of God, not man. . . . Continue to rob the white race in order to bribe the Asiatic and Negro and these people will overwhelm the white race and destroy all progress, religion, invention, art, and return us to the jungle. . . . Negro blood destroyed the civilization of Egypt, India, Phoenicia, Carthage, Greece, and it will destroy America!"   (35)

I put the literature into my pocket, to join the other samples. "If there's trouble, I ask, "where will it begin?"   (36)

"We don't condone violence," he says.   (37)

"But if—just suppose," I say.   (38)

He doesn't hesitate. "The red-neck," he says, "that's what you call 'em around here. Those fellows—and I'm one of them myself, just a red-neck that got educated—are the ones who will feel the rub. He is the one on the underside of the plank with nothing between him and the bare black ground. He's got to have something to give him pride. Just to be better than something."   (39)

To be better than something: so we are back to the pridefulness the yellow man had talked about. But no, there is more, something else.   (40)

There is the minister, a Baptist, an intellectual-looking man, a man whose face indicates conscience and thoughtfulness, pastor of a good church in a good district in a thriving city. "It is simple," he says. "It is a matter of God's will and revelation. I refer you to Acts 17—I don't remember the verse. This is the passage the integrationists are always quoting to prove that integration is Christian. But they won't quote it all. It's the end that counts."   (41)

I looked it up: *And hath made of one blood all nations of men for to dwell on all the face of the earth, and hath determined the times before appointed, and the bounds of their habitation.*   (42)

There is the very handsome lady of forty-five, charming and witty and gay, full of dramatic mimicry, a wonderful range of phrase, a quick sympathy, a totally captivating talker of the kind you still occasionally find among women of the Deep South, but never now in a woman under forty. She is sitting before the fire in the fine room, her brother, big and handsome but barefoot and rigid drunk, opposite her. But she gaily overrides that small difficulty ("Oh, don't mind him, he's just had a whole bottle of brandy. Been on a high-lonesome all by himself. But poor Jack, he feels better now.") She has been talking about the Negroes on her plantation,

and at last, about integration, but that only in one phrase, tossed off as gaily
and casually as any other of the evening, so casual as to permit no discussion: "But of course we have to keep the white race intact."   (43)

But the husband, much her senior, who has said almost nothing all evening, lifts his strong gizzled old face, and in kind of *sotto voce* growl, not
to her, not to me, not to anybody, utters: "In power—in power—you mean
the white race in power."   (44)

And I think of another Southerner, an integrationist, saying to me: "You
simply have to recognize a fact. In no county where the Negroes are two to
one is the white man going to surrender political power, not with the Negroes in those counties in their present condition. It's not a question of
being Southern. You put the same number of Yankee liberals in the same
county and in a week they'd be behaving the same way. Living with something and talking about it are two very different things, and living with
something is always the slow way."   (45)

And another, not an integrationist, from a black county, saying: "Yeah,
let 'em take over and in six months you'd be paying the taxes but a black
sheriff would be collecting 'em. You couldn't walk down the sidewalk. You'd
be communized, all right."   (46)

But is it power. Merely power? Or any of the other things suggested
thus far?   (47)

I think of a college professor in a section where about half the population is Negro. The college has no Negro students, but—"The heat is on," he
says. "But listen, brother," he says, "lots of our boys don't like it a bit. Not
a bit."   (48)

I ask would it be like the University of Alabama.   (49)

"It would be something, brother. I'll tell you that, brother. One of our
boys—been fooling around with an organization uptown—he came to me
and asked me to be sure to let him know when a nigger was coming, he and
some friends would stop that clock. But I didn't want to hear student talk.
I said, son, just don't tell me."   (50)

I asked what the faculty would do.   (51)

"Hide out, brother, hide out. And brother, I would, too."   (52)

Yes, he was a segregationist. I didn't have to ask him. Or ask his reasons,
for he was talking on, in his rather nasal voice—leaning happily back in his
chair in the handsome office, a spare, fiftyish man, dark-suited, rather
dressy, sharp-nosed, with some fringe-remnants of sandy hair on an elon-
gated, slightly freckled skull, rimless glasses on pale eyes: "Yeah, brother,
back in my county there was a long ridge running through the county, and
one side the ridge was good land, river bottom, and folks put on airs there
and held niggers, but on the other side of the ridge the ground so pore you
couldn't grow peas and nothing but pore white trash. So when the Civil War
came, the pore white trash, as the folks who put on airs called them, just

picked down the old rifle off the deer horns over the fireplace and joined the Federals coming down, just because they hated those fellows across the ridge. But don't get me wrong, brother. They didn't want any truck with niggers, either. To this day they vote Republican and hate niggers. It is just they hate niggers." (53)

Yes, they hate niggers, but I am in another room, the library of a plantation house, in Mississippi, and the planter is talking to me, leaning his length back at ease, speaking deliberately from his high-nosed, commanding face, the very figure of a Wade Hampton or Kirby Smith, only the gray uniform and cavalry boots not there, saying: "No, I don't hate Negroes. I never had a minute's trouble with one in my life, and never intend to. I don't believe in getting lathered up, and I don't intend to get lathered up. I simply don't discuss the question with anybody. But I'll tell you what I feel. I came out of the university with a lot of ideals and humanitarianism, and I stayed by it as long as I could. But I tell you now what has come out of thirty years of experience and careful consideration. I have a deep contempt for the Negro race as it exists here. It is not so much a matter of ability as of character. Character." (54)

He repeats the word. He is a man of character, it could never be denied. Of character and force. He is also a man of fine intelligence and good education. He reads Roman history. He collects books on the American West. He is widely traveled. He is unusually successful as a planter and businessman. He is a man of human warmth and generosity, and eminent justice. I overhear his wife, at this moment, talking to a Negro from the place, asking him if she can save some more money for him, to add to the hundred dollars she holds, trying to persuade him. (55)

The husband goes on: "It's not so much the hands on my place, as the lawyers and doctors and teachers and insurance men and undertakers—oh, yes, I've had dealings all around, or my hands have. The character just breaks down. It is not dependable. They pay lip service to the white man's ideals of conduct. They say, yes, I believe in honesty and truth and morality. But it is just lip service. Most of the time. I don't intend to get lathered up. This is just my private opinion. I believe in segregation, but I can always protect myself and my family. I dine at my club and my land is my own, and when I travel, the places I frequent have few if any Negroes. Not that I'd ever walk out of a restaurant, for I'm no professional Southerner. And I'd never give a nickel to the Citizens Council or anything like that. Nor have any of my friends, that I know of. That's townpeople stuff, anyway." (56)

Later on, he says: "For years, I thought I loved Negroes. And I loved their humor and other qualities. My father—he was a firster around here, first man to put glass windows in for them, first to give them a written monthly statement, first to do a lot to help them toward financial independence—well, my father, he used to look at me and say how it would be. He said, son, they will knock it out of you. Well, they did. I learned the grimness and the sadness."   (57)

And later, as we ride down the long row of the houses of the hands, he points to shreds of screening at windows, or here and there a broken screen door. "One of my last experiments," he says, dourly. "Three months, and they poked it out of the kitchen window so they could throw slops on the bare ground. They broke down the front door so they could spit tobacco juice out on the porch floor."   (58)

We ride on. We pass a nicely painted house, with a fenced dooryard, with flower beds, and flower boxes on the porch, and good, bright-painted porch furniture. I ask who lives there. "One of the hands," he says, "but he's got some energy and character. Look at his house. And he loves flowers. Has only three children, but when there's work he gets it done fast, and then finds some more to do. Makes $4,500 to $5,000 a year." Some old pride, or something from the lost days of idealism, comes back into his tone.   (59)

I ask what the other people on the place think of the tenant with the nice house.   (60)

"They think he's just lucky." And he mimics, a little bitterly, without any humor: "Boss, looks lak Jefferson's chillen, they jes picks faster'n mine. Caint he'p it, Boss."   (61)

I ask what Jefferson's color is.   (62)

"A real black man, a real Negro, all right. But he's got character."   (63)

I look down the interminable row of dingy houses, over the interminable flat of black earth toward the river.   (64)

William L. Shirer

(1904–   )

SHIRER *has had a distinguished career as a journalist and author. He has represented the* Chicago Tribune *and the Columbia Broadcasting System, among others, especially in the European theatre of operations during World War II. The Rise and Fall of the Third Reich won the National Book Award in 1961.*

◼ *A Turn of the Tide*

By THE BEGINNING of autumn 1941, Hitler believed that Russia was finished.
(1)

Within three weeks of the opening of the campaign, Field Marshal von Bock's Army Group Center, with thirty infantry divisions and fifteen panzer or motorized divisions, had pushed 450 miles from Bialystok to Smolensk. Moscow lay but 200 miles farther east along the high road which Napoleon had taken in 1812. To the north Field Marshal von Leeb's army group, twenty-one infantry and six armored divisions strong, was moving rapidly up through the Baltic States toward Leningrad. To the south Field Marshal von Rundstedt's army group of twenty-five infantry, four motorized, four mountain and five panzer divisions was advancing toward the Dnieper River and Kiev, capital of the fertile Ukraine, which Hitler coveted.   (2)

So *planmaessig* (according to plan), as the OKW communiqués put it, was the German progress along a thousand-mile front from the Baltic to the Black Sea, and so confident was the Nazi dictator that it would continue at an accelerated pace as one Soviet army after another was surrounded or dispersed, that on July 14, a bare three weeks after the invasion had begun, he issued a directive advising that the strength of the Army could be "considerably reduced in the near future" and that armament production would be concentrated on naval ships and Luftwaffe planes, especially the latter, for the conduct of the war against the last remaining enemy, Britain, and —he added—"against America should the case arise." By the end of September he instructed the High Command to prepare to disband forty infantry divisions so that this additional manpower could be utilized by industry.
(3)

Russia's two greatest cities, Leningrad, which Peter the Great had built as the capital on the Baltic, and Moscow, the ancient and now Bolshevik capital, seemed to Hitler about to fall. On September 18 he issued strict orders: "A capitulation of Leningrad or Moscow is not to be accepted, even if offered." What was to happen to them he made clear to his commanders in a directive of September 29:

> The Fuehrer has decided to have St. Petersburg [Leningrad] wiped off the fact of the earth.[1] The further existence of this large city is of no interest once Soviet Russia is overthrown . . .

[1] Emphasis in the original.

The intention is to close in on the city and raze it to the ground by artillery and by continuous air attack . . .

Requests that the city be taken over will be turned down, for *the problem of the survival of the population and of supplying it with food is one which cannot and should not be solved by us.* In this war for existence we have no interest in keeping even part of this great city's population.[2]   (4)

That same week, on October 3, Hitler returned to Berlin and in an address to the German people proclaimed the collapse of the Soviet Union. "I declare today, and I declare it without any reservation," he said, "that the enemy in the East has been struck down and will never rise again . . . Behind our troops there already lies a territory twice the size of the German Reich when I came to power in 1933."   (5)

When on October 8, Orel, a key city south of Moscow, fell, Hitler sent his press chief, Otto Dietrich, flying back to Berlin, to tell the correspondents of the world's leading newspapers there the next day that the last intact Soviet armies, those of Marshal Timoshenko, defending Moscow, were locked in two steel German pockets before the capital; that the southern armies of Marshal Budënny were routed and dispersed; and that sixty to seventy divisions of Marshal Voroshilov's army were surrounded in Leningrad.   (6)

"For all military purposes," Dietrich concluded smugly, "Soviet Russia is done with. The British dream of a two-front war is dead."   (7)

These public boasts of Hitler and Dietrich were, to say the least, premature.[3] In reality the Russians, despite the surprise with which they were taken on June 22, their subsequent heavy losses in men and equipment, their rapid withdrawal and the entrapment of some of their best armies, had begun in July to put up a mounting resistance such as the Wehrmacht had never encountered before. Halder's diary and the reports of such front-line commanders as General Guderian, who led a large panzer group on the central front, began to be peppered—and then laden—with accounts of severe fighting, desperate Russian stands and counter-attacks and heavy casualties to German as well as Soviet troops.   (8)

"The conduct of the Russian troops," General Blumentritt wrote later, "even in this first battle [for Minsk] was in striking contrast to the behavior

---

2 A few weeks later Goering told Ciano, "This year between twenty and thirty million persons will die of hunger in Russia. Perhaps it is well that it should be so, for certain nations must be decimated. But even if it were not, nothing can be done about it. It is obvious that if humanity is condemned to die of hunger, the last to die will be our two peoples . . . In the camps for Russian prisoners they have begun to eat each other." (*Ciano's Diplomatic Papers*, pp. 464–65.)

3 Not as premature, however, as the warnings of the American General Staff, which in July had confidentially informed American editors and Washington correspondents that the collapse of the Soviet Union was only a matter of a few weeks. It is not surprising that the declarations of Hitler and Dr. Dietrich early in October 1941 were widely believed in the United States and Britain as well as in Germany and elsewhere.

of the Poles and the Western Allies in defeat. Even when encircled the Russians stood their ground and fought." And there proved to be more of them, and with better equipment, than Adolf Hitler had dreamed was possible. Fresh Soviet divisions which German intelligence had no inkling of were continually being thrown into battle. "It is becoming ever clearer," Halder wrote in his diary on August 11, "that we underestimated the strength of the Russian colossus not only in the economic and transportation sphere but above all in the military. At the beginning we reckoned with some 200 enemy divisions and we have already identified 360. When a dozen of them are destroyed the Russians throw in another dozen. On this broad expanse our front is too thin. It has no depth. As a result, the repeated enemy attacks often meet with some success." Rundstedt put it bluntly to Allied interrogators after the war. "I realized," he said, "soon after the attack was begun that everything that had been written about Russia was nonsense." (9)

Several generals, Guderian, Blumentritt and Sepp Dietrich among them, have left reports expressing astonishment at their first encounter with the Russian T-34 tank, of which they had not previously heard and which was so heavily armored that the shells from the German antitank guns bounced harmlessly off it. The appearance of this panzer, Blumentritt said later, marked the beginning of what came to be called the "tank terror." Also, for the first time in the war, the Germans did not have the benefit of overwhelming superiority in the air to protect their ground troops and scout ahead. Despite the heavy losses on the ground in the first day of the campaign and in early combat, Soviet fighter planes kept appearing, like the fresh divisions, out of nowhere. Moreover, the swiftness of the German advance and the lack of suitable airfields in Russia left the German fighter bases too far back to provide effective cover at the front. "At several stages in the advance," General von Kleist later reported, "my panzer forces were handicapped through lack of cover overhead." (10)

There was another German miscalculation about the Russians which Kleist mentioned to Liddell Hart and which, of course, was shared by most of the other peoples of the West that summer. (11)

"Hopes of victory," Kleist said, "were largely built on the prospect that the invasion would produce a political upheaval in Russia . . . Too high hopes were built on the belief that Stalin would be overthrown by his own people if he suffered heavy defeats. The belief was fostered by the Fuehrer's political advisers." (12)

Indeed Hitler had told Jodl, "We have only to kick in the door and the whole rotten structure will come crashing down." (13)

The opportunity to kick in the door seemed to the Fuehrer to be at hand halfway through July when there occurred the first great controversy over strategy in the German High Command and led to a decision by the Fuehrer, over the protests of most of the top generals, which Halder thought proved to be "the greatest strategic blunder of the Eastern campaign." The issue was simple but fundamental. Should Bock's Army Group Center, the most powerful and so far the most successful of the three main German armies, push on the two hundred miles to Moscow from Smolensk, which it had reached on July 16? Or should the original plan, which Hitler had laid down in the December 18 directive, and which called for the main thrusts on the north and south flanks, be adhered to? In other words, was Moscow the prize goal, or Leningrad and the Ukraine?   (14)

The Army High Command, led by Brauchitsch and Halder and supported by Bock, whose central army group was moving up the main highway to Moscow, and by Guderian, whose panzer forces were leading it, insisted on an all-out drive for the Soviet capital. There was much more to their argument than merely stressing the psychological value of capturing the enemy capital. Moscow, they pointed out to Hitler, was a vital source of armament production and, even more important, the center of the Russian transportation and communications system. Take it, and the Soviets would not only be deprived of an essential source of arms but would be unable to move troops and supplies to the distant fronts, which thereafter would weaken, wither and collapse.   (15)

But there was a final conclusive argument which the generals advanced to the former corporal who was now their Supreme Commander. All their intelligence reports showed that the main Russian forces were now being concentrated before Moscow for an all-out defense of the capital. Just east of Smolensk a Soviet army of half a million men, which had extricated itself from Bock's double envelopment, was digging in to bar further German progress toward the capital.

> The center of gravity of Russian strength [Halder wrote in a report prepared for the Allies immediately after the war] was therefore in front of Army Group Center . . .
>
> The General Staff had been brought up with the idea that it must be the aim of an operation to defeat the military power of the enemy, and it therefore considered the next and most pressing task to be to defeat the forces of Timoshenko by concentrating all available forces at Army Group Center, to advance on Moscow, to take this nerve center of enemy resistance and to destroy the new enemy formations. The assembly for this attack had to be carried out as soon as possible because the season was advanced. Army Group North was in the meantime to fulfill its original mission and to try to contact the Finns. Army Group South was to advance farther East to tie down the strongest possible enemy force.
>
> . . . After oral discussions between the General Staff and the

> Supreme Command [OKW] had failed, the Commander in Chief
> of the Army [Brauchitsch] submitted a memorandum of the
> General Staff to Hitler. (16)

This, we learn from Halder's diary, was done on August 18. "The effect," says Halder, "was explosive." Hitler had his hungry eyes on the food belt and industrial areas of the Ukraine and on the Russian oil fields just beyond in the Caucasus. Besides, he thought he saw a golden opportunity to entrap Budënny's armies east of the Dnieper beyond Kiev, which still held out. He also wanted to capture Leningrad and join up with the Finns in the north. To accomplish these twin aims, several infantry and panzer divisions from Army Group Center would have to be detached and sent north and especially south. Moscow could wait. (17)

On August 21, Hitler hurled a new directive at his rebellious General Staff. Halder copied it out word for word in his diary the next day.

> The proposals of the Army for the continuation of the operations in the East do not accord with my intentions.
> The most important objective to attain before the onset of winter is not the capture of Moscow but the taking of the Crimea, the industrial and coal-mining areas of the Donets basin and the cutting off of Russian oil supplies from the Caucasus. In the north it is the locking up of Leningrad and the union with the Finns. (18)

The Soviet Fifth Army on the Dnieper in the south, whose stubborn resistance had annoyed Hitler for several days, must, he laid it down, be utterly destroyed, the Ukraine and the Crimea occupied, Leningrad surrounded and a junction with the Finns achieved. "Only then," he concluded, "will the conditions be created whereby Timoshenko's army can be attacked and successfully defeated."

> Thus [commented Halder bitterly] the aim of defeating decisively the Russian armies in front of Moscow was subordinated to the desire to obtain a valuable industrial area and to advance in the direction of Russian oil . . . Hitler now became obsessed with the idea of capturing both Leningrad and Stalingrad, for he persuaded himself that if these two "holy cities of Communism" were to fall, Russia would collapse. (19)

To add insult to injury to the field marshals and the generals who did not appreciate his strategic genius, Hitler sent what Halder called a "countermemorandum" (to that of the Army of the eighteenth), which the General Staff Chief described as "full of insults," such as stating that the Army High Command was full of "minds fossilized in out-of-date theories." (20)

"Unbearable! Unheard of! The limit!" Halder snorted in his diary the next day. He conferred all afternoon and evening with Field Marshal von Brauchitsch about the Fuehrer's "inadmissible" mixing into the business of the Army High Command and General Staff, finally proposing that the head of the Army and he himself resign their posts. "Brauchitsch refused," Halder noted, "because it wouldn't be practical and would change nothing." The gutless Field Marshal had already, as on so many other occasions, capitulated to the onetime corporal.   (21)

When General Guderian arrived at the Fuehrer's headquarters the next day, August 23, and was egged on by Halder to try to talk Hitler out of his disastrous decision, though the hard-bitten panzer leader needed no urging, he was met by Brauchitsch. "I forbid you," the Army Commander in Chief said, "to mention the question of Moscow to the Fuehrer. The operation to the south has been ordered. The problem now is simply how it is to be carried out. Discussion is pointless."   (22)

Nevertheless, when Guderian was ushered into the presence of Hitler —neither Brauchitsch nor Halder accompanied him—he disobeyed orders and argued as strongly as he could for the immediate assault on Moscow.

> Hitler let me speak to the end [Guderian later wrote]. He then described in detail the considerations which had led him to make a different decision. He said that the raw materials and agriculture of the Ukraine were vitally necessary for the future prosecution of the war. He spoke of the need of neutralizing the Crimea, "that Soviet aircraft carrier for attacking the Roumanian oil fields." For the first time I heard him use the phrase: "My generals know nothing about the economic aspects of war." . . . He had given strict orders that the attack on Kiev was to be the immediate strategic objective and all actions were to be carried out with that in mind. I here saw for the first time a spectacle with which I was later to become very familiar: all those present —Keitel, Jodl and others—nodded in agreement with every sentence that Hitler uttered, while I was left alone with my point of view . . .   (23)

But Halder had at no point in the previous discussions nodded his agreement. When Guderian saw him the next day and reported his failure to get Hitler to change his mind, he says the General Staff Chief "to my amazement suffered a complete nervous collapse, which led him to make accusations and imputations which were utterly unjustified."[5]   (24)

This was the most severe crisis in the German military High Command since the beginning of the war. Worse were to follow, with adversity.   (25)

---

[5] Halder, in his diary of August 24, gives quite a different version. He accuses Guderian of "irresponsibly" changing his mind after seeing Hitler and muses how useless it is to try to change a man's character. If he suffered, as Guderian alleges, "a complete nervous collapse," his pedantic diary notes that day indicate that he quickly recovered.

In itself Rundstedt's offensive in the south, made possible by the rein-forcement of Guderian's panzer forces and infantry divisions withdrawn from the central front, was, as Guderian put it, a great tactical victory. Kiev itself fell on September 19—German units had already penetrated 150 miles beyond it—and on the twenty-sixth the Battle of Kiev ended with the en-circlement and surrender of 665,000 Russian prisoners, according to the German claim. To Hitler it was "the greatest battle in the history of the world," but though it was a singular achievement some of his generals were more skeptical of its strategic significance. Bock's armorless army group in the center had been forced to cool its heels for two months along the Desna River just beyond Smolensk. The autumn rains, which would turn the Rus-sian roads into quagmires, were drawing near. And after them—the winter, the cold and the snow.   (26)

THE GREAT DRIVE ON MOSCOW

Reluctantly Hitler gave in to the urging of Brauchitsch, Halder and Bock and consented to the resumption of the drive on Moscow. But too late! Hal-der saw him on the afternoon of September 5 and now the Fuehrer, his mind made up, was in a hurry to get to the Kremlin. "Get started on the central front within eight to ten days," the Supreme Commander ordered. ("Impossible!" Halder exclaimed in his diary.) "Encircle them, beat and de-stroy them," Hitler added, promising to return to Army Group Center Gu-derian's panzer group, then still heavily engaged in the Ukraine, and add Reinhardt's tank corps from the Leningrad front. But it was not until the beginning of October that the armored forces could be brought back, re-fitted and made ready. On October 2 the great offensive was finally launched. "Typhoon" was the code name. A mighty wind, a cyclone, was to hit the Russians, destroy their last fighting forces before Moscow and bring the Soviet Union tumbling down.   (27)

But here again the Nazi dictator became a victim of his megalomania. Taking the Russian capital before winter came was not enough. He gave orders that Field Marshal von Leeb in the north was *at the same time* to capture Leningrad, make contact with the Finns beyond the city and drive on and cut the Murmansk railway. Also, at the same time, Rundstedt was to clear the Black Sea coast, take Rostov, seize the Maikop oil fields and push forward to Stalingrad on the Volga, thus severing Stalin's last link with the Caucasus. When Rundstedt tried to explain to Hitler that this meant an advance of more than four hundred miles beyond the Dnieper, with his left flank dangerously exposed, the Supreme Commander told him that the Rus-sians in the south were now incapable of offering serious resistance. Rund-stedt, who says that he "laughed aloud" at such ridiculous orders, was soon to find the contrary.   (28)

The German drive along the old road which Napoleon had taken to Moscow at first rolled along with all the fury of a typhoon. In the first fortnight of October, in what later Blumentritt called a "textbook battle," the Germans encircled two Soviet armies between Vyazma and Bryansk and claimed to have taken 650,000 prisoners along with 5,000 guns and 1,200 tanks. By October 20 German armored spearheads were within forty miles of Moscow and the Soviet ministries and foreign embassies were hastily evacuating to Kuibyshev on the Volga. Even the sober Halder, who had fallen off his horse and broken a collarbone and was temporarily hospitalized, now believed that with bold leadership and favorable weather Moscow could be taken before the severe Russian winter set in.   (29)

The fall rains, however, had commenced. *Rasputitza*, the period of mud, set in. The great army, moving on wheels, was slowed down and often forced to halt. Tanks had to be withdrawn from battle to pull guns and ammunition trucks out of the mire. Chains and couplings for this job were lacking and bundles of rope had to be dropped by Luftwaffe transport planes which were badly needed for lifting other military supplies. The rains began in mid-October and, as Guderian later remembered, "the next few weeks were dominated by the mud." General Blumentritt, chief of staff of Field Marshal von Kluge's Fourth Army, which was in the thick of the battle for Moscow, has vividly described the predicament.

> The infantryman slithers in the mud, while many teams of horses are needed to drag each gun forward. All wheeled vehicles sink up to their axles in the slime. Even tractors can only move with great difficulty. A large portion of our heavy artillery was soon stuck fast . . . The strain that all this caused our already exhausted troops can perhaps be imagined.   (30)

For the first time there crept into the diary of Halder and the reports of Guderian, Blumentritt and other German generals signs of doubt and then of despair. It spread to the lower officers and the troops in the field—or perhaps it stemmed from them. "And now, when Moscow was already almost in sight," Blumentritt recalled, "the mood both of commanders and troops began to change. Enemy resistance stiffened and the fighting became more bitter . . . Many of our companies were reduced to a mere sixty or seventy men." There was a shortage of serviceable artillery and tanks. "Winter," he says, "was about to begin, but there was no sign of winter clothing . . . Far behind the front the first partisan units were beginning to make their presence felt in the vast forests and swamps. Supply columns were frequently ambushed . . ."   (31)

Now, Blumentritt remembered, the ghosts of the Grand Army, which had taken this same road to Moscow, and the memory of Napoleon's fate began to haunt the dreams of the Nazi conquerors. The German generals began to read, or reread, Caulaincourt's grim account of the French conqueror's disastrous winter in Russia in 1812. (32)

Far to the south, where the weather was a little warmer but the rain and the mud were just as bad, things were not going well either. Kleist's tanks had entered Rostov at the mouth of the Don on November 21 amidst much fanfare from Dr. Goebbels' propaganda band that the "gateway to the Caucasus" had been opened. It did not remain open very long. Both Kleist and Rundstedt realized that Rostov could not be held. Five days later the Russians retook it and the Germans, attacked on both the northern and southern flanks, were in headlong retreat back fifty miles to the Mius River where Kleist and Rundstedt had wished in the first place to establish a winter line. (33)

The retreat from Rostov is another little turning point in the history of the Third Reich. Here was the first time that any Nazi army had ever suffered a major setback. "Our misfortunes began with Rostov," Guderian afterward commented; "that was the writing on the wall." It cost Field Marshal von Rundstedt, the senior officer in the German Army, his command. As he was retreating to the Mius:

> Suddenly an order came to me [he subsequently told Allied interrogators] from the Fuehrer: "Remain where you are, and retreat no further." I immediately wired back: "It is madness to attempt to hold. In the first place the troops cannot do it and in the second place if they do not retreat they will be destroyed. I repeat that this order be rescinded or that you find someone else." That same night the Fuehrer's reply arrived: "I am acceding to your request. Please give up your command." (34)

"I then," said Rundstedt, 'went home."[6] (35)

This mania for ordering distant troops to stand fast no matter what their peril perhaps saved the German Army from complete collapse in the shattering months ahead, though many generals dispute it, but it was to lead to Stalingrad and other disasters and to help seal Hitler's fate. (36)

---

[6] *"Groesste Aufregung* (greatest excitement) by the Fuehrer," Halder noted in his diary on November 30 in describing Rundstedt's retreat to the Mius and Hitler's dismissal of the Field Marshal. "The Fuehrer calls in Brauchitsch and hurls reproaches and abuse at him." Halder had begun his diary that day by noting the figures of German casualties up to November 26. "Total losses of the Eastern armies (not counting the sick), 743,112 officers and men—23 per cent of the entire force of 3.2 million."

On December 1, Halder recorded the replacement of Rundstedt by Reichenau, who still commanded the Sixth Army, which he had led in France and which had been having a hard time of it to the north of Kleist's armored divisions, which were retreating from Rostov.

"Reichenau phones the Fuehrer," Halder wrote, "and asks permission to withdraw tonight to the Mius line. Permission is given. So we are exactly where we were yesterday. But time and strength have been sacrificed and Rundstedt lost."

"The health of Brauchitsch," he added, "as the result of the continuing excitement is again causing anxiety." On November 10 Halder had recorded that the Army chief had suffered a severe heart attack.

Heavy snows and subzero temperatures came early that winter in Russia. Guderian noted the first snow on the night of October 6–7, just as the drive on Moscow was being resumed. It reminded him to ask headquarters again for winter clothing, especially for heavy boots and heavy wool socks. On October 12 he recorded the snow as still falling. On November 3 came the first cold wave, the thermometer dropping below the freezing point and continuing to fall. By the seventh Guderian was reporting the first "severe cases of frostbite" in his ranks and on the thirteenth that the temperature had fallen to 8 degrees below zero, Fahrenheit, and that the lack of winter clothing "was becoming increasingly felt." The bitter cold affected guns and machines as well as men.

> Ice was causing a lot of trouble [Guderian wrote] since the calks for the tank tracks had not yet arrived. The cold made the telescopic sights useless. In order to start the engines of the tanks fires had to be lit beneath them. Fuel was freezing on occasions and the oil became viscous . . . Each regiment [of the 112th Infantry Division] had already lost some 500 men from frostbite. As a result of the cold the machine guns were no longer able to fire and our 37-mm. antitank guns had proved ineffective against the [Russian] T-34 tank.   (37)

"The result," says Guderian, "was a panic which reached as far back as Bogorodsk. This was the first time that such a thing had occurred during the Russian campaign, and it was a warning that the combat ability of our infantry was at an end."   (38)

But not only of the infantry. On November 21 Halder scribbled in his diary that Guderian had telephoned to say that his panzer troops "had reached their end." This tough, aggressive tank commander admits that on this very day he decided to visit the commander of Army Group Center, Bock, and request that the orders he had received be changed, since he "could see no way of carrying them out." He was in a deep mood of depression, writing on the same day:

> The icy cold, the lack of shelter, the shortage of clothing, the heavy losses of men and equipment, the wretched state of our fuel supplies—all this makes the duties of a commander a misery, and the longer it goes on the more I am crushed by the enormous responsibility I have to bear.   (39)

In retrospect Guderian added:

> Only he who saw the endless expanse of Russian snow during this winter of our misery and felt the icy wind that blew across it, burying in snow every object in its path; who drove for hour

after hour through that no-man's land only at last to find too
thin shelter with insufficiently clothed, half-starved men; and
who also saw by contrast the well-fed, warmly clad and fresh Si-
berians, fully equipped for winter fighting . . . can truly judge the
events which now occurred.   (40)

Those events may now be briefly narrated, but not without first stressing
one point: terrible as the Russian winter was and granted that the Soviet
troops were naturally better prepared for it than the German, the main factor in what is now to be set down was not the weather but the fierce fighting
of the Red Army troops and their indomitable will not to give up. The diary
of Halder and the reports of the field commanders, which constantly express amazement at the extent and severity of Russian attacks and counter-
attacks and despair at the German setbacks and losses, are proof of that.
The Nazi generals could not understand why the Russians, considering the
nature of their tyrannical regime and the disastrous effects of the first German blows, did not collapse, as had the French and so many others with
less excuse.   (41)

"With amazement and disappointment," Blumentritt wrote, "we discovered in late October and early November that the beaten Russians
seemed quite unaware that as a military force they had almost ceased to
exist." Guderian tells of meeting an old retired Czarist general at Orel on
the road to Moscow.

> "If only you had come twenty years ago [he told the panzer
> General], we should have welcomed you with open arms. But now
> it's too late. We were just beginning to get on our feet, and now
> you arrive and throw us back twenty years so that we will have to
> start from the beginning all over again. Now we are fighting for
> Russia and in that cause we are all united.   (42)

Yet, as November approached its end amidst fresh blizzards and continued subzero temperatures, Moscow seemed within grasp to Hitler and
most of his generals. North, south and west of the capital German armies
had reached points within twenty to thirty miles of their goal. To Hitler
poring over the map at his headquarters far off in East Prussia the last
stretch seemed no distance at all. His armies had advanced five hundred
miles; they had only twenty to thirty miles to go. "One final heave," he told
Jodl in mid-November, "and we shall triumph." On the telephone to Halder
on November 22, Field Marshal von Bock, directing Army Group Center in
its final push for Moscow, compared the situation to the Battle of the
Marne, "where the last battalion thrown in decided the battle." Despite increased enemy resistance Bock told the General Staff Chief he believed
"everything was attainable." By the last day of November he was literally

throwing in his last battalion. The final all-out attack on the heart of the Soviet Union was set for the next day, December 1, 1941.   (43)

It stumbled on a steely resistance. The greatest tank force ever concentrated on one front: General Hoepner's Fourth Tank Group and General Hermann Hoth's Third Tank Group just north of Moscow and driving south, Guderian's Second Panzer Army just to the south of the capital and pushing north from Tula, Kluge's great Fourth Army in the middle and fighting its way due east through the forests that surrounded the city—on this formidable array were pinned Hitler's high hopes. By December 2 a reconnaissance battalion of the 258th Infantry Division had penetrated to Khimki, a suburb of Moscow, within sight of the spires of the Kremlin, but was driven out the next morning by a few Russian tanks and a motley force of hastily mobilized workers from the city's factories. This was the nearest the German troops ever got to Moscow; it was their first and last glimpse of the Kremlin.   (44)

Already on the evening of December 1, Bock, who was now suffering severe stomach cramps, had telephoned Halder to say that he could no longer "operate" with his weakened troops. The General Staff Chief had tried to cheer him on. "One must try," he said, "to bring the enemy down by a last expenditure of force. If that proves impossible then we will have to draw new conclusions." The next day Halder jotted in his diary: "Enemy resistance has reached its peak." On the following day, December 3, Bock was again on the phone to the Chief of the General Staff, who noted his message in his diary:

> Spearheads of the Fourth Army again pulled back because the flanks could not come forward . . . The moment must be faced when the strength of our troops is at an end.   (45)

When Bock spoke for the first time of going over to the defensive Halder tried to remind him that "the best defense was to stick to the attack."   (46)

It was easier said than done, in view of the Russians and the weather. The next day, December 4, Guderian, whose Second Panzer Army had been halted in its attempt to take Moscow from the south, reported that the thermometer had fallen to 31 degrees below zero. The next day it dropped another five degrees. His tanks, he said, were "almost immobilized" and he was threatened on his flanks and in the rear north of Tula.   (47)

December 5 was the critical day. Everywhere along the 200-mile semicircular front around Moscow the Germans had been stopped. By evening Guderian was notifying Bock that he was not only stopped but must pull back, and Bock was telephoning Halder that "his strength was at an end," and Brauchitsch was telling his Chief of the General Staff in despair that he was quitting as Commander in Chief of the Army. It was a dark and bitter day for the German generals.

> This was the first time [Guderian later wrote] that I had to take a decision of this sort, and none was more difficult . . . Our attack on Moscow had broken down. All the sacrifices and endurance of our brave troops had been in vain. We had suffered a grievous defeat. (48)

At Kluge's Fourth Army headquarters, Blumentritt, the chief of staff, realized that the turning point had been reached. Recalling it later, he wrote: "Our hopes of knocking Russia out of the war in 1941 had been dashed at the very last minute." (49)

The next day, December 6, General Georgi Zhukov, who had replaced Marshal Timoshenko as commander of the central front but six weeks before, struck. On the 200-mile front before Moscow he unleashed seven armies and two cavalry corps—100 divisions in all—consisting of troops that were either fresh or battle-tried and were equipped and trained to fight in the bitter cold and the deep snow. The blow which this relatively unknown general now delivered with such a formidable force of infantry, artillery, tanks, cavalry and planes, which Hitler had not faintly suspected existed, was so sudden and so shattering that the German Army and the Third Reich never fully recovered from it. For a few weeks during the rest of that cold and bitter December and on into January it seemed that the beaten and retreating German armies, their front continually pierced by Soviet breakthroughs, might disintegrate and perish in the Russian snows, as had Napoleon's Grand Army just 130 years before. At several crucial moments it came very close to that. Perhaps it was Hitler's granite will and determination and certainly it was the fortitude of the German soldier that saved the armies of the Third Reich from a complete debacle. (50)

But the failure was great. The Red armies had crippled but not destroyed. Moscow had not been taken, nor Leningrad nor Stalingrad nor the oil fields of the Caucasus; and the lifelines to Britain and America, to the north and to the south, remained open. For the first time in more than two years of unbroken military victories the armies of Hitler were retreating before a superior force. (51)

That was not all. The failure was greater than that. Halder realized this, at least later. "The myth of the invincibility of the German Army," he wrote, "was broken." There would be more German victories in Russia when another summer came around, but they could never restore the myth. December 6, 1941, then, is another turning point in the short history of the Third Reich and one of the most fateful ones. Hitler's power had reached its zenith; from now on it was to decline, sapped by the growing counterblows of the nations against which he had chosen to make aggressive war. (52)

A drastic shake-up in the German High Command and among the field commanders now took place. As the armies fell back over the icy roads and snowy fields before the Soviet counteroffensive, the heads of the German generals began to roll. Rundstedt, as we have already seen, was relieved of command of the southern armies because he had been forced to retreat from Rostov. Field Marshal von Bock's stomach pains became worse with the setbacks in December and he was replaced on December 18 by Field Marshal von Kluge, whose battered Fourth Army was being pushed back, forever, from the vicinity of Moscow. Even the dashing General Guderian, the originator of massive armored warfare which had so revolutionized modern battle, was cashiered—on Christmas Day—for ordering a retreat without permission from above. General Hoepner, an equally brilliant tank commander, whose Fourth Armored Group had come within sight of Moscow on the north and then been pushed back, was abruptly dismissed by Hitler on the same grounds, stripped of his rank and forbidden to wear a uniform. General Hans Count von Sponeck, who had received the Ritterkreuz for leading the airborne landings at The Hague the year before, received a severer chastisement for pulling back one division of his corps in the Crimea on December 29 after Russian troops had landed by sea behind him. He was not only summarily stripped of his rank but imprisoned, court-martialed and, at the insistence of Hitler, sentenced to death.[7]   (53)

Even the obsequious Keitel was in trouble with the Supreme Commander. Even he had enough sense to see during the first days of December that a general withdrawal around Moscow was necessary in order to avert disaster. But when he got up enough courage to say so to Hitler the latter turned on him and gave him a tongue-lashing, shouting that he was a "blockhead." Jodl found the unhappy OKW Chief a little later sitting at a desk writing out his resignation, a revolver at one side. Jodl quietly removed the weapon and persuaded Keitel—apparently without too much difficulty —to stay on and to continue to swallow the Fuehrer's insults, which he did, with amazing endurance, to the very end.   (54)

The strain of leading an army which could not always win under a Supreme Commander who insisted that it always do had brought about renewed heart attacks for Field Marshal von Brauchitsch, and by the time Zhukov's counteroffensive began he was determined to step down as Commander in Chief. He returned to headquarters from a trip to the receding front on December 15 and Halder found him "very beaten down." "Brauchitsch no longer sees any way out," Halder noted in his diary, "for the rescue of the Army from its desperate position." The head of the Army was at the end of his rope. He had asked Hitler on December 7 to relieve him

---

[7] He was not executed until after the July 1944 plot against Hitler, in which he was in no way involved.

and he renewed the request on December 17. It was formally granted two days later. What the Fuehrer really thought of the man he himself had named to head the Army he told to Goebbels three months later.

> The Fuehrer spoke of him [Brauchitsch] only in terms of contempt [Goebbels wrote in his diary on March 20, 1942]. A vain, cowardly wretch . . . and a nincompoop. (55)

To his cronies Hitler said of Brauchitsch, "He's no soldier; he's a man of straw. If Brauchitsch had remained at his post only for another few weeks, things would have ended in catastrophe." (56)

There was some speculation in Army circles as to who would succeed Brauchitsch, but it was as wide of the mark as the speculation years before as to who would succeed Hindenburg. On December 19 Hitler called in Halder and informed him that he himself was taking over as Commander in Chief of the Army. Halder could stay on as Chief of the General Staff if he wanted to—and he wanted to. But from now on, Hitler made it clear, he was personally running the Army, as he ran almost everything else in Germany.

> This little matter of operational command [Hitler told him] is something anyone can do. The task of the Commander in Chief of the Army is to train the Army in a National Socialist way. I know of no general who could do that, as I want it done. Consequently, I've decided to take over command of the Army myself. (57)

Hitler's triumph over the Prussian officer corps was thus completed. The former Vienna vagabond and ex-corporal was now head of state, Minister of War, Supreme Commander of the Armed Forces and Commander in Chief of the Army. The generals, as Halder complained—in his diary—were now merely postmen purveying Hitler's orders based on Hitler's singular conception of strategy. (58)

Actually the megalomaniacal dictator soon would make himself something even greater, legalizing a power never before held by any man—emperor, king or president—in the experience of the German Reichs. On April 26, 1942, he had his rubber-stamp Reichstag pass a law which gave him absolute power of life and death over every German and simply suspended any laws which might stand in the way of this. The words of the law have to be read to be believed.

> . . . In the present war, in which the German people are faced with a struggle for their existence or their annihilation, the Fuehrer must have all the rights postulated by him which serve to fur-

ther or achieve victory. Therefore—without being bound by existing legal regulations—in his capacity as Leader of the nation,
Supreme Commander of the Armed Forces, Head of Government and supreme executive chief, as Supreme Justice and
Leader of the Party—the Fuehrer must be in a position to force
with all means at his disposal every German, if necessary,
whether he be common soldier or officer, low or high official or
judge, leading or subordinate official of the party, worker or employer—to fulfill his duties. In case of violation of these duties,
the Fuehrer is entitled after conscientious examination, regardless of so-called well-deserved rights, to mete out due punishment and to remove the offender from his post, rank and position without introducing prescribed procedures.   (59)

Truly Adolf Hitler had become not only the Leader of Germany but the
Law. Not even in medieval times nor further back in the barbarous tribal
days had any German arrogated such tyrannical power, nominal and legal
as well as actual, to himself.   (60)

But even without this added authority, Hitler was absolute master of
the Army, of which he had now assumed direct command. Ruthlessly he
moved that bitter winter to stem the retreat of his beaten armies and to save
them from the fate of Napoleon's troops along the same frozen, snowbound
roads back from Moscow. He forbade any further withdrawals. The German
generals have long debated the merits of his stubborn stand—whether it
saved the troops from complete disaster or whether it compounded the
inevitable heavy losses. Most of the commanders have contended that if
they had been given freedom to pull back when their position became untenable they could have saved many men and much equipment and been in
a better position to re-form and even counterattack. As it was, whole divisions were frequently overrun or surrounded and cut to pieces when a
timely withdrawal would have saved them.   (61)

And yet some of the generals later reluctantly admitted that Hitler's iron
will in insisting that the armies stand and fight was his greatest accomplishment of the war in that it probably did save his armies from completely
disintegrating in the snow. This view is best summed up by General
Blumentritt.

Hitler's fanatical order that the troops must hold fast regardless in every position and in the most impossible circumstances
was undoubtedly correct. Hitler realized instinctively that any
retreat across the snow and ice must, within a few days, lead to
the dissolution of the front and that if this happened the Wehrmacht would suffer the same fate that had befallen the *Grande
Armée* . . . The withdrawal could only be carried out across the
open country since the roads and tracks were blocked with snow.
After a few nights this would prove too much for the troops, who

would simply lie down and die wherever they found themselves. There were no prepared positions in the rear into which they could be withdrawn, nor any sort of line to which they could hold on. (62)

General von Tippelskirch, a corps commander, agreed.

It was Hitler's one great achievement. At that critical moment the troops were remembering what they had heard about Napoleon's retreat from Moscow, and living under the shadow of it. If they had once begun a retreat, it might have turned into a panic flight. (63)

There was panic in the German Army, not only at the front but far in the rear at headquarters, and it is graphically recorded in Halder's diary. "Very difficult day!" he begins his journal on Christmas Day, 1941, and thereafter into the new year he repeats the words at the head of many a day's entry as he describes each fresh Russian breakthrough and the serious situation of the various armies.

December 29. Another critical day! . . . Dramatic long-distance telephone talk between Fuehrer and Kluge. Fuehrer forbids further withdrawal of northern wing of 4th Army. Very bad crisis by 9th Army where apparently the commanders have lost their heads. At noon an excited call from Kluge. 9th Army wishes to withdraw behind Rzhev . . .

January 2, 1942. A day of wild fighting! . . . Grave crisis by 4th and 9th Armies . . . Russian breakthrough north of Maloyaroslavets tears the front wide open and it's difficult to see at the moment how front can be restored . . . This situation leads Kluge to demand withdrawal of sagging front. Very stormy argument with Fuehrer, who however holds to his stand: The front will remain where it is regardless of consequences . . .

January 3. The situation has become more critical as the result of the breakthrough between Maloyaroslavets and Borovsk. Kuebler[8] and Bock very excited and demand withdrawal on the north front, which is crumbling. Again a dramatic scene by Fuehrer, who doubts courage of generals to make hard decisions. But troops simply don't hold their ground when it's 30 below zero. Fuehrer orders: He will personally decide if any more withdrawals necessary. . . . (64)

Not the Fuehrer but the Russian Army was by now deciding such matters. Hitler could force the German troops to stand fast and die, but he

---

8 General Kuebler had replaced Kluge on December 26 as commander of the Fourth Army when the latter took over Army Group Center. Though a tough soldier, he stood the strain only three weeks and then was relieved by General Heinrici.

could no more stop the Soviet advance than King Canute could prevent the tides from coming in. At one moment of panic some of the High Command officers suggested that perhaps the situation could be retrieved by the employment of poison gas. "Colonel Ochsner tries to talk me into beginning gas warfare against the Russians," Halder noted in his diary on January 7. Perhaps it was too cold. At any rate nothing came of the suggestion.   (65)

January 8 was "a very critical day," as Halder noted in his journal. "The breakthrough at Sukhinichi [southwest of Moscow] is becoming unbearable for Kluge. He is consequently insisting on withdrawing the 4th Army front." All day long the Field Marshal was on the phone to Hitler and Halder insisting on it. Finally, in the evening the Fuehrer reluctantly consented. Kluge was given permission to withdraw "step by step in order to protect his communications."   (66)

Step by step and sometimes more rapidly throughout that grim winter the German armies, which had planned to celebrate Christmas in Moscow, were driven back or forced by Russian encirclements and breakthroughs to retreat. By the end of February they found themselves from 75 to 200 miles from the capital. By the end of that freezing month Halder was noting in his diary the cost in men of the misfired Russian adventure. Total losses up to February 28, he wrote down, were 1,005,636, or 31 per cent of his entire force. Of these 202,251 had been killed, 725,642 wounded and 46,511 were missing. (Casualties from frostbite were 112,627.) This did not include the heavy losses among the Hungarians, Rumanians and Italians in Russia. (67)

With the coming of the spring thaws a lull came over the long front and Hitler and Halder began making plans for bringing up fresh troops and more tanks and guns to resume the offensive—at least on part of the front. Never again would they have the strength to attack all along the vast battle line. The bitter winter's toll and above all Zhukov's counteroffensive doomed that hope.   (68)

But Hitler, we now know, had realized long before that his gamble of conquering Russia—not only in six months but ever—had failed. In a diary entry of November 19, 1941, General Halder notes a long "lecture" of the Fuehrer to several officers of the High Command. Though his armies are only a few miles from Moscow and still driving hard to capture it, Hitler has abandoned hopes of striking Russia down this year and has already turned his thoughts to next year. Halder jotted down the Leader's ideas.

> Goals for next year. First of all the Caucasus. Objective: Russia's southern borders. Time: March to April. In the north after the close of this year's campaign, Vologda or Gorki,[9] but only at the end of May.

---

[9] Vologda, 300 miles northeast of Moscow, controlled the railway to Archangel. Gorki is 300 miles due *east* of the capital.

> Further goals for next year must remain open. They will de-
> pend on the capacity of our railroads. The question of later
> building an "East Wall" also remains open. (69)

No East Wall would be necessary if the Soviet Union were to be destroyed. Halder seems to have mulled over that as he listened to the Supreme Commander go on.

> On the whole [he concluded] one gets the impression that Hit-
> ler recognizes now that neither side can destroy the other and
> that this will lead to peace negotiations. (70)

This must have been a rude awakening for the Nazi conqueror who six
weeks before in Berlin had made a broadcast declaring "without any reservation" that Russia had been "struck down and would never rise again." His
plans had been wrecked, his hopes doomed. They were further dashed a
fortnight later, on December 6, when his troops began to be beaten back
from the suburbs of Moscow. (71)

The next day, Sunday, December 7, 1941, an event occurred on the other
side of the round earth that transformed the European war, which he had
so lightly provoked, into a world war, which, though he could not know it,
would seal his fate and that of the Third Reich. Japanese bombers attacked
Pearl Harbor. The next day[10] Hitler hurried back by train to Berlin from his
headquarters at Wolfsschanze. He had made a solemn secret promise to
Japan and the time had come to keep it—or break it. (72)

---

[10] Hitler's movements and whereabouts are noted in his daily calendar book, which is among the captured documents.

NARRATIVE, INCLUDING DESCRIPTION

Fictional Narrative

Philip Roth

(1933–)

ROTH won the National Book Award for fiction with his first book, Goodbye, Columbus and Five Short Stories *(1960). He published his first novel,* Letting Go, *in 1962. His latest novel,* When She Was Good *(1967), climbed quickly to the "Best Seller List" of the* New York Times Book Review. *Roth taught English at the University of Chicago before devoting his full time and talent to writing.*

■ *The Conversion of the Jews*

"YOU'RE A REAL one for opening your mouth in the first place," Itzie said. "What do you open your mouth all the time for?" (1)

"I didn't bring it up, Itz, I didn't," Ozzie said. (2)

"What do you care about Jesus Christ for anyway?" (3)

"I didn't bring up Jesus Christ. He did. I didn't even know what he was talking about. Jesus is historical, he kept saying. Jesus is historical." Ozzie mimicked the monumental voice of Rabbi Binder. (4)

"Jesus was a person that lived like you and me," Ozzie continued. "That's what Binder said—" (5)

"Yeah? . . . So what! What do I give two cents whether he lived or not. And what do you gotta open your mouth!" Itzie Lieberman favored closed-mouthedness, especially when it came to Ozzie Freedman's questions. Mrs. Freedman had to see Rabbi Binder twice before about Ozzie's questions and this Wednesday at four-thirty would be the third time. Itzie preferred

801

to keep *his* mother in the kitchen; he settled for behind-the-back subtleties such as gestures, faces, snarls and other less delicate barnyard noises.   (6)

"He was a real person, Jesus, but he wasn't like God, and we don't believe he is God." Slowly, Ozzie was explaining Rabbi Binder's position to Itzie, who had been absent from Hebrew School the previous afternoon. (7)

"The Catholics," Itzie said helpfully, "they believe in Jesus Christ, that he's God." Itzie Lieberman used "the Catholics" in its broadest sense—to include the Protestants.   (8)

Ozzie received Itzie's remark with a tiny head bob, as though it were a footnote, and went on. "His mother was Mary, and his father probably was Joseph," Ozzie said. "But the New Testament says his real father was God."   (9)

"His *real* father?"   (10)

"Yeah," Ozzie said, "that's the big thing, his father's supposed to be God."   (11)

"Bull."   (12)

"That's what Rabbi Binder says, that it's impossible—"   (13)

"Sure it's impossible. That stuff's all bull. To have a baby you gotta get laid," Itzie theologized. "Mary hadda get laid."   (14)

"That's what Binder says: 'The only way a woman can have a baby is to have intercourse with a man.'"   (15)

"He said *that*, Ozz?" For a moment it appeared that Itzie had put the theological question aside. "He said that, intercourse?" A little curled smile shaped itself in the lower half of Itzie's face like a pink mustache. "What you guys do, Ozz, you laugh or something?"   (16)

"I raised my hand."   (19)

"Yeah? Whatja say?"   (18)

"That's when I asked the question."   (19)

Itzie's face lit up. "Whatja ask about—intercourse?"   (20)

"No, I asked the question about God, how if He could create the heaven and earth in six days, and make all the animals and the fish and the light in six days—the light especially, that's what always gets me, that He could make the light. Making fish and animals, that's pretty good—"   (21)

"That's damn good." Itzie's appreciation was honest but unimaginative: it was as though God had just pitched a one-hitter.   (22)

"But making light . . . I mean when you think about it, it's really something," Ozzie said. "Anyway, I asked Binder if He could make all that in six days, and He could *pick* the six days he wanted right out of nowhere, why couldn't He let a woman have a baby without having intercourse." (23)

"You said intercourse, Ozz, to Binder?"   (24)

"Yeah."   (25)

"Right in class?"   (26)

"Yeah."   (27)

Itzie smacked the side of his head.   (28)

"I mean, no kidding around," Ozzie said, "that'd really be nothing. After all that other stuff, that'd practically be nothing."   (29)

Itzie considered a moment. "What'd Binder say?"   (30)

"He started all over again explaining how Jesus was historical and how he lived like you and me but he wasn't God. So I said I under*stood* that. What I wanted to know was different."   (31)

What Ozzie wanted to know was always different. The first time he had wanted to know how Rabbi Binder could call the Jews "The Chosen People" if the Declaration of Independence claimed all men to be created equal. Rabbi Binder tried to distinguish for him between political equality and spiritual legitimacy, but what Ozzie wanted to know, he insisted vehemently, was different. That was the first time his mother had to come. (32)

Then there was the plane crash. Fifty-eight people had been killed in a plane crash at La Guardia. In studying a casualty list in the newspaper his mother had discovered among the list of those dead eight Jewish names (his grandmother had nine but she counted Miller as a Jewish name); because of the eight she said the plane crash was "a tragedy." During free-discussion time on Wednesday Ozzie had brought to Rabbi Binder's attention this matter of "some of his relations" always picking out the Jewish names. Rabbi Binder had begun to explain cultural unity and some other things when Ozzie stood up at his seat and said that what he wanted to know was different. Rabbi Binder insisted that he sit down and it was then that Ozzie shouted that he wished all fifty-eight were Jews. That was the second time his mother came.   (33)

"And he kept explaining about Jesus being historical, and so I kept asking him. No kidding, Itz, he was trying to make me look stupid."   (34)

"So what he finally do?"   (35)

"Finally he starts screaming that I was deliberately simple-minded and a wise guy, and that my mother had to come, and this was the last time. And that I'd never get bar-mitzvahed if he could help it. Then, Itz, then he starts talking in that voice like a statue, real slow and deep, and he says that I better think over what I said about the Lord. He told me to go to his office and think it over." Ozzie leaned his body towards Itzie. "Itz, I thought it over for a solid hour, and now I'm convinced God could do it."   (36)

Ozzie had planned to confess his latest transgression to his mother as soon as she came home from work. But it was a Friday night in November and already dark, and when Mrs. Freedman came through the door she tossed off her coat, kissed Ozzie quickly on the face, and went to the kitchen table to light the three yellow candles, two for the Sabbath and one for Ozzie's father.   (37)

When his mother lit the candles she would move her two arms slowly towards her, dragging them through the air, as though persuading people whose minds were half made up. And her eyes would get glassy with tears. Even when his father was alive Ozzie remembered that her eyes had gotten glassy, so it didn't have anything to do with his dying. It had something to do with lighting the candles.   (38)

As she touched the flaming match to the unlit wick of a Sabbath candle, the phone rang, and Ozzie, standing only a foot from it, plucked it off the receiver and held it muffled to his chest. When his mother lit candles Ozzie felt there should be no noise; even breathing, if you could manage it, should be softened. Ozzie pressed the phone to his breast and watched his mother dragging whatever she was dragging, and he felt his own eyes get glassy. His mother was a round, tired, gray-haired penguin of a woman whose gray skin had begun to feel the tug of gravity and the weight of her own history. Even when she was dressed up she didn't look like a chosen person. But when she lit candles she looked like something better; like a woman who knew momentarily that God could do anything.   (39)

After a few mysterious minutes she was finished. Ozzie hung up the phone and walked to the kitchen table where she was beginning to lay the two places for the four-course Sabbath meal. He told her that she would have to see Rabbi Binder next Wednesday at four-thirty, and then he told her why. For the first time in their life together she hit Ozzie across the face with her hand.   (40)

All through the chopped liver and chicken soup part of the dinner Ozzie cried; he didn't have any appetite for the rest.   (41)

On Wednesday, in the largest of the three basement classrooms of the synagogue, Rabbi Marvin Binder, a tall, handsome, broad-shouldered man of thirty with thick strong-fibered black hair, removed his watch from his pocket and saw that it was four o'clock. At the rear of the room Yakov Blotnik, the seventy-one-year-old custodian, slowly polished the large window, mumbling to himself, unaware that it was four o'clock or six o'clock, Monday or Wednesday. To most of the students Yakov Blotnik's mumbling, along with his brown curly beard, scythe nose, and two heel-trailing black cats, made of him an object of wonder, a foreigner, a relic, towards whom they were alternately fearful and disrespectful. To Ozzie the mumbling had always seemed a monotonous, curious prayer; what made it curious was that old Blotnik had been mumbling so steadily for so many years, Ozzie suspected he had memorized the prayers and forgotten all about God. (42)

"It is now free-discussion time," Rabbi Binder said. "Feel free to talk about any Jewish matter at all—religion, family, politics, sports—"   (43)

There was silence. It was a gusty, clouded November afternoon and it did not seem as though there ever was or could be a thing called baseball.

So nobody this week said a word about that hero from the past, Hank Greenberg—which limited free discussion considerably.   (44)

And the soul-battering Ozzie Freedman had just received from Rabbi Binder had imposed its limitation. When it was Ozzie's turn to read aloud from the Hebrew book the rabbi had asked him petulantly why he didn't read more rapidly. He was showing no progress. Ozzie said he could read faster but that if he did he was sure not to understand what he was reading. Nevertheless, at the rabbi's repeated suggestion Ozzie tried, and showed a great talent, but in the midst of a long passage he stopped short and said he didn't understand a word he was reading, and started in again at a drag-footed pace. Then came the soul-battering.   (45)

Consequently when free-discussion time rolled around none of the students felt too free. The rabbi's invitation was answered only by the mumbling of feeble old Blotnik.   (46)

"Isn't there anything at all you would like to discuss?" Rabbi Binder asked again, looking at his watch. "No questions or comments?"   (47)

There was a small grumble from the third row. The rabbi requested that Ozzie rise and give the rest of the class the advantage of his thought.   (48)

Ozzie rose. "I forget it now," he said, and sat down in his place.   (49)

Rabbi Binder advanced a seat towards Ozzie and poised himself on the edge of the desk. It was Itzie's desk and the rabbi's frame only a dagger's-length away from his face snapped him to sitting attention.   (50)

"Stand up again, Oscar," Rabbi Binder said calmly, "and try to assemble your thoughts."   (51)

Ozzie stood up. All his classmates turned in their seats and watched as he gave an unconvincing scratch to his forehead.   (52)

"I can't assemble any," he announced, and plunked himself down.   (53)

"Stand up!" Rabbi Binder advanced from Itzie's desk to the one directly in front of Ozzie; when the rabbinical back was turned Itzie gave it five-fingers off the tip of his nose, causing a small titter in the room. Rabbi Binder was too absorbed in squelching Ozzie's nonsense once and for all to bother with titters. "Stand up, Oscar. What's your question about?"   (54)

Ozzie pulled a word out of the air. It was the handiest word. "Religion."   (55)

"Oh, now you remember?"   (56)

"Yes."   (57)

"What is it?"   (58)

Trapped, Ozzie blurted the first thing that came to him. "Why can't He make anything He wants to make!"   (59)

As Rabbi Binder prepared an answer, a final answer, Itzie, ten feet behind him, raised one finger on his left hand, gestured it meaningfully towards the rabbi's back, and brought the house down.   (60)

Binder twisted quickly to see what had happened and in the midst of the

commotion Ozzie shouted into the rabbi's back what he couldn't have
shouted to his face. It was a loud, toneless sound that had the timbre of
something stored inside for about six days.   (61)
   "You don't know! You don't know anything about God!"   (62)
The rabbi spun back towards Ozzie. "What?"   (63)
   "You don't know—you don't—"   (64)
   "Apologize, Oscar, apologize!" It was a threat.   (65)
   "You don't—"   (66)
Rabbi Binder's hand flicked out at Ozzie's cheek. Perhaps it had only
been meant to clamp the boy's mouth shut, but Ozzie ducked and the palm
caught him squarely on the nose.   (67)
   The blood came in a short, red spurt on to Ozzie's shirt front.   (68)
   The next moment was all confusion. Ozzie screamed, "You bastard, you
bastard!" and broke for the classroom door. Rabbi Binder lurched a step
backwards, as though his own blood had started flowing violently in the
opposite direction, then gave a clumsy lurch forward and bolted out the
door after Ozzie. The class followed after the rabbi's huge blue-suited back,
and before old Blotnik could turn from his window, the room was empty
and everyone was headed full speed up the three flights leading to the roof.
                                                                   (69)

   If one should compare the light of day to the life of man: sunrise to
birth; sunset—the dropping down over the edge—to death; then as Ozzie
Freedman wiggled through the trapdoor of the synagogue roof, his feet
kicking backwards bronco-style at Rabbi Binder's outstretched arms—at
that moment the day was fifty years old. As a rule, fifty or fifty-five reflects
accurately the age of late afternoons in November, for it is in that month,
during those hours, that one's awareness of light seems no longer a matter
of seeing, but of hearing: light begins clicking away. In fact, as Ozzie locked
shut the trapdoor in the rabbi's face, the sharp click of the bolt into the lock
might momentarily have been mistaken for the sound of the heavier gray
that had just throbbed through the sky.   (70)
   With all his weight Ozzie kneeled on the locked door; any instant he
was certain that Rabbi Binder's shoulder would fling it open, splintering the
wood into shrapnel and catapulting his body into the sky. But the door did
not move and below him he heard only the rumble of feet, first loud then
dim, like thunder rolling away.   (71)
   A question shot through his brain. "Can this be me?" For a thirteen-
year-old who had just labeled his religious leader a bastard, twice, it was
not an improper question. Louder and louder the question came to him—
"Is it me? Is it me?"—until he discovered himself no longer kneeling, but
racing crazily towards the edge of the roof, his eyes crying, his throat
screaming, and his arms flying everywhichway as though not his own. (72)

"Is it me? Is it me Me ME ME ME! *It has to be me—but is it!*"   (73)

It is the question a thief must ask himself the night he jimmies open his first window, and it is said to be the question with which bridegrooms quiz themselves before the altar.   (74)

In the few wild seconds it took Ozzie's body to propel him to the edge of the roof, his self-examination began to grow fuzzy. Gazing down at the street, he became confused as to the problem beneath the question: was it, is-it-me-who-called-Binder-a-bastard? or, is-it-me-prancing-around-on-the-roof? However, the scene below settled all, for there is an instant in any action when whether it is you or somebody else is academic. The thief crams the money in his pockets and scoots out the window. The bridegroom signs the hotel register for two. And the boy on the roof finds a streetful of people gaping at him, necks stretched backwards, faces up, as though he were the ceiling of the Hayden Planetarium. Suddenly you know it's you.   (75)

"Oscar! Oscar Freedman!" A voice rose from the center of the crowd, a voice that, could it have been seen, would have looked like the writing on scroll. "Oscar Freedman, get down from there. Immediately!" Rabbi Binder was pointing one arm stiffly up at him; and at the end of that arm, one finger aimed menacingly. It was the attitude of a dictator, but one—the eyes confessed all—whose personal valet had spit neatly in his face.   (76)

Ozzie didn't answer. Only for a blink's length did he look towards Rabbi Binder. Instead his eyes began to fit together the world beneath him, to sort out people from places, friends from enemies, participants from spectators. In little jagged starlike clusters his friends stood around Rabbi Binder, who was still pointing. The topmost point on a star compounded not of angels but of five adolescent boys was Itzie. What a world it was, with those stars below, Rabbi Binder below . . . Ozzie, who a moment earlier hadn't been able to control his own body, started to feel the meaning of the word control: he felt Peace and he felt Power.   (77)

"Oscar Freedman, I'll give you three to come down."   (78)

Few dictators give their subjects three to do anything; but, as always, Rabbi Binder only looked dictatorial.   (79)

"Are you ready, Oscar?"   (80)

Ozzie nodded his head yes, although he had no intention in the world—the lower one of the celestial one he'd just entered—of coming down even if Rabbi Binder should give him a million.   (81)

"All right then," said Rabbi Binder. He ran a hand through his black Samson hair as though it were the gesture prescribed for uttering the first digit. Then, with his other hand cutting a circle out of the small piece of sky around him, he spoke. "One!"   (82)

There was no thunder. On the contrary, at that moment, as though "one" was the cue for which he had been waiting, the world's least thunderous person appeared on the synagogue steps. He did not so much come out the synagogue door as lean out, onto the darkening air. He clutched at the doorknob with one hand and looked up at the roof.   (83)

"Oy!"   (84)

Yakov Blotnik's old mind hobbled slowly, as if on crutches, and though he couldn't decide precisely what the boy was doing on the roof, he knew it wasn't good—that is, it wasn't-good-for-the-Jews. For Yakov Blotnik life had fractionated itself simply: things were either good-for-the-Jews or no-good-for-the-Jews.   (85)

He smacked his free hand to his in-sucked cheek, gently. "Oy, Gut!" And then quickly as he was able, he jacked down his head and surveyed the street. There was Rabbi Binder (like a man at an auction with only three dollars in his pocket, he had just delivered a shaky "Two!"); there were the students, and that was all. So far it-wasn't-so-bad-for-the-Jews. But the boy had to come down immediately, before anybody saw. The problem: how to get the boy off the roof?   (86)

Anybody who has ever had a cat on the roof knows how to get him down. You call the fire department. Or first you call the operator and you ask her for the fire department. And the next thing there is great jamming of brakes and clanging of bells and shouting of instructions. And then the cat is off the roof. You do the same thing to get a boy off the roof.   (87)

That is, you do the same thing if you are Yakov Blotnik and you once had a cat on the roof.   (88)

When the engines, all four of them, arrived, Rabbi Binder had four times given Ozzie the count of three. The big hook-and-ladder swung around the corner and one of the firemen leaped from it, plunging headlong towards the yellow fire hydrant in front of the synagogue. With a huge wrench he began to unscrew the top nozzle. Rabbi Binder raced over to him and pulled at his shoulder.   (89)

"There's no fire . . ."   (90)

The fireman mumbled back over his shoulder and, heatedly, continued working at the nozzle.   (91)

"But there's no fire, there's no fire . . ." Binder shouted. When the fireman mumbled again, the rabbi grasped his face with both his hands and pointed it up at the roof.   (92)

To Ozzie it looked as though Rabbi Binder was trying to tug the fireman's head out of his body, like a cork from a bottle. He had to giggle at the picture they made: it was a family portrait—rabbi in black skullcap, fireman in red fire hat, and the little yellow hydrant squatting beside like a kid brother, bareheaded. From the edge of the roof Ozzie waved at the portrait, a one-handed, flapping, mocking wave; in doing it his right foot slipped from under him. Rabbi Binder covered his eyes with his hands. (93)

Firemen work fast. Before Ozzie had even regained his balance, a big, round, yellowed net was being held on the synagogue lawn. The firemen who held it looked up at Ozzie with stern, feelingless faces.   (94)

One of the firemen turned his head towards Rabbi Binder. "What, is the kid nuts or something?"   (95)

Rabbi Binder unpeeled his hands from his eyes, slowly, painfully, as if they were tape. Then he checked: nothing on the sidewalk, no dents in the net.   (96)

"Is he gonna jump, or what?" the fireman shouted.   (97)

In a voice not at all like a statue, Rabbi Binder finally answered. "Yes, Yes, I think so . . . He's been threatening to . . ."   (98)

Threatening to? Why, the reason he was on the roof, Ozzie remembered, was to get away; he hadn't even thought about jumping. He had just run to get away, and the truth was that he hadn't really headed for the roof as much as he'd been chased there.   (99)

"What's his name, the kid?"   (100)

"Freedman," Rabbi Binder answered. "Oscar Freedman."   (101)

The fireman looked up at Ozzie. "What is it with you, Oscar? You gonna jump, or what?"   (102)

Ozzie did not answer. Frankly, the question had just arisen.   (103)

"Look, Oscar, if you're gonna jump, jump—and if you're not gonna jump, don't jump. But don't waste our time, willya?"   (104)

Ozzie looked at the fireman and then at Rabbi Binder. He wanted to see Rabbi Binder cover his eyes one more time.   (105)

"I'm going to jump."   (106)

And then he scampered around the edge of the roof to the corner, where there was no net below, and he flapped his arms at his sides, swishing the air and smacking his palms to his trousers on the downbeat. He began screaming like some kind of engine, "Wheeeee . . . wheeeeee," and leaning way out over the edge with the upper half of his body. The firemen whipped around to cover the ground with the net. Rabbi Binder mumbled a few words to Somebody and covered his eyes. Everything happened quickly, jerkily, as in a silent movie. The crowd, which had arrived with the fire engines, gave out a long, Fourth-of-July fireworks oooh-aahhh. In the excitement no one had paid the crowd much heed, except, of course, Yakov Blotnik, who swung from the doorknob counting heads. "Fier und tsvantsik . . . finf und tsvantsik . . . Oy, Gut!" It wasn't like this with the cat.   (107)

Rabbi Binder peeked through his fingers, checked the sidewalk and net. Empty. But there was Ozzie racing to the other corner. The firemen raced with him but were unable to keep up. Whenever Ozzie wanted to he might jump and splatter himself upon the sidewalk, and by the time the firemen

scooted to the spot all they could do with their net would be to cover the
mess.   (108)
    "Wheeeee . . . wheeeee . . ."   (109)
    "Hey, Oscar," the winded fireman yelled, "What the hell is this, a game
or something?"   (110)
    "Wheeeee . . . wheeeee . . ."   (111)
    "Hey, Oscar—"   (112)
    But he was off now to the other corner, flapping his wings fiercely. Rabbi
Binder couldn't take it any longer—the fire engines from nowhere, the
screaming suicidal boy, the net. He fell to his knees, exhausted, and with
his hands curled together in front of his chest like a little dome, he pleaded,
"Oscar, stop it, Oscar. Don't jump, Oscar. Please come down . . . Please
don't jump."   (113)
    And further back in the crowd a single voice, a single young voice,
shouted a lone word to the boy on the roof.   (114)
    "Jump!"   (115)
    It was Itzie. Ozzie momentarily stopped flapping. (116)
    "Go ahead, Ozz—jump!" Itzie broke off his point of the star and cou-
rageously, with the inspiration not of a wise-guy but of a disciple, stood
alone. "Jump, Ozz, jump!"   (117)
    Still on his knees, his hands still curled, Rabbi Binder twisted his body
back. He looked at Itzie, then, agonizingly, back to Ozzie.   (118)
    "OSCAR, DON'T JUMP! PLEASE, DON'T JUMP . . . please, please . . ." (119)
    "Jump!" This time it wasn't Itzie but another point of the star. By the
time Mrs. Freedman arrived to keep her four-thirty appointment with
Rabbi Binder, the whole little upside down heaven was shouting and pleading for Ozzie to jump, and Rabbi Binder no longer was pleading with him
not to jump, but was crying into the dome of his hands.   (120)

    Understandably Mrs. Freedman couldn't figure out what her son was
doing on the roof. So she asked.   (121)
    "Ozzie, my Ozzie, what are you doing? My Ozzie, what is it?"   (122)
    Ozzie stopped wheeeeeing and slowed his arms down to a cruising flap,
the kind birds use in soft winds, but he did not answer. He stood against
the low, clouded, darkening sky—light clicked down swiftly now, as on a
small gear—flapping softly and gazing down at the small bundle of a woman
who was his mother.   (123)
    "What are you doing, Ozzie?" She turned towards the kneeling Rabbi
Binder and rushed so close that only a paper-thickness of dusk lay between
her stomach and his shoulders.   (124)
    "What is my baby doing?"   (125)
    Rabbi Binder gaped up at her but he too was mute. All that moved
was the dome of his hands; it shook back and forth like a weak pulse. (126)

"Rabbi, get him down! He'll kill himself. Get him down, my only baby . . ."   (127)

"I can't," Rabbi Binder said, "I can't . . . " and he turned his handsome head towards the crowd of boys behind him. "It's them. Listen to them."   (128)

And for the first time Mrs. Freedman saw the crowd of boys, and she heard what they were yelling.   (129)

"He's doing it for them. He won't listen to me. It's them." Rabbi Binder spoke like one in a trance.   (130)

"For them?"   (131)

"Yes."   (132)

"Why for them?"   (133)

"They want him to . . ."   (134)

Mrs. Freedman raised her two arms upward as though she were conducting the sky. "For them he's doing it!" And then in a gesture older than pyramids, older than prophets and floods, her arms came slapping down to her sides. "A martyr I have. Look!" She tilted her head to the roof. Ozzie was still flapping softly. "My martyr."   (135)

"Oscar, come down, *please*," Rabbi Binder groaned.   (136)

In a startlingly even voice Mrs. Freedman called to the boy on the roof. "Ozzie, come down, Ozzie. Don't be a martyr, my baby."   (137)

As though it were a litany, Rabbi Binder repeated her words. "Don't be a martyr, my baby. Don't be a martyr."   (138)

"Gawhead, Ozz—*be* a Martin!" It was Itzie. "Be a Martin, be a Martin," and all the voices joined in singing for Martindom, whatever *it* was. "Be a Martin, be a Martin . . ."   (139)

Somehow when you're on a roof the darker it gets the less you can hear. All Ozzie knew was that two groups wanted two new things: his friends were spirited and musical about what they wanted; his mother and the rabbi were even-toned, chanting, about what they didn't want. The rabbi's voice was without tears now and so was his mother's.   (140)

The big net stared up at Ozzie like a sightless eye. The big, clouded sky pushed down. From beneath it looked like a gray corrugated board. Suddenly, looking up into that unsympathetic sky, Ozzie realized all the strangeness of what these people, his friends, were asking: they wanted him to jump, to kill himself; they were singing about it now—it made them that happy. And there was an even greater strangeness: Rabbi Binder was on his knees, trembling. If there was a question to be asked now it was not "Is it me?" but rather "Is it us? . . . Is it us?"   (141)

Being on the roof, it turned out, was a serious thing. If he jumped would the singing become dancing? Would it? What would jumping stop? Yearningly, Ozzie wished he could rip open the sky, plunge his hands through,

and pull out the sun; and on the sun, like a coin, would be stamped JUMP or
DON'T JUMP.   (142)

Ozzie's knees rocked and sagged a little under him as though they were
setting him for a dive. His arms tightened, stiffened, froze, from shoulders
to fingernails. He felt as if each part of his body were going to vote as to
whether he should kill himself or not—and each part as though it were independent of *him*.   (143)

The light took an unexpected click down and the new darkness, like a
gag, hushed the friends singing for this and the mother and rabbi chanting
for that.   (144)

Ozzie stopped counting votes, and in a curiously high voice, like one
who wasn't prepared for speech, he spoke.   (145)

"Mamma?"   (146)

"Yes, Oscar."   (147)

"Mamma, get down on your knees, like Rabbi Binder."   (148)

"Oscar—"   (149)

"Get down on your knees," he said, "or I'll jump."   (150)

Ozzie heard a whimper, then a quick rustling, and when he looked down
where his mother had stood he saw the top of a head and beneath that a
circle of dress. She was kneeling beside Rabbi Binder.   (151)

He spoke again. "Everybody kneel." There was the sound of everybody
kneeling.   (152)

Ozzie looked around. With one hand he pointed towards the synagogue
entrance. "Make *him* kneel."   (153)

There was a noise, not of kneeling, but of body-and-cloth stretching.
Ozzie could hear Rabbi Binder saying in a gruff whisper, " . . . or he'll *kill*
himself," and when next he looked there was Yakov Blotnik off the doorknob and for the first time in his life upon his knees in the Gentile posture
of prayer.   (154)

As for the firemen—it is not as difficult as one might imagine to hold a
net taut while you are kneeling.   (155)

Ozzie looked around again; and then he called to Rabbi Binder.   (156)

"Rabbi?"   (157)

"Yes, Oscar."   (158)

"Rabbi Binder, do you believe in God."   (159)

"Yes."   (160)

"Do you believe God can do Anything?" Ozzie leaned his head out into
the darkness. "Anything?"   (161)

"Oscar, I think—"   (162)

"Tell me you believe God can do Anything."   (163)

There was a second's hesitation. Then: "God can do Anything."   (164)

"Tell me you believe God can make a child without intercourse." (165)

"He can."   (166)

"Tell me!"   (167)

"God," Rabbi Binder admitted, "can make a child without intercourse."
                                                                  (168)

"Mamma, you tell me."   (169)

"God can make a child without intercourse," his mother said.   (170)

"Make *him* tell me." There was no doubt who *him* was.   (171)

In a few moments Ozzie heard an old comical voice say something to the increasing darkness about God.   (172)

Next, Ozzie made everybody say it. And then he made them all say they believed in Jesus Christ—first one at a time, then all together.   (173)

When the catechizing was through it was the beginning of evening. From the street it sounded as if the boy on the roof might have sighed.
                                                                  (174)

"Ozzie?" A woman's voice dared to speak. "You'll come down now?"
                                                                  (175)

There was no answer, but the woman waited, and when a voice finally did speak it was thin and crying, and exhausted as that of an old man who has just finished pulling the bells.   (176)

"Mamma, don't you see—you shouldn't hit me. He shouldn't hit me. You shouldn't hit me about God, Mamma. You should never hit anybody about God—"   (177)

"Ozzie, please come down now."   (178)

"Promise me, promise me you'll never hit anybody about God."   (179)

He had asked only his mother, but for some reason everyone kneeling in the street promised he would never hit anybody about God.   (180)

Once again there was silence.   (181)

"I can come down now, Mamma," the boy on the roof finally said. He turned his head both ways as though checking the traffic lights. "Now I can come down . . ."   (182)

And he did, right into the center of the yellow net that glowed in the evening's edge like an overgrown halo.   (183)

Graham Greene

(1904–   )

GREENE has been accepted as one of the major Catholic writers of con-
temporary England. He has written children's books, plays, short stories,
and novels, and his works have been peculiarly susceptible to cinematic
translation. Some of his most popular titles have been these: The Basement
Room *(short stories, 1935)*, Brighton Rock *(1938)*, The Power and the
Glory *(Hawthorne prize, 1940)*, The Heart of the Matter *(1948)*, *and* The
Potting Shed *(play, 1957)*.

◼ *The Hint of an Explanation*

A LONG TRAIN journey on a late December evening, in this new version of
peace, is a dreary experience. I suppose that my fellow traveller and I could
consider ourselves lucky to have a compartment to ourselves, even though
the heating apparatus was not working, even though the lights went out
entirely in the frequent Pennine tunnels and were too dim anyway for us to
read our books without straining our eyes, and though there was no restaurant car to give at least a change of scene. It was when we were trying
simultaneously to chew the same kind of dry bun bought at the same station
buffet that my companion and I came together. Before that we had sat at
opposite ends of the carriage, both muffled to the chin in overcoats, both
bent low over type we could barely make out, but as I threw the remains
of my cake under the seat our eyes met, and he laid his book down.   (1)

By the time we were half-way to Bedwell Junction we had found an
enormous range of subjects for discussion; starting with buns and the
weather, we had gone on to politics, the government, foreign affairs, the
atom bomb, and, by an inevitable progression, God. We had not, however,

become either shrill or acid. My companion, who now sat opposite me, leaning a little forward, so that our knees nearly touched, gave such an impression of serenity that it would have been impossible to quarrel with him, however much our views differed, and differ they did profoundly.   (2)

I had soon realized I was speaking to a Catholic, to someone who believed—how do they put it?—in an omnipotent and omniscient Deity, while I was what is loosely called an Agnostic. I have a certain intuition (which I do not trust, founded as it may well be on childish experiences and needs) that a God exists, and I am surprised occasionally into belief by the extraordinary coincidences that beset our path like the traps set for leopards in the jungle, but intellectually I am revolted at the whole notion of such a God who can so abandon his creatures to the enormities of Free Will. I found myself expressing this view to my companion, who listened quietly and with respect. He made no attempt to interrupt: he showed none of the impatience or the intellectual arrogance I have grown to expect from Catholics; when the lights of a wayside station flashed across his face that had escaped hitherto the rays of the one globe working in the compartment, I caught a glimpse suddenly of—what? I stopped speaking, so strong was the impression. I was carried back ten years, to the other side of the great useless conflict, to a small town, Gisors in Normandy. I was again, for a moment, walking on the ancient battlements and looking down across the grey roofs, until my eyes for some reason lit on one grey stony "back" out of the many, where the face of a middle-aged man was pressed against a windowpane (I suppose that face has ceased to exist now, just as I believe the whole town with its medieval memories has been reduced to rubble). I remembered saying to myself with astonishment, "That man is happy—completely happy." I looked across the compartment at my fellow traveller, but his face was already again in shadow. I said weakly, "When you think what God—if there is a God—allows. It's not merely the physical agonies, but think of the corruption, even of children. . . ."   (3)

He said, "Our view is so limited," and I was disappointed at the conventionality of his reply. He must have been aware of my disappointment (it was as though our thoughts were huddled as closely as ourselves for warmth), for he went on, "Of course there is no answer here. We catch hints . . ." and then the train roared into another tunnel and the lights again went out. It was the longest tunnel yet; we went rocking down it, and the cold seemed to become more intense with the darkness like an icy fog (perhaps when one sense—of sight—is robbed of sensation, the others grow more sensitive). When we emerged into the mere grey of night and the globe lit up once more, I could see that my companion was leaning back on his seat.   (4)

I repeated his last words as a question, "Hints?"   (5)

"Oh, they mean very little in cold print—or cold speech," he said, shivering in his overcoat. "And they mean nothing at all to a human being other than the man who catches them. They are not scientific evidence—or evidence at all for that matter. Events that don't, somehow, turn out as they were intended—by the human actors I mean, or by the thing behind the human actors."   (6)

"The thing?"   (7)

"The word Satan is so anthropomorphic."   (8)

I had to lean forward now: I wanted to hear what he had to say. I am— I really am, God knows—open to conviction.   (9)

He said, "One's words are so crude, but I sometimes feel pity for that thing. It is so continually finding the right weapon to use against its Enemy and the weapon breaks in its own breast. It sometimes seems to me so— powerless. You said something just now about the corruption of children. It reminded me of something in my own childhood. You are the first person— except for one—that I have thought of telling it to, perhaps because you are anonymous. It's not a very long story, and in a way it's relevant."   (10)

I said, "I'd like to hear it."   (11)

"You mustn't expect too much meaning. But to me there seems to be a hint. That's all. A hint."   (12)

He went slowly on, turning his face to the pane, though he could have seen nothing real in the whirling world outside except an occasional signal lamp, a light in a window, a small country station torn backwards by our rush, picking his words with precision. He said, "When I was a child they taught me to serve at Mass. The church was a small one, for there were very few Catholics where I lived. It was a market town in East Anglia, surrounded by flat, chalky fields and ditches—so many ditches. I don't suppose there were fifty Catholics all told, and for some reason there was a tradition of hostility to us. Perhaps it went back to the burning of a Protestant martyr in the sixteenth century—there was a stone marking the place near where the meat stalls stood on Wednesdays. I was only half aware of the enmity, though I knew that my school nickname of Popey Martin had something to do with my religion, and I had heard that my father was nearly excluded from the Constitutional Club when he first came to the town.   (13)

"Every Sunday I had to dress up in my surplice and serve Mass. I hated it—I have always hated dressing up in any way (which is funny when you come to think of it), and I never ceased to be afraid of losing my place in the service and doing something which would put me to ridicule. Our services were at a different hour from the Anglican, and as our small, far-from-select band trudged out of the hideous chapel the whole of the townsfolk seemed to be on the way past to the proper church—I always thought of it as the proper church. We had to pass the parade of their eyes, indifferent, supercilious, mocking; you can't imagine how seriously religion can be taken in a small town, if only for social reasons."   (14)

"There was one man in particular; he was one of the two bakers in the town, the one my family did not patronize. I don't think any of the Catholics patronized him because he was called a free-thinker—an odd title, for, poor man, no one's thoughts were less free than his. He was hemmed in by his hatred—his hatred of us. He was very ugly to look at, with one wall-eye and a head the shape of a turnip, with the hair gone on the crown, and he was unmarried. He had no interests, apparently, but his baking and his hatred, though now that I am older I begin to see other sides to his nature —it did contain, perhaps, a certain furtive love. One would come across him suddenly sometimes on a country walk, especially if one were alone and it was Sunday. It was as if he rose from the ditches, and the smear of chalk on his clothes reminded one of the flour on his working overalls. He would have a stick in his hand and stab at the hedges, and if his mood were very black he would call out after one strange abrupt words like a foreign tongue —I know the meaning of those words, of course, now. Once the police went to his house because of what a boy said he'd seen, but nothing came of it except that the hate shackled him closer. His name was Blacker and he terrified me. (15)

"I think he had a particular hatred of my father—I don't know why. My father was manager of the Midland Bank, and it's possible that at some time Blacker may have had unsatisfactory dealings with the bank; my father was a very cautious man who suffered all his life from anxiety about money—his own and other people's. If I try and picture Blacker now I see him walking along a narrowing path between high windowless walls, and at the end of the path stands a small boy of ten—me. I don't know whether it's a symbolic picture or the memory of one of our encounters—our encounters somehow got more and more frequent. You talked just now about the corruption of children. That poor man was preparing to revenge himself on everything he hated—my father, the Catholics, the God whom people persisted in crediting—and that by corrupting me. He had evolved a horrible and ingenious plan. (16)

"I remember the first time I had a friendly word from him. I was passing his shop as rapidly as I could when I heard his voice call out with a kind of sly subservience as though he were an under servant. 'Master David,' he called, 'Master David,' and I hurried on. But the next time I passed that way he was at his door (he must have seen me coming) with one of those curly cakes in his hand that we called Chelsea buns. I didn't want to take it, but he made me, and then I couldn't be other than polite when he asked me to come into his parlour behind the shop and see something very special. (17)

"It was a small electric railway—a rare sight in those days, and he insisted on showing me how it worked. He made me turn the switches and stop and start it, and he told me that I could come in any morning and have a game with it. He used the word 'game' as though it were something secret, and it's true that I never told my family of this invitation and of how, perhaps twice a week those holidays, the desire to control that little railway became overpowering, and looking up and down the street to see if I were observed, I would dive into the shop."   (18)

Our larger, dirtier, adult train drove into a tunnel and the light went out. We sat in darkness and silence, with the noise of the train blocking our ears like wax. When we were through we didn't speak at once and I had to prick him into continuing. "An elaborate seduction," I said.   (19)

"Don't think his plans were as simple as that," my companion said, "or as crude. There was much more hate than love, poor man, in his make-up. Can you hate something you don't believe in? And yet he called himself a free-thinker. What an impossible paradox, to be free and to be so obsessed. Day by day all through those holidays his obsession must have grown, but he kept a grip; he bided his time. Perhaps that thing I spoke of gave him the strength and the wisdom. It was only a week from the end of the holidays that he spoke to me on what concerned him so deeply.   (20)

"I heard him behind me as I knelt on the floor, coupling two coaches. He said, 'You won't be able to do this, Master David, when school starts.' It wasn't a sentence that needed any comment from me any more than the one that followed. 'You ought to have it for your own, you ought,' but how skilfully and unemphatically he had sowed the longing, the idea of a possibility. . . . I was coming to his parlour every day now; you see, I had to cram every opportunity in before the hated term started again, and I suppose I was becoming accustomed to Blacker, to that wall-eye, that turnip head, that nauseating subservience. The Pope, you know, describes himself as 'the servant of the servants of God,' and Blacker—I sometimes think that Blacker was 'the servant of the servants of . . . ,' well, let it be.   (21)

"The very next day, standing in the doorway watching me play, he began to talk to me about religion. He said, with what untruth even I recognized, how much he admired the Catholics; he wished he could believe like that, but how could a baker believe? He accented 'a baker' as one might say a biologist, and the tiny train spun round the gauge 0 track. He said, 'I can bake the things you eat just as well as any Catholic can,' and disappeared into his shop. I hadn't the faintest idea what he meant. Presently he emerged again, holding in his hand a little wafer. 'Here,' he said, 'eat that and tell me. . . .' When I put it in my mouth I could tell that it was made in the same way as our wafers for communion—he had got the shape a little wrong, that was all—and I felt guilty and irrationally scared. 'Tell me,' he said, 'what's the difference?'   (22)

" 'Difference?' I asked.   (23)

" 'Isn't that just the same as you eat in church?'   (24)

"I said smugly, 'It hasn't been consecrated.' (25)

"He said, 'Do you think, if I put the two of them under a microscope, you could tell the difference?' (26)

"But even at ten I had the answer to that question. 'No,' I said, 'the— accidents don't change,' stumbling a little on the word 'accidents' which had suddenly conveyed to me the idea of death and wounds. (27)

"Blacker said with sudden intensity, 'How I'd like to get one of your ones in my mouth—just to see. . . .' (28)

"It may seem odd to you, but this was the first time that the idea of transsubstantiation really lodged in my mind. I had learned it all by rote; I had grown up with the idea. The Mass was as lifeless to me as the sentences in *De Bello Gallico;* communion a routine like drill in the school-yard, but here suddenly I was in the presence of a man who took it seriously, as seriously as the priest whom naturally one didn't count—it was his job. I felt more scared than ever. (29)

"He said, 'It's all nonsense, but I'd just like to have it in my mouth.' (30)

" 'You could if you were a Catholic,' I said naïvely. (31)

"He gazed at me with his one good eye, like a Cyclops. He said, 'You serve at Mass, don't you? It would be easy for you to get at one of those things. I tell you what I'd do—I'd swap this electric train for one of your wafers—consecrated, mind. It's got to be consecrated.' (32)

" 'I could get you one out of the box,' I said. I think I still imagined that his interest was a baker's interest—to see how they were made. (33)

" 'Oh, no,' he said, 'I want to see what your God tastes like.' (34)

" 'I couldn't do that.' (35)

" 'Not for a whole electric train, just for yourself? You wouldn't have any trouble at home. I'd pack it up and put a label inside that your dad could see: "For my bank manager's little boy from a grateful client." He'd be pleased as punch with that.' (36)

"Now that we are grown men it seems a trivial temptation, doesn't it? But try to think back to your own childhood. There was a whole circuit of rails there on the floor at our feet, straight rails and curved, and a little station with porters and passengers, a tunnel, a footbridge, a level crossing, two signals, buffers, of course—and, above all, a turntable. The tears of longing came into my eyes when I looked at the turntable. It was my favorite piece—it looked so ugly and practical and true. I said weakly, 'I wouldn't know how.' (37)

"How carefully he had been studying the ground! He must have slipped several times into Mass at the back of the church. It would have been no good, you understand, in a little town like that, presenting himself for communion. Everybody there knew him for what he was. He said to me, 'When you've been given communion you could just put it under your tongue a

moment. He serves you and the other boy first, and I saw you once go out
behind the curtain straight afterwards. You'd forgotten one of those little
bottles.'   (38)

" 'The cruet,' I said.   (39)

" 'Pepper and salt.' He grinned at me jovially, and I—well, I looked at
the little railway which I could no longer come and play with when term
started. I said, 'You'd just swallow it, wouldn't you?'   (40)

" 'Oh, yes,' he said. 'I'd just swallow it.'   (41)

"Somehow I didn't want to play with the train any more that day. I got
up and made for the door, but he detained me, gripping my lapel. He said,
'This will be a secret between you and me. Tomorrow's Sunday. You come
along here in the afternoon. Put it in an envelope and post it me. Monday
morning the train will be delivered bright and early.'   (42)

" 'Not tomorrow,' I implored him.   (43)

" 'I'm not interested in any other Sunday,' he said. 'It's your only chance.'
He shook me gently backwards and forwards. 'It will always have to be a
secret between you and me,' he said. 'Why, if anyone knew they'd take away
the train and there'd be me to reckon with. I'd bleed you something awful.
You know how I'm always about on Sunday walks. You can't avoid a man
like me. I crop up. You wouldn't ever be safe in your own house. I know
ways to get into houses when people are asleep.' He pulled me into the
shop after him and opened a drawer. In the drawer was an odd looking key
and a cut-throat razor. He said, "That's a master key that opens all locks and
that—that's what I bleed people with.' Then he patted my cheek with his
plump floury fingers and said, 'Forget it. You and me are friends.'   (44)

"That Sunday Mass stays in my head, every detail of it, as though it had
happened only a week ago. From the moment of the Confession to the moment of Consecration it had a terrible importance; only one other Mass has
ever been so important to me—perhaps not even one, for this was a solitary
Mass which would never happen again. It seemed as final as the last Sacra-
ment when the priest bent down and put the wafer in my mouth where I
knelt before the altar with my fellow server.   (45)

"I suppose I had made up my mind to commit this awful act—for, you
know, to us it must always seem an awful act—from the moment when I saw
Blacker watching from the back of the church. He had put on his best black
Sunday clothes and, as though he could never quite escape the smear of his
profession, he had a dab of dried talcum on his cheek, which he had presumably applied after using that cut-throat of his. He was watching me
closely all the time, and I think it was fear—fear of that terrible undefined
thing called bleeding—as much as covetousness that drove me to carry out
my instructions.   (46)

"My fellow server got briskly up and, taking the paten, preceded Father
Carey to the altar rail where the other communicants knelt. I had the Host

lodged under my tongue: it felt like a blister. I got up and made for the curtain to get the cruet that I had purposely left in the sacristy. When I was there I looked quickly round for a hiding place and saw an old copy of the *Universe* lying on a chair. I took the Host from my mouth and inserted it between two sheets—a little damp mess of pulp. Then I thought: perhaps Father Carey has put out the paper for a particular purpose and he will find the Host before I have time to remove it, and the enormity of my act began to come home to me when I tried to imagine what punishment I should incur. Murder is sufficiently trivial to have its appropriate punishment, but for this act the mind boggled at the thought of any retribution at all. I tried to remove the Host, but it stuck clammily between the pages, and in desperation I tore out a piece of the newspaper and, screwing the whole thing up, stuck it in my trousers pocket. When I came back through the curtain carrying the cruet my eyes met Blacker's. He gave me a grin of encouragement and unhappiness—yes, I am sure, unhappiness. Was it perhaps that the poor man was all the time seeking something incorruptible?   (47)

"I can remember little more of that day. I think my mind was shocked and stunned, and I was caught up too in the family bustle of Sunday. Sunday in a provincial town is the day for relations. All the family are at home, and unfamiliar cousins and uncles are apt to arrive, packed in the back seats of other people's cars. I remember that some crowd of the kind descended on us and pushed Blacker temporarily out of the foreground of my mind. There was somebody called Aunt Lucy, with a loud hollow laugh that filled the house with mechanical merriment like the sound of recorded laughter from inside a hall of mirrors, and I had no opportunity to go out alone even if I had wished to. When six o'clock came and Aunt Lucy and the cousins departed and peace returned, it was too late to go to Blacker's, and at eight it was my own bed-time.   (48)

"I think I had half forgotten what I had in my pocket. As I emptied my pocket the little screw of newspaper brought quickly back the Mass, the priest bending over me, Blacker's grin. I laid the packet on the chair by my bed and tried to go to sleep, but I was haunted by the shadows on the wall where the curtains blew, the squeak of furniture, the rustle in the chimney, haunted by the presence of God there on the chair. The Host had always been to me—well, the Host. I knew theoretically, as I have said, what I had to believe, but suddenly, as someone whistled in the road outside, whistled secretively, knowingly, to me, I knew that this which I had beside my bed was something of infinite value—something a man would pay for with his whole peace of mind, something that was so hated one could love it as one loves an outcast or a bullied child. These are adult words, and it was a child of ten who lay scared in bed, listening to the whistle from the road, Blacker's whistle, but I think he felt fairly clearly what I am describing now. That is what I meant when I said this Thing, whatever it is, that seizes every possible weapon against God, is always, everywhere, disappointed at the moment of success. It must have felt as certain of me as Blacker did. It must have felt certain too of Blacker. But I wonder, if one knew what happened later to that poor man, whether one would not find again that the weapon had been turned against its own breast. (49)

"At last I couldn't bear that whistle any more and got out of bed. I opened the curtains a little way, and there right under my window, the moonlight on his face, was Blacker. If I had stretched my hand down, his fingers reaching up could almost have touched mine. He looked up at me, flashing the one good eye, with hunger—I realize now that near-success must have developed his obsession almost to the point of madness. Desperation had driven him to the house. He whispered up at me. 'David, where is it?' (50)

"I jerked my head back at the room. 'Give it me,' he said. 'Quick. You shall have the train in the morning.' (51)

"I shook my head. He said, 'I've got the bleeder here, and the key. You'd better toss it down.' (52)

" 'Go away,' I said, but I could hardly speak for fear. (53)

" 'I'll bleed you first and then I'll have it just the same.' (54)

" 'Oh, no, you won't,' I said. I went to the chair and picked it—Him—up. There was only one place where He was safe. I couldn't separate the Host from the paper, so I swallowed both. The newsprint stuck like a prune skin to the back of my throat, but I rinsed it down with water from the ewer. Then I went back to the window and looked down at Blacker. He began to wheedle me. 'What have you done with it, David? What's the fuss? It's only a bit of bread,' looking so longingly and pleadingly up at me that even as a child I wondered whether he could really think that, and yet desire it so much. (55)

" 'I swallowed it,' I said. (56)

" 'Swallowed it?' (57)

" 'Yes,' I said. 'Go away.' (58)

"Then something happened which seems to me now more terrible than his desire to corrupt or my thoughtless act: he began to weep—the tears ran lopsidedly out of the one good eye and his shoulders shook. I only saw his face for a moment before he bent his head and strode off, the bald turnip head shaking, into the dark. When I think of it now, it's almost as if I had seen that Thing weeping for its inevitable defeat. It had tried to use me as a weapon, and now I had broken in its hands and it wept its hopeless tears through one of Blacker's eyes." (59)

The black furnaces of Bedwell Junction gathered around the line. The points switched and we were tossed from one set of rails to another. A spray of sparks, a signal light changing to red, tall chimneys jetting into the grey night sky, the fumes of steam from stationary engines—half the cold journey was over, and now remained the long wait for the slow cross-country train. I said, "It's an interesting story. I think I should have given Blacker what he wanted. I wonder what he would have done with it." (60)

"I really believe," my companion said, "that he would first of all have put it under his microscope—before he did all the other things I expect he had planned." (61)

"And the hints," I said. "I don't quite see what you mean by that." (62)

"Oh, well," he said vaguely, "you know for me it was an odd beginning, that affair, when you come to think of it," but I never should have known what he meant had not his coat, when he rose to take his bag from the rack, come open and disclosed the collar of a priest. (63)

I said, "I suppose you think you owe a lot to Blacker." (64)

"Yes," he said, "you see, I am a very happy man." (65)

Robert Penn Warren

(1905–   )

For a brief statement of facts about the author, see the headnote preceding his prose narrative piece "Segregation."

◼ *Blackberry Winter*

TO JOSEPH AND DAGMAR BEACH

It was getting into June and past eight o'clock in the morning, but there was a fire—even if it wasn't a big fire, just a fire of chunks—on the hearth of the big stone fireplace in the living room. I was standing on the hearth, almost into the chimney, hunched over the fire, working my bare toes slowly on the warm stone. I relished the heat which made the skin of my bare legs

warp and creep and tingle, even as I called to my mother, who was somewhere back in the dining room or kitchen, and said: "But it's June, I don't
have to put them on!"   (1)

"You put them on if you are going out," she called.   (2)

I tried to assess the degree of authority and conviction in the tone, but
at that distance it was hard to decide. I tried to analyze the tone, and then
I thought what a fool I had been to start out the back door and let her see
that I was barefoot. If I had gone out the front door or the side door she
would never have known, not till dinner time anyway, and by then the day
would have been half gone and I would have been all over the farm to see
what the storm had done and down to the creek to see the flood. But it had
never crossed my mind that they would try to stop you from going barefoot
in June, no matter if there had been a gully-washer and a cold spell.   (3)

Nobody had ever tried to stop me in June as long as I could remember,
and when you are nine years old, what you remember seems forever; for you
remember everything and everything is important and stands big and full
and fills up Time and is so solid that you can walk around and around it
like a tree and look at it. You are aware that time passes, that there is a
movement in time, but that is not what Time is. Time is not a movement,
a flowing, a wind then, but is, rather, a kind of climate in which things are,
and when a thing happens it begins to live and keeps on living and stands
solid in Time like the tree that you can walk around. And if there is a
movement, the movement is not Time itself, any more than a breeze is
climate, and all the breeze does is to shake a little the leaves on the tree
which is alive and solid. When you are nine, you know that there are things
that you don't know, but you know that when you know something you
know it. You know how a thing has been and you know that you can go
barefoot in June. You do not understand that voice from back in the kitchen
which says that you cannot go barefoot outdoors and run to see what has
happened and rub your feet over the wet shivery grass and make the perfect mark of your foot in the smooth, creamy, red mud and then muse upon
it as though you had suddenly come upon that single mark on the glistening
auroral beach of the world. You have never seen a beach, but you have read
the book and how the footprint was there.   (4)

The voice had said what it had said, and I looked savagely at the black
stockings and the strong, scuffed brown shoes which I had brought from my
closet as far as the hearth rug. I called once more, "But it's June," and
waited.   (5)

"It's June," the voice replied from far away, "but it's blackberry winter."
                                                                         (6)

I had lifted my head to reply to that, to make one more test of what was
in that tone, when I happened to see the man.   (7)

The fireplace in the living room was at the end; for the stone chimney was built, as in so many of the farmhouses in Tennessee, at the end of a gable, and there was a window on each side of the chimney. Out of the window on the north side of the fireplace I could see the man. When I saw the man I did not call out what I had intended, but, engrossed by the strangeness of the sight, watched him, still far off, come along the path by the edge of the woods.   (8)

What was strange was that there should be a man there at all. That path went along the yard fence, between the fence and the woods which came right down to the yard, and then on back past the chicken runs and on by the woods until it was lost to sight where the woods bulged out and cut off the back field. There the path disappeared into the woods. It led on back, I knew, through the woods and to the swamps, skirted the swamp where the big trees gave way to sycamores and water oaks and willows and tangled cane, and then led on to the river. Nobody ever went back there except people who wanted to gig frogs in the swamp or to fish in the river or to hunt in the woods, and those people, if they didn't have a standing permission from my father, always stopped to ask permission to cross the farm. But the man whom I now saw wasn't, I could tell even at that distance, a sportsman. And what would a sportsman have been doing down there after a storm? Besides, he was coming from the river, and nobody had gone down there that morning. I knew that for a fact, because if anybody had passed, certainly if a stranger had passed, the dogs would have made a racket and would have been out on him. But this man was coming up from the river and had come up through the woods. I suddenly had a vision of him moving up the grassy path in the woods, in the green twilight under the big trees, not making any sound on the path, while now and then, like drops off the eaves, a big drop of water would fall from a leaf or bough and strike a stiff oak leaf lower down with a small, hollow sound like a drop of water hitting tin. That sound, in the silence of the woods, would be very significant.   (9)

When you are a boy and stand in the stillness of woods, which can be so still that your heart almost stops beating and makes you want to stand there in the green twilight until you feel your very feet sinking into and clutching the earth like roots and your body breathing slow through its pores like the leaves—when you stand there and wait for the next drop to drop with its small, flat sound to a lower leaf, that sound seems to measure out something, to put an end to something, to begin something, and you cannot wait for it to happen and are afraid it will not happen, and then when it has happened, you are waiting again, almost afraid.   (10)

But the man whom I saw coming through the woods in my mind's eye did not pause and wait, growing into the ground and breathing with the enormous, soundless breathing of the leaves. Instead, I saw him moving in the green twilight inside my head as he was moving at that very moment along the path by the edge of the woods, coming toward the house. He was moving steadily, but not fast, with his shoulders hunched a little and his head thrust forward, like a man who has come a long way and has a long way to go. I shut my eyes for a couple of seconds, thinking that when I opened them he would not be there at all. There was no place for him to have come from, and there was no reason for him to come where he was coming, toward our house. But I opened my eyes, and there he was, and he was coming steadily along the side of the woods. He was not yet even with the back chicken yard. (11)

"Mama," I called. (12)

"You put them on," the voice said. (13)

"There's a man coming," I called, "out back." (14)

She did not reply to that, and I guessed that she had gone to the kitchen window to look. She would be looking at the man and wondering who he was and what he wanted, the way you always do in the country, and if I went back there now she would not notice right off whether or not I was barefoot. So I went back to the kitchen. (15)

She was standing by the window. "I don't recognize him," she said, not looking around at me. (16)

"Where could he be coming from?" I asked. (17)

"I don't know," she said. (18)

"What would he be doing down at the river? At night? In the storm?" (19)

She studied the figure out the window, then said. "Oh, I reckon maybe he cut across from the Dunbar place." (20)

That was, I realized, a perfectly rational explanation. He had not been down at the river in the storm, at night. He had come over this morning. You could cut across from the Dunbar place if you didn't mind breaking through a lot of elder and sassafras and blackberry bushes which had about taken over the old cross path, which nobody ever used any more. That satisfied me for a moment, but only for a moment. "Mama," I asked, "what would he be doing over at the Dunbar place last night?" (21)

Then she looked at me, and I knew I had made a mistake, for she was looking at my bare feet. "You haven't got your shoes on," she said. (22)

But I was saved by the dogs. That instant there was a bark which I recognized as Sam, the collie, and then a heavier, churning kind of bark which was Bully, and I saw a streak of white as Bully tore round the corner of the back porch and headed out for the man. Bully was a big, bone-white bull dog, the kind of dog that they used to call a farm bull dog but that you don't see any more, heavy chested and heavy headed, but with pretty long legs. He could take a fence as light as a hound. He had just cleared the white paling fence toward the woods when my mother ran out to the back porch and began calling, "Here you, Bully! Here you!" (23)

Bully stopped in the path, waiting for the man, but he gave a few more of those deep, gargling savage barks that reminded you of something down a stone-lined well. The red clay mud, I saw, was splashed up over his white chest and looked exciting, like blood. (24)

The man, however, had not stopped walking even when Bully took the fence and started at him. He had kept right on coming. All he had done was to switch a little paper parcel which he carried from the right hand to the left, and then reach into his pants pocket to get something. Then I saw the glitter and knew that he had a knife in his hand, probably the kind of mean knife just made for devilment and nothing else, with a blade as long as the blade of a frog-sticker, which will snap out ready when you press a button in the handle. That knife must have had a button in the handle, or else how could he have had the blade out glittering so quick and with just one hand? (25)

Pulling his knife against the dogs was a funny thing to do, for Bully was a big, powerful brute and fast, and Sam was all right. If those dogs had meant business, they might have knocked him down and ripped him before he got a stroke in. He ought to have picked up a heavy stick, something to take a swipe at them with and something which they could see and respect when they came at him. But he apparently did not know much about dogs. He just held the knife blade close against the right leg, low down, and kept on moving down the path. (26)

Then my mother had called, and Bully had stopped. So the man let the blade of the knife snap back into the handle, and dropped it into his pocket, and kept on coming. Many women would have been afraid with the strange man who they knew had that knife in his pocket. That is, if they were alone in the house with nobody but a nine-year-old boy. And my mother was alone, for my father had gone off, and Dellie, the cook, was down at her cabin because she wasn't feeling well. But my mother wasn't afraid. She wasn't a big woman, but she was clear and brisk about everything she did and looked everybody and everything right in the eye from her own blue eyes in her tanned face. She had been the first woman in the county to ride a horse astride (that was back when she was a girl and long before I was born), and I have seen her snatch up a pump gun and go out and knock a chicken hawk out of the air like a busted skeet when he came over her chicken yard. She was a steady and self-reliant woman, and when I think of her now after all the years she has been dead, I think of her brown hands, not big, but somewhat square for a woman's hands, with squarecut nails. They looked, as a matter of fact, more like a young boy's hands than a grown woman's. But back then it never crossed my mind that she would ever be dead. (27)

She stood on the back porch and watched the man enter the back gate, where the dogs (Bully had leaped back into the yard) were dancing and

muttering and giving sidelong glances back to my mother to see if she
meant what she had said. The man walked right by the dogs, almost brushing them, and didn't pay them any attention. I could see now that he wore
old khaki pants, and a dark wool coat with stripes in it, and a gray felt hat.
He had on a gray shirt with blue stripes in it, and no tie. But I could see a
tie, blue and reddish, sticking in his side coat-pocket. Everything was
wrong about what he wore. He ought to have been wearing blue jeans or
overalls, and a straw hat or an old black felt hat, and the coat, granting that
he might have been wearing a wool coat and not a jumper, ought not to
have had those stripes. Those clothes, despite the fact that they were old
enough and dirty enough for any tramp, didn't belong there in our back
yard, coming down the path, in Middle Tennessee, miles away from any
big town, and even a mile off the pike.   (28)

When he got almost to the steps, without having said anything, my
mother, very matter-of-factly, said, "Good morning."   (29)

"Good morning," he said, and stopped and looked her over. He did not
take off his hat, and under the brim you could see the perfectly unmemorable face, which wasn't old and wasn't young, or thick or thin. It was grayish and covered with about three days of stubble. The eyes were a kind of
nondescript, muddy hazel, or something like that, rather bloodshot. His
teeth, when he opened his mouth, showed yellow and uneven. A couple of
them had been knocked out. You knew that they had been knocked out, because there was a scar, not very old, there on the lower lip just beneath
the gap.   (30)

"Are you hunting work?" my mother asked him.   (31)

"Yes," he said—not "yes, mam"—and still did not take off his hat.   (32)

"I don't know about my husband, for he isn't here," she said, and didn't
mind a bit telling the tramp, or whoever he was, with the mean knife in his
pocket, that no man was around, "but I can give you a few things to do. The
storm has drowned a lot of my chicks. Three coops of them. You can gather
them up and bury them. Bury them deep so the dogs won't get at them. In
the woods. And fix the coops the wind blew over. And down yonder beyond
that pen by the edge of the woods are some drowned poults. They got out
and I couldn't get them in. Even after it started to rain hard. Poults haven't
got any sense."   (33)

"What are them things—poults?" he demanded, and spat on the brick
walk. He rubbed his foot over the spot, and I saw that he wore a black,
pointed-toe low shoe, all cracked and broken. It was a crazy kind of shoe to
be wearing in the country.   (34)

"Oh, they're young turkeys," my mother was saying. "And they haven't
got any sense. I oughtn't to try to raise them around here with so many
chickens, anyway. They don't thrive near chickens, even in separate pens.
And I won't give up my chickens." Then she stopped herself and resumed

briskly on the note of business. "When you finish that, you can fix my flower beds. A lot of trash and mud and gravel has washed down. Maybe you can save some of my flowers if you are careful." (35)

"Flowers," the man said, in a low, impersonal voice which seemed to have a wealth of meaning, but a meaning which I could not fathom. As I think back on it, it probably was not pure contempt. Rather, it was a kind of impersonal and distant marveling that he should be on the verge of grubbing in a flower bed. He said the word, and then looked off across the yard. (36)

"Yes, flowers," my mother replied with some asperity, as though she would have nothing said or implied against flowers. "And they were very fine this year." Then she stopped and looked at the man. "Are you hungry?" she demanded. (37)

"Yeah," he said. (38)

"I'll fix you something," she said, "before you get started." She turned to me. "Show him where he can wash up," she commanded, and went into the house. (39)

I took the man to the end of the porch where a pump was and where a couple of wash pans sat on a low shelf for people to use before they went into the house. I stood there while he laid down his little parcel wrapped in newspaper and took off his hat and looked around for a nail to hang it on. He poured the water and plunged his hands into it. They were big hands, and strong looking, but they did not have the creases and the earth-color of the hands of men who work outdoors. But they were dirty, with black dirt ground into the skin and under the nails. After he had washed his hands, he poured another basin of water and washed his face. He dried his face, and with the towel still dangling in his grasp, stepped over to the mirror on the house wall. He rubbed one hand over the stubble on his face. Then he carefully inspected his face, turning first one side and then the other, and stepped back and settled his striped coat down on his shoulders. He had the movements of a man who has just dressed up to go to church or a party—the way he settled his coat and smoothed it and scanned himself in the mirror. (40)

Then he caught my glance on him. He glared at me for an instant out of the bloodshot eyes, then demanded in a low, harsh voice, "What you looking at?" (41)

"Nothing," I managed to say, and stepped back a step from him. (42)

He flung the towel down, crumpled, on the shelf, and went toward the kitchen door and entered without knocking. (43)

My mother said something to him which I could not catch. I started to go in again, then thought about my bare feet, and decided to go back of the chicken yard, where the man would have to come to pick up the dead chicks. I hung around behind the chicken house until he came out. (44)

He moved across the chicken yard with a fastidious, not quite finicking motion, looking down at the curdled mud flecked with bits of chicken-droppings. The mud curled up over the soles of his black shoes. I stood back from him some six feet and watched him pick up the first of the drowned chicks. He held it up by one foot and inspected it.   (45)

There is nothing deader looking than a drowned chick. The feet curl in that feeble, empty way which back when I was a boy, even if I was a country boy who did not mind hog-killing or frog-gigging, made me feel hollow in the stomach. Instead of looking plump and fluffy, the body is stringy and limp with the fluff plastered to it, and the neck is long and loose like a little string of rag. And the eyes have that bluish membrane over them which makes you think of a very old man who is sick about to die.   (46)

The man stood there and inspected the chick. Then he looked all around as though he didn't know what to do with it.   (47)

"There's a great big old basket in the shed," I said, and pointed to the shed attached to the chicken house.   (48)

He inspected me as though he had just discovered my presence, and moved toward the shed.   (49)

"There's a spade there, too," I added.   (50)

He got the basket and began to pick up the other chicks, picking each one up slowly by a foot and then flinging it into the basket with a nasty, snapping motion. Now and then he would look at me out of the bloodshot eyes. Every time he seemed on the verge of saying something, but he did not. Perhaps he was building up to say something to me, but I did not wait that long. His way of looking at me made me so uncomfortable that I left the chicken yard.   (51)

Besides, I had just remembered that the creek was in flood, over the bridge, and that people were down there watching it. So I cut across the farm toward the creek. When I got to the big tobacco field I saw that it had not suffered much. The land lay right and not many tobacco plants had washed out of the ground. But I knew that a lot of tobacco round the country had been washed right out. My father had said so at breakfast.   (52)

My father was down at the bridge. When I came out of the gap in the osage hedge into the road, I saw him sitting on his mare over the heads of the other men who were standing around, admiring the flood. The creek was big here, even in low water; for only a couple of miles away it ran into the river, and when a real flood came, the red water got over the pike where it dipped down to the bridge, which was an iron bridge, and high over the floor and even the side railings of the bridge. Only the upper iron work would show, with the water boiling and frothing red and white around it. That creek rose so fast and so heavy because a few miles back it came down out of the hills, where the gorges filled up with water in no time when a rain came. The creek ran in a deep bed with limestone bluffs along both sides until it got within three quarters of a mile of the bridge, and when it came out from between those bluffs in flood it was boiling and hissing and steaming like water from a fire hose.   (53)

Whenever there was a flood, people from half the county would come down to see the sight. After a gully-washer there would not be any work to do anyway. If it didn't ruin your crop, you couldn't plow and you felt like taking a holiday to celebrate. If it did ruin your crop, there wasn't anything to do except to try to take your mind off the mortgage, if you were rich enough to have a mortgage, and if you couldn't afford a mortgage you needed something to take your mind off how hungry you would be by Christmas. So people would come down to the bridge and look at the flood. It made something different from the run of days.   (54)

There would not be much talking after the first few minutes of trying to guess how high the water was this time. The men and kids just stood around, or sat their horses or mules, as the case might be, or stood up in the wagon beds. They looked at the strangeness of the flood for an hour or two, and then somebody would say that he had better be getting on home to dinner and would start walking down the gray, puddled limestone pike, or would touch heel to his mount and start off. Everybody always knew what it would be like when he got down to the bridge, but people always came. It was like church or a funeral. They always came, that is, if it was summer and the flood unexpected. Nobody ever came down in winter to see high water.   (55)

When I came out of the gap in the bodock hedge, I saw the crowd, perhaps fifteen or twenty men and a lot of kids, and saw my father sitting his mare, Nellie Gray. He was a tall, limber man and carried himself well. I was always proud to see him sit a horse, he was so quiet and straight, and when I stepped through the gap of the hedge that morning, the first thing that happened was, I remember, the warm feeling I always had when I saw him up on a horse, just sitting. I did not go toward him, but skirted the crowd on the far side, to get a look at the creek. For one thing, I was not sure what he would say about the fact that I was barefoot. But the first thing I knew, I heard his voice calling, "Seth!"   (56)

I went toward him, moving apologetically past the men, who bent their large, red or thin, sallow faces above me. I knew some of the men, and knew their names, but because those I knew were there in a crowd, mixed with the strange faces, they seemed foreign to me, and not friendly. I did not look up at my father until I was almost within touching distance of his heel. Then I looked up and tried to read his face, to see if he was angry about my being barefoot. Before I could decide anything from that impassive, high-boned face, he had leaned over and reached a hand to me. "Grab on," he commanded.   (57)

I grabbed on and gave a little jump, and he said, "Up-see-daisy!" and whisked me, light as a feather, up to the pommel of his McClellan saddle. (58)

"You can see better up here," he said, slid back on the cantle a little to make me more comfortable, and then, looking over my head at the swollen, tumbling water, seemed to forget all about me. But his right hand was laid on my side, just above my thigh, to steady me. (59)

I was sitting there as quite as I could, feeling the faint stir of my father's chest against my shoulders as it rose and fell with his breath, when I saw the cow. At first, looking up the creek, I thought it was just another big piece of driftwood steaming down the creek in the ruck of water, but all at once a pretty good-size boy who had climbed part way up a telephone pole by the pike so that he could see better yelled out, "Golly-damn, look at that-air cow!" (60)

Everybody looked. It was a cow all right, but it might just as well have been driftwood; for it was dead as a chunk, rolling and rolling down the creek, appearing and disappearing, feet up or head up, it didn't matter which. (61)

The cow started up the talk again. Somebody wondered whether it would hit one of the clear places under the top girder of the bridge and get through or whether it would get tangled in the drift and trash that had piled against the upright girders and braces. Somebody remembered how about ten years before so much driftwood had piled up on the bridge that it was knocked off its foundations. Then the cow hit. It hit the edge of the drift against one of the girders, and hung there. For a few seconds it seemed as though it might tear loose, but then we saw that it was really caught. It bobbed and heaved on its side there in a slow, grinding, uneasy fashion. It had a yoke around its neck, the kind made out of a forked limb to keep a jumper behind fence. (62)

"She shore jumped one fence," one of the men said. (63)

And another: "Well, she done jumped her last one, fer a fack." (64)

Then they began to wonder about whose cow it might be. They decided it must belong to Milt Alley. They said that he had a cow that was a jumper, and kept her in a fenced-in piece of ground up the creek. I had never seen Milt Alley, but I knew who he was. He was a squatter and lived up the hills a way, on a shirt-tail patch of set-on-edge land, in a cabin. He was pore white trash. He had lots of children. I had seen the children at school, when they came. They were thin-faced, with straight, sticky-looking, dough-colored hair, and they smelled something like old sour buttermilk, not because they drank so much buttermilk but because that is the sort of smell which children out of those cabins tend to have. The big Alley boy drew dirty pictures and showed them to the little boys at school. (65)

That was Milt Alley's cow. It looked like the kind of cow he would have,

a scrawny, old, sway-backed cow, with a yoke around her neck. I wondered
if Milt Alley had another cow. (66)

"Poppa," I said, "do you think Milt Alley has got another cow?" (67)

"You say 'Mr. Alley,'" my father said quietly. (68)

"Do you think he has?" (69)

"No telling," my father said. (70)

Then a big gangly boy, about fifteen, who was sitting on a scraggly little
ole mule with a piece of croker sack thrown across the saw-tooth spine, and
who had been staring at the cow, suddenly said to nobody in particular,
"Reckin anybody ever et drownt cow?" (71)

He was the kind of boy who might just as well as not have been the son
of Milt Alley, with his faded and patched overalls ragged at the bottom of
the pants and the mud-stiff brogans hanging off his skinny, bare ankles at
the level of the mule's belly. He had said what he did, and then looked embarrassed and sullen when all the eyes swung at him. He hadn't meant to
say it, I am pretty sure now. He would have been too proud to say it, just
as Milt Alley would have been too proud. He had just been thinking out
loud, and the words had popped out. (72)

There was an old man standing there on the pike, an old man with a
white beard. "Son," he said to the embarrassed and sullen boy on the mule,
"you live long enough and you'll find a man will eat anything when the
time comes." (73)

"Time gonna come fer some folks this year," another man said. (74)

"Son," the old man said, "in my time I et things a man don't like to think
on. I was a sojer and I rode with Gin'l Forrest, and them things we et when
the time come. I tell you. I et meat what got up and run when you taken
out yore knife to cut a slice to put on the fire. You had to knock it down
with a carbeen butt, it was so active. That-air meat would jump like a bull-
frog, it was so full of skippers." (75)

But nobody was listening to the old man. The boy on the mule turned
his sullen sharp face from him, dug a heel into the side of the mule and
went off up the pike with a motion which made you think that any second
you would hear mule bones clashing inside that lank and scrofulous hide.
(76)

"Cy Dundee's boy," a man said, and nodded toward the figure going up
the pike on the mule. (77)

"Reckon Cy Dundee's young-uns seen times they'd settle fer drownt
cow," another man said. (78)

The old man with the beard peered at them both from his weak, slow
eyes, first at one and then at the other. "Live long enough," he said, "and
a man will settle fer what he kin git." (79)

Then there was silence again, with the people looking at the red, foam-
flecked water. (80)

My father lifted the bridle rein in his left hand, and the mare turned and walked around the group and up the pike. We rode on up to our big gate, where my father dismounted to open it and let me myself ride Nellie Gray through. When he got to the lane that led off from the drive about two hundred yards from our house, my father said, "Grab on." I grabbed on, and he let me down to the ground. "I'm going to ride down and look at my corn," he said. "You go on." He took the lane, and I stood there on the drive and watched him ride off. He was wearing cowhide boots and an old hunting coat, and I thought that that made him look very military, like a picture. That and the way he rode.   (81)

I did not go to the house. Instead, I went by the vegetable garden and crossed behind the stables, and headed down for Dellie's cabin. I wanted to go down and play with Jebb, who was Dellie's little boy about two years older than I was. Besides, I was cold. I shivered as I walked, and I had gooseflesh. The mud which crawled up between my toes with every step I took was like ice. Dellie would have a fire, but she wouldn't make me put on shoes and stockings.   (82)

Dellie's cabin was of logs, with one side, because it was on a slope, set on limestone chunks, with a little porch attached to it, and had a little whitewashed fence around it and a gate with plow-points on a wire to clink when somebody came in, and had two big white oaks in the yard and some flowers and a nice privy in the back with some honeysuckle growing over it. Dellie and Old Jebb, who was Jebb's father and who lived with Dellie and had lived with her for twenty-five years even if they never had got married, were careful to keep everything nice around their cabin. They had the name all over the community for being clean and clever Negroes. Dellie and Jebb were what they used to call "white-folks' niggers." There was a big difference between their cabin and the other two cabins farther down where the other tenants lived. My father kept the other cabins weatherproof, but he couldn't undertake to go down and pick up after the litter they strewed. They didn't take the trouble to have a vegetable patch like Dellie and Jebb or to make preserves from wild plum, and jelly from crab apple the way Dellie did. They were shiftless, and my father was always threatening to get shed of them. But he never did. When they finally left, they just up and left on their own, for no reason, to go and be shiftless somewhere else. Then some more came. But meanwhile they lived down there, Matt Rawson and his family, and Sid Turner and his, and I played with their children all over the farm when they weren't working. But when I wasn't around they were mean sometimes to Little Jebb. That was because the other tenants down there were jealous of Dellie and Jebb.   (83)

I was so cold that I ran the last fifty yards to Dellie's gate. As soon as I had entered the yard, I saw that the storm had been hard on Dellie's flowers. The yard was, as I have said, on a slight slope, and the water running across had gutted the flower beds and washed out all the good black woods-earth which Dellie had brought in. What little grass there was in the yard was plastered sparsely down on the ground, the way the drainage water had left it. It reminded me of the way the fluff was plastered down on the skin of the drowned chicks that the strange man had been picking up, up in my mother's chicken yard.   (84)

I took a few steps up the path to the cabin, and then I saw that the drainage water had washed a lot of trash and filth out from under Dellie's house. Up toward the porch, the ground was not clean any more. Old pieces of rag, two or three rusted cans, pieces of rotten rope, some hunks of old dog dung, broken glass, old paper, and all sorts of things like that had washed out from under Dellie's house to foul her clean yard. It looked just as bad as the yards of the other cabins, or worse. It was worse, as a matter of fact, because it was a surprise. I had never thought of all that filth being under Dellie's house. It was not anything against Dellie that the stuff had been under the cabin. Trash will get under any house. But I did not think of that when I saw the foulness which had washed out on the ground which Dellie sometimes used to sweep with a twig broom to make nice and clean.
                                                                                                     (85)

I picked my way past the filth, being careful not to get my bare feet on it, and mounted to Dellie's door. When I knocked, I heard her voice telling me to come in.   (86)

It was dark inside the cabin, after the daylight, but I could make out Dellie piled up in bed under a quilt, and Little Jebb crouched by the hearth, where a low fire simmered. "Howdy," I said to Dellie, "how you feeling?"   (87)

Her big eyes, the whites surprising and glaring in the black face, fixed on me as I stood there, but she did not reply. It did not look like Dellie, or act like Dellie, who would grumble and bustle around our kitchen, talking to herself, scolding me or Little Jebb, clanking pans, making all sorts of unnecessary noises and mutterings like an old-fashioned black steam thrasher engine when it has got up an extra head of steam and keeps popping the governor and rumbling and shaking on its wheels. But now Dellie just lay up there on the bed, under the patch-work quilt, and turned the black face, which I scarcely recognized, and glaring white eyes to me. (88)

"How you feeling?" I repeated.   (89)

"I'se sick," the voice said croakingly out of the strange black face which was not attached to Dellie's big, squat body, but stuck out from under a pile of tangled bedclothes. Then the voice added: "Mighty sick."   (90)

"I'm sorry," I managed to say.   (91)

The eyes remained fixed on me for a moment, then they left me and the head rolled back on the pillow. "Sorry," the voice said, in a flat way which wasn't question or statement of anything. It was just the empty word put

into the air with no meaning or expression, to float off like a feather or a
puff of smoke, while the big eyes, with the whites like the peeled white of
hard-boiled eggs, stared at the ceiling.   (92)

"Dellie," I said after a minute, "there's a tramp up at the house. He's got
a knife."   (93)

She was not listening. She closed her eyes.   (94)

I tiptoed over to the hearth where Jebb was and crouched beside him.
We begun to talk in low voices. I was asking him to get out his train and
play train. Old Jebb had put spool wheels on three cigar boxes and put wire
links between the boxes to make a train for Jebb. The box that was the
locomotive had the top closed and a length of broom stick for a smoke
stack. Jebb didn't want to get the train out, but I told him I would go home
if he didn't. So he got out the train, and the colored rocks, and fossils of
crinoid stems, and other junk he used for the load, and we began to push it
around, talking the way we thought trainmen talked, making a chuck-
chucking sound under the breath for the noise of the locomotive and now
and then uttering low, cautious toots for the whistle. We got so interested in
playing train that the toots got louder. Then, before he thought, Jebb gave
a good, loud *toot-toot,* blowing for a crossing.   (95)

"Come here," the voice said from the bed.   (96)

Jebb got up slow from his hands and knees, giving me a sudden, naked,
inimical look.   (97)

"Come here!" the voice said.   (98)

Jebb went to the bed. Dellie propped herself weakly up on one arm,
muttering, "Come closer."   (99)

Jebb stood closer.   (100)

"Last thing I do, I'm gonna do it," Dellie said. "Done tole you to be
quiet."   (101)

Then she slapped him. It was an awful slap, more awful for the kind of
weakness which it came from and brought to focus. I had seen her slap Jebb
before, but the slapping had always been the kind of easy slap you would
expect from a good-natured, grumbling Negro woman like Dellie. But this
was different. It was awful. It was so awful that Jebb didn't make a sound.
The tears just popped out and ran down his face, and his breath came
sharp, like gasps.   (102)

Dellie fell back. "Cain't even be sick," she said to the ceiling. "Git sick and
they won't even let you lay. They tromp all over you. Cain't even be sick."
Then she closed her eyes.   (103)

I went out of the room. I almost ran getting to the door, and I did run
across the porch and down the steps and across the yard, not caring
whether or not I stepped on the filth which had washed out from under the
cabin. I ran almost all the way home. Then I thought about my mother
catching me with the bare feet. So I went down to the stables.   (104)

I heard a noise in the crib, and opened the door. There was Big Jebb, sitting on an old nail keg, shelling corn into a bushel basket. I went in, pulling the door shut behind me, and crouched on the floor near him. I crouched there for a couple of minutes before either of us spoke, and watched him shelling the corn. (105)

He had very big hands, knotted and grayish at the joints, with calloused palms which seemed to be streaked with rust with the rust coming between the fingers to show from the back. His hands were so strong and tough that he could take a big ear of corn and rip the grains right off the cob with the palm of his hand, all in one motion, like a machine. "Work long as me," he would say, "and the good Lawd'll give you a hand lak cass-ion won't nuthin' hurt." And his hands did look like cast iron, old cast iron streaked with rust. (106)

He was an old man, up in his seventies, thirty years or more older than Dellie, but he was strong as a hill. He was a squat sort of man, heavy in the shoulders, with remarkably long arms, the kind of build they say the river natives have on the Congo from paddling so much in their boats. He had a round bullet-head, set on powerful shoulders. His skin was very black, and the thin hair on his head was now grizzled like tufts of old cotton batting. He had small eyes and a flat nose, not big, and the kindest and wisest old face in the world, the blunt, sad, wise face of an old animal peering tolerantly out on the goings-on of the merely human creatures before him. He was a good man, and I loved him next to my mother and father. I crouched there on the floor of the crib and watched him shell corn with the rusty cast-iron hands, while he looked down at me out of the little eyes set in the blunt face. (107)

"Dellie says she's might sick," I said. (108)

"Yeah," he said. (109)

"What's she sick from?" (110)

"Woman-mizry," he said. (111)

"What's woman-mizry?" (112)

"Hit comes on 'em," he said. "Hit just comes on 'em when the time comes." (113)

"What is it?" (114)

"Hit is the change," he said. "Hit is the change of life and time." (115)

"What changes?" (116)

"You too young to know." (117)

"Tell me." (118)

"Time come and you find out everthing." (119)

I knew that there was no use in asking him any more. When I asked him things and he said that, I always knew that he would not tell me. So I continued to crouch there and watch him. Now that I had sat there a little while, I was cold again. (120)

"What you shiver fer?" he asked me.   (121)

"I'm cold. I'm cold because it's blackberry winter," I said.   (122)

"Maybe 'tis and maybe 'tain't," he said.   (123)

"My mother says it is."   (124)

"Ain't sayen Miss Sallie doan know and ain't sayen she do. But folks
doan know everything."   (125)

"Why isn't it blackberry winter?"   (126)

"Too late fer blackberry winter. Blackberries done bloomed."   (127)

"She said it was."   (128)

"Blackberry winter just a leetle cold spell. Hit come and then hit go
away, and hit is growed summer of a sudden lak a gunshot. Ain't no tellen
hit will go way this time."   (129)

"It's June," I said.   (130)

"June," he replied with great contempt. "That what folks say. What June
mean? Maybe hit is come cold to stay."   (131)

"Why?"   (132)

"Cause this-here old yearth is tahrd. Hit is tahrd and ain't gonna perduce. Lawd let hit come rain one time forty days and forty nights, 'cause
He wus tahrd of sinful folks. Maybe this-here old yearth say to the Lawd,
Lawd, I done plum tahrd, Lawd, lemme rest. And Lawd say, Yearth, you
done yore best, you give 'em cawn and you give 'em taters, and all they
think on is they gut, and, Yearth, you kin take a rest."   (133)

"What will happen?"   (134)

"Folks will eat up everthing. The yearth won't perduce no more. Folks
cut down all the trees and burn 'em cause they cold, and the yearth won't
grow no more. I been tellen 'em. I been tellen folks. Sayen, maybe this year,
hit is the time. But they doan listen to me, how the yearth is tahrd. Maybe
this year they find out."   (135)

"Will everything die?"   (136)

"Everthing and everbody, hit will be so."   (137)

"This year?"   (138)

"Ain't no tellen. Maybe this year."   (139)

"My mother said it is blackberry winter," I said confidently, and got up.
                                                                             (140)

"Ain't sayen nuthin' again Miss Sallie," he said.   (141)

I went to the door of the crib. I was really cold now. Running, I had
got up a sweat and now I was worse.   (142)

I hung on the door, looking at Jebb, who was shelling corn again.   (143)

"There's a tramp came to the house," I said. I had almost forgotten the
tramp.   (144)

"Yeah."   (145)

"He came by the back way. What was he doing down there in the
storm?"   (146)

"They comes and they goes," he said, "and ain't no tellen." (147)

"He had a mean knife." (148)

"The good ones and the bad ones, they comes and they goes. Storm or sun, light or dark. They is folks and they comes and they goes lak folks." (149)

I hung on the door, shivering. (150)

He studied me a moment, then said, "You git on to the house. You ketch yore death. Then what yore mammy say?" (151)

I hesitated. (152)

"You git," he said. (153)

When I came to the back yard, I saw that my father was standing by the porch and the tramp was walking toward him. They began talking before I reached them, but I got there just as my father was saying, "I'm sorry, but I haven't got any work. I got all the hands on the place I need now. I won't need any extra until wheat thrashing." (154)

The stranger made no reply, just looked at my father. (155)

My father took out his leather coin purse, and got out a half-dollar. He held it toward the man. "This is for half a day," he said. (156)

The man looked at the coin, and then at my father, making no motion to take the money. But that was the right amount. A dollar a day was what you paid them back in 1910. And the man hadn't even worked half a day. (157)

Then the man reached out and took the coin. He dropped it into the right side pocket of his coat. Then he said, very slowly and without feeling: "I didn't want to work on your—farm." (158)

He used the word which they would have frailed me to death for using. (159)

I looked at my father's face and it was streaked white under the sunburn. Then he said, "Get off this place. Get off this place or I won't be responsible." (160)

The man dropped his right hand into his pants pocket. It was the pocket where he kept the knife. I was just about to yell to my father about the knife when the hand came back out with nothing in it. The man gave a kind of twisted grin, showing where the teeth had been knocked out above the new scar. I thought that instant how maybe he had tried before to pull a knife on somebody else and had got his teeth knocked out. (161)

So now he just gave that twisted, sickish grin out of the unmemorable, grayish face, and then spat on the brick path. The glob landed just about six inches from the toe of my father's right boot. My father looked down at it, and so did I. I thought that if the glob had hit my father's boot something would have happened. I looked down and saw the bright glob, and on one side of it my father's strong cowhide boots, with the brass eyelets and the leather thongs, heavy boots splashed with good red mud and set solid on the bricks, and on the other side the pointed-toe, broken, black shoes, on which the mud looked so sad and out of place. Then I saw one of the black shoes move a little, just a twitch first, then a real step backward. (162)

The man moved in a quarter circle to the end of the porch, with my father's steady gaze upon him all the while. At the end of the porch, the man reached up to the shelf where the wash pans were to get his little newspaper-wrapped parcel. Then he disappeared around the corner of the house and my father mounted the porch and went into the kitchen without a word. (163)

I followed around the house to see what the man would do. I wasn't afraid of him now, no matter if he did have the knife. When I got around in front, I saw him going out the yard gate and starting up the drive toward the pike. So I ran to catch up with him. He was sixty yards or so up the drive before I caught up. (164)

I did not walk right up even with him at first, but trailed him, the way a kid will, about seven or eight feet behind, now and then running two or three steps in order to hold my place against his longer stride. When I first came up behind him, he turned to give me a look, just a meaningless look, and then fixed his eyes up the drive and kept on walking. (165)

When we had got around the bend in the drive which cut the house from sight, and were going along by the edge of the woods, I decided to come up even with him. I ran a few steps, and was by his side, or almost, but some feet off to the right. I walked along in this position for a while, and he never noticed me. I walked along until we got within sight of the big gate that let on the pike. (166)

Then I said: "Where did you come from?" (167)

He looked at me then with a look which seemed almost suprised that I was there. Then he said, "It ain't none of yore business." (168)

We went on another fifty feet. (169)

Then I said, "Where are you going?" (170)

He stopped, studied me dispassionately for a moment, then suddenly took a step toward me and leaned his face down at me. The lips jerked back, but not in any grin, to show where the teeth were knocked out and to make the scar on the lower lip come white with the tension. (171)

He said: "Stop following me. You don't stop following me and I cut yore throat, you little son-of-a-bitch." (172)

Then he went on to the gate, and up the pike. (173)

That was thirty-five years ago. Since that time my father and mother have died. I was still a boy, but a big boy, when my father got cut on the blade of a mowing machine and died of lockjaw. My mother sold the place and went to town to live with her sister. But she never took hold after my father's death, and she died within three years, right in middle life. My aunt always said, "Sallie just died of a broken heart, she was so devoted." Dellie is dead, too, but she died, I heard, quite a long time after we sold the farm.

(174)

As for Little Jebb, he grew up to be a mean and ficey Negro. He killed another Negro in a fight and got sent to the penitentiary, where he is yet, the last I heard tell. He probably grew up to be mean and ficey from just being picked on so much by the children of the other tenants, who were jealous of Jebb and Dellie for being thrifty and clever and being white-folks' niggers.

(175)

Ole Jebb lived forever. I saw him ten years ago and he was about a hundred then, and not looking much different. He was living in town then, on relief—that was back in the Depression—when I went to see him. He said to me: "Too strong to die. When I was a young feller just comen on and seen how things wuz, I prayed the Lawd. I said, Oh, Lawd, gimme strength and meke me strong fer to do and to in-dure. The Lawd hearkened to my prayer. He give me strength. I was in-duren proud fer being strong and me much man. The Lawd give me my prayer and my strength. But now He done gone off and fergot me and left me alone with my strength. A man doan know what to pray fer, and him mortal."

(176)

Jebb is probably living yet, as far as I know.

(177)

That is what has happened since the morning when the tramp leaned his face down at me and showed his teeth and said: "Stop following me. You don't stop following me and I cut yore throat, you little son-of-a-bitch." That was what he said, for me not to follow him. But I did follow him, all the years.

(178)

John Steinbeck

(1902–   )

STEINBECK won the Pulitzer prize in 1940, the Nobel Prize for Literature in 1962, and was awarded the Presidential Medal of Freedom in 1964. Of Mice and Men *(1937) and* The Grapes of Wrath *(1939) are perhaps the most viable literary products of the efforts of the writers of the period to evaluate the human struggles for survival in the years of the Great Depression. Other significant titles in the Steinbeck canon include* Tortilla Flat *(1935),* Red Pony *(1937),* Cannery Row *(1945),* East of Eden *(1952),* Travels with Charley *(1962).*

■ *The Leader of the People*

ON SATURDAY afternoon Billy Buck, the ranch-hand, raked together the last of the old year's haystack and pitched small forkfuls over the wire fence to a few mildly interested cattle. High in the air small clouds like puffs of cannon smoke were driven eastward by the March wind. The wind could be heard whishing in the brush on the ridge crests, but no breath of it penetrated down into the ranch-cup.   (1)

The little boy, Jody, emerged from the house eating a thick piece of buttered bread. He saw Billy working on the last of the haystack. Jody tramped down scuffing his shoes in a way he had been told was destructive to good shoe-leather. A flock of white pigeons flew out of the black cypress tree as Jody passed, and circled the tree and landed again. A half-grown tortoise-shell cat leaped from the bunkhouse porch, galloped on stiff legs across the road, whirled and galloped back again. Jody picked up a stone to help the game along, but he was too late, for the cat was under the porch before the stone could be discharged. He threw the stone into the cypress tree and started the white pigeons on another whirling flight.   (2)

Arriving at the used-up haystack, the boy leaned against the barbed wire fence. "Will that be all of it, do you think?" he asked.   (3)

The middle-aged ranch-hand stopped his careful raking and stuck his fork into the ground. He took off his black hat and smoothed down his hair. "Nothing left of it that isn't soggy from ground moisture," he said. He replaced his hat and rubbed his dry leathery hands together.   (4)

"Ought to be plenty mice," Jody suggested.   (5)

"Lousy with them," said Billy. "Just crawling with mice."   (6)

"Well, maybe, when you get all through, I could call the dogs and hunt the mice."   (7)

"Sure, I guess you could," said Billy Buck. He lifted a forkful of the damp ground-hay and threw it into the air. Instantly three mice leaped out and burrowed frantically under the hay again.   (8)

Jody sighed with satisfaction. Those plump, sleek, arrogant mice were doomed. For eight months they had lived and multiplied in the haystack. They had been immune from cats, from traps, from poison and from Jody.

They had grown smug in their security, overbearing and fat. Now the time of disaster had come; they would not survive another day. (9)

Billy looked up at the top of the hills that surrounded the ranch. "Maybe you better ask your father before you do it," he suggested. (10)

"Well, where is he? I'll ask him now." (11)

"He rode up to the ridge ranch after dinner. He'll be back pretty soon." (12)

Jody slumped against the fence post. "I don't think he'd care." (13)

As Billy went back to his work he said ominously, "You'd better ask him anyway. You know how he is." (14)

Jody did know. His father, Carl Tiflin, insisted upon giving permission for anything that was done on the ranch, whether it was important or not. Jody sagged farther against the post until he was sitting on the ground. He looked up at the little puffs of wind-driven cloud. "Is it like to rain, Billy?" (15)

"It might. The wind's good for it, but not strong enough." (16)

"Well, I hope it don't rain until after I kill those damn mice." He looked over his shoulder to see whether Billy had noticed the mature profanity. Billy worked on without comment. (17)

Jody turned back and looked at the side-hill where the road from the outside world came down. The hill was washed with lean March sunshine. Silver thistles, blue lupins and a few poppies bloomed among the sage bushes. Halfway up the hill Jody could see Doubletree Mutt, the black dog, digging in a squirrel hole. He paddled for a while and then paused to kick bursts of dirt out between his hind legs, and he dug with an earnestness which belied the knowledge he must have had that no dog had ever caught a squirrel by digging in a hole. (18)

Suddenly, while Jody watched, the black dog stiffened, and backed out of the hole and looked up the hill toward the cleft in the ridge where the road came through. Jody looked up too. For a moment Carl Tiflin on horseback stood out against the pale sky and then he moved down the road toward the house. He carried something white in his hand. (19)

The boy started to his feet. "He's got a letter," Jody cried. He trotted away toward the ranch house, for the letter would probably be read aloud and he wanted to be there. He reached the house before his father did, and ran in. He heard Carl dismount from his creaking saddle and slap the horse on the side to send it to the barn where Billy would unsaddle it and turn it out. (20)

Jody ran into the kitchen. "We got a letter!" he cried. (21)

His mother looked up from a pan of beans. "Who has?" (22)

"Father has. I saw it in his hand." (23)

Carl strode into the kitchen then, and Jody's mother asked, "Who's the letter from, Carl?" (24)

He frowned quickly. "How did you know there was a letter?"   (25)

She nodded her head in the boy's direction. "Big-Britches Jody told me."   (26)

Jody was embarrassed.   (27)

His father looked down at him contemptuously. "He *is* getting to be a Big-Britches," Carl said. "He's minding everybody's business but his own. Got his big nose into everything."   (28)

Mrs. Tiflin relented a little. "Well, he hasn't enough to keep him busy. Who's the letter from?"   (29)

Carl still frowned on Jody. "I'll keep him busy if he isn't careful." He held out a sealed letter. "I guess it's from your father."   (30)

Mrs. Tiflin took a hairpin from her head and slit open the flap. Her lips pursed judiciously. Jody saw her eyes snap back and forth over the lines. "He says," she translated, "he says he's going to drive out Saturday to stay for a little while. Why, this is Saturday. The letter must have been delayed." She looked at the postmark. "This was mailed day before yesterday. It should have been here yesterday." She looked up questioningly at her husband, and then her face darkened angrily. "Now what have you got that look on you for? He doesn't come often."   (31)

Carl turned his eyes away from her anger. He could be stern with her most of the time, but when occasionally her temper arose, he could not combat it.   (32)

"What's the matter with you?" she demanded again.   (33)

In his explanation there was a tone of apology Jody himself might have used. "It's just that he talks," Carl said lamely. "Just talks."   (34)

"Well, what of it? You talk yourself."   (35)

"Sure I do. But your father only talks about one thing."   (36)

"Indians!" Jody broke in excitedly. "Indians and crossing the plains!"   (37)

Carl turned fiercely on him. "You get out, Mr. Big-Britches! Go on, now! Get out!"   (38)

Jody went miserably out the back door and closed the screen with elaborate quietness. Under the kitchen window his shamed, downcast eyes fell upon a curiously shaped stone, a stone of such fascination that he squatted down and picked it up and turned it over in his hands.   (39)

The voices came clearly to him through the open kitchen window. "Jody's damn well right," he heard his father say. "Just Indians and crossing the plains. I've heard that story about how the horses got driven off about a thousand times. He just goes on and on, and he never changes a word in the things he tells."   (40)

When Mrs. Tiflin answered her tone was so changed that Jody, outside the window, looked up from his study of the stone. Her voice had become soft and explanatory. Jody knew how her face would have changed to match the tone. She said quietly, "Look at it this way, Carl. That was the big thing in my father's life. He led a wagon train clear across the plains to the coast, and when it was finished, his life was done. It was a big thing to do, but it didn't last long enough. Look!" she continued, "it's as though he was born to do that, and after he finished it, there wasn't anything more for him to do but think about it and talk about it. If there'd been any farther west to go, he'd have gone. He's told me so himself. But at last there was the ocean. He lives right by the ocean where he had to stop." (41)

She had caught Carl, caught him and entangled him in her soft tone. (42)

"I've seen him," he agreed quietly. "He goes down and stares off west over the ocean." His voice sharpened a little. "And then he goes up to the Horseshoe Club in Pacific Grove, and he tells people how the Indians drove off the horses." (43)

She tried to catch him again. "Well, it's everything to him. You might be patient with him and pretend to listen." (44)

Carl turned impatiently away. "Well, if it gets too bad, I can always go down to the bunkhouse and sit with Billy," he said irritably. He walked through the house and slammed the front door after him. (45)

Jody ran to his chores. He dumped the grain to the chickens without chasing any of them. He gathered the eggs from the nests. He trotted into the house with the wood and interlaced it so carefully in the wood-box that two armloads seemed to fill it to overflowing. (46)

His mother had finished the beans by now. She stirred up the fire and brushed off the stove-top with a turkey wing. Jody peered cautiously at her to see whether any rancor toward him remained. "Is he coming today?" Jody asked. (47)

"That's what his letter said." (48)

"Maybe I better walk up the road to meet him." (49)

Mrs. Tiflin clanged the stove-lid shut. "That would be nice," she said. "He'd probably like to be met." (50)

"I guess I'll just do it then." (51)

Outside, Jody whistled shrilly to the dogs. "Come on up the hill," he commanded. The two dogs waved their tails and ran ahead. Along the road-side the sage had tender new tips. Jody tore off some pieces and rubbed them on his hands until the air was filled with the sharp wild smell. With a rush the dogs leaped from the road and yapped into the brush after a rabbit. That was the last Jody saw of them, for when they failed to catch the rabbit, they went back home. (52)

Jody plodded on up the hill toward the ridge top. When he reached the little cleft where the road came through, the afternoon wind struck him and blew up his hair and ruffled his shirt. He looked down on the little hills and ridges below and then out at the huge green Salinas Valley. He could see the white town of Salinas far out in the flat and the flash of its windows under the waning sun. Directly below him, in an oak tree, a crow congress had convened. The tree was black with crows all cawing at once.   (53)

Then Jody's eyes followed the wagon road down from the ridge where he stood, and lost it behind a hill, and picked it up again on the other side. On that distant stretch he saw a cart slowly pulled by a bay horse. It disappeared behind the hill. Jody sat down on the ground and watched the place where the cart would reappear again. The wind sang on the hilltops and the puff-ball clouds hurried eastward.   (54)

Then the cart came into sight and stopped. A man dressed in black dismounted from the seat and walked to the horse's head. Although it was so far away, Jody knew he had unhooked the check-rein, for the horse's head dropped forward. The horse moved on, and the man walked slowly up the hill beside it. Jody gave a glad cry and ran down the road toward them. The squirrels bumped along off the road, and a road-runner flirted its tail and raced over the edge of the hill and sailed out like a glider.   (55)

Jody tried to leap into the middle of his shadow at every step. A stone rolled under his foot and he went down. Around a little bend he raced, and there, a short distance ahead, were his grandfather and the cart. The boy dropped from his unseemly running and approached at a dignified walk.   (56)

The horse plodded stumble-footedly up the hill and the old man walked beside it. In the lowering sun their giant shadows flickered darkly behind them. The grandfather was dressed in a black broadcloth suit and he wore kid congress gaiters and a black tie on a short, hard collar. He carried his black slouch hat in his hand. His white beard was cropped close and his white eyebrows overhung his eyes like moustaches. The blue eyes were sternly merry. About the whole face and figure there was a granite dignity, so that every motion seemed an impossible thing. Once at rest, it seemed the old man would be stone, would never move again. His steps were slow and certain. Once made, no step could ever be retraced; once headed in a direction, the path would never bend nor the pace increase nor slow.   (57)

When Jody appeared around the bend, Grandfather waved his hat slowly in welcome, and he called, "Why, Jody! Come down to meet me, have you?"   (58)

Jody sidled near and turned and matched his step to the old man's step and stiffened his body and dragged his heels a little. "Yes, sir," he said. "We got your letter only today."   (59)

"Should have been here yesterday," said Grandfather. "It certainly should. How are all the folks?"   (60)

"They're fine, sir." He hesitated and then suggested shyly, "Would you like to come on a mouse hunt tomorrow, sir?"   (61)

"Mouse hunt, Jody?" Grandfather chuckled. "Have the people of this generation come down to hunting mice? They aren't very strong, the new people, but I hardly thought mice would be game for them."   (62)

"No, sir. It's just play. The haystack's gone. I'm going to drive out the mice to the dogs. And you can watch, or even beat the hay a little."   (63)

The stern, merry eyes turned down on him. "I see. You don't eat them, then. You haven't come to that yet."   (64)

Jody explained, "The dogs eat them, sir. It wouldn't be much like hunting Indians, I guess."   (65)

"No, not much—but then later, when the troops were hunting Indians and shooting children and burning teepees, it wasn't much different from your mouse hunt."   (66)

They topped the rise and started down into the ranch cup, and they lost the sun from their shoulders. "You've grown," Grandfather said. "Nearly an inch, I should say."   (67)

"More," Jody boasted. "Where they mark me on the door, I'm up more than an inch since Thanksgiving even."   (68)

Grandfather's rich throaty voice said, "Maybe you're getting too much water and turning to pith and stalk. Wait until you head out, and then we'll see."   (69)

Jody looked quickly into the old man's face to see whether his feelings should be hurt, but there was no will to injure, no punishing nor putting-in-your-place light in the keen blue eyes. "We might kill a pig," Jody suggested.   (70)

"Oh, no! I couldn't let you do that. You're just humoring me. It isn't the time and you know it."   (71)

"You know Riley, the big boar, sir?"   (72)

"Yes. I remember Riley well."   (73)

"Well, Riley ate a hole into that same haystack, and it fell down on him and smothered him."   (74)

"Pigs do that when they can," said Grandfather.   (75)

"Riley was a nice pig, for a boar, sir. I rode him sometimes, and he didn't mind."   (76)

A door slammed at the house below them, and they saw Jody's mother standing on the porch waving her apron in welcome. And they saw Carl Tiflin walking up from the barn to be at the house for the arrival.   (77)

The sun had disappeared from the hills by now. The blue smoke from the house chimney hung in flat layers in the purpling ranch-cup. The puff-ball clouds, dropped by the falling wind, hung listlessly in the sky.   (78)

Billy Buck came out of the bunkhouse and flung a wash basin of soapy water on the ground. He had been shaving in mid-week, for Billy held Grandfather in reverence, and Grandfather said that Billy was one of the few men of the new generation who had not gone soft. Although Billy was in middle age, Grandfather considered him a boy. Now Billy was hurrying toward the house too. (79)

When Jody and Grandfather arrived, the three were waiting for them in front of the yard gate. (80)

Carl said, "Hello, sir. We've been looking for you." (81)

Mrs. Tiflin kissed Grandfather on the side of his beard, and stood still while his big hand patted her shoulder. Billy shook hands solemnly, grinning under his straw moustache. "I'll put up your horse," said Billy, and he led the rig away. (82)

Grandfather watched him go, and then, turning back to the group, he said as he had said a hundred times before, "There's a good boy. I knew his father, old Mule-tail Buck. I never knew why they called him Mule-tail except he packed mules." (83)

Mrs. Tiflin turned and led the way into the house. "How long are you going to stay, Father? Your letter didn't say." (84)

"Well, I don't know. I thought I'd stay about two weeks. But I never stay as long as I think I'm going to." (85)

In a short while they were sitting at the white oilcloth table eating their supper. The lamp with the tin reflector hung over the table. Outside the dining-room windows the big moths battered softly against the glass. (86)

Grandfather cut his steak into tiny pieces and chewed slowly. "I'm hungry," he said. "Driving out here got my appetite up. It's like when we were crossing. We all got so hungry every night we could hardly wait to let the meat get done. I could eat about five pounds of buffalo meat every night." (87)

"It's moving around does it," said Billy. "My father was a government packer. I helped him when I was a kid. Just the two of us could about clean up a deer's ham." (88)

"I knew your father, Billy," said Grandfather. "A fine man he was. They called him Mule-tail Buck. I don't know why except he packed mules." (89)

"That was it," Billy agreed. "He packed mules." (90)

Grandfather put down his knife and fork and looked around the table. "I remember one time we ran out of meat—" His voice dropped to a curious low sing-song, dropped into a tonal groove the story had worn for itself. "There was no buffalo, no antelope, not even rabbits. The hunters couldn't even shoot a coyote. That was the time for the leader to be on the watch. I was the leader, and I kept my eyes open. Know why? Well, just the minute the people began to get hungry they'd start slaughtering the team oxen. Do you believe that? I've heard of parties that just ate up their draft cattle. Started from the middle and worked toward the ends. Finally they'd eat the lead pair, and then the wheelers. The leader of a party had to keep them from doing that." (91)

In some manner a big moth got into the room and circled the hanging kerosene lamp. Billy got up and tried to clap it between his hands. Carl struck with a cupped palm and caught the moth and broke it. He walked to the window and dropped it out. (92)

"As I was saying," Grandfather began again, but Carl interrupted him. "You'd better eat some more meat. All the rest of us are ready for our pudding." (93)

Jody saw a flash of anger in his mother's eyes. Grandfather picked up his knife and fork. "I'm pretty hungry, all right," he said. "I'll tell you about that later." (94)

When supper was over, when the family and Billy Buck sat in front of the fireplace in the other room, Jody anxiously watched Grandfather. He saw the signs he knew. The bearded head leaned forward; the eyes lost their sternness and looked wonderingly into the fire; the big lean fingers laced themselves on the black knees. "I wonder," he began, "I just wonder whether I ever told you how those thieving Piutes drove off thirty-five of our horses." (95)

"I think you did," Carl interrupted. "Wasn't it just before you went up into the Tahoe country?" (96)

Grandfather turned quickly toward his son-in-law. "That's right. I guess I must have told you that story." (97)

"Lots of times," Carl said cruelly, and he avoided his wife's eyes. But he felt the angry eyes on him, and he said, "'Course I'd like to hear it again." (98)

Grandfather looked back at the fire. His fingers unlaced and laced again. Jody knew how he felt, how his insides were collapsed and empty. Hadn't Jody been called a Big-Britches that very afternoon? He arose to heroism and opened himself to the term Big-Britches again. "Tell about Indians," he said softly. (99)

Grandfather's eyes grew stern again. "Boys always want to hear about Indians. It was a job for men, but boys want to hear about it. Well, let's see. Did I ever tell you how I wanted each wagon to carry a long iron plate?" (100)

Everyone but Jody remained silent. Jody said, "No. You didn't." (101)

"Well, when the Indians attacked, we always put the wagons in a circle and fought from between the wheels. I thought that if every wagon carried a long plate with rifle holes, the men could stand the plates on the outside of the wheels when the wagons were in the circle and they would be protected. It would save lives and that would make up for the extra weight of the iron. But of course the party wouldn't do it. No party had done it before and they couldn't see why they should go to the expense. They lived to regret it, too." (102)

Jody looked at his mother, and knew from her expression that she was

not listening at all. Carl picked at a callus on his thumb and Billy Buck
watched a spider crawling up the wall.   (103)

Grandfather's tone dropped into its narrative groove again. Jody knew
in advance exactly what words would fall. The story droned on, speeded up
for the attack, grew sad over the wounds, struck a dirge at the burials on
the great plains. Jody sat quietly watching Grandfather. The stern blue
eyes were detached. He looked as though he were not very interested in
the story himself.   (104)

When it was finished, when the pause had been politely respected as
the frontier of the story, Billy Buck stood up and stretched and hitched his
trousers. "I guess I'll turn in," he said. Then he faced Grandfather. "I've got
an old powder horn and a cap and ball pistol down to the bunkhouse. Did
I ever show them to you?"   (105)

Grandfather nodded slowly. "Yes, I think you did, Billy. Reminds me of
a pistol I had when I was leading the people across." Billy stood politely
until the little story was done, and then he said, "Good night," and went out
of the house.   (106)

Carl Tiflin tried to turn the conversation then. "How's the country between here and Monterey? I've heard it's pretty dry."   (107)

"It is dry," said Grandfather. "There's not a drop of water in the Laguna
Seca. But it's a long pull from '87. The whole country was powder then, and
in '61 I believe all the coyotes starved to death. We had fifteen inches of
rain this year."   (108)

"Yes, but it all came too early. We could do with some now." Carl's eye
fell on Jody. "Hadn't you better be getting to bed?"   (109)

Jody stood up obediently. "Can I kill the mice in the old haystack, sir?"
                                                                         (110)

"Mice? Oh! Sure, kill them all off. Billy said there isn't any good hay
left."   (111)

Jody exchanged a secret and satisfying look with Grandfather. "I'll kill
every one tomorrow," he promised.   (112)

Jody lay in his bed and thought of the impossible world of Indians and
buffaloes, a world that had ceased to be forever. He wished he could have
been living in the heroic time, but he knew he was not of heroic timber. No
one living now, save possibly Billy Buck, was worthy to do the things that
had been done. A race of giants had lived then, fearless men, men of a
staunchness unknown in this day. Jody thought of the wide plains and of
the wagons moving across like centipedes. He thought of Grandfather on a
huge white horse, marshaling the people. Across his mind marched the
great phantoms, and they marched off the earth and they were gone. (113)

He came back to the ranch for a moment, then. He heard the dull rushing sound that space and silence make. He heard one of the dogs, out in the

doghouse, scratching a flea and bumping his elbow against the floor with every stroke. Then the wind arose again and the black cypress groaned and Jody went to sleep. (114)

He was up half an hour before the triangle sounded for breakfast. His mother was rattling the stove to make the flames roar when Jody went through the kitchen. "You're up early," she said. "Where are you going?" (115)

"Out to get a good stick. We're going to kill the mice today." (116)

"Who is 'we'?" (117)

"Why, Grandfather and I." (118)

"So you've got him in it. You always like to have someone in with you in case there's blame to share." (119)

"I'll be right back," said Jody. "I want to have a good stick ready for after breakfast." (120)

He closed the screen door after him and went out into the cool blue morning. The birds were noisy in the dawn and the ranch cats came down from the hill like blunt snakes. They had been hunting gophers in the dark, and although the four cats were full of gopher meat, they sat in a semi-circle at the back door and mewed piteously for milk. Doubletree Mutt and Smasher moved sniffing along the edge of the brush, performing the duty with rigid ceremony, but when Jody whistled, their heads jerked up and their tails waved. They plunged down to him, wriggling their skins and yawning. Jody patted their heads seriously, and moved on to the weathered scrap pile. He selected an old broom handle and a short piece of inch-square scrap wood. From his pocket he took a shoelace and tied the ends of the sticks loosely together to make a flail. He whistled his new weapon through the air and struck the ground experimentally, while the dogs leaped aside and whined with apprehension. (121)

Jody turned and started down past the house toward the old haystack ground to look over the field of slaughter, but Billy Buck, sitting patiently on the back steps, called to him, "You better come back. It's only a couple of minutes till breakfast." (122)

Jody changed his course and moved toward the house. He leaned his flail against the steps. "That's to drive the mice out," he said. "I'll bet they're fat. I'll bet they don't know what's going to happen to them today." (123)

"No, nor you either," Billy remarked philosophically, "nor me, nor anyone." (124)

Jody was staggered by this thought. He knew it was true. His imagination twitched away from the mouse hunt. Then his mother came out on the back porch and struck the triangle, and all thoughts fell in a heap. (125)

Grandfather hadn't appeared at the table when they sat down. Billy nodded at his empty chair. "He's all right? He isn't sick?" (126)

"He takes a long time to dress," said Mrs. Tiflin. "He combs his whiskers and rubs up his shoes and brushes his clothes." (127)

Carl scattered sugar on his mush. "A man that's led a wagon train across the plains has got to be pretty careful how he dresses." (128)

Mrs. Tiflin turned on him. "Don't do that, Carl! Please don't!" There was more of threat than of request in her tone. And the threat irritated Carl. (129)

"Well, how many times do I have to listen to the story of the iron plates, and the thirty-five horses? That time's done. Why can't he forget it, now it's done?" He grew angrier while he talked, and his voice rose. "Why does he have to tell them over and over? He came across the plains. All right! Now it's finished. Nobody wants to hear about it over and over." (130)

The door into the kitchen closed softly. The four at the table sat frozen. Carl laid his mush spoon on the table and touched his chin with his fingers. (131)

Then the kitchen door opened and Grandfather walked in. His mouth smiled tightly and his eyes were squinted. "Good morning," he said, and he sat down and looked at his mush dish. (132)

Carl could not leave it there. "Did—did you hear what I said?" (133)

Grandfather jerked a little nod. (134)

"I don't know what got into me, sir. I didn't mean it. I was just being funny." (135)

Jody glanced in shame at his mother, and he saw that she was looking at Carl, and that she wasn't breathing. It was an awful thing that he was doing. He was tearing himself to pieces to talk like that. It was a terrible thing to him to retract a word, but to retract it in shame was infinitely worse. (136)

Grandfather looked sidewise. "I'm trying to get right side up," he said gently. "I'm not being mad. I don't mind what you said, but it might be true, and I would mind that." (137)

"It isn't true," said Carl. "I'm not feeling well this morning. I'm sorry I said it." (138)

"Don't be sorry, Carl. An old man doesn't see things sometimes. Maybe you're right. The crossing is finished. Maybe it should be forgotten, now it's done." (139)

Carl got up from the table. "I've had enough to eat. I'm going to work. Take your time, Billy!" He walked quickly out of the dining-room. Billy gulped the rest of his food and followed soon after. But Jody could not leave his chair. (140)

"Won't you tell any more stories?" Jody asked. (141)

"Why, sure I'll tell them, but only when—I'm sure people want to hear them." (142)

"I like to hear them, sir." (143)

"Oh! Of course you do, but you're a little boy. It was a job for men, but only little boys like to hear about it." (144)

Jody got up from his place. "I'll wait outside for you, sir. I've got a good stick for those mice." (145)

He waited by the gate until the old man came out on the porch. "Let's go down and kill the mice now," Jody called. (146)

"I think I'll just sit in the sun, Jody. You go kill the mice." (147)

"You can use my stick if you like." (148)

"No, I'll just sit here a while." (149)

Jody turned disconsolately away, and walked down toward the old hay-stack. He tried to whip up his enthusiasm with thoughts of the fat juicy mice. He beat the ground with his flail. The dogs coaxed and whined about him, but he could not go. Back at the house he could see Grandfather sitting on the porch, looking small and thin and black. (150)

Jody gave up and went to sit on the steps at the old man's feet. (151)

"Back already? Did you kill the mice?" (152)

"No, sir. I'll kill them some other day." (153)

The morning flies buzzed close to the ground and the ants dashed about in front of the steps. The heavy smell of sage slipped down the hill. The porch boards grew warm in the sunshine. (154)

Jody hardly knew when Grandfather started to talk. "I shouldn't stay here, feeling the way I do." He examined his strong old hands. "I feel as though the crossing wasn't worth doing." His eyes moved up the side-hill and stopped on a motionless hawk perched on a dead limb. "I tell those old stories, but they're not what I want to tell. I only know how I want people to feel when I tell them. (155)

"It wasn't Indians that were important, nor adventures, nor even getting out here. It was a whole bunch of people made into one big crawling beast. And I was the head. It was westering and westering. Every man wanted something for himself, but the big beast that was all of them wanted only westering. I was the leader, but if I hadn't been there, someone else would have been the head. The thing had to have a head. (156)

"Under the little bushes the shadows were black at white noonday. When we saw the mountains at last, we cried—all of us. But it wasn't getting here that mattered, it was movement and westering. (157)

"We carried life out here and set it down the way those ants carry eggs. And I was the leader. The westering was as big as God, and the slow steps that made the movement piled up and piled up until the continent was crossed. (158)

"Then we came down to the sea, and it was done." He stopped and wiped his eyes until the rims were red. "That's what I should be telling instead of stories." (159)

When Jody spoke, Grandfather started and looked down at him. "Maybe I could lead the people some day," Jody said.   (160)

The old man smiled. "There's no place to go. There's the ocean to stop you. There's a line of old men along the shore hating the ocean because it stopped them."   (161)

"In boats I might, sir."   (162)

"No place to go, Jody. Every place is taken. But that's not the worst—no, not the worst. Westering had died out of the people. Westering isn't a hunger any more. It's all done. Your father is right. It is finished." He laced his fingers on his knee and looked at them.   (163)

Jody felt very sad. "If you'd like a glass of lemonade I could make it for you."   (164)

Grandfather was about to refuse, and then he saw Jody's face. "That would be nice," he said. "Yes, it would be nice to drink a lemonade."   (165)

Jody ran into the kitchen where his mother was wiping the last of the breakfast dishes. "Can I have a lemon to make a lemonade for Grandfather?"   (166)

His mother mimicked—"And another lemon to make a lemonade for you."   (167)

"No ma'am. I don't want one."   (168)

"Jody! You're sick!" Then she stopped suddenly. "Take a lemon out of the cooler," she said softly. "Here, I'll reach the squeezer down to you."   (169)

Willa Cather

(1873–1947)

WILLA CATHER *tried briefly both journalism and teaching, but her heart lay with fiction. She reached her majority as a novelist when she turned her attention to the pioneers of her adopted Nebraska (O Pioneers! 1913; My Antonia, 1918) and the Catholic missionaries of New Mexico (Death Comes for the Archbishop, 1927). She was a very self-conscious artist, a self-consciousness which stimulated a collection of her stories,* Youth and the Bright Medusa *(1920), and her autobiographical sketches,* Not Under Forty *(1936).*

■ *The Sculptor's Funeral*

A GROUP of the townspeople stood on the station siding of a little Kansas town, awaiting the coming of the night train, which was already twenty minutes overdue. The snow had fallen thick over everything; in the pale starlight the line of bluffs across the wide, white meadows south of the town made soft, smoke-coloured curves against the clear sky. The men on the siding stood first on one foot and then on the other, their hands thrust deep into their trousers pockets, their overcoats open, their shoulders screwed up with the cold; and they glanced from time to time toward the southeast, where the railroad track wound along the river shore. They conversed in low tones and moved about restlessly, seeming uncertain as to what was expected of them. There was but one of the company who looked as if he knew exactly why he was there, and he kept conspicuously apart; walking to the far end of the platform, returning to the station door, then pacing up the track again, his chin sunk in the high collar of his overcoat, his burly shoulders drooping forward, his gait heavy and dogged. Presently he was approached by a tall, spare, grizzled man clad in a faded Grand Army suit, who shuffled out from the group and advanced with a certain deference, craning his neck forward until his back made the angle of a jack-knife three-quarters open.   (1)

"I reckon she's a-goin' to be pretty late agin to-night, Jim," he remarked in a squeaky falsetto. "S'pose it's the snow?"   (2)

"I don't know," responded the other man with a shade of annoyance, speaking from out an astonishing cataract of red beard that grew fiercely and thickly in all directions.   (3)

The spare man shifted the quill toothpick he was chewing to the other side of his mouth. "It ain't likely that anybody from the East will come with the corpse, I s'pose," he went on reflectively.   (4)

"I don't know," responded the other, more curtly than before.   (5)

"It's too bad he didn't belong to some lodge or other. I like an order funeral myself. They seem more appropriate for people of some repytation," the spare man continued, with an ingratiating concession in his shrill voice, as he carefully placed his toothpick in his vest pocket. He always carried the flag at the G. A. R. funerals in the town.   (6)

The heavy man turned on his heel, without replying, and walked up the siding. The spare man rejoined the uneasy group. "Jim's ez full ez a tick, ez ushel," he commented commiseratingly.   (7)

Just then a distant whistle sounded, and there was a shuffling of feet on the platform. A number of lanky boys, of all ages, appeared as suddenly and slimily as eels wakened by the crack of thunder; some came from the waiting-room, where they had been warming themselves by the red stove, or half asleep on the slat benches; others uncoiled themselves from baggage trucks or slid out of express wagons. Two clambered down from the driver's seat of a hearse that stood backed up against the siding. They straightened their stooping shoulders and lifted their heads, and a flash of momentary animation kindled their dull eyes at that cold, vibrant scream, the world-wide call for men. It stirred them like the note of a trumpet; just as it had often stirred the man who was coming home tonight, in his boyhood.　(8)

The night express shot, red as a rocket, from out the eastward marsh lands and wound along the river shore under the long lines of shivering poplars that sentinelled the meadows, the escaping steam hanging in grey masses against the pale sky and blotting out the Milky Way. In a moment the red glare from the headlight streamed up the snow-covered track before the siding and glittered on the wet, black rails. The burly man with the dishevelled red beard walked swiftly up the platform toward the approaching train, uncovering his head as he went. The group of men behind him hesitated, glanced questioningly at one another, and awkwardly followed his example. The train stopped, and the crowd shuffled up to the express car just as the door was thrown open, the man in the G. A. R. suit thrusting his head forward with curiosity. The express messenger appeared in the doorway, accompanied by a young man in a long ulster and travelling cap.　(9)

"Are Mr. Merrick's friends here?" inquired the young man.　(10)

The group on the platform swayed uneasily. Philip Phelps, the banker, responded with dignity: "We have come to take charge of the body. Mr. Merrick's father is very feeble and can't be about."　(11)

"Send the agent out here," growled the express messenger, "and tell the operator to lend a hand."　(12)

The coffin was got out of its rough-box and down on the snowy platform. The townspeople drew back enough to make room for it and then formed a close semicircle about it, looking curiously at the palm leaf which lay across the black cover. No one said anything. The baggage man stood by his truck, waiting to get at the trunks. The engine panted heavily, and the fireman dodged in and out among the wheels with his yellow torch and long oil-can, snapping the spindle boxes. The young Bostonian, one of the dead sculptor's pupils who had come with the body, looked about him helplessly. He turned to the banker, the only one of that black, uneasy, stoop-shouldered group who seemed enough of an individual to be addressed.　(13)

"None of Mr. Merrick's brothers are here?" he asked uncertainly.　(14)

The man with the red beard for the first time stepped up and joined the others. "No, they have not come yet; the family is scattered. The body will be taken directly to the house." He stooped and took hold of one of the handles of the coffin.   (15)

"Take the long hill road up, Thompson, it will be easier on the horses," called the liveryman as the undertaker snapped the door of the hearse and prepared to mount to the driver's seat.   (16)

Laird, the red-bearded lawyer, turned again to the stranger: "We didn't know whether there would be any one with him or not," he explained. "It's a long walk, so you'd better go up in the hack." He pointed to a single battered conveyance, but the young man replied stiffly: "Thank you, but I think I will go up with the hearse. If you don't object," turning to the undertaker, "I'll ride with you."   (17)

They clambered up over the wheels and drove off in the starlight up the long, white hill toward the town. The lamps in the still village were shining from under the low, snow-burdened roofs; and beyond, on every side, the plains reached out into emptiness, peaceful and wide as the soft sky itself, and wrapped in a tangible, white silence.   (18)

When the hearse backed up to a wooden sidewalk before a naked, weather-beaten frame house, the same composite, ill-defined group that had stood upon the station siding was huddled about the gate. The front yard was an icy swamp, and a couple of warped planks, extending from the sidewalk to the door, made a sort of rickety foot-bridge. The gate hung on one hinge, and was opened wide with difficulty. Steavens, the young stranger, noticed that something black was tied to the knob of the front door.   (19)

The grating sound made by the casket, as it was drawn from the hearse, was answered by a scream from the house; the front door was wrenched open, and a tall, corpulent woman rushed out bareheaded into the snow and flung herself upon the coffin, shrieking: "My boy, my boy! And this is how you've come home to me!"   (20)

As Steavens turned away and closed his eyes with a shudder of unutterable repulsion, another woman, also tall, but flat and angular, dressed entirely in black, darted out of the house and caught Mrs. Merrick by the shoulders, crying sharply: "Come, come, mother; you mustn't go on like this!" Her tone changed to one of obsequious solemnity as she turned to the banker: "The parlour is ready, Mr. Phelps."   (21)

The bearers carried the coffin along the narrow boards, while the undertaker ran ahead with the coffin-rests. They bore it into a large, unheated room that smelled of dampness and disuse and furniture polish, and set it down under a hanging lamp ornamented with jingling glass prisms and before a "Rogers group" of John Alden and Priscilla, wreathed with smilax. Henry Steavens stared about him with the sickening conviction that there had been a mistake, and that he had somehow arrived at the wrong destination. He looked at the clover-green Brussels, the fat plush upholstery, among the hand-painted china plaques and panels and vases, for some mark of identification,—for something that might once conceivably have belonged to Harvey Merrick. It was not until he recognized his friend in the crayon portrait of a little boy in kilts and curls, hanging above the piano, that he felt willing to let any of these people approach the coffin.   (22)

"Take the lid off, Mr. Thompson; let me see my boy's face," wailed the elder woman between her sobs. This time Steavens looked fearfully, almost beseechingly into her face, red and swollen under its masses of strong, black, shiny hair. He flushed, dropped his eyes, and then, almost incredulously, looked again. There was a kind of power about her face—a kind of brutal handsomeness, even; but it was scarred and furrowed by violence, and so coloured and coarsened by fiercer passions that grief seemed never to have laid a gentle finger there. The long nose was distended and knobbed at the end, and there were deep lines on either side of it; her heavy, black brows almost met across her forehead, her teeth were large and square, and set far apart—teeth that could tear. She filled the room; the men were obliterated, seemed tossed about like twigs in an angry water, and even Steavens felt himself being drawn into the whirlpool.   (23)

The daughter—the tall, raw-boned woman in crêpe, with a mourning comb in her hair which curiously lengthened her long face—sat stiffly upon the sofa, her hands, conspicuous for their large knuckles, folded in her lap, her mouth and eyes drawn down, solemnly awaiting the opening of the coffin. Near the door stood a mulatto woman, evidently a servant in the house, with a timid bearing and an emaciated face pitifully sad and gentle. She was weeping silently, the corner of her calico apron lifted to her eyes, occasionally suppressing a long, quivering sob. Steavens walked over and stood beside her.   (24)

Feeble steps were heard on the stairs, and an old man, tall and frail, odorous of pipe smoke, with shaggy, unkept grey hair and a dingy beard, tobacco stained about the mouth, entered uncertainly. He went slowly up to the coffin and stood rolling a blue cotton handkerchief between his hands, seeming so pained and embarrassed by his wife's orgy of grief that he had no consciousness of anything else.   (25)

"There, there, Annie, dear, don't take on so," he quavered timidly, putting out a shaking hand and awkwardly patting her elbow. She turned and sank upon his shoulder with such violence that he tottered a little. He did not even glance toward the coffin, but continued to look at her with a dull, frightened, appealing expression, as a spaniel looks at the whip. His sunken cheeks slowly reddened and burned with miserable shame. When his wife rushed from the room, her daughter strode after her with set lips. The servant stole up to the coffin, bent over it for a moment, and then slipped away to the kitchen, leaving Steavens, the lawyer, and the father to themselves. The old man stood looking down at his dead son's face. The sculptor's splendid head seemed even more noble in its rigid stillness than in life. The dark hair had crept down upon the wide forehead; the face seemed strangely long, but in it there was not that repose we expect to find in the faces of the dead. The brows were so drawn that there were two deep lines above the beaked nose, and the chin was thrust forward defiantly. It was as though the strain of life had been so sharp and bitter that death could not at once relax the tension and smooth the countenance into perfect peace—as though he were still guarding something precious, which might even yet be wrested from him. (26)

The old man's lips were working under his stained beard. He turned to the lawyer with timid deference: "Phelps and the rest are comin' back to set up with Harve, ain't they?" he asked. "Thank 'ee, Jim, thank 'ee." He brushed the hair back gently from his son's forehead. "He was a good boy, Jim; always a good boy. He was ez gentle ez a child and the kindest of 'em all—only we didn't none of us ever onderstand him." The tears trickled slowly down his beard and dropped upon the sculptor's coat. (27)

"Martin, Martin! Oh, Martin! come here," his wife wailed from the top of the stairs. The old man started timorously: "Yes, Annie, I'm coming." He turned away, hesitated, stood for a moment in miserable indecision; then reached back and patted the dead man's hair softly, and stumbled from the room. (28)

"Poor old man, I didn't think he had any tears left. Seems as if his eyes would have gone dry long ago. At his age nothing cuts very deep," remarked the lawyer. (29)

Something in his tone made Steavens glance up. While the mother had been in the room, the young man had scarcely seen any one else; but now, from the moment he first glanced into Jim Laird's florid face and blood-shot eyes, he knew that he had found what he had been heartsick at not finding before—the feeling, the understanding, that must exist in some one, even here. (30)

The man was red as his beard, with features swollen and blurred by dissipation, and a hot, blazing blue eye. His face was strained—that of a man who is controlling himself with difficulty—and he kept plucking at his beard with a sort of fierce resentment. Steavens, sitting by the window, watched him turn down the glaring lamp, still its jangling pendants with an angry gesture, and then stand with his hands locked behind him, staring down into the master's face. He could not help wondering what link there had been between the porcelain vessel and so sooty a lump of potter's clay. (31)

From the kitchen an uproar was sounding; when the dining-room door opened, the import of it was clear. The mother was abusing the maid for having forgotten to make the dressing for the chicken salad which had been prepared for the watchers. Steavens had never heard anything in the least like it; it was injured, emotional, dramatic abuse, unique and masterly in its excruciating cruelty, as violent and unrestrained as had been her grief of twenty minutes before. With a shudder of disgust the lawyer went into the dining-room and closed the door into the kitchen.   (32)

"Poor Roxy's getting it now," he remarked when he came back. "The Merricks took her out of the poor-house years ago; and if her loyalty would let her, I guess the poor old thing could tell tales that would curdle your blood. She's the mulatto woman who was standing in here a while ago, with her apron to her eyes. The old woman is a fury; there never was anybody like her. She made Harvey's life a hell for him when he lived at home; he was so sick ashamed of it. I never could see how he kept himself sweet."   (33)

"He was wonderful," said Steavens slowly, "wonderful; but until to-night I have never known how wonderful."   (34)

"That is the eternal wonder of it, anyway; that it can come even from such a dung heap as this," the lawyer cried, with a sweeping gesture which seemed to indicate much more than the four walls within which they stood.   (35)

"I think I'll see whether I can get a little air. The room is so close I am beginning to feel rather faint," murmured Steavens, struggling with one of the windows. The sash was stuck, however, and would not yield, so he sat down dejectedly and began pulling at his collar. The lawyer came over, loosened the sash with one blow of his red fist and sent the window up a few inches. Steavens thanked him, but the nausea which had been gradually climbing into his throat for the last half hour left him with but one desire— a desperate feeling that he must get away from this place with what was left of Harvey Merrick. Oh, he comprehended well enough now the quiet bitterness of the smile that he had seen so often on his master's lips!   (36)

Once when Merrick returned from a visit home, he brought with him a singularly feeling and suggestive bas-relief of a thin, faded old woman, sitting and sewing something pinned to her knee; while a full-lipped, full-blooded little urchin, his trousers held up by a single gallows, stood beside her, impatiently twitching her gown to call her attention to a butterfly he had caught. Steavens, impressed by the tender and delicate modelling of the thin, tired face, had asked him if it were his mother. He remembered the dull flush that had burned up in the sculptor's face.   (37)

The lawyer was sitting in a rocking-chair beside the coffin, his head thrown back and his eyes closed. Steavens looked at him earnestly, puzzled at the line of the chin, and wondering why a man should conceal a feature of such distinction under that disfiguring shock of beard. Suddenly, as though he felt the young sculptor's keen glance, Jim Laird opened his eyes.   (38)

"Was he always a good deal of an oyster?" he asked abruptly. "He was terribly shy as a boy."   (30)

"Yes, he was an oyster, since you put it so," rejoined Steavens. "Although he could be very fond of people, he always gave one the impression of being detached. He disliked violent emotion; he was reflective, and rather distrustful of himself—except, of course, as regarded his work. He was sure enough there. He distrusted men pretty thoroughly and women even more, yet somehow without believing ill of them. He was determined, indeed, to believe the best; but he seemed afraid to investigate." (40)

"A burnt dog dreads the fire," said the lawyer grimly, and closed his eyes. (41)

Steavens went on and on, reconstructing that whole miserable boyhood. All this raw, biting ugliness had been the portion of the man whose mind was to become an exhaustless gallery of beautiful impressions—so sensitive that the mere shadow of a poplar leaf flickering against a sunny wall would be etched and held there for ever. Surely, if ever a man had the magic word in his finger tips, it was Merrick. Whatever he touched, he revealed its holiest secret; liberated it from enchantment and restored it to its pristine loveliness. Upon whatever he had come in contact with, he had left a beautiful record of the experience—a sort of ethereal signature; a scent, a sound, a colour that was his own. (42)

Steavens understood now the real tragedy of his master's life; neither love nor wine, as many had conjectured; but a blow which had fallen earlier and cut deeper than anything else could have done—a shame not his, and yet so unescapably his, to hide in his heart from his very boyhood. And without—the frontier warfare; the yearning of a boy, cast ashore upon a desert of newness and ugliness and sordidness, for all that is chastened and old, and noble with traditions. (43)

At eleven o'clock the tall, flat woman in black announced that the watchers were arriving, and asked them to "step into the dining-room." As Steavens rose, the lawyer said dryly: "You go on—it'll be a good experience for you. I'm not equal to that crowd tonight; I've had twenty years of them." (44)

As Steavens closed the door after him he glanced back at the lawyer, sitting by the coffin in the dim light, with his chin resting on his hand. (45)

The same misty group that had stood before the door of the express car shuffled into the dining-room. In the light of the kerosene lamp they separated and became individuals. The minister, a pale, feeble-looking man with white hair and blond chin-whiskers, took his seat beside a small side table and placed his Bible upon it. The Grand Army man sat down behind the stove and tilted his chair back comfortably against the wall, fishing his quill toothpick from his waistcoat pocket. The two bankers, Phelps and Elder, sat off in a corner behind the dinner-table, where they could finish their discussion of the new usury law and its effect on chattel security loans. The real estate agent, an old man with a smiling, hypocritical face, soon joined them. The coal and lumber dealer and the cattle shipper sat on opposite sides of the hard coal-burner, their feet on the nickel-work. Steavens took a book from his pocket and began to read. The talk around him ranged through various topics of local interest while the house was quieting down. When it was clear that the members of the family were in bed, the Grand Army man hitched his shoulders and, untangling his long legs, caught his heels on the rounds of his chair. (46)

"S'pose there'll be a will, Phelps?" he queried in his weak falsetto. (47)

The banker laughed disagreeably, and began trimming his nails with a pearl-handled pocket-knife. (48)

"There'll scarcely be any need for one, will there?" he queried in his turn. (49)

The restless Grand Army man shifted his position again, getting his knees still nearer his chin. "Why, the ole man says Harve's done right well lately," he chirped. (50)

The other banker spoke up. "I reckon he means by that Harve ain't asked him to mortgage any more farms lately, so as he could go on with his education." (51)

"Seems like my mind don't reach back to a time when Harve wasn't bein' edycated," tittered the Grand Army man. (52)

There was a general chuckle. The minister took out his handkerchief and blew his nose sonorously. Banker Phelps closed his knife with a snap. "It's too bad the old man's sons didn't turn out better," he remarked with reflective authority. "They never hung together. He spent money enough on Harve to stock a dozen cattle-farms, and he might as well have poured it into Sand Creek. If Harve had stayed at home and helped nurse what little they had, and gone into stock on the old man's bottom farm, they might all have been well fixed. But the old man had to trust everything to tenants and was cheated right and left." (53)

"Harve never could have handled stock none," interposed the cattleman. "He hadn't it in him to be sharp. Do you remember when he bought Sander's mules for eight-year olds, when everybody in town knew that Sander's father-in-law give 'em to his wife for a wedding present eighteen years before, an' they was full-grown mules then?" (54)

The company laughed discreetly, and the Grand Army man rubbed his knees with a spasm of childish delight. (55)

"Harve never was much account for anything practical, and he shore was never fond of work," began the coal and lumber dealer. "I mind the last time he was home; the day he left, when the old man was out to the barn helpin' his hand hitch up to take Harve to the train, and Cal Moots was patchin' up the fence; Harve, he come out on the step and sings out, in his ladylike voice: 'Cal Moots, Cal Moots! please come cord my trunk.'" (56)

"That's Harve for you," approved the Grand Army man. "I kin hear him howlin' yet, when he was a big feller in long pants and his mother used to whale him with a rawhide in the barn for lettin' the cows git foundered in the cornfield when he was drivin' 'em home from pasture. He killed a cow of mine that-a-way onct—a pure Jersey and the best milker I had, an' the ole man had to put up for her. Harve, he was watchin' the sun set acrost the marshes when the anamile got away."   (57)

"Where the old man made his mistake was in sending the boy East to school," said Phelps, stroking his goatee and speaking in a deliberate, judicial tone. "There was where he got his head full of nonsense. What Harve needed, of all people, was a course in some first-class Kansas City business college."   (58)

The letters were swimming before Steavens's eyes. Was it possible that these men did not understand, that the palm on the coffin meant nothing to them? The very name of their town would have remained for ever buried in the postal guide had it not been now and again mentioned in the world in connection with Harvey Merrick's. He remembered what his master had said to him on the day of his death, after the congestion of both lungs had shut off any probability of recovery, and the sculptor had asked his pupil to send his body home. "It's not a pleasant place to be lying while the world is moving and doing and bettering," he had said with a feeble smile, "but it rather seems as though we ought to go back to the place we came from, in the end. The townspeople will come in for a look at me; and after they have had their say, I shan't have much to fear from the judgment of God!"   (59)

The cattleman took up the comment. "Forty's young for a Merrick to cash in; they usually hang on pretty well. Probably he helped it along with whisky."   (60)

"His mother's people were not long lived, and Harvey never had a robust constitution," said the minister mildly. He would have liked to say more. He had been the boy's Sunday-school teacher, and had been fond of him; but he felt that he was not in a position to speak. His own sons had turned out badly, and it was not a year since one of them had made his last trip home in the express car, shot in a gambling-house in the Black Hills.   (61)

"Nevertheless, there is no disputin' that Harve frequently looked upon the wine when it was red, also variegated, and it shore made an oncommon fool of him," moralized the cattleman.   (62)

Just then the door leading into the parlour rattled loudly and every one started involuntarily, looking relieved when only Jim Laird came out. The Grand Army man ducked his head when he saw the spark in his blue, blood-shot eye. They were all afraid of Jim; he was a drunkard, but he could twist the law to suit his client's needs as no other man in all western Kansas could do, and there were many who tried. The lawyer closed the door behind him, leaned back against it and folded his arms, cocking his head a little to one side. When he assumed this attitude in the court-room, ears were always pricked up, as it usually foretold a flood of withering sarcasm.   (63)

"I've been with you gentlemen before," he began in a dry, even tone, "when you've sat by the coffins of boys born and raised in this town; and, if I remember rightly, you were never any too well satisfied when you checked them up. What's the matter, anyhow? Why is it that reputable young men are as scarce as millionaires in Sand City? It might almost seem to a stranger that there was some way something the matter with your progressive town. Why did Ruben Sayer, the brightest young lawyer you ever turned out, after he had come home from the university as straight as a die, take to drinking and forge a check and shoot himself? Why did Bill Merrit's son die of the shakes in a saloon in Omaha? Why was Mr. Thomas's son, here, shot in a gambling-house? Why did young Adams burn his mill to beat the insurance companies and go to the pen?"   (64)

The lawyer paused and unfolded his arms, laying one clenched fist quietly on the table. "I'll tell you why. Because you drummed nothing but money and knavery into their ears from the time they wore knickerbockers; because you carped away at them as you've been carping here tonight, holding our friends Phelps and Elder up to them for their models, as our grandfathers held up George Washington and John Adams. But the boys were young, and raw at the business you put them to, and how could they match coppers with such artists as Phelps and Elder? You wanted them to be successful rascals; they were only unsuccessful ones—that's all the difference. There was only one boy ever raised in this borderland between ruffianism and civilization who didn't come to grief, and you hated Harvey Merrick more for winning out than you hated all the other boys who got under the wheels. Lord, Lord, how you did hate him! Phelps, here, is fond of saying that he could buy and sell us all out any time he's a mind to; but he knew Harve wouldn't have given a tinker's damn for his bank and all his cattle-farms put together; and a lack of appreciation, that way, goes hard with Phelps.   (65)

"Old Nimrod thinks Harve drank too much; and this from such as Nimrod and me!   (66)

"Brother Elder says Harve was too free with the old man's money—fell short in filial consideration, maybe. Well, we can all remember the very tone in which brother Elder swore his own father was a liar, in the county court; and we all know that the old man came out of that partnership with his son as bare as a sheared lamb. But maybe I'm getting personal, and I'd better be driving ahead at what I want to say."   (67)

The lawyer paused a moment, squared his heavy shoulders, and went on: "Harvey Merrick and I went to school together, back East. We were dead in earnest, and we wanted you all to be proud of us some day. We meant to be great men. Even I, and I haven't lost my sense of humour, gentlemen, I meant to be a great man. I came back here to practise, and I found you didn't in the least want me to be a great man. You wanted me to be a shrewd lawyer—oh, yes! Our veteran here wanted me to get him an increase of pension, because he had dyspepsia; Phelps wanted a new county survey that would put the widow Wilson's little bottom farm inside his south line; Elder wanted to lend money at 5 per cent a month, and get it collected; and Stark here wanted to wheedle old women up in Vermont into investing their annuities in real-estate mortgages that are not worth the paper they are written on. Oh, you needed me hard enough, and you'll go on needing me! (68)

"Well, I came back here and became the damned shyster you wanted me to be. You pretend to have some sort of respect for me; and yet you'll stand up and throw mud at Harvey Merrick, whose soul you couldn't dirty and whose hands you couldn't tie. Oh, you're a discriminating lot of Christians! There have been times when the sight of Harvey's name in some Eastern paper has made me hang my head like a whipped dog; and, again, times when I liked to think of him off there in the world, away from all this hog-wallow, climbing the big, clean up-grade he'd set for himself. (69)

"And we? Now that we've fought and lied and sweated and stolen, and hated as only the disappointed strugglers in a bitter, dead little Western town know how to do, what have we got to show for it? Harvey Merrick wouldn't have given one sunset over your marshes for all you've got put together, and you know it. It's not for me to say why, in the inscrutable wisdom of God, a genius should ever have been called from this place of hatred and bitter waters; but I want this Boston man to know that the drivel he's been hearing here tonight is the only tribute any truly great man could have from such a lot of sick, sidetracked, burnt-dog, land-poor sharks as the herepresent financiers of Sand City—upon which town may God have mercy!" (70)

The lawyer thrust out his hand to Steavens as he passed him, caught up his overcoat in the hall, and had left the house before the Grand Army man had had time to lift his ducked head and crane his long neck about at his fellows. (71)

Next day Jim Laird was drunk and unable to attend the funeral services. Steavens called twice at his office, but was compelled to start East without seeing him. He had a presentiment that he would hear from him again, and left his address on the lawyer's table; but if Laird found it, he never acknowledged it. The thing in him that Harvey Merrick had loved must have gone under ground with Harvey Merrick's coffin; for it never spoke again, and Jim got the cold he died of driving across the Colorado mountains to defend one of Phelps's sons who had got into trouble out there by cutting government timber. (72)

William Faulkner

(1897–1962)

FAULKNER, poet, novelist, and short story writer, was perhaps the most distinguished American author of the first half of the twentieth century; even if wrong the proposition is defensible. He won the Nobel Prize for Literature (1949), the National Book Gold Medal Award (1950), and the Pulitzer Prize (1954). Representative successes include The Sound and the Fury *(1929),* As I Lay Dying *(1930),* Light in August *(1932),* Go Down Moses and Other Stories *(1942).*

■ *Barn Burning*

THE STORE in which the Justice of the Peace's court was sitting smelled of cheese. The boy, crouched on his nail keg at the back of the crowded room, knew he smelled cheese, and more: from where he sat he could see the ranked shelves close-packed with the solid, squat, dynamic shapes of tin cans whose labels his stomach read, not from the lettering which meant nothing to his mind but from the scarlet devils and the silver curve of fish— this, the cheese which he knew he smelled and the hermetic meat which his intestines believed he smelled coming in intermittent gusts momentary and brief between the other constant one, the smell and sense just a little of fear because mostly of despair and grief, the old fierce pull of blood. He could not see the table where the Justice sat and before which his father and his father's enemy (*our enemy* he thought in that despair; *ourn! mine and hisn both! He's my father!*) stood, but he could hear them, the two of them that is, because his father had said no word yet:　　　　　　　　　　　　　(1)

"But what proof have you, Mr. Harris?"　　　　　　　　　　　　(2)

"I told you. The hog got into my corn. I caught it up and sent it back to him. He had no fence that would hold it. I told him so, warned him. The next time I put the hog in my pen. When he came to get it I gave him enough wire to patch up his pen. The next time I put the hog up and kept it. I rode down to his house and saw the wire I gave him still rolled on to the spool in his yard. I told him he could have the hog when he paid me a dollar pound fee. That evening a nigger came with the dollar and got the hog. He was a strange nigger. He said, 'He say to tell you wood and hay kin burn.' I said, 'What?' 'That whut he say to tell you,' the nigger said. 'Wood and hay kin burn.' That night my barn burned. I got the stock out but I lost the barn." (3)

"Where is the nigger? Have you got him?" (4)

"He was a strange nigger, I tell you. I don't know what became of him." (5)

"But that's not proof. Don't you see that's not proof?" (6)

"Get that boy up here. He knows." For a moment the boy thought too that the man meant his older brother until Harris said, "Not him. The little one. The boy," and, crouching, small for his age, small and wiry like his father, in patched and faded jeans even too small for him, with straight, uncombed, brown hair and eyes gray and wild as storm scud, he saw the men between himself and the table part and become a lane of grim faces, at the end of which he saw the Justice, a shabby, collarless, graying man in spectacles, beckoning him. He felt no floor under his bare feet; he seemed to walk beneath the palpable weight of the grim turning faces. His father, stiff in his black Sunday coat donned not for the trial but for the moving, did not even look at him. *He aims for me to lie,* he thought, again with that frantic grief and despair. *And I will have to do hit.* (7)

"What's your name, boy?" the Justice said. (8)

"Colonel Sartoris Snopes," the boy whispered. (9)

"Hey?" the Justice said. "Talk louder. Colonel Sartoris? I reckon anybody named for Colonel Sartoris in this country can't help but tell the truth, can they?" The boy said nothing. *Enemy! Enemy!* he thought; for a moment he could not even see, could not see that the Justice's face was kindly nor discern that his voice was troubled when he spoke to the man named Harris: "Do you want me to question this boy?" But he could hear, and during those subsequent long seconds while there was absolutely no sound in the crowded little room save that of quiet and intent breathing it was as if he had swung outward at the end of a grape vine, over a ravine, and at the top of the swing had been caught in a prolonged instant of mesmerized gravity, weightless in time. (10)

"No!" Harris said violently, explosively. "Damnation! Send him out of here!" Now time, the fluid world, rushed beneath him again, the voices coming to him again through the smell of cheese and sealed meat, the fear and despair and the old grief of blood: (11)

"This case is closed. I can't find against you, Snopes, but I can give you advice. Leave this country and don't come back to it."   (12)

His father spoke for the first time, his voice cold and harsh, level, without emphasis: "I aim to. I don't figure to stay in a country among people who . . ." he said something unprintable and vile, addressed to no one. (13)

"That'll do," the Justice said. "Take your wagon and get out of this country before dark. Case dismissed."   (14)

His father turned, and he followed the stiff black coat, the wiry figure walking a little stiffly from where a Confederate provost's man's musket ball had taken him in the heel on a stolen horse thirty years ago, followed the two backs now, since his older brother had appeared from somewhere in the crowd, no taller than the father but thicker, chewing tobacco steadily, between the two lines of grim-faced men and out of the store and across the worn gallery and down the sagging steps and among the dogs and half-grown boys in the mild May dust, where as he passed a voice hissed: (15)

"Barn burner!"   (16)

Again he could not see, whirling; there was a face in a red haze, moon-like, bigger than the full moon, the owner of it half again his size, he leaping in the red haze toward the face, feeling no blow, feeling no shock when his head struck the earth, scrabbling up and leaping again, feeling no blow this time either and tasting no blood, scrabbling up to see the other boy in full flight and himself already leaping into pursuit as his father's hand jerked him back, the harsh, cold voice speaking above him: "Go get in the wagon."

(17)

It stood in a grove of locusts and mulberries across the road. His two hulking sisters in their Sunday dresses and his mother and her sister in calico and sunbonnets were already in it, sitting on and among the sorry residue of the dozen and more movings which even the boy could remember—the battered stove, the broken beds and chairs, the clock inlaid with mother-of-pearl, which would not run, stopped at some fourteen minutes past two o'clock of a dead and forgotten day and time, which had been his mother's dowry. She was crying, though when she saw him she drew her sleeve across her face and began to descend from the wagon. "Get back," the father said.   (18)

"He's hurt. I got to get some water and wash his . . ."   (19)

"Get back in the wagon," his father said. He got in too, over the tail-gate. His father mounted to the seat where the older brother already sat and struck the gaunt mules two savage blows with the peeled willow, but without heat. It was not even sadistic; it was exactly that same quality which in later years would cause his descendants to over-run the engine before putting a motor car into motion, striking and reining back in the same movement. The wagon went on, the store with its quiet crowd of grimly watching men dropped behind; a curve in the road hid it. *Forever* he thought.

Maybe he's done satisfied now, now that he has . . . stopping himself, not to say it aloud even to himself. His mother's hand touched his shoulder. (20)

"Does hit hurt?" she said. (21)

"Naw," he said. "Hit don't hurt. Lemme be." (22)

"Can't you wipe some of the blood off before hit dries?" (23)

"I'll wash to-night," he said. "Lemme be, I tell you." (24)

The wagon went on. He did not know where they were going. None of them ever did or ever asked, because it was always somewhere, always a house of sorts waiting for them a day or two days or even three days away. Likely his father had already arranged to make a crop on another farm before he . . . Again he had to stop himself. He (the father) always did. There was something about his wolflike independence and even courage when the advantage was at least neutral which impressed strangers, as if they got from his latent ravening ferocity not so much a sense of dependability as a feeling that his ferocious conviction in the rightness of his own actions would be of advantage to all whose interest lay with his. (25)

That night they camped in a grove of oaks and beeches where a spring ran. The nights were still cool and they had a fire against it, of a rail lifted from a nearby fence and cut into lengths—a small fire, neat, niggard almost, a shrewd fire; such fires were his father's habit and custom always, even in freezing weather. Older, the boy might have remarked this and wondered why not a big one; why should not a man who had not only seen the waste and extravagance of war, but who had in his blood an inherent voracious prodigality with material not his own, have burned everything in sight? Then he might have gone a step farther and thought that that was the reason: that niggard blaze was the living fruit of nights passed during those four years in the woods hiding from all men, blue or gray, with his strings of horses (captured horses, he called them). And older still, he might have divined the true reason: that the element of fire spoke to some deep mainspring of his father's being, as the element of steel or of powder spoke to other men, as the one weapon for the preservation of integrity, else breath were not worth the breathing, and hence to be regarded with respect and used with discretion. (26)

But he did not think this now and he had seen those same niggard blazes all his life. He merely ate his supper beside it and was already half asleep over his iron plate when his father called him, and once more he followed the stiff back, the stiff and ruthless limp, up the slope and on to the starlit road where, turning, he could see his father against the stars but without face or depth—a shape black, flat, and bloodless as though cut from tin in the iron folds of the frockcoat which had not been made for him, the voice harsh like tin and without heat like tin: (27)

"You were fixing to tell them. You would have told him." He didn't answer. His father struck him with the flat of his hand on the side of the head, hard but without heat, exactly as he had struck the two mules at the store, exactly as he would strike either of them with any stick in order to kill a horse fly, his voice still without heat or anger: "You're getting to be a man. You got to learn. You got to learn to stick to your own blood or you ain't going to have any blood to stick to you. Do you think either of them, any man there this morning, would? Don't you know all they wanted was a chance to get at me because they knew I had them beat? Eh?" Later, twenty years later, he was to tell himself, "If I had said they wanted only truth, justice, he would have hit me again." But now he said nothing. He was not crying. He just stood there. "Answer me," his father said.   (28)

"Yes," he whispered. His father turned.   (29)

"Get on to bed. We'll be there to-morrow."   (30)

To-morrow they were there. In the early afternoon the wagon stopped before a paintless two-room house identical almost with the dozen others it had stopped before even in the boy's ten years, and again, as on the other dozen occasions, his mother and aunt got down and began to unload the wagon, although his two sisters and his father and brother had not moved.   (31)

"Likely hit ain't fitten for hawgs," one of the sisters said.   (32)

"Nevertheless, fit it will and you'll hog it and like it," his father said. "Get out of them chairs and help your Ma unload."   (33)

The two sisters got down, big, bovine, in a flutter of cheap ribbons; one of them drew from the jumbled wagon bed a battered lantern, the other a worn broom. His father handed the reins to the older son and began to climb stiffly over the wheel. "When they get unloaded, take the team to the barn and feed them." Then he said, and at first the boy thought he was still speaking to his brother: "Come with me."   (34)

"Me?" he said.   (35)

"Yes," his father said. "You."   (36)

"Abner," his mother said. His father paused and looked back—the harsh level stare beneath the shaggy, graying, irascible brows.   (37)

"I reckon I'll have a word with the man that aims to begin to-morrow owning me body and soul for the next eight months."   (38)

They went back up the road. A week ago—or before last night, that is—he would have asked where they were going, but not now. His father had struck him before last night but never before had he paused afterward to explain why; it was as if the blow and the following calm, outrageous voice still rang, repercussed, divulging nothing to him save the terrible handicap of being young, the light weight of his few years, just heavy enough to prevent his soaring free of the world as it seemed to be ordered but not heavy enough to keep him footed solid in it, to resist it and try to change the course of its events.   (39)

Presently he could see the grove of oaks and cedars and the other flowering trees and shrubs where the house would be, though not the house yet. They walked beside a fence massed with honeysuckle and Cherokee roses and came to a gate swinging open between two brick pillars, and now, beyond a sweep of drive, he saw the house for the first time and at that instant he forgot his father and the terror and despair both, and even when he remembered his father again (who had not stopped) the terror and despair did not return. Because, for all the twelve movings, they had sojourned until now in a poor country, a land of small farms and fields and houses, and he had never seen a house like this before. *Hit's big as a courthouse* he thought quietly, with a surge of peace and joy whose reason he could not have thought into words, being too young for that: *They are safe from him. People whose lives are a part of this peace and dignity are beyond his touch, be no more to them than a buzzing wasp: capable of stinging for a little moment but that's all; the spell of this peace and dignity rendering even the barns and stable and cribs which belong to it impervious to the puny flames he might contrive . . .* this, the peace and joy, ebbing for an instant as he looked again at the stiff black back, the stiff and implacable limp of the figure which was not dwarfed by the house, for the reason that it had never looked big anywhere and which now, against the serene columned backdrop, had more than ever that impervious quality of something cut ruthlessly from tin, depthless, as though, sidewise to the sun, it would cast no shadow. Watching him, the boy remarked the absolutely undeviating course which his father held and saw the stiff foot come squarely down in a pile of fresh droppings where a horse had stood in the drive and which his father could have avoided by a simple change of stride. But it ebbed only for a moment, though he could not have thought this into words either, walking on in the spell of the house, which he could even want but without envy, without sorrow, certainly never with that ravening and jealous rage which unknown to him walked in the ironlike black coat before him. *Maybe he will feel it too. Maybe it will even change him now from what maybe he couldn't help but be.*   (40)

They crossed the portico. Now he could hear his father's stiff foot as it came down on the boards with clocklike finality, a sound out of all proportion to the displacement of the body it bore and which was not dwarfed either by the white door before it, as though it had attained to a sort of vicious and ravening minimum not to be dwarfed by anything—the flat, wide, black hat, the formal coat of broadcloth which had once been black but which had now the friction-glazed greenish cast of the bodies of old house flies, the lifted sleeve which was too large, the lifted hand like a curled claw. The door opened so promptly that the boy knew the Negro must have been watching them all the time, an old man with neat grizzled hair, in a linen jacket, who stood barring the door with his body, saying, "Wipe yo foots, white man, fo you come in here. Major ain't home nohow." (41)

"Get out of my way, nigger," his father said, without heat too, flinging the door back and the Negro also and entering, his hat still on his head. And now the boy saw the prints of the stiff foot on the doorjamb and saw them appear on the pale rug behind the machinelike deliberation of the foot which seemed to bear (or transmit) twice the weight which the body compassed. The Negro was shouting "Miss Lula! Miss Lula!" somewhere behind them, then the boy, deluged as though by a warm wave by a suave turn of carpeted stair and a pendant glitter of chandeliers and a mute gleam of gold frames, heard the swift feet and saw her too, a lady—perhaps he had never seen her like before either—in a gray, smooth gown with lace at the throat and an apron tied at the waist and the sleeves turned back, wiping cake or biscuit dough from her hands with a towel as she came up the hall, looking not at his father at all but at the tracks on the blond rug with an expression of incredulous amazement. (42)

"I tried," the Negro cried. "I tole him to . . ." (43)

"Will you please go away?" she said in a shaking voice. "Major de Spain is not at home. Will you please go away?" (44)

His father had not spoken again. He did not speak again. He did not even look at her. He just stood stiff in the center of the rug, in his hat, the shaggy iron-gray brows twitching slightly above the pebble-colored eyes as he appeared to examine the house with brief deliberation. Then with the same deliberation he turned; the boy watched him pivot on the good leg and saw the stiff foot drag round the arc of the turning, leaving a final long and fading smear. His father never looked at it, he never once looked down at the rug. The Negro held the door. It closed behind them, upon the hysteric and indistinguishable woman-wail. His father stopped at the top of the steps and scraped his boot clean on the edge of it. At the gate he stopped again. He stood for a moment, planted stiffly on the stiff foot, looking back at the house. 'Pretty and white, ain't it?" he said. "That's sweat. Nigger sweat. Maybe it ain't white enough yet to suit him. Maybe he wants to mix some white sweat with it." (45)

Two hours later the boy was chopping wood behind the house within which his mother and aunt and the two sisters (the mother and aunt, not the two girls, he knew that; even at this distance and muffled by walls the flat loud voices of the two girls emanated an incorrigible idle inertia) were setting up the stove to prepare a meal, when he heard the hooves and saw the linen-clad man on a fine sorrel mare, whom he recognized even before he saw the rolled rug in front of the Negro youth following on a fat bay carriage horse—a suffused, angry face vanishing, still at full gallop, beyond the corner of the house where his father and brother were sitting in the two tilted chairs; and a moment later, almost before he could have put the axe down, he heard the hooves again and watched the sorrel mare go back out of the yard, already galloping again. Then his father began to shout one of the sisters' names, who presently emerged backward from the kitchen door dragging the rolled rug along the ground by one end while the other sister walked behind it. (46)

"If you ain't going to tote, go on and set up the wash pot," the first said. (47)

"You, Sarty!" the second shouted, "Set up the wash pot!" His father appeared at the door, framed against that shabbiness, as he had been against that other bland perfection, impervious to either, the mother's anxious face at his shoulder. (48)

"Go on," the father said. "Pick it up." The two sisters stooped, broad, lethargic; stooping, they presented an incredible expanse of pale cloth and a flutter of tawdry ribbons. (49)

"If I thought enough of a rug to have to git hit all the way from France I wouldn't keep hit where folks coming in would have to tromp on hit," the first said. They raised the rug. (50)

"Abner," the mother said. "Let me do it." (51)

"You go back and git dinner," his father said. "I'll tend to this." (52)

From the woodpile through the rest of the afternoon the boy watched them, the rug spread flat in the dust beside the bubbling wash-pot, the two sisters stooping over it with that profound and lethargic reluctance, while the father stood over them in turn, implacable and grim, driving them though never raising his voice again. He could smell the harsh homemade lye they were using; he saw his mother come to the door once and look toward them with an expression not anxious now but very like despair; he saw his father turn, and he fell to with the axe and saw from the corner of his eye his father raise from the ground a flattish fragment of field stone and examine it and return to the pot, and this time his mother actually spoke: 'Abner. Abner. Please don't. Please, Abner." (53)

Then he was done too. It was dusk; the whippoorwills had already begun. He could smell coffee from the room where they would presently eat the cold food remaining from the mid-afternoon meal, though when he entered the house he realized they were having coffee again probably because there was a fire on the hearth, before which the rug now lay spread over the backs of the two chairs. The tracks of his father's foot were gone. Where they had been were now long, water-cloudy scoriations resembling the sporadic course of a lilliputian moving machine. (54)

It still hung there while they ate the cold food and then went to bed, scattered without order or claim up and down the two rooms, his mother in one bed, where his father would later lie, the older brother in the other, himself, the aunt, and the two sisters on pallets on the floor. But his father was not in bed yet. The last thing the boy remembered was the depthless, harsh silhouette of the hat and coat bending over the rug and it seemed to him that he had not even closed his eyes when the silhouette was standing over him, the fire almost dead behind it, the stiff foot prodding him awake. "Catch up the mule," his father said.   (55)

When he returned with the mule his father was standing in the black door, the rolled rug over his shoulder. "Ain't you going to ride?" he said.
(56)

"No. Give me your foot."   (57)

He bent his knee into his father's hand, the wiry, surprising power flowed smoothly, rising, he rising with it, on to the mule's bare back (they had owned a saddle once; the boy could remember it though not when or where) and with the same effortlessness his father swung the rug up in front of him. Now in the starlight they retraced the afternoon's path, up the dusty road rife with honeysuckle, through the gate and up the black tunnel of the drive to the lightless house, where he sat on the mule and felt the rough warp of the rug drag across his thighs and vanish.   (58)

"Don't you want me to help?" he whispered. His father did not answer and now he heard again that stiff foot striking the hollow portico with that wooden and clocklike deliberation, that outrageous overstatement of the weight it carried. The rug, hunched, not flung (the boy could tell that even in the darkness) from his father's shoulder struck the angle of wall and floor with a sound unbelievably loud, thunderous, then the foot again, unhurried and enormous; a light came on in the house and the boy sat, tense, breathing steadily and quietly and just a little fast, though the foot itself did not increase its beat at all, descending the steps now; now the boy could see him.   (59)

"Don't you want to ride now?" he whispered. "We kin both ride now," the light within the house altering now, flaring up and sinking. *He's coming down the stairs now,* he thought. He had already ridden the mule up beside the horse block; presently his father was up behind him and he doubled the reins over and slashed the mule across the neck, but before the animal could begin to trot the hard, thin arm came round him, the hard, knotted hand jerking the mule back to a walk.   (60)

In the first red rays of the sun they were in the lot, putting plow gear on the mules. This time the sorrel mare was in the lot before he heard it at all, the rider collarless and even bareheaded, trembling, speaking in a shaking voice as the woman in the house had done, his father merely looking up once before stooping again to the hame he was buckling, so that the man on the mare spoke to his stooping back: (61)

"You must realize you have ruined that rug. Wasn't there anybody here, any of your women . . ." he ceased, shaking, the boy watching him, the older brother leaning now in the stable door, chewing, blinking slowly and steadily at nothing apparently. "It cost a hundred dollars. But you never had a hundred dollars. You never will. So I'm going to charge you twenty bushels of corn against your crop. I'll add it in your contract and when you come to the commissary you can sign it. That won't keep Mrs. de Spain quiet but maybe it will teach you to wipe your feet off before you enter her house again." (62)

Then he was gone. The boy looked at his father, who still had not spoken or even looked up again, who was now adjusting the logger-head in the hame. (63)

"Pap," he said. His father looked at him—the inscrutable face, the shaggy brows beneath which the gray eyes glinted coldly. Suddenly the boy went toward him, fast, stopping as suddenly. "You done the best you could!" he cried. "If he wanted hit done different why didn't he wait and tell you how? He won't git no twenty bushels! He won't git none! We'll gether hit and hide hit! I kin watch . . ." (64)

"Did you put the cutter back in the straight stock like I told you?" (65)

"No sir," he said. (66)

"Then go do it." (67)

That was Wednesday. During the rest of that week he worked steadily, at what was within his scope and some which was beyond it, with an industry that did not need to be driven nor even commanded twice; he had this from his mother, with the difference that some at least of what he did he liked to do, such as splitting wood with the half-size axe which his mother and aunt had earned, or saved money somehow, to present him with at Christmas. In company with the two older women (and on one afternoon, even one of the sisters), he built pens for the shoat and the cow which were a part of his father's contract with the landlord, and one afternoon, his father being absent, gone somewhere on one of the mules, he went to the field. (68)

They were running a middle buster now, his brother holding the plow straight while he handled the reins, and walking beside the straining mule, the rich black soil shearing cool and damp against his bare ankles, he thought *Maybe this is the end of it. Maybe even that twenty bushels that seems hard to have to pay for just a rug will be a cheap price for him to stop forever and always from being what he used to be;* thinking, dreaming now, so that his brother had to speak sharply to him to mind the mule: *Maybe he even won't collect the twenty bushels. Maybe it will all add up and balance and vanish—corn, rug, fire; the terror and grief, the being pulled two ways like between two teams of horses—gone, done with for ever and ever.* (69)

Then it was Saturday; he looked up from beneath the mule he was harnessing and saw his father in the black coat and hat. "Not that," his father said. "The wagon gear." And then, two hours later, sitting in the wagon bed behind his father and brother on the seat, the wagon accomplished a final curve, and he saw the weathered paintless store with its tattered tobacco and patent-medicine posters and the tethered wagons and saddle animals below the gallery. He mounted the gnawed steps behind his father and brother, and there again was the lane of quiet, watching faces for the three of them to walk through. He saw the man in spectacles sitting at the plank table and he did not need to be told this was a Justice of the Peace; he sent one glare of fierce, exultant, partisan defiance at the man in collar and cravat now, whom he had seen but twice before in his life, and that on a galloping horse, who now wore on his face an expression not of rage but of amazed unbelief which the boy could not have known was at the incredible circumstance of being sued by one of his own tenants, and came and stood against his father and cried at the Justice: "He ain't done it! He ain't burnt . . ." (70)

"Go back to the wagon," his father said. (71)

"Burnt?" the Justice said. "Do I understand this rug was burned too?" (72)

"Does anybody here claim it was?" his father said. "Go back to the wagon." But he did not, he merely retreated to the rear of the room, crowded as that other had been, but not to sit down this time, instead, to stand pressing among the motionless bodies, listening to the voices: (73)

"And you claim twenty bushels of corn is too high for the damage you did to the rug?" (74)

"He brought the rug to me and said he wanted the tracks washed out of it. I washed the tracks out and took the rug back to him." (75)

"But you didn't carry the rug back to him in the same condition it was in before you made the tracks on it." (76)

His father did not answer, and now for perhaps half a minute there was no sound at all save that of breathing, the faint, steady suspiration of complete and intent listening. (77)

"You decline to answer that, Mr. Snopes?" Again his father did not answer. "I'm going to find against you, Mr. Snopes. I'm going to find that you were responsible for the injury to Major de Spain's rug and hold you liable for it. But twenty bushels of corn seems a little high for a man in your circumstances to have to pay. Major de Spain claims it cost a hundred dollars. October corn will be worth about fifty cents. I figure that if Major de Spain can stand a ninety-five dollar loss on something he paid cash for, you can stand a five-dollar loss you haven't earned yet. I hold you in damages to Major de Spain to the amount of ten bushels of corn over and above your contract with him, to be paid to him out of your crop at gathering time. Court adjourned." (78)

It had taken no time hardly, the morning was but half begun. He thought they would return home and perhaps back to the field, since they

were late, far behind all other farmers. But instead his father passed on behind the wagon, merely indicating with his hand for the older brother to
follow with it, and he crossed the road toward the blacksmith shop opposite, pressing on after his father, overtaking him, speaking, whispering up at
the harsh, calm face beneath the weathered hat: "He won't git no ten
bushels neither. He won't git one. We'll . . ." until his father glanced for an
instant down at him, the face absolutely calm, the grizzled eyebrows
tangled above the cold eyes, the voice almost pleasant, almost gentle: (79)

"You think so? Well, we'll wait till October anyway." (80)

The matter of the wagon—the setting of a spoke or two and the tighten-
ing of the tires—did not take long either, the business of the tires accomplished by driving the wagon into the spring branch behind the shop and
letting it stand there, the mules nuzzling into the water from time to time,
and the boy on the seat with the idle reins, looking up the slope and through
the sooty tunnel of the shed where the slow hammer rang and where his
father sat on an upended cypress bolt, easily, either talking or listening, still
sitting there when the boy brought the dripping wagon up out of the branch
and halted it before the door. (81)

"Take them on to the shade and hitch," his father said. He did so and returned. His father and the smith and a third man squatting on his heels
inside the door were talking, about crops and animals; the boy, squatting
too in the ammoniac dust and hoof-parings and scales of rust, heard his
father tell a long and unhurried story out of the time before the birth of the
older brother even when he had been a professional horsetrader. And then
his father came up beside him where he stood before a tattered last year's
circus poster on the other side of the store, gazing rapt and quiet at the
scarlet horses, the incredible poisings and convolutions of tulle and tights
and the painted leers of comedians, and said, "It's time to eat." (82)

But not at home. Squatting beside his brother against the front wall, he
watched his father emerge from the store and produce from a paper sack a
segment of cheese and divide it carefully and deliberately into three with
his pocket knife and produce crackers from the same sack. They all three
squatted on the gallery and ate, slowly, without talking; then in the store
again, they drank from a tin dipper tepid water smelling of the cedar
bucket and of living beech trees. And still they did not go home. It was a
horse lot this time, a tall rail fence upon and along which men stood and sat
and out of which one by one horses were led, to be walked and trotted and
then cantered back and forth along the road while the slow swapping and
buying went on and the sun began to slant westward, they—the three of
them—watching and listening, the older brother with his muddy eyes and
his steady, inevitable tobacco, the father commenting now and then on certain of the animals, to no one in particular. (83)

It was after sundown when they reached home. They ate supper by lamplight, then, sitting on the doorstep, the boy watched the night fully accomplished, listening to the whippoorwills and the frogs, when he heard his mother's voice: "Abner! No! No! Oh, God. Oh, God. Abner!" and he rose, whirled, and saw the altered light through the door where a candle stub now burned in a bottle neck on the table and his father, still in the hat and coat, at once formal and burlesque as though dressed carefully for some shabby and ceremonial violence, emptying the reservoir of the lamp back into the five-gallon kerosene can from which it had been filled, while the mother tugged at his arm until he shifted the lamp to the other hand and flung her back, not savagely or viciously, just hard, into the wall, her hands flung out against the wall for balance, her mouth open and in her face the same quality of hopeless despair as had been in her voice. Then his father saw him standing in the door.   (84)

"Go to the barn and get that can of oil we were oiling the wagon with," he said. The boy did not move. Then he could speak.   (85)

"What . . ." he cried. "What are you . . ."   (86)

"Go get that oil," his father said. "Go."   (87)

Then he was moving, running, outside the house, toward the stable: this the old habit, the old blood which he had not been permitted to choose for himself, which had been bequeathed him willy nilly and which had run for so long (and who knew where, battening on what of outrage and savagery and lust) before it came to him. *I could keep on,* he thought. *I could run on and on and never look back, never need to see his face again. Only I can't. I can't,* the rusted can in his hand now, the liquid sploshing in it as he ran back to the house and into it, into the sound of his mother's weeping in the next room, and handed the can to his father.   (88)

"Ain't you going to even send a nigger?" he cried. "At least you sent a nigger before!"   (89)

This time his father didn't strike him. The hand came even faster than the blow had, the same hand which had set the can on the table with almost excruciating care flashing from the can toward him too quick for him to follow it, gripping him by the back of his shirt and on to tiptoe before he had seen it quit the can, the face stooping at him in breathless and frozen ferocity, the cold, dead voice speaking over him to the older brother who leaned against the table, chewing with that steady, curious, sidewise motion of cows: (90)

"Empty the can into the big one and go on. I'll ketch up with you." (91)

"Better tie him up to the bedpost," the brother said.   (92)

"Do like I told you," the father said. Then the boy was moving, his bunched shirt and the hard, bony hand between his shoulder-blades, his toes just touching the floor, across the room and into the other one, past the sisters sitting with **spread heavy** thighs in the two chairs over the cold

hearth, and to where his mother and aunt sat side by side on the bed, the
aunt's arms about his mother's shoulders.   (93)

"Hold him," the father said. The aunt made a startled movement. "Not
you," the father said. "Lennie. Take hold of him. I want to see you do it."
His mother took him by the wrist. "You'll hold him better than that. If he
gets loose don't you know what he is going to do? He will go up yonder."
He jerked his head toward the road. "Maybe I'd better tie him."   (94)

"I'll hold him," his mother whispered.   (95)

"See you do then." Then his father was gone, the stiff foot heavy and
measured upon the boards, ceasing at last.   (96)

Then he began to struggle. His mother caught him in both arms, he
jerking and wrenching at them. He would be stronger in the end, he knew
that. But he had no time to wait for it. "Lemme go!" he cried. "I don't want
to have to hit you!"   (97)

"Let him go!" the aunt said. "If he don't go, before God, I am going up
there myself!"   (98)

"Don't you see I can't?" his mother cried. "Sarty! Sarty! No! No! Help
me, Lizzie!"   (99)

Then he was free. His aunt grasped at him but it was too late. He
whirled, running, his mother stumbled forward on to her knees behind
him, crying to the nearer sister: "Catch him, Net! Catch him!" But that
was too late too, the sister (the sisters were twins, born at the same time, yet
either of them now gave the impression of being, encompassing as much
living meat and volume and weight as any other two of the family) not yet
having begun to rise from the chair, her head, face, alone merely turned,
presenting to him in the flying instant an astonishing expanse of young
female features untroubled by any surprise even, wearing only an expression of bovine interest. Then he was out of the room, out of the house, in
the mild dust of the starlit road and the heavy rifeness of honeysuckle, the
pale ribbon unspooling with terrific slowness under his running feet,
reaching the gate at last and turning in, running, his heart and lungs drumming, on up the drive toward the lighted house, the lighted door. He did
not knock, he burst in, sobbing for breath, incapable for the moment of
speech; he saw the astonished face of the Negro in the linen jacket without
knowing when the Negro had appeared.   (100)

"De Spain!" he cried, panted. "Where's . . ." then he saw the white man
too emerging from a white door down the hall. "Barn!" he cried. "Barn!"
                                                                    (101)

"What?" the white man said. "Barn?"   (102)
"Yes!" the boy cried. "Barn!"   (103)
"Catch him!" the white man shouted.   (104)

But it was too late this time too. The Negro grasped his shirt, but the entire sleeve, rotten with washing, carried away, and he was out that door too and in the drive again, and had actually never ceased to run even while he was screaming into the white man's face.   (105)

Behind him the white man was shouting, "My horse! Fetch my horse!" and he thought for an instant of cutting across the park and climbing the fence into the road, but he did not know the park nor how high the vine-massed fence might be and he dared not risk it. So he ran on down the drive, blood and breath roaring; presently he was in the road again though he could not see it. He could not hear either: the galloping mare was almost upon him before he heard her, and even then he held his course, as if the very urgency of his wild grief and need must in a moment more find him wings, waiting until the ultimate instant to hurl himself aside and into the weed-choked roadside ditch as the horse thundered past and on, for an instant in furious silhouette against the stars, the tranquil early summer night sky which, even before the shape of the horse and rider vanished, stained abruptly and violently upward: a long, swirling roar incredible and soundless, blotting the stars, and he springing up and into the road again, running again, knowing it was too late yet still running even after he heard the shot and, an instant later, two shots, pausing now without knowing he had ceased to run, crying "Pap! Pap!", running again before he knew he had begun to run, stumbling, tripping over something and scrabbling up again without ceasing to run, looking backward over his shoulder at the glare as he got up, running on among the invisible trees, panting, sobbing, "Father! Father!"   (106)

At midnight he was sitting on the crest of a hill. He did not know it was midnight and he did not know how far he had come. But there was no glare behind him now and he sat now, his back toward what he had called home for four days anyhow, his face toward the dark woods which he would enter when breath was strong again, small, shaking steadily in the chill darkness, hugging himself into the remainder of his thin, rotten shirt, the grief and despair now no longer terror and fear but just grief and despair. *Father. My father*, he thought. "He was brave!" he cried suddenly, aloud but not loud, no more than a whisper: "He was! He was in the war! He was in Colonel Sartoris' cav'ry!" not knowing that his father had gone to that war a private in the fine old European sense, wearing no uniform, admitting the authority of and giving fidelity to no man or army or flag, going to war as Malbrouck himself did: for booty—it meant nothing and less than nothing to him if it were enemy booty or his own.   (107)

The slow constellations wheeled on. It would be dawn and then sun-up after a while and he would be hungry. But that would be to-morrow and now he was only cold, and walking would cure that. His breathing was easier now and he decided to get up and go on, and then he found that he had been asleep because he knew it was almost dawn, the night almost over. He could tell that from the whippoorwills. They were everywhere now among the dark trees below him, constant and inflectioned and ceaseless, so that, as the instant for giving over to the day birds drew nearer and nearer, there was no interval at all between them. He got up. He was a little stiff, but walking would cure that too as it would the cold, and soon there would be the sun. He went on down the hill, toward the dark woods within which the liquid silver voices of the birds called unceasing—the rapid and urgent beating of the urgent and quiring heart of the late spring night. He did not look back. (108)

Ernest Hemingway

(1899–1961)

HEMINGWAY vied with William Faulkner for the accolade of most distinguished American novelist of the twentieth century. He received the Pulitzer Prize for fiction in 1953 and the Nobel Prize for Literature in 1954. Hemingway projected an image of the rugged individualist, serving as a war correspondent in Spain, China, and in Western Europe generally. He published his first book in 1923 (stories and poems) and achieved compelling critical visibility soon thereafter: The Sun Also Rises *(1926),* A Farewell to Arms *(1929),* Death in the Afternoon *(1932),* For Whom the Bell Tolls *(1940),* The Old Man and the Sea *(1952). Although Hemingway often undertook romantic and ritualistic themes and subjects, he was known for the clipped spareness of his verbal style.*

■ *After the Storm*

IT WASN'T about anything, something about making punch, and then we started fighting and I slipped and he had me down kneeling on my chest and choking me with both hands like he was trying to kill me and all the time I was trying to get the knife out of my pocket to cut him loose. Everybody was too drunk to pull him off me. He was choking me and hammering my head on the floor and I got the knife out and opened it up; and I cut the muscle right across his arm and he let go of me. He couldn't have held on if he wanted to. Then he rolled and hung onto that arm and started to cry and I said: (1)

"What the hell you want to choke me for?"   (2)

I'd have killed him. I couldn't swallow for a week. He hurt my throat bad.   (3)

Well, I went out of there and there were plenty of them with him and some came out after me and I made a turn and was down by the docks and I met a fellow and he said somebody killed a man up the street. I said "Who killed him?" and he said "I don't know who killed him but he's dead all right," and it was dark and there was water standing in the street and no lights and windows broke and boats all up in the town and trees blown down and everything all blown and I got a skiff and went out and found my boat where I had her inside of Mango Key and she was all right only she was full of water. So I bailed her out and pumped her out and there was a moon but plenty of clouds and still plenty rough and I took it down along; and when it was daylight I was off Eastern Harbor.   (4)

Brother, that was some storm. I was the first boat out and you never saw water like that was. It was just as white as a lye barrel and coming from Eastern Harbor to Sou'west Key you couldn't recognize the shore. There was a big channel blown right out through the middle of the beach. Trees and all blown out and a channel cut through and all the water white as chalk and everything on it; branches and whole trees and dead birds, and all floating. Inside the keys were all the pelicans in the world and all kinds of birds flying. They must have gone inside there when they knew it was coming.   (5)

I lay at Sou'west Key a day and nobody came after me. I was the first boat out and I seen a spar floating and I knew there must be a wreck and I started out to look for her. I found her. She was a three-masted schooner and I could just see the stumps of her spars out of water. She was in too deep water and I didn't get anything off of her. So I went on looking for something else. I had the start on all of them and I knew I ought to get whatever there was. I went on down over the sand-bars from where I left that three-masted schooner and I didn't find anything and I went on a long way. I was way out toward the quicksands and I didn't find anything so I went on. Then when I was in sight of the Rebecca Light I saw all kinds of birds making over something and I headed over for them to see what it was and there was a cloud of birds all right.   (6)

I could see something looked like a spar up out of the water and when I got over close the birds all went up in the air and stayed all around me. The water was clear out there and there was a spar of some kind sticking out

just above the water and when I come up close to it I saw it was all dark
under water like a long shadow and I came right over it and there under
water was a liner; just lying there all under water as big as the whole world.
I drifted over her in the boat. She lay on her side and the stern was deep
down. The port holes were all shut tight and I could see the glass shine in
the water and the whole of her; the biggest boat I ever saw in my life laying
there and I went along the whole length of her and then I went over and
anchored and I had the skiff on the deck forward and I shoved it down into
the water and sculled over with the birds all around me.   (7)

   I had a water glass like we use sponging and my hand shook so I could
hardly hold it. All the port holes were shut that you could see going along
over her but way down below near the bottom something must have been
open because there were pieces of things floating out all the time. You
couldn't tell what they were. Just pieces. That's what the birds were after.
You never saw so many birds. They were all around me; crazy yelling.   (8)

   I could see everything sharp and clear. I could see her rounded over and
she looked a mile long under the water. She was lying on a clear white bank
of sand and the spar was a sort of foremast or some sort of tackle that
slanted out of water the way she was laying on her side. Her bow wasn't
very far under. I could stand on the letters of her name on her bow and my
head was just out of water. But the nearest port hole was twelve feet down.
I could just reach it with the grains pole and I tried to break it with that but
I couldn't. The glass was too stout. So I sculled back to the boat and got a
wrench and lashed it to the end of the grains pole and I couldn't break it.
There I was looking down through the glass at the liner with everything in
her and I was the first one to her and couldn't get into her. She must
have had five million dollars worth in her.   (9)

   It made me shaky to think how much she must have in her. Inside the
port hole that was closest I could see something but I couldn't make it out
through the water glass. I couldn't do any good with the grains pole and I
took off my clothes and stood and took a couple of deep breaths and dove
over off the stern with the wrench in my hand and swam down. I could hold
on for a second to the edge of the port hole and I could see in and there
was a woman inside with her hair floating all out. I could see her floating
plain and I hit the glass twice with the wrench hard and I heard the noise
clink in my ears but it wouldn't break and I had to come up.   (10)

   I hung onto the dinghy and got my breath and then I climbed in and
took a couple of breaths and dove again. I swam down and took hold of
the edge of the port hole with my fingers and held it and hit the glass as
hard as I could with the wrench. I could see the woman floated in the water
through the glass. Her hair was tied once close to her head and it floated all
out in the water. I could see the rings on one of her hands. She was right up
close to the port hole and I hit the glass twice and I didn't even crack it.

When I came up I thought I wouldn't make it to the top before I'd have to
breathe.   (11)

   I went down once more and I cracked the glass, only cracked it, and
when I came up my nose was bleeding and I stood on the bow of the liner
with my bare feet on the letters of her name and my head just out and
rested there and then I swam over to the skiff and pulled up into it and sat
there waiting for my head to stop aching and looking down into the water
glass, but I bled so I had to wash out the water glass. Then I lay back in the
skiff and held my hand under my nose to stop it and I lay there with my
head back looking up and there was a million birds above and all around.
                                                                           (12)

   When I quit bleeding I took another look through the glass and then I
sculled over to the boat to try and find something heavier than the wrench
but I couldn't find a thing; not even a sponge hook. I went back and the
water was clearer all the time and you could see everything that floated out
over that white bank of sand. I looked for sharks but there weren't any. You
could have seen a shark a long way away. The water was so clear and the
sand white. There was a grapple for an anchor on the skiff and I cut it off
and went overboard and down with it. It carried me right down and past
the port hole and I grabbed and couldn't hold anything and went on down
and down, sliding along the curved side of her. I had to let go of the
grapple. I heard it bump once and it seemed like a year before I came up
through to the top of the water. The skiff was floated away with the tide
and I swam over to her with my nose bleeding in the water while I swam
and I was plenty glad there weren't sharks; but I was tired.   (13)

   My head felt cracked open and I lay in the skiff and rested and then I
sculled back. It was getting along in the afternoon. I went down once
more with the wrench and it didn't do any good. That wrench was too light.
It wasn't any good diving unless you had a big hammer or something
heavy enough to do good. Then I lashed the wrench to the grains pole
again and I watched through the water glass and pounded on the glass and
hammered until the wrench came off and I saw it in the glass, clear and
sharp, go sliding down along her and then off and down to the quicksand
and go in. Then I couldn't do a thing. The wrench was gone and I'd lost
the grapple so I sculled back to the boat. I was too tired to get the skiff
aboard and the sun was pretty low. The birds were all pulling out and
leaving her and I headed for Sou'west Key towing the skiff and the birds
going on ahead of me and behind me. I was plenty tired.   (14)

   That night it came on to blow and it blew for a week. You couldn't get
out to her. They come out from town and told me the fellow I'd had to cut
was all right except for his arm and I went back to town and they put me
under five hundred dollar bond. It came out all right because some of them,
friends of mine, swore he was after me with an ax, but by the time we got

back out to her the Greeks had blown her open and cleaned her out. They got the safe out with dynamite. Nobody ever knows how much they got. She carried gold and they got it all. They stripped her clean. I found her and I never got a nickel out of her. (15)

It was a hell of a thing all right. They say she was just outside of Havana harbor when the hurricane hit and she couldn't get in or the owners wouldn't let the captain chance coming in; they say he wanted to try; so she had to go with it and in the dark they were running with it trying to go through the gulf between Rebecca and Tortugas when she struck on the quicksands. Maybe her rudder was carried away. Maybe they weren't even steering. But anyway they couldn't have known they were quicksands and when she struck the captain must have ordered them to open up the ballast tanks so she'd lay solid. But it was quicksand she'd hit and when they opened the tank she went in stern first and then over on her beam ends. There were four hundred and fifty passengers and the crew on board of her and they must all have been aboard of her when I found her. They must have opened the tanks as soon as she struck and the minute she settled on it the quicksands took her down. Then her boilers must have burst and that must have been what made those pieces that came out. It was funny there weren't any sharks though. There wasn't a fish. I could have seen them on that clear white sand. (16)

Plenty of fish now though; jewfish, the biggest kind. The biggest part of her's under the sand now but they live inside of her; the biggest kind of jewfish. Some weigh three to four hundred pounds. Sometime we'll go out and get some. You can see the Rebecca light from where she is. They've got a buoy on her now. She's right at the end of the quicksand right at the edge of the gulf. She only missed going through by about a hundred yards. In the dark in the storm they just missed it; raining the way it was they couldn't have seen the Rebecca. Then they're not used to that sort of thing. The captain of a liner isn't used to scudding that way. They have a course and they tell me they set some sort of a compass and it steers itself. They probably didn't know where they were when they ran with that blow but they come close to making it. Maybe they'd lost the rudder though. Anyway there wasn't another thing for them to hit till they'd get to Mexico once they were in that gulf. Must have been something though when they struck in that rain and wind and he told them to open her tanks. Nobody could have been on deck in that blow and rain. Everybody must have been below. They couldn't have lived on deck. There must have been some scenes inside all right because you know she settled fast. I saw that wrench go into the sand. The captain couldn't have known it was quicksand when she struck unless he knew these waters. He just knew it wasn't rock. He must have seen it all up in the bridge. He must have known what it was about when she settled. I wonder how fast she made it. I wonder if the mate was there with him. Do you think they stayed inside the bridge or do you think they took it outside? They never found any bodies. Not a one. Nobody floating. They float a long way with life belts too. They must have took it inside. Well, the Greeks got it all. Everything. They must have come fast all right. They picked her clean. First there was the birds, then me, then the Greeks, and even the birds got more out of her than I did.   (17)

Ring Lardner

(1885–1933)

LARDNER began his career as a writer on the sports pages of Chicago and gradually attracted attention as a writer of short stories for three indelible qualities: complete mastery of the many varieties of racy American vernacular; concentration on everyday people as characters; an ironic humor which reveals the cruelty and stupidity of the average "anonymous" person. His range was very wide—from the baseball rookie (You Know Me, Al, 1926), to the movie magnate (The Love Nest, and Other Stories, 1926), to the song writers of Tin Pan Alley (June Moon, 1929, with George S. Kaufman).

■ *Haircut*

I GOT ANOTHER barber that comes over from Carterville and helps me out Saturdays, but the rest of the time I can get along all right alone. You can see for yourself that this ain't no New York City and besides that, the most of the boys works all day and don't have no leisure to drop in here and get themselves prettied up.   (1)

    You're a newcomer, ain't you? I thought I hadn't seen you round before. I hope you like it good enough to stay. As I say, we ain't no New York City or Chicago, but we have pretty good times. Not as good, though, since Jim

Kendall got killed. When he was alive, him and Hod Meyers used to keep this town in an uproar. I bet they was more laughin' done here than any town its size in America.   (2)

Jim was comical, and Hod was pretty near a match for him. Since Jim's gone, Hod tries to hold his end up just the same as ever, but it's tough goin' when you ain't got nobody to kind of work with.   (3)

They used to be plenty fun in here Saturdays. This place is jam-packed Saturdays, from four o'clock on. Jim and Hod would show up right after their supper, round six o'clock. Jim would set himself down in that big chair, nearest the blue spittoon. Whoever had been settin' in that chair, why they'd get up when Jim come in and give it to him.   (4)

You'd of thought it was a reserved seat like they have sometimes in a theayter. Hod would generally always stand or walk up and down, or some Saturdays, of course, he'd be settin' in this chair part of the time, gettin' a haircut.   (5)

Well, Jim would set there a w'ile without openin' his mouth only to spit, and then finally he'd say to me, "Whitey,"—my right name, that is, my right first name, is Dick, but everybody round here calls me Whitey—Jim would say, "Whitey, your nose looks like a rosebud tonight. You must of been drinkin' some of your aw de cologne."   (6)

So I'd say, "No, Jim, but you look like you'd been drinkin' somethin' of that kind or somethin' worse."   (7)

Jim would have to laugh at that, but then he'd speak up and say, "No, I ain't had nothin' to drink, but that ain't sayin' I wouldn't like somethin'. I wouldn't even mind if it was wood alcohol."   (8)

Then Hod Meyers would say, "Neither would your wife." That would set everybody to laughin' because Jim and his wife wasn't on very good terms. She'd of divorced him only they wasn't no chance to get alimony and she didn't have no way to take care of herself and the kids. She couldn't never understand Jim. He *was* kind of rough, but a good fella at heart. (9)

Him and Hod had all kinds of sport with Milt Sheppard. I don't suppose you've seen Milt. Well, he's got an Adam's apple that looks more like a mushmelon. So I'd be shavin' Milt and when I'd start to shave down here on his neck, Hod would holler, "Hey, Whitey, wait a minute! Before you cut into it, let's make up a pool and see who can guess closest to the number of seeds."   (10)

And Jim would say, "If Milt hadn't of been so hoggish, he'd of ordered a half a cantaloupe instead of a whole one and it might not of stuck in his throat."   (11)

All the boys would roar at this and Milt himself would force a smile, though the joke was on him. Jim certainly was a card!   (12)

There's his shavin' mug, settin' on the shelf, right next to Charley Vail's. "Charles M. Vail." That's the druggist. He comes in regular for his shave, three times a week. And Jim's is the cup next to Charley's. "James H. Kendall." Jim won't need no shavin' mug no more, but I'll leave it there just the same for old time's sake. Jim certainly was a character!   (13)

Years ago, Jim used to travel for a canned goods concern over in Carterville. They sold canned goods. Jim had the whole northern half of the State and was on the road five days out of every week. He'd drop in here Saturdays and tell his experiences for that week. It was rich.   (14)

I guess he paid more attention to playin' jokes than makin' sales. Finally the concern let him out and he come right home here and told everybody he'd been fired instead of sayin' he'd resigned like most fellas would of.
(15)

It was a Saturday and the shop was full and Jim got up out of that chair and says, "Gentlemen, I got an important announcement to make. I been fired from my job."   (16)

Well, they asked him if he was in earnest and he said he was and nobody could think of nothin' to say till Jim finally broke the ice himself. He says, "I been sellin' canned goods and now I'm canned goods myself." (17)

You see, the concern he'd been workin' for was a factory that made canned goods. Over in Carterville. And now Jim said he was canned himself. He was certainly a card!   (18)

Jim had a great trick that he used to play w'ile he was travelin'. For instance, he'd be ridin' on a train and they'd come to some little town like, well, like, we'll say, like Benton. Jim would look out the train window and read the signs on the stores.   (19)

For instance, they'd be a sign, "Henry Smith, Dry Goods." Well, Jim would write down the name and the name of the town and when he got to wherever he was goin' he'd mail back a postal card to Henry Smith at Benton and not sign no name to it, but he'd write on the card, well, somethin' like "Ask your wife about that book agent that spent the afternoon last week," or "Ask your Missus who kept her from gettin' lonesome the last time you was in Carterville." And he'd sign the card, "A Friend."   (20)

Of course, he never knew what really come of none of these jokes, but he could picture what *probably* happened and that was enough.   (21)

Jim didn't work very steady after he lost his position with the Carterville people. What he did earn, doin' odd jobs round town, why he spent pretty near all of it on gin and his family might of starved if the stores hadn't of carried them along. Jim's wife tried her hand at dressmakin', but they ain't nobody goin' to get rich makin' dresses in this town.   (22)

As I say, she'd of divorced Jim, only she seen that she couldn't support herself and the kids and she was always hopin' that some day Jim would cut out his habits and give her more than two or three dollars a week.   (23)

They was a time when she would go to whoever he was workin' for and ask them to give her his wages, but after she done this once or twice, he beat her to it by borrowin' most of his pay in advance. He told it all round town, how he had outfoxed his Missus. He certainly was a caution!   (24)

But he wasn't satisfied with just outwittin' her. He was sore the way she had acted, tryin' to grab off his pay. And he made up his mind he'd get even. Well, he waited till Evans's Circus was advertised to come to town. Then he told his wife and two kiddies that he was goin' to take them to the circus. The day of the circus, he told them he would get the tickets and meet them outside the entrance to the tent.   (25)

Well, he didn't have no intentions of bein' there or buyin' tickets or nothin'. He got full of gin and laid round Wright's poolroom all day. His wife and the kids waited and waited and of course he didn't show up. His wife didn't have a dime with her, or nowhere else, I guess. So she finally had to tell the kids it was all off and they cried like they wasn't never goin' to stop.   (26)

Well, it seems, w'ile they was cryin', Doc Stair came along and he asked what was the matter, but Mrs. Kendall was stubborn and wouldn't tell him, but the kids told him and he insisted on takin' them and their mother in the show. Jim found this out afterwards and it was one reason why he had it in for Doc Stair.   (27)

Doc Stair come here about a year and a half ago. He's a mighty hand-some young fella and his clothes always look like he has them made to order. He goes to Detroit two or three times a year and w'ile he's there he must have a tailor take his measure and then make him a suit to order. They cost pretty near twice as much, but they fit a whole lot better than if you just bought them in a store.   (28)

For a w'ile everybody was wonderin' why a young doctor like Doc Stair should come to a town like this where we already got old Doc Gamble and Doc Foote that's both been here for years and all the practice in town was always divided between the two of them.   (29)

Then they was a story got round that Doc Stair's gal had throwed him over, a gal up in the Northern Peninsula somewheres, and the reason he come here was to hide himself away and forget it. He said himself that he thought they wasn't nothin' like general practice in a place like ours to fit a man to be a good all round doctor. And that's why he'd came.   (30)

Anyways, it wasn't long before he was makin' enough to live on, though they tell me that he never dunned nobody for what they owed him, and the folks here certainly has got the owin' habit, even in my business. If I had all that was comin' to me for just shaves alone, I could go to Carterville and put up at the Mercer for a week and see a different picture every night. For instance, they's old George Purdy—but I guess I shouldn't ought to be gos-sipin'.   (31)

Well, last year, our coroner died, died of the flu. Ken Beatty, that was his name. He was the coroner. So they had to choose another man to be coroner in his place and they picked Doc Stair. He laughed at first and said he didn't want it, but they made him take it. It ain't no job that anybody would fight for and what a man makes out of it in a year would just about buy seeds for their garden. Doc's the kind, though, that can't say no to nothin' if you keep at him long enough.   (32)

But I was goin' to tell you about a poor boy we got here in town—Paul Dickson. He fell out of a tree when he was about ten years old. Lit on his head and it done somethin' to him and he ain't never been right. No harm in him, but just silly. Jim Kendall used to call him cuckoo; that's a name Jim had for anybody that was off their head, only he called people's head their bean. That was another of his gags, callin' head bean and callin' crazy people cuckoo. Only poor Paul ain't crazy, but just silly.   (33)

You can imagine that Jim used to have all kinds of fun with Paul. He'd send him to the White Front Garage for a left-handed monkey wrench. Of course they ain't no such a thing as a left-handed monkey wrench.   (34)

And once we had a kind of a fair here and they was a baseball game between the fats and the leans and before the game started Jim called Paul over and sent him way down to Schrader's hardware store to get a key for the pitcher's box.   (35)

They wasn't nothin' in the way of gags that Jim couldn't think up, when he put his mind to it.   (36)

Poor Paul was always kind of suspicious of people, maybe on account of how Jim had kept foolin' him. Paul wouldn't have much to do with anybody only his own mother and Doc Stair and a girl here in town named Julie Gregg. That is, she ain't a girl no more, but pretty near thirty or over. (37)

When Doc first come to town, Paul seemed to feel like here was a real friend and he hung around Doc's office most of the w'ile; the only time he wasn't there was when he'd go home to eat or sleep or when he seen Julie Gregg doin' her shoppin'.   (38)

When he looked out Doc's window and seen her, he'd run downstairs and join her and tag along with her to the different stores. The poor boy was crazy about Julie and she always treated him mighty nice and made him feel like he was welcome, though of course it wasn't nothin' but pity on her side.   (39)

Doc done all he could to improve Paul's mind and he told me once that he really thought the boy was gettin' better, that they was times when he was as bright and sensible as anybody else.   (40)

But I was goin' to tell you about Julie Gregg. Old Man Gregg was in the lumber business, but got to drinkin' and lost the most of his money and when he died, he didn't leave nothin' but the house and just enough insurance for the girl to skimp along on.   (41)

Her mother was a kind of a half invalid and didn't hardly ever leave the house. Julie wanted to sell the place and move somewheres else after the old man died, but the mother said she was born here and would die here. It was tough on Julie, as the young people round this town—well, she's too good for them.   (42)

She's been away to school and Chicago and New York and different places and they ain't no subject she can't talk on, where you take the rest of the young folks here and you mention anything to them outside of Gloria Swanson or Tommy Meighan and they think you're delirious. Did you see Gloria in Wages of Virtue? You missed somethin'!   (43)

Well, Doc Stair hadn't been here more than a week when he come in one day to get shaved and I recognized who he was as he had been pointed out to me, so I told him about my old lady. She's been ailin' for a couple of years and either Doc Gamble or Doc Foote, neither one, seemed to be helpin' her. So he said he would come out and see her, but if she was able to get out herself, it would be better to bring her to his office where he could make a completer examination.   (44)

So I took her to his office and w'ile I was waitin' for her in the reception room, in come Julie Gregg. When somebody comes in Doc Stair's office, they's a bell that rings in his inside office so as he can tell they's somebody to see him.   (45)

So he left my old lady inside and come out to the front office and that's the first time him and Julie met and I guess it was what they call love at first sight. But it wasn't fifty-fifty. This young fella was the slickest lookin' fella she'd ever seen in this town and she went wild over him. To him she was just a young lady that wanted to see the doctor.   (46)

She'd came on about the same business I had. Her mother had been doctorin' for years with Doc Gamble and Doc Foote and without no results. So she'd heard they was a new doc in town and decided to give him a try. He promised to call and see her mother that same day.   (47)

I said a minute ago that it was love at first sight on her part. I'm not only judgin' by how she acted afterwards but how she looked at him that first day in his office. I ain't no mind reader, but it was wrote all over her face that she was gone.   (48)

Now Jim Kendall, besides bein' a jokesmith and a pretty good drinker, well, Jim was quite a lady-killer. I guess he run pretty wild durin' the time he was on the road for them Carterville people, and besides that, he'd had a couple little affairs of the heart right here in town. As I say, his wife could of divorced him, only she couldn't.   (49)

But Jim was like the majority of men, and women, too, I guess. He wanted what he couldn't get. He wanted Julie Gregg and worked his head off tryin' to land her. Only he'd of said bean instead of head.   (50)

Well, Jim's habits and his jokes didn't appeal to Julie and of course he was a married man, so he didn't have no more chance than, well, than a rabbit. That's an expression of Jim's himself. When somebody didn't have no

chance to get elected or somethin', Jim would always say they didn't have
no more chance than a rabbit.   (51)

He didn't make no bones about how he felt. Right in here, more than
once, in front of the whole crowd, he said he was stuck on Julie and anybody that could get her for him was welcome to his house and his wife and
kids included. But she wouldn't have nothin' to do with him; wouldn't even
speak to him on the street. He finally seen he wasn't gettin' nowheres with
his usual line so he decided to try the rough stuff. He went right up to her
house one evenin' and when she opened the door he forced his way in and
grabbed her. But she broke loose and before he could stop her, she run in
the next room and locked the door and phoned to Joe Barnes. Joe's the
marshal. Jim could hear who she was phonin' to and he beat it before Joe
got there.   (52)

Joe was an old friend of Julie's pa. Joe went to Jim the next day and told
him what would happen if he ever done it again.   (53)

I don't know how the news of this little affair leaked out. Chances is that
Joe Barnes told his wife and she told somebody else's wife and they told
their husband. Anyways, it did leak out and Hod Meyers had the nerve to
kid Jim about it, right here in this shop. Jim didn't deny nothin' and kind of
laughed it off and said for us all to wait; that lots of people had tried to make
a monkey out of him, but he always got even.   (54)

Meanw'ile everybody in town was wise to Julie's bein' wild mad over
the Doc. I don't suppose she had any idear how her face changed when him
and her was together; of course she couldn't of, or she'd of kept away from
him. And she didn't know that we was all noticin' how many times she
made excuses to go up to his office or pass it on the other side of the
street and look up in his window to see if he was there. I felt sorry for her
and so did most other people.   (55)

Hod Meyers kept rubbin' it into Jim about how the Doc had cut him
out. Jim didn't pay no attention to the kiddin' and you could see he was
plannin' one of his jokes.   (56)

One trick Jim had was the knack of changin' his voice. He could make
you think he was a girl talkin' and he could mimic any man's voice. To show
you how good he was along this line, I'll tell you the joke he played on me
once.   (57)

You know, in most towns of any size, when a man is dead and needs a
shave, why the barber that shaves him soaks him five dollars for the job;
that is, he don't soak *him*, but whoever ordered the shave. I just charge
three dollars because personally I don't mind much shavin' a dead person.
They lay a whole lot stiller than live customers. The only thing is that you
don't feel like talkin' to them and you get kind of lonesome.   (58)

Well, about the coldest day we ever had here, two years ago last winter,
the phone rung at the house w'ile I was home to dinner and I answered the

phone and it was a woman's voice and she said she was Mrs. John Scott and her husband was dead and would I come out and shave him. (59)

Old John had always been a good customer of mine. But they live seven miles out in the country, on the Streeter road. Still I didn't see how I could say no. (60)

So I said I would be there, but would have to come in a jitney and it might cost three or four dollars besides the price of the shave. So she, or the voice, it said that was all right, so I got Frank Abbott to drive me out to the place and when I got there, who should open the door but old John himself! He wasn't no more dead than, well, than a rabbit. (61)

It didn't take no private detective to figure out who had played me this little joke. Nobody could of thought it up but Jim Kendall. He certainly was a card! (62)

I tell you this incident just to show you how he could disguise his voice and make you believe it was somebody else talkin'. I'd of swore it was Mrs. Scott had called me. Anyways, some woman. (63)

Well, Jim waited till he had Doc Stair's voice down pat; then he went after revenge. (64)

He called Julie up on a night when he knew Doc was over in Carterville. She never questioned but what it was Doc's voice. Jim said he must see her that night; he couldn't wait no longer to tell her somethin'. She was all excited and told him to come to the house. But he said he was expectin' an important long distance call and wouldn't she please forget her manners for once and come to his office. He said they couldn't nothin' hurt her and nobody would see her and he just *must* talk to her a little w'ile. Well, poor Julie fell for it. (65)

Doc always keeps a night light in his office, so it looked to Julie like they was somebody there. (66)

Meanw'ile Jim Kendall had went to Wright's poolroom, where they was a whole gang amusin' themselves. The most of them had drank plenty of gin, and they was a rough bunch even when sober. They was always strong for Jim's jokes and when he told them to come with him and see some fun they give up their card games and pool games and followed along. (67)

Doc's office is on the second floor. Right outside his door they's a flight of stairs leadin' to the floor above. Jim and his gang hid in the dark behind these stairs. (68)

Well, Julie come up to Doc's door and rung the bell and they was nothin' doin'. She rung it again and rung it seven or eight times. Then she tried the door and found it locked. Then Jim made some kind of a noise and she heard it and waited a minute, and then she says, "Is that you, Ralph?" Ralph is Doc's first name. (69)

They was no answer and it must of came to her all of a sudden that she'd been bunked. She pretty near fell downstairs and the whole gang after her.

They chased her all the way home, hollerin', "Is that you, Ralph?" and "Oh, Ralphie, dear, is that you?" Jim says he couldn't holler it himself, as he was laughin' too hard.   (70)

Poor Julie! She didn't show up here on Main Street for a long, long time afterward.   (71)

And of course Jim and his gang told everybody in town, everybody but Doc Stair. They was scared to tell him, and he might of never knowed only for Paul Dickson. The poor cuckoo, as Jim called him, he was here in the shop one night when Jim was still gloatin' yet over what he'd done to Julie. And Paul took in as much of it as he could understand and he run to Doc with the story.   (72)

It's a cinch Doc went up in the air and swore he'd make Jim suffer. But it was a kind of a delicate thing, because if it got out that he had beat Jim up, Julie was bound to hear of it and then she'd know that Doc knew and of course knowin' that he knew would make it worse for her than ever. He was goin' to do somethin', but it took a lot of figurin'.   (73)

Well, it was a couple days later when Jim was here in the shop again, and so was the cuckoo. Jim was goin' duck-shootin' the next day and had came in lookin' for Hod Meyers to go with him. I happened to know that Hod had went over to Carterville and wouldn't be home till the end of the week. So Jim said he hated to go alone and he guessed he would call it off. Then poor Paul spoke up and said if Jim would take him he would go along. Jim thought a w'ile and then he said, well, he guessed a half-wit was better than nothin'.   (74)

I suppose he was plottin' to get Paul out in the boat and play some joke on him, like pushin' him in the water. Anyways, he said Paul could go. He asked him had he ever shot a duck and Paul said no, he'd never even had a gun in his hands. So Jim said he could set in the boat and watch him and if he behaved himself, he might lend him his gun for a couple of shots. They made a date to meet in the mornin' and that's the last I seen of Jim alive.
                                                                        (75)

Next mornin', I hadn't been open more than ten minutes when Doc Stair come in. He looked kind of nervous. He asked me had I seen Paul Dickson. I said no, but I knew where he was, out duck-shootin' with Jim Kendall. So Doc says that's what he had heard, and he couldn't understand it because Paul had told him he wouldn't never have no more to do with Jim as long as he lived.   (76)

He said Paul had told him about the joke Jim had played on Julie. He said Paul had asked him what he thought of the joke and the Doc had told him that anybody that would do a thing like that ought not to be let live.
                                                                        (77)

I said it had been a kind of a raw thing, but Jim just couldn't resist no kind of a joke, no matter how raw. I said I thought he was all right at heart, but just bubblin' over with mischief. Doc turned and walked out. (78)

At noon he got a phone call from old John Scott. The lake where Jim and Paul had went shootin' is on John's place. Paul had come runnin' up to the house a few minutes before and said they'd been an accident. Jim had shot a few ducks and then give the gun to Paul and told him to try his luck. Paul hadn't never handled a gun and he was nervous. He was shakin' so hard that he couldn't control the gun. He let fire and Jim sunk back in the boat, dead. (79)

Doc Stair, bein' the coroner, jumped in Frank Abbott's flivver and rushed out to Scott's farm. Paul and old John was down on the shore of the lake. Paul had rowed the boat to shore, but they'd left the body in it, waitin' for Doc to come. (80)

Doc examined the body and said they might as well fetch it back to town. They was no use leavin' it there or callin' a jury, as it was a plain case of accidental shootin'. (81)

Personally I wouldn't never leave a person shoot a gun in the same boat I was in unless I was sure they knew somethin' about guns. Jim was a sucker to leave a new beginner have his gun, let alone a half-wit. It probably served Jim right, what he got. But still we miss him round here. He certainly was a card! (82)

Comb it wet or dry? (83)

Joseph Conrad

(1857–1924)

CONRAD *wrote his stories in "a borrowed tongue" in that he was born in Poland and exiled with his parents for a time in Northern Russia. In fact, he was twenty-one before he had the advantage of continuous contact with the English language. His novels and stories, which deal largely with the sea and outposts of the civilized world, are built upon twenty years' experience as a sailor. The moral dilemmas of individuals and the influence on one of his cultural heritage are recurrent subjects in his stories. Both critical and popular interest persists in such stories as* The "Nigger" of the Narcissus *(1898),* Lord Jim *(1900),* Heart of Darkness *(1902),* Nostromo *(1904), and* Victory *(1915).*

◼ *An Outpost of Progress*

I

THERE WERE TWO white men in charge of the trading station. Kayerts, the chief, was short and fat; Carlier, the assistant, was tall, with a large head and a very broad trunk perched upon a long pair of thin legs. The third man on the staff was a Sierra Leone nigger, who maintained that his name was Henry Price. However, for some reason or other, the natives down the river had given him the name of Makola, and it stuck to him through all his wanderings about the country. He spoke English and French with a warbling accent, wrote a beautiful hand, understood bookkeeping, and cherished in his innermost heart the worship of evil spirits. His wife was a negress from Loanda, very large and very noisy. Three children rolled about in sunshine before the door of his low, shed-like dwelling. Makola, taciturn and impenetrable, despised the two white men. He had charge of a small clay storehouse with a dried-grass roof, and pretended to keep a correct account of beads, cotton cloth, red kerchiefs, brass wire, and other trade goods it contained. Besides the storehouse and Makola's hut, there was only one large building in the cleared ground of the station. It was built neatly of reeds, with a verandah on all the four sides. There were three rooms in it. The one in the middle was the living-room, and had two rough tables and a few stools in it. The other two were the bedrooms for the white men. Each had a bedstead and a mosquito net for all furniture. The plank floor was littered with the belongings of the white men; open half-empty boxes, torn wearing apparel, old boots; all the things dirty, and all the things broken, that accumulate mysteriously round untidy men. There was also another dwelling-place some distance away from the buildings. In it, under a tall cross much out of the perpendicular, slept the man who had seen the beginning of all this; who had planned and had watched the construction of this outpost of progress. He had been, at home, an unsuccessful painter who, weary of pursuing fame on an empty stomach, had gone out there through high protections. He had been the first chief of that station. Makola had watched the energetic artist die of fever in the just finished house with his usual kind of "I told you so" indifference. Then, for a time, he dwelt alone with his family, his account books, and the Evil Spirit that rules the lands under the equator. He got on very well with his god. Perhaps he had propitiated him by a promise of more white men to play with, by and by. At any rate the director of the Great Trading Company, coming up in a steamer that resembled an enormous sardine box with a flat-roofed shed erected on it, found the station in good order, and Makola as usual quietly diligent. The director had the cross put up over the first agent's grave, and appointed Kayerts to the post. Carlier was told off as second in charge. The director was a man ruthless and efficient, who at times, but very imperceptibly, indulged in grim humour. He made a speech to Kayerts and Carlier, pointing out to them the promising aspect of their station. The nearest trading-post was about three hundred miles away. It was an exceptional opportunity for them to distinguish themselves and to earn percentages on the trade. This appointment was a favour done to beginners. Kayerts was moved almost to tears by his director's kindness. He would, he said, by doing his best, try to justify the flattering confidence, &c., &c. Kayerts had been in the Administration of the Telegraphs, and knew how to express himself correctly. Carlier, an ex-non-commissioned officer of cavalry in an army guaranteed from harm by several European Powers, was less impressed. If there were commissions to get, so much the better; and, trailing a sulky glance over the river, the forests, the impenetrable bush that seemed to cut off the station from the rest of the world, he muttered between his teeth, "We shall see, very soon." (1)

Next day, some bales of cotton goods and a few cases of provisions having been thrown on shore, the sardine-box steamer went off, not to return for another six months. On the deck the director touched his cap to the two agents, who stood on the bank waving their hats, and turning to an old servant of the Company on his passage to headquarters, said, "Look at those two imbeciles. They must be mad at home to send me such specimens. I told those fellows to plant a vegetable garden, build new storehouses and fences, and construct a landing-stage. I bet nothing will be done! They won't know how to begin. I always thought the station on this river useless, and they just fit the station!" (2)

"They will form themselves there," said the old stager with a quiet smile. (3)

"At any rate, I am rid of them for six months," retorted the director. (4)

The two men watched the steamer round the bend, then, ascending arm in arm the slope of the bank, returned to the station. They had been in this vast and dark country only a very short time, and as yet always in the midst of other white men, under the eye and guidance of their superiors. And now, dull as they were to the subtle influences of surroundings, they felt themselves very much alone, when suddenly left unassisted to face the wilderness; a wilderness rendered more strange, more incomprehensible by the mysterious glimpses of the vigorous life it contained. They were two perfectly insignificant and incapable individuals, whose existence is only rendered possible through the high organization of civilized crowds. Few men realize that their life, the very essence of their character, their capabilities and their audacities, are only the expression of their belief in the safety of their surroundings. The courage, the composure, the confidence; the emotions and principles; every great and every insignificant thought belongs not to the individual but to the crowd: to the crowd that believes blindly in the irresistible force of its institutions and of its morals, in the power of its police and of its opinion. But the contact with pure unmitigated savagery, with primitive nature and primitive man, brings sudden and profound trouble into the heart. To the sentiment of being alone of one's kind, to the clear perception of the loneliness of one's thoughts, of one's sensations—to the negation of the habitual, which is safe, there is added the affirmation of the unusual, which is dangerous; a suggestion of things vague, uncontrollable, and repulsive, whose discomposing intrusion excites the imagination and tries the civilized nerves of the foolish and the wise alike.   (5)

Kayerts and Carlier walked arm in arm, drawing close to one another as children do in the dark; and they had the same, not altogether unpleasant, sense of danger which one half suspects to be imaginary. They chatted persistently in familiar tones. "Our station is prettily situated," said one. The other assented with enthusiasm, enlarging volubly on the beauties of the situation. Then they passed near the grave. "Poor devil!" said Kayerts. "He died of fever, didn't he?" muttered Carlier, stopping short. "Why," retorted Kayerts, with indignation, "I've been told that the fellow exposed himself recklessly to the sun. The climate here, everybody says, is not at all worse than at home, as long as you keep out of the sun. Do you hear that, Carlier? I am chief here, and my orders are that you should not expose yourself to the sun!" He assumed his superiority jocularly, but his meaning was serious. The idea that he would, perhaps, have to bury Carlier and remain alone, gave him an inward shiver. He felt suddenly that this Carlier was more precious to him here, in the centre of Africa, than a brother could be anywhere else. Carlier, entering into the spirit of the thing, made a military salute and answered in a brisk tone, "Your orders shall be attended to, chief!" Then he burst out laughing, slapped Kayerts on the back and shouted, "We shall let life run easily here! Just sit still and gather in the ivory those savages will bring. This country has its good points, after all!" They both laughed loudly while Carlier thought: "That poor Kayerts; he is so fat and unhealthy. It would be awful if I had to bury him here. He is a man I respect." . . . Before they reached the verandah of their house they called one another "my dear fellow."   (6)

The first day they were very active, pottering about with hammers and nails and red calico, to put up curtains, make their house habitable and pretty; resolved to settle down comfortably to their new life. For them an impossible task. To grapple effectually with even purely material problems requires more serenity of mind and more lofty courage than people generally imagine. No two beings could have been more unfitted for such a struggle. Society, not from any tenderness, but because of its strange needs, had taken care of those two men, forbidding them all independent thought, all initiative, all departure from routine; and forbidding it under pain of death. They could only live on condition of being machines. And now, released from the fostering care of men with pens behind the ears, or of men with gold lace on the sleeves, they were like those lifelong prisoners who, liberated after many years, do not know what use to make of their freedom. They did not know what use to make of their faculties, being both, through want of practice, incapable of independent thought. (7)

At the end of two months Kayerts often would say, "If it was not for my Melie, you wouldn't catch me here." Melie was his daughter. He had thrown up his post in the Administration of the Telegraphs, though he had been for seventeen years perfectly happy there, to earn a dowry for his girl. His wife was dead, and the child was being brought up by his sisters. He regretted the streets, the pavements, the cafés, his friends of many years; all the things he used to see, day after day; all the thoughts suggested by familiar things—the thoughts effortless, monotonous, and soothing of a Government clerk; he regretted all the gossip, the small enmities, the mild venom, and the little jokes of Government offices. "If I had had a decent brother-in-law," Carlier would remark, "a fellow with a heart, I would not be here." He had left the army and had made himself so obnoxious to his family by his laziness and impudence, that an exasperated brother-in-law had made superhuman efforts to procure him an appointment in the Company as a second-class agent. Having not a penny in the world he was compelled to accept this means of livelihood as soon as it became quite clear to him that there was nothing more to squeeze out of his relations. He, like Kayerts, regretted his old life. He regretted the clink of sabre and spurs on a fine afternoon, the barrack-room witticisms, the girls of garrison towns; but, besides, he had also a sense of grievance. He was evidently a much ill-used man. This made him moody, at times. But the two men got on well together in the fellowship of their stupidity and laziness. Together they did nothing, absolutely nothing, and enjoyed the sense of the idleness for which they were paid. And in time they came to feel something resembling affection for one another. (8)

They lived like blind men in a large room, aware only of what came in contact with them (and of that only imperfectly), but unable to see the general aspect of things. The river, the forest, all the great land throbbing with life, were like a great emptiness. Even the brilliant sunshine disclosed nothing intelligible. Things appeared and disappeared before their eyes in an unconnected and aimless kind of way. The river seemed to come from nowhere and flow nowhither. It flowed through a void. Out of that void, at times, came canoes, and men with spears in their hands would suddenly crowd the yard of the station. They were naked, glossy black, ornamented with snowy shells and glistening brass wire, perfect of limb. They made an uncouth babbling noise when they spoke, moved in a stately manner, and sent quick, wild glances out of their startled, never-resting eyes. Those warriors would squat in long rows, four or more deep, before the verandah, while their chiefs bargained for hours with Makola over an elephant tusk. Kayerts sat on his chair and looked down on the proceedings, understanding nothing. He stared at them with his round blue eyes, called out to Carlier, "Here, look! look at that fellow there—and that other one, to the left. Did you ever see such a face? Oh, the funny brute!"   (9)

Carlier, smoking native tobacco in a short wooden pipe, would swagger up twirling his moustaches, and surveying the warriors with haughty indulgence, would say—   (10)

"Fine animals. Brought any bone? Yes? It's not any too soon. Look at the muscles of that fellow—third from the end. I wouldn't care to get a punch on the nose from him. Fine arms, but legs no good below the knee. Couldn't make cavalry men of them." And after glancing down complacently at his own shanks, he always concluded: "Pah! Don't they stink! You, Makola! Take that herd over to the fetish" (the storehouse was in every station called the fetish, perhaps because of the spirit of civilization it contained) "and give them up some of the rubbish you keep there. I'd rather see it full of bone than full of rags."   (11)

Kayerts approved.   (12)

"Yes, yes! Go and finish that palaver over there, Mr. Makola. I will come round when you are ready, to weigh the tusk. We must be careful." Then turning to his companion: "This is the tribe that lives down the river; they are rather aromatic. I remember, they had been once before here. D'ye hear that row? What a fellow has got to put up with in this dog of a country! My head is split."   (13)

Such profitable visits were rare. For days the two pioneers of trade and progress would look on their empty courtyard in the vibrating brilliance of vertical sunshine. Below the high bank, the silent river flowed on glittering and steady. On the sands in the middle of the stream, hippos and alligators sunned themselves side by side. And stretching away in all directions, surrounding the insignificant cleared spot of the trading post, immense forests, hiding fateful complications of fantastic life, lay in the eloquent silence of mute greatness. The two men understood nothing, cared for nothing but for the passage of days that separated them from the steamer's return. Their predecessor had left some torn books. They took up these wrecks of novels, and, as they had never read anything of the kind before, they were surprised and amused. Then during long days there were interminable and silly discussions about plots and personages. In the centre of Africa they made acquaintance of Richelieu and of d'Artagnan, of Hawk's Eye and of

Father Goriot, and of many other people. All these imaginary personages became subjects for gossip as if they had been living friends. They discounted their virtues, suspected their motives, decried their successes; were scandalized at their duplicity or were doubtful about their courage. The accounts of crimes filled them with indignation, while tender or pathetic passages moved them deeply. Carlier cleared his throat and said in a soldierly voice, "What nonsense!" Kayerts, his round eyes suffused with tears, his fat cheeks quivering, rubbed his bald head, and declared, "This is a splendid book. I had no idea there were such clever fellows in the world." They also found some old copies of a home paper. That print discussed what it was pleased to call "Our Colonial Expansion" in high-flown language. It spoke much of the rights and duties of civilization, of the sacredness of the civilizing work, and extolled the merits of those who went about bringing light, and faith and commerce to the dark places of the earth. Carlier and Kayerts read, wondered, and began to think better of themselves. Carlier said one evening, waving his hand about, "In a hundred years, there will be perhaps a town here. Quays, and warehouses, and barracks, and—and—billiard-rooms. Civilization, my boy, and virtue—and all. And then, chaps will read that two good fellows, Kayerts and Carlier, were the first civilized men to live in this very spot!" Kayerts nodded, "Yes, it is a consolation to think of that." They seemed to forget their dead predecessor; but, early one day, Carlier went out and replanted the cross firmly. "It used to make me squint whenever I walked that way," he explained to Kayerts over the morning coffee. "It made me squint, leaning over so much. So I just planted it upright. And solid, I promise you! I suspended myself with both hands to the cross-piece. Not a move. Oh, I did that properly."   (14)

At times Gobila came to see them. Gobila was the chief of the neighboring villages. He was a gray-headed savage, thin and black, with a white cloth round his loins and a mangy panther skin hanging over his back. He came up with long strides of his skeleton legs, swinging a staff as tall as himself, and, entering the common room of the station, would squat on his heels to the left of the door. There he sat, watching Kayerts, and now and then making a speech which the other did not understand. Kayerts, without interrupting his occupation, would from time to time say in a friendly manner: "How goes it, you old image?" and they would smile at one another. The two whites had a liking for that old and incomprehensible creature, and called him Father Gobila. Gobila's manner was paternal, and he seemed really to love all white men. They all appeared to him very young, indistinguishably alike (except for stature), and he knew that they were all brothers, and also immortal. The death of the artist, who was the first white man whom he knew intimately, did not disturb this belief, because he was firmly convinced that the white stranger had pretended to die and got himself buried for some mysterious purpose of his own, into which it was useless to inquire. Perhaps it was his way of going home to his own country? At any rate, these were his brothers, and he transferred his absurd affection to them. They returned it in a way. Carlier slapped him on the back, and recklessly struck off matches for his amusement. Kayerts was always ready to let him have a sniff at the ammonia bottle. In short, they behaved just like that other white creature that had hidden itself in a hole in the ground. Gobila considered them attentively. Perhaps they were the same being with the other—or one of them was. He couldn't decide—clear up that mystery; but he remained always very friendly. In consequence of that friendship the women of Gobila's village walked in single file through the reedy grass, bringing every morning to the station, fowls, and sweet potatoes, and palm wine, and sometimes a goat. The Company never provisions the stations fully, and the agents required those local supplies to live. They had them through the good-will of Gobila, and lived well. Now and then one of them had a bout of fever, and the other nursed him with gentle devotion. They did not think much of it. It left them weaker, and their appearance changed for the worse. Carlier was hollow-eyed and irritable. Kayerts showed a drawn, flabby face above the rotundity of his stomach, which gave him a weird aspect. But being constantly together, they did not notice the change that took place gradually in their appearance, and also in their dispositions.   (15)

Five months passed in that way.   (16)

Then, one morning, as Kayerts and Carlier, lounging in their chairs under the verandah, talked about the approaching visit of the steamer, a knot of armed men came out of the forest and advanced towards the station. They were strangers to that part of the country. They were tall, slight, draped classically from neck to heel in blue fringed cloths, and carried percussion muskets over their bare right shoulders. Makola showed signs of excitement, and ran out of the storehouse (where he spent all his days) to meet these visitors. They came into the courtyard and looked about them with steady, scornful glances. Their leader, a powerful and determined-looking negro with bloodshot eyes, stood in front of the verandah and made a long speech. He gesticulated much, and ceased very suddenly.   (17)

There was something in his intonation, in the sounds of the long sentences he used, that startled the two whites. It was like a reminiscence of something not exactly familiar, and yet resembling the speech of civilized men. It sounded like one of those impossible languages which sometimes we hear in our dreams.   (18)

"What lingo is that?" said the amazed Carlier. "In the first moment I fancied the fellow was going to speak French. Anyway, it is a different kind of gibberish to what we ever heard."   (19)

"Yes," replied Kayerts. "Hey, Makola, what does he say? Where do they come from? Who are they?"   (20)

But Makola, who seemed to be standing on hot bricks, answered hurriedly, "I don't know. They come from very far. Perhaps Mrs. Price will understand. They are perhaps bad men." (21)

The leader, after waiting for a while, said something sharply to Makola, who shook his head. Then the man, after looking round, noticed Makola's hut and walked over there. The next moment Mrs. Makola was heard speaking with great volubility. The other strangers—they were six in all—strolled about with an air of ease, put their heads through the door of the storeroom, congregated round the grave, pointed understandingly at the cross, and generally made themselves at home. (22)

"I don't like those chaps—and, I say, Kayerts, they must be from the coast; they've got firearms," observed the sagacious Carlier. (23)

Kayerts also did not like those chaps. They both, for the first time, became aware that they lived in conditions where the unusual may be dangerous, and that there was no power on earth outside of themselves to stand between them and the unusual. They became uneasy, went in and loaded their revolvers. Kayerts said, "We must order Makola to tell them to go away before dark." (24)

The strangers left in the afternoon, after eating a meal prepared for them by Mrs. Makola. The immense woman was excited, and talked much with the visitors. She rattled away shrilly, pointing here and there at the forests and at the river. Makola sat apart and watched. At times he got up and whispered to his wife. He accompanied the strangers across the ravine at the back of the station-ground, and returned slowly looking very thoughtful. When questioned by the white men he was very strange, seemed not to understand, seemed to have forgotten French—seemed to have forgotten how to speak altogether. Kayerts and Carlier agreed that the nigger had had too much palm wine. (25)

There was some talk about keeping a watch in turn, but in the evening everything seemed so quiet and peaceful that they retired as usual. All night they were disturbed by a lot of drumming in the villages. A deep, rapid roll near by would be followed by another far off—then all ceased. Soon short appeals would rattle out here and there, then all mingle together, increase, become vigorous and sustained, would spread out over the forest, roll through the night, unbroken and ceaseless, near and far, as if the whole land had been one immense drum booming out steadily an appeal to heaven. And through the deep and tremendous noise sudden yells that resembled snatches of songs from a madhouse darted shrill and high in discordant jets of sound which seemed to rush far above the earth and drive all peace from under the stars. (26)

Carlier and Kayerts slept badly. They both thought they had heard shots fired during the night—but they could not agree as to the direction. In the morning Makola was gone somewhere. He returned about noon with one of yesterday's strangers, and eluded all Kayerts' attempts to close with him: had become deaf apparently. Kayerts wondered. Carlier, who had been fishing off the bank, came back and remarked while he showed his catch, "The niggers seem to be in a deuce of a stir; I wonder what's up. I saw about fifteen canoes cross the river during the two hours I was there fishing." Kayerts, worried, said, "Isn't this Makola very queer to-day?" Carlier advised, "Keep all our men together in case of some trouble."   (27)

II

There were ten station men who had been left by the Director. Those fellows, having engaged themselves to the Company for six months (without having any idea of a month in particular and only a very faint notion of time in general), had been serving the cause of progress for upwards of two years. Belonging to a tribe from a very distant part of the land of darkness and sorrow, they did not run away, naturally supposing that as wandering strangers they would be killed by the inhabitants of the country; in which they were right. They lived in straw huts on the slope of a ravine overgrown with reedy grass, just behind the station buildings. They were not happy, regretting the festive incantations, the sorceries, the human sacrifices of their own land; where they also had parents, brothers, sisters, admired chiefs, respected magicians, loved friends, and other ties supposed generally to be human. Besides, the rice rations served out by the Company did not agree with them, being a food unknown to their land, and to which they could not get used. Consequently they were unhealthy and miserable. Had they been of any other tribe they would have made up their minds to die—for nothing is easier to certain savages than suicide—and so have escaped from the puzzling difficulties of existence. But belonging, as they did, to a warlike tribe with filed teeth, they had more grit, and went on stupidly living through disease and sorrow. They did very little work, and had lost their splendid physique. Carlier and Kayerts doctored them assiduously without being able to bring them back into condition again. They were mustered every morning and told off to different tasks—grass-cutting, fence-building, tree-felling, &c., &c., which no power on earth could induce them to execute efficiently. The two whites had practically very little control over them.   (28)

In the afternoon Makola came over to the big house and found Kayerts watching three heavy columns of smoke rising above the forests. "What is that?" asked Kayerts. "Some villages burn," answered Makola, who seemed to have regained his wits. Then he said abruptly: "We have got very little ivory; bad six months' trading. Do you like get a little more ivory?"   (29)

"Yes," said Kayerts, eagerly. He thought of percentages which were low. (30)

"Those men who came yesterday are traders from Loanda who have got more ivory than they can carry home. Shall I buy? I know their camp." (31)

"Certainly," said Kayerts. "What are those traders?" (32)

"Bad fellows," said Makola, indifferently. "They fight with people, and catch women and children. They are bad men, and got guns. There is a great disturbance in the country. Do you want ivory?" (33)

"Yes," said Kayerts. Makola said nothing for a while. Then: "Those workmen of ours are no good at all," he muttered, looking round. "Station in very bad order, sir. Director will growl. Better get a fine lot of ivory, then he say nothing." (34)

"I can't help it; the men won't work," said Kayerts. "When will you get that ivory?" (35)

"Very soon," said Makola. "Perhaps to-night. You leave it to me, and keep indoors, sir. I think you had better give some palm wine to our men to make a dance this evening. Enjoy themselves. Work better to-morrow. There's plenty palm wine—gone a little sour." (36)

Kayerts said "yes," and Makola, with his own hands, carried big calabashes to the door of his hut. They stood there till the evening, and Mrs. Makola looked into every one. The men got them at sunset. When Kayerts and Carlier retired, a big bonfire was flaring before the men's huts. They could hear their shouts and drumming. Some men from Gobila's village had joined the station hands, and the entertainment was a great success. (37)

In the middle of the night, Carlier waking suddenly, heard a man shout loudly; then a shot was fired. Only one. Carlier ran out and met Kayerts on the verandah. They were both startled. As they went across the yard to call Makola, they saw shadows moving in the night. One of them cried, "Don't shoot! It's me, Price." Then Makola appeared close to them. "Go back, go back, please," he urged, "you spoil all." "There are strange men about," said Carlier. "Never mind; I know," said Makola. Then he whispered, "All right. Bring ivory. Say nothing! I know my business." The two white men reluctantly went back to the house, but did not sleep. They heard footsteps, whispers, some groans. It seemed as if a lot of men came in, dumped heavy things on the ground, squabbled a long time, then went away. They lay on their hard beds and thought: "This Makola is invaluable." In the morning Carlier came out, very sleepy, and pulled at the cord of the big bell. The station hands mustered every morning to the sound of the bell. That morning nobody came. Kayerts turned out also, yawning. Across the yard they saw Makola come out of his hut, a tin basin of soapy water in his hand. Makola, a civilized nigger, was very neat in his person. He threw the soapsuds skilfully over a wretched little yellow cur he had, then turning his face to the agent's house, he shouted from the distance, "All the men gone last night!" (38)

They heard him plainly, but in their surprise they both yelled out together: "What!" Then they stared at one another. "We are in a proper fix now," growled Carlier. "It's incredible!" muttered Kayerts. "I will go to the huts and see," said Carlier, striding off. Makola coming up found Kayerts standing alone. (39)

"I can hardly believe it," said Kayerts, tearfully. "We took care of them as if they had been our children." (40)

"They went with the coast people," said Makola after a moment of hesitation. (41)

"What do I care with whom they went—the ungrateful brutes!" exclaimed the other. Then with sudden suspicion, and looking hard at Makola, he added: "What do you know about it?" (42)

Makola moved his shoulders, looking down on the ground. "What do I know? I think only. Will you come and look at the ivory I've got there? It is a fine lot. You never saw such." (43)

He moved towards the store. Kayerts followed him mechanically, thinking about the incredible desertion of the men. On the ground before the door of the fetish lay six splendid tusks. (44)

"What did you give for it?" asked Kayerts, after surveying the lot with satisfaction. (45)

"No regular trade," said Makola. "They brought the ivory and gave it to me. I told them to take what they most wanted in the station. It is a beautiful lot. No station can show such tusks. Those traders wanted carriers badly, and our men were no good here. No trade, no entry in books; all correct." (46)

Kayerts nearly burst with indignation. "Why!" he shouted, "I believe you have sold our men for these tusks!" Makola stood impassive and silent. "I—I—will—I," stuttered Kayerts. "You fiend!" he yelled out. (47)

"I did the best for you and the Company," said Makola, imperturbably. "Why you shout so much? Look at this tusk." (48)

"I dismiss you! I will report you—I won't look at the tusk. I forbid you to touch them. I order you to throw them into the river. You—you!" (49)

"You very red, Mr. Kayerts. If you are so irritable in the sun, you will get fever and die—like the first chief!" pronounced Makola impressively. (50)

They stood still, contemplating one another with intense eyes, as if they had been looking with effort across immense distances. Kayerts shivered. Makola had meant no more than he said, but his words seemed to Kayerts full of ominous menace! He turned sharply and went away to the house. Makola retired into the bosom of his family; and the tusks, left lying before the store, looked very large and valuable in the sunshine. (51)

Carlier came back on the verandah. "They're all gone, hey?" asked Kayerts from the far end of the common room in a muffled voice. "You did not find anybody?" (52)

"Oh, yes," said Carlier, "I found one of Gobila's people lying dead before the huts—shot through the body. We heard that shot last night." (53)

Kayerts came out quickly. He found his companion staring grimly over the yard at the tusks, away by the store. They both sat in silence for a while. Then Kayerts related his conversation with Makola. Carlier said nothing. At the midday meal they ate very little. They hardly exchanged a word that day. A great silence seemed to lie heavily over the station and press on their lips. Makola did not open the store; he spent the day playing with his children. He lay full-length on a mat outside his door, and the youngsters sat on his chest and clambered all over him. It was a touching picture. Mrs. Makola was busy cooking all day as usual. The white men made a somewhat better meal in the evening. Afterwards, Carlier smoking his pipe strolled over to the store; he stood for a long time over the tusks, touched one or two with his foot, even tried to lift the largest one by its small end. He came back to his chief, who had not stirred from the veran- dah, threw himself in the chair and said— (54)

"I can see it! They were pounced upon while they slept heavily after drinking all that palm wine you've allowed Makola to give them. A put-up job! See? The worst is, some of Gobila's people were there, and got carried off too, no doubt. The least drunk woke up, and got shot for his sobriety. This is a funny country. What will you do now?" (55)

"We can't touch it, of course," said Kayerts. (56)

"Of course not," assented Carlier. (57)

"Slavery is an awful thing," stammered out Kayerts in an unsteady voice. (58)

"Frightful—the sufferings," grunted Carlier with conviction. (59)

They believed their words. Everybody shows a respectful deference to certain sounds that he and his fellows can make. But about feelings people really know nothing. We talk with indignation or enthusiasm; we talk about oppression, cruelty, crime, devotion, self-sacrifice, virtue, and we know nothing real beyond the words. Nobody knows what suffering or sacrifice mean—except, perhaps the victims of the mysterious purpose of these illu- sions. (60)

Next morning they saw Makola very busy setting up in the yard the big scales used for weighing ivory. By and by Carlier said: "What's that filthy scoundrel up to?" and lounged out into the yard. Kayerts followed. They stood watching. Makola took no notice. When the balance was swung true, he tried to lift a tusk into the scale. It was too heavy. He looked up help- lessly without a word, and for a minute they stood round that balance as mute and still as three statues. Suddenly Carlier said: "Catch hold of the

other end, Makola—you beast!" and together they swung the tusk up. Kayerts trembled in every limb. He muttered, "I say! O! I say!" and putting his
hand in his pocket found there a dirty bit of paper and the stump of a pencil. He turned his back on the others, as if about to do something tricky,
and noted stealthily the weights which Carlier shouted out to him with
unnecessary loudness. When all was over Makola whispered to himself:
"The sun's very strong here for the tusks." Carlier said to Kayerts in a careless tone: "I say, chief, I might just as well give him a lift with this lot into
the store."   (61)

As they were going back to the house Kayerts observed with a sigh: "It
had to be done." And Carlier said: "It's deplorable, but, the men being
Company's men the ivory is Company's ivory. We must look after it." "I will
report to the Director, of course," said Kayerts. "Of course; let him decide,"
approved Carlier.   (62)

At midday they made a hearty meal. Kayerts sighed from time to time.
Whenever they mentioned Makola's name they always added to it an oppro-
brious epithet. It eased their conscience. Makola gave himself a half-holi-
day, and bathed his children in the river. No one from Gobila's villages
came near the station that day. No one came the next day, and the next, nor
for a whole week. Gobila's people might have been dead and buried for any
sign of life they gave. But they were only mourning for those they had lost
by the witchcraft of white men, who had brought wicked people into their
country. The wicked people were gone, but fear remained. Fear always remains. A man may destroy everything within himself, love and hate and
belief, and even doubt; but as long as he clings to life he cannot destroy
fear: the fear, subtle, indestructible, and terrible, that pervades his being;
that tinges his thoughts; that lurks in his heart; that watches on his lips the
struggle of his last breath. In his fear, the mild old Gobila offered extra
human sacrifices to all the Evil Spirits that had taken possession of his white
friends. His heart was heavy. Some warriors spoke about burning and killing, but the cautious old savage dissuaded them. Who could foresee the
woe those mysterious creatures, if irritated, might bring? They should be
left alone. Perhaps in time they would disappear into the earth as the first
one had disappeared. His people must keep away from them, and hope for
the best.   (63)

Kayerts and Carlier did not disappear, but remained above on this
earth, that, somehow, they fancied had become bigger and very empty. It
was not the absolute and dumb solitude of the post that impressed them so
much as an inarticulate feeling that something from within them was gone,
something that worked for their safety, and had kept the wilderness from
interfering with their hearts. The images of homes; the memory of people
like them, of men that thought and felt as they used to think and feel, receded into distances made indistinct by the glare of unclouded sunshine.

And out of the great silence of the surrounding wilderness, its very hope-lessness and savagery seemed to approach them nearer, to draw them gently, to look upon them, to envelop them with a solicitude irresistible, familiar, and disgusting.   (64)

Days lengthened into weeks, then into months. Gobila's people drummed and yelled to every new moon, as of yore, but kept away from the station. Makola and Carlier tried once in a canoe to open communications, but were received with a shower of arrows, and had to fly back to the station for dear life. That attempt set the country up and down the river into an uproar that could be very distinctly heard for days. The steamer was late. At first they spoke of delay jauntily, then anxiously, then gloomily. The matter was be-coming serious. Stores were running short. Carlier cast his lines off the bank, but the river was low, and the fish kept out in the stream. They dared not stroll far away from the station to shoot. Moreover, there was no game in the impenetrable forest. Once Carlier shot a hippo in the river. They had no boat to secure it, and it sank. When it floated up it drifted away, and Gobila's people secured the carcase. It was the occasion for a national holi-day, but Carlier had a fit of rage over it and talked about the necessity of exterminating all the niggers before the country could be made habitable. Kayerts mooned about silently; spent hours looking at the portrait of his Melie. It represented a little girl with long bleached tresses and a rather sour face. His legs were much swollen, and he could hardly walk. Carlier, undermined by fever, could not swagger any more, but kept tottering about, still with a devil-may-care air, as became a man who remembered his crack regiment. He had become hoarse, sarcastic, and inclined to say unpleasant things. He called it "being frank with you." They had long ago reckoned their percentages on trade, including in them that last deal of "this infamous Makola." They had also concluded not to say anything about it. Kayerts hesitated at first—was afraid of the Director.   (65)

"He has seen worse things done on the quiet," maintained Carlier, with a hoarse laugh. "Trust him! He won't thank you if you blab. He is no better than you or me. Who will talk if we hold our tongues? There is nobody here."   (66)

That was the root of the trouble! There was nobody there; and being left there alone with their weakness, they became daily more like a pair of accomplices than like a couple of devoted friends. They had heard nothing from home for eight months. Every evening they said, "To-morrow we shall see the steamer." But one of the Company's steamers had been wrecked, and the Director was busy with the other, relieving very distant and im-portant stations on the main river. He thought that the useless station, and the useless men, could wait. Meantime Kayerts and Carlier lived on rice boiled without salt, and cursed the Company, all Africa, and the day they were born. One must have lived on such diet to discover what ghastly

trouble the necessity of swallowing one's food may become. There was
literally nothing else in the station but rice and coffee; they drank the coffee
without sugar. The last fifteen lumps Kayerts had solemnly locked away in
his box, together with a half-bottle of Cognâc, "in case of sickness," he explained. Carlier approved. "When one is sick," he said, "any little extra like
that is cheering."   (67)

They waited. Rank grass began to sprout over the courtyard. The bell
never rang now. Days passed, silent, exasperating, and slow. When the two
men spoke, they snarled; and their silences were bitter, as if tinged by the
bitterness of their thoughts.   (68)

One day after a lunch of boiled rice, Carlier put down his cup untasted,
and said: "Hang it all! Let's have a decent cup of coffee for once. Bring out
that sugar, Kayerts!"   (69)

"For the sick," muttered Kayerts, without looking up.   (70)

"For the sick," mocked Carlier. "Bosh! . . . Well! I am sick."   (71)

"You are no more sick than I am, and I go without," said Kayerts in a
peaceful tone.   (72)

"Come! out with that sugar, you stingy old slave-dealer."   (73)

Kayerts looked up quickly. Carlier was smiling with marked insolence.
And suddenly it seemed to Kayerts that he had never seen that man before.
Who was he? He knew nothing about him. What was he capable of? There
was a surprising flash of violent emotion within him, as if in the presence of
something undreamt-of, dangerous, and final. But he managed to pronounce
with composure—   (74)

"That joke is in very bad taste. Don't repeat it."   (75)

"Joke!" said Carlier, hitching himself forward on his seat. "I am hungry
—I am sick—I don't joke! I hate hypocrites. You are a hypocrite. You are a
slave-dealer. I am a slave-dealer. There's nothing but slave-dealers in this
cursed country. I mean to have sugar in my coffee to-day, anyhow!"   (76)

"I forbid you to speak to me in that way," said Kayerts with a fair show
of resolution.   (77)

"You!—What?" shouted Carlier, jumping up.   (78)

Kayerts stood up also. "I am your chief," he began, trying to master the
shakiness of his voice.   (79)

"What?" yelled the other. "Who's chief? There's no chief here. There's
nothing here: there's nothing but you and I. Fetch the sugar—you pot-
bellied ass."   (80)

"Hold your tongue. Go out of this room," screamed Kayerts. "I dismiss
you—you scoundrel!"   (81)

Carlier swung a stool. All at once he looked dangerously in earnest.
"You flabby, good-for-nothing civilian—take that!" he howled.   (82)

Kayerts dropped under the table, and the stool struck the grass inner
wall of the room. Then, as Carlier was trying to upset the table, Kayerts in

desperation made a blind rush, head low, like a cornered pig would do, and over-turning his friend, bolted along the verandah, and into his room. He locked the door, snatched his revolver, and stood panting. In less than a minute Carlier was kicking at the door furiously, howling, "If you don't bring out that sugar, I will shoot you at sight, like a dog. Now then—one—two—three. You won't? I will show you who's the master." (83)

Kayerts thought the door would fall in, and scrambled through the square hole that served for a window in his room. There was then the whole breadth of the house between them. But the other was apparently not strong enough to break in the door, and Kayerts heard him running round. Then he also begin to run laboriously on his swollen legs. He ran as quickly as he could, grasping the revolver, and unable yet to understand what was happening to him. He saw in succession Makola's house, the store, the river, the ravine, and the low bushes; and he saw all those things again as he ran for the second time round the house. Then again they flashed past him. That morning he could not have walked a yard without a groan. (84)

And now he ran. He ran fast enough to keep out of sight of the other man. (85)

Then as, weak and desperate, he thought, "Before I finish the next round I shall die," he heard the other man stumble heavily, then stop. He stopped also. He had the back and Carlier the front of the house, as before. He heard him drop into a chair cursing, and suddenly his own legs gave way, and he slid down into a sitting posture with his back to the wall. His mouth was as dry as a cinder, and his face was wet with perspiration—and tears. What was it all about? He thought it must be a horrible illusion; he thought he was dreaming; he thought he was going mad! After a while he collected his senses. What did they quarrel about? That sugar! How absurd! He would give it to him—didn't want it himself. And he began scrambling to his feet with a sudden feeling of security. But before he had fairly stood upright, a commonsense reflection occurred to him and drove him back into despair. He thought: "If I give way now to that brute of a soldier, he will begin this horror again to-morrow—and the day after—every day—raise other pretensions, trample on me, torture me, make me his slave—and I will be lost! Lost! The steamer may not come for days—may never come." He shook so that he had to sit down on the floor again. He shivered forlornly. He felt he could not, would not move any more. He was completely distracted by the sudden perception that the position was without issue—that death and life had in a moment become equally difficult and terrible. (86)

All at once he heard the other push his chair back; and he leaped to his feet with extreme facility. He listened and got confused. Must run again! Right or left? He heard footsteps. He darted to the left, grasping his revolver, and at the very same instant, as it seemed to him, they came into violent collision. Both shouted with surprise. A loud explosion took place between them; a roar of red fire, thick smoke; and Kayerts, deafened and blinded, rushed back thinking: "I am hit—it's all over." He expected the other to come round—to gloat over his agony. He caught hold of an upright of the roof—"All over!" Then he heard a crashing fall on the other side of the house, as if somebody had tumbled headlong over a chair—then silence. Nothing more happened. He did not die. Only his shoulder felt as if it had been badly wrenched, and he had lost his revolver. He was disarmed and helpless! He waited for his fate. The other man made no sound. It was a stratagem. He was stalking him now! Along what side? Perhaps he was taking aim this very minute.   (87)

After a few moments of an agony frightful and absurd, he decided to go and meet his doom. He was prepared for every surrender. He turned the corner, steadying himself with one hand on the wall; made a few paces, and nearly swooned. He had seen on the floor, protruding past the other corner, a pair of turned-up feet. A pair of white naked feet in red slippers. He felt deadly sick, and stood for a time in profound darkness. Then Makola appeared before him, saying quietly: "Come along, Mr. Kayerts. He is dead." He burst into tears of gratitude; a loud, sobbing fit of crying. After a time he found himself sitting in a chair and looking at Carlier, who lay stretched on his back. Makola was kneeling over the body.   (88)

"Is this your revolver?" asked Makola, getting up.   (89)

"Yes," said Kayerts; then he added very quickly, "He ran after me to shoot me—you saw!"   (90)

"Yes, I saw," said Makola. "There is only one revolver; where's his?" (91)

"Don't know," whispered Kayerts in a voice that had become suddenly very faint.   (92)

"I will go and look for it," said the other, gently. He made the round along the verandah, while Kayerts sat still and looked at the corpse. Makola came back empty-handed, stood in deep thought, then stepped quietly into the dead man's room, and came out directly with a revolver, which he held up before Kayerts. Kayerts shut his eyes. Everything was going round. He found life more terrible and difficult than death. He had shot an unarmed man.   (93)

After meditating for a while, Makola said softly, pointing at the dead man who lay there with his right eye blown out—   (94)

"He died of fever." Kayerts looked at him with a stony stare. "Yes," repeated Makola, thoughtfully, stepping over the corpse, "I think he died of fever. Bury him to-morrow."   (95)

And he went away slowly to his expectant wife, leaving the two white men alone on the verandah.   (96)

Night came, and Kayerts sat unmoving on his chair. He sat quiet as if he had taken a dose of opium. The violence of the emotions he had passed through produced a feeling of exhausted serenity. He had plumbed in one short afternoon the depths of horror and despair, and now found repose in the conviction that life had no more secrets for him: neither had death! He sat by the corpse thinking; thinking very actively, thinking very new thoughts. He seemed to have broken loose from himself altogether. His old thoughts, convictions, likes and dislikes, things he respected and things he abhorred, appeared in their true light at last! Appeared contemptible and childish, false and ridiculous. He revelled in his new wisdom while he sat by the man he had killed. He argued with himself about all things under heaven with that kind of wrong-headed lucidity which may be observed in some lunatics. Incidentally he reflected that the fellow dead there had been a noxious beast anyway; that men died every day in thousands; perhaps in hundreds of thousands—who could tell?—and that in the number, that one death could not possibly make any difference; couldn't have any importance, at least to a thinking creature. He, Kayerts, was a thinking creature. He had been all his life, till that moment, a believer in a lot of nonsense like the rest of mankind—who are fools; but now he thought! He knew! He was at peace; he was familiar with the highest wisdom! Then he tried to imagine himself dead, and Carlier sitting in his chair watching him; and his attempt met with such unexpected success, that in a very few moments he became not at all sure who was dead and who was alive. This extraordinary achievement of his fancy startled him, however, and by a clever and timely effort of mind he saved himself just in time from becoming Carlier. His heart thumped, and he felt hot all over at the thought of that danger. Carlier! What a beastly thing! To compose his now disturbed nerves—and no wonder!—he tried to whistle a little. Then, suddenly, he fell asleep, or thought he had slept; but at any rate there was a fog, and somebody had whistled in the fog.   (97)

He stood up. The day had come, and a heavy mist had descended upon the land: the mist penetrating, enveloping, and silent; the morning mist of tropical lands; the mist that clings and kills; the mist white and deadly, immaculate and poisonous. He stood up, saw the body, and threw his arms above his head with a cry like that of a man who, waking from a trance, finds himself immured forever in a tomb. "Help! . . . My God!"   (98)

A shriek inhuman, vibrating and sudden, pierced like a sharp dart the white shroud of that land of sorrow. Three short, impatient screeches followed, and then, for a time, the fog-wreaths rolled on, undisturbed, through a formidable silence. Then many more shrieks, rapid and piercing, like the yells of some exasperated and ruthless creature, rent the air. Progress was calling to Kayerts from the river. Progress and civilization and all the virtues. Society was calling to its accomplished child to come, to be taken care of, to be instructed, to be judged, to be condemned; it called him to return to that rubbish heap from which he had wandered away, so that justice could be done.   (99)

Kayerts heard and understood. He stumbled out of the verandah, leaving the other man quite alone for the first time since they had been thrown there together. He groped his way through the fog, calling in his ignorance upon the invisible heaven to undo its work. Makola flitted by in the mist, shouting as he ran—   (100)

"Steamer! Steamer! They can't see. They whistle for the station. I go ring the bell. Go down to the landing, sir. I ring."   (101)

He disappeared. Kayerts stood still. He looked upwards; the fog rolled low over his head. He looked round like a man who has lost his way; and he saw a dark smudge, a cross-shaped stain, upon the shifting purity of the mist. As he began to stumble towards it, the station bell rang in a tumultuous peal its answer to the impatient clamour of the steamer.   (102)

The Managing Director of the Great Civilizing Company (since we know that civilization follows trade) landed first, and incontinently lost sight of the steamer. The fog down by the river was exceedingly dense; above, at the station, the bell rang unceasing and brazen.   (103)

The Director shouted loudly to the steamer: (104)

"There is nobody down to meet us; there may be something wrong, though they are ringing. You had better come, too!"   (105)

And he began to toil up the steep bank. The captain and the engine-driver of the boat followed behind. As they scrambled up the fog thinned, and they could see their Director a good way ahead. Suddenly they saw him start forward, calling to them over his shoulder:—"Run! Run to the house! I've found one of them. Run, look for the other!"   (106)

He had found one of them! And even he, the man of varied and startling experience, was somewhat discomposed by the manner of this finding. He stood and fumbled in his pockets (for a knife) while he faced Kayerts, who was hanging by a leather strap from the cross. He had evidently climbed the grave, which was high and narrow, and after tying the end of the strap to the arm, had swung himself off. His toes were only a couple of inches above the ground; his arms hung stiffly down; he seemed to be standing rigidly at attention, but with one purple cheek playfully posed on the shoulder. And, irreverently, he was putting out a swollen tongue at his Managing Director.   (107)

James Baldwin

(1924–   )

BALDWIN *was born and spent his childhood in the Harlem which he de-*
picts. His talent has been widely recognized and sponsored—by the Gug-
genheim Foundation (1954), the Partisan Review *(1956), the National In-*
stitute for Arts and Letters (1956), the Ford Foundation (1959). Active
in the Civil Rights movement, he is a member of the National Advisory
Board of CORE; and he is a member of the National Committee for a Sane
Nuclear Policy. He has published one play, Blues for Mr. Charlie *(1964),*
*several volumes of essays—*Notes of a Native Son *(1955),* Nobody Knows
My Name *(1960),* The Fire Next Time *(1963)—and several volumes of*
*fiction—*Go Tell It on the Mountain *(1953),* Giovanni's Room *(1958),* Another Country *(1962), and others.*

▣ *Sonny's Blues*

I READ ABOUT it in the paper, in the subway, on my way to work. I read it, and I couldn't believe it, and I read it again. Then perhaps I just stared at it, at the newsprint spelling out his name, spelling out the story. I stared at it in the swinging lights of the subway car, and in the faces and bodies of the people, and in my own face, trapped in the darkness which roared out-side.   (1)

It was not to be believed and I kept telling myself that, as I walked from the subway station to the high school. And at the same time I couldn't doubt it. I was scared, scared for Sonny. He became real to me again. A great block of ice got settled in my belly and kept melting there slowly all day long, while I taught my classes algebra. It was a special kind of ice. It kept melting, sending trickles of ice water all up and down my veins, but it never got less. Sometimes it hardened and seemed to expand until I felt my guts were going to come spilling out or that I was going to choke or scream. This would always be at a moment when I was remembering some specific thing Sonny had once said or done.   (2)

When he was about as old as the boys in my classes his face had been bright and open, there was a lot of copper in it; and he'd had wonderfully direct brown eyes, and great gentleness and privacy. I wondered what he looked like now. He had been picked up, the evening before, in a raid on an apartment downtown, for peddling and using heroin.   (3)

I couldn't believe it: but what I mean by that is that I couldn't find any room for it anywhere inside me. I had kept it outside me for a long time. I hadn't wanted to know. I had had suspicions, but I didn't name them, I kept putting them away. I told myself that Sonny was wild, but he wasn't crazy. And he'd always been a good boy, he hadn't ever turned hard or evil or disrespectful, the way kids can, so quick, so quick, especially in Harlem. I didn't want to believe that I'd ever see my brother going down, coming to nothing, all that light in his face gone out, in the condition I'd already seen so many others. Yet it had happened and here I was, talking about algebra to a lot of boys who might, every one of them for all I knew, be popping off needles every time they went to the head. Maybe it did more for them than algebra could.   (4)

I was sure that the first time Sonny had ever had horse, he couldn't have been much older than these boys were now. These boys, now, were living as we'd been living then, they were growing up with a rush and their heads bumped abruptly against the low ceiling of their actual possibilities. They were filled with rage. All they really knew were two darknesses, the darkness of their lives, which was now closing in on them, and the darkness of the movies, which had blinded them to that other darkness, and in which they now, vindictively, dreamed, at once more together than they were at any other time, and more alone.   (5)

When the last bell rang, the last class ended, I let out my breath. It seemed I'd been holding it for all that time. My clothes were wet—I may have looked as though I'd been sitting in a steam bath, all dressed up, all afternoon. I sat alone in the classroom a long time. I listened to the boys outside, downstairs, shouting and cursing and laughing. Their laughter struck me for perhaps the first time. It was not the joyous laughter which— God knows why—one associates with children. It was mocking and insular, its intent was to denigrate. It was disenchanted, and in this, also, lay the authority of their curses. Perhaps I was listening to them because I was thinking about my brother and in them I heard my brother. And myself.   (6)

One boy was whistling a tune, at once very complicated and very simple, it seemed to be pouring out of him as though he were a bird, and it sounded very cool and moving through all that harsh, bright air, only just holding its own through all those other sounds.   (7)

I stood up and walked over to the window and looked down into the courtyard. It was the beginning of the spring and the sap was rising in the boys. A teacher passed through them every now and again, quickly, as though he or she couldn't wait to get out of that courtyard, to get those boys out of their sight and off their minds. I started collecting my stuff. I thought I'd better get home and talk to Isabel.   (8)

The courtyard was almost deserted by the time I got downstairs. I saw this boy standing in the shadow of a doorway, looking just like Sonny. I almost called his name. Then I saw that it wasn't Sonny, but somebody we used to know, a boy from around our block. He'd been Sonny's friend. He'd never been mine, having been too young for me, and, anyway, I'd never liked him. And now, even though he was a grown-up man, he still hung around that block, still spent hours on the street corners, was always high and raggy. I used to run into him from time to time and he'd often work around to asking me for a quarter or fifty cents. He always had some real good excuse, too, and I always gave it to him, I don't know why.   (9)

But now, abruptly, I hated him. I couldn't stand the way he looked at me, partly like a dog, partly like a cunning child. I wanted to ask him what the hell he was doing in the school courtyard.   (10)

He sort of shuffled over to me, and he said, "I see you got the papers. So you already know about it."   (11)

"You mean about Sonny? Yes, I already know about it. How come they didn't get you?"   (12)

He grinned. It made him repulsive and it also brought to mind what he'd looked like as a kid. "I wasn't there. I stay away from them people."
                                                                        (13)

"Good for you." I offered him a cigarette and I watched him through the smoke. "You come all the way down here just to tell me about Sonny?" (14)

"That's right." He was sort of shaking his head and his eyes looked strange, as though they were about to cross. The bright sun deadened his damp dark brown skin and it made his eyes look yellow and showed up the dirt in his kinked hair. He smelled funky. I moved a little away from him and I said, "Well, thanks. But I already know about it and I got to get home."   (15)

"I'll walk you a little ways," he said. We started walking. There were a couple of kids still loitering in the courtyard and one of them said good-night to me and looked strangely at the boy beside me.   (16)

"What're you going to do?" he asked me. "I mean, about Sonny?"   (17)

"Look. I haven't seen Sonny for over a year, I'm not sure Im going to do anything. Anyway, what the hell *can* I do?"   (18)

"That's right," he said quickly, "ain't nothing you can do. Can't much help old Sonny no more, I guess." (19)

It was what I was thinking and so it seemed to me he had no right to say it. (20)

"I'm surprised at Sonny, though," he went on—he had a funny way of talking, he looked straight ahead as though he were talking to himself—"I thought Sonny was a smart boy, I thought he was too smart to get hung." (21)

"I guess he thought so too," I said sharply, "and that's how he got hung. And now about you? You're pretty goddamn smart, I bet." (22)

Then he looked directly at me, just for a minute. "I ain't smart," he said. "If I was smart, I'd have reached for a pistol a long time ago.' (23)

"Look. Don't tell *me* your sad story, if it was up to me, I'd give you one." Then I felt guilty—guilty, probably, for never having supposed that the poor bastard *had* a story of his own, much less a sad one, and I asked, quickly, "What's going to happen to him now?" (24)

He didn't answer this. He was off by himself some place. "Funny thing," he said, and from his tone we might have been discussing the quickest way to get to Brooklyn, "when I saw the papers this morning, the first thing I asked myself was if I had anything to do with it. I felt sort of responsible." (25)

I began to listen more carefully. The subway station was on the corner, just before us, and I stopped. He stopped, too. We were in front of a bar and he ducked slightly, peering in, but whoever he was looking for didn't seem to be there. The juke box was blasting away with something black and bouncy and I half watched the barmaid as she danced her way from the juke box to her place behind the bar. And I watched her face as she laughingly responded to something someone said to her, still keeping time to the music. When she smiled one saw the little girl, one sensed the doomed, still-struggling woman beneath the battered face of the semi-whore. (26)

"I never *give* Sonny nothing," the boy said finally, "but a long time ago I come to school high and Sonny asked me how it felt." He paused, I couldn't bear to watch him, I watched the barmaid, and I listened to the music which seemed to be causing the pavement to shake. "I told him it felt great." The music stopped, the barmaid paused and watched the juke box until the music began again. "It did." (27)

All this was carrying me some place I didn't want to go. I certainly didn't want to know how it felt. It filled everything, the people, the houses, the music, the dark, quicksilver barmaid, with menace; and this menace was their reality. (28)

"What's going to happen to him now?" I asked again. (29)

"They'll send him away some place and they'll try to cure him." He shook his head. "Maybe he'll even think he's kicked the habit. Then they'll let him loose"—he gestured, throwing his cigarette into the gutter. "That's all."   (30)

"What do you mean, that's *all*?"   (31)

But I knew what he meant.   (32)

"I *mean*, that's *all*." He turned his head and looked at me, pulling down the corners of his mouth. "Don't you know what I mean?" he asked, softly.
(33)

"How the hell *would* I know what you mean?" I almost whispered it, I don't know why.   (34)

"That's right," he said to the air, "how would *he* know what I mean?" He turned toward me again, patient and calm, and yet I somehow felt him shaking, shaking as though he were going to fall apart. I felt that ice in my guts again, the dread I'd felt all afternoon; and again I watched the bar-maid, moving about the bar, washing glasses, and singing. "Listen. They'll let him out and then it'll just start all over again. That's what I mean." (35)

"You mean—they'll let him out. And then he'll just start working his way back in again. You mean he'll never kick the habit. Is that what you mean?"
(36)

"That's right," he said, cheerfully. "*You* see what I mean."   (37)

"Tell me," I said it last, "why does he want to die? He must want to die, he's killing himself, why does he want to die?"   (38)

He looked at me in surprise. He licked his lips. "He don't want to die. He wants to live. Don't nobody want to die, ever."   (39)

Then I wanted to ask him—too many things. He could not have an-swered, or if he had, I could not have borne the answers. I started walking. "Well, I guess it's none of my business."   (40)

"It's going to be rough on old Sonny," he said. We reached the subway station. "This is your station?" he asked. I nodded. I took one step down. "Damn!" he said, suddenly. I looked up at him. He grinned again. "Damn it if I didn't leave all my money home. You ain't got a dollar on you, have you? Just for a couple of days, is all."   (41)

All at once something inside gave and threatened to come pouring out of me. I didn't hate him any more. I felt that in another moment I'd start crying like a child.   (42)

"Sure," I said. "Don't sweat." I looked in my wallet and didn't have a dollar, I only had a five. "Here," I said. "That hold you?"   (43)

He didn't look at it—he didn't want to look at it. A terrible, closed look came over his face, as though he were keeping the number on the bill a secret from him and me. "Thanks," he said, and now he was dying to see me go. "Don't worry about Sonny. Maybe I'll write him or something." (44)

"Sure," I said. "You do that. So long."   (45)

"Be seeing you," he said. I went on down the steps.   (46)

And I didn't write Sonny or send him anything for a long time. When I
finally did, it was just after my little girl died, he wrote me back a letter
which made me feel like a bastard.   (47)
    Here's what he said: (48)

> Dear brother,
>
>   You don't know how much I needed to hear from you. I
> wanted to write you many a time but I dug how much I must
> have hurt you and so I didn't write. But now I feel like a man
> who's been trying to climb up out of some deep, real deep and
> funky hole and just saw the sun up there, outside. I got to get
> outside.
>
>   I can't tell you much about how I got here. I mean I don't
> know how to tell you. I guess I was afraid of something or I
> was trying to escape from something and you know I have
> never been very strong in the head (smile). I'm glad Mama and
> Daddy are dead and can't see what's happened to their son and
> I swear if I'd known what I was doing I would never have hurt
> you so, you and a lot of other fine people who were nice to me
> and who believed in me.
>
>   I don't want you to think it had anything to do with me being
> a musician. It's more than that. Or maybe less than that. I can't
> get anything straight in my head down here and I try not to
> think about what's going to happen to me when I get outside
> again. Sometime I think I'm going to flip and *never* get outside
> and sometime I think I'll come straight back. I tell you one
> thing, though, I'd rather blow my brains out than go through this
> again. But that's what they all say, so they tell me. If I tell you
> when I'm coming to New York and if you could meet me, I sure
> would appreciate it. Give my love to Isabel and the kids and I
> was sure sorry to hear about little Gracie. I wish I could be like
> Mama and say the Lord's will be done, but I don't know it seems
> to me that trouble is the one thing that never does get stopped
> and I don't know what good it does to blame it on the Lord. But
> maybe it does some good if you believe it.
>
>   Your brother,
>   Sonny

Then I kept in constant touch with him and I sent him whatever I
could and I went to meet him when he came back to New York. When I saw
him many things I thought I had forgotten came flooding back to me. This
was because I had begun, finally, to wonder about Sonny, about the life that
Sonny lived inside. This life, whatever it was, had made him older and
thinner and it had deepened the distant stillness in which he had always
moved. He looked very unlike my baby brother. Yet, when he smiled, when

we shook hands, the baby brother I'd never known looked out from the depths of his private life, like an animal waiting to be coaxed into the light. (49)

"How you been keeping?" he asked me. (50)

"All right. And you?" (51)

"Just fine." He was smiling all over his face. "It's good to see you again." (52)

"It's good to see you." (53)

The seven years' difference in our ages lay between us like a chasm: I wondered if these years would ever operate between us as a bridge. I was remembering, and it made it hard to catch my breath, that I had been there when he was born; and I had heard the first words he had ever spoken. When he started to walk, he walked from our mother straight to me. I caught him just before he fell when he took the first steps he ever took in this world. (54)

"How's Isabel?" (55)

"Just fine. She's dying to see you." (56)

"And the boys?" (57)

"They're fine, too. They're anxious to see their uncle." (58)

"Oh, come on. You know they don't remember me." (59)

"Are you kidding? Of course they remember you." (60)

He grinned again. We got into a taxi. We had a lot to say to each other, far too much to know how to begin. (61)

As the taxi began to move, I asked, "You still want to go to India?" (62)

He laughed. "You still remember that. Hell, no. This place is Indian enough for me." (63)

"It used to belong to them," I said. (64)

And he laughed again. "They damn sure knew what they were doing when they got rid of it." (65)

Years ago, when he was around fourteen, he'd been all hipped on the idea of going to India. He read books about people sitting on rocks, naked, in all kinds of weather, but mostly bad, naturally, and walking barefoot through hot coals and arriving at wisdom. I used to say that it sounded to me as though they were getting away from wisdom as fast as they could. I think he sort of looked down on me for that. (66)

"Do you mind," he asked, "if we have the driver drive alongside the park? On the west side—I haven't seen the city in so long." (67)

"Of course not," I said. I was afraid that I might sound as though I were humoring him, but I hoped he wouldn't take it that way. (68)

So we drove along, between the green of the park and the stony, lifeless elegance of hotels and apartment buildings, toward the vivid, killing streets of our childhood. These streets hadn't changed, though housing projects jutted up out of them now like rocks in the middle of a boiling sea. Most of

the houses in which we had grown up had vanished, as had the stores from
which we had stolen, the basements in which we had first tried sex, the
rooftops from which we had hurled tin cans and bricks. But houses exactly
like the houses of our past yet dominated the landscape, boys exactly like
the boys we once had been found themselves smothering in these houses,
came down into the streets for light and air and found themselves encircled
by disaster. Some escaped the trap, most didn't. Those who got out always
left something of themselves behind, as some animals amputate a leg and
leave it in the trap. It might be said, perhaps, that I had escaped, after all,
I was a school teacher; or that Sonny had, he hadn't lived in Harlem for
years. Yet, as the cab moved uptown through streets which seemed, with a
rush, to darken with dark people, and as I covertly studied Sonny's face, it
came to me that what we both were seeking through our separate cab windows was that part of ourselves which had been left behind. It's always at
the hour of trouble and confrontation that the missing member aches. (69)

We hit 110th Street and started rolling up Lenox Avenue. And I'd known
this avenue all my life, but it seemed to me again, as it had seemed on the
day I'd first heard about Sonny's trouble, filled with a hidden menace which
was its very breath of life.   (70)

"We almost there," said Sonny.   (71)

"Almost." We were both too nervous to say anything more.   (72)

We live in a housing project. It hasn't been up long. A few days after it
was up it seemed uninhabitably new, now, of course, it's already rundown.
It looks like a parody of the good, clean, faceless life—God knows the people
who live in it do their best to make it a parody. The beat-looking grass
lying around isn't enough to make their lives green, the hedges will never
hold out the streets, and they know it. The big windows fool no one, they
aren't big enough to make space out of no space. They don't bother with
the windows, they watch the TV screen instead. The playground is most
popular with the children who don't play at jacks, or skip rope, or roller
skate, or swing, and they can be found in it after dark. We moved in partly
because it's not too far from where I teach, and partly for the kids; but it's
really just like the houses in which Sonny and I grew up. The same things
happen, they'll have the same things to remember. The moment Sonny and
I started into the house I had the feeling that I was simply bringing him
back into the danger he had almost died trying to escape.   (73)

Sonny has never been talkative. So I don't know why I was sure he'd be
dying to talk to me when supper was over the first night. Everything went
fine, the oldest boy remembered him, and the youngest boy liked him, and
Sonny had remembered to bring something for each of them; and Isabel,
who is really much nicer than I am, more open and giving, had gone to a lot
of trouble about dinner and was genuinely glad to see him. And she's always been able to tease Sonny in a way that I haven't. It was nice to see her

face so vivid again and to hear her laugh and watch her make Sonny laugh. She wasn't, or, anyway, she didn't seem to be, at all uneasy or embarrassed. She chatted as though there were no subject which had to be avoided and she got Sonny past his first, faint stiffness. And thank God she was there, for I was filled with that icy dread again. Everything I did seemed awkward to me, and everything I said sounded freighted with hidden meaning. I was trying to remember everything I'd heard about dope addiction and I couldn't help watching Sonny for signs. I wasn't doing it out of malice. I was trying to find out something about my brother. I was dying to hear him tell me he was safe.   (74)

"Safe!" my father grunted, whenever Mama suggested trying to move to a neighborhood which might be safer for children. "Safe, hell! Ain't no place safe for kids, nor nobody."   (75)

He always went on like this, but he wasn't, ever, really as bad as he sounded, not even on weekends, when he got drunk. As a matter of fact, he was always on the lookout for "something a little better," but he died before he found it. He died suddenly, during a drunken weekend in the middle of the war, when Sonny was fifteen. He and Sonny hadn't ever got on too well. And this was partly because Sonny was the apple of his father's eye. It was because he loved Sonny so much and was frightened for him, that he was always fighting with him. It doesn't do any good to fight with Sonny. Sonny just moves back, inside himself, where he can't be reached. But the principal reason that they never hit it off is that they were so much alike. Daddy was big and rough and loud-talking, just the opposite of Sonny, but they both had—that same privacy.   (76)

Mama tried to tell me something about this, just after Daddy died. I was home on leave from the army.   (77)

This was the last time I ever saw my mother alive. Just the same, this picture gets all mixed up in my mind with pictures I had of her when she was younger. The way I always see her is the way she used to be on a Sunday afternoon, say, when the old folks were talking after the big Sunday dinner. I always see her wearing pale blue. She'd be sitting on the sofa. And my father would be sitting in the easy chair, not far from her. And the living room would be full of church folks and relatives. There they sit, in chairs all around the living room, and the night is creeping up outside, but nobody knows it yet. You can see the darkness growing against the window-panes and you hear the street noises every now and again, or maybe the jangling beat of a tambourine from one of the churches close by, but it's real quiet in the room. For a moment nobody's talking, but every face looks darkening, like the sky outside. And my mother rocks a little from the waist, and my father's eyes are closed. Everyone is looking at something a child can't see. For a minute they've forgotten the children. Maybe a kid is lying on the rug, half asleep. Maybe somebody's got a kid in his lap and is absent-mindedly stroking the kid's head. Maybe there's a kid, quiet and big-eyed, curled up in a big chair in the corner. The silence, the darkness coming, and the darkness in the faces frightens the child obscurely. He hopes that the hand which strokes his forehead will never stop—will never die. He hopes that there will never come a time when the old folks won't be sitting around the living room, talking about where they've come from, and what they've seen, and what's happened to them and their kinfolk.   (78)

But something deep and watchful in the child knows that this is bound to end, is already ending. In a moment someone will get up and turn on the light. Then the old folks will remember the children and they won't talk any more that day. And when light fills the room, the child is filled with darkness. He knows that every time this happens he's moved just a little closer to that darkness outside. The darkness outside is what the old folks have been talking about. It's what they've come from. It's what they endure. The child knows that they won't talk any more because if he knows too much about what's happened to *them,* he'll know too much too soon, about what's going to happen to *him.*   (79)

The last time I talked to my mother, I remember I was restless. I wanted to get out and see Isabel. We weren't married then and we had a lot to straighten out between us.   (80)

There Mama sat, in black, by the window. She was humming an old church song, *Lord, you brought me from a long ways off.* Sonny was out somewhere. Mama kept watching the streets.   (81)

"I don't know," she said, "if I'll ever see you again, after you go off from here. But I hope you'll remember the things I tried to teach you."   (82)

"Don't talk like that," I said, and smiled. "You'll be here a long time yet."
(83)

She smiled, too, but she said nothing. She was quiet for a long time. And I said, "Mama, don't you worry about nothing. I'll be writing all the time, and you be getting the checks. . . ."   (84)

"I want to talk to you about your brother," she said, suddenly. "If anything happens to me he ain't going to have nobody to look out for him."
(85)

"Mama," I said, "ain't nothing going to happen to you *or* Sonny. Sonny's all right. He's a good boy and he's got good sense."   (86)

"It ain't a question of his being a good boy," Mama said, "nor of his having good sense. It ain't only the bad ones, nor yet the dumb ones that gets sucked under." She stopped, looking at me. "Your Daddy once had a brother," she said, and she smiled in a way that made me feel she was in pain. "You didn't never know that, did you?"   (87)

"No," I said, "I never knew that," and I watched her face.   (88)

"Oh, yes," she said, "your Daddy had a brother." She looked out of the window again. "I know you never saw your Daddy cry. But *I* did—many a time, through all these years." (89)

I asked her, "What happened to his brother? How come nobody's ever talked about him?" (90)

This was the first time I ever saw my mother look old. (91)

"His brother got killed," she said, "when he was just a little younger than you are now. I knew him. He was a fine boy. He was maybe a little full of the devil, but he didn't mean nobody no harm." (92)

Then she stopped and the room was silent, exactly as it had sometimes been on those Sunday afternoons. Mama kept looking out into the streets. (93)

"He used to have a job in the mill," she said, "and, like all young folks, he just liked to perform on Saturday nights. Saturday nights, him and your father would drift around to different places, go to dances and things like that, or just sit around with people they knew, and your father's brother would sing, he had a fine voice, and play along with himself on his guitar. Well, this particular Saturday night, him and your father was coming home from some place, and they were both a little drunk and there was a moon that night, it was bright like day. Your father's brother was feeling kind of good, and he was whistling to himself, and he had his guitar slung over his shoulder. They was coming down a hill and beneath them was a road that turned off from the highway. Well, your father's brother, being always kind of frisky, decided to run down this hill, and he did, with that guitar banging and clanging behind him, and he ran across the road, and he was making water behind a tree. And your father was sort of amused at him and he was still coming down the hill, kind of slow. Then he heard a car motor and that same minute his brother stepped from behind the tree, into the road, in the moonlight. And he started to cross the road. And your father started to run down the hill, he says he don't know why. This car was full of white men. They was all drunk, and when they seen your father's brother they let out a great whoop and holler and they aimed the car straight at him. They was having fun, they just wanted to scare him, the way they do sometimes, you know. But they was drunk. And I guess the boy, being drunk, too, and scared, kind of lost his head. By the time he jumped it was too late. Your father says he heard his brother scream when the car rolled over him, and he heard the wood of that guitar when it give, and he heard them strings go flying, and he heard them white men shouting, and the car kept on a-going and it ain't stopped till this day. And, time your father got down the hill, his brother weren't nothing but blood and pulp." (94)

Tears were gleaming on my mother's face. There wasn't anything I could say. (95)

"He never mentioned it," she said, "because I never let him mention it before you children. Your Daddy was like a crazy man that night and for many a night thereafter. He says he never in his life seen anything as dark as that road after the lights of that car had gone away. Weren't nothing, weren't nobody on that road, just your Daddy and his brother and that busted guitar. Oh, yes. Your Daddy never did really get right again. Till the day he died he weren't sure but that every white man he saw was the man that killed his brother."   (96)

She stopped and took out her handkerchief and dried her eyes and looked at me.   (97)

"I ain't telling you all this," she said, "to make you scared or bitter or to make you hate nobody. I'm telling you this because you got a brother. And the world ain't changed."   (98)

I guess I didn't want to believe this. I guess she saw this in my face. She turned away from me, toward the window again, searching those streets.
(99)

"But I praise my Redeemer," she said at last, "that He called your Daddy home before me. I ain't saying it to throw no flowers at myself, but, I declare, it keeps me from feeling too cast down to know I helped your father get safely through this world. Your father always acted like he was the roughest, strongest man on earth. And everybody took him to be like that. But if he hadn't had *me* there—to see his tears!"   (100)

She was crying again. Still, I couldn't move. I said, "Lord, Lord, Mama, I didn't know it was like that."   (101)

"Oh, honey," she said, "there's a lot that you don't know. But you are going to find it out." She stood up from the window and came over to me. "You got to hold on to your brother," she said, "and don't let him fall, no matter what it looks like is happening to him and no matter how evil you gets with him. You going to be evil with him many a time. But don't you forget what I told you, you hear?"   (102)

"I won't forget," I said. "Don't you worry, I won't forget. I won't let nothing happen to Sonny."   (103)

My mother smiled as though she were amused at something she saw in my face. Then, "You may not be able to stop nothing from happening. But you got to let him know you's *there*."   (104)

Two days later I was married, and then I was gone. And I had a lot of things on my mind and I pretty well forgot my promise to Mama until I got shipped home on a special furlough for her funeral.   (105)

And, after the funeral, with just Sonny and me alone in the empty kitchen, I tried to find out something about him.   (106)

"What do you want to do?" I asked him.   (107)

"I'm going to be a musician," he said.

For he had graduated, in the time I had been away, from dancing to the juke box to finding out who was playing what, and what they were doing with it, and he had bought himself a set of drums.   (108)

"You mean, you want to be a drummer?" I somehow had the feeling that being a drummer might be all right for other people but not for my brother Sonny.   (109)

"I don't think," he said, looking at me very gravely, "that I'll ever be a good drummer. But I think I can play a piano."   (110)

I frowned. I'd never played the role of the older brother quite so seriously before, had scarcely ever, in fact, *asked* Sonny a damn thing. I sensed myself in the presence of something I didn't really know how to handle, didn't understand. So I made my frown a little deeper as I asked: "What kind of musician do you want to be?"   (111)

He grinned. "How many kinds do you think there are?"   (112)

"Be *serious*," I said.   (113)

He laughed, throwing his head back, and then looked at me. "I *am* serious."   (114)

"Well, then, for Christ's sake, stop kidding around and answer a serious question. I mean, do you want to be a concert pianist, you want to play classical music and all that, or—or what?" Long before I finished he was laughing again. "For Christ's *sake*, Sonny!"   (115)

He sobered, but with difficulty. "I'm sorry. But you sound so—*scared!*" and he was off again.   (116)

"Well, you may think it's funny now, baby, but it's not going to be so funny when you have to make your living at it, let me tell you *that*." I was furious because I knew he was laughing at me and I didn't know why.   (117)

"No," he said, very sober now, and afraid, perhaps, that he'd hurt me, "I don't want to be a classical pianist. That isn't what interests me. I mean"— he paused, looking hard at me, as though his eyes would help me to understand, and then gestured helplessly, as though perhaps his hand would help—"I mean, I'll have a lot of studying to do, and I'll have to study *everything*, but, I mean, I want to play *with*—jazz musicians." He stopped. "I want to play jazz," he said.   (118)

Well, the word had never before sounded as heavy, as real, as it sounded that afternoon in Sonny's mouth. I just looked at him and I was probably frowning a real frown by this time. I simply couldn't see why on earth he'd want to spend his time hanging around nightclubs, clowning around on bandstands, while people pushed each other around a dance floor. It seemed—beneath him, somehow. I had never thought about it before, had never been forced to, but I suppose I had always put jazz musicians in a class with what Daddy called "good-time people."   (119)

"Are you *serious*?"   (120)

"Hell, *yes,* I'm serious."   (121)

He looked more helpless than ever, and annoyed, and deeply hurt. (122)

I suggested, helpfully: "You mean—like Louis Armstrong?"   (123)

His face closed as though I'd struck him. "No. I'm not talking about none of that old-time, down home crap."   (124)

"Well, look, Sonny, I'm sorry, don't get mad. I just don't altogether get it, that's all. Name somebody—you know, a jazz musician you admire." (125)

"Bird."   (126)

"Who?"   (127)

"Bird! Charlie Parker! Don't they teach you nothing in the goddamn army?"   (128)

I lit a cigarette. I was surprised and then a little amused to discover that I was trembling. "I've been out of touch," I said. "You'll have to be patient with me. Now. Who's this Parker character?"   (129)

"He's just one of the greatest jazz musicians alive," said Sonny, sullenly, his hands in his pockets, his back to me. "Maybe *the* greatest," he added, bitterly, "that's probably why *you* never heard of him."   (130)

"All right," I said, "I'm ignorant. I'm sorry. I'll go out and buy all the cat's records right away, all right?"   (131)

"It don't," said Sonny, with dignity, "make any difference to me. I don't care what you listen to. Don't do me no favors."   (132)

I was beginning to realize that I'd never seen him so upset before. With another part of my mind I was thinking that this would probably turn out to be one of those things kids go through and that I shouldn't make it seem important by pushing it too hard. Still, I didn't think it would do any harm to ask: "Doesn't all this take a lot of time? Can you make a living at it?" (133)

He turned back to me and half leaned, half sat, on the kitchen table. "Everything takes time," he said, "and—well, yes, sure, I can make a living at it. But what I don't seem to be able to make you understand is that it's the only thing I want to do."   (134)

"Well, Sonny," I said, gently, "you know people can't always do exactly what they *want* to do—"   (135)

"*No,* I don't know that," said Sonny, surprising me. "I think people *ought* to do what they want to do, what else are they alive for?"   (136)

"You getting to be a big boy," I said desperately, "it's time you started thinking about your future."   (137)

"I'm thinking about my future," said Sonny, grimly. "I think about it all the time."   (138)

I gave up. I decided, if he didn't change his mind, that we could always talk about it later. "In the meantime," I said, "you got to finish school." We had already decided that he'd have to move in with Isabel and her folks. I

knew this wasn't the ideal arrangement because Isabel's folks are inclined
to be dicty and they hadn't especially wanted Isabel to marry me. But I
didn't know what else to do. "And we have to get you fixed up at Isabel's."
(139)

There was a long silence. He moved from the kitchen table to the window. "That's a terrible idea. You know it yourself."   (140)

"Do you have a *better* idea?"   (141)

He just walked up and down the kitchen for a minute. He was as tall as
I was. He had started to shave. I suddenly had the feeling that I didn't
know him at all.   (142)

He stopped at the kitchen table and picked up my cigarettes. Looking at
me with a kind of mocking, amused defiance, he put one between his lips.
"You mind?"   (143)

"You smoking already?"   (144)

He lit the cigarette and nodded, watching me through the smoke. "I just
wanted to see if I'd have the courage to smoke in front of you." He grinned
and blew a great cloud of smoke to the ceiling. "It was easy." He looked at
my face. "Come on, now. I bet you was smoking at my age, tell the truth."
(145)

I didn't say anything but the truth was on my face, and he laughed. But
now there was something very strained in his laugh. "Sure. And I bet that
ain't all you was doing."   (146)

He was frightening me a little. "Cut the crap," I said. "We already decided that you was going to go and live at Isabel's. Now what's got into you
all of a sudden?"   (147)

"*You* decided it," he pointed out. "*I* didn't decide nothing." He stopped
in front of me, leaning against the stove, arms loosely folded. "Look,
brother. I don't want to stay in Harlem no more, I really don't." He was
very earnest. He looked at me, then over toward the kitchen window. There
was something in his eyes I'd never seen before, some thoughtfulness, some
worry all his own. He rubbed the muscle of one arm. "It's time I was getting
out of here."   (148)

"Where do you want to *go*, Sonny?"   (149)

"I want to join the army. Or the navy, I don't care. If I say I'm old
enough, they'll believe me."   (150)

Then I got mad. It was because I was so scared. "You must be crazy.
You goddamn fool, what the hell do you want to go and join the *army* for?"
(151)

"I just told you. To get out of Harlem."   (152)

"Sonny, you haven't even finished *school*. And if you really want to be
a musician, how do you expect to study if you're in the *army*?"   (153)

He looked at me, trapped, and in anguish. "There's ways. I might be

able to work out some kind of deal. Anyway, I'll have the G.I. Bill when I
come out."   (154)

"*If* you come out." We stared at each other. "Sonny, please. Be reasonable. I know the setup is far from perfect. But we got to do the best we can."
(155)

"I ain't learning nothing in school," he said. "Even when I go." He
turned away from me and opened the window and threw his cigarette out
into the narrow alley. I watched his back. "At least, I ain't learning nothing you'd want me to learn." He slammed the window so hard I thought the
glass would fly out, and turned back to me. "And I'm sick of the stink of
these garbage cans!"   (156)

"Sonny," I said, "I know how you feel. But if you don't finish school
now, you're going to be sorry later that you didn't." I grabbed him by the
shoulders. "And you only got another year. It ain't so bad. And I'll come
back and I swear I'll help you do *whatever* you want to do. Just try to put
up with it till I come back. Will you please do that? For me?"   (157)

He didn't answer and he wouldn't look at me.   (158)

"Sonny. You hear me?"   (159)

He pulled away. "I hear you. But you never hear anything *I* say." (160)

I didn't know what to say to that. He looked out of the window and then
back at me. "OK," he said, and sighed. "I'll try."   (161)

Then I said, trying to cheer him up a little, "They got a piano at Isabel's.
You can practice on it."   (162)

And as a matter of fact, it did cheer him up for a minute. "That's right,"
he said to himself. "I forgot that." His face relaxed a little. But the worry,
the thoughtfulness, played on it still, the way shadows play on a face which
is staring into the fire.   (163)

But I thought I'd never hear the end of that piano. At first, Isabel
would write me, saying how nice it was that Sonny was so serious about his
music and how, as soon as he came in from school, or wherever he had been
when he was supposed to be at school, he went straight to that piano and
stayed there until suppertime. And, after supper, he went back to that piano
and stayed there until everybody went to bed. He was at the piano all day
Saturday and all day Sunday. Then he bought a record player and started
playing records. He'd play one record over and over again, all day long
sometimes, and he'd improvise along with it on the piano. Or he'd play one
section of the record, one chord, one change, one progression, then he'd do
it on the piano. Then back to the record. Then back to the piano.   (164)

Well, I really don't know how they stood it. Isabel finally confessed that
it wasn't like living with a person at all, it was like living with sound. And
the sound didn't make any sense to her, didn't make any sense to any of
them—naturally. They began, in a way, to be afflicted by this presence that

was living in their home. It was as though Sonny were some sort of god, or monster. He moved in an atmosphere which wasn't like theirs at all. They fed him and he ate, he washed himself, he walked in and out of their door; he certainly wasn't nasty or unpleasant or rude, Sonny isn't any of those things; but it was as though he were all wrapped up in some cloud, some fire, some vision all his own; and there wasn't any way to reach him.   (165)

At the same time, he wasn't really a man yet, he was still a child, and they had to watch out for him in all kinds of ways. They certainly couldn't throw him out. Neither did they dare to make a great scene about that piano because even they dimly sensed, as I sensed, from so many thousands of miles away, that Sonny was at that piano playing for his life.   (166)

But he hadn't been going to school. One day a letter came from the school board and Isabel's mother got it—there had, apparently, been other letters but Sonny had torn them up. This day, when Sonny came in, Isabel's mother showed him the letter and asked where he'd been spending his time. And she finally got it out of him that he'd been down in Greenwich Village, with musicians and other characters, in a white girl's apartment. And this scared her and she started to scream at him and what came up, once she began—though she denies it to this day—was what sacrifices they were making to give Sonny a decent home and how little he appreciated it.   (167)

Sonny didn't play the piano that day. By evening, Isabel's mother had calmed down but then there was the old man to deal with, and Isabel herself. Isabel says she did her best to be calm but she broke down and started crying. She says she just watched Sonny's face. She could tell, by watching him, what was happening with him. And what was happening was that they penetrated his cloud, they had reached him. Even if their fingers had been a thousand times more gentle than human fingers ever are, he could hardly help feeling that they had stripped him naked and were spitting on that nakedness. For he also had to see that his presence, that music, which was life or death to him, had been torture for them and that they had endured it, not at all for his sake, but only for mine. And Sonny couldn't take that. He can take it a little better today than he could then but he's still not very good at it and, frankly, I don't know anybody who is.   (168)

The silence of the next few days must have been louder than the sound of all the music ever played since time began. One morning, before she went to work, Isabel was in his room for something and she suddenly realized that all of his records were gone. And she knew for certain that he was gone. And he was. He went as far as the navy would carry him. He finally sent me a postcard from some place in Greece and that was the first I knew that Sonny was still alive. I didn't see him any more until we were both back in New York and the war had long been over.   (169)

He was a man by then, of course, but I wasn't willing to see it. He came by the house from time to time, but we fought almost every time we met. I didn't like the way he carried himself, loose and dreamlike all the time, and I didn't like his friends, and his music seemed to be merely an excuse for the life he led. It sounded just that weird and disordered.   (170)

Then we had a fight, a pretty awful fight, and I didn't see him for months. By and by I looked him up, where he was living, in a furnished room in the Village, and I tried to make it up. But there were lots of other people in the room and Sonny just lay on his bed, and he wouldn't come downstairs with me, and he treated these other people as though they were his family and I weren't. So I got mad and then he got mad, and then I told him that he might just as well be dead as live the way he was living. Then he stood up and he told me not to worry about him any more in life, that he *was* dead as far as I was concerned. Then he pushed me to the door and the other people looked on as though nothing were happening, and he slammed the door behind me. I stood in the hallway, staring at the door. I heard somebody laugh in the room and then the tears came to my eyes. I started down the steps, whistling to keep from crying, I kept whistling to myself, *You going to need me, baby, one of these cold, rainy days.*   (171)

I read about Sonny's trouble in the spring. Little Grace died in the fall. She was a beautiful little girl. But she only lived a little over two years. She died of polio and she suffered. She had a slight fever for a couple of days, but it didn't seem like anything and we just kept her in bed. And we would certainly have called the doctor, but the fever dropped, she seemed to be all right. So we thought it had just been a cold. Then, one day, she was up, playing, Isabel was in the kitchen fixing lunch for the two boys when they'd come in from school, and she heard Grace fall down in the living room. When you have a lot of children you don't always start running when one of them falls, unless they start screaming or something. And, this time, Grace was quiet. Yet, Isabel says that when she heard that *thump* and then that silence, something happened in her to make her afraid. And she ran to the living room and there was little Grace on the floor, all twisted up, and the reason she hadn't screamed was that she couldn't get her breath. And when she did scream, it was the worst sound, Isabel says, that she'd ever heard in all her life, and she still hears it sometimes in her dreams. Isabel will sometimes wake me up with a low, moaning, strangled sound and I have to be quick to awaken her and hold her to me and where Isabel is weeping against me seems a mortal wound.   (172)

I think I may have written Sonny the very day that little Grace was buried. I was sitting in the living room in the dark, by myself, and I suddenly thought of Sonny. My trouble made his real.   (173)

One Saturday afternoon, when Sonny had been living with us, or, anyway, been in our house, for nearly two weeks, I found myself wandering aimlessly about the living room, drinking from a can of beer, and trying to

work up the courage to search Sonny's room. He was out, he was usually
out whenever I was home, and Isabel had taken the children to see their
grandparents. Suddenly I was standing still in front of the living room window, watching Seventh Avenue. The idea of searching Sonny's room made
me still. I scarcely dared to admit to myself what I'd be searching for. I
didn't know what I'd do if I found it. Or if I didn't.   (174)

On the sidewalk across from me, near the entrance to a barbecue joint,
some people were holding an old-fashioned revival meeting. The barbecue
cook, wearing a dirty white apron, his conked hair reddish and metallic in
the pale sun, and a cigarette between his lips, stood in the doorway, watching them. Kids and older people paused in their errands and stood there,
along with some older men and a couple of very tough-looking women who
watched everything that happened on the avenue, as though they owned it,
or were maybe owned by it. Well, they were watching this, too. The revival
was being carried on by three sisters in black, and a brother. All they had
were their voices and their Bibles and a tambourine. The brother was tes-
tifying and while he testified two of the sisters stood together, seeming to
say, amen, and the third sister walked around with the tambourine outstretched and a couple of people dropped coins into it. Then the brother's
testimony ended and the sister who had been taking up the collection
dumped the coins into her palm and transferred them to the pocket of her
long black robe. Then she raised both hands, striking the tambourine
against the air, and then against one hand, and she started to sing. And the
two other sisters and the brother joined in.   (175)

It was strange, suddenly, to watch, though I had been seeing these street
meetings all my life. So, of course, had everybody else down there. Yet, they
paused and watched and listened and I stood still at the window. *"Tis the
old ship of Zion,"* they sang, and the sister with the tambourine kept a
steady, jangling beat, *"it has rescued many a thousand!"* Not a soul under
the sound of their voices was hearing this song for the first time, not one of
them had been rescued. Nor had they seen much in the way of rescue work
being done around them. Neither did they especially believe in the holiness
of the three sisters and the brother, they knew too much about them, knew
where they lived, and how. The woman with the tambourine, whose voice
dominated the air, whose face was bright with joy, was divided by very
little from the woman who stood watching her, a cigarette between her
heavy, chapped lips, her hair a cuckoo's nest, her face scarred and swollen
from many beatings, and her black eyes glittering like coal. Perhaps they
both knew this, which was why, when, as rarely, they addressed each other,
they addressed each other as Sister. As the singing filled the air the watching, listening faces underwent a change, the eyes focusing on something
within; the music seemed to soothe a poison out of them; and time seemed,
nearly, to fall away from the sullen, belligerent, battered faces, as though

they were fleeing back to their first condition, while dreaming of their last. The barbecue cook half shook his head and smiled, and dropped his cigarette and disappeared into his joint. A man fumbled in his pockets for change and stood holding it in his hand impatiently, as though he had just remembered a pressing appointment further up the avenue. He looked furious. Then I saw Sonny, standing on the edge of the crowd. He was carrying a wide, flat notebook with a green cover, and it made him look, from where I was standing, almost like a schoolboy. The coppery sun brought out the copper in his skin, he was very faintly smiling, standing very still. Then the singing stopped, the tambourine turned into a collection plate again. The furious man dropped in his coins and vanished, so did a couple of the women, and Sonny dropped some change in the plate, looking directly at the woman with a little smile. He started across the avenue, toward the house. He has a slow, loping walk, something like the way Harlem hipsters walk, only he's imposed on this his own half-beat. I had never really noticed it before.   (176)

I stayed at the window, both relieved and apprehensive. As Sonny disappeared from my sight, they began singing again. And they were still singing when his key turned in the lock.   (177)

"Hey," he said.   (178)

"Hey, yourself. You want some beer?"   (179)

"No. Well, maybe." But he came up to the window and stood beside me, looking out. "What a warm voice," he said.   (180)

They were singing *If I could only hear my mother pray again!*   (181)

"Yes," I said, "and she can sure beat that tambourine."   (182)

"But what a terrible song," he said, and laughed. He dropped his notebook on the sofa and disappeared into the kitchen. "Where's Isabel and the kids?"   (183)

"I think they went to see their grandparents. You hungry?"   (184)

"No." He came back into the living room with his can of beer. "You want to come some place with me tonight?"   (185)

I sensed, I don't know how, that I couldn't possibly say no. "Sure. Where?"   (186)

He sat down on the sofa and picked up his notebook and started leafing through it. "I'm going to sit in with some fellows in a joint in the Village." (187)

"You mean, you're going to play, tonight?"   (188)

"That's right." He took a swallow of his beer and moved back to the window. He gave me a sidelong look. "If you can stand it."   (189)

"I'll try," I said.   (190)

He smiled to himself and we both watched as the meeting across the way broke up. The three sisters and the brother, heads bowed, were singing *God be with you till we meet again.* The faces around them were very quiet.

Then the song ended. The small crowd dispersed. We watched the three women and the lone man walk slowly up the avenue. (191)

"When she was singing before," said Sonny, abruptly, "her voice reminded me for a minute of what heroin feels like sometimes—when it's in your veins. It makes you feel sort of warm and cool at the same time. And distant. And—and sure." He sipped his beer, very deliberately not looking at me. I watched his face. "It makes you feel—in control. Sometimes you've got to have that feeling." (192)

"Do you?" I sat down slowly in the easy chair. (193)

"Sometimes." He went to the sofa and picked up his notebook again. "Some people do." (194)

"In order," I asked, "to play?" And my voice was very ugly, full of contempt and anger. (195)

"Well"—he looked at me with great, troubled eyes, as though, in fact, he hoped his eyes would tell me things he could never otherwise say—"they *think* so. And *if* they think so—!" (196)

"And what do *you* think?" I asked. (197)

He sat on the sofa and put his can of beer on the floor. "I don't know," he said, and I couldn't be sure if he were answering my question or pursuing his thoughts. His face didn't tell me. "It's not so much to *play*. It's to *stand* it, to be able to make it at all. On any level." He frowned and smiled: "In order to keep from shaking to pieces." (198)

"But these friends of yours," I said, "they seem to shake themselves to pieces pretty goddamn fast." (199)

"Maybe." He played with the notebook. And something told me that I should curb my tongue, that Sonny was doing his best to talk, that I should listen. "But of course you only know the ones that've gone to pieces. Some don't—or at least they haven't *yet* and that's just about all *any* of us can say." He paused. "And then there are some who just live, really, in hell, and they know it and they see what's happening and they go right on. I don't know." He sighed, dropped the notebook, folded his arms. "Some guys, you can tell from the way they play, they on something *all* the time. And you can see that, well, it makes something real for them. But of course," he picked up his beer from the floor and sipped it and put the can down again, "they *want* to, too, you've got to see that. Even some of them that say they don't—*some*, not all." (200)

"And what about you?" I asked—I couldn't help it. "What about you? Do *you* want to?" (201)

He stood up and walked to the window and remained silent for a long time. Then he sighed. "Me," he said. Then: "While I was downstairs before, on my way here, listening to that woman sing, it struck me all of a sudden how much suffering she must have had to go through—to sing like that. It's *repulsive* to think you have to suffer that much." (202)

I said: "But there's no way not to suffer—is there, Sonny?"   (203)

"I believe not," he said and smiled, "but that's never stopped anyone from trying." He looked at me. "Has it?" I realized, with this mocking look, that there stood between us, forever, beyond the power of time or forgiveness, the fact that I had held silence—so long!—when he had needed human speech to help him. He turned back to the window. "No, there's no way not to suffer. But you try all kinds of ways to keep from drowning in it, to keep on top of it, and to make it seem—well, like *you*. Like you did something, all right, and now you're suffering for it. You know?" I said nothing. "Well you know," he said, impatiently, "why *do* people suffer? Maybe it's better to do something to give it a reason, *any* reason."   (204)

"But we just agreed," I said, "that there's no way not to suffer. Isn't it better, then, just to—take it?"   (205)

"But nobody just takes it," Sonny cried, "that's what I'm telling you! *Everybody* tries not to. You're just hung up on the *way* some people try— it's not *your* way!"   (206)

The hair on my face began to itch, my face felt wet. "That's not true," I said, "that's not true. I don't give a damn what other people do, I don't even care how they suffer. I just care how *you* suffer." And he looked at me. "Please believe me," I said, "I don't want to see you—die—trying not to suffer."   (207)

"I won't," he said, flatly, "die trying not to suffer. At least, not any faster than anybody else."   (208)

"But there's no need," I said, trying to laugh, "is there? in killing yourself."   (209)

I wanted to say more, but I couldn't. I wanted to talk about will power and how life could be—well, beautiful. I wanted to say that it was all within; but was it? or, rather, wasn't that exactly the trouble? And I wanted to promise that I would never fail him again. But it would all have sounded— empty words and lies.   (210)

So I made the promise to myself and prayed that I would keep it. (211)

"It's terrible sometimes, inside," he said, "that's what's the trouble. You walk these streets, black and funky and cold, and there's not really a living ass to talk to, and there's nothing shaking, and there's no way of getting it out—that storm inside. You can't talk it and you can't make love with it, and when you finally try to get with it and play it, you realize *nobody's* listening. So *you've* got to listen. You got to find a way to listen."   (212)

And then he walked away from the window and sat on the sofa again, as though all the wind had suddenly been knocked out of him. "Sometimes you'll do *anything* to play, even cut your mother's throat." He laughed and looked at me. "Or your brother's." Then he sobered. "Or your own." Then: "Don't worry. I'm all right now and I think I'll *be* all right. But I can't forget

—where I've been. I don't mean just the physical place I've been, I mean
where I've *been*. And *what* I've been."   (213)

"What have you been, Sonny?" I asked.   (214)

He smiled—but sat sideways on the sofa, his elbow resting on the back,
his fingers playing with his mouth and chin, not looking at me. "I've been
something I didn't recognize, didn't know I could be. Didn't know anybody
could be." He stopped, looking inward, looking helplessly young, looking
old. "I'm not talking about it now because I feel *guilty* or anything like that
—maybe it would be better if I did, I don't know. Anyway, I can't really
talk about it. Not to you, not to anybody," and now he turned and faced me.
"Sometimes, you know, and it was actually when I was most *out* of the
world, I felt that I was in it, that I was *with* it, really, and I could play or
I didn't really have to *play*, it just came out of me, it was there. And I don't
know how I played, thinking about it now, but I know I did awful things,
those times, sometimes, to people. Or it wasn't that I *did* anything to them—
it was that they weren't real." He picked up the beer can; it was empty; he
rolled it between his palms: "And other times—well, I needed a fix, I needed
to find a place to lean, I needed to clear a space to *listen*—and I couldn't
find it, and I—went crazy, I did terrible things to *me*, I was terrible *for* me."
He began pressing the beer can between his hands, I watched the metal begin to give. It glittered, as he played with it, like a knife, and I was afraid
he would cut himself, but I said nothing. "Oh well. I can never tell you. I
was all by myself at the bottom of something, stinking and sweating and
crying and shaking, and I smelled it, you know? *my* stink, and I thought I'd
die if I couldn't get away from it and yet, all the same, I knew that everything I was doing was just locking me in with it. And I didn't know," he
paused, still flattening the beer can, "I didn't know, I still *don't* know, something kept telling me that maybe it was good to smell your own stink, but I
didn't think that *that* was what I'd been trying to do—and—who can stand
it?" and he abruptly dropped the ruined beer can, looking at me with a
small, still smile, and then rose, walking to the window as though it were
the lodestone rock. I watched his face, he watched the avenue. "I couldn't
tell you when Mama died—but the reason I wanted to leave Harlem so bad
was to get away from drugs. And then, when I ran away, that's what I was
running from—really. When I came back, nothing had changed, *I* hadn't
changed, I was just—older." And he stopped, drumming with his fingers on
the windowpane. The sun had vanished, soon darkness would fall. I
watched his face. "It can come again," he said, almost as though speaking to
himself. Then he turned to me. "It can come again," he repeated. "I just
want you to know that."   (215)

"All right," I said, at last. "So it can come again, All right."   (216)

He smiled, but the smile was sorrowful. "I had to try to tell you," he said.   (217)

"Yes," I said. "I understand that."   (218)

"You're my brother," he said, looking straight at me, and not smiling at all.   (219)

"Yes," I repeated, "yes. I understand that."   (220)

He turned back to the window, looking out. "All that hatred down there," he said, "all that hatred and misery and love. It's a wonder it doesn't blow the avenue apart."   (221)

We went to the only nightclub on a short, dark street, downtown. We squeezed through the narrow, chattering, jam-packed bar to the entrance of the big room, where the bandstand was. And we stood there for a moment, for the lights were very dim in this room and we couldn't see. Then, "Hello, boy," said a voice and an enormous black man, much older than Sonny or myself, erupted out of all that atmospheric lighting and put an arm around Sonny's shoulder. "I been sitting right here," he said, "waiting for you."   (222)

He had a big voice, too, and heads in the darkness turned toward us.

Sonny grinned and pulled a little away, and said, "Creole, this is my brother. I told you about him."   (224)

Creole shook my hand. "I'm glad to meet you, son," he said, and it was clear that he was glad to meet me *there*, for Sonny's sake. And he smiled, "You got a real musician in *your* family," and he took his arm from Sonny's shoulder and slapped him, lightly, affectionately, with the back of his hand.   (225)

"Well. Now I've heard it all," said a voice behind us. This was another musician, and a friend of Sonny's, a coal-black, cheerful-looking man, built close to the ground. He immediately began confiding to me, at the top of his lungs, the most terrible things about Sonny, his teeth gleaming like a lighthouse and his laugh coming up out of him like the beginning of an earthquake. And it turned out that everyone at the bar knew Sonny, or almost everyone; some were musicians, working there, or nearby, or not working, some were simply hangers-on, and some were there to hear Sonny play. I was introduced to all of them and they were all very polite to me. Yet, it was clear that, for them, I was only Sonny's brother. Here, I was in Sonny's world. Or, rather: his kingdom. Here, it was not even a question that his veins bore royal blood.   (226)

They were going to play soon and Creole installed me, by myself, at a table in a dark corner. Then I watched them, Creole, and the little black man, and Sonny, and the others, while they horsed around, standing just below the bandstand. The light from the bandstand spilled just a little short of them and, watching them laughing and gesturing and moving about, I had the feeling that they, nevertheless, were being most careful not to step into that circle of light too suddenly: that if they moved into the light too suddenly, without thinking, they would perish in flame. Then, while I watched, one of them, the small, black man, moved into the light and crossed the bandstand and started fooling around with his drums. Then—being funny and being, also, extremely ceremonious—Creole took Sonny by the arm and led him to the piano. A woman's voice called Sonny's name and a few hands started clapping. And Sonny, also being funny and being ceremonious, and so touched, I think, that he could have cried, but neither hiding it nor showing it, riding it like a man, grinned, and put both hands to his heart and bowed from the waist.   (227)

Creole then went to the bass fiddle and a lean, very bright-skinned brown man jumped up on the bandstand and picked up his horn. So there they were, and the atmosphere on the bandstand and in the room began to change and tighten. Someone stepped up to the microphone and announced them. Then there were all kinds of murmurs. Some people at the bar shushed others. The waitress ran around, frantically getting in the last orders, guys and chicks got closer to each other, and the lights on the bandstand, on the quartet, turned to a kind of indigo. Then they all looked different there. Creole looked about him for the last time, as though he were making certain that all his chickens were in the coop, and then he—jumped and struck the fiddle. And there they were.   (228)

All I know about music is that not many people ever really hear it. And even then, on the rare occasions when something opens within, and the music enters, what we mainly hear, or hear corroborated, are personal, private, vanishing evocations. But the man who creates the music is hearing something else, is dealing with the roar rising from the void and imposing order on it as it hits the air. What is evoked in him, then, is of another order, more terrible because it has no words, and triumphant, too, for that same reason. And his triumph, when he triumphs, is ours. I just watched Sonny's face. His face was troubled, he was working hard, but he wasn't with it. And I had the feeling that, in a way, everyone on the bandstand was waiting for him, both waiting for him and pushing him along. But as I began to watch Creole, I realized that it was Creole who held them all back. He had them on a short rein. Up there, keeping the beat with his whole body, wailing on the fiddle, with his eyes half closed, he was listening to everything, but he was listening to Sonny. He was having a dialogue with Sonny. He wanted Sonny to leave the shoreline and strike out for the deep water. He was Sonny's witness that deep water and drowning were not the same thing—he had been there, and he knew. And he wanted Sonny to know. He was waiting for Sonny to do the things on the keys which would let Creole know that Sonny was in the water.   (229)

And, while Creole listened, Sonny moved, deep within, exactly like someone in torment. I had never before thought of how awful the relation-ship must be between the musician and his instrument. He has to fill it, this instrument, with the breath of life, his own. He has to make it do what he wants it to do. And a piano is just a piano. It's made out of so much wood and wires and little hammers and big ones, and ivory. While there's only so much you can do with it, the only way to find this out is to try; to try and make it do everything.   (230)

And Sonny hadn't been near a piano for over a year. And he wasn't on much better terms with his life, not the life that stretched before him now. He and the piano stammered, started one way, got scared, stopped; started another way, panicked, marked time, started again; then seemed to have found a direction, panicked again, got stuck. And the face I saw on Sonny I'd never seen before. Everything had been burned out of it, and, at the same time, things usually hidden were being burned in, by the fire and fury of the battle which was occurring in him up there.   (231)

Yet, watching Creole's face as they neared the end of the first set, I had the feeling that something had happened, something I hadn't heard. Then they finished, there was scattered applause, and then, without an instant's warning, Creole started into something else, it was almost sardonic, it was *Am I Blue*. And, as though he commanded, Sonny began to play. Something began to happen. And Creole let out the reins. The dry, low, black man said something awful on the drums, Creole answered, and the drums talked back. Then the horn insisted, sweet and high, slightly detached perhaps, and Creole listened, commenting now and then, dry, and driving, beautiful and calm and old. Then they all came together again, and Sonny was part of the family again. I could tell this from his face. He seemed to have found, right there beneath his fingers, a damn brand-new piano. It seemed that he couldn't get over it. Then, for awhile, just being happy with Sonny, they seemed to be agreeing with him that brand-new pianos certainly were a gas.
                                                                      (232)

Then Creole stepped forward to remind them that what they were play-ing was the blues. He hit something in all of them, he hit something in me, myself, and the music tightened and deepened, apprehension began to beat the air. Creole began to tell us what the blues were all about. They were not about anything very new. He and his boys up there were keeping it new, at the risk of ruin, destruction, madness, and death, in order to find new ways to make us listen. For, while the tale of how we suffer, and how we are de-lighted, and how we may triumph is never new, it always must be heard. There isn't any other tale to tell, it's the only light we've got in all this dark-ness.   (233)

And this tale, according to that face, that body, those strong hands on those strings, has another aspect in every country, and a new depth in every generation. Listen, Creole seemed to be saying, listen. Now these are

Sonny's blues. He made the little black man on the drums know it, and the bright, brown man on the horn. Creole wasn't trying any longer to get Sonny in the water. He was wishing him Godspeed. Then he stepped back, very slowly, filling the air with the immense suggestion that Sonny speak for himself.   (234)

Then they all gathered around Sonny and Sonny played. Every now and again one of them seemed to say, amen. Sonny's fingers filled the air with life, his life. But that life contained so many others. And Sonny went all the way back, he really began with the spare, flat statement of the opening phrase of the song. Then he began to make it his. It was very beautiful because it wasn't hurried and it was no longer a lament. I seemed to hear with what burning he had made it his, with what burning we had yet to make it ours, how we could cease lamenting. Freedom lurked around us and I understood, at last, that he could help us to be free if we would listen, that he would never be free until we did. Yet, there was no battle in his face now. I heard what he had gone through, and would continue to go through until he came to rest in earth. He had made it his: that long line, of which we knew only Mama and Daddy. And he was giving it back, as everything must be given back, so that, passing through death, it can live forever. I saw my mother's face again, and felt, for the first time, how the stones of the road she had walked on must have bruised her feet. I saw the moonlit road where my father's brother died. And it brought something else back to me, and carried me past it, I saw my little girl again and felt Isabel's tears again, and I felt my own tears begin to rise. And I was yet aware that this was only a moment, that the world waited outside, as hungry as a tiger, and that trouble stretched above us, longer than the sky.   (235)

Then it was over. Creole and Sonny let out their breath, both soaking wet, and grinning. There was a lot of applause and some of it was real. In the dark, the girl came by and I asked her to take drinks to the bandstand. There was a long pause, while they talked up there in the indigo light and after awhile I saw the girl put a Scotch and milk on top of the piano for Sonny. He didn't seem to notice it, but just before they started playing again, he sipped from it and looked toward me, and nodded. Then he put it back on top of the piano. For me, then, as they began to play again, it glowed and shook above my brother's head like the very cup of trembling.

                                                                                    (236)

James Joyce

(1882–1941)

JOYCE was one of the major products of the Irish Renaissance in litera-
ture. Born near Dublin and educated by the Jesuits, he struggled long to
free himself of cultural provincialism and intellectual dogmatism, spending
most of his adult life on the Continent. His principal works are Dubliners
(1914), Portrait of the Artist as a Young Man *(1916), and* Ulysses *(1922).*
Joyce was throughout his life a literary experimentalist, and no two of his
works have closely comparable styles.

◼ *The Dead*

LILY, THE CARETAKER's daughter, was literally run off her feet. Hardly had
she brought one gentleman into the little pantry behind the office on the
ground floor and helped him off with his overcoat than the wheezy hall-
door bell clanged again and she had to scamper along the bare hallway to
let in another guest. It was well for her she had not to attend to the ladies
also. But Miss Kate and Miss Julia had thought of that and had converted
the bathroom upstairs into a ladies' dressing-room. Miss Kate and Miss Julia
were there, gossiping and laughing and fussing, walking after each other to
the head of the stairs, peering down over the banisters and calling down to
Lily to ask her who had come.   (1)

It was always a great affair, the Misses Morkan's annual dance. Everybody who knew them came to it, members of the family, old friends of the
family, the members of Julia's choir, any of Kate's pupils that were grown
up enough, and even some of Mary Jane's pupils too. Never once had it
fallen flat. For years and years it had gone off in splendid style, as long as
anyone could remember; ever since Kate and Julia, after the death of their
brother Pat, had left the house in Stoney Batter and taken Mary Jane, their

only niece, to live with them in the dark, gaunt house on Usher's Island, the upper part of which they had rented from Mr. Fulham, the corn-factor on the ground floor. That was a good thirty years ago if it was a day. Mary Jane, who was then a little girl in short clothes, was now the main prop of the household, for she had the organ in Haddington Road. She had been through the Academy and gave a pupils' concert every year in the upper room of the Antient Concert Rooms. Many of her pupils belonged to the better-class families on the Kingstown and Dalkey line. Old as they were, her aunts also did their share. Julia, though she was quite grey, was still the leading soprano in Adam and Eve's, and Kate, being too feeble to go about much, gave music lessons to beginners on the old square piano in the back room. Lily, the caretaker's daughter, did housemaid's work for them. Though their life was modest, they believed in eating well; the best of everything: diamond-bone sirloins, three-shilling tea and the best bottled stout. But Lily seldom made a mistake in the orders, so that she got on well with her three mistresses. They were fussy, that was all. But the only thing they would not stand was back answers. (2)

Of course, they had good reason to be fussy on such a night. And then it was long after ten o'clock and yet there was no sign of Gabriel and his wife. Besides they were dreadfully afraid that Freddy Malins might turn up screwed. They would not wish for worlds that any of Mary Jane's pupils should see him under the influence; and when he was like that it was some-times very hard to manage him. Freddy Malins always came late, but they wondered what could be keeping Gabriel: and that was what brought them every two minutes to the banisters to ask Lily had Gabriel or Freddy come. (3)

"O, Mr. Conroy," said Lily to Gabriel when she opened the door for him, "Miss Kate and Miss Julia thought you were never coming. Good-night, Mrs. Conroy." (4)

"I'll engage they did," said Gabriel, "but they forget that my wife here takes three mortal hours to dress herself." (5)

He stood on the mat, scraping the snow from his goloshes, while Lily led his wife to the foot of the stairs and called out: (6)

"Miss Kate, here's Mrs. Conroy." (7)

Kate and Julia came toddling down the dark stairs at once. Both of them kissed Gabriel's wife, said she must be perished alive, and asked was Gabriel with her. (8)

"Here I am as right as the mail, Aunt Kate! Go on up. I'll follow," called out Gabriel from the dark. (9)

He continued scraping his feet vigorously while the three women went upstairs, laughing, to the ladies' dressing-room. A light fringe of snow lay like a cape on the shoulders of his overcoat and like toecaps on the toes of his goloshes; and, as the buttons of his overcoat slipped with a squeaking noise through the snow-stiffened frieze, a cold, fragrant air from out-of-doors escaped from crevices and folds.   (10)

"Is it snowing again, Mr. Conroy?" asked Lily.   (11)

She had preceded him into the pantry to help him off with his overcoat. Gabriel smiled at the three syllables she had given his surname and glanced at her. She was a slim, growing girl, pale in complexion and with hay-coloured hair. The gas in the pantry made her look still paler. Gabriel had known her when she was a child and used to sit on the lowest step nursing a rag doll.   (12)

"Yes, Lily," he answered, "and I think we're in for a night of it."   (13)

He looked up at the pantry ceiling, which was shaking with the stamping and shuffling of feet on the floor above, listened for a moment to the piano and then glanced at the girl, who was folding his overcoat carefully at the end of a shelf.   (14)

"Tell me, Lily," he said in a friendly tone, "do you still go to school?"
                              (15)

"O no, sir," she answered. "I'm done schooling this year and more." (16)

"O, then," said Gabriel gaily, "I suppose we'll be going to your wedding one of these fine days with your young man, eh?"   (17)

The girl glanced back at him over her shoulder and said with great bitterness: (18)

"The men that is now is only all palaver and what they can get out of you."   (19)

Gabriel coloured, as if he felt he had made a mistake and, without looking at her, kicked off his goloshes and flicked actively with his muffler at his patent-leather shoes.   (20)

He was a stout, tallish young man. The high colour of his cheeks pushed upwards even to his forehead, where it scattered itself in a few formless patches of pale red; and on his hairless face there scintillated restlessly the polished lenses and the bright gilt rims of the glasses which screened his delicate and restless eyes. His glossy black hair was parted in the middle and brushed in a long curve behind his ears where it curled slightly beneath the groove left by his hat.   (21)

When he had flicked lustre into his shoes he stood up and pulled his waistcoat down more tightly on his plump body. Then he took a coin rapidly from his pocket.   (22)

"O Lily," he said, thrusting it into her hands, "it's Christmas-time, isn't it? Just . . . here's a little. . . ."   (23)

He walked rapidly towards the door.   (24)

"O no, sir," cried the girl, following him. "Really, sir, I wouldn't take it.'
                              (25)

"Christmas-time! Christmas-time!" said Gabriel, almost trotting to the stairs and waving his hand to her in deprecation.   (26)

The girl, seeing that he had gained the stairs, called out after him: (27)
"Well, thank you, sir." (28)

He waited outside the drawing-room door until the waltz should finish,
listening to the skirts that swept against it and to the shuffling of feet. He
was still discomposed by the girl's bitter and sudden retort. It had cast a
gloom over him which he tried to dispel by arranging his cuffs and the bows
of his tie. He then took from his waistcoat pocket a little paper and glanced
at the headings he had made for his speech. He was undecided about the
lines from Robert Browning, for he feared they would be above the heads
of his hearers. Some quotation that they would recognise from Shakespeare
or from the Melodies would be better. The indelicate clacking of the men's
heels and the shuffling of their soles reminded him that their grade of culture differed from his. He would only make himself ridiculous by quoting
poetry to them which they could not understand. They would think that he
was airing his superior education. He would fail with them just as he had
failed with the girl in the pantry. He had taken up a wrong tone. His whole
speech was a mistake from first to last, an utter failure. (29)

Just then his aunts and his wife came out of the ladies' dressing-room.
His aunts were two small, plainly dressed old women. Aunt Julia was an
inch or so the taller. Her hair, drawn low over the tops of her ears, was
grey; and grey also, with darker shadows, was her large flaccid face.
Though she was stout in build and stood erect, her slow eyes and parted
lips gave her the appearance of a woman who did not know where she was
or where she was going. Aunt Kate was more vivacious. Her face, healthier
than her sister's, was all puckers and creases, like a shrivelled red apple, and
her hair, braided in the same old-fashioned way, had not lost its ripe nut
colour. (30)

They both kissed Gabriel frankly. He was their favourite nephew, the
son of their dead elder sister, Ellen, who had married T. J. Conroy of the
Port and Docks. (31)

"Gretta tells me you're not going to take a cab back to Monkstown to-
night, Gabriel," said Aunt Kate. (32)

"No," said Gabriel, turning to his wife, "we had quite enough of that last
year, hadn't we? Don't you remember, Aunt Kate, what a cold Gretta got
out of it? Cab windows rattling all the way, and the east wind blowing in
after we passed Merrion. Very jolly it was. Gretta caught a dreadful cold."
(33)

Aunt Kate frowned severely and nodded her head at every word. (34)
"Quite right, Gabriel, quite right," she said. "You can't be too careful."
(35)

"But as for Gretta there," said Gabriel, "she'd walk home in the snow if
she were let." (36)

Mrs. Conroy laughed. (37)

"Don't mind him, Aunt Kate," she said. "He's really an awful bother, what with green shades for Tom's eyes at night and making him do the dumb-bells, and forcing Eva to eat the stirabout. The poor child! And she simply hates the sight of it! . . . O, but you'll never guess what he makes me wear now!"   (38)

She broke out into a peal of laughter and glanced at her husband, whose admiring and happy eyes had been wandering from her dress to her face and hair. The two aunts laughed heartily, too, for Gabriel's solicitude was a standing joke with them.   (39)

"Goloshes!" said Mrs. Conroy. "That's the latest. Whenever it's wet underfoot I must put on my goloshes. To-night even, he wanted me to put them on, but I wouldn't. The next thing he'll buy me will be a diving suit."   (40)

Gabriel laughed nervously and patted his tie reassuringly, while Aunt Kate nearly doubled herself, so heartily did she enjoy the joke. The smile soon faded from Aunt Julia's face and her mirthless eyes were directed towards her nephew's face. After a pause she asked: (41)

"And what are goloshes, Gabriel?"   (42)

"Goloshes, Julia!" exclaimed her sister. "Goodness me, don't you know what goloshes are? You wear them over your . . . over your boots, Gretta, isn't it?"   (43)

"Yes," said Mrs. Conroy. "Guttapercha things. We both have a pair now. Gabriel says everyone wears them on the continent."   (44)

"O, on the continent," murmured Aunt Julia, nodding her head slowly.
                                                                            (45)

Gabriel knitted his brows and said, as if he were slightly angered: (46)

"It's nothing very wonderful, but Gretta thinks it very funny because she says the word reminds her of Christy Minstrels."   (47)

"But tell me, Gabriel," said Aunt Kate, with brisk tact. "Of course, you've seen about the room. Gretta was saying . . ."   (48)

"O, the room is all right," replied Gabriel. "I've taken one in the Gresham."   (49)

"To be sure," said Aunt Kate, "by far the best thing to do. And the children, Gretta, you're not anxious about them?"   (50)

"O, for one night," said Mrs. Conroy. "Besides, Bessie will look after them."   (51)

"To be sure," said Aunt Kate again. "What a comfort it is to have a girl like that, one you can depend on! There's that Lily, I'm sure I don't know what has come over her lately. She's not the girl she was at all."   (52)

Gabriel was about to ask his aunt some questions on this point, but she broke off suddenly to gaze after her sister, who had wandered down the stairs and was craning her neck over the banisters.   (53)

"Now, I ask you," she said almost testily, "where is Julia going? Julia! Julia! Where are you going?" (54)

Julia, who had gone half way down one flight, came back and announced blandly: (55)

"Here's Freddy." (56)

At the same moment a clapping of hands and a final flourish of the pianist told that the waltz had ended. The drawing-room door was opened from within and some couples came out. Aunt Kate drew Gabriel aside hurriedly and whispered into his ear: (57)

"Slip down, Gabriel, like a good fellow and see if he's all right, and don't let him up if he's screwed. I'm sure he's screwed. I'm sure he is." (58)

Gabriel went to the stairs and listened over the banisters. He could hear two persons talking in the pantry. Then he recognised Freddy Malins' laugh. He went down the stairs noisily. (59)

"It's such a relief," said Aunt Kate to Mrs. Conroy, "that Gabriel is here. I always feel easier in my mind when he's here. . . . Julia, there's Miss Daly and Miss Power will take some refreshment. Thanks for your beautiful waltz, Miss Daly. It made lovely time." (60)

A tall wizen-faced man, with a stiff grizzled moustache and swarthy skin, who was passing out with his partner, said: (61)

"And may we have some refreshment, too, Miss Morkan?" (62)

"Julia," said Aunt Kate summarily, "and here's Mr. Browne and Miss Furlong. Take them in, Julia, with Miss Daly and Miss Power." (63)

"I'm the man for the ladies," said Mr. Browne, pursing his lips until his moustache bristled and smiling in all his wrinkles. "You know, Miss Morkan, the reason they are so fond of me is—" (64)

He did not finish his sentence, but, seeing that Aunt Kate was out of earshot, at once led the three young ladies into the back room. The middle of the room was occupied by two square tables placed end to end, and on these Aunt Julia and the caretaker were straightening and smoothing a large cloth. On the sideboard were arrayed dishes and plates, and glasses and bundles of knives and forks and spoons. The top of the closed square piano served also as a sideboard for viands and sweets. At a smaller sideboard in one corner two young men were standing, drinking hop-bitters. (65)

Mr. Browne led his charges thither and invited them all, in jest, to some ladies' punch, hot, strong and sweet. As they said they never took anything strong, he opened three bottles of lemonade for them. Then he asked one of the young men to move aside, and, taking hold of the decanter, filled out for himself a goodly measure of whisky. The young men eyed him respectfully while he took a trial sip. (66)

"God help me," he said, smiling, "it's the doctor's orders." (67)

His wizened face broke into a broader smile, and the three young ladies laughed in musical echo to his pleasantry, swaying their bodies to and fro, with nervous jerks of their shoulders. The boldest said: (68)

"O, now, Mr. Browne, I'm sure the doctor never ordered anything of the kind."   (69)

Mr. Browne took another sip of his whisky and said, with sidling mimicry: (70)

"Well, you see, I'm like the famous Mrs. Cassidy, who is reported to have said: 'Now, Mary Grimes, if I don't take it, make me take it, for I feel I want it.'"   (71)

His hot face had leaned forward a little too confidentially and he had assumed a very low Dublin accent so that the young ladies, with one instinct, received his speech in silence. Miss Furlong, who was one of Mary Jane's pupils, asked Miss Daly what was the name of the pretty waltz she had played; and Mr. Browne, seeing that he was ignored, turned promptly to the two young men who were more appreciative.   (72)

A red-faced young woman, dressed in pansy, came into the room, excitedly clapping her hands and crying: (73)

"Quadrilles! Quadrilles!"   (74)

Close on her heels came Aunt Kate, crying: (75)

"Two gentlemen and three ladies, Mary Jane!"   (76)

"O, here's Mr. Bergin and Mr. Kerrigan," said Mary Jane. "Mr. Kerrigan, will you take Miss Power? Miss Furlong, may I get you a partner, Mr. Bergin. O, that'll just do now."   (77)

"Three ladies, Mary Jane," said Aunt Kate.   (78)

The two young gentlemen asked the ladies if they might have the pleasure, and Mary Jane turned to Miss Daly.   (79)

"O, Miss Daly, you're really awfully good, after playing for the last two dances, but really we're so short of ladies to-night."   (80)

"I don't mind in the least, Miss Morkan."   (81)

"But I've a nice partner for you, Mr. Bartell D'Arcy, the tenor. I'll get him to sing later on. All Dublin is raving about him."   (82)

"Lovely voice, lovely voice!" said Aunt Kate.   (83)

As the piano had twice begun the prelude to the first figure Mary Jane led her recruits quickly from the room. They had hardly gone when Aunt Julia wandered slowly into the room, looking behind her at something. (84)

"What is the matter, Julia?" asked Aunt Kate anxiously. "Who is it?"
                                                                             (85)

Julia, who was carrying in a column of table-napkins, turned to her sister and said, simply, as if the question had surprised her: (86)

"It's only Freddy, Kate, and Gabriel with him."   (87)

In fact right behind her Gabriel could be seen piloting Freddy Malins across the landing. The latter, a young man of about forty, was of Gabriel's size and build, with very round shoulders. His face was fleshy and pallid, touched with colour only at the thick hanging lobes of his ears and at the wide wings of his nose. He had coarse features, a blunt nose, a convex and receding brow, tumid and protruded lips. His heavy-lidded eyes and the disorder of his scanty hair made him look sleepy. He was laughing heartily in a high key at a story which he had been telling Gabriel on the stairs and at the same time rubbing the knuckles of his left fist backwards and forwards into his left eye. (88)

"Good-evening, Freddy," said Aunt Julia. (89)

Freddy Malins bade the Misses Morkan good-evening in what seemed an offhand fashion by reason of the habitual catch in his voice and then, seeing that Mr. Browne was grinning at him from the sideboard, crossed the room on rather shaky legs and began to repeat in an undertone the story he had just told to Gabriel. (90)

"He's not so bad, is he?" said Aunt Kate to Gabriel. (91)

Gabriel's brows were dark but he raised them quickly and answered: (92)

"O, no, hardly noticeable." (93)

"Now, isn't he a terrible fellow!" she said. "And his poor mother made him take the pledge on New Year's Eve. But come on, Gabriel, into the drawing-room." (94)

Before leaving the room with Gabriel she signalled to Mr. Browne by frowning and shaking her forefinger in warning to and fro. Mr. Browne nodded in answer and, when she had gone, said to Freddy Malins: (95)

"Now, then, Teddy, I'm going to fill you out a good glass of lemonade just to buck you up." (96)

Freddy Malins, who was nearing the climax of his story, waved the offer aside impatiently but Mr. Browne, having first called Freddy Malins' attention to a disarray in his dress, filled out and handed him a full glass of lemonade. Freddy Malins' left hand accepted the glass mechanically, his right hand being engaged in the mechanical readjustment of his dress. Mr. Browne, whose face was once more wrinkling with mirth, poured out for himself a glass of whisky while Freddy Malins exploded, before he had well reached the climax of his story, in a kink of high-pitched bronchitic laughter and, setting down his untasted and overflowing glass, began to rub the knuckles of his left fist backwards and forwards into his left eye, repeating words of his last phrase as well as his fit of laughter would allow him. (97)

Gabriel could not listen while Mary Jane was playing her Academy piece, full of runs and difficult passages, to the hushed drawing-room. He liked music but the piece she was playing had no melody for him and he doubted whether it had any melody for the other listeners, though they had begged Mary Jane to play something. Four young men, who had come from the refreshment-room to stand in the doorway at the sound of the piano, had gone away quietly in couples after a few minutes. The only persons who seemed to follow the music were Mary Jane herself, her hands racing along the key-board or lifted from it at the pauses like those of a priestess in momentary imprecation, and Aunt Kate standing at her elbow to turn the page.   (98)

Gabriel's eyes, irritated by the floor, which glittered with beeswax under the heavy chandelier, wandered to the wall above the piano. A picture of the balcony scene in *Romeo and Juliet* hung there and beside it was a picture of the two murdered princes in the Tower which Aunt Julia had worked in red, blue and brown wools when she was a girl. Probably in the school they had gone to as girls that kind of work had been taught for one year. His mother had worked for him as a birthday present a waistcoat of purple tabinet, with little foxes' heads upon it, lined with brown satin and having round mulberry buttons. It was strange that his mother had had no musical talent though Aunt Kate used to call her the brains carrier of the Morkan family. Both she and Julia had always seemed a little proud of their serious and matronly sister. Her photograph stood before the pier-glass. She held an open book on her knees and was pointing out something in it to Constantine who, dressed in a man-o'-war suit, lay at her feet. It was she who had chosen the names of her sons for she was very sensible of the dignity of family life. Thanks to her, Constantine was now senior curate in Balbriggan and, thanks to her, Gabriel himself had taken his degree in the Royal University. A shadow passed over his face as he remembered her sullen opposition to his marriage. Some slighting phrases she had used still rankled in his memory; she had once spoken of Gretta as being country cute and that was not true of Gretta at all. It was Gretta who had nursed her during all her last long illness in their house at Monkstown.   (99)

He knew that Mary Jane must be near the end of her piece for she was playing again the opening melody with runs of scales after every bar and while he waited for the end the resentment died down in his heart. The piece ended with a trill of octaves in the treble and a final deep octave in the bass. Great applause greeted Mary Jane as, blushing and rolling up her music nervously, she escaped from the room. The most vigorous clapping came from the four young men in the doorway who had gone away to the refreshment-room at the beginning of the piece but had come back when the piano had stopped.   (100)

Lancers were arranged. Gabriel found himself partnered with Miss Ivors. She was a frank-mannered talkative young lady, with a freckled face and prominent brown eyes. She did not wear a low-cut bodice and the large brooch which was fixed in the front of her collar bore on it an Irish device and motto.   (101)

When they had taken their places she said abruptly: (102)

"I have a crow to pluck with you." (103)

"With me?" said Gabriel. (104)

She nodded her head gravely. (105)

"What is it?" asked Gabriel, smiling at her solemn manner. (106)

"Who is G. C.?" answered Miss Ivors, turning her eyes upon him. (107)

Gabriel coloured and was about to knit his brows, as if he did not understand, when she said bluntly: (108)

"O, innocent Amy! I have found out that you write for *The Daily Express*. Now, aren't you ashamed of yourself?" (109)

"Why should I be ashamed of myself?" asked Gabriel, blinking his eyes and trying to smile. (110)

"Well, I'm ashamed of you," said Miss Ivors frankly. "To say you'd write for a paper like that. I didn't think you were a West Briton." (111)

A look of perplexity appeared on Gabriel's face. It was true that he wrote a literary column every Wednesday in *The Daily Express*, for which he was paid fifteen shillings. But that did not make him a West Briton surely. The books he received for review were almost more welcome than the paltry cheque. He loved to feel the covers and turn over the pages of newly printed books. Nearly every day when his teaching in the college was ended he used to wander down the quays to the second-hand booksellers, to Hickey's on Bachelor's Walk, to Webb's or Massey's on Aston's Quay, or to O'Clohissey's in the by-street. He did not know how to meet her charge. He wanted to say that literature was above politics. But they were friends of many years' standing and their careers had been parallel, first at the University and then as teachers: he could not risk a grandiose phrase with her. He continued blinking his eyes and trying to smile and murmured lamely that he saw nothing political in writing reviews of books. (112)

When their turn to cross had come he was still perplexed and inattentive. Miss Ivors promptly took his hand in a warm grasp and said in a soft friendly tone: (113)

"Of course, I was only joking. Come, we cross now." (114)

When they were together again she spoke of the University question and Gabriel felt more at ease. A friend of hers had shown her his review of Browning's poems. That was how she had found out the secret: but she liked the review immensely. Then she said suddenly: (115)

"O, Mr. Conroy, will you come for an excursion to the Aran Isles this summer? We're going to stay there a whole month. It will be splendid out in the Atlantic. You ought to come. Mr. Clancy is coming, and Mr. Kilkelly and Kathleen Kearney. It would be splendid for Gretta too if she'd come. She's from Connacht, isn't she?" (116)

"Her people are," said Gabriel shortly. (117)

"But you will come, won't you?" said Miss Ivors, laying her warm hand eagerly on his arm. (118)

"The fact is," said Gabriel, "I have just arranged to go——"   (119)

"Go where?" asked Miss Ivors.   (120)

"Well, you know, every year I go for a cycling tour with some fellows and so——"   (121)

"But where?" asked Miss Ivors.   (122)

"Well, we usually go to France or Belgium or perhaps Germany," said Gabriel awkwardly.   (123)

"And why do you go to France and Belgium," said Miss Ivors, "instead of visiting your own land?"   (124)

"Well," said Gabriel, "it's partly to keep in touch with the languages and partly for a change."   (125)

"And haven't you your own language to keep in touch with—Irish?" asked Miss Ivors.   (126)

"Well," said Gabriel, "if it comes to that, you know, Irish is not my language."   (127)

Their neighbours had turned to listen to the cross-examination. Gabriel glanced right and left nervously and tried to keep his good humour under the ordeal which was making a blush invade his forehead.   (128)

"And haven't you your own land to visit," continued Miss Ivors, "that you know nothing of, your own people, and your own country?"   (129)

"O, to tell you the truth," retorted Gabriel suddenly, "I'm sick of my own country, sick of it!"   (130)

"Why?" asked Miss Ivors.   (131)

Gabriel did not answer for his retort had heated him.   (132)

"Why?" repeated Miss Ivors.   (133)

They had to go visiting together and, as he had not answered her, Miss Ivors said warmly: (134)

"Of course, you've no answer."   (135)

Gabriel tried to cover his agitation by taking part in the dance with great energy. He avoided her eyes for he had seen a sour expression on her face. But when they met in the long chain he was surprised to feel his hand firmly pressed. She looked at him from under her brows for a moment quizzically until he smiled. Then, just as the chain was about to start again, she stood on tiptoe and whispered into his ear: (136)

"West Briton!"   (137)

When the lancers were over Gabriel went away to a remote corner of the room where Freddy Malins' mother was sitting. She was a stout feeble old woman with white hair. Her voice had a catch in it like her son's and she stuttered slightly. She had been told that Freddy had come and that he was nearly all right. Gabriel asked her whether she had had a good crossing. She lived with her married daughter in Glasgow and came to Dublin on a visit once a year. She answered placidly that she had had a beautiful crossing and that the captain had been most attentive to her. She spoke also of the beautiful house her daughter kept in Glasgow, and of all the friends they had there. While her tongue rambled on Gabriel tried to banish from his mind all memory of the unpleasant incident with Miss Ivors. Of course the girl or woman, or whatever she was, was an enthusiast but there was a time for all things. Perhaps he ought not to have answered her like that. But she had no right to call him a West Briton before people, even in joke. She had tried to make him ridiculous before people, heckling him and staring at him with her rabbit's eyes. (138)

He saw his wife making her way towards him through the waltzing couples. When she reached him she said into his ear: (139)

"Gabriel, Aunt Kate wants to know won't you carve the goose as usual. Miss Daly will carve the ham and I'll do the pudding." (140)

"All right," said Gabriel. (141)

"She's sending in the younger ones first as soon as this waltz is over so that we'll have the table to ourselves." (142)

"Were you dancing?" asked Gabriel. (143)

"Of course I was. Didn't you see me? What row had you with Molly Ivors?" (144)

"No row. Why? Did she say so?" (145)

"Something like that. I'm trying to get that Mr. D'Arcy to sing. He's full of conceit, I think." (146)

"There was no row," said Gabriel moodily, "only she wanted me to go for a trip to the west of Ireland and I said I wouldn't." (147)

His wife clasped her hands excitedly and gave a little jump. (148)

"O, do go, Gabriel," she cried. "I'd love to see Galway again." (149)

"You can go if you like," said Gabriel coldly. (150)

She looked at him for a moment, then turned to Mrs. Malins and said: (151)

"There's a nice husband for you, Mrs. Malins." (152)

While she was threading her way back across the room Mrs. Malins, without adverting to the interruption, went on to tell Gabriel what beautiful places there were in Scotland and beautiful scenery. Her son-in-law brought them every year to the lakes and they used to go fishing. Her son-in-law was a splendid fisher. One day he caught a beautiful big fish and the man in the hotel cooked it for their dinner. (153)

Gabriel hardly heard what she said. Now that supper was coming near he began to think again about his speech and about the quotation. When he saw Freddy Malins coming across the room to visit his mother Gabriel left the chair free for him and retired into the embrasure of the window. The room had already cleared and from the back room came the clatter of plates and knives. Those who still remained in the drawing-room seemed tired of dancing and were conversing quietly in little groups. Gabriel's warm trembling fingers tapped the cold pane of the window. How cool it must be outside! How pleasant it would be to walk out alone, first along by the river and then through the park! The snow would be lying on the branches of the trees and forming a bright cap on the top of the Wellington Monument. How much more pleasant it would be there than at the supper-table! (154)

He ran over the headings of his speech: Irish hospitality, sad memories, the Three Graces, Paris, the quotation from Browning. He repeated to himself a phrase he had written in his review: "One feels that one is listening to a thought-tormented music." Miss Ivors had praised the review. Was she sincere? Had she really any life of her own behind all her propagandism? There had never been any ill-feeling between them until that night. It unnerved him to think that she would be at the supper-table, looking up at him while he spoke with her critical quizzing eyes. Perhaps she would not be sorry to see him fail in his speech. An idea came into his mind and gave him courage. He would say, alluding to Aunt Kate and Aunt Julia: "Ladies and Gentlemen, the generation which is now on the wane among us may have had its faults but for my part I think it had certain qualities of hospitality, of humour, of humanity, which the new and very serious and hypereducated generation that is growing up around us seems to me to lack." Very good: that was one for Miss Ivors. What did he care that his aunts were only two ignorant old women? (155)

A murmur in the room attracted his attention. Mr. Browne was advancing from the door, gallantly escorting Aunt Julia, who leaned upon his arm, smiling and hanging her head. An irregular musketry of applause escorted her also as far as the piano and then, as Mary Jane seated herself on the stool, and Aunt Julia, no longer smiling, half turned so as to pitch her voice fairly into the room, gradually ceased. Gabriel recognised the prelude. It was that of an old song of Aunt Julia's—*Arrayed for the Bridal.* Her voice, strong and clear in tone, attacked with great spirit the runs which embellish the air and though she sang very rapidly she did not miss even the smallest of the grace notes. To follow the voice, without looking at the singer's face, was to feel and share the excitement of swift and secure flight. Gabriel applauded loudly with all the others at the close of the song and loud applause was borne in from the invisible supper-table. It sounded so genuine that a little colour struggled into Aunt Julia's face as she bent to replace in the music-stand the old leather-bound song-book that had her initials on the cover. Freddy Malins, who had listened with his head perched sideways to hear her better, was still applauding when everyone else had ceased and talking animatedly to his mother who nodded her head gravely and slowly in acquiescence. At last, when he could clap no more, he stood up suddenly and hurried across the room to Aunt Julia whose hand he seized and held in both his hands, shaking it when words failed him or the catch in his voice proved too much for him. (156)

"I was just telling my mother," he said, "I never heard you sing so well, never. No, I never heard your voice so good as it is to-night. Now! Would you believe that now? That's the truth. Upon my word and honour that's the truth. I never heard your voice sound so fresh and so . . . so clear and fresh, never." (157)

Aunt Julia smiled broadly and murmured something about compliments as she released her hand from his grasp. Mr. Browne extended his open hand towards her and said to those who were near him in the manner of a showman introducing a prodigy to an audience: (158)

"Miss Julia Morkan, my latest discovery!" (159)

He was laughing very heartily at this himself when Freddy Malins turned to him and said: (160)

"Well, Browne, if you're serious you might make a worse discovery. All I can say is I never heard her sing half so well as long as I am coming here. And that's the honest truth." (161)

"Neither did I," said Mr. Browne. "I think her voice has greatly improved." (162)

Aunt Julia shrugged her shoulders and said with meek pride: (163)

"Thirty years ago I hadn't a bad voice as voices go." (164)

"I often told Julia," said Aunt Kate emphatically, "that she was simply thrown away in that choir. But she never would be said by me." (165)

She turned as if to appeal to the good sense of the others against a refractory child while Aunt Julia gazed in front of her, a vague smile of reminiscence playing on her face. (166)

"No," continued Aunt Kate, "she wouldn't be said or led by anyone, slaving there in that choir night and day, night and day. Six o'clock on Christmas morning! And all for what?" (167)

"Well, isn't it for the honour of God, Aunt Kate?" asked Mary Jane, twisting round on the piano-stool and smiling. (168)

Aunt Kate turned fiercely on her niece and said: (169)

"I know all about the honour of God, Mary Jane, but I think it's not at all honourable for the pope to turn out the women of the choirs that have slaved there all their lives and put little whippersnappers of boys over their heads. I suppose it is for the good of the Church if the pope does it. But it's not just, Mary Jane, and it's not right." (170)

She had worked herself into a passion and would have continued in defence of her sister for it was a sore subject with her but Mary Jane, seeing that all the dancers had come back, intervened pacifically: (171)

"Now, Aunt Kate, you're giving scandal to Mr. Browne who is of the other persuasion." (172)

Aunt Kate turned to Mr. Browne, who was grinning at this allusion to his religion, and said hastily: (173)

"O, I don't question the pope's being right. I'm only a stupid old woman

and I wouldn't presume to do such a thing. But there's such a thing as common everyday politeness and gratitude. And if I were in Julia's place I'd tell
that Father Healey straight up to his face . . ."   (174)

"And besides, Aunt Kate," said Mary Jane, "we really are all hungry and
when we are hungry we are all very quarrelsome."   (175)

"And when we are thirsty we are also quarrelsome," added Mr. Browne.
(176)

"So that we had better go to supper," said Mary Jane, "and finish the
discussion afterwards."   (177)

On the landing outside the drawing-room Gabriel found his wife and
Mary Jane trying to persuade Miss Ivors to stay for supper. But Miss Ivors,
who had put on her hat and was buttoning her cloak, would not stay. She
did not feel in the least hungry and she had already overstayed her time.
(178)

"But only for ten minutes, Molly," said Mrs. Conroy. "That won't delay
you."   (179)

"To take a pick itself," said Mary Jane, "after all your dancing."   (180)

"I really couldn't," said Miss Ivors.   (181)

"I am afraid you didn't enjoy yourself at all," said Mary Jane hopelessly.
(182)

"Ever so much, I assure you," said Miss Ivors, "but you really must let
me run off now."   (183)

"But how can you get home?" asked Mrs. Conroy.   (184)·

"O, it's only two steps up the quay."   (185)

Gabriel hesitated a moment and said: (186)

"If you will allow me, Miss Ivors, I'll see you home if you are really
obliged to go."   (187)

But Miss Ivors broke away from them.   (188)

"I won't hear of it," she cried. "For goodness' sake go in to your suppers
and don't mind me. I'm quite well able to take care of myself."   (189)

"Well, you're the comical girl, Molly," said Mrs. Conroy frankly.   (190)

"*Beannacht libh*," cried Miss Ivors, with a laugh, as she ran down the
staircase.   (191)

Mary Jane gazed after her, a moody puzzled expression on her face,
while Mrs. Conroy leaned over the banisters to listen for the hall-door.
Gabriel asked himself was he the cause of her abrupt departure. But she did
not seem to be in ill humour: she had gone away laughing. He stared
blankly down the staircase.   (192)

At the moment Aunt Kate came toddling out of the supper-room, almost
wringing her hands in despair.   (193)

"Where is Gabriel?" she cried. "Where on earth is Gabriel? There's
everyone waiting in there, stage to let, and nobody to carve the goose!"
(194)

"Here I am, Aunt Kate!" cried Gabriel, with sudden animation, "ready to carve a flock of geese, if necessary." (195)

A fat brown goose lay at one end of the table and at the other end, on a bed of creased paper strewn with sprigs of parsley, lay a great ham, stripped of its outer skin and peppered over with crust crumbs, a neat paper frill round its shin and beside this was a round of spiced beef. Between these rival ends ran parallel lines of side-dishes: two little minsters of jelly, red and yellow; a shallow dish full of blocks of blancmange and red jam, a large green leaf-shaped dish with a stalk-shaped handle, on which lay bunches of purple raisins and peeled almonds, a companion dish on which lay a solid rectangle of Smyrna figs, a dish of custard topped with grated nutmeg, a small bowl full of chocolates and sweets wrapped in gold and silver papers and a glass vase in which stood some tall celery stalks. In the centre of the table there stood, as sentries to a fruit-stand which upheld a pyramid of oranges and American apples, two squat old-fashioned decanters of cut glass, one containing port and the other dark sherry. On the closed square piano a pudding in a huge yellow dish lay in waiting and behind it were three squads of bottles of stout and ale and minerals, drawn up according to the colours of their uniforms, the first two black, with brown and red labels, the third and smallest squad white, with transverse green sashes. (196)

Gabriel took his seat boldly at the head of the table and, having looked to the edge of the carver, plunged his fork firmly into the goose. He felt quite at ease now for he was an expert carver and liked nothing better than to find himself at the head of a well-laden table. (197)

"Miss Furlong, what shall I send you?" he asked. "A wing or a slice of the breast?" (198)

"Just a small slice of the breast." (199)

"Miss Higgins, what for you?" (200)

"O, anything at all, Mr. Conroy." (201)

While Gabriel and Miss Daly exchanged plates of goose and plates of ham and spiced beef Lily went from guest to guest with a dish of hot floury potatoes wrapped in a white napkin. This was Mary Jane's idea and she had also suggested apple sauce for the goose but Aunt Kate had said that plain roast goose without any apple sauce had always been good enough for her and she hoped she might never eat worse. Mary Jane waited on her pupils and saw that they got the best slices and Aunt Kate and Aunt Julia opened and carried across from the piano bottles of stout and ale for the gentlemen and bottles of minerals for the ladies. There was a great deal of confusion and laughter and noise, the noise of orders and counter-orders, of knives and forks, of corks and glass-stoppers. Gabriel began to carve second helpings as soon as he had finished the first round without serving himself. Everyone protested loudly so that he compromised by taking a long draught of stout for he had found the carving hot work. Mary Jane settled down quietly to her supper but Aunt Kate and Aunt Julia were still toddling round the table, walking on each other's heels, getting in each other's way and giving each other unheeded orders. Mr. Browne begged of them to sit down and eat their suppers and so did Gabriel but they said there was time enough, so that, at last, Freddy Malins stood up and, capturing Aunt Kate, plumped her down on her chair amid general laughter.   (202)

When everyone had been well served Gabriel said, smiling: (203)

"Now, if anyone wants a little more of what vulgar people call stuffing let him or her speak."   (204)

A chorus of voices invited him to begin his own supper and Lily came forward with three potatoes which she had reserved for him.   (205)

"Very well," said Gabriel amiably, as he took another preparatory draught, "kindly forget my existence, ladies and gentlemen, for a few minutes."   (206)

He set to his supper and took no part in the conversation with which the table covered Lily's removal of the plates. The subject of talk was the opera company which was then at the Theatre Royal. Mr. Bartell D'Arcy, the tenor, a dark-complexioned young man with a smart moustache, praised very highly the leading contralto of the company but Miss Furlong thought she had a rather vulgar style of production. Freddy Malins said there was a negro chieftain singing in the second part of the Gaiety pantomime who had one of the finest tenor voices he had ever heard.   (207)

"Have you heard him?" he asked Mr. Bartell D'Arcy across the table.
                    (208)

"No," answered Mr. Bartell D'Arcy carelessly.   (209)

"Because," Freddy Malins explained, "now I'd be curious to hear your opinion of him. I think he has a grand voice."   (210)

"It takes Teddy to find out the really good things," said Mr. Browne familiarly to the table.   (211)

"And why couldn't he have a voice too?" asked Freddy Malins sharply. "Is it because he's only a black?"   (212)

Nobody answered this question and Mary Jane led the table back to the legitimate opera. One of her pupils had given her a pass for *Mignon*. Of course it was very fine, she said, but it made her think of poor Georgina Burns. Mr. Browne could go back farther still, to the old Italian companies that used to come to Dublin—Tietjens, Ilma de Murzka, Campanini, the great Trebelli Giuglini, Ravelli, Aramburo. Those were the days, he said, when there was something like singing to be heard in Dublin. He told too of how the top gallery of the old Royal used to be packed night after night, of how one night an Italian tenor had sung five encores to *Let me like a Soldier fall*, introducing a high C every time, and of how the gallery boys would sometimes in their enthusiasm unyoke the horses from the carriage of some great *prima donna* and pull her themselves through the streets to her hotel. Why did they never play the grand old operas now, he asked, *Dinorah, Lucrezia Borgia?* Because they could not get the voices to sing them: that was why. (213)

"O, well," said Mr. Bartell D'Arcy, "I presume there are as good singers to-day as there were then." (214)

"Where are they?" asked Mr. Browne defiantly. (215)

"In London, Paris, Milan," said Mr. Bartell D'Arcy warmly. "I suppose Caruso, for example, is quite as good, if not better than any of the men you have mentioned." (216)

"Maybe so," said Mr. Browne. "But I may tell you I doubt it strongly." (217)

"O, I'd give anything to hear Caruso sing," said Mary Jane. (218)

"For me," said Aunt Kate, who had been picking a bone, "there was only one tenor. To please me, I mean. But I suppose none of you ever heard of him." (219)

"Who was he, Miss Morkan?" asked Mr. Bartell D'Arcy politely. (220)

"His name," said Aunt Kate, "was Parkinson. I heard him when he was in his prime and I think he had then the purest tenor voice that was ever put into a man's throat." (221)

"Strange," said Mr. Bartell D'Arcy. "I never even heard of him." (222)

"Yes, yes, Miss Morkan is right," said Mr. Browne. "I remember hearing of old Parkinson but he's too far back for me." (223)

"A beautiful, pure, sweet, mellow English tenor," said Aunt Kate with enthusiasm. (224)

Gabriel having finished, the huge pudding was transferred to the table. The clatter of forks and spoons began again. Gabriel's wife served out spoonfuls of the pudding and passed the plates down the table. Midway down they were held up by Mary Jane, who replenished them with raspberry or orange jelly or with blancmange and jam. The pudding was of Aunt Julia's making and she received praises for it from all quarters. She herself said that it was not quite brown enough. (225)

"Well, I hope, Miss Morkan," said Mr. Browne, "that I'm brown enough for you because, you know, I'm all brown." (226)

All the gentlemen, except Gabriel, ate some of the pudding out of compliment to Aunt Julia. As Gabriel never ate sweets the celery had been left for him. Freddy Malins also took a stalk of celery and ate it with his pudding. He had been told that celery was a capital thing for the blood and he was just then under doctor's care. Mrs. Malins, who had been silent all through the supper, said that her son was going down to Mount Melleray in a week or so. The table then spoke of Mount Melleray, how bracing the air was down there, how hospitable the monks were and how they never asked for a penny-piece from their guests. (227)

"And do you mean to say," asked Mr. Browne incredulously, "that a chap can go down there and put up there as if it were a hotel and live on the fat of the land and then come away without paying anything?"   (228)

"O, most people give some donation to the monastery when they leave," said Mary Jane.   (229)

"I wish we had an institution like that in our Church," said Mr. Browne candidly.   (230)

He was astonished to hear that the monks never spoke, got up at two in the morning and slept in their coffins. He asked what they did it for. (231)

"That's the rule of the order," said Aunt Kate firmly.   (232)

"Yes, but why?" asked Mr. Browne.   (233)

Aunt Kate repeated that it was the rule, that was all. Mr. Browne still seemed not to understand. Freddy Malins explained to him, as best he could, that the monks were trying to make up for the sins committed by all the sinners in the outside world. The explanation was not very clear for Mr. Browne grinned and said: (234)

"I like that idea very much but wouldn't a comfortable spring bed do them as well as a coffin?"   (235)

"The coffin," said Mary Jane, "is to remind them of their last end."   (236)

As the subject had grown lugubrious it was buried in a silence of the table during which Mrs. Malins could be heard saying to her neighbour in an indistinct undertone: (237)

"They are very good men, the monks, very pious men."   (238)

The raisins and almonds and figs and apples and oranges and chocolates and sweets were now passed about the table and Aunt Julia invited all the guests to have either port or sherry. At first Mr. Bartell D'Arcy refused to take either but one of his neighbours nudged him and whispered something to him upon which he allowed his glass to be filled. Gradually as the last glasses were being filled the conversation ceased. A pause followed, broken only by the noise of the wine and by unsettlings of chairs. The Misses Morkan, all three, looked down at the tablecloth. Someone coughed once or twice and then a few gentlemen patted the table gently as a signal for silence. The silence came and Gabriel pushed back his chair and stood up.   (239)

The patting at once grew louder in encouragement and then ceased altogether. Gabriel leaned his ten trembling fingers on the tablecloth and smiled nervously at the company. Meeting a row of upturned faces he raised his eyes to the chandelier. The piano was playing a waltz tune and he could hear the skirts sweeping against the drawing-room door. People, perhaps, were standing in the snow on the quay outside, gazing up at the lighted windows and listening to the waltz music. The air was pure there. In the distance lay the park where the trees were weighted with snow. The

Wellington Monument wore a gleaming cap of snow that flashed westward over the white field of Fifteen Acres. (240)

He began: (241)

"Ladies and Gentlemen, (242)

"It has fallen to my lot this evening, as in years past, to perform a very pleasing task but a task for which I am afraid my poor powers as a speaker are all too inadequate." (243)

"No, no!" said Mr. Browne. (244)

"But, however that may be, I can only ask you to-night to take the will for the deed and to lend me your attention for a few moments while I endeavour to express to you in words what my feelings are on this occasion. (245)

"Ladies and Gentlemen, it is not the first time that we have gathered together under this hospitable roof, around this hospitable board. It is not the first time that we have been the recipients—or perhaps, I had better say, the victims—of the hospitality of certain good ladies." (246)

He made a circle in the air with his arm and paused. Everyone laughed or smiled at Aunt Kate and Aunt Julia and Mary Jane who all turned crimson with pleasure. Gabriel went on more boldly: (247)

"I feel more strongly with every recurring year that our country has no tradition which does it so much honour and which it should guard so jealously as that of its hospitality. It is a tradition that is unique as far as my experience goes (and I have visited not a few places abroad) among the modern nations. Some would say, perhaps, that with us it is rather a failing than anything to be boasted of. But granted even that, it is, to my mind, a princely failing, and one that I trust will long be cultivated among us. Of one thing, at least, I am sure. As long as this one roof shelters the good ladies aforesaid—and I wish from my heart it may do so for many and many a long year to come—the tradition of genuine warm-hearted courteous Irish hospitality, which our forefathers have handed down to us and which we in turn must hand down to our descendants, is still alive among us." (248)

A hearty murmur of assent ran round the table. It shot through Gabriel's mind that Miss Ivors was not there and that she had gone away discourteously: and he said with confidence in himself: (249)

"Ladies and Gentlemen, (250)

"A new generation is growing up in our midst, a generation actuated by new ideas and new principles. It is serious and enthusiastic for these new ideas and its enthusiasm, even when it is misdirected, is, I believe, in the main sincere. But we are living in a sceptical and, if I may use the phrase, a thought-tormented age: and sometimes I fear that this new generation, educated or hypereducated as it is, will lack those qualities of humanity, of hospitality, of kindly humour which belonged to an older day. Listening to-night to the names of all those great singers of the past it seemed to me,

I must confess, that we were living in a less spacious age. Those days might, without exaggeration, be called spacious days: and if they are gone beyond recall let us hope, at least, that in gatherings such as this we shall still speak of them with pride and affection, still cherish in our hearts the memory of those dead and gone great ones whose fame the world will not willingly let die."   (251)

"Hear, hear!" said Mr. Browne loudly.   (252)

"But yet," continued Gabriel, his voice falling into a softer inflection, "there are always in gatherings such as this sadder thoughts that will recur to our minds: thoughts of the past, of youth, of changes, of absent faces that we miss here to-night. Our path through life is strewn with many such sad memories: and were we to brood upon them always we could not find the heart to go on bravely with our work among the living. We have all of us living duties and living affections which claim, and rightly claim, our strenuous endeavours.   (253)

"Therefore, I will not linger on the past. I will not let any gloomy moralising intrude upon us here to-night. Here we are gathered together for a brief moment from the bustle and rush of our everyday routine. We are met here as friends, in the spirit of good-fellowship, as colleagues, also to a certain extent, in the true spirit of *camaraderie,* and as the guests of—what shall I call them?—the Three Graces of the Dublin musical world."   (254)

The table burst into applause and laughter at this allusion. Aunt Julia vainly asked each of her neighbours in turn to tell her what Gabriel had said.   (255)

"He says we are the Three Graces, Aunt Julia," said Mary Jane.   (256)

Aunt Julia did not understand but she looked up, smiling, at Gabriel, who continued in the same vein: (257)

"Ladies and Gentlemen,   (258)

"I will not attempt to play to-night the part that Paris played on another occasion. I will not attempt to choose between them. The task would be an invidious one and one beyond my poor powers. For when I view them in turn, whether it be our chief hostess herself, whose good heart, whose too good heart, has become a byword with all who know her, or her sister, who seems to be gifted with perennial youth and whose singing must have been a surprise and a revelation to us all to-night, or, last but not least, when I consider our youngest hostess, talented, cheerful, hard-working and the best of nieces, I confess, Ladies and Gentlemen, that I do not know to which of them I should award the prize."   (259)

Gabriel glanced down at his aunts and, seeing the large smile on Aunt Julia's face and the tears which had risen to Aunt Kate's eyes, hastened to his close. He raised his glass of port gallantly, while every member of the company fingered a glass expectantly, and said loudly: (260)

"Let us toast them all three together. Let us drink to their health, wealth, long life, happiness and prosperity and may they long continue to hold the proud and self-won position which they hold in their profession and the position of honour and affection which they hold in our hearts."　　(261)

All the guests stood up, glass in hand, and turning towards the three seated ladies, sang in unison, with Mr. Browne as leader:

> "For they are jolly gay fellows,
> For they are jolly gay fellows,
> For they are jolly gay fellows,
> Which nobody can deny."　　(262)

Aunt Kate was making frank use of her handkerchief and even Aunt Julia seemed moved. Freddy Malins beat time with his pudding-fork and the singers turned towards one another, as if in melodious conference, while they sang with emphasis:

> "Unless he tells a lie,
> Unless he tells a lie."　　(263)

Then, turning once more towards their hostesses, they sang:

> "For they are jolly gay fellows,
> For they are jolly gay fellows,
> For they are jolly gay fellows,
> Which nobody can deny."　　(264)

The acclamation which followed was taken up beyond the door of the supper-room by many of the other guests and renewed time after time, Freddy Malins acting as officer with his fork on high.　　(265)

The piercing morning air came into the hall where they were standing so that Aunt Kate said:　　(266)

"Close the door, somebody. Mrs. Malins will get her death of cold."　　(267)

"Browne is out there, Aunt Kate," said Mary Jane.　　(268)

"Browne is everywhere," said Aunt Kate, lowering her voice.　　(269)

Mary Jane laughed at her tone.　　(270)

"Really," she said archly, "he is very attentive."　　(271)

"He has been laid on here like the gas," said Aunt Kate in the same tone, "all during the Christmas."　　(272)

She laughed herself this time good-humouredly and then added quickly:　　(273)

"But tell him to come in, Mary Jane, and close the door. I hope to goodness he didn't hear me."　　(274)

At that moment the hall-door was opened and Mr. Browne came in from the doorstep, laughing as if his heart would break. He was dressed in a long green overcoat with mock astrakhan cuffs and collar and wore on his

head an oval fur cap. He pointed down the snow-covered quay from where
the sound of shrill prolonged whistling was borne in.   (275)

"Teddy will have all the cabs in Dublin out," he said.   (276)

Gabriel advanced from the little pantry behind the office, struggling into
his overcoat and, looking round the hall, said: (277)

"Gretta not down yet?"   (278)

"She's getting on her things, Gabriel," said Aunt Kate.   (279)

"Who's playing up there?" asked Gabriel.   (280)

"Nobody. They're all gone."   (281)

"O no, Aunt Kate," said Mary Jane. "Bartell D'Arcy and Miss O'Callaghan aren't gone yet."   (282)

"Someone is fooling at the piano anyhow," said Gabriel.   (283)

Mary Jane glanced at Gabriel and Mr. Browne and said with a shiver:
                                                                         (284)

"It makes me feel cold to look at you two gentlemen muffled up like
that. I wouldn't like to face your journey home at this hour."   (285)

"I'd like nothing better this minute," said Mr. Browne stoutly, "than a
rattling fine walk in the country or a fast drive with a good spanking goer
between the shafts."   (286)

"We used to have a very good horse and trap at home," said Aunt Julia
sadly.   (287)

"The never-to-be-forgotten Johnny," said Mary Jane, laughing.   (288)

Aunt Kate and Gabriel laughed too.   (289)

"Why, what was wonderful about Johnnny?" asked Mr. Browne.   (290)

"The late lamented Patrick Morkan, our grandfather, that is," explained
Gabriel, "commonly known in his later years as the old gentleman, was a
glue-boiler."   (291)

"O, now, Gabriel," said Aunt Kate, laughing, "he had a starch mill."
                                                                         (292)

"Well, glue or starch," said Gabriel, "the old gentleman had a horse by
the name of Johnny. And Johnny used to work in the old gentleman's mill,
walking round and round in order to drive the mill. That was all very well:
but now comes the tragic part about Johnny. One fine day the old gentleman thought he'd like to drive out with the quality to a military review in
the park."   (293)

"The Lord have mercy on his soul," said Aunt Kate compassionately.
                                                                         (294)

"Amen," said Gabriel. "So the old gentleman, as I said, harnessed Johnny
and put on his very best tall hat and his very best stock collar and drove out
in grand style from his ancestral mansion somewhere near Back Lane, I
think."   (295)

Everyone laughed, even Mrs. Malins, at Gabriel's manner and Aunt
Kate said: (296)

"O, now, Gabriel, he didn't live in Back Lane, really. Only the mill was there." (297)

"Out from the mansion of his forefathers," continued Gabriel, "he drove with Johnny. And everything went on beautifully until Johnny came in sight of King Billy's statue: and whether he fell in love with the horse King Billy sits on or whether he thought he was back again in the mill, anyhow he began to walk round the statue." (298)

Gabriel paced in a circle round the hall in his goloshes amid the laughter of the others. (299)

"Round and round he went," said Gabriel, "and the old gentleman, who was a very pompous old gentleman, was highly indignant. 'Go on, sir! What do you mean, sir? Johnny! Johnny! Most extraordinary conduct! Can't understand the horse!'" (300)

The peals of laughter which followed Gabriel's imitation of the incident was interrupted by a resounding knock at the hall door. Mary Jane ran to open it and let in Freddy Malins. Freddy Malins, with his hat well back on his head and his shoulders humped with cold, was puffing and steaming after his exertions. (301)

"I could only get one cab," he said. (302)

"O, we'll find another along the quay," said Gabriel. (303)

"Yes," said Aunt Kate. "Better not keep Mrs. Malins standing in the draught." (304)

Mrs. Malins was helped down the front steps by her son and Mr. Browne and, after many manœuvres, hoisted into the cab. Freddy Malins clambered in after her and spent a long time settling her on the seat, Mr. Browne helping him with advice. At last she was settled comfortably and Freddy Malins invited Mr. Browne into the cab. There was a good deal of confused talk, and then Mr. Browne got into the cab. The cabman settled his rug over his knees, and bent down for the address. The confusion grew greater and the cabman was directed differently by Freddy Malins and Mr. Browne, each of whom had his head out through a window of the cab. The difficulty was to know where to drop Mr. Browne along the route, and Aunt Kate, Aunt Julia and Mary Jane helped the discussion from the door-step with cross-directions and contradictions and abundance of laughter. As for Freddy Malins he was speechless with laughter. He popped his head in and out of the window every moment to the great danger of his hat, and told his mother how the discussion was progressing, till at last Mr. Browne shouted to the bewildered cabman above the din of everybody's laughter: (305)

"Do you know Trinity College?" (306)

"Yes, sir," said the cabman. (307)

"Well, drive bang up against Trinity College gates," said Mr. Browne, "and then we'll tell you where to go. You understand now?" (308)

"Yes, sir," said the cabman. (309)

"Make like a bird for Trinity College." (310)

"Right, sir," said the cabman. (311)

The horse was whipped up and the cab rattled off along the quay amid a chorus of laughter and adieus. (312)

Gabriel had not gone to the door with the others. He was in a dark part of the hall gazing up the staircase. A woman was standing near the top of the first flight, in the shadow also. He could not see her face but he could see the terracotta and salmon-pink panels of her skirt which the shadow made appear black and white. It was his wife. She was leaning on the banisters, listening to something. Gabriel was surprised at her stillness and strained his ear to listen also. But he could hear little save the noise of laughter and dispute on the front steps, a few chords struck on the piano and a few notes of a man's voice singing. (313)

He stood still in the gloom of the hall, trying to catch the air that the voice was singing and gazing up at his wife. There was grace and mystery in her attitude as if she were a symbol of something. He asked himself what is a woman standing on the stairs in the shadow, listening to distant music, a symbol of. If he were a painter he would paint her in that attitude. Her blue felt hat would show off the bronze of her hair against the darkness and the dark panels of her skirt would show off the light ones. *Distant Music* he would call the picture if he were a painter. (314)

The hall-door was closed; and Aunt Kate, Aunt Julia and Mary Jane came down the hall, still laughing. (315)

"Well, isn't Freddy terrible?" said Mary Jane. "He's really terrible." (316)

Gabriel said nothing but pointed up the stairs towards where his wife was standing. Now that the hall-door was closed the voice and the piano could be heard more clearly. Gabriel held up his hand for them to be silent. The song seemed to be in the old Irish tonality and the singer seemed uncertain both of his words and of his voice. The voice, made plaintive by distance and by the singer's hoarseness, faintly illuminated the cadence of the air with words expressing grief:

> "O, the rain falls on my heavy locks
> And the dew wets my skin,
> My babe lies cold . . ." (317)

"O," exclaimed Mary Jane. "It's Bartell D'Arcy singing and he wouldn't sing all the night. O, I'll get him to sing a song before he goes." (318)

"O, do, Mary Jane," said Aunt Kate. (319)

Mary Jane brushed past the others and ran to the staircase, but before she reached it the singing stopped and the piano was closed abruptly. (302)

"O, what a pity! she cried. "Is he coming down, Gretta?"   (321)

Gabriel heard his wife answer yes and saw her come down towards them. A few steps behind her were Mr. Bartell D'Arcy and Miss O'Callaghan.   (322)

"O, Mr. D'Arcy," cried Mary Jane, "it's downright mean of you to break off like that when we were all in raptures listening to you."   (323)

"I have been at him all the evening," said Miss O'Callaghan, "and Mrs. Conroy, too, and he told us he had a dreadful cold and couldn't sing." (324)

"O, Mr. D'Arcy," said Aunt Kate, "now that was a great fib to tell." (325)

"Can't you see that I'm as hoarse as a crow?" said Mr. D'Arcy roughly.   (326)

He went into the pantry hastily and put on his overcoat. The others, taken aback by his rude speech, could find nothing to say. Aunt Kate wrinkled her brows and made signs to the others to drop the subject. Mr. D'Arcy stood swathing his neck carefully and frowning.   (327)

"It's the weather," said Aunt Julia, after a pause.   (328)

"Yes, everybody has colds," said Aunt Kate readily, "everybody." (329)

"They say," said Mary Jane, "we haven't had snow like it for thirty years; and I read this morning in the newspapers that the snow is general all over Ireland."   (330)

"I love the look of snow," said Aunt Julia sadly.   (331)

"So do I," said Miss O'Callaghan. "I think Christmas is never really Christmas unless we have the snow on the ground."   (332)

"But poor Mr. D'Arcy doesn't like the snow," said Aunt Kate, smiling.   (333)

Mr. D'Arcy came from the pantry, fully swathed and buttoned, and in a repentant tone told them the history of his cold. Everyone gave him advice and said it was a great pity and urged him to be very careful of his throat in the night air. Gabriel watched his wife, who did not join in the conversation. She was standing right under the dusty fanlight and the flame of the gas lit up the rich bronze of her hair, which he had seen her drying at the fire a few days before. She was in the same attitude and seemed unaware of the talk about her. At last she turned towards them and Gabriel saw that there was colour on her cheeks and that her eyes were shining. A sudden tide of joy went leaping out of his heart.   (334)

"Mr. D'Arcy," she said, "what is the name of that song you were singing?"   (335)

"It's called *The Lass of Aughrim*," said Mr. D'Arcy, "but I couldn't remember it properly. Why? Do you know it?"   (336)

"*The Lass of Aughrim*," she repeated. "I couldn't think of the name."   (337)

"It's a very nice air," said Mary Jane. "I'm sorry you were not in voice to-night."   (338)

"Now, Mary Jane," said Aunt Kate, "don't annoy Mr. D'Arcy. I won't have him annoyed." (339)

Seeing that all were ready to start she shepherded them to the door, where good-night was said: (340)

"Well, good-night, Aunt Kate, and thanks for the pleasant evening." (341)

"Good-night, Gabriel. Good-night, Gretta!" (342)

"Good-night, Aunt Kate, and thanks ever so much. Good-night, Aunt Julia." (343)

"O, good-night, Gretta, I didn't see you." (344)

"Good-night, Mr. D'Arcy. Good-night, Miss O'Callaghan." (345)

"Good-night, Miss Morkan." (346)

"Good-night, again." (347)

"Good-night, all. Safe home." (348)

"Good-night. Good night." (349)

The morning was still dark. A dull, yellow light brooded over the houses and the river; and the sky seemed to be descending. It was slushy underfoot; and only streaks and patches of snow lay on the roofs, on the parapets of the quay and on the area railings. The lamps were still burning redly in the murky air and, across the river, the palace of the Four Courts stood out menacingly against the heavy sky. (350)

She was walking on before him with Mr. Bartell D'Arcy, her shoes in a brown parcel tucked under one arm and her hands holding her skirt up from the slush. She had no longer any grace of attitude, but Gabriel's eyes were still bright with happiness. The blood went bounding along his veins; and the thoughts went rioting through his brain, proud, joyful, tender, valorous. (351)

She was walking on before him so lightly and so erect that he longed to run after her noiselessly, catch her by the shoulders and say something foolish and affectionate into her ear. She seemed to him so frail that he longed to defend her against something and then to be alone with her. Moments of their secret life together burst like stars upon his memory. A heliotrope envelope was lying beside his breakfast-cup and he was caressing it with his hand. Birds were twittering in the ivy and the sunny web of the curtain was shimmering along the floor: he could not eat for happiness. They were standing on the crowded platform and he was placing a ticket inside the warm palm of her glove. He was standing with her in the cold, looking in through a grated window at a man making bottles in a roaring furnace. It was very cold. Her face, fragrant in the cold air, was quite close to his; and suddenly he called out to the man at the furnace: (352)

"Is the fire hot, sir?" (353)

But the man could not hear with the noise of the furnace. It was just as well. He might have answered rudely. (354)

A wave of yet more tender joy escaped from his heart and went coursing in warm flood along his arteries. Like the tender fire of stars moments of their life together, that no one knew of or would ever know of, broke upon and illumined his memory. He longed to recall to her those moments, to make her forget the years of their dull existence together and remember only their moments of ecstasy. For the years, he felt, had not quenched his soul or hers. Their children, his writing, her household cares had not quenched all their souls' tender fire. In one letter that he had written to her then he had said: "Why is it that words like these seem to me so dull and cold? Is it because there is no word tender enough to be your name?" (355)

Like distant music these words that he had written years before were borne towards him from the past. He longed to be alone with her. When the others had gone away, when he and she were in the room in the hotel, then they would be alone together. He would call her softly: (356)

"Gretta!"   (357)

Perhaps she would not hear at once: she would be undressing. Then something in his voice would strike her. She would turn and look at him. . . .
(358)

At the corner of Winetavern Street they met a cab. He was glad of its rattling noise as it saved him from conversation. She was looking out of the window and seemed tired. The others spoke only a few words, pointing out some building or street. The horse galloped along wearily under the murky morning sky, dragging his old rattling box after his heels, and Gabriel was again in a cab with her, galloping to catch the boat, galloping to their honeymoon.   (359)

As the cab drove across O'Connell Bridge Miss O'Callaghan said:

"They say you never cross O'Connell Bridge without seeing a white horse."   (360)

"I see a white man this time," said Gabriel.   (361)

"Where?" asked Mr. Bartell D'Arcy.   (362)

Gabriel pointed to the statue, on which lay patches of snow. Then he nodded familiarly to it and waved his hand.   (363)

"Good-night, Dan," he said gaily.   (364)

When the cab drew up before the hotel, Gabriel jumped out and, in spite of Mr. Bartell D'Arcy's protest, paid the driver. He gave the man a shilling over his fare. The man saluted and said: (365)

"A prosperous New Year to you, sir."   (366)

"The same to you," said Gabriel cordially.   (367)

She leaned for a moment on his arm in getting out of the cab and while standing at the curbstone, bidding the others good-night. She leaned lightly on his arm, as lightly as when she had danced with him a few hours before. He had felt proud and happy then, happy that she was his, proud of her grace and wifely carriage. But now, after the kindling again of so many memories, the first touch of her body, musical and strange and perfumed, sent through him a keen pang of lust. Under cover of her silence he pressed her arm closely to his side, and, as they stood at the hotel door, he felt that they had escaped from their lives and duties, escaped from home and friends and run away together with wild and radiant hearts to a new adventure.   (368)

An old man was dozing in a great hooded chair in the hall. He lit a candle in the office and went before them to the stairs. They followed him in silence, their feet falling in soft thuds on the thickly carpeted stairs. She mounted the stairs behind the porter, her head bowed in the ascent, her frail shoulders curved as with a burden, her skirt girt tightly about her. He could have flung his arms about her hips and held her still, for his arms were trembling with desire to seize her and only the stress of his nails against the palms of his hands held the wild impulse of his body in check. The porter halted on the stairs to settle his guttering candle. They halted, too, on the steps below him. In the silence Gabriel could hear the falling of the molten wax into the tray and the thumping of his own heart against his ribs.   (369)

The porter led them along a corridor and opened a door. Then he set his unstable candle down on a toilet-table and asked at what hour they were to be called in the morning.   (370)

"Eight," said Gabriel.   (371)

The porter pointed to the tap of the electric-light and began a muttered apology, but Gabriel cut him short.   (372)

"We don't want any light. We have light enough from the street. And I say," he added, pointing to the candle, "you might remove that handsome article, like a good man."   (373)

The porter took up his candle again, but slowly, for he was surprised by such a novel idea. Then he mumbled good-night and went out. Gabriel shot the lock to.   (374)

A ghastly light from the street lamp lay in a long shaft from one window to the door. Gabriel threw his overcoat and hat on a couch and crossed the room towards the window. He looked down into the street in order that his emotion might calm a little. Then he turned and leaned against a chest of drawers with his back to the light. She had taken off her hat and cloak and was standing before a large swinging mirror, unhooking her waist. Gabriel paused for a few moments, watching her, and then said: (375)

"Gretta!"   (376)

She turned away from the mirror slowly and walked along the shaft of light towards him. Her face looked so serious and weary that the words would not pass Gabriel's lips. No, it was not the moment yet.   (377)

"You looked tired," he said.   (378)

"I am a little," she answered.   (379)

"You don't feel ill or weak?" (380)

"No, tired: that's all." (381)

She went on to the window and stood there, looking out. Gabriel waited again and then, fearing that diffidence was about to conquer him, he said abruptly: (382)

"By the way, Gretta!" (383)

"What is it?" (384)

"You know that poor fellow Malins?" he said quickly. (385)

"Yes. What about him?" (386)

"Well, poor fellow, he's a decent sort of chap, after all," continued Gabriel in a false voice. "He gave me back that sovereign I lent him, and I didn't expect it, really. It's a pity he wouldn't keep away from that Browne, because he's not a bad fellow, really." (387)

He was trembling now with annoyance. Why did she seem so abstracted? He did not know how he could begin. Was she annoyed, too, about something? If she would only turn to him or come to him of her own accord! To take her as she was would be brutal. No, he must see some ardour in her eyes first. He longed to be master of her strange mood. (388)

"When did you lend him the pound?" she asked, after a pause. (389)

Gabriel strove to restrain himself from breaking out into brutal language about the sottish Malins and his pound. He longed to cry to her from his soul, to crush her body against his, to overmaster her. But he said: (390)

"O, at Christmas, when he opened that little Christmas-card shop in Henry Street." (391)

He was in such a fever of rage and desire that he did not hear her come from the window. She stood before him for an instant, looking at him strangely. Then, suddenly raising herself on tiptoe and resting her hands lightly on his shoulders, she kissed him. (392)

"You are a very generous person, Gabriel," she said. (393)

Gabriel, trembling with delight at her sudden kiss and at the quaintness of her phrase, put his hands on her hair and began smoothing it back, scarcely touching it with his fingers. The washing had made it fine and brilliant. His heart was brimming over with happiness. Just when he was wishing for it she had come to him of her own accord. Perhaps her thoughts had been running with his. Perhaps she had felt the impetuous desire that was in him, and then the yielding mood had come upon her. Now that she had fallen to him so easily, he wondered why he had been so diffident. (394)

He stood, holding her head between his hands. Then, slipping one arm swiftly about her body and drawing her towards him, he said softly: (395)

"Gretta, dear, what are you thinking about?" (396)

She did not answer nor yield wholly to his arm. He said again, softly: (397)

"Tell me what it is, Gretta. I think I know what is the matter. Do I know?" (398)

She did not answer at once. Then she said in an outburst of tears: (399)

"O, I am thinking about that song, *The Lass of Aughrim.*" (400)

She broke loose from him and ran to the bed and, throwing her arms across the bed-rail, hid her face. Gabriel stood stock-still for a moment in astonishment and then followed her. As he passed in the way of the cheval-glass he caught sight of himself in full length, his broad, well-filled shirt-front, the face whose expression always puzzled him when he saw it in a mirror, and his glimmering gilt-rimmed eye-glasses. He halted a few paces from her and said: (401)

"What about the song? Why does that make you cry?" (402)

She raised her head from her arms and dried her eyes with the back of her hand like a child. A kinder note than he had intended went into his voice. (403)

"Why, Gretta?" he asked. (404)

"I am thinking about a person long ago who used to sing that song." (405)

"And who was the person long ago?" asked Gabriel, smiling. (406)

"It was a person I used to know in Galway when I was living with my grandmother," she said. (407)

The smile passed away from Gabriel's face. A dull anger began to gather again at the back of his mind and the dull fires of his lust began to glow angrily in his veins. (408)

"Someone you were in love with?" he asked ironically. (409)

"It was a young boy I used to know," she answered, "named Michael Furey. He used to sing that song, *The Lass of Aughrim.* He was very delicate." (410)

Gabriel was silent. He did not wish her to think that he was interested in this delicate boy. (411)

"I can see him so plainly," she said, after a moment. "Such eyes as he had: big, dark eyes! And such an expression in them—an expression!" (412)

"O, then, you are in love with him?" said Gabriel. (413)

"I used to go out walking with him," she said, "when I was in Galway." (414)

A thought flew across Gabriel's mind. (415)

"Perhaps that was why you wanted to go to Galway with that Ivors girl?" he said coldly. (416)

She looked at him and asked in surprise: (417)

"What for?" (418)

Her eyes made Gabriel feel awkward. He shrugged his shoulders and said: (419)

"How do I know? To see him, perhaps." (420)

She looked away from him along the shaft of light towards the window in silence. (421)

"He is dead," she said at length. "He died when he was only seventeen. Isn't it a terrible thing to die so young as that?" (422)

"What was he?" asked Gabriel, still ironically. (423)

"He was in the gasworks," she said. (424)

Gabriel felt humiliated by the failure of his irony and by the evocation of this figure from the dead, a boy in the gasworks. While he had been full of memories of their secret life together, full of tenderness and joy and desire, she had been comparing him in her mind with another. A shameful consciousness of his own person assailed him. He saw himself as a ludicrous figure, acting as a pennyboy for his aunts, a nervous, well-meaning sentimentalist, orating to vulgarians and idealising his own clownish lusts, the pitiable fatuous fellow he had caught a glimpse of in the mirror. Instinctively he turned his back more to the light lest she might see the shame that burned upon his forehead. (425)

He tried to keep up his tone of cold interrogation, but his voice when he spoke was humble and indifferent. (426)

"I suppose you were in love with this Michael Furey, Gretta," he said. (427)

"I was great with him at that time," she said. (428)

Her voice was veiled and sad. Gabriel, feeling now how vain it would be to try to lead her whither he had purposed, caressed one of her hands and said, also sadly: (429)

"And what did he die of so young, Gretta? Consumption, was it?" (430)

"I think he died for me," she answered. (431)

A vague terror seized Gabriel at this answer, as if, at that hour when he had hoped to triumph, some impalpable and vindictive being was coming against him, gathering forces against him in its vague world. But he shook himself free of it with an effort of reason and continued to caress her hand. He did not question her again, for he felt that she would tell him of herself. Her hand was warm and moist: it did not respond to his touch, but he continued to caress it just as he had caressed her first letter to him that spring morning. (432)

"It was in the winter," she said, "about the beginning of the winter when I was going to leave my grandmother's and come up here to the convent. And he was ill at the time in his lodgings in Galway and wouldn't be let out, and his people in Oughterard were written to. He was in decline, they said, or something like that. I never knew rightly." (433)

She paused for a moment and sighed. (434)

"Poor fellow," she said. "He was very fond of me and he was such a gentle boy. We used to go out together, walking, you know, Gabriel, like the way they do in the country. He was going to study singing only for his health. He had a very good voice, poor Michael Furey." (435)

"Well; and then?" asked Gabriel. (436)

"And then when it came to the time for me to leave Galway and come up to the convent he was much worse and I wouldn't be let see him so I wrote him a letter saying I was going up to Dublin and would be back in the summer, and hoping he would be better then." (437)

She paused for a moment to get her voice under control, and then went on: (438)

"Then the night before I left, I was in my grandmother's house in Nuns' Island, packing up, and I heard gravel thrown up against the window. The window was so wet I couldn't see, so I ran downstairs as I was and slipped out the back into the garden and there was the poor fellow at the end of the garden, shivering." (439)

"And did you not tell him to go back?" asked Gabriel. (440)

"I implored of him to go home at once and told him he would get his death in the rain. But he said he did not want to live. I can see his eyes as well as well! He was standing at the end of the wall where there was a tree." (441)

"And did he go home?" asked Gabriel. (442)

"Yes, he went home. And when I was only a week in the convent he died and he was buried in Oughterard, where his people came from. O, the day I heard that, that he was dead!" (443)

She stopped, choking with sobs, and, overcome by emotion, flung herself face downward on the bed, sobbing in the quilt. Gabriel held her hand for a moment longer, irresolutely, and then, shy of intruding on her grief, let it fall gently and walked quietly to the window. (444)

She was fast asleep. (445)

Gabriel, leaning on his elbow, looked for a few moments unresentfully on her tangled hair and half-open mouth, listening to her deep-drawn breath So she had had that romance in her life: a man had died for her sake. It hardly pained him now to think how poor a part he, her husband, had played in her life. He watched her while she slept, as though he and she had never lived together as man and wife. His curious eyes rested long upon her face and on her hair: and, as he thought of what she must have been then, in that time of her first girlish beauty, a strange, friendly pity for her entered his soul. He did not like to say even to himself that her face was no longer beautiful, but he knew that it was no longer the face for which Michael Furey had braved death. (446)

Perhaps she had not told him all the story. His eyes moved to the chair over which she had thrown some of her clothes. A petticoat string dangled to the floor. One boot stood upright, its limp upper fallen down: the fellow of it lay upon its side. He wondered at his riot of emotions of an hour before. From what had it proceeded? From his aunt's supper, from his own foolish speech, from the wine and dancing, the merry-making when saying good-night in the hall, the pleasure of the walk along the river in the snow. Poor Aunt Julia! She, too, would soon be a shade with the shade of Patrick Morkan and his horse. He had caught that haggard look upon her face for a moment when she was singing *Arrayed for the Bridal*. Soon, perhaps, he would be sitting in that same drawing-room, dressed in black, his silk hat on his knees. The blinds would be drawn down and Aunt Kate would be sitting beside him, crying and blowing her nose and telling him how Julia had died. He would cast about in his mind for some words that might console her, and would find only lame and useless ones. Yes, yes: that would happen very soon. (447)

The air of the room chilled his shoulders. He stretched himself cautiously along under the sheets and lay down beside his wife. One by one, they were all becoming shades. Better pass boldly into that other world, in the full glory of some passion, than fade and wither dismally with age. He thought of how she who lay beside him had locked in her heart for so many years that image of her lover's eyes when he had told her that he did not wish to live. (448)

Generous tears filled Gabriel's eyes. He had never felt like that himself towards any woman, but he knew that such a feeling must be love. The tears gathered more thickly in his eyes and in the partial darkness he imagined he saw the form of a young man standing under a dripping tree. Other forms were near. His soul had approached that region where dwell the vast hosts of the dead. He was conscious of, but could not apprehend, their wayward and flickering existence. His own identity was fading out into a grey impalpable world: the solid world itself, which these dead had one time reared and lived in, was dissolving and dwindling. (449)

A few light taps upon the pane made him turn to the window. It had begun to snow again. He watched sleepily the flakes, silver and dark, falling obliquely against the lamplight. The time had come for him to set out on his journey westward. Yes, the newspapers were right: snow was general all over Ireland. It was falling on every part of the dark central plain, on the treeless hills, falling softly upon the Bog of Allen and, farther westward, softly falling into the dark mutinous Shannon waves. It was falling, too, upon every part of the lonely churchyard on the hill where Michael Furey lay buried. It lay thickly drifted on the crooked crosses and headstones, on the spears of the little gate, on the barren thorns. His soul swooned slowly as he heard the snow falling faintly through the universe and faintly falling, like the descent of their last end, upon all the living and the dead. (450)

Glossary of
Rhetorical Terms
and
Comprehension
Questions

Glossary

Abstract words. One aspect of diction, and therefore of style, which critics find measurable is the relative use an author makes of abstract, general terms as opposed to concrete, specific terms. *Abstract words* are used to name abstract ideas or concepts. For example, Michael Harrington, in "The Two Nations," speaks of "spirit," "aspiration," "vision," "élan," "responsibility," "potential." *Concrete words,* which tend to predominate in narrative and descriptive writing, are used to name objects which can be perceived through the senses—for example, the sights and smells in Robert Penn Warren's "Blackberry Winter." There are also generic (or general) words as distinct from specific words. The words *athlete, golfer, Arnold Palmer* move from the general to the specific. *Athlete* is general, but not abstract; *athletics* is abstract. One type of word is not better than another type. Each is appropriate in its proper place, though most rhetoricians have a decided prejudice in favor, at least, of a good deal of practice on the part of youthful writers in the use of specific, concrete words. See T. S. Eliot's discussion of the terms in "The Perfect Critic," ¶9, and Orwell's discussion of the meaninglessness of many abstract words (¶8) and of the relationship between originality, vividness, and concreteness (¶11) in "Politics and the English Language." Margaret Mead, in "The Education of the Samoan Child," makes notable use of concrete words in describing an aspect of primitive culture. Twain, in "That Farm of My Uncle John's," ¶'s and 22 and *passim,* makes massive use of concrete, specific words, as does Sandburg, on a slighter scale, in "The Boyhood of Lincoln," *passim.*

Action. *Action* is one of the essential ingredients of narrative: something happens to people. It may be simple and uncomplicated—events clearly recorded and interpreted—or it may be complex and subject to various interpretations, as in Shirer's "A Turn of the Tide." Action on the level of ideas, as in Merton's "God's Will at Columbia," records incidents but subordinates them to changes in thought and belief. Warren, in "Segregation," relates ideas to a variety of personalities—shows how they act or propose to act in the face of integration.

Allusion. An *allusion* is an indirect reference, as distinct from a direct reference. For example, T. S. Eliot refers to Matthew Arnold directly in the opening paragraph of "The Perfect Critic." In the closing paragraph, he alludes to Arnold, without mentioning him by name, through Arnold's well-known distinction between "ages of criticism and ages of creativeness." A writer who makes abundant use of allusions is said to have a highly or richly allusive style. Obviously such a writer must make certain assumptions about the erudition of his audience since any miscalculation on this score would cause a serious breakdown in communication. Trilling, in "Freud and Literature," alludes to Shakespeare's *Hamlet* in ¶10 ("Gildensterns") and to Mithridates, King of Pontus (¶41). Huxley, in "Science and God: The Naturalistic Approach," alludes to Matthew Arnold in ¶7 ("a power, not ourselves") and to Lord Macaulay in ¶14 ("As every schoolboy knows"); however, he *refers* to Swift in ¶16. Russell, in "A Free Man's Worship," ¶16, alludes to Shakespeare's *Macbeth*.

Ambiguity. *Ambiguity* is a term used to describe a situation, expression, or line of thought which has two or more possible meanings or interpretations. In writing, ambiguity may be unintentional or intentional. Unintentional ambiguity leaves the exact meaning of the author obscure and indistinct. Intentional ambiguity, which is very common in literature, may be a play on words (see **PUN**) or a reflection of the author's sense of the complex nature of reality. Cleanth Brooks, in "Wordsworth and the Paradox of the Imagination," draws attention to Wordsworth's use of ambiguity in his "Ode"—especially in ¶'s 16, 19, and 47; in ¶49 he distinguishes between *ambiguity* and *confusion*. See also **PARADOX** and **IRONY**.

Analogy. An *analogy* is an extended comparison (see **METAPHOR, SIMILE**) by which an unfamiliar process or situation is clarified by being likened to a familiar process or situation. Analogy is often useful in exposition and persuasion; it is highly suspect in argument. In "Why Nations Decline," ¶1, Morgenthau discredits the "biological analogy" as a way of accounting for the decline of nations; but in ¶34 he draws an analogy between "ossified empires" and the dinosaur. Newman's uses of analogies in ¶'s 16–19 and 21 of "Literature" are valid because the terms of the analogies (Shakespeare and Cicero; the other arts and the art of literature) are compatible, and the analogies are not carried beyond a point of relevance. Analogies are found in ¶'s 7 and 27 of Arnold's "The Study of Poetry." Pater draws an analogy between good logic and good writing in ¶15 of "Style." Besides drawing a distinction between *metaphor* and *analogy* (¶'s 37–39), Illo, in "The Rhetoric of Malcolm X," uses analogies in ¶'s 33 (drawn from Malcolm X) and 50 (Malcolm X–Hamlet). McLuhan, in "Television: The Timid Giant," uses analogy frequently—e.g., ¶'s 20, 24, 49. See also Barzun, "Conversation, Manners, and the Home," ¶'s 2 and 60–61; Janson, "The Artist and His Public," ¶'s 3 and 14. Emerson, in "The American Scholar," uses analogies so plentifully that his essay might almost be said to be developed by the "analogical" method: see ¶'s 1, 12, 17, 18, 23, 24, 25, 27, 28, 34, 36, 39. Ruth Benedict, in "The Diversity of Cultures," ¶'s 6–7, makes an elaborate and excellent use of analogy ("cultural life" and "speech"). Hitler, in "Nation and Race," ¶'s 3 and 7, uses *false* analogies between "races" and "species." See also Lippmann, "The Pursuit of Liberty," ¶37; Hook, "The Conflict of Freedoms," ¶'s 9, 10, 15, 19; Frankel, "Ideals and Idols of Democracy," ¶1. See also Freud, "Repression," ¶'s 3, 4, 11, 18; Huxley, "Science and God: The Naturalistic Approach," ¶'s 11, 13–15, 16; Watts, "Sitting Quietly, Doing Nothing," ¶'s 5–10 and *passim;* Lewis, "The Abolition of Man," ¶'s 6, 9, 12 18; Tillich, "Man and History," ¶13; Twain, "That Farm of My Uncle John's," ¶2; Kazin, "School Days at Brownsville," ¶'s 8, 9; Sandburg, "The Boyhood of Lincoln," ¶25; Faulkner, "Barn Burning," ¶10.

Antithesis. One formula of argument, frequently associated with the philosopher Hegel and his followers, proceeds by a method of reconciliation of opposites: *antithesis, thesis, synthesis.* A brief but clear illustration will be found in the first footnote in Webb's "The Boom Hypothesis of Modern History." A somewhat vague but perceptible use of this dialectic appears in Emerson's "The American Scholar": *antithesis* (¶'s 13–14), *thesis* (¶'s 15–18), *synthesis,* (¶'s 19–20). It is to be found, also, in Bruner's "Motives for Learning," ¶2. See especially Mao Tse-Tung's "Methods of Thinking and Methods of Work," ¶'s 3, 15, 18, 19–21, and *passim* for a special application of dialectic. Toynbee shapes his essay, "Christianity and Civilization," on a formula of antithesis–thesis–synthesis.

Argument. *Argument* is one of the five major forms of discourse (**EXPOSITION, PERSUASION, NARRATION, DESCRIPTION**). Like *persuasion,* argument attempts to move the reader from one point to another point; unlike persuasion, which is calculated to evoke overt action, argument's principal aim is conviction, to move the reader's *mind* from one point to another. And, of course, argument makes full use of the methods of expository analysis. The following terms are relevant to argument, but are discussed separately in this glossary: *proposition, issue, evidence, induction, deduction, analogy, syllogism, fallacy, non sequitur, hasty generalization, equivocation, begging the question, ignoring the question.*

Argument and persuasion are frequently combined. The following essays, for example, have substantial elements of both argument and persuasion in them: Harrington's "The Two Nations"; Emerson's "The American Scholar"; Bestor's "The College of *Liberal* Arts and Sciences." An element of persuasion, though not at all gross, can be found in Hutchins' "The Higher Learning"—"a return to intellect" and a new emphasis in education and scholarship. McGinley ("Suburbia: Of Thee I Sing") and McCarthy ("America the Beautiful") want only to change people's views. It is men's view of the world that Ruth Benedict wishes to correct in "The Diversity of Cultures."

Sidney Hook's "The Conflict of Freedoms" provides, *in parvo*, an illustration of the traditional structure of argument:

I   Introduction (¶'s 1–6)
   A. Exordium (¶1)
   B. Exposition or Narration (¶'s 2–5)
   C. Proposition (¶6)
   D. Division of Proofs (¶6)
II   Proof (¶'s 7–19)
   A. Confirmation (¶'s 7–11)
   B. Refutation (¶'s 12–19)
III   End (¶20)
   A. Summary
   B. Conclusion

Dewey's "Science and Free Culture" provides, in action, a brief lexicon of some of the major elements of argument.

Balanced Sentence. A *balanced sentence* is a sentence containing parallel elements (phrases, clauses) of comparable length and grammatical structure. It is an effective stylistic device if it is handled with euphony and variety, as it is in Newman's essay "Literature," ¶'s 32–34 and *passim*, and in Russell's "A Free Man's Worship," ¶3 and *passim*.

Begging the Question. *Begging the question* is one of the more common logic traps or fallacies. The author takes for granted what requires proof, he makes a false or incomplete assumption, or he argues in a circle. In each case the proposition (major or minor) "goes begging." In a real sense, Hitler's whole essay is an example of question-begging, but see especially ¶28, in which he exemplifies *all three ways* of begging the question.

Beginning, Middle, and End.   (See **STRUCTURE.**)

Cause and Effect. *Cause and effect* is one of the principal methods of expository analysis. Like other methods, it is the natural, formal result of the way in which the human mind asks questions and seeks answers: Why? Because.

One may emphasize one cause and several effects; one cause and one effect; several causes and one effect; several causes and several effects; a sequence, or chain, of causes and effects. He may also stress a major cause and a major effect, with subsidiary and supportive causes and effects. This is essentially the task Webb sets himself in "The Boom Hypothesis of Modern History," as illustrated in ¶5. There, also, Webb implies his intention of avoiding the major fallacy of cause and effect: *post hoc, ergo propter hoc*—after the event in time, hence because of it. Webb's phrase is "after the discoveries and because of them." Hitler, in "Nation and Race," falls into this trap in ¶11. Morgenthau, in "Why Nations Decline," is concerned throughout with assigning, however tentatively, numerous possible causes for one effect. Galbraith uses the method in ¶12 of "The Concept of the Conventional Wisdom." In ¶7 of "Politics and the English Language," Orwell uses a series of one cause/one effect relationships. McLuhan, in "Television: The Timid Giant," uses cause/effect, separately or in combination with other methods, in ¶'s 4, 7, 15, 16, 27, 30–34, 38, 41–46, 50–52, 55, 57–64, 65–69. See also Mumford, "Architecture as Symbol," ¶'s 3, 6, 27; Brooks, "Conclusion," ¶5 (what *caused* the "transfiguration" and what were its *effects*); Bruner, "Motives for Learning," ¶'s 11, 13–15; Tawney, "Rights and Functions," ¶'s 3, 5, 7, 11; Frankel, "Ideals and Idols of Democracy," ¶31; Myrdal, "A Methodological Note on Valuations and Beliefs," ¶'s 7–9, 12, 13, 14–16, 22; Dewey, "Science and Free Culture," ¶'s 9–12, 31–35; Huxley, "Science and God: The Naturalistic Approach," ¶40.

Characters. *Characters* are the people to whom things happen in **NARRATIVE** or about whom **DESCRIPTION** is written. A character may be minor or major according to his central relevance to the narrative and the attention the author gives him. The principal character in a narrative is called the *protagonist*. In general, persons are "characterized" in narrative by a combination of some or all of the following methods: physical description, involvement in action, manner of speaking, explicit authorial analysis, and the "reputation" they have among other characters in the story. Warren, in "Segregation," depends largely on physical description and mannerisms of thought and expression to characterize the persons he interviews. The gallery of locals which Willa Cather creates in "The Sculptor's Funeral" is put together by individual physical descriptions, by identification with a "misty group," by the quality of their thoughts and expressions, and by the attitude of the two principals (Steavens and Laird) toward them.

Classification and Division. *Classification and division* is another method of expository analysis. According to Aldous Huxley, "The first and indispensable condition of systematic thought is classification." *Classification* is the process by which species are "classed" with their genus. *Division* is the opposite side of the same coin: the process by which general classes are broken down into their several parts. They may be used separately, but the use of one implies the relevance of the other. "How to Detect Propaganda" is an illustration of both: it is division in the sense that the species ("devices") of propaganda are broken down and analyzed; it is classification in that these devices are being classified under the general heading of "propaganda devices." The worth of the method is usually tested by three criteria: (a) clarity, (b) discreteness, (c) inclusiveness. In ¶'s 5–8 of "Politics and the English Language," Orwell divides into species a general class of "tricks by means of which the work of prose-construction is habitually dodged." In ¶2 of "The Artist and His Public," Janson makes a division of the "unspoken assumptions" in the "roadblock" between expert and layman. In ¶'s 16–24 of "The Greenwich Village Idea," Cowley breaks the system of Greenwich Village ideas down into their several implicit propositions. The over-all method of Emerson's "The American Scholar," ¶'s 8–30, is *classification/division*: the major "influences" (division) in the making of a scholar (classification). Note also Emerson's generalizations about the role of *classification* in learning, ¶8. See Bestor, "The College of *Liberal* Arts and Sciences," ¶'s 11, 13, 14–16. The fundamental purpose of Linton's "Race" is *classification/division*—see esp. ¶'s 38–48. See also Hook's "The Conflict of Freedoms," ¶'s 7–10, 17; Frankel's "Ideals and Idols of Democracy," ¶'s 13, 15, 25, 42; Huxley's "Science and God: The Naturalistic Approach," ¶'s 3, 18–29, 33.

Climax. The *climax* of a story is the point of highest emotional tension, in which the conflicts developed in the story are brought to focal action. For example, the climax in Greene's "The Hint of an Explanation" occurs in

¶ 55, when David swallows the purloined host. In Warren's "Blackberry Winter," the plot climaxes in ¶'s 161–162, in the confrontation between the boy's father and the stranger. In Steinbeck's "The Leader of the People," the climax occurs in ¶'s 131–139; in Joyce's "The Dead," in ¶'s 423–436.

Colloquial Language. (See **LEVELS OF USAGE.**)

Comparison and Contrast. Yet another method of expository analysis, *comparison and/or contrast*, like cause and effect, may be used in several patterns: the exposition may be devoted entirely to a delineation of the points in which two persons, objects, events, or systems are alike; or it may be devoted to the point in which they differ; or, again, the emphasis may include both similarities and differences. In general, two principles should be observed in formal comparisons and/or contrasts: (a) the objects dealt with should belong to the same class; (b) the points of comparison and/or contrast should be specific and precise. In general, this method is used to elucidate the unfamiliar through the familiar or at least to point up generally ignored aspects of the familiar. For a contrast between certain English or European attitudes and those of Americans, see Brogan's essay, "America Is Made," ¶'s 9, 10, 11. See, also, Newman's essay, "Literature," ¶'s 8–9; Arnold's "The Study of Poetry," ¶26; Trilling's "Freud and Literature," ¶'s 21–23; Illo's "The Rhetoric of Malcolm X," ¶'s 4–5; McLuhan's "Television: The Timid Giant," ¶'s 11–12, 15, 29, 31, 36–37, 39–40, 53–54, 57–64; Janson's, "The Artist and His Public," ¶'s 5 and 6; Cowley's "The Greenwich Village Idea," ¶6; Bestor's "The College of *Liberal* Arts and Sciences," ¶'s 3 and 7; Mead's "The Education of the Samoan Child," *passim*, in which the education of boys and girls is continuously compared and contrasted; Tawney's "Rights and Functions," ¶'s 4, 7–8, 9; Bryson's "On Deceiving the Public for the Public Good," ¶'s 12–13, 17, 27; Frankel's "Ideals and Idols of Democracy," ¶6; Whitehead's "The Origins of Modern Science," ¶'s 3, 16, 18; Dewey's "Science and Free Culture," ¶'s 24–25; Huxley's "Science and God: The Naturalistic Approach," ¶'s 16–17, 32–45, 45–47, 48–49; Niebuhr's "The Conflict Between Individual and Social Morality," ¶'s 1–2, 23–24; Tillich's "Man and History," ¶'s 12, 14.

Concrete Words. (See **ABSTRACT WORDS.**)

Contrast. (See **COMPARISON.**)

Corollary. A *corollary* is a deduction or inference which follows naturally upon and in consequence of the establishment of a proposition—"If this is true, then so is that." See ¶'s 2–3 of Webb's "The Boom Hypothesis of Modern History."

Deduction. *Deduction* is a term generally used as synonymous with *deductive reasoning*, although technically a deduction is the result or product of the process of deductive reasoning. The term is paired necessarily with *induction*, or *inductive reasoning*. Together they represent the two major ways in which the mind reaches generalizations or conclusions. Induction moves from the particular to the general and is frequently associated with empirical science; deduction moves from the general to the particular and is frequently associated with abstract philosophy. (In fact, it is sometimes held that science and philosophy were divorced when Bacon popularized empiricism or induction as the "exclusive" method of modern science.) Induction is a method by which experimental data (controlled observation) are used as a basis for generalization: having observed a representative number of examples of a phenomenon, we reach a conclusion (generalization) about all phenomena of the same class. Obviously we cannot examine *all* examples; hence we take the *inductive leap* on the basis of a convincing number of examples and settle for *probability* rather than *certainty*. Deduction takes a generalization and comes to a knowledge of the unknown through the known. Its principal formula is the syllogism. Obviously the two ways of thinking overlap: a conclusion inductively arrived at may be used as the major premise of a syllogism. (See **SYLLOGISM**.)

Hutchins' essay "The Higher Learning" can be profitably read as a critique of intellectual methodology. Too many scientists, he argues, suffer from the paralysis of data-gathering (induction carried to a ponderous extreme); and although he dissociates himself from so complete an abstractionist as Descartes, Hutchins holds that the intellect should formulate the propositions which experiment verifies or modifies or discredits. In other words, *deduction* is a method of thinking, induction a technique of testing. Linton, in "Race," ¶9, uses a series of deductions to speculate about certain conditions of pre-historic man. John XXIII, in "Relations Between Individuals and the Public Authorities Within a Single State," proceeds throughout by deduction. Toynbee, in "Christianity and Civilization," exposes his inductive methodology when he proposes to test his hypothesis by examining "every instance" (¶10).

Definition. *Definition* is one of the basic methods of expository analysis, its purpose being to assign to a term or concept or type clear and meaningful identification. *Formal* definitions can be stated in a single sentence:

A = B + C. In his essay "Literature," Newman uses a formal definition in ¶10: "Literature is the personal use or exercise of language." Like all correct formal definitions, the subject and the predicate nominative in Newman's sentence are interchangeable. *Rhetorical* definitions are more extended—frequently requiring a full paragraph or even a full essay, and the author is relatively free to choose his own method of elaboration *so long as it is thoroughly relevant*. Newman's definition of *style* in his essay, ¶'s 10–11, is *rhetorical*. Arnold's definition of a classic—"The Study of Poetry," ¶7—is *formal*. In "Style," Pater uses *formal definitions* in ¶'s 4, 7, 14 and *rhetorical definitions* in ¶'s 7, 14, 26, and 27 and *passim*, his whole essay in a sense being a rhetorical definition. T. S. Eliot, in "The Perfect Critic," makes frequent use of *formal* definition—e.g., of "free intelligence" (¶13) and of the end of enjoyment of poetry (¶17); in ¶18, Eliot uses a sequence of *formal* definitions to construct a *rhetorical* definition of criticism; in "Toward a Pluralistic Criticism," Cargill begins with *formal* definitions of the function of the critic and the meaning of the past (¶1) and ends with a *formal* definition of the role of the critic and scholar (¶14); in "How to Detect Propaganda," seven propaganda devices are defined by a combination of *formal* and *rhetorical* definitions; in "Politics and the English Language," ¶'s 5–8, *rhetorical* definitions are given of four "tricks" of slovenly writers; in "The Rhetoric of Malcolm X," Illo uses *formal* definitions in ¶'s 2 ("jurisprudence," "primal intelligence," "love," "man"), 3 ("rhetoric"), 4 ("great orator"), 8 ("declination"), and elsewhere. In "Television: The Timid Giant," McLuhan is pervasively concerned with establishing a vocabulary or defining terms; more specifically, he uses *formal* definitions in ¶'s 11 ("gestalt"), 13 ("tactility"), 16 ("synesthesia"), 19 ("TV"), and *rhetorical* definition is a basic part of the methodology of ¶'s 53–54 and 57–64. In "Conversation, Manners, and the Home," Barzun uses formal definitions in ¶'s 1 ("conversation"), 16 ("shuffling"), 34 ("maridauvage"), and *rhetorical* definition in ¶17 ("to *personalize*"). See also Mumford, "Architecture as Symbol," ¶25; Janson, "The Artist and His Public," ¶'s 2, 4, 5 (*formal definitions*) and ¶3 (*rhetorical definition*); Brooks, "Conclusion," ¶4 (the "role" of literary New England); Bestor, "The College of *Liberal* Arts and Sciences," ¶'s 9, 12, 31; Drucker, "The Education Revolution," ¶'s 22, 36. A special use of definition is *definition of terms*, usually formal definitions: for example, Linton, "Race," ¶30. A combination of *formal* and *rhetorical* definition appears in Tawney's "Rights and Functions," ¶1. See also Lippmann, "The Pursuit of Liberty," ¶14; Hook, "The Conflict of Freedoms," ¶'s 3, 4, 7, 10; Frankel, "Ideals and Idols of Democracy," ¶'s 1, 15; Myrdal, "A Methodological Note on Valuations and Beliefs," ¶'s 1, 4, 17; Dewey, "Science and Free Culture," ¶24; Freud, "Repression," *passim*; Huxley, "Science and God: The Naturalistic Approach," ¶'s 1, 4, 16; Lewis, "The Abolition of Man," ¶11; Maritain, "The Crisis of Modern Humanism," ¶1; Tillich, "Man and History," ¶'s 1, 2, 7, 10.

Dénouement. The *dénouement*, or resolution, of a story is the "tidying up" which takes place after the **CLIMAX**, in which unanswered questions are answered, punishments and rewards are meted out, the "end" is confirmed. In short stories, the dénouement is often very brief, sometimes implicit rather than explicit. In Roth's "The Conversion of the Jews," the dénouement is Ozzie's act of diving into the firemen's net. In Greene's "The Hint of an Explanation," the resolution takes place in ¶'s 60–65; in Warren's "Blackberry Winter," the mop-up takes place in ¶'s 174–178; in Joyce's "The Dead," in ¶'s 437–443.

Description. *Description* is one of the major forms of discourse (along with **ARGUMENT** and **PERSUASION, EXPOSITION,** and **NARRATIVE). Its** purpose is to enable the reader, in his mind's eye, to *see* a scene, a person, an object, or a situation. Usually imaginative description contains the following qualities: a **DOMINANT IMPRESSION,** a consistent **POINT OF VIEW,** and **VIVIDNESS.** (See each of these terms in the glossary for specific illustrations. For further terms which description shares with narrative, see also **CHARACTERS, SETTING, SYMBOL, TONE.**)

Dialectic. (See **ANTITHESIS.**)

Dilemma. In argument or in a situation, a person finds himself faced with a dilemma when the alternatives ("horns") between which he has to choose tell, or seem to tell, equally against him. Morgenthau's lecture "Why Nations Decline" is shot through with a sense of the dilemma presented by the topic, and he specifies a celebrated dilemma in ¶'s 11 and 12. Margaret Mead describes the "dilemma" of a Samoan youth in ¶'s 19–22 of "The Education of a Samoan Child."

Division. (See **CLASSIFICATION AND DIVISION.)**

Dominant Impression All writing should convey to the reader a single, unified impression. Therefore, in general terms, the author's **TONE** is related to the *dominant impression* which his writing gives. The term is specifically used, however, in the context of *description*: the author tries to impress upon the reader a basic image, with physical characteristics and emotional overtones. For example, Twain, in "That Farm of My Uncle John's," is trying to persuade the reader that "It was a heavenly place for a boy. . . ." That is the way he feels about it; that is the way he wants the reader to feel about it. Kazin, on the other hand, in "School Days at Brownsville," announces in the second sentence his sense of "sickness" and "fear" as the dominant impression of his narrative, expanding it (¶'s 13–15) to "something severe, frightening, obscene." The dominant impression Orwell gets and gives of "Marrakech" is of the "invisibility" of the people (¶21) in the context of a brown, waterless, bestial life.

Effect. (See **CAUSE AND EFFECT.**)

Equivocation. One of the common fallacies in argument, *equivocation* is the use of the same term in two different senses or meanings. Drucker, for example, in "The Educational Revolution," is guilty of two different meanings of "the highly educated"—one meaning to have had a good many years of formal education (*passim*), the other meaning (¶36) "people who can formulate, understand and support purposeful, principled, courageous [international] policies." In ¶29 of "Nation and Race," Hitler is guilty of a combination of *equivocation* and *begging the question:* he takes for granted what requires proof, and he shifts his definition of "Aryan."

Euphony. See "Introduction," p. xv. An extraordinarily pat example of euphony can be found in Newman's essay "Literature," ¶'s 32–34. Two conditions accentuated Newman's emphasis on euphony: (1) in ¶7, he insists that literature "addresses itself, in its primary idea, to the ear, not to the eye"; (2) he has literally written something to be spoken and heard—a lecture.

Evidence. *Evidence,* in argument, is the raw material of proof. In general, evidence is divided into two categories—evidence of fact and evidence of opinion—as reasoning is divided into induction and deduction. Factual evidence cannot be argued; it can only be verified beyond reasonable doubt. Opinion lies at the very heart of argument. As evidence, however, opinion must carry with it the weight of authority and trustworthiness. In "The Higher Learning," for example, Hutchins cites the opinions of authorities most likely to be acceptable to the scientists who are his principal antagonists: Whitehead, Bertrand Russell, William Stanley Jevons, Jules Henri Poincare, Claude Bernard, John Dewey. Drucker, on the other hand ("The Educational Revolution"), makes broad use of the evidence of facts, ¶'s 11–18. Ruth Benedict also uses factual evidence as her singular method of proof in "The Diversity of Cultures." Rachel Carson, in "And No Birds Sing," combines through evidence of opinion (the Midwest housewife as well as the curator at the Museum of Natural History) and evidence of fact (statistical as well as inferential).

Example. *Example* is another one of the basic methods of expository analysis. It is the method of evidence by which instances are provided to give credibility and persuasiveness to a generalization. Mark Twain uses a mass of concrete, vivid details to "prove" that his uncle's farm "was a heavenly place for a boy" ("That Farm of My Uncle John's"); Hans Morgenthau combines the method of cause and effect with the method of example throughout "Why Nations Decline" to give clarity and force to his generalizations. His basic formula in the essay is this: nations decline (a) because (b) for example. Galbraith, in "The Concept of the Conventional Wisdom," uses the method, combined with *process analysis*, in ¶'s 20–24. Newman, in "Literature," uses example (instances, illustrations) in ¶'s 2–5, 13, 21, 23. The pervasive method of Arnold's "The Study of Poetry" is that of example, but see especially ¶10. Other illustrations are these: Trilling, "Freud and Literature," ¶'s 4, 11, 32; Cargill, "Toward a Pluralistic Criticism," ¶'s 3 and 6; Orwell, "Politics and the English Language," ¶3 and, in combination with other methods, ¶'s 5–8; Illo, "The Rhetoric of Malcolm X," ¶7; McLuhan, "Television: The Timid Giant," ¶'s 5, 7, 10, 22, 24, 29, 65–69; Janson, "The Artist and His Public," ¶'s 8, 9, 10; Bryson, "On Deceiving the Public for the Public Good," ¶'s 6–7; Whitehead, "The Origins of Modern Science," ¶'s 2, 15, 23; Huxley, "Science and God: The Naturalistic Approach," ¶'s 40, 41–44; Toynbee, "Christianity and Civilization," ¶9; Niebuhr, "The Conflict Between Individual and Social Morality," ¶'s 6, 18, 19.

Exposition. One of the five major forms of discourse (**DESCRIPTION, ARGUMENT, NARRATIVE,** and **PERSUASION**), it is the aim, of exposition, to explain or clarify a subject. See the first section of this volume.

Figurative Language. (See **METAPHOR, PERSONIFICATION,** and **SIMILE.**)

Hypothesis. A *hypothesis*, sometimes called a "working hypothesis," is a tentative supposition provisionally adopted to explain certain facts or to aid in their investigation. Professor Webb uses the term very explicitly and carefully in "The Boom Hypothesis of Modern History," as do Linton, "Race," ¶4, and Toynbee, "Christianity and Civilization," ¶10.

Imagery. *Imagery* is a broad term for the use of concrete visual detail in writing—the use of *images*, which we recognize as the root of the word "imagination." More specifically, however, the term is associated with figurative language, especially **METAPHOR.**

Induction. (See **DEDUCTION.**)

In medias res. Especially in narrative writing, jumping right "into the middle of things," without introductory exposition or stage-setting, is known as using the technique of *in medias res*. All of the fictional narratives in this volume illustrate this technique. So also do some of the factual narratives—those by Orwell, for example, and by Shirer.

Irony. *Irony*, a widely used rhetorical device in all literature, is of two kinds, *verbal* and *situational*. *Verbal irony* results from a discrepancy between the literal meaning of a statement and the author's or speaker's actual intention. *Situational irony* is the result of a reversal in the expected outcome. Ring Lardner's "Haircut" is a vivid example of *situational irony*: the listener, or reader, reverses the speaker's intended impression. Brooks, in "Wordsworth and the Paradox of the Imagination," points up examples of *situational irony* in ¶'s 21, 25, 30–31, 39; and Williamson, in "How to Write Like a Social Scientist," ¶'s 14–19, provides an extended example of *verbal irony*. Barzun's tone, in "Conversation, Manners, and the Home," is frequently ironic, and he uses the technique vividly in ¶'s 13, 14, 34 and esp. 61. See also Brooks, "Conclusion," ¶6; Cowley, "The Greenwich Village Idea," ¶'s 28, 33, 34. The most brutally ironic story in this volume is Conrad's "An Outpost of Progress."

Issue. An *issue* is a minor proposition essential to the support of the main proposition. All minor propositions are supportive; minor propositions considered crucial to the proof of the major proposition are an issue. In "The Diversity of Cultures," Ruth Benedict sets forth two major propositions (summary, ¶34), which she must argue separately. She then selects minor propositions in support; these are issues in the sense that, having selected them from a larger sample, she rests the validity of her argument on her ability to validate these. For example, in support of her first proposition she makes cultural diversity on matters of adolescence, warfare, and marriage *issues.*

Levels of Usage. Language, like punishment, fits the crime. Very *formal English,* pure of diction and severe of sentence, is most appropriate to the highest efforts of scholarship and statesmanship. *Informal English* is the standard level of the generality of educated people. *Colloquial English* is often identical with *informal English:* it is the language of conversation and social intercourse—idiomatic and relaxed. *Slang,* which is always being created and replaced, is the more or less flippant but often colorful and effective language of the "new generation." *Local English* is made up of expressions and combinations common to a given locale or region.

Severe standards of usage, except on very formal occasions, have generally broken down. For example, the contraction is now completely respectable.

The Romantic movement in poetry, the rise of fiction, and the increasing visibility of American literature have all served to bring forward the language actually spoken by men. Examples of slang and localisms abound in the fictional narratives in this volume. See especially Lardner's "Haircut," in which the whole style of the story depends upon the representative local speech of the narrator. In the factual narratives, too, one finds it. For example, Sandburg lets the Indiana pioneers speak their own language without apology in "The Boyhood of Lincoln."

Metaphor. A *metaphor is* one of the forms of figurative language in which one object is illuminated by association (or comparison) with another, the association being more immediate than in *simile* in that the instrument of comparison (*like, as*) is omitted. For example, Mary McCarthy in "America the Beautiful," ¶20: "Europe is the unfinished negative of which America is the proof." For example, John W. Gardner, in "Tyranny Without a Tyrant," ¶1: "tides," "surface currents," "merest whitecaps," and ¶22: "it was a sort of parlor car in which we rode." The most elaborate discussion of metaphor in this volume is Brooks' "Wordsworth and the Paradox of the Imagination," especially ¶'s 16, 17, 18, 30. Cargill, in "Toward a Pluralistic Criticism," ¶'s 5 and 6, uses an elaborate cluster of metaphors, and even so nonornamental a writer as Williamson uses a comparable cluster in "How to Write Like a Social Scientist," ¶'s 5–6. In "Politics and the English Language," Orwell not only uses metaphors (e.g., ¶5), but defines "the sole aim" of metaphors and shows the relationship between "mixed metaphors" and mixed-up thoughts (¶12). See also Mumford, "Architecture as Symbol,"

¶8 ("paper flowers"); Hutchins, "The Higher Learning," ¶7 ("green word") and ¶9 ("blizzards of data"); Bruner, "Motives for Learning," ¶12: *mixed metaphor;* Marx and Engels, "The Communist Manifesto," ¶'s 2, 3, 124; Tawney, "Rights and Functions," ¶7; Whitehead, "The Origins of Modern Science," ¶'s 4, 5, 43; Toynbee, "Christianity and Civilization," ¶22; Tillich, "Man and History," ¶14; Kazin, "School Days at Brownsville," ¶1.

Methods of Expository Analysis. Elsewhere in this glossary, the chief *methods of expository analysis* are described and illustrated: *definition, classification and division, example, comparison and contrast,* including *analogy, cause and effect, process* or *function.* One can find numerous examples of each of these in a more or less clear and singular form; but it is still true that they more frequently appear in various combinations because rhetoric, being in practice more informal than formal, more flexible than rigid, readily yields to functional combinations. Thus, in ¶16 of "Style," Pater combines *comparison/contrast, rhetorical definition, process analysis,* and *example.* In "Television: The Timid Giant," McLuhan frequently uses two or more methods in combination: ¶'s 5 and 65–69, *example* and *cause/effect;* 7, *example* and *process analysis;* 15 and 31, *cause/effect* and *comparison/ contrast;* 29, *example* and *comparison/contrast;* 39–40, *process analysis* and *comparison/contrast;* 53–54, *definition, example,* and *comparison/contrast;* 57–64, *comparison/contrast, cause/effect,* and *definition.* Mumford, in "Architecture as Symbol," combines *example* with *comparison/contrast* and *cause/effect* (¶3) and *example* with *cause/effect* (¶22). Bruner, in "Motives for Learning," combines *cause/effect* and *example* in ¶'s 10 and 16. Marx and Engels, "The Communist Manifesto," combine *example* with *cause/effect* (¶'s 15–25) and *process analysis* with *classification/division* (¶111). Tawney, in "Rights and Functions," combines *cause/effect* with *process analysis* (¶3), *cause/effect* with *comparison/contrast* (¶'s 4 and 7); Lippmann, in "The Pursuit of Liberty," ¶25, combines *example* and *cause/effect;* Bryson, in "On Deceiving the Public for the Public Good," ¶3, combines *example* with *process analysis* and *cause/effect* and, in ¶9, *definition* with *comparison/ contrast;* Frankel, in "Ideals and Idols of Democracy," ¶15, combines *definition* with *classification/division;* Myrdal, in "A Methodological Note on Valuations and Beliefs," combines *definition* with *comparison/contrast* (¶1), *process analysis* with *comparison/contrast* (¶5), *process analysis* with *cause/effect* (¶'s 7–9, 11, 13, 14–16, 22, 23–28), *comparison/contrast* with *cause/effect* (¶12); Whitehead, in "The Origins of Modern Science," combines *cause/effect, process analysis,* and *comparison/contrast* (¶14), and *comparison/contrast, classification/division, cause/effect* (¶37–40); Carson, in "And No Birds Sing," combines *process analysis* with *example* (¶35); Freud, in "Repression," combines *example, process analysis,* and *com-*

parison/contrast (¶'s 22–27); Huxley, in "Science and God: The Natural-istic Approach," interweaves *classification/division,* (implicit) *analogy,* and *definition* (¶'s 18–29) and interweaves *comparison/contrast, classification/ division, process analysis, cause/effect,* and *example* (¶'s 32–49); Lewis, in "The Abolition of Man" combines *comparison/contrast* with *classification/ division* (¶6) and *comparison/contrast* with *process analysis* and *cause/ effect* (¶16); Toynbee, in "Christianity and Civilization," ¶13, combines *example* with *process analysis;* Niebuhr, in "The Conflict Between Individ-ual and Social Morality," ¶'s 7 and 20: combines *example* with *cause/effect,* ¶10: *comparison/contrast* with *cause/effect,* ¶'s 21–22: *classification/divi-sion* with *process analysis.*

Narrative. *Narrative,* like **DESCRIPTION, ARGUMENT, PERSUASION,** and **EXPOSITION,** is one of the major forms of discourse. Its purpose is to let the reader know what happened. Therefore, all narrative is an exposition of action. Narrative may be factual (biography, history, auto-biography) or it may be fictional (a tale, a short story, a novel). The last section of this volume contains examples of both types. For illustrations of particular aspects and techniques of narrative, see **ACTION, CHARAC-TERS, DÉNOUEMENT, IN MEDIAS RES, PLOT, POINT OF VIEW, SETTING, SYMBOL, THEME, TONE, TURNING-POINT.**

Non Sequitur. In argument, a *non sequitur* is a fallacy in which the conclu-sion "does not follow" from the premises. In "The Two Nations," Michael Harrington is pointing up two examples of *non sequitur* in the reasoning of Robert Lampmam: ¶'s 30–31 and 34–35. In ¶11 of "Nation and Race," Hitler provides a blatant example.

Paradox. A *paradox* is a statement or situation which, contrary to common or expected opinion, is apparently contradictory but in fact true. In "Style," Pater points up the idea that his apparently *subjective* prose and theory of prose is in fact *impersonal* (¶'s 28–29). In "Wordsworth and the Paradox of the Imagination," Brooks stresses the concept throughout, but very point-edly in ¶'s 20, 21, 27. In "Toward a Pluralistic Criticism," Cargill sees our love of books as paradoxical against our increasing divorce from the past (¶1). See also Janson, "The Artist and His Public," ¶'s 9 and 14; Hutchins,

"The Higher Learning," ¶8; Bryson, "On Deceiving the Public for the Public Good," ¶30; Niebuhr, "The Conflict Between Individual and Social Morality," ¶14. See also **AMBIGUITY** and **IRONY.**

Parody. *Parody* is an imitation or mimicry of another's writing, or of a type of writing to emphasize its weakness or mannerisms. Newman parodies "fine writing" in ¶12 of "Literature." Orwell, in ¶10 of "Politics and the English Language," parodies what he calls "modern English."

Personification. A *personification* is a figure of speech through which human characteristics are attributed to non-human organisms, abstract concepts, or inanimate objects. For example, Michael Harrington, "The Two Nations," ¶16: "the environment . . . counsels."

Persuasion. One of the five major forms of discourse (**EXPOSITION, NARRATIVE, DESCRIPTION,** and **ARGUMENT**), *presuasion* is sometimes confused with argument. Argument seeks to convince someone that something is true; persuasion seeks to do the same thing. But there is a real, though not an exclusive, difference between them. Argument appeals rigorously to reason, persuasion appeals pervasively to emotion; argument attempts to *affect* judgment, persuasion attempts to *effect* action. Good argument can be judged by traditional tests of validity; there is only one acid test of persuasion: did it get the job done. Both forms have both a reputable and a disreputable history: literature, in its broadest sense, is rich in examples of bad argument and superb persuasion, or of good argument and the basest kind of propaganda. And the two forms overlap: elements of each can usually be detected in the other. In persuasion, however, the predetermined end is explicit; in argument, if there is indeed an end beyond understanding, the end is implicit. The end of propaganda is action, and hence the "propaganda devices" outlined and characterized in "How to Detect Propaganda" might also be called "persuasion devices" in a pure form. Michael Harrington's "The Two Nations" is a clear example of argument and persuasion in a meaningful combination. Emerson's "The American Scholar" is a compelling example of persuasion, where the clear object is *action* and the method largely one of emotional and imaginative appeal. Rachel Carson's "And No Birds Sing" is an example of persuasion employing a substantial argumentative framework: she got immediate action from both the public and the Government.

Plot. E. M. Forster, in *Aspects of the Novel*, has put *plot* into context as follows: "Let us define a plot. We have defined a story as a narrative of events arranged in their time sequence. A plot is also a narrative of events, the emphasis falling on causality. 'The king died and then the queen died' is a story. 'The king died and then the queen died of grief' is a plot. The time-sequence is preserved, but the sense of causality overshadows it. Or again: 'The queen died, no one knew why, until it was discovered that it was through grief at the death of the king.' This is a plot with mystery in it."

Forster is right in his emphasis on causality, although such terms as **CLIMAX** and **RESOLUTION** are also relevant, at least to the working out of *plot*.

Among the factual narratives in this volume, the one which comes closest perhaps to *plot* as one of the essential ingredients in fictional narrative is "Discovery of a Father," by Sherwood Anderson. But although the boy undergoes change as a result of action, this is recorded as a simple experience, not as a complication having various stages and in need of authorial resolution.

Point of View. *Point of view* sometimes means attitude or conviction. In **DESCRIPTION** and **NARRATIVE**, it has a more technical meaning. In both of these, the *point of view* can be established if these questions can be answered: who is the narrator? where does he "stand" (literally and figuratively)? what is his frame of mind? For example, in "School Days in Brownsville," the narrator is Kazin himself (these are his experiences); he is "standing" in the courtyard of the public school he attended; he is "sick with all [his] old fear of it." On a still more technical level, in fictional writing a distinction must be drawn between the "narrator" and the author. Here by *point of view* we mean, as Percy Lubbock said, "The relation in which the narrator stands to the story." There are several "angles" from which a narrator may tell a story: (1) he may tell a story in which he was intricately involved as a character using the first person ("I"); (2) he may tell a story in which he was not involved as a participant, but about which he knows the "facts," using the first person; (3) he may tell a story, using the third person ("he," "it," "they"), about which he knows everything, inner and outer, is "omniscient"; (4) he may tell a story, using the third person, about which he knows something, but not everything, more about one character, for example, than about another. Sherwood Anderson's "Discovery of a Father" is an example of the first of these, as are the other autobiographical narratives under the heading of "Factual Narrative." Anderson's use of this technique is especially noteworthy since the narrator (the "I"), although he reveals the true character of his father, does not himself understand it. George Orwell, in "Marrakech," uses the second, both as narrator and describer: his participation in the life of Marrakech is as the reader's "seeing eye." Warren, in a similar manner, in "Segregation," provides the reader with a guided tour of opinion and personality in the South. Philip Roth, in "The Conversion of the Jews," uses the fourth "angle of vision" itemized above. In "The Hint of an Explanation," we have two narrators—an "outer" and an "inner." The outer narrator tells the reader what he saw and heard in the first person (the second technique itemized above); the inner narrator tells his listener the facts and "hints" at an explanation of them (the first technique itemized above). John Steinbeck, in "The Leader of the People," uses basically the fourth technique, though he occasionally enters into Jody's thoughts and feelings as an omniscient narrator. This is also the technique of Faulkner's "Barn Burning." "After the Storm" is a monologue, therefore entirely in the first person, stripped of all interpretive commentary. The point of view used in Willa Cather's "The Sculptor's Funeral" is a variation of the technique used by Steinbeck and Faulkner. Ring Lardner, in "Haircut," has the raw story told according to the second technique itemized above, but it is clear throughout that the author is critical of the narrator. In "Sonny's Blues," Baldwin uses a first person point of view similar to Lardner's except that the narrator's illumination at the end is more explicit. Conrad ("An Outpost of Progress") uses the third-person omniscient point of view. Joyce, in "The Dead," uses the third-person omniscient point of view, with Gabriel as the reader's guide through the story.

Post Hoc, Ergo Propter Hoc. (See **CAUSE AND EFFECT.**)

Process Analysis. One of the basic methods of expository analysis, *process analysis* outlines how something functions, how something is made, how something is (or should be) done—"something" here to include ideologies and systems as well as mechanical processes. Michael Harrington, in "The Two Nations," ¶'s 43–53, uses a method of process analysis in outlining the kind of anti-poverty program the nation needs. Galbraith, in "The Concept of the Conventional Wisdom," ¶'s 20–24, uses it to show how changed circumstances fracture accepted ideas and lead to another set of accepted ideas. In "Style," Pater uses the method in ¶13 to show how the artist winnows his vocabulary. Trilling, in "Freud and Literature," ¶'s 3–8, traces the culmination of Romanticist literature in Freud. "How to Detect Propaganda" is, in its over-all skeletal intention, an example of process analysis: "You can detect propaganda by learning these devices and applying them to the media of communication." Williamson's "How to Write Like a Social Scientist," ¶'s 14–19, provides a more fully developed example, as does

Orwell in ¶19 of "Politics and the English Language." McLuhan, in "Television: The Timid Giant," uses the method alone or in combination in ¶'s 7, 39–40. The dominant method in Mumford's "Architecture as Symbol," ¶'s 11–19, is process analysis, occasionally combined with other methods such as **EXAMPLE.** See also Janson, "The Artist and His Public," ¶4; Brooks, "Conclusion," ¶2; Mead, "The Education of the Samoan Child," *passim;* Linton, "Race," ¶'s 7, 31–33; Marx and Engels, "The Communist Manifesto," ¶'s 10–12, 37–43, 164–171; Myrdal, "A Methodological Note on Valuations and Beliefs," ¶'s 2, 4, 7–9, 14–16, 22–28; Carson, "And No Birds Sing," ¶'s 7, 13; Freud, "Repression," ¶12; Huxley, "Science and God: The Naturalistic Approach," ¶'s 30–31, 34–37; Tillich, "Man and History," ¶3.

Proposition. A *proposition* is a "clear, singular statement of a point of view" in argument—"what the argument's all about." The *main proposition* is the central assertion about which the argument revolves. In Mary McCarthy's "America the Beautiful," for example, the main proposition is stated at the end of ¶5: "The virtue of American civilization is that it is unmaterialistic." An argumentative essay may also contain two or more *minor propositions,* or supporting assertions. Examples of the rather numerous minor propositions in McCarthy's essay are these: The American feels the "things" that surround him "to be irrelevant to him" (¶6); Americans tolerate intolerable material conditions (¶9); the American "lives sparely and thinly" among his possessions (¶11). Barzun, in "Conversation, Manners, and the Home," draws attention (¶19) to the proposition "that for true sociability being agreeable is not enough. . . ." See also Janson, "The Artist and His Public," ¶14—"that works of art exist in order to be liked rather than to be debated"; Benedict, "The Diversity of Cultures," ¶34—that the diversity of cultures results "from the ease with which societies elaborate or reject possible aspects of existence" and "even more [from] a complex interweaving of cultural traits."

Pun. A *pun* is a play on words with similar sounds but different meanings, usually for a witty effect. Mary McCarthy concludes her essay "America the Beautiful" with a pun more wry than witty: "posterity is not around the corner." Illo, in "The Rhetoric of Malcolm X," uses puns having the general effect of neologisms: "warfare state" (¶20) and "Newspeak" (¶35). McLuhan uses puns in "Television: The Timid Giant"—for example, "Paared down" (¶3) and (from Joyce) "sobconscious" (¶11). In a footnote to ¶54, Barzun ("Conversation, Manners, and the Home") cites a devastatingly modern pun of Cyril Connolly's: "a womb with a view."

Resolution. (See **DÉNOUEMENT.**)

Rhetorical Question. A *rhetorical question* is a question which is asked, not for an answer, but for a dramatic, vivid effect. See the concluding paragraph of Michael Harrington's "The Two Nations." See also ¶28 of Arnold's "The Study of Poetry" and ¶2 of Cargill's "Toward a Pluralistic Criticism."

Rhythm. In prose as in poetry, *rhythm* is the result of controlled cadences of stressed and unstressed syllables; having to do with sound (on the inner or the outer ear), it is an aspect of **EUPHONY.** Except in emotive oratory, modern prose style tends to stress an easy conversational rhythm, without much calculated variation. For an example of a masterful use of rhythm as it was used in English prose for three centuries, see Newman's "Literature," ¶'s 32–34. See, also, Pater's "Style," ¶6 and the footnote; Russell's "A Free Man's Worship," ¶3 and *passim;* Niebuhr's "The Conflict Between Individual and Social Morality," ¶'s 1 and 14.

Setting. The *setting* of a story includes those elements of "staging" in which the action takes place, including time and place and atmosphere. The setting of Warren's "Blackberry Winter" is a day in June 1910 in Middle Tennessee after a flood and during a cold snap. Physical environment is so important in this story that it takes on symbolic significance.

Simile. A *simile* is a figure of speech in which an object is explicity compared with another by the use of *like* or *as* to make the first object clearer and more vivid. For example, in Gardner's "Tyranny Without a Tyrant," ¶21—"like cogs in the machine" and "like grains of sand in a bucket"; in Eliot's "The Perfect Critic," ¶4—"like the leaves of an artichoke"; in Orwell's "Politics and the English Language," ¶12—"like tea leaves blocking a sink," ¶16—"like soft snow," ¶17—"like cavalry horses"; in Mumford's "Architecture as Symbol," ¶20—"like delicate seedlings"; in Brooks' "Conclusion," ¶8–an elaborate combination of simile and metaphor–and ¶'s 9–10; in Emerson's "The American Scholar," where *similes* and *metaphors* are used profusely: ¶'s 1, 15, 17, 26, 31, 33, 35, 36, 41 (some of the *similes*, e.g., ¶'s 26, 31, can also be read as *analogies*); in Lippmann's "The Pursuit of Liberty," ¶12; in Huxley's, "Science and God: The Naturalistic Approach," ¶40 (a startling example); in Kazin's "School Days at Brownsville," ¶'s 1, 10; in Merton's "God's Will at Columbia," ¶10; in Greene's "The Hint of an Explanation," ¶'s 3, 4, 32, 47, 48, 55.

Structure. By *structure* one usually means the unified arrangement of the parts of a piece of writing, a quality of order described by Aristotle as "beginning, middle, end." The *beginning* should achieve two ends: let the reader know where he (and therefore the narrator) stands and where he is going; the *middle* provides the series of incidents and other experiences which fulfil the promise of the beginning; the *end,* implicitly or explicitly, abruptly or as a more elaborate "summing up," satisfies the reader that what was promised in the beginning was actually delivered. Kazin, for example, in "School Days in Brownsville," takes his stand with the reader in the courtyard of the public school which he attended, and through an appeal to the senses (especially sight, sound, and smell), strengthened by figures of speech, evokes a parade of feelings and incidents which make believable his remembrance of sickness and fear. In the last paragraph, he brings the narrative back to the courtyard and re-states the dominant symbol —that of the "white, thinly ruled, official record book."

Style. See "Introduction," p. xv. See also Newman, "Literature" and Pater, "Style."

Syllogism. The *syllogism* is the basic formula of deductive reasoning. A syllogism consists of three parts, expressed or implied: a major premise, a minor premise, and a conclusion. If one accepts the premises as valid, he must accept the conclusion—hence the importance of scrutinizing the premises carefully. In the first place, the major premise must include *all possible cases* to which it is applied. Secondly, the minor premise must distribute its terms so as not to falsify the utility of the major premise. For example:

> All men (A) must die (B).
> Robin Redbreast (C) must die (B).
> Therefore, Robin Redbreast (C) is a man (A).

The terms of the minor premise are falsely distributed; hence the conclusion is false. The subject of the major premise is inverted in the minor premise.

> All men (A) must die (B).
> Martin Luther King (C) is a man (A).
> Therefore, Martin Luther King (C) must die (B).

The syllogism is derived from the basic Euclidian formula: two things equal to the same thing are equal to each other. But they must be *truly* equal.

The following examples from the text are further clarifications of syllogistic principles. Our quarrel with Phyllis McGinley's argument in "Suburbia: Of Thee I Sing" is that its minor premise is invalid:

> I like the suburbs;
> What I like others should like;
> Therefore, others should like the suburbs.

Amongst the implied syllogisms in Newman's essay "Literature," ¶'s 8–9, the following is easily recognizable:

> All literature is essentially a personal work.
> Euclid's *Elements* is not a personal work.
> Therefore, Euclid's *Elements* is not literature.

It should be noted that here both the minor premise and the conclusion are stated in the negative—hence, the valid departure from the ordinary distribution of the middle term. George Orwell draws attention to a prevailing implicit syllogism in ¶1 of "Politics and the English Language." Made explicit, it would read as follows:

> A decadent civilization is inevitably
> accompanied by a decadent language;
> Our civilization is decadent;
> Therefore, our language is decadent.

In "Conversation, Manners, and the Home," ¶'s 7–8, Barzun draws attention to alternate syllogisms. In "The Higher Learning," Hutchins proceeds by the technique of implied syllogism—for example, ¶15. Hitler's essay "Nation and Race" is riddled with examples of *faulty* syllogisms, but see esp. ¶19, sentence beginning, "Anyone, for example, who really desired the victory of the pacifistic idea. . . ." John XXIII, in "Relations Between Individuals and the Public Authorities Within a Single State," evolves his principles syllogistically. For example:

> ¶2   The moral order is the source of right reason;
> Legitimate authority is an expression of right reason;
> Therefore, legitimate authority is an expression of moral order.

> ¶3   The dignity of man derives from reason and free will;
> Irresponsible authority ignores reason and free will;
> Therefore, irresponsible authority ignores the dignity of man.

See also Lippmann, "The Pursuit of Liberty," ¶26; Toynbee, "Christianity and Civilization," ¶'s 21 and 22.

Symbol. Both the word and the meaning of *symbol* are from the Greek: *sign.* There are, of course, religious symbols, patriotic symbols, literary symbols, and so forth. In literature, a symbol is an object which has a definite, recognizable identity on a literal level, as well as another meaning which the author, through a context of verbal suggestion, gives it. A symbol gains its vividness and force from its appropriateness and from the subtle suggestiveness of the author's handling of it. Cleanth Brooks, for example, points out a pattern of symbols in Wordsworth's "Ode" in his essay "Wordsworth and the Paradox of the Imagination," especially ¶'s 16 and 18. Mumford, in "Architecture as Symbol," deals with architecture as a reflection of integrative and disintegrative forces in society at large. Kazin, in "School Days at Brownsville," elevates the "white, thinly ruled, official record book" to the level of symbol, giving it coercive, familial, sexual and religious associations. An action may also have symbolic significance, frequently by association with religious ritual. The naked swim in the darkness, amid rain and lightning, in Sherwood Anderson's "Discovery of a Father" has both its literal meaning and a suggestion of baptismal ritual. At the end of Roth's "The Conversion of the Jews," the firemen's net takes on symbolic qualities as Ozzie's "halo." In Greene's "The Hint of an Explanation," Blacker's threat of "bleeding" David is symbolic, suggesting the blood of Christ, sacrifice, martyrdom. Warren's "Blackberry Winter" is rich in symbols—the flood itself, the filth washed from under Dellie's house, Old Jebb (a latter-day Tithonus), and so forth. Steinbeck's "The Leader of the People" is not as ritualistic as Warren's story, but most of the details of the "ranch-cup" in which the action takes place fit into a symbolic context, especially, for example, the mice. Baldwin's "Sonny's Blues" operates throughout on the literal as well as the symbolic (or parabolic) level. Conrad's "An Outpost of Progress" is rich in symbols—the cross, for example, and the mist.

Synthesis. (See **ANTITHESIS.**)

Theme. The *theme* of a story is its meaning, its "moral," the comment on the nature of life which it posits. A story may have several motifs, but the *theme* is the statement about reality which unifies the various characters, actions, and sub-themes. A theme is not truly separable from a story in that fiction is woven of experience—a simple statement of meaning is never equivalent to the story itself. However, for discussion purposes, the "moral" of a story, like the moral of a parable, can be identified. A clear distinction should be made between the theme and the *subject-matter* of a story. The subject-matter is the raw material (setting, characters, incidents, subjects touched upon) of the story, through which the theme is examined. "Religion," for example, is not the theme of Roth's "The Conversion of the Jews"; religion is an aspect of the subject-matter. The theme might be paraphrased something like this: If an innocent really wanted to "know something about God," he would probably be persecuted even by his religion's ministers and might even have to push the matter to rebellion and the edge of martyrdom to get them to drop their rituals and clichés and listen. This is probably a fair statement of the theme of Warren's "Blackberry Winter": At a moment in the life of a boy—even in a single day—events can happen which make the aspects of the world, of life, fundamentally different—the big and the solid and the knowable become small and fluid and incomprehensible.

Thesis. The *thesis* of a piece of writing is the statement of the major proposition or assertion that it sets forth. The thesis is to the essay as a whole what the topic sentence is to the single paragraph. (For a special use of the term *thesis*, see **ANTITHESIS.**)

The thesis of Mary McCarthy's "America the Beautiful" is summed up in ¶4: "that the visible and material America is not the real or the only one."

Tone. *Tone* is at once a very elusive and a very genuine aspect of style. The "tone of voice" which we "hear" in a piece of writing is an important reflection of an author's attitude toward his subject and of his attitude toward his audience. In a very real sense, then, tone is inseparable from the very meaning an author attempts to communicate. An excellent example of the interpenetration of these qualities is Brogan's essay "America Is Made," written in a light, somewhat unsympathetic tone of irony undoubtedly more congenial to the English than to the American ear. The tone of the narrator in Willa Cather's "The Sculptor's Funeral" is one of incredulous shock and moral outrage, conveyed principally by Steavens and Laird, but also by the author's characterization of the gallery of characters, including the figures of speech with which she reveals them. The tone of the narrator in Ring Lardner's "Haircut" is summed up in the repeated "Jim certainly was a character!" but behind it is an authorial tone of deep irony.

Turning-Point. The *turning-point* of a story is that point at which the action takes a decisive turn. (Not to be confused with **CLIMAX.**) In most stories the turning-point occurs near the middle, as it usually occurs in the third act of a five-act play. We don't yet know how matters will end, but we do know that there is no returning to the old set of givens. For example, the *turning-point* in Roth's "The Conversion of the Jews" is the scene in which

Ozzie charges Binder with ignorance about God, gets his nose bloodied, calls him a bastard, and escapes to the roof. From this point of crisis we move *toward* the climax. The turning-point in Greene's "The Hint of an Explanation" occurs in ¶40; in Warren's "Blackberry Winter," in ¶'s 102–104; in Faulkner's "Barn Burning," in ¶88; in Baldwin's "Sonny's Blues," in ¶168; in Conrad's "An Outpost of Progress," in ¶60; in Joyce's "The Dead," in ¶'s 233–253, Gabriel's after-dinner speech.

Vividness. *Vividness* is a quality of all writing that is lively and fresh. The term is also used in a more restricted sense to indicate a quality of *descriptive writing* in which lifelike mental images are evoked to help the reader "see" the thing described. Devices for achieving vividness include the use of **FIGURATIVE LANGUAGE** and **CONCRETE WORDS** and a broad appeal to all five senses. Perhaps the selection in the text which most thoroughly appeals to the concrete and the sensuous is Twain's "That Farm of My Uncle John's," though Sandburg uses the same techniques throughout "The Boyhood of Lincoln." Orwell, in "Marrakech," achieves vividness by the force of the examples chosen (flies after corpses returning to restaurants) and by simple, visual figures of speech ("lines of women, bent double like inverted capital L's").

John Kenneth Galbraith   *The Concept of the Conventional Wisdom*

1. What does Galbraith mean by "conventional wisdom"?
2. Why has the *acceptable* the tactical advantage over the *relevant*? Why especially in economic and social behavior?
3. What factors contribute to the acceptability of ideas? Why do acceptable ideas have great stability?
4. In paragraph 8, Galbraith remarks, "To proclaim the need for new ideas has served, in some measure, as a substitute for them." What does he mean? How is this statement applicable to social science scholarship?

Why do people like to have said what they approve? In what way is this articulation a religious rite?

Why are events the enemy of conventional wisdom? Under what circumstances will a conventional idea die? What illustrations does Galbraith submit to support his contention? What part do men like Adam Smith and John Maynard Keynes play in this process?

What positive function in the field of social comment does conventional wisdom serve? What disabilities does a system based on conventional wisdom have?

David Riesman   *New Standards for Old:*
From Conspicuous Consumption to Conspicuous Production

Why are companies finding it more difficult to recruit salesmen? In what way is the growing desire to be part of a group antagonistic to the character of the salesman or entrepreneur? Why do many companies have compulsive retirement at a certain age?

How does the author illustrate his thesis about the changing relationship of the individual to the group by reference to Willy Loman and Howard Wagner?

What is Veblen's thesis? What is the relationship between it and Riesman's contention that today people tend to seek group identification?

How has what the author terms the "bounteousness of modern industry" helped make conspicuous consumption obsolete? What part has been played by education, mass media, relaxation of standards?

How are foundations utilized by the wealthy to evade conspicuous consumption? Why does Riesman term the federal government "the biggest foundation of all . . ."? How are children also a means to evade conspicuous consumption?

What is conspicuous production? How is it manifested? What factors have influenced its development?

What is the thesis of this essay? In what paragraph is it clearly articulated?

Why does the tone of the final paragraph differ from that of the rest of this essay?

Comprehension
Questions

Walter Prescott Webb   *The Boom Hypothesis of Modern History*

1. What is Webb's boom hypothesis?
2. What does he mean by the frontier? Metropolis?
3. In what way does the author consider the modern age an abnormal one?
4. In paragraph 5 Webb speaks of the "change of ratios" as the force that precipitated the boom. Explain.
5. What part did society's acquisitive instinct have in the boom?
6. Why can't we measure the quantity of goods during the period of history spoken of?
7. Why does the author consider 1930 as the crucial year?
8. What implication for the future is inherent in Webb's argument? See the second, third, and last paragraphs.

Sir Dennis William Brogan   *America is Made*

1. What economic reasons did the pioneer have for "selling" America? How did the Supreme Court Decision spoken of in paragraph 3 further intensify this booster spirit? Why was pessimism considered treason?
2. What are the two interpretations made of the term "receiver" in paragraph 4? What point does Brogan make in this paragraph?
3. In what way is the farmer a participant in "the web of speculation, of optimism, of boosting . . ."? The local banker? The local doctor?
4. How did towns attempt to anchor a settler permanently?
5. The author makes specific contrast between English and American traits. What are they? Whom do these contrasts favor?
6. What connection does Brogan make between credit and publicity?
7. Why was the national spirit tougher on economic and political dissenters than on religious dissenters? Why is there still intolerance of individual eccentricity?
8. Why does Brogan characterize 1929 as a crucial year?
9. What evidence is there to show that the audience for whom this essay is intended is more English than American?
10. What is the purpose of this essay?

Mary McCarthy   *America the Beautiful*

1. Why couldn't the visitor be shown what was truly American?
2. What does the author mean by conditions? Why don't they represent the real America?
3. What deceives Europeans into believing that Americans are materialistic?
4. Miss McCarthy states in paragraph 8, "Americans build skyscrapers: Le Corbusier worships them." Explain.
5. What arguments does the author advance to prove the unmaterialistic character of American life? Explain her contention that for early Americans "the purchase of a bathtub was the exercise of a spiritual right." What is the significance of the subtitle of this essay?
6. Why don't the majority of Americans enjoy their possessions? Why are minority groups exceptions?
7. What similarity does Miss McCarthy see between the nation with its new bomb and the Consumer with his new Buick? Why does she fear that Americans won't be able not to use the bomb?
8. What does the author mean by dissociated condition of Americans? What explanation does she offer for this condtion?
9. What are the true ingredients of the American character?
10. Explain Miss McCarthy's contention that "Columbus . . . passed on" and "the explorers have failed to see us."
11. Explain her statement that "Europe is the unfinished negative of which America is the proof."

Lewis Mumford   *The Suburban Way of Life*

1. What evidence is there that the suburb is almost as old as the city itself?
2. What was the purpose of the original creators of the suburb? What are the characteristics of this historical suburb?
3. What effect did the romantic impulse have on suburban development? Why were the architects and the planners of the early romantic movement more scientific and rational than their modern counterparts?
4. What are the characteristics of the modern suburb? In what way is it a caricature both of the historic city and the archetypal suburban refuge?
5. Mumford speaks of the loss suffered by those who left the city. What is he referring to?
6. What positive effect has the suburb had on urban development? What alternative does the author offer to the universal suburb or the universal megalopolis?

Phyllis McGinley   *Suburbia: Of Thee I Sing*

1. What clichés about suburban life does the author attack?
2. According to Miss McGinley, what are the virtues of suburbia? What are the defects of the city? country?

---

3. In paragraph 9, the writer remarks that compromise is Manor "the pleasant place it is." What does she mean?
4. Miss McGinley and Lewis Mumford in "The Suburba in their attitude toward the modern suburb. Yet her suburb closely match his. What specific examples can y
5. What is the purpose of this essay? How does thi Mumford's? How do the two authors differ in th evidence?

Hans J. Morgenthau   *Why Nations*

1. Why does Morgenthau believe any analogy betw nations and natural-science data misleading?
2. Why does he suggest we approach the topic of th a considerable degree of humility . . ."?
3. Explain the author's contention that technologic often determine the rise and fall of nations. How surrender at Munich as support? What other proof
4. What are the three typical mistakes nations mak their power in comparison with the power of ot is given in each case?
5. What is the "gap" Morganthau speaks of in para nations is implicit in his analysis?
6. Why may this essay be characterized as undogm:
7. What techniques does the author use that make of his material?

Michael Harrington   *The 1*

1. Why does Harrington refer to the poor in *I*
2. Why hasn't welfare legislation helped the real'
3. Explain Harrington's contention that the po
4. Why does he criticize even those liberals poor?
5. Which of Lampman's arguments does the he counter each of them? Why does he rej "case poverty"?
6. At various points in his essay, Harringto passion to end poverty. What does he meat
7. Why can't state, city or private agencie can the federal government? Why must of the two political parties for an effecti

John W. Gardner　*Tyranny Without A Tyrant*

1. Why is Gardner so concerned with the fate of the individual?

2. What is the "new and streamlined tyranny" facing the individual today? What does the author mean by the "tyranny of formula"?

3. Why is there no tyrant in the tyranny Gardner speaks of? In what respect is this situation more difficult to deal with than if there actually were a dictator who manipulated his people?

4. In paragraphs 6–15, the author details three errors clouding the present problem of the relationship of the individual to society. What are they?

5. Why do individuals conform? How has specialization aided people's wish to conform?

6. In paragraph 27, Gardner speaks of the individual's "instinct for his own survival." What does he mean? What evidence does he submit?

7. How does large-scale organization enlarge the individual's freedom? What does Gardner mean by "organizing for freedom"?

8. Compare Gardner's and Brogan's ideas concerning the reasons why people conform.

John Henry Newman　*Literature*

1. In paragraph 2, Newman sets forth the three propositions he intends to refute in the rest of his essay. What are they? What is the relationship of paragraphs 4 and 5 to paragraph 2?

2. Why does literature imply writing, not speaking? What syllogism does Newman use in paragraph 8 to demonstrate that literature is essentially a personal work?

3. What distinction does he make between literature and science?

4. Explain Newman's contention that "style is a thinking out into language." How does he use this thesis to disprove those critics, especially of classical writers, who believe fine writing is merely ornamental? How does Newman support his point of view by reference to Cicero?

5. What analogy does the author use in paragraph 21? Why?

6. What defense does Newman make against the doctrine that easy translation is the test of good writing? What analogies does he include to illustrate his point?

7. What contentions about Scripture does Newman refute in section 8? What supporting arguments does he offer? At what point does Scripture enter the realm of science?

8. What is the purpose of section 10?

Matthew Arnold　*The Study of Poetry*

1. For what occasion did Arnold write this essay? Where in the selection does he reveal his purpose?

2. What does Arnold conceive the function of poetry to be? In what way is poetry more important than science, religion and philosophy?

3. Why is Arnold so concerned with high standards in poetry?

4. What does he mean by the historic estimate of poetry? Personal estimate? Why are both of these approaches false? Why are both fallacies natural?

5. What analogy does the author make in paragraph 7? Why?

6. What is the touchstone theory advanced in paragraph 10?

7. In paragraph 10, Arnold indicates that "tact" is required to use this method of evaluation. What does he mean?

8. What is Arnold's estimate of French romance poetry? Why?

9. Why does he praise Chaucer's poetry? What is a classic? Why isn't Chaucer a classic?

10. In paragraph 22, Arnold deals with Shakespeare and Milton. Why is his discussion so cursory?

11. In what way did the age in which Dryden and Pope live help mold their work? What is Arnold's attitude toward their prose? Their poetry?

12. The author states that the position of the poet Gray is "singular." What does he mean?

13. In what way does Burns's Scotch world help deny him the role of a classic? What evidence does Arnold give that the personal estimate of Burns's poetry was the dominant critical approach? What differences does he see between the work of Burns and Chaucer?

14. Why doesn't Arnold deal with the poetry of Byron, Shelley and Wordsworth?

15. In what way are the attitudes of Arnold and Newman toward literature similar?

Walter Pater   *Appreciations*

1. According to the author, what is the aim of literary criticism?

2. What does Pater say is the purpose of his essay? What is the relationship of paragraphs 1 and 2 to this purpose?

3. What distinction does Pater make between external fact and a writer's "sense of fact"? When does the historian become the artist?

4. What is the difference between fine art and serviceable art? What is literary art? When may we call literary art *good*? When does good art become great art?

5. According to Pater, why did his age prefer imaginative prose to poetry?

6. What does he mean by the term *scholar*? Why is the literary artist a scholar "by necessity"? Why is the artist's appeal directed toward the scholar?

7. Explain Pater's contention in paragraph 12 that "all art does but consist in the removal of surplusage. . ."

8. What is *mind* in style? *Soul* in style?

9. Why does Pater refer to Flaubert as "the martyr of literary style"?

10. What is the function of tact or taste in relationship to style?

11. How does Pater support his view that style is not mere subjectivity? In what sense is style "impersonal"?

12. Compare the ideas in this selection with those in Newman's essay "Literature."

Thomas Stearns Eliot   *The Perfect Critic*

1. What is impressionistic criticism? Why is Eliot opposed to it?

2. In what way are Symons' critical comments about *Antony and Cleopatra* in paragraph 3 impressionistic? Why, according to Eliot, can't such impressions be called either false or true?

3. Why is Swinburne more of a critic in his criticism than Symons? Why is the artist a better critic than the non-artist?

4. What is the "abstract style in criticism"? Why is Eliot opposed to it? Why is the statement in paragraph 1 that poetry is "the most highly organized form of intellectual activity" an example of abstract criticism?

5. How have the "corruption" of professional philosophers and the accumulation of knowledge in the seventeenth century helped in the development of abstract criticism?

6. What is Eliot's concept of literary criticism? What qualities must the "perfect critic" have?

7. What is Eliot's attitude toward the following as literary critics: Coleridge, Arnold, Aristotle, Horace, Campion, Dryden, Remy de Gourmont?

Lionel Trilling   *Freud and Literature*

1. What support does Trilling give to his contention that "psychoanalysis is one of the culminations of the Romanticist literature of the nineteenth century"?

2. Why is it difficult to assess the exact influence of Freud on literature? What has been the general beneficial effect of Freud on literary criticism?

3. What evidence does Trilling provide to show Freud to be a rationalistic positivist?

4. Why, according to Trilling, does Freud speak about art with "contempt"?

5. What common elements do dream and neurosis have with art? What differences?

6. What limits and limitations of psychoanalysis in art was Freud aware of? What two things did he believe the analytical method could accomplish in art?

7. Explain why Trilling states that "there is no single meaning to any work of art . . ." How does he use this contention to rebut both James and Freud?

8. In what way can psychoanalysis help in interpreting literature? Explain Trilling's statement that Alexander's essay on *Henry IV* "has the tact to *accept* the play. . ."

9. What three contributions has Freud made to the understanding or the practice of art?

10. What is the purpose of this essay? What is the function of each of its four parts in relation to this purpose?

11. What is the tone of this essay?

Cleanth Brooks *Wordsworth and the Paradox of the Imagination*

1. What method does Brooks use to analyze Wordsworth's poem? Refer to specific phrases in paragraphs 1, 2, 3 and 8 that indicate his intention. Why does he forfeit the help Wordsworth's letters, notes and other poems might give to understand the Ode?

2. What is ambiguity? What is ambiguous about the child's vision? What are the two interpretations of the word *visionary*?

3. What is a paradox? Explain the paradox involving the child's vision and the common daylight in paragraph 13.

4. What analogy does Brooks make between the moon and sun, and the child? See paragraphs 14, 17 and 18 in particular.

5. Why does Brooks analyze Stanza V immediately after examining Stanzas I and II?

6. What is symbolism? What is meant by the "central symbolism of light" in Stanza V? What is ambiguous about this symbol?

7. What is ambiguous about Wordsworth's use of darkness as a symbol? What two "modes of perception" does the poet speak of?

8. What is irony? What is ironic about the child's desires and actions in this world? What is ironical about Stanza VI? What is the "ironic shock" Brooks speaks of in paragraph 39?

9. What relationship does the poet make between hearing and vision in Stanza III?

10. What ambiguities are involved in Wordsworth's use of earth?

11. Why does Brooks consider Stanza VII a failure?

12. What are realist and projective doctrines? How are these doctrines reconciled in the poem? What is the theme of the poem?

13. Why does Brooks believe the solution of the poem a weakness?

14. In paragraph 12, Brooks states that "Freud's brilliant accounts resemble science less that they do poems. . ." Compare this statement with Trilling's comments concerning Freud and literature.

15. What would be the attitude of Eliot, Pater, Arnold and Trilling towards Brooks' method of treating Wordsworth's poems?

Oscar Cargill *Toward a Pluralistic Criticism*

1. How does Cargill emphasize the importance of the past? How did the literature of the twenties and trends in the academies tend to undermine the influence of the past?

2. What were the new critics reacting against? What do they conceive the function of criticism to be? What criticisms of the new critics does Cargill

make? Explain his statement in paragraph 3, "We rape from frame and setting to adorn our tales or to trigger a specious erudition." What contribution to literary criticism have the new critics made?

3. What distinction does the author make between scholars and critics? What is his attitude toward the research scholar? To what end does he use Edel's biographical study of Henry James?

4. What is the approach of Freudian criticism? Archetypal? Moral? What is Cargill's attitude toward each?

5. What is the significance of the title of the essay? Explain Cargill's feeling that the literary critic's role should be that of "both scholar and critic."

6. What would be Arnold's reaction to Cargill's opening remark: "The function of the critic and scholar is to make the past functional, for unless it can be used, it is deader than death itself."

7. Compare Cargill's theory of literary criticism with that of Pater, Eliot, Trilling, and Brooks.

8. Why is this selection placed last in the series of essays concerned with literary criticism?

9. What evidence is there that this essay is well organized?

Institute for Propaganda Analysis *How to Detect Propaganda*

1. What is propaganda?
2. What is the nature of each of the seven common propaganda devices?
3. What do all seven devices have in common?
4. Why is Card Stacking the hardest propaganda device to detect?
5. What is the tone of this article?

Samuel T. Williamson *How to Write Like a Social Scientist*

1. What is the main point of this essay? Why is Williamson so concerned with the writing of social scientists?

2. Why are the author's "rules" ironic? What are the real rules implicit in his irony?

3. What is the source of Williamson's examples of "pedantic Choctaw"? What effect do these examples have on the force of his argument?

4. What are the characteristics of Williamson's style?

5. What is the tone of the essay?

George Orwell *Politics and the English Language*

1. What is the main thesis of this selection? In which paragraphs is it articulated?

2. Regarding the decline of language, what does Orwell mean by "an effect can become a cause"? What basis for hope does he offer in this connection?

3. Explain the meaning of dying metaphors, operators or verbal false limbs, pretentious diction, meaningless words. What examples does the author offer for each of these errors?

4. In paragraph 10, Orwell parodies a Biblical selection. In what way is the original a superior piece of writing?

5. Why do people tend to use ready-made phrases?

6. What important questions should a careful writer ask himself? What are the key rules he should follow? How does the last of these rules show Orwell as undogmatic?

7. Explain the author's contention that political speech and writing are "largely the defense of the indefensible."

8. Explain Orwell's remark that "all issues are political issues. . ."

John Illo *The Rhetoric of Malcolm X*

1. How does Illo define rhetoric? What does he see as its function?

2. Explain the author's statement in paragraph 3 that "rhetoric is in fact poeticized logic. . ." What difference, however, does he discern between the orator and poet?

3. What is Illo's attitude toward the American Establishment? Why? What evidence does he provide to support his point-of-view?

4. What was Malcolm's main accomplishment? Why was he an effective rhetorician? What rhetorical devices did he employ?

5. What was Malcolm's "central message"? How did his position on race differ from that of other Negro leaders?

6. What was Malcolm's main weakness?

7. What is the tone of Illo's remarks about Malcolm, especially in paragraphs 49 and 50?

8. What distinction does Illo make between analogy and metaphor? Why did Malcolm prefer the former? Why did he prefer the paragraph to the sentence?

9. What are the main subdivisions of this essay? What is the function of paragraphs 1–4? paragraphs 5–6? paragraph 7?

10 Is the title of this essay appropriate? Review the contents of the selection before answering.

11. Compare the similarity of ideas in this essay (especially in paragraphs 5 and 11) and those in Orwell's "Politics and the English Language."

Marshall McLuhan *Television The Timid Giant*

1. How does the TV image differ from film or photo? Why is the TV image a mosaic?

2. What effect does the low-intensity or definition of the TV image have on viewer participation? Why? Why is this participation "profoundly" tactile? Why is the effect of television an "electric extension of our central nervous system. . ."?

3. Why is television characterized as a cool medium? Explain McLuhan's contention in paragraph 6 that "TV has cooled Cuba down." Why is television called "The Timid Giant"?

4. Why is the radio characterized as a hot medium? Explain the comment in paragraph 6 that "Radio is the medium for frenzy. . ."

5. Why did radio have a profound effect on Europe but not on the United States or England?

6. Define *Synesthesia*. How has television had a synesthetic effect on the United States and England?

7. In what way is print like the movie and the comicstrip form like television? What is meant by "the homogenizing power of typography. . ."? How has print technology affected our education and our industrial and political life?

8. How has television's in-depth participation affected the following: loyalty to the consumer package, adolescence, paperbacks, the automobile, baseball, football, dialectical speech?

9. In paragraphs 14 and 28, McLuhan rebuts critics who would censor television because of scenes of violence. What is his point? Explain the meaning of the phrase, "the medium is the message."

Jacques Barzun *Conversation, Manners, and the Home*

1. What does Barzun mean by manners?

2. What distinction does he make between the exchange and the sifting of opinion?

3. What effect have democratic manners had on conversation? Why don't democratic manners tolerate contradiction in conversation?

4. Why is the statement in paragraph 7 a *syllogism*?

5. Why does the democrat have an unconscious fear of intellect? How does the intellect impede the democrat's desire to be philanthropic?

6. What distinction does Barzun make between intellectual shuffling and being self-aware?

7. According to the author, how does the individual strengthen the intellect?

8. How does a "surfeit of personality" impede conversation?

9. Explain Barzun's contention that conversation is "the antithesis of education."

10. What distinction does he make between vanity and pride?

11. What point is Barzun making in paragraph 31 in his quotations from the circular and the column?

12. In what way has the novel taught intellectuals their anti-intellectualism and their "diffident gestures of the spirit"?

13. Why does Barzun take modern youth to task?

14. Why does he criticize the self-centered family?

15. Why don't democratic manners favor highly organized speech?

16. Select statements illustrating Barzun's use of irony.
17. Explain the relationship among the three key words in the title of this essay.
18. Into what major divisions can this article be divided?

Lewis Mumford *Architecture as Symbol*

1. In what way is architecture a symbol?
2. Explain Mumford's belief in paragraph 4 that architecture "endows with special significance the impulses and ideas that shape it. . ."
3. Why was the nineteenth century a "period of disintegration" from an architectural point-of-view? What does Mumford mean in stating that architecture was dead in the social sense from the sixteenth to the twentieth centuries?
4. What were the contributions of the following to architecture: Morris, Richardson, Wright, Le Corbusier?
5. What were the strong and weak points of L'Art Nouveau?
6. What was the influence of gardening on architecture?
7. What is the tone of this article? Is it appropriate for the author's purpose?

H. W. Janson *The Artist and His Public*

1. What is the purpose of this essay? How does the organization of the essay help accomplish its aim?
2. Why is it difficult to devise a rating scale for art?
3. Although Janson admits the difficulty of defining art, he does provide certain guidelines. What are they? Why is Picasso's *Bull's Head* art?
4. Why is the making of a work of art analogous to the process of giving birth? How does Janson illustrate by reference to Michaelangelo's *St. Matthew*?
5. Why does the author characterize the making of a work of art as "a strange and risky business. . ."?
6. How does the creator differ from the craftsman?
7. Explain Janson's statement that "originality is always relative. . ." How does he illustrate this point by reference to the *Thorn Puller* and the *Battle of Sea Gods*?
8. What distinction does the author make between copying and representing? How does he illustrate this distinction by reference to Manet's *Luncheon on The Grass*?
9. What is tradition? What is its relation to the artist's "leap of the imagination"?
10. What are applied arts? What is their purpose? What is their relation to art and craft?

Van Wyck Brooks *The Flowering of New England, Conclusion*

1. What is a culture cycle? What is its pattern?
2. In what way was the movement of mind in New England a cultural cycle?

3. How does Brooks characterize the New England writers at the zenith of their cycle? Explain his remark that these writers possessed "an extra-literary sanction."

4. Why was it inevitable that the West react against New England? What was the effect of this reaction on the reputations of the popular and esoteric New England writers?

5. What aspects of Thoreau, Hawthorne and Emerson does the author stress?

6. What are the chief characteristics of Brooks' style? What stylistic differences are there in several sections of this essay, especially in Brooks' descriptions of Thoreau, Hawthorne and Emerson?

Malcolm Cowley   *The Greenwich Village Idea*

1. Who were the inhabitants of Grub Street? Why did Pope attack them?

2. What distinction does Cowley make between Grub Street and Bohemia?

3. What influence did Murger's books, *Scenes de la Vie de Bohême* have on Grub Street and Bohemia?

4. What is ironic about the position of the Villagers and that of the *Saturday Evening Post* in the years following World War I?

5. Explain the author's contention that Greenwich Village "was also a doctrine." What are the main points of this system of ideas?

6. Why was the business—Christian ethic—substantially a production ethic? Why was there a need to switch to a consumption ethic?

7. How did the Greenwich Village idea prove useful to a consumption ethic? What is ironic in this situation?

8. What caused the revolution in morals? What part did the Village play in this revolution?

9. Explain the idea that if Greenwich Villages was dying, "it was dying of success."

Ralph Waldo Emerson   *The American Scholar*

1. What is Emerson's overall purpose in this selection? How does the order of the essay contribute to this purpose? What devices does the author use to achieve his aim?

2. How does Emerson define the word *scholar*? What does he mean that at his worst the scholar "tends to become a mere thinker, or, still worse, the parrot of other men's thinking"?

3. How does nature influence the mind? Emerson states that nature "resembles [men's] own spirit. . ." Explain.

4. What is the value of books? At what point do they do man a disservice? Explain the comment in paragraph 16 that "genius is always sufficiently the enemy of genius by over-influence."

5. What should be the proper function of a college education?

6. Why must the scholar be a man of action? What is the value of action? Explain Emerson's remark in paragraph 28 that "character is higher than intellect."

7. What are the duties of the scholar? Why must he be both free and brave?

8. What is the main idea of paragraphs 35 and 36? Explain the statement in paragraph 36, "It is one soul which animates all men." Why does Emerson view the literature of Goethe, Wordsworth and Carlyle as a hopeful sign?

9. What is Emerson's purpose in speaking of the American scholar and not just the scholar in general? Explain his contention in paragraph 44 that "we have listened too long to the courtly muses of Europe."

Arthur Bestor   *The College of Liberal Arts and Sciences*

1. What is Bestor's purpose in this essay?

2. How does secondary instruction differ from university education in America?

3. In what sense is the undergraduate college of England and America a transitional institution?

4. How does the liberal arts college prepare for the fulfillment of the motto *E pluribus unum*?

5. What does Bestor mean by "ways of thinking"? Give examples.

6. How does vocational or professional training differ from a liberal education?

7. What criticism does Bestor make of the free-elective system?

8. What is the author's proposal for improving liberal arts education?

9. How does Bestor use the threshold theory in this plan?

10. Read Barzun's "Conversation, Manners, and the Home." What significant ideas concerning education are stressed in it and in this selection?

Robert Maynard Hutchins   *The Higher Learning*

1. In what way has our misuse of facts made us anti-intellectual?

2. Why does Hutchins favor Newton and Galileo over Descartes and Bacon? What is the purpose of the quotations in paragraphs 20–23?

3. What does Hutchins see wrong with university education? Why is he especially critical of the role of science? Why does he consider character, personality and facts to be the "three worst words" in education?

4. What should be the purpose of university education? Explain Hutchin's statement in paragraph 27 that "a well-planned university course is a wide sweep of generality." What should be the purpose of scholarship?

5. What relationship does Hutchins point to between the university and society? What similarity is there between Hutchins' concept of the proper role of the teacher and that of Emerson?

Peter F. Drucker   *The Educational Revolution*

1. Prior to the twentieth century, why couldn't society afford many educated people? What is the "iron law" referred to in paragraph 7? What is the relationship of this "law" to manual labor?

2. What has caused the educational revolution? In what way are educated people the capital of a developed society?

3. How has the educational revolution been a force in automation?

4. Why will society have to make all jobs "meaningful and capable of satisfying an educated man"?

5. How has the educational revolution had an impact on world economy?

6. What are the political implications of educational inequality between nations?

7. In paragraph 36, Drucker speaks of the need for "highly educated people." What does he mean? Compare this concept of the educated man with that of Hutchins.

Jerome S. Bruner   *Motives for Learning*

1. What distinction does Bruner make between short-run and long-run development of interest? What may be the effect of such devices as films and audio-visual aids? Why is the possible problem resulting from the use of such devices compounded by "an entertainment-oriented, mass-communications culture. . ."? Why does the author insist on the need for "active autonomy of of attention. . ."?

2. What should motives for learning be based on?

3. What has been ambivalent about America's attitude toward education? What factors have helped Americans become aware of the content and quality of education?

4. What two trends in the educational system will be accelerated? What is meritocracy? Why is it likely that baring any planning, these trends will lead to meritocracy?

5. What will be the undesirable effects of meritocracy?

6. What measures does Bruner offer to prevent the ill effects of meritocracy?

Margaret Mead   *The Education of the Samoan Child*

1. Why is the relative rather than actual age of the child important?

2. What is the nature of the child's education until he is four or five years old?

3. In what ways is the education of girls from about six to puberty less comprehensive than boys of the same age? In this age group, why do boys organize more efficiently than girls?

4. Of what does the girl's education from puberty on consist? Why does Dr. Mead call the age of seventeen the "best period" of a girl's life?

5. What effect has government schooling had on the native household?

6. What is the *Aumaga*? a *matai*? the *Fono*? What are responsibilities of the seventeen-year-old boy? What dilemma faces him at this age?

7. What is the tone of this article? Why is it appropriate to the purpose of the article?

Ruth Benedict *The Diversity of Cultures*

1. What are the two main propositions of this essay? What issues does Miss Benedict develop to support each of them?

2. In paragraph 6, the author draws an analogy between speech and culture. What is her point?

3. What distinction does Miss Benedict make between biological and social puberty?

4. Define totemism and shaman.

5. What evidence is there that this selection follows a pattern of induction?

6. What is the overall purpose of the essay? See in particular, paragraphs 4, 5, 25, 30, 32, 33, 45 and especially 46.

7. Rhetorically speaking, how does this essay differ from that of Margaret Mead?

Ralph Linton *Race*

1. What is the purpose of paragraphs 1–4?

2. What is hybridization? The concept of primary types? What is Linton's attitude toward each?

3. What evidence is there that all existing human varieties belong to the same species?

4. How does Linton explain the existence of present human varieties?

5. What is the function of paragraph 9?

6. What is natural selection? Why doesn't it account for all changes in physical types?

7. What connection do variations in skin color have with natural environment?

8. What is social selection? How does it influence diversity of human types?

9. Why is it almost impossible for any group to maintain absolute purity of blood? Why aren't hybrid people inferior to pure-bred ones?

10. What is ironic about the position of those Europeans who believe in the superiority of pure strains? To whom is Linton obviously referring?

11. What is a breed? How are norms for physical characteristics arrived at? What is an ideal physical type?

12. What is a race? What is a stock? What are the stocks and the races that comprise each? Why is the Mongoloid stock the most difficult to define?

13. Why are breeds "genuine biological entities and races and stocks 'abstractions'"? Why is Linton so cautious in using classifications?

Adolf Hitler   *Nation and Race*

1. What does Hitler mean by race? How does his view differ from Linton's?

2. How does Hitler support his contention that mixing of races lowers the level of the higher one? What analogies from nature does he draw upon? What historical "experience" does he submit? How does Linton's view on hybridization differ from Hitler's?

3. How does Hitler use the theory of natural selection as an argument for aggression? How do Linton's views on natural selection differ from Hitler's?

4. Explain Hitler's idea that war is necessary for "pacifism."

5. What distinction does Hitler make between culture-bearing and culture-creating races?

6. How does cultural perfection depend on *one* race? Why does Hitler mention the myth of Prometheus? Explain Hitler's remarks in paragraph 43 that "the progress of humanity is like climbing an endless ladder. . . ."

7. What propaganda devices does Hitler use? Refer to "How to Detect Propaganda."

Karl Marx and Friedrich Engels   *The Communist Manifesto*

1. What is the purpose of Part I? To whom is it addressed?

2. How has the "epoch of the bourgeoisie" simplified class antagonisms?

3. *The Manifesto* suggests that bourgeoisie tyranny is worse than feudal tyranny. In what way?

4. Explain the statement in paragraph 28 that modern bourgeoisie society is "the sorcerer, who is no longer able to control the powers of the nether world whom he has called up by his spells." What is meant by "the epidemic of overproduction"?

5. In what way are the bourgeoisie a commodity?

6. Explain the contention in paragraph 39 that "every class struggle is a political struggle."

7. What is the purpose of Section II? To whom is it addressed? What arguments against Communism are advanced by the bourgeoisie? How is each answered?

8. What is the purpose of Section III? To whom is it addressed? Define the following movements and tell why each is considered inadequate: feudal socialism, clerical socialism, petty bourgeoisie socialism, critical-utopian socialism and Communism.

9. What is the purpose of Part IV? To whom is it addressed? Why is it so brief?

Mao Tse-Tung   *Methods of Thinking and Methods of Work*

1. In paragraph 7, Mao speaks of two stages in the process of cognition. What are they? In what way is the first stage inductive?

2. What is Mao's attitude toward idealism and metaphysics. Why?

3. Explain the statement in paragraph 19 that "the law of the unity of opposites is the fundamental law of the universe."

4. What effect do subjectivity, one-sidedness and superficiality have on thinking?

5. Of what does the art of leadership consist?

Pope John XXIII *Relations Between Individuals and the Public Authorities Within A Single State*

1. Why is society necessary? What is its purpose? In what way does civil authority derive from God? How does this divine source act as a check on the power of authority?

2. What are the implications of the statement in paragraph 6 that if civil authorities go against the moral orders "neither the laws made nor the authorizations granted can be binding on the consciences of the citizens. . ."?

3. How is the doctrine of civil authority set forth in this essay "fully consonant with any truly democratic regime"?

4. What are the essentials of the common good?

5. What are the responsibilities of civil authority? Why must it give special attention to social and economic progress of the individual? Why especially in the modern world?

6. What should be the relationship between the state and the individual in the field of economics?

7. What are the responsibilities of individuals in society?

8. What is the implication of paragraph 31?

9. What is liberal about this essay's point-of-view?

R. H. Tawney *Rights and Functions*

1. What is a function? What is the responsibility of the agent in relationship to a function? How did the history of England prior to 1700 reflect this agent-function relationship? What caused this relationship to break up?

2. What change in thought concerning function and agent occurred in the eighteenth century? Explain the statement in paragraph 4 that "God had been thrust into the frigid altitudes of infinite space."

3. How did private rights and interests replace the function of Church and State? Why did society resemble "a giant joint-stock company"? What does Tawney mean by the "mysticism of reason" that acted as a substitute for God in the eighteenth century?

4. Explain the contention in paragraph 8 that it was not the right to liberty that appealed to the English, but "the expediency of liberty. . ." How did Smith and Bentham link the exercise of individual rights and the public good?

5. What criticism of utilitarianism does Tawney make? What does he mean in stating the Liberal Movement of the eighteenth century "was important to disarm the new ogre of industrialism"?

6. Contrast Pope John's concept of the proper functioning of society with practice in the eighteenth century.

7. What is the relevance of "The Communist Manifesto" to the eighteenth century concept of the sanctity of property and unrestricted individualism in economics?

Walter Lippmann   *The Pursuit of Liberty*

1. What is the main idea of this essay?

2. In what way is liberty established by laws and usages?

3. Explain Lippmann's contention that man's pursuit of liberty has not been motivated by "an ideological predilection."

4. What is the proper role of liberalism in society? Why isn't liberalism the doctrine of laissez faire? How does the liberal differ from the anarchist?

5. In paragraph 15, Lippmann uses an analogy between men and society and runners in a race. What is his point?

6. Explain the comment in paragraph 23 that "the division of labor was not invented by economists. . . ."

7. Why can't modern society be made to conform to a preconceived system of operation? What is Lippmann's attitude toward Plato's *Republic*? Why?

8. What is the proper function of statesmen and society?

9. Compare Lippmann's and Tawney's attitude toward the "classic liberals."

Lyman Bryson   *On Deceiving the Public for the Public Good*

1. What are the "great collectives" Bryson speaks of in paragraph 1? What effect do they have on our lives?

2. Why does the author feel that "our unpredictability is part of our human charm"?

3. Bryson states that a leader is an "embodied suggestion." What does he mean? How does he illustrate by reference to Hitler?

4. What is the purpose of political life? How is the leader's function related to this purpose?

5. What are the *closed* and *open* theories of freedom?

6. Bryson maintains that nations must first place themselves under spiritual domination before they can dominate others. What does he mean? How does he illustrate by reference to Rome and Britain on one hand and Greece and France on the other?

7. What evidence does the author provide to illustrate that love of free inquiry does not destroy the power of a great nation?

8. Put in Kantian terms, what choices face all nations? Which choice is incompatible with democracy? Why?

9. In what way is the purpose of a leader bound up with the Kantian choice?
10. Why aren't freedom and power antithetical? What support does Bryson give to demonstrate that significant cultural achievements generally have not paralleled great material power?
11. Why is the answer to the question "Should a leader deceive the public for the public?" really a choice in political action?
12. Contrast the attitudes of Bryson and Lippmann toward the function of a leader in society.

Sidney Hook   *The Conflict of Freedoms*

1. What is political freedom? When is a government called *free*? What are "the processes by which political consent is won"? What is their relation to political freedom?
2. What are the *absolute* and *admonitions* views of freedom? What is Hook's position? What three reasons does he offer for his point of view?
3. What do *true* and *apparent* freedom have in common? What does Hook mean in paragraph 8 by the "fetish of the abstraction. . ."? Why does he distinguish between common usage and common sense in relation to freedom?
4. Why is it logically impossible to have absolute freedom?
5. Explain how freedoms of which we approve may conflict. How does Hook use the paradigm case in paragraph 13 to support his view?
6. What does Hook mean by stating freedoms are *strategic*? What two arguments against his own position does he raise? Why? How does he counter each of them?
7. Trace the organization of this essay by dividing it into paragraph sections.
8. Why do Hook and Lippmann disapprove of Plato's political philosophy?
9. Compare Hook's attitude toward absolute freedom with Lippmann's.

Charles Frankel   *Ideals and Idols of Democracy*

1. What are the two democratic traditions of which Frankel speaks? Why is the tension between them really a "family quarrel"?
2. Why is democracy an "acquired" taste?
3. What are the four ideals of political democracy? Explain each.
4. Why does the ideal of government-by-consent require a social system?
5. Why do the practical conditions for making an open society work lie outside of legal formalities?
6. What is the American dream? Explain Frankel's statement that every society has its own "mad dream."
7. What are private governments? What is their function?
8. What is an idol? What three idols does Frankel mention? Why is each an idol?
9. Why is democracy really rule-by-minorities?

10. How does democracy depend on political blocs and pressure groups?

11. Why does democracy require ideas?

12. Into what paragraph division do the ideas in this essay fall?

13. Is Frankel's essay more disturbing than reassuring? Why?

Gunnar Myrdal   *A Methodological Note on Valuations and Beliefs*

1. What are *beliefs*? *Valuations*? *Opinions*?

2. What is the "psychological interrelation" between beliefs and valuations?

3. Why do a person's valuations conflict? Explain Myrdal's contention that valuations "refer to different levels of the moral personality."

4. What are *rationalizations*? Define *behavior*.

5. Why are the valuations on the higher, more general plane invoked in moral criticism?

6. What is the result if specific attitudes run counter to general moral principles? What may result if there is an attempt to reinterpret or change general moral valuations?

7. What is moral escapism?

8. Why is society moving increasingly in the direction of more general valuations?

9. How are beliefs the "building stones" for a person's valuations? What is the purpose of education?

10. Why does the author criticize Sumner's concept of mores?

11. What are revolutions or explosions as used by Myrdal? Why do they keep occurring in modern society?

12. What criticism does Myrdal make of Marx?

13. How may cynicism lead to "a revulsion to fascism and pagan gods" in an opinion catharsis?

Alfred North Whitehead   *The Origins of Modern Science*

1. What is the overall purpose of this essay?

2. What differences does the author point out between the Reformation and the rise of science? Why does he make this contrast?

3. What contribution did Greece make to modern science? Explain the remark in paragraph 16 that "the minds of the Greeks" were infected with an eager generality."

4. In what way was the Greek view of nature essentially dramatic?

5. What does Whitehead mean by the historical spirit? How did the Greeks "damp down" this spirit? In what way were the Reformation and scientific movements aspects of the historical revolt? Why was the revolt an anti-intellectual movement?

6. What parallel does the author see between the Greek tragedians' vision of fate and the scientific vision? Explain the statement in paragraph 27 that "the laws of physics are the decree of fate."

7. How did the Stoics influence medieval thought?

8. What was the most significant contribution of medievalism to the development of the scientific movement? What was the source of this contribution?

9. What comparison does Whitehead draw between the sixth century in Italy and the sixteenth?

10. What was the "final ingredient" needed for the rise of science, which was provided by the rise of Naturalism in the late Middle Ages?

11. Explain the author's comment that science has now reached a turning point. What two methods for "purification" of ideas lie open to it?

12. What is Whitehead's solution to the problem of the direction science should take?

John Dewey   *Science and Free Culture*

1. How has science hindered rather than aided democracy?

2. How have governments exercised direct and indirect control over science? Explain the remark in paragraph 8 that "a kind of positive halo surrounds scientific endeavors."

3. How has the demand for direct social control of scientific investigations been unknowingly intensified by scientists themselves?

4. How does Dewey counter the assertion that desires are fixed?

5. Explain the idea in paragraph 22 that "science operates as part of folklore, not just as science."

6. What is the scientific attitude? Why does it go against human impulses?

7. In what way is the fate of democracy tied up with the need to spread the scientific attitude? How is the problem of spreading the scientific attitude related to economics? Education? Art? Religion? Morality?

8. What does Dewey see as the responsibility of scientists? What is the relationship of science and a free culture?

9. What criticisms of education in America does Dewey make? Compare and contrast his views with those of Hutchins.

Sir Arthur S. Eddington   *Man's Place in the Universe*

1. What is Eddington's purpose in writing this essay?

2. Why is it difficult to estimate the number of stars in the universe?

3. What is the Galactic System? How does it differ from our local star-cloud?

4. Why is the sun referred to as a "humble unit"? Why is the sun labelled "a respectable middle-class citizen"?

5. Why does Eddington speak of our world as insignificant?

6. How did the sidereal universe begin? What evidence is there that evolution has not reached the same development in all parts of this universe?

7. What two speculations does the author speak of in paragraph 9? Why have they been rejected?

8. Why would Venus be a possible place for life similar to ours to exist? Why does Eddington say in paragraph 14 that Venus is "a world which is all ocean—where fishes are supreme"?

9. How was the moon formed? Why isn't it an ordinary satellite?

10. What is the make-up of Mars? What proof of seasonal change on Mars is there?

11. Why does Eddington refer to the solar system as a "freak"? What point does he make in paragraph 25 using the star/tennis ball analogy?

12. What is the tone of the article?

Isaac Asimov *Over the Edge of the Universe*

1. What is the overall purpose of this essay?

2. Define spectrum. What is a red-shift? Violet-shift?

3. What were the findings of Slipher? Humanson? What is Hubble's Law?

4. What is the purpose of paragraph 8?

5. What are the big-bang and continuous creation theories of the universe?

6. What is the time machine Asimov speaks of in paragraph 8?

7. What is the purpose of paragraph 19? Paragraph 26?

8. What were the contributions of Jansky? Baade? Ryle?

9. What are quasars? Why do they puzzle astronomers? How did information about quasars favor the big-bang theory? What discovery in 1966 further strengthened the big-bang theory?

10. Why does the continuous creation theory provide for a "godlike vision" and the big-bang theory force men "to face an inevitable end"? What is the purpose of the final paragraph?

11. What is the tone of this article? Contrast it with that of Eddington's selection.

Rachel Carson *And No Birds Sing*

1. What is the author's intention in this essay?

2. Why is the Dutch elm disease difficult to destroy?

3. How are the robins destroyed by the Dutch elm disease?

4. What pragmatic argument does Miss Carson advance to save the birds?

5. What is ironical about the whole program of spraying the elms?

6. What alternatives does the author offer to spraying with insecticides?

7. How do the robin and eagle sequences differ in their use of evidence?

8. This essay is well organized. Trace the development of the ideas to their climax.

9. Statistics can make very dry reading. How does Miss Carson avoid this pitfall?

10. In what way are this essay and the one by Asimov similar?

Sigmund Freud *Repression*

1. What is repression? Why is flight from an instinct impossible? What is condemnation? Why is repression between flight and condemnation?

2. Freud states in paragraph 6 that repression "causes pleasure in one part of the mind and 'pain' in another." Explain.

3. What is primal repression? What is its purpose? What is repression proper? Why is it termed an after-expulsion?

4. What is instinct presentation? What does Freud mean in paragraph 11 that it "ramifies like a fungus . . ." if withdrawn from consciousness by repression?

5. Under what circumstances will derivatives of what was repressed have access to the conscious part of the mind?

6. What is cathexis? What is its relationship to repression? How does an increase of cathexis operate in the same way as "an approach to the unconscious . . ."?

7. How is repression mobile?

8. What is charge of affect? What is anxiety? What is their relationship?

9. What is a substitute-formation? Symptom? What causes both?

10. What is anxiety-hysteria? How does Freud illustrate by animal-phobia? Why does he term the repression in animal-phobia "radically unsuccessful"?

11. What is conversion-hysteria? How does it differ from anxiety-hysteria?

12. What is obsessional neurosis? How does repression in this case make use of a reaction-formation? Why is the "final form" of repression in the obsessional neurosis "a sterile and never-ending struggle"?

13. What is the tone of this article?

Sir Julian Huxley *"Science and God": The Naturalistic Approach*

1. In what way are gods "empirical facts"?

2. What are the three "possible" ways of defining the nature of gods? What ways does Huxley see as impossible? Why?

3. Which definition of gods does the author accept? Why?

4. What is scientific naturalism? What evidence does Huxley provide to illustrate that the "absolutist" approach in natural science has been replaced by scientific naturalism?

5. How do gods resemble scientific hypotheses? How do they differ?

6. What is mythological thought? How are gods products of mythological thought?

7. What is magical thinking? What is its relationship to man's infantile phase? What is the projective mode of organizing mythological thought? How is it related to the infant's development? What is the mythological mode of organizing mythological thought?

8. What parallels are there between the evolution of gods and biological evolution of organisms? What examples are provided to illustrate each stage of the evolution of gods?

9. Huxley states that the so-called conflict between science and religion is really the result of competition between science and religion. Explain what other competition gods have had to face.
10. Huxley states in paragraph 53 that "it will soon be impossible for an intelligent, educated man or woman to believe in a god . . ." Why?

Bertrand Russell *A Free Man's Worship*

1. Why does Russell refer to the world as "alien and inhuman . . ."?
2. What is the "strange mystery" he speaks of in paragraph 4?
3. What is Russell's attitude toward conventional religion? Why?
4. In paragraph 9, the author states that "indignation is still a bondage . . ." In what way?
5. Explain Russell's view in paragraph 9 what wisdom is found "in the submission of our desires but not in our thoughts." Why is "renunciation" essential to wisdom? Why must the "self" die before ideals can be realized?
6. In what way can man "transform and refashion the unconscious universe . . ." through the imagination. Why does the past have "such magical power"?
7. According to Russell, what is man's responsibility to man?
8. What are the stylistic characteristics of this essay? Is the style appropriate for Russell's purpose? Why?
9. How do Russell and Huxley differ in the kind of supporting material each uses for his main idea?

Alan W. Watts *"Sitting Quietly, Doing Nothing"*

1. What is the purpose of this essay? What rhetorical devices does the author rely most heavily on to achieve his aim?
2. Explain Watts' statement in paragraph 1 that "the mind must stop trying to act upon itself . . ."
3. What is "natural sincerity"? How is this sincerity illustrated by the saying "In walking, just walk. In sitting, just sit"? How is trying to be natural an "affectation"?
4. How does Watts use the furnace/thermostat image to explain human self-consciousness? How may "feed-back" lead to human anxiety?
5. Explain the idea in paragraph 12 that "reflection is also action . . ."
6. What is the Unborn? Why is "sitting quietly, doing nothing" essential to Zen? Why is a second thought really just a mirror reflected image?
7. Under what circumstances may Zen be "a very dangerous medicine . . ."?
8. Explain the remark in paragraph 25 that "the Zen experience is more of conclusion than a premise."
9. Explain the contention in paragraph 26 that "Zen lies beyond the ethical standpoint . . ." What relationship does Watts point out between Zen and Confucianism?

C. S. Lewis *The Abolition of Man*

1. Explain Lewis' remark in paragraph 2, "If I pay you to carry me, I am not therefore myself a strong man."
2. In paragraph 2, the author redefines man's power over nature to "a power possessed by some men . . ." What does he mean?
3. Define *conditioners.* Why does each advance of power over nature won by man leave him "weaker as well as stronger"? How can the general also be the prisoner?
4. What two significant differences does Lewis see between past attempts to mold man and the one he describes? What is the Tao? How does it differ from the values determined by the conditioners?
5. What leads Lewis to conclude that the conditioners will be motivated by their own pleasure? In what way will they be subject to nature? What is the magician's bargain the author speaks of in paragraph 12?
6. Explain Lewis' contention in paragraph 17 that "the serious magical endeavor and the serious scientific endeavor are twins . . ." Why was the modern scientific movement "born in an unhealthy neighborhood and at an inauspicious hour"?
7. What solution does Lewis offer for the problem he describes in this essay?
8. What is the tone of this selection?

Jacques Maritain *The Crisis of Modern Humanism*

1. What is Maritain's definition of humanism?
2. What is the defect of classical humanism? What is an anthropocentric concept of man and culture?
3. What is the fallacy the author speaks of in paragraph 5?
4. What is the *"irrationalist tidal wave"* referred to in paragraph 9? What is its relationship to classical humanism? What is *counter-humanism?* Why is Nietzsche spoken of as "Poor Nietzsche"?
5. Why is Maritain critical of Marxism? Explain why in Marxism it is "reason itself which decapitates reason."
6. What is *"humanism of the Incarnation"*? How does it contrast with classical humanism?

Arnold J. Toynbee *Christianity and Civilization*

1. What are the three main topics of this essay? What idea underlies all of them?
2. How does Toynbee answer the charge that Christianity was the destroyer of civilization? What fallacy in Gibbon's thinking does he see?
3. What is the "chrysalis" view of Christianity? What evidence is there for this view? Why does Toynbee reject it?
4. To what relationship between religion and civilization does the author subscribe? Why? Explain the religion/chariot analogy in paragraph 14.

5. What parallels does Toynbee point out between the Graeco-Roman civilization and ours?

6. What is the "worship of Leviathan"? What is the author's attitude toward Communism? Democracy? In what way have we been living on "spiritual capital"?

7. Toynbee states it is not necessary that one higher religion replace another. Why?

8. Why doesn't Toynbee believe that the establishment of a world-wide, enduring Christian Church would mean the establishment of the Kingdom of Heaven on earth? What does he mean by "Caesar will always have work to do . . ."? What is his purpose in speaking of the Sacrifice of the Mass and the Hierarchy?

9. What relationship does Toynbee point out between Christianity and progress? Explain the statement in paragraph 29 "Seeking God is itself a social act." How would the Church Militant aid social progress?

10. Explain Toynbee's remark in paragraph 38 that "a pagan soul, no less than a Christian soul, has ultimate salvation within its reach . . ."

11. What similarity of ideas are there in the essays of Toynbee, Maritain and Lewis?

Reinhold Niebuhr *The Conflict Between Individual and Social Morality*

1. What is religious morality? Political morality? In what way do they conflict? Why is this conflict "not absolute"?

2. How has religious morality been cultivated by religion?

3. What is rational morality? Why is it utilitarian? Why is it "within limits, possible"? Why is it not as realistic as either religious or political morality?

4. What dangers are there resulting from inner restraint being placed on self-assertion by religion?

5. Explain Neibuhr's statement that the religious ideal "in its purest form" is unrelated to social justice? Why isn't religious idealism necessarily socially effective? How may religious idealism lead to social good? What evidence does the author provide to show that the use of religious idealism in group relations has not been effective?

6. Why does Niebuhr conclude that we should accept dualism in morals? Why are both individual moral discipline and idealism still needed in group relations?

7. What contrast does Niebuhr make between the middle ages and our own age?

8. Why does Niebuhr ask for "a sublime madness in the soul"? Why is reason also needed?

Paul Tillich *Man and History*

1. What distinction does Tillich make between history and historical consciousness?

2. What is tradition? When does an occurrence become an historical event?

3. What does Tillich mean by "symbolic vision"? How does this vision influence the scholar's approach to historical facts? Why doesn't this influence conflict with the methods of historical research?

4. What are the four characteristics of human history? What difference is there between human and other history? In what way is natural history an analogue to history but not history proper?

5. What distinction does the author point to between prehistorical and historical man? Why can't we fix the moment when one became the other?

6. What is posthistory? What possibilities for the future of mankind does Tillich describe?

7. What is a state? What are *eros* relationships? What is the connection between these relationships and the state?

8. What is "vocational consciousness"? What examples of this consciousness does Tillich give? How does he use the rise of Nayism to illustrate the importance of "vocational consciousness"?

9. Explain the remark in paragraph 23 that "the aim of history does not lie in history" and the statement in paragraph 24 that "history is the history of groups."

10. Why does Tillich maintain that "the question of whether individuals or 'masses' determine history must be replaced by an exact description of their interplay"?

Martin Buber *Postscript*

1. What does Buber mean by the *I - Thou* relationship between men? Why does he term full mutuality a "grace"? Explain the limitation of mutuality in teacher/pupil and psychotherapist/patient relationships.

2. What is the *I - Thou* relationship between man and God? Why is it necessary to say that "God is *also* a Person"? Why does Buber stress that God is an *absolute* Person? Why don't *I - Thou* relationships between men interfere with man's *I - Thou* relationship with God?

3. What is the "threshold of mutuality" involved in the *I - Thou* relationship between man and animal?

4. What reciprocity does the plant give to man's action toward it? Why does Buber term this sphere of activity *pre-threshold* or *preliminal*?

5. What is the *superliminal*? What is the spirit which is "to hand"? What examples does Buber provide? What does Buber mean by spirit "not to hand"?

Narrative: *Factual and Fictional*

Narrative writing—unlike exposition and argument, for example—is essentially experiential; that is, it recreates, in a highly selective way, an experience (event, episode) in the private or public history of a man or group of men. Narrative writing has significant meaning, of course, as the classical fables and parables clearly show; but its method of pointing up that meaning is very special. Although it requires very careful reading indeed, it does not yield to the kinds of "tests of cognition" which the above questions are intended to supply. Hence the following suggestions for mastering the narrative selections:

First, study the following terms in the "Glossary of Rhetorical Terms": *action, characters, climax, dénouement, description, dominant impression, in medias res, narrative, plot, point of view, setting, structure, symbol, theme, tone, turning-point, vividness*. These terms will provide you with a basic vocabulary for talking about narrative, especially if you will examine the illustrations of each term to be found in the text itself.

Second, apply to each of the narrative selections these *most basic* questions:

1. Who are the people in the narrative who do things and to whom things happen? (*Characters*)
2. What is the pattern of actions in which there is a cause-effect relationship? (*Action/Plot*)
3. When and where do the events of the narrative take place? (*Setting*)
4. What is the "angle of vision" from which the narrator views the events and relates them to the reader—as observer, as participant, as a combination of the two? (*Point of view*)
5. What "tone of voice" does the narrator use in telling his story? Is he sympathetic, ambiguous, authoritarian, ironic? (*Tone*)
6. To what extent does the narrator enrich his story by associating it with the motifs of his culture? Are there ritualistic icons or traditions through which he expands the relevance of his narrative? (*Symbol*)
7. What is the central, unifying concept, idea, or "moral" which the author intends his story to convey? What "criticism of life"—system of values—is he exposing? (*Theme*)

If you can answer these seven questions about each of the narratives in this volume, you are well prepared to participate in a classroom dialogue about them. If you have some clear idea about the other, more technical, terms in the glossary, you are reading to guide the discussion.

Index of Authors